INTERACTIVE CASEBOOK SERIES℠

CIVIL PROCEDURE

A Contemporary Approach

FIFTH EDITION

_____

A. Benjamin Spencer
PROFESSOR OF LAW
UNIVERSITY OF VIRGINIA SCHOOL OF LAW

_____

WEST
ACADEMIC
PUBLISHING

Interactive Casebook Series^{SM} is a servicemark registered in the U.S. Patent Trademark Office.

© West, a Thomson business, 2007, 2008
© 2011 Thomson Reuters
© 2014, 2015 LEG, Inc. d/b/a West Academic
© 2018 LEG, Inc. d/b/a West Academic
    444 Cedar Street, Suite 700
    St. Paul, MN 55101
    1-877-888-1330

West, West Academic Publishing, and West Academic are trademarks of West Publishing Corporation, used under license.

Printed in the United States of America

ISBN: 978-1-63460-790-2

For Marlette, Bella, Mya, James, Mary Alice, Emma, Alyssa, Adam, Philip, and Sophia

PREFACE TO THE FIFTH EDITION

THIS FIFTH EDITION OF *Civil Procedure: A Contemporary Approach* fully incorporates the 2015 amendments to the Federal Rules of Civil Procedure, as well as a few case law developments since the 2015 publication date of the Revised Fourth Edition. Two particularly noteworthy new cases that are included in this edition are the Supreme Court's personal jurisdiction decisions in *Bristol-Myers Squibb Co. v. Superior Court*, 137 S. Ct. 1773 (2017) (elaborating on specific jurisdiction), and *BNSF Railway Co. v. Tyrrell*, 137 S. Ct. 1549 (2017) (remarking on general jurisdiction). This edition, like the one that preceded it, integrates references to online assessment tools in the CasebookPlus platform. These consist of a bank of 300 multiple-choice questions that provide comprehensive assessment of the topics covered in this book, with detailed feedback consisting of explanations for both correct and incorrect responses. This feature provides an unparalleled opportunity to engage with the material actively as the course progresses and permits students and professors to determine the extent to which the material is being learned. The bank of questions will also serve as excellent preparation for the civil procedure component of the Multistate Bar Exam, which was added to the MBE in February 2015. Finally, in what is a significant change, the material pertaining to notice and service of process are removed from Chapters 2 and 6, respectively, and consolidated into a new Chapter 2. Personal jurisdiction, which previously made up Chapter 2, is redesignated as Chapter 1 (former Chapter 1 is now an "Overview").

I am very grateful to all of you who use this casebook, and to those of you who have provided much needed feedback. My hope is that the book continues to serve the needs of students by presenting federal civil procedure in a clear, straightforward, and engaging manner. Thanks to my wonderful wife, Marlette, who helps to make it all happen with her love and support, managing our nine children while I spent numerous hours working on this revision. I thank her for everything that she does to enable me to do what I do.

A.B.S., February 2018

Preface to the First Editon

THIS CASEBOOK HAD ITS ORIGINS in my desire to provide students with a learning resource more in tune with the ways that law students think and learn today. The current generation of law students has come of age in a highly technologically-sophisticated environment, with the heavy use of laptop computers and the Internet dominating the educational experience. Today it is commonplace to see 100% of the students in a classroom typing away at their computers as professors give their lectures (although many are using their computers for other distractions). The vast majority of legal research resources are now online, meaning students are much more accustomed to using electronic materials downloaded into their computers than they are with fumbling through clunky physical texts. Thus, although it is necessary for law schools to continue to inculcate in students the ability to consult hard copy materials when appropriate, it is also necessary to update the manner in which reading material is transmitted to students within law school courses.

This book was designed with the contemporary law student in mind. That focus is reflected in the content and style of the book as well as in its features. The primary purpose of a casebook is to serve as an effective learning tool for students, not as a hornbook for budding practitioners or a comprehensive treatise on the subject. Thus, here you will find a focused presentation of the core concepts central to a basic first-year education in federal civil procedure. The information is presented in a manner that is clear and easy to understand. Rather than masses of undifferentiated text, you will find the material identified and separated by headings and various text boxes that help bring the material off the page. The online version of the book should be particularly useful in enabling you to engage the material. It is extensively hyperlinked to a vast range of online resources that will enhance your learning experience such as Westlaw® legal materials, special documents, and informational Web sites. I hope that you find this book to be extremely user-friendly and facilitative of developing a full understanding and appreciation of this subject matter. If you come up with suggestions for how this book can be even more useful for students or more effective in fulfilling its mission, please do not hesitate to contact me with your thoughts.

I must thank my wife, Marlette, for tirelessly taking care of our household while I was compelled to spend increasing amounts of time away working on the completion of this book. I also must thank my mother and father for their moral support for this project. More directly, this book would not have been possible without the able research assistance of David Killion, Lesley McCall, Capri Miller, and Briton Nelson. My wonderful assistant, Elizabeth Garrett, was also amazing in providing me with editorial and administrative assistance every step of the way. Special thanks to my Dean, Rod Smolla, for giving me the encouragement and resources I needed to produce this casebook. Finally, I am indebted to all of my colleagues at Richmond and elsewhere who took the time to review these materials or simply to support me through this process; I hope that one day I am able to repay the favor.

A.B.S., March 2007

The cases presented in this book have been edited. A set of asterisks (* * *) appear where I have removed material from the text of an opinion. Footnotes have been largely removed from the opinions. However, where footnotes appear their original numbering is retained. Footnotes of my own creation are indicated by a raised asterisk (*) and followed with a bracketed notation of authorship ([Ed.]). Where the author of an opinion uses a raised asterisk to refer to a footnote, the asterisk will be retained and bracketed information regarding authorship of the footnote will follow to distinguish these notes from the notes that I insert.

Table of Contents

CHAPTER SIX *Pleading*   457

CHAPTER SEVEN *Joinder of Claims and Parties*   573

CHAPTER TEN *Trials*

Table of Cases

The principal cases are in bold type. Cases cited or discussed in the text are in roman type. References are to pages. Cases cited in principal cases and within other quoted materials are not included.

CIVIL PROCEDURE

A Contemporary Approach

FIFTH EDITION

Overview

WELCOME TO CIVIL PROCEDURE. Although this is likely the course about which you are most apprehensive simply based on word of mouth or fear of the unknown, you should have no special concerns about your ability to learn and master this subject. Certainly, civil procedure stands apart from your other first-year courses because it likely connects the least with your prior life experiences. Experience has already probably given you a cursory understanding of contracts, property, torts, and criminal law—the stuff of every basic first-year law school curriculum. As a result of this seeming familiarity, most students approach these other subjects feeling as if they at least have a grasp of what they will be learning more about and why those things matter.

Not so much so with civil procedure. This subject is not something that most people ordinarily encounter in their daily lives, although our lives are certainly impacted heavily by it. Civil procedure, in a nutshell, refers to the body of rules, statutes, and doctrines that govern where and how private suits are initiated, litigated, and resolved by litigants, their attorneys, and the courts. The subject addresses questions such as:

- Where may I file suit against a particular person? May the case be filed in federal or state court? What documents do I have to file to initiate and proceed with my case?

- What law applies to the suit?

- How can I get information from my adversary in this case, if at all?

- Can multiple defendants be sued at the same time in the same case?

- If someone has been sued, can that person sue the plaintiff back? Can a defendant bring other parties into the action?

- I don't like the jury's verdict; can I ask the judge to give me a different result? Can I appeal the judge's decision? Can I relitigate my case in a different court?

These topics and many more will be covered as you proceed through your study of civil procedure.

In this Introduction, we will first walk through the basic features of this casebook so that you understand how to get the most out of it as you go through the course. Then we will turn to an overview of the American judicial system and a brief outline of the path that a case takes as it proceeds from the initial selection of a proper court through the appeals process.

A. Features of This Casebook

The whole purpose of this casebook is to facilitate your ability to access and to absorb the material so that you can succeed as a student and ultimately as a lawyer. As you will soon learn, however, law school is about more than simply learning information; it is about developing certain types of analytical skills that are important to the practice of law. Thus, in civil procedure as in all of your courses, you will have to develop the ability to engage legal materials such as constitutional provisions, cases, statutes, and rules and pull from them principles and doctrines that you can apply to hypothetical and eventually real-world situations as they are presented to you. Legal analysis is both the ability to understand the principles and doctrines that flow from various legal sources and the ability to apply those principles to future cases. Law school coursework facilitates the acquisition and refinement of your legal analytical skills by presenting core concepts primarily through the legal sources from which they are derived rather than by pulling those concepts out and spoon-feeding them to you.

That said, your understanding of the material is critical; there is no point in a course or a casebook that never successfully *teaches* you what you need to know about a subject. The purpose of taking civil procedure is for you appreciate the full range of procedural issues that must be addressed when you have to prosecute or defend against a lawsuit. At the end of this course, you should be able to figure out, for example, whether a court is a proper one in which a case may be brought, whether the court can and should enter summary judgment for a particular party, and whether and how you can challenge a determination made by the judge or the jury in a case.

This casebook is designed to strike the proper balance between presenting the information in a way that is understandable and doing so by gently nudging you to delve into the material to discover many of the important principles for yourself with ample guidance along the way. Toward that end, this casebook departs from the approach and appearance of the traditional casebooks you will likely experience in your other courses. Every feature has been designed with one purpose in mind: the facilitation of student learning. Here are the main features of this book:

1. Text Boxes

Throughout the book, you will find various text boxes on either side of the page that are intended to provide information that will aid in your understanding of a case, draw your attention to important or noteworthy matters that deserve special attention, or cause you to think more deeply about an issue or question arising from the material. The categories of text boxes are as follows:

 What's That? These boxes will explain the meaning of special legal terms that appear in the main text. Definitions may be accessed in the electronic casebook by mousing over underlined terms in the text.

 Take Note! Here you will be prompted to take special notice of what is being discussed in a case or something interesting that deserves further thought or attention.

 Food for Thought. These boxes will pose questions that prompt you to think about various issues raised by the material.

 Make the Connection. When concepts or discussions that pertain to information covered in other law school courses appear in a case or elsewhere in this text, often you will find this text box to indicate the course in which you can study those topics. Here you may also be prompted to connect information in the current case to material that you have covered elsewhere in this course.

 FYI. A self-explanatory category that shares useful or simply interesting information relevant to material in the text.

 Practice Pointer. Here you will find advice relevant to legal practice, typically inspired by the actions (or inaction) of legal counsel in the cases or simply prompted by an important issue being discussed.

 It's Latin to Me! The law is fond of Latin terms and phrases; when you encounter these in the text for the first time, this box will explain their meaning.

 Go Online! If there are relevant online resources that are worth consulting in relation to any matter being discussed, these boxes will direct you to them.

 For More Information. These boxes point you to additional resources to consult for more information on a subject.

 Major Themes. In the Executive Summaries at the end of each chapter, you will find here a discussion of some of the deeper themes and issues pertaining to the topic covered in that chapter.

 Test Your Knowledge. These boxes, also located in each Executive Summaries section, contain hyperlinks to online assessment questions that will help you test your understanding of the material in each chapter.

2. Electronic Casebook with Hyperlinks

Perhaps one of the more unique features of this casebook is the availability of an accompanying electronic version containing hyperlinked text. The entire casebook is available electronically in a format that you can highlight and search with ease. Additionally, the electronic version of this book is fully hyperlinked to many different resources:

a.   Cases, Statutes, and Articles

Older law review articles that do not appear on Westlaw will be linked to PDF versions at HeinOnline (http://home.heinonline.org/).

Case citations, statutes, rules, constitutional provisions, and most law review articles are hyperlinked to Westlaw. Simply click on the link and students with Westlaw accounts will be able to sign on and view the complete versions of the linked source.

b.   CasebookPlus™ Assessment Questions

Throughout this book at the end of each chapter, you will find a Review box that mentions CasebookPlus. Click on the associated links to access relevant multiple-choice questions that will help you assess your understanding of the concepts covered in that chapter. You can use these as a review at the end of the chapter or access the questions as you go through each topic. Your professor may also be interested in having you answer certain questions as you cover each topic in your course.

c.   Online Materials

As you see in the text box above, whenever a website is referred to in the text, it will be presented as a live hyperlink that you can click to visit the indicated site online.

d.   Names of Justices and Other Judges

The names of Supreme Court Justices (and at times some of the lower court judges) are hyperlinked to biographical information about them when their names appear as authors of or signatories to an opinion in a case (example: CARDOZO). Take time to look at this information to develop an appreciation for the background of each Justice; such information can at times prove useful in understanding a Justice's perspective, style, or jurisprudence. When other names are highlighted, such as influential English jurists (example: Lord Ellenborough), the link will take you to websites presenting their biographical information.

e. Court Websites

Whenever a court is referenced in a case, its name will be hyperlinked to that court's website (example: <u>U.S. Court of Appeals for the Fifth Circuit</u>). You can visit these sites to get a better idea of the court's place within the judicial system or its geographical location, which can be important to understanding some cases. Both federal and state courts will be hyperlinked throughout the text.

f. Organizational or Governmental Websites

There will be times when organizations of various kinds (governmental, corporate, or non-profit) will appear in the text as litigants or third parties or as agencies that previously handled the case (example: <u>Securities and Exchange Commission</u>). When appropriate, these will be hyperlinked to their respective websites so that you can learn more about the organization, either to aid in your understanding of a case or sometimes simply to obtain interesting trivia that will broaden your view of the parties that are involved in a dispute.

g. Internal Cross-References

When other sections or chapters are referred to in the text, they will be hyperlinked so that clicking on them will immediately take you to that portion of the case-book (example: <u>Chapter 4</u>). Additionally, the table of contents is hyperlinked so that you can easily access portions of the book by clicking on the page number of interest.

h. *FLEX* Cases

When a case of some significance to an issue is mentioned or discussed, but is not included as a principal case in this book, you will occasionally find after the citation to the case a hyperlinked indication that the case is a "*FLEX* Case" (example: [*FLEX Case 3.A*]). Clicking on this link will take you to an edited version of the case that your professor may assign for you to read. You may also want to review these cases on your own to explore further the issues that they raise.

3. Case Excerpts

The cases as they appear in the text are edited versions that omit portions of the opinion that are of lesser importance to the lesson at hand. Full versions of the cases may be accessed easily by clicking on the associated hyperlinked case citation that you will find in the caption of the case.

Given that some text and most footnotes from the judicial opinions

Take Note!

The bottom line is this: This casebook was not designed to contain vast pages of useless material that you would likely ignore or skip through. Rather, the material you will find in these pages is limited to things that you should be reading in order to learn and understand the topics being presented.

are edited out, it should be clear that the material that is *included* in this casebook is important or at least relevant. Thus, if a footnote is reproduced within a case, it is there for a reason. You should read the footnote and try to identify why the information contained within the note is relevant or important. The same goes for concurring and dissenting opinions. If such opinions appear along with the case, you need to read them and try to understand the contributions they can make to your understanding of the case or the issues raised therein.

4. Statutes and Rules

Although you can find the Federal Rules of Civil Procedure and important provisions from Title 28 of the U.S. Code when you click on the hyperlinked references in the text (example: 28 U.S.C. § 1331), when important rules or statutes are being discussed in detail you will find the rule or statute excerpted directly in the text as follows:

FRCP 1. Scope and Purpose.

These rules govern the procedure in all civil actions and proceedings in the United States district courts * * * . They should be construed, administered, and employed by the court and the parties to secure the just, speedy, and inexpensive determination of every action and proceeding.

The aim here is to bring your attention to important statutory language in context, without distracting you away from the main text.

5. Points for Discussion, Hypotheticals, and Perspective & Analysis

At various points in this book—mostly after the principal case excerpts—there will be a Points for Discussion section that will feature focused questions that you should consider and be able to answer. Also, here you will find further explanation or discussion of the issues raised in the case or by a particular rule or statute. These sections are critical to read because in them you will often find the detailed presentation of information that builds on and explicates concepts presented in the principal case or discusses other important components of the subject under discussion. Also in these sections you will at times find one or two hypothetical problems to test your understanding of the concepts and ability to apply them to new factual situations.

Finally, when a topic has been the subject of some amount of scholarly discussion or debate, there may be a shaded area entitled Perspective & Analysis. Under this heading, you will find the presentation of an issue followed by an extended excerpt from a scholarly writing on the matter. These debates and perspectives are important because they can help deepen your knowledge of a topic and enhance your appreciation of its significance to larger concerns.

6. Executive Summaries

At the end of each chapter, there will be an Executive Summary that summarizes the main top-level points covered by the chapter, notes two or three deeper themes or issues that relate to the chapter's topic, and presents a few additional resources that you may consult if you are interested in learning more about the topics covered in that chapter. Use these summaries to make sure that you take away from each chapter what you were supposed to have learned. If you discover gaps in your understanding, either refer back to the relevant section of the chapter for review, meet with your professor for discussion, or consult the additional resources to read more about the topic.

Take Note!

Keep in mind that the top-level summary that you will find in the Executive Summaries is hardly comprehensive or of sufficient depth to provide you with everything you need to know about the topic. Rather, it is simply a global summation of key points as a way of bringing your review of a chapter to a close.

B. Introduction to U.S. Judicial Systems

As you already know, in the United States the federal government consists of three branches: the legislative branch (Congress), the executive branch (the President), and the judicial branch (the Supreme Court and inferior federal courts). Our concern here is the federal judiciary, which for the most part derives its existence and authority from <u>Article III of the U.S. Constitution</u> and from legislation and rules enacted or acceded to by the other two branches. In this section, we will review the structure of the federal judiciary, its relationship to the separate judicial systems of the states, and the system through which procedural rules governing federal civil practice are developed and promulgated.

FYI

Although we will spend most of our time in this course concerning ourselves with practice and procedure in these trial level courts, we will typically be doing so by reading cases decided by federal appellate courts. This is so because it is mainly the appellate courts that authoritatively articulate the law that governs procedure in these lower courts.

Federal District Courts

The federal judicial system consists of a hierarchical group of courts divided based on geography and jurisdiction. The main entry points into the system are the <u>United States district courts</u>, which serve as the trial courts where most cases are filed initially. There are 94 federal judicial districts covering each of the states, the District of Columbia, and the various territories of the United States. Every state has at least one federal judicial district, and several have more than one. However, it is worth noting that no district crosses state lines or embraces multiple states.* Within these districts, there can be multiple judges, who may be located in different courthouses spread throughout the district in various "divisions" of the district.

Our major initial focus in this casebook will be on identifying when one may bring a suit in the federal district courts and which among these courts may properly hear the case. The topics of personal jurisdiction, subject matter jurisdiction, and venue each address these issues and will be introduced more fully below.

FYI

Under Article III of the U.S Constitution, federal judges serving on the district courts, the U.S. Courts of Appeals, and the U.S. Supreme Court (and judges on the Court of International Trade) hold lifetime appointments and may not have their salaries decreased during their tenure. However, this status does not apply to judges of courts constituted under alternate constitutional provisions, such as U.S. Bankruptcy Courts, which are constituted under Article I, or the District Court of the Virgin Islands, which is constituted under Article IV. Puerto Rico's U.S. District Court, on the other hand, is constituted under Article III. For a discussion of the distinctions between the various types of tribunals, see James E. Pfander, Article I Tribunals, Article III Courts, and the Judicial Power of the United States, 118 Harv. L. Rev. 643 (2004).

U.S. Courts of Appeals

Appeals from the federal district courts are heard by various U.S. Courts of Appeals that are organized into geographical regions called "circuits." There are 12 regional circuits and one subject-matter-oriented circuit referred to as the U.S. Court of Appeals for the Federal Circuit (located in Washington, D.C., and designed primarily to hear patent appeals). The regional circuits covering the states and the U.S. territories are numbered 1 through 11, while the District of Columbia has its own circuit called the U.S. Court of Appeals for the D.C. Circuit. The topic of appeals from the district courts to these appeals courts will be covered more fully in Chapter 11.

The circuit courts consist of multiple judges who hear appeals initially as three-judge panels, contrasted with federal district court judges who typically handle cases on their own. Appeals from district courts are presented and argued to these courts both through written briefs (supported by trial court record material) and through oral arguments before the deciding panel. Under special circumstances, a party who loses before the panel may seek reconsideration by all of the active circuit judges sitting on that court, a process referred to as a rehearing *en banc*.[†]

---

* The District of Wyoming is an exception to this statement; it is comprised of the entire state of Wyoming and those portions of Yellowstone National Park situated in Montana and Idaho. [Ed.]

† Because of the large number of judges serving on the Ninth Circuit, it holds its rehearings *en banc* not with all of the active circuit judges but with a subset of that group. [Ed.]

Below, you will find a map that illustrates the division of the United States into federal districts and circuits. Note that the U.S. Court of Appeals for the First Circuit not only includes the upper New England states, but also embraces Puerto Rico and hears appeals from the federal district court in that U.S. territory. Similarly, the U.S. Court of Appeals for the Third Circuit hears appeals from the federal district court located in the U.S. Virgin Islands.

Map of U.S. Circuits and Federal Judicial Districts

Source: Administrative Office of the U.S. Courts

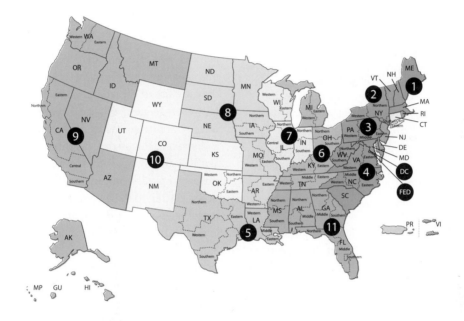

The Supreme Court of the United States

The Supreme Court of the United States sits at the top of the U.S. judicial system. Cases decided by the circuit courts may be presented to the Supreme Court for review, but its review of such cases is largely discretionary. Litigants seeking review submit a petition for *certiorari* to the Supreme Court; if the Court decides to take the case, it grants the petition. *See* 28 U.S.C. § 1254(1).

The Supreme Court also has the authority to review the decisions of the court of last resort in each of the states, the District of Columbia, Puerto Rico, and the U.S. Virgin Islands to the extent they involve issues of federal law. *See* 28 U.S.C. §§ 1257, 1258, 1260. State courts are fully competent to hear cases based on federal law or involving federal law to some degree. When those courts decide matters of federal law, litigants who disagree with what the state's highest court has said on the matter may seek review on the federal issue by the Supreme Court. Again, this review is discretionary, meaning that if the Supreme Court denies review, the state court's ruling on the issue will stand.

State Judicial Systems

The states, the District of Columbia, and the U.S. territories have their own systems of courts that are completely separate from the federal system and from one another. They are typically organized in a manner similar to what we see in the federal system, with a series of trial courts, intermediate appellate courts, and a court or courts of last resort. However, not all states have multiple intermediate appellate courts, and several states have no intermediate appeals court (Montana is an example).

Go Online!

The National Center for State Courts has a very useful application that provides information about the structure of the court system in each of the 50 states, the District of Columbia, and U.S. Territories. *See* http://www.ncsc.org/sco.

State trial courts are courts of general jurisdiction that ordinarily may hear all types of cases, whether they are based on federal or state law. However, states will also typically have specialized lower courts to hear a discrete category of disputes such as those involving domestic relations, probate matters, or small claims. As noted earlier, to the extent that federal legal issues are resolved by state courts and reviewed by a state's highest court, those determinations can be reviewed by the U.S. Supreme Court. It is worth emphasizing, though, that the U.S. Supreme Court has no jurisdiction to review state court determinations on matters of *state* law. Thus, for example, if the Pennsylvania Supreme Court decided that a traffic stop, vehicle search, and arrest violated the Pennsylvania Constitution, the U.S. Supreme Court could not review or question that determination. On the other hand, if the Pennsylvania Supreme Court ruled that the same incident violated the Fourth Amendment of the U.S. Constitution, the U.S. Supreme Court would have full authority to accept an appeal of that decision and reverse it if it disagreed with the Pennsylvania high court on the Fourth Amendment issue.

The Federal Rulemaking Process

The rules and doctrines governing civil practice before the federal courts come from many different sources, including constitutional provisions, federal statutes, and a special set of rules called the Federal Rules of Civil Procedure. This body of law and the judicial opinions interpreting it make up most of what we refer to as civil procedure. Although you no doubt have a good understanding of what constitutional provisions and federal statutes are and where they come from, what are these "Federal Rules of Civil Procedure" and where do they come from?

The Federal Rules of Civil Procedure were adopted in 1938 and drafted by a special committee comprised of judges, practitioners, and law professors appointed for the task. Today, these rules are revised regularly pursuant to a process that Congress established in the Rules Enabling Act, 28 U.S.C. §§ 2071–2077. Briefly, the process begins with consideration of proposed rule changes by the Advisory Committee on Civil Rules. After conducting hearings and receiving comments on the proposed amendments, the Advisory Committee may approve certain changes and recommend their adoption to the Committee on Rules of Practice and Procedure of the Judicial Conference, typically referred to as the Standing Committee. If the Standing Committee approves of the changes, it recommends their approval to the Judicial Conference, which then may accept or reject the amendments. Next, those amendments adopted by the Judicial Conference are sent to the U.S. Supreme Court for its approval. If the Court approves, it transmits the changes to Congress by May 1 of the year in which the amendments are to take effect. Congress then has seven months to reject the changes; if it fails to do so, the amendments become effective on December 1 of that year.

Why do you think that Congress established this system for promulgating and amending the Federal Rules? To learn more about the federal rulemaking process, visit the Federal Rulemaking homepage at the U.S. Courts website (www. uscourts.gov).

C. An Outline of a Civil Action

This casebook and most likely your course will be organized to track the progression of a lawsuit from start to finish. Let's now take a moment to go through each stage to highlight the topics and issues that we will be covering during the course. To get us started, take a look at the litigation diagram that is shown below. This diagram will be reproduced at the beginning of each chapter.

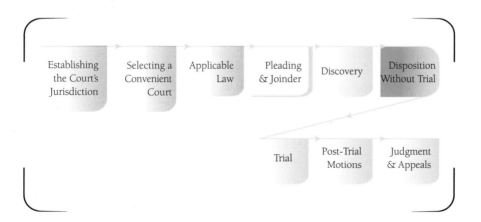

As we go through these phases of civil litigation, keep in mind that this is a broad, linear overview of the course of a civil action in the federal system. As we get to each topic in the chapters, the complications, nuances, and alternative twists and turns that are possible will be addressed.

1. Selecting a Proper Court

When an aggrieved person wants to pursue legal action against someone, that person must initially determine where she may file her lawsuit. A prospective plaintiff must decide between state and federal court (or possibly a foreign court), and then among those courts she must determine geographically where to file suit, meaning, for example, in Georgia federal court, California federal court, or Oklahoma state court. These are not simply strategic choices that may be freely made at the discretion of our fictitious plaintiff. Rather, there are statutes, rules, and legal doctrines that limit the authority of various courts to adjudicate disputes of a certain kind or to render judgments that will bind certain individuals. These limitations on the adjudicatory authority of courts are generally referred to as limits on a court's jurisdiction. There are two aspects of jurisdiction that we will consider in this casebook: personal jurisdiction and subject matter jurisdiction. Providing proper notice of a lawsuit is also an aspect of establishing a court's jurisdiction that we will cover as well. Finally, selecting a proper court entails identifying courts that are a proper "venue" under applicable statutes.

a. Personal Jurisdiction

Personal jurisdiction addresses itself to questions about the authority of a court to exercise power over an individual or entity and adjudicate their rights. For example, if you are from California and I am from Minnesota, and we collide on a highway in Illinois, can California courts exercise personal jurisdiction over me as a defendant in any resulting lawsuit? Can California courts exercise jurisdiction over you as a defendant in such a lawsuit? These are important questions because when a court lacks personal jurisdiction over a party, any resulting judgment it enters against that party will not be binding and enforceable. Thus, in choosing where to file a lawsuit, litigants along with their attorneys must identify those courts that would be able to exercise personal jurisdiction over each of the defendants in the action. In our study of this topic—which is covered in Chapter 1—we will explore how courts determine whether they have personal jurisdiction over parties in a case.

b. Notice

Before a court may exercise jurisdiction over a defendant, that person or entity must have been properly notified of the action. There are constitutional and rule-based aspects to this notification requirement. The Due Process Clauses of the Fifth and Fourteenth Amendments to the U.S. Constitution are the sources of the constitutional notice requirement, while Rule 4 of the Federal Rules of Civil Procedure sets forth the details regarding how parties may be notified of actions brought against them in the Federal Courts. Notice is covered in Chapter 2.

c. Subject Matter Jurisdiction

Courts must also have competency to hear a case, meaning they are authorized to adjudicate disputes of a particular kind. Subject matter jurisdiction rules address this issue. Thus, if *A* wishes to sue *B* for $2,000 based on damage that *B* caused to *A*'s car, whether a federal court can hear that case is determined with reference to the law of federal subject matter jurisdiction. Federal courts are empowered to hear and resolve only certain limited types of cases, meaning not all disputes may be brought in the federal courts. Sorting out which suits may and may not be brought in the federal courts will be our focus when we cover this topic in Chapter 3.

d. Venue

In addition to these jurisdictional limitations on a court's authority, there are rules of convenience that further determine the proper court that may hear a case within a judicial system. These venue rules resolve questions such as whether a case may be brought in the Southern District of Texas, or the Central District of California, or both, or neither. Venue rules focus on the location of the parties and the events giving rise to the dispute to identify those judicial districts in which the action may be pursued conveniently. We will consider federal venue rules and the rules governing the transfer or dismissal of cases based on venue concerns in Chapter 4.

2. Applicable Law

Another preliminary matter that we will consider—although this matter may arise at any point within a case—is what law should apply to the issues that are raised in the dispute. There are two dimensions to this question: (1) whether state or federal law should apply and (2) if state law applies, which state's law applies. Here we are concerned primarily with the former question.

Make the Connection

The question of which state's law to apply when state law governs an issue will not be covered in this book. Deciding between competing state laws is a topic that you can study in a **Conflict of Laws** course.

When a federal court is adjudicating a dispute involving the alleged negligence of the defendant, should the federal court apply a particular state's law of negligence or is there some federal law of negligence that the court should apply? Or, when deciding whether certain material is protected by the attorney-client privilege, does the federal court look to federal or state law to make that determination? These are the types of choice-of-law questions that are addressed by what has come to be known as the *Erie* Doctrine, named for the seminal Supreme Court case of *Erie Railroad Co. v. Tompkins*, 304 U.S. 64 (1938). We will cover this topic in Chapter 5.

3. Pleading & Joinder

Once a litigant has selected a proper court, she must file and serve a complaint to initiate the action. What information must appear in this complaint? How much detail regarding what happened is necessary? Can the plaintiff amend her complaint if it needs to be changed in some way? Once served, the defendant may file an answer or may respond first by raising any of a number of special defenses or objections by motion. What are these defenses and what information must be in the defendant's answer? Many rules govern these pleadings and motions, and these will be covered in Chapter 6.

Related to pleadings is the matter of how a lawsuit may be shaped with respect to claims and parties. Can multiple claims be asserted in a single lawsuit or must separate actions be pursued? Can a plaintiff sue multiple defendants simultaneously within the same action? Can nonparties try to intervene in a case and make themselves parties? Can nonparties be forced to join in a lawsuit, either as plaintiffs or defendants? What if millions of plaintiffs all have the same claim against a common defendant; when can they unite as a group to sue the defendant jointly as a class? Each of these questions pertains to joinder, the topic of Chapter 7.

4. Discovery

After the lawsuit has been suitably filed and shaped, the parties eventually engage in a process of compelled information exchange called discovery. This process is meant to give the parties access to all available relevant information to enable them to build their respective cases. The American system is designed to prevent litigants from being able to conceal information that might prove useful in a case, but the ability to discover the information in the possession of one's adversary is not limitless. In Chapter 8, we will discuss the scope of civil discovery in the federal system, the devices that are available for obtaining information during an action, and the mechanisms that have been established to resolve the inevitable disputes that can arise in this context.

5. Trials & Disposition Without Trial

After discovery has progressed to some extent (or, in some instances, much earlier) the case may be preemptively concluded short of a trial through a negotiated settlement or through the entry of summary judgment, a judicial ruling that there is no genuine, material factual dispute between the parties warranting a trial.

Alternatively, a court may direct the parties into an alternative dispute resolution (ADR) process that ends up resolving the case without trial. Finally, it is possible that a defendant will fail entirely to appear or defend itself in an action, which can result in the court having to enter a default judgment. These and other means by which an action may conclude without proceeding to trial will be treated in Chapter 9.

In the event that a case does proceed to trial, one critical issue that will be our focus here is the role of the jury. Determining whether a jury rather than a judge may decide an issue, the role of the jury in the federal system, the rules surrounding the selection of members of a jury, and the phases of a jury trial will feature in the first half of Chapter 10. The second half of the chapter will turn to the rules surrounding courts' ability to preempt or reverse the verdict of the jury or set aside the verdict to order a new trial or other post-trial relief.

6. Judgments & Appeals

The final chapter of this book, Chapter 11, covers several matters pertaining to judgments.

a. Securing & Enforcing Judgments

First is the matter of securing an anticipated judgment at the outset of a case. For example, if the defendant has limited assets and you would like to make sure that those assets are available to satisfy the judgment you hope to obtain in a suit, there are mechanisms available for securing those assets provisionally. Similarly, a plaintiff who seeks a judgment preventing a defendant from taking some allegedly harmful action will need a means of preserving the status quo pending the court's determination of the matter. Otherwise, the defendant will be free to take the feared action while the court spends time figuring out whether to prohibit it. These concerns are addressed by various provisional remedies that will be covered in Chapter 11. At the other end of the process, once a party has obtained a final enforceable judgment it must be executed if the prevailing party expects to obtain the relief won. This enforcement process will also be covered in Chapter 11.

b. Appellate Review

Earlier we briefly alluded to appeals that may be taken from the federal district courts up to the various circuit courts. Strict rules limit the point at which any given decision may be challenged before an appellate tribunal. *See* 28 U.S.C. §§ 1291, 1292. Thus, while a final judgment entered on a jury verdict may be appealable, a ruling by a trial judge that certain documents must be produced during discovery typically may not be appealed. What is the difference between the two types of determinations that results in their disparate amenability to appeal? What are the rules governing what types of decisions may be appealed and the point at which they may be appealed? Also important in this regard is the manner in which federal appeals courts exercise their reviewing authority. Are they free to second-guess the decisions of lower court judges by substituting their own views, or do they owe some deference to the views of the trial court? All of these issues surrounding appellate review will be treated in Chapter 11.

c. Preclusion Doctrine

Chapter 11 concludes with a consideration of preclusion doctrine, the body of law that governs the extent to which previous determinations of claims or issues preclude the relitigation of those matters or closely related matters in subsequent lawsuits. The principal doctrines here—referred to as claim preclusion (*res judicata*) and issue preclusion (collateral estoppel)—will be covered in detail.

D. Recurring Themes

As you embark on your study of civil procedure, keep in mind that you are not just studying a collection of rules and doctrines that you are supposed to memorize. Although you are studying the nuts and bolts of the federal civil justice system in the United States, never lose sight of the bigger picture. The rules that you will be learning form a *system*, a system with a design and a purpose, a system with certain costs and benefits, and a system that has an impact on the ability to resolve disputes or vindicate rights that have been transgressed.

Thus, when you confront a topic, you should not only seek to understand how to apply the rule to specific fact patterns; you should also wonder how the topic fits within the larger context of a lawsuit, how the doctrines developed within that topic affect people's ability to assert valid claims, the costs that the rule or doctrine imposes on litigants attempting to prosecute or defend against an action, and the real-life consequences of procedural doctrines for individual litigants and society at large. Ask yourself why a rule is written a certain way. What goals were the rulemakers or courts trying to achieve in shaping the rule or doctrine in a particular fashion? If this rule were written differently, what impact would that have on litigants? On the system? On other procedural rules? Who benefits and who is harmed by this rule or legal decision? Ask these questions at every turn to deepen your appreciation of the meaning and import of the rules of procedure.

Finally, keep the following recurring themes in mind as you progress through this subject:

Federalism. We live in a federal system, meaning that certain limited authority is given to our national government with the remaining power reserved to the states. How does *federalism* impact federal civil procedure?

The distinction between law and equity. Our system is inherited from the civil justice system of England that existed at the time our nation was founded. Part of that legacy is the historical distinction between *law* and *equity*. Courts at law used juries, had rigid pleading and limited joinder, and were capable of awarding money damages as relief. The equity courts—which arose out of a need to provide redress for those who could not attain relief from the law courts—lacked juries, embraced open-ended procedure that permitted expansive joinder of claims and parties, permitted discovery, exalted the discretion of the judge or chancellor to do justice in individual cases, and were empowered to award nonmonetary or equitable relief to litigants such as injunctions or the return of wrongfully-taken property. The Federal Rules of Civil Procedure merged law and equity into a single system, bringing many of equity's unconstrained procedures into the combined system. *See* Stephen N. Subrin, *How Equity Conquered Common Law: The Federal Rules of Civil Procedure in Historical Perspective*, 135 U. Pa. L. Rev. 909 (1987) (describing the history of the Federal Rules of Civil Procedure and how equity procedure dominated in the merged system). What impact does this legacy of the distinction between law and equity have on how civil procedure rules are designed and interpreted today? How are courts to determine which matters may be resolved by a jury and which may be handled by the judge under a merged system?

Judicial discretion. In our system, judges are given enormous discretion at each stage of the litigation process to control party conduct, to eliminate issues or claims from the case, or to prevent matters from being decided by the jury. How do the rules provide for and constrain such discretion? Are there areas where judicial discretion is too extensive? Does judicial discretion undermine consistency, predictability, and fairness in how procedural rules and doctrines are interpreted and applied? What role, if any, does appellate review (or its mere availability) play in constraining discretion and in guiding how judges resolve the procedural issues before them?

Fairness versus efficiency. Some of the rules and procedural doctrines that you will be studying will seem to favor the interests of access, fairness, and justice while other rules and decisions will appear more concerned with promoting efficiency, predictability, or at times procedural formality. When should the values of fairness prevail over those of efficiency? Can rules be crafted and interpreted in a way that reconciles these competing policy interests?

These themes, and others, will be reflected in the material that follows. Try to keep them in mind as you consider each topic. I sincerely hope that you find this book engaging, informative, and accessible. We now turn to our consideration of federal civil procedure.

CHAPTER ONE

Personal Jurisdiction

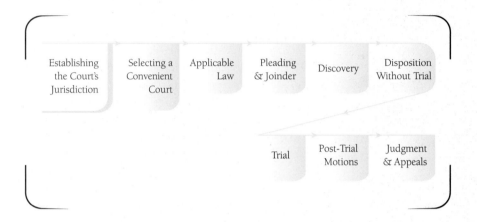

Introduction

BEFORE A COURT MAY ENTERTAIN a civil action and render a binding judgment, it must have jurisdiction to adjudicate the claims in question. There are two aspects of a court's jurisdiction to adjudicate: jurisdiction over the parties to the dispute (personal jurisdiction) and jurisdiction over the subject matter of the dispute (subject matter jurisdiction). This chapter will focus on the first type of jurisdiction, while Chapter 3 will cover the second type.

One of the first tasks you will face as a lawyer trying to identify a court in which to initiate a lawsuit is to find a court that has the power to exercise personal jurisdiction* over the defendant or defendants in the case. Without the authority to exercise such jurisdiction, the court does not have the power to render a binding judgment that defendants will be obliged to obey. The focus of this chapter is to review the legal framework that governs the determination of the scope of a court's personal jurisdiction and how we as lawyers can figure out whether a given court has personal jurisdiction over the defendants in any given case.

---

* Although the power of courts to adjudicate claims against particular defendants is referred to most commonly as personal jurisdiction, it also might at times be referred to as territorial jurisdiction. [Ed.]

Personal Jurisdiction in the Federal Courts

Although our main concern throughout this casebook is civil procedure in the federal system, in this chapter we will spend a great deal of time learning about the statutory and constitutional limits on personal jurisdiction that constrain state courts. Why is this so if personal jurisdiction in the federal courts is our main concern? The reason is that under the Federal Rules of Civil Procedure, the scope of personal jurisdiction in the federal courts is most often determined by the scope of personal jurisdiction in the courts of the state where the federal court is located. This linkage is set forth in Federal Rule 4(k)(1)(A), which reads: "Serving a summons or filing a waiver of service establishes personal jurisdiction over a defendant who is subject to the jurisdiction of a court of general jurisdiction in the state where the district court is located." FED. R. CIV. P. 4(k)(1)(A). (Rule 4(k) contains other provisions governing personal jurisdiction in the federal courts, which we will cover in Section E below.)

Practice Pointer

Because a court lacking the power to exercise jurisdiction over the defendant may not render a binding judgment against that defendant, one of your initial tasks if you represent the defendant should be to determine whether the court selected by the plaintiff has proper jurisdiction over your client for the claims asserted. The process by which one may raise a challenge to a court's exercise of personal jurisdiction will be covered in Chapter 6.

Given the language of Rule 4(k)(1)(A), the personal jurisdiction analysis for a case in federal court will typically be no different than such an analysis would be were the case in state court. Hence, in this chapter, we will review the standards that govern the determination of personal jurisdiction in state courts.

Food for Thought

As you learn more about personal jurisdiction and about the judicial system in the United States, think about whether it makes sense to limit the personal jurisdictional reach of federal courts to that of host states. *See* A. Benjamin Spencer, *Nationwide Personal Jurisdiction for Our Federal Courts*, 87 DENVER L. REV. 325 (2010).

A. Historical Roots of the Doctrine

Our review of personal jurisdiction doctrine begins with the primary case in which the Supreme Court articulated its vision of the proper jurisdictional reach of state courts, *Pennoyer v. Neff*. After gaining an understanding of the foundational principles of personal jurisdiction articulated in *Pennoyer*, we will turn in Section B to the modern doctrine of personal jurisdiction established by *International Shoe Co. v. Washington* and subsequent cases.

1. The Traditional Bases of Personal Jurisdiction

Pennoyer v. Neff

Supreme Court of the United States
95 U.S. (5 Otto) 714 (1877)

ERROR to the Circuit Court of the United States for the District of Oregon.

MR. JUSTICE FIELD delivered the opinion of the court.

This action was brought by Neff [then a resident of California] against Pennoyer for the recovery of a tract of land [with an alleged value of $15,000] situated in Multnomah County, Oregon. Pennoyer, in his answer, denied Neff's title and right to possession, and set up a title in himself. * * * [T]he cause was tried by the court, and a special verdict given, upon which judgment was rendered in favor of Neff; whereupon Pennoyer sued out this writ of error.

The plaintiff asserts title to the premises by a patent of the United States issued to him in 1866, under the act of Congress of Sept. 27, 1850, usually known as the Donation Law of Oregon. The defendant claims to have acquired the premises under a sheriff's deed, made upon a sale of the property on execution issued upon a judgment recovered against the plaintiff in one of the circuit courts of the State. The case turns upon the validity of this judgment.

Make the Connection

Enforcement of judgments through execution and other aspects of securing and enforcing judgments are discussed in Chapter 11.

It appears from the record that the judgment was rendered in February, 1866, in favor of J.H. Mitchell, for less than $300, including costs, in an action brought by him upon a demand for services as an attorney; that, at the time the action was commenced and the judgment rendered, the defendant therein, the plaintiff here, was a non-resident of the State that he was not personally served with process, and did not appear therein; and that the judgment was entered upon his default in not answering the complaint, upon a constructive service of summons by publication. [In the action by Mitchell against Neff, jurisdiction was established and notice was given by publication of the summons for six successive weeks in the

Pacific Christian Advocate, a weekly newspaper of general circulation published in Multnomah County, Oregon.]

The Code of Oregon provides for such service when an action is brought against a non-resident and absent defendant, who has property within the State. It also provides, where the action is for the recovery of money or damages, for the attachment of the property of the non-resident. * * * In the case against the plaintiff, the property here in controversy sold under the judgment rendered was not attached, nor in any way brought under the jurisdiction of the court. Its first connection with the case was caused by a levy of the execution. It was not, therefore, disposed of pursuant to any adjudication, but only in enforcement of a personal judgment, having no relation to the property, rendered against a non-resident without service of process upon him in the action, or his appearance therein. The court below did not consider that an attachment of the property was essential to its jurisdiction or to the validity of the sale, but held that the judgment was invalid from defects in the affidavit upon which the order of publication was obtained, and in the affidavit by which the publication was proved.

What's That?

A *collateral attack* is an attack on a judgment other than through a direct appeal in the initial action. Why was a collateral attack rather than a direct appeal undertaken by Neff?

[The Court rejected this ground for rendering the judgment invalid by concluding that a challenge to the affidavit could only be made in a direct appeal, not in a collateral attack on the judgment as was present here.] * * * [I]t was also contended in that court, and is insisted upon here, that the judgment in the State court against the plaintiff was void for want of personal service of process on him, or of his appearance in the action in which it was rendered and that the premises in controversy could not be subjected to the payment of the demand of a resident creditor except by a proceeding *in rem*; that is, by a direct proceeding against the property for that purpose. If these positions are sound, the ruling of the Circuit Court as to the invalidity of that judgment must be sustained, notwithstanding our dissent from the reasons upon which it was made. And that they are sound would seem to follow from two well-established principles of public law respecting the jurisdiction of an independent State over persons and property. The several States of the Union are not, it is true, in every respect independent, many of the right and powers which originally belonged to them being now vested in the government created by the Constitution. But, except as restrained and limited by that instrument, they possess and exercise

What's That?

Civil status, as used here, refers primarily to marital and parental status. What point is the Court making here about the authority of a state to determine the civil status of its inhabitants?

the authority of independent States, and the principles of public law to which we have referred are applicable to them. One of these principles is, that every State possesses exclusive jurisdiction and sovereignty over persons and property within its territory. As a consequence, every State has the power to determine for itself the civil status and capacities of its inhabitants; to prescribe the subjects upon which they may contract, the forms and solemnities with which their contracts shall be executed, the rights and obligations arising from them, and the mode in which their validity shall be determined and their obligations enforced; and also they regulate the manner and conditions upon which property situated within such territory, both personal and real, may be acquired, enjoyed, and transferred. The other principle of public law referred to follows from the one mentioned; that is, that no State can exercise direct jurisdiction and authority over persons or property without its territory. The several States are of equal dignity and authority, and the independence of one implies the exclusion of power from all others. And so it is laid down by jurists, as an elementary principle, that the laws of one State have no operation outside of its territory, except so far as is allowed by comity; and that no tribunal established by it can extend its process beyond that territory so as to subject either persons or property to its decisions. 'Any exertion of authority of this sort beyond this limit,' says Story, 'is a mere nullity, and incapable of binding such persons or property in any other tribunals.'

What's That?

Comity is a term that refers to the recognition that one government affords to the legislative, executive, or judicial acts of another government, not out of obligation, but out of mutual respect and the desire for reciprocity.

But as contracts made in one State may be enforceable only in another State, and property may be held by non-residents, the exercise of the jurisdiction which every State is admitted to possess over persons and property within its own territory will often affect persons and property without it. To any influence exerted in this way by a State affecting persons resident or property situated elsewhere, no objection can be justly taken; whilst any direct exertion of authority upon them, in an attempt to give ex-territorial operation to its laws, or to enforce an ex-territorial jurisdiction by its tribunals, would be deemed an encroachment upon the independence of the State in which the persons are domiciled or the property is situated, and be resisted as usurpation.

Thus the State, through its tribunals, may compel persons domiciled within its limits to execute, in pursuance of their contracts respecting property elsewhere situated, instruments in such form * * * as to transfer the title, so far as such formalities can be complied with; and the exercise of this jurisdiction in no manner interferes with the supreme control over the property by the State within which it is situated.

So the State, through its tribunals, may subject property situated within its limits owned by non-residents to the payment of the demand of its own citizens against them; and the exercise of this jurisdiction in no respect infringes upon the sovereignty of the State where the owners are domiciled. Every State owes protection to its own citizens; and, when non-residents deal with them, it is a legitimate and just exercise of authority to hold and appropriate any property owned by such non-residents to satisfy the claims of its citizens. It is in virtue of the State's jurisdiction over the property of the non-resident situated within its limits that its tribunals can inquire into that non-resident's obligations to its own citizens, and the inquiry can then be carried only to the extent necessary to control the disposition of the property. If the non-resident [has] no property in the State, there is nothing upon which the tribunals can adjudicate. * * *

* * * If, without personal service, judgments *in personam*, obtained *ex parte* against non-residents and absent parties, upon mere publication of process, which, in the great majority of cases, would never be seen by the parties interested, could be upheld and enforced, they would be the constant instruments of fraud and oppression. Judgments for all sorts of claims upon contracts and for torts, real or pretended, would be thus obtained, under which property would be seized, when the evidence of the transactions upon which they were founded, if they ever had any existence, had perished.

It's Latin to Me!

Ex parte is a Latin phrase that refers to proceedings before a judge that involve one party without notice to or the participation of other interested parties.

Substituted service by publication, or in any other authorized form, may be sufficient to inform parties of the object of proceedings taken where property is once brought under the control of the court by seizure or some equivalent act. The law assumes that property is always in the possession of its owner, in person or by agent; and it proceeds upon the theory that its seizure will inform him, not only that it is taken into the custody of the court, but that he must look to any proceedings authorized by law upon such seizure for its condemnation and sale.

Such service may also be sufficient in cases where the object of the action is to reach and dispose of property in the State, or of some interest therein, by enforcing a contract or a lien respecting the same, or to partition it among different owners, or, when the public is a party, to condemn and

Food for Thought

The Court here indicates instances in which service by publication may be an acceptable means of giving notice of and initiating an action. Why does the Court treat notice by publication as permissible in these cases but not in the present case? What distinction is the Court making?

appropriate it for a public purpose. In other words, such service may answer in all actions which are substantially proceedings *in rem*. But where the entire object of the action is to determine the personal rights and obligations of the defendants, that is, where the suit is merely *in personam*, constructive service in this form upon a non-resident is ineffectual for any purpose. Process from the tribunals of one State cannot run into another State, and summon parties there domiciled to leave its territory and respond to proceedings against them. Publication of process or notice within the State where the tribunal sits cannot create any greater obligation upon the non-resident to appear. Process sent to him out of the State, and process published within it, are equally unavailing in proceedings to establish his personal liability.

The want of authority of the tribunals of a State to adjudicate upon the obligations of non-residents, where they have no property within its limits, is not denied by the court below: but the position is assumed, that, where they have property within the State, it is immaterial whether the property is in the first instance brought under the control of the court by attachment or some other equivalent act, and afterwards applied by its judgment to the satisfaction of demands against its owner; or such demands be first established in a personal action, and the property of the non-resident be afterwards seized and sold on execution. But the answer to this position has already been given in the statement, that the jurisdiction of the court to inquire into and determine his obligations at all is only incidental to its jurisdiction over the property. Its jurisdiction in that respect cannot be made to depend upon facts to be ascertained after it has tried the cause and rendered the judgment. If the judgment be previously void, it will not become valid by the subsequent discovery of property of the defendant, or by his subsequent acquisition of it. The judgment, if void when rendered, will always remain void: it cannot occupy the doubtful position of being valid if property be found, and void if there be none. * * *

The force and effect of judgments rendered against non-residents without personal service of process upon them, or their voluntary appearance, have been the subject of frequent consideration in the courts of the United States and of the several States, as attempts have been made to enforce such judgments in States other than those in which they were rendered, under the provision of the Constitution requiring that 'full faith and credit shall be given in each State to the public acts, records, and judicial proceedings of every other State;' and the act of Congress providing for the mode of authenticating such acts, records, and proceedings, and declaring that, when thus authenticated, 'they shall have such faith and credit given to them in every court within the United States as they have by law or usage in the courts of the State from which they are or shall or [sic] taken.' In the earlier cases, it was supposed that the act gave to all judgments the same effect in other States which they had by law in the State where rendered. But this view was afterwards qualified so as to make the act applicable only when the court rendering the judgment had jurisdiction of the parties and of the subject-matter, and not to preclude an inquiry into the jurisdiction of the court in which the judgment was rendered, or the right of the State itself to exercise authority over the person or the subject-matter. * * *

* * *

Since the adoption of the Fourteenth Amendment to the Federal Constitution, the validity of such judgments may be directly questioned, and their enforcement in the State resisted, on the ground that proceedings in a court of justice to determine the personal rights and obligations of parties over whom that court has no jurisdiction do not constitute due process of law. Whatever difficulty may be experienced in giving to those terms a definition which will embrace every permissible exertion of power affecting private rights, and exclude such as is forbidden, there can be no doubt of their meaning when applied to judicial proceedings. They then mean a course of legal proceedings according to those rules and principles which have been established in our systems of jurisprudence for the protection and enforcement of private rights. To give such proceedings any validity, there must be a tribunal competent by its constitution—that is, by the law of its creation—to pass upon the subject-matter of the suit; and, if that involves merely a determination of the personal liability of the defendant, he must be brought within its jurisdiction by service of process within the State, or his voluntary appearance.

Except in cases affecting the personal *status* of the plaintiff, and cases in which that mode of service may be considered to have been assented to in advance, as hereinafter mentioned, the substituted service of process by publication, allowed by the law of Oregon and by similar laws in other States, where actions are brought against non-residents, is effectual only where, in connection with process against the person for commencing the action, property in the State is brought under the control of the court, and subjected to its disposition by process adapted to that purpose, or where the judgment is sought as a means of reaching such property or affecting some interest therein; in other words, where the action is in the nature of a proceeding *in rem*. * * *

It is true that, in a strict sense, a proceeding *in rem* is one taken directly against property, and has for its object the disposition of the property, without reference to the title of individual claimants; but, in a larger and more general sense, the terms are applied to actions between parties, where the direct object is to reach and dispose of property owned by them, or of some interest therein. Such are cases commenced by attachment against the property of debtors, or instituted to partition real estate, foreclose a mortgage, or enforce a lien. So far as they affect property in the State, they are substantially proceedings *in rem* in the broader sense which we have mentioned. * * *

It follows from the views expressed that the personal judgment recovered in the State court of Oregon against the plaintiff herein, then a non-resident of the State, was without any validity, and did not authorize a sale of the property in controversy.

To prevent any misapplication of the views expressed in this opinion, it is proper to observe that we do not mean to assert, by any thing we have said, that a State may not authorize proceedings to determine the *status* of one of its citizens towards a non-resident, which would be binding within the State, though made without service of process or personal notice to the non-resident. The jurisdiction which every State possesses to determine the civil *status* and capacities of all its inhabitants involves authority to prescribe the conditions on which proceedings affecting them may be commenced and carried on within its territory. The State, for example, has absolute right to prescribe the conditions upon which the marriage relation between its own citizens shall be created, and the causes for which it may be dissolved. One of the parties guilty of acts for which, by the law of the State, a dissolution may be granted, may have removed to a State where no dissolution is permitted. The complaining party would, therefore, fail if a divorce were sought in the State of the defendant; and if application could not be made to the tribunals of the complainant's domicile in such case, and proceedings be there instituted without personal service of process or personal notice to the offending party, the injured citizen would be without redress.

Neither do we mean to assert that a State may not require a non-resident entering into a partnership or association within its limits, or making contracts enforceable there, to appoint an agent or representative in the State to receive service of process and notice in legal proceedings instituted with respect to such partnership, association, or contracts, or to designate a place where such service may be made and notice given, and provide, upon their failure, to make such appointment or to designate such place that service may be made upon a public officer designated for that purpose, or in some other prescribed way, and that judgments rendered upon such service may not be binding upon the non-residents both within and without the State. * * * Nor do we doubt that a State, on creating corporations or other institutions for pecuniary or charitable purposes, may provide a mode in which their conduct may be investigated, their obligations enforced, or their charters revoked, which shall require other than personal service upon their officers or members. Parties becoming members of such corporations or institutions would hold their interest subject to the conditions prescribed by law.

In the present case, there is no feature of this kind, and, consequently, no consideration of what would be the effect of such legislation in enforcing the contract of a non-resident can arise. The question here respects only the validity of a money judgment rendered in one State, in an action upon a simple contract against the resident of another, without service of process upon him, or his appearance therein.

Judgment affirmed.

[The dissenting opinion of JUSTICE HUNT is omitted.]

Points for Discussion

a. Procedural History

Be sure to understand the procedural history of this case. There were two relevant legal proceedings here. Who were the parties and what were the claims and outcomes in each proceeding? What was the key issue that the Supreme Court had to resolve in the case before it? Linda Silberman's article, Shaffer v. Heitner: *The End of an Era*, 53 N.Y.U. L. REV. 33, 44 n.53 (1978), contains a helpful summary of the facts and procedural background of *Pennoyer*.

b. Types of Territorial Jurisdiction

The *Pennoyer* Court distinguished several types of territorial jurisdiction. *In personam* jurisdiction refers to a court's jurisdiction over a person or entity in an action against that party. Why, according to the Court in *Pennoyer*, did the Oregon court fail to obtain *in personam* jurisdiction over Neff?

> **FYI**
>
> Students interested in learning more about the colorful personalities of the litigants in *Pennoyer v. Neff* should consult Wendy Collins Perdue, *Sin, Scandal, and Substantive Due Process: Personal Jurisdiction and Pennoyer Reconsidered*, 62 WASH. L. REV. 479, 480–90 (1987). Also, note that Pennoyer went on to become the eighth Governor of Oregon.

A proceeding that is *in rem* determines the status of property within the court's jurisdiction. A court exercising *in rem* jurisdiction has power only over the property and its disposition; the court lacks power over any of the property's owners. Eminent domain actions or actions to condemn a property would be examples of true *in rem* proceedings. *See* JACK H. FRIEDENTHAL ET AL., CIVIL PROCEDURE § 3.8, at 116 (4th ed. 2005). Closely related to true *in rem* proceedings are *quasi-in-rem* type I actions that seek to resolve competing claims related to a property. For example, if *P* claims title to land in possession of *D*—an out-of-state resident—*P* could initiate a quiet title action in a court with jurisdiction over the property to determine who owns the land as between *P* and *D*. *P* would simply have the court seize or attach the property on a preliminary showing of a colorable claim entitling *P* to relief.

> **Make the Connection**
>
> A *quiet title action* is a proceeding in which a plaintiff seeks to establish title to land with respect to other adverse claimants. You may study such actions further in your first-year **Property** course.

What is the rationale for permitting a court to exercise jurisdiction over property without being able to exercise *in personam* jurisdiction over its owner?

A third category of jurisdiction mentioned in *Pennoyer* is *quasi-in-rem* type II jurisdiction, a type of jurisdiction that gives a court authority to render judgment against a person but limits recovery in the action to the value of property owned by that person within the court's geographical jurisdiction. *See, e.g., Harris v. Balk,* 198 U.S. 215 (1905) (upholding *quasi-in-rem* jurisdiction based on the attachment of debt located within the court's jurisdiction). In effect, attachment of the

> ### It's Latin to Me!
>
> As you will soon discover, Latin terminology permeates the legal lexicon. The three categories of territorial jurisdiction illustrate this fact:
>
> - *In rem* means "against a thing"
> - *In personam* means "against a person"
> - *Quasi in rem* means "as if against a thing"

property is used as a basis for jurisdiction and satisfaction of any ensuing judgment, but the property itself need not be related to the subject matter of the dispute. Can you identify a situation in which this type of *quasi-in-rem* jurisdiction would be appropriate? Could Mitchell have done anything differently to use *quasi-in-rem* jurisdiction to obtain Neff's land?

The Court in *Pennoyer* indicates that different types of notice are acceptable for the various categories of territorial jurisdiction. For example, the Court states, "[W]here the suit is merely *in personam*, constructive service in this form upon a non-resident is ineffectual for any purpose." Why do you think the different types of jurisdiction require or permit different degrees of notice?

c. The Rule of *Pennoyer*

Pennoyer served as the foundation of the constitutional law of personal jurisdiction until the Court's next major statement on the matter in *International Shoe Co. v. Washington,* 326 U.S. 310 (1945) [*infra* at p. 35]. What rule does the *Pennoyer* Court announce as constraining the scope of a court's territorial jurisdiction? Central to *Pennoyer*'s constitutional analysis were references to the Due Process Clause of the Fourteenth Amendment and the Full Faith and Credit Clause of Article IV of the U.S. Constitution. How do each of these provisions relate to personal jurisdiction according to the *Pennoyer* Court? The Court also appeared to base its holding in part on a respect for the proper limits on state sovereign authority. What role did such limits play in shaping the Court's view of jurisdiction?

d. Applications of *Pennoyer*

Transient Presence. Under *Pennoyer*, may a court exercise personal jurisdiction based on service on a defendant who is simply passing through the state briefly? *See Grace v. MacArthur,* 170 F. Supp. 442, 447 (E.D. Ark. 1959) (upholding personal jurisdiction in Arkansas based on service on a defendant while a passenger on an airplane flying over Arkansas airspace). As will be seen later in this chapter, service of process within the forum state remains a viable basis for establishing personal jurisdiction over *natural persons* (not entities) to this day. *See* <u>Burnham v. Superior Court of Cal., County of Marin, 495 U.S. 604, 608–609 (1990)</u>.

State Citizens. Imagine that a citizen of the state in which the case is being litigated (referred to as the *forum state*) is served with process in an action while he is outside of the state's boundaries. Is such service effective to establish personal jurisdiction under *Pennoyer*? *See* <u>Milliken v. Meyer, 311 U.S. 457, 462 (1940)</u> ("Domicile in the state is alone sufficient to bring an absent defendant within the reach of the state's jurisdiction for purposes of a personal judgment by means of appropriate substituted service."). Note that an individual's status as a citizen of a state is determined with reference to their domicile, which refers to the state where a person lives and intends to remain for an indefinite period of time. *See* <u>Miss. Band of Choctaw Indians v. Holyfield, 490 U.S. 30, 48 (1989)</u> ("[D]omicile is established by physical presence in a place in connection with a certain state of mind concerning one's intent to remain there."). An individual real person is always subject to personal jurisdiction in his or her state of domicile. *See* <u>Good-year Dunlop Tires Operations, S.A. v. Brown, 594 U.S 915, 924 (2011)</u> ("For an individual, the paradigm forum for the exercise of general jurisdiction is the individual's domicile. . . .").

Hypo 1.1

Martha, disowned by her family, has moved to Iowa and bought a farm. She is very happy in her new home. Unfortunately, she has a difficult former business partner, Samuel, who believes that Martha owes him money from a failed venture in Delaware. Samuel has sued Martha in Iowa. At the time, Martha was in the Hamptons (NY) visiting family and friends, and so Samuel arranged for Martha to be served with process while she was there. Would the exercise of personal jurisdiction over Martha in Iowa courts be constitutional in this case?

Consent. In *Pennoyer* the Court indicated that either in-state service or one's voluntary appearance was required to assert *in personam* jurisdiction over a defendant. Another way of conceptualizing voluntary appearance is as consent. In other words, one who voluntarily appears before a court is consenting to the

FYI

Nonresident plaintiffs—by filing their claims with a court—may be regarded as having consented to the jurisdiction of the court for any claims that may be filed against them within the same proceeding. *See* <u>Adam v. Saenger, 303 U.S. 59, 67–68 (1938)</u> ("The plaintiff having . . . submitted himself to the jurisdiction of the court, there is nothing arbitrary or unreasonable in treating him as being there for all purposes for which justice to the defendant requires his presence.").

jurisdiction of that court. The *Pennoyer* Court also appeared to endorse the notion that states could extract consent to jurisdiction from various types of entities such as partnerships or corporations. What circumstances did the Court identify as those in which such extracted consent would be permissible?

2. Stretching *Pennoyer* in the Early Twentieth Century

Pennoyer was decided during the era of <u>covered wagons</u> and the <u>horse and buggy</u>, a time when interstate travel was more difficult, and thus, relatively infrequent. However, in the decades after *Pennoyer*, major developments in the national economy—such as the advent of more advanced corporate structures and technological innovations such as the telephone and the automobile—threatened the viability of the jurisdictional doctrine propounded by the *Pennoyer* Court. The early twentieth century witnessed a dramatic increase in interstate travel and communications, with businesses increasingly operating across state lines. Thus, it was more likely that persons or entities from one state would travel through or engage in activities within another state, thereby increasing the likelihood that these out-of-staters would be drawn into interstate litigation.

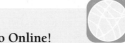

Go Online!

For a good overview of the full array of technological advances witnessed during the course of the first half of the twentieth century in the United States, go online and view Wikipedia's article entitled <u>20th Century</u>.

How could the courts apply *Pennoyer*'s requirement of presence or consent in this new context in which nonresidents might cause harm within the state but not be found within its boundaries for purposes of serving them with process in any ensuing lawsuit? This became the central jurisdictional problem of the early twentieth century. Does *Pennoyer* contain any seeds of an approach one might take to obtaining jurisdiction over an absent nonresident alleged to have caused harm within a state? The next case addresses these questions.

Hess v. Pawloski

Supreme Court of the United States
274 U.S. 352 (1927)

In Error to the Superior Court of Worcester County, Massachusetts.

Mr. Justice BUTLER delivered the opinion of the Court.

This action was brought by defendant in error to recover damages for personal injuries.[*] The declaration alleged that plaintiff in error negligently and wantonly

Take Note!

The Court here uses the terms "defendant in error" and "plaintiff in error" to describe the parties in the case. What do these terms mean? Which term refers to which party? Be sure to sort this out before your classroom discussion of the case.

drove a motor vehicle on a public highway in Massachusetts, and that by reason thereof the vehicle struck and injured defendant in error. Plaintiff in error is a resident of Pennsylvania. No personal service was made on him, and no property belonging to him was attached. The service of process was made in compliance with chapter 90, General Laws of Massachusetts * * * the material parts of which follow:

* * * [T]he operation by a nonresident of a motor vehicle on a public way in the commonwealth * * * shall be deemed equivalent to an appointment by such nonresident of the registrar or his successor in office, to be his true and lawful attorney upon whom may be served all lawful processes in any action or proceeding against him, growing out of any accident or collision in which said nonresident may be involved while operating a motor vehicle on such a way, and said acceptance or operation shall be a signification of his agreement that any such process against him which is so served shall be of the same legal force and validity as if served on him personally. Service of such process shall be made by leaving a copy of the process * * * in the hands of the registrar * * * and such service shall be sufficient service upon the said nonresident: Provided, that notice of such service and a copy of the process are forthwith sent by registered mail by the plaintiff to the defendant, and the defendant's return receipt and the plaintiff's affidavit of compliance herewith are appended to the writ and entered with the declaration. * * *

Plaintiff in error appeared specially for the purpose of contesting jurisdiction, and filed an answer in abatement and moved to dismiss on the ground that the service of process, if sustained, would deprive him of his property without due

---

[*] The victim was between nine and ten years of age at the time of the accident. [Ed.]

process of law, in violation of the Fourteenth Amendment. The court overruled the answer in abatement and denied the motion. The <u>Supreme Judicial Court</u> held the statute to be a valid exercise of the police power, and affirmed the order. At the trial the contention was renewed and again denied. Plaintiff in error excepted. The jury returned a verdict for defendant in error. The exceptions were overruled by the Supreme Judicial Court. Thereupon the superior court entered judgment. The writ of error was allowed by the Chief Justice of that court.

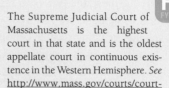

The Supreme Judicial Court of Massachusetts is the highest court in that state and is the oldest appellate court in continuous existence in the Western Hemisphere. *See* http://www.mass.gov/courts/court-info/sjc/about/.

The question is whether the Massachusetts enactment contravenes the due process clause of the Fourteenth Amendment.

The process of a court of one state cannot run into another and summon a party there domiciled to respond to proceedings against him. Notice sent outside the state to a nonresident is unavailing to give jurisdiction in an action against him personally for money recovery. <u>*Pennoyer v. Neff*, 95 U.S. 714 (1877)</u>. There must be actual service within the state of notice upon him or upon some one authorized to accept service for him. A personal judgment rendered against a nonresident, who has neither been served with process nor appeared in the suit, is without validity. The mere transaction of business in a state by nonresident natural persons does not imply consent to be bound by the process of its courts. The power of a state to exclude foreign corporations, although not absolute, but qualified, is the ground on which such an implication is supported as to them. But a state may not withhold from nonresident individuals the right of doing business therein. The privileges and immunities clause of the Constitution (<u>section 2, art. 4</u>), safeguards to the citizens of one state the right 'to pass through, or to reside in any other state for purposes of trade, agriculture, professional pursuits, or otherwise.' And it prohibits state legislation discriminating against citizens of other states.

Motor vehicles are dangerous machines, and, even when skillfully and carefully operated, their use is attended by serious dangers to persons and property. In the public interest the state may make and enforce regulations reasonably calculated to promote care on the part of all, residents and nonresidents alike, who use its highways. The measure in question operates to require a nonresident to answer for his conduct in the state where arise causes of action alleged against him, as well as to provide for a claimant a convenient method by which he may sue to enforce his rights. Under the statute the implied consent is limited to proceedings growing out of accidents or collisions on a highway in which the nonresident may be involved. It is required that he shall actually receive and receipt for notice of the service and a copy of the process. And it contemplates such continuances as may be found necessary to give reasonable time and opportunity for defense. It makes no hostile discrimination against nonresidents, but tends to put them on the same footing as residents. Literal and precise equality in respect of this matter is not attainable; it is not required. The state's power to regulate the use of its highways extends to their use by nonresidents as well as by residents. And, in advance of the operation of a motor vehicle on its highway by a nonresident, the state may require him to appoint one of its officials as his agent on whom process may be served in proceedings growing out of such use. *Kane v. New Jersey,* 242 U.S. 160, 167 (1916). That case recognized power of the state to exclude a nonresident until the formal appointment is made. And, having the power so to exclude, the state may declare that the use of the highway by the nonresident is the equivalent of the appointment of the registrar as agent on whom process may be served. The difference between the formal and implied appointment is not substantial, so far as concerns the application of the due process clause of the Fourteenth Amendment.

Judgment affirmed.

Points for Discussion

a. Implied Consent

In *Hess*, the Court approved of the use of implied consent as a means of exerting personal jurisdiction over nonresident motorists who cause accidents within another state. Is the notion of implied consent consistent with the Court's opinion in *Pennoyer*? Does the implied consent doctrine have applicability outside of the nonresident motorist context?

Take Note!

Although implied consent is embraced in *Hess* as a basis for permitting the exercise of personal jurisdiction, the Court will move toward a different construct when it establishes the modern form of the doctrine in *International Shoe*, the next principal case in this text.

A consent theory was also used by courts to justify jurisdiction over foreign (foreign here meaning out-of-state) corporations. Initially, a corporation's express consent to the appointment of an in-state agent for service of process was required but eventually courts embraced the same notion of implied consent highlighted in *Hess*.

b. The "Doing Business" Approach

Because the concept of implied consent was an uncomfortable legal fiction, courts turned to the notion of presence—borrowing from the other wing of the *Pennoyer* rule—as a means of analyzing whether courts could exercise jurisdiction over foreign corporations. Presence was inferred from the fact that the corporation could be said to be "doing business" within the state, a concept that turned out to provide more of a conclusion than an analytical framework. *See* Philadelphia & Reading Ry. Co. v. McKibbin, 243 U.S. 264, 265 (1917) ("A foreign corporation is amenable to process . . . in the absence of consent, only if it is doing business within the state in such manner and to such extent as to warrant the inference that it is present there."); Int'l Harvester Co. v. Kentucky, 234 U.S. 579, 583, 589 (1914) ("[I]t is essential to the rendition of a personal judgment that the corporation be 'doing business' within the state. . . . We are satisfied that the presence of a corporation within a state necessary to the service of process is shown when it appears that the corporation is there carrying on business in such sense as to manifest its presence within the state . . . ."). How does one determine whether a corporation is doing business in a state? Courts were not uniform in their approach to this question.

The imprecision and malleability of the doing business concept remained and ultimately generated enough foment and jurisdictional unpredictability that the need for the Supreme Court to step in and clear up the doctrinal confusion had intensified by the mid-twentieth century. *See* Philip B. Kurland, *The Supreme Court, the Due Process Clause and the In Personam Jurisdiction of State Courts—From* Pennoyer *to* Denckla: *A Review*, 25 U. CHI. L. REV. 569, 586 (1958) (describing personal jurisdiction doctrine as having been "in so bad a state of disrepair" that "the time had long since passed" for the Court to "set its house in order in this field"). The Court set about doing just that in International Shoe Co. v. Washington, our next case.

B. Modern Personal Jurisdiction Doctrine

International Shoe Co. v. State of Washington

Supreme Court of the United States
326 U.S. 310 (1945)

Appeal from the Supreme Court of the State of Washington.

MR. CHIEF JUSTICE STONE delivered the opinion of the Court.

The questions for decision are (1) whether, within the limitations of the due process clause of the Fourteenth Amendment, appellant, a Delaware corporation, has by its activities in the State of Washington rendered itself amenable to proceedings in the courts of that state to recover unpaid contributions to the state unemployment compensation fund exacted by state statutes and (2) whether the state can exact those contributions consistently with the due process clause of the Fourteenth Amendment.

The statutes in question set up a comprehensive scheme of unemployment compensation, the costs of which are defrayed by contributions required to be made by employers to a state unemployment compensation fund. The contributions are a specified percentage of the wages payable annually by each employer for his employees' services in the state. The assessment and collection of the contributions and the fund are administered by respondents. Section 14(c) of the Act authorizes respondent Commissioner to issue an order and notice of assessment of delinquent contributions upon prescribed personal service of the notice upon the employer if found within the state, or, if not so found, by mailing the notice to the employer by <u>registered mail</u> at his last known address. That section also authorizes the Commissioner to collect the assessment by distraint if it is not paid within ten days after service of the notice. * * * [T]he order of assessment may be administratively reviewed by an appeal tribunal within the office of unemployment upon petition of the employer, and this determination is * * * made subject to judicial review on questions of law by the state Superior Court, with further right of appeal in the state Supreme Court as in other civil cases.

Take Note!

Take note of the adjudicative process set forth here. These orders by the Commissioner are not challenged initially in a trial court, but rather in a state administrative agency. Be sure to understand the path this dispute took to get to the Supreme Court.

In this case notice of assessment for the years in question was personally served upon a sales solicitor employed by appellant in the State of Washington, and a copy of the notice was mailed by registered mail to appellant at its address in St. Louis, Missouri. Appellant appeared specially before the office of unemployment and moved to set aside the order and notice of assessment on the ground that the service upon appellant's salesman was not proper service upon appellant; that appellant was not a corporation of the State of Washington and was not doing business within the state; that it had no agent within the state upon whom service could be made; and that appellant is not an employer and does not furnish employment within the meaning of the statute.

The motion was heard on evidence and a stipulation of facts by the appeal tribunal which denied the motion and ruled that respondent Commissioner was entitled to recover the unpaid contributions. That action was affirmed by the Commissioner; both the Superior Court and the Supreme Court affirmed. Appellant in each of these courts assailed the statute as applied, as a violation of the due process clause of the Fourteenth Amendment, and as imposing a constitutionally prohibited burden on interstate commerce. The cause comes here on appeal, * * * appellant assigning as error that the challenged statutes as applied infringe the due process clause of the Fourteenth Amendment and the commerce clause.

The facts as found by the appeal tribunal and accepted by the state Superior Court and Supreme Court, are not in dispute. Appellant is a Delaware corporation having its principal place of business in St. Louis, Missouri, and is engaged in the manufacture and sale of shoes and other footwear. It maintains places of business in several states, other than Washington, at which its manufacturing is carried on and from which its merchandise is distributed interstate through several sales units or branches located outside the State of Washington.

FYI

You may be wondering why many corporations that otherwise have no connection with Delaware are incorporated there. The perception that Delaware has more favorable laws governing corporations mostly explains this phenomenon. Delaware's official website for its Division of Corporations (http://www.corp.delaware.gov/) touts this and other benefits of choosing Delaware as a corporate home.

Appellant has no office in Washington and makes no contracts either for sale or purchase of merchandise there. It maintains no stock of merchandise in that state and makes there no deliveries of goods in intrastate commerce. During the years from 1937 to 1940, now in question, appellant employed eleven to thirteen salesmen under direct supervision and control of sales managers located in St. Louis. These salesmen resided in Washington; their principal activities were confined to that state; and they were compensated by commissions based upon the amount of their sales. The commissions for each year totaled more than $31,000. Appellant supplies its salesmen with a line of samples, each consisting of one shoe of a pair, which they display to prospective purchasers. On occasion they rent permanent sample rooms, for exhibiting samples, in business buildings, or rent rooms in hotels or business buildings temporarily for that purpose. The cost of such rentals is reimbursed by appellant.

The authority of the salesmen is limited to exhibiting their samples and soliciting orders from prospective buyers, at prices and on terms fixed by appellant. The salesmen transmit the orders to appellant's office in St. Louis for acceptance or rejection, and when accepted the merchandise for filling the orders is shipped f.o.b. from points outside Washington to the purchasers within the state. All the merchandise shipped into Washington is invoiced at the place of shipment from which collections are made. No salesman has authority to enter into contracts or to make collections.

What's That?

F.o.b. is an abbreviation for *free on board.* This is a shipping term indicating that the seller pays shipping costs and is responsible for the goods until they are delivered to the buyer's carrier or vessel, at which point the seller's delivery is complete and the buyer becomes responsible for the goods.

The Supreme Court of Washington was of opinion that the regular and systematic solicitation of orders in the state by appellant's salesmen, resulting in a continuous flow of appellant's product into the state, was sufficient to constitute doing business in the state so as to make appellant amenable to suit in its courts. But it was also of opinion that there were sufficient additional activities shown to bring the case within the rule frequently stated, that solicitation within a state by the agents of a foreign corporation plus some additional activities there are sufficient to render the corporation amenable to suit brought in the courts of the state to enforce an obligation arising out of its activities there. The court found such additional activities in the salesmen's display of samples sometimes in permanent display rooms, and the salesmen's residence within the state, continued over a period of years, all resulting in a substantial volume of merchandise regularly shipped by appellant to purchasers within the state. * * *

Appellant * * * insists that its activities within the state were not sufficient to manifest its 'presence' there and that in its absence the state courts were without jurisdiction, that consequently it was a denial of due process for the state to subject appellant to suit. It refers to those cases in which it was said that the mere solicitation of orders for the purchase of goods within a state, to be accepted without the state and filled by shipment of the purchased goods interstate, does not render the corporation seller amenable to suit within the state. And appellant further argues that since it was not present within the state, it is a denial of due process to subject it to taxation or other money exaction. It thus denies the power of the state to lay the tax or to subject appellant to a suit for its collection.

Historically the jurisdiction of courts to render judgment *in personam* is grounded on their de facto power over the defendant's person. Hence his presence within the territorial jurisdiction of court was prerequisite to its rendition of a judgment personally binding him. <u>Pennoyer v. Neff, 95 U.S. 714 (1877)</u>. But now that the capias ad respondendum has given way to personal service of summons or other form of notice, due process requires only that in order to subject a defendant to a judgment *in personam*, if he be not present within the territory of the forum, he have certain minimum contacts with it such that the maintenance of the suit does not offend 'traditional notions of fair play and substantial justice.' <u>Milliken v. Meyer, 311 U.S. 457, 463 (1940)</u>. *See* <u>Holmes</u>, J., in <u>McDonald v. Mabee, 243 U.S. 90, 91 (1917)</u>.

Make the Connection

The "corporate personality" referred to in this paragraph is the corporation, which is a business entity treated as a legal person—distinct from its shareholders and individual officers and directors—that exists indefinitely. This is a concept you will study further in a basic **Corporations** or **Business Associations** course.

Since the corporate personality is a fiction, although a fiction intended to be acted upon as though it were a fact, it is clear that unlike an individual its 'presence' without, as well as within, the state of its origin can be manifested only by activities carried on in its behalf by those who are authorized to act for it. To say that the corporation is so far 'present' there as to satisfy due process requirements, for purposes of taxation or the maintenance of suits against it in the courts of the state, is to beg the question to be decided. For the terms 'present' or 'presence' are used merely to symbolize those activities of the corporation's agent within the state which courts will deem to be sufficient to satisfy the demands of due process. Those demands may be met by such contacts of the corporation with the state of the forum as make it reasonable, in the context of our federal system of government, to require the corporation to defend the particular suit which is brought there. An 'estimate of the inconveniences' which would result to the corporation from a trial away from its 'home' or principal place of business is relevant in this connection.

'Presence' in the state in this sense has never been doubted when the activities of the corporation there have not only been continuous and systematic, but also give rise to the liabilities sued on, even though no consent to be sued or authorization to an agent to accept service of process has been given. Conversely it has been generally recognized that the casual presence of the corporate agent or even his conduct of single or isolated items of activities in a state in the corporation's behalf are not enough to subject it to suit on causes of action unconnected with the activities there. To require the corporation in such circumstances to defend the suit away from its home or other jurisdiction where it carries on more substantial activities has been thought to lay too great and unreasonable a burden on the corporation to comport with due process.

While it has been held in cases on which appellant relies that continuous activity of some sorts within a state is not enough to support the demand that the corporation be amenable to suits unrelated to that activity there have been instances in which the continuous corporate operations within a state were thought so substantial and of such a nature as to justify suit against it on causes of action arising from dealings entirely distinct from those activities.

Finally, although the commission of some single or occasional acts of the corporate agent in a state sufficient to impose an obligation or liability on the corporation has not been thought to confer upon the state authority to enforce it, other such acts, because of their nature and quality and the circumstances of their commission, may be deemed sufficient to render the corporation liable to suit. *Cf. Kane v. New Jersey*, 242 U.S. 160 (1916); *Hess v. Pawloski*, 274 U.S. 352 (1927). True, some of the decisions holding the corporation amenable to suit have been supported by resort to the legal fiction that it has given its consent to service and suit, consent being implied from its presence in the state through the acts of its authorized agents. But more realistically it may be said that those authorized acts were of such a nature as to justify the fiction.

It is evident that the criteria by which we mark the boundary line between those activities which justify the subjection of a corporation to suit, and those which do not, cannot be simply mechanical or quantitative. The test is not merely, as has sometimes been suggested, whether the activity, which the corporation has seen fit to procure through its agents in another state, is a little more or a little less. Whether due process is satisfied must depend rather upon the quality and nature of the activity in relation to the fair and orderly administration of the laws which it was the purpose of the due process clause to insure. That clause does not contemplate that a state may make binding a judgment *in personam* against an individual or corporate defendant with which the state has no contacts, ties, or relations. *Cf. Pennoyer v. Neff*.

But to the extent that a corporation exercises the privilege of conducting activities within a state, it enjoys the benefits and protection of the laws of that state. The exercise of that privilege may give rise to obligations; and, so far as those obligations arise out of or are connected with the activities within the state, a procedure which requires the corporation to respond to a suit brought to enforce them can, in most instances, hardly be said to be undue.

Applying these standards, the activities carried on in behalf of appellant in the State of Washington were neither irregular nor casual. They were systematic and continuous throughout the years in question. They resulted in a large volume of interstate business, in the course of which appellant received the benefits and protection of the laws of the state, including the right to resort to the courts for the enforcement of its rights. The obligation which is here sued upon arose out of those very activities. It is evident that these operations establish sufficient contacts or ties with the state of the forum to make it reasonable and just according to our traditional conception of fair play and substantial justice to permit the state to enforce the obligations which appellant has incurred there. Hence we cannot say that the maintenance of the present suit in the State of Washington involves an unreasonable or undue procedure.

We are likewise unable to conclude that the service of the process within the state upon an agent whose activities establish appellant's 'presence' there was not sufficient notice of the suit, or that the suit was so unrelated to those activities as to make the agent an inappropriate vehicle for communicating the notice. It is enough that appellant has established such contacts with the state that the particular form of substituted service adopted there gives reasonable assurance that the notice will be actual. Nor can we say that the mailing of the notice of suit to appellant by registered mail at its home office was not reasonably calculated to apprise appellant of the suit. * * *

Appellant having rendered itself amenable to suit upon obligations arising out of the activities of its salesmen in Washington, the state may maintain the present suit *in personam* to collect the tax laid upon the exercise of the privilege of employing appellant's salesmen within the state. For Washington has made one of those activities, which taken together establish appellant's 'presence' there for purposes of suit, the taxable event by which the state brings appellant within the reach of its taxing power. The state thus has constitutional power to lay the tax and to subject appellant to a suit to recover it. The activities which establish its 'presence' subject it alike to taxation by the state and to suit to recover the tax.

Affirmed.

Mr. Justice JACKSON took no part in the consideration or decision of this case.

Mr. Justice BLACK delivered the following opinion.

* * *

* * * The Court * * * has engaged in an unnecessary discussion in the course of which it has announced vague Constitutional criteria applied for the first time to the issue before us. It has thus introduced uncertain elements confusing the simple pattern and tending to curtail the exercise of State powers to an extent not justified by the Constitution.

* * *

I believe that the Federal Constitution leaves to each State, without any 'ifs' or 'buts', a power to tax and to open the doors of its courts for its citizens to sue corporations whose agents do business in those States. Believing that the Constitution gave the States that power, I think it a judicial deprivation to condition its exercise upon this Court's notion of 'fairplay', however appealing that term may be. Nor can I stretch the meaning of due process so far as to authorize this Court to deprive a State of the right to afford judicial protection to its citizens on the ground that it would be more 'convenient' for the corporation to be sued somewhere else.

There is a strong emotional appeal in the words 'fair play', 'justice', and 'reasonableness.' But they were not chosen by those who wrote the original Constitution or the Fourteenth Amendment as a measuring rod for this Court to use in invalidating State or Federal laws passed by elected legislative representatives. No one, not even those who most feared a democratic government, ever formally proposed that courts should be given power to invalidate legislation under any such elastic standards. Express prohibitions against certain types of legislation are found in the Constitution, and under the long settled practice, courts invalidate laws found to conflict with them. This requires interpretation, and interpretation, it is true, may result in extension of the Constitution's purpose. But that is no reason for reading the due process clause so as to restrict a State's power to tax and sue those whose activities affect persons and businesses within the State, provided proper service can be had. * * *

Points for Discussion

a. The *International Shoe* Approach

In what way does the Court in *International Shoe* depart from and revise the jurisdictional standard set forth in *Pennoyer*? What is the approach to analyzing personal jurisdiction that the *International Shoe* Court announces here and how does it differ from the "doing business" approach?

Take Note!

Note that although *International Shoe* involved a corporation as the defendant, the Supreme Court has subsequently affirmed that the minimum contacts analysis applies equally to cases involving individual defendants. *Kulko v. Superior Court*, 436 U.S. 84, 92 (1978).

In *International Shoe*, the Court states that in order for a state to exercise jurisdiction over a defendant, the defendant must "have certain minimum contacts with it such that the maintenance of the suit does not offend 'traditional notions of fair play and substantial justice.' " What does this statement mean? How does the Court elaborate on this phrase? Does the minimum contacts approach provide a workable standard for courts to apply to determine personal jurisdiction in specific cases? Does this approach represent an improvement, at least in terms of clarity and predictability, on the doing business approach?

b. Specific and General Jurisdiction

In the text of its opinion, the *International Shoe* Court makes the distinction between cases in which the defendant's contacts "give rise to the liabilities sued on" and actions in which those contacts are "unrelated" to the allegations in the suit. Courts and commentators have come to use the term specific jurisdiction to refer to cases involving forum contacts that are related to the claims asserted in the action and the term general jurisdiction for suits involving only unrelated forum state contacts. What does the Court say in *International Shoe* about the circumstances under which a defendant's contacts will suffice to support jurisdiction in each of these contexts?

It is worth noting here that the Supreme Court has used the phrases "related to" or "arises out of" interchangeably to describe the nature of the connection between a defendant's contacts and the underlying cause of action in the specific jurisdiction context. *See Helicopteros Nacionales de Colombia, S.A. v. Hall*, 466 U.S. 408, 415 n.10 (1984). Lower courts have split on the issue of what type of relationship suffices. *Compare Bird v. Parsons*, 289 F.3d 865, 875 (6th Cir. 2002) ("If a defendant's contacts with the forum state are related to the operative facts of the controversy, then an action will be deemed to have arisen from those contacts."), *with Doe v. Unocal Corp.*, 248 F.3d 915, 924 (9th Cir. 2001) (applying a "but for" test to determine whether a cause of action arises out of forum contacts). Thus, in practice, some sensitivity to this issue may be necessary depending upon the approach taken by the circuit in which jurisdiction is being sought.

c. State Sovereignty and the Minimum Contacts Standard

State sovereignty figured prominently in *Pennoyer* as a basis for the Court's conclusion that a state's assertion of personal jurisdiction required in-state presence or consent. Is the minimum contacts approach of *International Shoe* similarly rooted in notions of state sovereignty or do other factors—such as fairness and convenience—feature more prominently? What are the interests that the Court is trying to protect with its revised jurisdictional doctrine?

The Court seems to indicate that a sort of quid pro quo is at work here when it connects a defendant's receipt of "benefits" from operating within a state to a concomitant "obligation" to submit to that court's jurisdiction. Is this concept reminiscent of the theory of implied consent articulated in *Hess* above? Note that although the *International Shoe* approach would affirm the outcome in *Hess*, the implied consent rationale featured in *Hess* is no longer valid after *International Shoe*.

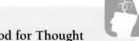

Food for Thought

Can you articulate how the *Hess* result can be reached using the *International Shoe* analysis?

d. Justice Black's Opinion

What is Justice Black's quarrel with the principal opinion in *International Shoe*? Do you share his concerns and agree with his views of the meaning of due process?

e. The Analytical Framework Established by *International Shoe*

Be sure to understand the nature of the jurisdictional analysis created by *International Shoe*. To test your understanding of the case, consider the following hypothetical problems:

Hypo 1.2

A truck owned by ABC, Inc. (a State A corporation based in State B), and driven by one of its employees traveled through State C on its way to State D to deliver some merchandise there. While in State C, the truck collided with a car driven by a rancher, who was injured in the accident. The rancher filed suit against ABC in State C, alleging negligence by the ABC truck driver. Assuming the ABC truck driver was acting within the scope of employment when the accident occurred, would the exercise of personal jurisdiction over ABC in State C courts be constitutional in this case?

Hypo 1.3

In State A there lives a former employee of a corporation who once lived and worked for the company in its State B headquarters (the corporation is also incorporated in State B). The former employee initiated an action against the corporation in State A federal court, asserting a claim for wrongful termination. To achieve service of process, the former employee served the driver of one of the corporation's delivery trucks while it was stopped at a gas station in State A. Would the exercise of personal jurisdiction over the corporation in State A courts be constitutional in this case?

C. Specific Jurisdiction: Applying the Minimum Contacts Analysis

Just as litigants constantly battled over the precise meaning of "doing business" prior to *International Shoe*, in the wake of *International Shoe* there was much litigation over the meaning of the term "minimum contacts" and the degree of contacts necessary to support an assertion of personal jurisdiction. Before we turn to a consideration of the Supreme Court's line of cases that address this issue, it is important first to understand the proper relation of the doctrine of *International Shoe* to the actual assertion of jurisdiction within state courts.

1. State "Long-Arm" Statutes: The Statutory Authority for Personal Jurisdiction

a. The Role of Long-Arm Statutes in a Jurisdictional Analysis

International Shoe was a decision that articulated the constitutional limits on exercises of personal jurisdiction, holding that jurisdiction is constitutionally permissible in circumstances where it can be said that the defendant has minimum contacts with the forum state such that the exercise of jurisdiction is fair and reasonable. The *International Shoe* decision did not, however, mandate that state courts actually exercise jurisdiction to the fullest extent permitted by the Constitution. Whether states would exercise personal jurisdiction over a defendant in any given case was solely a decision for each state to make and they were free to assert merely some or all of the jurisdictional authority the *International Shoe* Court indicated was available to them.

States identify the range of circumstances in which they wish to exercise personal jurisdiction over defendants through jurisdictional statutes (often referred to as long-arm statutes). A personal jurisdiction analysis must typically begin with these statutes because they determine—as a matter of state statutory law—whether the court at issue has the authority to exercise jurisdiction over the defendant.

Once it is determined that such statutory authority indeed exists, it then becomes necessary to determine whether—as a matter of federal constitutional law—the Constitution indeed permits an assertion of personal jurisdiction under such circumstances. *See, e.g.,* Gray v. Am. Radiator & Standard Sanitary Corp., 176 N.E.2d 761 (Ill. 1961).

b. The Types of Long-Arm Statutes

Long-arm statutes are similar to the Massachusetts nonresident motorist statute in Hess v. Pawloski that treated the operation of a motor vehicle within the state as equivalent to the appointment of a certain state official as the operator's agent for service of process. After the notion of implied consent embodied in the Massachusetts statute was validated by the Court in *Hess*, states were encouraged to enact similar statutes and to expand the reach of such statutes beyond motor vehicle activity to other activities within the state.

The decision in *International Shoe*, though repudiating implied consent in favor of the minimum contacts approach, only accelerated and expanded this trend of states reaching out to assert jurisdiction over nonresidents. *International Shoe* identified the broad contours of the circumstances under which the assertion of jurisdiction over nonresidents would be constitutionally permissible. States sought to give these circumstances more specificity by promulgating long-arm statutes that articulated the specific circumstances under which they would attempt to subject defendants to personal jurisdiction in their courts. Many states did this by enumerating jurisdiction-triggering contacts specifically. New York's long-arm statute illustrates this approach:

> **FYI**
>
> To see a comprehensive presentation of the long-arm statutes from each of the states (as of 2003) compiled by the law firm of Vedder Price, click here.

N.Y. Civil Practice Law & Rules: § 302.

Personal jurisdiction by acts of non-domiciliaries

(a) **Acts which are the basis of jurisdiction.** As to a cause of action arising from any of the acts enumerated in this section, a court may exercise personal jurisdiction over any non-domiciliary, or his executor or administrator, who in person or through an agent:

   1.   transacts any business within the state or contracts anywhere to supply goods or services in the state; or

   2.   commits a tortious act within the state, except as to a cause of action for defamation of character arising from the act; or

> 3. commits a tortious act without the state causing injury to person or property within the state, except as to a cause of action for defamation of character arising from the act, if he
>
>   (i) regularly does or solicits business, or engages in any other persistent course of conduct, or derives substantial revenue from goods used or consumed or services rendered, in the state, or
>
>   (ii) expects or should reasonably expect the act to have consequences in the state and derives substantial revenue from interstate or international commerce; or
>
> 4. owns, uses or possesses any real property situated within the state.
>
>   * * *

Under an enumerated act statute of this kind, if the defendant has not engaged in any conduct set forth in the statute, then the courts of the state will not be able to exercise jurisdiction over that defendant, even if such an exercise of jurisdiction would be constitutional. Why do you think a state would leave out situations in which it does not wish to exercise personal jurisdiction? **Figure 1.1** illustrates the relationship between enumerated act long-arm statutes and the constitutional scope of personal jurisdiction.

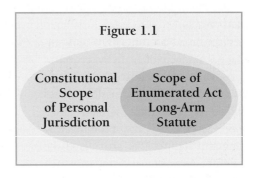

States that have not opted for the enumerated act approach have decided that they are interested in asserting personal jurisdiction to the fullest extent permissible under the U.S. Constitution. Thus, these states have promulgated statutes to that effect by using language such as one will find in Rhode Island's long-arm statute:

R.I. General Laws: § 9–5–33(a).

Jurisdiction over foreign corporations and over nonresident individuals, partnerships, or associations

(a) Every foreign corporation, every individual not a resident of this state or his or her executor or administrator, and every partnership or association, composed of any person or persons not such residents, that shall have the necessary minimum contacts with the state of Rhode Island, shall be subject to the jurisdiction of the state of Rhode Island, and the courts of this state shall hold such foreign corporations and such nonresident individuals or their executors or administrators, and such partnerships or associations amenable to suit in Rhode Island in every case not contrary to the provisions of the constitution or laws of the United States.

Notwithstanding this distinction between the enumerated act model and the Rhode Island model for long-arm statutes, many states having what appear on their face to be enumerated act statutes have nonetheless interpreted those statutes to allow personal jurisdiction to the fullest extent permitted under the Constitution. Oklahoma provides but one example of this phenomenon. *See Fields v. Volkswagen of Am., Inc.*, 555 P.2d 48, 52 (Okla. 1976) ("The intention in Oklahoma is to extend the jurisdiction of Oklahoma courts over non-residents to the outer limits permitted by the due process requirements of the United States Constitution."); *see also Woodring v. Hall*, 438 P.2d 135, 141 (Kan. 1968) (holding that Kansas's long-arm statute enumerating specific acts "reflects a conscientious state policy to assert jurisdiction over nonresident defendants to the extent permitted by the due process clause of the Fourteenth Amendment to the Constitution of the United States").

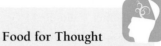

Food for Thought

Does this practice of state courts interpreting enumerated act long-arm statutes to extend to the limits of due process make any sense? *See* Douglas D. McFarland, *Dictum Run Wild: How Long-Arm Statutes Extended to the Limits of Due Process*, 84 B.U. L. Rev. 491, 538–40 (2004).

When a state has a long-arm statute that either follows the Rhode Island model or has been interpreted to extend jurisdiction to the full limits of due process, the standard two-step process of analyzing the statutory and constitutional authority to exercise jurisdiction collapses into a single-step constitutional analysis. *See, e.g., Batton v. Tenn. Farmers Mut. Ins. Co.*, 736 P.2d 2, 4 (Ariz. 1987) ("[T]his two-step inquiry [looking first at the long-arm rule and then at due process] is redundant because our interpretation extends [the Arizona long-arm statute] to the permissible limits of due process.").

2. Minimum Contacts: The Constitutional Authority for Personal Jurisdiction

Turning to the constitutional analysis established by *International Shoe*, the next two cases illustrate the Supreme Court's early efforts to clarify the scope of its new minimum contacts doctrine.

McGee v. International Life Insurance Co.

Supreme Court of the United States
355 U.S. 220 (1957)

Opinion of the Court by MR. JUSTICE BLACK, announced by MR. JUSTICE DOUGLAS.

Petitioner, Lulu B. McGee, recovered a judgment in a California state court against respondent, International Life Insurance Company, on a contract of insur-

What's That?

In cases before the Supreme Court on a petition for *certiorari*, the party who is challenging the ruling of the previous court is referred to as the *petitioner* and the responding party is the *respondent*. These terms bear no necessary relationship to which party was the plaintiff or defendant in the trial court.

ance. Respondent was not served with process in California but by registered mail at its principal place of business in Texas. The California court based its jurisdiction on a state statute which subjects foreign corporations to suit in California on insurance contracts with residents of that State even though such corporations cannot be served with process within its borders.

Unable to collect the judgment in California petitioner went to Texas where she filed suit on the judgment in a Texas court. But the Texas courts refused to enforce her judgment holding it was void under the Fourteenth Amendment because service of process outside California could not give the courts of that State jurisdiction over respondent. * * *

The material facts are relatively simple. In 1944, Lowell Franklin, a resident of California, purchased a life insurance policy from the Empire Mutual Insurance Company, an Arizona corporation. In 1948 the respondent agreed with Empire Mutual to assume its insurance obligations. Respondent then mailed a reinsurance certificate to Franklin in California offering to insure him in accordance with the terms of the policy he held with Empire Mutual. He accepted this offer and from that time until his death in 1950 paid premiums by mail from his California home to respondent's Texas office. Petitioner Franklin's mother was the beneficiary under the policy. She sent proofs of his death to the respondent but it refused to pay claiming that he had committed suicide. It appears that neither Empire Mutual nor respondent has ever had any office or agent in California. And so far as the record before us shows, respondent has never solicited or done any insurance business in California apart from the policy involved here.

Since *Pennoyer v. Neff*, 95 U.S. 714 (1877), this Court has held that the Due Process Clause of the Fourteenth Amendment places some limit on the power of state courts to enter binding judgments against persons not served with process within their boundaries. But just where this line of limitation falls has been the subject of prolific controversy, particularly with respect to foreign corporations. In a continuing process of evolution this Court accepted and then abandoned 'consent,' 'doing business,' and 'presence' as the standard for measuring the extent of state judicial power over such corporations. More recently in <u>International Shoe Co. v. State of Washington, 326 U.S. 310 (1945)</u> the Court decided that "due process requires only that in order to subject a defendant to a judgment *in personam*, if he be not present within the territory of the forum, he have certain minimum contacts with it such that the maintenance of the suit does not offend 'traditional notions of fair play and substantial justice.' "

Looking back over this long history of litigation a trend is clearly discernible toward expanding the permissible scope of state jurisdiction over foreign corporations and other nonresidents. In part this is attributable to the fundamental transformation of our national economy over the years. Today many commercial transactions touch two or more States and may involve parties separated by the full continent. With this increasing nationalization of commerce has come a great increase in the amount of business conducted by mail across state lines. At the same time modern transportation and communication have made it much less burdensome for a party sued to defend himself in a State where he engages in economic activity.

Food for Thought

The Court here acknowledges a trend of expanding the permissible scope of state jurisdiction over nonresidents. Given that constitutional personal jurisdiction doctrine is based on the Due Process Clause—a provision that does not change—how is it that the permissible scope of jurisdiction can change over time? Is it that the Due Process Clause is supposed to be malleable and accommodating of new circumstances or is it that the Court was overly narrow in its previous interpretation of what the clause would allow?

Turning to this case we think it apparent that the Due Process Clause did not preclude the California court from entering a judgment binding on respondent. It is sufficient for purposes of due process that the suit was based on a contract which had substantial connection with that State. The contract was delivered in California, the premiums were mailed from there and the insured was a resident of that State when he died. It cannot be denied that California has a manifest interest in providing effective means of redress for its residents when their insurers refuse to pay claims. These residents would be at a severe disadvantage if they were forced to follow the insurance company to a distant State in order to hold it legally accountable. When claims were small or moderate individual claimants frequently could not afford the cost of bringing an action in a foreign forum—thus in effect making the company judgment proof. Often the crucial witnesses—as here on the company's defense of suicide—will be found in the insured's locality. Of course there may be inconvenience to the insurer if it is held amenable to suit in California where it had this contract but certainly nothing which amounts to a denial of due process. There is no contention that respondent did not have adequate notice of the suit or sufficient time to prepare its defenses and appear.

* * *

The judgment is reversed and the cause is remanded * * * for further proceedings not inconsistent with this opinion.

It is so ordered.

Hanson v. Denckla

Supreme Court of the United States
357 U.S. 235 (1958)

Mr. Chief Justice Warren delivered the opinion of the Court.

This controversy concerns the right to $400,000, part of the corpus of a trust established in Delaware by a settlor who later became domiciled in Florida. One group of claimants, 'legatees,' urge that this property passed under the residuary clause of the settlor's will, which was admitted to probate in Florida. The Florida courts have sustained this position. Other claimants, 'appointees' and 'beneficiaries,' contend that the property passed pursuant to the settlor's exercise of the *inter vivos* power of appointment created in the deed of trust. The Delaware courts adopted this position and refused to accord full faith and credit to the Florida determination because the Florida court had not acquired jurisdiction over an indispensable party, the Delaware trustee. * * *

Take Note!

Although the date of this case (1958) indicates that *Hanson* was decided in the year following *McGee*, both cases were decided during the same Term by the same Justices. Think about whether the results in each case are consistent with one another.

Make the Connection

A *trust* is an entity created to hold assets for the benefit of persons or other entities. Trusts are a subject you may study either in your **Property** course or a course on **Trusts & Estates**.

The trust whose validity is contested here was created in 1935. Dora Browning Donner, then a domiciliary of Pennsylvania, executed a trust instrument in Delaware naming the

Wilmington Trust Co., of Wilmington, Delaware, as trustee. The corpus was composed of securities. Mrs. Donner reserved the income for life, and stated that the remainder should be paid to such persons or upon such trusts as she should appoint by *inter vivos* or testamentary instrument. The trust agreement provided that Mrs. Donner could change the trustee, and that she could amend, alter or revoke the agreement at any time. * * * A few days after the trust was established Mrs. Donner exercised her power of appointment. That appointment was replaced by another in 1939. Thereafter she left Pennsylvania, and in 1944 became domiciled in Florida, where she remained until her death in 1952. Mrs. Donner's will

It's Latin to Me!

Corpus is Latin for "body" and refers to the property for which a trustee is responsible. *Inter vivos* is Latin for "between the living" and refers to property conveyed not by a will but during the conveyor's lifetime.

was executed Dec. 3, 1949. On that same day she executed the *inter vivos* power of appointment whose terms are at issue here. * * * [S]he appointed the sum of $200,000 to each of two trusts previously established with another Delaware trustee, the Delaware Trust Co. * * *

The two trusts with the Delaware Trust Co. were created in 1948 by Mrs. Donner's daughter, Elizabeth Donner Hanson, for the benefit of Elizabeth's children, Donner Hanson and Joseph Donner Winsor. In identical terms they provide that the income not required for the beneficiary's support should be accumulated to age 25, when the beneficiary should be paid 1/4 of the corpus and receive the income from the balance for life. * * *

Mrs. Donner died Nov. 20, 1952. Her will, which was admitted to probate in Florida, named Elizabeth Donner Hanson as executrix. * * * After disposing of personal and household effects, Mrs. Donner's will directed that the balance of her property (the $1,000,000 appointed from the Delaware trust) be paid in equal parts to two trusts for the benefit of her daughters Katherine N. R. Denckla and Dorothy B. R. Stewart.

This controversy grows out of the residuary clause that created the last mentioned trusts. * * * Residuary legatees Denckla and Stewart, already the recipients of over $500,000 each, urge that the power of appointment over the $400,000 appointed to sister Elizabeth's children was not 'effectively exercised' and that the property should accordingly pass to them. Fourteen months after Mrs. Donner's death these parties petitioned a Florida chancery court for a declaratory judgment 'concerning what property passes under the residuary clause' of the will. Personal service was had upon the following defendants: (1) executrix Elizabeth Donner Hanson, (2) beneficiaries Donner Hanson and Joseph Donner Winsor, and (3) potential beneficiary William Donner Roosevelt, also one of Elizabeth's children. * * * About a dozen other defendants were nonresidents and could not be personally served. These included the Wilmington Trust Co. ('trustee'), the Delaware Trust Co. (to whom the $400,000 had been paid shortly after Mrs. Donner's death), certain individuals who were potential successors in interest to complainants Denckla and Stewart, and most of the named appointees in Mrs. Donner's 1949 appointment. A copy of the pleadings and a 'Notice to Appear and Defend' were sent to each of these defendants by ordinary mail, and notice was published locally as required by the Florida statutes dealing with constructive service. * * *

The appearing defendants (Elizabeth Donner Hanson and her children) moved to dismiss the suit because the exercise of jurisdiction over indispensable parties, the Delaware trustees, would offend Section 1 of the Fourteenth Amendment [the Due Process Clause]. The Chancellor ruled that he lacked jurisdiction over these nonresident defendants because no personal service was had and because the trust corpus was outside the territorial jurisdiction of the court. The cause was dismissed as to them. As far as parties before the court were concerned, however, he ruled that the power of appointment was testamentary and void under the applicable Florida law. In a decree dated Jan. 14, 1955, he ruled that the $400,000 passed under the residuary clause of the will.

After the Florida litigation began, but before entry of the decree, the executrix instituted a declaratory judgment action in Delaware to determine who was entitled to participate in the trust assets held in that State. Except for the addition of beneficiary Winsor and several appointees, the parties were substantially the same as in the Florida litigation. * * * All of the trust companies, beneficiaries, and legatees except Katherine N. R. Denckla, appeared and participated in the litigation. After the Florida court enjoined executrix Hanson from further participation, her children pursued their own interests. When the Florida decree was entered the legatees unsuccessfully urged it as *res judicata* of the Delaware dispute. In a decree * * * the Delaware Chancellor ruled that the trust and power of appointment were valid under the applicable Delaware law * * * .

It's Latin to Me!

Res judicata, which is Latin for "a thing adjudicated," is a doctrine that prevents the relitigation of matters that a tribunal has already authoritatively decided. This topic will be covered in Chapter 11.

Alleging that she would be bound by the Delaware decree, the executrix moved the Florida Supreme Court to remand with instructions to dismiss the Florida suit then pending on appeal. * * * The motion was denied. The Florida Supreme Court affirmed its Chancellor's conclusion that Florida law applied to determine the validity of the trust and power of appointment. Under that law the trust was invalid * * *. The Chancellor's conclusion that there was no jurisdiction over the trust companies and other absent defendants was reversed. The court ruled that jurisdiction to construe the will carried with it 'substantive' jurisdiction 'over the persons of the absent defendants' * * * .

[On the issue of whether Delaware was obligated to give full faith and credit to the Florida decree, the Delaware courts ruled that the Florida decree was] not binding for purposes of full faith and credit because the Florida court had no personal jurisdiction over the trust companies and no jurisdiction over the trust *res*.

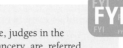

In Delaware, judges in the Court of Chancery are referred to as Chancellors. Delaware's chancery court is the tribunal that deals with disputes involving trusts and estates, as well as internal corporate matters. More information on Delaware's court system is available at www.courts.delaware.gov/Courts. Although Florida appears to have had a similar arrangement at the time, it no longer has chancery courts within its system. *See* www.ncsconline.org/D_Research/CT_Struct/state_inc.asp?STATE=FL.

The issues for our decision are, first, whether Florida erred in holding that it had jurisdiction over the nonresident defendants, and second, whether Delaware erred in refusing full faith and credit to the Florida decree. * * *

* * * Appellees [argue] for *in personam* jurisdiction over the Delaware trustee. They urge that the circumstances of this case amount to sufficient affiliation with the State of Florida to empower its courts to exercise personal jurisdiction over this nonresident defendant. Principal reliance is placed upon <u>McGee v. International Life Ins. Co., 355 U.S. 220 (1957)</u>. In *McGee* the Court noted the trend of expanding personal jurisdiction over nonresidents. As technological progress has increased the flow of commerce between States, the need for jurisdiction over nonresidents has undergone a similar increase. At the same time, progress in communications and transportation has made the defense of a suit in a foreign tribunal less burdensome. In response to these changes, the requirements for personal jurisdiction over non-residents have evolved from the rigid rule of <u>Pennoyer v. Neff</u>, to the flexible standard of *International Shoe Co. v. State of Washington*. But it is a mistake to assume that this trend heralds the eventual demise of all restrictions on the personal jurisdiction of state courts. Those restrictions are more than a guarantee of immunity from inconvenient or distant litigation. They are a consequence of territorial limitations on the power of the respective States. However minimal the burden of defending in a foreign tribunal, a defendant may not be called upon to do so unless he has had the 'minimal contacts' with that State that are a prerequisite to its exercise of power over him.

We fail to find such contacts in the circumstances of this case. The defendant trust company has no office in Florida, and transacts no business there. None of the trust assets has ever been held or administered in Florida, and the record discloses no solicitation of business in that State either in person or by mail.

The cause of action in this case is not one that arises out of an act done or transaction consummated in the forum State. In that respect, it differs from *McGee v. International Life Ins. Co.* * * * . In *McGee*, the nonresident defendant solicited a reinsurance agreement with a resident of California. The offer was accepted in that State, and the insurance premiums were mailed from there until the insured's death. Noting the interest California has in providing effective redress for its residents when nonresident insurers refuse to pay claims on insurance they have solicited in that State, the Court upheld jurisdiction because the suit 'was based on a contract which had substantial connection with that State.' In contrast, this action involves the validity of an agreement that was entered without any connection with the forum State. The agreement was executed in Delaware by a trust company incorporated in that State and a settlor domiciled in Pennsylvania. The first relationship Florida had to the agreement was years later when the settlor became domiciled there, and the trustee remitted the trust income to her in that State. From Florida Mrs. Donner carried on several bits of trust administration that may be compared to the mailing of premiums in *McGee*. But the record discloses no instance in which the trustee performed any acts in Florida that bear the same relationship to the agreement as the solicitation in *McGee*. Consequently, this suit cannot be said to be one to enforce an obligation that arose from a privilege the defendant exercised in Florida. This case is also different from *McGee* in that there the State had enacted special legislation * * * to exercise what *McGee* called its 'manifest interest' in providing effective redress for citizens who had been injured by nonresidents engaged in an activity that the State treats as exceptional and subjects to special regulation.

The execution in Florida of the powers of appointment under which the beneficiaries and appointees claim does not give Florida a substantial connection with the contract on which this suit is based. * * * The unilateral activity of those who claim some relationship with a nonresident defendant cannot satisfy the requirement of contact with the forum State. The application of that rule will vary with the quality and nature of the defendant's activity, but it is essential in each case that there be some act by which the defendant purposefully avails itself of the privilege of conducting activities within the forum State, thus invoking the benefits and protections of its laws. *International Shoe Co. v. State of Washington*. The settlor's execution in Florida of her power of appointment cannot remedy the absence of such an act in this case.

It is urged that because the settlor and most of the appointees and beneficiaries were domiciled in Florida the courts of that State should be able to exercise personal jurisdiction over the nonresident trustees. This is a nonsequitur [sic]. With personal jurisdiction over the executor, legatees, and appointees, there is nothing in federal law to prevent Florida from adjudicating concerning the respective rights and liabilities of those parties. But Florida has not chosen to do so. As we understand its law, the trustee is an indispensable party over whom the court must acquire jurisdiction before it is empowered to enter judgment in a proceeding affecting the validity of a trust. It does not acquire that jurisdiction by being the 'center of gravity' of the controversy, or the most convenient location for litigation. The issue is personal jurisdiction, not choice of law. It is resolved in this case by considering the acts of the trustee. As we have indicated, they are insufficient to sustain the jurisdiction. * * *

* * * The same reasons that compel reversal of the Florida judgment require affirmance of the Delaware one. Delaware is under no obligation to give full faith and credit to a Florida judgment invalid in Florida because [it is] offensive to the Due Process Clause of the Fourteenth Amendment. * * *

The judgment of the Delaware Supreme Court is affirmed, and the judgment of the Florida Supreme Court is reversed and the cause is remanded for proceedings not inconsistent with this opinion.

It is so ordered.

MR. JUSTICE BLACK, whom MR. JUSTICE BURTON and MR. JUSTICE BRENNAN join, dissenting.

* * *

In light of the foregoing circumstances it seems quite clear to me that there is nothing in the Due Process Clause which denies Florida the right to determine whether Mrs. Donner's appointment was valid * * * . This disposition, which was designed to take effect after her death, had very close and substantial connections with that State. Not only was the appointment made in Florida by a domiciliary of Florida, but the primary beneficiaries also lived in that State. In my view it could hardly be denied that Florida had sufficient interest so that a court with jurisdiction might properly apply Florida law, if it chose, to determine whether the appointment was effectual. True, the question whether the law of a State can be applied to a transaction is different from the question whether the courts of that State have jurisdiction to enter a judgment, but the two are often closely related and to a substantial degree depend upon similar considerations. It seems to me that where a transaction has as much relationship to a State as Mrs. Donner's appointment had to Florida its courts ought to have power to adjudicate controversies arising out of that transaction, unless litigation there would impose such a heavy and disproportionate burden on a nonresident defendant that it would offend what this Court has referred to as 'traditional notions of fair play and substantial justice.' So far as the nonresident defendants here are concerned I can see nothing which approaches that degree of unfairness. Florida, the home of the principal contenders for Mrs. Donner's largess, was a reasonably convenient forum for all. Certainly there is nothing fundamentally unfair in subjecting the corporate trustee to the jurisdiction of the Florida courts. It chose to maintain business relations with Mrs. Donner in that State for eight years, regularly communicating with her with respect to the business of the trust including the very appointment in question.

Florida's interest in the validity of Mrs. Donner's appointment is made more emphatic by the fact that her will is being administered in that State. It has traditionally been the rule that the State where a person is domiciled at the time of his death is the proper place to determine the validity of his will, to construe its provisions and to marshal and distribute his personal property. * * *

[The dissenting opinion by MR. JUSTICE DOUGLAS is omitted.]

Points for Discussion

a. Lessons from *McGee* and *Hanson*

McGee involved an isolated contact—an insurance contract with a forum resident—in a suit on that contract. How did the Court apply the minimum contacts test to analyze these facts of *McGee*? What were the relevant forum contacts in *Hanson* and how did the court apply the minimum contacts analysis to those contacts?

What further development of the *International Shoe* minimum contacts doctrine occurs in *McGee* and *Hanson*? One important development to note is the *McGee* Court's consideration of factors such as the forum state's interest, the interests of persons pursuing such claims, the inconvenience to the defendant, and the location of witnesses as relevant to the jurisdictional analysis. Another important development to note is *Hanson* Court's emphasis on state sovereignty as part of the theoretical underpinning for its jurisdictional doctrine: "[R]estrictions on the personal jurisdiction of state courts . . . are more than a guarantee of immunity from inconvenient or distant litigation. They are a consequence of territorial limitations on the power of the respective States." What elements of the minimum contacts analysis reflect a concern for state sovereignty? In *McGee* and in *Hanson*, which interests seem to hold more sway, state sovereignty or fairness? The *Hanson* Court also developed personal jurisdiction doctrine by clarifying how to determine whether one's forum state contacts count for purposes of establishing personal jurisdiction:

> The unilateral activity of those who claim some relationship with a nonresi-
> dent defendant cannot satisfy the requirement of contact with the forum
> State. The application of that rule will vary with the quality and nature of
> the defendant's activity, but it is essential in each case that there be some
> act by which the defendant purposefully avails itself of the privilege of

conducting activities within the forum State, thus invoking the benefits and protections of its laws.

Hanson, 357 U.S. at 253. See if you understand the contours of the minimum contacts doctrine in the wake of *Hanson* and *McGee* by trying the following hypothetical problem:

Hypo 1.4

A customer from State A purchased a ladder from a local hardware store based in State A. Afterwards, the customer moved to State B. The following month, the customer returned to State A for a visit, told the owner of the hardware store about the move to State B, and bought a chain saw. Back in State B, the customer was injured while standing on the ladder attempting to trim a tree with the chain saw. The ladder collapsed and the chain saw cut him badly.

The customer initiated an action against the owner of the hardware store in State B federal court alleging that both the stepladder and the chain saw were defective. May the State B federal court constitutionally exercise personal jurisdiction over the owner in this case?

b. Distinguishing *McGee* and *Hanson*

The facts of these two cases are similar in that an out-of-state defendant is in a business relationship with forum residents. How does the Court distinguish the facts of *Hanson* from those of *McGee* to reach a different outcome? Is the Court's distinction persuasive? If Mrs. Donner had been alive and wanted to sue the trustees in Florida for a dispute regarding the trust, do you think the Court would have upheld jurisdiction in Florida? If so, why did the Court not uphold Florida jurisdiction in *Hanson*? Does the fact that there was a competing judgment from another state bear on this question?

McGee indicated that the forum state's interest in providing a forum for resolving the suit was a factor in determining whether personal jurisdiction was proper. Each state in *McGee* and *Hanson* had some interest in the subject matter of the underlying lawsuits. Which state had a stronger interest in the respective disputes resolved in *McGee* and *Hanson*, California or Florida? What about the relative strengths of the interests of Delaware and Florida in *Hanson*; was Delaware's interest stronger than Florida's? Do the jurisdictional outcomes in *McGee* and *Hanson* align with the strength of each state's interest? If not, what other factors are entering the analysis to produce a different outcome than a pure interest analysis would suggest?

c. The Winners and Losers in *McGee* and *Hanson*

As a practical matter, what were the personal outcomes in these two cases? The Court's decision in *McGee* meant that an insurance beneficiary was able to collect on her judgment against an insurer for its failure to pay insurance proceeds due. The decision in *Hanson* meant that the decedent's two grandchildren were able to keep their $400,000 inheritance from being taken by their aunts who already shared an inheritance of $1 million. Do you think that these prospective outcomes had any impact on the Court's decision on the jurisdictional issues? If the Court had held in *Hanson*, for example, that the Florida judgment was valid and entitled to respect by Delaware courts, the Donner grandchildren would have been disinherited, a result some may not have viewed as just. Does the minimum contacts doctrine allow for such considerations to come into play?

d. Technological Innovation and Jurisdiction

The Court in *McGee* referred to technological and economic changes in society that had, by that time, facilitated greater interstate travel and eased the burdens of defending suits outside of one's home state. How did these developments factor into the Court's interpretation of the minimum contacts doctrine and its application to the facts of that case? Given the rapid technological innovation that characterizes life in the twenty-first century, and the utility of particular advances such as the Internet and instant electronic communications, think about what impact societal advances should have on personal jurisdiction analysis, if any, in view of the role accorded to such advances by the Court in *McGee*.

World-Wide Volkswagen Corp. v. Woodson

Supreme Court of the United States
444 U.S. 286 (1980)

MR. JUSTICE WHITE delivered the opinion of the Court.

* * *

I

Respondents Harry and Kay Robinson purchased a new Audi automobile from petitioner Seaway Volkswagen, Inc. (Seaway), in Massena, N.Y., in 1976. The following year the Robinson family, who resided in New York, left that State for a new home in Arizona. As they passed through the State of Oklahoma, another car struck their Audi in the rear, causing a fire which severely burned Kay Robinson and her two children.

The Robinsons subsequently brought a products-liability action in the <u>District Court for Creek County, Okla.</u>, claiming that their injuries resulted from defective design and placement of the Audi's gas tank and fuel system. They joined as defendants the automobile's manufacturer, Audi NSU Auto Union Aktiengesellschaft (Audi); its importer Volkswagen of America, Inc. (Volkswagen); its regional distributor, petitioner World-Wide Volkswagen Corp. (World-Wide); and its retail dealer, petitioner Seaway. Seaway and World-Wide entered special appearances, claiming that Oklahoma's exercise of jurisdiction over them would offend the limitations on the State's jurisdiction imposed by the Due Process Clause of the Fourteenth Amendment.

Take Note!

Notice that Audi and Volkswagen did not challenge jurisdiction here. Why do you think that is so?

The facts presented to the District Court showed that World-Wide is incorporated and has its business office in New York. It distributes vehicles, parts, and accessories, under contract with Volkswagen, to retail dealers in New York, New Jersey, and Connecticut. Seaway, one of these retail dealers, is incorporated and has its place of business in New York. Insofar as the record reveals, Seaway and World-Wide are fully independent corporations whose relations with each other and with Volkswagen and Audi are contractual only. Respondents adduced no evidence that either World-Wide or Seaway does any business in Oklahoma, ships or sells any products to or in that State, has an agent to receive process there, or purchases advertisements in any media calculated to reach Oklahoma. In fact, as respondents' counsel conceded at oral argument there was no showing that any automobile sold by World-Wide or Seaway has ever entered Oklahoma with the single exception of the vehicle involved in the present case.

Despite the apparent paucity of contacts between petitioners and Oklahoma, the District Court rejected their constitutional claim and reaffirmed that ruling in denying petitioners' motion for reconsideration. Petitioners then sought a writ of prohibition in the <u>Supreme Court of Oklahoma</u> to restrain the District Judge, respondent Charles S. Woodson, from exercising *in personam* jurisdiction over them. They renewed their contention that, because they had no "minimal contacts" with the State of Oklahoma, the actions of the District Judge were in violation of their rights under the Due Process Clause.

Take Note!

The judge referred to in the text is the "Woodson" that appears in the caption in this case. Why is the judge a party rather than the Robinsons?

The Supreme Court of Oklahoma denied the writ, holding that personal jurisdiction over petitioners was authorized by Oklahoma's "long-arm" statute. Okla. Stat., Tit. 12, § 1701.03(a)(4) (1971).[7] Although the court noted that the proper approach was to test jurisdiction against both statutory and constitutional standards, its analysis did not distinguish these questions, probably because [Oklahoma's long-arm statute] has been interpreted as conferring jurisdiction to the limits permitted by the United States Constitution. The court's rationale was contained in the following paragraph:

> "In the case before us, the product being sold and distributed by the petitioners is by its very design and purpose so mobile that petitioners can foresee its possible use in Oklahoma. This is especially true of the distributor, who has the exclusive right to distribute such automobile in New York, New Jersey and Connecticut. The evidence presented below demonstrated that goods sold and distributed by the petitioners were used in the State of Oklahoma, and under the facts we believe it reasonable to infer, given the retail value of the automobile, that the petitioners derive substantial income from automobiles which from time to time are used in the State of Oklahoma. This being the case, we hold that under the facts presented, the trial court was justified in concluding that the petitioners derive substantial revenue from goods used or consumed in this State." * * *

II

The Due Process Clause of the Fourteenth Amendment limits the power of a state court to render a valid personal judgment against a nonresident defendant. A judgment rendered in violation of due process is void in the rendering State and is not entitled to full faith and credit elsewhere. Due process requires that the defendant be given adequate notice of the suit, and be subject to the personal jurisdiction of the court. In the present case, it is not contended that notice was inadequate; the only question is whether these particular petitioners were subject to the jurisdiction of the Oklahoma courts.

As has long been settled, and as we reaffirm today, a state court may exercise personal jurisdiction over a nonresident defendant only so long as there exist "minimum contacts" between the defendant and the forum State. The concept of minimum contacts, in turn, can be seen to perform two related, but distinguishable, functions. It protects the defendant against the burdens of litigating in a distant or inconvenient forum. And it acts to ensure that the States through their courts,

---

[7]   This subsection provides: "A court may exercise personal jurisdiction over a person, who acts directly or by an agent, as to a cause of action or claim for relief arising from the person's . . . causing tortious injury in this state by an act or omission outside this state if he regularly does or solicits business or engages in any other persistent course of conduct, or derives substantial revenue from goods used or consumed or services rendered, in this state . . . ." * * * [This provision has since been repealed. Ed.]

do not reach out beyond the limits imposed on them by their status as coequal sovereigns in a federal system.

The protection against inconvenient litigation is typically described in terms of "reasonableness" or "fairness." We have said that the defendant's contacts with the forum State must be such that maintenance of the suit "does not offend 'traditional notions of fair play and substantial justice.'" The relationship between the defendant and the forum must be such that it is "reasonable . . . to require the corporation to defend the particular suit which is brought there." Implicit in this emphasis on reasonableness is the understanding that the burden on the defendant, while always a primary concern, will in an appropriate case be considered in light of other relevant factors, including the forum State's interest in adjudicating the dispute, see *McGee v. International Life Ins. Co., 355 U.S. 220 (1957)*; the plaintiff's interest in obtaining convenient and effective relief, at least when that interest is not adequately protected by the plaintiff's power to choose the forum; the interstate judicial system's interest in obtaining the most efficient resolution of controversies; and the shared interest of the several States in furthering fundamental substantive social policies.

The limits imposed on state jurisdiction by the Due Process Clause, in its role as a guarantor against inconvenient litigation, have been substantially relaxed over the years. As we noted in *McGee*, this trend is largely attributable to a fundamental transformation in the American economy:

> "Today many commercial transactions touch two or more States and may involve parties separated by the full continent. With this increasing nationalization of commerce has come a great increase in the amount of business conducted by mail across state lines. At the same time modern transportation and communication have made it much less burdensome for a party sued to defend himself in a State where he engages in economic activity."

The historical developments noted in *McGee*, of course, have only accelerated in the generation since that case was decided.

Nevertheless, we have never accepted the proposition that state lines are irrelevant for jurisdictional purposes, nor could we, and remain faithful to the principles of interstate federalism embodied in the Constitution. The economic interdependence of the States was foreseen and desired by the Framers. In the Commerce Clause, they provided that the Nation was to be a common market, a "free trade unit" in which the States are debarred from acting as separable economic entities. But the Framers also intended that the States retain many essential attributes of sovereignty, including, in particular, the sovereign power to try causes in their courts. The sovereignty of each State, in turn, implied a limitation on the sovereignty of all of its sister States—a limitation express or implicit in both the original scheme of the Constitution and the Fourteenth Amendment.

Hence, even while abandoning the shibboleth that "[t]he authority of every tribunal is necessarily restricted by the territorial limits of the State in which it is established," *Pennoyer v. Neff, 95 U.S. 714, 720 (1877)*, we emphasized that the reasonableness of asserting jurisdiction over the defendant must be assessed "in the context of our federal system of government," *International Shoe*, and stressed that the Due Process Clause ensures not only fairness, but also the "orderly administration of the laws," *id.* * * *

Thus, the Due Process Clause "does not contemplate that a state may make binding a judgment *in personam* against an individual or corporate defendant with which the state has no contacts, ties, or relations." *International Shoe, 326 U.S. 310, 319 (1945)*. Even if the defendant would suffer minimal or no inconvenience from being forced to litigate before the tribunals of another State; even if the forum State has a strong interest in applying its law to the controversy; even if the forum State is the most convenient location for litigation, the Due Process Clause, acting as an instrument of interstate federalism, may sometimes act to divest the State of its power to render a valid judgment. *Hanson v. Denckla, 357 U.S. 235 (1958)*.

III

Applying these principles to the case at hand we find in the record before us a total absence of those affiliating circumstances that are a necessary predicate to any exercise of state-court jurisdiction. Petitioners carry on no activity whatsoever in Oklahoma. They close no sales and perform no services there. They avail themselves of none of the privileges and benefits of Oklahoma law. They solicit no business there either through salespersons or through advertising reasonably calculated to reach the State. Nor does the record show that they regularly sell cars at wholesale or retail to Oklahoma customers or residents or that they indirectly, through others, serve or seek to serve the Oklahoma market. In short, respondents seek to base jurisdiction on one, isolated occurrence and whatever inferences can be drawn therefrom: the fortuitous circumstance that a single Audi automobile, sold in New York to New York residents, happened to suffer an accident while passing through Oklahoma.

It is argued, however, that because an automobile is mobile by its very design and purpose it was "foreseeable" that the Robinsons' Audi would cause injury in Oklahoma. Yet "foreseeability" alone has never been a sufficient benchmark for personal jurisdiction under the Due Process Clause. In *Hanson v. Denckla*, it was no doubt foreseeable that the settlor of a Delaware trust would subsequently move to Florida and seek to exercise a power of appointment there; yet we held that Florida courts could not constitutionally exercise jurisdiction over a Delaware trustee that had no other contacts with the forum State. * * *

If foreseeability were the criterion * * * [e]very seller of chattels would in effect appoint the chattel his agent for service of process. His amenability to suit would travel with the chattel. * * *

This is not to say, of course, that foreseeability is wholly irrelevant. But the foreseeability that is critical to due process analysis is not the mere likelihood that a product will find its way into the forum State. Rather, it is

What's That?

A *chattel* is simply a legal term for movable physical property.

that the defendant's conduct and connection with the forum State are such that he should reasonably anticipate being haled into court there. The Due Process Clause, by ensuring the "orderly administration of the laws," gives a degree of predictability to the legal system that allows potential defendants to structure their primary conduct with some minimum assurance as to where that conduct will and will not render them liable to suit.

When a corporation "purposefully avails itself of the privilege of conducting activities within the forum State," *Hanson v. Denckla*, it has clear notice that it is subject to suit there, and can act to alleviate the risk of burdensome litigation by procuring insurance, passing the expected costs on to customers, or, if the risks are too great, severing its connection with the State. Hence if the sale of a product of a manufacturer or distributor such as Audi or Volkswagen is not simply an isolated occurrence, but arises from the efforts of the manufacturer or distributor to serve directly or indirectly, the market for its product in other States, it is not unreasonable to subject it to suit in one of those States if its allegedly defective merchandise has there been the source of injury to its owner or to others. The forum State does not exceed its powers under the Due Process Clause if it asserts personal jurisdiction over a corporation that delivers its products into the stream of commerce with the expectation that they will be purchased by consumers in the forum State.

But there is no such or similar basis for Oklahoma jurisdiction over World-Wide or Seaway in this case. Seaway's sales are made in Massena, N.Y. World-Wide's market, although substantially larger, is limited to dealers in New York, New Jersey, and Connecticut. * * * It is foreseeable that the purchasers of automobiles sold by World-Wide and Seaway may take them to Oklahoma. But the mere "unilateral activity of those who claim some relationship with a nonresident defendant cannot satisfy the requirement of contact with the forum State." *Hanson v. Denckla*.

In a variant on the previous argument, it is contended that jurisdiction can be supported by the fact that petitioners earn substantial revenue from goods used in Oklahoma. * * * While this inference seems less than compelling on the facts * * *, we need not question the court's factual findings in order to reject its reasoning.

This argument seems to make the point that the purchase of automobiles in New York, from which the petitioners earn substantial revenue, would not occur *but for* the fact that the automobiles are capable of use in distant States like Oklahoma. Respondents observe that the very purpose of an automobile is to travel, and that travel of automobiles sold by petitioners is facilitated by an extensive chain of Volkswagen service centers throughout the country, including some in Oklahoma.[12] However, financial benefits accruing to the defendant from a collateral relation to the forum State will not support jurisdiction if they do not stem from a constitutionally cognizable contact with that State. In our view, whatever marginal revenues petitioners may receive by virtue of the fact that their products are capable of use in Oklahoma is far too attenuated a contact to justify that State's exercise of *in personam* jurisdiction over them.

Because we find that petitioners have no "contacts, ties, or relations" with the State of Oklahoma, the judgment of the Supreme Court of Oklahoma is

Reversed.

[The dissenting opinions of JUSTICE MARSHALL and JUSTICE BLACKMUN are omitted.]

JUSTICE BRENNAN, dissenting.

The Court holds that the Due Process Clause of the Fourteenth Amendment bars the States from asserting jurisdiction over the defendants in these two cases. In each case the Court so decides because it fails to find the "minimum contacts" that have been required since *International Shoe Co. v. Washington*, 326 U.S. 310, 316 (1945). Because I believe that the Court reads *International Shoe* and its progeny too narrowly, and because I believe that the standards enunciated by those cases may already be obsolete as constitutional boundaries, I dissent.

I

The Court's opinions focus tightly on the existence of contacts between the forum and the defendant. In so doing, they accord too little weight to the strength of the forum State's interest in the case and fail to explore whether there would be any actual inconvenience to the defendant. The essential inquiry in locating the constitutional limits on state-court jurisdiction over absent defendants is whether the particular exercise of jurisdiction offends " 'traditional notions of fair play and substantial justice.' " The clear focus in *International Shoe* was on fairness and rea-sonableness. The Court specifically declined to establish a mechanical test based on the quantum of contacts between a State and the defendant * * * . * * *

Surely *International Shoe* contemplated that the significance of the contacts necessary to support jurisdiction would diminish if some other consideration helped

---

[12] As we have noted, petitioners earn no direct revenues from these service centers.

establish that jurisdiction would be fair and reasonable. The interests of the State and other parties in proceeding with the case in a particular forum are such considerations. *McGee v. International Life Ins. Co., 355 U.S. 220, 223 (1957)*, for instance, accorded great importance to a State's "manifest interest in providing effective means of redress" for its citizens.

Another consideration is the actual burden a defendant must bear in defending the suit in the forum. Because lesser burdens reduce the unfairness to the defendant, jurisdiction may be justified despite less significant contacts. The burden, of course, must be of constitutional dimension. Due process limits on jurisdiction do not protect a defendant from all inconvenience of travel * * * . Instead, the constitutionally significant "burden" to be analyzed relates to the mobility of the defendant's defense. For instance, if having to travel to a foreign forum would hamper the defense because witnesses or evidence or the defendant himself were immobile, or if there were a disproportionately large number of witnesses or amount of evidence that would have to be transported at the defendant's expense, or if being away from home for the duration of the trial would work some special hardship on the defendant, then the Constitution would require special consideration for the defendant's interests.

* * *

II

* * * I would find that the forum State has an interest in permitting the litigation to go forward, the litigation is connected to the forum, the defendant is linked to the forum, and the burden of defending is not unreasonable. Accordingly, I would hold that it is neither unfair nor unreasonable to require these defendants to defend in the forum State.

* * *

B

In [this case] the interest of the forum State and its connection to the litigation is strong. The automobile accident underlying the litigation occurred in Oklahoma. The plaintiffs were hospitalized in Oklahoma when they brought suit. Essential witnesses and evidence were in Oklahoma. The State has a legitimate interest in enforcing its laws designed to keep its highway system safe, and the trial can proceed at least as efficiently in Oklahoma as anywhere else.

The petitioners are not unconnected with the forum. Although both sell automobiles within limited sales territories, each sold the automobile which in fact was driven to Oklahoma where it was involved in an accident.[8] It may be true, as the Court suggests, that each sincerely intended to limit its commercial impact to the limited territory, and that each intended to accept the benefits and protection of the laws only of those States within the territory. But obviously these were unrealistic hopes that cannot be treated as an automatic constitutional shield.[9]

An automobile simply is not a stationary item or one designed to be used in one place. An automobile is *intended* to be moved around. Someone in the business of selling large numbers of automobiles can hardly plead ignorance of their mobility or pretend that the automobiles stay put after they are sold. It is not merely that a dealer in automobiles foresees that they will move. The dealer actually intends that the purchasers will use the automobiles to travel to distant States where the dealer does not directly "do business." The sale of an automobile does *purposefully* inject the vehicle into the stream of interstate commerce so that it can travel to distant States. * * *

Furthermore, an automobile seller derives substantial benefits from States other than its own. A large part of the value of automobiles is the extensive, nationwide network of highways. Significant portions of that network have been constructed by and are maintained by the individual States, including Oklahoma. The States, through their highway programs, contribute in a very direct and important way to the value of petitioners' businesses. Additionally, a network of other related dealerships with their service departments operates throughout the country under the protection of the laws of the various States, including Oklahoma, and enhances the value of petitioners' businesses by facilitating their customers' traveling.

Thus, the Court errs in its conclusion that "petitioners have *no* 'contacts, ties, or relations' " with Oklahoma. There obviously are contacts, and, given Oklahoma's connection to the litigation, the contacts are sufficiently significant to make it fair and reasonable for the petitioners to submit to Oklahoma's jurisdiction.

III

It may be that affirmance of the judgments in these cases would approach the outer limits of *International Shoe*'s jurisdictional principle. But that principle, with its almost exclusive focus on the rights of defendants, may be outdated. * * * *International Shoe* inherited its defendant focus from *Pennoyer v. Neff*, 95 U.S. 714

---

[8] On the basis of this fact the state court inferred that the petitioners derived substantial revenue from goods used in Oklahoma. The inference is not without support. Certainly, were use of goods accepted as a relevant contact, a plaintiff would not need to have an exact count of the number of petitioners' cars that are used in Oklahoma.

[9] Moreover, imposing liability in this case would not so undermine certainty as to destroy an automobile dealer's ability to do business. According jurisdiction does not expand liability except in the marginal case where a plaintiff cannot afford to bring an action except in the plaintiff's own State. In addition, these petitioners are represented by insurance companies. They not only could, but did, purchase insurance to protect them should they stand trial and lose the case. The costs of the insurance no doubt are passed on to customers.

(1878), and represented the last major step this Court has taken in the long process of liberalizing the doctrine of personal jurisdiction. Though its flexible approach represented a major advance, the structure of our society has changed in many significant ways since *International Shoe* was decided in 1945. * * *

As the Court acknowledges both the nationalization of commerce and the ease of transportation and communication have accelerated in the generation since 1957. The model of society on which the *International Shoe* Court based its opinion is no longer accurate. Business people, no matter how local their businesses, cannot assume that goods remain in the business'[s] locality. * * *

In answering the question whether or not it is fair and reasonable to allow a particular forum to hold a trial binding on a particular defendant, the interests of the forum State and other parties loom large in today's world and surely are entitled to as much weight as are the interests of the defendant. The "orderly administration of the laws" provides a firm basis for according some protection to the interests of plaintiffs and States as well as of defendants. Certainly, I cannot see how a defendant's right to due process is violated if the defendant suffers no inconvenience.

The conclusion I draw is that constitutional concepts of fairness no longer require the extreme concern for defendants that was once necessary. Rather, * * * minimum contacts must exist "among the parties, the contested transaction, and the forum State."[15] The contacts between any two of these should not be determinative. * * * Assuming that a State gives a nonresident defendant adequate notice and opportunity to defend, I do not think the Due Process Clause is offended merely because the defendant has to board a plane to get to the site of the trial.

The Court's opinion * * * suggests that the defendant ought to be subject to a State's jurisdiction only if he has contacts with the State "such that he should reasonably anticipate being haled into court there."[18] There is nothing unreasonable or unfair, however, about recognizing commercial reality. Given the tremendous mobility of goods and people, and the inability of businessmen to control where goods are taken by customers (or retailers), I do not think that the defendant should be in complete control of the geographical stretch of his amenability to suit. * * * When an action in fact causes injury in another State, the actor should be prepared to answer for it there unless defending in that State would be unfair for some reason other than that a state boundary must be crossed.

---

[15] In some cases, the inquiry will resemble the inquiry commonly undertaken in determining which State's law to apply. That it is fair to apply a State's law to a nonresident defendant is clearly relevant in determining whether it is fair to subject the defendant to jurisdiction in that State.

[18] The Court suggests that this is the critical foreseeability rather than the likelihood that the product will go to the forum State. But the reasoning begs the question. A defendant cannot know if his actions will subject him to jurisdiction in another State until we have declared what the law of jurisdiction is.

In effect the Court is allowing defendants to assert the sovereign rights of their home States. * * * I would not abolish limits on jurisdiction or strip state boundaries of all significance; I would still require the plaintiff to demonstrate sufficient contacts among the parties, the forum, and the litigation to make the forum a reasonable State in which to hold the trial.

I would also, however, strip the defendant of an unjustified veto power over certain very appropriate fora—a power the defendant justifiably enjoyed long ago when communication and travel over long distances were slow and unpredictable and when notions of state sovereignty were impractical and exaggerated. But I repeat that that is not today's world. If a plaintiff can show that his chosen forum State has a sufficient interest in the litigation (or sufficient contacts with the defendant), then the defendant who cannot show some real injury to a constitutionality protected interest, should have no constitutional excuse not to appear.[21]

The plaintiffs * * * brought suit in a forum with which they had significant contacts and which had significant contacts with the litigation. I am not convinced that the defendants would suffer any "heavy and disproportionate burden" in defending the suits. Accordingly, I would hold that the Constitution should not shield the defendants from appearing and defending in the plaintiffs' chosen fora.

Points for Discussion

a. Minimum Contacts After *World-Wide Volkswagen*

The majority opinion indicates that "[t]he concept of minimum contacts . . . can be seen to perform two related, but distinguishable, functions," which it identifies as protecting defendants against burdensome, inconvenient litigation and enforcing a respect for interstate federalism and the limits on state sovereign authority. How does the Court in *World-Wide Volkswagen* develop the minimum contacts analysis to protect these two distinct interests?

In elaborating on the nature of contacts one must have with the forum state, the *World-Wide Volkswagen* Court emphasized the importance of a defendant being able to "reasonably anticipate being haled into court" there, which can be said to be the case when the defendant "purposefully avails itself of the privilege of conducting activities within the forum state." The roots of these understandings can be found in *Hanson*.

With respect to the concept of "reasonableness" within the jurisdictional analysis, the *World-Wide Volkswagen* Court identified an array of relevant considerations,

---

[21] Frequently, of course, the defendant will be able to influence the choice of forum through traditional doctrines, such as venue or *forum non conveniens*, permitting the transfer of litigation.

including the interests of the defendant, the plaintiff, the forum state, other states, and the "interstate judicial system." The incorporation of these factors into the analysis is largely the legacy of *McGee*. Together, the *World-Wide Volkswagen* Court's understanding of minimum contacts and reasonableness gives shape to the modern doctrine of specific personal jurisdiction in place today.

b. Practical Outcome

After concluding that Oklahoma could not exercise personal jurisdiction over World-Wide and Seaway, the absence of those two defendants made it possible to remove the case from Oklahoma state court to federal district court in Oklahoma. [Removal of cases from state to federal court is a subject covered in Chapter 3.] After removal, the Robinsons lost their case when the federal jury returned a verdict for the defendants. This was quite unfortunate for the Robinsons, given the horrible injuries they suffered in the accident:

> Since Kay Robinson had been trapped in the burning car the longest . . . [s]he had burns on forty-eight percent of her body . . . . Most of her fingers were amputated, and she had severe scarring over the entire upper part of her body. Eva and Kay also suffered severe psychological trauma both from the ordeal and from their permanent disfigurement.

Charles W. Adams, World-Wide Volkswagen v. Woodson—*The Rest of The Story*, 72 NEB. L. REV. 1122, 1126 (1993).

Indications at the time were that a jury in Oklahoma state court would have been more likely to rule in the Robinson's favor, which is probably why the Robinsons initially sought to have their case tried in the state court. Is such forum shopping in an effort to seek or avoid a certain court because of the probable impact on your client's case a legitimate strategy that attorneys and litigants should pursue? Should courts take these considerations into account when determining jurisdictional questions?

c. State Sovereignty and Personal Jurisdiction

Although the *World-Wide Volkswagen* Court gave prominence to state sovereignty interests in articulating the contours of the minimum contacts analysis it applied, the Court soon after issued an opinion in another case that called into question the role that state sovereignty plays in jurisdictional analysis:

> The personal jurisdiction requirement recognizes and protects an individual liberty interest. It represents a restriction on judicial power not as a matter of sovereignty, but as a matter of individual liberty. * * * The restriction on state sovereign power described in *World-Wide Volkswagen Corp.*, however, must be seen as ultimately a function of the individual liberty interest preserved by the Due Process Clause. That Clause is the only source of the personal jurisdiction requirement and the Clause itself makes no mention

of federalism concerns. Furthermore, if the federalism concept operated as an independent restriction on the sovereign power of the court, it would not be possible to waive the personal jurisdiction requirement: Individual actions cannot change the powers of sovereignty, although the individual can subject himself to powers from which he may otherwise be protected.

Ins. Corp. of Ireland v. Compagnie des Bauxites de Guinee, 456 U.S. 694, 702, 703 n.10 (1982) (White, J.). Justice White, the author of *World-Wide Volkswagen* was also the author of *Insurance Corp. of Ireland*. Are his views on the role of federalism and state sovereignty in a personal jurisdiction analysis consistent in both cases? Do you agree with his assessment that the limits of interstate federalism place no independent constraint on the scope of a state's ability to exercise jurisdiction over nonresident defendants?

d. Justice Brennan's Dissent

What is Justice Brennan's concern with the majority's approach in *World-Wide Volkswagen*? What vision of the minimum contacts test does he propose? Which view of the doctrine is more in line with the original analysis conceived by the Court in *International Shoe*?

e. *Kulko v. Superior Court*

Kulko v. Superior Court, 436 U.S. 84 (1978), a case that pre-dates *World-Wide Volkswagen*, is similar to that case in that the Court rejected jurisdiction over the defendant based on the unilateral activity of the plaintiff affiliating herself with the forum state. Specifically, in *Kulko* the divorced mother of two children brought an action in California—where the mother and children resided—against the children's father—who resided in New York—for full custody of the children and an increase in child support. Kulko, the father, made a special appearance to challenge California's jurisdiction on the ground that he was not a resident of California and lacked sufficient minimum contacts with the state under *International Shoe Co. v. Washington*. Here is an excerpt from Justice Marshall's opinion for the Court:

Take Note!

Note that here as in *World-Wide Volkswagen* the court is a party in the caption of the case before the Supreme Court. Can you figure out why this is so?

The "purposeful act" that the California Supreme Court believed did warrant the exercise of personal jurisdiction over appellant in California was [Kulko's] "actively and fully [consenting] to [his daughter] living in California for the school year . . . and . . . [sending] her to California for that purpose." We cannot accept the proposition that appellant's acquiescence in [his daughter's] desire to live with her mother conferred jurisdiction over appellant in the California courts in this action. A father who agrees, in the interests of family harmony and his children's preferences, to allow them to spend more time in California than was required under a separation agreement can hardly be said to have "purposefully availed himself" of the "benefits and protections" of California's laws.

Nor can we agree with the assertion of the court below that the exercise of *in personam* jurisdiction here was warranted by the financial benefit appellant derived from his daughter's presence in California for nine months of the year. * * * [T]his circumstance, even if true, does not support California's assertion of jurisdiction here. Any diminution in appellant's household costs resulted, not from the child's presence in California, but rather from her absence from appellant's home.

* * *

The circumstances in this case clearly render "unreasonable" California's assertion of personal jurisdiction. There is no claim that appellant has visited physical injury on either property or persons within the State of California. The cause of action herein asserted arises, not from the defendant's commercial transactions in interstate commerce, but rather from his personal, domestic relations. It thus cannot be said that appellant has sought a commercial benefit from solicitation of business from a resident of California * * *.

Finally, basic considerations of fairness point decisively in favor of appellant's State of domicile as the proper forum for adjudication of this case, whatever the merits of appellee's underlying claim. It is appellant who has remained in the State of the marital domicile, whereas it is appellee who has moved across the continent. * * * As noted above, appellant did no more than acquiesce in the stated preference of one of his children to live with her mother in California. This single act is surely not one that a reasonable parent would expect to result in the substantial financial burden and personal strain of litigating a child-support suit in a forum 3,000 miles away, and we therefore see

Food for Thought

Consider the practical outcome of this decision: Kulko's ex-wife will be unable to sue him where she lives but will have to travel to Kulko's home state (New York in this case) to seek custody and increased child support payments. Is that fair? Can this opinion be criticized for belittling the significance of domestic relations cases and devaluing the interests of mothers seeking to provide for their children? *See* ROY L. BROOKS, CRITICAL PROCEDURE 44–47 (1998).

no basis on which it can be said that appellant could reasonably have anticipated being "haled before a [California] court."

How did the Court view Kulko's contacts with California? Did the Court give enough weight to those contacts?

Given California's particularly strong interest in the custodial fate of the children in this case as California residents and in the sufficiency of their financial support, what justifies the rejection of jurisdiction over Kulko here, inconvenience to the defendant? Should the defendant's convenience concerns be given such weight?

f. *Keeton v. Hustler Magazine, Inc.*

Not long after *World-Wide Volkswagen*, in a decision that was unanimous as to the result, the Supreme Court decided <u>Keeton v. Hustler Magazine, Inc., 465 U.S. 770 (1984)</u> [*FLEX* Case 1.A]. In *Keeton*, the Court upheld the assertion of personal jurisdiction in a libel case where neither of the parties was from the forum state (New Hampshire) but the defamatory material in question was circulated there. Based on the fact that the defendant had a "regular circulation of magazines" in New Hampshire and the plaintiff's "cause of action arises out of the very activity being conducted, in part, in New Hampshire," the Court had no difficultly concluding that Hustler Magazine could "reasonably anticipate" being sued there and that permitting jurisdiction would not be unfair.

Food for Thought

The plaintiff in *Keeton* brought her suit in New Hampshire only because it was time-barred by the statutes of limitations in all of the other states. Was the Court right to give little weight to this fact in its jurisdictional analysis? The Court also gave little weight to the fact that the plaintiff had no connection with New Hampshire other than publication of the defamation there. Should the plaintiff's lack of a connection matter?

g. The *Calder* "Effects" Test

The same day that *Keeton* was decided, the Court issued its opinion in <u>Calder v. Jones, 465 U.S. 783 (1984)</u> [*FLEX* Case 1.B] another personal jurisdiction case involving a libel claim. In *Calder*, the Court was faced with a jurisdictional challenge from the writer and editor (two different people) of the offending article rather than the publication itself. Citing the intentional tortious actions of the defendants, the fact that they "expressly aimed" those actions at the forum state—California—by targeting a plaintiff who lived and worked there, and their knowledge that "the brunt of that injury" would be felt by the plaintiff in California, Justice Rehnquist—for a unanimous Court—found the exercise of personal jurisdiction to be permissible. The test set forth in *Calder* is often referred to as the "effects" test because of Justice Rehnquist's statement that "[j]urisdiction over petitioners is therefore proper in California based on the 'effects' of their Florida conduct in California."

Lower courts have had mixed reactions to the *Calder* decision. Some have given *Calder* a broad interpretation, *see, e.g.*, *Carteret Sav. Bank, FA v. Shushan, 954 F.2d 141, 148 (3d Cir. 1992)* ("Under the effects test, a court may exercise personal jurisdiction over a nonresident defendant who acts outside the forum state to cause an effect upon the plaintiff within the forum state."), while others have restricted the effects test to those situations in which the defendant has "expressly aimed" its tortious conduct at the forum state with knowledge that the plaintiff is likely to suffer harm there, *see, e.g.*, *Schwarzenegger v. Fred Martin Motor Co., 374 F.3d 797, 803 (9th Cir. 2004)*. Under the latter view, courts have used the express aiming requirement to ensure that the defendant actually intended to direct its tortious activity specifically at the forum and that the forum was the "focal point" of the tortious conduct and the place where the "brunt of the harm" occurred. *See Fielding v. Hubert Burda Media, Inc., 415 F.3d 419, 425, 427 (5th Cir. 2005)*. Which view is more in accord with the opinion in *Calder? See* A. Benjamin Spencer, *Terminating* Calder: *"Effects" Based Jurisdiction in the Ninth Circuit after* Schwarzenegger v. Fred Martin Motor Co., 26 WHITTIER L. REV. 197 (2004).

In 2014, the Supreme Court decided *Walden v. Fiore, 134 S. Ct. 1115 (2014)* [*FLEX Case 1.C*], which provides a further discussion of *Calder* and illustrates the limits of its "effects" test. *See id.* at 1124–25 (holding that mere knowledge of plaintiffs' connections with the forum state and potential to suffer harm there are insufficient to provide minimum contacts over an out-of-state intentional tortfeasor).

Burger King Corp. v. Rudzewicz

Supreme Court of the United States
471 U.S. 462 (1985)

JUSTICE BRENNAN delivered the opinion of the Court.

I.A

Burger King Corporation is a Florida corporation whose principal offices are in Miami. * * *

* * *

The instant litigation grows out of Burger King's termination of one of its franchisees * * * . The appellee John Rudzewicz, a Michigan citizen and resident, is the senior partner in a Detroit accounting firm. In 1978, he was approached by Brian

MacShara, the son of a business acquaintance, who suggested that they jointly apply to Burger King for a franchise in the Detroit area. MacShara proposed to serve as the manager of the restaurant if Rudzewicz would put up the investment capital; in exchange, the two would evenly share the profits. * * *

* * *

[Their restaurant] facility apparently enjoyed steady business during the summer of 1979, but patronage declined after a recession began later that year. Rudzewicz and MacShara soon fell far behind in their monthly payments to Miami. Headquarters sent notices of default, and an extended period of negotiations began among the franchisees, the Birmingham district office, and the Miami headquarters. After several Burger King officials in Miami had engaged in prolonged but ultimately unsuccessful negotiations with the franchisees by mail and by telephone, headquarters terminated the franchise and ordered Rudzewicz and MacShara to vacate the premises. They refused and continued to occupy and operate the facility as a Burger King restaurant.

B

Burger King commenced the instant action in the <u>United States District Court for the Southern District of Florida</u> in May 1981, invoking that court's diversity jurisdiction pursuant to <u>28 U.S.C. § 1332(a)</u> and its original jurisdiction over federal trademark disputes pursuant to <u>§ 1338(a)</u>. Burger King alleged that Rudzewicz and MacShara had breached their franchise obligations "within [the jurisdiction of] this district court" by failing to make the required payments "at plaintiff's place of business in Miami, Dade County, Florida," and also charged that they were tortiously infringing its trademarks and service marks through their continued, unauthorized operation as a Burger King restaurant. Burger King sought damages, injunctive relief, and costs and attorney's fees. Rudzewicz and MacShara entered special appearances and argued, *inter alia*, that because they were Michigan residents and because Burger King's claim did not "arise" within the Southern District of Florida, the District Court lacked personal jurisdiction over them. The District Court denied their motions * * * . * * *

It's Latin to Me!

Inter alia is simply a Latin phrase that means "among other things." Its use indicates that the argument made was only one among several presented by the party, the others not being relevant to the issue in this case.

[The court entered judgment against Rudzewicz and MacShara on the merits. A divided panel of the <u>Eleventh Circuit</u> reversed the judgment, concluding that the District Court could not properly exercise personal jurisdiction over Rudzewicz pursuant to the Florida long-arm statute.]

II.A

* * *

We have noted several reasons why a forum legitimately may exercise personal jurisdiction over a nonresident who "purposefully directs" his activities toward forum residents. A State generally has a "manifest interest" in providing its residents with a convenient forum for redressing injuries inflicted by out-of-state actors. Moreover, where individuals "purposefully derive benefit" from their interstate activities, it may well be unfair to allow them to escape having to account in other States for consequences that arise proximately from such activities; the Due Process Clause may not readily be wielded as a territorial shield to avoid interstate obligations that have been voluntarily assumed. And because "modern transportation and communications have made it much less burdensome for a party sued to defend himself in a State where he engages in economic activity," it usually will not be unfair to subject him to the burdens of litigating in another forum for disputes relating to such activity. *McGee v. International Life Insurance Co., 355 U.S. 220, 223 (1957)*.

Notwithstanding these considerations, the constitutional touchstone remains whether the defendant purposefully established "minimum contacts" in the forum State. Although it has been argued that foreseeability of causing *injury* in another State should be sufficient to establish such contacts there when policy considerations so require, the Court has consistently held that this kind of foreseeability is not a "sufficient benchmark" for exercising personal jurisdiction. *World-Wide Volkswagen Corp. v. Woodson, 444 U.S. 286, 295 (1980)*. Instead, "the foreseeability that is critical to due process analysis . . . is that the defendant's conduct and connection with the forum State are such that he should reasonably anticipate being haled into court there." * * *

This "purposeful availment" requirement ensures that a defendant will not be haled into a jurisdiction solely as a result of "random," "fortuitous," or "attenuated" contacts, or of the "unilateral activity of another party or a third person." Jurisdiction is proper, however, where the contacts proximately result from actions by the defendant *himself* that create a "substantial connection" with the forum State. Thus where the defendant "deliberately" has engaged in significant activities within a State, or has created "continuing obligations" between himself and residents of the forum, he manifestly has availed himself of the privilege of conducting business there, and because his activities are shielded by "the benefits and protections" of the forum's laws it is presumptively not unreasonable to require him to submit to the burdens of litigation in that forum as well.

* * *

Once it has been decided that a defendant purposefully established minimum contacts within the forum State, these contacts may be considered in light of other factors to determine whether the assertion of personal jurisdiction would comport with "fair play and substantial justice." Thus courts in "appropriate case[s]" may evaluate "the burden on the defendant," "the forum State's interest in adjudicating the dispute," "the plaintiff's interest in obtaining convenient and effective relief," "the interstate judicial system's interest in obtaining the most efficient resolution of controversies," and the "shared interest of the several States in furthering fundamental substantive social policies." World-Wide Volkswagen Corp. v. Woodson, 444 U.S. 286, 292 (1980). These considerations sometimes serve to establish the reasonableness of jurisdiction upon a lesser showing of minimum contacts than would otherwise be required. On the other hand, where a defendant who purposefully has directed his activities at forum residents seeks to defeat jurisdiction, he must present a compelling case that the presence of some other considerations would render jurisdiction unreasonable. Most such considerations usually may be accommodated through means short of finding jurisdiction unconstitutional. For example, the potential clash of the forum's law with the "fundamental substantive social policies" of another State may be accommodated through application of the forum's choice-of-law rules. Similarly, a defendant claiming substantial inconvenience may seek a change of venue. Nevertheless, minimum requirements inherent in the concept of "fair play and substantial justice" may defeat the reasonableness of jurisdiction even if the defendant has purposefully engaged in forum activities. As we previously have noted, jurisdictional rules may not be employed in such a way as to make litigation "so gravely difficult and inconvenient" that a party unfairly is at a "severe disadvantage" in comparison to his opponent.

B

(1)

Applying these principles to the case at hand, we believe there is substantial record evidence supporting the District Court's conclusion that the assertion of personal jurisdiction over Rudzewicz in Florida for the alleged breach of his franchise agreement did not offend due process. At the outset, we note a continued division among lower courts respecting whether and to what extent a contract can constitute a "contact" for purposes of due process analysis. If the question is whether an individual's contract with an out-of-state party *alone* can automatically establish sufficient minimum contacts in the other party's home forum, we believe the answer clearly is that it cannot. The Court long ago rejected the notion that personal jurisdiction might turn on "mechanical" tests, or on "conceptualistic . . . theories of the place of contracting or of performance." Instead, we have emphasized the need for a "highly realistic" approach that recognizes that a "contract" is "ordinarily but an intermediate step serving to tie up prior business negotiations with future consequences which themselves are the real object of the business transaction." It is these factors—prior negotiations and contemplated future consequences, along with the terms of the contract and the parties' actual course of dealing—that must be evaluated in determining whether the defendant purposefully established minimum contacts within the forum.

In this case, no physical ties to Florida can be attributed to Rudzewicz other than MacShara's brief training course in Miami. Rudzewicz did not maintain offices in Florida and, for all that appears from the record, has never even visited there. Yet this franchise dispute grew directly out of "a contract which had a *substantial* connection with that State." *McGee v. International Life Insurance Co.*, 355 U.S., at 223 (emphasis added). Eschewing the option of operating an independent local enterprise, Rudzewicz deliberately "reach[ed] out beyond" Michigan and negotiated with a Florida corporation for the purchase of a long-term franchise and the manifold benefits that would derive from affiliation with a nationwide organization. Upon approval, he entered into a carefully structured 20-year relationship that envisioned continuing and wide-reaching contacts with Burger King in Florida. In light of Rudzewicz' voluntary acceptance of the long-term and exacting regulation of his business from Burger King's Miami headquarters, the "quality and nature" of his relationship to the company in Florida can in no sense be viewed as "random," "fortuitous," or "attenuated." Rudzewicz' refusal to make the contractually required payments in Miami, and his continued use of Burger King's trademarks and confidential business information after his termination, caused foreseeable injuries to the corporation in Florida. For these reasons it was, at the very least, presumptively reasonable for Rudzewicz to be called to account there for such injuries.

The Court of Appeals concluded, however, that in light of the supervision emanating from Burger King's district office in Birmingham, Rudzewicz reasonably believed that "the Michigan office was for all intents and purposes the embodiment of Burger King" and that he therefore had no "reason to anticipate a Burger King suit outside of Michigan." This reasoning overlooks substantial record evidence indicating that Rudzewicz most certainly knew that he was affiliating himself with an enterprise based primarily in Florida. The contract documents themselves emphasize that Burger King's operations are conducted and supervised from the Miami headquarters, that all relevant notices and payments must be sent there, and that the agreements were made in and enforced from Miami. Moreover, the parties' actual course of dealing repeatedly confirmed that decisionmaking authority was vested in the Miami headquarters and that the district office served largely as an intermediate link between the headquarters and the franchisees. When problems arose over building design, site-development fees, rent computation, and the defaulted payments, Rudzewicz and MacShara learned that the Michigan office was powerless to resolve their disputes and could only channel their communications to Miami. Throughout these disputes, the Miami headquarters and the Michigan franchisees carried on a continuous course of direct communications by mail and by telephone, and it was the Miami headquarters that made the key negotiating decisions out of which the instant litigation arose.

Moreover, we believe the Court of Appeals gave insufficient weight to provisions in the various franchise documents providing that all disputes would be governed by Florida law. The franchise agreement, for example, stated:

"This Agreement shall become valid when executed and accepted by BKC at Miami, Florida; it shall be deemed made and entered into in the State of Florida and shall be governed and construed under and in accordance with the laws of the State of Florida. The choice of law designation does not require that all suits concerning this Agreement be filed in Florida."

The Court of Appeals reasoned that choice-of-law provisions are irrelevant to the question of personal jurisdiction, relying on *Hanson v. Denckla* for the proposition that "the center of gravity for choice-of-law purposes does not necessarily confer the sovereign prerogative to assert jurisdiction." This reasoning misperceives the import of the quoted proposition. The Court in *Hanson* and subsequent cases has emphasized that choice-of-law *analysis*—which focuses on all elements of a transaction, and not simply on the defendant's conduct—is distinct from minimum-contacts jurisdictional analysis—which focuses at the threshold solely on the defendant's purposeful connection to the forum. Nothing in our cases, however, suggests that a choice-of-law *provision* should be ignored in considering whether a defendant has "purposefully invoked the benefits and protections of a State's laws" for jurisdictional purposes. Although such a provision standing alone would be insufficient to confer jurisdiction, we believe that, when combined with the 20-year interdependent relationship Rudzewicz established with Burger King's Miami headquarters, it reinforced his deliberate affiliation with the forum State and the reasonable foreseeability of possible litigation there. As Judge Johnson argued in his dissent below, Rudzewicz "purposefully availed himself of the benefits and protections of Florida's laws" by entering into contracts expressly providing that those laws would govern franchise disputes.

Food for Thought

The franchise agreement in Burger King had a choice-of-law clause indicating that Florida law governed the contract. What role does this provision play in the Court's personal jurisdiction analysis here?

(2)

Nor has Rudzewicz pointed to other factors that can be said persuasively to outweigh the considerations discussed above and to establish the *unconstitutionality* of Florida's assertion of jurisdiction. We cannot conclude that Florida had no "legitimate interest in holding [Rudzewicz] answerable on a claim related to" the contacts he had established in that State. * * * [T]he Court of Appeals' assertion that the Florida litigation "severely impaired [Rudzewicz's] ability to call Michigan witnesses who might be essential to his defense and counterclaim" is wholly without support in the record. And even to the extent that it is inconvenient for a party who has minimum contacts with a forum to litigate there, such considerations most frequently can be accommodated through a change of venue. Although the Court has suggested that inconvenience may at some point become so substantial as to achieve *constitutional* magnitude, this is not such a case.

What's That?

Venue is a doctrine that determines which among the federal districts may serve as a forum for a case. Venue and *change of venue* are topics that will be covered in Chapter 4.

The Court of Appeals also concluded, however, that the parties' dealings involved "a characteristic disparity of bargaining power" and "elements of surprise," and that Rudzewicz "lacked fair notice" of the potential for litigation in Florida because the contractual provisions suggesting to the contrary were merely "boilerplate declarations in a lengthy printed contract." Rudzewicz presented many of these arguments to the District Court, contending that Burger King was guilty of misrepresentation, fraud, and duress; that it gave insufficient notice in its dealings with him; and that the contract was one of adhesion. After a 3-day bench trial, the District Court found that Burger King had made no misrepresentations, that Rudzewicz and MacShara "were and are experienced and sophisticated businessmen," and that "at no time" did they "ac[t] under economic duress or disadvantage imposed by" Burger King. * * *

Make the Connection

These arguments, including the assertions of *misrepresentation*, *fraud*, and *duress* are all defenses to the enforceability of a contract that you will study in a **Contracts** course.

III

Notwithstanding these considerations, the Court of Appeals apparently believed that it was necessary to reject jurisdiction in this case as a prophylactic measure, reasoning that an affirmance of the District Court's judgment would result in the exercise of jurisdiction over "out-of-state consumers to collect payments due on modest personal purchases" and would "sow the seeds of default judgments against franchisees owing smaller debts." We share the Court of Appeals' broader concerns and therefore reject any talismanic jurisdictional formulas; "the facts of each case must [always] be weighed" in determining whether personal jurisdiction would comport with "fair play and substantial justice." The "quality and nature" of an interstate transaction may sometimes be so "random," "fortuitous," or "attenuated" that it cannot fairly be said that the potential defendant "should reasonably anticipate being haled into court" in another jurisdiction. We also have emphasized that jurisdiction may not be grounded on a contract whose terms have been obtained through "fraud, undue influence, or overweening bargaining power" and whose application would render litigation "so gravely difficult and inconvenient that [a party] will for all practical purposes be deprived of his day in court."

* * *

For the reasons set forth above, however, these dangers are not present in the instant case. Because Rudzewicz established a substantial and continuing relationship with Burger King's Miami headquarters, received fair notice from the contract documents and the course of dealing that he might be subject to suit in Florida, and has failed to demonstrate how jurisdiction in that forum would otherwise be fundamentally unfair, we conclude that the District Court's exercise of jurisdiction pursuant to [the Florida long-arm statute] did not offend due process. The judgment of the Court of Appeals is accordingly reversed, and the case is remanded for further proceedings consistent with this opinion.

It is so ordered.

JUSTICE POWELL took no part in the consideration or decision of this case.

JUSTICE STEVENS, with whom JUSTICE WHITE joins, dissenting.

In my opinion there is a significant element of unfairness in requiring a franchisee to defend a case of this kind in the forum chosen by the franchisor. It is undisputed that appellee maintained no place of business in Florida, that he had no employees in that State, and that he was not licensed to do business there. Appellee did not prepare his French fries, shakes, and hamburgers in Michigan, and then deliver them into the stream of commerce "with the expectation that they [would] be purchased by consumers in" Florida. To the contrary, appellee did business only in Michigan, his business, property, and payroll taxes were payable in that State, and he sold all of his products there.

Throughout the business relationship, appellee's principal contacts with appellant were with its Michigan office. Notwithstanding its disclaimer the Court seems ultimately to rely on nothing more than standard boilerplate language contained in various documents to establish that appellee " 'purposefully availed himself of the benefits and protections of Florida's laws.' " Such superficial analysis creates a potential for unfairness not only in negotiations between franchisors and their franchisees but, more significantly, in the resolution of the disputes that inevitably arise from time to time in such relationships.

* * *

Accordingly, I respectfully dissent.

Points for Discussion

a.   Minimum Contacts After *Burger King*

Justice Brennan, the dissenter in *World-Wide Volkswagen*, is now the author of the Court's opinion in *Burger King*. Does he take the opportunity to infuse some of his views of the minimum contacts doctrine evident in his *World-Wide Volkswagen* dissent into his analysis here? Some have described Brennan's approach to analyzing the two wings of the minimum contacts test (the purposeful availment prong and the reasonableness prong) as a "sliding-scale" approach, wherein a greater showing for one prong of the test can make up for a lesser showing for the other prong. Does such an approach make sense? Is it consistent with the Court's original articulation of the doctrine in *International Shoe* or with the doctrine as articulated in *World-Wide Volkswagen*?

b.   Brennan's Contract-Plus Analysis

In his *Burger King* opinion, Justice Brennan seemed to reject the notion that a contractual relationship with a forum resident alone is sufficient to confer jurisdiction over a non-resident in the forum: "If the question is whether an individual's contract with an out-of-state party *alone* can automatically establish sufficient minimum contacts in the other party's home forum, we believe the answer clearly is that it cannot." Is this statement consistent with the Court's holding in *McGee* or has *McGee* been overruled? If a contractual relationship alone is insufficient, what additional factors did Justice Brennan identify as justifying Florida's assertion of jurisdiction in *Burger King*? What role did the presence of a Florida choice-of-law provision in the contract play in Justice Brennan's determination that jurisdiction was proper in Florida? Many have referred to Justice Brennan's minimum contacts analysis in this case as a "contract-plus" analysis. *See, e.g.*, *Ganis Corp. v. Jackson, 822 F.2d 194, 197 (1st Cir. 1987)*. What elements in your view make up this contract-plus analysis? Will contracts always have these so-called "plus" elements?

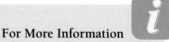

> **For More Information**
>
> To read more analysis of Justice Brennan's contract-plus approach, see Pamela J. Stephens, *The Single Contract as Minimum Contacts: Justice Brennan "Has it His Way,"* 28 WM. & MARY L. REV. 89, 109–10 (1986).

c.   The Defendant's Burden of Proof

Although plaintiffs firmly carry the burden of establishing personal jurisdiction over a defendant, Justice Brennan here indicates that once the plaintiff establishes that the defendant has purposefully availed itself of the forum, the burden is on the defendant to then demonstrate that the assertion of jurisdiction would be unreasonable:

"[W]here a defendant who purposefully has directed his activities at forum residents seeks to defeat jurisdiction, he must present a compelling case that the presence of some other considerations would render jurisdiction unreasonable." *Burger King*, 471 U.S. at 477. Is this burden-shifting approach appropriate?

———————

Specific jurisdiction, as we have seen, requires certain minimum contacts with the forum state. In the context of modern commerce, it frequently occurs that a defendant's product may end up in—and cause harm in—a state indirectly through third parties. Determining under what circumstances such indirect contacts with a state could warrant the exercise of specific jurisdiction is the question that the Supreme Court took up in the next two cases.

Asahi Metal Industry Co. v. Superior Court

Supreme Court of the United States
480 U.S. 102 (1987)

JUSTICE O'CONNOR announced the judgment of the Court and delivered the unanimous opinion of the Court with respect to Part I, the opinion of the Court with respect to Part II-B, in which THE CHIEF JUSTICE, JUSTICE BRENNAN, JUSTICE WHITE, JUSTICE MARSHALL, JUSTICE BLACKMUN, JUSTICE POWELL, and JUSTICE STEVENS join, and an opinion with respect to Parts II-A and III, in which THE CHIEF JUSTICE, JUSTICE POWELL, and JUSTICE SCALIA join.

Take Note!

This is a fractured ruling in which no opinion garnered the support of a majority of the Justices. What impact does that fact have on the state of the law as pronounced within the opinions? Be sure to sort out where each Justice stands in this case.

This case presents the question whether the mere awareness on the part of a foreign defendant that the components it manufactured, sold, and delivered outside the United States would reach the forum State in the stream of commerce constitutes "minimum contacts" between the defendant and the forum State such that the exercise of jurisdiction "does not offend 'traditional notions of fair play and substantial justice.' "

I

On September 23, 1978, on Interstate Highway 80 in Solano County, California, Gary Zurcher lost control of his Honda motorcycle and collided with a tractor. Zurcher was severely injured, and his passenger and wife, Ruth Ann Moreno, was killed. In September 1979, Zurcher filed a product liability action in the <u>Superior Court of the State of California in and for the County of Solano</u>. Zurcher alleged that the 1978 accident was caused by a sudden loss of air and an explosion in the rear tire of the motorcycle, and alleged that the motorcycle tire, tube, and sealant were defective. Zurcher's complaint named, *inter alia*, Cheng Shin Rubber Industrial Co., Ltd. (Cheng Shin), the Taiwanese manufacturer of the tube. Cheng Shin in turn filed a cross-complaint seeking indemnification from its codefendants and from petitioner, Asahi Metal Industry Co., Ltd. (Asahi), the manufacturer of the tube's valve assembly. Zurcher's claims against Cheng Shin and the other defendants were eventually settled and dismissed, leaving only Cheng Shin's indemnity action against Asahi.

Take Note!

The presence of these multiple claims and settlements can be confusing. Try drawing a diagram to identify each of the various actions, what they alleged, and the parties that remain after certain claims are settled and dismissed.

California's long-arm statute authorizes the exercise of jurisdiction "on any basis not inconsistent with the Constitution of this state or of the United States." Asahi moved to quash Cheng Shin's service of summons, arguing the State could not exert jurisdiction over it consistent with the <u>Due Process Clause</u> of the Fourteenth Amendment.

* * * Asahi is a Japanese corporation. It manufactures tire valve assemblies in Japan and sells the assemblies to Cheng Shin, and to several other tire manufacturers, for use as components in finished tire tubes. Asahi's sales to Cheng Shin took place in Taiwan. The shipments from Asahi to Cheng Shin were sent from Japan to Taiwan. Cheng Shin bought and incorporated into its tire tubes 150,000 Asahi valve assemblies in 1978; 500,000 in 1979; 500,000 in 1980; 100,000 in 1981; and 100,000 in 1982. Sales to Cheng Shin accounted for 1.24 percent of Asahi's income in 1981 and 0.44 percent in 1982. Cheng Shin alleged that approximately 20 percent of its sales in the United States are in California. Cheng Shin purchases valve assemblies from other suppliers as well, and sells finished tubes throughout the world.

* * * An affidavit of a manager of Cheng Shin whose duties included the purchasing of component parts stated: "In discussions with Asahi regarding the purchase of valve stem assemblies the fact that my Company sells tubes throughout the world and specifically the United States has been discussed. I am informed and believe that Asahi was fully aware that valve stem assemblies sold to my Company and to others would end up throughout the United States and in California." An affidavit of the president of Asahi, on the other hand, declared that Asahi "has never contemplated that its limited sales of tire valves to Cheng Shin in Taiwan would subject it to lawsuits in California." The record does not include any contract between Cheng Shin and Asahi.

Primarily on the basis of the above information, the Superior Court denied the motion to quash summons, stating: "Asahi obviously does business on an international scale. It is not unreasonable that they defend claims of defect in their product on an international scale." * * *

We granted certiorari, and now reverse.

II

A

* * * Most recently we have reaffirmed the oft-quoted reasoning of <u>Hanson v. Denckla, 357 U.S. 235, 253 (1958)</u>, that minimum contacts must have a basis in "some act by which the defendant purposefully avails itself of the privilege of conducting activities within the forum State, thus invoking the benefits and protections of its laws." <u>Burger King, 471 U.S. 462, 475 (1985)</u>. "Jurisdiction is proper . . . where the contacts proximately result from actions by the defendant *himself* that create a 'substantial connection' with the forum State."

Applying the principle that minimum contacts must be based on an act of the defendant, the Court in <u>World-Wide Volkswagen Corp. v. Woodson, 444 U.S. 286 (1980)</u>, rejected the assertion that a consumer's unilateral act of bringing the defendant's product into the forum State was a sufficient constitutional basis for personal jurisdiction over the defendant. It had been argued in *World-Wide Volkswagen* that because an automobile retailer and its wholesale distributor sold a product mobile by design and purpose, they could foresee being haled into court in the distant States into which their customers might drive. The Court rejected this concept of foreseeability as an insufficient basis for jurisdiction under the Due Process Clause. The Court disclaimed, however, the idea that "foreseeability is wholly irrelevant" to personal jurisdiction, concluding that "[t]he forum State does not exceed its powers under the Due Process Clause if it asserts personal jurisdiction over a corporation that delivers its products into the stream of commerce with the expectation that they will be purchased by consumers in the forum State."

* * *

In *World-Wide Volkswagen* itself, the state court sought to base jurisdiction not on any act of the defendant, but on the foreseeable unilateral actions of the consumer. Since *World-Wide Volkswagen*, lower courts have been confronted with cases in which the defendant acted by placing a product in the stream of commerce, and the stream eventually swept defendant's product into the forum State, but the defendant did nothing else to purposefully avail itself of the market in the forum State. Some courts have understood the Due Process Clause, as interpreted in *World-Wide Volkswagen*, to allow an exercise of personal jurisdiction to be based on no more than the defendant's act of placing the product in the stream of commerce. Other courts have understood the Due Process Clause and the above-quoted language in *World-Wide Volkswagen* to require the action of the defendant to be more purposefully directed at the forum State than the mere act of placing a product in the stream of commerce.

The reasoning of the Supreme Court of California in the present case illustrates the former interpretation of *World-Wide Volkswagen*. The Supreme Court of California held that, because the stream of commerce eventually brought some valves Asahi sold Cheng Shin into California, Asahi's awareness that its valves would be sold in California was sufficient to permit California to exercise jurisdiction over Asahi consistent with the requirements of the Due Process Clause. The Supreme Court of California's position was consistent with those courts that have held that mere foreseeability or awareness was a constitutionally sufficient basis for personal jurisdiction if the defendant's product made its way into the forum State while still in the stream of commerce.

Other courts, however, have understood the Due Process Clause to require something more than that the defendant was aware of its product's entry into the forum State through the stream of commerce in order for the State to exert jurisdiction over the defendant. * * *

We now find this latter position to be consonant with the requirements of due process. The "substantial connection" between the defendant and the forum State necessary for a finding of minimum contacts must come about by *an action of the defendant purposefully directed toward the forum State*. The placement of a product into the stream of commerce, without more, is not an act of the defendant purposefully directed toward the forum State. Additional conduct of the defendant may indicate an intent or purpose to serve the market in the forum State, for example, designing the product for the market in the forum State, advertising in the forum State, establishing channels for providing regular advice to customers in the forum State, or marketing the product through a distributor who has agreed to serve as the sales agent in the forum State. But a defendant's awareness that the stream of commerce may or will sweep the product into the forum State does not convert the mere act of placing the product into the stream into an act purposefully directed toward the forum State.

Assuming, *arguendo*, that respondents have established Asahi's awareness that some of the valves sold to Cheng Shin would be incorporated into tire tubes sold in California, respondents have not demonstrated any action by Asahi to purposefully avail itself of the California market. * * * It has no office, agents, employees, or property in California. It does not advertise or otherwise solicit business in California. * * * On the basis of these facts, the exertion of personal jurisdiction over Asahi by the Superior Court of California exceeds the limits of due process.

It's Latin to Me!

Arguendo is a Latin term that means "for the sake of argument." Its use here indicates that the Court is addressing a point that has not been established, but showing that even if it had been established it would not have affected the Court's ultimate conclusion.

B

* * *

We have previously explained that the determination of the reasonableness of the exercise of jurisdiction in each case will depend on an evaluation of several factors. A court must consider the burden on the defendant, the interests of the forum State, and the plaintiff's interest in obtaining relief. It must also weigh in its determination "the interstate judicial system's interest in obtaining the most efficient resolution of controversies; and the shared interest of the several States in furthering fundamental substantive social policies." *World-Wide Volkswagen.*

A consideration of these factors in the present case clearly reveals the unreasonableness of the assertion of jurisdiction over Asahi, even apart from the question of the placement of goods in the stream of commerce.

Certainly the burden on the defendant in this case is severe. Asahi has been commanded by the Supreme Court of California not only to traverse the distance between Asahi's headquarters in Japan and the Superior Court of California in and for the County of Solano, but also to submit its dispute with Cheng Shin to a foreign nation's judicial system. The unique burdens placed upon one who must defend oneself in a foreign legal system should have significant weight in assessing the reasonableness of stretching the long arm of personal jurisdiction over national borders.

When minimum contacts have been established, often the interests of the plaintiff and the forum in the exercise of jurisdiction will justify even the serious burdens placed on the alien defendant. In the present case, however, the interests of the plaintiff and the forum in California's assertion of jurisdiction over Asahi are slight. All that remains is a claim for indemnification asserted by Cheng Shin, a Taiwanese corporation, against Asahi. The transaction on which the indemnification claim is based took place in Taiwan; Asahi's components were shipped from Japan to Taiwan. Cheng Shin has not demonstrated that it is more convenient for it to litigate its indemnification claim against Asahi in California rather than in Taiwan or Japan.

Because the plaintiff is not a California resident, California's legitimate interests in the dispute have considerably diminished. The Supreme Court of California argued that the State had an interest in "protecting its consumers by ensuring that foreign manufacturers comply with the state's safety standards." The State Supreme Court's definition of California's interest, however, was overly broad. The dispute between Cheng Shin and Asahi is primarily about indemnification rather than safety standards. Moreover, it is not at all clear at this point that California law should govern the question whether a Japanese corporation should indemnify a Taiwanese corporation on the basis of a sale made in Taiwan and a shipment of goods from Japan to Taiwan. The possibility of being haled into a California court as a result of an accident involving Asahi's components undoubtedly creates an additional deterrent to the manufacture of unsafe components; however, similar pressures will be placed on Asahi by the purchasers of its components as long as those who use Asahi components in their final products, and sell those products in California, are subject to the application of California tort law.

Make the Connection

An *indemnification* claim seeks reimbursement from a party for losses incurred as a result of that party's actions. This is a concept you should cover in **Torts**.

World-Wide Volkswagen also admonished courts to take into consideration the interests of the "several States," in addition to the forum State, in the efficient judicial resolution of the dispute and the advancement of substantive policies. In the present case, this advice calls for a court to consider the procedural and substantive policies of other *nations* whose interests are affected by the assertion of jurisdiction by the California court. The procedural and substantive interests of other nations in a state court's assertion of jurisdiction over an alien defendant will differ from case to case. In every case, however, those interests, as well as the Federal interest in Government's foreign relations policies, will be best served by a careful inquiry into the reasonableness of the assertion of jurisdiction in the particular case, and an unwillingness to find the serious burdens on an alien defendant outweighed by minimal interests on the part of the plaintiff or the forum State. "Great care and reserve should be exercised when extending our notions of personal jurisdiction into the international field."

Considering the international context, the heavy burden on the alien defendant, and the slight interests of the plaintiff and the forum State, the exercise of personal jurisdiction by a California court over Asahi in this instance would be unreasonable and unfair.

III

Because the facts of this case do not establish minimum contacts such that the exercise of personal jurisdiction is consistent with fair play and substantial justice, the judgment of the Supreme Court of California is reversed, and the case is remanded for further proceedings not inconsistent with this opinion.

It is so ordered.

Justice Brennan, with whom Justice White, Justice Marshall, and Justice Blackmun join, concurring in part and concurring in the judgment.

I do not agree with the interpretation in Part II-A of the stream-of-commerce theory, nor with the conclusion that Asahi did not "purposely avail itself of the California market." I do agree, however, with the Court's conclusion in Part II-B that the exercise of personal jurisdiction over Asahi in this case would not comport with "fair play and substantial justice." This is one of those rare cases in which "minimum requirements inherent in the concept of 'fair play and substantial justice' . . . defeat the reasonableness of jurisdiction even [though] the defendant has purposefully engaged in forum activities." *Burger King Corp. v. Rudzewicz*, 471 U.S. 462, 477–478 (1985). I therefore join Parts I and II-B of the Court's opinion, and write separately to explain my disagreement with Part II-A.

Part II-A states that "a defendant's awareness that the stream of commerce may or will sweep the product into the forum State does not convert the mere act of placing the product into the stream into an act purposefully directed toward the forum State." Under this view, a plaintiff would be required to show "[a]dditional conduct" directed toward the forum before finding the exercise of jurisdiction over the defendant to be consistent with the Due Process Clause. I see no need for such a showing, however. The stream of commerce refers not to unpredictable currents or eddies, but to the regular and anticipated flow of products from manufacture to distribution to retail sale. As long as a participant in this process is aware that the final product is being marketed in the forum State, the possibility of a lawsuit there cannot come as a surprise. Nor will the litigation present a burden for which there is no corresponding benefit. A defendant who has placed goods in the stream of commerce benefits economically from the retail sale of the final product in the forum State, and indirectly benefits from the State's laws that regulate and facilitate commercial activity. These benefits accrue regardless of whether that participant directly conducts business in the forum State, or engages in additional conduct directed toward that State. * * *

JUSTICE STEVENS, with whom JUSTICE WHITE and JUSTICE BLACKMUN join, concurring in part and concurring in the judgment.

The judgment of the Supreme Court of California should be reversed for the reasons stated in Part II-B of the Court's opinion. While I join Parts I and II-B, I do not join Part II-A for two reasons. First, it is not necessary to the Court's decision. An examination of minimum contacts is not always necessary to determine whether a state court's assertion of personal jurisdiction is constitutional. Part II-B establishes, after considering the factors set forth in *World-Wide Volkswagen Corp. v. Woodson*, *444 U.S. 286, 292 (1980)*, that California's exercise of jurisdiction over Asahi in this case would be "unreasonable and unfair." This finding alone requires reversal; this case fits within the rule that "minimum requirements inherent in the concept of 'fair play and substantial justice' may defeat the reasonableness of jurisdiction even if the defendant has purposefully engaged in forum activities." *Burger King*. Accordingly, I see no reason in this case for the plurality to articulate "purposeful direction" or any other test as the nexus between an act of a defendant and the forum State that is necessary to establish minimum contacts.

Second, even assuming that the test ought to be formulated here, Part II-A mis-applies it to the facts of this case. The plurality seems to assume that an unwavering line can be drawn between "mere awareness" that a component will find its way into the forum State and "purposeful availment" of the forum's market. Over the course of its dealings with Cheng Shin, Asahi has arguably engaged in a higher quantum of conduct than "[t]he placement of a product into the stream of commerce, without more. . . ." Whether or not this conduct rises to the level of purposeful availment requires a constitutional determination that is affected by the volume, the value, and the hazardous character of the components. In most circumstances I would be inclined to conclude that a regular course of dealing that results in deliveries of over 100,000 units annually over a period of several years would constitute "purposeful availment" even though the item delivered to the forum State was a standard product marketed throughout the world.

J. McIntyre Machinery, Ltd. v. Nicastro

Supreme Court of the United States
131 S. Ct. 2780 (2011)

JUSTICE KENNEDY announced the judgment of the Court and delivered an opinion, in which THE CHIEF JUSTICE, JUSTICE SCALIA, and JUSTICE THOMAS join.

* * *

I

This case arises from a products-liability suit filed in New Jersey state court. Robert Nicastro seriously injured his hand while using a metal-shearing machine manufactured by J. McIntyre Machinery, Ltd. (J. McIntyre). The accident occurred in New Jersey, but the machine was manufactured in England, where J. McIntyre is incorporated and operates. The question here is whether the New Jersey courts have jurisdiction over J. McIntyre, notwithstanding the fact that the company at no time either marketed goods in the State or shipped them there. Nicastro was a plaintiff in the New Jersey trial court and is the respondent here; J. McIntyre was a defendant and is now the petitioner.

At oral argument in this Court, Nicastro's counsel stressed three primary facts in defense of New Jersey's assertion of jurisdiction over J. McIntyre.

First, an independent company agreed to sell J. McIntyre's machines in the United States. J. McIntyre itself did not sell its machines to buyers in this country beyond the U.S. distributor, and there is no allegation that the distributor was under J. McIntyre's control. Second, J. McIntyre officials attended annual conventions for the scrap recycling industry to advertise J. McIntyre's machines alongside the distributor. The conventions took place in various States, but never in New Jersey. Third, no more than four machines (the record suggests only one), including the machine that caused the injuries that are the basis for this suit, ended up in New Jersey.

In addition to these facts emphasized by petitioner, the New Jersey Supreme Court noted that J. McIntyre held both United States and European patents on its recycling technology. 201 N.J., at 55. It also noted that the U.S. distributor "structured [its] advertising and sales efforts in accordance with" J. McIntyre's "direction and guidance whenever possible," and that "at least some of the machines were sold on consignment to" the distributor. *Id., at 55, 56* (internal quotation marks omitted).

In light of these facts, the New Jersey Supreme Court concluded that New Jersey courts could exercise jurisdiction over petitioner without contravention of the Due Process Clause. Jurisdiction was proper, in that court's view, because the injury occurred in New Jersey; because petitioner knew or reasonably should have known "that its products are distributed through a nationwide distribution system that might lead to those products being sold in any of the fifty states"; and because petitioner failed to "take some reasonable step to prevent the distribution of its products in this State." _Id., at 77._

* * *

II

The Due Process Clause protects an individual's right to be deprived of life, liberty, or property only by the exercise of lawful power. Cf. _Giaccio v. Pennsylvania, 382 U.S. 399, 403 (1966)_ (The Clause "protect[s] a person against having the Government impose burdens upon him except in accordance with the valid laws of the land"). * * *

A court may subject a defendant to judgment only when the defendant has sufficient contacts with the sovereign "such that the maintenance of the suit does not offend 'traditional notions of fair play and substantial justice.' " _International Shoe Co. v. Washington, 326 U.S. 310, 316 (1945)_ (quoting _Milliken v. Meyer, 311 U.S. 457, 463 (1940)_). Freeform notions of fundamental fairness divorced from traditional practice cannot transform a judgment rendered in the absence of authority into law. As a general rule, the sovereign's exercise of power requires some act by which the defendant "purposefully avails itself of the privilege of conducting activities within the forum State, thus invoking the benefits and protections of its laws," _Hanson v. Denckla, 357 U.S. 235, 253 (1958)_, though in some cases, as with an intentional tort, the defendant might well fall within the State's authority by reason of his attempt to obstruct its laws. In products-liability cases like this one, it is the defendant's purposeful availment that makes jurisdiction consistent with "traditional notions of fair play and substantial justice."

A person may submit to a State's authority in a number of ways. There is, of course, explicit consent. _E.g., Insurance Corp. of Ireland v. Compagnie des Bauxites de Guinee, 456 U.S. 694, 703 (1982)_. Presence within a State at the time suit commences through service of process is another example. _See Burnham v. Superior Court of Cal., County of Marin, 495 U.S. 604, 608–609 (1990)_. Citizenship or domicile—or, by analogy, incorporation or principal place of business for corporations—also indicates general submission to a State's powers. _Goodyear Dunlop Tires Operations, S.A. v. Brown_ [131 S. Ct. 2846 (2011)]. Each of these examples reveals circumstances, or a course of conduct, from which it is proper to infer an intention to benefit from and thus an intention to submit to the laws of the forum State. Cf. _Burger King Corp. v. Rudzewicz, 471 U.S. 462, 476 (1985)_. These examples support exercise of the general jurisdiction of the State's courts and allow the State to resolve both matters that originate within the State and those based on activities and events elsewhere. _Helicopteros Nacionales de Colombia, S.A. v. Hall, 466 U.S. 408, 414, and n.9 (1984)_.

By contrast, those who live or operate primarily outside a State have a due process right not to be subjected to judgment in its courts as a general matter.

There is also a more limited form of submission to a State's authority for disputes that "arise out of or are connected with the activities within the state." *International Shoe Co., supra,* at 319. Where a defendant "purposefully avails itself of the privilege of conducting activities within the forum State, thus invoking the benefits and protections of its laws," *Hanson, supra,* at 253, it submits to the judicial power of an otherwise foreign sovereign to the extent that power is exercised in connection with the defendant's activities touching on the State. In other words, submission through contact with and activity directed at a sovereign may justify specific jurisdiction "in a suit arising out of or related to the defendant's contacts with the forum." *Helicopteros, supra,* at 414, n.8; see also *Goodyear.*

The imprecision arising from <u>*Asahi Metal Industry Co. v. Superior Court of Cal., Solano Cty.,* 480 U.S. 102 (1987),</u> for the most part, results from its statement of the relation between jurisdiction and the "stream of commerce." The stream of commerce, like other metaphors, has its deficiencies as well as its utility. It refers to the movement of goods from manufacturers through distributors to consumers, yet beyond that descriptive purpose its meaning is far from exact. This Court has stated that a defendant's placing goods into the stream of commerce "with the expectation that they will be purchased by consumers within the forum State" may indicate purposeful availment. <u>*World-Wide Volkswagen Corp. v. Woodson,* 444 U.S. 286, 298 (1980)</u> (finding that expectation lacking). But that statement does not amend the general rule of personal jurisdiction. It merely observes that a defendant may in an appropriate case be subject to jurisdiction without entering the forum—itself an unexceptional proposition—as where manufacturers or distributors "seek to serve" a given State's market. *Id.,* at 295. The principal inquiry in cases of this sort is whether the defendant's activities manifest an intention to submit to the power of a sovereign. In other words, the defendant must "purposefully avai[l] itself of the privilege of conducting activities within the forum State, thus invoking the benefits and protections of its laws." *Hanson, supra,* at 253; *Insurance Corp., supra,* at 704–705 ("[A]ctions of the defendant may amount to a legal submission to the jurisdiction of the court"). Sometimes a defendant does so by sending its goods rather than its agents. The defendant's transmission of goods permits the exercise of jurisdiction only where the defendant can be said to have targeted the forum; as a general rule, it is not enough that the defendant might have predicted that its goods will reach the forum State.

Food for Thought

Here Justice Kennedy indicates that the defendant must have targeted the forum for there to be jurisdiction. Does he indicate here or elsewhere in the opinion how that determination is made? Did Justice O'Connor offer a method in her *Asahi* opinion?

In *Asahi,* an opinion by Justice Brennan for four Justices outlined a different approach. It discarded the central concept of sovereign authority in favor of considerations of fairness and foreseeability. As that concurrence contended, "jurisdiction premised on the placement of a product into the stream of commerce [without more] is consistent with the Due Process Clause," for "[a]s long as a participant in this process is aware that the final product is being marketed in the forum State, the possibility of a lawsuit there cannot come as a surprise." 480 U.S., at 117 (opinion concurring in part and concurring in judgment). It was the premise of the concurring opinion that the defendant's ability to anticipate suit renders the assertion of jurisdiction fair. In this way, the opinion made foreseeability the touchstone of jurisdiction.

The standard set forth in Justice Brennan's concurrence was rejected in an opinion written by Justice O'Connor; but the relevant part of that opinion, too, commanded the assent of only four Justices, not a majority of the Court. That opinion stated: "The 'substantial connection' between the defendant and the forum State necessary for a finding of minimum contacts must come about by an action of the defendant purposefully directed toward the forum State. The placement of a product into the stream of commerce, without more, is not an act of the defendant purposefully directed toward the forum State." *Id., at 112.*

Since *Asahi* was decided, the courts have sought to reconcile the competing opinions. But Justice Brennan's concurrence, advocating a rule based on general notions of fairness and foreseeability, is inconsistent with the premises of lawful judicial power. This Court's precedents make clear that it is the defendant's actions, not his expectations, that empower a State's courts to subject him to judgment.

The conclusion that jurisdiction is in the first instance a question of authority rather than fairness explains, for example, why the principal opinion in *Burnham* "conducted no independent inquiry into the desirability or fairness" of the rule that service of process within a State suffices to establish jurisdiction over an otherwise foreign defendant. 495 U.S., at 621. As that opinion explained, "[t]he view developed early that each State had the power to hale before its courts any individual who could be found within its borders." *Id., at 610.* Furthermore, were general fairness considerations the touchstone of jurisdiction, a lack of purposeful availment might be excused where carefully crafted judicial procedures could otherwise protect the defendant's interests, or where the plaintiff would suffer substantial hardship if forced to litigate in a foreign forum. That such considerations have not been deemed controlling is instructive. *See, e.g., World-Wide Volkswagen, supra,* at 294.

Two principles are implicit in the foregoing. First, personal jurisdiction requires a forum-by-forum, or sovereign-by-sovereign, analysis. The question is whether a defendant has followed a course of conduct directed at the society or economy existing within the jurisdiction of a given sovereign, so that the sovereign has the power to subject the defendant to judgment concerning that conduct. Personal jurisdiction, of course, restricts "judicial power not as a matter of sovereignty, but as a matter of individual liberty," for due process protects the individual's right to be subject only to lawful power. <u>Insurance Corp., 456 U.S., at 702</u>. But whether a judicial judgment is lawful depends on whether the sovereign has authority to render it.

The second principle is a corollary of the first. Because the United States is a distinct sovereign, a defendant may in principle be subject to the jurisdiction of the courts of the United States but not of any particular State. This is consistent with the premises and unique genius of our Constitution. Ours is "a legal system unprecedented in form and design, establishing two orders of government, each with its own direct relationship, its own privity, its own set of mutual rights and obligations to the people who sustain it and are governed by it." <u>U.S. Term Limits, Inc. v. Thornton, 514 U.S. 779, 838 (1995)</u> (KENNEDY, J., concurring). For jurisdiction, a litigant may have the requisite relationship with the United States Government but not with the government of any individual State. That would be an exceptional case, however. If the defendant is a domestic domiciliary, the courts of its home State are available and can exercise general jurisdiction. And if another State were to assert jurisdiction in an inappropriate case, it would upset the federal balance, which posits that each State has a sovereignty that is not subject to unlawful intrusion by other States. Furthermore, foreign corporations will often target or concentrate on particular States, subjecting them to specific jurisdiction in those forums.

It must be remembered, however, that although this case and *Asahi* both involve foreign manufacturers, the undesirable consequences of Justice Brennan's approach are no less significant for domestic producers. The owner of a small Florida farm might sell crops to a large nearby distributor, for example, who might then distribute them to grocers across the country. If foreseeability were the controlling criterion, the farmer could be sued in Alaska or any number of other States' courts without ever leaving town. And the issue of foreseeability may itself be contested so that significant expenses are incurred just on the preliminary issue of jurisdiction. Jurisdictional rules should avoid these costs whenever possible.

The conclusion that the authority to subject a defendant to judgment depends on purposeful availment, consistent with Justice O'Connor's opinion in *Asahi,* does not by itself resolve many difficult questions of jurisdiction that will arise in particular cases. The defendant's conduct and the economic realities of the market the defendant seeks to serve will differ across cases, and judicial exposition will, in common-law fashion, clarify the contours of that principle.

III

In this case, petitioner directed marketing and sales efforts at the United States. * * * Here the question concerns the authority of a New Jersey state court to exercise jurisdiction, so it is petitioner's purposeful contacts with New Jersey, not with the United States, that alone are relevant.

Respondent has not established that J. McIntyre engaged in conduct purposefully directed at New Jersey. Recall that respondent's claim of jurisdiction centers on three facts: The distributor agreed to sell J. McIntyre's machines in the United States; J. McIntyre officials attended trade shows in several States but not in New Jersey; and up to four machines ended up in New Jersey. The British manufacturer had no office in New Jersey; it neither paid taxes nor owned property there; and it neither advertised in, nor sent any employees to, the State. Indeed, after discovery the trial court found that the "defendant does not have a single contact with New Jersey short of the machine in question ending up in this state." These facts may reveal an intent to serve the U.S. market, but they do not show that J. McIntyre purposefully availed itself of the New Jersey market.

It is notable that the New Jersey Supreme Court appears to agree, for it could "not find that J. McIntyre had a presence or minimum contacts in this State—in any jurisprudential sense—that would justify a New Jersey court to exercise jurisdiction in this case." 201 N.J., at 61. The court nonetheless held that petitioner could be sued in New Jersey based on a "stream-of-commerce theory of jurisdiction." *Ibid.* As discussed, however, the stream-of-commerce metaphor cannot supersede either the mandate of the Due Process Clause or the limits on judicial authority that Clause ensures. The New Jersey Supreme Court also cited "significant policy reasons" to justify its holding, including the State's "strong interest in protecting its citizens from defective products." *Id., at 75*. That interest is doubtless strong, but the Constitution commands restraint before discarding liberty in the name of expediency.

* * *

Due process protects petitioner's right to be subject only to lawful authority. At no time did petitioner engage in any activities in New Jersey that reveal an intent to invoke or benefit from the protection of its laws. New Jersey is without power to adjudge the rights and liabilities of J. McIntyre, and its exercise of jurisdiction would violate due process. The contrary judgment of the New Jersey Supreme Court is

Reversed.

JUSTICE BREYER, with whom JUSTICE ALITO joins, concurring in the judgment.

The Supreme Court of New Jersey adopted a broad understanding of the scope of personal jurisdiction based on its view that "[t]he increasingly fast-paced globalization of the world economy has removed national borders as barriers to trade." *Nicastro v. McIntyre Machinery America, Ltd.,* 201 N.J. 48, 52 (2010). I do not doubt that there have been many recent changes in commerce and communication, many of which are not anticipated by our precedents. But this case does not present any of those issues. So I think it unwise to announce a rule of broad applicability without full consideration of the modern-day consequences.

In my view, the outcome of this case is determined by our precedents. Based on the facts found by the New Jersey courts, respondent Robert Nicastro failed to meet his burden to demonstrate that it was constitutionally proper to exercise jurisdiction over petitioner J. McIntyre Machinery, Ltd. (British Manufacturer), a British firm that manufactures scrap-metal machines in Great Britain and sells them through an independent distributor in the United States (American Distributor). On that basis, I agree with the plurality that the contrary judgment of the Supreme Court of New Jersey should be reversed.

I

* * *

None of our precedents finds that a single isolated sale, even if accompanied by the kind of sales effort indicated here, is sufficient. Rather, this Court's previous holdings suggest the contrary. The Court has held that a single sale to a customer who takes an accident-causing product to a different State (where the accident takes place) is not a sufficient basis for asserting jurisdiction. See <u>World-Wide Volkswagen Corp. v. Woodson, 444 U.S. 286 (1980)</u>. And the Court, in separate opinions, has strongly suggested that a single sale of a product in a State does not constitute an adequate basis for asserting jurisdiction over an out-of-state defendant, even if that defendant places his goods in the stream of commerce, fully aware (and hoping) that such a sale will take place. See <u>Asahi Metal Industry Co. v. Superior Court of Cal., Solano Cty., 480 U.S. 102, 111, 112 (1987)</u> (opinion of O'Connor, J.) (requiring "something more" than simply placing "a product into the stream of commerce," even if defendant is "awar[e]" that the stream "may or will sweep the product into the forum State"); <u>id., at 117</u> (Brennan, J., concurring in part and concurring in judgment) (jurisdiction should lie where a sale in a State is part of "the regular and anticipated flow" of commerce into the State, but not where that sale is only an "edd[y]," *i.e.,* an isolated occurrence).

Here, the relevant facts found by the New Jersey Supreme Court show no "regular . . . flow" or "regular course" of sales in New Jersey; and there is no "something more," such as special state-related design, advertising, advice, marketing, or anything else. Mr. Nicastro, who here bears the burden of proving jurisdiction, has shown no specific effort by the British Manufacturer to sell in New Jersey. He has introduced no list of potential New Jersey customers who might, for example, have regularly attended trade shows. And he has not otherwise shown that the British Manufacturer "purposefully avail[ed] itself of the privilege of conducting activities" within New Jersey, or that it delivered its goods in the stream of commerce "with the expectation that they will be purchased" by New Jersey users. *World-Wide Volkswagen, supra,* at 297–298 (internal quotation marks omitted).

* * *

Accordingly, on the record present here, resolving this case requires no more than adhering to our precedents.

II

I would not go further. Because the incident at issue in this case does not implicate modern concerns, and because the factual record leaves many open questions, this is an unsuitable vehicle for making broad pronouncements that refashion basic jurisdictional rules.

* * *

JUSTICE GINSBURG, with whom JUSTICE SOTOMAYOR and JUSTICE KAGAN join, dissenting.

A foreign industrialist seeks to develop a market in the United States for machines it manufactures. It hopes to derive substantial revenue from sales it makes to United States purchasers. Where in the United States buyers reside does not matter to this manufacturer. Its goal is simply to sell as much as it can, wherever it can. It excludes no region or State from the market it wishes to reach. But, all things considered, it prefers to avoid products liability litigation in the United States. To that end, it engages a U.S. distributor to ship its machines stateside. Has it succeeded in escaping personal jurisdiction in a State where one of its products is sold and causes injury or even death to a local user?

Under this Court's pathmarking precedent in *International Shoe Co. v. Washington*, 326 U.S. 310 (1945), and subsequent decisions, one would expect the answer to be unequivocally, "No." But instead, six Justices of this Court, in divergent opinions, tell us that the manufacturer has avoided the jurisdiction of our state courts, except perhaps in States where its products are sold in sizeable quantities. Inconceivable as it may have seemed yesterday, the splintered majority today "turn[s] the clock back to the days before modern long-arm statutes when a manufacturer, to avoid being haled into court where a user is injured, need only Pilate-like wash its hands of a product by having independent distributors market it." Weintraub, *A Map Out of the Personal Jurisdiction Labyrinth*, 28 U.C. DAVIS L. REV. 531, 555 (1995).

I

On October 11, 2001, a three-ton metal shearing machine severed four fingers on Robert Nicastro's right hand. Alleging that the machine was a dangerous product defectively made, Nicastro sought compensation from the machine's manufacturer, J. McIntyre Machinery Ltd. (McIntyre UK). Established in 1872 as a United Kingdom corporation, and headquartered in Nottingham, England, McIntyre UK "designs, develops and manufactures a complete range of equipment for metal recycling." The company's product line, as advertised on McIntyre UK's Web site, includes "metal shears, balers, cable and can recycling equipment, furnaces, casting equipment and . . . the world's best aluminium dross processing and cooling system." McIntyre UK holds both United States and European patents on its technology.

The machine that injured Nicastro, a "McIntyre Model 640 Shear," sold in the United States for $24,900 in 1995, and features a "massive cutting capacity." According to McIntyre UK's product brochure, the machine is "use[d] throughout the [w]orld." * * * Nicastro operated the 640 Shear in the course of his employment at Curcio Scrap Metal (CSM) in Saddle Brook, New Jersey. CSM's owner, Frank Curcio, "first heard of [McIntyre UK's] machine while attending an Institute of Scrap Metal Industries [(ISRI)] convention in Las Vegas in 1994 or 1995, where [McIntyre UK] was an exhibitor." * * *

McIntyre UK representatives attended every ISRI convention from 1990 through 2005. These annual expositions were held in diverse venues across the United States; in addition to Las Vegas, conventions were held 1990–2005 in New Orleans, Orlando, San Antonio, and San Francisco. McIntyre UK's president, Michael Pownall, regularly attended ISRI conventions. He attended ISRI's Las Vegas convention the year CSM's owner first learned of, and saw, the 640 Shear. McIntyre UK exhibited its products at ISRI trade shows, the company acknowledged, hoping to reach "anyone interested in the machine from anywhere in the United States."

* * *

From at least 1995 until 2001, McIntyre UK retained an Ohio-based company, McIntyre Machinery America, Ltd. (McIntyre America), "as its exclusive distributor for the entire United States." *Nicastro v. McIntyre Machinery America, Ltd.,* 399 N.J. Super. 539, 558 (App. 2008). Though similarly named, the two companies were separate and independent entities with "no commonality of ownership or management." *Id., at 545.* In invoices and other written communications, McIntyre America described itself as McIntyre UK's national distributor, "America's Link" to "Quality Metal Processing Equipment" from England.

In a November 23, 1999 letter to McIntyre America, McIntyre UK's president spoke plainly about the manufacturer's objective in authorizing the exclusive distributorship: "All we wish to do is sell our products in the [United] States—and get paid!" * * *

Over the years, McIntyre America distributed several McIntyre UK products to U.S. customers, including, in addition to the 640 Shear, McIntyre UK's "Niagara" and "Tardis" systems, wire strippers, and can machines. In promoting McIntyre UK's products at conventions and demonstration sites and in trade journal advertisements, McIntyre America looked to McIntyre UK for direction and guidance. To achieve McIntyre UK's objective, *i.e.,* "to sell [its] machines to customers throughout the United States," 399 N.J. Super., at 548, "the two companies [were acting] closely in concert with each other," *ibid.* McIntyre UK never instructed its distributor to avoid certain States or regions of the country; rather, as just noted, the manufacturer engaged McIntyre America to attract customers "from anywhere in the United States."

In sum, McIntyre UK's regular attendance and exhibitions at ISRI conventions was surely a purposeful step to reach customers for its products "anywhere in the United States." At least as purposeful was McIntyre UK's engagement of McIntyre America as the conduit for sales of McIntyre UK's machines to buyers "throughout the United States." Given McIntyre UK's endeavors to reach and profit from the United States market as a whole, Nicastro's suit, I would hold, has been brought in a forum entirely appropriate for the adjudication of his claim. He alleges that McIntyre UK's shear machine was defectively designed or manufactured and, as a result, caused injury to him at his workplace. The machine arrived in Nicastro's New Jersey workplace not randomly or fortuitously, but as a result of the U.S. connections and distribution system that McIntyre UK deliberately arranged. On what sensible view of the allocation of adjudicatory authority could the place of Nicastro's injury within the United States be deemed off limits for his products liability claim against a foreign manufacturer who targeted the United States (including all the States that constitute the Nation) as the territory it sought to develop?

II

* * * [T]he constitutional limits on a state court's adjudicatory authority derive from considerations of due process, not state sovereignty. * * * [I]n *International Shoe* itself, and decisions thereafter, the Court has made plain that legal fictions, notably "presence" and "implied consent," should be discarded, for they conceal the actual bases on which jurisdiction rests. *See* 326 U.S., at 316, 318. "[T]he relationship among the defendant, the forum, and the litigation" determines whether due process permits the exercise of personal jurisdiction over a defendant, *Shaffer,* 433 U.S., at 204, and "fictions of implied consent" or "corporate presence" do not advance the proper inquiry, *id.,* at 202. *See also Burnham v. Superior Court of Cal., County of Marin,* 495 U.S. 604, 618, 110 S.Ct. 2105, 109 L.Ed.2d 631 (1990) (plurality opinion) (*International Shoe* "cast . . . aside" fictions of "consent" and "presence").

* * * [T]he plurality's notion that consent is the animating concept draws no support from controlling decisions of this Court. Quite the contrary, the Court has explained, a forum can exercise jurisdiction when its contacts with the controversy are sufficient; invocation of a fictitious consent, the Court has repeatedly said, is unnecessary and unhelpful. *See, e.g., Burger King Corp. v. Rudzewicz,* 471 U.S. 462, 472, 105 S.Ct. 2174, 85 L.Ed.2d 528 (1985) (Due Process Clause permits "forum . . . to assert specific jurisdiction over an out-of-state defendant who has not consented to suit there"); <u>McGee v. International Life Ins. Co., 355 U.S. 220, 222, 78 S.Ct. 199, 2 L.Ed.2d 223 (1957)</u> ("[T]his Court [has] abandoned 'consent,' 'doing business,' and 'presence' as the standard for measuring the extent of state judicial power over [out-of-state] corporations.").[5]

III

* * *

The modern approach to jurisdiction over corporations and other legal entities, ushered in by *International Shoe,* gave prime place to reason and fairness. Is it not fair and reasonable, given the mode of trading of which this case is an example, to require the international seller to defend at the place its products cause injury? Do not litigational convenience and choice-of-law considerations point in that direction? On what measure of reason and fairness can it be considered undue to require McIntyre UK to defend in New Jersey as an incident of its efforts to develop a market for its industrial machines anywhere and everywhere in the United States? Is not the burden on McIntyre UK to defend in New Jersey fair, *i.e.,* a reasonable cost of transacting business internationally, in comparison to the burden on Nicastro to go to Nottingham, England to gain recompense for an injury he sustained using McIntyre's product at his workplace in Saddle Brook, New Jersey?

McIntyre UK dealt with the United States as a single market. Like most foreign manufacturers, it was concerned not with the prospect of suit in State X as opposed to State Y, but rather with its subjection to suit anywhere in the United States. As a McIntyre UK officer wrote in an e-mail to McIntyre America: "American law—who needs it?!" If McIntyre UK is answerable in the United States at all, is it not "perfectly appropriate to permit the exercise of that jurisdiction . . . at the place of injury"? *See* Degnan & Kane, <u>The Exercise of Jurisdiction Over and Enforcement of Judgments Against Alien Defendants, 39 Hastings L.J. 799, 813–815 (1988)</u> (noting that "[i]n the international order," the State that counts is the United States, not its component States, and that the fair place of suit within the United States is essentially a question of venue).

In sum, McIntyre UK, by engaging McIntyre America to promote and sell its machines in the United States, "purposefully availed itself" of the United States market nationwide, not a market in a single State or a discrete collection of States. McIntyre UK thereby availed itself of the market of all States in which its products were sold by its exclusive distributor. "Th[e] 'purposeful availment' requirement," this Court has explained, simply "ensures that a defendant will not be haled into a jurisdiction solely as a result of 'random,' 'fortuitous,' or 'attenuated' contacts."

---

[5] The plurality's notion that jurisdiction over foreign corporations depends upon the defendant's "submission," seems scarcely different from the long-discredited fiction of implied consent. It bears emphasis that a majority of this Court's members do not share the plurality's view.

Burger King, 471 U.S., at 475. Adjudicatory authority is appropriately exercised where "actions by the defendant *himself*" give rise to the affiliation with the forum. *Ibid.* How could McIntyre UK not have intended, by its actions targeting a national market, to sell products in the fourth largest destination for imports among all States of the United States and the largest scrap metal market?

Food for Thought

Justice Ginsburg finds purposeful availment under these facts while Justice Kennedy does not. What accounts for the difference? Have they articulated different tests or do they view the facts differently?

* * *

IV.A

While this Court has not considered in any prior case the now-prevalent pattern presented here—a foreign-country manufacturer enlisting a U.S. distributor to develop a market in the United States for the manufacturer's products—none of the Court's decisions tug against the judgment made by the New Jersey Supreme Court. McIntyre contends otherwise, citing *World-Wide Volkswagen*, and *Asahi Metal Industry Co. v. Superior Court of Cal., Solano Cty., 480 U.S. 102 (1987)*.

* * *

Notably, the foreign manufacturer of the Audi in *World-Wide Volkswagen* did not object to the jurisdiction of the Oklahoma courts and the U.S. importer abandoned its initially stated objection. 444 U.S., at 288, and n.3. And most relevant here, the Court's opinion indicates that an objection to jurisdiction by the manufacturer or national distributor would have been unavailing. To reiterate, the Court said in *World-Wide Volkswagen* that, when a manufacturer or distributor aims to sell its product to customers in several States, it is reasonable "to subject it to suit in [any] one of those States if its allegedly defective [product] has there been the source of injury." *Id.*, at 297.

Asahi arose out of a motorcycle accident in California. Plaintiff, a California resident injured in the accident, sued the Taiwanese manufacturer of the motorcycle's tire tubes, claiming that defects in its product caused the accident. The tube manufacturer cross-claimed against Asahi, the Japanese maker of the valve assembly, and Asahi contested the California courts' jurisdiction. By the time the case reached this Court, the injured plaintiff had settled his case and only the indemnity claim by the Taiwanese company against the Japanese valve-assembly manufacturer remained.

The decision was not a close call. The Court had before it a foreign plaintiff, the Taiwanese manufacturer, and a foreign defendant, the Japanese valve-assembly maker, and the indemnification dispute concerned a transaction between those parties that occurred abroad. All agreed on the bottom line: The Japanese valve-assembly manufacturer was not reasonably brought into the California courts to litigate a dispute with another foreign party over a transaction that took place outside the United States.

* * *

* * * Asahi, unlike McIntyre UK, did not itself seek out customers in the United States, it engaged no distributor to promote its wares here, it appeared at no tradeshows in the United States, and, of course, it had no Web site advertising its products to the world. Moreover, Asahi was a component-part manufacturer with "little control over the final destination of its products once they were delivered into the stream of commerce." It was important to the Court in *Asahi* that "those who use Asahi components in their final products, and sell those products in California, [would be] subject to the application of California tort law." 480 U.S., at 115 (majority opinion). To hold that *Asahi* controls this case would, to put it bluntly, be dead wrong.

* * *

For the reasons stated, I would hold McIntyre UK answerable in New Jersey for the harm Nicastro suffered at his workplace in that State using McIntyre UK's shearing machine. While I dissent from the Court's judgment, I take heart that the plurality opinion does not speak for the Court, for that opinion would take a giant step away from the "notions of fair play and substantial justice" underlying *International Shoe.* 326 U.S., at 316 (internal quotation marks omitted).

———————————

Points for Discussion

a. The Law After *Asahi*

No entire opinion in *Asahi* garnered the support of a majority of the Justices. This is unfortunate because the disparate opinions propound quite distinct views of how personal jurisdiction should be analyzed in stream-of-commerce cases. How would you describe the differing tests articulated by Justice O'Connor and Justice Brennan? What precedential effect should be given to the various opinions in *Asahi*, if any?

Food for Thought

The division among the Justices in *Asahi* left lower courts free to follow the test put forth in either of the two principal opinions. *Compare, e.g., Luv N' care, Ltd. v. Insta-Mix, Inc, 438 F.3d 465, 470 (5th Cir. 2006)* (following the Brennan approach), *with Fortis Corporate Ins. v. Viken Ship Mgmt., 450 F.3d 214, 220 (6th Cir. 2006)* (following the O'Connor approach). Which approach is more consistent with the Supreme Court's prior precedents?

Although the Justices were not in general agreement, there was majority support for the Court's analysis in Part II-B of the opinion, in which the Court analyzed the reasonableness of California's assertion of jurisdiction. The five factors used here, often referred to as the *Asahi* factors, are central to this analysis and comprise the substance of the reasonableness prong of personal jurisdiction analysis today.

b. The Law After *McIntyre*

As in Asahi, the Justices in McIntyre were unable to resolve the question before them with a majority opinion. Thus, even though the Court agreed to hear the appeal in McIntyre most likely for the purpose of resolving the split created by Asahi, it failed to do so. What then is the state of the stream-of-commerce doctrine after McIntyre? See, e.g., *AFTG-TG, L.L.C. v. Nuvoton Tech. Corp., 689 F.3d 1358, 1363 (Fed. Cir. 2012)* ("Because McIntyre did not produce a majority opinion, we must follow the narrowest holding among the plurality opinions in that case. The narrowest holding is that which can be distilled from Justice Breyer's concurrence—that the law remains the same after McIntyre." (citing *Marks v. United States, 430 U.S. 188, 193 (1977)*)). *See also Williams v. Romarm, SA, 756 F.3d 777, 784 (D.C.*

Food for Thought

In *Marks v. United States* the Supreme Court stated, "When a fragmented Court decides a case and no single rationale explaining the result enjoys the assent of five Justices, the holding of the Court may be viewed as that position taken by those Members who concurred in the judgments on the narrowest grounds."

Cir. 2014) (embracing Justice Breyer's concurrence as the narrowest of the *McIntyre* opinions). Courts in other circuits have treated *McIntyre*'s lack of any majority as indicative of no change to prior doctrine. *See, e.g., Ainsworth v. Moffett Eng'g, Ltd., 716 F.3d 174, 179 (5th Cir. 2013)* (applying its pre-*McIntyre* stream-of-commerce precedent based on the conclusion that *McIntyre* failed to alter the Supreme Court's existing stream-of-commerce framework); *Wireless Environment, LLC v. HooToo.com, Inc., No. 1:15CV1215, 2016 WL 4530617, at *3 (N.D. Ohio Aug. 30, 2016)* ("Since the Supreme Court in *Nicastro* did not resolve the circuit split . . . the Sixth Circuit's 'stream of commerce plus' approach . . . continues to control.").

Even though five Justices failed to settle on an agreed approach to analyzing stream-of-commerce cases, is there at least a majority *against* any of the two competing approaches in *Asahi*? Be sure to understand each of the perspectives offered by the three competing opinions in *McIntyre*. For a good discussion of the opinions in *McIntyre*, see Adam N. Steinman, *The Lay of the Land: Examining the Three Opinions in* J. McIntyre Machinery, Ltd. v. Nicastro, 63 S.C. L. REV. 481 (2012).

Hypo 1.5, which follows, tests your understanding of and ability to apply the various approaches to the stream-of-commerce analysis featured in Asahi and McIntyre.

Hypo 1.5

Mini Gun, Inc., a Wyoming corporation, manufactures tiny guns that are used in the manufacture of G.I. George, a doll that looks like a soldier. The dolls in turn are manufactured by HB Toys, a Texas corporation, which distributes them in the southwestern United States. Mini Gun has no control whatsoever over where HB Toys chooses to sell the G.I. George dolls, but it knows from payments it has received over the last ten years that HB Toys has been selling 1,000 dolls a year in New Mexico. Mini Gun's contract with HB Toys calls for it to be paid based on the number of dolls sold. In New Mexico, a toddler swallows the gun of a G.I. George doll and suffers personal injuries.

The child's parents sue Mini Gun in New Mexico, which has a long-arm statute authorizing jurisdiction to the constitutional limit. May New Mexico courts exercise personal jurisdiction over Mini Gun in this products-liability action?

The most recent statement of the Supreme Court on the minimum contacts test for personal jurisdiction came in the next case, where there Court upheld the notion that due process requires a connection between plaintiffs' claims and a state to permit the courts of that state to adjudicate those claims.

Bristol-Myers Squibb Co. v. Superior Court

Supreme Court of the United States
137 S. Ct. 1773 (2017)

JUSTICE ALITO delivered the opinion of the Court.

More than 600 plaintiffs, most of whom are not California residents, filed this civil action in a California state court against Bristol-Myers Squibb Company (BMS), asserting a variety of state-law claims based on injuries allegedly caused by a BMS drug called Plavix. The California Supreme Court held that the California courts have specific jurisdiction to entertain the nonresidents' claims. We now reverse.

I.A

BMS, a large pharmaceutical company, is incorporated in Delaware and headquartered in New York, and it maintains substantial operations in both New York and New Jersey. Over 50 percent of BMS's work force in the United States is employed in those two States.

BMS also engages in business activities in other jurisdictions, including California. Five of the company's research and laboratory facilities, which employ a total of around 160 employees, are located there. BMS also employs about 250 sales representatives in California and maintains a small state-government advocacy office in Sacramento.

One of the pharmaceuticals that BMS manufactures and sells is Plavix, a prescription drug that thins the blood and inhibits blood clotting. BMS did not develop Plavix in California, did not create a marketing strategy for Plavix in California, and did not manufacture, label, package, or work on the regulatory approval of the product in California. BMS instead engaged in all of these activities in either New York or New Jersey. But BMS does sell Plavix in California. Between 2006 and 2012, it sold almost 187 million Plavix pills in the State and took in more than $900 million from those sales. This amounts to a little over one percent of the company's nationwide sales revenue.

B

A group of plaintiffs—consisting of 86 California residents and 592 residents from 33 other States—filed eight separate complaints in California Superior Court, alleging that Plavix had damaged their health. All the complaints asserted 13 claims under California law, including products liability, negligent misrepresentation, and misleading advertising claims. The nonresident plaintiffs did not allege that they obtained Plavix through California physicians or from any other California source;

nor did they claim that they were injured by Plavix or were treated for their injuries in California.

Asserting lack of personal jurisdiction, BMS moved to quash service of summons on the nonresidents' claims, but the California Superior Court denied this motion * * * . * * *

[After petitioning the California Court of Appeal for a writ of mandate,] [t]he Court of Appeal * * * went on to find that the California courts had specific jurisdiction over the nonresidents' claims against BMS.

What's That?

A writ of mandate is an order of a court to an inferior court to compel it to do something that the law requires. In some states, it is a mechanism provided for achieving interlocutory (*i.e.* immediate) appeals of adverse determinations on threshold issues such as personal jurisdiction.

The California Supreme Court affirmed. The court * * * was divided on the question of specific jurisdiction. The majority applied a "sliding scale approach to specific jurisdiction." Under this approach, "the more wide ranging the defendant's forum contacts, the more readily is shown a connection between the forum contacts and the claim." Applying this test, the majority concluded that "BMS's extensive contacts with California" permitted the exercise of specific jurisdiction "based on a less direct connection between BMS's forum activities and plaintiffs' claims than might otherwise be required." This attenuated requirement was met, the majority found, because the claims of the nonresidents were similar in several ways to the claims of the California residents (as to which specific jurisdiction was uncontested). The court noted that "[b]oth the resident and nonresident plaintiffs' claims are based on the same allegedly defective product and the assertedly misleading marketing and promotion of that product." And while acknowledging that "there is no claim that Plavix itself was designed and developed in [BMS's California research facilities]," the court thought it significant that other research was done in the State.

* * *

We granted certiorari to decide whether the California courts' exercise of jurisdiction in this case violates the Due Process Clause of the Fourteenth Amendment.

II.A

It has long been established that the Fourteenth Amendment limits the personal jurisdiction of state courts. Because "[a] state court's assertion of jurisdiction exposes defendants to the State's coercive power," it is "subject to review for compatibility with the Fourteenth Amendment's Due Process Clause," *Goodyear Dunlop Tires*

Operations, S.A. v. Brown, 564 U.S. 915, 918, 131 S.Ct. 2846, 180 L.Ed.2d 796 (2011), which "limits the power of a state court to render a valid personal judgment against a nonresident defendant," *World-Wide Volkswagen,* 100 S.Ct. 559 [(1980)]. The primary focus of our personal jurisdiction inquiry is the defendant's relationship to the forum State. See *Walden v. Fiore,* 134 S.Ct. 1115, 1121–1123 (2014); *Phillips Petroleum Co. v. Shutts,* 472 U.S. 797, 806–807 (1985).

* * *

* * * In order for a state court to exercise specific jurisdiction, "the *suit* " must "aris[e] out of or relat[e] to the defendant's contacts with the *forum.*" *Daimler AG v. Bauman,*134 S.Ct. 746 (2014) (internal quotation marks omitted; emphasis added); see *Burger King Corp. v. Rudzewicz,* 471 U.S. 462, 472–473 (1985); *Helicopteros Nacionales de Colombia, S.A. v. Hall,* 466 U.S. 408, 414 (1984). In other words, there must be "an affiliation between the forum and the underlying controversy, principally, [an] activity or an occurrence that takes place in the forum State and is therefore subject to the State's regulation." *Goodyear,* 564 U.S., at 919, 131 S.Ct. 2846 (internal quotation marks and brackets omitted). For this reason, "specific jurisdiction is confined to adjudication of issues deriving from, or connected with, the very controversy that establishes jurisdiction." (internal quotation marks omitted).

B

In determining whether personal jurisdiction is present, a court must consider a variety of interests. These include "the interests of the forum State and of the plaintiff in proceeding with the cause in the plaintiff's forum of choice." *Kulko v. Superior Court of Cal., City and County of San Francisco,* 436 U.S. 84, 92 (1978); see *Daimler,* 134 S.Ct., at 762, n. 20; *Asahi Metal Industry Co. v. Superior Court of Cal., Solano Cty.,* 480 U.S. 102, 113 (1987); *World-Wide Volkswagen,* 444 U.S., at 292. But the "primary concern" is "the burden on the defendant." *Id., at 292.* Assessing this burden obviously requires a court to consider the practical problems resulting from litigating in the forum, but it also encompasses the more abstract matter of submitting to the coercive power of a State that may have little legitimate interest in the claims in question. As we have put it, restrictions on personal jurisdiction "are more than a guarantee of immunity from inconvenient or distant litigation. They are a consequence of territorial limitations on the power of the respective States." *Hanson v. Denckla,* 357 U.S. 235, 251 (1958). "[T]he States retain many essential attributes of sovereignty, including, in particular, the sovereign power to try causes in their courts. The sovereignty of each State . . . implie[s] a limitation on the sovereignty of all its sister States." *World-Wide Volkswagen,* 444 U.S., at 293. And at times, this federalism interest may be decisive. As we explained in *World-Wide Volkswagen,* "[e]ven if the defendant would suffer minimal or no inconvenience from being forced to litigate before the tribunals of another State; even if the forum State has a strong interest in applying its law to the controversy; even if the forum State is the most convenient location for litigation, the Due Process Clause, acting as an instrument of interstate federalism, may sometimes act to divest the State of its power to render a valid judgment." *Id., at 294*.

III.A

Our settled principles regarding specific jurisdiction control this case. In order for a court to exercise specific jurisdiction over a claim, there must be an "affiliation between the forum and the underlying controversy, principally, [an] activity or an occurrence that takes place in the forum State." *Goodyear, 564 U.S., at 919* (internal quotation marks and brackets in original omitted). When there is no such connection, specific jurisdiction is lacking regardless of the extent of a defendant's unconnected activities in the State. See *id., at 931, n. 6* ("[E]ven regularly occurring sales of a product in a State do not justify the exercise of jurisdiction over a claim unrelated to those sales").

For this reason, the California Supreme Court's "sliding scale approach" is difficult to square with our precedents. Under the California approach, the strength of the requisite connection between the forum and the specific claims at issue is relaxed if the defendant has extensive forum contacts that are unrelated to those claims. Our cases provide no support for this approach, which resembles a loose and spurious form of general jurisdiction. For specific jurisdiction, a defendant's general connections with the forum are not enough. As we have said, "[a] corporation's 'continuous activity of some sorts within a state . . . is not enough to support the demand that the corporation be amenable to suits unrelated to that activity.' " *Id., at 927, 131 S.Ct. 2846* (quoting *International Shoe, 326 U.S., at 318, 66 S.Ct. 154*).

What's That?

General jurisdiction is a form of "all-purpose" jurisdiction that a court may exercise over a person or entity in its home state, without any need for a connection between the claims and that state. General jurisdiction is covered in the next section of this chapter.

The present case illustrates the danger of the California approach. The State Supreme Court found that specific jurisdiction was present without identifying any adequate link between the State and the nonresidents' claims. As noted, the nonresidents were not prescribed Plavix in California, did not purchase Plavix in California, did not ingest Plavix in California, and were not injured by Plavix in California. The mere fact that *other* plaintiffs were prescribed, obtained, and ingested Plavix in California—and allegedly sustained the same injuries as did the nonresidents—does not allow the State to assert specific jurisdiction over the nonresidents' claims. As we have explained, "a defendant's relationship with a . . . third party, standing alone, is an insufficient basis for jurisdiction." *Walden, 134 S.Ct., at 1123*. This remains true even when third parties (here, the plaintiffs who reside in California) can bring claims similar to those brought by the nonresidents. Nor is it sufficient—or even relevant—that BMS conducted research in California on matters unrelated to Plavix. What is needed—and what is missing here—is a connection between the forum and the specific claims at issue.

Our decision in *Walden, supra,* illustrates this requirement. In that case, Nevada plaintiffs sued an out-of-state defendant for conducting an allegedly unlawful search of the plaintiffs while they were in Georgia preparing to board a plane bound for Nevada. We held that the Nevada courts lacked specific jurisdiction even though the plaintiffs were Nevada residents and "suffered foreseeable harm in Nevada." *Id., 134 S.Ct., at 1124.* Because the "*relevant* conduct occurred entirely in Georgi[a] . . . the mere fact that [this] conduct affected plaintiffs with connections to the forum State d[id] not suffice to authorize jurisdiction." *Id., 134 S.Ct., at 1126* (emphasis added).

In today's case, the connection between the nonresidents' claims and the forum is even weaker. The relevant plaintiffs are not California residents and do not claim to have suffered harm in that State. In addition, as in *Walden,* all the conduct giving rise to the nonresidents' claims occurred elsewhere. It follows that the California courts cannot claim specific jurisdiction. See *World-Wide Volkswagen, supra, at 295* (finding no personal jurisdiction in Oklahoma because the defendant "carr[ied] on no activity whatsoever in Oklahoma" and dismissing "the fortuitous circumstance that a single Audi automobile, sold [by defendants] in New York to New York residents, happened to suffer an accident while passing through Oklahoma" as an "isolated occurrence").

B

The nonresidents maintain that two of our cases support the decision below, but they misinterpret those precedents. [The Court went on to indicate how neither *Keeton v. Hustler Magazine, Inc., 465 U.S. 770 (1984),* nor *Phillips Petroleum Co. v. Shutts, 472 U.S. 797 (1985),* provide any support for the nonresidents' position].

C

In a last ditch contention, respondents contend that BMS's "decision to contract with a California company [McKesson] to distribute [Plavix] nationally" provides a sufficient basis for personal jurisdiction. But as we have explained, "[t]he requirements of *International Shoe* . . . must be met as to each defendant over whom a state court exercises jurisdiction." *Rush v. Savchuk, 444 U.S. 320, 332 (1980)*; see *Walden, 134 S.Ct., at 1123* ("[A] defendant's relationship with a . . . third party, standing alone, is an insufficient basis for jurisdiction"). In this case, it is not alleged that BMS engaged in relevant acts together with McKesson in California. Nor is it alleged that BMS is derivatively liable for McKesson's conduct in California. And the nonresidents "have adduced no evidence to show how or by whom the Plavix they took was distributed to the pharmacies that dispensed it to them." The bare fact that

BMS contracted with a California distributor is not enough to establish personal jurisdiction in the State.

IV

Our straightforward application in this case of settled principles of personal jurisdiction will not result in the parade of horribles that respondents conjure up. Our decision does not prevent the California and out-of-state plaintiffs from joining together in a consolidated action in the States that have general jurisdiction over BMS. BMS concedes that such suits could be brought in either New York or Delaware. Alternatively, the plaintiffs who are residents of a particular State—for example, the 92 plaintiffs from Texas and the 71 from Ohio—could probably sue together in their home States. In addition, since our decision concerns the due process limits on the exercise of specific jurisdiction by a State, we leave open the question whether the Fifth Amendment imposes the same restrictions on the exercise of personal jurisdiction by a federal court. See *Omni Capital Int'l, Ltd. v. Rudolf Wolff & Co.*, 484 U.S. 97, 102, n. 5 (1987).

* * *

The judgment of the California Supreme Court is reversed, and the case is remanded for further proceedings not inconsistent with this opinion.

It is so ordered.

JUSTICE SOTOMAYOR, dissenting.

Three years ago, the Court imposed substantial curbs on the exercise of general jurisdiction in its decision in *Daimler AG v. Bauman*, 134 S.Ct. 746 (2014). Today, the Court takes its first step toward a similar contraction of specific jurisdiction by holding that a corporation that engages in a nationwide course of conduct cannot be held accountable in a state court by a group of injured people unless all of those people were injured in the forum State.

I fear the consequences of the Court's decision today will be substantial. The majority's rule will make it difficult to aggregate the claims of plaintiffs across the country whose claims may be worth little alone. It will make it impossible to bring a nationwide mass action in state court against defendants who are "at home" in different States. And it will result in piecemeal litigation and the bifurcation of claims. None of this is necessary. A core concern in this Court's personal jurisdiction cases is fairness. And there is nothing unfair about subjecting a massive corporation to suit in a State for a nationwide course of conduct that injures both forum residents and nonresidents alike. [Justice Sotomayor went on to conclude that BMS was subject to specific jurisdiction in California on the nonresidents' claims because it had purposefully availed itself of California, the nonresidents' claims were related to the claims of the California residents given that they were based on similar conduct by BMS, and the assertion of jurisdiction would be reasonable.]

* * *

It "does not offend 'traditional notions of fair play and substantial justice,' " *International Shoe*, 326 U.S., at 316, 66 S.Ct. 154 to permit plaintiffs to aggregate claims arising out of a single nationwide course of conduct in a single suit in a single State where some, but not all, were injured. But that is exactly what the Court holds today is barred by the Due Process Clause.

This is not a rule the Constitution has required before. I respectfully dissent.

Points for Discussion

a.   The Outcome in *Bristol-Myers Squibb*

The majority in *Bristol-Myers Squibb* seemed to have no difficulty concluding that there was no specific jurisdiction over the claims of nonresident plaintiffs whose claims lacked any connection to the forum state, California. Do you agree that this result is straightforward and compelled by the Court's precedents, or do you sympathize with Justice Sotomayor's perspective expressed in her dissent? What are the consequences of this decision for the nonresident plaintiffs? Are their prospects for obtaining relief against BMS doomed by the decision?

b.   Specific Jurisdiction Doctrine After *Bristol-Myers Squibb*

What does the doctrine of specific jurisdiction look like in the wake of *Bristol-Myers Squibb*? The Court made clear that to support specific jurisdiction, "the suit must arise out of or relate to the defendant's contacts with the forum." Additionally, the Court affirmed that the reasonableness of jurisdiction is a consideration, but that the "burden on the defendant" is a "primary consideration" in relation to other considerations such as the interests of the forum state and the plaintiff. Lastly, the Court stated that limitations on state sovereignty were a source of the due process limitations on personal jurisdiction, not merely considerations of fairness. How do these views jibe with previous articulations of specific jurisdiction doctrine by the Court?

At bottom, it seems clear that the Court will not permit a state court to exercise specific jurisdiction over claims that are unrelated to connections that the defendant has with that state. Do you have a clear sense of what the standard is for determining whether a claim "relates to" the defendant's forum state contacts? What if the facts of *Bristol-Myers Squibb* were different and showed that BMS developed its entire Plavix marketing strategy in California and all Plavix advertising nationally emanated out of California? Do you think that would be sufficient to permit California courts to exercise specific jurisdiction over the claims of nonresidents who purchased, ingested, and were harmed by Plavix outside of California?

c. Vicarious Personal Jurisdiction?

In *Bristol-Myers Squibb* the nonresident plaintiffs largely relied on the fact that their claims were identical to the claims of the plaintiffs who were California residents. The Court squarely rejected the idea that claims that independently would not qualify for specific personal jurisdiction could somehow be eligible for jurisdiction based merely on the fact that there were coplaintiffs whose claims did qualify for specific jurisdiction:

> The mere fact that other plaintiffs were prescribed, obtained, and ingested Plavix in California—and allegedly sustained the same injuries as did the nonresidents—does not allow the State to assert specific jurisdiction over the nonresidents' claims. As we have explained, "a defendant's relationship with a . . . third party, standing alone, is an insufficient basis for jurisdiction." *Walden*, 134 S.Ct., at 1123. This remains true even when third parties (here, the plaintiffs who reside in California) can bring claims similar to those brought by the nonresidents.

This result is not surprising. It is an established principle that when a plaintiff relies on specific jurisdiction, she must establish that jurisdiction is proper for "each claim asserted against a defendant." *Action Embroidery Corp. v. Atl. Embroidery, Inc.*, 368 F.3d 1174, 1180 (9th Cir. 2004); *see also Phillips Exeter Academy v. Howard Phillips Fund*, 196 F.3d 284, 289 (1st Cir. 1999) ("Questions of specific jurisdiction are always tied to the particular claims asserted."); 5B C. WRIGHT & A. MILLER, FED. PRAC. & PROC. § 1351 n.30 (3d ed. 2004) ("There is no such thing as supplemental specific personal jurisdiction; if separate claims are pled, specific personal jurisdiction must independently exist for each claim and the existence of personal jurisdiction for one claim will not provide the basis for another claim.").

3. Modern Challenge: Personal Jurisdiction Based on Internet Contacts

The *Asahi* case was decided long before the dawn of the Information Age, a period that would see the development of pervasive personal computing, instant electronic communications, and a global network called the Internet that would change the world forever. These dramatic technological advances have had an enormous impact on all aspects of civil litigation, including personal jurisdiction doctrine.

As human activity has migrated into the online world, instances of actionable wrongdoing mediated through the Internet have come with it. Just as one could defame Shirley Jones via the circulation of a print newspaper in real space, today the same defamatory comments can be circulated instantly to the entire world via cyberspace. Fraud is quite at home in the online environment, where people are bombarded daily with fraudulent email schemes that inevitably seek to separate their victims from some portion of their hard-earned money. Or, more simply, an online retailer may have no physical operations within a jurisdiction but regularly sells and distributes products to customers there through its website; disputes between such sellers and their customers will ultimately arise in such a context as often as, if not more frequently than, they do in the physical world.

Go Online!

Email fraud is so pervasive that the FBI keeps track of this activity. Visit https://www.ic3.gov/crimeschemes.asp to see a website maintained by the FBI's Cyber Investigations unit that updates the public on the latest Internet crime schemes.

When a defendant's contacts with a forum state are mediated through the Internet, what standards should courts use to evaluate these contacts? How should the issue of purposeful availment be evaluated when the defendant's contacts with a state consist of websites that are available everywhere in the world and thus in every state in the country? Can the minimum contacts analysis be applied to such virtual contacts or does that test require some modification for this medium? Consider these questions as you read the next case.

Young v. New Haven Advocate

U.S. Court of Appeals for the Fourth Circuit
315 F.3d 256 (4th Cir. 2002)

MICHAEL, CIRCUIT JUDGE.

The question in this appeal is whether two Connecticut newspapers and certain of their staff (sometimes, the "newspaper defendants") subjected themselves to personal jurisdiction in Virginia by posting on the Internet news articles that, in the context of discussing the State of Connecticut's policy of housing its prisoners in Virginia institutions, allegedly defamed the warden of a Virginia prison. Our recent decision in *ALS Scan, Inc. v. Digital Service Consultants, Inc.*, 293 F.3d 707 (4th Cir. 2002), supplies the standard for determining a court's authority to exercise personal jurisdiction over an out-of-state person who places information on the Internet. Applying that standard, we hold that a court in Virginia cannot constitutionally exercise jurisdiction over the Connecticut-based newspaper defendants because they did not manifest an intent to aim their websites or the posted articles at a Virginia audience. Accordingly, we reverse the district court's order denying the defendants' motion to dismiss for lack of personal jurisdiction.

I.

Sometime in the late 1990s the State of Connecticut was faced with substantial overcrowding in its maximum security prisons. To alleviate the problem, Connecticut contracted with the Commonwealth of Virginia to house Connecticut prisoners in Virginia's correctional facilities. Beginning in late 1999 Connecticut transferred about 500 prisoners, mostly African-American and Hispanic, to the Wallens Ridge State Prison, a "supermax" facility in Big Stone Gap, Virginia. The plaintiff, Stanley Young, is the warden at Wallens Ridge. Connecticut's arrangement to incarcerate a sizeable number of its offenders in Virginia prisons provoked considerable public debate in Connecticut. Several Connecticut legislators openly criticized the policy, and there were demonstrations against it at the state capitol in Hartford.

Connecticut newspapers, including defendants the *New Haven Advocate* (the Advocate) and the *Hartford Courant* (the Courant), began reporting on the controversy. On March 30, 2000, the Advocate published a news article, written by one of its reporters, defendant Camille Jackson, about the transfer of Connecticut inmates to Wallens Ridge. The article discussed the allegedly harsh conditions at the Virginia prison and pointed out that the long trip to southwestern Virginia made visits by prisoners' families difficult or impossible. In the middle of her lengthy article, Jackson mentioned a class action that inmates transferred from Connecticut had filed against Warden Young and the Connecticut Commissioner of Corrections. The inmates alleged a lack of proper hygiene and medical care and the denial of religious privileges at Wallens Ridge. Finally, a paragraph at the end of the article reported that a Connecticut state senator had expressed concern about the presence of Confederate Civil War memorabilia in Warden Young's office. At about the same time the Courant published three columns, written by defendant-reporter Amy Pagnozzi, questioning the practice of relocating Connecticut inmates to Virginia prisons. The columns reported on letters written home by inmates who alleged cruelty by prison guards. In one column Pagnozzi called Wallens Ridge a "cut-rate gulag." Warden Young was not mentioned in any of the Pagnozzi columns.

On May 12, 2000, Warden Young sued the two newspapers, their editors (Gail Thompson and Brian Toolan), and the two reporters for libel in a diversity action filed in the Western District of Virginia. He claimed that the newspapers' articles imply that he "is a racist who advocates racism" and that he "encourages abuse of inmates by the guards" at Wallens Ridge. Young alleged that the newspapers circulated the allegedly defamatory articles throughout the world by posting them on their Internet websites.

The newspaper defendants filed motions to dismiss the complaint under Federal Rule of Civil Procedure 12(b)(2) on the ground that the district court lacked personal jurisdiction over them. In support of the motions the editor and reporter from each newspaper provided declarations establishing the following undisputed facts. The Advocate is a free newspaper published once a week in New Haven, Connecticut. It is distributed in New Haven and the surrounding area, and some of its content is published on the Internet. The Advocate has a small number of subscribers, and none of them are in Virginia. The Courant is published daily in Hartford, Connecticut. The newspaper is distributed in and around Hartford, and some of its content is published on the Internet. When the articles in question were published, the Courant had eight mail subscribers in Virginia. Neither newspaper solicits subscriptions from Virginia residents. No one from either newspaper, not even the reporters, traveled to Virginia to work on the articles about Connecticut's prisoner transfer policy. The two reporters, Jackson of the Advocate and Pagnozzi of the Courant, made a few telephone calls into Virginia to gather some information for the articles. Both interviewed by telephone a spokesman for the Virginia Department of Corrections. All other interviews were done with people located in Connecticut. The two reporters wrote their articles in Connecticut. The individual defendants (the reporters and editors) do not have any traditional contacts with the Commonwealth of Virginia. They do not live in Virginia, solicit any business there, or have any assets or business relationships there. The newspapers do not have offices or employees in Virginia, and they do not regularly solicit or do business in Virginia. Finally, the newspapers do not derive any substantial revenue from goods used or services rendered in Virginia.

In responding to the declarations of the editors and reporters, Warden Young pointed out that the newspapers posted the allegedly defamatory articles on Internet websites that were accessible to Virginia residents. In addition, Young provided copies of assorted print-outs from the newspapers' websites. For the Advocate, Young submitted eleven pages from newhavenadvocate.com and newmassmedia.com for January 26, 2001. The two pages from newhavenadvocate.com are the Advocate's homepage, which includes links to articles about the "Best of New Haven" and New Haven's park police. The nine pages from newmassmedia.com, a website maintained by the publishers of the Advocate, consist of classified advertising from that week's newspapers and instructions on how to submit a classified ad. The listings include advertisements for real estate rentals in New Haven and Guilford, Connecticut, for roommates wanted and tattoo services offered in Hamden, Connecticut, and for a bassist needed by a band in West Haven, Connecticut. For the Courant, Young provided nine pages from hartfordcourant.com and ctnow.com for January 26, 2001. The hartfordcourant.com homepage characterizes the website as a "source of news and entertainment in and about Connecticut." A page soliciting advertising in the Courant refers to "exposure for your message in this market" in the "best medium in the state to deliver your advertising message." The pages from ctnow.com, a website produced by the Courant, provide news stories from that day's edition of the Courant, weather reports for Hartford and New Haven, Connecticut, and links to sites for the University of Connecticut and Connecticut state government. The website promotes its online advertising as a "source for jobs in Connecticut." The website printouts provided for January 26, 2001, do not have any content with a connection to readers in Virginia.

The district court denied the newspaper defendants' motions to dismiss, concluding that it could exercise personal jurisdiction over them under Virginia's long-arm statute because "the defendants' Connecticut-based Internet activities constituted an act leading to an injury to the plaintiff in Virginia." The district court also held that the defendants' Internet activities were sufficient to satisfy the requirements of constitutional due process. With our permission the newspaper defendants are taking this interlocutory appeal. The facts relating to jurisdiction are undisputed, and the district court's decision that it has personal jurisdiction over these defendants presents a legal question that we review de novo.

II.

A.

A federal court may exercise personal jurisdiction over a defendant in the manner provided by state law. Because Virginia's long-arm statute extends personal jurisdiction to the extent permitted by the Due Process Clause, see *English & Smith v. Metzger, 901 F.2d 36, 38 (4th Cir.1990)*, "the statutory inquiry necessarily merges with the constitutional inquiry, and the two inquiries essentially become one." The question, then, is whether the defendant has sufficient "minimum contacts with [the forum] such that the maintenance of the suit does not offend 'traditional notions of fair play and substantial justice.' " *International Shoe Co. v. Washington, 326 U.S. 310, 316 (1945)*. * * * Warden Young argues only for specific jurisdiction, so we limit our discussion accordingly. When a defendant's contacts with the forum state "are also the basis for the suit, those contacts may establish specific jurisdiction." In determining whether specific jurisdiction exists, we traditionally ask (1) whether the defendant purposefully availed itself of the privileges of conducting activities in the forum state, (2) whether the plaintiff's claim arises out of the defendant's forum-related activities, and (3) "whether the exercise of personal jurisdiction over the defendant would be constitutionally reasonable." * * *

B.

We turn to whether the district court can exercise specific jurisdiction over the newspaper defendants, namely, the two newspapers, the two editors, and the two reporters. To begin with, we can put aside the few Virginia contacts that are not Internet based because Warden Young does not rely on them. Thus, Young does not claim that the reporters' few telephone calls into Virginia or the Courant's eight Virginia subscribers are sufficient to establish personal jurisdiction over those defendants. Nor did the district court rely on these traditional contacts.

Warden Young argues that the district court has specific personal jurisdiction over the newspaper defendants (hereafter, the "newspapers") because of the following contacts between them and Virginia: (1) the newspapers, knowing that Young was a Virginia resident, intentionally discussed and defamed him in their articles, (2) the newspapers posted the articles on their websites, which were accessible in Virginia, and (3) the primary effects of the defamatory statements on Young's reputation were felt in Virginia. Young emphasizes that he is not arguing that jurisdiction is proper in any location where defamatory Internet content can be accessed, which would be anywhere in the world. Rather, Young argues that personal jurisdiction is proper in Virginia because the newspapers understood that their defamatory articles, which were available to Virginia residents on the Internet, would expose Young to public hatred, contempt, and ridicule in Virginia, where he lived and worked. As the district court put it, "[t]he defendants were all well aware of the fact that the plaintiff was employed as a warden within the Virginia correctional system and resided in Virginia," and they "also should have been aware that any harm suffered by Young from the circulation of these articles on the Internet would primarily occur in Virginia."

Young frames his argument in a way that makes one thing clear: if the newspapers' contacts with Virginia were sufficient to establish personal jurisdiction, those contacts arose solely from the newspapers' Internet-based activities. Recently, in *ALS Scan* we discussed the challenges presented in applying traditional jurisdictional principles to decide when "an out-of-state citizen, through electronic contacts, has conceptually 'entered' the State via the Internet for jurisdictional purposes." *ALS Scan, 293 F.3d at 713*. There, we held that "specific jurisdiction in the Internet context may be based only on an out-of-state person's Internet activity directed at [the forum state] and causing injury that gives rise to a potential claim cognizable in [that state]." We noted that this standard for determining specific jurisdiction based on Internet contacts is consistent with the one used by the Supreme Court in *Calder v. Jones, 465 U.S. 783 (1984)*. *Calder*, though not an Internet case, has particular relevance here because it deals with personal jurisdiction in the context of a libel suit. In *Calder* a California actress brought suit there against, among others, two Floridians, a reporter and an editor who wrote and edited in Florida a National Enquirer article claiming that the actress had a problem with alcohol. The Supreme Court held that California had jurisdiction over the Florida residents because "California [was] the focal point both of the story and of the harm suffered." *Calder, 465 U.S. at 789*. The writers' "actions were expressly aimed at California," the Court said, "[a]nd they knew that the brunt of [the potentially devastating] injury would be felt by [the actress] in the State in which she lives and works and in which the National Enquirer has its largest circulation," 600,000 copies. *Calder, 465 U.S. at 789–90*.

Warden Young argues that *Calder* requires a finding of jurisdiction in this case simply because the newspapers posted articles on their Internet websites that discussed the warden and his Virginia prison, and he would feel the effects of any libel in Virginia, where he lives and works. *Calder* does not sweep that broadly, as we have recognized. For example, in *ESAB Group, Inc. v. Centricut, Inc.*, 126 F.3d 617, 625–26 (4th Cir. 1997), we emphasized how important it is in light of *Calder* to look at whether the defendant has expressly aimed or directed its conduct toward the forum state. We said that "[a]lthough the place that the plaintiff feels the alleged injury is plainly relevant to the [jurisdictional] inquiry, it must ultimately be accompanied by the defendant's own [sufficient minimum] contacts with the state if jurisdiction . . . is to be upheld." We thus had no trouble in concluding in *ALS Scan* that application of *Calder* in the Internet context requires proof that the out-of-state defendant's Internet activity is expressly targeted at or directed to the forum state. In *ALS Scan* we went on to adapt the traditional standard for establishing specific jurisdiction so that it makes sense in the Internet context. We "conclude[d] that a State may, consistent with due process, exercise judicial power over a person outside of the State when that person (1) directs electronic activity into the State, (2) with the manifested intent of engaging in business or other interactions within the State, and (3) that activity creates, in a person within the State, a potential cause of action cognizable in the State's courts." *ALS Scan*, 293 F.3d at 714.

When the Internet activity is, as here, the posting of news articles on a website, the *ALS Scan* test works more smoothly when parts one and two of the test are considered together. We thus ask whether the newspapers manifested an intent to direct their website content—which included certain articles discussing conditions in a Virginia prison—to a Virginia audience. As we recognized in *ALS Scan*, "a person's act of placing information on the Internet" is not sufficient by itself to "subject[ ] that person to personal jurisdiction in each State in which the information is accessed." Otherwise, a "person placing information on the Internet would be subject to personal jurisdiction in every State," and the traditional due process principles governing a State's jurisdiction over persons outside of its borders would be subverted. *See also GTE New Media Servs. Inc. v. BellSouth Corp.*, 199 F.3d 1343, 1350 (D.C. Cir. 2000). Thus, the fact that the newspapers' websites could be accessed anywhere, including Virginia, does not by itself demonstrate that the newspapers were intentionally directing their website content to a Virginia audience. Something more than posting and accessibility is needed to "indicate that the [newspapers] purposefully (albeit electronically) directed [their] activity in a substantial way to the forum state," Virginia. *Panavision Int'l, L.P. v. Toeppen*, 141 F.3d 1316, 1321 (9th Cir. 1998). The newspapers must, through the Internet postings, manifest an intent to target and focus on Virginia readers.

We therefore turn to the pages from the newspapers' websites that Warden Young placed in the record, and we examine their general thrust and content. The overall content of both websites is decidedly local, and neither newspaper's website contains advertisements aimed at a Virginia audience. For example, the website that distributes the Courant, ctnow.com, provides access to local (Connecticut) weather and traffic information and links to websites for the University of Connecticut and Connecticut state government. The Advocate's website features stories focusing on New Haven, such as one entitled "The Best of New Haven." In sum, it appears that these newspapers maintain their websites to serve local readers in Connecticut, to expand the reach of their papers within their local markets, and to provide their local markets with a place for classified ads. The websites are not designed to attract or serve a Virginia audience.

Food for Thought

The court here indicates that the website must be found to target a Virginia audience in order to support jurisdiction. What is the court's basis for this requirement and is such a requirement consistent with *Calder*?

We also examine the specific articles Young complains about to determine whether they were posted on the Internet with the intent to target a Virginia audience. The articles included discussions about the allegedly harsh conditions at the Wallens Ridge prison, where Young was warden. One article mentioned Young by name and quoted a Connecticut state senator who reported that Young had Confederate Civil War memorabilia in his office. The focus of the articles, however, was the Connecticut prisoner transfer policy and its impact on the transferred prisoners and their families back home in Connecticut. The articles reported on and encouraged a public debate in Connecticut about whether the transfer policy was sound or practical for that state and its citizens. Connecticut, not Virginia, was the focal point of the articles.

The facts in this case establish that the newspapers' websites, as well as the articles in question, were aimed at a Connecticut audience. The newspapers did not post materials on the Internet with the manifest intent of targeting Virginia readers. Accordingly, the newspapers could not have "reasonably anticipate[d] being haled into court [in Virginia] to answer for the truth of the statements made in their article[s]." In sum, the newspapers do not have sufficient Internet contacts with Virginia to permit the district court to exercise specific jurisdiction over them.[*]

We reverse the order of the district court denying the motions to dismiss for lack of personal jurisdiction.

REVERSED.

---

[*] Because the newspapers did not intentionally direct Internet activity to Virginia, and jurisdiction fails on that ground, we have no need to explore the last part of the *ALS Scan* inquiry, that is, whether the challenged conduct created a cause of action in Virginia. *See ALS Scan,* 293 F.3d at 714. [Footnote by the court]

Points for Discussion

a. The Contemporary Approach to Personal Jurisdiction Based on Internet Contacts

Because the Supreme Court has yet to address personal jurisdiction doctrine based on online conduct, *see Walden v. Fiore*, 134 S. Ct. 1115, 1125 (2014) ("We leave questions about virtual contacts for another day."), *Young* is provided as an example of how the federal appeals courts have evolved an approach to determining the propriety of specific jurisdiction based on forum state contacts mediated through the Internet. Early attempts by courts to wrestle with this issue produced mixed approaches initially. Some courts applied a traditional jurisdictional analysis, not regarding Internet-mediated contacts as deserving of a special test but, rather, evaluating the nature and quality of the Internet activity to determine whether the defendant had purposefully availed itself of the forum sufficiently to create minimum contacts, followed by an ordinary analysis of the reasonableness of jurisdiction. *See, e.g., Inset Sys., Inc. v. Instruction Set, Inc.,* 937 F. Supp. 161 (D. Conn. 1996) [*FLEX Case 1.D*] (finding minimum contacts based on Web-based advertising and a toll-free phone number available within the forum state).

Another district court took a different approach. In *Zippo Mfg. Co. v. Zippo Dot Com, Inc.,* 952 F. Supp. 1119 (W.D. Pa. 1997) [*FLEX Case 1.E*], the court developed a novel approach to analyzing Web-based activities by classifying them as passive, active, or interactive and attaching jurisdictional consequences to each category. Thus, if a website were considered passive, personal jurisdiction could not be based on it, whereas if a website were active, personal jurisdiction would be appropriate. Interactive sites could support jurisdiction depending on the level of interactivity and the commercial nature of the site. Does this approach seem sound? Is it consistent with the Supreme Court's minimum contacts cases?

After *Zippo*, the federal appeals courts began embracing its approach, modifying it in the manner seen in *Young*. The Ninth Circuit, for example, in *Cybersell, Inc. v. Cybersell, Inc.,* 130 F.3d 414 (9th Cir. 1997), indicated that websites that simply advertise or solicit sales were "passive" and thus could not support an assertion of personal jurisdiction without " 'something more' to indicate that the defendant purposefully (albeit electronically) directed his activity in a substantial way to the forum state." *Id. at 418*.

Indeed, most circuits have adapted the *Zippo* test by infusing it with some requirement of intentional, forum-specific "targeting" or "express aiming" as the "something more" that the *Cybersell* court alluded to. *See, e.g., Fatouros v. Lambrakis,* 627 Fed. Appx. 84, 88 (3d Cir. 2015) ("Fatouros did not present a prima facie case that the defendants purposefully availed themselves of conducting activity in New Jersey by directly targeting their activities or postings to the state, knowingly interacting with residents of New Jersey via their activities or postings, or through sufficient other related contacts.") (internal quotation marks and brackets omitted); *Cossaboon v. Me. Med. Ctr.*, 600 F.3d 25, 35 (1st Cir. 2010) ("[F]or website activity to support the exercise of personal jurisdiction, 'something more is necessary, such as interactive features which allow the successful online ordering of the defendant's products.' " (quoting *McBee v. Delica Co.*, 417 F.3d 107, 124 (1st Cir. 2005))); *ALS Scan, Inc. v. Digital Serv. Consultants, Inc.*, 293 F.3d 707, 714 (4th Cir. 2002) (requiring, as a prerequisite to jurisdiction, that a website be directed at the forum and also mandating a specific intent to engage in business or other interactions within the forum state). *See also, e.g., Louis Vuitton Malletier, S.A. v. Mosseri*, 736 F.3d 1339, 1358 (11th Cir. 2013) ("[P]urposeful availment for due process was shown here because, in addition to his fully interactive 'pendoza.com' website accessible in Florida, Mosseri had other contacts with Florida—through selling and distributing infringing goods through his website to Florida consumers—and the cause of action here derives directly from those contacts."). Why do you think courts have required "something more" beyond the presence of a website to support a finding of minimum contacts? Is such a requirement appropriate?

Practice Pointer

Because the Supreme Court has not resolved how Internet contacts should be analyzed for purposes of determining personal jurisdiction there is some room for argument in this area, although practitioners will have to be cognizant of the binding circuit precedent covering the jurisdiction in which their cases are being heard.

—Perspective & Analysis—

Several scholars have criticized the circuit courts' embrace of the *Zippo* approach as a response to analyzing virtual contacts. Here is an excerpt from an article articulating that perspective:

> [The] body of Internet-jurisdiction jurisprudence [has] several shortcomings. First, the prevalent tests for evaluating jurisdiction based on network-mediated contacts wrongly presume that Internet activity is directed at no particular place simply because it is accessible globally. Thus, courts have required additional indicia of state-specific targeting before they permit a finding of purposeful availment. This stringent requirement is inappropriate given the ordinarily ubiquitous nature of Internet activity. Second, the prevalent approaches have overemphasized Web sites and their level of "interactivity." However, a Web site's interactivity minimally implicates whether a defendant's wrongful conduct is purposefully directed at a state in a manner that would support a finding of purposeful availment under traditional principles. More importantly, this irrelevant litmus test for Web sites has essentially disqualified all Web sites that are deemed "passive" from supporting personal jurisdiction, a result that is clearly extreme and inconsistent with what a traditional analysis would suggest.

A. Benjamin Spencer, *Jurisdiction and the Internet: Returning to Traditional Principles to Analyze Network-Mediated Contacts*, 2006 U. ILL. L. REV. 71, 75.

b.   **The Express Aiming Approach &** *Calder*

Young involved an allegation of libel mediated through the Internet. As the *Young* court noted, the plaintiff's assertion of libel made this case similar in some respects to the Supreme Court case of *Calder v. Jones*. Given the similar fact patterns, how did the *Young* court distinguish *Calder* to obtain a different result in this case? Is the analysis of the court in *Young* consistent with the principles articulated in *Calder*?

c.   **The Need for Internet-Specific Jurisdictional Tests**

In both *Zippo* and circuit cases such as *Young v. New Haven Advocate*, the courts articulated and applied personal jurisdiction tests that were specially crafted for Internet jurisdiction fact patterns. Why do you think that courts have felt compelled to develop these Internet-specific tests to analyze assertions of personal jurisdiction based on virtual contacts? Is it possible to analyze *Young* or any other Internet case using the traditional jurisdictional analysis developed by the Supreme Court in *International Shoe* and its progeny? What would be the result in *Young* if a traditional personal jurisdiction analysis were applied to the facts of that case? The Seventh Circuit, in *Illinois v. Hemi Group LLC*, 622 F.3d 754, 758–59 (7th Cir. 2010), noted its express rejection of the *Zippo* approach in favor of the traditional personal jurisdiction analysis:

> We wish to point out that we have done the entire minimum contacts analysis without resorting to the sliding scale approach first developed in *Zippo Mfg. Co. v. Zippo Dot Com, Inc.*, 952 F. Supp. 1119, 1124 (W.D. Pa. 1997). This was not by mistake. Although several other circuits have explicitly adopted the sliding scale approach, *see Tamburo v. Dworkin*, 601 F.3d 693, 703 n.7 (7th Cir. 2010) (collecting cases), our court has expressly declined to do so. In *Tamburo*, we said that we were hesitant "to fashion a special jurisdictional test for Internet-based cases." *Id.* That case dealt specifically with an intentional tort (defamation) committed over the Internet and through e-mail. Long before the Internet became a medium for defamation, the Supreme Court in *Calder v. Jones* had decided the relevant jurisdictional standard for intentional torts that cross state lines. We concluded that "the principles articulated [in *Calder*] can be applied to cases involving tortious conduct committed over the Internet." *Tamburo*, 601 F.3d at 703.
>
> We reach the same conclusion here. *Zippo's* sliding scale was always just short-hand for determining whether a defendant had established sufficient minimum contacts with a forum to justify exercising personal jurisdiction over him in the forum state. But we think that the traditional due process inquiry described earlier is not so difficult to apply to cases involving Internet contacts that courts need some sort of easier-to-apply categorical test.

Which approach makes the most sense to you? Try analyzing the next hypothetical problem using both a traditional analysis and the Internet-specific approach currently embraced by many of the circuit courts.

Hypo 1.6

A California company, Software.com, sells a product called Winnows, a computer operating system. Software.com accepts orders for its product through its website and has sold the software through its website in all fifty states. Belinda Buffett, a Nebraska resident who is the inventor of similar software, sues Software.com in Nebraska state court for copyright infringement. Assume a long-arm statute that permits jurisdiction to the constitutional limit. May Nebraska courts exercise personal jurisdiction over Software.com?

D. Alternatives to Specific Jurisdiction

The preceding section dealt with specific jurisdiction cases, that is, cases in which the purported forum contacts bore some relation to the claims asserted in the action and formed the basis for an exercise of personal jurisdiction over the defendant. Specific jurisdiction is the most common form of territorial jurisdiction asserted by courts and thus is the area in which the law of personal jurisdiction is most developed.

In this section we turn to those other types of cases involving territorial jurisdiction that do not fall within this category. This section will address the doctrines of general jurisdiction, *in rem* jurisdiction, transient jurisdiction, and jurisdiction based on consent.

---

1. General Jurisdiction

Under what circumstances may a defendant be subjected to personal jurisdiction within a state based wholly on contacts having no relation to the underlying claims being asserted, a type of jurisdiction referred to as general jurisdiction? The Supreme Court first addressed this issue in *Perkins v. Benguet Consolidated Mining Co.*, 342 U.S. 437 (1952) [*FLEX Case 1.F*]. There, the Court was faced with an attempt to exercise jurisdiction in Ohio over a Philippine mining company forced to relocate is corporate activities to Ohio due to the occupation of the Islands by the Japanese during World War II. Although the claims asserted against the defendant were not related to its Ohio activities, the Court concluded that personal jurisdiction was permissible based on the company's continuous and systematic headquarters-like operations in Ohio.

The Court next addressed general jurisdiction in *Helicopteros Nacionales de Colombia, S.A. v. Hall*, 466 U.S. 408 (1984) [*FLEX Case 1.G*]. There, the Court declined to permit general jurisdiction in Texas in a suit arising out of a helicopter accident in Peru. The defendant's contacts in Texas included negotiation of the helicopter service agreement, the purchase of helicopters and parts from a Texas company, the training of helicopter pilots in Texas, the technical training of management and maintenance personnel in Texas, and the use of a Texas bank for payments under the contract. The Court concluded that these contacts were not the kind of substantial, continuous and systematic contacts the Court found to exist in *Perkins*.

With the Supreme Court having concluded that the defendant's contacts with the forum state were sufficient for general jurisdiction in *Perkins* but not in *Helicopteros*, lower courts were left trying to define the gray area in between, developing their own understandings of what level of forum state contacts could suffice to support jurisdiction in a case unrelated to those contacts. *See, e.g., Tamburo v. Dworkin, 601 F.3d 693, 701 (7th Cir. 2010)* ("A defendant with 'continuous and systematic' contacts with a state is subject to general jurisdiction there in any action, even if the action is unrelated to those contacts. The threshold for general jurisdiction is high; the contacts must be sufficiently extensive and pervasive to approximate physical presence."); *Fraser v. Smith, 594 F.3d 842, 850 (11th Cir. 2010)* ("We thus conclude that the contacts in this case were not sufficiently pervasive, continuous, and systematic to establish general jurisdiction over [the defendant]."); *Metcalfe v. Renaissance Marine, Inc., 566 F.3d 324, 334 (3d Cir. 2009)* ("If the defendant maintains continuous and substantial forum affiliations, then general jurisdiction exists."); *Doe v. Unocal Corp., 248 F.3d 915, 923 (9th Cir. 2001)* ("If the defendant's activities in the forum are substantial, continuous and systematic, general jurisdiction is available.").

The Court largely resolved this uncertainty in *Goodyear Dunlop Tires Operations, S.A. v. Brown, 564 U.S. 915 (2011)* [*FLEX Case 1.H*]. Goodyear involved an accident involving the parents of children from North Carolina who were killed in an accident in France while riding on a bus using Goodyear tires. The parents brought suit in North Carolina against various Goodyear subsidiaries that manufacture tires primarily for sale in European and Asian markets. However, a significant number of their tires—none of which were the kind involved in the accident—were distributed within North Carolina. The Supreme Court rejected the decision of the North Carolina Court of Appeals permitting personal jurisdiction under these circumstances. After stating that "the paradigm forum for the exercise of general jurisdiction is the individual's domicile; for a corporation, it is an equivalent place, one in which the corporation is fairly regarded as at home," *id. at 924*, the Court concluded that the Goodyear subsidiaries "are in no sense at home in North Carolina." The Court added, "A corporation's 'continuous activity of some sorts within a state' . . . 'is not enough to support the demand that the corporation be amenable to suits unrelated to that activity.' " *Id. at 927* (quoting *Int'l Shoe, 326 U.S. at 318*).

What standard for exercising general jurisdiction comes out of this line of cases? Is general jurisdiction for entities limited strictly to circumstances like *Perkins*, where headquarters-like activity renders the company at home or do these cases leave room for other conditions where general jurisdiction might be warranted? The next case is the Supreme Court's most recent decision addressing the scope of general jurisdiction.

Daimler AG v. Bauman

Supreme Court of the United States
134 S. Ct. 746 (2014)

JUSTICE GINSBURG delivered the opinion of the Court.

This case concerns the authority of a court in the United States to entertain a claim brought by foreign plaintiffs against a foreign defendant based on events occurring entirely outside the United States. * * *

I

In 2004, plaintiffs (respondents here) filed suit in the United States District Court for the Northern District of California, alleging that MB Argentina collaborated with Argentinian state security forces to kidnap, detain, torture, and kill plaintiffs and their relatives during the military dictatorship in place there from 1976 through 1983, a period known as Argentina's "Dirty War." Based on those allegations, plaintiffs asserted claims under the Alien Tort Statute, 28 U.S.C. § 1350, and the Torture Victim Protection Act of 1991, 106 Stat. 73, note following 28 U.S.C. § 1350, as well as claims for wrongful death and intentional infliction of emotional distress under the laws of California and Argentina. The incidents recounted in the complaint center on MB Argentina's plant in Gonzalez Catan, Argentina; no part of MB Argentina's alleged collaboration with Argentinian authorities took place in California or anywhere else in the United States.

Plaintiffs' operative complaint names only one corporate defendant: Daimler, the petitioner here. Plaintiffs seek to hold Daimler vicariously liable for MB Argentina's alleged malfeasance. Daimler is a German *Aktiengesellschaft* (public stock company) that manufactures Mercedes-Benz vehicles in Germany and has its headquarters in Stuttgart. At times relevant to this case, MB Argentina was a subsidiary wholly owned by Daimler's predecessor in interest.

Daimler moved to dismiss the action for want of personal jurisdiction. Opposing the motion, plaintiffs submitted declarations and exhibits purporting to demonstrate the presence of Daimler itself in California. Alternatively, plaintiffs maintained that jurisdiction over Daimler could be founded on the California contacts of MBUSA, a distinct corporate entity that, according to plaintiffs, should be treated as Daimler's agent for jurisdictional purposes.

MBUSA, an indirect subsidiary of Daimler, is a Delaware limited liability corporation. MBUSA serves as Daimler's exclusive importer and distributor in the United States, purchasing Mercedes-Benz automobiles from Daimler in Germany, then importing those vehicles, and ultimately distributing them to independent dealerships located throughout the Nation. Although MBUSA's principal place of business is in New Jersey, MBUSA has multiple California-based facilities, including a regional office in Costa Mesa, a Vehicle Preparation Center in Carson, and a Classic Center in Irvine. According to the record developed below, MBUSA is the largest supplier of luxury vehicles to the California market. In particular, over 10% of all sales of new vehicles in the United States take place in California, and MBUSA's California sales account for 2.4% of Daimler's worldwide sales.

The relationship between Daimler and MBUSA is delineated in a General Distributor Agreement, which sets forth requirements for MBUSA's distribution of Mercedes-Benz vehicles in the United States. That agreement established MBUSA as an "independent contracto[r]" that "buy[s] and sell[s] [vehicles] . . . as an independent business for [its] own account." The agreement "does not make [MBUSA] . . . a general or special agent, partner, joint venturer or employee of DAIMLERCHRYSLER or any DaimlerChrysler Group Company"; MBUSA "ha[s] no authority to make binding obligations for or act on behalf of DAIMLERCHRYSLER or any DaimlerChrysler Group Company." *Ibid.*

After allowing jurisdictional discovery on plaintiffs' agency allegations, the District Court granted Daimler's motion to dismiss. Daimler's own affiliations with California, the court first determined, were insufficient to support the exercise of all-purpose jurisdiction over the corporation. Next, the court declined to attribute MBUSA's California contacts to Daimler on an agency theory, concluding that plaintiffs failed to demonstrate that MBUSA acted as Daimler's agent.

The Ninth Circuit at first affirmed the District Court's judgment. Addressing solely the question of agency, the Court of Appeals held that plaintiffs had not shown the existence of an agency relationship of the kind that might warrant attribution of MBUSA's contacts to Daimler. Judge Reinhardt dissented. In his view, the agency test was satisfied and considerations of "reasonableness" did not bar the exercise of jurisdiction. Granting plaintiffs' petition for rehearing, the panel withdrew its initial opinion and replaced it with one authored by Judge Reinhardt, which elaborated on reasoning he initially expressed in dissent.

Daimler petitioned for rehearing and rehearing en banc, urging that the exercise of personal jurisdiction over Daimler could not be reconciled with this Court's decision in *Goodyear Dunlop Tires Operations, S.A. v. Brown*, 564 U.S. ___, 131 S.Ct. 2846 (2011). Over the dissent of eight judges, the Ninth Circuit denied Daimler's petition.

We granted certiorari to decide whether, consistent with the Due Process Clause of the Fourteenth Amendment, Daimler is amenable to suit in California courts for claims involving only foreign plaintiffs and conduct occurring entirely abroad.

II

Federal courts ordinarily follow state law in determining the bounds of their jurisdiction over persons. See FED. RULE CIV. PROC. 4(k)(1)(A) (service of process is effective to establish personal jurisdiction over a defendant "who is subject to the jurisdiction of a court of general jurisdiction in the state where the district court is located"). Under California's long-arm statute, California state courts may exercise personal jurisdiction "on any basis not inconsistent with the Constitution of this state or of the United States." Cal. Civ. Proc. Code Ann. § 410.10 (West 2004). California's long-arm statute allows the exercise of personal jurisdiction to the full extent permissible under the U. S. Constitution. We therefore inquire whether the Ninth Circuit's holding comports with the limits imposed by federal due process. See, *e.g., Burger King Corp. v. Rudzewicz, 471 U.S. 462, 464 (1985)*.

III

In *Pennoyer v. Neff, 95 U.S. 714 (1878)*, decided shortly after the enactment of the Fourteenth Amendment, the Court held that a tribunal's jurisdiction over persons reaches no farther than the geographic bounds of the forum. See *id.,* at 720 ("The authority of every tribunal is necessarily restricted by the territorial limits of the State in which it is established."). See also *Shaffer v. Heitner, 433 U.S. 186, 197 (1977)* (Under *Pennoyer,* "any attempt 'directly' to assert extraterritorial jurisdiction over persons or property would offend sister States and exceed the inherent limits of the State's power."). In time, however, that strict territorial approach yielded to a less rigid understanding, spurred by "changes in the technology of transportation and communication, and the tremendous growth of interstate business activity." *Burnham v. Superior Court of Cal., County of Marin, 495 U.S. 604, 617 (1990)* (opinion of SCALIA, J.).

"The canonical opinion in this area remains *International Shoe* [*Co. v. Washington*], *326 U.S. 310* [(1945)], in which we held that a State may authorize its courts to exercise personal jurisdiction over an out-of-state defendant if the defendant has 'certain minimum contacts with [the State] such that the maintenance of the suit does not offend "traditional notions of fair play and substantial justice." *Goodyear, 131 S.Ct., at 2853* (quoting *International Shoe, 326 U.S., at 316, 66 S.Ct. 154*). Following *International Shoe,* "the relationship among the defendant, the forum, and the litigation, rather than the mutually exclusive sovereignty of the States on which the rules of *Pennoyer* rest, became the central concern of the inquiry into personal jurisdiction." *Shaffer, 433 U.S., at 204.*

International Shoe's conception of "fair play and substantial justice" presaged the development of two categories of personal jurisdiction. The first category is represented by *International Shoe* itself, a case in which the in-state activities of the corporate defendant "ha[d] not only been continuous and systematic, but also g[a]ve rise to the liabilities sued on." 326 U.S., at 317. *International Shoe* recognized, as well, that "the commission of some single or occasional acts of the corporate agent in a state" may sometimes be enough to subject the corporation to jurisdiction in that State's tribunals with respect to suits relating to that in-state activity. *Id., at 318.* Adjudicatory authority of this order, in which the suit "aris[es] out of or relate[s] to the defendant's contacts with the forum," *Helicopteros Nacionales de Colombia, S.A. v. Hall,* 466 U.S. 408, 414, n. 8 (1984), is today called "specific jurisdiction."

International Shoe distinguished between, on the one hand, exercises of specific jurisdiction, as just described, and on the other, situations where a foreign corporation's "continuous corporate operations within a state [are] so substantial and of such a nature as to justify suit against it on causes of action arising from dealings entirely distinct from those activities." 326 U.S., at 318, 66 S.Ct. 154. As we have since explained, "[a] court may assert general jurisdiction over foreign (sister-state or foreign-country) corporations to hear any and all claims against them when their affiliations with the State are so 'continuous and systematic' as to render them essentially at home in the forum State." *Goodyear,* 131 S.Ct., at 2851.

Since *International Shoe,* "specific jurisdiction has become the centerpiece of modern jurisdiction theory, while general jurisdiction [has played] a reduced role." *Goodyear,* 131 S.Ct., at 2854 (quoting Twitchell, The Myth of General Jurisdiction, 101 Harv.L.Rev. 610, 628 (1988)). *International Shoe's* momentous departure from *Pennoyer's* rigidly territorial focus, we have noted, unleashed a rapid expansion of tribunals' ability to hear claims against out-of-state defendants when the episode-in-suit occurred in the forum or the defendant purposefully availed itself of the forum. * * *

Our post-*International Shoe* opinions on general jurisdiction, by comparison, are few. "[The Court's] 1952 decision in *Perkins v. Benguet Consol. Mining Co.* remains the textbook case of general jurisdiction appropriately exercised over a foreign corporation that has not consented to suit in the forum." *Goodyear,* 131 S.Ct., at 2856 (internal quotation marks and brackets omitted). The defendant in *Perkins,* Benguet, was a company incorporated under the laws of the Philippines, where it operated gold and silver mines. Benguet ceased its mining operations during the Japanese occupation of the Philippines in World War II; its president moved to Ohio, where he kept an office, maintained the company's files, and oversaw the company's activities. *Perkins v. Benguet Consol. Mining Co.,* 342 U.S. 437, 448 (1952). The plaintiff, an Ohio resident, sued Benguet on a claim that neither arose in Ohio nor related to the corporation's activities in that State. We held that the Ohio courts could exercise general jurisdiction over Benguet without offending due process. *Ibid.* That was so, we later noted, because "Ohio was the corporation's principal, if temporary, place of business." *Keeton v. Hustler Magazine, Inc.,* 465 U.S. 770, 780, n. 11 (1984).

The next case on point, *Helicopteros,* 466 U.S. 408, arose from a helicopter crash in Peru. Four U.S. citizens perished in that accident; their survivors and representatives brought suit in Texas state court against the helicopter's owner and operator, a Colombian corporation. That company's contacts with Texas were confined to "sending its chief executive officer to Houston for a contract-negotiation session; accepting into its New York bank account checks drawn on a Houston bank; purchasing helicopters, equipment, and training services from [a Texas-based helicopter company] for substantial sums; and sending personnel to [Texas] for training." *Id., at 416.* Notably, those contacts bore no apparent relationship to the accident that gave rise to the suit. We held that the company's Texas connections did not resemble the "continuous and systematic general business contacts . . . found to exist in *Perkins.*" *Ibid.* "[M]ere purchases, even if occurring at regular intervals," we clarified, "are not enough to warrant a State's assertion of *in personam* jurisdiction over a nonresident corporation in a cause of action not related to those purchase transactions." *Id., at 418.*

Most recently, in *Goodyear,* we answered the question: "Are foreign subsidiaries of a United States parent corporation amenable to suit in state court on claims unrelated to any activity of the subsidiaries in the forum State? " 131 S.Ct., at 2850. That case arose from a bus accident outside Paris that killed two boys from North Carolina. The boys' parents brought a wrongful-death suit in North Carolina state court alleging that the bus's tire was defectively manufactured. The complaint named as defendants not only The Goodyear Tire and Rubber Company (Goodyear), an Ohio corporation, but also Goodyear's Turkish, French, and Luxembourgian subsidiaries. Those foreign subsidiaries, which manufactured tires for sale in Europe and Asia, lacked any affiliation with North Carolina. A small percentage of tires manufactured by the foreign subsidiaries were distributed in North Carolina, however, and on that ground, the North Carolina Court of Appeals held the subsidiaries amenable to the general jurisdiction of North Carolina courts.

We reversed, observing that the North Carolina court's analysis "elided the essential difference between case-specific and all-purpose (general) jurisdiction." 131 S.Ct., at 2855. Although the placement of a product into the stream of commerce "may bolster an affiliation germane to *specific* jurisdiction," we explained, such contacts "do not warrant a determination that, based on those ties, the forum has *general* jurisdiction over a defendant." 131 S.Ct., at 2857. As *International Shoe* itself teaches, a corporation's "continuous activity of some sorts within a state is not enough to support the demand that the corporation be amenable to suits unrelated to that activity." 326 U.S., at 318. Because Goodyear's foreign subsidiaries were "in no sense at home in North Carolina," we held, those subsidiaries could not be required to submit to the general jurisdiction of that State's courts. 131 S.Ct., at

2857. See also *J. McIntyre Machinery, Ltd. v. Nicastro,* 131 S.Ct. 2780, 2797–2798 (2011) (GINSBURG, J., dissenting) (noting unanimous agreement that a foreign manufacturer, which engaged an independent U.S.-based distributor to sell its machines throughout the United States, could not be exposed to all-purpose jurisdiction in New Jersey courts based on those contacts).

As is evident from *Perkins, Helicopteros,* and *Goodyear,* general and specific jurisdiction have followed markedly different trajectories post-*International Shoe.* Specific jurisdiction has been cut loose from *Pennoyer's* sway, but we have declined to stretch general jurisdiction beyond limits traditionally recognized. As this Court has increasingly trained on the "relationship among the defendant, the forum, and the litigation," *Shaffer,* 433 U.S., at 204, *i.e.,* specific jurisdiction, general jurisdiction has come to occupy a less dominant place in the contemporary scheme.[11]

IV

With this background, we turn directly to the question whether Daimler's affiliations with California are sufficient to subject it to the general (all-purpose) personal jurisdiction of that State's courts. In the proceedings below, the parties agreed on, or failed to contest, certain points we now take as given. Plaintiffs have never attempted to fit this case into the *specific* jurisdiction category. Nor did plaintiffs challenge on appeal the District Court's holding that Daimler's own contacts with California were, by themselves, too sporadic to justify the exercise of general jurisdiction. While plaintiffs ultimately persuaded the Ninth Circuit to impute MBUSA's California contacts to Daimler on an agency theory, at no point have they maintained that MBUSA is an alter ego of Daimler.

Daimler, on the other hand, failed to object below to plaintiffs' assertion that the California courts could exercise all-purpose jurisdiction over MBUSA. But see Brief for Petitioner 23, n. 4 (suggestion that in light of *Goodyear,* MBUSA may not be amenable to general jurisdiction in California); Brief for United States as *Amicus Curiae* 16, n. 5 (hereinafter U.S. Brief) (same). We will assume then, for purposes of this decision only, that MBUSA qualifies as at home in California.

A

In sustaining the exercise of general jurisdiction over Daimler, the Ninth Circuit relied on an agency theory, determining that MBUSA acted as Daimler's agent for jurisdictional purposes and then attributing MBUSA's California contacts to Daimler. The Ninth Circuit's agency analysis derived from Circuit precedent considering principally whether the subsidiary "performs services that are sufficiently important to the foreign corporation that if it did not have a representative to perform them,

---

[11] As the Court made plain in *Goodyear* and repeats here, general jurisdiction requires affiliations "so 'continuous and systematic' as to render [the foreign corporation] essentially at home in the forum State." 564 U.S., at ___, 131 S.Ct., at 2851, i.e., comparable to a domestic enterprise in that State.

the corporation's own officials would undertake to perform substantially similar services." 644 F.3d, at 920 (quoting *Doe v. Unocal Corp.*, 248 F.3d 915, 928 (C.A.9 2001); emphasis deleted).

This Court has not yet addressed whether a foreign corporation may be subjected to a court's general jurisdiction based on the contacts of its in-state subsidiary. Daimler argues, and several Courts of Appeals have held, that a subsidiary's jurisdictional contacts can be imputed to its parent only when the former is so dominated by the latter as to be its alter ego. The Ninth Circuit adopted a less rigorous test based on what it described as an "agency" relationship. Agencies, we note, come in many sizes and shapes: "One may be an agent for some business purposes and not others so that the fact that one may be an agent for one purpose does not make him or her an agent for every purpose." 2A C. J. S., Agency § 43, p. 367 (2013) (footnote omitted). A subsidiary, for example, might be its parent's agent for claims arising in the place where the subsidiary operates, yet not its agent regarding claims arising elsewhere. The Court of Appeals did not advert to that prospect. But we need not pass judgment on invocation of an agency theory in the context of general jurisdiction, for in no event can the appeals court's analysis be sustained.

The Ninth Circuit's agency finding rested primarily on its observation that MBUSA's services were "important" to Daimler, as gauged by Daimler's hypothetical readiness to perform those services itself if MBUSA did not exist. Formulated this way, the inquiry into importance stacks the deck, for it will always yield a pro-jurisdiction answer: "Anything a corporation does through an independent contractor, subsidiary, or distributor is presumably something that the corporation would do 'by other means' if the independent contractor, subsidiary, or distributor did not exist." 676 F.3d, at 777 (O'Scannlain, J., dissenting from denial of rehearing en banc). The Ninth Circuit's agency theory thus appears to subject foreign corporations to general jurisdiction whenever they have an in-state subsidiary or affiliate, an outcome that would sweep beyond even the "sprawling view of general jurisdiction" we rejected in *Goodyear*, 131 S.Ct., at 2856.

B

Even if we were to assume that MBUSA is at home in California, and further to assume MBUSA's contacts are imputable to Daimler, there would still be no basis to subject Daimler to general jurisdiction in California, for Daimler's slim contacts with the State hardly render it at home there.

Goodyear made clear that only a limited set of affiliations with a forum will render a defendant amenable to all-purpose jurisdiction there. "For an individual, the paradigm forum for the exercise of general jurisdiction is the individual's domicile; for a corporation, it is an equivalent place, one in which the corporation is fairly regarded as at home." 131 S.Ct., at 2853–2854 (citing Brilmayer et al., A General Look at General Jurisdiction, 66 Texas L.Rev. 721, 728 (1988)). With respect to a corporation, the place of incorporation and principal place of business are "paradig[m] . . . bases for general jurisdiction." *Id.*, at 735. See also Twitchell, 101 Harv. L.Rev., at 633. Those affiliations have the virtue of being unique—that is, each ordinarily indicates only one place—as well as easily ascertainable. Cf. *Hertz Corp. v. Friend, 559 U.S. 77, 94 (2010)* ("Simple jurisdictional rules . . . promote greater predictability."). These bases afford plaintiffs recourse to at least one clear and certain forum in which a corporate defendant may be sued on any and all claims.

Goodyear did not hold that a corporation may be subject to general jurisdiction *only* in a forum where it is incorporated or has its principal place of business; it simply typed those places paradigm all-purpose forums. Plaintiffs would have us look beyond the exemplar bases *Goodyear* identified, and approve the exercise of general jurisdiction in every State in which a corporation "engages in a substantial, continuous, and systematic course of business." Brief for Respondents 16–17, and nn. 7–8. That formulation, we hold, is unacceptably grasping.

As noted, the words "continuous and systematic" were used in *International Shoe* to describe instances in which the exercise of *specific* jurisdiction would be appropriate. See 326 U.S., at 317, 66 S.Ct. 154 (jurisdiction can be asserted where a corporation's in-state activities are not only "continuous and systematic, but also give rise to the liabilities sued on"). Turning to all-purpose jurisdiction, in contrast, *International Shoe* speaks of "instances in which the continuous corporate operations within a state [are] so substantial and of such a nature as to justify suit . . . *on causes of action arising from dealings entirely distinct from those activities.*" *Id.*, at 318, 66 S.Ct. 154 (emphasis added). See also Twitchell, Why We Keep Doing Business With Doing-Business Jurisdiction, 2001 U. Chi. Legal Forum 171, 184 (*International Shoe* "is clearly not saying that dispute-blind jurisdiction exists whenever 'continuous and systematic' contacts are found."). Accordingly, the inquiry under *Goodyear* is not whether a foreign corporation's in-forum contacts can be said to be in some sense "continuous and systematic," it is whether that corporation's "affiliations with the State are so 'continuous and systematic' as to render [it] essentially at home in the forum State." 131 S.Ct., at 2851. [19]

Here, neither Daimler nor MBUSA is incorporated in California, nor does either entity have its principal place of business there. If Daimler's California activities sufficed to allow adjudication of this Argentina-rooted case in California, the same global reach would presumably be available in every other State in which MBUSA's sales are sizable. Such exorbitant exercises of all-purpose jurisdiction would scarcely permit

---

[19] We do not foreclose the possibility that in an exceptional case, see, e.g., *Perkins*, a corporation's operations in a forum other than its formal place of incorporation or principal place of business may be so substantial and of such a nature as to render the corporation at home in that State. But this case presents no occasion to explore that question, because Daimler's activities in California plainly do not approach that level. It is one thing to hold a corporation answerable for operations in the forum State, quite another to expose it to suit on claims having no connection whatever to the forum State.

out-of-state defendants "to structure their primary conduct with some minimum assurance as to where that conduct will and will not render them liable to suit." *Burger King Corp., 471 U.S., at 472* (internal quotation marks omitted).

It was therefore error for the Ninth Circuit to conclude that Daimler, even with MBUSA's contacts attributed to it, was at home in California, and hence subject to suit there on claims by foreign plaintiffs having nothing to do with anything that occurred or had its principal impact in California.[20]

C

* * *

The Ninth Circuit * * * paid little heed to the risks to international comity its expansive view of general jurisdiction posed. Other nations do not share the uninhibited approach to personal jurisdiction advanced by the Court of Appeals in this case. In the European Union, for example, a corporation may generally be sued in the nation in which it is "domiciled," a term defined to refer only to the location of the corporation's "statutory seat," "central administration," or "principal place of business." European Parliament and Council Reg. 1215/2012, Arts. 4(1), and 63(1),

---

[20] To clarify in light of Justice SOTOMAYOR's opinion concurring in the judgment, the general jurisdiction inquiry does not "focu[s] solely on the magnitude of the defendant's in-state contacts." General jurisdiction instead calls for an appraisal of a corporation's activities in their entirety, nationwide and worldwide. A corporation that operates in many places can scarcely be deemed at home in all of them. Otherwise, "at home" would be synonymous with "doing business" tests framed before specific jurisdiction evolved in the United States. Nothing in *International Shoe* and its progeny suggests that "a particular quantum of local activity" should give a State authority over a "far larger quantum of . . . activity" having no connection to any in-state activity.

Justice SOTOMAYOR would reach the same result, but for a different reason. Rather than concluding that Daimler is not at home in California, Justice SOTOMAYOR would hold that the exercise of general jurisdiction over Daimler would be unreasonable "in the unique circumstances of this case." In other words, she favors a resolution fit for this day and case only. True, a multipronged reasonableness check was articulated in *Asahi, 480 U.S., at 113–114*, but not as a free-floating test. Instead, the check was to be essayed when specific jurisdiction is at issue. See also *Burger King Corp. v. Rudzewicz, 471 U.S. 462, 476–478 (1985)*. First, a court is to determine whether the connection between the forum and the episode-in-suit could justify the exercise of specific jurisdiction. Then, in a second step, the court is to consider several additional factors to assess the reasonableness of entertaining the case. When a corporation is genuinely at home in the forum State, however, any second-step inquiry would be superfluous.

Justice SOTOMAYOR fears that our holding will "lead to greater unpredictability by radically expanding the scope of jurisdictional discovery." But it is hard to see why much in the way of discovery would be needed to determine where a corporation is at home. Justice SOTOMAYOR's proposal to import *Asahi*'s "reasonableness" check into the general jurisdiction determination, on the other hand, would indeed compound the jurisdictional inquiry. The reasonableness factors identified in *Asahi* include "the burden on the defendant," "the interests of the forum State," "the plaintiff's interest in obtaining relief," "the interstate judicial system's interest in obtaining the most efficient resolution of controversies," "the shared interest of the several States in furthering fundamental substantive social policies," and, in the international context, "the procedural and substantive policies of other nations whose interests are affected by the assertion of jurisdiction." 480 U.S., at 113–115 (some internal quotation marks omitted). Imposing such a checklist in cases of general jurisdiction would hardly promote the efficient disposition of an issue that should be resolved expeditiously at the outset of litigation.

2012 O.J. (L. 351) 7, 18. See also *id.*, Art. 7(5), 2012 O.J. 7 (as to "a dispute *arising out of the operations of a branch, agency or other establishment,*" a corporation may be sued "in the courts for the place where the branch, agency or other establishment is situated" (emphasis added)). The Solicitor General informs us, in this regard, that "foreign governments' objections to some domestic courts' expansive views of general jurisdiction have in the past impeded negotiations of international agreements on the reciprocal recognition and enforcement of judgments." U.S. Brief 2 (citing Juenger, The American Law of General Jurisdiction, 2001 U. Chi. Legal Forum 141, 161–162). See also U.S. Brief 2 (expressing concern that unpredictable applications of general jurisdiction based on activities of U.S.-based subsidiaries could discourage foreign investors); Brief for Respondents 35 (acknowledging that "doing business" basis for general jurisdiction has led to "international friction"). Considerations of international rapport thus reinforce our determination that subjecting Daimler to the general jurisdiction of courts in California would not accord with the "fair play and substantial justice" due process demands. *International Shoe,* 326 U.S., at 316 (quoting *Milliken v. Meyer,* 311 U.S. 457, 463 (1940)).

For the reasons stated, the judgment of the United States Court of Appeals for the Ninth Circuit is

Reversed.

Justice Sotomayor, concurring in the judgment.

* * *

I

* * *

Our personal jurisdiction precedents call for a two-part analysis. The contacts prong asks whether the defendant has sufficient contacts with the forum State to support personal jurisdiction; the reasonableness prong asks whether the exercise of jurisdiction would be unreasonable under the circumstances. *Burger King Corp. v. Rudzewicz,* 471 U.S. 462, 475–478 (1985). As the majority points out, all of the cases in which we have applied the reasonableness prong have involved specific as opposed to general jurisdiction. Whether the reasonableness prong should apply in the general jurisdiction context is therefore a question we have never decided, and it is one on which I can appreciate the arguments on both sides. But it would be imprudent to decide that question in this case given that respondents have failed to argue against the application of the reasonableness prong during the entire 8-year history of this litigation. As a result, I would decide this case under the reasonableness prong without foreclosing future consideration of whether that prong should be limited to the specific jurisdiction context.

We identified the factors that bear on reasonableness in *Asahi Metal Industry Co. v. Superior Court of Cal., Solano Cty.*, 480 U.S. 102 (1987): "the burden on the defendant, the interests of the forum State," "the plaintiff's interest in obtaining relief" in the forum State, and the interests of other sovereigns in resolving the dispute. *Id., at 113–114.* We held in *Asahi* that it would be "unreasonable and unfair" for a California court to exercise jurisdiction over a claim between a Taiwanese plaintiff and a Japanese defendant that arose out of a transaction in Taiwan, particularly where the Taiwanese plaintiff had not shown that it would be more convenient to litigate in California than in Taiwan or Japan. *Id., at 114.*

The same considerations resolve this case. It involves Argentine plaintiffs suing a German defendant for conduct that took place in Argentina. Like the plaintiffs in *Asahi,* respondents have failed to show that it would be more convenient to litigate in California than in Germany, a sovereign with a far greater interest in resolving the dispute. *Asahi* thus makes clear that it would be unreasonable for a court in California to subject Daimler to its jurisdiction.

* * *

III

* * *

A

Until today, our precedents had established a straightforward test for general jurisdiction: Does the defendant have "continuous corporate operations within a state" that are "so substantial and of such a nature as to justify suit against it on causes of action arising from dealings entirely distinct from those activities"? *International Shoe Co. v. Washington,* 326 U.S. 310, 318 (1945); see also *Helicopteros Nacionales de Colombia, S.A. v. Hall,* 466 U.S. 408, 416 (1984) (asking whether defendant had "continuous and systematic general business contacts"). In every case where we have applied this test, we have focused solely on the magnitude of the defendant's in-state contacts, not the relative magnitude of those contacts in comparison to the defendant's contacts with other States. * * * Just as in *Perkins* and *Helicopteros,* our opinion in *Goodyear* did not identify the defendants' contacts outside of the forum State, but focused instead on the defendants' lack of offices, employees, direct sales, and business operations within the State.

This approach follows from the touchstone principle of due process in this field, the concept of reciprocal fairness. When a corporation chooses to invoke the benefits and protections of a State in which it operates, the State acquires the authority to subject the company to suit in its courts. See *International Shoe,* 326 U.S., at 319 ("[T]o the extent that a corporation exercises the privilege of conducting activities within a state, it enjoys the benefits and protection of the laws of that state" such that an "obligatio[n] arise[s]" to respond there to suit); *J. McIntyre Machinery, Ltd. v. Nicastro*, 131 S.Ct. 2780, 2796–2797 (2011) (plurality opinion) (same principle for general jurisdiction). The majority's focus on the extent of a corporate defendant's out-of-forum contacts is untethered from this rationale. After all, the degree to which a company intentionally benefits from a forum State depends on its interactions with that State, not its interactions elsewhere. An article on which the majority relies (and on which *Goodyear* relied as well, 131 S.Ct., at 2853–2854) expresses the point well: "We should not treat defendants as less amenable to suit merely because they carry on more substantial business in other states . . . . [T]he amount of activity elsewhere seems virtually irrelevant to . . . the imposition of general jurisdiction over a defendant." Brilmayer et al., A General Look at General Jurisdiction, 66 Texas L.Rev. 721, 742 (1988).

Had the majority applied our settled approach, it would have had little trouble concluding that Daimler's California contacts rise to the requisite level, given the majority's assumption that MBUSA's contacts may be attributed to Daimler and given Daimler's concession that those contacts render MBUSA "at home" in California.

* * *

Because I would reverse the Ninth Circuit's decision on the narrower ground that the exercise of jurisdiction over Daimler would be unreasonable in any event, I respectfully concur in the judgment only.

———————

Points for Discussion

a. General Jurisdiction in *Daimler*

What are the parameters for exercising general jurisdiction as presented by the *Daimler* Court? Does its view of the standard for general jurisdiction diverge in any meaningful way from what it laid out in *Goodyear*? There has been disagreement on this point. *See* Brooke A. Weedon, *New Limits on General Personal Jurisdiction: Examining the Retroactive Application of* Daimler *in Long-Pending Cases*, 72 Wash. & Lee L. Rev. 1549, 1551–52 (2015) ("Some argue that *Daimler* created a much stricter test for general jurisdiction than was previously in existence, but others counter that the *Daimler* decision simply restated the existing *Goodyear* rule."). What is your view?

In *Daimler*, the Court stated, "*Goodyear* did not hold that a corporation may be subject to general jurisdiction *only* in a forum where it is incorporated or has its principal place of business; it simply typed those places paradigm all-purpose forums." Does *Daimler* provide any insight into what other types of contacts might be able to subject a corporation to general jurisdiction besides its headquarters or situs of incorporation? What about for entities besides corporations, which are not incorporated in a location but "organized" as partnerships, limited liability companies, or other non-corporate entities? Do you at least have a clear sense from *Daimler* of what types of contacts *will not* suffice for general jurisdiction?

Finally, it is important to recognize that when making the "at home" assessment, the *Daimler* Court indicated that "the general jurisdiction inquiry does not focus solely on the magnitude of the defendant's in-state contacts." *Daimler, 134 S.Ct. at 762, n.20*. Instead, the analysis "calls for an

Food for Thought

Should a defendant who maintains a constant presence in a state via a website and through Web-generated sales activity to forum residents be subject to general jurisdiction in that state? *See, e.g., Tamburo v. Dworkin, 601 F.3d 693, 701 (7th Cir. 2010)* (stating that "the maintenance of a public Internet website" is insufficient, "without more, to establish general jurisdiction").

appraisal of a corporation's activities in their entirety"; "[a] corporation that operates in many places can scarcely be deemed at home in all of them." *Id.* How should these remarks be interpreted? What is likely meant here is that although an entity's forum contacts may be quite extensive when viewed in isolation, if—when viewed in the context of their contacts globally—the contacts appear to be less central to the entity, the forum in question is not likely to be considered its home. See *BNSF Railway Co. v. Tyrrell, 137 S. Ct. 1549, 1559 (2017)* [*FLEX Case 1.I*] (holding that although "BNSF has over 2,000 miles of railroad track and more than 2,000 employees in Montana," such contacts were insufficient to render it at home there to support general jurisdiction).

b. General Jurisdiction After *Daimler*

The circuit courts have tended to acknowledge *Daimler*'s allowance for general jurisdiction beyond the paradigm circumstances, although this allowance appears to be little more than a theoretical possibility. *See* Alan M. Trammell, *A Tale of Two Jurisdictions*, 68 VAND. L. REV. 501, 521 (2015) (noting that, after *Daimler*, "[a] corporation likely is subject to general jurisdiction only in a state where it has incorporated or maintains its principal place of business" despite an exception being "theoretically possible"). For example, the Second Circuit indicated that, "in our view *Daimler* established that, except in a truly 'exceptional' case, a corporate defendant may be treated as 'essentially at home' only where it is incorporated or maintains its principal place of business—the 'paradigm' cases." *Brown v. Lockheed Martin, 814 F.3d 619, 627 (2d Cir. 2016)* (noting also that this reading of *Daimler* accords with the interpretations of the Seventh, Ninth, and Fifth Circuits).

However, the Tenth Circuit appears to read *Daimler* more broadly: "BNYM [one of the litigants] argues *Daimler* limited general jurisdiction to a corporation's state of incorporation or principal place of business, except in exceptional circumstances not present in this case. *Daimler*, like *Goodyear*, did not limit general jurisdiction in this manner." *Am. Fidelity Assurance Co. v. Bank of N.Y. Mellon*, 810 F.3d 1234, 1237 (10th Cir. 2016).

Based on the entire body of Supreme Court precedent on this topic, it appears that the paradigm cases are likely to dominate the general jurisdiction space, with circumstances such as were presented in *Perkins*—de facto, headquarters-like activity—warranting a finding of general jurisdiction beyond the location of a company's official headquarters or places of incorporation or organization. *See Daimler*, 134 S. Ct. at 761 n.19 ("[I]n an exceptional case, see, e.g., *Perkins*, a corporation's operations in a forum other than its formal place of incorporation or principal place of business may be so substantial and of such a nature as to render the corporation at home in that State."). Indeed, the Court recently affirmed in *BNSF Railway Co. v. Tyrrell*, 137 S. Ct. 1549 (2017) [*FLEX Case 1.1*] that the "exceptional circumstance" spoken of in *Daimler* should be measured by the circumstances present in *Perkins*. *See id. at 1558* ("The exercise of general jurisdiction is not limited to these forums; in an 'exceptional case,' a corporate defendant's operations in another forum 'may be so substantial and of such a nature as to render the corporation at home in that State.' We suggested that *Perkins v. Benguet Consol. Mining Co.*, exemplified such a case." (quoting *Daimler*, 134 S. Ct. at 761 n.19)); *see also id.* at 1561 (Sotomayor, J., concurring in part and dissenting in part) (stating that the *BNSF* Court's "opinion here could be understood to limit that exception to the exact facts of *Perkins*"). Simply having "continuous activity" and even "extensive forum contacts" will not suffice for general jurisdiction if the activity is unrelated to the suit. *See Bristol-Myers Squibb Co. v. Superior Court*, 137 S. Ct. 1773, 1781 (2017) ("As we have said, "[a] corporation's 'continuous activity of some sorts within a state . . . is not enough to support the demand that the corporation be amenable to suits unrelated to that activity.' " (quoting *Goodyear Dunlop Tires Operations, S.A. v. Brown*, 564 U.S. 915, 927 (2011))).

2. Power over Property

Thus far we have ignored cases in which jurisdiction is predicated on the attachment of property within the forum state. This type of jurisdiction, which can be either *in rem* or *quasi-in-rem*, was last touched on during our consideration of *Pennoyer v. Neff*. After *Pennoyer*, the Supreme Court held in *International Shoe* that the constitutionality of a state's assertion of jurisdiction depends upon the defendant having "minimum contacts" with the forum such that the exercise of jurisdiction over it will be fair and reasonable. Does the minimum contacts requirement apply to assertions of jurisdiction based on property? In the next case, the Supreme Court addressed and resolved this question.

Shaffer v. Heitner

Supreme Court of the United States
433 U.S. 186 (1977)

MR. JUSTICE MARSHALL delivered the opinion of the Court.

The controversy in this case concerns the constitutionality of a Delaware statute that allows a court of that State to take jurisdiction of a lawsuit by sequestering any property of the defendant that happens to be located in Delaware. Appellants contend that the sequestration statute as applied in this case violates the Due Process Clause of the Fourteenth Amendment both because it permits the state courts to

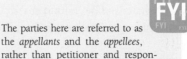

The parties here are referred to as the *appellants* and the *appellees*, rather than petitioner and respondent. The former terms are used here because this case was before the Court under its appellate jurisdiction, which obligated the Supreme Court to hear appeals from the final judgments of states' highest courts. This appellate jurisdiction was abolished by an amendment to 28 U.S.C. § 1257 in 1988.

exercise jurisdiction despite the absence of sufficient contacts among the defendants, the litigation, and the State of Delaware and because it authorizes the deprivation of defendants' property without providing adequate procedural safeguards. We find it necessary to consider only the first of these contentions.

I

Appellee Heitner, a nonresident of Delaware, is the owner of one share of stock in the Greyhound Corp., a business incorporated under the laws of Delaware with its principal place of business in Phoenix, Ariz. On May 22, 1974, he filed a shareholder's derivative suit in the Court of Chancery for New Castle County, Del., in which he named as defendants Greyhound, its wholly owned subsidiary Greyhound Lines, Inc.,[1] and 28 present or former officers or directors of one or both of the corporations. In essence, Heitner alleged that the individual defendants had violated their duties to Greyhound by causing it and its subsidiary to engage in actions that resulted in the corpora-

Make the Connection

A *shareholder's derivative suit* is an action by a shareholder on behalf of a corporation against the corporation's officers and/or directors alleging a breach of some duty they owed to the corporation. This is a topic you will likely cover in a basic **Corporations** course.

---

[1] Greyhound Lines, Inc., is incorporated in California and has its principal place of business in Phoenix, Ariz. [Currently, Greyhound Lines, Inc. is incorporated in Delaware and headquartered in Texas. The Greyhound Corporation divested itself of Greyhound Lines, Inc. in 1987 and changed its name to The Dial Corporation, which is now a subsidiary of German company Henkel AG & Co. Ed.]

tions being held liable for substantial damages in a private antitrust suit and a large fine in a criminal contempt action. The activities which led to these penalties took place in Oregon.

Simultaneously with his complaint, Heitner filed a motion for an order of sequestration of the Delaware property of the individual defendants [consisting of 82,000 shares of Greyhound stock plus stock options owned by the defendants. No defendants were Delaware residents.]

The requested sequestration order was signed the day the motion was filed. Pursuant to that order, the sequestrator "seized" approximately 82,000 shares of Greyhound common stock belonging to 19 of the defendants, and options belonging to another 2 defendants. These seizures were accomplished by placing "stop transfer" orders or their equivalents on the books of the Greyhound Corp. So far as the record shows, none of the certificates representing the seized property was physically present in Delaware. The stock was considered to be in Delaware, and so subject to seizure, by virtue of <u>Del. Code Ann., Tit. 8, § 169 (1975)</u>, which makes Delaware the situs of ownership of all stock in Delaware corporations.

All 28 defendants were notified of the initiation of the suit by certified mail directed to their last known addresses and by publication in a New Castle County [Delaware] newspaper. The 21 defendants whose property was seized (hereafter referred to as appellants) responded by entering a special appearance for the purpose of moving to quash service of process and to vacate the sequestration order. They contended that the *ex parte* sequestration procedure did not accord them due process of law and that the property seized was not capable of attachment in Delaware. In addition, appellants asserted that under the rule of <u>International Shoe Co. v. Washington, 326 U.S. 310 (1945)</u>, they did not have sufficient contacts with Delaware to sustain the jurisdiction of that State's courts.

The Court of Chancery rejected these arguments * * * On appeal, the Delaware Supreme Court affirmed the judgment of the Court of Chancery. * * *

II

The Delaware courts rejected appellants' jurisdictional challenge by noting that this suit was brought as a *quasi in rem* proceeding. Since *quasi in rem* jurisdiction is traditionally based on attachment or seizure of property present in the jurisdiction, not on contacts between the defendant and the State, the courts considered appellants' claimed lack of contacts with Delaware to be unimportant. This categorical analysis assumes the continued soundness of the conceptual structure founded on the century-old case of <u>Pennoyer v. Neff, 95 U.S. 714 (1878)</u>. * * *

From our perspective, the importance of *Pennoyer* is not its result, but the fact that its principles and corollaries derived from them became the basic elements of the constitutional doctrine governing state-court jurisdiction. As we have noted, under *Pennoyer* state authority to adjudicate was based on the jurisdiction's power over either persons or property. This fundamental concept is embodied in the very vocabulary which we use to describe judgments. If a court's jurisdiction is based on its authority over the defendant's person, the action and judgment are denominated "*in personam*" and can impose a personal obligation on the defendant in favor of the plaintiff. If jurisdiction is based on the court's power over property within its territory, the action is called "*in rem*" or

Take Note!

Note that here Justice Marshall provides a good review of the meanings of and distinctions between the terms *in personam*, *in rem*, and *quasi in rem*.

"*quasi in rem*." The effect of a judgment in such a case is limited to the property that supports jurisdiction and does not impose a personal liability on the property owner, since he is not before the court. In *Pennoyer's* terms, the owner is affected only "indirectly" by an *in rem* judgment adverse to his interest in the property subject to the court's disposition.

By concluding that "[t]he authority of every tribunal is necessarily restricted by the territorial limits of the State in which it is established," *Pennoyer* sharply limited the availability of *in personam* jurisdiction over defendants not resident in the forum State. If a nonresident defendant could not be found in a State, he could not be sued there. On the other hand, since the State in which property was located was considered to have exclusive sovereignty over that property, *in rem* actions could proceed regardless of the owner's location. Indeed, since a State's process could not reach beyond its borders, this Court held after *Pennoyer* that due process did not require any effort to give a property owner personal notice that his property was involved in an *in rem* proceeding.

The *Pennoyer* rules generally favored nonresident defendants by making them harder to sue. This advantage was reduced, however, by the ability of a resident plaintiff to satisfy a claim against a nonresident defendant by bringing into court any property of the defendant located in the plaintiff's State. * * *

[After *International Shoe*] the relationship among the defendant, the forum, and the litigation, rather than the mutually exclusive sovereignty of the States on which the rules of *Pennoyer* rest, became the central concern of the inquiry into personal jurisdiction. The immediate effect of this departure from *Pennoyer's* conceptual apparatus was to increase the ability of the state courts to obtain personal jurisdiction over nonresident defendants.

No equally dramatic change has occurred in the law governing jurisdiction *in rem*. There have, however, been intimations that the collapse of the *in personam* wing of *Pennoyer* has not left that decision unweakened as a foundation for *in rem* jurisdiction. Well-reasoned lower court opinions have questioned the proposition that the presence of property in a State gives that State jurisdiction to adjudicate rights to the property regardless of the relationship of the underlying dispute and the property owner to the forum. The overwhelming majority of commentators have also rejected *Pennoyer*'s premise that a proceeding "against" property is not a proceeding against the owners of that property. Accordingly, they urge that the "traditional notions of fair play and substantial justice" that govern a State's power to adjudicate *in personam* should also govern its power to adjudicate personal rights to property located in the State.

Although this Court has not addressed this argument directly, we have held that property cannot be subjected to a court's judgment unless reasonable and appropriate efforts have been made to give the property owners actual notice of the action. <u>Mullane v. Central Hanover Bank & Trust Co., 339 U.S. 306 (1950)</u>. This conclusion recognizes, contrary to *Pennoyer*, that an adverse judgment *in rem* directly affects the property owner by divesting him of his rights in the property before the court. It is clear, therefore, that the law of state-court jurisdiction no longer stands securely on the foundation established in *Pennoyer*. We think that the time is ripe to consider whether the standard of fairness and substantial justice set forth in *International Shoe* should be held to govern actions *in rem* as well as *in personam*.

III

The case for applying to jurisdiction *in rem* the same test of "fair play and substantial justice" as governs assertions of jurisdiction *in personam* is simple and straightforward. It is premised on recognition that "[t]he phrase, 'judicial jurisdiction over a thing', is a customary elliptical way of referring to jurisdiction over the interests of persons in a thing." This recognition leads to the conclusion that in order to justify an exercise of jurisdiction *in rem*, the basis for jurisdiction must be sufficient to justify exercising "jurisdiction over the interests of persons in a thing." The standard for determining whether an exercise of jurisdiction over the interests of persons is consistent with the Due Process Clause is the minimum-contacts standard elucidated in *International Shoe*.

This argument, of course, does not ignore the fact that the presence of property in a State may bear on the existence of jurisdiction by providing contacts among the forum State, the defendant, and the litigation. For example, when claims to the property itself are the source of the underlying controversy between the plaintiff and the defendant, it would be unusual for the State where the property is located not to have jurisdiction. In such cases, the defendant's claim to property located in the State would normally indicate that he expected to benefit from the State's protection of his interest. The State's strong interests in assuring the marketability of property within its borders and in providing a procedure for peaceful resolution of disputes about the possession of that property would also support jurisdiction, as would the likelihood that important records and witnesses will be found in the State. The presence of property may also favor jurisdiction in cases such as suits for injury suffered on the land of an absentee owner, where the defendant's ownership of the property is conceded but the cause of action is otherwise related to rights and duties growing out of that ownership.

It appears, therefore, that jurisdiction over many types of actions which now are or might be brought *in rem* would not be affected by a holding that any assertion of state-court jurisdiction must satisfy the *International Shoe* standard.[30] For the type of *quasi in rem* action typified by * * * the present case, however, accepting the proposed analysis would result in significant change. These are cases where the property which now serves as the basis for state-court jurisdiction is completely unrelated to the plaintiff's cause of action. Thus, although the presence of the defendant's property in a State might suggest the existence of other ties among the defendant, the State, and the litigation, the presence of the property alone would not support the State's jurisdiction. If those other ties did not exist, cases over which the State is now thought to have jurisdiction could not be brought in that forum.

Since acceptance of the *International Shoe* test would most affect this class of cases, we examine the arguments against adopting that standard as they relate to this category of litigation. Before doing so, however, we note that this type of case also presents the clearest illustration of the argument in favor of assessing assertions of jurisdiction by a single standard. For in cases such as * * * this one, the only role played by the property is to provide the basis for bringing the defendant into court. Indeed, the express purpose of the Delaware sequestration procedure is to compel the defendant to enter a personal appearance. In such cases, if a direct assertion of personal jurisdiction over the defendant would violate the Constitution, it would seem that an indirect assertion of that jurisdiction should be equally impermissible.

The primary rationale for treating the presence of property as a sufficient basis for jurisdiction to adjudicate claims over which the State would not have jurisdiction if *International Shoe* applied is that a wrongdoer "should not be able to avoid payment of his obligations by the expedient of removing his assets to a place where he is not subject to an *in personam* suit." Restatement § 66, Comment a. This justification, however, does not explain why jurisdiction should be recognized without regard to

What's That?

The "Restatement" is short for Restatement of Law and refers to a series of volumes authored by the American Law Institute (www.ali.org) that present a comprehensive statement of the law in a given area. They have frequently been cited by courts.

---

[30] We do not suggest that jurisdictional doctrines other than those discussed in text, such as the particularized rules governing adjudications of status, are inconsistent with the standard of fairness.

whether the property is present in the State because of an effort to avoid the owner's obligations. Nor does it support jurisdiction to adjudicate the underlying claim. At most, it suggests that a State in which property is located should have jurisdiction to attach that property, by use of proper procedures, as security for a judgment being sought in a forum where the litigation can be maintained consistently with *International Shoe*. Moreover, we know of nothing to justify the assumption that a debtor can avoid paying his obligations by removing his property to a State in which his creditor cannot obtain personal jurisdiction over him. * * *

It might also be suggested that allowing *in rem* jurisdiction avoids the uncertainty inherent in the *International Shoe* standard and assures a plaintiff of a forum. We believe, however, that the fairness standard of *International Shoe* can be easily applied in the vast majority of cases. * * *

We are left, then, to consider the significance of the long history of jurisdiction based solely on the presence of property in a State. Although the theory that territorial power is both essential to and sufficient for jurisdiction has been undermined, we have never held that the presence of property in a State does not automatically confer jurisdiction over the owner's interest in that property. This history must be considered as supporting the proposition that jurisdiction based solely on the presence of property satisfies the demands of due process, but it is not decisive. "[T]raditional notions of fair play and substantial justice" can be as readily offended by the perpetuation of ancient forms that are no longer justified as by the adoption of new procedures that are inconsistent with the basic values of our constitutional heritage. The fiction that an assertion of jurisdiction over property is anything but an assertion of jurisdiction over the owner of the property supports an ancient form without substantial modern justification. Its continued acceptance would serve only to allow state-court jurisdiction that is fundamentally unfair to the defendant.

Food for Thought

In what ways is jurisdiction based solely on the presence of property in a state "fundamentally unfair to the defendant?" If such jurisdiction is the only way a plaintiff may proceed against a defendant, should that fact be considered in evaluating the fairness of the assertion of jurisdiction?

We therefore conclude that all assertions of state-court jurisdiction must be evaluated according to the standards set forth in *International Shoe* and its progeny.

IV

The Delaware courts based their assertion of jurisdiction in this case solely on the statutory presence of appellants' property in Delaware. Yet that property is not the subject matter of this litigation, nor is the underlying cause of action related to the property. Appellants' holdings in Greyhound do not, therefore, provide contacts with Delaware sufficient to support the jurisdiction of that State's courts over appellants. If it exists, that jurisdiction must have some other foundation.

Appellee Heitner did not allege and does not now claim that appellants have ever set foot in Delaware. Nor does he identify any act related to his cause of action as having taken place in Delaware. Nevertheless, he contends that appellants' positions as directors and officers of a corporation chartered in Delaware provide sufficient "contacts, ties, or relations" with that State to give its courts jurisdiction over appellants in this stockholder's derivative action. This argument is based primarily on what Heitner asserts to be the strong interest of Delaware in supervising the management of a Delaware corporation. That interest is said to derive from the role of Delaware law in establishing the corporation and defining the obligations owed to it by its officers and directors. In order to protect this interest, appellee concludes, Delaware's courts must have jurisdiction over corporate fiduciaries such as appellants.

This argument is undercut by the failure of the Delaware Legislature to assert the state interest appellee finds so compelling. Delaware law bases jurisdiction, not on appellants' status as corporate fiduciaries, but rather on the presence of their property in the State. Although the sequestration procedure used here may be most frequently used in derivative suits against officers and directors, the authorizing statute evinces no specific concern with such actions. Sequestration can be used in any suit against a nonresident, and reaches corporate fiduciaries only if they happen to own interests in a Delaware corporation, or other property in the State. But as Heitner's failure to secure jurisdiction over seven of the defendants named in his complaint demonstrates, there is no necessary relationship between holding a position as a corporate fiduciary and owning stock or other interests in the corporation. If Delaware perceived its interest in securing jurisdiction over corporate fiduciaries to be as great as Heitner suggests, we would expect it to have enacted a statute more clearly designed to protect that interest.

Moreover, even if Heitner's assessment of the importance of Delaware's interest is accepted, his argument fails to demonstrate that Delaware is a fair forum for this litigation. The interest appellee has identified may support the application of Delaware law to resolve any controversy over appellants' actions in their capacities as officers and directors. But we have rejected the argument that if a State's law can properly be applied to a dispute, its courts necessarily have jurisdiction over the parties to that dispute. * * *

Appellee suggests that by accepting positions as officers or directors of a Delaware corporation, appellants performed the acts required by *Hanson v. Denckla*. He notes that Delaware law provides substantial benefits to corporate officers and directors, and that these benefits were at least in part the incentive for appellants to assume their positions. It is, he says, "only fair and just" to require appellants, in return for these benefits, to respond in the State of Delaware when they are accused of misusing their power.

But like Heitner's first argument, this line of reasoning establishes only that it is appropriate for Delaware law to govern the obligations of appellants to Greyhound and its stockholders. It does not demonstrate that appellants have "purposefully avail(ed themselves) of the privilege of conducting activities within the forum State," *Hanson v. Denckla, supra,* in a way that would justify bringing them before a Delaware tribunal. Appellants have simply had nothing to do with the State of Delaware. Moreover, appellants had no reason to expect to be haled before a Delaware court. Delaware, unlike some States, has not enacted a statute that treats acceptance of a directorship as consent to jurisdiction in the State. And "[i]t strains reason . . . to suggest that anyone buying securities in a corporation formed in Delaware 'impliedly consents' to subject himself to Delaware's . . . jurisdiction on any cause of action." Appellants, who were not required to acquire interests in Greyhound in order to hold their positions, did not by acquiring those interests surrender their right to be brought to judgment only in States with which they had had "minimum contacts."

> **FYI**
>
> The Delaware legislature took the Court up on its suggestion and within thirteen days of this decision amended its laws to provide that nonresident directors of Delaware corporations shall be deemed to have consented to the appointment of the corporation's registered agent in Delaware or the Secretary of State as his or her agent for service of process. *See* 10 Del. Code § 3114.

The Due Process Clause "does not contemplate that a state may make binding a judgment . . . against an individual or corporate defendant with which the state has no contacts, ties, or relations." *International Shoe Co. v. Washington*.

Delaware's assertion of jurisdiction over appellants in this case is inconsistent with that constitutional limitation on state power. The judgment of the Delaware Supreme Court must, therefore, be reversed.

It is so ordered.

MR. JUSTICE REHNQUIST took no part in the consideration or decision of this case.

MR. JUSTICE POWELL, concurring.

I agree that the principles of *International Shoe Co. v. Washington*, should be extended to govern assertions of *in rem* as well as *in personam* jurisdiction in a state court. I also agree that neither the statutory presence of appellants' stock in Delaware nor their positions as directors and officers of a Delaware corporation can provide sufficient contacts to support the Delaware courts' assertion of jurisdiction in this case.

I would explicitly reserve judgment, however, on whether the ownership of some forms of property whose situs is indisputably and permanently located within a State may, without more, provide the contacts necessary to subject a defendant to jurisdiction within the State to the extent of the value of the property. In the case of real property, in particular, preservation of the common-law concept of *quasi in rem* jurisdiction arguably would avoid the uncertainty of the general *International Shoe* standard without significant cost to " 'traditional notions of fair play and substantial justice.' "

Subject to the foregoing reservation, I join the opinion of the Court.

MR. JUSTICE STEVENS, concurring in the judgment.

* * *

One who purchases shares of stock on the open market can hardly be expected to know that he has thereby become subject to suit in a forum remote from his residence and unrelated to the transaction. As a practical matter, the Delaware sequestration statute creates an unacceptable risk of judgment without notice. Unlike the 49 other States, Delaware treats the place of incorporation as the situs of the stock, even though both the owner and the custodian of the shares are elsewhere. Moreover, Delaware denies the defendant the opportunity to defend the merits of the suit unless he subjects himself to the unlimited jurisdiction of the court. Thus, it coerces a defendant either to submit to personal jurisdiction in a forum which could not otherwise obtain such jurisdiction or to lose the securities which have been attached. If its procedure were upheld, Delaware would, in effect, impose a duty of inquiry on every purchaser of securities in the national market. For unless the purchaser ascertains both the State of incorporation of the company whose shares he is buying, and also the idiosyncrasies of its law, he may be assuming an unknown risk of litigation. I therefore agree with the Court that on the record before us no adequate basis for jurisdiction exists and that the Delaware statute is unconstitutional on its face.

How the Court's opinion may be applied in other contexts is not entirely clear to me. I agree with Mr. Justice POWELL that it should not be read to invalidate *quasi in rem* jurisdiction where real estate is involved. I would also not read it as invalidating other long-accepted methods of acquiring jurisdiction over persons with adequate notice of both the particular controversy and the fact that their local activities might subject them to suit. My uncertainty as to the reach of the opinion, and my fear that it purports to decide a great deal more than is necessary to dispose of this case, persuade me merely to concur in the judgment.

MR. JUSTICE BRENNAN, concurring in part and dissenting in part.

I join Parts I-III of the Court's opinion. I fully agree that the minimum-contacts analysis developed in *International Shoe* represents a far more sensible construct for the exercise of state-court jurisdiction than the patchwork of legal and factual fictions that has been generated from the decision in *Pennoyer v. Neff*. It is precisely because the inquiry into minimum contacts is now of such overriding importance, however, that I must respectfully dissent from Part IV of the Court's opinion.

* * *

II

* * * I am convinced that as a general rule a state forum has jurisdiction to adjudicate a shareholder derivative action centering on the conduct and policies of the directors and officers of a corporation chartered by that State. Unlike the Court, I therefore would not foreclose Delaware from asserting jurisdiction over appellants were it persuaded to do so on the basis of minimum contacts.

It is well settled that a derivative lawsuit as presented here does not inure primarily to the benefit of the named plaintiff. Rather, the primary beneficiaries are the corporation and its owners, the shareholders. * * *

Viewed in this light, the chartering State has an unusually powerful interest in insuring the availability of a convenient forum for litigating claims involving a possible multiplicity of defendant fiduciaries and for vindicating the State's substantive policies regarding the management of its domestic corporations. I believe that our cases fairly establish that the State's valid substantive interests are important considerations in assessing whether it constitutionally may claim jurisdiction over a given cause of action.

In this instance, Delaware can point to at least three interrelated public policies that are furthered by its assertion of jurisdiction. First, the State has a substantial interest in providing restitution for its local corporations that allegedly have been victimized by fiduciary misconduct, even if the managerial decisions occurred outside the State. The importance of this general state interest in assuring restitution for its own residents previously found expression in cases that went outside the then-prevailing due process framework to authorize state-court jurisdiction over nonresident motorists who injure others within the State. More recently, it has led States to seek and to acquire jurisdiction over nonresident tortfeasors whose purely out-of-state activities produce domestic consequences. Second, state courts have legitimately read their jurisdiction expansively when a cause of action centers in an area in which the forum State possesses a manifest regulatory interest. * * * [T]he conduct of corporate fiduciaries is just such a matter in which the policies and interests of the domestic forum are ordinarily presumed to be paramount. Finally, a State like Delaware has a recognized interest in affording a convenient forum for supervising and overseeing the affairs of an entity that is purely the creation of that State's law. * * *

To be sure, the Court is not blind to these considerations. It notes that the State's interests "may support the application of Delaware law to resolve any controversy over appellants' actions in their capacities as officers and directors." But this, the Court argues, pertains to choice of law, not jurisdiction. I recognize that the jurisdictional and choice-of-law inquiries are not identical. But I would not compartmentalize thinking in this area quite so rigidly as it seems to me the Court does today, for both inquiries "are often closely related and to a substantial degree depend upon similar considerations." * * * At the minimum, the decision that it is fair to bind a defendant by a State's laws and rules should prove to be highly relevant to the fairness of permitting that same State to accept jurisdiction for adjudicating the controversy. * * *

Make the Connection

Choice of law refers to the question of which jurisdiction's law should apply in a case. You can study this topic further in a **Conflict of Laws** course. We will study choice of law in a limited sense in Chapter 5 when we consider the doctrine guiding the choice between applying federal or state law when a case is in federal court.

I, therefore, would approach the minimum-contacts analysis differently than does the Court. Crucial to me is the fact that appellants voluntarily associated themselves with the State of Delaware, "invoking the benefits and protections of its laws" by entering into a long-term and fragile relationship with one of its domestic corporations. They thereby elected to assume powers and to undertake responsibilities wholly derived from that State's rules and regulations, and to become eligible for those benefits that Delaware law makes available to its corporations' officials. While it is possible that countervailing issues of judicial efficiency and the like might clearly favor a different forum, they do not appear on the meager record before us; and, of course, we are concerned solely with "minimum" contacts, not the "best" contacts. I thus do not believe that it is unfair to insist that appellants make themselves available to suit in a competent forum that Delaware might create for vindication of its important public policies directly pertaining to appellants' fiduciary associations with the State.

Points for Discussion

a. The Outcome in *Shaffer*

The Court in *Shaffer* held that Delaware could not exercise jurisdiction over current and former directors of a Delaware corporation in an action alleging violations of their fiduciary duties owed to that corporation. Doesn't Delaware have a particularly strong interest in litigating disputes alleging that corporate directors have violated duties owed to Delaware corporations as Justice Brennan suggests? What was the majority's view on this issue? Why was jurisdiction not appropriate on that basis?

b. Jurisdiction and Property After *Shaffer*

Prior to *Shaffer*, the understanding was that the presence of property within a state alone was a sufficient basis for a state's exercise of jurisdiction over that property, either in a dispute involving the property (*in rem* or *quasi-in-rem* type I jurisdiction) or in an unrelated suit, but only to the extent of the value of the property (*quasi-in-rem* type II jurisdiction). How did *Shaffer* alter this landscape? Do either *in rem* or *quasi-in-rem* jurisdiction survive *Shaffer*? *See, e.g.*, <u>Caesars World, Inc. v. Caesars-Palace.com, 112 F. Supp. 2d 502, 504 (E.D. Va. 2000)</u> (concluding that *Shaffer's* minimum contacts requirement applies only to assertions of *quasi-in-rem* type II jurisdiction). *See also* <u>Shaffer v. Heitner, 433 U.S. 186, 210 n.36 (1977)</u> (affirming the continuing validity of jurisdiction based on property in the judgment-enforcement context). If assertions of jurisdiction based on property now must satisfy the minimum contacts test of *International Shoe*, how does such an analysis proceed?

Hypo 1.7

A bank in State A lent money to a borrower domiciled in State A. When the loan became due, the borrower failed to pay. After that time, the borrower inherited property in State B. The bank initiated an action against the borrower on the debt in a court of State B. To obtain jurisdiction over the borrower in State B, the bank attached the borrower's State B property as is permitted under State B law. May State B constitutionally exercise personal jurisdiction over the borrower in this case?

Hypo 1.8

A client from State A hired a lawyer from State B to handle the client's purchase of real property located in State B. The lawyer did so, but the client failed to pay the lawyer's fees. The lawyer initiated an action in State B federal court, attaching the State B property in question (as is permitted under State B law) to get jurisdiction. Is jurisdiction in the State B federal court over the client constitutional in this case?

Hypo 1.9

Neff, who has never been to Oregon, bought some property in Oregon from Pennoyer. Mitchell claims that the land belongs to him and that Pennoyer did not have proper title to convey the land. Mitchell initiated a quiet title action in Oregon state court against Neff to determine the proper owner of the land; he attached the property (as is permitted under Oregon law) to get jurisdiction. Is jurisdiction constitutional in Oregon?

c. *In Rem* Jurisdiction in Cybersquatting Cases

The practice of registering someone else's trademark as a domain name has been outlawed through the Anticybersquatting and Consumer Protection Act (ACPA). The statute provides that the trademark owners may initiate *in rem* civil actions for violations of the ACPA in the district in which the domain name is registered, but only if the plaintiff is unable to obtain personal jurisdiction over the offending domain name registrant. 15 U.S.C. § 1125(d)(2)(A). Thus, jurisdiction in such cases would be *in rem*, based solely on the presence of the domain name registration in the forum state. If the registrant of the domain name otherwise has no contacts with the forum state, would the exercise of jurisdiction on the basis of the domain name presence alone be constitutional in light of *Shaffer*? *See Harrods Ltd. v. Sixty Internet Domain Names, 302 F.3d 214, 225 (4th Cir. 2002)* ("[B]ecause claims to the property itself are the source of the underlying controversy, and because Virginia has important interests in exercising jurisdiction over that property . . . , we conclude that courts in Virginia, the state where the Domain Names are registered, may constitutionally exercise *in rem* jurisdiction over them." (internal quotation marks and citation omitted)).

3. Transient Jurisdiction

If, according to the Court in *Shaffer*, "all assertions of state-court jurisdiction must be evaluated according to the standards set forth in *International Shoe*," do cases such as *Grace v. MacArthur, 170 F. Supp. 442 (E.D. Ark. 1959)*, which upheld the exercise of jurisdiction based solely on the service of process on the defendant within the state, have any continuing validity? That is, after *Shaffer*, would it be constitutional to exercise personal jurisdiction over defendants for any cause of action based purely on in-state service of process, so-called "tag" or transient jurisdiction? The next case takes up that question.

> **FYI**
>
> Recall that in *Grace v. MacArthur* [discussed after *Pennoyer v. Neff* in this casebook], the defendant was served with process while a passenger on an airplane during the time the plane was flying over the forum state's (Arkansas) airspace. Does upholding the assertion of jurisdiction on such a basis make sense to you?

Burnham v. Superior Court

Supreme Court of the United States
495 U.S. 604 (1990)

JUSTICE SCALIA announced the judgment of the Court and delivered an opinion in which THE CHIEF JUSTICE and JUSTICE KENNEDY join, and in which JUSTICE WHITE joins with respect to Parts I, II-A, II-B, and II-C.

The question presented is whether the Due Process Clause of the Fourteenth Amendment denies California courts jurisdiction over a nonresident, who was personally served with process while temporarily in that State, in a suit unrelated to his activities in the State.

Take Note!

Justice Scalia's opinion carries the approval of only three other Justices, making it merely a plurality opinion rather than a majority opinion. What does that mean for the precedential effect of the opinion?

I

Petitioner Dennis Burnham married Francie Burnham in 1976 in West Virginia. In 1977 the couple moved to New Jersey, where their two children were born. In July 1987 the Burnhams decided to separate. They agreed that Mrs. Burnham, who intended to move to California, would take custody of the children. Shortly before Mrs. Burnham departed for California that same month, she and petitioner agreed that she would file for divorce on grounds of "irreconcilable differences."

In October 1987, petitioner filed for divorce in New Jersey state court on grounds of "desertion." Petitioner did not, however, obtain an issuance of summons against his wife and did not attempt to serve her with process. Mrs. Burnham, after unsuccessfully demanding that petitioner adhere to their prior agreement to submit to an "irreconcilable differences" divorce, brought suit for divorce in California state court * * * .

In late January, petitioner visited southern California on business, after which he went north to visit his children [during which time] petitioner was served with a California court summons and a copy of Mrs. Burnham's divorce petition. He then returned to New Jersey.

Later that year, petitioner made a special appearance in the California Superior Court, moving to quash the service of process on the ground that the court lacked personal jurisdiction over him because his only contacts with California were a few short visits to the State for the purposes of conducting business and visiting his children. The Superior Court denied the motion, and the California Court of Appeal denied mandamus relief, rejecting petitioner's contention that the Due Process Clause prohibited California courts from asserting jurisdiction over him because he lacked "minimum contacts" with the State. The court held it to be "a valid jurisdictional predicate for *in personam* jurisdiction" that the "defendant [was] present in the forum state and personally served with process." We granted certiorari.

> ### It's Latin to Me!
>
> *Mandamus* is a Latin term meaning "we command" and refers to a writ issued by a superior court compelling a lower court or official to act (or refrain from acting) in a certain way.

II.A

* * * To determine whether the assertion of personal jurisdiction is consistent with due process, we have long relied on the principles traditionally followed by American courts in marking out the territorial limits of each State's authority. That criterion was first announced in <u>Pennoyer v. Neff, 95 U.S. 714, 722 (1878)</u>, in which we stated that due process "mean[s] a course of legal proceedings according to those rules and principles which have been established in our systems of jurisprudence for the protection and enforcement of private rights," including the "well-established principles of public law respecting the jurisdiction of an independent State over persons and property." In what has become the classic expression of the criterion, we said in <u>International Shoe Co. v. Washington, 326 U.S. 310 (1945)</u>, that a state court's assertion of personal jurisdiction satisfies the Due Process Clause if it does not violate " 'traditional notions of fair play and substantial justice.' " Since *International Shoe*, we have only been called upon to decide whether these "traditional notions" permit States to exercise jurisdiction over absent defendants in a manner that deviates from the rules of jurisdiction applied in the 19th century. We have held such deviations permissible, but only with respect to suits arising out of the absent defendant's contacts with the State. The question we must decide today is whether due process requires a similar connection between the litigation and the defendant's contacts with the State in cases where the defendant is physically present in the State at the time process is served upon him.

B

Among the most firmly established principles of personal jurisdiction in American tradition is that the courts of a State have jurisdiction over nonresidents who are physically present in the State. The view developed early that each State had the power to hale before its courts any individual who could be found within its borders, and that once having acquired jurisdiction over such a person by properly serving him with process, the State could retain jurisdiction to enter judgment against him, no matter how fleeting his visit. That view had antecedents in English common-law practice, which sometimes allowed "transitory" actions, arising out of events outside the country, to be maintained against seemingly nonresident defendants who were present in England. * * *

Decisions in the courts of many States in the 19th and early 20th centuries held that personal service upon a physically present defendant sufficed to confer jurisdiction, without regard to whether the defendant was only briefly in the State or whether the cause of action was related to his activities there. * * * Most States, moreover, had statutes or common-law rules that exempted from service of process individuals who were brought into the forum by force or fraud or who were there as a party or witness in unrelated judicial proceedings. These exceptions obviously rested upon the premise that service of process conferred jurisdiction. * * * [A]s far as we have been able to determine, not one American case from the period (or, for that matter, not one American case until 1978) held, or even suggested, that in-state personal service on an individual was insufficient to confer personal jurisdiction. * * *

Take Note!

Justice Scalia here discusses traditional exceptions to the rule that permits jurisdiction based on in-state personal service: immunity for parties and witnesses in unrelated litigation and immunity for those induced into the forum through fraud. These exceptions generally remain valid today. See N. Light Tech., Inc. v. N. Lights Club, 236 F.3d 57, 62 (1st Cir. 2001); 4A C. WRIGHT, A. MILLER & A. STEINMAN, FED. PRAC. & PROC. §§ 1076–1081 (4th ed. 2015).

This American jurisdictional practice is, moreover, not merely old; it is continuing. It remains the practice of, not only a substantial number of the States, but as far as we are aware all the States and the Federal Government * * * . We do not know of a single state or federal statute, or a single judicial decision resting upon state law, that has abandoned in-state service as a basis of jurisdiction. Many recent cases reaffirm it.

C

Despite this formidable body of precedent, petitioner contends, in reliance on our decisions applying the *International Shoe* standard, that in the absence of "continuous and systematic" contacts with the forum, a nonresident defendant can be subjected to judgment only as to matters that arise out of or relate to his contacts with the forum. This argument rests on a thorough misunderstanding of our cases.

The view of most courts in the 19th century was that a court simply could not exercise *in personam* jurisdiction over a nonresident who had not been personally served with process in the forum. *Pennoyer v. Neff*, while renowned for its statement of the principle that the Fourteenth Amendment prohibits such an exercise of jurisdiction, in fact set that forth only as dictum and decided the case (which involved a judgment rendered more than two years before the Fourteenth Amendment's ratification) under "well-established principles of public law." Those principles, embodied in the Due Process Clause, required * * * that when proceedings "involv[e] merely a determination of the personal liability of the defendant, he must be brought within [the court's] jurisdiction by service of process within the State, or his voluntary appearance." * * *

Later years, however, saw the weakening of the *Pennoyer* rule. In the late 19th and early 20th centuries, changes in the technology of transportation and communication, and the tremendous growth of interstate business activity, led to an "inevitable relaxation of the strict limits on state jurisdiction" over nonresident individuals and corporations. States required, for example, that nonresident corporations appoint an in-state agent upon whom process could be served as a condition of transacting business within their borders, and provided in-state "substituted service" for nonresident motorists who caused injury in the State and left before personal service could be accomplished, *see, e.g., Kane v. New Jersey, 242 U.S. 160 (1916); Hess v. Pawloski, 274 U.S. 352 (1927)*. We initially upheld these laws under the Due Process Clause on grounds that they complied with *Pennoyer's* rigid requirement of either "consent," or "presence." As many observed, however, the consent and presence were purely fictional. Our opinion in *International Shoe* cast those fictions aside and made explicit the underlying basis of these decisions: Due process does not necessarily require the States to adhere to the unbending territorial limits on jurisdiction set forth in *Pennoyer*. The validity of assertion of jurisdiction over a nonconsenting defendant who is not present in the forum depends upon whether "the quality and nature of [his] activity" in relation to the forum renders such jurisdiction consistent with " 'traditional notions of fair play and substantial justice.' " Subsequent cases have derived from the *International Shoe* standard the general rule that a State may dispense with in-forum personal service on nonresident defendants in suits arising out of their activities in the State. * * *

Nothing in *International Shoe* or the cases that have followed it, however, offers support for the very different proposition petitioner seeks to establish today: that a defendant's presence in the forum is not only unnecessary to validate novel, nontraditional assertions of jurisdiction, but is itself no longer sufficient to establish jurisdiction. That proposition is unfaithful to both elementary logic and the foundations of our due process jurisprudence. The distinction between what is needed to support novel procedures and what is needed to sustain traditional ones is fundamental * * * .

The short of the matter is that jurisdiction based on physical presence alone constitutes due process because it is one of the continuing traditions of our legal system that define the due process standard of "traditional notions of fair play and substantial justice." That standard was developed by analogy to "physical presence," and it would be perverse to say it could now be turned against that touchstone of jurisdiction.

D

Petitioner's strongest argument, though we ultimately reject it, relies upon our decision in *Shaffer v. Heitner, 433 U.S. 186 (1977)*. * * *

It goes too far to say, as petitioner contends, that *Shaffer* compels the conclusion that a State lacks jurisdiction over an individual unless the litigation arises out of his activities in the State. *Shaffer*, like *International Shoe*, involved jurisdiction over an absent defendant, and it stands for nothing more than the proposition that when the "minimum contact" that is a substitute for physical presence consists of property ownership it must, like other minimum contacts, be related to the litigation. Petitioner wrenches out of its context our statement in *Shaffer* that "all assertions of state-court jurisdiction must be evaluated according to the standards set forth in *International Shoe* and its progeny." When read together with the two sentences that preceded it, the meaning of this statement becomes clear:

> "The fiction that an assertion of jurisdiction over property is anything but an assertion of jurisdiction over the owner of the property supports an ancient form without substantial modern justification. Its continued acceptance would serve only to allow state-court jurisdiction that is fundamentally unfair to the defendant.

> "We *therefore conclude* that all assertions of state-court jurisdiction must be evaluated according to the standards set forth in *International Shoe* and its progeny." (emphasis added).

Shaffer was saying, in other words, not that all bases for the assertion of *in personam* jurisdiction (including, presumably, in-state service) must be treated alike and subjected to the "minimum contacts" analysis of *International Shoe*; but rather that *quasi in rem* jurisdiction, that fictional "ancient form," and *in personam* jurisdiction, are really one and the same and must be treated alike—leading to the conclusion that *quasi in rem* jurisdiction, i.e., that form of *in personam* jurisdiction based upon a "property ownership" contact and by definition unaccompanied by personal, in-state service, must satisfy the litigation-relatedness requirement of *International Shoe*. The logic of *Shaffer*'s holding—which places all suits against absent nonresidents on the same constitutional footing, regardless of whether a separate Latin label is attached to one particular basis of contact—does not compel the conclusion that physically present defendants must be treated identically to absent ones. As we have demonstrated at length, our tradition has treated the two classes of defendants quite differently, and it is unreasonable to read *Shaffer* as casually obliterating that distinction. *International Shoe* confined its "minimum contacts" requirement to situations in which the defendant "be not present within the territory of the forum," and nothing in *Shaffer* expands that requirement beyond that.

It is fair to say, however, that while our holding today does not contradict *Shaffer*, our basic approach to the due process question is different. We have conducted no independent inquiry into the desirability or fairness of the prevailing in-state service rule, leaving that judgment to the legislatures that are free to amend it; for our purposes, its validation is its pedigree, as the phrase "traditional notions of fair play and substantial justice" makes clear. *Shaffer* did conduct such an independent inquiry, asserting that " 'traditional notions of fair play and substantial justice' can be as readily offended by the perpetuation of ancient forms that are no longer justified as by the adoption of new procedures that are inconsistent with the basic values of our constitutional heritage." Perhaps that assertion can be sustained when the "perpetuation of ancient forms" is engaged in by only a very small minority of the States. Where, however, as in the present case, a jurisdictional principle is both firmly approved by tradition and still favored, it is impossible to imagine what standard we could appeal to for the judgment that it is "no longer justified." While in no way receding from or casting doubt upon the holding of *Shaffer* or any other case, we reaffirm today our time-honored approach. For new procedures, hitherto unknown, the Due Process Clause requires analysis to determine whether "traditional notions of fair play and substantial justice" have been offended. But a doctrine of personal jurisdiction that dates back to the adoption of the Fourteenth Amendment and is still generally observed unquestionably meets that standard.

III

A few words in response to Justice BRENNAN's opinion concurring in the judgment: It insists that we apply "contemporary notions of due process" to determine the constitutionality of California's assertion of jurisdiction. But our analysis today comports with that prescription, at least if we give it the only sense allowed by our precedents. The "contemporary notions of due process" applicable to personal jurisdiction are the enduring "traditional notions of fair play and substantial justice" established as the test by *International Shoe*. By its very language, that test is satisfied if a state court adheres to jurisdictional rules that are generally applied and have always been applied in the United States.

But the concurrence's proposed standard of "contemporary notions of due process" requires more: It measures state-court jurisdiction not only against traditional doctrines in this country, including current state-court practice, but also against each Justice's subjective assessment of what is fair and just. Authority for that seductive standard is not to be found in any of our personal jurisdiction cases. It is, indeed, an outright break with the test of "traditional notions of fair play and substantial justice," which would have to be reformulated "our notions of fair play and substantial justice."

The subjectivity, and hence inadequacy, of this approach becomes apparent when the concurrence tries to explain why the assertion of jurisdiction in the present case meets its standard of continuing-American-tradition-plus-innate-fairness. Justice BRENNAN lists the "benefits" Mr. Burnham derived from the State of California—the fact that, during the few days he was there, "[h]is health and safety [were] guaranteed by the State's police, fire, and emergency medical services; he [was] free to travel on the State's roads and waterways; he likely enjoy[ed] the fruits of the State's economy." Three days' worth of these benefits strike us as powerfully inadequate to establish, as an abstract matter, that it is "fair" for California to decree the ownership of all Mr. Burnham's worldly goods acquired during the 10 years of his marriage, and the custody over his children. * * * Even less persuasive are the other "fairness" factors alluded to by Justice BRENNAN. * * *

There is, we must acknowledge, one factor mentioned by Justice BRENNAN that both relates distinctively to the assertion of jurisdiction on the basis of personal in-state service and is fully persuasive—namely, the fact that a defendant voluntarily present in a particular State has a "reasonable expectatio[n]" that he is subject to suit there. By formulating it as a "reasonable expectation" Justice BRENNAN makes that seem like a "fairness" factor; but in reality, of course, it is just tradition masquerading as "fairness." The only reason for charging Mr. Burnham with the reasonable expectation of being subject to suit is that the States of the Union assert adjudicatory jurisdiction over the person, and have always asserted adjudicatory jurisdiction over the person, by serving him with process during his temporary physical presence in their territory. That continuing tradition, which anyone entering California should have known about, renders it "fair" for Mr. Burnham, who voluntarily entered California, to be sued there for divorce—at least "fair" in the limited sense that he has no one but himself to blame. Justice BRENNAN's long journey is a circular one, leaving him, at the end of the day, in complete reliance upon the very factor he sought to avoid: The existence of a continuing tradition is not enough, fairness also must be considered; fairness exists here because there is a continuing tradition.

While Justice BRENNAN's concurrence is unwilling to confess that the Justices of this Court can possibly be bound by a continuing American tradition that a particular procedure is fair, neither is it willing to embrace the logical consequences of that refusal—or even to be clear about what consequences (logical or otherwise) it does embrace. Justice BRENNAN says that "[f]or these reasons [i.e., because of the reasonableness factors enumerated above], as a rule the exercise of personal jurisdiction over a defendant based on his voluntary presence in the forum will satisfy the requirements of due process." The use of the word "rule" conveys the reassuring feeling that he is establishing a principle of law one can rely upon—but of course he is not. Since Justice BRENNAN's only criterion of constitutionality is "fairness," the phrase "as a rule" represents nothing more than his estimation that, usually, all the elements of "fairness" he discusses in the present case will exist. But what if they do not? Suppose, for example, that a defendant in Mr. Burnham's situation enjoys not three days' worth of California's "benefits," but 15 minutes' worth. Or suppose we remove one of those "benefits"— "enjoy[ment of] the fruits of the State's economy"—by positing that Mr. Burnham had not come to California on business, but only to visit his children. * * * [D]espite the fact that he manages to work the word "rule" into his formulation, Justice BRENNAN's approach does not establish a rule of law at all, but only a "totality of the circumstances" test, guaranteeing what traditional territorial rules of jurisdiction were designed precisely to avoid: uncertainty and litigation over the preliminary issue of the forum's competence. It may be that those evils, necessarily accompanying a freestanding "reasonableness" inquiry, must be accepted at the margins, when we evaluate nontraditional forms of jurisdiction newly adopted by the States. But that is no reason for injecting them into the core of our American practice, exposing to such a "reasonableness" inquiry the ground of jurisdiction that has hitherto been considered the very baseline of reasonableness, physical presence.

The difference between us and Justice BRENNAN has nothing to do with whether "further progress [is] to be made" in the "evolution of our legal system." It has to do with whether changes are to be adopted as progressive by the American people or decreed as progressive by the Justices of this Court. Nothing we say today prevents individual States from limiting or entirely abandoning the in-state-service basis of jurisdiction. And nothing prevents an overwhelming majority of them from doing so, with the consequence that the "traditional notions of fairness" that this Court applies may change. But the States have overwhelmingly declined to adopt such limitation or abandonment, evidently not considering it to be progress. The question is whether, armed with no authority other than individual Justices' perceptions of fairness that conflict with both past and current practice, this Court can compel the States to make such a change on the ground that "due process" requires it. We hold that it cannot.

* * *

Because the Due Process Clause does not prohibit the California courts from exercising jurisdiction over petitioner based on the fact of in-state service of process, the judgment is

Affirmed.

JUSTICE WHITE, concurring in part and concurring in the judgment.

I join Parts I, II-A, II-B, and II-C of JUSTICE SCALIA's opinion and concur in the judgment of affirmance. The rule allowing jurisdiction to be obtained over a nonresident by personal service in the forum State, without more, has been and is so widely accepted throughout this country that I could not possibly strike it down, either on its face or as applied in this case, on the ground that it denies due process of law guaranteed by the Fourteenth Amendment. * * *

JUSTICE BRENNAN, with whom JUSTICE MARSHALL, JUSTICE BLACKMUN, and JUSTICE O'CONNOR join, concurring in the judgment.

I agree with Justice SCALIA that the Due Process Clause of the Fourteenth Amendment generally permits a state court to exercise jurisdiction over a defendant if he is served with process while voluntarily present in the forum State. I do not perceive the need, however, to decide that a jurisdictional rule that " 'has been immemorially the actual law of the land,' " automatically comports with due process simply by virtue of its "pedigree." Although I agree that history is an important factor in establishing whether a jurisdictional rule satisfies due process requirements, I cannot agree that it is the only factor such that all traditional rules of jurisdiction are, ipso facto, forever constitutional. Unlike Justice SCALIA, I would undertake an "independent inquiry into the . . . fairness of the prevailing in-state service rule." I therefore concur only in the judgment.

I

I believe that the approach adopted by Justice SCALIA's opinion today—reliance solely on historical pedigree—is foreclosed by our decisions in *International Shoe Co. v. Washington, 326 U.S. 310 (1945)*, and *Shaffer v. Heitner, 433 U.S. 186 (1977)*. In *International Shoe*, we held that a state court's assertion of personal jurisdiction does not violate the Due Process Clause if it is consistent with " 'traditional notions of fair play and substantial justice.' " In *Shaffer*, we stated that "all assertions of state-court jurisdiction must be evaluated according to the standards set forth in *International Shoe* and its progeny." The critical insight of *Shaffer* is that all rules of jurisdiction, even ancient ones, must satisfy contemporary notions of due process. No longer were we content to limit our jurisdictional analysis to pronouncements that "[t]he foundation of jurisdiction is physical power," and that "every State possesses exclusive jurisdiction and sovereignty over persons and property within its territory." *Pennoyer v. Neff, 95 U.S. 714, 722 (1878)*. While acknowledging that "history must be considered as supporting the proposition that jurisdiction based solely on the presence of property satisfie[d] the demands of due process," we found that this factor could not be "decisive." We recognized that " '[t]raditional notions of fair play and substantial justice' can be as readily offended by the perpetuation of ancient forms that are no longer justified as by the adoption of new procedures that are inconsistent with the basic values of our constitutional heritage." I agree with this approach and continue to believe that "the minimum-contacts analysis developed in *International Shoe* . . . represents a far more sensible construct for the exercise of state-court jurisdiction than the patchwork of legal and factual fictions that has been generated from the decision in *Pennoyer v. Neff*."

While our holding in *Shaffer* may have been limited to *quasi in rem* jurisdiction, our mode of analysis was not. Indeed, that we were willing in *Shaffer* to examine anew the appropriateness of the *quasi in rem* rule—until that time dutifully accepted by American courts for at least a century—demonstrates that we did not believe that the "pedigree" of a jurisdictional practice was dispositive in deciding whether it was consistent with due process. * * * If we could discard an "ancient form without substantial modern justification" in *Shaffer*, we can do so again. * * *

II

Tradition, though alone not dispositive, is of course relevant to the question whether the rule of transient jurisdiction is consistent with due process.[7] Tradition is salient not in the sense that practices of the past are automatically reasonable today; indeed, under such a standard, the legitimacy of transient jurisdiction would be called into question because the rule's historical "pedigree" is a matter of intense debate. The rule was a stranger to the common law and was rather weakly implanted in American jurisprudence "at the crucial time for present purposes: 1868, when the Fourteenth Amendment was adopted." For much of the 19th century, American courts did not uniformly recognize the concept of transient jurisdiction, and it appears that the transient rule did not receive wide currency until well after our decision in *Pennoyer v. Neff*.

Rather, I find the historical background relevant because, however murky the jurisprudential origins of transient jurisdiction, the fact that American courts have announced the rule for perhaps a century * * * provides a defendant voluntarily present in a particular State today "clear notice that [he] is subject to suit" in the forum. * * * The transient rule is consistent with reasonable expectations and is entitled to a strong presumption that it comports with due process. "If I visit another State, . . . I knowingly assume some risk that the State will exercise its power over my property or my person while there. My contact with the State, though minimal, gives rise to predictable risks." Thus, proposed revisions to the *Restatement (Second) of Conflict of Laws* § 28, provide that "[a] state has power to exercise judicial jurisdiction over an individual who is present within its territory unless the individual's relationship to the state is so attenuated as to make the exercise of such jurisdiction unreasonable."

By visiting the forum State, a transient defendant actually "avail[s]" himself, of significant benefits provided by the State. His health and safety are guaranteed by the State's police, fire, and emergency medical services; he is free to travel on the State's roads and waterways; he likely enjoys the fruits of the State's economy as well. Moreover, the Privileges and Immunities Clause of Article IV prevents a state government from discriminating against a transient defendant by denying him the

---

[7] I do not propose that the "contemporary notions of due process" to be applied are no more than "each Justice's subjective assessment of what is fair and just." Rather, the inquiry is guided by our decisions beginning with *International Shoe Co. v. Washington*, 326 U.S. 310 (1945), and the specific factors that we have developed to ascertain whether a jurisdictional rule comports with "traditional notions of fair play and substantial justice."

protections of its law or the right of access to its courts. Subject only to the doctrine of *forum non conveniens*, an out-of-state plaintiff may use state courts in all circumstances in which those courts would be available to state citizens. Without transient jurisdiction, an asymmetry would arise: A transient would have the full benefit of the power of the forum State's courts as a plaintiff while retaining immunity from their authority as a defendant.

> **It's Latin to Me!**
>
> *Forum non conveniens* is Latin for "an unsuitable forum" and refers to the doctrine under which a court dismisses a case because the case would more conveniently be tried in another forum in a separate judicial system. We will be studying this doctrine in Chapter 4.

The potential burdens on a transient defendant are slight. "[M]odern transportation and communications have made it much less burdensome for a party sued to defend himself" in a State outside his place of residence. That the defendant has already journeyed at least once before to the forum—as evidenced by the fact that he was served with process there—is an indication that suit in the forum likely would not be prohibitively inconvenient. Finally, any burdens that do arise can be ameliorated by a variety of procedural devices. For these reasons, as a rule the exercise of personal jurisdiction over a defendant based on his voluntary presence in the forum will satisfy the requirements of due process.* * *

In this case, it is undisputed that petitioner was served with process while voluntarily and knowingly in the State of California. I therefore concur in the judgment.

JUSTICE STEVENS, concurring in the judgment.

As I explained in my separate writing, I did not join the Court's opinion in *Shaffer v. Heitner*, 433 U.S. 186 (1977), because I was concerned by its unnecessarily broad reach. The same concern prevents me from joining either Justice SCALIA's or Justice BRENNAN's opinion in this case. For me, it is sufficient to note that the historical evidence and consensus identified by Justice SCALIA, the considerations of fairness identified by Justice BRENNAN, and the common sense displayed by Justice WHITE, all combine to demonstrate that this is, indeed, a very easy case.* Accordingly, I agree that the judgment should be *affirmed*.

───────────────

* Perhaps the adage about hard cases making bad law should be revised to cover easy cases. [Footnote by Justice Stevens]

Points for Discussion

a. The Law After *Burnham*

Take another look at the alignment of the Justices in *Burnham*. Notice that although all the Justices agreed on the outcome in the case, no opinion was supported by a majority. What, then, is the state of the law regarding transient jurisdiction after *Burnham*? Although no majority view of the rationale is articulated in *Burnham*, what is clear after *Burnham* is that jurisdiction based solely on in-state service—sometimes referred to as "transient" or "tag" jurisdiction—is constitutionally valid. Is it clear that jurisdiction would still be valid in cases like *Grace v. MacArthur, 170 F. Supp. 442 (E.D. Ark. 1959)*, where the defendant was served with process while flying over the forum jurisdiction's airspace?

Can transient jurisdiction be applied beyond the individual context, to corporations or partnerships? *Burnham* did not address this issue and lower courts have reached varying conclusions, although the weight of authority appears to be in favor of limiting transient jurisdiction to natural persons. *Compare Oyuela v. Seacor Marine (Nigeria), Inc., 290 F. Supp. 2d 713, 720 (E.D. La. 2003)* ("*Burnham's* reassertion of the general validity of transient jurisdiction provides no indication that it should only apply to natural persons. Prior case law suggests that service of process upon a corporate agent provides a sufficient basis to assert jurisdiction over nonresident corporations."), *with Golden Scorpio Corp. v. Steel Horse Saloon I, 2009 WL 976598, at *3 n.4 (D. Ariz. Apr. 9, 2009)* ("[I]t appears that the physical presence theory is limited to circumstances where service of process was made upon a natural person who was physically within the forum state when served and who is himself or herself a defendant in the action."). *See also* 4A C. WRIGHT, A. MILLER, & A. STEINMAN, FED. PRAC. & PROC. § 1102 (4th ed. 2015) ("Service made upon a corporation, partnership, or other unincorporated association simply by delivering process to a corporate or comparable officer who happens to reside or be physically present in the state at the time the documents are served will not be effective to establish in personam jurisdiction . . ."); *Nehemiah v. Athletics Congress of U.S.A., 765 F.2d 42, 46 (3d Cir. 1985)* ("[W]e now conclude that due process considerations preclude effecting personal jurisdiction over an unincorporated association merely by in-state service on its agent.").

Does *Burnham* signal a return to the territoriality of *Pennoyer* that had seemingly been rebuked by the Court in *Shaffer*? Is *Burnham* consistent with *Shaffer*?

b. Justice Brennan's Concurring Opinion

By now you should be well versed in the practice of evaluating Justice Brennan's opinions in personal jurisdiction cases. What is Justice Brennan's quarrel with Justice Scalia's reasoning in *Burnham*? Justice Brennan attempts to justify the constitutionality of transient jurisdiction by analyzing it under the purposeful availment and reasonableness prongs of the minimum contacts test. Is his analysis convincing? What problems can you identify with his analysis?

c. Justice Scalia's Style of Analysis

What is your view of Justice Scalia's approach to analyzing the constitutionality of in-state service? Should history and tradition control the issue in the manner he insists or should evolving standards of fairness govern the inquiry? *See* Martin H. Redish, *Tradition, Fairness, and Personal Jurisdiction: Due Process and Constitutional Theory After* Burnham v. Superior Court, 22 RUTGERS L.J. 675 (1991) (criticizing Justice Scalia's approach to due process in *Burnham*). How persuasive are Justice Scalia's arguments compared with those of Justice Brennan? Does Justice Scalia's tone suggest that more is at issue than the constitutionality of transient jurisdiction?

---

4. Consent

When studying *Pennoyer v. Neff* earlier in the chapter, we learned that there was a consent exception to the in-state service or voluntary appearance requirements established in that case. Although the reform of personal jurisdiction doctrine that took place in *International Shoe* did repudiate *Hess's* implied consent as a constitutional basis for jurisdiction, it did not eliminate actual consent as a permissible basis for exercising personal jurisdiction over defendants. Express consent can serve to force plaintiffs to litigate their disputes in a particular forum. The next case illustrates this point.

Carnival Cruise Lines, Inc. v. Shute

Supreme Court of the United States
499 U.S. 585 (1991)

JUSTICE BLACKMUN delivered the opinion of the Court.

In this admiralty case we primarily consider whether the United States Court of Appeals for the Ninth Circuit correctly refused to enforce a forum-selection clause contained in tickets issued by petitioner Carnival Cruise Lines, Inc., to respondents Eulala and Russel Shute.

I

What's That?

Admiralty cases are those heard in the federal courts involving maritime contracts, torts, injuries, or offenses. The Federal Rules of Civil Procedure apply to such cases with limited exceptions.

The Shutes, through an Arlington, Wash., travel agent, purchased passage for a 7-day cruise on petitioner's ship, the *Tropicale*. * * * The face of each ticket, at its left-hand lower corner, contained this admonition:

"SUBJECT TO CONDITIONS OF CONTRACT ON LAST PAGES IMPOR-
TANT! PLEASE READ CONTRACT-ON LAST PAGES 1, 2, 3" App. 15.

The following appeared on "contract page 1" of each ticket:

"TERMS AND CONDITIONS OF PASSAGE CONTRACT TICKET

. . . . .

"3. (a) The acceptance of this ticket by the person or persons named hereon
as passengers shall be deemed to be an acceptance and agreement by each
of them of all of the terms and conditions of this Passage Contract Ticket.

. . . . .

"8. It is agreed by and between the passenger and the Carrier that all disputes and matters whatsoever arising under, in connection with or incident
to this Contract shall be litigated, if at all, in and before a Court located
in the State of Florida, U.S.A., to the exclusion of the Courts of any other
state or country."

The last quoted paragraph is the forum-selection clause at issue.

II

Respondents boarded the *Tropicale* in Los Angeles, Cal. The ship sailed to
Puerto Vallarta, Mexico, and then returned to Los Angeles. While the ship was in
international waters off the Mexican coast, respondent Eulala Shute was injured
when she slipped on a deck mat during a guided tour of the ship's galley. Respondents filed suit against petitioner in the United States District Court for the Western
District of Washington, claiming that Mrs. Shute's injuries had been caused by the
negligence of Carnival Cruise Lines and its employees.

Petitioner moved for summary
judgment, contending that the forum
clause in respondents' tickets required
the Shutes to bring their suit against
petitioner in a court in the State of
Florida. * * *

Turning to the forum-selection
clause, the Court of Appeals acknowledged that a court concerned with the

What's That?

Summary judgment refers to the pretrial resolution of a claim or defense
because there is no issue of material fact and the movant is entitled
to judgment as a matter of law. This
topic will be covered in Chapter 9.

enforceability of such a clause must begin its analysis with *The Bremen v. Zapata
Off-Shore Co., 407 U.S. 1 (1972)*, where this Court held that forum-selection clauses,
although not "historically . . . favored," are "prima facie valid." The appellate court

concluded that the forum clause should not be enforced because it "was not freely bargained for." As an "independent justification" for refusing to enforce the clause, the Court of Appeals noted that there was evidence in the record to indicate that "the Shutes are physically and financially incapable of pursuing this litigation in Florida" and that the enforcement of the clause would operate to deprive them of their day in court and thereby contravene this Court's holding in *The Bremen.* * * *

III

* * *

Within this context, respondents urge that the forum clause should not be enforced because, contrary to this Court's teachings in *The Bremen*, the clause was not the product of negotiation, and enforcement effectively would deprive respondents of their day in court. * * *

IV.

A

Both petitioner and respondents argue vigorously that the Court's opinion in *The Bremen* governs this case, and each side purports to find ample support for its position in that opinion's broad-ranging language. This seeming paradox derives in large part from key factual differences between this case and *The Bremen*, differences that preclude an automatic and simple application of *The Bremen*'s general principles to the facts here.

In *The Bremen*, this Court addressed the enforceability of a forum-selection clause in a contract between two business corporations. An American corporation, Zapata, made a contract with Unterweser, a German corporation, for the towage of Zapata's oceangoing drilling rig from Louisiana to a point in the Adriatic Sea off the coast of Italy. The agreement provided that any dispute arising under the contract was to be resolved in the London Court of Justice. After a storm in the Gulf of Mexico seriously damaged the rig, Zapata ordered Unterweser's ship to tow the rig to Tampa, Fla., the nearest point of refuge. Thereafter, Zapata sued Unterweser in admiralty in federal court at Tampa. Citing the forum clause, Unterweser moved to dismiss. The District Court denied Unterweser's motion, and the Court of Appeals for the Fifth Circuit, sitting en banc on rehearing, and by a sharply divided vote, affirmed.

This Court vacated and remanded, stating that, in general, "a freely negotiated private international agreement, unaffected by fraud, undue influence, or overweening bargaining power, such as that involved here, should be given full effect." The Court further generalized that "in the light of present-day commercial realities and expanding international trade we conclude that the forum clause should control absent a strong showing that it should be set aside." The Court did not define precisely the circumstances that would make it unreasonable for a court to enforce a forum clause. Instead, the Court discussed a number of factors that made it reasonable to enforce the clause at issue in *The Bremen* and that, presumably, would be pertinent in any determination whether to enforce a similar clause. * * *

In applying *The Bremen*, the Court of Appeals in the present litigation took note of the foregoing "reasonableness" factors and rather automatically decided that the forum-selection clause was unenforceable because, unlike the parties in *The Bremen*, respondents are not business persons and did not negotiate the terms of the clause with petitioner. * * *

The Bremen concerned a "far from routine transaction between companies of two different nations contemplating the tow of an extremely costly piece of equipment from Louisiana across the Gulf of Mexico and the Atlantic Ocean, through the Mediterranean Sea to its final destination in the Adriatic Sea." These facts suggest that, even apart from the evidence of negotiation regarding the forum clause, it was entirely reasonable for the Court in *The Bremen* to have expected Unterweser and Zapata to have negotiated with care in selecting a forum for the resolution of disputes arising from their special towing contract.

In contrast, respondents' passage contract was purely routine and doubtless nearly identical to every commercial passage contract issued by petitioner and most other cruise lines. In this context, it would be entirely unreasonable for us to assume that respondents—or any other cruise passenger—would negotiate with petitioner the terms of a forum-selection clause in an ordinary commercial cruise ticket. Common sense dictates that a ticket of this kind will be a form contract the terms of which are not subject to negotiation, and that an individual purchasing the ticket will not have bargaining parity with the cruise line. But by ignoring the crucial differences in the business contexts in which the respective contracts were executed, the Court of Appeals' analysis seems to us to have distorted somewhat this Court's holding in *The Bremen*.

In evaluating the reasonableness of the forum clause at issue in this case, we must refine the analysis of *The Bremen* to account for the realities of form passage contracts. As an initial matter, we do not adopt the Court of Appeals' determination that a nonnegotiated forum-selection clause in a form ticket contract is never enforceable simply because it is not the subject of bargaining. Including a reasonable forum clause in a form contract of this kind well may be permissible for several reasons: First, a cruise line has a special interest in limiting the fora in

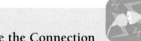

Make the Connection

Evaluating the reasonableness and enforceability of form contracts that were not the product of negotiation is a subject you will likely take up in your first-year **Contracts** course.

which it potentially could be subject to suit. Because a cruise ship typically carries passengers from many locales, it is not unlikely that a mishap on a cruise could subject the cruise line to litigation in several different fora. Additionally, a clause establishing *ex ante* the forum for dispute resolution has the salutary effect of dispelling any confusion about where suits arising from the contract must be brought and defended, sparing litigants the time and expense of pretrial motions to determine the correct forum and conserving judicial resources that otherwise would be devoted to deciding those motions. Finally, it stands to reason that passengers who purchase tickets containing a forum clause like that at issue in this case benefit in the form of reduced fares reflecting the savings that the cruise line enjoys by limiting the fora in which it may be sued.

We also do not accept the Court of Appeals' "independent justification" for its conclusion that *The Bremen* dictates that the clause should not be enforced because "[t]here is evidence in the record to indicate that the Shutes are physically and financially incapable of pursuing this litigation in Florida." * * * [W]e conclude that [respondents] have not satisfied the "heavy burden of proof," required to set aside the clause on grounds of inconvenience.

It bears emphasis that forum-selection clauses contained in form passage contracts are subject to judicial scrutiny for fundamental fairness. In this case, there is no indication that petitioner set Florida as the forum in which disputes were to be resolved as a means of discouraging cruise passengers from pursuing legitimate claims. * * * Similarly, there is no evidence that petitioner obtained respondents' accession to the forum clause by fraud or overreaching. Finally, respondents have conceded that they were given notice of the forum provision and, therefore, presumably retained the option of rejecting the contract with impunity. In the case before us, therefore, we conclude that the Court of Appeals erred in refusing to enforce the forum-selection clause. * * *

The judgment of the Court of Appeals is reversed.

It is so ordered.

JUSTICE STEVENS, with whom JUSTICE MARSHALL joins, dissenting.

The Court prefaces its legal analysis with a factual statement that implies that a purchaser of a Carnival Cruise Lines passenger ticket is fully and fairly notified about the existence of the choice of forum clause in the fine print on the back of the ticket. Even if this implication were accurate, I would disagree with the Court's analysis. But, given the Court's preface, I begin my dissent by noting that only the most meticulous passenger is likely to become aware of the forum-selection provision. * * *

Of course, many passengers, like the respondents in this case will not have an opportunity to read paragraph 8 until they have actually purchased their tickets. By this point, the passengers will already have accepted the condition set forth in paragraph 16(a), which provides that "[t]he Carrier shall not be liable to make any refund to passengers in respect of . . . tickets wholly or partly not used by a passenger." Not knowing whether or not that provision is legally enforceable, I assume that the average passenger would accept the risk of having to file suit in Florida in the event of an injury, rather than canceling—without a refund—a planned vacation at the last minute. * * *

* * *

The Bremen, which the Court effectively treats as controlling this case, had nothing to say about stipulations printed on the back of passenger tickets. That case involved the enforceability of a forum-selection clause in a freely negotiated international agreement between two large corporations * * * . * * *

I respectfully dissent.

———————————

Points for Discussion

a.   The Outcome in *Carnival Cruise Lines*

Carnival Cruise Lines stands for the proposition that defendants may consent to jurisdiction prior to the initiation of a lawsuit, through forum-selection clauses for example, and that such agreements will ordinarily be binding and enforced by federal courts if consistent with fundamental fairness. *See Smith v. Doe*, 991 F. Supp. 781, 783 (E.D. La. 1998) ("Under [*Carnival Cruise Lines*], forum selection clauses are prima facie valid and will be enforced unless the resisting party shows insufficient notice of the forum selection clause or that the clause is fundamentally unfair."). Do you agree with the Court's assessment of the fairness of the forum-selection clause in *Carnival Cruise Lines*? What is the impact of the Court's holding in *Carnival Cruise Lines* on the plaintiffs in the case? Is it fair that they will have to travel to Florida to litigate their claims against Carnival? Do you think the Shutes were aware of the forum-selection clause and its implications when they purchased their tickets or used them for travel? Should that matter?

b.   The Law Governing the Enforceability of Forum-Selection Clauses

Although *Carnival Cruise Lines* established that as a matter of federal law, forum-selection clauses are presumptively valid and enforceable, the case did not address the question of whether federal or state law governs this issue in federal court. This is a question that must be asked because—as you will learn in your study of the *Erie* doctrine in Chapter 5—federal courts are directed to apply the relevant state substantive law when exercising diversity jurisdiction. However, a majority of the federal appeals courts have held that forum selection is a procedural issue and thus federal law governs. *See, e.g., Alliance Health Group, LLC v. Bridging Health Options, LLC*, 553 F.3d 397, 399 (5th Cir. 2008) ("Federal law applies to determine the enforceability of forum selection clauses in both diversity and federal question cases."); *Wong v. PartyGaming Ltd.*, 589 F.3d 821, 828 (6th Cir. 2009) (citing the six other circuits applying federal law to determine the validity of forum-selection clauses and holding that "in this diversity suit, the enforceability of the forum selection clause is governed by federal law").* The Seventh and Tenth Circuits disagree. See Abbott Labs. v. Takeda Pharms. Co., 476 F.3d 421, 423 (7th Cir. 2007) ("Simplicity argues for determining the validity . . . of a forum selection clause . . . by reference to the law of the jurisdiction whose law governs the rest of the contract . . . ."); Yavuz v. 61 MM, Ltd., 465 F.3d 418, 428 (10th Cir. 2006) ("We see no particular reason . . . why a forum-selection clause . . . should be singled out as a provision not to be interpreted in accordance with the law chosen by the contracting parties."). Note that forum-selection clauses also have implications for determining venue, a topic covered in Chapter 4. See Atl. Marine Constr. Co. v. U.S. Dist. Court for W. Dist. of Texas, 134 S. Ct. 568 (2013).

c.   Consent in Other Contexts

State Registration Statutes. The Court in *Pennoyer* indicated that corporations could be made to consent to jurisdiction as a condition of doing business within a state. What if the corporation registers to do business within the state without providing express consent to jurisdiction there? May such registration be treated as consent to jurisdiction? The majority view seems to be that mere registration will not suffice. See, e.g., Ratliff v. Cooper Labs., Inc., 444 F.2d 745, 748 (4th Cir.), cert. denied, 404 U.S. 948 (1971) (holding that due process would not permit registration to do business to serve as the basis for an exercise of jurisdiction over a corporation for disputes arising out of out-of-state conduct). That said, some courts may still adhere to the view that appointment of an agent in the state to accept personal service may be treated as consent to personal jurisdiction in that state, based on the arguably out-dated pre-*International Shoe* case of Pa. Fire Ins. Co. v. Gold Issue Mining & Milling Co., 243 U.S. 93 (1917), which held that a foreign corporation's execution of "a power of attorney that made service on the superintendent the equivalent of personal service" in compliance with a Missouri statute subjected the corporation to jurisdiction there based on corporate consent. See, e.g., Bane v. Netlink, Inc., 925 F.2d 637, 640–41 (3d Cir. 1991) (holding that registration constituted consent to suit on any cause of action); see also Restatement (Second) Conflict of Laws § 44 ("A state has power to exercise judicial jurisdiction over a foreign corporation which has authorized an agent or a public official to accept service of process in actions brought against the corporation in the state as to all causes of action to which the authority of the agent or official to accept service extends.").

If a state requires corporations to appoint an agent for service of process within the state, some courts have upheld jurisdiction over the corporation in disputes both related and unrelated to activity within the forum. See, e.g., Knowlton v. Allied Van Lines, Inc., 900 F.2d 1196, 1200 (8th Cir. 1990) ("[A]ppointment of an agent for service of process under § 303.10 gives consent to the jurisdiction of Minnesota courts for any cause of action, whether or not arising out of activities within the state. Such consent is a valid basis of personal jurisdiction, and resort to minimum-contacts or due-process analysis to justify the jurisdiction is unnecessary."). Other

---

* The Second, Third, Fifth, Eighth, Ninth, and Eleventh Circuits each apply federal law to evaluate the validity of forum-selection clauses. [Ed.]

courts have rejected the validity of this approach. *See, e.g., Consol. Dev. Corp. v. Sherritt, Inc.*, 216 F.3d 1286, 1293 (11th Cir. 2000) ("Courts of appeals that have addressed this issue have rejected the argument that appointing a registered agent is sufficient to establish general personal jurisdiction over a corporation."); *Wenche Siemer v. Learjet Acquisition Corp.*, 966 F.2d 179, 183 (5th Cir. 1992) ("[A] foreign corporation that properly complies with the Texas registration statute only consents to personal jurisdiction where such jurisdiction is constitutionally permissible."); *Sandstrom v. ChemLawn Corp.*, 904 F.2d 83, 89 (1st Cir. 1990) (indicating that a mere license to do business and the designation of an agent for service of process within the forum state is insufficient to confer general jurisdiction).

Do the cases finding registration in a state sufficient to confer jurisdiction retain any validity after the Court's general jurisdiction decision in *Daimler AG v. Bauman*, 134 S. Ct. 746 (2014)? *See, e.g., Perez v. Air and Liquid Systems Corp.*, 2016 WL 7049153, at *7–*9 (S.D. Ill. Dec. 2, 2016) (discussing impact of *Daimler* on cases treating corporate registration as sufficient to confer general jurisdiction). The key here may be an analysis of the registration statute at issue to determine whether it sufficiently put the corporation on notice that it was consenting to jurisdiction through the act of registering an agent. *See id.*

Consent by Estoppel. Another type of "consent" may occur when a defendant is non-cooperative in a court's effort to determine whether personal jurisdiction exists. *Insurance Corp. of Ireland v. Compagnie des Bauxites de Guinee*, 456 U.S. 694, 706 (1982), illustrates this rule. In that case, when the defendants refused to comply with discovery orders instructing them to produce information pertaining to their forum connections, the district court entered a presumptive finding that the defendants were subject to the jurisdiction of the district court. The Supreme Court upheld this sanction on the ground that the defendants had submitted to the jurisdiction of the court for the limited purpose of challenging jurisdiction, which in turn meant that the defendants agreed "to abide by that court's determination on the issue of jurisdiction" and the court's effort to discover whether jurisdiction was proper. *Id. at 706.*

From *Insurance Corp. of Ireland* we learn then that defendants who make a limited appearance for the purpose of contesting jurisdiction will thereby be bound by an adverse determination on that issue and will have to proceed with defending the case (although they may challenge the jurisdictional ruling on appeal from the final judgment). A defendant interested in avoiding that possibility would have to ignore

Practice Pointer

Personal jurisdiction and choice-of-law matters are standard issues that should be addressed in most commercial contracts. As a practitioner, be sure to consider these issues and draft clear, enforceable provisions that will effectuate your client's desires in these areas in the event of a dispute.

the proceedings altogether and collaterally attack any ensuing judgment when the plaintiff seeks to enforce it.

d. Forum-Selection Clauses Versus Choice-of-Law Clauses

Keep in mind the distinction between a forum-selection clause and a choice-of-law clause. Forum-selection clauses identify the court in which disputes arising under the contract must be litigated, serving to prevent personal jurisdiction challenges when the clause is upheld. Choice-of-law clauses identify the law that will govern disputes arising under the contract and say nothing about the forum in which such a dispute must be litigated. The franchise agreement at issue in *Burger King v. Rudzewicz* provides an example of a contract that contained a choice-of-law clause but not a forum-selection clause. Why do you think a contract would contain one type of clause but not the other?

———————————

E. Personal Jurisdiction in the Federal Courts

As discussed at the beginning of this chapter, Federal Rule 4(k) outlines the scope of personal jurisdiction in the federal courts. Here is the text of Rule 4(k):

Rule 4(k). Territorial Limits of Effective Service.

(1) *In General.* Serving a summons or filing a waiver of service establishes personal jurisdiction over a defendant:

(A) who is subject to the jurisdiction of a court of general jurisdiction in the state where the district court is located;

(B) who is a party joined under Rule 14 or 19 and is served within a judicial district of the United States and not more than 100 miles from where the summons was issued; or

(C) when authorized by a federal statute.

(2) *Federal Claim Outside State-Court Jurisdiction.* For a claim that arises under federal law, serving a summons or filing a waiver of service establishes personal jurisdiction over a defendant if:

(A) the defendant is not subject to jurisdiction in any state's courts of general jurisdiction; and

(B) exercising jurisdiction is consistent with the United States Constitution and laws.

In most cases, Rule 4(k)(1)(A) will be the relevant provision because the conditions for invoking the other portions of the rule are less frequently present. Thus, the jurisdictional reach of the federal courts will typically be coextensive with the territorial reach of the states in which those courts are respectively located. Why do you think the federal rules constrain the jurisdiction of the federal district courts in this way? Should federal courts be so constrained, particularly in light of the existence of venue limitations on where cases may be heard? [Venue is discussed in Chapter 4.] See A. Benjamin Spencer, *Nationwide Personal Jurisdiction for Our Federal Courts*, 87 DENV. U. L. REV. 325, 325 (2010) (arguing that Rule 4(k) "should be amended to provide that district courts have personal jurisdiction over all defendants who have constitutionally sufficient contacts with the United States, leaving a refined venue doctrine to attend to matters relating to the convenience and propriety of litigating a matter in one particular district versus another").

Although Rule 4(k)(1)(A) will govern in most instances, one must become familiar with the other provisions in the rule in order to be able to identify those situations in which they, and not Rule 4(k)(1)(A), apply. These provisions are discussed below.

Points for Discussion

a. Rule 4(k)(1)(B)—The "100-mile Bulge Rule"

Rule 4(k)(1)(B), also referred to as the "100-mile Bulge Rule," only applies to efforts to assert personal jurisdiction over parties joined to the action under Rule 14 or Rule 19 (see Chapter 7) *and* may only be invoked when such parties can be served process within 100 miles of the courthouse where the action is being litigated, so long as service occurs within the United States. This provision is useful for serving local Rule 14 or Rule 19 parties in federal districts with courthouses adjacent to state borders such as the Southern District of New York (located across the river from New Jersey), or the U.S. District Court for the District of Columbia.

What's That?

Rule 14 permits defending parties in an action to assert claims against nonparties to an action to allege their responsibility for some or all of the claims being asserted against the defending party. *Rule 19* permits the court to force certain nonparties to become part of an action because of some prejudicial impact their absence will have on the parties or matters at issue in the case. These rules are covered in Chapter 7.

b. Rule 4(k)(1)(C)—Federal Statutory Authorization

Rule 4(k)(1)(C) indicates that personal jurisdiction in the federal courts can depart from the limits of their host states in cases where there is a federal statute that authorizes jurisdiction of a different scope. Although there are several statutes that do contain special service of process provisions that permit federal courts to exercise personal jurisdiction on a nationwide (or sometimes worldwide) basis rather than based on forum state contacts, such provisions are not the norm.

For More Information

For examples of statutes that confer nationwide or worldwide personal jurisdiction on the federal courts, see 15 U.S.C.A. § 25 (Clayton Act); 29 U.S.C.A. § 1132(e)(2) (ERISA); 15 U.S.C.A. § 78aa (Securities and Exchange Act of 1934).

When nationwide service provisions are applicable, what standards should govern the constitutionality of an assertion of jurisdiction? Keep in mind that when not tied to the jurisdictional reach of states, the Fifth Amendment's Due Process Clause applies and a defendant's contacts with the forum state lose their relevance. Instead, courts look for minimum contacts with the United States as a whole to evaluate the constitutionality of jurisdiction. *See, e.g., Pinker v. Roche Holdings, Ltd.*, 292 F.3d 361, 369 (3d Cir. 2002) ("[A] federal court's personal jurisdiction may be assessed on the basis of the defendant's national contacts when the plaintiff's claim rests on a federal statute authorizing nationwide service of process."); *SEC v. Carrillo*, 115 F.3d 1540, 1544 (11th Cir. 1997) ("We agree with the rule applied by the other circuits and hereby hold that the applicable forum for minimum contacts purposes is the United States in cases where, as here, the court's personal jurisdiction is invoked based on a federal statute authorizing nationwide or worldwide service of process."); *Busch v. Buchman, Buchman & O'Brien, Law Firm*, 11 F.3d 1255, 1258 (5th Cir. 1994) ("[W]hen a federal court is attempting to exercise personal jurisdiction over a defendant in a suit based upon a federal statute providing for nationwide service of process, the relevant inquiry is whether the defendant had minimum contacts with the United States."). Can you identify the rationale for looking only at contacts with the United States as a whole in such circumstances?

Some courts independently assess the reasonableness of personal jurisdiction under the *Asahi* factors in this context, even after finding that the defendant has minimum contacts with the United States. *See, e.g., Republic of Panama v. BCCI Holdings (Luxembourg) S.A.*, 119 F.3d 935, 947 & n.23 (11th Cir. 1997) (stating that "[a] defendant's 'minimum contacts' with the United States do not . . . automatically satisfy the due process requirements of the Fifth Amendment," because "[t]here are circumstances, although rare, in which a defendant may have sufficient contacts with the United States as a whole but still will be unduly burdened by the assertion of jurisdiction in a faraway and inconvenient forum" and noting that in making this statement "we depart from the reasoning and holdings of the majority of our sister circuits").

c. Rule 4(k)(2)

Finally, Rule 4(k)(2) is a fallback provision—promulgated in response to the case of *Omni Capital Int'l v. Rudolf Wolff & Co.*, 484 U.S. 97 (1987)—that simply covers a situation in which a defendant has minimum contacts with all of the United States but not with any particular state. Note, however, that this provision is only available for claims arising under federal law (see Chapter 3) and is only available when no state would be able to exercise personal jurisdiction. When seeking to invoke Rule 4(k)(2), should the plaintiff bear the burden of establishing that the defendant is not amenable to jurisdiction in any state? Or should the defendant have to establish that it is subject to jurisdiction in a particular state? *Compare BP Chems. Ltd. v. Formosa Chem. & Fibre Corp.*, 229 F.3d 254, 259 (3d Cir. 2000) (holding that the plaintiff bears the burden), *with ISI Int'l, Inc. v. Borden Ladner Gervais L.L.P.*, 256 F.3d 548, 552 (7th Cir. 2001) (placing the burden on defendants either to name a state having jurisdiction or be subject to application of Rule 4(k)(2)).

d. Challenging Personal Jurisdiction in Federal Court

Throughout this chapter you have been exposed to the concept of a special appearance as the means by which a defendant has challenged personal jurisdiction. Defendants in federal court who wish to challenge jurisdiction do not, strictly speaking, make a "special appearance." Rather, the Federal Rules of Civil Procedure provide two principal means for an appearing defendant to raise such a challenge. First, the defendant may make a motion, under Rule 12(b)(2), to dismiss the action for lack of personal jurisdiction. The defendant must make this motion initially before other responses are offered, although the Federal Rules also require that any motion challenging personal jurisdiction must be consolidated with a challenge to venue or service of process if any such challenges are to be made. FED. R. CIV. P. 12(g) & (h). If the defendant does not want to raise a personal jurisdiction challenge before filing an answer, the Federal Rules permit defendants to include such challenges in their answer. But keep in mind that a personal jurisdiction defense can only be raised for the first time in the answer if no other defenses have been asserted previously. Raising defenses by motion or in the answer will be addressed more fully in Chapter 6.

e. Pendent Personal Jurisdiction

Personal jurisdiction must be proper over the defendant with respect to each claim in an action. *See* 16 MOORE'S FEDERAL PRACTICE § 108.42[1], at 108–54 to 108–55 (2012) ("Several circuits have taken the view that the determination of specific personal jurisdiction is a claim-specific inquiry . . . . Thus, a conclusion that the court has personal jurisdiction over one defendant as to a particular claim does not necessarily mean that the court has personal jurisdiction over that same defendant as to other claims by the same plaintiff."

Pendent personal jurisdiction is a controversial, sometimes-recognized federal court common law doctrine that gives courts—under very limited circumstances—the discretion to exercise personal jurisdiction over claims that would not independently qualify for personal jurisdiction. 4A C. WRIGHT, A. MILLER & A. STEINMAN, FED. PRAC. & PROC. § 1069.7 (4th ed. 2015) ("[I]f pendent personal jurisdiction exists, it must be properly understood to be a federal common law doctrine."). Pendent personal jurisdiction is only possible when the claims lacking an independent basis for personal jurisdiction arise out of a common nucleus of operative facts as a claim over which the court does have personal jurisdiction; it is principally (but not exclusively) employed when there is a federal claim over which the court has nationwide jurisdiction based on a special statutory provision that also had supplemental claims attached to it. *See, e.g., Action Embroidery Corp. v. Atl. Embroidery, Inc.*, 368 F.3d 1174, 1180 (9th Cir. 2004) ("Pendent personal jurisdiction is typically found where one or more federal claims for which there is nationwide personal jurisdiction are combined in the same suit with one or more state or federal claims for which there is not nationwide personal jurisdiction."). *See also SunCoke Energy Inc. v. MAN Ferrostaal AG*, 563 F.3d 211, 221 (6th Cir. 2009) (Rogers, J., dissenting) (" '[P]endent personal jurisdiction' has been sparingly permitted in federal diversity cases, and the district court has discretion whether or not to exercise it.") (citation omitted); 4A C. WRIGHT, A. MILLER & A. STEINMAN, FED. PRAC. & PROC. § 1069.7 (4th ed. 2015) ("Pendent personal jurisdiction can play a role in cases where federal question subject matter jurisdiction exists based on a federal statute with a provision for nationwide service of process.").

Food for Thought

Why might the doctrine of pendent personal jurisdiction be controversial? Recall that personal jurisdiction is claim specific. On what authority—consistent with due process—may a court hear a claim over which it admittedly lacks an independent basis for personal jurisdiction? Might the answer be different for state versus federal courts? Does the doctrine survive the Court's decision in *Bristol-Myers Squibb Co. v. Superior Court*, 137 S. Ct. 1773 (2017)?

To be clear, the doctrine of pendent personal jurisdiction *is not* used to exercise personal jurisdiction over the claims of some plaintiffs based on jurisdiction that exists over the claims of other coplaintiffs in the action. *See Bristol-Myers Squibb Co. v. Superior Court*, 228 Cal.App.4th 605 (2014) (" '[P]endent personal jurisdiction' has no bearing on the analysis of whether claims by non-resident plaintiffs, that is, different plaintiffs, may proceed with those of resident plaintiffs."), *reversed on other grounds, Bristol-Myers Squibb Co. v. Superior Court*, 137 S. Ct. 1773 (2017). *See also Bristol-Myers Squibb Co. v. Superior Court*, 137 S. Ct. 1773, 1781 (2017) ("The mere fact that other plaintiffs were prescribed, obtained, and ingested Plavix in California—and allegedly sustained the same injuries as did the nonresidents—does not allow the State to assert specific jurisdiction over the nonresidents' claims.").

Executive Summary

■ **The Requirement of Personal Jurisdiction.** A court must have personal jurisdiction over a defendant to render a binding judgment against it.

■ **Personal Jurisdiction in State Courts.** The personal jurisdiction of state courts is defined by the terms of their respective jurisdictional statutes and confined by the limits of due process.

■ **The Constitutional Standard.** The standard for evaluating the constitutionality of a state's assertion of personal jurisdiction is the minimum contacts analysis of *International Shoe*, which the Court has refined to mean that the defendant must have purposeful contacts with the forum state and the assertion of jurisdiction must not be unreasonable.

■ **The *Asahi* Reasonableness Factors.** The reasonableness of an assertion of personal jurisdiction is assessed with reference to the five-factored test applied in *Asahi*.

■ **General Jurisdiction.** Courts may exercise jurisdiction based on unrelated forum state contacts for individuals in their state of domicile and for entities in those places they are fairly regarded as at home, such as the states where their headquarters are located or they are incorporated.

Major Themes

Keep in mind several overarching themes at work within the doctrine of personal jurisdiction:

a. *Societal Advances*—to what extent should social, economic, and technological evolution impact personal jurisdiction doctrine?

b. *State Sovereignty*—what role, if any, does state sovereignty play in the doctrine of personal jurisdiction?

c. *Predictability*—to what extent has jurisdictional doctrine enabled parties to predict where their conduct will subject them to jurisdiction?

d. *Impact of Decisions*—in each decision, there are real-life consequences for parties and the viability of their claims or their ability to defend against claims. To what extent does or should personal jurisdiction doctrine account for the "justice" of forcing one party to travel to prosecute or defend its case?

■ **Traditional Exceptions.** Although all assertions of personal jurisdiction are subject to the minimum contacts analysis of *International Shoe*, various traditional exceptions to this analysis remain valid, such as the in-state service and consent exceptions. Assertions of jurisdiction based on property are not exempt from the minimum contacts standard, but the analysis will invariably lead to the conclusion that jurisdiction in a true *in rem* or *quasi-in-rem* type I case is consistent with that standard.

■ **Personal Jurisdiction in Federal Court.** Personal jurisdiction in the federal courts is generally limited to the scope of personal jurisdiction of their host states. However, Rule 4(k) provides alternatives that may be applicable in some situations.

For More Information

Students interested in studying personal jurisdiction or notice further may consult the following resources:

- 4 C. WRIGHT, A. MILLER & A STEINMAN, FED. PRAC. & PROC. CIV. § 1064 *et seq.* (4th ed. 2015) (Personal Jurisdiction).

- Linda S. Mullenix, *Personal Jurisdiction Stops Here: Cabining the Extraterritorial Reach of American Courts,* 45 U. TOL. L. REV. 705 (2014).

———————————

Test Your Knowledge

To assess your understanding of the material in this chapter, click here to take a quiz.

CHAPTER TWO

Notice

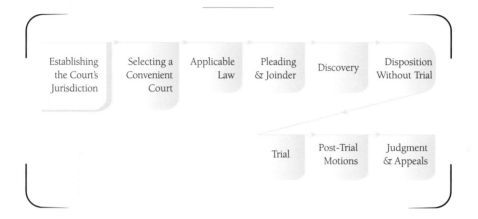

Establishing the Court's Jurisdiction → Selecting a Convenient Court → Applicable Law → Pleading & Joinder → Discovery → Disposition Without Trial → Trial → Post-Trial Motions → Judgment & Appeals

Introduction

IN ADDITION TO BEING ABLE to exercise personal jurisdiction over a party in an action, proper notice of the action must be given to the party before a court's exercise of jurisdiction will be effective. *See, e.g., Mid-Continent Wood Products, Inc. v. Harris,* 936 F.2d 297, 301 (7th Cir. 1991) ("This court has long recognized that valid service of process is necessary in order to assert personal jurisdiction over a defendant."). In the absence of proper notice, any judgment rendered against the party may be subject to challenge and denied recognition. As with personal jurisdiction, there are constitutional and statutory aspects to the notice requirement, with the constitutional dimension being similarly derived from due process. This chapter will explore both aspects of the notice requirement for civil cases in the federal courts.

A. The Constitutional Notice Requirement

The constitutional notice requirement is rooted in the Due Process Clauses of the Fifth and Fourteenth Amendments. The statutory notice requirement in the federal courts is found in Rule 4 of the Federal Rules of Civil Procedure, which sets forth the rules for service of process. Because service in compliance with Rule 4 generally presents no constitutional issues, most issues regarding the constitutionality of notice come up in the context of complying with state statutes. In the case that follows, the Supreme Court articulated the foundational constitutional standard for evaluating the propriety of various notice regimes.

Mullane v. Central Hanover Bank & Trust

Supreme Court of the United States
339 U.S. 306 (1950)

MR. JUSTICE JACKSON delivered the opinion of the Court.

This controversy questions the constitutional sufficiency of notice to beneficiaries on judicial settlement of accounts by the trustee of a common trust fund established under the New York Banking Law. The New York Court of Appeals considered and overruled objections that the statutory notice contravenes requirements of the Fourteenth Amendment and that by allowance of the account beneficiaries were deprived of property without due process of law. * * *

Common trust fund legislation is addressed to a problem appropriate for state action. Mounting overheads have made administration of small trusts undesirable to corporate trustees. In order that donors and testators of moderately sized trusts may not be denied the service of corporate fiduciaries, the District of Columbia and some thirty states other than New York have permitted pooling small trust estates into one fund for investment administration. The income, capital gains, losses and expenses of the collective trust are shared by the constituent trusts in proportion to their contribution. By this plan, diversification of risk and economy of management can be extended to those whose capital standing alone would not obtain such advantage.

Statutory authorization for the establishment of such common trust funds is provided in the New York Banking Law. Under this Act a trust company may, with approval of the State Banking Board, establish a common fund and, within prescribed limits, invest therein the assets of an unlimited number of estates, trusts or other funds of which it is trustee. Each participating trust shares ratably in the common fund, but exclusive management and control is in the trust company as trustee, and neither a fiduciary nor any beneficiary of a participating trust is deemed to have ownership in any particular asset or investment of this common fund. The trust company must keep fund assets separate from its own, and in its fiduciary capacity may not deal with itself or any affiliate. Provisions are made for accountings twelve to fifteen months after the establishment of a fund and triennially thereafter. The decree in each such judicial settlement of accounts is made binding and conclusive as to any matter set forth in the account upon everyone having any interest in the common fund or in any participating estate, trust or fund.

In January, 1946, Central Hanover Bank and Trust Company established a common trust fund in accordance with these provisions, and in March, 1947, it petitioned the <u>Surrogate's Court</u> for settlement of its first account as common trustee. During the accounting period a total of 113 trusts, approximately half *inter vivos* and half testamentary, participated in the common trust fund, the gross capital of which was nearly three million dollars. The record does not show the number or residence of the beneficiaries, but they were many and it is clear that some of them were not residents of the State of New York.

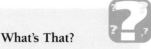

What's That?

The New York Surrogate's Court "hears cases involving the affairs of decedents, including the probate of wills and the administration of estates. It also handles adoptions." *See* www.courts.state.ny.us/courts/nyc/surrogates/index.shtml.

The only notice given beneficiaries of this specific application was by publication in a local newspaper in strict compliance with the minimum requirements of <u>N.Y. Banking Law § 100–c(12)</u>: "After filing such petition (for judicial settlement of its account) the petitioner shall cause to be issued by the court in which the petition is filed and shall publish not less than once in each week for four successive weeks in a newspaper to be designated by the court a notice or citation addressed generally without naming them to all parties interested in such common trust fund and in such estates, trusts or funds mentioned in the petition, all of which may be described in the notice or citation only in the manner set forth in said petition and without setting forth the residence of any such decedent or donor of any such estate, trust or fund." Thus the only notice required, and the only one given, was by newspaper publication setting forth merely the name and address of the trust company, the name and the date of establishment of the common trust fund, and a list of all participating estates, trusts or funds.

At the time the first investment in the common fund was made on behalf of each participating estate, however, the trust company, pursuant to the requirements of <u>§ 100–c(9)</u>, had notified by mail each person of full age and sound mind whose name and address was then known to it and who was "entitled to share in the income therefrom * * * (or) * * * who would be entitled to share in the principal if the event upon which such estate, trust or fund will become distributable should have occurred at the time of sending such notice." Included in the notice was a copy of those provisions of the Act relating to the sending of the notice itself and to the judicial settlement of common trust fund accounts.

Upon the filing of the petition for the settlement of accounts, appellant was, by order of the court pursuant to <u>§ 100–c(12)</u>, appointed special guardian and attorney for all persons known or unknown not otherwise appearing who had or might thereafter have any interest in the income of the common trust fund; and appellee Vaughan was appointed to represent those similarly interested in the principal. There were no other appearances on behalf of any one interested in either interest or principal.

Take Note!

Who is the appellant and who is the appellee in this case? What is the difference between the interests they were appointed to represent? Why do you think these two interest groups need separate representation?

Appellant appeared specially, objecting that notice and the statutory provisions for notice to beneficiaries were inadequate to afford due process under the Fourteenth Amendment, and therefore that the court was without jurisdiction to render a final and binding decree. Appellant's objections were entertained and overruled, the Surrogate holding that the notice required and given was sufficient. A final decree accepting the accounts has been entered, affirmed by the Appellate Division of the Supreme Court, and by the Court of Appeals of the State of New York.

The effect of this decree, as held below, is to settle "all questions respecting the management of the common fund." We understand that every right which beneficiaries would otherwise have against the trust company, either as trustee of the common fund or as trustee of any individual trust, for improper management of the common trust fund during the period covered by the accounting is sealed and wholly terminated by the decree.

> The New York Court system uses unusual names for its various units with its general trial courts denominated Supreme Courts and its highest appellate court being the Court of Appeals. Visit the New York State Court System website for more information.

We are met at the outset with a challenge to the power of the State— the right of its courts to adjudicate at all as against those beneficiaries who reside without the State of New York. It is contended that the proceeding is one *in personam* in that the decree affects neither title to nor possession of any *res*, but adjudges only personal rights of the beneficiaries to surcharge their trustee for negligence or breach of trust. Accordingly, it is said, under the strict doctrine of *Pennoyer v. Neff* the Surrogate is without jurisdiction as to nonresidents upon whom personal service of process was not made.

Distinctions between actions *in rem* and those *in personam* are ancient and originally expressed in procedural terms what seems really to have been a distinction in the substantive law of property under a system quite unlike our own. The legal recognition and rise in economic importance of incorporeal or intangible forms of property have upset the ancient simplicity of property law and the clarity of its distinctions, while new forms of proceedings have confused the old procedural classification. American courts have sometimes classed certain actions as *in rem* because personal service of process was not required, and at other times have held personal service of process not required because the action was *in rem*.

Judicial proceedings to settle fiduciary accounts have been sometimes termed *in rem*, or more indefinitely *quasi in rem*, or more vaguely still, 'in the nature of a proceeding *in rem*.' It is not readily apparent how the courts of New York did or would classify the present proceeding, which has some characteristics and is wanting in some features of proceedings both *in rem* and *in personam*. But in any event we think that the requirements of the Fourteenth Amendment to the Federal Constitution do not depend upon a classification for which the standards are so elusive and confused generally and which, being primarily for state courts to define, may and do vary from state to state. Without disparaging the usefulness of distinctions between actions *in rem* and those *in personam* in many branches of law, or on other issues, or the reasoning which underlies them, we do not rest the power of the State to resort to constructive service in this proceeding upon how its courts or this Court may regard this historic antithesis. It is sufficient to observe that, whatever the technical definition of its chosen procedure, the interest of each state in providing means to close trusts that exist by the grace of its laws and are administered under the supervision of its courts is so insistent and rooted in custom as to establish beyond doubt the right of its courts to determine the interests of all claimants, resident or nonresident, provided its procedure accords full opportunity to appear and be heard.

Quite different from the question of a state's power to discharge trustees is that of the opportunity it must give beneficiaries to contest. Many controversies have raged about the cryptic and abstract words of the Due Process Clause but there can be no doubt that at a minimum they require that deprivation of life, liberty or property by adjudication be preceded by notice and opportunity for hearing appropriate to the nature of the case.

In two ways this proceeding does or may deprive beneficiaries of property. It may cut off their rights to have the trustee answer for negligent or illegal impairments of their interests. Also, their interests are presumably subject to diminution in the proceeding by allowance of fees and expenses to one who, in their names but without their knowledge, may conduct a fruitless

Make the Connection

The Due Process Clause has been used for many different purposes, including the provision of basic procedural protections such as the right to notice and hearing, as a basis for incorporating the Bill of Rights against the states, and as the source for unenumerated substantive rights. The debate surrounding the proper interpretation of the Due Process Clause is something you may be exposed to in a **Constitutional Law** course.

or uncompensatory contest. Certainly the proceeding is one in which they may be deprived of property rights and hence notice and hearing must measure up to the standards of due process.

Personal service of written notice within the jurisdiction is the classic form of notice always adequate in any type of proceeding. But the vital interest of the State in bringing any issues as to its fiduciaries to a final settlement can be served only if interests or claims of individuals who are outside of the State can somehow be determined. A construction of the Due Process Clause which would place impossible or impractical obstacles in the way could not be justified.

Against this interest of the State we must balance the individual interest sought to be protected by the Fourteenth Amendment. This is defined by our holding that "The fundamental requisite of due process of law is the opportunity to be heard." This right to be heard has little reality or worth unless one is informed that the matter is pending and can choose for himself whether to appear or default, acquiesce or contest.

The Court has not committed itself to any formula achieving a balance between these interests in a particular proceeding or determining when constructive notice may be utilized or what test it must meet. Personal service has not in all circumstances been regarded as indispensable to the process due to residents, and it has more often been held unnecessary as to nonresidents. * * *

An elementary and fundamental requirement of due process in any proceeding which is to be accorded finality is notice reasonably calculated, under all the circumstances, to apprise interested parties of the pendency of the action and afford them an opportunity to present their objections. The notice must be of such nature as reasonably to convey the required information and it must afford a reasonable time for those interested to make their appearance. But if with due regard for the practicalities and peculiarities of the case these conditions are reasonably met the constitutional requirements are satisfied. * * *

But when notice is a person's due, process which is a mere gesture is not due process. The means employed must be such as one desirous of actually informing the absentee might reasonably adopt to accomplish it. The reasonableness and hence the constitutional validity of any chosen method may be defended on the ground that it is in itself reasonably certain to inform those affected, or, where conditions do not reasonably permit such notice, that the form chosen is not substantially less likely to bring home notice than other of the feasible and customary substitutes.

It would be idle to pretend that publication alone, as prescribed here, is a reliable means of acquainting interested parties of the fact that their rights are before the courts. It is not an accident that the greater number of cases reaching this Court on the question of adequacy of notice have been concerned with actions founded on process constructively served through local newspapers. Chance alone brings to the attention of even a local resident an advertisement in small type inserted in the back pages of a newspaper, and if he makes his home outside the area of the newspaper's normal circulation the odds that the information will never reach him are large indeed. The chance of actual notice is further reduced when as here the notice required does not even name those whose attention it is supposed to attract, and does not inform acquaintances who might call it to attention. In weighing its sufficiency on the basis of equivalence with actual notice we are unable to regard this as more than a feint.

Nor is publication here reinforced by steps likely to attract the parties' attention to the proceeding. It is true that publication traditionally has been acceptable as notification supplemental to other action which in itself may reasonably be expected to convey a warning. The ways of an owner with tangible property are such that he usually arranges means to learn of any direct attack upon his possessory or proprietary rights. Hence, libel of a ship, attachment of a chattel or entry upon real estate in the name of law may reasonably be expected to come promptly to the owner's attention. When the state within which the owner has located such property seizes it for some reason, publication or posting affords an additional measure of notification. A state may indulge the assumption that one who has left tangible property in the state either has abandoned it, in which case proceedings against it deprive him of nothing, or that he has left some caretaker under a duty to let him know that it is being jeopardized. * * *

In the case before us there is, of course, no abandonment. On the other hand these beneficiaries do have a resident fiduciary as caretaker of their interest in this property. But it is their caretaker who in the accounting becomes their adversary. Their trustee is released from giving notice of jeopardy, and no one else is expected to do so. Not even the special guardian is required or apparently expected to communicate with his ward and client, and, of course, if such a duty were merely transferred from the trustee to the guardian, economy would not be served and more likely the cost would be increased.

This Court has not hesitated to approve of resort to publication as a customary substitute in another class of cases where it is not reasonably possible or practicable to give more adequate warning. Thus it has been recognized that, in the case of persons missing or unknown, employment of an indirect and even a probably futile means of notification is all that the situation permits and creates no constitutional bar to a final decree foreclosing their rights.

Those beneficiaries represented by appellant whose interests or whereabouts could not with due diligence be ascertained come clearly within this category. As to them the statutory notice is sufficient. However great the odds that publication will never reach the eyes of such unknown parties, it is not in the typical case much more likely to fail than any of the choices open to legislators endeavoring to prescribe the best notice practicable.

Nor do we consider it unreasonable for the State to dispense with more certain notice to those beneficiaries whose interests are either conjectural or future or, although they could be discovered upon investigation, do not in due course of business come to knowledge of the common trustee. Whatever searches might be required in another situation under ordinary standards of diligence, in view of the character of the proceedings and the nature of the interests here involved we think them unnecessary. We recognize the practical difficulties and costs that would be attendant on frequent investigations into the status of great numbers of beneficiaries, many of whose interests in the common fund are so remote as to be ephemeral; and we have no doubt that such impracticable and extended searches are not required in the name of due process. The expense of keeping informed from day to day of substitutions among even current income beneficiaries and presumptive remaindermen, to say nothing of the far greater number of contingent beneficiaries, would impose a severe burden on the plan, and would likely dissipate its advantages. These are practical matters in which we should be reluctant to disturb the judgment of the state authorities.

Accordingly we overrule appellant's constitutional objections to published notice insofar as they are urged on behalf of any beneficiaries whose interests or addresses are unknown to the trustee.

As to known present beneficiaries of known place of residence, however, notice by publication stands on a different footing. Exceptions in the name of necessity do not sweep away the rule that within the limits of practicability notice must be such as is reasonably calculated to reach interested parties. Where the names and post office addresses of those affected by a proceeding are at hand, the reasons disappear for resort to means less likely than the mails to apprise them of its pendency.

The trustee has on its books the names and addresses of the income beneficiaries represented by appellant, and we find no tenable ground for dispensing with a serious effort to inform them personally of the accounting, at least by ordinary mail to the record addresses. Certainly sending them a copy of the statute months and perhaps years in advance does not answer this purpose. The trustee periodically remits their income to them, and we think that they might reasonably expect that with or apart from their remittances word might come to them personally that steps were being taken affecting their interests.

We need not weigh contentions that a requirement of personal service of citation on even the large number of known resident or nonresident beneficiaries would, by reasons of delay if not of expense, seriously interfere with the proper administration of the fund. Of course personal service even without the jurisdiction of the issuing authority serves the end of actual and personal notice, whatever power of compulsion it might lack. However, no such service is required under the circumstances. This type of trust presupposes a large number of small interests. The individual interest does not stand alone but is identical with that of a class. The rights of each in the integrity of the fund and the fidelity of the trustee are shared by many other beneficiaries. Therefore notice reasonably certain to reach most of those interested in objecting is likely to safeguard the interests of all, since any objections sustained would inure to the benefit of all. We think that under such circumstances reasonable risks that notice might not actually reach every beneficiary are justifiable. * * *

The statutory notice to known beneficiaries is inadequate, not because in fact it fails to reach everyone, but because under the circumstances it is not reasonably calculated to reach those who could easily be informed by other means at hand. However it may have been in former times, the mails today are recognized as an efficient and inexpensive means of communication. Moreover, the fact that the trust company has been able to give mailed notice to known beneficiaries at the time the common trust fund was established is persuasive that postal notification at the time of accounting would not seriously burden the plan.

* * *

We hold the notice of judicial settlement of accounts required by the New York Banking Law § 100–c(12) is incompatible with the requirements of the Fourteenth Amendment as a basis for adjudication depriving known persons whose whereabouts are also known of substantial property rights. Accordingly the judgment is reversed and the cause remanded for further proceedings not inconsistent with this opinion.

Reversed.

MR. JUSTICE DOUGLAS took no part in the consideration or decision of this case.

[The dissenting opinion of JUSTICE BURTON is omitted.]

Points for Discussion

a. The *Mullane* Standard

What standard does the Court announce in *Mullane* for evaluating the propriety of notice in any given situation? *See Schroeder v. City of New York*, 371 U.S. 208 (1962); *Walker v. City of Hutchinson*, 352 U.S. 112 (1956). Are there different standards for the different groups in the case? How does the Court explain the reason for the difference?

The Court seems to stop short of requiring the best notice possible. What is the Court's justification for a lesser standard?

b. *In Rem* **Actions**

Under *Mullane*, may notice vary according to whether an action is *in personam*, *in rem*, or *quasi in rem*? Do such distinctions make sense?

c. Applying *Mullane*

Mullane's notice standard calls for a highly fact-specific inquiry, making it somewhat difficult to predict whether the Court will uphold the constitutionality of notice in any given case. Indeed, the Court more recently has varied in its own application of the *Mullane* standard when determining the extent to which state and federal officials must attempt to notify property owners before the government deprives them of that property through various legal processes. The next two cases highlight the tension in this area.

────────

Dusenbery v. United States

Supreme Court of the United States
534 U.S. 161 (2002)

CHIEF JUSTICE REHNQUIST delivered the opinion of the Court.

This case concerns the adequacy of the means employed by the Federal Bureau of Investigation (FBI) to provide notice to a federal prisoner of his right to contest the administrative forfeiture of property seized during the execution of a search warrant for the residence where he was arrested.

* * *

To effect * * * a forfeiture, the [Controlled Substances Act] required the [FBI] to send written notice of the seizure together with information on the applicable forfeiture procedures to each party who appeared to have an interest in the property. It also required the publication for at least three successive weeks of a similar notice in a newspaper of general circulation in the judicial district in which the forfeiture proceeding was brought. The FBI sent letters of its intention to forfeit the cash [belonging to the federal prisoner] by certified mail addressed to petitioner care of the Federal Correctional Institution (FCI) in Milan, Michigan, where he was then incarcerated; to the address of the residence where petitioner was arrested; and to an address in Randolph, Ohio, the town where petitioner's mother lived. It placed the requisite legal notice in three consecutive Sunday editions of the Cleveland Plain Dealer. Similar practices were followed with respect to the proposed forfeiture of the car. The FBI received no response to these notices within the time allotted, and so declared the items administratively forfeited. An FBI agent turned over the cash to the United States Marshals Service on December 13, 1988.

Nearly five years later, petitioner moved in the District Court pursuant to * * * the Federal Rules of Criminal Procedure seeking return of all the property and funds seized in his criminal case. * * * The District Court denied the motion * * * . * * *

The Court of Appeals for the Sixth Circuit vacated the District Court's judgment and remanded for further proceedings. * * *

Following remand, the District Court entered an order allowing discovery and subsequently presided over a telephone deposition of James Lawson, an Inmate Systems Officer who began to work in the mailroom at FCI Milan early in 1988 and who had submitted an affidavit in the case. Lawson testified that he signed the certified mail receipt for the FBI's notice to petitioner regarding the cash. He also testified about the procedures within FCI Milan for accepting, logging, and delivering certified mail addressed to inmates. Lawson explained that the procedure would have been for him to log the mail in, for petitioner's "Unit Team" to sign for it, and for it then to be given to petitioner. But he said that a paper trail no longer existed because the Bureau of Prisons (BOP) had a policy of holding prison logbooks for only one year after they were closed.

Both parties moved for summary judgment. The District Court ruled that the Government's sending of notice by certified mail to petitioner's place of incarceration satisfied his due process rights as to the cash. The Court of Appeals affirmed. Citing *Mullane v. Central Hanover Bank & Trust Co., 339 U.S. 306 (1950)*, it held that the Government's notice of the cash forfeiture comported with due process even in the absence of proof that the mail actually reached petitioner.

* * *

The Due Process Clause of the Fifth Amendment prohibits the United States, as the Due Process Clause of the Fourteenth Amendment prohibits the States, from depriving any person of property without "due process of law." From these "cryptic and abstract words," we have determined that individuals whose property interests are at stake are entitled to "notice and an opportunity to be heard."

* * *

We think *Mullane* supplies the appropriate analytical framework. * * * Since *Mullane* was decided, we have regularly turned to it when confronted with questions regarding the adequacy of the method used to give notice. * * *

* * *

Was the notice in this case "reasonably calculated under all the circumstances" to apprise petitioner of the pendency of the cash forfeiture? The Government here carried its burden of showing the following procedures had been used to give notice. The FBI sent certified mail addressed to petitioner at the correctional facility where he was incarcerated. At that facility, prison mailroom staff traveled to the city post office every day to obtain all the mail for the institution, including inmate mail. The staff signed for all certified mail before leaving the post office. Once the mail was transported back to the facility, certified mail was entered in a logbook maintained in the mailroom. A member of the inmate's Unit Team then signed for the certified mail to acknowledge its receipt before removing it from the mailroom, and either a Unit Team member or another staff member distributed the mail to the inmate during the institution's "mail call."

Petitioner does not seriously contest the FBI's use of the postal service to send its certified letter to him, a method our cases have recognized as adequate for known addressees when we have found notice by publication insufficient. Instead, he argues that the notice was insufficient because due process generally requires "actual notice" to interested parties prior to forfeiture, which he takes to mean actual receipt of notice. For this proposition he cites *Mennonite Bd. of Missions v. Adams, 462 U.S. 791, 796–797 (1983)*. But the only sentence in *Mennonite* arguably supporting petitioner's view appears in a footnote. That sentence reads: "Our cases have required the State to make efforts to provide actual notice to all interested parties comparable to the efforts that were previously required only in *in personam* actions." It does not say that the State *must provide* actual notice, but that it *must attempt to provide* actual notice. Since *Mennonite* concluded that mailed notice of a pending tax sale to a mortgagee of record was constitutionally sufficient, the sentence is at best inconclusive dicta for the view petitioner espouses.

We note that none of our cases cited by either party has required actual notice in proceedings such as this. Instead, we have allowed the Government to defend the "reasonableness and hence the constitutional validity of any chosen method . . . on the ground that it is in itself reasonably certain to inform those affected." *Mullane*.

Petitioner argues that because he was housed in a federal prison at the time of the forfeiture, the FBI could have made arrangements with the BOP to assure the delivery of the notice in question to him. But it is hard to see why such a principle would not also apply, for example, to members of the Armed Forces both in this country and overseas. Undoubtedly the Government could make a special effort in any case (just as it did in the movie "Saving Private Ryan") to assure that a particular piece of mail reaches a particular individual who is in one way or another in the custody of the Government. It could, for example, have allowed petitioner to make an escorted visit to the post office himself in order to sign for his letter. But the Due Process Clause does not require such heroic efforts by the Government; it requires only that the Government's effort be "reasonably calculated" to apprise a party of the pendency of the action; " '[t]he criterion is not the possibility of conceivable injury but the just and reasonable character of the requirements . . . .") *Mullane*.

Nor does the Due Process Clause require the Government to substitute the procedures proposed by petitioner for those in place at FCI Milan in 1988. See Brief for Petitioner 17 (suggesting that the Government could send the notice to a prison official with a request that a prison employee watch the prisoner open the notice, cosign a receipt, and mail the signed paper back to the agency from which it came). The suggested procedures would work primarily to bolster the Government's ability to establish that the prisoner actually received notice of the forfeiture, a problem petitioner perceives to be the FCI Milan's procedures' primary defect. But as we have noted above, our cases have never required actual notice. The facts of the present case, moreover, illustrate the difficulty with such a requirement. The letter in question was sent to petitioner in 1988, but the claim of improper notice was first asserted in 1993. What might be reasonably fresh in the minds of all parties had the question arisen contemporaneously will surely be stale five years later. The issue would often turn on disputed testimony as to whether the letter was in fact delivered to petitioner. The title to property should not depend on such vagaries.

Food for Thought

Are these apt scenarios for the Court to use to debunk the petitioner's argument? Is the petitioner suggesting that the Government undertake "heroic" efforts to deliver him notice or something much more mundane? What simple extra steps might the Government have taken to deliver notice to the petitioner if it had been truly concerned with getting notice to him?

Justice GINSBURG's dissent does not contend, as petitioner does, that due process could be satisfied in this case only with actual notice. It makes an alternative argument that the FBI's notice was constitutionally flawed because it was " 'substantially less likely to bring home notice' than a feasible substitute,"—namely, the methods used currently by the BOP, which generally require an inmate to sign a logbook acknowledging delivery. Just how requiring the *end recipient* to sign for a piece of mail substantially improves the reliability of the delivery procedures *leading up to* that person's receipt, Justice GINSBURG's dissent does not persuasively explain. * * *

* * *

Here, the use of the mail addressed to petitioner at the penitentiary was clearly acceptable for much the same reason we have approved mailed notice in the past. Short of allowing the prisoner to go to the post office himself, the remaining portion of the delivery would necessarily depend on a system in effect within the prison itself relying on prison staff. We think the FBI's use of the system described in detail above was "reasonably calculated, under all the circumstances, to apprise [petitioner] of the pendency of the action." *Mullane*. Due process requires no more.

The judgment of the Court of Appeals is

Affirmed.

JUSTICE GINSBURG, with whom JUSTICE STEVENS, JUSTICE SOUTER, and JUSTICE BREYER join, dissenting.

     "'The fundamental requisite of due process of law is the opportunity to be heard.' This right to be heard has little reality or worth unless one is informed that the matter is pending and can choose for himself whether to appear or default, acquiesce or contest." *Mullane v. Central Hanover Bank & Trust Co.*, 339 U.S. 306, 314 (1950). Today's decision diminishes the safeguard of notice, affording an opportunity to be heard, before one is deprived of property. As adequate to notify prisoners that the Government seeks forfeiture of their property, the Court condones a procedure too lax to reliably ensure that a prisoner will receive a legal notice sent to him. The Court does so despite the Government's total control of a prison inmate's location, and the evident feasibility of tightening the notice procedure "as [would] one desirous of actually informing [the prisoner]." Because the Court, without warrant in fact or law, approves a procedure "less likely to bring home notice" than a feasible alternative, I dissent. * * *

Jones v. Flowers

Supreme Court of the United States
547 U.S. 220 (2006)

CHIEF JUSTICE ROBERTS delivered the opinion of the Court.

     Before a State may take property and sell it for unpaid taxes, the Due Process Clause of the Fourteenth Amendment requires the government to provide the owner "notice and opportunity for hearing appropriate to the nature of the case." *Mullane v. Central Hanover Bank & Trust Co.*, 339 U.S. 306, 313 (1950). We granted certiorari to determine whether, when notice of a tax sale is mailed to the owner and returned undelivered, the government must take additional reasonable steps to provide notice before taking the owner's property.

What's That?

A *tax sale* is the sale of property because of the nonpayment of taxes due.

I

In 1967, petitioner Gary Jones purchased a house at <u>717 North Bryan Street in Little Rock, Arkansas</u>. He lived in the house with his wife until they separated in 1993. Jones then moved into an apartment in Little Rock, and his wife continued to live in the North Bryan Street house. Jones paid his mortgage each month for 30 years, and the mortgage company paid Jones' property taxes. After Jones paid off his mortgage in 1997, the property taxes went unpaid, and the property was certified as delinquent.

In April 2000, respondent Mark Wilcox, the <u>Commissioner of State Lands</u> (Commissioner), attempted to notify Jones of his tax delinquency, and his right to redeem the property, by mailing a certified letter to Jones at the North Bryan Street address. The packet of information stated that unless Jones redeemed the property, it would be subject to public sale two years later on April 17, 2002. Nobody was home to sign for the letter, and nobody appeared at the post office to retrieve the letter within the next 15 days. The post office returned the unopened packet to the Commissioner marked "unclaimed."

Two years later, and just a few weeks before the public sale, the Commissioner published a notice of public sale in the Arkansas Democrat Gazette. No bids were submitted, which permitted the State to negotiate a private sale of the property. Several months later, respondent Linda Flowers submitted a purchase offer. The Commissioner mailed another certified letter to Jones at the North Bryan Street address, attempting to notify him that his house would be sold to Flowers if he did not pay his taxes. Like the first letter, the second was also returned to the Commissioner marked "unclaimed." Flowers purchased the house, which the parties stipulated in the trial court had a fair market value of $80,000, for $21,042.15. Immediately after the 30-day period for postsale redemption passed, Flowers had an unlawful detainer notice delivered to the property. The notice was served on Jones' daughter, who contacted Jones and notified him of the tax sale.

Jones filed a lawsuit in Arkansas state court against the Commissioner and Flowers, alleging that the Commissioner's failure to provide notice of the tax sale and of Jones' right to redeem resulted in the taking of his property without due process. The

Make the Connection

The "taking" complained of here is in reference to the *Takings Clause* of the Constitution, the Fifth Amendment provision that prohibits the government from taking private property for public use without fair compensation. You may study this provision further in a **Constitutional Law** or possibly a **Property** course.

Commissioner and Flowers moved for summary judgment on the ground that the two unclaimed letters sent by the Commissioner were a constitutionally adequate attempt at notice, and Jones filed a cross-motion for summary judgment. The trial court granted summary judgment in favor of the Commissioner and Flowers. It concluded that the Arkansas tax sale statute, which set forth the notice procedure followed by the Commissioner, complied with constitutional due process requirements.

Jones appealed, and the Arkansas Supreme Court affirmed the trial court's judgment. The court noted our precedent stating that due process does not require actual notice, *see Dusenbery v. United States*, 534 U.S. 161 (2002), and it held that attempting to provide notice by certified mail satisfied due process in the circumstances presented. * * *

II.

A

Due process does not require that a property owner receive actual notice before the government may take his property. Rather, we have stated that due process requires the government to provide "notice reasonably calculated, under all the circumstances, to apprise interested parties of the pendency of the action and afford them an opportunity to present their objections." *Mullane*. The Commissioner argues that once the State provided notice reasonably calculated to apprise Jones of the impending tax sale by mailing him a certified letter, due process was satisfied. The Arkansas statutory scheme is reasonably calculated to provide notice, the Commissioner continues, because it provides for notice by certified mail to an address that the property owner is responsible for keeping up to date. The Commissioner notes * * * that the Arkansas scheme exceeds constitutional requirements by requiring the Commissioner to use certified mail.

It is true that this Court has deemed notice constitutionally sufficient if it was reasonably calculated to reach the intended recipient when sent. *See, e.g., Dusenbery*; *Mullane*. In each of these cases, the government attempted to provide notice and heard nothing back indicating that anything had gone awry, and we stated that "[t]he reasonableness and hence the constitutional validity of [the] chosen method may be defended on the ground that it is in itself reasonably certain to inform those affected." But we have never addressed whether due process entails further responsibility when the government becomes aware prior to the taking that its attempt at notice has failed. * * * The question presented is whether such knowledge on the government's part is a "circumstance and condition" that varies the "notice required." * * *

In *Mullane*, we stated that "when notice is a person's due . . . [t]he means employed must be such as one desirous of actually informing the absentee might reasonably adopt to accomplish it," and that assessing the adequacy of a particular form of notice requires balancing the "interest of the State" against "the individual interest sought to be protected by the Fourteenth Amendment." * * *

We do not think that a person who actually desired to inform a real property owner of an impending tax sale of a house he owns would do nothing when a certified letter sent to the owner is returned unclaimed. If the Commissioner prepared a stack of letters to mail to delinquent taxpayers, handed them to the postman, and then watched as the departing postman accidentally dropped the letters down a storm drain, one would certainly expect the Commissioner's office to prepare a new stack of letters and send them again. No one "desirous of actually informing" the owners would simply shrug his shoulders as the letters disappeared and say "I tried." Failure to follow up would be unreasonable, despite the fact that the letters were reasonably calculated to reach their intended recipients when delivered to the postman.

By the same token, when a letter is returned by the post office, the sender will ordinarily attempt to resend it, if it is practicable to do so. This is especially true when, as here, the subject matter of the letter concerns such an important and irreversible prospect as the loss of a house. * * * [T]he State * * * had good reason to suspect when the notice was returned that Jones was "no better off than if the notice had never been sent." Deciding to take no further action is not what someone "desirous of actually informing" Jones would do; such a person would take further reasonable steps if any were available. * * *

It is certainly true, as the Commissioner and Solicitor General contend, that the failure of notice in a specific case does not establish the inadequacy of the attempted notice; in that sense,

The *Solicitor General* is the official who argues before the Supreme Court on behalf of the United States government in all cases in which the U.S. is a party and in cases where the U.S. has been granted permission to participate. *See* http://www.usdoj.gov/osg/.

the constitutionality of a particular procedure for notice is assessed *ex ante*, rather than *post hoc*. But if a feature of the State's chosen procedure is that it promptly provides additional information to the government about the effectiveness of notice, it does not contravene the *ex ante* principle to consider what the government does with that information in assessing the adequacy of the chosen procedure. After all, the State knew *ex ante* that it would promptly learn whether its effort to effect notice through certified mail had succeeded. It would not be inconsistent with the approach the Court has taken in notice cases to ask, with respect to a procedure under which telephone calls were placed to owners, what the State did when no one answered. Asking what the State does when a notice letter is returned unclaimed is not substantively different. * * *

It's Latin to Me!

Ex ante is Latin for "from before" and refers to how matters might have appeared beforehand rather than in hindsight. *Post hoc*, Latin for "after this," has the opposite meaning of *ex ante*; it refers to a hindsight perspective.

Mr. Jones should have been more diligent with respect to his property, no question. People must pay their taxes, and the government may hold citizens accountable for tax delinquency by taking their property. But before forcing a citizen to satisfy his debt by forfeiting his property, due process requires the government to provide adequate notice of the impending taking.

B

In response to the returned form suggesting that Jones had not received notice that he was about to lose his property, the State did nothing. For the reasons stated, we conclude the State should have taken additional reasonable steps to notify Jones, if practicable to do so. * * *

We think there were several reasonable steps the State could have taken. * * *

The Solicitor General argues that requiring further effort when the government learns that notice was not delivered will cause the government to favor modes of providing notice that do not generate additional information—for example, starting (and stopping) with regular mail instead of certified mail. We find this unlikely, as we have no doubt that the government repeatedly finds itself being asked to prove that notice was sent and received. Using certified mail provides the State with documentation of personal delivery and protection against false claims that notice was never received. That added security, however, comes at a price—the State also learns when notice has *not* been received. We conclude that, under the circumstances presented, the State cannot simply ignore that information in proceeding to take and sell the owner's property * * *.

* * *

The dissent forcefully articulates some basic principles about constitutionally required notice, principles from which we have no intention to depart. In particular, we disclaim any "new rule" that is "contrary to *Dusenbery* and a significant departure from *Mullane*." In *Dusenbery*, the Government was aware that someone at the prison had signed for the prisoner's notice letter, and we determined that this attempt at notice was adequate, despite the fact that the State could have made notice more likely by requiring the prisoner to sign for the letter himself. In this case, of course, the notice letter was returned to the Commissioner, informing him that his attempt at notice had failed. * * *

The Commissioner's effort to provide notice to Jones of an impending tax sale of his house was insufficient to satisfy due process given the circumstances of this case. The judgment of the Arkansas Supreme Court is reversed, and the case is remanded for proceedings not inconsistent with this opinion.

It is so ordered.

JUSTICE ALITO took no part in the consideration or decision of this case.

JUSTICE THOMAS, with whom JUSTICE SCALIA and JUSTICE KENNEDY join, dissenting.

* * *

Adopting petitioner's arguments, the Court holds today that "when mailed notice of a tax sale is returned unclaimed, the State must take additional reasonable steps to attempt to provide notice to the property owner before selling his property, if it is practicable to do so." The Court concludes that it was practicable for Arkansas to take additional steps here * * *. Because, under this Court's precedents, the State's notice methods clearly satisfy the requirements of the Due Process Clause, I respectfully dissent.

I

* * *

The methods of notice employed by Arkansas were reasonably calculated to inform petitioner of proceedings affecting his property interest and thus satisfy the requirements of the Due Process Clause. The State mailed a notice by certified letter to the address provided by petitioner. The certified letter was returned to the State marked "unclaimed" after three attempts to deliver it. The State then published a notice of public sale containing redemption information in the Arkansas Democrat Gazette newspaper. After Flowers submitted a purchase offer, the State sent yet another certified letter to petitioner at his record address. That letter, too, was returned to the State marked "unclaimed" after three delivery attempts.

Arkansas' attempts to contact petitioner by certified mail at his "record address," without more, satisfy due process. *Dusenbery*; *see also Mullane*. Because the notices were sent to the address provided by petitioner himself, the State had an especially sound basis for determining that notice would reach him. Moreover, Arkansas exceeded the constitutional minimum by additionally publishing notice in a local newspaper. Due process requires nothing more—and certainly not here, where petitioner had a statutory duty to pay his taxes and to report any change of address to the state taxing authority.

* * *

Points for Discussion

a. Reconciling *Dusenbery* and *Jones*

The outcomes in *Dusenbery* and *Jones* can appear to be contradictory. In *Dusenbery*, the Court found that the government's delivery of notice to the mail room at the prison where the party to be notified was incarcerated was sufficient, even though the inmate was in the very same government's custody and thus could have been notified in a manner more certain to have reached him. In *Jones* on the other hand, the government sent notice via certified mail on two separate occasions, efforts that were deemed insufficient given the government's notice of their failure.

Are these two cases inconsistent with one another or can they be reconciled? What might explain the seemingly opposed outcomes? Note the change in personnel on the Court between the two rulings.

b. Actual Notice

In *Dusenbery*, the Court disclaims any notion that actual notice is a requirement of due process. What if it can be shown that the party to be notified actually received notice? Will proof of actual notice validate the constitutionality of the procedures used to achieve such notice in that case? Consider <u>*Wuchter v. Pizzutti*, 276 U.S. 13 (1928)</u>, in which the Court held that a state's nonresident motorist statute was unconstitutional because it failed to require the Secretary of State to notify nonresidents of the commencement of actions against them, even though in the case before it, the defendant had actually received notice.

c. Constitutional Notice After *Jones*

Since *Jones*, the Court has not moved further in the direction suggested by *Dusenbery*, which had appeared to presage a more narrow view of the notice obligations under *Mullane*. *Jones* seems to portend a broader view of *Mullane* that takes its language at face value: What would a person who really wants to notify a party do? It is clear that in both cases one who was truly desirous of notifying the respective property owners would have done more. The core holding of *Jones*, however, is that when the government receives an indication that its attempt at notice has failed, additional reasonable steps to provide notice must be taken if available. *See, e.g.,* <u>*Linn Farms and Timber Ltd. P'ship v. Union Pac. R.R. Co.*, 2010 WL 2179132, at *1 (E.D. Ark. May 25, 2010)</u> (holding that the Arkansas Commissioner of State Lands should have obtained a correct address for the defendant and re-sent notice after his original letter was sent by certified mail but was returned and stamped "Not Deliverable As Addressed—Unable To Forward"). What additional steps in *Jones* could the government have taken to effect notice? Try the next two hypothetical problems to test your understanding of the constitutional notice requirement.

Hypo 2.1

An attorney from State A helped a client from State B purchase property in State A. The two corresponded regularly through the mail as they were working on the deal. The attorney ultimately arranged the purchase of the land for the client, but the client failed to pay the attorney's legal fees.

The attorney sued the client in State A state court, serving notice by publication in a local State A newspaper as allowed under State A law. The client has now approached you for advice on whether the notice by publication is constitutionally sufficient. What is your advice?

Hypo 2.2

An attorney from State A helped a client from State B purchase property in State A. The two corresponded regularly through the mail as they were working on the deal. The attorney ultimately arranged the purchase of the land for the client, but the client failed to pay the attorney's legal fees. The attorney sued the client in State A state court, sending notice by certified mail to the client's last known address. After the mail was returned to the attorney marked "undelivered," the attorney published notice of the suit in a local State A newspaper as is permitted under State A law. The client never learned of the case and the court entered a default judgment in favor of the attorney.

When the attorney attempted to enforce the default judgment in State B, the client attacked the judgment by arguing that notice in the State A case was constitutionally defective. How should the court rule with respect to the client's challenge?

B. Statutory Notice: Service of Process

After a civil action has been filed in federal court, the plaintiff must have the summons and complaint served on the defendants in the case. Although service is the plaintiff's responsibility, these documents cannot actually be delivered by a party in the case and must be done by someone who is at least 18 years old. FED R. CIV. P. 4(c). This means process servers or paralegals are typically used to serve process; it is not good practice for attorneys in the case to do so because they may later be called to testify about service if a dispute arises.

The summons and the complaint together are referred to as the process. Local rules may also require that additional forms be attached to the complaint, such as a civil cover sheet. *See,*

Go Online

A *summons* is a document that orders the defendant to appear in court and respond to the plaintiff's allegations. Rule 4(a) sets forth the requirements for the summons, which must be prepared by the plaintiff. The United States Courts' website includes a link to a form ("Summons in a Civil Action") that plaintiffs may use for this purpose. *See* www.uscourts.gov/FormsAndFees/Forms/CourtFormsByCategory.aspx.

e.g. U.S. Dist. Ct., N.D. Cal., Civ. R. 3–2(a). The Federal Rules establish very specific guidelines governing how service of process is to be accomplished. These requirements are set forth in Rule 4.

Serving Individuals

Let us start by considering Rule 4(e), which governs service on individual defendants:

FRCP 4(e). Serving an Individual
Within a Judicial District of the United States.

(e)   Serving an Individual Within a Judicial District of the United States. Unless federal law provides otherwise, an individual—other than a minor, an incompetent person, or a person whose waiver has been filed—may be served in a judicial district of the United States by:

  (1)   following state law for serving a summons in an action brought in courts of general jurisdiction in the state where the district court is located or where service is made; or

  (2)   doing any of the following:

    (A)   delivering a copy of the summons and of the complaint to the individual personally;

    (B)   leaving a copy of each at the individual's dwelling or usual place of abode with someone of suitable age and discretion who resides there; or

    (C)   delivering a copy of each to an agent authorized by appointment or by law to receive service of process.

Take Note!

Parties cannot serve the summons and complaint; it must be done by a person 18 years of age or older who is not a party. FED. R. CIV. P. 4(c)(2). Generally, it is not a good practice for a party's attorney to serve process because of the potential need for the process server to provide testimony in the event of a dispute over service. That said, service by one's counsel in the case is permissible. *See Trustees of Local Union No. 727 Pension Fund v. Perfect Parking, 126 F.R.D. 48, 52 (N.D. Ill. 1989)* ("While service by counsel for plaintiff may not be the most preferable method, service by counsel is proper.").

This provision boils down to permitting service in accordance with the law of the state in which the case is pending or where service is achieved, or personal service on the individual defendant, her abode (with conditions), or her agent. When state-law sanctioned methods of service are used, they must comport with the minimum requisites of federal due process. *See, e.g., Hickory Travel Sys., Inc. v. TUI AG, 213 F.R.D. 547, 552 (N.D. Cal. 2003)* ("Federal law, in the form of due process limitations, may become relevant if state law is highly permissive in allowing service . . . ."). The due process limitations are those developed by the Supreme Court in <u>*Mullane v. Central Hanover Bank & Trust,* 339 U.S. 306 (1950)</u>, and its progeny. Moreover, if the individual defendant to be served is a minor or a legally incompetent person being served within the United States, state law governing service on such individuals in the state where service is made *must* be employed. FED. R. CIV. P. 4(g).

When serving process at a defendant's "dwelling or usual place of abode" it must be left with someone who resides there, although courts have found that doorpersons and apartment managers reside at the buildings where they are on duty for purposes of Rule 4(e)(2)(B). *See, e.g. <u>Hartford Fire Ins. Co. v. Perinovic,</u> 152 F.R.D. 128 (N.D. Ill. 1993)* (approving service on apartment doorman). Also, when effecting service of process at the defendant's dwelling it must be given to a person who is of "suitable age and discretion," which does not require service on an adult but rather requires that the person receiving the documents be sufficiently mature to understand the importance of passing them along to the defendant. *See, e.g., Universal Prop. and Cas. Ins. Co. v. Melendez-Grant*, No. 2:12-cv-02660-DCN, <u>2013 WL 3550445</u>, at *2 (D.S.C. July 11, 2013) (approving service on the defendant's 11-year-old son); <u>*Metro. Life Ins. Co. v. Hunter,* No. 1:12-cv-01009, 2013 WL 2156326, at *2 (E.D. Va. May 15, 2013)</u> (finding that service on defendant's 16-year-old son was proper under Rule 4(e)(2)).

Food for Thought

What should count as one's "abode" for purposes of Rule 4(e)? May a person have multiple abodes? *See, e.g., <u>Nat'l Dev. Co. v. Triad Holding Corp., 930 F.2d 253, 257 (2d Cir. 1991)</u>* (permitting multiple residences under the Rule 4 and allowing service on the place where the defendant was actually living at the time of service).

Note that <u>Rule 4(e)</u> only governs service on individuals who can be located within the United States. Note also that the defendant's agent for service of process may be one that she has personally appointed or one that is authorized to be such an agent by law. The agent must be one that was appointed for the specific purpose of receiving process, with the burden being on the plaintiff to prove that an agency relationship existed between the defendant and the individual who accepted service. *See, e.g., <u>McCain v. California Highway Patrol,</u> 2011 WL 5169372 (E.D. Ca. Oct. 28, 2011)* (leaving documents with desk officer not authorized to accept service on behalf of other officers did not comply with Rule 4(e)(2)(C) because neither California law nor CHP policy indicated that such persons were authorized agents for such purpose); <u>*Nyholm v. Pryce,* 259 F.R.D. 101, 104 (D.N.J. 2009)</u> ("Plaintiff has offered no evidence to show that Officers Pryce and/or Stillwell expressly designated the 'Hall, Associate Administrator' to serve as their agent for acceptance of process.").

Serving Entities

Service on corporations or other entities within the United States is governed by Rule 4(h)(1), which in turn refers the reader back to Rule 4(e)(1) (permitting service in accordance with state law) but also provides an additional means of service: "by delivering a copy of the summons and of the complaint to an officer, a managing or general agent, or any other agent authorized by appointment or by law to receive service of process and—if the agent is one authorized by statute and the statute so requires—by also mailing a copy of each to the defendant. . . ." FED. R. CIV. P. 4(h)(1)(B).

Take Note!

Note that here, unlike when individual defendants are being served, if the corporate agent for service of process is authorized by law rather than appointment to receive service, the rule requires that a copy of the summons and complaint be mailed to the defendant in addition to being delivered to that agent. Why do you think this is so?

Courts have interpreted the term "delivering" to mean hand delivery, not mail. *Osorio v. Emily Morgan Enters., LLC*, No. Civ.A.SA04CA0179–XR, 2005 WL 589620, at *2 (W.D. Tex. Mar.14, 2005) ("The latter part of Rule 4(h)(1) does not provide for service of process upon corporations by mail as a matter of federal procedure."). Also, the summons and complaint cannot simply be delivered to any employee of the company, including a receptionist; rather, if not delivered to the registered agent of the company, the documents must be delivered to an officer or managing agent, *i.e.* individuals who have authority to manage the daily operations of the organization such as a CEO, president, or corporate secretary. *See, e.g.*, *Jackson v. Schryver Med. Sales & Marketing*, No. 07-cv-01371-WYD-KMT, 2008 WL 3878023, at *3 (D. Colo. Aug. 20, 2008) ("It is clear that the plaintiff did not comply with Rule 4(h)(1)(B) since it is undisputed the receptionist at the office of Schryver Medical on December 24, 2008 was not 'an officer, a managing or general agent or any other agent authorized by appointment or by law to receive service of process.' "). Do not forget, however, that under Rule 4(h)(1) entities may also be served according to state law, which may permit service via methods not expressly authorized by other provisions of Rule 4(h).

Service Outside the United States

Service on individuals and corporations located outside of the United States is more complicated. Rule 4(f) sets up a loosely tripartite structure governing how such persons and corporations should be served. First,

Practice Pointer

The U.S. State Department website contains extensive information about serving legal documents abroad. The website should be one of your first points of reference if you face such a task. *See* Service of Process, https://travel.state.gov/content/travel/en/legal-considerations/judicial/service-of-process.html.

service can be made pursuant to the terms of an international treaty such as the <u>Hague Convention on the Service Abroad of Judicial and Extrajudicial Documents</u> (or the <u>Inter-American Convention on Letters Rogatory</u>), which establishes a detailed regime for transmitting such documents to persons found within foreign countries. Fed. R. Civ. P. 4(f)(1).

Second, in the absence of an international agreement, service can be made within the foreign country in one of three ways: (1) in the manner defendants are ordinarily served within those countries for suits in their regular courts; (2) as directed by that country in response to a letter rogatory from the U.S. court requesting instruction on service; or, for individual defendants, (3) through in-hand service of process or by "any form of mail that the clerk addresses and sends to the individual and that requires a signed receipt," provided the foreign country does not prohibit such service. Fed. R. Civ. P. 4(f)(2).

What's That?

A *letter rogatory* is a formal letter from a court to an authority within a foreign government that seeks guidance and cooperation in an effort to further some judicial task the court is trying to accomplish.

Third, <u>Rule 4(f)</u> includes a provision that permits service "by other means not prohibited by international agreement, as the court orders." Fed. R. Civ. P. 4(f)(3). Should plaintiffs be able to serve defendants pursuant to this last catch-all provision without first making an effort to serve pursuant to the other means outlined earlier in the Rule? The next case addresses this issue.

Rio Properties, Inc. v. Rio International Interlink

U.S. Court of Appeals for the Ninth Circuit
<u>284 F.3d 1007 (9th Cir. 2002)</u>

Trott, Circuit Judge.

Las Vegas hotel and casino operator Rio Properties, Inc. ("RIO") sued Rio International Interlink ("RII"), a foreign Internet business entity, asserting various statutory and common law trademark infringement claims. The district court entered default judgment against RII for failing to comply with the court's discovery orders. RII now appeals the sufficiency of the service of process, effected via email and regular mail pursuant to <u>Federal Rule of Civil Procedure 4(f)(3)</u>, the district court's exercise of personal jurisdiction, and ultimately, the entry of default judgment and the award of attorneys' fees and costs. * * * [W]e affirm the district court's decision.

BACKGROUND

What's That?

Attorneys' fees are the amount of money that a losing party may be ordered to pay its adversary to compensate it for the cost of legal representation incurred in litigating against the losing party. Under what is known as the *American rule*, losing parties do not ordinarily have to pay attorneys' fees but may be ordered to do so under special circumstances.

RIO owns the RIO All Suite Casino Resort, the "Best Hotel Value in the World" according to Travel and Leisure Magazine. * * * In addition to its elegant hotel, RIO's gambling empire consists of the Rio Race & Sports Book, which allows customers to wager on professional sports. To protect its exclusive rights in the "RIO" name, RIO registered numerous trademarks with the United States Patent and Trademark Office. When RIO sought to expand its presence onto the Internet, it registered the domain name, www.playrio.com. At that address, RIO operates a website that informs prospective customers about its hotel and allows those enticed by Lady Luck to make reservations.

RII is a Costa Rican entity that participates in an Internet sports gambling operation, doing business variously as Rio International Sportsbook, Rio Online Sportsbook, or Rio International Sports. RII enables its customers to wager on sporting events online or via a 1-800 telephone number. Far from a penny ante operation, RII grosses an estimated $3 million annually.

RIO became aware of RII's existence by virtue of RII's advertisement in the Football Betting Guide '98 Preview. RIO later discovered, in the Nevada edition of the Daily Racing Form, another RII advertisement which invited customers to visit RII's website, www.riosports.com. RII also ran radio spots in Las Vegas as part of its comprehensive marketing strategy.

Upon learning of RII, RIO fired off an epistle demanding that RII cease and desist from operating the www.riosports.com website. Although RII did not formally respond, it promptly disabled the objectionable website. Apparently not ready to cash in its chips, RII soon activated the URL http://www.betrio.com to host an identical sports gambling operation. Perturbed, RIO filed the present action alleging various trademark infringement claims and seeking to enjoin RII from the continued use of the name "RIO."

To initiate suit, RIO attempted to locate RII in the United States for service of process. RIO discovered that RII claimed an address in Miami, Florida when it registered the allegedly infringing domain names. As it turned out, however, that address housed only RII's international courier, IEC, which was not authorized to accept service on RII's behalf. Nevertheless, IEC agreed to forward the summons and complaint to RII's Costa Rican courier.

After sending a copy of the summons and complaint through IEC, RIO received a telephone call from Los Angeles attorney John Carpenter ("Carpenter") inquiring about the lawsuit. Apparently, RII received the summons and complaint from IEC and subsequently consulted Carpenter about how to respond.

Carpenter indicated that RII provided him with a partially illegible copy of the complaint and asked RIO to send him a complete copy. RIO agreed to resend the complaint and, in addition, asked Carpenter to accept service for RII; Carpenter politely declined. Carpenter did, however, request that RIO notify him upon successful completion of service of process on RII.

Food for Thought

The opinion reveals that RII actually received a copy of the complaint from IEC. If RII received the summons and complaint and has actual notice of the lawsuit, how is it able to challenge the sufficiency of service as it is doing here?

Thus thwarted in its attempt to serve RII in the United States, RIO investigated the possibility of serving RII in Costa Rica. Toward this end, RIO searched international directory databases looking for RII's address in Costa Rica. These efforts proved fruitless however; the investigator learned only that RII preferred communication through its email address, email@betrio.com, and received snail mail, including payment for its services, at the IEC address in Florida.

Unable to serve RII by conventional means, RIO filed an emergency motion for alternate service of process. RII opted not to respond to RIO's motion. The district court granted RIO's motion, and pursuant to <u>Federal Rules of Civil Procedure 4(h)(2) and 4(f)(3)</u>, ordered service of process on RII through the mail to Carpenter and IEC and via RII's email address, email@betrio.com.

Court order in hand, RIO served RII by these court-sanctioned methods. RII filed a motion to dismiss for insufficient service of process and lack of personal jurisdiction. The parties fully briefed the issues, and the district court denied RII's motion without a hearing. RII then filed its answer, denying RIO's allegations and asserting twenty-two affirmative defenses.

As the case proceeded, RIO propounded discovery requests and interrogatories on RII. RIO granted RII two informal extensions of time in which to respond. Nonetheless, RII's eventual responses were almost entirely useless, consisting largely of the answer "N/A," ostensibly meaning "Not Applicable." After additional futile attempts to elicit good faith responses from RII, RIO brought a motion to compel discovery. In granting RIO's motion, the district court warned that in the event RII failed to comply, monetary sanctions would be an insufficient remedy and that "preclusive sanctions" would be awarded. When RII failed to comply with the district court's discovery order, RIO moved for terminating sanctions.

Although RII belatedly complied, in part, with RIO's discovery request, the district court granted RIO's motion for sanctions and entered default judgment against RII. Citing RII's reprehensible conduct and bad faith, the district court additionally directed RII to pay reasonable attorneys' fees and costs to RIO in the amount of $88,761.50 and $7,859.52 respectively.

RII now appeals the sufficiency of the court-ordered service of process, the district court's exercise of personal jurisdiction as well as the propriety of the default judgment, and the award of attorneys' fees and costs.

DISCUSSION

I. Alternative Service Of Process

A. Applicability of Rule 4(f)(3)

We review for an abuse of discretion the district court's decision regarding the sufficiency of service of process. *Walker v. Sumner*, 14 F.3d 1415, 1422 (9th Cir. 1994). Federal Rule of Civil Procedure 4(h)(2) authorizes service of process on a foreign business entity in the manner prescribed by Rule 4(f) for individuals. The subsection of Rule 4(f) relevant to our decision, Rule 4(f)(3), permits service in a place not within any judicial district of the United States "by . . . means not prohibited by international agreement as may be directed by the court."

As obvious from its plain language, service under Rule 4(f)(3) must be (1) directed by the court; and (2) not prohibited by international agreement. No other limitations are evident from the text. In fact, as long as court-directed and not prohibited by an international agreement, service of process ordered under Rule 4(f)(3) may be accomplished in contravention of the laws of the foreign country.

RII argues that Rule 4(f) should be read to create a hierarchy of preferred methods of service of process. RII's interpretation would require that a party attempt service of process by those methods enumerated in Rule 4(f)(2), including by diplomatic channels and letters rogatory, before petitioning the court for alternative relief under Rule 4(f)(3). We find no support for RII's position. No such requirement is found in the Rule's text, implied by its structure, or even hinted at in the advisory committee notes.

By all indications, court-directed service under Rule 4(f)(3) is as favored as service available under Rule 4(f)(1)[4] or Rule 4(f)(2). Indeed, Rule 4(f)(3) is one of three separately numbered subsections in Rule 4(f), and each subsection is separated from the one previous merely by the simple conjunction "or." Rule 4(f)(3) is not subsumed within or in any way dominated by Rule 4(f)'s other subsections; it stands

---

[4] A federal court would be prohibited from issuing a Rule 4(f)(3) order in contravention of an international agreement, including the Hague Convention referenced in Rule 4(f)(1). The parties agree, however, that the Hague Convention does not apply in this case because Costa Rica is not a signatory.

independently, on equal footing. Moreover, no language in Rules 4(f)(1) or 4(f)(2) indicates their primacy, and certainly Rule 4(f)(3) includes no qualifiers or limitations which indicate its availability only after attempting service of process by other means.

The advisory committee notes ("advisory notes") bolster our analysis. Beyond stating that service ordered under Rule 4(f)(3) must comport with constitutional notions of due process and must not be prohibited by international agreement, the advisory notes indicate the availability of alternate service of process under Rule 4(f)(3) without first attempting service by other means. Specifically, the advisory notes suggest that in cases of "urgency," Rule 4(f)(3) may allow the district court to order a "special method of service," even if other methods of service remain incomplete or unattempted.

What's That?

Advisory committee notes are commentary prepared by the Advisory Committee on Civil Rules—the entity that drafts amendments to the Federal Rules—designed to clarify or explain the rules. What weight should these notes be given when interpreting the Federal Rules? For more information about the rulemaking process, visit http://www.uscourts.gov/rulesand policies/rules.aspx.

Thus, examining the language and structure of Rule 4(f) and the accompanying advisory committee notes, we are left with the inevitable conclusion that service of process under Rule 4(f)(3) is neither a "last resort" nor "extraordinary relief." It is merely one means among several which enables service of process on an international defendant.

RII argues that *Graval v. P.T. Bakrie & Bros.*, 986 F. Supp. 1326, 1330 (C.D. Cal. 1996), requires attempted service by other methods, including through diplomatic channels or rogatory, before resort to court-ordered service under Rule 4(f)(3). The court in *Graval* believed that Rule 4(f)(3) was "intended as a last resort, only to be employed when there are no other feasible alternatives." Yet, the court in *Graval* erroneously based this belief on an advisory committee note pertaining solely to Rule 4(f)(2), which simply does not apply to Rule 4(f)(3). Indeed, *Graval*'s interpretation of Rule 4(f) is indefensible; it is unsupported by Rule 4(f)'s language and structure or by any proper reading of the advisory committee notes. Nor does any other case interpreting Rule 4(f)(3) or its predecessor endorse *Graval*'s interpretation. Thus, we disapprove of the statements in *Graval* which would require attempted service by all feasible alternatives before service under Rule 4(f)(3) is allowed. Instead, we hold that Rule 4(f)(3) is an equal means of effecting service of process under the Federal Rules of Civil Procedure, and we commit to the sound discretion of the district court the task of determining when the particularities and necessities of a given case require alternate service of process under Rule 4(f)(3).

Applying this proper construction of <u>Rule 4(f)(3)</u> and its predecessor, trial courts have authorized a wide variety of alternative methods of service including publication, ordinary mail, mail to the defendant's last known address, delivery to the defendant's attorney, <u>telex</u>, and most recently, email.

In this case, RIO attempted to serve RII by conventional means in the United States. Although RII claimed an address in Florida, that address housed only IEC, RII's international courier, which refused to accept service of process on RII's behalf. RII's attorney, Carpenter, who was specifically consulted in this matter, also declined to accept service of process. RIO's private investigator subsequently failed to discover RII's whereabouts in Costa Rica. Thus unable to serve RII, RIO brought an emergency motion to effectuate alternative service of process.

Contrary to RII's assertions, RIO need not have attempted every permissible means of service of process before petitioning the court for alternative relief. Instead, RIO needed only to demonstrate that the facts and circumstances of the present case necessitated the district court's intervention. Thus, when RIO presented the district court with its inability to serve an elusive international defendant, striving to evade service of process, the district court properly exercised its discretionary powers to craft alternate means of service. We expressly agree with the district court's handling of this case and its use of <u>Rule 4(f)(3)</u> to ensure the smooth functioning of our courts of law.

B. Reasonableness of the Court Ordered Methods of Service

Even if facially permitted by <u>Rule 4(f)(3)</u>, a method of service of process must also comport with constitutional notions of due process. To meet this requirement, the method of service crafted by the district court must be "reasonably calculated, under all the circumstances, to apprise interested parties of the pendency of the action and afford them an opportunity to present their objections." <u>*Mullane v. Central Hanover Bank & Trust Co.*, 339 U.S. 306, 314 (1950)</u>.

Make the Connection

The court here engages in a *Mullane* analysis, which we covered at the beginning of this chapter. Take this opportunity to refresh your understanding of the concepts and analysis arising from the *Mullane* line of cases.

Without hesitation, we conclude that each alternative method of service of process ordered by the district court was constitutionally acceptable. In our view, each method of service was reasonably calculated, under these circumstances, to apprise RII of the pendency of the action and afford it an opportunity to respond.

In particular, service through IEC was appropriate because RII listed IEC's address as its own when registering the allegedly infringing domain name. The record also reflects that RII directed its customers to remit payment to IEC's address. Moreover, when RIO sent a copy of the summons and complaint to RII through IEC, RII received it. All told, this evidence indicates that RII relied heavily upon IEC to operate its business in the United States and that IEC could effectively pass information to RII in Costa Rica.

Service upon Carpenter was also appropriate because he had been specifically consulted by RII regarding this lawsuit. He knew of RII's legal positions, and it seems clear that he was in contact with RII in Costa Rica. Accordingly, service to Carpenter was also reasonably calculated in these circumstances to apprise RII of the pendency of the present action.

Finally, we turn to the district court's order authorizing service of process on RII by email at email@betrio.com. We acknowledge that we tread upon untrodden ground. The parties cite no authority condoning service of process over the Internet or via email, and our own investigation has unearthed no decisions by the United States Courts of Appeals dealing with service of process by email and only one case anywhere in the federal courts. Despite this dearth of authority, however, we do not labor long in reaching our decision. Considering the facts presented by this case, we conclude not only that service of process by email was proper—that is, reasonably calculated to apprise RII of the pendency of the action and afford it an opportunity to respond—but in this case, it was the method of service most likely to reach RII.

To be sure, the Constitution does not require any particular means of service of process, only that the method selected be reasonably calculated to provide notice and an opportunity to respond. *See Mullane, 339 U.S. at 314.* In proper circumstances, this broad constitutional principle unshackles the federal courts from anachronistic methods of service and permits them entry into the technological renaissance. * * *

Although communication via email and over the Internet is comparatively new, such communication has been zealously embraced within the business community. RII particularly has embraced the modern e-business model and profited immensely from it. In fact, RII structured its business such that it could be contacted only via its email address. RII listed no easily discoverable street address in the United States or in Costa Rica. Rather, on its website and print media, RII designated its email address as its preferred contact information.

* * * If any method of communication is reasonably calculated to provide RII with notice, surely it is email—the method of communication which RII utilizes and prefers. In addition, email was the only court-ordered method of service aimed directly and instantly at RII, as opposed to methods of service effected through intermediaries like IEC and Carpenter. Indeed, when faced with an inter-

national e-business scofflaw, playing hide-and-seek with the federal court, email may be the only means of effecting service of process. Certainly in this case, it was a means reasonably calculated to apprise RII of the pendency of the lawsuit, and the Constitution requires nothing more.

Citing *WAWA, Inc. v. Christensen*, No. 99-1454, 1999 WL 557936, at *1 (E.D. Pa. July 29, 1999) (unpublished), RII contends that email is never an approved method of service under Rule 4. We disagree. In *WAWA*, the plaintiff attempted to serve the defendant via email absent a court order. Although RII is correct that a plaintiff may not generally resort to email service on his own initiative, in this case * * *, email service was properly ordered by the district court using its discretion under Rule 4(f)(3).

Despite our endorsement of service of process by email in this case, we are cognizant of its limitations. In most instances, there is no way to confirm receipt of an email message. * * * We note, however, that, except for the provisions recently introduced into Rule 5(b), email service is not available absent a Rule 4(f)(3) court decree. Accordingly, we leave it to the discretion of the district court to balance the limitations of email service against its benefits in any particular case. In our case, the district court performed the balancing test admirably, crafting methods of service reasonably calculated under the circumstances to apprise RII of the pendency of the action.[8]

* * *

For the reasons delineated above, we affirm the district court's decision in all respects.

Points for Discussion

a.   International Service Under Rule 4(f)

In light of *Rio Properties*, may plaintiffs immediately avail themselves of Rule 4(f)(3) and obtain a court order authorizing a special type of service or are there some prerequisites to the availability of a Rule 4(f)(3) order? If such prerequisites exist, what are they?

Although Rule 4(f)(3) may not include an exhaustion requirement, it may be a good practice to demonstrate that service by other means is difficult or unavailable. See, e.g., *Bravetti v. Liu*, No. 3:12-cv-7492-MAS-TJB, 2013 WL 6501740, at *3 (D.N.J. Dec. 11, 2013) ("Courts can grant Rule 4(f)(3) requests even where a plain-

---

[8]   Notably, RII does not argue that it did not receive notice of the present lawsuit or that such notice was incomplete, delayed or in any way prejudicial to its ability to respond effectively and in a timely manner.

tiff does not show that the other means are unduly burdensome or impossible. Yet, it is helpful to plaintiff's case to show some measure of difficulty in effecting service by usual means."); *MorningStar v. Dejun*, No. CV 11-00655 DDP (VBKx), 2013 WL 502474, at * 1. (C.D. Cal. Feb. 8, 2013) (permitting alternative service under Rule 4(f)(3) "where Plaintiffs have attempted to serve the Foreign Defendants through the Hague Convention for over a year, with no success"). Indeed, in *Rio Properties* the court indicated that "RIO needed only to demonstrate that the facts and circumstances of the present case necessitated the district court's intervention," which it did by showing its inability to serve the defendant via other means. *Rio Properties, 284 F.3d* at 1016.

Food for Thought

Those who take a closer look at the process for achieving service abroad under the Hague Convention might find it to be fairly cumbersome. See, e.g., Eric Porterfield, *Too Much Process, Not Enough Service: International Service of Process Under The Hague Service Convention*, 86 TEMP. L. REV. 331 (2014). Why do you think international service seems to be so difficult? Should it be simplified or are their concerns that warrant a cautious approach?

Further, if service is to be made within a country that is a signatory to the Hague Service Convention, it must be done using the mechanisms approved in that treaty; these requirements cannot be circumvented simply by recourse to Rule 4(f)(3). *Volkswagenwerk AG v. Schlunk*, 486 U.S. 694, 706 (1988) (holding that the Hague Convention is "the exclusive means of valid service" for entities in countries that are signatories to the Hague Convention). Compare with *Blockbuster, LLC v. Grupo Mizbe, S.A.,* NO. 13-62042-CIV, 2015 WL 12712061, at *1 (S.D. Fla. July 22, 2015) ("The Inter-American Convention, unlike the Hague Convention, does not purport to provide the exclusive means of effecting service of process between the signatories."). If the address of the defendant is unknown, however, the Hague Convention does not apply. Convention on Service Abroad of Judicial and Extrajudicial Documents in Civil and Commercial Matters (Hague Service Convention) art. 1, Nov. 15, 1965, 20 U.S.T. 361. Neither does it apply if service is done within the United States or within a country that is not a signatory to the Convention.

Recently, in *Water Splash, Inc. v. Menon, 137 S. Ct. 1504 (2017)*, the Supreme Court clarified that under The Hague Convention, service by mail is not prohibited. The Court concluded as follows:

> In short, the traditional tools of treaty interpretation unmistakably demonstrate that Article 10(a) encompasses service by mail. To be clear, this does not mean that the Convention affirmatively authorizes service by mail. Article 10(a) simply provides that, as long as the receiving state does not object, the Convention does not "interfere with . . . the freedom" to serve

documents through postal channels. In other words, in cases governed by the Hague Service Convention, service by mail is permissible if two conditions are met: first, the receiving state has not objected to service by mail; and second, service by mail is authorized under otherwise-applicable law.

Id. at 1513.

b. Actual Notice

In *Rio Properties* the defendant, RII, received actual notice of the pendency of the lawsuit and copies of the summons and the complaint. Nevertheless, RII was able to challenge the sufficiency of service. Why is this so? *See, e.g., Jean-Louis v. Superior Maitenance Company*, 3:16-cv-00200-RLY-MPB, 2016 WL 7179373, at *1 (S.D. Ind. Dec. 9, 2016) ("A defendant's actual notice of litigation is insufficient to satisfy the requirements for service of process set forth in Rule 4."); *In re TFT-LCD (Flat Panel) Antitrust Litig.*, Nos. M 07–1827 SI, C 09–1115 SI, 2009 WL 4874872, at *2 (N.D. Cal. Oct. 6, 2009) ("[I]t is well-established that a defendant's actual notice of pending litigation is not sufficient to satisfy the requirements of Rule 4." (collecting appellate decisions)). Should the Federal Rules be amended to provide that proof of actual notice will suffice to ratify whatever means of service was employed? Why or why not?

c. Waiver of Service

RII was deliberately evading service in *Rio Properties*, as is made clear by the fact that it had knowledge of the lawsuit but nonetheless persisted in forcing Rio Properties to engage in all manner of expensive efforts to achieve service on RII in the United States and abroad.

In an effort to address the issue of defendants ceaselessly attempting to dodge service of process, and the associated delay and high costs resulting from such evasion, the Federal Rules were amended in 1993 to encourage defendants—except for minors or incompetents—to waive formal service of process and accept service by mail. This encouragement is achieved by offering defendants who waive formal service additional time to respond to the complaint—60 days (90 days for defendants outside the United States) instead of the ordinary 21 days. FED. R. CIV. P. 4(d)(3); 12(a)(1)(A)(i). As further incentive, defendants located in the U.S. are threatened with having to cover the costs incurred in effecting formal service, *see, e.g., U.S. Engine Production, Inc. v. AGCS Marine Ins. Co.*, 769 F. Supp. 2d 626, 629 (S.D.N.Y. 2011) (indicating that "costs incurred in effecting service" and reasonable attorney fees incurred in making the motion to collect such costs are reimbursable under Rule 4(d)(2) but not "any attorneys' fees incurred in the process of effecting service"), unless the defendant can convince the court that it had a good cause for not agreeing to waive formal service. FED. R. CIV. P. 4(d)(2). *See, e.g., Mason Tenders District Council Pension Fund v. Messera*, No. 95 Civ. 9341, 1997 WL 221200, *6

(S.D.N.Y. Apr. 1, 1997) (finding good cause to deny costs when the waiver request failed to include a self-addressed stamped envelope pursuant to Rule 4(2)(G) [now 4(d)(1)(C)]); *Henry v. Glaize Md. Orchards, Inc.*, 103 F.R.D. 589, 590 (D. Md. 1984) (holding that good cause exists to avoid the imposition of process serving fees when defendant does not actually receive summons and complaint by mail).

Rule 4(d) sets forth a number of detailed requirements that plaintiffs must satisfy to provide a defendant with a proper request that the defendant waive formal service of the summons and complaint. The defendant has no obligation to respond to a request for waiver, in which case the plaintiff should proceed to achieve service through whatever means is authorized under remaining parts of Rule 4. However, non-waiving defendants found within the U.S. then become subject to the obligation to cover the plaintiff's cost of service as noted above. If the defendant does agree to waive formal service, Rule 4(d)(5) makes it clear that such a waiver does not also amount to a waiver of any objection to personal jurisdiction or venue.

d. Service via Modern Methods of Communication

In *Rio Properties* the plaintiff had to get special permission to serve RII via email. Such service by the court's permission is only provided for under the Rule 4 when serving a defendant in a foreign country, *see* FED. R. CIV. P. 4(f)(3). Otherwise, Rule 4 does not approve of serving process via email, fax, and private delivery services such as FedEx and UPS, although applicable state service rules may permit such alternative methods. *See, e.g., Aevoe Corp. v. Pace,* No. C 11-3215, 2011 WL 3904133 at *2 (N.D. Cal. Sept. 6, 2011) (accessing California service rules under Rule 4(e)(1), which in turn allowed service "in a manner reasonably calculated to give actual notice to the party," and permitting service by email after a demonstration that diligence had been exercised in attempting to achieve service by alternate means). The Federal Rules permit (with consent) the use of email for the service of various pleadings and papers, once an action has commenced, but that rule does not cover initial service of the summons and complaint. *See* FED. R. CIV. P. 5(b)(2)(E).

Take Note!

Any method selected by a court for effecting service of process must satisfy the constitutional due process standard set forth in *Mullane* and its progeny. *See Chanel, Inc. v. Zhixian,* 2010 WL 1740695, at *3 (S.D. Fla. Apr. 29, 2010).

What do you think accounts for the reluctance of the federal rulemakers to embrace email, fax, and private delivery services as acceptable means of achieving formal service of the summons and complaint? *See* John N. Murphy, III, Note, *From Snail Mail to E-Mail: The Steady Evolution of Service of Process,* 19 ST. JOHN'S J. LEGAL COMMENT. 73, 76 (2004) (examining the evolution of service of process that has led to the increased acceptance of service via email in certain situations); Jeremy A. Colby, *You've Got Mail: The Modern Trend Towards Universal Electronic Service of Process*, 51 Buff. L. Rev. 337, 376–81 (2003) (arguing that the trend towards electronic service will eventually become the rule rather than the exception in light of increasing globalization and technological advancements).

> **FYI**
> In 2008 an Australian court permitted service of legal documents via Facebook. *See Legal Papers Served via Facebook*, news.bbc.co.uk/2/hi/7785004.stm. When do you think U.S. courts will be comfortable permitting service using online social networks or other novel communications technologies?

Should service of process ever be permitted via social media platforms, such as Facebook, Twitter, or Snapchat? *See, e.g., Ferrarese v. Shaw*, 164 F. Supp. 3d 361, 368 (E.D.N.Y. 2016) ("Plaintiff is Ordered [based on accessing New York law via Rule 4(e)(1)] to attempt service of process of the summons and petition by all of the following methods: (1) by sending copies of the summons and petition by certified mail, return receipt requested to defendant's last known address and to defendant's sister at this address; (2) by emailing a copy of the summons and petition to the email address tatashaw@gmail.com; and (3) by sending a Facebook message to Tata Shaw, which is linked to the Tata Shaw Facebook page, that contains a copy of the summons and petition."); *United States v. Mohammad*, 249 F.Supp. 3d 450, 454 (D.D.C. 2007) ("After customary means of service [abroad] proved ineffective, on August 27, 2015, this Court granted the government's motion, under Rule 4(f)(3) of the Federal Rules of Civil Procedure, for substituted service of process, and authorized the government to serve process upon the defendant by means of email and Facebook message."). *See also* Angela Upchurch, *"Hacking" Service of Process: Using Social Media To Provide Constitutionally Sufficient Notice of Process,* 38 U. Ark. Little Rock L. Rev. 559 (2016) (exploring the permissibility of service via social media under the constitutional standard for notice).

e. Serving Foreign States

When the defendant is a foreign state or component thereof, Rule 4(j) directs that the service provisions of the Foreign Sovereign Immunities Act, 28 U.S.C. § 1608, apply. For foreign states, there is a hierarchy of permissible methods, including service according to any special arrangement between the plaintiff and the foreign state, pursuant to any applicable

> **Take Note!**
> Any method selected by a court for effecting service of process must satisfy the constitutional due process standard set forth in *Mullane* and its progeny. *See Chanel, Inc. v. Zhixian*, 2010 WL 1740695, at *3 (S.D. Fla. Apr. 29, 2010).

international convention on the service of documents, by clerk of the court to the head of the state's ministry of foreign affairs and translated into their language, or by the clerk to the U.S. State Department, which is to use diplomatic channels to transmit the documents. 28 U.S.C. § 1608(a). Agencies or instrumentalities of foreign states have a distinct set of service methods that apply to them. *See* 28 U.S.C. § 1608(b) (providing for service, *inter alia*, per special arrangement, international treaty, court order, or as directed by the foreign authority). *See also, e.g.,* Democratic Republic of Congo v. FG Hemisphere Assocs., 508 F.3d 1062 (D.C. Cir. 2007) (illustrating application of § 1608).

f.   Time for Service

Under Rule 4(m) a plaintiff serving a complaint within the United States must do so within 90 days after the complaint is filed or risk dismissal of the action without prejudice (meaning the complaint can be refiled). If the plaintiff fails to complete service within the time period required by Rule 4(m), an extension can be obtained if "good cause" is shown, FED. R. CIV. P. 4(m), although some courts may entertain an extension of the time in the absence of a good cause showing, *see, e.g.,* Zapata v. City of New York, 502 F.3d 192, 196 (2d Cir. 2007). Good cause to extend the time period could include evidence of evasive activity by the party to be served, financial limitations of the serving party, or errors by the process server. *See, e.g.,* Coleman v. Milwaukee Bd. of Sch. Dirs., 290 F.3d 932, 934 (7th Cir. 2002) ("Good cause means a valid reason for delay, such as the defendant's evading service.").

Take Note!

The deadline for achieving service set forth in Rule 4(m) does not apply to service abroad pursuant to Rule 4(f). FED. R. CIV. P. 4(m) ("This subdivision (m) does not apply to service in a foreign country under Rule 4(f) . . . .").

Executive Summary

■ **Constitutional Notice Requirement.** Valid jurisdiction depends on appropriate notice, which in turn requires "notice reasonably calculated, under all the circumstances, to apprise interested parties of the pendency of the action and afford them an opportunity to present their objections." *Mullane v. Cent. Hanover Bank & Trust.*

■ **Service of Process.** Complaints in civil actions must be served according to the provisions outlined in Rule 4, which includes authorization for use of state-approved methods of service under certain circumstances. Any state methods employed must be consistent with the *Mullane* standard.

Major Themes

Keep in mind the following themes relating to notice in the federal courts:

a. *Reasonableness Under the Circumstances.*—The *Mullane* standard does not require the absolute best possible notice; rather, the circumstances will dictate what level of notice is reasonable. Relying on a method of service known to have failed will is unreasonable and will not suffice.

b. *Form over Function.*—Often, methods of notice are challenged as insufficient by defendants who have received actual notice of the action. Thus, one must remember that actual notice is typically not what matters here. Rather, what is important is that the method of notice was consistent with applicable rules regarding service and with the constitutional standard outlined in *Mullane*.

c. *State Methods.*—Although Rule 4 may be limited in the methods of service it permits, do not forget that in most cases it permits recourse to state law methods of service, which may be much more broad in what they permit.

■ **International Service.** Service abroad must be done pursuant to any applicable treaty, such as the Hague Convention. However, judges retain the ability to order alternative methods under Rule 4(f)(3) under certain circumstances, provided such methods are consistent with the *Mullane* standard. FED. R. CIV. P. 4(f).

■ **Waiver of Service.** Formal service may be dispensed with if a defendant agrees to waive service under Rule 4(d). Waiving service comes with more time to respond (60 days within the U.S. and 90 days if responding from outside of the U.S.), while failure to waive subjects defendants served in the United States to the possibility of having to pay for the expense of formal service. FED. R. CIV. P. 4(d).

For More Information

Students interested in studying notice and service of process further may consult the following resources:

- 4A C. Wright, A. Miller & A Steinman, Fed. Prac. & Proc. Civ. § 1074 *et seq.* (4th ed. 2015) (Constitutional Notice Requirement).

- 4A C. Wright, A. Miller & A Steinman, Fed. Prac. & Proc. Civ. §§ 1089–1118 (4th ed. 2015) (Manner of Service).

Test Your Knowledge

To assess your understanding of the material in this chapter, click here to take a quiz.

CHAPTER THREE

Subject Matter Jurisdiction

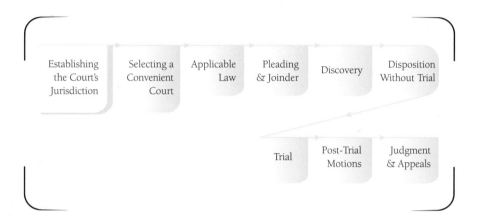

Introduction

RECALL THAT A COURT'S POWER to hear a case is not only determined by the requirement that it have personal jurisdiction over the parties, but also by the requirement that the court have subject matter jurisdiction over the type of case before it. Although state courts are mainly courts of general jurisdiction* that can hear cases involving any subject—including most matters arising under federal law—the federal courts are courts of limited jurisdiction that may only hear cases of a kind that they are affirmatively authorized to hear. The U.S. Constitution strictly limits the types of cases that fall within the judicial power exercised by the federal courts, and Congress has further limited the courts' power by authorizing inferior federal courts to hear only a subset of what the Constitution otherwise permits. Only those types of cases falling within the terms of the various statutes conferring federal subject matter jurisdiction may be heard by these federal courts.

The study of federal subject matter jurisdiction is important for several reasons. As an attorney representing a client interested in initiating a lawsuit, you must be able to determine whether your case may (or must) be brought in federal court. On

---

* Do not confuse this use of the term "general jurisdiction" with the concept as it is used in the context of personal jurisdiction. [Ed.]

the other hand, if you represent a defendant sued in federal court, you will need to know whether the case was properly brought there. Finally, if you represent a defendant in a state court suit, you will have to determine whether the case may be removed to federal court.

The Constitutional Framework

To understand subject matter jurisdiction, we first need to look at the constitutional provision that establishes the outer limits of the subject matter jurisdiction of the federal courts. That provision is <u>Article III, § 2 of the U.S. Constitution</u>:

<u>U.S. Constitution, Article III, § 2</u>

Section 2. The judicial Power shall extend to all Cases, in Law and Equity, arising under this Constitution, the Laws of the United States, and Treaties made, or which shall be made, under their Authority;—to all Cases affecting Ambassadors, other public Ministers and Consuls;—to all Cases of admiralty and maritime Jurisdiction;—to Controversies to which the United States shall be a Party;—to Controversies between two or more States;—between a State and Citizens of another State;—between Citizens of different States;—between Citizens of the same State claiming Lands under Grants of different States, and between a State, or the Citizens thereof, and foreign States, Citizens or Subjects.

Within this clause, we find that Article III extends the judicial power of the federal courts to nine categories of cases:

The Judicial Power Under Article III

1. Cases arising under the Constitution, federal statutes, and treaties;

2. Cases affecting Ambassadors, other public Ministers, and Consuls;

3. Cases of admiralty and maritime Jurisdiction;

4. Controversies in which the United States is a party;

5. Controversies between two or more States;

6. Controversies between a State and Citizens of another State;

7. Controversies between Citizens of different States;

8. Controversies between Citizens of the same State claiming Lands under Grants of different States; and

9. Controversies between a State, or the Citizens thereof, and foreign States, Citizens or Subjects.

Although Article III *authorizes* federal jurisdiction in these types of cases, the traditional understanding has been that jurisdiction is not actually *conferred* on the lower federal courts (those other than the U.S. Supreme Court) by this constitutional provision. Congress must confer this authority on the lower federal courts in order for them to be empowered to hear such cases. *See Cary v. Curtis, 44 U.S. 236, 245 (1845)* ("[T]he judicial power of the United States . . . is . . . dependent for its distribution and organization, and for the modes of its exercise, entirely upon the action of Congress, who possess the sole power of creating the tribunals (inferior to the Supreme Court) . . . and of investing them with jurisdiction . . . ."). *But see* A. Benjamin Spencer, *The Judicial Power and the Inferior Federal Courts: Exploring the Constitutional Vesting Thesis*, 46 GA. L. REV. 1, 46 (2011) ("[E]ven though the Supreme Court's embrace of the view that Congress may limit the jurisdiction of inferior federal courts is of ancient lineage, the proposition has never satisfactorily been established by the Court."). This is more than a mere theoretical distinction; there is a gap between the scope of the judicial power under the Constitution and what Congress has decided to confer upon lower federal courts. **Figure 3.1** illustrates this concept.

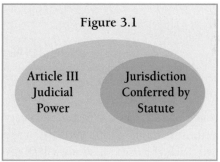

Figure 3.1

Article III Judicial Power

Jurisdiction Conferred by Statute

Congress has enacted such jurisdiction-conferring legislation, which is codified mostly in various parts of Title 28 of the U.S. Code. In this chapter, we will focus on those provisions conferring diversity jurisdiction, federal question jurisdiction, supplemental jurisdiction, and removal jurisdiction on the federal courts.[*]

A. Diversity Jurisdiction

Congress has given the federal courts jurisdiction over lawsuits between citizens from different states and cases involving U.S. citizens and aliens through the federal diversity statute, 28 U.S.C. § 1332:

---

[*] The fact that these types of subject matter jurisdiction are the focus of first-year civil procedure courses should not obscure from your view the existence of other bases for federal subject matter jurisdiction, including admiralty jurisdiction, 28 U.S.C. § 1333, interpleader jurisdiction, 28 U.S.C. § 1335, and jurisdiction in cases involving the United States as a party, 28 U.S.C. §§ 1345, 1346. [Ed.]

Diversity Jurisdiction: 28 U.S.C. § 1332

(a)   The district courts shall have original jurisdiction of all civil actions where the matter in controversy exceeds the sum or value of $75,000, exclusive of interest and costs, and is between—

(1)   citizens of different States;

(2)   citizens of a State and citizens or subjects of a foreign state, except that the district courts shall not have original jurisdiction under this subsection of an action between citizens of a State and citizens or subjects of a foreign state who are lawfully admitted for permanent residence in the United States and are domiciled in the same State;

(3)   citizens of different States and in which citizens or subjects of a foreign state are additional parties; and

(4)   a foreign state, defined in section 1603(a) of this title, as plaintiff and citizens of a State or of different States.

* * *

(e)   The word "States", as used in this section, includes the Territories, the District of Columbia, and the Commonwealth of Puerto Rico.

Under the federal diversity statute, diversity jurisdiction exists if two general conditions are met: (1) there is diversity of citizenship in one of the ways set forth in the statute, and (2) the jurisdictional amount-in-controversy requirement is satisfied. Each of these conditions will be reviewed in turn.

1. The Diversity-of-Citizenship Requirement

The requirement in § 1332 that the dispute be between "citizens of different states" is referred to as the ***diversity-of-citizenship*** requirement. Although it might seem that determining whether a suit is between citizens of different states should be a relatively simple matter, there are a couple of issues surrounding the determination: (1) figuring out a party's citizenship for diversity purposes and (2) understanding whether the right type of diversity exists. The next case, *Mas v. Perry*, focuses on the first of these concerns.

Mas v. Perry

U.S. Court of Appeals for the Fifth Circuit
489 F.2d 1396 (5th Cir. 1974)

AINSWORTH, CIRCUIT JUDGE:

Appellees Jean Paul Mas, a citizen of France, and Judy Mas were married at her home in Jackson, Mississippi. Prior to their marriage, Mr. and Mrs. Mas were graduate assistants, pursuing coursework as well as performing teaching duties, for approximately nine months and one year, respectively, at Louisiana State University in Baton Rouge, Louisiana. Shortly after their marriage, they returned to Baton Rouge to resume their duties as graduate assistants at LSU. They remained in Baton Rouge for approximately two more years, after which they moved to Park Ridge, Illinois. At the time of the trial in this case, it was their intention to return to Baton Rouge while Mr. Mas finished his studies for the degree of Doctor of Philosophy. Mr. and Mrs. Mas were undecided as to where they would reside after that.

Take Note!

Unlike personal jurisdiction, subject matter jurisdiction cannot be waived, meaning any party or the court may question its existence for the first time before, during, or after the case proceeds through adjudication at the district court level. However, parties who have had a full and fair opportunity to litigate the subject matter jurisdiction question will not—with limited exceptions—be able to challenge it in a collateral attack. *See Ins. Corp. of Ireland v. Compagnie des Bauxites de Guinee, 456 U.S. 694, 702 n.9 (1982).*

Upon their return to Baton Rouge after their marriage, appellees rented an apartment from appellant Oliver H. Perry, a citizen of Louisiana. This appeal arises from a final judgment entered on a jury verdict awarding $5,000 to Mr. Mas and $15,000 to Mrs. Mas for damages incurred by them as a result of the discovery that their bedroom and bathroom contained "two-way" mirrors and that they had been watched through them by the appellant during three of the first four months of their marriage.

At the close of the appellees' case at trial, appellant made an oral motion to dismiss for lack of jurisdiction. The motion was denied by the district court. Before this Court, appellant challenges the final judgment below solely on jurisdictional grounds, contending that appellees failed to prove diversity of citizenship among the parties and that the requisite jurisdictional amount is lacking with respect to Mr. Mas. Finding no merit to these contentions, we affirm. Under section 1332(a)(2), the federal judicial power extends to the claim of Mr. Mas, a citizen of France, against the appellant, a citizen of Louisiana. Since we conclude that Mrs. Mas is a citizen of Mississippi for diversity purposes, the district court also properly had jurisdiction under section 1332(a)(1) of her claim.

It has long been the general rule that complete diversity of parties is required in order that diversity jurisdiction obtain; that is, no party on one side may be a citizen of the same State as any party on the other side. *Strawbridge v. Curtiss, 7 U.S. 267 (1806)*. This determination of one's State Citizenship for diversity purposes is controlled by federal law, not by the law of any State. As is the case in other areas of federal jurisdiction, the diverse citizenship among adverse parties must be present at the time the complaint is filed. Jurisdiction is unaffected by subsequent changes in the citizenship of the parties. The burden of pleading the diverse citizenship is upon the party invoking federal jurisdiction; and if the diversity jurisdiction is properly challenged, that party also bears the burden of proof.

Take Note!

This paragraph is full of statements setting forth the law on several matters pertaining to diversity jurisdiction. These legal principles—particularly the complete diversity requirement—are important to know, so make a note of them.

To be a citizen of a State within the meaning of section 1332, a natural person must be both a citizen of the United States, and a domiciliary of that State. For diversity purposes, citizenship means domicile; mere residence in the State is not sufficient. A person's domicile is the place of "his true, fixed, and permanent home and principal establishment, and to which he has the intention of returning whenever he is absent therefrom. . . ." A change of domicile may be effected only by a combination of two elements: (a) taking up residence in a different domicile with (b) the intention to remain there.

It is clear that at the time of her marriage, Mrs. Mas was a domiciliary of the State of Mississippi. While it is generally the case that the domicile of the wife—and, consequently, her State citizenship for purposes of diversity jurisdiction—is deemed to be that of her husband, we find no precedent for extending this concept to the situation here, in which the husband is a citizen of a foreign state but resides in the United States. Indeed, such a fiction would work absurd results on the facts before us. If Mr. Mas were considered a domiciliary of France—as he would be since he had lived in Louisiana as a student-

FYI

Although the rule tying a wife's domicile to that of her husband was the rule at common law, the modern trend is to recognize that husbands and wives can have different domiciles. *See* RESTATEMENT (SECOND) OF CONFLICT OF LAWS § 21 cmt. b (Am. Law Inst. rev. 1988).

teaching assistant prior to filing this suit—then Mrs. Mas would also be deemed a domiciliary, and thus, fictionally at least, a citizen of France. She would not be a citizen of any State and could not sue in a federal court on that basis; nor could she invoke the alienage jurisdiction to bring her claim in federal court, since she is not an alien. On the other hand, if Mrs. Mas's domicile were Louisiana, she would become a Louisiana citizen for diversity purposes and could not bring suit with her husband against appellant, also a Louisiana citizen, on the basis of diversity jurisdiction. These are curious results under a rule arising from the theoretical identity of person and interest of the married couple.

An American woman is not deemed to have lost her United States citizenship solely by reason of her marriage to an alien. Similarly, we conclude that for diversity purposes a woman does not have her domicile or State citizenship changed solely by reason of her marriage to an alien.

Mrs. Mas's Mississippi domicile was disturbed neither by her year in Louisiana prior to her marriage nor as a result of the time she and her husband spent at LSU after their marriage, since for both periods she was a graduate assistant at LSU. Though she testified that after her marriage she had no intention of returning to her parents' home in Mississippi, Mrs. Mas did not effect a change of domicile since she and Mr. Mas were in Louisiana only as students and lacked the requisite intention to remain there. Until she acquires a new domicile, she remains a domiciliary, and thus a citizen, of Mississippi.[2] * * *

Thus the power of the federal district court to entertain the claims of appellees in this case stands on two separate legs of diversity jurisdiction: a claim by an alien against a State citizen; and an action between citizens of different States. We also note, however, the propriety of having the federal district court entertain a spouse's action against a defendant, where the district court already has jurisdiction over a claim, arising from the same transaction, by the other spouse against the same defendant. In the case before us, such a result is particularly desirable. The claims of Mr. and Mrs. Mas arise from the same operative facts, and there was almost complete interdependence between their claims with respect to the proof required and the issues raised at trial. Thus, since the district court had jurisdiction of Mr. Mas's action, sound judicial administration militates strongly in favor of federal jurisdiction of Mrs. Mas's claim.

Affirmed.

---

[2] The original complaint in this case was filed within several days of Mr. and Mrs. Mas's realization that they had been watched through the mirrors, quite some time before they moved to Park Ridge, Illinois. Because the district court's jurisdiction is not affected by actions of the parties subsequent to the commencement of the suit, the testimony concerning Mr. and Mrs. Mas's moves after that time is not determinative of the issue of diverse citizenship, though it is of interest insofar as it supports their lack of intent to remain permanently in Louisiana.

Points for Discussion

a. Determining Citizenship

Individuals. As revealed in *Mas v. Perry*, the key to determining the citizenship of individuals for purposes of evaluating the existence of diversity jurisdiction is to identify their respective states of domicile. The court in *Mas* repeated the definition of this concept: residence within a state (or U.S. territory) coupled with the intention to remain there for an indefinite period of time. *Mississippi Band of Choctaw Indians v. Holyfield*, 490 U.S. 30, 48 (1989) ("For adults, domicile is established by physical presence in a place in connection with a certain state of mind concerning one's intent to remain there."); *id.* ("Since most minors are legally incapable of forming the requisite intent to establish a domicile, their domicile is determined by that of their parents."); 13E C. WRIGHT & A. MILLER, FED. PRAC. & PROC. § 3615 (4th ed. 2015) (discussing various circumstances under which a minor's domicile is based on the father or the mother). A person cannot have multiple domiciles, even though she may have multiple residences. Also, once a person establishes a domicile, that is not changed until domicile is established in a new place, which requires the coincidence of residency and the requisite intent. Finally, to be considered a citizen of an American state within the meaning of the diversity statute, the individual must be a U.S. Citizen. *See Newman-Green, Inc. v. Alfonzo-Larrain*, 490 U.S. 826, 828 (1989) ("In order to be a citizen of a State within the meaning of the diversity statute, a natural person must both be a citizen of the United States and be domiciled within the State.").

Hypo 3.1

Carly, a native of New York, lived her entire life in New York until she went off to college. She attended college in California, but always intended to return to New York after she graduated, even though she voted in California elections while in school there. Upon graduation, Carly decided to go to law school in Washington, D.C., and relocated to a new apartment there. Now her plans were to complete law school and return to New York after graduation to take the bar exam and then seek employment with a New York law firm.

During Carly's second year of law school, while driving her car she hit a pedestrian on M Street in downtown Washington, killing him instantly. The victim's widow, Laurelle (a lifelong D.C. resident), filed a wrongful-death action in the U.S. District Court for the District of Columbia for $1 million. Carly moved to dismiss the action for lack of subject matter jurisdiction, arguing that no diversity exists. How should the court rule on the motion?

Corporations. A different approach is taken to determine the citizenship of corporations for purposes of the diversity statute. Under 28 U.S.C. § 1332(c)(1), "[A] corporation shall be deemed to be a citizen of every State and foreign state by which it has been incorporated and of the State or foreign state where it has its principal place of business . . . ." Thus, unlike individuals, a corporation can be a citizen of two (or more) states. Indeed, it is important to understand that for diversity jurisdiction purposes a corporation is a citizen of *all* of the places where it has citizenship; one cannot simply pick and choose a citizenship to count when analyzing diversity. For example, if a corporation has its principal place of business in New York City and is incorporated in France, it is a citizen of both New York and France, and *both* citizenships must be counted in assessing diversity of citizenship.

Take Note!

The Supreme Court has decided that a national bank, which obtains its corporate charter from the federal government rather than any state, is a citizen only of the state in which the bank has its main office. *See Wachovia Bank v. Schmidt*, 546 U.S. 303 (2006).

How is the principal place of business for a corporation determined? The Supreme Court answered that question in *Hertz Corp. v. Friend*, 559 U.S. 77 (2010) [*FLEX Case 3.A*]:

> The federal diversity jurisdiction statute provides that "a corporation shall be deemed to be a citizen of any State by which it has been incorporated *and of the State where it has its principal place of business.*" 28 U.S.C. § 1332(c)(1) (emphasis added). We seek here to resolve different interpretations that the Circuits have given this phrase. In doing so, we place primary weight upon the need for judicial administration of a jurisdictional statute to remain as simple as possible. And we conclude that the phrase "principal place of business" refers to the place where the corporation's high level officers direct, control, and coordinate the corporation's activities. Lower federal courts have often metaphorically called that place the corporation's "nerve center." We believe that the "nerve center" will typically be found at a corporation's headquarters.

As the Court indicated, prior to *Hertz* the circuits had been split on the proper interpretation of "principal place of business" in 28 U.S.C. § 1332(c)(1). There were three prevailing approaches that the Circuits followed: (1) the *nerve center* test (locus of corporate decision making authority and overall control), (2) the *corporate activities* test (location of a corporation's production or service activities), and (3) the *total activity* test (a hybrid of the previous two approaches). *See Capitol Indem. Corp. v. Russellville Steel Co.*, 367 F.3d 831, 835–36 (8th Cir. 2004) (describing each of the three tests). *Hertz* made clear that the nerve center test is the correct approach. Does this interpretation of "principal place of business" make the most sense? How is a corporation's nerve center—*i.e.*, its headquarters—supposed to be determined? *See Hertz*, 130 S. Ct. at 1194 ("[I]f the bulk of a company's business activities visible to the public take place in New Jersey, while its top officers direct those activities just across the river in New York, the 'principal place of business' is New York."). Are there any problems that you can foresee that might accompany the use of the nerve center test to determine corporate citizenship?

Unincorporated Associations. Entities such as partnerships, limited liability companies, and labor unions are not treated like corporations for diversity purposes but rather are treated as a collection of individuals. Thus, the citizenship of such entities tracks the citizenship of all constituent members of the organization. *See Lincoln Prop. Co. v. Roche, 546 U.S. 81, 84 n.1 (2005)* ("[F]or diversity purposes, a partnership entity, unlike a corporation, does not rank as a citizen[.]"); *Carden v. Arkoma Assocs., 494 U.S. 185, 189 (1990)* (same); *see also, e.g., GMAC Commercial Credit L.L.C. v. Dillard Dep't Stores, Inc., 357 F.3d 827, 828–29 (8th Cir. 2004)* (concluding that a limited liability company is assigned the citizenship of its members because of its close resemblance to a limited partnership); *Conk v. Richards & O'Neil, L.L.P., 77 F. Supp. 2d 956, 960 (S.D. Ind. 1999)* (holding that the citizenship of a limited liability partnership for diversity jurisdiction depends on the citizenship of all of its partners). Is such treatment of these organizations fair and rational? What are the practical consequences of such a rule? What is the basis for treating corporations differently than unincorporated entities?

Legal Representatives. Take note of the fact that under 28 U.S.C. § 1332(c)(2), "the legal representative of the estate of a decedent shall be deemed to be a citizen only of the same State as the decedent, and the legal representative of an infant or incompetent shall be deemed to be a citizen only of the same State as the infant or incompetent." What do you think is the rationale for this rule?

Class Actions. Class actions (covered in Chapter 7) are actions brought by a representative plaintiff on behalf of absent class members under Federal Rule 23. When determining diversity of citizenship for class actions, only the citizenship of the named class representatives are to be considered, not the citizenship of the unnamed class members. *See Devlin v. Scardelletti, 536 U.S. 1, 10 (2002)*. Why do you think that only the named class representatives are considered for the purpose of determining diversity of citizenship?

b. The Complete Diversity Requirement

In *Strawbridge v. Curtiss, 7 U.S. 267 (1806)*, the Supreme Court—per Chief Justice Marshall—held that under the statute authorizing diversity jurisdiction, to satisfy the diversity of citizenship requirement there must be what has come to be referred to as complete diversity, meaning that where citizens of the same state appear on both sides of a dispute, diversity jurisdiction is unavailable. Thus, for example, in a suit by a plaintiff from New York against two defendants, one from

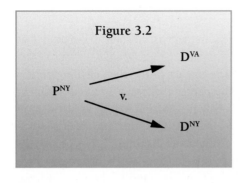

Figure 3.2

Virginia and the other from New York, there would not be complete diversity and thus diversity jurisdiction would be unavailable. This array of parties would appear as reflected in **Figure 3.2**.

Because there was some debate as to whether *Strawbridge* stood for the proposition that the complete diversity rule was a constitutional requirement, the Supreme Court, in *State Farm Fire & Cas. Co. v. Tashire*, 386 U.S. 523, 531 (1967), clarified that Chief Justice Marshall was only construing the language of the diversity statute rather than articulating a constitutional limitation on diversity jurisdiction. Thus, Article III permits the extension of federal jurisdiction to cases where parties from the same state are on both sides of the dispute so long as at least one plaintiff is diverse from at least one defendant, a circumstance referred to as **minimal diversity**. In the above example, although the presence of New Yorkers on both sides of the suit would destroy complete diversity, the presence of the Virginian does create minimal diversity. Keep in mind, however, that the diversity statute, 28 U.S.C. § 1332(a) continues to be interpreted to require complete diversity; minimal diversity—though constitutionally permissible—will not suffice in the ordinary case.

Take Note!

Under Rule 21, courts have authority to preserve complete diversity by dismissing a non-diverse party without prejudice, so long as that party is not an indispensable party as defined by Rule 19. *See Newman-Green, Inc. v. Alfonzo-Larrain*, 490 U.S. 826, 834 n.7 (1989). Rule 19, which addresses compulsory party joinder, is covered in Chapter 7.

Although minimal diversity is insufficient under the general diversity statute, Congress has availed itself of the ability to confer federal jurisdiction in cases

For More Information

For examples of statutes that require only minimal diversity as a basis for federal jurisdiction, see 28 U.S.C. § 1335 (Interpleader); 28 U.S.C. § 1369 (Multiparty, multiforum jurisdiction); 28 U.S.C. § 1332(d) (Class Action Fairness Act).*

involving only minimal diversity through statutes covering specific types of cases. Thus, if an action is initiated under an act requiring only minimal diversity, the presence of co-citizens on either side of the controversy will not undermine jurisdiction so long as there is at least one pair of adversaries from two different states.

c. The Time-of-Filing Rule

Whether the diversity of citizenship requirement is satisfied is a matter that is determined at the time that the complaint is filed. *Grupo Dataflux v. Atlas Global Grp., L.P.*, 541 U.S. 567, 569–70 (2004). The impact of the **time-of-filing rule** is that subsequent changes in citizenship of the parties that result in the destruction of complete diversity do not undermine diversity jurisdiction so long as jurisdiction

> **Example 3.1**
>
> P^{NY} v. D^{VA}. VA defendant moves to New York after the action is filed in federal court to create P^{NY} v. D^{NY}. Diversity jurisdiction is not undermined because there was complete diversity at the time of filing.

was proper at the time the action was filed. *See* **Example 3.1**. Does such a rule make sense? Conversely, there is an exception to the time-of-filing rule that permits a court to exercise jurisdiction over a dispute that initially *lacked* complete diversity if the jurisdictional defect is subsequently cured by the dismissal of the party that destroyed complete diversity. *See Grupo Dataflux*, 541 U.S. at 572.

However, post-filing changes in citizenship of the parties cannot cure a lack of diversity that existed at the time of filing. *Id.* at 575. Does this distinction make sense?

d. Collusive Joinder

Efforts to manipulate the citizenship of the parties in an effort to create (not destroy) diversity by "improperly or collusively" naming parties in the action—such as by assigning your claim to someone else, for example—are prohibited under 28 U.S.C. § 1359. *See Kramer v. Caribbean Mills, Inc.*, 394 U.S. 823, 828 (1969) (finding a non-diverse party's attempt to create diversity jurisdiction by assigning its claim to a diverse party to be a violation of 28 U.S.C. § 1359).

e. The Domestic Relations Exception

Federal courts may not hear cases seeking the issuance of a divorce, an award of spousal support, or child custody decrees. *Ankenbrandt v. Richards*, 504 U.S. 689 (1992). Why do you think this is so? The *Ankenbrandt* Court explained the rationale for the rule as follows:

> [O]ur conclusion . . . is . . . supported by sound policy considerations. Issuance of decrees of this type not infrequently involves retention of jurisdiction by the court and deployment of social workers to monitor compliance. As a matter of judicial economy, state courts are more eminently suited to work of this type than are federal courts, which lack the close association with state and local government organizations dedicated to handling issues that arise out of conflicts over divorce, alimony, and child custody decrees. Moreover, as a matter of

judicial expertise, it makes far more sense to retain the rule that federal courts lack power to issue these types of decrees because of the special proficiency developed by state tribunals over the past century and a half in handling issues that arise in the granting of such decrees.

Id. at 703–04. Is this judicially-created exception to diversity jurisdiction justified? See *Perspective & Analysis* below.

—Perspective & Analysis—

Some scholars have argued that the domestic relations exception to federal jurisdiction is not justified and have asserted that the exception reflects the low importance placed on women's issues at the federal level:

> What underlies both this lack of interest in and opposition to jurisdiction over gender-related injuries is the usually unstated and widely shared assumption that women are not relevant to the federal courts. This assumption, in turn, is fueled by an association of women with roles traditionally governed by state law (marriage, childbearing, and family care—oversimplified, a "private" world) and a corresponding association of the federal courts not with such "domestic" concerns but rather with commerce, constitutional law, federal statutory enforcement (oversimplified, a "public" world) in which men predominate.

Judith Resnik, *"Naturally" Without Gender: Women, Jurisdiction, and the Federal Courts*, 66 N.Y.U. L. Rev. 1682, 1696 (1991).

---

f. The Probate Matters Exception

Under the so-called "probate exception" to federal diversity jurisdiction, federal courts may not probate or annul a will, administer a decedent's estate, or dispose of property that is in the custody of a probate court. *Markham v. Allen,* 326 U.S. 490, 494 (1946). However, the federal courts may in some cases decide matters that do involve a state's probate laws so long as the courts are not being asked to engage in one of the activities covered by the probate matters exception described above. See *Marshall v. Marshall,* 547 U.S. 293, 310–12 (2006).

FYI

In *Marshall v. Marshall*, the petitioner was Vicki Lynn Marshall, who was better known as Anna Nicole Smith, a well-known actress and model who died in 2007. She was victorious in this case, in which the Supreme Court ruled that she could sue her deceased husband's son in federal court for tortious interference with her expected gift from her husband.

2. Alienage Jurisdiction

Before moving on to a discussion of the amount-in-controversy requirement, it is worth pausing to consider the special rules surrounding ***alienage jurisdiction***, which is a special class of diversity jurisdiction involving non-U.S. citizens ("aliens") as litigants. Recall that the diversity statute, 28 U.S.C. § 1332, provides for jurisdiction over suits involving aliens when the action involves "citizens of a State and citizens or subjects of a foreign state" or "citizens of different States and in which citizens or subjects of a foreign state are additional parties."

Thus, the statute permits diversity jurisdiction over cases involving aliens when they are aligned against a U.S. citizen or when they are simply additional parties to an action that already involves adversaries who are U.S. citizens. *See, e.g.*, *Samincorp, Inc. v. Southwire Co.*, 531 F. Supp. 1, 2–3 (N.D. Ga. 1980) (holding that diversity jurisdiction was not destroyed by the fact that subjects of a foreign state were additional parties on both sides of the action); *see also* 13E C. WRIGHT, A. MILLER & E. COOPER, FED. PRAC. & PROC. JURIS. 3D § 3604 ("[T]he language of Section 1332(a)(3) is broad enough to allow aliens to be additional parties on both sides of the dispute. Under this interpretation, jurisdiction would exist if a New Yorker, and a Canadian, sued a Californian, and a German . . . .").

However, the language of the statute does not permit aliens to be adversaries without the presence of U.S. citizens on *both sides* of the case, meaning there is no diversity jurisdiction over cases involving only an alien versus another alien, *see, e.g.*, *Universal Licensing Corp. v. Paola del Lungo S.p.A.*, 293 F.3d 579, 581 (2d Cir. 2002), or cases involving an alien against an alien and a U.S. citizen, *see Ed & Fred, Inc. v. Puritan Marine Ins. Underwriters Corp.*, 506 F.2d 757, 758 (5th Cir. 1975). **Table 3.1**, which assumes the amount in controversy requirement is satisfied, illustrates these limitations:

Table 3.1

Parties	Jurisdiction?
P^{VA} + French Citizen v. D^{NY} + German Citizen	Yes
P^{VA} v. German Citizen	Yes
P^{VA} v. D^{NY} + German Citizen	Yes
French Citizen v. German Citizen	No
French Citizen v. D^{NY} + German Citizen	No
P^{VA} + French Citizen v. D^{NY} + French Citizen	Yes

Note the final entry in the table, which clarifies that there is no requirement that aliens in the action be citizens of different foreign states; having fellow citizens of a common foreign country on both sides of an action will not destroy the diversity created by the citizenship of the parties who are U.S. citizens.

An important part of doing a proper analysis here is recognizing that entities— including corporations—can be citizens of multiple places, in which case each location is counted for the diversity analysis. Thus, if a corporation is incorporated in London and headquartered in New York, it is a citizen both of the United Kingdom and of New York. What this means is that if the aforementioned corporation sues or is sued by an alien in federal court, there will not be any diversity jurisdiction because there will be alien citizenship on both sides of the dispute without a U.S. citizen also on both sides. **Figure 3.3** illustrates this point.

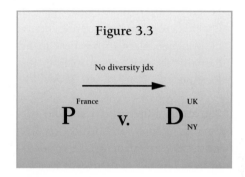

Figure 3.3

No diversity jdx

France   UK
P   v.   D
                      NY

Points for Discussion

a. Permanent Resident Aliens

What happens if the alien involved in the action happens to be a permanent resident alien living in the United States? According to the diversity statute "the district courts shall not have original jurisdiction under this subsection of an action between citizens of a State and citizens or subjects of a foreign state who are lawfully admitted for permanent residence in the United States and are domiciled in the same State." 28 U.S.C. § 1332(a)(2). Thus, even though there ordinarily would be jurisdiction between a U.S. citizen domiciled in a U.S. state and an alien, if that alien has permanent resident status and is domiciled in that same state, there can be no diversity jurisdiction under § 1332(a)(2). Note, however, that permanent resident aliens are still treated as aliens when aligned against other aliens or U.S. citizens domiciled in different states. Thus, an action by a permanent resident alien from France residing in Connecticut against a foreign company based in Germany would not qualify for diversity jurisdiction because there would be aliens on both sides of the action without U.S. citizen coparties on both sides. **Figure 3.4** illustrates this point.

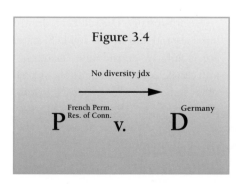

Figure 3.4

No diversity jdx

French Perm.   Germany
P Res. of Conn.   v.   D

Again, to be clear, the permanent resident alien status of a party is completely meaningless for purposes of diversity jurisdiction unless their adversary is a U.S. citizen *from that same State*. Otherwise, ignore the permanent resident status and treat them as you would any other alien. Permanent resident alien status does not turn that alien into a U.S. citizen for diversity purposes.

Hypo 3.2

Javier, a citizen of Arizona, was scheduled to have a business meeting in Phoenix, Arizona, with representatives of Alliance, a French Company with its principal place of business in France. Alliance graciously sent a driver, Bernard, to pick Javier up from his home to drive Javier to the meeting's location.

Bernard is a French citizen who relocated to the United States to work full time in Arizona for Alliance. He lives in Arizona and has recently acquired status as a permanent U.S. resident. Unfortunately, after picking up Javier from his home, Bernard was in a car accident in which Javier was severely injured. Javier brings suit in federal court in Arizona against Bernard and Alliance. Does this action satisfy the diversity of citizenship requirement of § 1332?

---

b. Stateless Persons & Entities

A final note on alienage jurisdiction: actions involving non-U.S. citizens who are not citizens or subjects of any foreign state—so-called "stateless" persons—do not qualify for federal diversity jurisdiction under 28 U.S.C. § 1332. *See Blair Holdings Corp. v. Rubinstein,* 133 F. Supp. 496, 501–02 (S.D.N.Y. 1955); 13E C. WRIGHT, A. MILLER & E. COOPER, FED. PRAC. & PROC. JURIS. 3d § 3604 ("[T]here is no jurisdiction over a suit between a citizen of the United States and a person who is not a citizen of any country.").

Go Online

The stateless person involved in *Blair Holdings* was the holder of a "Nansen Passport," a document issued by the League of Nations to stateless refugees during the mid-20th century. For more information, visit http://en.wikipedia.org/wiki/Nansen_passport.

Additionally, U.S. citizens domiciled abroad and not in any U.S. state are similarly considered "stateless" and can be considered neither citizens of a state nor aliens. *See Newman-Green, Inc. v. Alfonzo-Larrain,* 490 U.S. 826, 828 (1989) ("In order to be a citizen of a State within the meaning of the diversity statute, a natural person must be both a citizen of the United States *and* be domiciled within the State. The problem in this case is that Bettison, although a

United States citizen, has no domicile in any State. He is therefore 'stateless' for purposes of § 1332(a)(3)." (emphasis in original)); *Cresswell v. Sullivan & Cromwell*, 922 F.2d 60 (2d Cir. 1990) ("United States citizens who are domiciled abroad are neither citizens of any state of the United States nor citizens or subjects of a foreign state, and § 1332(a) does not provide that the courts have jurisdiction over a suit to which such persons are parties.").

> **FYI**
>
> For purposes of diversity jurisdiction, dual citizens of the United States and another country are treated as U.S. citizens. *See Frett-Smith v. Vanterpool,* 511 F.3d 396, 400 (3d Cir. 2008) ("[F]or purposes of diversity jurisdiction, only the American nationality of a dual national is recognized.").

Finally, American Indian Tribes, as domestic sovereigns, are not considered citizens of any state and thus cannot sue or be sued in diversity. *Romanella v. Hayward*, 114 F.3d 15, 16 (2d Cir. 1997) ("[A]n Indian tribe is not a citizen of any state for purposes of diversity jurisdiction."). However, federal question jurisdiction remains a possibility. *See, e.g.*, *Beneficial Nat'l Bank v. Anderson*, 539 U.S. 1, 8 n.4 (2003). ("This Court has also held that federal courts have subject-matter jurisdiction to hear possessory land claims under state law brought by Indian tribes because of the uniquely federal 'nature and source of the possessory rights of Indian tribes.) (quoting *Oneida Indian Nation of N.Y. State v. County of Oneida*, 414 U.S. 661, 667 (1974))). *See also* 28 U.S.C. § 1362 (granting jurisdiction over claims by federally recognized Indian tribes asserting claims under the Constitution, laws, or treaties of the United States).

The presence of any of the various kinds of stateless persons or entities mentioned above as parties in an action will destroy diversity and undermine the diversity jurisdiction of a court. *See, e.g.*, *Frazier v. Brophy*, 358 Fed. App'x 212, 213 (2d Cir. 2009) ("Because an Indian Tribe is not a citizen of any state, the Oneida Nation's presence as a party bars a federal court from hearing the matter under its diversity jurisdiction.").

3. The Amount-in-Controversy Requirement

Once diversity of citizenship is established, the amount in controversy between the parties must *exceed* $75,000. 28 U.S.C. § 1332(a). How is the amount in controversy determined?

Del Vecchio v. Conseco, Inc.

U.S. Court of Appeals for the Seventh Circuit
230 F.3d 974 (7th Cir. 2000)

DIANE P. WOOD, CIRCUIT JUDGE.

At one time, Elio Del Vecchio held a $5,000 whole life insurance policy issued by Bankers National Life Insurance Company (Bankers Life). Many years later, he turned it in and replaced it with a $10,000 universal life policy. He thought, in essence, that he could transform the $5,000 policy into the $10,000 policy for free. When that turned out not to be true, he sued Conseco, Bankers Life, and Great American Reserve Insurance Company for defrauding him by inducing him to make the trade. Del Vecchio's suit was brought on behalf of himself and other purchasers of the defendants' life insurance products who had been similarly defrauded.

> **FYI**
>
> The amount-in-controversy requirement when Congress first granted diversity jurisdiction in the Judiciary Act of 1789 was $500. Congress has successively raised this amount to $2,000 in 1887, to $3,000 in 1911, to $10,000 in 1958, to $50,000 in 1988, and to $75,000 in 1996, a rate of growth that outstrips the inflation rate for the same period.

Because we find that the federal courts do not have jurisdiction over this case, it must be dismissed on that basis. * * * The district court granted the defendants' motion for summary judgment on the basis that the statutes of limitations for Del Vecchio's various claims had run. Del Vecchio appeals.

II

In his complaint, Del Vecchio asserted that federal jurisdiction was proper under 28 U.S.C. § 1332 * * * . But in order to support jurisdiction under § 1332, two requirements must be satisfied: complete diversity of citizenship between the plaintiffs and the defendants, and the proper amount in controversy (now and when Del Vecchio sued, more than $75,000). Del Vecchio's problem is not the citizenship requirement, as the parties are clearly diverse * * * . Rather, Del Vecchio's difficulty lies in meeting the amount in controversy requirement.

Snyder v. Harris, 394 U.S. 332 (1969), held that FED. R. CIV. P. 23 does not alter the general rule that multiple persons' claims cannot be combined to reach the minimum amount in controversy. * * * [A]s we now explain, Del Vecchio's suit cannot proceed under *Snyder*.

Del Vecchio's complaint included the following allegations about the amount in controversy:

The amount-in-controversy exceeds $75,000, exclusive of interests and costs. Specifically, Plaintiff has alleged unjust enrichment and seeks the imposition of a constructive trust. As a result, he has an undivided interest in the full recovery in this action, which will substantially exceed the necessary jurisdictional amount.

From the language of his pleading, it appears that Del Vecchio was trying to evade *Snyder* by framing the amount in controversy in terms of what the defendants would have at stake if the class action were certified: their total unjust enrichment over which Del Vecchio seeks the imposition of a constructive trust. (Presumably, he is proposing to act as the trustee for the other class members.) Del Vecchio's theory, however, amounts to a complete end-run around the principles enunciated in *Snyder.* While this court has adopted the "either viewpoint" approach (that is, the amount in controversy can be determined from either the plaintiff's or the defendant's viewpoint), we have none-

> **What's That?**
>
> Class actions are suits in which named representative plaintiffs proceed on behalf of similarly situated—but absent—others. *See* FED. R. CIV. P. 23. Class actions will be discussed in Chapter 7.

theless maintained that "[w]hatever the form of relief sought, each plaintiff's claim must be held separate from each other plaintiff's claim from both the plaintiff's and the defendant's standpoint." That means, for Del Vecchio, that the amount in controversy from the defendants' point of view is the amount they risk paying him, not the amount they might have to pay the entire class.

Furthermore, this case does not fit into the narrow exceptions to the anti-aggregation rule recognized by the *Snyder* Court. It is not a case where there is one res at issue, such as an estate. In those cases, it is proper to consider the value of the entire res for purposes of determining jurisdiction, for even if several plaintiffs have a claim to it, the recovery is nonetheless a unitary whole that must then be divided. This is not such a situation, as each of the insureds Del Vecchio wants to represent is entitled to his or her own separate recovery. Under *Snyder,* Del Vecchio simply cannot satisfy the amount in controversy requirement by framing it in terms of the aggregate amount by which Bankers Life and the other defendants have been unjustly enriched through their insurance contracts with the various unnamed class members.

Noting this problem with jurisdiction, and our duty to dismiss the case if jurisdiction is lacking, we asked the parties to submit supplemental briefing regarding the amount in controversy. Del Vecchio responded by claiming that not only he, but each and every class member, would be able to assert such high punitive damages in good faith that each class member individually would meet the amount required by § 1332, and that the total amount in controversy has ballooned to $1.5 billion. The defendant insurance companies also appear to rely on the availability of punitive damages, as we explain below, though they principally complain that everyone proceeded in good faith below and that they do not wish to lose their favorable judgment on the merits.

We have no quarrel in principle with the idea that punitive damages may sometimes be taken into account in deciding whether the proper amount is in controversy. As we have written before:

> [w]here punitive damages are required to satisfy the jurisdictional amount in a diversity case, a two-part inquiry is necessary. The first question is whether punitive damages are recoverable as a matter of state law. If the answer is yes, the court has subject matter jurisdiction unless it is clear "beyond a legal certainty that the plaintiff would under no circumstances be entitled to recover the jurisdictional amount."

> Generally, we give plaintiffs the benefit of the doubt in these matters, but a complaint will be dismissed if it "appear[s] to a legal certainty that the claim is really for less than the jurisdictional amount." And a claim for actual damages that vastly exceeds the apparent amount at stake * * * and asserts a right to punitive damages at the far upper end of the possible distribution of outcomes must be assessed critically; otherwise, the statutory limits on federal court jurisdiction could be undermined.

Make the Connection

Fraud is a **Tort** concept that refers to an intentional deception that causes harm to the plaintiff. *Breach of fiduciary duty* is the violation of a legal obligation to act for another's benefit. You will most likely encounter this latter concept in a basic **Corporations** course, but you may cover it in **Torts** or **Trusts & Estates** as well.

Indiana does allow the award of punitive damages for fraud and breach of fiduciary duty, and so the first of the two requirements mentioned above is met. Whether we have jurisdiction, then, depends on whether, "to a legal certainty," we are convinced that Del Vecchio is not entitled to damages sufficient to meet the amount in controversy requirement. In cases where the defendants contest punitive damage allegations, we require the plaintiff to support its claim with "competent proof," lest fanciful claims for punitive damages end up defeating the statute's requirement of a particular amount in controversy. Here, in the lower court the defendants were certainly challenging Del Vecchio's substantive claims to entitlement to punitive damages; their accommodating attitude did not arise until their supplemental briefs on appeal, at which point they found themselves in the slightly odd position of urging that Del Vecchio indeed had substantial claims for both actual and punitive damages. We think it appropriate to review the new punitive damage allegations with the same level of scrutiny that we would give such allegations had they been contested for jurisdictional purposes below.

The defendants now assert that Del Vecchio's compensatory damages could be as much as $15,000: $5,000 for the policy he traded in and $10,000 for the policy he bought. The defendants then reason that because Del Vecchio's complaint includes claims for which Indiana law provides punitive damages may be available, it is entirely possible that punitive damages exceeding $60,000 would be awarded. This, we assume, is not because they are conceding that their behavior might rationally be seen by anyone as sufficiently culpable to deserve such an award; it is only an observation that a 4 to 1 ratio of punitive to compensatory damages is not uncommon for these sorts of claims under Indiana law.

Food for Thought

Why do you think the defendants here are arguing in favor of federal jurisdiction on appeal, something you might ordinarily expect defendants to oppose? What benefit might they derive from a finding that diversity jurisdiction exists?

This seems like sheer speculation to us, however, and we do not find it a persuasive reason to conclude that Del Vecchio individually has alleged a claim exceeding $75,000 in value. And in any event, it is Del Vecchio who bears the burden of proving that the case is properly in federal court, as it is he who is trying to invoke federal jurisdiction. But his theory of jurisdiction fares no better than that of the defendants. Originally, Del Vecchio took an approach similar to theirs. In his motion in opposition to summary judgment, Del Vecchio listed two types of damages: the shortfall between the cash value guaranteed by the policy and the actual cash value (which between 1994 and 1997 amounted to $4,879) and the failure of the defendants to pay interest on the policy at fair market rate (no figure is given for this amount, but given the small dollar amounts at stake, it cannot be substantial). Being very generous on the up-side, Del Vecchio's total damages under this theory hover somewhere between $5,000 and $10,000—plainly far short of what he needs.

In his supplemental brief on appeal, Del Vecchio abandons this theory for an entirely different tack. He now asserts * * * that his compensatory damages amount to a mere $600, which represents the amount of the cash value lost between the years 1988 and 1996. On top of that modest figure, he claims that a punitive damage award in the * * * amount of $75,000 (a ratio of 125 to 1) would be appropriate here. * * *

Although it is not unheard of for Indiana courts to uphold punitive damage awards that exceed the underlying compensatory awards by several multiples, a multiplier of 125 lies at the very outer edge of awards that have been allowed. * * * "[A] punitive damage recovery in such a large multiple of a compensatory recovery as 125 times stretches the normal ratio, and would face certain remittitur. Considering the nature of their claim and the amount of the potential compensatory damage awards on that claim, a punitive damages recovery if rendered for the amount necessary to exceed $75,000 would be excessive." * * * [Del Vecchio's] individual claim does not meet the requirement of § 1332 that more than $75,000 must be at stake * * * .

What's That?

Remittitur refers to the judicial reduction of a jury award because it exceeds an acceptable amount. The Supreme Court has indicated that excessive punitive damages awards are subject to remittitur under the Due Process Clause. *See* BMW of N. Am., Inc. v. Gore, 517 U.S. 559, 568 (1996).

III

While we are not unsympathetic to the waste of effort represented by a case that has been fully litigated in the wrong court, both the Supreme Court and we ourselves have noted time and again that subject matter jurisdiction is a fundamental limitation on the power of a federal court to act. Once it appears, as it has here, that subject matter jurisdiction is lacking, only one path lies open to us. We hereby VACATE the order dismissing the action on the merits and REMAND the case with orders to dismiss it for want of federal subject matter jurisdiction.

Points for Discussion

a.   The Basic Amount-in-Controversy Requirement

For a claim to qualify for diversity jurisdiction, it must satisfy the amount-in-controversy requirement of 28 U.S.C. § 1332. This cannot ordinarily be done with the assistance of the defendant's counterclaim. *See, e.g.,* Davis v. Mutual of Omaha Ins. Co., 290 F. Supp. 217 (W.D. Mo. 1968) (where plaintiff's complaint does not involve the jurisdictional amount, defendant's counterclaim could not supply it).

Be sure to recognize that the diversity statute requires that the amount in controversy *exceed* $75,000. Thus, claims for $75,000 will be jurisdictionally insufficient. *See* Freeland v. Liberty Mut. Fire Ins. Co., 632 F.3d 250 (6th Cir. 2011). Also, as *Del Vecchio* makes clear, although punitive damages may be included and the amount of the plaintiff's total claim for damages controls the analysis, the amount claimed must be made in good faith; only when it appears "to a legal certainty" that the claim is actually for a jurisdictionally insufficient amount should a court dismiss the matter on jurisdictional grounds. St. Paul Mercury Indem. Co. v. Red Cab Co., 303 U.S.

283, 288–89 (1938); *see also Kalick v. Nw. Airlines Corp.*, 372 F. App'x 317, 321–22 (3d Cir. 2010) (denying jurisdiction where plaintiff claimed $1,433.59 in compensatory damages and $161,600 in punitive damages based on the likelihood that the punitive damages amount was unconstitutionally excessive); *Geographic Expeditions, Inc. v. Estate of Lhotka ex rel. Lhotka*, 599 F.3d 1102, 1108 (9th Cir. 2010) (finding that a $16,831 contractual damages cap did not create a "legal certainty" of an insufficient amount in controversy; "[J]ust because a defendant might have a valid defense that will reduce recovery to below the jurisdictional amount does not mean the defendant will ultimately prevail on that defense"). Did the court in *Del Vecchio* adhere to this standard?

Food for Thought

Why do you think Congress has imposed an amount-in-controversy requirement for diversity cases? Note that Congress abolished the amount-in-controversy requirement for federal question cases (discussed below) in 1980.

b.   Exclusion of Interest and Costs

Section 1332 states that the amount in controversy must be calculated "exclusive of interest and costs." It is important to understand that the interest referred to here is not the contract interest one pays on a loan, nor is it the type of interest that my be imposed by statute as a penalty. *See, e.g., Watson v. Provident Life & Acc. Ins. Co.*, 2009 WL 1437823, at *5 (N.D. Tex. May 22, 2009) (treating statutory interest as damages or a penalty based on legislative intent). Rather, excluded interest is the prejudgment interest a plaintiff seeks to compensate it for any delay in payment on a debt due. *See, e.g., Sauer v. Prudential Ins. Co. of Am.*, 2011 WL 5117772, *2 (C.D. Cal. Oct. 28, 2011) ("[P]rejudgment interest [is] expressly prohibited from inclusion in the amount in controversy requirement."); *Wilmoth v. Celadon Trucking Services, Inc.*, 2015 WL 1537209, at *2 (S.D. Ind. Apr. 6, 2015) ("[I]nterest that becomes due because of a delay in payment . . . should be exclude[d] from the amount in controversy requirement.").

The costs that are excluded from the amount-in-controversy calculation are those of the kind referenced in 28 U.S.C. § 1920, such as clerk's fees, docket fees, or fees for printing, copying and procuring witnesses. *See, e.g., Waller v. Wal-Mart Stores, Inc.*, 2002 WL 34504722, at *2 (N.D. Tex. Mar. 4, 2002) ("[C]opying costs are taxable costs under 28 U.S.C. § 1920(4) and thus, under the express provisions of § 1332(a), cannot be considered in determining the amount in controversy."). Attorneys' fees are not excluded as costs and may thus be included in the amount-in-controversy determination. *Guglielmino v. McKee Foods Corp.*, 506 F.3d 696, 700 (9th Cir. 2007) ("Section 1332(a)'s amount-in-controversy requirement excludes only 'interest and costs' and therefore includes attorneys' fees.").

c. Injunction Cases

How should courts measure the amount in controversy when injunctive relief is being sought rather than damages? Courts primarily look either at the value of the relief to the plaintiff or at the cost such relief would impose on the defendant. *See McCarty v. Amoco Pipeline Co.*, 595 F.2d 389, 391–92 (7th Cir. 1979) (discussing the various approaches to valuing injunctive relief); *see also Leonard v. Enter. Rent a Car*, 279 F.3d 967, 973 (11th Cir. 2002) ("The value of injunctive or declaratory relief for amount in controversy purposes is the monetary value of the object of the litigation that would flow to the plaintiffs if the injunction were granted.").

d. Aggregation

To what extent may a plaintiff or plaintiffs combine or aggregate their claims against a single defendant or multiple defendants to reach the jurisdictionally required amount? There is only one true circumstance where separate claims may be aggregated to satisfy the amount-in-controversy requirement: A party may aggregate its multiple claims against another party. *Snyder v. Harris*, 394 U.S. 332, 335 (1969) ("Aggregation has been permitted only [ ] in cases in which a single plaintiff seeks to aggregate two or more of his own claims against a single defendant . . . ."). In **Figure 3.5**, the plaintiff is permitted to add the two separate claims—regardless of whether they are related or unrelated to one another—to satisfy section 1332's amount-in-controversy requirement.

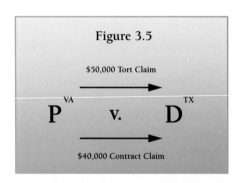

Figure 3.5

$50,000 Tort Claim

VA   TX
P   v.   D

$40,000 Contract Claim

Unlike an individual plaintiff, multiple plaintiffs may not add their claims together for purposes of calculating the amount in controversy.[*] *Snyder*, 394 U.S. at 335 ("The traditional judicial interpretation under all of these statutes [granting diversity jurisdiction] has been from the beginning that the separate and distinct claims of two or more plaintiffs cannot be aggregated in order to satisfy the jurisdictional amount requirement."). Neither may a party aggregate separate and distinct claims it asserts against multiple defendants. *Citizens' Bank of Louisiana v. Cannon*, 164 U.S. 319, 322 (1896) ("[J]urisdiction cannot be conferred . . . by joining in one bill against distinct defendants claims no one of which reached the jurisdictional amount."); *Jewell v. Grain Dealers Mut. Ins. Co.*, 290 F.2d 11, 13 (5th Cir. 1961) ("[W]here a suit is brought against several defendants asserting claims

---

[*] Here we are only talking about the prohibition against aggregating damages to reach the required jurisdictional amount (greater than $75,000). Multiple plaintiffs may join together to pursue distinct but factually-related claims against a common defendant under Rule 20. This and other joinder rules will be discussed in Chapter 7. [Ed.]

against each of them which are separate and distinct, the test of jurisdiction is the amount of each claim, and not their aggregate." (citations and internal quotation marks omitted)).

In addition to the circumstance where a single party may aggregate its distinct claims against another party, courts will refer to two other instances where aggregation is permitted, but this can be confusing for students because aggregation is not really happening there. The first is when multiple parties assert claims based on a common undivided interest, such as joint ownership of property. For example, if two people own a $100,000 house as joint tenants (as opposed to as tenants in common), and the defendant is alleged to have burned down that house, the claim of the two homeowners is not $50,000 each but a

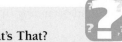

What's That?

Joint tenancy is a type of ownership where each owner owns 100% of the property, whereas *tenancy in common* is a type of ownership where each owner owns a distinct, alienable percentage or share of the property. You will study these and other types of ownership in a **Property** course.

common, undivided $100,000. No aggregation is occurring here, but courts will use the language of aggregation to refer to this situation as an example of when it is permitted. <u>Snyder, 394 U.S. at 335</u> ("Aggregation has been permitted . . . in cases in which two or more plaintiffs unite to enforce a single title or right in which they have a common and undivided interest."). Students should not confuse the aforementioned situation with an action where multiple plaintiffs assert separate but related claims against a common defendant; the fact that two plaintiffs have claims that arise out of the same incident or contract does not make them claims that arise out of a common, undivided interest. Thus, such claims may not be aggregated to reach the jurisdictional amount.

The other additional circumstance when courts will say that aggregation is permitted is when a plaintiff asserts claims against a multiple defendants based on joint-and-several liability. *See, e.g.* <u>Morrison v. Allstate Indem. Co., 228 F.3d 1255, 1263 n. 7 (11th Cir. 2000)</u> ("Claims against multiple defendants can only be aggregated when the defendants are jointly liable to the plaintiff."). But in truth, it is not that the plaintiff in such a case has two, say, $50,000 claims against each of two defendants but, rather, that the plaintiff has one $100,000 claim against each of the defendants, jointly and severally. This does not mean that the plaintiff is seeking a total of $200,000; it simply means that each defendant could

Make the Connection

You will study joint-and-several liability in a **Torts** course.

be held responsible individually for the entirety of the $100,000 claim regardless of each defendant's share of the liability.

Note that these restrictions on aggregation are based on interpretations of the diversity statute and are not constitutional in nature, meaning Congress is free to alter or deviate from them through legislation. Do these rules make sense? Can you identify situations in which each rule would apply? The following hypos test your understanding of these principles.

Hypo 3.3

John initiated an action in federal court against George for defamation, seeking $45,000 in damages. In the same action John also asserted a claim against George for breach of contract, seeking $40,000 in damages. John is a citizen of Massachusetts. George is a citizen of Texas. George moves to dismiss the action for lack of subject matter jurisdiction. How should the court rule on the motion?

Hypo 3.4

A car driver and passenger from State A were hit by a truck and severely injured. The car driver and the passenger initiated an action in State A federal court, as co-plaintiffs, against the truck driver, a State B citizen, for negligence arising from the car accident. The car driver sought $50,000 in damages, while the passenger sought $30,000 in damages. May the court exercise subject matter jurisdiction over the two claims in this action?

As the court in *Del Vecchio* noted, the Supreme Court in <u>*Snyder v. Harris*, 394 U.S. 332 (1969)</u>, held that <u>Rule 23</u>—which provides for class actions—does not overcome the rule against multiple plaintiffs being able to aggregate their claims to reach the jurisdictional amount. The Court also has ruled that under the diversity statute and <u>Rule 23</u>, even if a class consists of members whose claims do satisfy the jurisdictional amount, other class members with jurisdictionally insufficient claims could not piggyback on the qualifying claims. <u>*Zahn v. Int'l Paper Co.*, 414 U.S. 291, 294–95 (1973)</u>. However, in <u>*Exxon Mobil Corp. v. Allapattah Services, Inc.*, 545 U.S. 546 (2005)</u>, the Court

Food for Thought

If class action plaintiffs seek punitive damages, should the aggregate amount be considered for purposes of satisfying the amount-in-controversy requirement? *See* <u>*Smith v. GTE Corp.*, 236 F.3d 1292, 1304 (11th Cir. 2001)</u> ("[T]he class claim for punitive damages . . . may not be viewed in the aggregate for amount in controversy purposes, but instead must be divided pro rata among each class member.").

held that under the federal supplemental jurisdiction statute, <u>28 U.S.C. § 1367</u>, insufficient claims may enjoy federal jurisdiction on the basis of jurisdictionally sufficient claims asserted by fellow plaintiffs. The supplemental jurisdiction statute will be covered in more detail below in <u>Section C</u>.

Although most circuits have concluded that a plaintiff's claim may not be aggregated with a defendant's counterclaim to satisfy the amount-in-controversy requirement, both the Third and Tenth Circuits have allowed it if the counterclaim is compulsory. *See <u>Spectacor Management Grp. v. Brown</u>, 131 F.3d 120 (3rd Cir. 1997)* (compulsory counterclaim filed by defendant will satisfy jurisdictional amount if defendant elects not to file a motion to dismiss); <u>*Geoffrey E. Macpherson, Ltd. v. Brine-cell, Inc.*, 98 F.3d 1241, 1245 n.2 (10th Cir. 1996)</u> (defendant's compulsory counterclaim can be included in jurisdictional amount). But, this is the minority approach. *See, e.g., <u>Cent. Associated Carriers v. Nickelberry</u>, 995 F. Supp. 1031, 1036 (W.D. Mo. 1998)* ("[T]he logical and majority rule is that the question of jurisdictional amount is based upon the plaintiff's Petition or Complaint and jurisdiction cannot be invoked by the filing of a counterclaim in the jurisdictional amount, even though such counterclaim is compulsory under state law.").* 14AA C. WRIGHT, A. MILLER & E. COOPER, FED. PRAC. & PROC. § <u>3706</u> (4th ed. 2011); 14C C. WRIGHT, A. MILLER, E. COOPER & J. STEINMAN, FED. PRAC. & PROC. § <u>3725.3</u> (4th ed. 2009).

What's That?

A *compulsory counterclaim* is a claim that a defendant has against a plaintiff that arises out of the same transaction or occurrence as the plaintiff's claim against that defendant. These must be asserted or they are waived. Rule 13(a) governs these claims and will be covered in <u>Chapter 7</u> (Joinder).

e.   The Need for Diversity Jurisdiction

It is often said that diversity jurisdiction was originally conceived as a means of providing out-of-state litigants with a neutral forum that would be free from the biases state courts were feared to have in favor of their own citizens. Does this rationale still justify diversity jurisdiction? See *Perspective & Analysis* below. Although the amount-in-controversy requirement has increased over the years to its present amount, Congress has not seen fit to abolish diversity jurisdiction, even though diversity cases consume a good portion of the judicial resources of the federal courts.

---

* The Fifth Circuit in <u>*Liberty Mut. Ins. Co. v. Horton*, 275 F.2d 148 (5th Cir. 1960)</u>, *aff'd*, <u>367 U.S. 348 (1961)</u>, appeared to embrace this rule as well, although it has not since applied the rule and lower courts within the Fifth Circuit have cast doubt on its continuing viability. *See, e.g., <u>Thrash v. New England Mut. Life Ins. Co.</u>, 534 F. Supp. 2d 691, 695 n.2 (S.D. Miss. 2008)* ("The Fifth Circuit's decision in *Horton* was rendered nearly fifty years ago, and in that time, only one other Fifth Circuit case has cited *Horton* for the proposition that the counterclaim and main claim may be aggregated to satisfy the amount in controversy, and even [there], the counterclaim was itself in an amount in excess of the jurisdictional minimum, and the reference to the aggregation rule recited in *Horton* appeared as dictum.").

—Perspective & Analysis—

What is the rationale for continuing to entertain state-law disputes in federal courts based on diversity jurisdiction? Would federal courts be better served by focusing on matters of federal concern? Here is one commentator's argument in favor of abolishing diversity jurisdiction:

> The most straightforward reason to eliminate diversity jurisdiction [is because doing so] will significantly reduce the caseload problem in the federal courts. . . . [A] number of additional reasons support [abolishing diversity jurisdiction]. *First,* . . . no other major class of cases has a weaker claim on federal juridical resources. . . . *Second,* . . . [f]ederal courts are capable of deciding state law questions, but they offer no special advantages in such cases; . . . the state courts have greater expertise and authority. . . . *Third,* diversity jurisdiction is frequently a source of friction between state and federal courts. . . . *Fourth,* . . . complex procedural problems . . . make it more expensive and time-consuming to litigate diversity cases.

Larry Kramer, *Diversity Jurisdiction*, 1990 BYU L. Rev. 97, 102–05.

f. The Class Action Fairness Act

In 2005, Congress passed the Class Action Fairness Act ("CAFA"), which extends federal jurisdiction to class actions in which there are at least 100 class members, class members' claims in the aggregate total more than $5,000,000, and any class member is diverse from any defendant (minimal diversity). Why do you think Congress expanded federal jurisdiction in this way? The Class Action Fairness Act will be discussed in greater detail in Chapter 7.

For More Information

To learn more about the Class Action Fairness Act, see Alan B. Morrison, *Removing Class Actions to Federal Court: A Better Way to Handle the Problem of Overlapping Class Actions,* 57 STAN. L. REV. 1521 (2005). *See also* S. REP. No. 109–14, 109th Cong., 1st Sess. 2005, 2005 U.S.C.C.A.N. 3, 2005 WL 627977 (Feb. 28, 2005).

B. Federal Question Jurisdiction

In the previous section, we looked at the scope of federal courts' power to hear cases involving some degree of diversity of citizenship among the parties. In this section we turn to federal question jurisdiction, the authority of federal courts to hear cases involving federal constitutional, statutory, or treaty law. Article III, § 2 of the Constitution extends the judicial power "to all Cases, in Law and Equity, arising under this Constitution, the Laws of the United States, and Treaties . . . ."

As discussed earlier, Article III is not self-executing but rather simply sets forth the broad contours of judicial authority that Congress may assign to lower federal courts as it sees fit. Although Congress did so to a limited extent when, for example, it gave federal courts jurisdiction over patent and copyright cases, *see* Act of Feb. 15, 1819, ch. 19, 3 Stat. 481, and actions under the revenue laws, *see* Act of Mar. 2, 1833, ch. 57, 4 Stat. 632, it was not until 1875 that Congress enacted legislation conferring jurisdiction over all federal law cases on lower federal courts. *See* Act of Mar. 3, 1875, ch. 137, § 1, 18 Stat. 470. Today, this grant of authority can be found in the general federal question statute, 28 U.S.C. § 1331, which reads as follows:

Federal Question Jurisdiction: 28 U.S.C. § 1331

The district courts shall have original jurisdiction of all civil actions arising under the Constitution, laws, or treaties of the United States.

1. The Constitutional Standard

Although the language of the statute is nearly identical to the language used in Article III, the Supreme Court has interpreted the two passages differently. The Court in *Osborn v. Bank of the United States*, 22 U.S. 738 (1824), provided its interpretation of Article III through an opinion by Chief Justice Marshall:

Osborn v. Bank of the United States

Supreme Court of the United States
22 U.S. (9 Wheat.) 738 (1824)

MR. CHIEF JUSTICE MARSHALL delivered the opinion of the Court

[The Bank of the United States sued in federal court to obtain an injunction restraining an Ohio state official (Osborn) from collecting a tax on the Bank that the Bank felt was unconstitutional. The federal statute creating the Bank authorized federal jurisdiction in all cases involving the Bank. The question before the Court here was whether that statutory grant was constitutional under Article III.]

FYI

The abbreviated word located within the citation for *Osborn* refers to the name of the Reporter of Decisions at the time, Henry Wheaton. More information on the Reporters of Decisions is available at en.wikipedia. org/wiki/U.S._Supreme_Court_ Reporter_of_Decisions.

When a Bank sues, the first question which presents itself, and which lies at the foundation of the cause, is, has this legal entity a right to sue? Has it a right to come, not into this Court particularly, but into any Court? This depends on a law of the United States. The next question is, has this being a right to make this particular contract? If this question be decided in the negative, the cause is determined against the plaintiff; and this question, too, depends entirely on a law of the United States. These are important questions, and they exist in every possible case. The right to sue, if decided once, is decided for ever; but the power of Congress was exercised antecedently to the first decision on that right, and if it was constitutional then, it cannot cease to be so, because the particular question is decided. It may be revived at the will of the party, and most probably would be renewed, were the tribunal to be changed. But the question respecting the right to make a particular contract, or to acquire a particular property, or to sue on account of a particular injury, belongs to every particular case, and may be renewed in every case. The question forms an original ingredient in every cause. Whether it be in fact relied on or not, in the defence, it is still a part of the cause, and may be relied on. The right of the plaintiff to sue, cannot depend on the defence which the defendant may choose to set up. His right to sue is anterior to that defence, and must depend on the state of things when the action is brought. The questions which the case involves, then, must determine its character, whether those questions be made in the cause or not.

The appellants say, that the case arises on the contract; but the validity of the contract depends on a law of the United States, and the plaintiff is compelled, in every case, to show its validity. The case arises emphatically under the law. The act of Congress is its foundation. The contract could never have been made, but under the authority of that act. The act itself is the first ingredient in the case, is its origin, is that from which every other part arises. That other questions may also arise, as the execution of the contract, or its performance, cannot change the case, or give it any other origin than the charter of incorporation. The action still originates in, and is sustained by, that charter.

———————

Points for Discussion

a. *Osborn*'s View of Article III

According to Chief Justice Marshall in *Osborn*, under Article III Congress may confer jurisdiction whenever a federal question forms an "ingredient" of the claim. As later explained by Justice Frankfurter, the "arising under" clause of Article III as interpreted by the Court in *Osborn* gives Congress the flexibility to confer federal question jurisdiction "whenever there exists in the background some federal proposition that might be challenged, despite the remoteness of the likelihood of actual presentation of such a federal question." *Textile Workers Union of Am. v. Lincoln Mills of Ala.*, 353 U.S. 448, 471 (1957) (Frankfurter, J., dissenting). Keep in mind, however, that this language from *Osborn* offers an interpretation of the scope and meaning of Article III, not of legislation conferring jurisdiction on the federal courts (the federal question jurisdiction statute was not enacted until 1875. *See* Act of Mar. 3, 1875, § 1, 18 Stat. 470).

b. Interpreting § 1331

Because the federal question jurisdiction statute contains similar "arising under" language interpreted by the Court in *Osborn*, legitimate questions arose as to whether the scope of the statute was coterminous with the grant of Article III. In other words, under the federal question statute, does federal question jurisdiction exist in any case where federal law is involved in some way? In the cases that follow, the Supreme Court addresses the meaning of § 1331 and its relationship with Article III.

---

2. The "Well-Pleaded Complaint" Rule

Louisville & Nashville Railroad Co. v. Mottley

Supreme Court of the United States
211 U.S. 149 (1908)

APPEAL from the Circuit Court of the United States for the Western District of Kentucky * * * .

The appellees (husband and wife), being residents and citizens of Kentucky, brought this suit in equity in the circuit court of the United States for the western district of Kentucky against the appellant, a railroad company and a citizen of the same state. The object of the suit was to compel the specific performance of [a] contract * * * .

The bill alleged that in September, 1871, plaintiffs, while passengers upon the defendant railroad, were injured by the defendant's negligence, and released their respective claims for damages in consideration of the agreement for transportation during their lives, expressed in the contract. It is alleged that the contract was performed by the defendant up to January 1, 1907, when the defendant declined to renew the passes. The bill then alleges

> **FYI**
>
> The Circuit Court mentioned here is not one of the U.S. Courts of Appeals in existence today but rather is one of a now-abolished system of courts that until 1911 served as special courts hearing federal criminal cases, suits between citizens of different states, and civil suits initiated by the United States. These courts had no separate judges; rather, Supreme Court Justices "rode circuit" by traveling to their assigned circuit to hear cases along with district judges.

that the refusal to comply with the contract was based solely upon that part of the act of Congress of June 29, 1906 * * * , which forbids the giving of free passes or free transportation. The bill further alleges: First, that the act of Congress referred to does not prohibit the giving of passes under the circumstances of this case; and, second, that, if the law is to be construed as prohibiting such passes, it is in conflict with the 5th Amendment of the Constitution, because it deprives the plaintiffs of their property without due process of law. The defendant demurred to the bill. The judge of the circuit court overruled the demurrer, entered a decree for the relief prayed for, and the defendant appealed directly to this court.

MR. JUSTICE MOODY, after making the foregoing statement, delivered the opinion of the court:

Two questions of law were raised by the demurrer to the bill, were brought here by appeal, and have been argued before us. They are, first, whether that part of the act of Congress of June 29, 1906 * * *, which forbids the giving of free passes or the collection of any different compensation for transportation of passengers than that specified in the tariff filed, makes it unlawful to perform a contract for transportation of persons who, in good faith, before the passage of the act, had accepted such contract in satisfaction of a valid cause of action against the railroad; and, second, whether the statute, if it should be construed to render such a contract unlawful, is in violation of the 5th Amendment of the Constitution of the United States. We do not deem it necessary, however, to consider either of these questions, because, in our opinion, the court below was without jurisdiction of the cause. Neither party has questioned that jurisdiction, but it is the duty of this court to see to it that the jurisdiction of the circuit court, which is defined and limited by statute, is not exceeded. * * *

Take Note!

Here, the Court considers the jurisdictional question even though neither of the parties raised the issue before the Supreme Court or in the lower courts. How can the Court do this? *See* FED R. CIV. P. 12(h)(3); *Ruhrgas AG v. Marathon Oil Co.,* 526 U.S. 574, 583 (1999).

There was no diversity of citizenship, and it is not and cannot be suggested that there was any ground of jurisdiction, except that the case was a "suit . . . arising under the Constitution or laws of the United States." It is the settled interpretation of these words, as used in this statute, conferring jurisdiction, that a suit arises under the Constitution and laws of the United States only when the plaintiff's statement of his own cause of action shows that it is based upon those laws or that Constitution. It is not enough that the plaintiff alleges some anticipated defense to his cause of action, and asserts that the defense is invalidated by some provision of the Constitution of the United States. Although such allegations show that very likely, in the course of the litigation, a question under the Constitution would arise, they do not show that the suit, that is, the plaintiff's original cause of action, arises under the Constitution. In *Tennessee v. Union & Planters' Bank*, 152 U.S. 454, the plaintiff, the state of Tennessee, brought suit in the circuit court of the United States to recover from the defendant certain taxes alleged to be due under the laws of the state. The plaintiff alleged that the defendant claimed an immunity from the taxation by virtue of its charter, and that therefore the tax was void, because in violation of the provision of the Constitution of the United States, which forbids any state from passing a law impairing the obligation of contracts. The cause was held to be beyond the jurisdiction of the circuit court, the court saying, by Mr. Justice Gray (p. 464): "A suggestion of one party, that the other will or may set up a claim under the Constitution or laws of the United States, does not make the suit one arising under that Constitution or those laws." Again, in *Boston & M. Consol. Copper & S. Min. Co. v. Montana Ore Purchasing Co.*, 188 U.S. 632, the plaintiff brought suit in the circuit court of the United States for the conversion of copper ore and for an injunction against its continuance. The plaintiff then alleged, for the purpose of showing jurisdiction, in substance, that the defendant would set up in defense certain laws of the United States. The cause was held to be beyond the jurisdiction of the circuit court, the court saying, by Mr. Justice Peckham:

> "It would be wholly unnecessary and improper, in order to prove complainant's cause of action, to go into any matters of defense which the defendants might possibly set up, and then attempt to reply to such defense, and thus, if possible, to show that a Federal question might or probably would arise in the course of the trial of the case. To allege such defense and then make an answer to it before the defendant has the opportunity to itself plead or prove its own defense is inconsistent with any known rule of pleading, so far as we are aware, and is improper.

> "The rule is a reasonable and just one that the complainant in the first instance shall be confined to a statement of its cause of action, leaving to the defendant to set up in his answer what his defense is, and, if anything more than a denial of complainant's cause of action, imposing upon the defendant the burden of proving such defense.

> "Conforming itself to that rule, the complainant would not, in the assertion or proof of its cause of action, bring up a single Federal question. The presentation of its cause of action would not show that it was one arising under the Constitution or laws of the United States.["]

* * *

* * * The application of this rule to the case at bar is decisive against the jurisdiction of the circuit court.

Points for Discussion

a. The "Well-Pleaded Complaint" Rule

Mottley sets forth what has come to be referred to as the "well-pleaded complaint" rule, which holds that to qualify for statutory federal question jurisdiction, the presence of a federal question must appear in the plaintiff's presentation of its case in the context of a "well-pleaded" complaint, that is, one that limits itself to a statement of its own cause of action.

Thus, under the well-pleaded complaint rule, federal questions appearing only as defenses raised in response to a complaint will not suffice to warrant federal question jurisdiction. Neither will allegations in the complaint that simply anticipate and articulate potential federal law defenses serve as grounds for federal jurisdiction; only plaintiffs' affirmative statements of their claims will be considered. *See Taylor v. Anderson, 234 U.S. 74, 75–76 (1914).*

Is the well-pleaded complaint rule, which constrains the scope of statutory federal question jurisdiction, a constitutionally-required limitation? In other words, is the Court interpreting the scope of statutory federal question jurisdiction to be more narrow than the scope of the constitutional grant of such jurisdiction?

—Perspective & Analysis—

Several scholars have argued that the well-pleaded complaint rule needlessly prevents federal courts from looking at dispositive federal defenses to determine whether a case truly "arises under" federal law and thus frustrates the true purposes of the federal question jurisdiction statute. Here is an excerpt from an article articulating that perspective:

> Despite its great age and the federal courts' now-uniform acceptance of it, the well-pleaded complaint rule should be abandoned. . . . The well-pleaded complaint rule focuses entirely upon which pleading properly contains a federal issue alleged to be dispositive of the controversy. As a result of this tunnel vision, many cases containing important federal issues must now be adjudicated in the state courts * * *.

> * * *

> The well-pleaded complaint rule also fails to honor the purposes for which federal jurisdiction was created. Since the drafting of the Constitution, judges and scholars have recognized the desirability of federal adjudication of questions of federal law, both to avoid state hostility to federal law and to ensure reasonable uniformity in its interpretation and application. The well-pleaded complaint rule in no respect serves either of these goals.

Donald L. Doernberg, *There's No Reason for It; It's Just Our Policy: Why the Well-Pleaded Complaint Rule Sabotages the Purposes of Federal Question Jurisdiction*, 38 HASTINGS L.J. 597, 662–63 (1987).

b. Master-of-the-Complaint Rule

The Supreme Court has emphasized that the well-pleaded complaint rule "makes the plaintiff the master of the claim; he or she may avoid federal [question] jurisdiction by exclusive reliance on state law." *Caterpillar Inc. v. Williams*, 482 U.S. 386, 392 (1987) (citing *The Fair v. Kohler Die & Specialty Co.*, 228 U.S. 22, 25 (1913) (Holmes, J.) ("Of course, the party who brings a suit is master to decide what law he will rely upon . . . .")); *see also Standard Fire Ins. Co. v. Knowles*, 568 U.S. 588 (2013) [*FLEX* Case 3.D] ("Knowles also points out that federal courts permit individual plaintiffs, who are the masters of their complaints, to avoid removal to federal court, and to obtain a remand to state court, by stipulating to amounts at issue that fall below the federal jurisdictional requirement. That is so.").

c. The Artful Pleading Doctrine

Although the plaintiff is the master of her complaint, courts will not permit the plaintiff to manipulate federal jurisdiction through "artful pleading." Artful pleading can entail efforts both to avoid federal jurisdiction and to obtain it. Artful pleading that seeks to invoke federal jurisdiction occurs when a plaintiff asserting state-law claims attempts to anticipate and refute federal law defenses in the complaint as a means of making the claim appear to raise a federal question.

The Declaratory Judgment Act, 28 U.S.C. §§ 2201–02, is particularly facilitative of such artful pleading, as it enables parties to seek an affirmative declaration that a particular federal defense is not valid. *See* Arthur R. Miller, *Artful Pleading: A Doctrine in Search of Definition*, 76 TEX. L. REV. 1781, 1783 (1998) ("The term 'artful pleading,' . . . described an attempt by the plaintiff to create federal question jurisdiction through the anticipation and inclusion of a federal defense on the face of its complaint in an action brought under the Declaratory Judgment Act."). However, because use of the Declaratory Judgment Act in this way would expand federal jurisdiction beyond the limits imposed by the well-pleaded complaint rule, the Supreme Court in *Skelly Oil Co. v. Phillips Petroleum Co.*, 339 U.S. 667 (1950), rejected the practice and reaffirmed the vitality of the well-pleaded complaint rule. *See id. at 672* (" '[A] suggestion of one party, that the other will or may set up a claim under the Constitution or laws of the United States, does not make the suit one arising under that Constitution or those laws.) (quoting *Tennessee v. Union & Planters' Bank*, 152 U.S. 454, 464 (1894))).

Plaintiffs seeking to avoid federal jurisdiction by pleading state-law claims, in state court, in areas in which federal law preempts state law will not succeed. Courts will disre-

Make the Connection

Preemption refers to the principle that federal law can supersede applicable state law where the two conflict. This is a concept you may study in a **Federal Courts** or a **Constitutional Law** course.

gard the allegation of state-law claims and treat them as arising under the federal law that occupies the field, making them removable to federal court. This is known as the ***complete preemption*** doctrine, and it applies when "the pre-emptive force of a statute is so 'extraordinary' that it 'converts an ordinary state common-law complaint into one stating a federal claim for purposes of the well-pleaded complaint rule.' " *Caterpillar Inc. v. Williams, 482 U.S. 386, 393 (1987)* (quoting *Metro. Life Ins. Co. v. Taylor, 481 U.S. 58, 65 (1987)*).

d. Federal Question Jurisdiction Based on Counterclaims?

For More Information

To learn more about the issue of counterclaims and federal question jurisdiction, see Christopher A. Cotropia, *Counterclaims, the Well-Pleaded Complaint, and Federal Jurisdiction*, 33 HOFSTRA L. REV. 1 (2004).

Based on the well-pleaded complaint rule, the Supreme Court has held that the presentation of federal questions in counterclaims asserted in response to the initial complaint will not provide a basis for asserting federal question jurisdiction over the original claims. *Holmes Grp., Inc. v. Vornado Air Circulation Sys., Inc., 535 U.S. 826 (2002)*. Note that there certainly can be federal question jurisdiction over counterclaims. The point being made here is that the presence of federal counterclaims by the defendant cannot confer federal question jurisdiction on the plaintiff's claims. What do you think the rationale is for the Court's rejection of federal question jurisdiction based on federal counterclaims? Would defendants have too great an ability to undermine the plaintiff's choice of a state forum if counterclaims were permitted to create federal jurisdiction over the plaintiff's claims (thus making the case removable to federal court)?

What's That?

A party may *remove* a case from state to federal court if the plaintiff's case qualifies for federal subject matter jurisdiction. Removal jurisdiction is covered fully in Section D below.

Hypo 3.5

ABC Corp. (FL) sued Ed (FL), its former employee, for business libel, a tort claim. The action was brought in federal court and alleges that Ed falsely reported to a federal agency that ABC was using substandard materials on a federal construction project.

Ed filed an answer, admitting that he made a report to the agency but alleging that his report was protected by the First Amendment to the U.S. Constitution. Ed also filed a counterclaim against ABC based on the Federal Whistleblower Act, which authorizes damages for anyone who is dismissed or disciplined for reporting fraud on the federal government. Ed moves to dismiss ABC's claim for lack of subject matter jurisdiction. Result?

---

3. The Essential Federal Element Requirement

Determining whether a federal question exists in actions brought under federal law is a relatively simple matter provided the well-pleaded complaint rule is satisfied. However, a more difficult question presents itself when state-law claims are asserted that require the determination of federal legal issues for their ultimate resolution. To illustrate this situation, assume A asserts a claim against B for breach of fiduciary duty—a state-law claim—on the ground that B's conduct violated federal securities laws. If B is found to have violated federal securities laws, A will prevail in her claim; if B is found not to have violated such laws, A will lose. Thus, A's claim depends on a determination of a matter of federal law. Do these types of claims "arise under" federal law such as to support the exercise of federal question jurisdiction?

One answer to this question came from Justice Oliver Wendell Holmes in *American Well Works Co. v. Layne & Bowler Co.*, 241 U.S. 257 (1916), in which he stated, "A suit arises under the law that creates the cause of action." *Id.* at 260. This formulation has been referred to as the Holmes "creation test." Thus, in our example above, according to the Holmes creation test, the suit would not arise under federal law since state law created the cause of action.

But, the Supreme Court has also embraced a more expansive view of the scope of arising-under jurisdiction, as exemplified in *Smith v. Kansas City Title & Trust Co.*, 255 U.S. 180 (1921). In *Smith*, a shareholder sued his corporation seeking to enjoin the corporation from investing in bonds issued under the Federal Farm Loan Act. The shareholder claimed that the Act was unconstitutional, thus making the investment illegal under governing Missouri banking law. Although federal law did not create the claim that the shareholder now asserted, the Court in *Smith* found that the plaintiff's entitlement to relief depended upon determining the constitutionality of the Act, a federal issue. This dependency, said the Court, sufficed to bring the case within the jurisdiction of the district court.

Notwithstanding its holding in *Smith*, the Court in *Moore v. Chesapeake & Ohio Railway Co.*, 291 U.S. 205 (1934), denied federal jurisdiction in an action brought under a state's employer liability law that barred findings of contributory negligence or assumption of risk where the employer's actions were found to have violated any state or federal employee safety statute, even though the plaintiff claimed that the defendant's actions had violated just such a federal statute. How can *Moore* be reconciled with *Smith*?

The Court attempted to clarify when federal question jurisdiction would exist over state-law claims dependent upon the resolution of federal issues years later in the case of <u>Merrell Dow Pharmaceuticals Inc. v. Thompson, 478 U.S. 804 (1986)</u> [<u>FLEX Case 3.B</u>]. In *Merrell Dow* the plaintiffs asserted several tort claims for birth defects that their children received allegedly as a result of the consumption of <u>Benedectin</u> during the plaintiffs' pregnancies. The plaintiffs asserted that the defendants' violations of the Federal Food, Drug, and Cosmetic Act (FDCA) was the direct and proximate cause of their injuries, a claim that caused the defendant Merrell Dow to remove the case to federal court on the basis of federal question jurisdiction. Clarifying its pronouncement in the earlier case of <u>Franchise Tax Board of State of California v. Construction Laborers Vacation Trust, 463 U.S. 1 (1983)</u>, that the presence of "substantial, disputed" questions of federal law sufficed to support federal question jurisdiction, the Court in *Merrell Dow* concluded that the claims did not arise under federal law. The Court reached this conclusion in large part because Congress had determined that there should be no federal private cause of action under the FDCA. Such a determination, the Court concluded, "is tantamount to a congressional conclusion that the presence of a claimed violation of the statute as an element of a state cause of action is insufficiently 'substantial' to confer federal-question jurisdiction." <u>Merrell Dow, 478 U.S. at 814</u>.

Make the Connection

Contributory negligence is a **Tort** concept that refers to plaintiffs' degree of responsibility for contributing to the circumstances that gave rise to the harms they accuse defendants of causing; this serves as a complete defense that bars a plaintiff's recovery in some states. *Assumption of risk*—also a **Tort** concept—is a defense that bars plaintiffs from recovering for an injury resulting from a voluntary exposure to a known and appreciated danger.

What standard did the Court set forth in *Merrell Dow* for determining whether a state-law claim invoking federal law issues arises under federal law? Although it was clear that the federal issue in the claim had to be "substantial," it was not clear after *Merrell Dow* whether the absence of a federal private right of action was fatal to federal question jurisdiction. The Supreme Court addressed this issue in the next case.

Grable & Sons Metal Prods., Inc. v. Darue Engineering & Mfg.

Supreme Court of the United States
545 U.S. 308 (2005)

JUSTICE SOUTER delivered the opinion of the Court.

The question is whether want of a federal cause of action to try claims of title to land obtained at a federal tax sale precludes removal to federal court of a state action with non-diverse parties raising a disputed issue of federal title law. We answer no, and hold that the national interest in providing a federal forum for federal tax litigation is sufficiently substantial to support the exercise of federal question jurisdiction over the disputed issue on removal, which would not distort any division of labor between the state and federal courts, provided or assumed by Congress.

I

In 1994, the Internal Revenue Service seized Michigan real property belonging to petitioner Grable & Sons Metal Products, Inc., to satisfy Grable's federal tax delinquency. Title 26 U.S.C. § 6335 required the IRS to give notice of the seizure, and there is no dispute that Grable received actual notice by certified mail before the IRS sold the property to respondent Darue Engineering & Manufacturing. Although Grable also received notice of the sale itself, it did not exercise its statutory right to redeem the property within 180 days of the sale, § 6337(b)(1), and after that period had passed, the Government gave Darue a quitclaim deed, § 6339.

Five years later, Grable brought a quiet title action in state court, claiming that Darue's record title was invalid because the IRS had failed to notify Grable of its seizure of the property in the exact manner required by § 6335(a), which provides that written notice must be "given by the Secretary to the owner of the property [or] left at his usual place of abode or business." Grable said that the statute required personal service, not service by certified mail.

Darue removed the case to Federal District Court as presenting a federal question, because the claim of title depended on the interpretation of the notice statute in the federal tax law. The District Court declined to remand the case at Grable's behest after finding that the "claim does pose a significant question of federal law," * * * and ruling that Grable's lack of a federal right of action to enforce its claim against Darue did not bar the exercise of federal jurisdiction. * * *

The Court of Appeals for the Sixth Circuit affirmed. On the jurisdictional question, the panel thought it sufficed that the title claim raised an issue of federal law that had to be resolved, and implicated a substantial federal interest (in construing federal tax law). * * * We granted certiorari on the jurisdictional question * * * to resolve a split within the Courts of Appeals on whether *Merrell Dow Pharmaceuticals*

Inc. v. Thompson, 478 U.S. 804 (1986), always requires a federal cause of action as a condition for exercising federal-question jurisdiction. We now affirm.

II

Darue was entitled to remove the quiet title action if Grable could have brought it in federal district court originally, 28 U.S.C. § 1441(a), as a civil action "arising under the Constitution, laws, or treaties of the United States," § 1331. This provision for federal-question jurisdiction is invoked by and large by plaintiffs pleading a cause of action created by federal law * * * . There is, however, another longstanding, if less frequently encountered, variety of federal "arising under" jurisdiction, this Court having recognized for nearly 100 years that in certain cases federal question jurisdiction will lie over state-law claims that implicate significant federal issues. The doctrine captures the commonsense notion that a federal court ought to be able to hear claims recognized under state law that nonetheless turn on substantial questions of federal law, and thus justify resort to the experience, solicitude, and hope of uniformity that a federal forum offers on federal issues.

The classic example is *Smith v. Kansas City Title & Trust Co.*, 255 U.S. 180 (1921), a suit by a shareholder claiming that the defendant corporation could not lawfully buy certain bonds of the National Government because their issuance was unconstitutional. Although Missouri law provided the cause of action, the Court recognized federal-question jurisdiction because the principal issue in the case was the federal constitutionality of the bond issue. *Smith* thus held, in a somewhat generous statement of the scope of the doctrine, that a state-law claim could give rise to federal-question jurisdiction so long as it "appears from the [complaint] that the right to relief depends upon the construction or application of [federal law]."

The *Smith* statement has been subject to some trimming to fit earlier and later cases recognizing the vitality of the basic doctrine, but shying away from the expansive view that mere need to apply federal law in a state-law claim will suffice to open the "arising under" door. * * * It has in fact become a constant refrain in such cases that federal jurisdiction demands not only a contested federal issue, but a substantial one, indicating a serious federal interest in claiming the advantages thought to be inherent in a federal forum. *E.g.*, *Merrell Dow*, 478 U.S. at 814, and n.12.

But even when the state action discloses a contested and substantial federal question, the exercise of federal jurisdiction is subject to a possible veto. For the federal issue will ultimately qualify for a federal forum only if federal jurisdiction is consistent with congressional judgment about the sound division of labor between state and federal courts governing the application of § 1331. * * * Because arising-under jurisdiction to hear a state-law claim always raises the possibility of upsetting the state-federal line drawn (or at least assumed) by Congress, the presence of a disputed federal issue and the ostensible importance of a federal forum are never necessarily dispositive; there must always be an assessment of any disruptive portent in exercising federal jurisdiction.

These considerations have kept us from stating a "single, precise, all-embracing" test for jurisdiction over federal issues embedded in state-law claims between nondiverse parties. We have not kept them out simply because they appeared in state raiment, * * * but neither have we treated "federal issue" as a password opening federal courts to any state action embracing a point of federal law. Instead, the question is, does a state-law claim necessarily raise a stated federal issue, actually disputed and substantial, which a federal forum may entertain without disturbing any congressionally approved balance of federal and state judicial responsibilities.

III

A

This case warrants federal jurisdiction. [Under the applicable state law] Grable's state complaint must specify "the facts establishing the superiority of [its] claim," and Grable has premised its superior title claim on a failure by the IRS to give it adequate notice, as defined by federal law. Whether Grable was given notice within the meaning of the federal statute is thus an essential element of its quiet title claim, and the meaning of the federal statute is actually in dispute; it appears to be the only legal or factual issue contested in the case. * * * The Government has a strong interest in the "prompt and certain collection of delinquent taxes," and the ability of the IRS to satisfy its claims from the property of delinquents requires clear terms of notice to allow buyers like Darue to satisfy themselves that the Service has touched the bases necessary for good title. The Government thus has a direct interest in the availability of a federal forum to vindicate its own administrative action, and buyers (as well as tax delinquents) may find it valuable to come before judges used to federal tax matters. Finally, because it will be the rare state title case that raises a contested matter of federal law, federal jurisdiction to resolve genuine disagreement over federal tax title provisions will portend only a microscopic effect on the federal-state division of labor.

* * *

B

Merrell Dow * * * is not to the contrary. *Merrell Dow* considered a state tort claim resting in part on the allegation that the defendant drug company had violated a federal misbranding prohibition, and was thus presumptively negligent under Ohio law. The Court assumed that federal law would have to be applied to resolve the claim, but after closely examining the strength of the federal interest at stake and the implications of opening the federal forum, held federal jurisdiction unavailable. Congress had not provided a private federal cause of action for violation of the federal branding requirement, and the Court found "it would . . . flout, or at least undermine, congressional intent to conclude that federal courts might nevertheless exercise federal-question jurisdiction and provide remedies for violations of that federal statute solely because the violation . . . is said to be a . . . 'proximate cause' under state law."

Because federal law provides for no quiet title action that could be brought against Darue, Grable argues that there can be no federal jurisdiction here, stressing some broad language in *Merrell Dow* (including the passage just quoted) that on its face supports Grable's position. But * * * *Merrell Dow* cannot be read whole as overturning decades of precedent, as it would have done by * * * converting a federal cause of action from a sufficient condition for federal-question jurisdiction into a necessary one.

* * *

* * * *Merrell Dow* should be read in its entirety as treating the absence of a federal private right of action as evidence relevant to, but not dispositive of, the "sensitive judgments about congressional intent" that § 1331 requires. The absence of any federal cause of action affected *Merrell Dow*'s result [in] two ways. The Court saw the fact as worth some consideration in the assessment of substantiality. But its primary importance emerged when the Court treated the combination of no federal cause of action and no preemption of state remedies for misbranding as an important clue to Congress's conception of the scope of jurisdiction to be exercised under § 1331. * * * [I]f the federal labeling standard without a federal cause of action could get a state claim into federal court, so could any other federal standard without a federal cause of action. And that would have meant a tremendous number of cases.

> **FYI**
> Note here that the Court indicates that the presence of a federal right of action is a "sufficient condition for federal-question jurisdiction." Although this is true in most circumstances, the Court has identified an extremely rare exception to this rule. *See Shoshone Mining Co. v. Rutter*, 177 U.S. 505, 507 (1900).

One only needed to consider the treatment of federal violations generally in garden variety state tort law. "The violation of federal statutes and regulations is commonly given negligence per se effect in state tort proceedings." A general rule of exercising federal jurisdiction over state claims resting on federal mislabeling and other statutory violations would thus have heralded a potentially enormous shift of

> **FYI**
> *Negligence per se* is a **Tort** concept that treats proof of a statutory violation as conclusive proof of a party's negligence. An alternative would be to treat a statutory violation merely as *evidence* of negligence, not conclusive proof of it.

traditionally state cases into federal courts. Expressing concern over the "increased volume of federal litigation," and noting the importance of adhering to "legislative intent," *Merrell Dow* thought it improbable that the Congress, having made no provision for a federal cause of action, would have meant to welcome any state-law tort case implicating federal law "solely because the violation of the federal statute is said to [create] a rebuttable presumption [of negligence] . . . under state law." In this situation, no welcome mat meant keep out. *Merrell Dow*'s analysis thus fits within the framework of examining the importance of having a federal forum for the issue, and the consistency of such a forum with Congress's intended division of labor between state and federal courts.

As already indicated, however, a comparable analysis yields a different jurisdictional conclusion in this case. Although Congress also indicated ambivalence in this case by providing no private right of action to Grable, it is the rare state quiet title action that involves contested issues of federal law. Consequently, jurisdiction over actions like Grable's would not materially affect, or threaten to affect, the normal currents of litigation. Given the absence of threatening structural consequences and the clear interest the Government, its buyers, and its delinquents have in the availability of a federal forum, there is no good reason to shirk from federal jurisdiction over the dispositive and contested federal issue at the heart of the state-law title claim.

IV

The judgment of the Court of Appeals, upholding federal jurisdiction over Grable's quiet title action, is affirmed.

It is so ordered.

JUSTICE THOMAS, concurring.

The Court faithfully applies our precedents interpreting 28 U.S.C. § 1331 to authorize federal-court jurisdiction over some cases in which state law creates the cause of action but requires determination of an issue of federal law. In this case, no one has asked us to overrule those precedents and adopt the rule Justice Holmes set forth in *American Well Works*, limiting § 1331 jurisdiction to cases in which federal law creates the cause of action pleaded on the face of the plaintiff's complaint. In an appropriate case, and perhaps with the benefit of better evidence as to the original meaning of § 1331's text, I would be willing to consider that course.

Jurisdictional rules should be clear. Whatever the virtues of the *Smith* standard, it is anything but clear. * * * Whatever the vices of the *American Well Works* rule, it is clear. Moreover, it accounts for the "vast majority" of cases that come within § 1331 under our current case law—further indication that trying to sort out which cases fall within the smaller *Smith* category may not be worth the effort it entails.

Accordingly, I would be willing in appropriate circumstances to reconsider our interpretation of § 1331.

Points for Discussion

a. The *Grable* Standard

The *Grable* Court indicated that the key question in determining whether state-law claims involving federal issues qualify for federal question jurisdiction is "does a state-law claim necessarily raise a stated federal issue, actually disputed and substantial, which a federal forum may entertain without disturbing any congressionally approved balance of federal and state judicial responsibilities?" How does one determine whether a federal issue is "substantial" or whether there is "any congressionally approved balance of federal and state judicial responsibilities" that might be disturbed by the exercise of federal jurisdiction? *See, e.g., R.I. Fishermen's All., Inc. v. R.I. Dep't of Envtl. Mgmt.*, 585 F.3d 42 (1st Cir. 2009) (finding the federal issue involved—the compliance with federally-sanctioned interstate compacts—to be substantial and that suits under the state law in question would be rare); *Broder v. Cablevision Sys. Corp.*, 418 F.3d 187 (2d Cir. 2005) (regarding the federal issues in the case as pertaining to a "complex regulatory scheme" raising questions that "are not clearly insubstantial" and finding that claims involving these issues would be relatively rare). The *Merrell Dow* Court appeared to use the absence of a private right of action in a federal statute as evidence that the issue was insufficiently substantial to support federal jurisdiction. How did the *Grable* Court differ in its approach to this question?

Do you believe that the *Grable* standard provides the "clear" jurisdictional rule that Justice Thomas wishes to see? In his concurrence, Justice Thomas states that he would be willing to limit federal question jurisdiction to those matters embraced by Justice Holmes's creation test. What would be the implications of limiting federal question jurisdiction to claims created by federal law? The Supreme Court has the authority to review state court determinations of federal legal questions and thus important federal issues embedded in state-law claims would still have some chance of receiving federal review in this manner. Given the availability of such review, would there be any disadvantages to fully embracing the Holmes creation test? For a discussion of the history behind federal question jurisdiction and a suggestion that this history is more consistent with the broader understanding of federal "arising under" jurisdiction reflected in *Grable*, see Ann Woolhandler & Michael G. Collins, *Federal Question Jurisdiction and Justice Holmes*, 84 NOTRE DAME L. REV. 2151 (2010).

b. *Empire HealthChoice Assurance Inc. v. McVeigh*

In the Term following *Grable*, the Court had occasion to apply the *Grable* standard to a suit by a federal health insurance carrier against an injured beneficiary for reimbursement after the beneficiary recovered for his injuries in a state-court action against a third party that caused the accident. In *Empire HealthChoice Assurance Inc. v. McVeigh, 547 U.S. 677 (2006)*, the health plan carrier argued that federal jurisdiction was proper because, in part, the rights sued upon were rooted in a federal contract between the carrier and the federal government authorizing the carrier to provide health coverage for federal employees. The relevant federal statute in *Empire HealthChoice* that authorized these federal contracts also authorized federal court jurisdiction for coverage or benefits claims against the United States but not for claims by health plan carriers against beneficiaries for reimbursement. The Court concluded that federal question jurisdiction was not proper. Is this result consistent with your understanding of *Grable*?

c. **Federal Question Jurisdiction After *Grable***

Although the Court in *Grable* declined to move to a full embrace of the Holmes creation test and affirmed the embedded federal element wing of federal question jurisdiction, *Grable* should not be read as an endorsement of a broad, sweeping view of the scope of federal question jurisdiction. To the contrary, in *Grable* the Court wrote that it had "sh[ied] away from the expansive view that mere need to apply federal law in a state-law claim will suffice to open the 'arising under' door" and that such cases require "sensitive judgments about congressional intent." Thus, in *Gunn v. Minton*, 568 U.S. 251 (2013) [*FLEX* Case 3.C], the Court declined to find federal question jurisdiction over a state legal malpractice action simply because the resolution of a federal patent issue was necessary to resolution of the claim. As the Court explained, "[I]t is not enough that the federal issue be significant to the particular parties in the immediate suit . . . . The substantiality inquiry under *Grable* looks instead to the importance of the issue to the federal system as a whole." *Id.* at 1066. The Court concluded that the hypothetical patent question—which related to whether a court would have accepted a patent argument the attorney never made— was not important to patent law generally; it also concluded that permitting a state court to opine on the question would not undermine the ability of federal courts to resolve real patent cases. *Id.* at 1067.

Similarly, lower federal courts have not hesitated to reject federal jurisdiction over claims that involve insubstantial federal issues or that would engage the federal courts in resolving matters Congress wanted to see resolved in other ways. *See, e.g., Kalick v. Nw. Airlines Corp.*, 372 F. App'x 317, 320 (3d Cir. 2010) ("[I]t does not appear from Kalick's complaint that the interpretation of the federal regulation is in dispute, only whether NWA abided by the regulations. Kalick cannot simply cite to a federal regulation that does not give rise to a private cause of action in order to satisfy federal subject matter jurisdiction."); *Budget Prepay, Inc. v. AT&T Corp.,*

605 F.3d 273, 281 (5th Cir. 2010) (holding that obligations in a federal statutory provision that could be contracted around could not be described as substantial and finding that federal jurisdiction would disrupt the scheme of "cooperative federalism" erected by the statute).

C. Supplemental Jurisdiction

Thus far we have been studying statutes that confer **original jurisdiction** on the federal courts, meaning that claims that qualify for jurisdiction under these statutes may be brought initially in federal court, independent of any other claims. For example, an action asserting a violation of federal securities law would fall within the original jurisdiction of the federal courts because it qualifies for federal question jurisdiction under 28 U.S.C. § 1331.

If a claim does not fall within the original jurisdiction of the federal courts, either through the diversity statute or through the general federal question statute (or one of the special federal-jurisdiction-conferring statutes),* then it will not be possible to assert that claim on its own in federal court. However, if a plaintiff asserts such a non-qualifying claim in conjunction with a separate claim that *does* fall within the original jurisdiction of the federal courts, it is possible that a federal court will be able to assert supplemental jurisdiction over the non-qualifying claim or claims based on their ability to "piggyback" on the claims that do qualify for federal jurisdiction. The doctrine of supplemental jurisdiction is concerned with the circumstances under which federal courts may exercise jurisdiction over these *supplemental claims* that would not otherwise qualify for federal subject matter jurisdiction were they asserted in isolation.

The forerunners of supplemental jurisdiction were the judicially-created doctrines of pendent jurisdiction—which addressed the ability of plaintiffs to add non-qualifying claims to qualifying claims that they asserted—and ancillary jurisdiction—which referred to the jurisdiction extended over non-qualifying claims by plaintiffs or defendants asserted as counterclaims, crossclaims, or third-party claims. In 1990, these separate doctrines were codified together in the federal supplemental jurisdiction stat-

What's That?

Counterclaims (claims by defending parties against their aggressors), *crossclaims* (claims against coparties), and *third-party claims* (claims against nonparties) are joinder concepts covered in Chapter 7.

---

* Title 28 contains additional bases for federal subject matter jurisdiction beyond diversity and federal question cases. *See, e.g.*, 28 U.S.C. § 1333 (admiralty and maritime cases); 28 U.S.C. § 1334 (bankruptcy cases); 28 U.S.C. §§ 1345, 1346 (United States as a party). [Ed.]

ute, 28 U.S.C. § 1367. However, to understand fully how supplemental jurisdiction works, we must first review the line of Supreme Court cases prior to 1990 that shaped the contours of pendent and ancillary jurisdiction because those cases ultimately gave rise to, and help us to interpret, the federal supplemental jurisdiction statute.

1. The Constitutional Standard

United Mine Workers of America v. Gibbs

Supreme Court of the United States
383 U.S. 715 (1966)

MR. JUSTICE BRENNAN delivered the opinion of the Court.

Respondent Paul Gibbs was awarded compensatory and punitive damages in this action against petitioner United Mine Workers of America (UMW) for alleged violations of § 303 of the Labor Management Relations Act, and of the common law of Tennessee. The case grew out of the rivalry between the United Mine Workers and the Southern Labor Union over representation of workers in the southern Appalachian coal fields. Tennessee Consolidated Coal Company, not a party here, laid off 100 miners of the UMW's Local 5881 when it closed one of its mines in southern Tennessee during the spring of 1960. Late that summer, Grundy Company, a wholly owned subsidiary of Consolidated, hired respondent as mine superintendent to attempt to open a new mine on Consolidated's property at nearby Gray's Creek through use of members of the Southern Labor Union. As part of the arrangement, Grundy also gave respondent a contract to haul the mine's coal to the nearest railroad loading point.

On August 15 and 16, 1960, armed members of Local 5881 forcibly prevented the opening of the mine, threatening respondent and beating an organizer for the rival union. The members of the local believed Consolidated had promised them the jobs at the new mine; they insisted that if anyone would do the work, they would. At this time, no representative of the UMW, their international union, was present. George Gilbert, the UMW's field representative for the area including Local 5881, was away at Middlesboro, Kentucky, attending an Executive Board meeting when the members of the local discovered Grundy's plan; he did not return to the area until late in the day of August 16. There was uncontradicted testimony that he first learned of the violence while at the meeting, and returned with explicit instructions from his international union superiors to establish a limited picket line, to prevent any further violence, and to see to it that the strike did not spread to neighboring mines. There was no further violence at the mine site; a picket line was maintained there for nine months; and no further attempts were made to open the mine during that period.

Respondent lost his job as superintendent, and never entered into performance of his haulage contract. He testified that he soon began to lose other trucking contracts and mine leases he held in nearby areas. Claiming these effects to be the result of a concerted union plan against him, he sought recovery not against Local 5881 or its members, but only against petitioner, the international union. The suit was brought in the <u>United States District Court for the Eastern District of Tennessee</u>, and jurisdiction was premised on allegations of secondary boycotts under § 303. The state law claim, for which jurisdiction was based upon the doctrine of pendent jurisdiction, asserted "an unlawful conspiracy and an unlawful boycott aimed at him and (Grundy) to maliciously, wantonly and willfully interfere with his contract of employment and with his contract of haulage."

The trial judge refused to submit to the jury the claims of pressure intended to cause mining firms other than Grundy to cease doing business with Gibbs; he found those claims unsupported by the evidence. The jury's verdict was that the UMW had violated both § 303 and state law. Gibbs was awarded $60,000 as damages under the employment contract and $14,500 under the haulage contract; he was also awarded $100,000 punitive damages. On motion, the trial court set aside the award of damages with respect to the haulage contract on the ground that damage was unproved. It also held that union pressure on Grundy to discharge respondent as supervisor would constitute only a primary dispute with Grundy, as respondent's employer, and hence was not cognizable as a claim under § 303. Interference with the employment relationship was cognizable as a state claim, however, and a remitted award was sustained on the state law claim. The <u>Court of Appeals for the Sixth Circuit</u> affirmed. We granted certiorari. We reverse.

I.

A threshold question is whether the District Court properly entertained jurisdiction of the claim based on Tennessee law. * * * The Court held in <u>Hurn v. Oursler, 289 U.S. 238 (1933)</u>, that state law claims are appropriate for federal court determination if they form a separate but parallel ground for relief also sought in a substantial claim based on federal law. The Court distinguished permissible from non-permissible exercises of federal judicial power over state law claims by contrasting "a case where two distinct grounds in support of a single cause of action are alleged, one only of which presents a federal question, and a case where two separate and distinct causes of action are alleged, one only of which is federal in character. In the former, where the federal question averred is not plainly wanting in substance, the federal court, even though the federal ground be not established, may nevertheless retain and dispose of the case upon the non-federal ground; in the latter it may not do so upon the nonfederal cause of action." The question is into which category the present action fell.

Hurn was decided in 1933, before the unification of law and equity by the Federal Rules of Civil Procedure. At the time, the meaning of "cause of action" was a subject of serious dispute * * * .

* * *

With the adoption of the Federal Rules of Civil Procedure and the unified form of action, FED. R. CIV. P. 2, much of the controversy over "cause of action" abated. The phrase remained as the keystone of the *Hurn* test, however, and, as commentators have noted, has been the source of considerable confusion. Under the Rules, the impulse is toward entertaining the broadest possible scope of action consistent with fairness to the parties; joinder of claims, parties and remedies is strongly encouraged. Yet because the *Hurn* question involves issues of jurisdiction as well as convenience, there has been some tendency to limit its application to cases in which the state and federal claims are, as in *Hurn*, "little more than the equivalent of different epithets to characterize the same group of circumstances."

This limited approach is unnecessarily grudging. Pendent jurisdiction, in the sense of judicial power, exists whenever there is a claim "arising under (the) Constitution, the Laws of the United States, and Treaties made,

> The Court's reference to the "unification of law and equity" refers to the abolition of the old procedural distinctions between actions at law and suits at equity that was accomplished in the federal system by the adoption of Rule 2 in 1938. For a good discussion of the merger of law and equity in the federal system, and an argument that equity came out ahead in the process, see Stephen N. Subrin, *How Equity Conquered Common Law: The Federal Rules of Civil Procedure in Historical Perspective*, 135 U. PA. L. REV. 909 (1987).

or which shall be made, under their Authority * * *," U.S. Const. art. III, § 2, and the relationship between that claim and the state claim permits the conclusion that the entire action before the court comprises but one constitutional "case." The federal claim must have substance sufficient to confer subject matter jurisdiction on the court. The state and federal claims must derive from a common nucleus of operative fact. But if, considered without regard to their federal or state character, a plaintiff's claims are such that he would ordinarily be expected to try them all in one judicial proceeding, then, assuming substantiality of the federal issues, there is power in federal courts to hear the whole.

That power need not be exercised in every case in which it is found to exist. It has consistently been recognized that pendent jurisdiction is a doctrine of discretion, not of plaintiff's right. Its justification lies in considerations of judicial economy, convenience and fairness to litigants; if these are not present a federal court should hesitate to exercise jurisdiction over state claims, even though bound to apply state law to them, *Erie R.R. Co. v. Tompkins*, 304 U.S. 64 (1938). Needless decisions of state law should be avoided both as a matter of comity and to promote justice between the parties, by procuring for them a surer-footed reading of applicable law. Certainly, if the federal claims are dismissed before trial, even though not insubstantial in a jurisdictional sense, the state claims should be dismissed as well. Similarly, if it appears that the state issues substantially predominate, whether in terms of proof, of the scope of

What's That?

Erie R.R. Co. v. Tompkins is a major case that serves as the foundation for the law concerning whether to apply state or federal law to a given issue in federal court. We will study this case and its progeny in Chapter 5.

the issues raised, or of the comprehensiveness of the remedy sought, the state claims may be dismissed without prejudice and left for resolution to state tribunals. There may, on the other hand, be situations in which the state claim is so closely tied to questions of federal policy that the argument for exercise of pendent jurisdiction is particularly strong. In the present case, for example, the allowable scope of the

state claim implicates the federal doctrine of pre-emption; while this interrelationship does not create statutory federal question jurisdiction, *Louisville & N.R. Co. v. Mottley*, 211 U.S. 149 (1908), its existence is relevant to the exercise of discretion. Finally, there may be reasons independent of jurisdictional considerations, such as the likelihood of jury confusion in treating divergent legal theories of relief, that would justify separating state and federal claims for trial, FED. R. CIV. P. 42(b). If so, jurisdiction should ordinarily be refused.

The question of power will ordinarily be resolved on [the basis of] the pleadings. But the issue whether pendent jurisdiction has been properly assumed is one which remains open throughout the litigation. Pretrial procedures or even the trial itself may reveal a substantial hegemony of state law claims, or likelihood of jury confusion, which could not have been anticipated at the pleading stage. Although it will of course be appropriate to take account in this circumstance of the already completed course of the litigation, dismissal of the state claim might even then be merited. For example, it may appear that the plaintiff was well aware of the nature of his proofs and the relative importance of his claims; recognition of a federal court's wide latitude to decide ancillary questions of state law does not imply that it must tolerate a litigant's effort to impose upon it what is in effect only a state law case. Once it appears that a state claim constitutes the real body of a case, to which the federal claim is only an appendage, the state claim may fairly be dismissed.

We are not prepared to say that in the present case the District Court exceeded its discretion in proceeding to judgment on the state claim. * * * [T]he state and federal claims arose from the same nucleus of operative fact and reflected alternative remedies. Indeed, the verdict sheet sent in to the jury authorized only one award of damages, so that recovery could not be given separately on the federal and state claims. * * *

* * *

[Part II omitted.]

Reversed.

THE CHIEF JUSTICE took no part in the decision of this case.

[The concurring opinion by JUSTICE HARLAN, joined by JUSTICE CLARK, is omitted.]

Points for Discussion

a. The *Gibbs* Standard

In *Gibbs*, the Court identifies the circumstances under which federal courts may exercise jurisdiction over state-law claims that do not qualify on their own for federal jurisdiction but are related to claims asserted in the action that do qualify. What relationship does the Court announce must exist between non-qualifying claims and related qualifying claims?

The Court states that, "The state and federal claims must derive from a common nucleus of operative fact." What does this mean? What is the constitutional authority for the exercise of jurisdiction over these claims that otherwise would not qualify for federal jurisdiction? Are there good policy reasons why courts or litigants would want such non-qualifying state-law claims to be heard along with related claims that do qualify for federal jurisdiction?

b. Where Is the Statute?

Earlier in this chapter it was noted that a proper exercise of federal jurisdiction depends upon the presence of constitutional *and* statutory authority. Although *Gibbs* elaborates on the constitutional standard that governs whether a federal court may entertain state-law claims that on their own do not qualify for federal jurisdiction, no statutory authority for doing so appears to be in the picture (remember that *Gibbs* occurs well before enactment of the federal supplemental jurisdiction statute). Is there statutory authority for the Court's authorization of jurisdiction over such non-qualifying claims? If not, what is the basis for the Court's extension of jurisdiction to these claims?

c. The Discretionary Nature of Pendent Jurisdiction

In *Gibbs*, Justice Brennan made it clear that the power to exercise pendent jurisdiction "need not be exercised in every case in which it is found to exist," indicating that the doctrine was discretionary in nature. What criteria did Justice

Brennan announce to aid in the determination of whether courts should exercise discretion not to exercise pendent or ancillary jurisdiction?

———————————

2. Pendent and Ancillary Jurisdiction After *Gibbs*

In *Gibbs*, the Court faced a plaintiff who asserted a qualifying federal law claim and a non-qualifying state-law claim against the same defendant, the classic pendent jurisdiction scenario. Did the *Gibbs* doctrine permit federal courts to exercise jurisdiction when a plaintiff seeks to assert a qualifying federal claim against one defendant and a non-qualifying state claim against a different party?

a. *Aldinger v. Howard*: Pendent Parties Attached to Federal Question Claims

The Court addressed this situation—which describes **pendent party jurisdiction**—in *Aldinger v. Howard*, 427 U.S. 1 (1976), although it failed to address its constitutionality and focused only on whether Congress had precluded the exercise of pendent party jurisdiction in the circumstances present in the case. In *Aldinger*, the plaintiff alleged federal civil rights violations against several officers and sued the county that employed the officers under state law. The litigants were not diverse, so the plaintiff sought to base federal jurisdiction over the entire case on the federal question jurisdiction enjoyed by the civil rights claim and argued for pendent jurisdiction over the state-law claim against the county under the *Gibbs* "common nucleus of operative fact" standard. **Figure 3.6** illustrates, in the abstract, the circumstance at issue in *Aldinger*.

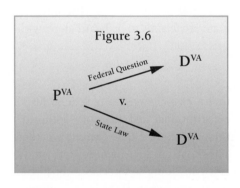

Figure 3.6

The Supreme Court rejected the attempt to establish pendent jurisdiction over the state-law claim based on its interpretation of the civil rights statute at issue in the case, 42 U.S.C. § 1983. Specifically, because § 1983 had been interpreted to exclude counties from the reach of federal causes of action for constitutional violations by state officers, the Court concluded that Congress implicitly negated the idea that state claims against counties could be heard on a pendent party jurisdiction basis in federal court. The Court announced, however, that congressional silence on the matter would leave a presumption in favor of pendent party jurisdiction intact and thus left open the possibility that "[o]ther statutory grants and other alignments of parties and claims might call for a different result." *Aldinger*, 427 U.S. at 18.

b. *Owen Equipment & Erection Co. v. Kroger*: Pendent Parties Attached to Diversity Claims

The Court revisited the issue but under slightly different circumstances in <u>*Owen Equipment & Erection Co. v. Kroger*, 437 U.S. 365 (1978)</u>. In *Kroger*, a plaintiff asserted a qualifying state tort claim based on diversity jurisdiction, and the defendant in response asserted an indemnity claim against a third party not diverse from the plaintiff. **Figure 3.7** illustrates, in the abstract, the arrangement of parties and claims at issue in *Owen Equipment*.

> In 1978, after *Aldinger*, the Supreme Court held that municipalities, like counties and other local governmental units, are amenable to suit under the Civil Rights Act. *See* <u>*Monell v. Dep't of Soc. Servs.*, 436 U.S. 658, 690 (1978)</u>. This holding, had it been available at the time of the suit in *Aldinger*, would have eliminated the need for the plaintiff to rely on state-law claims to proceed against the county.

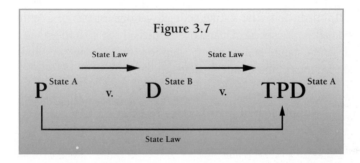

When the plaintiff amended his complaint to assert a state-law claim against the third party, he argued that there should be pendent party jurisdiction over the claim against the third party since there could be no diversity jurisdiction. The Court rejected this effort, arguing that <u>28 U.S.C. § 1332</u>—the federal diversity statute—and its accompanying complete diversity requirement must be read to preclude assertions of pendent jurisdiction in such situations. Why do you think the Court reached this conclusion?

c. *Finley v. United States*: Pendent Parties Attached to FTCA Claims

In 1989, in <u>*Finley v. United States*, 490 U.S. 545 (1989)</u>, the Court had to decide whether a plaintiff asserting tort claims against the United States under the <u>Federal Tort Claims Act</u> (FTCA) could use pendent party jurisdiction to assert a state law tort claim against a city government in the same case. The Court, per Justice Scalia, held that pendent party jurisdiction was impermissible under the circumstances because Congress had not affirmatively authorized such jurisdiction under the FTCA. This holding contradicted the suggestion in *Aldinger* that pendent party jurisdiction, if constitutional, was presumptively permissible unless Congress negated the presumption. Justice Scalia's opinion turned this presumption on its head by indicating that such jurisdiction was presumptively impermissible unless Congress affirmatively authorized it, a move that elicited a sharp dissent by Justice Stevens. Which view is more consistent with the notion that the federal courts are courts of limited jurisdiction under our Constitution?

3. Modern Supplemental Jurisdiction Doctrine

a. The Supplemental Jurisdiction Statute

Importantly, as the Court rejected pendent party jurisdiction based on its interpretation of the FTCA in *Finley*, Justice Scalia wrote, "[w]hatever we say regarding the scope of jurisdiction conferred by a particular statute can of course be changed by Congress." *Finley, 490 U.S. at 556*. Congress responded to this invitation in 1990 by promulgating 28 U.S.C. § 1367, the federal supplemental jurisdiction statute, in an effort to codify principles of ancillary and pendent jurisdiction into what is now called supplemental jurisdiction. The statute codified various aspects of existing doctrine, but also modified some aspects of it and overturned others. To understand the supplemental jurisdiction statute and its relationship to prior case law, we should consider the two main sections of the statute separately.

Supplemental Jurisdiction: 28 U.S.C. § 1367(a)

(a)   Except as provided in subsections (b) and (c) or as expressly provided otherwise by Federal statute, in any civil action of which the district courts have original jurisdiction, the district courts shall have supplemental jurisdiction over all other claims that are so related to claims in the action within such original jurisdiction that they form part of the same case or controversy under Article III of the United States Constitution. Such supplemental jurisdiction shall include claims that involve the joinder or intervention of additional parties.

Two things are noteworthy in this provision. First, the language of § 1367(a) provides for supplemental jurisdiction over all claims that form part of the same Article III "case or controversy." As such, the statute incorporates the *Gibbs* "common nucleus of operative fact" standard. Second, the final sentence provides for supplemental jurisdiction over claims involving the joinder or intervention of additional parties, authorizing pendent party jurisdiction at least as a general matter. What impact does this language have on *Finley*?

Although § 1367(a) is generous in its grant of jurisdiction by extending jurisdiction over "all other claims" that are sufficiently related according to the standard of *Gibbs*, § 1367(a) is not the end of the matter. That provision must be read in conjunction with the immediately following provision, § 1367(b), which identifies those classes of claims that cannot qualify for supplemental jurisdiction, notwithstanding the fact that they may have satisfied the requirements of § 1367(a). Thus, it is critical to evaluate a claim under § 1367(a) *and* (b) before concluding that any claims not independently qualifying for federal subject matter jurisdiction do in fact qualify for supplemental jurisdiction. Here is the language of § 1367(b):

> ### Supplemental Jurisdiction: 28 U.S.C. § 1367(b)
>
> (b)   In any civil action of which the district courts have original jurisdiction founded solely on section 1332 of this title, the district courts shall not have supplemental jurisdiction under subsection (a) over claims by plaintiffs against persons made parties under Rule 14, 19, 20, or 24 of the Federal Rules of Civil Procedure, or over claims by persons proposed to be joined as plaintiffs under Rule 19 of such rules, or seeking to intervene as plaintiffs under Rule 24 of such rules, when exercising supplemental jurisdiction over such claims would be inconsistent with the jurisdictional requirements of section 1332.

What does this language mean? First-year law students often find this language difficult to parse. To understand just exactly what § 1367(b) says, it is helpful to break it down into three parts:

The first portion of § 1367(b) identifies the categories of cases in which its remaining provisions will be a consideration. Section 1367(b) only addresses itself to civil actions in which original jurisdiction is based "solely on section 1332," the federal diversity statute. Thus, in cases where the original jurisdiction of the federal court is founded on federal question jurisdiction (28 U.S.C. § 1331)—or another basis for federal jurisdiction such as admiralty (*see* 28 U.S.C. § 1333) or bankruptcy (*see* 28 U.S.C. § 1334)—or there are both diversity-based claims and federal question claims in the action, § 1367(b) does not apply.

The second section of § 1367(b) to consider is the portion identifying a set of "claims by plaintiffs" that do not qualify for supplemental jurisdiction in the context of a case where original jurisdiction is based solely on diversity jurisdiction. Those disqualified claims are by plaintiffs against the following parties:

Third Parties—claims by plaintiffs against parties impleaded under Rule 14;

Necessary Parties—claims by plaintiffs against parties joined under Rule 19;

Permissive Parties—claims by plaintiffs against parties joined under Rule 20; and

> **What's That?**
>
> The rules mentioned here—Rules 14, 19, 20, & 24—are each rules concerning joinder of parties. They will be covered fully in Chapter 7.

Intervening Parties—claims by plaintiffs against parties intervening under Rule 24.

If a prospective supplemental claim is one that falls within any of these categories, it will not be eligible for supplemental jurisdiction if it is seeking to piggyback only on a diversity claim. **Hypos 3.6** & **3.7** test your understanding of this portion of the rule:

Hypo 3.6

A State A shopkeeper filed a complaint against a State B supplier in State A federal court based on the supplier's failure to deliver goods to the shopkeeper in a timely fashion. The shopkeeper is seeking $100,000 in damages. After receiving the shopkeeper's complaint, the supplier filed a third-party complaint against the delivery company, a State B corporation headquartered in State B, alleging that the delivery company is partially responsible for the delay and thus should be liable for 50% of any liability the supplier is found to have to the shopkeeper (assume that in State A, joint tortfeasors may be subject to contribution claims).

May the court exercise subject matter jurisdiction over the supplier's claim against the delivery company?

Hypo 3.7

An entrepreneur from State A initiated an action in federal court against a competitor from State B for tortious interference with prospective business advantage, a state law claim, seeking $100,000 in damages. In the same complaint, the entrepreneur also asserted a claim against a business owner for defamation under state law arising out of the same incident that formed the basis for the entrepreneur's tortious interference claim against the competitor. The business owner resides in State C but also has a summer home in State A, where service of process was delivered. The entrepreneur seeks $40,000 in damages for the defamation claim against the business owner. The rule that permits the competitor and the business owner to be sued together is Rule 20, thus making them parties joined under Rule 20.

May the court exercise subject matter jurisdiction over the entrepreneur's claim against the business owner?

The third and final section of § 1367(b) sets forth the other types of claims that will not qualify for supplemental jurisdiction in diversity-only cases. Those disqualified claims are:

- **Rule 19 Plaintiffs**—claims by plaintiffs joined under Rule 19;

- **Rule 24 Plaintiffs**—claims by plaintiffs who intervene under Rule 24.

Thus, if the qualifying claims in an action are based on diversity jurisdiction, supplemental jurisdiction will not extend to these other claims.

Hypo 3.8

Mary (VA) brought an action against Lindsey (NY) for $500,000 on a breach of contract claim in New York federal court. Carl (NY) intervened as a plaintiff under Rule 24 to assert a claim against Lindsey for $25,000, also for breach of contract.

Does the New York federal court have jurisdiction over Carl's claim against Lindsey?

The supplemental jurisdiction statute—28 U.S.C. § 1367—governs all assertions of supplemental jurisdiction, incorporating the *Gibbs* standard for the relationship between qualifying and non-qualifying claims. As you work on developing a complete understanding of the operation of § 1367(b), try to identify the ways in which the provision alters the post-*Gibbs* line of cases reviewed above. In other words, how would *Aldinger*, *Kroger*, and *Finley* be decided under the supplemental jurisdiction statute?

b. Interpretive Difficulties with § 1367

Note that § 1367(b) is very specific about the types of claims disqualified from supplemental jurisdiction under its provisions. However, such specificity has not prevented questions from arising regarding the proper interpretation of the statute. Specifically, questions arose concerning whether § 1367(b) overruled *Zahn v. International Paper Co.*, 414 U.S. 291 (1973), a case in which the Supreme Court held that each plaintiff in a class action individually had to satisfy the amount-in-controversy requirement of § 1332(a). Under § 1367(b), it appears that if one plaintiff asserts a qualifying diversity claim, other claims of co-plaintiffs that do not meet the amount-in-controversy requirement would qualify for supplemental jurisdiction because they would be part of the same case or controversy, *see* § 1367(a), and § 1367(b) makes no mention of disqualifying claims asserted by plaintiffs joined under Rule 20 (permissive joinder) or Rule 23 (joinder of plaintiffs as a class action). A circuit split developed on this issue, leading the Supreme Court to step in and resolve the matter in the following case.

Exxon Mobil Corp. v. Allapattah Services, Inc.

Supreme Court of the United States
545 U.S. 546 (2005)

JUSTICE KENNEDY delivered the opinion of the Court.

These consolidated cases present the question whether a federal court in a diversity action may exercise supplemental jurisdiction over additional plaintiffs whose claims do not satisfy the minimum amount-in-controversy requirement, provided the claims are part of the same case or controversy as the claims of plaintiffs who do allege a sufficient amount in controversy. Our decision turns on the correct interpretation of 28 U.S.C. § 1367. The question has divided the Courts of Appeals, and we granted certiorari to resolve the conflict. * * *

What's That?

The Court here refers to *consolidated cases*. When multiple cases present the same legal issue for resolution by the Court, the Court may order the cases to be consolidated and will hear and resolve them together, issuing an opinion or set of opinions that are applicable to the group.

I

In 1991, about 10,000 Exxon dealers filed a class-action suit against the Exxon Corporation in the United States District Court for the Northern District of Florida. The dealers alleged an intentional and systematic scheme by Exxon under which they were overcharged for fuel purchased from Exxon. The plaintiffs invoked the District Court's § 1332(a) diversity jurisdiction. After a unanimous jury verdict in favor of the plaintiffs, the District Court certified the case for interlocutory review, asking whether it had properly exercised § 1367 supplemental jurisdiction over the claims of class members who did not meet the jurisdictional minimum amount in controversy.

The Court of Appeals for the Eleventh Circuit upheld the District Court's extension of supplemental jurisdiction to these class members. *Allapattah Services, Inc. v. Exxon Corp.*, 333 F.3d 1248 (2003). "[W]e find," the court held, "that § 1367 clearly and unambiguously provides district courts with the authority in diversity class actions to exercise supplemental jurisdiction over the claims of class members who do not meet the minimum amount in controversy as long as the district court has original jurisdiction over the claims of at least one of the class representatives." This decision accords with the views of the Courts of Appeals for the Fourth, Sixth, and Seventh Circuits. The Courts of Appeals for the Fifth and Ninth Circuits, adopting a similar analysis of the statute, have held that in a diversity class action the unnamed class members need not meet the amount-in-controversy requirement, provided the named class members do. * * *

In the other case now before us [Rosario Ortega v. Star-Kist, 370 F.3d 124 (2004)] the Court of Appeals for the First Circuit took a different position on the meaning of § 1367(a). In that case, a 9-year-old girl sued Star-Kist in a diversity action in the United States District Court for the District of Puerto Rico, seeking damages for unusually severe injuries she received when she sliced her finger on a tuna can. Her family joined in the suit, seeking damages for emotional distress and certain medical expenses. The District Court granted summary judgment to Star-Kist, finding that none of the plaintiffs met the minimum amount-in-controversy requirement. The Court of Appeals for the First Circuit, however, ruled that the injured girl, but not her family members, had made allegations of damages in the requisite amount.

The Court of Appeals then addressed whether, in light of the fact that one plaintiff met the requirements for original jurisdiction, supplemental jurisdiction over the remaining plaintiffs' claims was proper under § 1367. The court held that § 1367 authorizes supplemental jurisdiction only when the district court has original jurisdiction over the action, and that in a diversity case original jurisdiction is lacking if one plaintiff fails to satisfy the amount-in-controversy requirement. * * * The Court of Appeals for the First Circuit's view of § 1367 is, however, shared by the Courts of Appeal for the Third, Eighth, and Tenth Circuits, and the latter two Courts of Appeals have expressly applied this rule to class actions.

II

A

The district courts of the United States, as we have said many times, are "courts of limited jurisdiction. They possess only that power authorized by Constitution and statute." In order to provide a federal forum for plaintiffs who seek to vindicate federal rights, Congress has conferred on the district courts original jurisdiction in federal-question cases—civil actions that arise under the Constitution, laws, or treaties of the United States. 28 U.S.C. § 1331. In order to provide a neutral forum for what have come to be known as diversity cases, Congress also has granted district courts original jurisdiction in civil actions between citizens of different States, between U.S. citizens and foreign citizens, or by foreign states against U.S. citizens. § 1332. To ensure that diversity jurisdiction does not flood the federal courts with minor disputes, § 1332(a) requires that the matter in controversy in a diversity case exceed a specified amount, currently $75,000.

Although the district courts may not exercise jurisdiction absent a statutory basis, it is well established—in certain classes of cases—that, once a court has original jurisdiction over some claims in the action, it may exercise supplemental jurisdiction over additional claims that are part of the same case or controversy. The leading modern case for this principle is *United Mine Workers of America v. Gibbs*, 383 U.S. 715 (1966). In *Gibbs*, the plaintiff alleged the defendant's conduct violated both federal and state law. The District Court, *Gibbs* held, had original jurisdiction over the action based on the federal claims. *Gibbs* confirmed that the District Court had the additional power (though not the obligation) to exercise supplemental jurisdiction over related state claims that arose from the same Article III case or controversy.

As we later noted, the decision allowing jurisdiction over pendent state claims in *Gibbs* did not mention, let alone come to grips with, the text of the jurisdictional statutes and the bedrock principle that federal courts have no jurisdiction without statutory authorization. *Finley v. United States*, 490 U.S. 545, 548 (1989). In *Finley*, we nonetheless reaffirmed and rationalized *Gibbs* and its progeny by inferring from it the interpretive principle that, in cases involving supplemental jurisdiction over additional claims between parties properly in federal court, the jurisdictional statutes should be read broadly, on the assumption that in this context Congress intended to authorize courts to exercise their full Article III power to dispose of an entire action before the court [which] comprises but one constitutional "case."

We have not, however, applied *Gibbs'* expansive interpretive approach to other aspects of the jurisdictional statutes. For instance, we have consistently interpreted § 1332 as requiring complete diversity: In a case with multiple plaintiffs and multiple defendants, the presence in the action of a single plaintiff from the same State as a single defendant deprives the district court of original diversity jurisdiction over the entire action. *Strawbridge v. Curtiss*, 7 U.S. 267 (1806); *Owen Equipment & Erection Co. v. Kroger*, 437 U.S. 365 (1978). The complete diversity requirement is not mandated by the Constitution, *State Farm Fire & Casualty Co. v. Tashire*, 386 U.S. 523, 530–31 (1967), or by the plain text of § 1332(a). The Court, nonetheless, has adhered to the complete diversity rule in light of the purpose of the diversity requirement, which is to provide a federal forum for important disputes where state courts might favor, or be perceived as favoring, home-state litigants. The presence of parties from the same State on both sides of a case dispels this concern, eliminating a principal reason for conferring § 1332 jurisdiction over any of the claims in the action. * * * In order for a federal court to invoke supplemental jurisdiction under *Gibbs*, it must first have original jurisdiction over at least one claim in the action. Incomplete diversity destroys original jurisdiction with respect to all claims, so there is nothing to which supplemental jurisdiction can adhere.

In contrast to the diversity requirement, most of the other statutory prerequisites for federal jurisdiction, including the federal-question and amount-in-controversy requirements, can be analyzed claim by claim. True, it does not follow by necessity from this that a district court has authority to exercise supplemental jurisdiction over all claims provided there is original jurisdiction over just one. Before the enactment of § 1367, the Court declined in contexts other than the pendent-claim instance to follow *Gibbs'* expansive approach to interpretation of the jurisdictional statutes. The Court took a more restrictive view of the proper interpretation of these statutes in so-called pendent-party cases involving supplemental jurisdiction over claims involving additional parties—plaintiffs or defendants—where the district courts would lack original jurisdiction over claims by each of the parties standing alone.

Thus, with respect to plaintiff-specific jurisdictional requirements, the Court held in *Clark v. Paul Gray, Inc.*, 306 U.S. 583 (1939), that every plaintiff must separately satisfy the amount-in-controversy requirement. Though *Clark* was a federal-question case, at that time federal-question jurisdiction had an amount-in-controversy requirement analogous to the amount-in-controversy requirement for diversity cases. "Proper practice," *Clark* held, "requires that where each of several plaintiffs is bound to establish the jurisdictional amount with respect to his own claim, the suit should be dismissed as to those who fail to show that the requisite amount is involved." The Court reaffirmed this rule, in the context of a class action brought invoking § 1332(a) diversity jurisdiction, in *Zahn v. International Paper Co.*, 414 U.S. 291 (1973). It follows "inescapably" from *Clark*, the Court held in *Zahn*, that "any plaintiff without the jurisdictional amount must be dismissed from the case, even though others allege jurisdictionally sufficient claims."

The Court took a similar approach with respect to supplemental jurisdiction over claims against additional defendants that fall outside the district courts' original jurisdiction. In *Aldinger v. Howard*, 427 U.S. 1 (1976), the plaintiff brought a 42 U.S.C. § 1983 action against county officials in district court pursuant to the statutory grant of jurisdiction in 28 U.S.C. § 1343(3). The plaintiff further alleged the court had supplemental jurisdiction over her related state-law claims against the county, even though the county was not suable under § 1983 and so was not subject to § 1343(3)'s original jurisdiction. The Court held that supplemental jurisdiction could not be exercised because Congress, in enacting § 1343(3), had declined (albeit implicitly) to extend federal jurisdiction over any party who could not be sued under the federal civil rights statutes. "Before it can be concluded that [supplemental] jurisdiction [over additional parties] exists," *Aldinger* held, "a federal court must satisfy itself not only that Article III permits it, but that Congress in the statutes conferring jurisdiction has not expressly or by implication negated its existence."

In *Finley v. United States*, 490 U.S. 545 (1989), we confronted a similar issue in a different statutory context. The plaintiff in *Finley* brought a Federal Tort Claims Act negligence suit against the Federal Aviation Administration in District Court, which had original jurisdiction under § 1346(b). The plaintiff tried to add related claims against other defendants, invoking the District Court's supplemental jurisdiction over so-called pendent parties. We held that the District Court lacked a sufficient statutory basis for exercising supplemental jurisdiction over these claims. Relying primarily on *Zahn*, *Aldinger*, and *Kroger*, we held in *Finley* that "a grant of jurisdiction over claims involving particular parties does not itself confer jurisdiction over additional claims by or against different parties." While *Finley* did not "limit or impair" *Gibbs'* liberal approach to interpreting the jurisdictional statutes in the context of supplemental jurisdiction over additional claims involving the same parties, *Finley* nevertheless declined to extend that interpretive assumption to claims involving additional parties. * * *

As the jurisdictional statutes existed in 1989, then, here is how matters stood: First, the diversity requirement in § 1332(a) required complete diversity; absent complete diversity, the district court lacked original jurisdiction over all of the claims in the action. Second, if the district court had original jurisdiction over at least one claim, the jurisdictional statutes implicitly authorized supplemental jurisdiction over all other claims between the same parties arising out of the same Article III case or controversy. *Gibbs.* Third, even when the district court had original jurisdiction over one or more claims between particular parties, the jurisdictional statutes did not authorize supplemental jurisdiction over additional claims involving other parties. *Clark*; *Zahn*; *Finley.*

Food for Thought

The Court writes, "it is just as important not to adopt an artificial construction that is narrower than what the text provides." However, earlier in the opinion the Court noted its own interpretation of § 1332 as requiring "complete diversity," even though such a requirement is not compelled by the language of Article III or § 1332. Is the Court living up to its own standard for interpreting jurisdictional statutes?

B

In *Finley* we emphasized that "[w]hatever we say regarding the scope of jurisdiction conferred by a particular statute can of course be changed by Congress." 490 U.S. at 556. In 1990, Congress accepted the invitation. It * * * enacted § 1367, the provision which controls these cases. * * *

All parties to this litigation and all courts to consider the question agree that § 1367 overturned the result in *Finley*. There is no warrant, however, for assuming that § 1367 did no more than to overrule *Finley* and otherwise to codify the existing state of the law of supplemental jurisdiction. We must not give jurisdictional statutes a more expansive interpretation than their text warrants, but it is just as important not to adopt an artificial construction that is narrower than what the text provides. No sound canon of interpretation requires Congress to speak with extraordinary clarity in order to modify the rules of federal jurisdiction within appropriate

What's That?

Canons of interpretation or *construction* are "a set of background norms and conventions that are used by courts when interpreting statutes." James J. Brudney & Corey Ditslear, *Canons of Construction and the Elusive Quest for Neutral Reasoning*, 58 VAND. L. REV. 1 (2005).

constitutional bounds. Ordinary principles of statutory construction apply. In order to determine the scope of supplemental jurisdiction authorized by § 1367, then, we must examine the statute's text in light of context, structure, and related statutory provisions.

Section 1367(a) is a broad grant of supplemental jurisdiction over other claims within the same case or controversy, as long as the action is one in which the district courts would have original jurisdiction. The last sentence of § 1367(a) makes it clear that the grant of supplemental jurisdiction extends to claims involving joinder or intervention of additional parties. The single question before us, therefore, is whether a diversity case in which the claims of some plaintiffs satisfy the amount-in-controversy requirement, but the claims of others plaintiffs do not, presents a "civil action of which the district courts have original jurisdiction." If the answer is yes, § 1367(a) confers supplemental jurisdiction over all claims, including those that do not independently satisfy the amount-in-controversy requirement, if the claims are part of the same Article III case or controversy. If the answer is no, § 1367(a) is inapplicable and, in light of our holdings in *Clark* and *Zahn*, the district court has no statutory basis for exercising supplemental jurisdiction over the additional claims.

We now conclude the answer must be yes. When the well-pleaded complaint contains at least one claim that satisfies the amount-in-controversy requirement, and there are no other relevant jurisdictional defects, the district court, beyond all question, has original jurisdiction over that claim. The presence of other claims in the complaint, over which the district court may lack original jurisdiction, is of no moment. If the court has original jurisdiction over a single claim in the complaint, it has original jurisdiction over a "civil action" within the meaning of § 1367(a), even if the civil action over which it has jurisdiction comprises fewer claims than were included in the complaint. Once the court determines it has original jurisdiction over the civil action, it can turn to the question whether it has a constitutional and statutory basis for exercising supplemental jurisdiction over the other claims in the action.

Section 1367(a) commences with the direction that §§ 1367(b) and (c), or other relevant statutes, may provide specific exceptions, but otherwise § 1367(a) is a broad jurisdictional grant, with no distinction drawn between pendent-claim and pendent-party cases. In fact, the last sentence of § 1367(a) makes clear that the provision grants supplemental jurisdiction over claims involving joinder or intervention of additional parties. The terms of § 1367 do not acknowledge any distinction between pendent jurisdiction and the doctrine of so-called ancillary jurisdiction. Though the doctrines of pendent and ancillary jurisdiction developed separately as a historical matter, the Court has recognized that the doctrines are "two species of the same generic problem," *Kroger*. Nothing in § 1367 indicates a congressional intent to recognize, preserve, or create some meaningful, substantive distinction between the jurisdictional categories we have historically labeled pendent and ancillary.

If § 1367(a) were the sum total of the relevant statutory language, our holding would rest on that language alone. The statute, of course, instructs us to examine § 1367(b) to determine if any of its exceptions apply, so we proceed to that section. While § 1367(b) qualifies the broad rule of § 1367(a), it does not withdraw supplemental jurisdiction over the claims of the additional parties at issue here. The specific exceptions to § 1367(a) contained in § 1367(b), moreover, provide additional support for our conclusion that § 1367(a) confers supplemental jurisdiction over these claims. Section 1367(b), which applies only to diversity cases, withholds supplemental jurisdiction over the claims of plaintiffs proposed to be joined as indispensable parties under Federal Rule of Civil Procedure 19, or who seek to intervene pursuant to Rule 24. Nothing in the text of § 1367(b), however, withholds supplemental jurisdiction over the claims of plaintiffs permissively joined under Rule 20 (like the additional plaintiffs in *Ortega*) or certified as class-action members pursuant to Rule 23 (like the additional plaintiffs in *Exxon*). The natural, indeed the necessary, inference is that § 1367 confers supplemental jurisdiction over claims by Rule 20 and Rule 23 plaintiffs. This inference, at least with respect to Rule 20 plaintiffs, is strengthened by the fact that § 1367(b) explicitly excludes supplemental jurisdiction over claims against defendants joined under Rule 20.

> **FYI**
> Each of these rules mentioned here (Rules 19, 20, 23, & 24) will be covered fully in Chapter 7, which deals with joinder. In brief, Rule 20 permits plaintiffs to sue within the same action if they assert related claims, and Rule 23 permits plaintiffs to proceed as a class when a number of detailed requirements are satisfied.

We cannot accept the view, urged by some of the parties, commentators, and Courts of Appeals, that a district court lacks original jurisdiction over a civil action unless the court has original jurisdiction over every claim in the complaint. As we understand this position, it requires assuming either that all claims in the complaint must stand or fall as a single, indivisible "civil action" as a matter of definitional necessity—what we will refer to as the "indivisibility theory"—or else that the inclusion of a claim or party falling outside the district court's original jurisdiction somehow contaminates every other claim in the complaint, depriving the court of original jurisdiction over any of these claims—what we will refer to as the "contamination theory."

The indivisibility theory is easily dismissed, as it is inconsistent with the whole notion of supplemental jurisdiction. If a district court must have original jurisdiction over every claim in the complaint in order to have "original jurisdiction" over a "civil action," then in *Gibbs* there was no civil action of which the district court could assume original jurisdiction under § 1331, and so no basis for exercising supplemental jurisdiction over any of the claims. The indivisibility theory is further belied by our practice—in both federal-question and diversity cases—of allowing federal courts to cure jurisdictional defects by dismissing the offending parties rather than dismissing the entire action. *Clark*, for example, makes clear that claims that are jurisdictionally defective as to amount in controversy do not destroy original jurisdiction over other claims. If the presence of jurisdictionally problematic claims in the complaint meant the district court was without original jurisdiction over the single, indivisible civil action before it, then the district court would have to dismiss the whole action rather than particular parties.

We also find it unconvincing to say that the definitional indivisibility theory applies in the context of diversity cases but not in the context of federal-question cases. The broad and general language of the statute does not permit this result. The contention is premised on the notion that the phrase "original jurisdiction of all civil actions" means different things in § 1331 and § 1332. It is implausible, however, to say that the identical phrase means one thing (original jurisdiction in all actions where at least one claim in the complaint meets the following requirements) in § 1331 and something else (original jurisdiction in all actions where every claim in the complaint meets the following requirements) in § 1332.

The contamination theory, as we have noted, can make some sense in the special context of the complete diversity requirement because the presence of non-diverse parties on both sides of a lawsuit eliminates the justification for providing a federal forum. The theory, however, makes little sense with respect to the amount-in-controversy requirement, which is meant to ensure that a dispute is sufficiently important to warrant federal-court attention. The presence of a single nondiverse party may eliminate the fear of bias with respect to all claims, but the presence of a claim that falls short of the minimum amount in controversy does nothing to reduce the importance of the claims that do meet this requirement.

* * *

We also reject the argument * * * that while the presence of additional claims over which the district court lacks jurisdiction does not mean the civil action is outside the purview of § 1367(a), the presence of additional parties does. The basis for this distinction is not altogether clear, and it is in considerable tension with statutory text. Section 1367(a) applies by its terms to any civil action of which the district courts have original jurisdiction, and the last sentence of § 1367(a) expressly contemplates that the court may have supplemental jurisdiction over additional parties. So it cannot be the case that the presence of those parties destroys the court's original jurisdiction, within the meaning of § 1367(a), over a civil action otherwise properly before it. Also, § 1367(b) expressly withholds supplemental jurisdiction in diversity cases over claims by plaintiffs joined as indispensable parties under Rule 19. If joinder of such parties were sufficient to deprive the district court of original jurisdiction over the civil action within the meaning of § 1367(a), this specific limitation on supplemental jurisdiction in § 1367(b) would be superfluous. The argument that the presence of additional parties removes the civil action from the scope of § 1367(a) also would mean that § 1367 left the *Finley* result undisturbed. * * * Yet all concede that one purpose of § 1367 was to change the result reached in *Finley*.

Finally, it is suggested that our interpretation of § 1367(a) creates an anomaly regarding the exceptions listed in § 1367(b): It is not immediately obvious why Congress would withhold supplemental jurisdiction over plaintiffs joined as parties "needed for just adjudication" under Rule 19 but would allow supplemental jurisdiction over plaintiffs permissively joined under Rule 20. The omission of Rule 20 plaintiffs from the list of exceptions in § 1367(b) may have been an "unintentional drafting gap." If that is the case, it is up to Congress rather than the courts to fix it. The omission may seem odd, but it is not absurd. An alternative explanation for the different treatment of Rule 19 and Rule 20 is that Congress was concerned that extending supplemental jurisdiction to Rule 19 plaintiffs would allow circumvention of the complete diversity rule: A nondiverse plaintiff might be omitted intentionally from the original action, but joined later under Rule 19 as a necessary party. The contamination theory described above, if applicable, means this ruse would fail, but Congress may have wanted to make assurance double sure. More generally, Congress may have concluded that federal jurisdiction is only appropriate if the district court would have original jurisdiction over the claims of all those plaintiffs who are so essential to the action that they could be joined under Rule 19.

* * *

And so we circle back to the original question. When the well-pleaded complaint in district court includes multiple claims, all part of the same case or controversy, and some, but not all, of the claims are within the court's original jurisdiction, does the court have before it "any civil action of which the district courts have original jurisdiction"? It does. Under § 1367, the court has original jurisdiction over the civil action comprising the claims for which there is no jurisdictional defect. No other reading of § 1367 is plausible in light of the text and structure of the jurisdictional statute. Though the special nature and purpose of the diversity requirement mean that a single nondiverse party can contaminate every other claim in the lawsuit, the contamination does not occur with respect to jurisdictional defects that go only to the substantive importance of individual claims.

Food for Thought

The Court asserts that "[n]o other reading of § 1367 is plausible in light of the text and structure of the jurisdictional statute." Is this an overstatement? Both dissents present extensive arguments in favor of contrary interpretations of § 1367. Do their views lack plausibility?

It follows from this conclusion that the threshold requirement of § 1367(a) is satisfied in cases, like those now before us, where some, but not all, of the plaintiffs in a diversity action allege a sufficient amount in controversy. We hold that § 1367 by its plain text overruled *Clark* and *Zahn* and authorized supplemental jurisdiction over all claims by diverse parties arising out of the same Article III case or controversy, subject only to enumerated exceptions not applicable in the cases now before us.

C

The proponents of the alternative view of § 1367 insist that the statute is at least ambiguous and that we should look to other interpretive tools, including the legislative history of § 1367, which supposedly demonstrate Congress did not intend § 1367 to overrule *Zahn*. We can reject this argument at the very outset simply because § 1367 is not ambiguous. For the reasons elaborated above, interpreting § 1367 to foreclose supplemental jurisdiction over plaintiffs in diversity cases who do not meet the minimum amount in controversy is inconsistent with the text, read in light of other statutory provisions and our established jurisprudence. Even if we were to stipulate, however, that the reading these proponents urge upon us is textually plausible, the legislative history cited to support it would not alter our view as to the best interpretation of § 1367.

Those who urge that the legislative history refutes our interpretation rely primarily on the House Judiciary Committee Report on the Judicial Improvements Act. * * * The Report * * * remarked that § 1367(b) "is not intended to affect the jurisdictional requirements of [§ 1332] in diversity only-class actions, as those requirements were interpreted prior to *Finley*," citing, without further elaboration, *Zahn* * * * . * * *

As we have repeatedly held, the authoritative statement is the statutory text, not the legislative history or any other extrinsic material. Extrinsic materials have a role in statutory interpretation only to the extent they shed a reliable light on the enacting Legislature's understanding of otherwise ambiguous terms. Not all extrinsic materials are reliable sources of insight into legislative understandings, however, and legislative history in particular is vulnerable to two serious criticisms. First, legislative history is itself often murky, ambiguous, and contradictory. * * * Second, judicial reliance on legislative materials like committee reports, which are not themselves subject to the requirements of Article I, may give unrepresentative committee members—or, worse yet, unelected staffers and lobbyists—both the power and the incentive to attempt strategic manipulations of legislative history to secure results they were unable to achieve through the statutory text. We need not comment here on whether these problems are sufficiently prevalent to render legislative history inherently unreliable in all circumstances, a point on which Members of this Court have disagreed. It is clear, however, that in this instance both criticisms are right on the mark.

First of all, the legislative history of § 1367 is far murkier than selective quotation from the House Report would suggest. The text of § 1367 is based substantially on a draft proposal contained in a Federal Court Study Committee working paper, which was drafted by a Subcommittee chaired by Judge Posner. While the Subcommittee explained, in language echoed by the House Report, that its proposal "basically restores the law as it existed prior to *Finley*," it observed in a footnote that its proposal would overrule *Zahn* and that this would be a good idea. Although the Federal Courts Study Committee did not expressly adopt the Subcommittee's specific reference to *Zahn*, it neither explicitly disagreed with the Subcommittee's conclusion that this was the best reading of the proposed text nor substantially modified the proposal to avoid this result. Therefore, even if the House Report could fairly be read to reflect an understanding that the text of § 1367 did not overrule *Zahn*, the Subcommittee Working Paper on which § 1367 was based reflected the opposite understanding. The House Report is no more authoritative than the Subcommittee Working Paper. The utility of either can extend no further than the light it sheds on how the enacting Legislature understood the statutory text. Trying to figure out how to square the Subcommittee Working Paper's understanding with the House Report's understanding, or which is more reflective of the understanding of the enacting legislators, is a hopeless task.

Food for Thought

Under what circumstances should courts be able to consider a statute's legislative history as an aid to interpreting the statute? *See* Stephen Breyer, *On the Uses of Legislative History in Interpreting Statutes*, 65 S. CAL. L. REV. 845 (1992).

Second, the worst fears of critics who argue legislative history will be used to circumvent the Article I process were realized in this case. The telltale evidence is the statement, by three law professors who participated in drafting § 1367 that § 1367 "on its face" permits "supplemental jurisdiction over claims of class members that do not satisfy section 1332's jurisdictional amount requirement, which would overrule [*Zahn*]. [There is] a disclaimer of intent to accomplish this result in the legislative history . . . . It would have been better had the statute dealt explicitly with this problem, and the legislative history was an attempt to correct the oversight." Rowe, Burbank, & Mengler, *Compounding or Creating Confusion About Supplemental Jurisdiction? A Reply to Professor Freer*, 40 EMORY L.J. 943, 960, n.90 (1991). The professors were frank to concede that if one refuses to consider the legislative history, one has no choice but to "conclude that section 1367 has wiped *Zahn* off the books." So there exists an acknowledgment, by parties who have detailed, specific knowledge of the statute and the drafting process, both that the plain text of § 1367 overruled *Zahn* and that language to the contrary in the House Report was a post hoc attempt to alter that result. One need not subscribe to the wholesale condemnation of legislative history to refuse to give any effect to such a deliberate effort to amend a statute through a committee report.

In sum, even if we believed resort to legislative history were appropriate in these cases—a point we do not concede—we would not give significant weight to the House Report. The distinguished jurists who drafted the Subcommittee Working Paper, along with three of the participants in the drafting of § 1367, agree that this provision, on its face, overrules *Zahn*. This accords with the best reading of the statute's text, and nothing in the legislative history indicates directly and explicitly that Congress understood the phrase "civil action of which the district courts have original jurisdiction" to exclude cases in which some but not all of the diversity plaintiffs meet the amount-in-controversy requirement.

* * *

The judgment of the Court of Appeals for the Eleventh Circuit [in *Exxon*] is affirmed. The judgment of the Court of Appeals for the First Circuit [in *Ortega*] is reversed, and the case is remanded for proceedings consistent with this opinion.

It is so ordered.

JUSTICE STEVENS, with whom JUSTICE BREYER joins, dissenting.

Justice GINSBURG's carefully reasoned [dissenting] opinion, demonstrates the error in the Court's rather ambitious reading of this opaque jurisdictional statute. She also has demonstrated that "ambiguity" is a term that may have different meanings for different judges, for the Court has made the remarkable declaration that its reading of the statute is so obviously correct—and Justice GINSBURG's so obviously wrong—that the text does not even qualify as "ambiguous." Because ambiguity is apparently in the eye of the beholder, I remain convinced that it is unwise to treat the ambiguity *vel non* of a statute as deter-

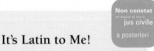

It's Latin to Me!

Vel non is Latin for "or not." Thus, Justice Steven's use of the term here means "it is unwise to treat the ambiguity [or non-ambiguity] of the statute as determinative . . . ."

Non constat
ex aequo et bono
jus civile
a posteriori

minative of whether legislative history is consulted. Indeed, I believe that we as judges are more, rather than less, constrained when we make ourselves accountable to all reliable evidence of legislative intent.

* * *

The sweeping purpose that the Court's decision imputes to Congress bears no resemblance to the House Report's description of the statute. But this does not seem to trouble the Court, for its decision today treats statutory interpretation as a pedantic exercise, divorced from any serious attempt at ascertaining congressional intent. Of course, there are situations in which we do not honor Congress' apparent intent unless that intent is made "clear" in the text of a statute—in this way, we can be certain that Congress considered the issue and intended a disfavored outcome. But that principle provides no basis for discounting the House Report, given that our cases have never recognized a presumption in favor of expansive diversity jurisdiction.

The Court's reasons for ignoring this virtual billboard of congressional intent are unpersuasive. That a subcommittee of the Federal Courts Study Committee believed that an earlier, substantially similar version of the statute overruled *Zahn*, only high-lights the fact that the statute is ambiguous. What is determinative is that the House Report explicitly rejected that broad reading of the statutory text. Such a report has special significance as an indicator of legislative intent. In Congress, committee reports are normally considered the authoritative explication of a statute's text and purposes, and busy legislators and their assistants rely on that explication in casting their votes.

The Court's second reason—its comment on the three law professors who par-ticipated in drafting § 1367—is similarly off the mark. In the law review article that the Court refers to, the professors were merely saying that the text of the statute was susceptible to an overly broad (and simplistic) reading, and that clarification in the House Report was therefore appropriate. Significantly, the reference to *Zahn* in the House Report does not at all appear to be tacked-on or out of place; indeed, it is wholly consistent with the Report's broader explanation of Congress' goal of overruling *Finley* and preserving pre-*Finley* law. To suggest that these professors participated in a "deliberate effort to amend a statute through a committee report," reveals an unrealistic view of the legislative process, not to mention disrespect for three law professors who acted in the role of public servants. To be sure, legislative history can be manipulated. But, in the situation before us, there is little reason to fear that an unholy conspiracy of "unrepresentative committee members," law professors, and "unelected staffers and lobbyists," endeavored to torpedo Congress' attempt to overrule (without discussion) two longstanding features of this Court's diversity jurisprudence.

After nearly 20 pages of complicated analysis, which explores subtle doctrinal nuances and coins various neologisms, the Court announces that § 1367 could not reasonably be read another way. That conclusion is difficult to accept. Given Justice GINSBURG's persuasive account of the statutory text and its jurisprudential backdrop, and given the uncommonly clear legislative history, I am confident that the majority's interpretation of § 1367 is mistaken. I respectfully dissent.

JUSTICE GINSBURG, with whom JUSTICE STEVENS, JUSTICE O'CONNOR, and JUSTICE BREYER join, dissenting.

These cases present the question whether Congress, by enacting 28 U.S.C. § 1367, overruled this Court's decisions in *Clark* and *Zahn*. *Clark* held that, when federal-court jurisdiction is predicated on a specified amount in controversy, each plaintiff joined in the litigation must independently meet the jurisdictional amount requirement. *Zahn* confirmed that in class actions governed by Federal Rule of Civil Procedure 23(b)(3), "[e]ach [class member] . . . must satisfy the jurisdictional amount, and any [class member] who does not must be dismissed from the case."

Section 1367, all agree, was designed to overturn this Court's decision in *Finley v. United States.* * * * What more § 1367 wrought is an issue on which courts of appeals have sharply divided. The Court today holds that § 1367 * * * notably enlarges federal diversity jurisdiction. The Court reads § 1367 to overrule *Clark* and *Zahn*, thereby allowing access to federal court by co-plaintiffs or class members who do not meet the now in excess of $75,000 amount-in-controversy requirement, so long as at least one co-plaintiff, or the named class representative, has a jurisdictionally sufficient claim.

The Court adopts a plausibly broad reading of § 1367, a measure that is hardly a model of the careful drafter's art. There is another plausible reading, however, one less disruptive of our jurisprudence regarding supplemental jurisdiction. If one reads § 1367(a) to instruct, as the statute's text suggests, that the district court must first have "original jurisdiction" over a "civil action" before supplemental jurisdiction can attach, then *Clark* and *Zahn* are preserved, and supplemental jurisdiction does not open the way for joinder of plaintiffs, or inclusion of class members, who do not independently meet the amount-in-controversy requirement. For the reasons that follow, I conclude that this narrower construction is the better reading of § 1367.

I

A

* * *

[I]n federal-question cases before § 1367's enactment, the Court recognized pendent-claim jurisdiction, *Gibbs*, but not pendent-party jurisdiction, *Finley*. As to ancillary jurisdiction, the Court adhered to the limitation that in diversity cases, throughout the litigation, all plaintiffs must remain diverse from all defendants. *See Kroger.* * * *

II

A

Section 1367, by its terms, operates only in civil actions "of which the district courts have original jurisdiction." The "original jurisdiction" relevant here is diversity-of-citizenship jurisdiction, conferred by § 1332. The character of that jurisdiction is the essential backdrop for comprehension of § 1367.

The Constitution broadly provides for federal-court jurisdiction in controversies "between Citizens of different States." U.S. Const. art. III, § 2, cl. 1. This Court has read that provision to demand no more than "minimal diversity," i.e., so long as one party on the plaintiffs' side and one party on the defendants' side are of diverse citizenship, Congress may authorize federal courts to exercise diversity jurisdiction. *See State Farm Fire & Casualty Co. v. Tashire*, 386 U.S. 523, 530–31 (1967). Further, the Constitution includes no amount-in-controversy limitation on the exercise of federal jurisdiction. But from the start, Congress, as its measures have been construed by this Court, has limited federal court exercise of diversity jurisdiction in two principal ways. First, unless Congress specifies otherwise, diversity must be "complete," i.e., all parties on plaintiffs' side must be diverse from all parties on defendants' side. *Strawbridge v. Curtiss*, 7 U.S. 267 (1806). Second, each plaintiff's stake must independently meet the amount-in-controversy specification: "When two or more plaintiffs, having separate and distinct demands, unite for convenience and economy in a single suit, it is essential that the demand of each be of the requisite jurisdictional amount."

The statute today governing federal court exercise of diversity jurisdiction in the generality of cases, § 1332, like all its predecessors, incorporates both a diverse-citizenship requirement and an amount-in-controversy specification. As to the latter, the statute reads: "The district courts shall have original jurisdiction [in diversity-of-citizenship cases] where the matter in controversy exceeds the sum . . . of $75,000." § 1332(a). This Court has long held that, in determining whether the amount-in-controversy requirement has been satisfied, a single plaintiff may aggregate two or more claims against a single defendant, even if the claims are unrelated. But in multiparty cases, including class actions, we have * * * adhered to the nonaggregation rule * * *.

This Court most recently addressed "[t]he meaning of [§ 1332's] 'matter in controversy' language" in *Zahn*. *Zahn*, like *Snyder* decided four years earlier, was a class action. In *Snyder*, no class member had a claim large enough to satisfy the jurisdictional amount. But in *Zahn*, the named plaintiffs had such claims. Nevertheless, the Court declined to depart from its "longstanding construction of the 'matter in controversy' requirement of § 1332." The *Zahn* Court stated:

> "*Snyder* invoked the well-established rule that each of several plaintiffs asserting separate and distinct claims must satisfy the jurisdictional-amount requirement if his claim is to survive a motion to dismiss. This rule plainly mandates not only that there may be no aggregation and that the entire case must be dismissed where none of the plaintiffs claims [meets the amount-in-controversy requirement] but also requires that any plaintiff without the jurisdictional amount must be dismissed from the case, even though others allege jurisdictionally sufficient claims."

The rule that each plaintiff must independently satisfy the amount-in-controversy requirement, unless Congress expressly orders otherwise, was thus the solidly established reading of § 1332 when Congress enacted the Judicial Improvements Act of 1990, which added § 1367 to Title 28.

B

These cases present the question whether Congress abrogated the nonaggregation rule long tied to § 1332 when it enacted § 1367. * * * The Court should assume, as it ordinarily does, that Congress legislated against a background of law already in place and the historical development of that law. Here, that background is the statutory grant of diversity jurisdiction, the amount-in-controversy condition that Congress, from the start, has tied to the grant, and the nonaggregation rule this Court has long applied to the determination of the "matter in controversy."

* * *

The Court is unanimous in reading § 1367(a) to permit pendent-party jurisdiction in federal-question cases, and thus, to overrule *Finley*. * * *

The Court divides, however, on the impact of § 1367(a) on diversity cases controlled by § 1332. Under the majority's reading, § 1367(a) permits the joinder of related claims cut loose from the nonaggregation rule that has long attended actions under § 1332. Only the claims specified in § 1367(b) would be excluded from § 1367(a)'s expansion of § 1332's grant of diversity jurisdiction. And because § 1367(b) contains no exception for joinder of plaintiffs under Rule 20 or class actions under Rule 23, the Court concludes, *Clark* and *Zahn* have been overruled.

The Court's reading is surely plausible, especially if one detaches § 1367(a) from its context and attempts no reconciliation with prior interpretations of § 1332's amount-in-controversy requirement. But § 1367(a)'s text, as the First Circuit held, can be read another way, one that would involve no rejection of *Clark* and *Zahn*.

As explained by the First Circuit in *Ortega* * * * , § 1367(a) addresses "civil action[s] of which the district courts have original jurisdiction," a formulation that, in diversity cases, is sensibly read to incorporate the rules on joinder and aggregation tightly tied to § 1332 at the time of § 1367's enactment. On this reading, a complaint must first meet that "original jurisdiction" measurement. If it does not, no supplemental jurisdiction is authorized. If it does, § 1367(a) authorizes "supplemental jurisdiction" over related claims. In other words, § 1367(a) would preserve undiminished, as part and parcel of § 1332 "original jurisdiction" determinations, both the "complete diversity" rule and the decisions restricting aggregation to arrive at the amount in controversy. Section 1367(b)'s office, then, would be "to prevent the erosion of the complete diversity [and amount-in-controversy] requirement[s] that might otherwise result from an expansive application of what was once termed the doctrine of ancillary jurisdiction." In contrast to the Court's construction of § 1367, which draws a sharp line between the diversity and amount-in-controversy components of § 1332; the interpretation presented here does not sever the two jurisdictional requirements.

The more restrained reading of § 1367 just outlined would yield affirmance of the First Circuit's judgment in *Ortega*, and reversal of the Eleventh Circuit's judgment in *Exxon*. It would not discard entirely, as the Court does, the judicially developed doctrines of pendent and ancillary jurisdiction as they existed when *Finley* was decided. Instead, it would recognize § 1367 essentially as a codification of those doctrines, placing them under a single heading, but largely retaining their substance, with overriding *Finley* the only basic change * * * . * * *

The less disruptive view I take of § 1367 also accounts for the omission of Rule 20 plaintiffs and Rule 23 class actions in § 1367(b)'s text. If one reads § 1367(a) as a plenary grant of supplemental jurisdiction to federal courts sitting in diversity, one would indeed look for exceptions in § 1367(b). Finding none for permissive joinder of parties or class actions, one would conclude that Congress effectively, even if unintentionally, overruled *Clark* and *Zahn*. But if one recognizes that the nonaggregation rule delineated in *Clark* and *Zahn* forms part of the determination whether "original jurisdiction" exists in a diversity case, then plaintiffs who do not meet the amount-in-controversy requirement would fail at the § 1367(a) threshold. Congress would have no reason to resort to a § 1367(b) exception to turn such plaintiffs away from federal court, given that their claims, from the start, would fall outside the court's § 1332 jurisdiction.

* * *

What is the utility of § 1367(b) under my reading of § 1367(a)? Section 1367(a) allows parties other than the plaintiff to assert reactive claims once entertained under the heading ancillary jurisdiction. As earlier observed, § 1367(b) stops plaintiffs from circumventing § 1332's jurisdictional requirements by using another's claim as a hook to add a claim that the plaintiff could not have brought in the first instance. *Kroger* is the paradigm case. There, the Court held that ancillary jurisdiction did not extend to a plaintiff's claim against a nondiverse party who had been impleaded by the defendant under Rule 14. Section 1367(b), then, is corroborative of § 1367(a)'s coverage of claims formerly called ancillary, but provides exceptions to assure that accommodation of added claims would not fundamentally alter "the jurisdictional requirements of section 1332."

While § 1367's enigmatic text defies flawless interpretation, the precedent-preservative reading, I am persuaded, better accords with the historical and legal context of Congress' enactment of the supplemental jurisdiction statute, and the established limits on pendent and ancillary jurisdiction. It does not attribute to Congress a jurisdictional enlargement broader than the one to which the legislators adverted and it follows the sound counsel that "close questions of [statutory] construction should be resolved in favor of continuity and against change."

* * *

For the reasons stated, I would hold that § 1367 does not overrule *Clark* and *Zahn*. I would therefore affirm the judgment of the Court of Appeals for the First Circuit and reverse the judgment of the Court of Appeals for the Eleventh Circuit.

Points for Discussion

a. What Was the Disagreement Among the Justices?

There was a clear split among the Justices regarding the correct interpretation of § 1367. The crux of the dispute was whether there could be "original jurisdiction" in a diversity-only case in which only one claim among several satisfied the jurisdictional amount-in-controversy requirement. Can you articulate the competing views on this issue expressed by the Justices in this case? Which side has the better argument? Does the statute's failure to mention claims by plaintiffs joined under Rule 20 or Rule 23 tip the balance in either side's favor?

b. Statutory Interpretation and Legislative History

Another critical area of disagreement was whether the statute was ambiguous such as to warrant reference to its legislative history. A general rule when interpreting statutes is that the legislative history should not be consulted unless there is an ambiguity on the face of the statute in need of clarification. *See Barnhill v. Johnson*, 503 U.S. 393, 401 (1992) ("[A]ppeals to statutory history are well taken only to resolve 'statutory ambiguity.) (citing *Toibb v. Radloff*, 501 U.S. 157, 162 (1991))); *Blum v. Stenson*, 465 U.S. 886, 896 (1984) ("Where, as here, resolution of a question of federal law turns on a statute and the intention of Congress, we look first to the statutory language and then to the legislative history if the statutory language is unclear."). Is § 1367 ambiguous, as the dissents argue, with respect to whether supplemental jurisdiction extends to jurisdictionally insufficient claims by Rule 20 or 23 plaintiffs in diversity-only cases? If not, what role should the legislative history play if it appears to be at odds with the plain language of the statute? Should courts be constrained to stick with the statutory language notwithstanding legislative intent that goes in the opposite direction? Which side had the better argument for its mode of statutory interpretation in this case?

> **For More Information**
>
> The propriety of consulting legislative history as an aid in interpreting statutes is a matter of hot debate among the Supreme Court Justices and legal scholars. Students interested in reading more on this issue should consult Abner S. Greene, *The Missing Step of Textualism*, 74 FORDHAM L. REV. 1913 (2006) and ANTONIN SCALIA, A MATTER OF INTERPRETATION (1997).

Justice Ginsburg conceded that both the majority's and her interpretation of § 1367 were plausible but argued that her view was "better." How should the Court choose between two plausible interpretations of a statute? If one view depends on reference to legislative history and the other does not, is one view privileged over the other?

—Perspective & Analysis—

As already noted, the proper use of legislative history in interpreting statutes is the subject of much debate. Here is the perspective of one scholar who opposes the practice:

> [T]he widespread use of legislative history . . . has had major adverse effects. . . . Judges . . . are increasingly reluctant to accept responsibility for making difficult policy decisions or to offer reasoned justifications upon which they might later be criticized. Legislative history provides these people with an "out." They can use it to deflect responsibility onto past Congresses. The only justifications they need offer are the past Congresses' supposed intents. Members of Congress can make law by "manufacturing" legislative history, thereby evading the Constitutional requirements for legislating that assure that laws receive the appropriate representative consent. This, plus the inability to predict how courts and agencies will use legislative history, have stripped Congress of a large measure of the control over the laws that the Constitution intends it to have.

W. David Slawson, *Legislative History and the Need to Bring Statutory Interpretation Under the Rule of Law,* 44 STAN. L. REV. 383, 383–84 (1992).

---

c. Impact on Class Actions

What is the impact of *Allapattah* on class action practice, particularly in light of the enactment of the Class Action Fairness Act of 2005 discussed above? CAFA permits aggregation of jurisdictionally insufficient claims to achieve a separate $5 million-plus amount-in-controversy requirement for multistate class actions. Under § 1367, however, class members whose claims do not aggregate to that amount can still obtain supplemental jurisdiction over their claims so long as at least one class plaintiff asserts a claim worth more than $75,000. The impact of *Allapattah* then is that recourse to CAFA to obtain federal jurisdiction is only necessary when no claimant has a claim above $75,000, a fairly common occurrence in modern class action practice. *See Brill v. Countrywide Home Loans, Inc.,* 427 F.3d 446 (7th Cir. 2005) (holding that CAFA removal jurisdiction was appropriate when each claimant sought only $1,500 but total claim would thereby

For More Information

For a summary of the impact of the Class Action Fairness Act, *Exxon Mobil v. Allapattah*, and *Grable* on class actions, see Gregory P. Joseph, *Federal Class Action Jurisdiction After CAFA,* Exxon Mobil *and* Grable, 8 DEL. L. REV. 157 (2006).

exceed $5 million); *Chavis v. Fidelity Warranty Servs., Inc.*, 415 F. Supp. 2d 620 (D.S.C. 2006) (finding federal removal jurisdiction appropriate under CAFA where the maximum individual claim is $50,000 but maximum total claim easily exceeds $5 million). Prior to *Allapattah*, CAFA would have been of greater utility in bringing cases into federal court because the then-prevailing rule from *Zahn* that every single claim in a joint action had to satisfy the $75,000-plus amount-in-controversy requirement precluded many class actions from qualifying for federal jurisdiction; CAFA's relaxed standards would have circumvented this limitation in cases where the claims aggregated to more than $5 million. However, the Supreme Court through *Allapattah* stole much of CAFA's thunder by removing the barrier to federal jurisdiction that *Zahn* had imposed and that CAFA was designed in part to overcome.

d. Impact on Claims by Rule 20 Plaintiffs

Allapattah did not just address itself to the ability of class action plaintiffs to obtain supplemental jurisdiction over their claims. The case also discussed the ability of courts to exercise supplemental jurisdiction over claims asserted by plaintiffs joined under Rule 20. **Hypo 3.9** tests your understanding of this aspect of the decision:

Hypo 3.9

In New Jersey federal court, Martin (DE) and Franklin (PA) sued Rhonda (NJ) for breach of a contract between the three parties. Martin is seeking $150,000 in damages, while Franklin is seeking $25,000 in damages. The rule that permits Martin and Franklin to sue jointly is Rule 20, thus making them both parties joined under Rule 20.

Does the New Jersey federal court have jurisdiction over Franklin's claim against Rhonda?

e. Discretionary Denial of Supplemental Jurisdiction

Recall that the Court in *Gibbs* indicated that the exercise of pendent jurisdiction was discretionary and that courts, for various articulated reasons, could decline to exercise such jurisdiction. The federal supplemental jurisdiction statute, per § 1367(c), adheres to this approach by codifying, to a certain extent, the discretionary aspect of the doctrine and the criteria for determining whether to decline supplemental jurisdiction.

Supplemental Jurisdiction: <u>28 U.S.C. § 1367(c)</u>

(c)   The district courts may decline to exercise supplemental jurisdiction over a claim under subsection (a) if—

(1)   the claim raises a novel or complex issue of State law,

(2)   the claim substantially predominates over the claim or claims over which the district court has original jurisdiction,

(3)   the district court has dismissed all claims over which it has original jurisdiction, or

(4)   in exceptional circumstances, there are other compelling reasons for declining jurisdiction.

Does this language strictly incorporate the *Gibbs* factors or is there a difference? How should the final provision, permitting courts to decline supplemental jurisdiction for "other compelling reasons" be interpreted? <u>*Metro Fdn. Contractors, Inc. v. Arch Ins. Co.*, 498 Fed. Appx. 98, 103 (2d Cir. 2012)</u> ("courts have found that "exceptional circumstances" exist for declining jurisdiction under § 1367(c)(4) where the claims in federal court are duplicative of claims already asserted in parallel state court proceedings."); <u>*Alexander v. Byrd*, 2014 WL 5449626, at *10 (W.D. Tenn. Oct. 24, 2014)</u> ("Courts and commentators have recognized that the potential for jury confusion can be a sufficiently compelling reason for declining jurisdiction under § 1367(c)(4)." (citations and internal quotation marks omitted)). For a discussion of discretionary denials of supplemental jurisdiction, see <u>*Exec. Software N. Am., Inc. v. U.S. Dist. Court*, 24 F.3d 1545, 1556–59 (9th Cir. 1994)</u>, *rev'd on other grounds sub nom. Calif. Dep't of Water Res. v. Powerex Corp.*, 533 F.3d 1087, 1091 (9th Cir. 2008); Rachel Ellen Hinkle, *The Revision of 28 U.S.C. § 1367(c) and the Debate over the District Court's Discretion to Decline Supplemental Jurisdiction*, <u>69 TENN. L. REV. 111 (2001)</u>.

If the supplemental claims are dismissed, § 1367(d) provides that the "period of limitations for" refiling in state court a state claim so dismissed "shall be tolled while the claim is pending [in federal court] and for a period of 30 days after it is dismissed unless State law provides for a longer tolling period." The Supreme Court has interpreted this provision to mean that the statute of limitations period stops running while the supplemental claims are in federal court, and the time clock "starts running again when the tolling period ends, picking up where it left off." <u>*Artis v. District of Columbia*, No. 16-460, 2018 WL 491524 (2018)</u>.

D. Removal Jurisdiction

The jurisdiction conferred on the federal courts through the federal question, diversity, and supplemental jurisdiction statutes gives federal courts jurisdiction that is *concurrent* with the jurisdiction of state courts. *See* Mims v. Arrow Fin. Servs., LLC, 565 U.S. 368, 377 (2012) ("In cases 'arising under' federal law, we note, there is a deeply rooted presumption in favor of concurrent state court jurisdiction, rebuttable if Congress affirmatively ousts the state courts of jurisdiction over a particular federal claim.") (citation and internal quotation marks omitted). Thus, plaintiffs have the option of filing, in state court, claims that would otherwise qualify for federal jurisdiction under these statutes. However, if a plaintiff does file such claims in state court, a different federal statute enables defendants to **remove** the entire case into federal court, provided a series of requirements for invoking the removal jurisdiction of the federal courts is met. In this section of the chapter, we will cover the myriad requirements for getting cases into federal courts by invoking their removal jurisdiction.

1. General Standards of Removability

The circumstances in which a defendant or defendants may remove a case to federal court are covered by statute. The general standards for removal appear in 28 U.S.C. § 1441:

Removal of Civil Actions: 28 U.S.C. § 1441(a)

(a) * * * [A]ny civil action brought in a State court of which the district courts of the United States have original jurisdiction, may be removed by the defendant or the defendants, to the district court of the United States for the district and division embracing the place where such action is pending.

How do courts or parties determine whether a case falls within the "original jurisdiction" of the federal district courts for purposes of invoking removal jurisdiction? Does the well-pleaded complaint rule of *Mottley* (discussed in Section B.2 above) apply in the removal context? The following case explores this issue.

Hays v. Bryan Cave L.L.P.

U.S. Court of Appeals for the Seventh Circuit
446 F.3d 712 (7th Cir. 2006)

POSNER, CIRCUIT JUDGE.

This is a case of some novelty but little difficulty. The plaintiff brought suit in an Illinois court, charging the defendants, a law firm and its lawyers who had represented him in a federal criminal case with legal malpractice under Illinois common law. The defendants removed the case to federal district court on the ground that it really arose under federal law because, as the district court ruled in refusing to remand the case, the resolution of a malpractice claim growing out of the defense of a federal criminal case would "require a substantial evaluation of applicable federal law," specifically a determination of the meaning and scope of the federal criminal statutes under which Hays had been convicted.

Having accepted jurisdiction of the case, the district judge dismissed it on the merits, precipitating this appeal, in which Hays contends that the district court never obtained jurisdiction because the suit was not removable. * * *

The standard applied by the district judge in deciding to deny the motion to remand was incorrect. A defendant might have defenses based on federal law to claims that arose only under state law, and it might be predictable at the outset that most of the time and the other resources consumed in the litigation would be devoted to those defenses. Yet * * * a case filed in state court under state law cannot be removed to federal court on the basis that there are defenses based on federal law. *Louisville & Nashville R.R. v. Mottley*, 211 U.S. 149, 152 (1908). What is true is that if federal law creates the claim on which the plaintiff is suing, the fact that he has omitted from his complaint any reference to federal law will not defeat removal. *Franchise Tax Bd. v. Construction Laborers Vacation Trust*, 463 U.S. 1, 22–23 (1983). As the cases say, the plaintiff cannot abrogate the defendant's right of removal by "artful pleading." So for example if a suit is filed in state court charging a fiduciary with a breach of his fiduciary duty, and the defendant is an ERISA [Employee Retirement Income Security Act] fiduciary, the case is removable to federal court even if the complaint does not mention ERISA. Because ERISA displaces all state law within its scope, such a case necessarily arises under federal law, namely under ERISA, and so is removable despite the complaint's reticence.

That is not the case here. Nothing in federal law prevents a disappointed litigant in a federal case from suing his lawyer under state malpractice law. The elements of legal malpractice in Illinois (as elsewhere)—"an attorney-client relationship, a duty arising from that relationship, a breach of that duty, and actual damages or injury proximately caused by that breach," plus, if the case in which the alleged malpractice occurred was a criminal case, that the defendant was actually innocent—are independent of the law under which the suit that the defendant lawyer is alleged to have muffed was brought. Issues concerning the meaning of that law are quite likely to arise in such a malpractice action, but there is nothing unusual about a court having to decide issues that arise under the law of other jurisdictions; otherwise there would be no field called "conflict of laws" and no rule barring removal of a case from state to federal court on the basis of a federal defense. * * *

Cases that arise under federal law are removable to federal court, though filed originally in state court, in order to limit forum shopping. For otherwise, in any area of concurrent federal-state jurisdiction, plaintiffs would have a free choice of whether the suit would be litigated in state court or in federal court. With removal on the basis of the federal nature of the plaintiff's claim possible, either side can choose to litigate in federal court, while if removal were possible on the basis of a federal defense, defendants would have the exclusive choice of forum in any case in which a nonfrivolous federal defense could be pleaded.

The judgment of the district court is vacated with directions to remand the case to the state court in which it was filed.

VACATED AND REMANDED.

Points for Discussion

a. Removal Under 28 U.S.C. § 1441(a)

From § 1441(a) and *Hays*, we learn that to be removable, an action must be one that would fall within the original jurisdiction of the federal courts, consistent with the requirements of the well-pleaded complaint rule and the artful pleading doctrine. That means that the plaintiff must have been able to initiate the civil action in federal court originally—based on matters found within the complaint—which would be the case if the action was comprised of at least one claim that qualified for federal jurisdiction either through diversity jurisdiction, federal question jurisdiction, or another statute conferring federal subject matter jurisdiction. Additional claims properly falling within the supplemental jurisdiction of the federal courts are treated as part of the "civil action" that may be removed under § 1441(a). *See, e.g.,* *Gossmeyer v. McDonald,* 128 F.3d 481, 488 (7th Cir. 1997) (holding that removal of the state defamation claim against an anonymous informant whose tip instigated the investigation out of which the federal constitutional claim arose was proper).

To determine whether a claim falls within the original jurisdiction of the federal courts, one simply has to go through the jurisdictional analyses for the various types of subject matter jurisdiction. Thus, if trying to determine whether claims A, B, & C are removable, it is necessary to analyze claims A, B, & C separately to see if they would qualify for federal question jurisdiction, diversity jurisdiction, supplemental jurisdiction, or some other basis for federal jurisdiction had they been filed in federal court initially. If the claims meet the requirements for federal jurisdiction, the action is removable under § 1441(a), subject to the provisions limiting removability discussed below.

When figuring out the amount in controversy for a claim removed based on diversity jurisdiction, the amount stated in the initial state-court complaint is used, unless nonmonetary relief is sought or the claim comes from a state not requiring the amount in controversy to be stated in a complaint, in which case the notice of removal may assert the amount in controversy. 28 U.S.C. § 1446(c)(2). Under such circumstances, the district court must find by a preponderance of the evidence that the amount in controversy exceeds the requisite jurisdictional amount in 28 U.S.C. § 1332(a).

Take Note!

Because removal analysis includes a determination of whether claims qualify for federal jurisdiction, every removal question you will face potentially also involves a regular subject matter jurisdiction analysis.

Keep in mind that for all of these subject matter jurisdiction determinations, the relevant time to make the assessment is the time of removal, not the time at which the case was originally filed in state court. *See Caterpillar, Inc. v. Lewis,* 519 U.S. 61, 73 (1996) (referring to the "requirement that the case be fit for federal adjudication at the time the removal petition is filed"). That said, if federal subject matter jurisdiction becomes proper by the time of judgment, that can cure any jurisdictional defect that may have existed at the time of removal. *Id.* at 75–76.

b. Removability Based on Claims by Non-Plaintiffs?

An otherwise nonremovable case does not become removable simply if the defendant asserts counterclaims that fall within the original jurisdiction of the federal courts. The well-pleaded complaint rule precludes reference to claims by defendants when determining the removability of a case. *See, e.g., Redevelopment Agency v. Alvarez,* 288 F. Supp. 2d 1112, 1115 (C.D. Cal. 2003) ("For both removal and original jurisdiction, the federal question must be presented by the plaintiff's complaint as it stands at the time of removal. Removal, therefore, cannot be based on a counterclaim or cross-claim raising a federal question." (citing *Metro Ford Truck Sales, Inc. v. Ford Motor Co.,* 145 F.3d 320, 327 (5th Cir. 1998))). Removal must be based on the plaintiff's case. *See, e.g., Cardello v. CRC Indus., Inc.,* 432 F. Supp. 2d 555, 557 (W.D. Pa. 2006) ("[F]or removal, the federal question must appear on the face of the complaint unaided by the answer or petition for removal."). Thus, whether the defendant raises federal defenses or counterclaims is irrelevant to the removal analysis.

c. Manipulation to Affect Removability

What if the plaintiff, after a case is removed to federal court, decides to amend her complaint to eliminate the basis for federal jurisdiction; must the case then be remanded to state court? *See St. Paul Mercury Indem. Co. v. Red Cab Co.*, 303 U.S. 283 (1938) (holding that the plaintiff's post-removal reduction of its claim below the requisite jurisdictional amount did not deprive the federal court of jurisdiction); *Hatcher v. Lowe's Home Ctrs., Inc.*, 718 F. Supp. 2d 684, 688 (E.D. Va. 2010) ("Once a district court's jurisdiction attaches at the time of removal—as it did here—post-removal amendments, 'which reduce the amount recoverable, whether beyond the plaintiff's control or the result of his volition, do not oust the district court's jurisdiction.' " (quoting *St. Paul Mercury*, 303 U.S. at 293)).

It is also possible that a plaintiff may name a non-diverse party as a co-defendant in an action in state court simply to defeat the removability of the case. If the co-defendant is a "sham defendant," the case may still be removed and the sham defendant ignored, but only if that defendant was fraudulently joined, meaning there is no possibility that the plaintiff could recover from that party. *In re Prempro Prods. Liab. Litig.*, 591 F. 3d 613, 620 (8th Cir. 2010) ("Fraudulent joinder occurs when a plaintiff files a frivolous or illegitimate claim against a non-diverse defendant solely to prevent removal. When determining if a party has been fraudulently joined, a court considers whether there is any reasonable basis in fact or law to support a claim against a nondiverse defendant."); *see also Padilla v. AT&T Corp.*, 697 F. Supp. 2d 1156, 1158–60 (C.D. Cal. 2009) ("[R]emoval is proper despite the presence of a non-diverse defendant where that defendant is a fraudulently joined or sham defendant. . . . The words fraud and sham imply a degree of chicanery or deceit, and a state court plaintiff engaging in a common strategy of pleading broadly does not engage in a fraud or sham.").

—Perspective & Analysis—

Why would plaintiffs file cases that could have been brought in federal court in state court? This question touches on the issue of forum shopping:

> Reasons for avoiding federal court range from the mundane (greater familiarity with state procedure) to the strategic (greater likelihood of securing justice for clients). In most states, local judges are elected by the very people whose disputes they will hear, motivating speedy and fair adjudication. Federal judges are appointed for life, and their courts are clogged with criminal cases. * * *

> To reduce their burgeoning dockets, federal courts have increasingly engaged in stringent control of discovery, aggressive encouragement of settlement, and more frequent granting of summary judgment. As a result, litigation in federal court is more expensive and time-consuming. Moreover, plaintiffs whose cases are removed to federal court are substantially less successful than those who originally file there. Finally, but significantly, lawsuits in federal court are increasingly being consolidated into multidistrict, pretrial litigation proceedings, where they often languish for years.

Erik B. Walker, *Keep Your Case in State Court*, 40 TRIAL 22, 22 (Sept. 2004).

If a plaintiff attempts to plead a claim on state-law grounds when the law governing the matter is exclusively federal, courts will treat the claim as one arising under federal law. "Under this so-called 'complete preemption doctrine,' a plaintiff's state cause of action may be recast as a federal claim for relief, making its removal by the defendant proper on the basis of federal question jurisdiction." *Vaden v. Discover Bank*, 556 U.S. 49, 61 (2009) (citation and emendations omitted).

Finally, plaintiffs might attempt to manipulate removability in the class action context by asserting up front that their class will seek less than the amount in controversy required by the applicable statute. This is what the plaintiff attempted in *Standard Fire Insurance Co. v. Knowles*, 568 U.S. 588 (2013) [*FLEX Case 3.D*]. There, the plaintiff was a class representative in a case the defendants sought to remove under the Class Action Fairness Act, which permits removal of class actions that seek more than $5 million in the aggregate (as well as satisfy other requirements outlined in 28 U.S.C. § 1332(d), to be discussed later in this chapter as well as in Chapter 7). The class representative sought to avoid removal by stipulating that the class "will not at any time during this case . . . seek damages for the class . . . in excess of $5,000,000 in the aggregate." *Id. at 1347*. The Supreme Court held that because the class had yet to be certified, the putative class representative could not bind the class to this stipulation, leaving the lower court obligated to calculate the amount in controversy without regard to the offered stipulation. *Id. at 1350*. How does this holding jibe with the idea that a plaintiff is the master of her complaint?

d.   Limits on Removability Imposed by 28 U.S.C. § 1441(b)

Although § 1441(a) sets forth the general standard for removability, it is not the end of the matter. Section 1441(b) goes on to qualify the circumstances under which a claim will be removable in non-federal-question cases:

> **Removal based on diversity of citizenship: 28 U.S.C. § 1441(b)(2)**
>
> (b)(2)   A civil action otherwise removable solely on the basis of the jurisdiction under section 1332(a) of this title may not be removed if any of the parties in interest properly joined and served as defendants is a citizen of the State in which such action is brought.

Section 1441(b) of the removal statute tells us that notwithstanding the provisions of § 1441(a), an action solely based on diversity jurisdiction is not removable if any defendant is a citizen of the state in which the plaintiff initiated the action. This principle is sometimes referred to as the ***forum-state defendant rule***. Keep in mind that when claims arising under federal law are present, the citizenship of the defendants does not affect the removability of the case to federal court.

e.   No Removal from Federal to State Court

It is worth emphasizing that removal can only occur from a state court to a federal court; there is no provision in the federal statutes governing removal that enables litigants to remove cases initially filed in federal court to state court. Parties interested in litigating a federal court case in state court would have to have the federal case dismissed and then pursue the matter in state court. For example, claims before district courts based on supplemental jurisdiction may be dismissed if the discretionary factors of § 1367(c) suggest that the district court should decline jurisdiction over such claims. 28 U.S.C. § 1367(c). District courts may also decline jurisdiction over a case on *forum non conveniens* grounds or on the basis that the federal court should yield to a state court under various abstention doctrines. The same holds true for litigants in one state court interested in moving the case to another state court: As separate judicial systems, there is no provision for transferring a civil case from one state court to another and thus state judges would have to rely on the same doctrines of *forum non conveniens* and abstention to achieve such a result.

Make the Connection

Abstention doctrines allow federal courts to refrain or "abstain" from hearing cases that would be better heard in state court for various reasons. You may study these doctrines further in a **Federal Courts** course or a **Complex Litigation** course.

f.   Removal of Additional Claims

What happens when there are claims within the civil action that fail to qualify for diversity, federal question, or supplemental jurisdiction? Can those claims be removed along with the rest of the case? The removal statute contains a provision that addresses this issue:

Joinder of Federal law claims and State law claims:
28 U.S.C. § 1441(c)

(1)   If a civil action includes—

(A)   a claim arising under the Constitution, laws, or treaties of the United States (within the meaning of section 1331 of this title), and

(B)   a claim not within the original or supplemental jurisdiction of the district court or a claim that has been made nonremovable by statute,

the entire action may be removed if the action would be removable without the inclusion of the claim described in subparagraph (B).

(2)   Upon removal of an action described in paragraph (1), the district court shall sever from the action all claims described in paragraph (1)(B) and shall remand the severed claims to the State court from which the action was removed. Only defendants against whom a claim described in paragraph (1)(A) has been asserted are required to join in or consent to the removal under paragraph (1).

Thus, when non-qualifying claims are removed to federal court along with federal question claims, the proper course is for the federal court to remand the non-qualifying claims to state court. Note that 28 U.S.C. § 1441(c) permits removal and then severance and remand only in the presence of removable federal question claims. How should courts handle non-qualifying claims removed along with claims based on diversity jurisdiction? *See, e.g.*, *Vinson v. Schneider Nat'l Carriers, Inc.*, 942 F. Supp. 2d 630 (N.D. Tex. 2013) ("Congress, in amending section 1441(c), elected not to allow severance and remand of a nonremovable claim with respect to an action removed on the basis of diversity of citizenship. The plain language of the statute allows a court to sever only the nonremovable claim and remand it to state court if the action also includes a claim under 28 U.S.C. § 1331, that is, one based on a federal question."). If there are claims that qualify for diversity jurisdiction and claims that do not qualify for any form of federal subject matter jurisdiction, the entire action is non-removable and, if removed, subject to remand in its entirety. *See Horn v. Kmart Corp.*, 2007 WL 1138473 (S.D. Ohio 2007) (where basis of removal was diversity jurisdiction, court remanded case finding that "the language of 1441(c) suggests that the entire case be remanded"); *Riverside Transp., Inc. v. Bellsouth Telecom., Inc.*, 847 F. Supp. 453 (M.D. La. 1994) (holding that because § 1441(c) excludes diversity cases, court had to remand entire action when some members of class action did not meet amount-in-controversy requirement).

2. Removal & Remand Procedures

There are a host of additional procedural requirements governing the removal process; these are set forth in 28 U.S.C. § 1441, § 1446 (procedure for removal), and § 1447 (procedures after removal). The most noteworthy of these procedural requirements are reviewed below.

a.   Who Can Remove a Case?

Under the general federal removal statute, only defendants may remove cases to federal court. *See Shamrock Oil & Gas Corp. v. Sheets*, 313 U.S. 100 (1941) (holding a state-court plaintiff against whom the defendant had filed a counterclaim could not remove the action to federal court under the statutory predecessor to § 1441(a)). Why do you think this is so? As already mentioned, the statute requires that in cases where the basis for removal is diversity jurisdiction, no defendant may be a citizen of the forum state. 28 U.S.C. § 1441(b)(2). Can you identify the rationale behind this limi-

Food for Thought

Should third-party defendants be able to remove cases to federal court? *See, e.g.*, *Hamilton v. Aetna Life & Cas. Co.*, 5 F.3d 642 (2d Cir. 1993) ("Only true defendants have removal rights: plaintiffs defending counterclaims and third-party defendants may not remove an action, and their consent is not required for removal if all the true defendants consent.").

tation? Further, when an action is removed under § 1441(a), all properly joined and served defendants must agree to the removal (referred to as the ***defendant-unanimity rule***). 28 U.S.C. § 1446(b)(2)(A). Note that if non-qualifying claims are removed along with federal question claims under § 1441(c), only the defendants to federal question claims must consent to the removal. Note also that there is a special removal statute for patent claims, under which any party—including plaintiffs—may remove the action. 28 U.S.C. § 1454.

b.   How Is a Case Removed?

To remove a case, a defendant simply must file a ***notice of removal*** "in the district court of the United States for the district and division within which such action is pending." 28 U.S.C. § 1446(a). Promptly after filing the notice of removal, the removing defendant must give written notice to all adverse parties and file a copy of the notice with the clerk of the state court from which the case was removed, which achieves the removal and divests the state court of jurisdiction. 28 U.S.C. § 1446(d). Consideration of the propriety of the removal is handled by the federal court to which the case is removed, not the state court where the case was filed.

Because defendants may be sensitive about waiving personal jurisdiction, it is important to note that filing a notice of removal does not constitute a waiver of any challenge to personal jurisdiction. *Morris & Co. v. Skandinavia Ins. Co.*, 279 U.S. 405, 409 (1929) ("Petitioner suggests that, by removal of the case to the federal court, objection to jurisdiction over the person of respondent was waived. Our decisions are to the contrary."); *Silva v. City of Madison*, 69 F.3d 1368, 1376 (7th Cir. 1995) ("This right [to object to the court's personal jurisdiction] is not waived by filing a petition for removal to federal court."); *McDowell v. Tankinetics, Inc.*, 2012 WL 828509, at *4 (W.D. Mo. Mar. 8, 2012) ("[R]equiring a defendant to include all potential defenses in a notice of removal or considering defenses not included to be waived would appear to run counter to Rule 12. Under Rule 12, a defense is only waived if it is not included in a responsive pleading or set forth in a motion to dismiss."). That said, stating one's personal jurisdiction challenge in the notice of removal is a belt-and-suspenders approach taken by some practitioners just to be safe. *See McDowell*, 2012 WL 828509, at *4. ("[D]espite the clear discussion of waiver of a defense under Rule 12, Defendants covered all bases by specifically indicating in their Notice of Removal that they did not intend to waive personal jurisdiction by removing this case to federal court."); *see also Fink v. Swisshelm*, 182 F.R.D. 630, 631 (D. Kan. 1998) ("Defendant alleges that he had not been served with process when the Court entered default and that it consequently lacks personal jurisdiction over him and has no lawful authority to enter default. Defendant's argument ignores the fact that on May 27, 1998, he voluntarily entered an appearance in this case by filing his Notice Of Removal To The United States District Court For The District Of Kansas." (citing D. Kan. Rule 5.1(d), which provides that appearances may be entered in notice of removal by listing of counsel and party represented)).

c. When Can a Case Be Removed?

Each defendant in an action has 30 days after receipt of service of the complaint to file a notice of removal with the federal court. 28 U.S.C. § 1446(b). If a case is non-removable initially, but subsequently becomes removable because of a change in parties or amendments to the complaint, a defendant can remove such a case within 30 days of receiving notice of the fact that the case is now removable. *Id.* Thus, the propriety of removal jurisdiction is measured at the time of the filing of the notice of removal, not the complaint. *Caterpillar Inc. v. Lewis*, 519 U.S. 61, 68–69 (1996) ("In a case not originally removable, a defendant who receives a pleading or other paper indicating the postcommencement satisfaction of federal jurisdictional requirements—for example, by reason of the dismissal of a nondiverse party—may remove the case to federal court within 30 days of receiving such information."); *Harris v. Bankers Life & Cas. Co.*, 425 F.3d 689, 695–96 (9th Cir. 2005) (holding that the 30-day period for filing a notice of removal commenced when the plaintiff abandoned the claim against non-diverse defendant, rendering diversity complete, not with the original complaint, which did not indicate complete diversity).

One caveat to this "time of removal" rule is that if a case was initially non-removable because of a lack of diversity, and the parties subsequently become diverse due to the relocation of the defendant, courts generally will not treat such claims as now removable on the basis of diversity jurisdiction. *See* 14B C. WRIGHT, A. MILLER, E. COOPER & J. STEINMAN, FED. PRAC. & PROC. § 3723 (4th ed. 2009) ("The purpose of requiring diversity to exist at both times apparently is to prevent a non-diverse defendant from acquiring a new domicile after commencement of the state court suit and then removing on the basis of the newly created diversity of citizenship."). Courts take conflicting approaches to removability when the plaintiff is the relocating party. *See id.* (citing cases).

Practice Pointer

Given the possibility of waiving your client's right to remove the case to federal court, as an attorney representing a defendant in state court you should give early consideration to whether the claims filed against your client are removable before launching a more general defense in the state court.

It is possible for a defendant to waive its right to removal "by proceeding to defend the action in state court or otherwise invoking the processes of that court." *Brown v. Demco, Inc.*, 792 F.2d 478, 481 (5th Cir. 1986) (citing *Schell v. Food Mach. Corp.*, 87 F.2d 385, 388 (5th Cir. 1937)). "The waiver must be clear and indicate a specific, positive intent to proceed in state court." *Jacko v. Thorn Americas, Inc.*, 121 F. Supp. 2d 574, 576 (E.D. Tex. 2000).

Notwithstanding the rule providing for 30 days to remove a case that subsequently becomes removable, there is a 1-year limitation on the removal of cases based on diversity jurisdiction, meaning that diversity cases may not be removed more than one year after the filing of the complaint in the action. 28 U.S.C. § 1446(b). What should a court do if a plaintiff in a diversity action intentionally waits to amend its claim to make the action removable one year and one day after the filing of the complaint? The removal statute provides that if the court "finds that the plaintiff has acted in bad faith in order to prevent a defendant from removing the action," such as, for example, if "the plaintiff deliberately failed to disclose the actual amount in controversy to prevent removal," the 1-year limitation will not apply. 28 U.S.C. § 1446(c).

d.   What Procedures Govern Remand?

Although the filing of a notice of removal removes a case immediately, other parties do have the opportunity to contest the removal by making a motion to remand a case to state court. Unless they are seeking remand based on a claim that the federal court lacks subject matter jurisdiction over the case, parties have 30 days after the filing of the notice of removal to seek a remand or their ability to do so is waived. 28 U.S.C. § 1447(c). Notwithstanding this 30-day deadline, the Federal Rules require

Take Note!

The Supreme Court has held that a district court's order remanding a case to state court after declining to exercise supplemental jurisdiction under 28 U.S.C. § 1367(c) is not a remand based on a lack of subject matter jurisdiction. *Carlsbad Tech., Inc. v. HIF Bio, Inc., 556 U.S. 635 (2009)*. Thus, such remand orders are appealable.

defendants who have yet to answer the complaint prior to removal to present an answer or other defense within 21 days after service of the initial complaint or 7 days after the filing of the notice of removal, whichever is longer. FED. R. CIV. P. 81(c)(2)(A)–(C).

If the federal court decides to remand the case to state court based on a defect in removal procedure or a lack of subject matter jurisdiction, the defendant may ordinarily not appeal that order. 28 U.S.C. § 1447(d); *Kircher v. Putnam Funds Trust, 547 U.S. 633, 640–42 (2006)* (indicating that remands based on grounds listed in § 1447(c)—*e.g.*, defective removal procedure or lack of subject matter jurisdic-

What's That?

A *final judgment* is a judgment that leaves nothing open to further dispute and conclusively resolves the dispute between the parties, unless it is reversed or set aside on appeal. This should be distinguished from *interlocutory orders*, which are interim decisions made by a court and are generally not appealable until after a final judgment is entered. *See* 28 U.S.C. §§ 1291, 1292. Final judgments are discussed in Chapter 11.

tion—are not appealable but remands based on other discretionary grounds are reviewable (citing *Thermtron Prods., Inc. v. Hermansdorfer, 423 U.S. 336, 345–46 (1976)))*, *abrogated on other grounds by Quackenbush v. Allstate Ins. Co., 517 U.S. 706 (1996)*. However, if a court denies a motion for remand, such a denial is reviewable, but only on appeal of the final judgment in the case. *See, e.g.*, *Caterpillar Inc. v. Williams, 482 U.S. 386, 390–91 (1987)*. Why do you think there is this disparity in the appealability of remand determinations?

In the event of a remand, the party that sought remand may be entitled to costs and attorneys' fees associated with the removal. *See* 28 U.S.C. § 1447(c); *Martin v. Franklin Capital Corp.*, 546 U.S. 132, 136 (2005) (holding that the award of attorneys' fees on remand depends on whether there was an "objectively reasonable basis for removal" notwithstanding the fact that the case has been remanded).

e. Class Action Fairness Act

The Class Action Fairness Act ("CAFA"), Pub. L. No. 109–2, 119 Stat. 4 (2005), extends federal jurisdiction to certain large class actions in which the aggregate amount in controversy exceeds $5 million. Qualifying class actions are removable under special removal procedures promulgated with CAFA and codified at 28 U.S.C. § 1453. Here are the highlights of these special class action removal provisions, which one commentator has referred to as "red-carpet removal." *See* Adam N. Steinman, *Sausage-Making, Pigs' Ears, and Congressional Expansions of Federal Jurisdiction: Exxon Mobil v. Allapattah and Its Lessons for the Class Action Fairness Act*, 81 WASH. L. REV. 279, 290–93 (2006):

"Red-Carpet" Removal Under CAFA

- CAFA actions are removable "without regard to whether any defendant is a citizen of the State in which the action is brought";

- CAFA authorizes removal "by any defendant without the consent of all defendants";

- Class actions removed under CAFA are not subject to the one-year time limit on removability that ordinarily applies to diversity cases; and

- Class actions removed under CAFA are not subject to the ordinary bar against appellate review of remand orders.

---

f. Special Removal Statutes

There are other statutes that provide for removal of cases in special circumstances in addition to § 1441. *See, e.g.*, 28 U.S.C. § 1443 (special removal statute for claims arising under any law providing for civil rights). For example, 28 U.S.C. § 1442 gives federal officers the ability to remove both civil and criminal cases in which they are involved, while § 1441 provides only for the removal of civil cases. Unlike other defendants, under § 1442 a federal officer can remove a case even if the plaintiff could not have filed the case in federal court in the first instance. Additionally, although removals under § 1441 are subject to the well-pleaded complaint rule, removals under § 1442 are not. *Jefferson Cnty. v. Acker*, 527 U.S. 423, 431 (1999). Finally, whereas all defendants must consent to removal under § 1441, a federal officer or agency defendant can unilaterally remove a case under § 1442. *See Durham v. Lockheed Martin Corp.*, 445 F.3d 1247, 1253 (9th Cir. 2006).

There are also express prohibitions against the removal of some actions, which are found in 28 U.S.C. § 1445 (precluding the removal of certain claims against railroads and carriers, workers' compensation claims, and claims under the Violence Against Women Act). Why might these claims be denied removal jurisdiction when they can qualify for federal question or diversity jurisdiction? *See also, e.g.*, 15 U.S.C. § 3612 ("No case arising under this chapter [dealing with condominium conversion abuse claims] and brought in any State court of competent jurisdiction shall be removed to any court of the United States, except where any officer or employee of the United States in his official capacity is a party.").

Practice Pointer

As noted in the text, there can be special removal provisions beyond the removal statute, such as within the Federal Arbitration Act, *see* 9 U.S.C. § 205 (providing for removal to federal court when the subject matter of an action relates to an international arbitration agreement), or the Price-Anderson Act, *see* 42 U.S.C. § 2210(n)(2) (making claims arising out of nuclear incidents removable from state to federal court). Be sure to check for such provisions when confronting the possibility of removal to federal court.

If claims made non-removable by statute are present in an action filed in state court and there are no federal question claims, the entire action is non-removable and, if removed, subject to remand in its entirety. This is because § 1441(c) only permits the removal, severance, and remand of non-removable claims when federal question claims are present. *See, e.g.*, *Husk v. E.I. Du Pont De Nemours & Co.*, 842 F. Supp. 895, 897–98 n.2 (S.D. W.Va. 1994) (in removed case containing claim under § 1445(c) and other state law claims, concluding that, because plaintiff's complaint did not raise a federal question, "28 U.S.C. §§ 1331 and 1441(c) thus prohibit this Court from assuming jurisdiction over the case, and it must be remanded").

Executive Summary

- **Article III.** Article III of the Constitution sets the outer limits of federal subject matter jurisdiction; Congress ultimately must confer such jurisdiction on lower federal courts before it may be exercised, making them courts of limited jurisdiction. Congress has conferred some but not all of the jurisdictional authority contained within Article III.

- **Diversity Jurisdiction.** 28 U.S.C. § 1332 gives federal courts jurisdiction over cases between citizens of different states where the amount in controversy exceeds $75,000. Cases between U.S. citizens and aliens involving the requisite amount also fall within the diversity jurisdiction of the federal courts. Citizenship is determined with reference to an individual's domicile, while for corporations it is determined by their state of incorporation and principal place of business, which the Supreme Court has held refers to their headquarters. Citizenship for other collective entities is tied to the citizenship of their constituent members.

Major Themes

The following are some key themes that emerge from the subject matter jurisdiction material:

a. *Limited Jurisdiction*—the federal courts are courts of limited jurisdiction, meaning that a federal court may not hear a case unless there is constitutional and statutory authority to do so.

b. *Forum Shopping*—the rules governing federal jurisdiction may not be manipulated to achieve or avoid federal jurisdiction. The well-pleaded complaint rule and the artful pleading doctrines police this conduct.

c. *Expanding Federal Jurisdiction*—recent cases such as *Grable* and *Allapattah*, plus the enactment of CAFA, have expanded federal court jurisdiction.

■ **Federal Question Jurisdiction.** Federal courts have jurisdiction over all civil actions arising under federal law under 28 U.S.C. § 1331. This grant of jurisdiction has been deemed to be narrower than the scope of such jurisdiction under the Constitution. A claim arises under federal law if it necessarily raises a substantial federal issue that appears on the face of the plaintiff's well-pleaded complaint.

■ **Supplemental Jurisdiction.** Under 28 U.S.C. § 1367, federal courts may hear claims that do not fall within the original jurisdiction of the federal courts if they share a common nucleus of operative fact with a claim in the action that does fall within the original jurisdiction of the federal courts, provided such supplemental claims are not barred explicitly from enjoying supplemental jurisdiction by one of the exceptions enumerated in § 1367(b).

■ **Removal Jurisdiction.** When a plaintiff files her case in state court, any defendant (except when any defendant is a forum resident in diversity cases) may remove that case to federal court if there is some basis for exercising federal subject matter jurisdiction over the claims in the case. All defendants must agree to removal and the notice of removal must be filed with the federal court within 30 days of the receipt of notice of the removability of the action. Remands on grounds other than a lack of subject matter jurisdiction must be sought within 30 days of the filing of the notice of removal.

For More Information

Students interested in obtaining more information about subject matter jurisdiction may consult the following resources:

- 13D C. WRIGHT, A. MILLER, E. COOPER & R. FREER, FED. PRAC. & PROC. § 3561 *et seq.* (3d ed. 2008) (federal question jurisdiction).
- 13E C. WRIGHT, A. MILLER & E. COOPER, FED. PRAC. & PROC. § 3601 *et seq.* (3d ed. 2009) (diversity jurisdiction).
- 13D C. WRIGHT, A. MILLER & R. FREER, FED. PRAC. & PROC. § 3567 *et seq.* (4th ed. 2008) (supplemental jurisdiction).
- 14B C. WRIGHT, A. MILLER, E. COOPER & J. STEINMAN, FED. PRAC. & PROC. § 3721 *et seq.* (4th ed. 2009) (removal jurisdiction).

Test Your Knowledge

To assess your understanding of the material in this chapter, click here to take a quiz.

CHAPTER FOUR

Venue

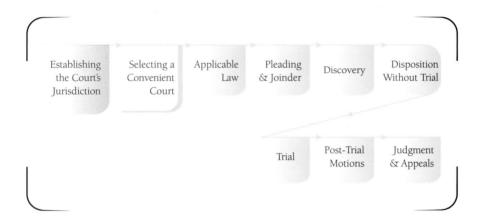

THE CONCEPT OF VENUE IS similar to personal jurisdiction—the subject of Chapter 1—in that it pertains to the geographical area within which a civil action may be brought. However, venue is not concerned with the constitutional and statutory limits of a court's jurisdiction over parties in an action, but with identifying the most sensible and convenient locales or "venues" within a system in which to litigate a case. In other words, rules of venue function as a means of allocating judicial business among different locations within the same judicial system. When a case is to be filed in federal court, federal venue rules govern which districts within the federal system are sufficiently related to the parties or to the dispute such that they would each serve as a convenient forum in which to litigate the case.

> A *judicial system* refers to the court system within the government of a particular sovereign. Thus, the federal courts are a separate judicial system from the courts of Virginia, which in turn are a separate judicial system from the courts of Georgia. Venue rules determine the proper court within a single judicial system, not across different systems.

Thus, after finding a court that is able to exercise personal jurisdiction over the parties in the action (*see* Chapter 1) and subject matter jurisdiction over the claims raised in the dispute (*see* Chapter 3), the next step in choosing a proper forum within the federal system is to identify the particular federal district or districts where the case may be brought.* This chapter considers the standards governing venue in the federal system as well as the conditions under which an action may be transferred from one venue to another or dismissed altogether when the preferred venue lies outside the federal system.

A. Original Venue

Proper venue in the federal system is determined by various provisions of Title 28 of the U.S. Code. After reviewing these basic provisions and how they are interpreted and applied generally, we will briefly consider how the venue rules deal with more complex cases involving multiple claims.

1. The Basic Venue Rules

Venue in the federal system is primarily a matter of statutory law. Ordinary cases are governed by the general venue statute, 28 U.S.C. § 1391:

Venue Generally. 28 U.S.C. § 1391.

(b) Venue in general.—A civil action may be brought in—

(1) a judicial district in which any defendant resides, if all defendants are residents of the State in which the district is located;

(2) a judicial district in which a substantial part of the events or omissions giving rise to the claim occurred, or a substantial part of property that is the subject of the action is situated; or

(3) if there is no district in which an action may otherwise be brought as provided in this section, any judicial district in which any defendant is subject to the court's personal jurisdiction with respect to such action. (d) Residency of corporations in States with multiple districts.—For purposes of venue under this chapter, in a State which has more than one judicial district and in which a defendant that is a corporation is subject to personal jurisdiction at the time an action is commenced, such corporation shall be deemed to reside in any district in that State within which its contacts would be sufficient to subject it to personal jurisdiction if that district were a separate State, and, if there is no such district, the corporation shall be deemed to reside in the district within which it has the most significant contacts.

---

* If a case is being brought within a state court, state venue rules will have to be consulted to identify the court within that state's judicial system that serves as the proper venue for that case. Here we focus only on the rules governing venue in the federal system. [Ed.]

(c) **Residency.** — For all venue purposes —

    (1) a natural person, including an alien lawfully admitted for permanent residence in the United States, shall be deemed to reside in the judicial district in which that person is domiciled;

    (2) an entity with the capacity to sue and be sued in its common name under applicable law, whether or not incorporated, shall be deemed to reside, if a defendant, in any judicial district in which such defendant is subject to the court's personal jurisdiction with respect to the civil action in question * * * and

    (3) a defendant not resident in the United States may be sued in any judicial district, and the joinder of such a defendant shall be disregarded in determining where the action may be brought with respect to other defendants.

(d) **Residency of corporations in States with multiple districts.** — For purposes of venue under this chapter, in a State which has more than one judicial district and in which a defendant that is a corporation is subject to personal jurisdiction at the time an action is commenced, such corporation shall be deemed to reside in any district in that State within which its contacts would be sufficient to subject it to personal jurisdiction if that district were a separate State, and, if there is no such district, the corporation shall be deemed to reside in the district within which it has the most significant contacts.

Before attempting to parse this provision, let us take a look at a case that illustrates how courts interpret and apply the general venue statute.

Surface Supplied Inc. v. Kirby Morgan Dive Systems, Inc.

U.S. District Court for the Northern District of California
2013 WL 2355446 (N.D. Cal. May 29, 2013)

MAXINE M. CHESNEY, DISTRICT JUDGE.

Before the Court is defendant Kirby Morgan Dive Systems, Inc.'s ("Kirby Morgan") motion, filed April 5, 2013, to dismiss the above-titled action * * *.

BACKGROUND

Plaintiff Surface Supplied Inc. ("Surface Supplied") is a California corporation, established on June 30, 2011, whose principal place of business is the Northern District of California, and whose three employees reside in said district. [Defendant Kirby Morgan's "principal facilities" and all but one of its employees are located in the Central District of California.] Surface Supplied "is engaged in the business of research, design, development and manufacture of digital gas analyzer and depth gauge products . . . for the commercial diving industry." Surface Supplied's products are "alpha stage products," and, to date, none have been sold.

Surface Supplied maintains a website "on which it describes the external specifications of its products," but through which it does not "sell or offer [them] for sale." On the home page of its website, Surface Supplied has used a "cropped version" of "a public domain and well known photograph of an underwater water diver against a backdrop of an American flag." On three occasions in 2011, Surface Supplied used the cropped version in advertisements appearing in the national publication *Underwater Magazine,* and on one occasion in the national publication, *Marine Technology Report,* which publications were distributed to consumers in the Central District [of California]. Surface Supplied also "maintains a presence on the social media sites Facebook and Twitter" on which it has used a photograph of "a fully outfitted diver standing on seaside rocks." Surface Supplied's products are engraved with a logo of a "highly fanciful abstract image of a helmet." Surface Supplied has also "digitally superimposed this logo over a picture of a tee shirt, which has been displayed on its website and social media sites," but Surface Supplied "has never printed or distributed any tee shirt bearing this logo."

On January 22, 2013, Kirby Morgan, a corporation that sells commercial diving helmets and surface gas controllers and analyzers sent Surface Supplied a cease and desist letter, by which letter Kirby Morgan accused Surface Supplied of infringing its trademarks by "using images and representations of Kirby Morgan's helmets on its website, Facebook page, t-shirts, Twitter and on the panels of Surface Supplied's gas analyzer equipment" and demanded that Surface Supplied cease its use of the infringing images. The letter also demanded an answer no later than February 1, 2013, and stated, "If Kirby Morgan does not receive a suitable response by the aforementioned date, the company will have no choice but to take appropriate legal action which may include immediately seeking a temporary restraining order . . . ."

Thereafter, Surface Supplied requested, and Kirby Morgan granted, a one week extension to February 8, 2013. In lieu of replying, however, Surface Supplied, on February 8, 2013, filed the instant action, seeking a declaration of non-infringement of Kirby Morgan's federally registered trademarks. Thereafter, on March 15, 2013, Kirby Morgan filed an action in the Central District [of California], alleging, *inter alia,* federal trademark infringement claims against Surface Supplied. *See Kirby Morgan Dive Systems, Inc. v. Surface Supplied, Inc.,* No. 13–1862 (C.D. Cal. filed Mar. 15, 2013) ("Central District action").

Practice Pointer

Notice that Surface Supplied preempted the threatened action by Kirby Morgan by taking the initiative and filing a declaratory judgment action first. This permitted Surface Supply to attempt to control the location of the action, which is the subject of the procedural dispute addressed by this opinion. Were Surface Supplied's actions appropriate?

DISCUSSION

Kirby Morgan moves for dismissal of the instant action pursuant to the Court's equitable powers under the Declaratory Judgment Act, 28 U.S.C. §§ 2201 and 2202 * * *.

I. Motion to Dismiss

What's That?

The Declaratory Judgment Act gives district courts discretion to entertain cases within their jurisdiction that seek a declaration of legal rights rather than any affirmative relief. Doing so is discretionary, and courts may decline such actions.

"The exercise of jurisdiction under . . . 28 U.S.C. § 2201(a), is committed to the sound discretion of the federal district courts[;][e]ven if the district court has subject matter jurisdiction, it is not required to exercise its authority to hear the case." *Huth v. Hartford Ins. Co. of the Midwest,* 298 F.3d 800, 802 (9th Cir. 2002). Kirby Morgan argues the instant action is an anticipatory suit that should be dismissed in light of Kirby Morgan's later-filed Central District action. In opposition, Surface Supplied argues venue is not proper in the Central District. This Court will not exercise its discretion to dismiss the instant action if the action in the Central District is not properly venued therein, and, consequently, the Court first addresses that issue.

Take Note!

Notice how the venue challenge comes into play here: Venue in the Northern District action is not being challenged but, rather, Surface Supplied is challenging venue in the Central District action. Be sure to understand how the question of venue in the Central District action is relevant to the dismissal motion in the Northern District action.

Venue is proper in:

(1)   a judicial district in which any defendant resides, if all defendants are residents of the State in which the district is located;

(2)   a judicial district in which a substantial part of the events or omissions giving rise to the claim occurred, or a substantial part of property that is the subject of the action is situated; or

(3)   if there is no district in which an action may otherwise be brought as provided in this section, any judicial district in which any defendant is subject to the court's personal jurisdiction with respect to such action.

See 28 U.S.C. § 1391(b). Kirby Morgan argues venue is proper in the Central District pursuant to the first two subsections of § 1391(b). The Court addresses each in turn.

A. Judicial District in Which Any Defendant Resides

"A civil action may be brought in . . . a judicial district in which any defendant resides, if all defendants are residents of the State in which the district is located." *See* 28 U.S.C. § 1391(b)(1). Surface Supplied is the defendant in the Central District action, and, consequently, for purposes of determining venue for said action, the Court must determine whether Surface Supplied resides in the Central District. "[I]n a State which has more than one judicial district and in which a defendant that is a corporation is subject to personal jurisdiction at the time an action is commenced, such corporation shall be deemed to reside in any district in that State within which its contacts would be sufficient to subject it to personal jurisdiction if that district were a separate State . . . ." *See* 28 U.S.C. § 1391(d). As a "California corporation" with its "principal place of business" in California, Surface Supplied is subject to personal jurisdiction in California, a state having more than one judicial district; consequently, the Court next considers whether Surface Supplied would be subject to personal jurisdiction in the Central District if such district were a separate state.

"Where, as here, there is no applicable federal statute governing personal jurisdiction, the district court applies the law of the state in which the district court sits." *See Schwarzenegger v. Fred Martin Motor Co.*, 374 F.3d 797, 800 (9th Cir. 2004). "Because California's long-arm jurisdictional statute is coextensive with federal due process requirements, the jurisdictional analyses under state law and federal due process are the same." *See id.* at 800–01.

"There are two types of personal jurisdiction, specific and general." * * * Surface Supplied's only contacts with the Central District are its advertisements in national magazines, its passive website, and its accounts on Facebook and Twitter [and thus insufficient to support general jurisdiction]. The Court thus turns to specific jurisdiction.

The Ninth Circuit has articulated a three-prong test for analyzing specific jurisdiction:

(1) The non-resident defendant must purposefully direct his activities or consummate some transaction with the forum or resident thereof; or perform some act by which he purposefully avails himself of the privilege of conducting activities in the forum, thereby invoking the benefits and protections of its laws;

(2) the claim must be one which arises out of or relates to the defendant's forum-related activities; and

(3) the exercise of jurisdiction must comport with fair play and substantial justice, i.e. it must be reasonable.

Yahoo! Inc. v. La Ligue Contre Le Racisme Et L'Antisemitisme, 433 F.3d 1199, 1205–06 (9th Cir. 2006) (en banc). Under the first prong, a party "purposefully avails itself of the forum if its contacts with the forum are attributable to (1) intentional acts; (2) expressly aimed at the forum; (3) causing harm, the brunt of which is suffered—and which the defendant knows is likely to be suffered—in the forum." *See Rio Properties, Inc. v. Rio Int'l Interlink,* 284 F.3d 1007, 1019 (9th Cir.2002) (citing *Calder v. Jones,* 465 U.S. 783, 788–89 (1984)).

The maintenance of a passive website alone does not constitute purposeful availment, *see Cybersell, Inc. v. Cybersell, Inc.,* 130 F.3d 414, 418–20 (9th Cir. 1997); rather, " 'something more' [is] required to indicate that the defendant purposefully directed its activity in a substantial way to the forum," *see Rio Properties,* 284 F.3d at 1020 (quoting *Cybersell,* 130 F.3d at 418). Here, Kirby Morgan argues Surface Supplied's advertising in *Underwater Magazine* and *Marine Technology Report* and its presence on Facebook and Twitter constitute the "something more" required to show purposeful availment.

Advertisements that "specifically target[ ] consumers" in a forum constituting a trademark holder's principal place of business can constitute the requisite "something more." *See Rio Properties, Inc.,* 284 F.3d at 1020 (holding advertisements that "demonstrate[d] an insistent marketing campaign directed toward" forum constituted purposeful availment). Advertising in national publications or on Facebook and Twitter, however, is not sufficient to support a finding of purposeful availment. *See Cascade Corp. v. Hiab-Foco AB,* 619 F.2d 36, 37–38 (9th Cir. 1980) (finding no specific jurisdiction where defendant patent holder advertised in "national publications" circulated in forum, visited forum on two occasions, and mailed accusatory letters to plaintiff in forum).

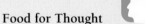

Food for Thought

Recall the discussion of jurisdiction in the Internet context in Chapter 1 and note the requirement for "something more" beyond an Internet presence in a state to support purposeful availment. Would an analysis under *Calder v. Jones,* 465 U.S. 783 (1984) yield a different conclusion, given the Central District action alleges trademark infringement?

Accordingly, Surface Supplied would not be subject to personal jurisdiction in the Central District were such district a separate state, and, consequently, 28 U.S.C. § 1391(b)(1) does not provide for venue therein.

B. Judicial District in Which a Substantial Part of Events or Omissions Giving Rise to the Claim Occurred

"A civil action may be brought in . . . a judicial district in which a substantial part of the events or omissions giving rise to the claim occurred." *See* 28 U.S.C. § 1391(b)(2). The "events or omissions giving rise to the claim[s]" in the Central

District action are the design and use of Surface Supplied's logo and other images that Kirby Morgan alleges infringes its trademarks. As all of Surface Supplied's activities occurred in the Northern District of California, it cannot be said that a substantial part of the events or omissions giving rise to the claims occurred in the Central District. Section 1391(b)(2) thus does not provide for venue in the Central District.

Accordingly, the Court will deny Kirby Morgan's motion to dismiss.

* * *

Points for Discussion

a. Three Introductory Points

Before getting into the nuts and bolts of how to conduct an analysis under the general venue statute, it is important to clarify three significant points:

The possibility of multiple proper venues. First, the venue statute is not designed to give you one venue or the best venue. Rather, several possible venues may come out of an analysis under § 1391. For example, if all the defendants reside in State A, but a substantial part of the events underlying the action happened in State B, then venue would be proper in any federal judicial district within those states where the defendants all reside or where the relevant events occurred. When multiple venues are proper, the plaintiff is free to select among any of the options, constrained only by the need to select a district court that could exercise personal jurisdiction over all the defendants. This means that to a certain degree, plaintiffs are able to engage in forum shopping, *i.e.*, seeking the most strategically advantageous forum for litigating the action. The plaintiff's selection, however, is subject to the right of parties to transfer the action to another venue, a topic covered in Section B of this chapter below.

Recent amendments to the venue statutes. Several provisions of the federal venue statutes were amended on December 7, 2011 by the Federal Courts Jurisdiction and Venue Clarification Act (JVCA). A principal reform was to eliminate the duplicative provisions of § 1391(a) & (b). The standards formerly set forth in these separate provisions are now found in § 1391(b) alone. Also, what used to appear in § 1391(c) now appears in § 1391(d), with what was in § 1391(d) now appearing in § 1391(c)(3). You will need to make note of these numbering changes when researching cases that predate the JVCA. Minor substantive clarifications were introduced throughout various parts of the venue statutes as well. For a very brief synopsis of the legislation, see THE THIRD BRANCH NEWS, *Long-Awaited Act Clarifies Venue and Jurisdiction* (December 2011).

The fallback provisions. Section 1391(b)(3)—which is referred to as the *fallback provision*—permits venue in any district having personal jurisdiction over any defendant only if "there is no district in which an action may otherwise be brought." That means that application of the previous two subdivisions, (b)(1) and (b)(2) have failed to yield *any* proper venue. This does not mean that venue can be obtained under one of the fallback provisions if an analysis under the first two subdivisions fails to produce a particularly desired venue. If an analysis under the first two subdivisions identifies any proper venue, even one that fails to match a desired locale, there is no recourse to the fallback provision. *See Daniel v. Am. Bd. of Emergency Med., 428 F.3d 408, 434 (2d Cir. 2005)* ("[V]enue may be based on [(b)(3)] only if venue cannot be established in another district pursuant to any other venue provision."). In what circumstances might you imagine that the fallback provision would be available for laying venue?

b. Analysis Under § 1391

Now, let's parse the venue statute to clarify how it lays venue in actions filed in federal court. Beginning with subdivision (b)(1), this provision indicates that venue is proper in "a judicial district in which any defendant resides, if all defendants are residents of the State in which the district is located." Thus, in an action by *A*

Take Note!

Note that a plaintiff must ordinarily establish proper venue as to each claim and each defendant. *See* 14D C. WRIGHT & A. MILLER, FED. PRAC. & PROC. § 3808 (4th ed. 2013).

against *B* and *C*, where *B* resides in the Eastern District of Virginia and *C* resides in the Western District of Virginia, venue would be proper under (b)(1) in either the Eastern or the Western Districts of Virginia, the state the defendants have in common. Notice that here we are paying no attention to the plaintiff's state of residence. Why do you think the plaintiff's residence is irrelevant to a venue analysis under the general venue statute?

Go Online

A map showing the current boundaries of the federal districts can be viewed by visiting http://www.uscourts.gov/uscourts/images/CircuitMap.pdf.

What if the defendants reside in a state that has more than one federal judicial district? Refer back to the discussion of federal judicial districts in the Overview at the beginning of this book. In states having only one district, the boundaries of the district are coextensive with those of the state, and thus defendants who all reside in such states will be amenable to suit in the district that covers that state, without regard to where within the state they reside. However, in states with multiple judicial districts, venue analysis under § 1391(b)(1) must identify both the defendants' state of residence and the district within that state in which the defendants reside. This is the analysis featured in the *Surface Supplied* case above.

Hypo 4.1

In an action by *X* against *Y* and *Z* (two individuals), where *X* lives in the Northern district of New York, *Y* lives in the Southern District of New York and *Z* lives in the Eastern District of New York, what would be the available proper venue or venues under 1391(b)(1)?

Subdivision (b)(2) provides that venue is proper in "a judicial district in which a substantial part of the events or omissions giving rise to the claim occurred, or a substantial part of property that is the subject of the action is situated." 28 U.S.C. § 1391(b)(2). How is it determined where a "substantial" portion of the events or omissions underlying the claim occurred? *See, e.g., Gulf Ins. Co. v. Glasbrenner,* 417 F.3d 353, 357 (2d Cir. 2005) ("[F]or venue to be proper, *significant* events or omissions *material* to the plaintiff's claim must have occurred in the district in question, even if other material events occurred elsewhere."); *First of Mich. Corp. v. Bramlet,* 141 F.3d 260, 263 (6th Cir. 1998) (holding that "proper venue is not limited to the district where the most substantial event giving rise to the complaint arose" but instead that "the plaintiff may file his complaint in any forum where a substantial part of the events or omissions giving rise to the claim arose"). Should the defendant's experience of harm be considered an "event" giving rise to the claim for purposes of (b)(2)? *See Estate of Abtan v. Blackwater Lodge & Training Ctr.,* 611 F. Supp. 2d 1, 8 (D.D.C. 2009) ("In tort cases, when determining whether a substantial part of the events or omissions giving rise to the plaintiff's claim occurred . . . in a particular district for purposes of § 1391(b)(2), . . . courts focus on . . . the place where the allegedly tortious actions occurred and the place where the harms were felt." (internal quotations and citations omitted)). How was this analysis conducted by the court in *Surface Supplied* above?

Notice that the events or omissions that are analyzed are limited to those "giving rise to" the claim. What connection should exist between events or omissions and the claim before treating those events or omissions as giving rise to the claim? Should events and omissions only count if they were essential to the existence of the claim under the relevant substantive law? *Daniel v. Am. Bd. of Emergency Med.,* 428 F.3d 408, 433 (2d Cir. 2005) ("When material acts or omissions within the forum bear a close nexus to the claims, they are properly deemed 'significant' and, thus, substantial, but when a close nexus is lacking, so too is the substantiality necessary to support venue."); *Jenkins Brick Co. v. Bremer,* 321 F.3d 1366, 1371 (11th Cir. 2003) ("Only the events that directly give rise to a claim are relevant. And of the places where the events have taken place, only those locations hosting a 'substantial part' of the events are to be considered [for determining venue].").

Again, if it turns out that an analysis under subdivision (b)(1) and (b)(2) reveal no proper venue in any federal district, recourse may be had to the fallback provision of § 1391(b)(3).

c. Determining Residency for Purposes of Venue

Thus far, we have simply asserted that the defendants were residents of a given state. However, an important question is how residency is determined for purposes of venue. Recall that for personal jurisdiction and diversity jurisdiction, the relevant consideration for individuals was their state of citizenship, which was in turn determined by domicile. For corporations, state citizenship for purposes of diversity jurisdiction meant their states of incorporation and the state of their principal place of business. Yet another set of rules covered the citizenship of non-corporate entities such as voluntary associations and partnerships. *See* Chapter 3. The rules for determining the residency of these types of parties are reviewed below.

Individuals. The 2011 Jurisdiction and Venue Clarification Act amended § 1391(c) to make clear that an individual's residency for venue purposes is his or her domicile, something that was not explicit in the previous version of this statute. Recall from our discussion of domicile in Chapter 3 that domicile is the place where a person is physically located and intends to remain for an indefinite period of time. Note also that domicile is purely a concept for individual real persons, not entities.

Corporations. Under 28 U.S.C. § 1391(d) (formerly § 1391(c)), corporations are residents of any district where they are subject to personal jurisdiction. If the state has more than one district, then a corporation is a resident of any district in which it could be subject to personal jurisdiction were that district a state. How does one analyze personal jurisdiction with respect to federal judicial districts? *See, e.g., Honor Plastic Indus. Co. v. Lollicup USA, Inc.,* 2006 WL 2792812, at *5 (E.D. Cal. Sept. 28, 2006) ("Title 28 U.S.C. § 1391(c) [now § 1391(d)] says any corporate defendant 'shall be deemed to reside in any judicial district in which it is subject to personal jurisdiction at the time the action is commenced.' This effectively turns the venue question

Food for Thought

Where can a corporation be said to reside within the state where it is incorporated, when such states have multiple federal districts? *Compare Jackson v. Fugro Geoservices, Inc.,* 2005 WL 3543929, at *1–2 (E.D. La. Nov. 30, 2005) (treating a corporation as a resident of all districts in the state), *with Horizon Mktg v. Kingdom Int'l. Ltd.,* 244 F. Supp. 2d 131, 138 (E.D.N.Y. 2003) (treating a corporation as only resident in the district of its official corporate address within the state), *with Tranor v. Brown,* 913 F. Supp. 388, 390 (E.D. Pa. 1996) ("[V]enue does not lie against a corporation in a multi-district state solely because of its corporate status. . . . [Section 1391] ensures that corporate defendants cannot be sued in districts within their state of incorporation with which they have no contacts." (citations omitted)).

into a personal jurisdiction analysis, treating the Eastern District of California as a state."). *See also QRG, Ltd. v. Nartron Corp.,* 2006 WL 2583626, at *3 (W.D. Pa. Sept. 7, 2006) (engaging in § 1391(c) [now § 1391(d)] analysis). How did the court in *Surface Supplied,* above, engage in this analysis?

Because corporate residency is tied to personal jurisdiction, multiple possible residencies exist beyond the corporation's place of incorporation and principal place of business—locales that would confer general jurisdiction over the corporation. All districts within which a corporation would be subject to specific jurisdiction for the civil action in question would also be districts in which a corporation resides for venue purposes.

Hypo 4.2

Bernard fell ill after consuming spinach from Williams Farms and sold by Wholesome Markets. Williams Farms is not a corporation but is rather the name under which Pete Williams, a California resident, does business. He ships the spinach grown on his farm to retail outlets throughout the United States including Wholesome Markets. Wholesome Markets is a Delaware corporation with its principal place of business in New York. It operates grocery stores in each of the 50 states. Bernard purchased the spinach that made him sick at the Wholesome Markets store in his home neighborhood in Portland, Oregon.

Bernard initiated an action against Williams and Wholesome Markets for negligence in the U.S. District Court for the District of Oregon. Williams moves to dismiss for improper venue. Should the court grant the motion?

Hypo 4.3

Bernard, an Oregon citizen, fell ill in Texas after consuming spinach from Osage Farms and sold by Wholesome Markets (Bernard purchased the spinach in Texas). Osage Farms is a Delaware corporation operating from a farm in Los Angeles, California (the Central District of California). Osage ships the spinach grown on its farm to retail outlets throughout the United States including Wholesome Markets. Wholesome Markets is a Delaware corporation with its principal place of business in New York. It operates grocery stores in each of the 50 states. Bernard purchased the spinach that made him sick at the Wholesome Markets store in Houston, Texas (Southern District of Texas) during a business trip. Bernard initiated an action against Osage Farms and Wholesome Markets for negligence in the U.S. District Court for the District of Oregon. Osage moves to dismiss for improper venue. Should the court grant the motion?

Unincorporated Entities. The Supreme Court has held that for purposes of a venue analysis, the residence of an unincorporated association such as a partnership or trade union is "determined by looking to the residence of the association itself rather than that of its individual members." *Denver & Rio Grande W.R.R. Co. v. Bhd. of R.R. Trainmen*, 387 U.S. 556, 559 (1967). The 2011 Jurisdiction and Venue Clarification Act codifies this treatment of unincorporated entities as defendants by providing that they reside "in any judicial district in which such defendant is subject to the court's personal jurisdiction with respect to the civil action in question." 28 U.S.C. § 1391(c)(2). Why do you think this is the case? What justifies looking at the association to determine residence for purposes of venue but looking at individual members to determine citizenship for purposes of diversity jurisdiction?

d.   Venue in Removed Cases

The language of the general removal statute (*see* Chapter 3) indicates the federal district in which removed cases must be heard, in effect making those federal districts the proper venue for removed cases. *See* 28 U.S.C. § 1441(a); *Polizzi v. Cowles Magazines, Inc.*, 345 U.S. 663, 665–66 (1953) ("The venue of removed actions is governed by 28 U.S.C.A. § 1441(a). . . . Section 1441(a) expressly provides that the proper venue of a removed action is 'the district court of the United States for the district and division embracing the place where such action is pending.' "). Thus, for removed cases, a separate analysis under the venue statutes is unnecessary and challenges to venue as improper are unavailable, provided the district indicated in § 1441(a) is where the removed case is now being heard. *See* 28 U.S.C. § 1390(c) ("This chapter shall not determine the district court to which a civil action pending in a State court may be removed . . . ."); *Lundahl v. Pub. Storage Mgmt., Inc.*, 62 Fed. App'x 217, 218–19 (10th Cir. 2003) ("[R]emoval venue is controlled by 28 U.S.C. § 1441(a) which provides that cases may be removed to 'the district court of the United States for the district and division embracing the place where such action is pending.' Thus, the dismissal based on § 1391(b) was improvidently granted, and venue in the federal district court for the district of Utah is proper."); *Godfredson v. JBC Legal Grp., P.C.*, 387 F. Supp. 2d 543, 555 (E.D.N.C. 2005) ("28 U.S.C. § 1391 does not apply when, as here, defendants remove a case to federal court from state court.").

e.   Venue for Alien Defendants

The general venue statute contains a special provision governing the determination of venue in actions against aliens. Section 1391(c)(3)—formerly 1391(d)—states, "a defendant not resident in the United States may be sued in any judicial district . . . ." Thus, if there is a defendant who is not a U.S. citizen, or, presumably, a U.S. citizen domiciled abroad, that defendant may be sued in any federal district court anywhere in the country (as far as venue is concerned; personal jurisdiction and subject matter jurisdiction would be separate matters). This provision also applies to foreign corporations lacking a U.S. residency, not just individuals. *See* *Go-Video, Inc. v. Akai Elec. Co.*, 885 F.2d 1406, 1410–11 (9th Cir. 1989); *O.S.C. Corp. v. Toshiba Am., Inc.*, 491 F.2d

1064, 1068 (9th Cir. 1974) ("[U]nder section 1391(d) as an alien corporation it can be sued in any district."). If an alien (or non-U.S. resident) is one of several defendants, they are disregarded for purposes of determining venue with respect to the U.S. resident defendants. 28 U.S.C. § 1391(c)(3).

f. Venue and Personal Jurisdiction

Venue and personal jurisdiction are not the same thing. Venue can be proper in a district but that same court can lack personal jurisdiction. *See, e.g.*, *World-Wide Volkswagen v. Woodson*, 444 U.S. 286 (1980). Alternatively, a court may be able to exercise personal jurisdiction over a defendant but venue may be improper there. *See* **Example 4.1**.

> **Example 4.1**
>
> P^{FL} v. D^{DE} & D^{NY}. All events giving rise to P's claim arose in California. Under the general venue statute, although D^{DE} would be subject to personal jurisdiction in Delaware and D^{NY} would be subject to personal jurisdiction in New York, venue would not be proper in either state but would be proper in the relevant district in California.

The distinction between the two concepts does not mean that they will not often coincide, however. Indeed, because entities reside in any district in which they are subject to personal jurisdiction for purposes of venue, when a court has personal jurisdiction over all the defendants, and all the defendants are entities, venue will always be proper there because by definition all defendants will "reside" in that jurisdiction. *See* **Example 4.2**. Of course, when there is only one defendant and that defendant is an entity, venue is proper wherever that defendant could be subjected to personal jurisdiction.

g. Challenging Venue

If a defendant feels that the district in which the plaintiff has brought the action is improper under the applicable venue statute, the proper vehicle for challenging venue is a ***motion to dismiss for improper venue***. *See* FED. R. CIV. P. 12(b)(3). This is one of the waivable defenses, meaning that under the Federal Rules the motion must be made in a defendant's initial response to the plaintiff's complaint or it is waived. *See* FED. R. CIV. P. 12(g) & (h). The rules governing the waivable defenses will be covered in greater detail in Chapter 6.

> **Example 4.2**
>
> Polly wants to sue ABC, Inc. and XYZ Corp. in California federal court. ABC has substantial operations related to the suit in the Northern District of California and XYZ has the same level of operations in the Southern District of California. Because both defendants are corporations and they would each be subject to personal jurisdiction in the districts where they have related corporate operations, the defendants all reside within the same state (California) and venue would be proper in either the Northern or Southern Districts of California.

h. Venue and Forum-Selection Clauses

Federal courts must enforce mandatory forum-selection clauses unless the objecting party can "clearly show that enforcement would be unreasonable and unjust, or that the clause [is] invalid for such reasons as fraud or overreaching." *M/S Bremen v. Zapata Off-Shore Co.*, 407 U.S. 1, 15 (1972). Thus, a valid forum-selection clause can serve as the basis for making venue proper based on consent. *See, e.g.*, *Martin Eng'g Co. v. Nark*, No. 12 C 8891, 2013 WL 4501410, at *4 (N.D. Ill. Aug. 22, 2013) ("Because the Court finds the forum selection clause at issue to be permissive, providing consent for the claim to be brought in Illinois, venue in this District is proper. Therefore, Defendant cannot claim improper venue and move for dismissal under Rule 12(b)(3) . . . ."). However, a forum-selection clause cannot serve as the basis for a dismissal for improper

What's That?

Forum non conveniens is a common law doctrine permitting the dismissal of cases so that they may be filed in a more appropriate forum outside of the federal system.

venue if venue is otherwise proper under a federal statute. *See Atl. Marine Constr. Co. v. U.S. Dist. Court for the W. Dist. of Tex.*, 134 S. Ct. 568, 577 (2013) ("Section 1406(a) and Rule 12(b)(3) allow dismissal only when venue is 'wrong' or 'improper.' Whether venue is 'wrong' or 'improper' depends exclusively on whether the court in which the case was brought satisfies the requirements of federal venue laws, and those provisions say nothing about a forum-selection clause."). The proper remedy when a case is filed in a venue not conforming with that indicated by a valid forum-selection clause is a motion to transfer the case under 28 U.S.C. § 1404 or a motion to dismiss for *forum non conveniens*. *Id.* at 579 ("Section 1404(a) therefore provides a mechanism for enforcement of forum-selection clauses that point to a particular federal district."); *id.* at 580 ("[T]he appropriate way to enforce a forum-selection clause pointing to a state or foreign forum is through the doctrine of *forum non conveniens*.").

2. Pendent Venue

Thus far we have considered actions in which venue was proper for each claim under the general venue statue. What happens in cases where there are multiple claims against multiple defendants filed in a particular forum, some of which are properly venued in that forum and others that are not? The next case wrestles with this situation.

PKWare v. Meade

U.S. District Court, Eastern District of Wisconsin
79 F. Supp. 2d 1007 (E.D. Wis. 2000)

ADELMAN, DISTRICT JUDGE.

Plaintiff PKWare, Inc. is a Milwaukee company which develops and licenses various software products. Plaintiff is the originator of certain software known as PKZIP software, and owns a patent, trademarks and copyrights on some of the technology related to the software. Defendant Timothy L. Meade is an Ohio resident in the business of translating and reselling software. In September 1992 plaintiff and Meade entered into a contract (the "agreement") under which Meade would convert some of plaintiff's software so that it could be used in environments other than those for which it was designed. At the time Meade entered into the agreement he was a sole proprietor doing business under the name "Ascent Solutions." In 1993 Meade incorporated his business in Ohio under the name Ascent Solutions, Inc. ("ASI") and became ASI's majority shareholder, president and CEO.

Make the Connection

False designation of origin involves the use of some mark or design in connection with a product that gives an erroneous impression of the source of the product. This is a trademark concept that would be covered in an **Intellectual Property** course.

In 1999 plaintiff commenced this action against both defendants alleging a variety of claims under both state and federal law. These claims include (1) breach of contract, (2) copyright infringement, (3) patent infringement, (4) trademark infringement, (5) false designation of origin, (6) common law trademark infringement, (7) common law unfair competition, (8) dilution of mark, and (9) breach of duty of good faith and fair dealing. Pursuant to FED. R. CIV. P. 12(b)(2) and 12(b)(3), defendants moved to dismiss for lack of personal jurisdiction and improper venue * * * . I now address defendants' motions.

I. Factual Background

Plaintiff alleges that "on information and belief some time after the effective date of the Agreement, Meade . . . purported to assign his rights and duties under the Agreement to [ASI]." The agreement, however, provides that neither party may assign it without the other party's written consent. The record contains no evidence that Meade

What's That?

According to *Black's Law Dictionary*, allegations based on information and belief are those "based on second-hand information that the declarant believes to be true." Rule 11 permits parties to make allegations on this basis.

formally assigned his interest to ASI or that plaintiff consented in writing to such an assignment. The parties agree, however, that ASI performed Meade's responsibilities under the agreement. Further ASI does not dispute that it was a party to the agreement despite Meade's having signed it while he was a sole proprietor. ASI agrees that it had a "business relationship [with] PKWare . . . from September 1992 to the present."

Under the agreement Meade was to convert or "port" plaintiff's software so that it could have wider use. Porting is generally accomplished by rewriting a component of the software known as source code. Upon completion of the porting Meade was to send PKWare copies of the resulting software known under the agreement as "Resulting Programs and Software Collections." Also, under the agreement plaintiff granted Meade a license to resell the converted software in return for a thirty percent royalty which was to be paid monthly. Under the agreement Meade could license the source code to third parties and subcontract the conversion work with plaintiff's consent but was responsible for the work of subcontractors. Meade's royalty payments were to be accompanied by monthly reports setting forth the sales for each environment for which the software had been converted during the period that the agreement was in effect. Defendants sent plaintiff some royalty payments and sales reports.

Meade and plaintiff negotiated the agreement after lengthy communications by telephone, e-mail and writings between Meade in Ohio and plaintiff in Wisconsin. During the course of the agreement Meade communicated with plaintiff's employees about matters related to the agreement on numerous occasions via telephone and e-mail. Meade also visited Milwaukee once to attempt to hire one of plaintiff's employees, Steven Burg, during which visit and subsequently "the ongoing relationship between PKWare and ASI was occasionally discussed." The agreement provided that it would be governed by Wisconsin law.

ASI operates an interactive website with an on-line store where users from around the world can place orders for ASI products including some PKZIP products and other software. ASI sells software products all over the world including in Wisconsin. ASI has also provided products and/or services to at least eighty-six different customers in Wisconsin over the course of the last several years with the majority of these sales occurring in the Eastern District of Wisconsin. ASI also advertises on the internet search engine "AltaVista" and in ComputerWorld magazine and the SciTech Science catalogue, all of which have Wisconsin subscribers. * * *

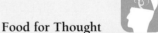

Food for Thought

The court has listed here the defendants' contacts with the forum state, Wisconsin. Based on your understanding of personal jurisdiction, do you think that the court—which is located in Wisconsin—has personal jurisdiction over the defendants?

III. Venue

Defendants argue that venue is improper in this judicial district. The burden of showing that venue is proper is on the plaintiff. *Grantham v. Challenge-Cook Bros., Inc.*, 420 F.2d 1182, 1184 (7th Cir. 1969). For venue to lie it must be proper as to both defendants and as to all claims. *Payne v. Marketing Showcase, Inc.*, 602 F. Supp. 656, 658 (N.D. Ill. 1985); Georgene M. Vairo, *Determination of Proper Venue*, in 17 MOORE'S FEDERAL PRACTICE § 110.05 (Daniel R. Coquillette et al. eds., 3d ed. 1997). Here, plaintiff brings a breach of contract and other state law claims as well as federal claims for trademark, copyright and patent infringement. Because of the variety of plaintiff's claims, several venue statutes are relevant.

Take Note!

The court here states a general rule: In the face of a defendant's challenge to venue, it is the plaintiff who has the burden of showing that venue is proper, not the defendant who must show that venue is improper. Why do you think the burden is allocated in this way?

A. State Law Claims and Federal Trademark Claims

Venue for plaintiff's state law claims is governed by the general venue statute, 28 U.S.C. § 1391. The same is true of plaintiff's federal trademark related claims because the Lanham Act has no special venue provision. *Woodke v. Dahm,* 70 F.3d 983 (8th Cir. 1995). Section 1391(b) provides that where, as here, subject matter jurisdiction is not founded solely on diversity, venue exists in "(1) a judicial district where any defendant resides, if all defendants reside in the same State, [or] (2) a judicial district in which a substantial part of the events or omissions giving rise to the claim occurred." ASI can be regarded as residing in this district because, under 28 U.S.C. § 1391(c), a corporation is deemed to reside in a district in which it is subject to personal jurisdiction.[*] Meade, however, is not a corporation and resides in Ohio. Therefore, venue is not proper as to either defendant under § 1391(b)(1).

However, § 1391(b)(2) provides that venue exists in this district if "a substantial part of the events or omissions giving rise to the claim occurred" here. Section 1391(b)(2) is the result of a 1990 amendment which changed the law to the extent that prior law had encouraged an approach that a claim could generally arise in only one venue. Under the amended law, however, venue may be proper in more than one district as long as a "substantial" part of the key events or omissions occurred in the district. In determining where substantial parts of the underlying events occurred I focus on the activities of the defendant and not those of the plaintiff.

---

[*] In an omitted portion of the opinion, the court concluded that personal jurisdiction was proper with respect to ASI in Wisconsin. [Ed.]

In applying the "substantial part" test provided in amended § 1391(b)(2) to breach of contract cases, courts consider a number of factors including where the conduct underlying the breach occurred and where performance under the contract was to take place. *Consolidated Ins. Co. v. Vanderwoude*, 876 F. Supp. 198, 202 (N.D. Ind. 1995). The "substantial part of the events or omissions" standard may be satisfied by a communication transmitted or not transmitted to or from the district in which the cause of action was filed, given a sufficient relationship between the communication and the cause of action. In contract cases courts have held that the delivery or non-delivery of goods and the payment or non-payment of money were significant events providing a basis for venue in the district where they were to occur. *See* *American Carpet Mills v. Gunny Corp.*, 649 F.2d 1056, 1059 (5th Cir. 1981) (place where goods were to be delivered was place of performance); *Gardner Eng'g Corp. v. Page Eng'g Co.*, 484 F.2d 27, 33 (8th Cir. 1973) (venue existed at site where delivery was to be made); *Decker Coal Co. v. Commonw. Edison Co.*, 805 F.2d 834, 843–44 (9th Cir. 1986) (venue for claim based on breach of contract is in place of intended performance rather than place of repudiation); *Oce-Industries, Inc. v. Coleman*, 487 F. Supp. 548, 552 (N.D. Ill. 1980) (place where orders accepted and payment to be made important for venue purposes).

In the present case defendants were obliged under the agreement to deliver copies of software, make royalty payments and send sales reports to plaintiff in this district and allegedly failed to do so. Defendants were also supposed to obtain approval for sublicensing and distributing in this district and allegedly failed to do so. Further, defendants allegedly attempted unsuccessfully to cure their default here. These alleged failures constitute a substantial part of the events or omissions giving rise to plaintiff's claim. Thus, based on the facts of the case and the foregoing authority, it is reasonable to conclude that venue exists in this district with respect to plaintiff's state law and trademark claims.

B. Federal Copyright Claims

Title 28 U.S.C. § 1400(a) governs venue in copyright claims and provides that venue is proper in a district in which the defendant "resides" or "may be found." Under this provision, a defendant "may be found" in a district if the defendant is subject to personal jurisdiction in that forum. Because I have found that defendants are subject to personal jurisdiction here venue is proper under 28 U.S.C. § 1400(a) with respect to plaintiff's copyright claims.

Take Note!

As mentioned earlier, there are special venue statutes that govern certain types of cases. When these statutes apply, they indicate proper venues for their respective claims. Thus, the court here applies the special statute governing venue in federal copyright claims and the patent action venue provision to the patent infringement claim below.

C. Patent Infringement Claim

Title 28 U.S.C. § 1400(b) governs plaintiff's patent infringement claim. It provides that an action may be brought in a district "where the defendant resides or where the defendant has committed acts of infringement and has a regular and established place of business."

1. Claim Against ASI

It is not disputed that ASI has no "regular and established place of business" in this district. The question, therefore, is whether for § 1400(b) purposes ASI "resides" in the Eastern District of Wisconsin. [The court went on to conclude that ASI did reside in the Eastern District of Wisconsin under a now invalidated interpretation of 28 U.S.C. § 1400(b). *See TC Heartland LLC v. Kraft Food Group Brands LLC,* 137 S. Ct. 1514 (2017).]

2. Meade

Section 1400(b) also governs venue with respect to plaintiff's patent infringement claim against Meade. Meade is not a corporation and resides in Ohio. Venue, therefore, is not proper here under the "resides" clause of § 1400(b) and will only lie under § 1400(b) if Meade "committed acts of infringement" and has a "regular and established place of business" in this district. "Having a 'regular and established place of business' involves more than 'doing business.' " *Brunswick Corp. v. Suzuki Motor Co.,* 575 F. Supp. 1412, 1423 (E.D. Wis. 1983). Meade does not have a regular and established place of business in this judicial district. He neither owns nor rents property, nor employs sales agents here. Therefore, venue is not proper in this district under § 1400(b) with respect to the patent infringement claim against Meade.

Plaintiff, however, asks the court to exercise pendent venue over the improperly venued claim. Meade objects pointing out both that patent infringement claims are governed exclusively by § 1400(b) and that venue must generally be established for each separate cause of action. Courts have sometimes relied on a theory of pendent venue analogous to the doctrine of supplemental jurisdiction. *See, e.g., Travis v. Anthes Imperial Ltd.,* 473 F.2d 515, 528–29 (8th Cir. 1973) (when venue is proper on federal claims, it is also proper on pendent state claims); *Beattie v. United States,* 756 F.2d 91, 101 (D.C. Cir. 1984) (the doctrine of "pendent venue" is now well established). Generally, pendent venue will be applied if a court may also exercise supplemental jurisdiction.

However, there is no practical reason to limit the application of pendent venue to pendent jurisdiction cases, and judges have recognized this by utilizing pendent venue in other situations. In *Zenith Radio Corp. v. Matsushita Elec. Ind. Co.,* 402 F. Supp. 262 (E.D. Pa. 1975), plaintiff brought claims under two different federal statutes, one of which was properly venued and one of which was not. The court retained jurisdiction of both, holding that it would be senseless to bifurcate the case by dismissing or transferring some counts while retaining the others, since the facts underlying both claims were essentially the same. See also *Seamon v. Upham*, 563 F. Supp. 396, 399 (E.D. Tex. 1983), where the court noted that pendent venue could be exercised if it furthered the goals of judicial economy, convenience and fairness to the litigants.

However, courts have been less willing to accept venue of a claim for patent infringement based on the doctrine of pendent venue. Patent infringement cases are governed by a specific venue statute, § 1400(b), and courts have expressed the view that application of the doctrine of pendent venue is inconsistent with the specific requirements of the statute. *See Bradford Novelty Co. v. Manheim*, 156 F. Supp. 489, 491 (S.D.N.Y. 1957) (Congress saw fit to narrowly confine the venue provisions applicable to this type of action). The Supreme Court's comments about § 1400(b) also counsel caution in regard to applying pendent venue to patent infringement cases. *See Schnell v. Peter Eckrich & Sons*, 365 U.S. 260, 264 (1961) ("The requirement of venue is specific and unambiguous; it is not one of those vague principles which, in the interest of some overriding policy, is to be given a liberal construction."). Additionally, no Seventh Circuit case authorizes the application of pendent venue in this case.

Thus, I decline to apply the doctrine of pendent venue to plaintiff's patent infringement claim against Meade. Therefore, venue with respect to the claim is improper in this district. Pursuant to FED. R. CIV. P. 12(b)(3), Meade has moved to dismiss this claim. His motion will be granted.

* * *

Points for Discussion

a. Pendent Venue

When a plaintiff asserts multiple claims in an action, venue must ordinarily be proper for each of those claims. *Centerville ALF, Inc. v. Balanced Care Corp.*, 197 F. Supp. 2d 1039, 1046 (S.D. Ohio 2002) ("Plaintiffs bear the burden of establishing that venue is proper . . . and must demonstrate that venue is proper for each claim asserted in their complaint."). However, many courts have recognized an exception to this general rule in the doctrine of pendent venue, according to which venue may be proper with respect to an improperly venued claim if the claim is joined to a properly venued claim, and the claims arise out of a common nucleus of operative fact. 14D C. WRIGHT, A. MILLER, E. COOPER & R. FREER, FED. PRAC. & PROC. § 3808 (4th ed. 2013). *See also High River Ltd. P'ship v. Mylan Lab., Inc.*, 353 F. Supp. 2d 487, 493 (M.D. Pa. 2005) ("Pendent venue is an exception to the rule that venue must be established for each cause of action asserted in the complaint."). *But see McCaskey v.*

Cont'l Airlines, Inc., 133 F. Supp. 2d 514, 525 (S.D. Tex. 2001) ("Simply put, there is no pendant [sic] venue under 28 U.S.C. § 1391(a)(2).").

What do you think is the rationale for this judicially-recognized exception? Is the notion of pendent venue consistent with the general venue statute? With respect to claims governed by specialized venue statutes, should the doctrine of pendent venue be available to lay venue in forums not approved by those statutes? *See, e.g., Price v. Countrywide Home Loans, Inc.,* 2005 WL 2354348, at *5–6 (S.D. Ga. Sept. 26, 2005). For a thorough discussion of pendent venue doctrine, see Richard Corn, *Pendent Venue: A Doctrine in Search of a Theory*, 68 U. CHI. L. REV. 931 (2001).

b. Venue for Subsequently Joined Claims

How should courts assess venue for claims that are asserted against the original parties by way of counterclaims, crossclaims, or by outsiders seeking to intervene in the case? Generally speaking, courts have not required an independent assessment of venue for such additional claims. *See* 14D C. WRIGHT, A. MILLER, E. COOPER & R. FREER, FED. PRAC. & PROC. § 3808 (4th ed. 2013) ("When these additional claims are asserted against parties to the original suit, the better view is that no venue objection should be entertained. . . . The action already has been "brought" in that district court and venue should not be lost by the subsequent expansion of the case among the same parties.").

Conventional wisdom also holds that third-party defendants lack an ability to challenge venue with respect to the claims asserted against them. *See* 6 C. WRIGHT, A. MILLER, & M. KANE, FED. PRAC & PROC., § 1445 (3d. ed. 2010) ("According to existing case law, the statutory venue limitations have no application to Rule 14 claims even if they would require the third-party action to be heard in another district had it been brought as an independent action."). However, venue challenges should remain available for any additional unrelated claims asserted against third-party defendants under Rule 18(a). *Lehman v. Revolution Portfolio LLC,* 166 F.3d 389, 394 (1st Cir. 1999) (indicating that "[the Rule 18(a)] authorization is subject only to the usual requirements of jurisdiction and venue").

c. Special Venue Statutes

The general venue statute, by its own terms, applies "except as otherwise provided by law." As illustrated in *PKWare*, there are indeed other venue provisions for specific types of cases that might trump the general venue provisions of § 1391 when they apply. *See, e.g.,* 28 U.S.C. § 1400 (copyright and patent cases).[*]

---

[*] The Supreme Court recently interpreted the term "resides" in 28 U.S.C. § 1400(b) to be limited—for corporations—to their states of incorporation. *TC Heartland LLC v. Kraft Food Group Brands LLC,* 137 S. Ct. 1514 (2017). This was notwithstanding the fact that the general venue statute—28 U.S.C. § 1391(d)—defines the term "resides" more broadly than that for all venue purposes under Chapter 87 of Title 28, of which the patent venue statute is a part.

Thus, in assessing venue it is important first to determine whether one of these special statutes applies before moving on to an analysis of venue under the general venue statute. Note, however, that the alien venue provision, § 1391(c)(3) (formerly § 1391(d)), itself trumps special venue statutes. *See Brunette Mach. Works, Ltd. v. Kockum Indus., Inc., 406 U.S. 706, 714 (1972)* (holding that § 1391(d) [now § 1391(c)(3)] is "a declaration of the long-established rule that suits against aliens are wholly outside the operation of all the federal venue laws, general and special"). Courts have also held that

Take Note!

Special venue provisions can also be found within substantive statutory provisions themselves. *See, e.g.,* 15 U.S.C. § 22 (Clayton Act) (providing for venue in antitrust cases).

when the general venue statute and the special venue statute are not in conflict, and the special venue statute is not exclusive, litigants may be able to lay venue by satisfying either standard that applies. *See* 14D C. WRIGHT, A. MILLER, E. COOPER & R. FREER, FED. PRAC. & PROC. § 3808 n.4 (4th ed. 2013) ("This conclusion results from the Supreme Court's holding that special venue statutes will supplant the general venue provision only if such restrictive intent is indicated in the specialized statute.") (citing *Pure Oil Co. v. Suarez, 384 U.S. 202 (1966)*)).

B. Change of Venue

What happens if the court where the plaintiff files its case is not a proper venue under the applicable venue statute? Or, what recourse does a defendant have if she simply finds the selected venue to be too inconvenient, even though venue may be proper? Taking the latter situation first, federal law provides courts with the power to *transfer* cases to another federal judicial district—even though venue in the first district may be proper—on the ground that doing so is "in the interest of justice" and better for the "convenience of parties and witnesses":

> **Change of Venue: 28 U.S.C. § 1404(a)**
>
> (a) For the convenience of parties and witnesses, in the interest of justice, a district court may transfer any civil action to any other district or division where it might have been brought or to any district or division to which all parties have consented.

Thus, a defendant who feels that the plaintiff's chosen venue is too inconvenient or otherwise unduly burdensome may seek a transfer of the case to another federal judicial district (or division within the initially chosen district).

Take Note!

Both § 1404 and § 1406 below permit transfer to a "district." A district refers to one of the federal judicial districts discussed above. Thus, under the federal venue transfer statutes, an action may not be transferred from federal court to a state court.

On the other hand, if the plaintiff initially files an action in a forum that is not a proper venue under the applicable venue statute, then the defendant may still seek to transfer the case but pursuant to a separate change of venue provision, 28 U.S.C. 1406:

Curing Defective Venue: 28 U.S.C. § 1406(a)

(a) The district court of a district in which is filed a case laying venue in the wrong division or district shall dismiss, or if it be in the interest of justice, transfer such case to any district or division in which it could have been brought.

Note that a court may dismiss a case for improper venue under 28 U.S.C. § 1406 as an alternative to transferring the case. Keep in mind, however, that dismissals pursued under § 1406 may be waived if not raised under the circumstances required for seeking a dismissal for improper venue under Rule 12(b)(3). *See, e.g.*, *Smart v. Goord*, 21 F. Supp. 2d 309, 318 n.6 (S.D.N.Y. 1998) ("Waiver of objection to improper venue only pertains to a motion to dismiss or transfer on the basis of improper venue pursuant to 28 U.S.C. § 1406(a), not to a motion to transfer for convenience and the interest of justice pursuant to 28 U.S.C. § 1404(a).").

In this section, we will cover two issues presented by these venue transfer provisions: (1) To which federal districts may an action be transferred, and (2) What standards govern transfer under § 1404 and § 1406?

1. Determining Available Transferee Courts

Hoffman v. Blaski[*]

Supreme Court of the United States
363 U.S. 335 (1960)

MR. JUSTICE W̲H̲I̲T̲T̲A̲K̲E̲R̲ delivered the opinion of the Court.

* * *

The instant cases present the question whether a District Court, in which a civil action has been properly brought, is empowered by § 1404(a) to transfer the action, on the motion of the defendant, to a district in which the plaintiff did not have a *right* to bring it.

Respondents, Blaski and others, residents of Illinois, brought this patent infringement action in the United States District Court for the Northern District of Texas against one Howell and a Texas corporation controlled by him, alleging that the defendants are residents of, and maintain their only place of business in, the City of Dallas, in the Northern District of Texas, where they are infringing respondents' patents. After being served with process and filing their answer, the defendants moved, under § 1404(a), to transfer the action to the United States District Court for the Northern District of Illinois.[3] Respondents objected to the transfer on the ground that, inasmuch as the defendants did not reside, maintain a place of business, or infringe the patents in, and could not have been served with process in, the Illinois district, the courts of that district lacked venue over the action[4] and ability to command jurisdiction over the defendants; that therefore that district was not a forum in which the respondents had a right to bring the action, and, hence, the court was without power to transfer it to that district. Without mentioning that objection or the question it raised, the District Court found that "the motion should be granted for the convenience of the parties and witnesses in the interest of justice," and ordered the case transferred to the Illinois district. Thereupon, respondents moved in the Fifth Circuit for leave to file a petition for a writ of mandamus directing the vacation of that order. That court, holding that "(t)he purposes for which

---

[*] This case was resolved along with a companion case, *Sullivan v. Behimer*, which raised the same question as *Hoffman v. Blaski*. Discussion of the facts of *Sullivan* is omitted here. [Ed.]

[2] The asserted basis of the motion was that trial of the action in the Illinois District Court would be more convenient to the parties and witnesses and in the interest of justice because several actions involving the validity of these patents were then pending in that court, and that pretrial and discovery steps taken in those actions had developed a substantial amount of evidence that would be relevant and useful in this action. Defendants also stated in the motion that, if and when the case be so transferred, they would waive all objections to the venue of the Illinois District Court over the action and would enter their appearance in the action in that court.

[3] *See* 28 U.S.C. § 1400(b).

§ 1404(a) was enacted would be unduly circumscribed if a transfer could not be made 'in the interest of justice' to a district where the defendants not only waive venue but to which they seek the transfer," denied the motion.

Upon receipt of a certified copy of the pleadings and record, the Illinois District Court assigned the action to Judge Hoffman's calendar. Respondents promptly moved for an order remanding the action on the ground that the Texas District Court did not have power to make the transfer order and, hence, the Illinois District Court was not thereby vested with jurisdiction of the action. After expressing his view that the "weight of reason and logic" favored "retransfer of this case to Texas," Judge Hoffman, with misgivings, denied the motion. Respondents then filed in the Seventh Circuit a petition for a writ of mandamus directing Judge Hoffman to reverse his order. After hearing and rehearing, the Seventh Circuit, holding that "(w)hen Congress provided (in § 1404(a)) for transfer (of a civil action) to a district 'where it might have been brought,' it is hardly open to doubt but that it referred to a district where the plaintiff * * * had a right to bring the case," and that respondents did not have a *right* to bring this action in the Illinois district, granted the writ, one judge dissenting.

* * *

Petitioners' "thesis" and sole claim is that § 1404(a), being remedial, should be broadly construed, and, when so construed, the phrase "where it might have been brought" should be held to relate not only to the time of the bringing of the action, but also to the time of the transfer; and that "if at such time the transferee forum has the power to adjudicate the issues of the action, it is a forum in which the action might *then* have been brought." (Emphasis added.) They argue that in the interim between the bringing of the action and the filing of a motion to transfer it, the defendants may move their residence to, or, if corporations, may begin the transaction of business in, some other district, and, if such is done, the phrase "where it might have been brought" should be construed to empower the District Court to transfer the action, on motion of the defendants, to such other district; and that, similarly, if, as here, the defendants move to transfer the action to some other district and consent to submit to the jurisdiction of such other district, the latter district should be held one "in which the action might *then* have been brought." (Emphasis added.)

We do not agree. We do not think the § 1404(a) phrase "where it might have been brought" can be interpreted to mean, as petitioners' theory would required, "where it may now be rebrought, with defendants' consent." This Court has said, in a different context, that § 1404(a) is "unambiguous, direct [and] clear," *Ex parte Collett, 337 U.S. 55, 58 (1949)*, and that "the unequivocal words of § 1404(a) and the legislative history * * * (establish) that Congress indeed meant what it said." *United States v. National City Lines, Inc., 337 U.S. 78, 84 (1949)*. * * * [W]e think the dissenting opinion of Judges Hastie and McLaughlin in *Paramount Pictures, Inc. v. Rodney, 186 F.2d 111, 119 (3d Cir. 1951)*, correctly answered this contention:

But we do not see how the conduct of a defendant after suit has been instituted can add to the forums where 'it might have been brought.' In the normal meaning of words this language of Section 1404(a) directs the attention of the judge who is considering a transfer to the situation which existed when suit was instituted.

It is not to be doubted that the transferee courts, like every District Court, had jurisdiction to entertain actions of the character involved, but it is obvious that they did not acquire jurisdiction over these particular actions when they were brought in the transferor courts. The transferee courts could have acquired jurisdiction over these actions only if properly brought in those courts, or if validly transferred thereto under § 1404(a). Of course, venue, like jurisdiction over the person, may be waived. A defendant, properly served with process by a court having subject matter jurisdiction, waives venue by failing seasonably to assert it, or even simply by making default. But the power of a District Court under § 1404(a) to transfer an action to another district is made to depend not upon the wish or waiver of the defendant but, rather, upon whether the transferee district was one in which the action "might have been brought" by the plaintiff.

The thesis urged by petitioners would not only do violence to the plain words of § 1404(a), but would also inject gross discrimination. That thesis, if adopted, would empower a District Court, upon a finding of convenience, to transfer an action to any district desired by the defendants and in which they were willing to waive their statutory defenses as to venue and jurisdiction over their persons, regardless of the fact that such transferee district was not one in which the action "might have been brought" by the plaintiff. Conversely, that thesis would not permit the court, upon motion of the plaintiffs and a like showing of convenience, to transfer the action to the same district, without the consent and waiver of venue and personal jurisdiction defenses by the defendants. Nothing in § 1404(a), or in its legislative history, suggests such a unilateral objective and we should not, under the guise of interpretation, ascribe to Congress any such discriminatory purpose.

* * *

Inasmuch as the respondents (plaintiffs) did not have a right to bring these actions in the respective transferee districts, it follows that the judgments of the Court of Appeals were correct and must be affirmed.

Affirmed.

[A concurrence by Justice Stewart and dissents by Justices Frankfurter, Harlan, and Brennan have been omitted.]

Atlantic Marine Constr. Co. v. U.S. Dist. Court, W.D. Tex.

Supreme Court of the United States
134 S. Ct. 568 (2013)

JUSTICE ALITO delivered the opinion of the Court.

The question in this case concerns the procedure that is available for a defendant in a civil case who seeks to enforce a forum-selection clause. We reject petitioner's argument that such a clause may be enforced by a motion to dismiss under 28 U.S.C. § 1406(a) or Rule 12(b)(3) of the Federal Rules of Civil Procedure. Instead, a forum-selection clause may be enforced by a motion to transfer under § 1404(a), which provides that "[f]or the convenience of parties and witnesses, in the interest of justice, a district court may transfer any civil action to any other district or division where it might have been brought or to any district or division to which all parties have consented." When a defendant files such a motion, we conclude, a district court should transfer the case unless extraordinary circumstances unrelated to the convenience of the parties clearly disfavor a transfer. In the present case, both the District Court and the Court of Appeals misunderstood the standards to be applied in adjudicating a § 1404(a) motion in a case involving a forum-selection clause, and we therefore reverse the decision below.

I

Petitioner Atlantic Marine Construction Co., a Virginia corporation with its principal place of business in Virginia, entered into a contract with the United States Army Corps of Engineers to construct a child-development center at Fort Hood in the Western District of Texas. Atlantic Marine then entered into a subcontract with respondent J-Crew Management, Inc., a Texas corporation, for work on the project. This subcontract included a forum-selection clause, which stated that all disputes between the parties "shall be litigated in the Circuit Court for the City of Norfolk, Virginia, or the United States District Court for the Eastern District of Virginia, Norfolk Division."

When a dispute about payment under the subcontract arose, however, J-Crew sued Atlantic Marine in the Western District of Texas, invoking that court's diversity jurisdiction. Atlantic Marine moved to dismiss the suit, arguing that the forum-selection clause rendered venue in the Western District of Texas "wrong" under § 1406(a) and "improper" under Federal Rule of Civil Procedure 12(b)(3). In the alternative, Atlantic Marine moved to transfer the case to the Eastern District of Virginia under § 1404(a). J-Crew opposed these motions.

The District Court denied both motions. It first concluded that § 1404(a) is the exclusive mechanism for enforcing a forum-selection clause that points to another federal forum. The District Court then held that Atlantic Marine bore the burden of establishing that a transfer would be appropriate under § 1404(a) and that the court would "consider a nonexhaustive and nonexclusive list of public and private interest factors," of which the "forum-selection clause [was] only one such factor." Giving particular weight to its findings that "compulsory process will not be available for the majority of J-Crew's witnesses" and that there would be "significant expense for those willing witnesses," the District Court held that Atlantic Marine had failed to carry its burden of showing that transfer "would be in the interest of justice or increase the convenience to the parties and their witnesses."

Atlantic Marine petitioned the Court of Appeals for a writ of mandamus directing the District Court to dismiss the case under § 1406(a) or to transfer the case to the Eastern District of Virginia under § 1404(a). The Court of Appeals denied Atlantic Marine's petition because Atlantic Marine had not established a "clear and indisputable" right to relief. *See Cheney v. United States Dist. Court for D. C.*, 542 U. S. 367, 381 (2004) (mandamus "petitioner must satisfy the burden of showing that [his] right to issuance of the writ is clear and indisputable" (internal quotation marks omitted; brackets in original)). Relying on *Stewart Organization, Inc. v. Ricoh Corp.*, 487 U. S. 22 (1988), the Court of Appeals agreed with the District Court that § 1404(a) is the exclusive mechanism for enforcing a forum-selection clause that points to another federal forum when venue is otherwise proper in the district where the case was brought.[2] The court stated, however, that if a forum-selection clause points to a nonfederal forum, dismissal under Rule 12(b)(3) would be the correct mechanism to enforce the clause because § 1404(a) by its terms does not permit transfer to any tribunal other than another federal court. The Court of Appeals then concluded that the District Court had not clearly abused its discretion in refusing to transfer the case after conducting the balance-of-interests analysis required by § 1404(a). That was so even though there was no dispute that the forum-selection clause was valid. We granted certiorari.

II

Atlantic Marine contends that a party may enforce a forum-selection clause by seeking dismissal of the suit under § 1406(a) and Rule 12(b)(3). We disagree. Section 1406(a) and Rule 12(b)(3) allow dismissal only when venue is "wrong" or "improper." Whether venue is "wrong" or "improper" depends exclusively on whether the court in which the case was brought satisfies the requirements of federal venue laws, and those provisions say nothing about a forum-selection clause.

A

* * * When venue is challenged, the court must determine whether the case falls within one of the three categories set out in § 1391(b). If it does, venue is proper; if

---

[2] Venue was otherwise proper in the Western District of Texas because the subcontract at issue in the suit was entered into and was to be performed in that district. *See United States ex rel. J-Crew Management, Inc. v. Atlantic Marine Constr. Co.*, 2012 WL 8499879, *5 (WD Tex., Apr. 6, 2012) (citing 28 U.S.C. § 1391(b)(2)).

it does not, venue is improper, and the case must be dismissed or transferred under § 1406(a). Whether the parties entered into a contract containing a forum-selection clause has no bearing on whether a case falls into one of the categories of cases listed in § 1391(b). As a result, a case filed in a district that falls within § 1391 may not be dismissed under § 1406(a) or Rule 12(b)(3).

* * *

Our holding * * * finds support in *Stewart,* 487 U. S. 22. As here, the parties in *Stewart* had included a forum-selection clause in the relevant contract, but the plaintiff filed suit in a different federal district. The defendant had initially moved to transfer the case or, in the alternative, to dismiss for improper venue under § 1406(a), but by the time the case reached this Court, the defendant had abandoned its § 1406(a) argument and sought only transfer under § 1404(a). We rejected the plaintiff's argument that state law governs a motion to transfer venue pursuant to a forum-selection clause, concluding instead that "federal law, specifically 28 U. S. C. § 1404(a), governs the District Court's decision whether to give effect to the parties' forum-selection clause." We went on to explain that a "motion to transfer under § 1404(a) . . . calls on the district court to weigh in the balance a number of case-specific factors" and that the "presence of a forum-selection clause . . . will be a significant factor that figures centrally in the district court's calculus."

The question whether venue in the original court was "wrong: under § 1406(a) was not before the Court, but we wrote in a footnote that "[t]he parties do not dispute that the District Court properly denied the motion to dismiss the case for improper venue under 28 U. S. C. § 1406(a) because respondent apparently does business in the Northern District of Alabama. *See* 28 U. S. C. § 1391(c) (venue proper in judicial district in which corporation is doing business)." In other words, because § 1391 made venue proper, venue could not be "wrong" for purposes of § 1406(a). Though *dictum*, the Court's observation supports the holding we reach today. A contrary view would all but drain *Stewart* of any significance. If a forum-selection clause rendered venue in all other federal courts "wrong," a defendant could always obtain automatic dismissal or transfer under § 1406(a) and would not have any reason to resort to § 1404(a). *Stewart's* holding would be limited to the presumably rare case in which the defendant inexplicably fails to file a motion under § 1406(a) or Rule 12(b)(3).

B

Although a forum-selection clause does not render venue in a court "wrong" or "improper" within the meaning of § 1406(a) or Rule 12(b)(3), the clause may be enforced through a motion to transfer under § 1404(a). That provision states that "[f]or the convenience of parties and witnesses, in the interest of justice, a district court may transfer any civil action to any other district or division where it might have been brought or to any district or division to which all parties have consented." Unlike § 1406(a), § 1404(a) does not condition transfer on the initial forum's being "wrong." And it permits transfer to any district where venue is also proper (*i.e.*, "where [the case] might have been brought") or to any other district to which the parties have agreed by contract or stipulation.

Section 1404(a) therefore provides a mechanism for enforcement of forum-selection clauses that point to a particular federal district. And for the reasons we address in Part III, *infra*, a proper application of § 1404(a) requires that a forum-selection clause be "given controlling weight in all but the most exceptional cases." *Stewart, supra,* at 33 (KENNEDY, J., concurring).

Atlantic Marine argues that § 1404(a) is not a suitable mechanism to enforce forum-selection clauses because that provision cannot provide for transfer when a forum-selection clause specifies a state or foreign tribunal and we agree with Atlantic Marine that the Court of Appeals failed to provide a sound answer to this problem. The Court of Appeals opined that a forum-selection clause pointing to a nonfederal forum should be enforced through Rule 12(b)(3), which permits a party to move for dismissal of a case based on "improper venue." 701 F. 3d, at 740. As Atlantic Marine persuasively argues, however, that conclusion cannot be reconciled with our construction of the term "improper venue" in § 1406 to refer only to a forum that does not satisfy federal venue laws. If venue is proper under federal venue rules, it does not matter for the purpose of Rule 12(b)(3) whether the forum-selection clause points to a federal or a nonfederal forum.

Instead, the appropriate way to enforce a forum-selection clause pointing to a state or foreign forum is through the doctrine of *forum non conveniens.* Section 1404(a) is merely a codification of the doctrine of *forum non conveniens* for the subset of cases in which the transferee forum is within the federal court system; in such cases, Congress has replaced the traditional remedy of outright dismissal with transfer. *See Sinochem Int'l Co. v. Malaysia Int'l Shipping Corp.,* 549 U.S. 422, 430 (2007) ("For the federal court system, Congress has codified the doctrine . . ."); *see also* notes following § 1404 (Historical and Revision Notes) (Section 1404(a) "was drafted in accordance with the doctrine of forum non conveniens, permitting transfer to a more convenient forum, even though the venue is proper"). For the remaining set of cases calling for a nonfederal forum, § 1404(a) has no application, but the residual doctrine of *forum non conveniens* "has continuing application in federal courts." *Sinochem,* 549 U.S., at 430 (internal quotation marks and brackets omitted); *see also ibid.* (noting that federal courts invoke *forum non conveniens* "in cases where the alternative forum is abroad, and perhaps in rare instances where a state or territorial court serves litigational convenience best" (internal quotation marks and citation omitted)). And because both § 1404(a) and the *forum non conveniens* doctrine from which it derives entail the same balancing-of-interests standard, courts should evaluate a forum-selection clause pointing to a nonfederal forum in the same way that they evaluate a forum-selection clause pointing to a federal forum.

C

An *amicus* before the Court argues that a defendant in a breach-of-contract action should be able to obtain dismissal under Rule 12(b)(6) if the plaintiff files suit in a district other than the one specified in a valid forum-selection clause. Petitioner, however, did not file a motion under Rule 12(b)(6), and the parties did not brief the Rule's application to this case at any stage of this litigation. We therefore will not consider it. Even if a defendant could use Rule 12(b)(6) to enforce a forum-selection clause, that would not change our conclusions that § 1406(a) and Rule 12(b)(3) are not proper mechanisms to enforce a forum-selection clause and that § 1404(a) and the *forum non conveniens* doctrine provide appropriate enforcement mechanisms.

III

Although the Court of Appeals correctly identified § 1404(a) as the appropriate provision to enforce the forum-selection clause in this case, the Court of Appeals erred in failing to make the adjustments required in a § 1404(a) analysis when the transfer motion is premised on a forum-selection clause. When the parties have agreed to a valid forum-selection clause, a district court should ordinarily transfer the case to the forum specified in that clause.[5] Only under extraordinary circumstances unrelated to the convenience of the parties should a § 1404(a) motion be denied. And no such exceptional factors appear to be present in this case.

A

In the typical case not involving a forum-selection clause, a district court considering a § 1404(a) motion (or a *forum non conveniens* motion) must evaluate both the convenience of the parties and various public-interest considerations.[6] Ordinarily, the district court would weigh the relevant factors and decide whether, on balance, a transfer would serve "the convenience of parties and witnesses" and otherwise promote 'the interest of justice.' § 1404(a).

The calculus changes, however, when the parties' contract contains a valid forum-selection clause, which "represents the parties' agreement as to the most

---

[5] Our analysis presupposes a contractually valid forum-selection clause.

[6] Factors relating to the parties' private interests include 'relative ease of access to sources of proof; availability of compulsory process for attendance of unwilling, and the cost of obtaining attendance of willing, witnesses; possibility of view of premises, if view would be appropriate to the action; and all other practical problems that make trial of a case easy, expeditious and inexpensive.' *Piper Aircraft Co. v. Reyno,* 454 U. S. 235, 241, n. 6 (1981) (internal quotation marks omitted). Public-interest factors may include 'the administrative difficulties flowing from court congestion; the local interest in having localized controversies decided at home; [and] the interest in having the trial of a diversity case in a forum that is at home with the law.' Ibid. (internal quotation marks omitted). The Court must also give some weight to the plaintiffs' choice of forum. See *Norwood v. Kirkpatrick,* 349 U. S. 29, 32 (1995).

proper forum." _Stewart, 487 U. S., at 31_. The "enforcement of valid forum-selection clauses, bargained for by the parties, protects their legitimate expectations and furthers vital interests of the justice system." _Id., at 33_ (KENNEDY, J., concurring). For that reason, and because the overarching consideration under § 1404(a) is whether a transfer would promote "the interest of justice," "a valid forum-selection clause [should be] given controlling weight in all but the most exceptional cases." _Id., at 33_ (same). The presence of a valid forum-selection clause requires district courts to adjust their usual § 1404(a) analysis in three ways.

First, the plaintiff's choice of forum merits no weight. Rather, as the party defying the forum-selection clause, the plaintiff bears the burden of establishing that transfer to the forum for which the parties bargained is unwarranted. Because plaintiffs are ordinarily allowed to select whatever forum they consider most advantageous (consistent with jurisdictional and venue limitations), we have termed their selection the "plaintiff's venue privilege." _Van Dusen, 376 U. S., at 635_. But when a plaintiff agrees by contract to bring suit only in a specified forum—presumably in exchange for other binding promises by the defendant—the plaintiff has effectively exercised its "venue privilege" before a dispute arises. Only that initial choice deserves deference, and the plaintiff must bear the burden of showing why the court should not transfer the case to the forum to which the parties agreed.

Second, a court evaluating a defendant's § 1404(a) motion to transfer based on a forum-selection clause should not consider arguments about the parties' private interests. When parties agree to a forum-selection clause, they waive the right to challenge the preselected forum as inconvenient or less convenient for themselves or their witnesses, or for their pursuit of the litigation. A court accordingly must deem the private-interest factors to weigh entirely in favor of the preselected forum. As we have explained in a different but "instructive" context, _Stewart, supra_, at 28, "[w]hatever 'inconvenience' [the parties] would suffer by being forced to litigate in the contractual forum as [they] agreed to do was clearly foreseeable at the time of contracting." _The Bremen v. Zapata Off-Shore Co., 407 U. S. 1, 17–18 (1972); see also Stewart, supra_, at 33 (KENNEDY, J., concurring) (stating that _Bremen's_ "reasoning applies with much force to federal courts sitting in diversity").

As a consequence, a district court may consider arguments about public-interest factors only. Because those factors will rarely defeat a transfer motion, the practical result is that forum-selection clauses should control except in unusual cases. Although it is "conceivable in a particular case" that the district court "would refuse to transfer a case notwithstanding the counterweight of a forum-selection clause," _Stewart, supra_, at 30–31, such cases will not be common.

Third, when a party bound by a forum-selection clause flouts its contractual obligation and files suit in a different forum, a § 1404(a) transfer of venue will not carry with it the original venue's choice-of-law rules—a factor that in some circumstances may affect public-interest considerations. *See Piper Aircraft Co. v. Reyno,* 454 U. S. 235, 241, n. 6 (1981) (listing a court's familiarity with the "law that must govern the action" as a potential factor). A federal court sitting in diversity ordinarily must follow the choice-of-law rules of the State in which it sits. *See Klaxon Co. v. Stentor Elec. Mfg. Co.,* 313 U. S. 487, 494–496 (1941). However, we previously identified an exception to that principle for § 1404(a) transfers, requiring that the state law applicable in the original court also apply in the transferee court. *See Van Dusen,* 376 U. S., at 639. We deemed that exception necessary to prevent "defendants, properly subjected to suit in the transferor State," from "invok[ing] § 1404(a) to gain the benefits of the laws of another jurisdiction . . . ." *Id., at 638; see Ferens v. John Deere Co.,* 494 U. S. 516, 522 (1990) (extending the *Van Dusen* rule to § 1404(a) motions by plaintiffs).

The policies motivating our exception to the *Klaxon* rule for § 1404(a) transfers, however, do not support an extension to cases where a defendant's motion is premised on enforcement of a valid forum-selection clause. *See Ferens, supra,* at 523. To the contrary, those considerations lead us to reject the rule that the law of the court in which the plaintiff inappropriately filed suit should follow the case to the forum contractually selected by the parties. In *Van Dusen,* we were concerned that, through a § 1404(a) transfer, a defendant could "defeat the state-law advantages that might accrue from the exercise of [the plaintiff's] venue privilege." 376 U. S., at 635. But as discussed above, a plaintiff who files suit in violation of a forum-selection clause enjoys no such "privilege" with respect to its choice of forum, and therefore it is entitled to no concomitant "state-law advantages." Not only would it be inequitable to allow the plaintiff to fasten its choice of substantive law to the venue transfer, but it would also encourage gamesmanship. Because "§ 1404(a) should not create or multiply opportunities for forum shopping," *Ferens, supra,* at 523, we will not apply the *Van Dusen* rule when a transfer stems from enforcement of a forum-selection clause: The court in the contractually selected venue should not apply the law of the transferor venue to which the parties waived their right.[8]

When parties have contracted in advance to litigate disputes in a particular forum, courts should not unnecessarily disrupt the parties' settled expectations. A forum-selection clause, after all, may have figured centrally in the parties' negotia-

---

[8] For the reasons detailed above, see Part II-B, *supra,* the same standards should apply to motions to dismiss for *forum non conveniens* in cases involving valid forum-selection clauses pointing to state or foreign forums. We have noted in contexts unrelated to forum-selection clauses that a defendant 'invoking *forum non conveniens* ordinarily bears a heavy burden in opposing the plaintiff's chosen forum.' *Sinochem Int'l Co. v. Malaysia Int'l Shipping Co.,* 549 U. S. 422, 430 (2007). That is because of the 'hars[h] result' of that doctrine: Unlike a § 1404(a) motion, a successful motion under *forum non conveniens* requires dismissal of the case. *Norwood,* 349 U. S., at 32. That inconveniences plaintiffs in several respects and even 'makes it possible for [plaintiffs] to lose out completely, through the running of the statute of limitations in the forum finally deemed appropriate.' *Id., at 31* (internal quotation marks omitted). Such caution is not warranted, however, when the plaintiff has violated a contractual obligation by filing suit in a forum other than the one specified in a valid forum-selection clause. In such a case, dismissal would work no injustice on the plaintiff.

tions and may have affected how they set monetary and other contractual terms; it may, in fact, have been a critical factor in their agreement to do business together in the first place. In all but the most unusual cases, therefore, 'the interest of justice' is served by holding parties to their bargain.

B

The District Court's application of § 1404(a) in this case did not comport with these principles. The District Court improperly placed the burden on Atlantic Marine to prove that transfer to the parties' contractually preselected forum was appropriate. As the party acting in violation of the forum-selection clause, J-Crew must bear the burden of showing that public-interest factors overwhelmingly disfavor a transfer.

The District Court also erred in giving weight to arguments about the parties' private interests, given that all private interests, as expressed in the forum-selection clause, weigh in favor of the transfer. The District Court stated that the private-interest factors "militat[e] against a transfer to Virginia" because "compulsory process will not be available for the majority of J-Crew's witnesses" and there will be "significant expense for those willing witnesses." But when J-Crew entered into a contract to litigate all disputes in Virginia, it knew that a distant forum might hinder its ability to call certain witnesses and might impose other burdens on its litigation efforts. It nevertheless promised to resolve its disputes in Virginia, and the District Court should not have given any weight to J-Crew's current claims of inconvenience.

The District Court also held that the public-interest factors weighed in favor of keeping the case in Texas because Texas contract law is more familiar to federal judges in Texas than to their federal colleagues in Virginia. That ruling, however, rested in part on the District Court's belief that the federal court sitting in Virginia would have been required to apply Texas' choice-of-law rules, which in this case pointed to Texas contract law. But for the reasons we have explained, the transferee court would apply Virginia choice-of-law rules. It is true that even these Virginia rules may point to the contract law of Texas, as the State in which the contract was formed. But at minimum, the fact that the Virginia court will not be required to apply Texas choice-of-law rules reduces whatever weight the District Court might have given to the public-interest factor that looks to the familiarity of the transferee court with the applicable law. And, in any event, federal judges routinely apply the law of a State other than the State in which they sit. We are not aware of any exceptionally arcane features of Texas contract law that are likely to defy comprehension by a federal judge sitting in Virginia.

* * *

We reverse the judgment of the Court of Appeals for the Fifth Circuit. Although no public-interest factors that might support the denial of Atlantic Marine's motion to transfer are apparent on the record before us, we remand the case for the courts below to decide that question.

It is so ordered.

———————

Points for Discussion

a. Proper Transferee Districts Under § 1404 & § 1406

Under *Hoffman*, only those districts where the plaintiff could have initially filed the action properly, without consent of the defendant, are permissible transferee courts for purposes of § 1404. However, the 2011 Jurisdiction and Venue Clarification Act (JVCA) amended § 1404(a) to permit a transfer "to any district or division to which all parties have consented." Does this language overrule *Hoffman* completely? If not, what is the continuing relevance of the case, if any? Under what circumstances would all parties, including the plaintiff, have consented to litigating in a district? *See, e.g., Atl. Marine Constr. Co. v. U.S. Dist. Court for W. Dist. of Tex.*, 134 S. Ct. 568, 579 (2013) (noting that the jurisdiction identified in a forum-selection clause would be a district to which all parties have consented under 1404(a)). To which districts may a case be transferred under § 1406, which limits transferee districts to those where the case "could have been brought"?

> **FYI**
>
> The JVCA also amended § 1404 to bar transferring cases to th District Courts for Guam, the Northern Mariana Islands, and the Virgin Islands. 28 U.S.C. § 1404(d). A similar amendment was not made to § 1406.

b. Forum-Selection Clauses

Parties to contracts are free to identify the forum in which any disputes that arise under the contract will be litigated. If a plaintiff initiates an action in a federal judicial district different from the one identified in a governing forum-selection clause, the defendant may seek to enforce the forum-selection clause by a motion to transfer under § 1404(a). *See Atl. Marine*, 134 S. Ct. at 579 ("Although a forum-selection clause does not render venue in a court 'wrong' or 'improper' within the meaning of § 1406(a) or Rule 12(b)(3), the clause may be enforced through a motion to transfer under § 1404(a)."). Indeed, as the Court held in *Atlantic Marine*,

> **Take Note!**
>
> The Supreme Court in *Atlantic Marine* expressly did not consider the question of whether a defendant can seek dismissal under Rule 12(b)(6) if the plaintiff files suit in a district other than the one specified in a valid forum-selection clause.

when forum-selection clauses are the basis for a § 1404 transfer motion, "a district court should transfer the case unless extraordinary circumstances unrelated to the convenience of the parties clearly disfavor a transfer." *Id.* at 575. However, if the forum-selection clause points to a state or foreign court as the agreed forum for a dispute, the appropriate way to enforce such a clause would be through the doctrine of *forum non conveniens, see id.* at 580, a topic covered later in this chapter.

c. Transfers in the Absence of Personal Jurisdiction

It is quite possible that a plaintiff will file an action in a federal district court that is an improper venue and lacks personal jurisdiction over the defendants. Should the district court be able to transfer the case even though it lacks jurisdiction over the defendants, or should the court only be able to dismiss the action for lack of personal jurisdiction and permit the plaintiff to refile in another court? *See* 28 U.S.C. § 1631 (permitting transfers in the absence of jurisdiction); *Goldlawr, Inc. v. Heiman,* 369 U.S. 463, 466 (1962) ("The language of § 1406(a) is amply broad enough to authorize the transfer of cases, however wrong the plaintiff may have been in filing his case as to venue, whether the court in which it was filed had personal jurisdiction over the defendants or not.").

Alternatively, when the initial venue is improper, what if the prospective transferee court has proper venue but would lack personal jurisdiction over the defendant? In that case, per *Hoffman,* the court would not be one "where it might have been brought" and thus the case could not be transferred there. Is the transferor court required to determine the amenability of the defendant to personal jurisdiction before granting a transfer? Which party should bear the burden on this issue? *See Mellor v. Moe,* 2006 WL 1644877, at *1 n.2 (D.N.J. June 14, 2006) (noting that "a finding of personal jurisdiction over [the defendant] in the proposed transferee court is a prerequisite to transfer pursuant to 28 U.S.C. § 1406(a)," and that the moving party must present proof that personal jurisdiction is proper in the transferee court).

d. Multidistrict Litigation

There is a special venue provision that enables cases to be transferred outside of § 1404 or § 1406 to any federal district court selected by a special panel of judges who are appointed to oversee such transfers. Under 28 U.S.C. § 1407, civil actions sharing common questions of fact pending in different federal districts may be transferred to any district for consolidated pretrial proceedings. Such transfers are determined and implemented by a special body called the Judicial Panel on Multidistrict Litigation (JPML). If there is a trial in such cases, however, they are to be remanded to their respective original transferor courts. See *Lexecon Inc. v. Milberg Weiss Bershad Hynes & Lerach,* 523 U.S. 26 (1998).

Go Online

Students interested in learning more about the JPML can visit its website at www.jpml.uscourts.gov.

2. Standards for Venue Transfers

Having reviewed the methods of identifying proper transferee courts, we now turn to a consideration of the standards that transferor courts use to determine whether a case should be transferred. These standards are illustrated in the two cases that follow.

Smith v. Colonial Penn Insurance Co.

U.S. District Court for the Southern District of Texas
943 F. Supp. 782 (S.D. Tex. 1996)

KENT, DISTRICT JUDGE.

> **FYI**
>
> Judge Kent, the author of this opinion, was impeached by the U.S. House of Representatives after being criminally charged for sexually harassing his employees. He resigned rather than face conviction and removal from office by the Senate and subsequently was sentenced to 33 months imprisonment for obstructing the criminal investigation into his sexual misconduct. *See* en.wikipedia. org/wiki/Samuel_B._Kent.

This is a breach of contract case based on an insurance contract entered into by Plaintiff and Defendant. Now before the Court is Defendant's October 11, 1996 Motion to Transfer Venue from the Galveston Division to the Houston Division of the United States District Court for the Southern District of Texas pursuant to 28 U.S.C. § 1404(a). For the reasons set forth below, the Motion is DENIED.

Section 1404(a) provides: "For the convenience of parties and witnesses, in the interest of justice, a district court may transfer any civil action to any other district or division where it might have been brought." 28 U.S.C. § 1404(a). The defendant bears the burden of demonstrating to the District Court that it should, in its sound discretion, decide to transfer the action. The Court weighs the following factors to decide whether a transfer is warranted: the availability and convenience of witnesses and parties, the location of counsel, the location of books and records, the cost of obtaining attendance of witnesses and other trial expenses, the place of the alleged wrong, the possibility of delay and prejudice if transfer is granted, and the plaintiff's choice of forum, which is generally entitled to great deference.

> **Take Note!**
>
> In this paragraph, the court sets forth several factors that are relevant to a determination of whether a transfer is warranted. Make a note of these factors because they can help give substance to your analysis of whether a transfer would be "in the interest of justice" or promote the convenience of the parties and witnesses.

Defendant's request for a transfer of venue is centered around the fact that Galveston does not have a commercial airport into which Defendant's employees and corporate representatives may fly and out of which they may be expediently whisked to the federal courthouse in Galveston. Rather, Defendant contends that it will be faced with the huge "inconvenience" of flying into Houston and <u>driving less than forty miles to the Galveston courthouse</u>, an act that will "encumber" it with "unnecessary driving time and expenses." The Court certainly does not wish to encumber any litigant with such an onerous burden.

The Court, being somewhat familiar with the Northeast, notes that perceptions about travel are different in that part of the country than they are in Texas. A litigant in that part of the country could cross several states in a few hours and might be shocked at having to travel fifty miles to try a case, but in this vast state of Texas, such a travel distance would not be viewed with any surprise or consternation. Defendant should be assured that it is not embarking on a

Take Note!

Although the plaintiff has the burden of showing that venue is proper in the face of a challenge to venue, when a defendant seeks a change of venue, that defendant bears the burden of demonstrating that the court should transfer the case. Why do you think the burden is allocated in this way?

three-week-long trip via covered wagons when it travels to Galveston. Rather, Defendant will be pleased to discover that the highway is paved and lighted all the way to Galveston, and thanks to the efforts of this Court's predecessor, <u>Judge Roy Bean</u>, the trip should be free of rustlers, hooligans, or vicious varmints of unsavory kind. Moreover, the speed limit was recently increased to seventy miles per hour on most of the road leading to Galveston, so Defendant should be able to hurtle to justice at lightning speed. To assuage Defendant's worries about the inconvenience of the drive, the Court notes that <u>Houston's Hobby Airport</u> is located about equal drivetime from downtown Houston and the Galveston courthouse. Defendant will likely find it an easy, traffic-free ride to Galveston as compared to a congested, construction-riddled drive to downtown Houston. The Court notes that any inconvenience suffered in having to drive to Galveston may likely be offset by the peacefulness of the ride and the scenic beauty of the sunny isle.

The convenience of the witnesses and the parties is generally a primary concern of this Court when considering transfer motions. However, vague statements about the convenience of unknown and unnamed witnesses is insufficient to convince this

Food for Thought

The court makes the argument that modern innovations that make travel and communications more convenient undermine the defendants' arguments regarding the inconvenience of traveling to Galveston rather than Houston. Is this a valid point? Couldn't one make the same argument about traveling to anywhere in the country, that as long as it only takes a flight and a cab ride to get there, convenience is not an issue? At what point does travel become sufficiently inconvenient to warrant a transfer in this "age of convenient travel"?

Court that the convenience of the witnesses and the parties would be best served by transferring venue. In the Court's view, even if all the witnesses, documents, and evidence relevant to this case were located within walking distance of the Houston Division courthouse, the inconvenience caused by retaining the case in this Court would be minimal at best in this age of convenient travel, communication, discovery, and trial testimony preservation. The Galveston Division courthouse is only about fifty miles from the Houston Division courthouse. "[I]t is not as if the key witnesses will be asked to travel to the wilds of Alaska or the furthest reaches on the Continental United States."

As to Defendant's argument that Houston might also be a more convenient forum for Plaintiff, the Court notes that Plaintiff picked Galveston as her forum of choice even though she resides in San Antonio. Defendant argues that flight travel is available between Houston and San Antonio but is not available between Galveston and San Antonio, again because of the absence of a commercial airport. Alas, this Court's kingdom for a commercial airport! The Court is unpersuaded by this argument because it is not this Court's concern how Plaintiff gets here, whether it be by plane, train, automobile, horseback, foot, or on the back of a huge Texas jackrabbit, as long as Plaintiff is here at the proper date and time. Thus, the Court declines to disturb the forum chosen by the Plaintiff and introduce the likelihood of delay inherent in any transfer simply to avoid the insignificant inconvenience that Defendant may suffer by litigating this matter in Galveston rather than Houston.

For the reasons stated above, Defendant's Motion to Transfer is hereby DENIED.

Bolivia v. Philip Morris Companies, Inc.

U.S. District Court for the Southern District of Texas
39 F. Supp. 2d 1008 (S.D. Tex. 1999)

KENT, DISTRICT JUDGE.

Take Note!

The judge in this case, Judge Kent is the same judge that decided the previous case, *Smith v. Colonial Penn Ins. Co.* Ask yourself whether Judge Kent's determination in this case is consistent with his resolution of the previous case.

Plaintiff, the Republic of Bolivia, brings this action to recover from numerous tobacco companies various health care costs it allegedly incurred in treating illnesses its residents suffered as a result of tobacco use. This action was originally filed in the District Court of Brazoria County, Texas * * * and removed to this Court on February 19, 1999, by certain Defendants alleging jurisdiction under 28 U.S.C. § 1331 and 28 U.S.C. § 1332. For the following reasons, the Court exercises its authority and discretion pursuant to 28 U.S.C. § 1404(a) to sua sponte TRANSFER this case to the United States District Court for the District of Columbia.

This is one of at least six similar actions brought by foreign governments in various courts throughout the United States. The governments of Guatemala, Panama, Nicaragua, Thailand, Venezuela, and Bolivia have filed suit in the geographically diverse locales of Washington, D.C., Puerto Rico, Texas, Louisiana, and Florida, in both state and federal courts. Why none of these countries seems to have a court system their own governments have confidence in is a mystery to this Court. Moreover, given the tremendous number of United States jurisdictions encompassing fascinating and exotic places, the Court can hardly imagine why the Republic of Bolivia elected to file suit in the veritable hinterlands of Brazoria County, Texas. The Court seriously doubts whether Brazoria County has ever seen a live Bolivian . . . even on the Discovery Channel. Though only here by removal, this humble Court by the sea is certainly flattered by what must be the worldwide renown of rural Texas courts for dispensing justice with unparalleled fairness and alacrity, apparently in common discussion even on the mountain peaks of Bolivia! Still, the Court would be remiss in accepting an obligation for which it truly does not have the necessary resources. Only one judge presides in the Galveston Division—which currently has before it over seven hundred cases and annual civil filings exceeding such number—and that judge is presently burdened with a significant personal situation which diminishes its ability to always give the attention it would like to all of its daunting docket obligations, despite genuinely heroic efforts to do so. And, while Galveston is indeed an international seaport, the capacity of this Court to address the complex and sophisticated issues of international law and foreign relations presented by this case is dwarfed by that of its esteemed colleagues in the District of Columbia who deftly address such awesome tasks as a matter of course. Indeed, this Court, while doing its very best to address the more prosaic matters routinely before it, cannot think of a Bench better versed and more capable of handling precisely this type of case, which requires a high level of expertise in international matters. In fact, proceedings brought by the Republic of Guatemala are currently well underway in that Court in a related action, and there is a request now before the Judicial Panel on Multidistrict Litigation to transfer to the United States District Court for the District of Columbia all six tobacco actions brought by foreign governments, ostensibly for consolidated treatment. Such a Bench, well-populated with genuinely renowned intellects, can certainly better bear and share the burden of

Food for Thought

Should the size of the court's docket or the judge's personal problems be legitimate grounds for transferring a case away from a proper venue selected by the plaintiff?

multidistrict litigation than this single judge division, where the judge moves his lips when he reads. . . .

* * * [I]t is the Court's opinion that the District of Columbia, located in this Nation's capital, is a much more logical venue for the parties and witnesses in this action because, among other things, Plaintiff has an embassy in Washington, D.C., and thus a physical presence and governmental representatives there, whereas there isn't even a Bolivian restaurant anywhere near here! * * * [T]he Court is virtually certain that Bolivia is not within the four counties over which this Court presides, even though the words Bolivia and Brazoria are a lot alike and caused some real, initial confusion until the Court conferred with its law clerks. Thus, it is readily apparent, even from an outdated globe such as that possessed by this Court, that Bolivia, a hemisphere away, ain't in south-central Texas, and that, at the very least, the District of Columbia is a more appropriate venue (though Bolivia isn't located there either). Furthermore, as this Judicial District bears no significant relationship to any of the matters at issue, and the judge of this Court simply loves cigars, the Plaintiff can be expected to suffer neither harm nor prejudice by a transfer to Washington, D.C., a Bench better able to rise to the smoky challenges presented by this case, despite the alleged and historic presence there of countless "smoke-filled" rooms. Consequently, pursuant to 28 U.S.C. § 1404(a), for the convenience of parties and witnesses, and in the interest of justice, this case is hereby TRANSFERRED to the United States District Court for the District of Columbia.

Points for Discussion

a.   Standards for Deciding Whether to Transfer

FYI

When a § 1404 transfer is sought pursuant to a forum-selection clause, the Supreme Court has instructed that the clause is to be given controlling weight, meaning the plaintiff's choice of forum is given no weight and the convenience interests of the parties and witnesses are similarly ignored. *Atlantic Marine Const. Co., Inc. v. U.S. Dist. Court for Western Dist. of Texas*, 134 S. Ct. 568, 581–82 (2013). Transfers under these circumstances can only be defeated if there are public-interest factors such as court congestion or a special need to have localized controversies decided at home in courts familiar with the applicable law. *Id.* at 581 n.6.

What standards did the court use to evaluate whether a venue transfer was appropriate? Where do you think the court got these considerations from since they are not in the statute? Section 1404 permits transfers whenever it is "in the interest of justice" to do so, consistent with convenience to the parties and witnesses; is such a standard too indeterminate? *See Perspective & Analysis* below. Do you think that Judge Kent was justified in denying a transfer in *Smith* but forcing a transfer, *sua sponte*, in *Philip Morris*? These cases involved transfers under § 1404(a). Should the standards that apply to transfers under § 1406(a) be the same? *See Sinclair v. Kleindienst,* 711 F.2d 291, 294 (D.C. Cir. 1983) (finding it "in the interests of justice" to allow transfer under § 1406(a) where cause of action would be barred by statute of limitations without a transfer, personal jurisdiction could be obtained over defendants, and venue is proper in transferee court); *Loeb v. Bank of Am.,* 254 F. Supp. 2d 581, 588 (E.D. Pa. 2003) ("[T]he standard for transfer pursuant to § 1404(a) is lower than the standard for transfer pursuant to § 1406(a) . . . ."). See 14D C. WRIGHT, A. MILLER, E. COOPER & R. FREER, FED. PRAC. & PROC. § 3808 (4th ed. 2013) for a fuller discussion of the factors courts use to evaluate whether a transfer is in the interest of justice.

—Perspective & Analysis—

Scholars have criticized the "in the interest of justice" standard of the venue transfer statute as so open-ended that it fosters unpredictability and delay in the handling of motions to transfer:

> [T]he law governing section 1404 motions . . . is in chaos. The ad hoc balancing employed by the district courts precludes any prediction on whether a particular transfer motion will succeed. This lack of standards invites a defendant to seek a transfer even when the plaintiff has chosen a reasonable forum. Today, the motion to transfer often has little relationship to the "interests of justice." Instead, such motions have become a vehicle for defendant delay and an increasing burden on the already backlogged federal courts.

David E. Steinberg, *The Motion to Transfer and the Interests of Justice,* 66 NOTRE DAME L. REV. 443, 446–47 (1990).

b. "Divisions" Within Districts

Note that in *Smith* the issue was whether the court would transfer the case from the "Galveston Division" to the "Houston Division" of the United States District Court for the Southern District of Texas. Divisions are simply administrative sub-units within federal districts divided by geographical location. Both of the federal venue transfer provisions apply to transfers to other divisions within a district and the same standards governing whether to grant a transfer to another district apply.

c. Why Allow Transfers at All?

Shouldn't plaintiffs be entitled to bring and keep their case in the forum of their choice if it is a proper venue under the applicable venue statute? *See In re Nat'l Presto Indus., Inc.,* 347 F.3d 662, 664 (7th Cir. 2003). If an action is brought in a jurisdiction having personal jurisdiction over all defendants, why should courts permit a change of venue?

d. What Law Applies After a Transfer?

When diversity actions are litigated in federal court, the court follows the choice-of-law rules for the state in which it sits to determine which state's law to apply. Once a case is transferred to a different federal district court in another state pursuant to § 1404(a), should the transferee court apply the law that would have applied had the case remained with the transferor court or is it free to apply the choice-of-law rules applicable within the transferee court's state? The Supreme Court has stated that state-law claims transferred under § 1404(a) are to be governed by the same law that would have been applicable in the transferor courts. *See Ferens v. John Deere Co., 494 U.S. 516 (1990); Van Dusen v. Barrack, 376 U.S. 612 (1964). See also* Note, *Choice of Law in Federal Court After Transfer of Venue,* 63 CORNELL L. REV. 149, 156 (1977).

> **FYI**
>
> When a court has to resolve the substance of a dispute based on state law, it first has to determine which state's substantive law to apply. Courts make this determination by reference to the forum state's choice-of-law rules.

However, if the § 1404 transfer was made pursuant to a forum-selection clause, the *Van Dusen* rule will not apply, meaning the law that would have applied in the transferor court will not follow the case to the transferee district identified in the forum-selection clause. *See Atl. Marine Constr. Co. v. U.S. Dist. Court for W. Dist. of Tex., 134 S. Ct. 568, 582 (2013)* ("[W]hen a party bound by a forum-selection clause flouts its contractual obligation and files suit in a different forum, a § 1404(a) transfer of venue will not carry with it the original venue's choice-of-law rules . . . ."). Similarly, if a case is transferred under § 1406 because it was filed in an improper venue initially, the *Van Dusen* rule will not apply. *See GBJ Corp. v. E. Ohio Paving Co., 139 F.3d 1080, 1085 (6th Cir.1998)* ("Rather, it was transferred under 28 U.S.C. § 1406(a), because of improper venue and a lack of jurisdiction. When a case is transferred on that basis, the choice-of-law rules of the transfer*ee* court apply." (emphasis in original)).

In federal question cases, courts are to apply governing federal law, which can vary among the district courts depending upon which federal circuit embraces their district. When a case is transferred under § 1404(a) from a district in one circuit to another district in a different circuit, which circuit's law should the transferee court apply? *See In re Korean Air Lines Disaster of Sept. 1, 1983, 829 F.2d 1171 (D.C. Cir. 1987)* (indicating that transferee court is not bound by transferor circuit law).

C. Forum Non Conveniens

As we have just learned, the federal change of venue provisions only permit the transfer of a case to another federal court. However, it may sometimes be the case that the forum that would be more just or convenient is not within the federal system. What mechanism is available to federal courts once they have determined that a case before them would be better located in a court outside of the federal system, such as a state court or a court in a foreign country? The next case involves the doctrine of *forum non conveniens*, a common-law (judicially-created or non-statutory) doctrine for handling cases that would be better tried in a different judicial system.

Piper Aircraft Co. v. Reyno

Supreme Court of the United States
454 U.S. 235 (1981)

JUSTICE MARSHALL delivered the opinion of the Court.

These cases arise out of an air crash that took place in Scotland. Respondent, acting as representative of the estates of several Scottish citizens killed in the accident, brought wrongful-death actions against petitioners that were ultimately transferred to the United States District Court for the Middle District of Pennsylvania. Petitioners moved to dismiss on the ground of *forum non conveniens*. After noting that an alternative forum existed in Scotland, the District Court granted their motions. The

> **Make the Connection**
>
> *Wrongful-death actions* are suits by the survivors of a person who has been killed (or by the representative of the decedent's estate) that seek compensation for the loss of that person's life. You may study this cause of action further in your first-year **Torts** course.

United States Court of Appeals for the Third Circuit reversed. The Court of Appeals based its decision, at least in part, on the ground that dismissal is automatically barred where the law of the alternative forum is less favorable to the plaintiff than the law of the forum chosen by the plaintiff. * * *

I.A

In July 1976, a small commercial aircraft crashed in the Scottish highlands during the course of a charter flight from Blackpool to Perth. The pilot and five passengers were killed instantly. The decedents were all Scottish subjects and residents, as are their heirs and next of kin. There were no eyewitnesses to the accident. At the time of the crash the plane was subject to Scottish air traffic control.

The aircraft, a twin-engine Piper Aztec, was manufactured in Pennsylvania by petitioner Piper Aircraft Co. (Piper). The propellers were manufactured in Ohio by petitioner Hartzell Propeller, Inc. (Hartzell). At the time of the crash the aircraft was registered in Great Britain and was owned and maintained by Air Navigation and Trading Co., Ltd. (Air Navigation). It was operated by McDonald Aviation, Ltd. (McDonald), a Scottish air taxi service. Both Air Navigation and McDonald were organized in the United Kingdom. The wreckage of the plane is now in a hangar in Farnsborough, England.

The British Department of Trade investigated the accident shortly after it occurred. A preliminary report found that the plane crashed after developing a spin, and suggested that mechanical failure in the plane or the propeller was responsible. At Hartzell's request, this report was reviewed by a three-member Review Board, which held a 9-day adversary hearing attended by all interested parties. The Review Board found no evidence of defective equipment and indicated that pilot error may have contributed to the accident. The pilot, who had obtained his commercial pilot's license only three months earlier, was flying over high ground at an altitude considerably lower than the minimum height required by his company's operations manual.

In July 1977, a California probate court appointed respondent Gaynell Reyno administratrix of the estates of the five passengers. Reyno is not related to and does not know any of the decedents or their survivors; she was a legal secretary to the attorney who filed this lawsuit. Several days after her appointment, Reyno commenced separate wrongful-death actions against Piper and Hartzell in the Superior Court of California, claiming negligence and strict liability. Air Navigation, McDonald, and the estate of the pilot are not parties to this litigation.

Food for Thought

Why is the attorney's legal secretary being used as the administratrix in this case? Does this arrangement raise any concerns for you?

The survivors of the five passengers whose estates are represented by Reyno filed a separate action in the United Kingdom against Air Navigation, McDonald, and the pilot's estate. Reyno candidly admits that the action against Piper and Hartzell was filed in the United States because its laws regarding liability, capacity to sue, and damages are more favorable to her position than are those of Scotland. Scottish law does not recognize strict liability in tort. Moreover, it permits wrongful-death actions only when brought by a decedent's relatives. The relatives may sue only for "loss of support and society."

Make the Connection

Strict liability is a **Tort** concept that refers to the rule that permits liability to be established based solely upon a showing of causation, without having to establish fault or culpability.

On petitioners' motion, the suit was removed to the <u>United States District Court for the Central District of California</u>. Piper then moved for transfer to the United States District Court for the Middle District of Pennsylvania, pursuant to <u>28 U.S.C. § 1404(a)</u>. Hartzell moved to dismiss for lack of personal jurisdiction, or in the alternative, to transfer.[5] In December 1977, the District Court quashed service on Hartzell and transferred the case to the Middle District of Pennsylvania. Respondent then properly served process on Hartzell.

B

In May 1978, after the suit had been transferred, both Hartzell and Piper moved to dismiss the action on the ground of *forum non conveniens*. The District Court granted these motions in October 1979. It relied on the balancing test set forth by this Court in <u>Gulf Oil Corp. v. Gilbert, 330 U.S. 501 (1947)</u> * * * . In those decisions, the Court stated that a plaintiff's choice of forum should rarely be disturbed. However, when an alternative forum has jurisdiction to hear the case, and when trial in the chosen forum would "establish . . . oppressiveness and vexation to a defendant . . . out of all proportion to plaintiff's convenience," or when the "chosen forum [is] inappropriate because of considerations affecting the court's own administrative and legal problems," the court may, in the exercise of its sound discretion, dismiss the case. To guide trial court discretion, the Court provided a list of "private interest factors" affecting the convenience of the litigants, and a list of "public interest factors" affecting the convenience of the forum. <u>Gilbert, 330 U.S. at 508–09</u>.[6]

* * * [T]he District Court analyzed the facts of [this case]. It began by observing that an alternative forum existed in Scotland; Piper and Hartzell had agreed to submit to the jurisdiction of the Scottish courts and to waive any statute of limitations defense that might be available. It then stated that plaintiff's choice of forum was entitled to little weight. The court recognized that a plaintiff's choice ordinarily deserves substantial deference. It noted, however, that Reyno "is a representative of foreign citizens and residents seeking a forum in the United States because of the more liberal rules concerning products liability law," and that "the courts have been less solicitous when the plaintiff is not an American citizen or resident, and particularly when the foreign citizens seek to benefit from the more liberal tort rules provided for the protection of citizens and residents of the United States."

---

[5] The District Court concluded that it could not assert personal jurisdiction over Hartzell consistent with due process. However, it decided not to dismiss Hartzell because the corporation would be amenable to process in Pennsylvania.

[6] The factors pertaining to the private interests of the litigants included the "relative ease of access to sources of proof; availability of compulsory process for attendance of unwilling, and the cost of obtaining attendance of willing, witnesses; possibility of view of premises, if view would be appropriate to the action; and all other practical problems that make trial of a case easy, expeditious and inexpensive." <u>Gilbert, 330 U.S. at 508</u>. The public factors bearing on the question included the administrative difficulties flowing from court congestion; the "local interest in having localized controversies decided at home"; the interest in having the trial of a diversity case in a forum that is at home with the law that must govern the action; the avoidance of unnecessary problems in conflict of laws, or in the application of foreign law; and the unfairness of burdening citizens in an unrelated forum with jury duty. <u>Id. at 509</u>.

The District Court next examined several factors relating to the private interests of the litigants, and determined that these factors strongly pointed towards Scotland as the appropriate forum. Although evidence concerning the design, manufacture, and testing of the plane and propeller is located in the United States, the connections with Scotland are otherwise "overwhelming." The real parties in interest are citizens of Scotland, as were all the decedents. Witnesses who could testify regarding the maintenance of the aircraft, the training of the pilot, and the investigation of the accident-all essential to the defense-are in Great Britain. Moreover, all witnesses to damages are located in Scotland. Trial would be aided by familiarity with Scottish topography, and by easy access to the wreckage.

The District Court reasoned that because crucial witnesses and evidence were beyond the reach of compulsory process, and because the defendants would not be able to implead potential Scottish third-party defendants, it would be "unfair to make Piper and Hartzell proceed to trial in this forum." The survivors had brought separate actions in Scotland against the pilot, McDonald, and Air Navigation. "[I]t would be fairer to all parties and less costly if the entire case was presented to one jury with available testimony from all relevant witnesses." Although the court recognized that if trial were held in the United States, Piper and Hartzell could file indemnity or contribution actions against the Scottish defendants, it believed that there was a significant risk of inconsistent verdicts.

What's That?

The term *implead* means to bring a nonparty into the action (thereby making it a third-party defendant) under Rule 14, which will be covered in Chapter 7.

The District Court concluded that the relevant public interests also pointed strongly towards dismissal. The court determined that Pennsylvania law would apply to Piper and Scottish law to Hartzell if the case were tried in the Middle District of Pennsylvania.[8] As a result, "trial in this forum would be hopelessly complex and confusing for a jury." In addition, the court noted that it was unfamiliar with Scottish law and thus would have to rely upon experts from that country. The court also found that the trial would be enormously costly and time-consuming; that it would be unfair to burden citizens with jury duty when the Middle District

---

[8] Under *Klaxon v. Stentor Electric Mfg. Co.,* 313 U.S. 487 (1941), a court ordinarily must apply the choice-of-law rules of the State in which it sits. However, where a case is transferred pursuant to 28 U.S.C. § 1404(a), it must apply the choice-of-law rules of the State from which the case was transferred. *Van Dusen v. Barrack,* 376 U.S. 612 (1964). Relying on these two cases, the District Court concluded that California choice-of-law rules would apply to Piper, and Pennsylvania choice-of-law rules would apply to Hartzell. It further concluded that California applied a "governmental interests" analysis in resolving choice-of-law problems, and that Pennsylvania employed a "significant contacts" analysis. The court used the "governmental interests" analysis to determine that Pennsylvania liability rules would apply to Piper, and the "significant contacts" analysis to determine that Scottish liability rules would apply to Hartzell.

of Pennsylvania has little connection with the controversy; and that Scotland has a substantial interest in the outcome of the litigation.

In opposing the motions to dismiss, respondent contended that dismissal would be unfair because Scottish law was less favorable. The District Court explicitly rejected this claim. It reasoned that the possibility that dismissal might lead to an unfavorable change in the law did not deserve significant weight; any deficiency in the foreign law was a "matter to be dealt with in the foreign forum."

C

On appeal, the United States Court of Appeals for the Third Circuit reversed and remanded for trial. The decision to reverse appears to be based on two alternative grounds. First, the Court held that the District Court abused its discretion in conducting the *Gilbert* analysis. Second, the Court held that dismissal is never appropriate where the law of the alternative forum is less favorable to the plaintiff.

The Court of Appeals began its review of the District Court's *Gilbert* analysis by noting that the plaintiff's choice of forum deserved substantial weight, even though the real parties in interest are nonresidents. It then rejected the District Court's balancing of the private interests. It found that Piper and Hartzell had failed adequately to support their claim that key witnesses would be unavailable if trial were held in the United States: they had never specified the witnesses they would call and the testimony these witnesses would provide. The Court of Appeals gave little weight to the fact that Piper and Hartzell would not be able to implead potential Scottish third-party defendants, reasoning that this difficulty would be "burdensome" but not "unfair." Finally, the court stated that resolution of the suit would not be significantly aided by familiarity with Scottish topography, or by viewing the wreckage.

The Court of Appeals also rejected the District Court's analysis of the public interest factors. It found that the District Court gave undue emphasis to the application of Scottish law: "the mere fact that the court is called upon to determine and apply foreign law does not present a legal problem of the sort which would justify the dismissal of a case otherwise properly before the court." In any event, it believed that Scottish law need not be applied. After conducting its own choice-of-law analysis, the Court of Appeals determined that American law would govern the actions against both Piper and Hartzell. The same choice-of-law analysis apparently led it to conclude that Pennsylvania and Ohio, rather than Scotland, are the jurisdictions with the greatest policy interests in the dispute, and that all other public interest factors favored trial in the United States.

The Court of Appeals concluded as part of its choice-of-law analysis that the United States had the greatest policy interest in the dispute. It apparently believed that this conclusion necessarily implied that the *forum non conveniens* public interest factors pointed toward trial in the United States.

In any event, it appears that the Court of Appeals would have reversed even if the District Court had properly balanced the public and private interests. The court stated:

> [I]t is apparent that the dismissal would work a change in the applicable law so that the plaintiff's strict liability claim would be eliminated from the case. But . . . a dismissal for forum non conveniens, like a statutory transfer, "should not, despite its convenience, result in a change in the applicable law." Only when American law is not applicable, or when the foreign jurisdiction would, as a matter of its own choice of law, give the plaintiff the benefit of the claim to which she is entitled here, would dismissal be justified.

In other words, the court decided that dismissal is automatically barred if it would lead to a change in the applicable law unfavorable to the plaintiff.

* * *

II

The Court of Appeals erred in holding that plaintiffs may defeat a motion to dismiss on the ground of *forum non conveniens* merely by showing that the substantive law that would be applied in the alternative forum is less favorable to the plaintiffs than that of the present forum. The possibility of a change in substantive law should ordinarily not be given conclusive or even substantial weight in the *forum non conveniens* inquiry.

* * *

In fact, if conclusive or substantial weight were given to the possibility of a change in law, the *forum non conveniens* doctrine would become virtually useless. Jurisdiction and venue requirements are often easily satisfied. As a result, many plaintiffs are able to choose from among several forums. Ordinarily, these plaintiffs will select that forum whose choice-of-law rules are most advantageous. Thus, if the possibility of an unfavorable change in substantive law is given substantial weight in the *forum non conveniens* inquiry, dismissal would rarely be proper.

* * *

The Court of Appeals' approach is not only inconsistent with the purpose of the *forum non conveniens* doctrine, but also poses substantial practical problems. If the possibility of a change in law were given substantial weight, deciding motions to dismiss on the ground of *forum non conveniens* would become quite difficult. Choice-of-law analysis would become extremely important, and the courts would frequently be required to interpret the law of foreign jurisdictions. First, the trial court would have to determine what law would apply if the case were tried in the chosen forum, and what law would apply if the case were tried in the alternative forum. It would then have to compare the rights, remedies, and procedures available under the law that would be applied in each forum. Dismissal would be appropriate only if the court concluded that the law applied by the alternative forum is as favorable to the plaintiff as that of the chosen forum. The doctrine of *forum non conveniens*, however, is designed in part to help courts avoid conducting complex exercises in comparative law. As we stated in *Gilbert*, the public interest factors point towards dismissal where the court would be required to "untangle problems in conflict of laws, and in law foreign to itself."

Upholding the decision of the Court of Appeals would result in other practical problems. At least where the foreign plaintiff named an American manufacturer as defendant, a court could not dismiss the case on grounds of *forum non conveniens* where dismissal might lead to an unfavorable change in law. The American courts, which are already extremely attractive to foreign plaintiffs,[18] would become even more attractive. The flow of litigation into the United States would increase and further congest already crowded courts. * * *

We do not hold that the possibility of an unfavorable change in law should never be a relevant consideration in a *forum non conveniens* inquiry. Of course, if the remedy provided by the alternative forum is so clearly inadequate or unsatisfactory that it is no remedy at all, the unfavorable change in law may be given substantial weight; the district court may conclude that dismissal would not be in the interests of justice.[22] In these cases, however, the remedies that would be provided by the Scottish courts do not fall within this category. Although the relatives of the decedents may not be able to rely on a strict liability theory, and although their potential damages award may be smaller, there is no danger that they will be deprived of any remedy or treated unfairly.

---

[18] First, all but 6 of the 50 American States—Delaware, Massachusetts, Michigan, North Carolina, Virginia, and Wyoming—offer strict liability. * * * [S]trict liability remains primarily an American innovation. Second, the tort plaintiff may choose, at least potentially, from among 50 jurisdictions if he decides to file suit in the United States. Each of these jurisdictions applies its own set of malleable choice-of-law rules. Third, jury trials are almost always available in the United States, while they are never provided in civil law jurisdictions. * * * Fourth, unlike most foreign jurisdictions, American courts allow contingent attorney's fees, and do not tax losing parties with their opponents' attorney's fees. Fifth, discovery is more extensive in American than in foreign courts.

[22] At the outset of any *forum non conveniens* inquiry, the court must determine whether there exists an alternative forum. Ordinarily, this requirement will be satisfied when the defendant is "amenable to process" in the other jurisdiction. *Gilbert, 330 U.S. at 506–507*. In rare circumstances, however, where the remedy offered by the other forum is clearly unsatisfactory, the other forum may not be an adequate alternative, and the initial requirement may not be satisfied. Thus, for example, dismissal would not be appropriate where the alternative forum does not permit litigation of the subject matter of the dispute.

III

The Court of Appeals also erred in rejecting the District Court's *Gilbert* analysis. The Court of Appeals stated that more weight should have been given to the plaintiff's choice of forum, and criticized the District Court's analysis of the private and public interests. However, the District Court's decision regarding the deference due plaintiff's choice of forum was appropriate. Furthermore, we do not believe that the District Court abused its discretion in weighing the private and public interests.

Take Note!

The Court here indicates that the district court did not abuse its discretion. Make note that this is a reference to the standard of review applicable here: the district court's application of the *Gilbert* factors is entitled to deference and may only be overturned by appellate courts if the district court abused its discretion. *See* Part III.B of the Opinion below. Contrast this with the de novo standard of review, which permits appellate courts to make their own independent analysis of the matter at hand without giving any deference to the district court's analysis. Why do you think an abuse of discretion standard is appropriate for the review of a district court's application of the *Gilbert* factors? Standards of review will be covered more fully in Chapter 11.

A

The District Court acknowledged that there is ordinarily a strong presumption in favor of the plaintiff's choice of forum, which may be overcome only when the private and public interest factors clearly point towards trial in the alternative forum. It held, however, that the presumption applies with less force when the plaintiff or real parties in interest are foreign.

The District Court's distinction between resident or citizen plaintiffs and foreign plaintiffs is fully justified. In <u>Koster [v. Lumbermens Mut. Cas. Co., 330 U.S. 518 (1947)</u>] the Court indicated that a plaintiff's choice of forum is entitled to greater deference when the plaintiff has chosen the home forum.[23] When the home forum has been chosen, it is reasonable to assume that this choice is convenient. When the plaintiff is foreign, however, this assumption is much less reasonable. Because the central purpose of any *forum non conveniens* inquiry is to ensure that the trial is convenient, a foreign plaintiff's choice deserves less deference.

---

[23] In *Koster*, we stated that "[i]n any balancing of conveniences, a real showing of convenience by a plaintiff who has sued in his home forum will normally outweigh the inconvenience the defendant may have shown." * * * [T]he lower federal courts have routinely given less weight to a foreign plaintiff's choice of forum. A citizen's forum choice should not be given dispositive weight, however. Citizens or residents deserve somewhat more deference than foreign plaintiffs, but dismissal should not be automatically barred when a plaintiff has filed suit in his home forum. As always, if the balance of conveniences suggests that trial in the chosen forum would be unnecessarily burdensome for the defendant or the court, dismissal is proper.

B

The *forum non conveniens* determination is committed to the sound discretion of the trial court. It may be reversed only when there has been a clear abuse of discretion; where the court has considered all relevant public and private interest factors, and where its balancing of these factors is reasonable, its decision deserves substantial deference. Here, the Court of Appeals expressly acknowledged that the standard of review was one of abuse of discretion. In examining the District Court's analysis of the public and private interests, however, the Court of Appeals seems to have lost sight of this rule, and substituted its own judgment for that of the District Court.

(1)

In analyzing the private interest factors, the District Court stated that the connections with Scotland are "overwhelming." This characterization may be somewhat exaggerated. Particularly with respect to the question of relative ease of access to sources of proof, the private interests point in both directions. As respondent emphasizes, records concerning the design, manufacture, and testing of the propeller and plane are located in the United States. She would have greater access to sources of proof relevant to her strict liability and negligence theories if trial were held here. However, the District Court did not act unreasonably in concluding that fewer evidentiary problems would be posed if the trial were held in Scotland. A large proportion of the relevant evidence is located in Great Britain.

The Court of Appeals found that the problems of proof could not be given any weight because Piper and Hartzell failed to describe with specificity the evidence they would not be able to obtain if trial were held in the United States. It suggested that defendants seeking *forum non conveniens* dismissal must submit affidavits identifying the witnesses they would call and the testimony these witnesses would provide if the trial were held in the alternative forum. Such detail is not necessary. Piper and Hartzell have moved for dismissal precisely because many crucial witnesses are located beyond the reach of compulsory process, and thus are difficult to identify or interview. Requiring extensive investigation would defeat the purpose of their motion. Of course, defendants must provide enough information to enable the District Court to balance the parties' interests. Our examination of the record convinces us that sufficient information was provided here. Both Piper and Hartzell submitted affidavits describing the evidentiary problems they would face if the trial were held in the United States.

The District Court correctly concluded that the problems posed by the inability to implead potential third-party defendants clearly supported holding the trial in Scotland. Joinder of the pilot's estate, Air Navigation, and McDonald is crucial to the presentation of petitioners' defense. If Piper and Hartzell can show that the accident was caused not by a design defect, but rather by the negligence of the pilot, the plane's owners, or the charter company, they will be relieved of all liability. It is true, of course, that if Hartzell and Piper were found liable after a trial in the United States, they could institute an action for indemnity or contribution against these parties in Scotland. It would be far more convenient, however, to resolve all claims in one trial. The Court of Appeals rejected this argument. Forcing petitioners to rely on actions for indemnity or contributions would be "burdensome" but not "unfair." Finding that trial in the plaintiff's chosen forum would be burdensome, however, is sufficient to support dismissal on grounds of *forum non conveniens*.

(2)

The District Court's review of the factors relating to the public interest was also reasonable. On the basis of its choice-of-law analysis, it concluded that if the case were tried in the Middle District of Pennsylvania, Pennsylvania law would apply to Piper and Scottish law to Hartzell. It stated that a trial involving two sets of laws would be confusing to the jury. It also noted its own lack of familiarity with Scottish law. Consideration of these problems was clearly appropriate under *Gilbert*; in that case we explicitly held that the need to apply foreign law pointed towards dismissal. The Court of Appeals found that the District Court's choice-of-law analysis was incorrect, and that American law would apply to both Hartzell and Piper. Thus, lack of familiarity with foreign law would not be a problem. Even if the Court of Appeals' conclusion is correct, however, all other public interest factors favored trial in Scotland.

Scotland has a very strong interest in this litigation. The accident occurred in its airspace. All of the decedents were Scottish. Apart from Piper and Hartzell, all potential plaintiffs and defendants are either Scottish or English. As we stated in *Gilbert*, there is "a local interest in having localized controversies decided at home." 330 U.S. at 509. Respondent argues that American citizens have an interest in ensuring that American manufacturers are deterred from producing defective products, and that additional deterrence might be obtained if Piper and Hartzell were tried in the United States, where they could be sued on the basis of both negligence and strict liability. However, the incremental deterrence that would be gained if this trial were held in an American court is likely to be insignificant. The American interest in this accident is simply not sufficient to justify the enormous commitment of judicial time and resources that would inevitably be required if the case were to be tried here.

IV

The Court of Appeals erred in holding that the possibility of an unfavorable change in law bars dismissal on the ground of *forum non conveniens*. It also erred in rejecting the District Court's *Gilbert* analysis. The District Court properly decided that the presumption in favor of the respondent's forum choice applied with less than maximum force because the real parties in interest are foreign. It did not act unreasonably in deciding that the private interests pointed towards trial in Scotland. Nor did it act unreasonably in deciding that the public interests favored trial in Scotland. Thus, the judgment of the Court of Appeals is

Reversed.

JUSTICE POWELL took no part in the decision of these cases.

JUSTICE O'CONNOR took no part in the consideration or decision of these cases.

[The concurring opinion of JUSTICE WHITE and the dissenting opinion of JUSTICE STEVENS joined by JUSTICE BRENNAN are omitted.]

Points for Discussion

a. Standards for Deciding Whether to Dismiss for *Forum Non Conveniens*

Forum non conveniens is a common-law (judicially-created) doctrine that is applied when it would be more convenient for a case to be heard in an alternative forum that is located outside of the judicial system in which the case is currently pending. For federal courts, this means that the more convenient forum is located outside of the United States, or less frequently, in a state court within the United States.

If a litigant believes that the case would be more conveniently tried outside of the federal court system, it may seek a dismissal of the case on *forum non conveniens* grounds via a motion. Courts are also empowered to dismiss a case based on *forum non conveniens* on their own initiative without a motion. *See, e.g.,* Wong v. PartyGaming Ltd., 589 F.3d 821, 824–25, 830 (6th Cir. 2009) (upholding the district court's decision to dismiss the action *sua sponte* on forum non conveniens grounds).

Based on what you read in *Piper Aircraft*, what are the requirements for dismissing a case on *forum non conveniens* grounds? What role do the factors set forth by the Court in Gulf Oil Corp. v. Gilbert, 330 U.S. 501 (1947), and quoted by the *Piper Aircraft* Court in footnote 6 play in the analysis? What role did the Court indicate that the plaintiff's choice of forum should have in the analysis?

b. An Adequate Alternative Forum

An important element of granting a *forum non conveniens* dismissal is that there is an adequate alternate forum where the plaintiff may proceed with the case. What issues are relevant to determining whether an *adequate* alternate forum exists?

See Wenzel v. Marriott Int'l, Inc., No. 13 Civ. 8335(AT), 2014 WL 6603414, at *4 (S.D.N.Y. Nov. 17, 2014) ("A forum will usually be adequate so long as it permits litigation of the subject matter of the dispute, provides adequate procedural safeguards and the remedy available in the alternative forum is not so inadequate as to amount to no remedy at all." (citation and internal quotation marks omitted)). In *Piper Aircraft* the Court rejected using the fact that less favorable substantive law would apply as a basis for denying a *forum non conveniens* dismissal. Do you agree with that decision?

Consider whether the decision in this case would have changed if Scotland did not permit recovery for wrongful death under these circumstances or if its legal system failed to provide basic due process protections available in the United States. Alternatively, what if the damages for wrongful death in Scotland were capped at an unusually low figure, such as $10,000 per person; would Scotland still be viewed as an adequate alternate forum? *See Gonzalez v. Chrysler Corp.*, 301 F.3d 377, 382–83 (5th Cir. 2002) (holding that the adequacy analysis for *forum non conveniens* dismissals may not include an evaluation of whether it makes economic sense for the plaintiff to proceed in an alternate foreign jurisdiction). At what point should differences in substantive law impact the *forum non conveniens* analysis?

c. *Forum Non Conveniens* Dismissals Prior to Jurisdictional Determinations

The Supreme Court has determined that courts need not resolve other threshold objections—such as whether the court has subject matter jurisdiction or personal jurisdiction—prior to addressing a defendant's *forum non conveniens* motion and dismissing the case on that basis. *Sinochem Int'l Co. v. Malaysia Int'l Shipping Corp.*, 549 U.S. 422 (2007).

d. After Dismissal

What happens after a court dismisses a case on *forum non conveniens* grounds? Plaintiffs then have the option to refile their cases in the alternate forum. However, there could be difficulties associated with doing so. For example, the alternate forum may lack personal jurisdiction over the defendant or the statute of limitations period may have run. When there is a possibility or probability that the plaintiff will face such challenges to refiling its case in the wake of a *forum non conveniens* dismissal, the dismissing court typically will dismiss the case only on the condition that the defendant will not contest the ability of the subsequent court to hear the case. *See, e.g.*, *Pollux Holding, Ltd. v. Chase Manhattan Bank*, 329 F.3d 64 (2d Cir. 2003), *cert. denied*, 540 U.S. 1149 (2004) (affirming district court's dismissal of case filed in New York against defendant British bank, when defendant had agreed as a condition to submit to the jurisdiction of British courts).

Do courts have authority to impose such conditions on defendants when granting *forum non conveniens* dismissals if they have not first determined whether they have subject matter jurisdiction over the claims and personal jurisdiction over the defendants, a determination the Supreme Court in *Sinochem* said courts do not have to make? The Court avoided this issue in *Sinochem* itself. *See Sinochem, 549 U.S. at 435* ("We . . . need not decide whether a court conditioning a *forum non conveniens* dismissal on the waiver of jurisdictional or limitations defenses in the foreign forum must first determine its own authority to adjudicate the case.").

Practice Pointer

As counsel for a plaintiff facing a *forum non conveniens* dismissal, be sure to pursue and secure conditions of the dismissal from the court that require the defendant to waive all jurisdictional, venue, statute of limitations, and other challenges to the ability of a subsequent court to hear your client's case.

If a federal court dismisses a claim on *forum non conveniens* grounds in favor of litigating the case in the court of another country, may the plaintiff refile the case in a state court instead? If the plaintiff does so, may the defendant get a federal court injunction prohibiting the state court action as contrary to the previous *forum non conveniens* dismissal? *See Chick Kam Choo v. Exxon Corp., 486 U.S. 140, 149 (1988)* (rejecting such an injunction entered after a federal *forum non conveniens* dismissal and holding that state court was free to conduct its own *forum non conveniens* analysis because "whether the Texas state courts are an appropriate forum for [the plaintiff's] Singapore law claims has not yet been litigated").

e. *Forum Non Conveniens* **and the** *Erie* **Doctrine**

As you will learn in Chapter 5, under the doctrine of *Erie R.R. Co. v. Tompkins, 304 U.S. 64 (1938)*, federal courts sitting in diversity are obligated to apply the substantive state law that would be applied to a claim in the state where the federal court hearing the case is located. Does this requirement apply to the law of *forum non conveniens*? In other words, when hearing claims based on state law may federal courts follow federal *forum non conveniens* doctrine or must they apply the relevant state approach to *forum non conveniens*? The Supreme Court has suggested, but not held, that the federal law of *forum non conveniens* is a procedural doctrine that federal courts must apply but that state courts may ignore. *See Am. Dredging Co. v. Miller, 510 U.S. 443, 453 (1994)* (stating that "*forum non conveniens* . . . is procedural rather than substantive").

Executive Summary

■ **Basic Venue.** 28 U.S.C. § 1391 is the general venue statute. Careful application of its provisions is necessary to determine whether venue is proper in cases where the statute applies.

■ **Special Venue Statutes.** When there are special venue statutes that apply, they generally serve to supplement the general venue statute unless the special statute is exclusive or somehow conflicts with the general venue statute.

Major Themes

Keep in mind two overarching themes at work within the area of venue:

a. *Forum Shopping*—the venue statute may often give plaintiffs an array of proper venues in which to file their actions. Although this decision will ultimately be constrained in part by personal jurisdiction considerations, plaintiffs here have some ability to identify the forum that is best for their interests from a strategic perspective.

b. *Defendant Veto*—although the defendant does not have an absolute "veto" over the forum selection of the plaintiff, the venue transfer provisions along with the doctrine of *forum non conveniens* do enable the defendant to attempt to convince the court that the action should be heard in a court other than that selected initially by the plaintiff.

■ **Pendent Venue.** Although venue must be proper with respect to each claim, many courts recognize the concept of *pendent venue*, which will permit proper venue for one claim to establish proper venue for all claims that share a common nucleus of operative fact. This, however, is not a universally accepted principle.

■ **Change of Venue (Transfer).** 28 U.S.C. § 1404 permits courts to transfer a properly venued case to another federal district or division in which the case could have been brought initially, if doing so furthers the convenience of the witnesses and parties and is in the interests of justice. 28 U.S.C. § 1406 permits courts to transfer improperly venued cases to other federal districts where they could have been brought if the interests of justice suggest that such a transfer is warranted.

■ **Applicable Law After Transfer.** When state law claims are transferred from *proper* venues, the law that would have applied in the transferor court applies in the transferee court. When federal question claims are transferred, the transferee court is generally not bound by the circuit law of the transferor court.

■ *Forum Non Conveniens.* When the analysis of the *Gilbert* private and public interest factors indicates that a more appropriate and adequate alternate forum exists for the action, but the alternate forum is within a separate judicial system, a court may dismiss the case on *forum non conveniens* grounds. When doing so, courts typically will condition the dismissal on the defendant agreeing to permit the case to be litigated in the alternate forum, waiving any jurisdictional or other challenges to the alternate court's authority to adjudicate the dispute.

For More Information

Students interested in obtaining more information about venue may consult the following resources:

- 14D C. WRIGHT, A. MILLER, E. COOPER & R. FREER, FED. PRAC. & PROC. § 3808 *et seq.* (4th ed. 2013).

- Mary Garvey Algero, *In Defense of Forum Shopping: A Realistic Look at Selecting a Venue*, 78 NEB. L. REV. 79 (1999).

- Kimberly Jade Norwood, *Shopping for a Venue: The Need for More Limits on Choice*, 50 U. MIAMI L. REV. 267 (1996).

Test Your Knowledge

To assess your understanding of the material in this chapter, click here to take a quiz.

CHAPTER FIVE

The Erie *Doctrine*
State Law in Federal Courts

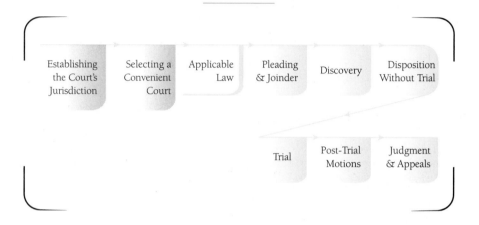

THUS FAR WE HAVE COVERED the various rules, doctrines, and statutes that provide the framework for identifying the proper court for litigating a case within the federal system. The doctrines of personal jurisdiction and subject matter jurisdiction are used to determine which court or courts have the power and authority to hear a case. Venue doctrine concerns itself with identifying a convenient forum that serves the interests of the parties and the witnesses involved in a case.

Now we turn to what many consider to be a more nettlesome issue, that matter of which law—state versus federal—must be applied to various matters under consideration within a federal court. This is a question that is relevant only when a federal court is considering claims not arising under federal law; in that circumstance federal law generally applies to all of the issues surrounding federal claims. However, when a federal court hears non-federal claims through its diversity or supplemental jurisdiction, such as contract or tort claims, what law should it apply, state law or federal law?

Take Note!

A mild warning is in order here. The *Erie* doctrine is one of the more complicated topics you will cover in Civil Procedure. It will be helpful to pay close attention to what the Court says in each of the cases below and to try to understand the contribution to (or alteration of) the doctrine made by each case. A complete picture of the doctrine will likely not emerge until the final cases in the line are covered.

In this chapter, we will cover the doctrine that federal courts use to make this determination, the *Erie* doctrine, so named for the seminal Supreme Court case— Erie Railroad Co. v. Tompkins, 304 U.S. 64 (1938)—that laid the groundwork for how these vertical* choice-of-law matters are resolved to this day.

A. Applicable Law Prior to *Erie*

The starting point for the study of the *Erie* doctrine must actually begin before *Erie*, with consideration of a statute called the Rules of Decision Act ("RDA") and with a review of the Supreme Court's early view of what the RDA said about applicable law in federal courts. The RDA—which was enacted in 1789 as a component of the Judiciary Act of 1789—today is codified at 28 U.S.C. § 1652:

State Laws as Rules of Decision: 28 U.S.C. § 1652

The laws of the several states, except where the Constitution or treaties of the United States or Acts of Congress otherwise require or provide, shall be regarded as rules of decision in civil actions in the courts of the United States, in cases where they apply.

Does this statute make clear the circumstances under which state law applies in civil actions in federal courts? It does make clear that the terms of the RDA are only applicable when the Constitution, federal statutes, or treaties do not apply. Thus, the RDA is inapplicable to federal question claims, where the relevant governing law is the federal statutory or constitutional provision at issue. What about non-federal claims? The RDA points to the "laws of the several states," but what does that mean? The laws enacted by a state's legislature? The pronouncements of a state's courts? Common law doctrines in force within a state? The next case presents the Supreme Court's early interpretation of the RDA and its initial response to each of these questions.

Swift v. Tyson

Supreme Court of the United States
41 U.S. (16 Pet.) 1 (1842)

[Tyson, a New Yorker, tendered a bill of exchange (a negotiable instrument akin to a check) to some land speculators as payment for land that Tyson thought the speculators owned. The speculators then used Tyson's bill of exchange to pay off a pre-existing debt to Swift. When Swift attempted to "cash" Tyson's bill of exchange,

---

* Determinations of whether to apply one state's law versus that of another state is a *horizontal* choice-of-law issue that is covered in a **Conflict of Laws** course. In this book the focus will be on the vertical choice-of-law issue of whether federal or state law should be applied when a case is in federal court. [Ed.]

Tyson refused to honor it because, as it turned out, the speculators did not own the land they had purported to sell to Tyson, leading Tyson to argue that he was under no obligation to honor the bill of exchange because it was procured by fraud. Swift sued Tyson in federal court based on diversity jurisdiction to collect on the bill. Under prevailing law, "bona fide" holders of such bills, who acquired them for valuable consideration without knowledge of the fraud, were entitled to payment on the bills. However, under New York contract law, a pre-existing debt did not constitute valuable consideration, meaning that fraud tainting the transaction would be a legitimate defense for Tyson and he would not have to pay on the bill. The question before the Supreme Court was whether it was obliged to defer to New York's view regarding pre-existing debt as valuable consideration or free to develop its own view of the matter.]

STORY, JUSTICE, delivered the opinion of the court.

There is no doubt, that a *bona fide* holder of a negotiable instrument, for a valuable consideration, without any notice of facts which impeach its validity, as between the antecedent parties, if he takes it under an endorsement made before the same becomes due, holds the title unaffected by these facts, and may recover thereon, although, as between the antecedent parties, the transaction may be without any legal validity. This is a doctrine so long and so well established,

Make the Connection

The concept of a *bona fide holder for value* is a central concept covered in a **Commercial Paper** course, a subject typically tested on state bar exams.

and so essential to the security of negotiable paper, that it is laid up among the fundamentals of the law, and requires no authority or reasoning to be now brought in its support. * * *

What's That?

Consideration is a **Contracts** concept and refers to something of value given in exchange for a promise. Consideration is ordinarily necessary for a promise to become a binding, enforceable contract.

In the present case, the plaintiff is a *bona fide* holder, without notice, for what the law deems a good and valid consideration, that is, for a preexisting debt; and the only real question in the cause is, whether, under the circumstances of the present case, such a pre-existing debt constitutes a valuable consideration, in the sense of the general rule applicable to negotiable instruments. We say, under the circumstances of the present case, for the acceptance having been made in New York, the argument on behalf of the defendant is, that the contract is to be treated as a New York contract, and therefore, to be governed by the laws of New York, as expounded by its courts, as well upon general principles, as by the express provisions of the 34th section of the Judiciary Act of 1789, ch. 20 [The Rules of Decision Act]. And then it is further contended, that by the law of New York, as thus expounded by its courts, a pre-existing debt does not constitute, in the sense of the general rule, a valuable consideration applicable to negotiable instruments.

* * *

But, admitting the doctrine to be fully settled in New York, it remains to be considered, whether it is obligatory upon this court, if it differs from the principles established in the general commercial law. It is observable, that the courts of New York do not found their decisions upon this point, upon any local statute, or positive, fixed or ancient local usage; but they deduce the doctrine from the general principles of commercial law. It is, however, contended, that the [Rules of Decision Act] furnishes a rule obligatory upon this court to follow the decisions of the state tribunals in all cases to which they apply. That section provides "that the laws of the several states, except where the Constitution, treaties or statutes of the United States shall otherwise require or provide, shall be regarded as rules of decision, in trials at common law, in the courts of the United States, in cases where they apply." In order to maintain the argument, it is essential, therefore, to hold, that the word "laws," in this section, includes within the scope of its meaning, the decisions of the local tribunals. In the ordinary use of language, it will hardly be contended, that the deci-sions of courts constitute laws. They are, at most, only evidence of what the laws are, and are not, of themselves, laws. They are often re-examined, reversed and qualified by the courts themselves, whenever they are found to be either defective, or ill-founded, or otherwise incorrect. The laws of a state are more usually understood to mean the rules and enactments pro-mulgated by the legislative authority thereof, or long-established local cus-

Take Note!

The term *local* as used here does not refer to local municipalities or other political subdivisions within states— the more common understanding of the term—but rather refers to the states themselves, "local" law and courts rather than federal.

toms having the force of laws. In all the various cases, which have hitherto come before us for decision, this court have [*sic*] uniformly supposed, that the true inter-pretation of the [Rules of Decision Act] limited its application to state laws, strictly local, that is to say, to the positive statutes of the state, and the construction thereof adopted by the local tribunals, and to rights and titles to things having a permanent locality, such as the rights and titles to real estate, and other matters immovable and intra-territorial in their nature and character. It never has been supposed by us, that the section did apply, or was designed to apply, to questions of a more general nature, not at all dependent upon local statutes or local usages of a fixed and perma-nent operation, as, for example, to the construction of ordinary contracts or other written instruments, and especially to questions of general commercial law, where the state tribunals are called upon to perform the like functions as ourselves, that is, to ascertain, upon general reasoning and legal analogies, what is the true exposition of the contract or instrument, or what is the just rule furnished by the principles of commercial law to govern the case. And we have not now the slightest difficulty in holding, that this section, upon its true intendment and construction, is strictly limited to local statutes and local usages of the character before stated, and does not extend to contracts and other instruments of a commercial nature, the true interpretation and effect whereof are to be sought, not in the decisions of the local tribunals, but in the general principles and doctrines of commercial jurisprudence. Undoubtedly, the decisions of the local tribunals upon such subjects are entitled to, and will receive, the most deliberate attention and respect of this court; but they cannot furnish positive rules, or conclusive authority, by which our own judgments are to be bound up and governed. The law respecting negotiable instruments may be truly declared * * * to be in a great measure, not the law of a single country only, but of the commercial world. * * *

It becomes necessary for us, therefore, upon the present occasion, to express our own opinion of the true result of the commercial law upon the question now before us. And we have no hesitation in saying, that a pre-existing debt does constitute a valuable consideration, in the sense of the general rule already stated, as applicable to negotiable instruments. Assuming it to be true * * * that the holder of a negotiable instrument is unaffected with the equities between the antecedent parties, of which he has no notice, only where he receives it in the usual course of trade and business, for a valuable consideration, before it becomes due; we are prepared to say, that receiving it in payment of, or as security for, a pre-existing debt, is according to the known usual course of trade and business. And why, upon principle, should not a pre-existing debt be deemed such a valuable consideration? It is for the benefit and convenience of the commercial world, to give as wide an extent as practicable to the credit and circulation of negotiable paper, that it

Take Note!

Notice that the Court here seeks to explain the policy rationale behind the rule it is following and applying. Why do you think the policy behind the rule is important? What role does and should policy play in guiding a court's discernment of what the law is or should be and whether to apply the rule in the case before it?

may pass not only as security for new purchases and advances, made upon the transfer thereof, but also in payment of, and as security for, pre-existing debts. The creditor is thereby enabled to realize or to secure his debt, and thus may safely give a prolonged credit, or forbear from taking any legal steps to enforce his rights. The debtor also has the advantage of making his negotiable securities of equivalent value to cash. But establish the opposite conclusion, that negotiable paper cannot be applied in payment of, or as security for, pre-existing debts, without letting in all the equities between the original and antecedent parties, and the value and circulation of such securities must be essentially diminished, and the debtor driven to the embarrassment of making a sale thereof, often at a ruinous discount, to some third person, and then, by circuity, to apply the proceeds to the payment of his debts. What, indeed, upon such a doctrine, would become of that large class of cases, where new notes are given by the same or by other parties, by way of renewal or security to banks, in lieu of old securities discounted by them, which have arrived at maturity? Probably, more than one-half of all bank transactions in our country, as well as those of other countries, are of this nature. The doctrine would strike a fatal blow at all discounts of negotiable securities for pre-existing debts. * * *

[A concurring opinion by JUSTICE CATRON is omitted.]

Points for Discussion

a. The Holding of *Swift*

What conclusion did the Court reach regarding the meaning of the phrase "[t]he laws of the several states" in the Rules of Decision Act? Does the Court's reading of the RDA make sense? What alternative readings of the phrase can you imagine?

b. The Common Law

The Court in *Swift* rejected the idea that the RDA obligated it to adhere to the common law decisions of state courts in resolving non-federal claims. What was the basis for this position? To understand this view, it is important to note that at the time of *Swift*, the prevailing view of the common law was that there was one "true" body of common law that transcended state boundaries, and that all judges—both state and federal—were in the same business of trying to ascertain that law. Thus, judicial opinions in which judges conveyed their understandings of the common law were not viewed themselves to be "law" but rather were viewed as mere expressions of courts' opinions about what the common law was. How were courts under this view expected to identify the common law? How did the Court in *Swift* come to its understanding of the relevant common law governing the commercial transactions and negotiable instruments at issue in the case?

Food for Thought

Might the Court have been mistaken to interpret "[t]he laws of the several states" to refer to the obligation to apply an individual state's statutory law in federal diversity actions? *See* WILFRED J. RITZ, REWRITING THE HISTORY OF THE JUDICIARY ACT OF 1789: EXPOSING MYTHS, CHALLENGING PREMISES, AND USING NEW EVIDENCE 148 (1990) ("American law is to be found in the 'laws of the several states' viewed as a group of eleven states in 1789, and not viewed separately and individually. It is not a direction to apply the law of a particular state, for if it had been so intended, the section would have referred to the 'laws of the respective states.' ").

c. Nationalizing the Economy

Justice Story's opinion prominently features a discussion of the policy concerns that underlaid the rule he was articulating and applying in *Swift*. Part of his concern was that the country not only needed to have a reliable system of banking and commercial paper but that there needed to be uniform rules governing these matters in order to promote the growth of interstate commerce and the development of a truly national economy rather than a balkanized collection of local economies. Should such considerations factor into a judge's effort to identify or develop the law? What would the impact have been had the Court made a contrary decision?

d. Federal General Common Law

In the wake of *Swift*, federal courts proceeded to make independent assessments of the common law (developing what was referred to as **federal general common law**) as did their state court counterparts, leading to the rise of distinct bodies of law in which a state court might have one view of the common law rule governing an issue and a federal court located within the same state would have another, contrary view. Because state and federal courts have overlapping jurisdiction, a dispute could be governed by two completely different legal rules depending upon whether the dispute was litigated in state or federal court. What potential problems might arise under such circumstances? Might litigants under such a regime be able to select a particular forum based on which law governed in each? Would all litigants equally be able to choose between state and federal forums for litigating their cases?

B. Establishing the *Erie* Doctrine

As you might imagine, the use of federal general common law for disputes in federal court, but state common law—which could differ—in state court actually undermined the legal uniformity that the *Swift* Court had hoped to encourage. In the next case, the Court revisited the rule of *Swift* and laid the foundation for the modern doctrine governing vertical choice-of-law matters in the United States.

Erie Railroad Co. v. Tompkins

Supreme Court of the United States
304 U.S. 64 (1938)

MR. JUSTICE BRANDEIS delivered the opinion of the Court.

The question for decision is whether the oft-challenged doctrine of *Swift v. Tyson* shall now be disapproved.

Tompkins, a citizen of Pennsylvania, was injured on a dark night by a passing freight train of the Erie Railroad Company while walking along its right of way at Hughestown in that state. He claimed that the accident occurred through negligence in the operation, or maintenance, of the train; that he was rightfully on the premises as licensee because on a commonly used beaten footpath which ran for a short distance alongside the tracks; and that he was struck by something which looked like a door projecting from one of the moving cars. To enforce that claim he brought an action in the federal court for Southern New York, which had jurisdiction because the company is a corporation of that state. It denied liability; and the case was tried by a jury.

What's That?

A *right of way* is a right to pass through another's property.

The Erie insisted that its duty to Tompkins was no greater than that owed to a trespasser. It contended, among other things, that its duty to Tompkins, and hence its liability, should be determined in accordance with the Pennsylvania law; that under the law of Pennsylvania, as declared by its highest court, persons who use pathways along the railroad right of way—that is, a longitudinal pathway as distinguished from a crossing—are to be deemed trespassers; and that the railroad is not liable for injuries to undiscovered trespassers resulting from its negligence, unless it be wanton or willful. Tompkins denied that any such rule had been established by the decisions of the Pennsylvania courts; and contended that, since there was no statute of the state on the subject, the railroad's duty and liability is to be determined in federal courts as a matter of general law.

The trial judge refused to rule that the applicable law precluded recovery. The jury brought in a verdict of $30,000; and the judgment entered thereon was affirmed by the Circuit Court of Appeals, which held that it was unnecessary to consider whether the law of Pennsylvania was as contended, because the question was one not of local, but of general, law, and that "upon questions of general law the federal courts are free, in absence of a local statute, to exercise their independent judgment as to what the law is; and it is well settled that the question of the responsibility of a railroad for injuries caused by its servants is one of general law." * * *

The Erie had contended that application of the Pennsylvania rule was required, among other things, by section 34 of the Federal Judiciary Act of September 24, 1789 [the Rules of Decision Act], which provides: "The laws of the several States, except where the Constitution, treaties, or statutes of the United States otherwise require or provide, shall be regarded as rules of decision in trials at common law, in the courts of the United States, in cases where they apply."

Because of the importance of the question whether the federal court was free to disregard the alleged rule of the Pennsylvania common law, we granted certiorari.

First. <u>Swift v. Tyson, 41 U.S. (16 Pet.) 1 (1842)</u>, held that federal courts exercising jurisdiction on the ground of diversity of citizenship need not, in matters of general jurisprudence, apply the unwritten law of the state as declared by its highest court; that they are free to exercise an independent judgment as to what the common law of the state is—or should be * * * .

* * * The federal courts assumed, in the broad field of "general law," the power to declare rules of decision which Congress was confessedly without power to enact as statutes. Doubt was repeatedly expressed as to the correctness of the construction given section 34, and as to the soundness of the rule which it introduced. But it was the more recent research of a competent scholar, who examined the original document, which established that the construction given to it by the Court was erroneous; and that the purpose of the section was merely to make certain that, in all matters except those in which some federal law is controlling, the federal courts exercising jurisdiction in diversity of citizenship cases would apply as their rules of decision the law of the state, unwritten as well as written.[5]

Food for Thought

The research mentioned here unearthed a previously undiscovered earlier draft of the RDA, which included the following language: "[T]he Statute law of the several States in force for the time being and their unwritten or common law now in use . . ., except where [federal law] shall otherwise require or provide, shall be regarded as rules of decision in the trials at common law in the courts of the United States in cases where they apply." Justice Brandeis took this as an indication that the final version of the RDA must be read to include state common law decisions as part of the law that federal courts sitting in diversity must apply. Do you agree with Justice Brandeis's view of how this legislative history should shape one's interpretation of the RDA?

Criticism of the doctrine became widespread after the decision of <u>Black & White Taxicab & Transfer Co. v. Brown & Yellow Taxicab & Transfer Co., 276 U.S. 518 (1928)</u>. There, Brown & Yellow, a Kentucky corporation owned by Kentuckians, and the Louisville & Nashville Railroad, also a Kentucky corporation, wished that the former should have the exclusive privilege of soliciting passenger and baggage transportation at the Bowling Green, Ky., Railroad station; and that the Black & White, a competing Kentucky corporation, should be prevented from interfering with that privilege. Knowing that such a contract would be void under the common law of Kentucky, it was arranged that the Brown & Yellow reincorporate under the law of Tennessee, and that the contract with the railroad should be executed there. The suit was then brought by the Tennessee corporation in the federal court for Western Kentucky to enjoin competition by the Black & White; an injunction issued by the District Court

---

[5] Charles Warren, *New Light on the History of the Federal Judiciary Act of 1789*, 37 Harv. L. Rev. 49, 51–52, 81–88, 108 (1923).

was sustained by the Court of Appeals; and this Court, citing many decisions in which the doctrine of Swift & Tyson had been applied, affirmed the decree.

Second. Experience in applying the doctrine of *Swift v. Tyson*, had revealed its defects, political and social; and the benefits expected to flow from the rule did not accrue. Persistence of state courts in their own opinions on questions of common law prevented uniformity; and the impossibility of discovering a satisfactory line of demarcation between the province of general law and that of local law developed a new well of uncertainties.

On the other hand, the mischievous results of the doctrine had become apparent. Diversity of citizenship jurisdiction was conferred in order to prevent apprehended discrimination in state courts against those not citizens of the state. *Swift v. Tyson* introduced grave discrimination by noncitizens against citizens. It made rights enjoyed under the unwritten "general law" vary according to whether enforcement was sought in the state or in the federal court; and the privilege of selecting the court in which the right should be determined was conferred upon the noncitizen.[9] Thus, the doctrine rendered impossible equal protection of the law. In attempting to promote uniformity of law throughout the United States, the doctrine had prevented uniformity in the administration of the law of the state.

Take Note!

The Court here is walking through some of the difficulties that arose as a result of the *Swift* doctrine. Make a note of these and ask how these concerns factor into the Court's view of applicable law in federal courts in this case and in subsequent cases in the *Erie* line.

The discrimination resulting became in practice far-reaching. This resulted in part from the broad province accorded to the so-called "general law" as to which federal courts exercised an independent judgment. In addition to questions of purely commercial law, "general law" was held to include the obligations under contracts entered into and to be performed within the state, the extent to which a carrier operating within a state may stipulate for exemption from liability for his own negligence or that of his employee; the liability for torts committed within the state upon persons resident or property located there, even where the question of liability depended upon the scope of a property right conferred by the state; and the right to exemplary or punitive damages. Furthermore, state decisions construing local deeds, mineral conveyances, and even devises of real estate, were disregarded.

---

[9] It was even possible for a nonresident plaintiff defeated on a point of law in the highest court of a State nevertheless to win out by taking a nonsuit and renewing the controversy in the federal court.

In part the discrimination resulted from the wide range of persons held entitled to avail themselves of the federal rule by resort to the diversity of citizenship jurisdiction. Through this jurisdiction individual citizens willing to remove from their own state and become citizens of another might avail themselves of the federal rule. And, without even change of residence, a corporate citizen of the state could avail itself of the federal rule by reincorporating under the laws of another state, as was done in the Taxicab Case.

Food for Thought

Justice Brandeis says that the *Swift v. Tyson* approach is unconstitutional. In what way was the *Swift* interpretation of the RDA "unconstitutional"?

The injustice and confusion incident to the doctrine of *Swift v. Tyson* have been repeatedly urged as reasons for abolishing or limiting diversity of citizenship jurisdiction. Other legislative relief has been proposed.[21] If only a question of statutory construction were involved, we should not be prepared to abandon a doctrine so widely applied throughout nearly a century. But the unconstitutionality of the course pursued has now been made clear, and compels us to do so.

Food for Thought

Justice Brandeis states here, "There is no federal general common law." Yet on the same day as he issued his opinion in *Erie*, he issued an opinion in another case in which he wrote, "[W]hether the water of an interstate stream must be apportioned between the two States is a question of 'federal common law' upon which neither the statutes nor the decisions of either State can be conclusive." *Hinderlider v. La Plata River & Cherry Creek Ditch Co., 304 U.S. 92 (1938)*. Is he being inconsistent, or is there a distinction to be made?

Third. Except in matters governed by the Federal Constitution or by acts of Congress, the law to be applied in any case is the law of the state. And whether the law of the state shall be declared by its Legislature in a statute or by its highest court in a decision is not a matter of federal concern. There is no federal general common law. Congress has no power to declare substantive rules of common law applicable in a state whether they be local in their nature or "general," be they commercial law or a part of the law of torts. And no clause in the Constitution purports to confer such a power upon the federal courts. As stated by Mr. Justice Field when protesting in *Baltimore & O.R. Co. v. Baugh, 149 U.S. 368 (1893)*, against ignoring the Ohio common law of fellow-servant liability:

---

[21] Thus, bills which would abrogate the doctrine of *Swift v. Tyson* have been introduced. State statutes on conflicting questions of "general law" have also been suggested.

I am aware that what has been termed the general law of the country—which is often little less than what the judge advancing the doctrine thinks at the time should be the general law on a particular subject—has been often advanced in judicial opinions of this court to control a conflicting law of a state. I admit that learned judges have fallen into the habit of repeating this doctrine as a convenient mode of brushing aside the law of a state in conflict with their views. And I confess that, moved and governed by the authority of the great names of those judges, I have, myself, in many instances, unhesitatingly and confidently, but I think now erroneously, repeated the same doctrine. But, notwithstanding the great names which may be cited in favor of the doctrine, and notwithstanding the frequency with which the doctrine has been reiterated, there stands, as a perpetual protest against its repetition, the constitution of the United States, which recognizes and preserves the autonomy and independence of the states— independence in their legislative and independence in their judicial departments. Supervision over either the legislative or the judicial action of the states is in no case permissible except as to matters by the constitution specifically authorized or delegated to the United States. Any interference with either, except as thus permitted, is an invasion of the authority of the state, and, to that extent, a denial of its independence.

The fallacy underlying the rule declared in *Swift v. Tyson* is made clear by Mr. Justice Holmes. The doctrine rests upon the assumption that there is "a transcendental body of law outside of any particular State but obligatory within it unless and until changed by statute," that federal courts have the power to use their judgment as to what the rules of common law are; and that in the federal courts "the parties are entitled to an independent judgment on matters of general law":

> "But law in the sense in which courts speak of it today does not exist without some definite authority behind it. The common law so far as it is enforced in a State, whether called common law or not, is not the common law generally but the law of that State existing by the authority of that State without regard to what it may have been in England or anywhere else. * * *

> "The authority and only authority is the State, and if that be so, the voice adopted by the State as its own (whether it be of its Legislature or of its Supreme Court) should utter the last word."

Thus the doctrine of *Swift v. Tyson* is, as Mr. Justice Holmes said, "an unconstitutional assumption of powers by the Courts of the United States which no lapse of time or respectable array of opinion should make us hesitate to correct." In disapproving that doctrine we do not hold unconstitutional section 34 of the Federal Judiciary Act of 1789 or any other act of Congress. We merely declare that in applying the doctrine this Court and the lower courts have invaded rights which in our opinion are reserved by the Constitution to the several states.

Make the Connection

When the Court speaks of powers "reserved by the Constitution to the several states," it is referring to the Tenth Amendment to the Constitution, a central federalism-protecting provision in our system of government. You can study this amendment further in a **Federal Courts** course or a **Constitutional Law** course.

Fourth. The defendant contended that by the common law of Pennsylvania as declared by its highest court * * * , the only duty owed to the plaintiff was to refrain from willful or wanton injury. The plaintiff denied that such is the Pennsylvania law. In support of their respective contentions the parties discussed and cited many decisions of the Supreme Court of the state. The Circuit Court of Appeals ruled that the question of liability is one of general law; and on that ground declined to decide the issue of state law. As we hold this was error, the judgment is reversed and the case remanded to it for further proceedings in conformity with our opinion.

FYI
Justice Cardozo had a heart attack in late 1937 and he suffered a stroke in early 1938. He died on July 9, 1938.

Reversed.

MR. JUSTICE CARDOZO took no part in the consideration or decision of this case.

MR. JUSTICE BUTLER (dissenting).

* * *

Defendant's petition for writ of certiorari presented two questions: Whether its duty toward plaintiff should have been determined in accordance with the law as found by the highest court of Pennsylvania, and whether the evidence conclusively showed plaintiff guilty of contributory negligence. Plaintiff contends that, as always heretofore held by this Court, the issues of negligence and contributory negligence are to be determined by general law against which local decisions may not be held conclusive; that defendant relies on a solitary Pennsylvania case of doubtful applicability, and that, even if the decisions of the courts of that state were deemed controlling, the same result would have to be reached.

Make the Connection

Contributory negligence is a doctrine that bars a plaintiff from recovery if she is partly to blame for the harm she has suffered. You will study this concept in your first-year **Torts** course.

No constitutional question was suggested or argued below or here. And as a general rule, this Court will not consider any question not raised below and presented by the petition. Here it does not decide either of the questions presented, but, changing the rule of decision in force since the foundation of the government, remands the case to be adjudged according to a standard never before deemed permissible.

The opinion just announced states that: "The question for decision is whether the oft-challenged doctrine of *Swift v. Tyson* shall now be disapproved."

* * *

The doctrine of that case has been followed by this Court in an unbroken line of decisions. So far as appears, it was not questioned until more than 50 years later, and then by a single judge. *Baltimore & O.R. Co. v. Baugh*, 149 U.S. 368, 390 (1893). * * *

* * *

While amendments to section 34 have from time to time been suggested, the section stands as originally enacted. Evidently Congress has intended throughout the years that the rule of decision as construed should continue to govern federal courts in trials at common law. The opinion just announced suggests that Mr. Warren's research has established that from the beginning this Court has erroneously construed section 34. But that author's "New Light on the History of the Federal Judiciary Act of 1789" does not purport to be authoritative, and was intended to be no more than suggestive. The weight to be given to his discovery has never been discussed at this bar. * * *

Food for Thought

Does the fact that Congress never amended the RDA to overturn the Court's interpretation of the statute in *Swift* indicate Congress's approval of that interpretation? If so, does that undermine Justice Brandeis's use of the Warren research cited in footnote 5?

This Court has often emphasized its reluctance to consider constitutional questions and that legislation will not be held invalid as repugnant to the fundamental law if the case may be decided upon any other ground. In view of grave consequences liable to result from erroneous exertion of its power to set aside legislation, the Court should move cautiously, seek assistance of counsel, act only after ample deliberation, show that the question is before the Court, that its decision cannot be avoided by construction of the statute assailed or otherwise, indicate precisely the principle or provision of the Constitution held to have been transgressed, and fully disclose the reasons and authorities found to warrant the conclusion of invalidity. These safeguards against the improvident use of the great power to invalidate legislation are so well-grounded and familiar that * * * citation of authority to support them is no longer necessary.

So far as appears, no litigant has ever challenged the power of Congress to establish the rule as construed. It has so long endured that its destruction now without appropriate deliberation cannot be justified. There is nothing in the opinion to suggest that consideration of any constitutional question is

Food for Thought

Justice Butler here presents a series of principles that should guide the Court in deciding constitutional questions. Are these sound guidelines? Did the majority adhere to these admonitions here? If not, does that failure undermine the strength of the decision?

necessary to a decision of the case. By way of reasoning, it contains nothing that requires the conclusion reached. Admittedly, there is no authority to support that conclusion. Against the protest of those joining in this opinion, the Court declines to assign the case for reargument. It may not justly be assumed that the labor and argument of counsel for the parties would not disclose the right conclusion and aid the Court in the statement of reasons to support it. Indeed, it would have been appropriate to give Congress opportunity to be heard before divesting it of power to prescribe rules of decision to be followed in the courts of the United States.

The course pursued by the Court in this case is repugnant to the Act of Congress of August 24, 1937, 50 Stat. 751, 28 U.S.C.A. § 17 and note, 349a, 380a and note, 401. It declares that:

Whenever the constitutionality of any Act of Congress affecting the public interest is drawn in question in any court of the United States in any suit or proceeding to which the United States, or any agency thereof, or any officer or employee thereof, as such officer or employee, is not a party, the court having jurisdiction of the suit or proceeding shall certify such fact to the Attorney General. In any such case the court shall permit the United States to intervene and become a party for presentation of evidence * * * and argument upon the question of the constitutionality of such Act. In any such suit or proceeding the United States shall, subject to the applicable provisions of law, have all the rights of a party and the liabilities of a party as to court costs to the extent necessary for a proper presentation of the facts and law relating to the constitutionality of such Act.

That provision extends to this Court. If defendant had applied for and obtained the writ of *certiorari* upon the claim that, as now held, Congress has no power to prescribe the rule of decision, section 34 as construed, it would have been the duty of this Court to issue the prescribed certificate to the Attorney General in order that the United States might intervene and be heard on the constitutional question. Within the purpose of the statute and its true intent and meaning, the constitutionality of that measure has been "drawn in question." Congress intended to give the United States the right to be heard in every case involving constitutionality of an act affecting the public interest. In view of the rule that, in the absence of challenge of constitutionality, statutes will not here be invalidated on that ground, the Act of August 24, 1937 extends to cases where constitutionality is first "drawn in question" by the Court. * * *

* * * [T]he Court states that it does not hold section 34 unconstitutional, but merely that, in applying the doctrine of *Swift v. Tyson* construing it, this Court and the lower courts have invaded rights which are reserved by the Constitution to the several states. But, plainly through the form of words employed, the substance of the decision appears; it strikes down as unconstitutional section 34 as construed by our decisions; it divests the Congress of power to prescribe rules to be followed by federal courts when deciding questions of general law. In that broad field it compels this and the lower federal courts to follow decisions of the courts of a particular state.

I am of opinion that the constitutional validity of the rule need not be considered, because under the law, as found by the courts of Pennsylvania and generally throughout the country, it is plain that the evidence required a finding that plaintiff was guilty of negligence that contributed to cause his injuries, and that the judgment below should be reversed upon that ground.

Mr. Justice McReynolds, concurs in this opinion.

Mr. Justice Reed (concurring in part).

I concur in the conclusion reached in this case, in the disapproval of the doctrine of *Swift v. Tyson*, and in the reasoning of the majority opinion, except in so far as it relies upon the unconstitutionality of the "course pursued" by the federal courts.

The "doctrine of *Swift v. Tyson*," as I understand it, is that the words "the laws," as used in section 34, line 1, of the Federal Judiciary Act of September 24, 1789, do not include in their meaning "the decisions of the local tribunals." * * *

To decide the case now before us and to "disapprove" the doctrine of *Swift v. Tyson* requires only that we say that the words 'the laws' include in their meaning the decisions of the local tribunals. As the majority opinion shows, by its reference to Mr. Warren's research[ ] and the first quotation from Mr. Justice Holmes, that this Court is now of the view that "laws" includes "decisions," it is unnecessary to go further and declare that the "course pursued" was "unconstitutional," instead of merely erroneous.

The "unconstitutional" course referred to in the majority opinion is apparently the ruling in *Swift v. Tyson* that the supposed omission of Congress to legislate as to the effect of decisions leaves federal courts free to interpret general law for themselves. I am not at all sure whether, in the absence of federal statutory direction, federal courts would be compelled to follow state decisions. There was sufficient doubt about the matter in 1789 to induce the first Congress to legislate. No former opinions of this Court have passed upon it. * * * If the opinion commits this Court to the position that the Congress is without power to declare what rules of substantive law shall govern the federal courts, that conclusion also seems questionable. The line between procedural and substantive law is hazy, but no one doubts federal power over procedure. The Judiciary Article [III], and the "necessary and proper" clause of article 1, § 8, may fully authorize legislation, such as this section of the Judiciary Act.

In this Court, *stare decisis*, in statutory construction, is a useful rule, not an inexorable command. It seems preferable to overturn an established construction of an act of Congress, rather than, in the circumstances of this case, to interpret the Constitution. * * *

> ### It's Latin to Me!
>
> *Stare decisis* is Latin for "to stand by things decided" and refers to the judicially-created doctrine of adhering to precedent.

Points for Discussion

a. The Constitutional Discussion in *Erie*

What is the precise nature of the constitutional decision announced by Justice Brandeis in *Erie*? Although he disclaims that he is declaring the RDA itself to be unconstitutional, he does declare the rule of *Swift* to be unconstitutional, holding that it is unconstitutional for Congress or the federal courts "to declare substantive rules of common law applicable in a state." What constitutional provision or provisions are violated by federal judicial or congressional declarations of substantive rules of common law? Are there any constitutional provisions that can be read to authorize such declarations on the part of Congress or the federal courts?

> ### Food for Thought
>
> Was the constitutional discussion in *Erie* necessary or was it simply dicta? *See* Charles E. Clark, *State Law in the Federal Courts: The Brooding Omnipresence of* Erie v. Tompkins, 55 YALE L.J. 267, 278 (1946) ("[Brandeis's constitutional statement] has always puzzled commentators, who have been wont to consider the statement as dictum . . . . The opinion carefully refrains from terming the rules of decision act unconstitutional . . . .").

The concurring and dissenting Justices took Justice Brandeis to task for even reaching and resolving the constitutional question because it was not presented to the Court for consideration and argued before it. The concurring Justices also felt that the constitutional holding was not necessary to resolution of the case. Should either of these points have prevented Justice Brandeis from raising any constitutional concerns as he did? What considerations do you think prompted Justice Brandeis to reach the constitutional question over the dissenters' objections?

Keep in mind that the Court generally adheres to a practice of avoiding constitutional questions that are not necessary to resolution of a case. *Three Affiliated Tribes of Fort Berthold Reservation v. Wold Eng'g, P.C.*, 467 U.S. 138, 157 (1984) ("It is a fundamental rule of judicial restraint, however, that this Court will not reach constitutional questions in advance of the necessity of deciding them."). Under what circumstances should the Court reach and resolve constitutional questions that may be embedded within a case? Do you think the circumstances prior to *Erie* warranted resolution of the constitutional question presented by the facts of *Erie*?

b.   The Holding of *Erie*

Beyond its declaration that the approach of *Swift* was unconstitutional, what is the affirmative holding of *Erie*? In other words, if the Court rejected *Swift's* interpretation of the RDA as excluding state court common law decisions, what is the *Erie* Court's interpretation of the RDA? What are the potential implications of this interpretation?

Keep in mind that *Erie's* holding applies to non-federal claims being heard in federal court, which, as we learned in Chapter 3, can occur either through an exercise of diversity jurisdiction or supplemental jurisdiction. Thus, when federal question jurisdiction is the basis for hearing the claim, reference to the rule of *Erie* is unnecessary.

c.   The Rationale Behind *Erie*

What policy interests led the Court to overrule *Swift* and migrate to the new view of the RDA announced in *Erie*? Recall that the *Swift* Court was concerned with promoting national uniformity in the law and fostering the development of a national economy. What impact might the *Erie* decision have on those matters?

The *Erie* Court also mentions problems that arose under the *Swift* regime as an impetus behind rejecting the rule of that case. What were those problems and how does the rule of *Erie* overcome them?

—Perspective & Analysis—

Justice Brandeis described the manipulation of federal jurisdiction or forum shopping in order to bring one's case under a preferable set of common law legal rules as a major problem caused by the Swift regime. Some scholars have argued that this concern, which has come to dominate modern Erie jurisprudence, should not be the central policy concern that animates the doctrine:

> [A]nxious about its implications, the Roosevelt Court vigorously enforced its anti-forum-shopping interpretation of *Erie* while ignoring Brandeis's constitutional language . . . . In turning the Court away from *Erie's* constitutional foundation, [Justice] Frankfurter's role was pivotal. . . . By substituting a monolithic "anti-forum shopping" policy for the broader social concerns that had animated Brandeis, Frankfurter identified *Erie* with a practical purpose that was not only narrow but rigid and ultimately formalistic. [Frankfurter] focused the "*Erie* doctrine" on one type of forum shopping and on one particular goal. It thereby ignored the broader concerns with unfair and abusive litigation tactics that had engaged Brandeis and helped inform his thinking about *Swift* and diversity jurisdiction.

EDWARD A. PURCELL, JR., BRANDEIS AND THE PROGRESSIVE CONSTITUTION: *ERIE*, THE JUDICIAL POWER AND THE POLITICS OF THE FEDERAL COURTS IN TWENTIETH CENTURY AMERICA 202–16 (2000).

d. Substance Versus Procedure

The *Erie* Court indicated that Congress and the federal courts lack the authority to declare and impose "substantive" rules of common law applicable within the states. Does this leave the door open for federal lawmaking in the area of *procedural* rules that would govern such matters in federal diversity cases, even if federal courts cannot develop general substantive common law rules to apply in such cases? What does Justice Reed say about this issue in his opinion?

If *Erie* permits the application of federal procedural rules in diversity cases but not federal substantive common law rules, how does one draw the line distinguishing one from the other? Justice Reed states, "The line between procedural and substantive law is hazy." *Erie, 304 U.S. at 91* (Reed, J., concurring). Is the difference between substance and procedure a real distinction, or at least one that can be reasonably discerned?

e. Federal Common Law After *Erie*

In *Erie*, Justice Brandeis indicated, "There is no federal general common law." However, you should understand that there remains federal common law, which refers to federal decisional law in areas of national concern. This " 'new' federal common law addresses 'subjects within national legislative power where Congress has so directed' or where the basic scheme of the Constitution so demands." *Am. Elec. Power Co. v. Connecticut, 131 S. Ct. 2527, 2535 (2011)* (quoting Friendly, *In*

Praise of Erie—*And of the New Federal Common Law*, 39 N.Y.U. L. REV. 383, 383, 422 (1964)); *see also* <u>Maersk Inc. v. F & S Distrib. Co.</u>, No. CV 00-12168, 2001 WL 1875852, at *1 (C.D. Ca. Mar. 28, 2001) ("Federal common law exists where (1) necessary to protect federal proprietary interests in suits involving the United States or its officers, <u>Clearfield Trust Co. v. United States, 318 U.S. 363, 366–67 (1943)</u>; (2) Congress has given federal courts the power to develop substantive law, <u>Pilot Life Ins. Co. v. Dedeaux, 481 U.S. 41, 56 (1987)</u>; or (3) there is a significant conflict between some federal policy or interest and the use of state law, <u>O'Melveny & Myers v. FDIC, 512 U.S. 79, 82 (1994)</u>."). The Supreme Court has indicated that this power is exercised with reticence, adopting appropriate state law or waiting for Congress to speak on the matter. *Am. Elec. Power*, 131 S. Ct. at 2537 ("Absent a demonstrated need for a federal rule of decision, the Court has taken the prudent course of adopting the readymade body of state law as the federal rule of decision until Congress strikes a different accommodation." (citation and internal quotation marks omitted)).

Food for Thought

Does the Rules of Decision Act contemplate any kind of federal common law, general, "new," or otherwise? *See* Martin Redish, *The Federal Courts in the Political Order: Judicial Jurisdiction and American Political Theory* (1991) (arguing that the notion of substantive federal common law violates the Rules of Decision Act).

Examples of areas where federal common law applies include interstate disputes, *see* <u>Illinois v. Milwaukee, 406 U.S. 91, 103 (1972)</u> ("When we deal with air and water in their ambient or interstate aspects, there is a federal common law."); enforcement of collective-bargaining agreements under the Labor Management Relations Act, *see* <u>Textile Workers v. Lincoln Mills of Ala., 353 U.S. 448, 456 (1957)</u> (recognizing a federal common-law claim for breach of a CBA under the LMRA); maritime law, *see* <u>Yamaha Motor Corp., U.S.A. v. Calhoun, 516 U.S. 199 (1996)</u> (describing maritime law as "a species of judge-made federal common law"); the preclusive effect of federal court judgments, *see* <u>Semtek Int'l Inc. v. Lockheed Martin Corp., 531 U.S. 497, 507–08 (2001)</u> (holding that the preclusive effect of a federal-court judgment is determined by federal common law); and the law of international relations, *see* <u>In re Estate of Ferdinand E. Marcos Human Rights Litig., 978 F.2d 493, 502 (9th Cir. 1992)</u> ("It is . . . well settled that the law of nations is part of federal common law."); *see also* <u>Jumara v. State Farm Ins. Co., 55 F.3d 873, 877 (3d Cir. 1995)</u> ("Because questions of venue and the enforcement of forum-selection clauses are essentially procedural, rather than substantive, in nature, federal law applies in diversity cases irrespective of *Erie*.").

C. Development of the *Erie* Doctrine

The substance/procedure divide suggested in *Erie* turned out to form the heart of what courts would struggle with in the wake of *Erie* as they attempted to apply it to particular cases. That is, given *Erie*'s admonition to apply substantive state law— including state common law judicial decisions—to the resolution of non-federal claims being heard in federal court, courts had to identify whether a particular state legal rule was indeed "substantive" or "procedural."

For example, if a state legal rule required that a question be resolved by a judge but federal law indicated that resolution of the same issue must be by a jury, is that a procedural or substantive matter? Or to provide another example, if a claim is barred as untimely under state law but not under federal law, is that a substantive or procedural matter? The answers to these questions are important; if these are procedural matters then the state rules may be ignored, potentially leading to significantly different outcomes between cases brought in federal and state court.

Combine this difficulty with an additional wrinkle: 1938, the year that *Erie* was decided, was also the year in which the Federal Rules of Civil Procedure became effective. In light of *Erie*, would it be permissible to apply this new body of federal law (the Federal Rules) and other federal "procedural" law to the resolution of non-federal claims being heard in federal court?

In the line of cases that follow, the Supreme Court worked its way through these issues, trying to develop a principled approach to determining whether state legal rules were substantive or procedural and thus whether federal courts hearing non-federal claims were obliged to apply those rules.

Guaranty Trust Co. of New York v. York

Supreme Court of the United States
326 U.S. 99 (1945)

Mr. Justice Frankfurter delivered the opinion of the Court.

* * *

In May, 1930, Van Sweringen Corporation issued notes to the amount of $30,000,000. Under an indenture of the same date, petitioner, Guaranty Trust Co., was named trustee with power and obligations to enforce the rights of the noteholders in the assets of the Corporation and of the Van Sweringen brothers. In October, 1930, petitioner, with other banks, made large advances to companies affiliated with the Corporation and wholly controlled by the Van Sweringens. In October, 1931, when it was apparent that the Corporation could not meet its obligations, Guaranty co-operated in a plan for the purchase of the outstanding notes on the basis of cash for 50% of the face value of the notes and twenty shares of Van Sweringen Corporation's stock for each $1,000 note. This exchange offer remained open until December 15, 1931.

Respondent York received $6,000 of the notes as a gift in 1934, her donor not having accepted the offer of exchange. In April, 1940, three accepting noteholders began suit against petitioner, charging fraud and misrepresentation. Respondent's application to intervene in that suit was denied, and summary judgment in favor of Guaranty was affirmed. After her dismissal from [that] litigation, respondent * * * began the present proceedings.

Make the Connection

A *breach of trust* refers to a trustee's violation of its fiduciary duties, such as the duty of loyalty or the duty of candor. You can study fiduciary duties further in a **Corporations** course.

[This] suit, instituted as a class action on behalf of non-accepting noteholders and brought in a federal court solely because of diversity of citizenship, is based on an alleged breach of trust by Guaranty in that it failed to protect the interests of the noteholders in assenting to the exchange offer and failed to disclose its self-interest when sponsoring the offer. Petitioner moved for summary judgment, which was granted * * * . On appeal, the Circuit Court of Appeals * * * held that in a suit brought on the equity side of a federal district court that court is not required to apply the State statute of limitations that would govern like suits in the courts of a State where the federal court is sitting even though the exclusive basis of federal jurisdiction is diversity of citizenship. * * *

In view of the basis of the decision below, it is not for us to consider whether the New York statute would actually bar this suit were it brought in a State court. Our only concern is with the holding that the federal courts in a suit like this are not bound by local law.

What's That?

The *equity side* refers to when the federal court hears suits for remedies other than damages such as injunctions, specific performance, or imposition of a constructive trust.

We put to one side the considerations relevant in disposing of questions that arise when a federal court is adjudicating a claim based on a federal law. Our problem only touches transactions for which rights and obligations are created by one of the States, and for the assertion of which, in case of diversity of the citizenship of the parties, Congress has made a federal court another available forum.

Our starting point must be the policy of federal jurisdiction which *Erie R.R. Co. v. Tompkins,* 304 U.S. 64 (1938) embodies. In overruling *Swift v. Tyson, Erie* did not merely overrule a venerable case. It overruled a particular way of looking at law which dominated the judicial process long after its inadequacies had been laid bare. Law was conceived as a "brooding omnipresence" of Reason, of which decisions were merely evidence and not themselves the controlling formulations. Accordingly, federal courts deemed themselves free to ascertain what Reason, and therefore Law, required wholly independent of authoritatively declared State law, even in cases where a legal right as the basis for relief was created by State authority and could not be created by federal authority and the case got into a federal court merely because it was "between Citizens of different States" under Art. III, § 2 of the Constitution of the United States.

The reference to a "brooding omnipresence" is a quote from Justice Holmes in *Southern Pacific Co. v. Jensen,* 244 U.S. 205, 222 (1917) (Holmes, J., dissenting), in which he wrote, "The common law is not a brooding omnipresence in the sky, but the articulate voice of some sovereign or quasi sovereign that can be identified."

This impulse to freedom from the rules that controlled State courts regarding State-created rights was so strongly rooted in the prevailing views concerning the nature of law, that the federal courts almost imperceptibly were led to mutilating construction even of the explicit command given to them by Congress to apply State law in cases purporting to enforce the law of a State. See § 34 of the Judiciary Act of 1789, 1 Stat. 73 [the Rules of Decision Act]. * * *

Food for Thought

If the *Swift* interpretation of the Rules of Decision Act was such a "mutilating construction" of that statute, why did Congress acquiesce in the interpretation and not enact clarifying legislation as it has done in other instances where it felt that the Court's interpretation of a statute was mistaken?

* * *

In exercising their jurisdiction on the ground of diversity of citizenship, the federal courts, in the long course of their history, have not differentiated in their regard for State law between actions at law and suits in equity. Although § 34 of the Judiciary Act of 1789 directed that the "laws of the several States * * * shall be regarded as rules of decision in trials of common law * * *," this was deemed, consistently for over a hundred years, to be merely declaratory of what would in any event have governed the federal courts and therefore was equally applicable to equity suits.

What's That?

The *law side* refers to when the federal court hears actions at law seeking money damages as relief. This contrasts with the *equity side* as defined above. This distinction is a remnant of the separate court systems that handled each type of matter in England. The Federal Rules abolish this distinction in the federal system, but in many different areas the distinction still has an impact, such as determining whether one is entitled to a jury.

Indeed, it may fairly be said that the federal courts gave greater respect to State-created "substantive rights," in equity than they gave them on the law side, because rights at law were usually declared by State courts and as such increasingly flouted by extension of the doctrine of *Swift v. Tyson*, while rights in equity were frequently defined by legislative enactment and as such known and respected by the federal courts.

Partly because the States in the early days varied greatly in the manner in which equitable relief was afforded and in the extent to which it was available, Congress provided that "the forms and modes of proceeding in suits * * * of equity" would conform to the settled uses of courts of equity. Section 2, 1 Stat. 275. But this enactment gave the federal courts no power that they would not have had in any event when courts were given "cognizance," by the first Judiciary Act, of "equity." From the beginning there has been a good deal of talk in the cases that federal equity is a separate legal system. And so it is, properly understood. The suits in equity of which the federal courts have had "cognizance" ever since 1789 constituted the body of law which had been transplanted to this country from the English Court of Chancery. But this system of equity "derived its doctrines, as well as its powers, from its mode of giving relief." In giving federal courts "cognizance" of equity suits in cases of diversity jurisdiction, Congress never gave, nor did the federal courts ever claim, the power to deny substantive rights created by State law or to create substantive rights denied by State law.

This does not mean that whatever equitable remedy is available in a State court must be available in a diversity suit in a federal court, or conversely, that a federal court may not afford an equitable remedy not available in a State court. Equitable relief in a federal court is of course subject to restrictions: the suit must be within the traditional scope of equity as historically evolved in the English Court of Chancery; a plain, adequate and complete remedy at law must be wanting; explicit Congressional curtailment of equity powers must be respected; the constitutional right to trial by jury cannot be evaded, *Whitehead v. Shattuck*, 138 U.S. 146 (1891). That a State may authorize its courts to give equitable relief unhampered by any or all such restrictions cannot remove these fetters from the federal courts. State law cannot define the remedies which a federal court must give simply because a federal court in diversity jurisdiction is available as an alternative tribunal to the State's courts. Contrariwise, a federal court may afford an equitable remedy for a substantive right recognized by a State even though a State court cannot give it. Whatever contradiction or confusion may be produced by a medley of judicial phrases severed

Take Note!

The Court here is articulating the restrictions on equity jurisdiction in the federal courts. The preeminent restriction—that equity is unavailable when an adequate remedy exists at law (money damages)—is a direct transplant from English practice. The others—no equity in the face of Congressional curtailment and no evasion of the jury right—are restrictions unique to the American system.

from their environment, the body of adjudications concerning equitable relief in diversity cases leaves no doubt that the federal courts enforced State-created substantive rights if the mode of proceeding and remedy were consonant with the traditional body of equitable remedies, practice and procedure, and in so doing they were enforcing rights created by the States and not arising under any inherent or statutory federal law.

* * *

And so this case reduces itself to the narrow question whether, when no recovery could be had in a State court because the action is barred by the statute of limitations, a federal court in equity can take cognizance of the suit because there is diversity of citizenship between the parties. Is the outlawry, according to State law, of a claim created by the States a matter of "substantive rights" to be respected by a federal court of equity when that court's jurisdiction is dependent on the fact that there is a State-created right, or is such statute of "a mere remedial character," which a federal court may disregard?

Matters of "substance" and matters of "procedure" are much talked about in the books as though they defined a great divide cutting across the whole domain of law. But, of course, "substance" and "procedure" are the same keywords to very different problems. Neither "substance" nor "procedure" represents the same invariants. Each implies different variables depending upon the particular problem for which it is used. And the different problems are only distantly related at best, for the terms are in common use in connection with situations turning on such different considerations as those that are relevant to questions pertaining to *ex post facto* legislation, the impairment of the obligations of contract, the enforcement of federal rights in the State courts and the multitudinous phases of the conflict of laws.

Here we are dealing with a right to recover derived not from the United States but from one of the States. When, because the plaintiff happens to be a nonresident,

Take Note!

The Court states that federal courts sitting in diversity are "only another court of the State." Is this a fair characterization of the status of federal courts when they hear diversity claims?

such a right is enforceable in a federal as well as in a State court, the forms and mode of enforcing the right may at times, naturally enough, vary because the two judicial systems are not identic. But since a federal court adjudicating a state-created right solely because of the diversity of citizenship of the parties is for that purpose, in effect, only another court of the State, it cannot afford recovery if the right to

recover is made unavailable by the State nor can it substantially affect the enforcement of the right as given by the State.

And so the question is not whether a statute of limitations is deemed a matter of "procedure" in some sense. The question is whether such a statute concerns merely the manner and the means by which a right to recover, as recognized by the State, is enforced, or whether such statutory limitation is a matter of substance in the aspect that alone is relevant to our problem, namely, does it significantly affect the result of a litigation for a federal court to disregard a law of a State that would be controlling in an action upon the same claim by the same parties in a State court?

It is therefore immaterial whether statutes of limitation are characterized either as "substantive" or "procedural" in State court opinions in any use of those terms unrelated to the specific issue before us. *Erie R.R. Co. v. Tompkins* was not an endeavor to formulate scientific legal terminology. It expressed a policy that touches vitally the proper distribution of judicial power between State and federal courts. In essence, the intent of that decision was to insure that, in all cases where a federal court is exercising jurisdiction solely because of the diversity of citizenship of the parties, the outcome of the litigation in the federal court should be substantially the same, so far as legal rules determine the outcome of a litigation, as it would be if tried in a State court. The nub of the policy that underlies *Erie R.R. Co. v. Tompkins* is that for the same transaction the accident of a suit by a non-resident litigant in a federal court instead of in a State court a block away, should not lead to a substantially different result. And so, putting to one side abstractions regarding "substance" and "procedure," we have held that in diversity cases the federal courts must follow the law of the State as to burden of proof, as to conflict of laws, and as to contributory negligence. *Erie R.R. Co. v. Tompkins* has been applied with an eye alert to essentials in avoiding disregard of State law in diversity cases in the federal courts. A policy so important to our federalism must be kept free from entanglements with analytical or terminological niceties.

Plainly enough, a statute that would completely bar recovery in a suit if brought in a State court bears on a State-created right vitally and not merely formally or negligibly. As to consequences that so intimately affect recovery or non-recovery a federal court in a diversity case should follow State law. * * *

Food for Thought

The Court here seems to minimize the importance of the substance/procedure divide in aiding in the determination of whether a federal court must follow state legal rules in diversity cases. What approach does the Court offer in its place? Is the Court's view here properly rooted in *Erie* or is it an innovation?

* * *

To make an exception to *Erie R.R. Co. v. Tompkins* on the equity side of a federal court is to reject the considerations of policy which, after long travail, led to that decision. Judge Augustus N. Hand thus summarized below the fatal objection to such inroad upon *Erie R.R. Co. v. Tompkins*: "In my opinion it would be a mischievous practice to disregard state statutes of limitation whenever federal courts think that the result of adopting them may be inequitable. Such procedure would promote the choice of United States rather than of state courts in order to gain the advantage of different laws. The main foundation for the criticism of *Swift v. Tyson* was that a litigant in cases where federal jurisdiction is based only on diverse citizenship may obtain a more favorable decision by suing in the United States courts."

Diversity jurisdiction is founded on assurance to non-resident litigants of courts free from susceptibility to potential local bias. The Framers of the Constitution, according to Marshall, entertained "apprehensions" lest distant suitors be subjected to local bias in State courts, or, at least, viewed with "indulgence the possible fears and apprehensions" of such suitors. *Bank of U.S. v. Deveaux*, 9 U.S. 61, 87 (1809) (Marshall, C.J.). And so Congress afforded out-of-state litigants another tribunal, not another body of law. The operation of a double system of conflicting laws in the same State is plainly hostile to the reign of law. Certainly, the fortuitous circumstance of residence out of a State of one of the parties to a litigation ought not to give rise to a discrimination against others equally concerned but locally resident. The source of substantive rights enforced by a federal court under diversity jurisdiction, it cannot be said too often, is the law of the States. Whenever that law is authoritatively declared by a State, whether its voice be the legislature or its highest court, such law ought to govern in litigation founded on that law, whether the forum of application is a State or a federal court and whether the remedies be sought at law or may be had in equity.

* * *

The judgment is reversed and the case is remanded for proceedings not inconsistent with this opinion.

So ordered.

MR. JUSTICE ROBERTS and MR. JUSTICE DOUGLAS took no part in the consideration or decision of this case.

MR. JUSTICE RUTLEDGE [joined by MR. JUSTICE MURPHY]

I dissent. If the policy of judicial conservatism were to be followed in this case, which forbids deciding constitutional and other important questions hypothetically or prematurely, I would favor remanding the cause to the Court of Appeals for determination of the narrow and comparatively minor question whether, under the applicable local law, the cause of action has been barred by lapse of time. That question has not been decided, may be determined in respondent's favor, and in that event the important question affecting federal judicial power now resolved, in a manner contrary to all prior decision here, will have been determined without substantial ultimate effect upon the litigation.

But the Court conceives itself confronted with the necessity for making that determination and in doing so overturns a rule of decision which has prevailed in the federal courts from almost the beginning. I am unable to assent to that decision * * *. One may give full adherence to the rule of *Erie R.R. Co. v. Tompkins*, and its extension to cases in equity in so far as they affect clearly substantive rights, without conceding or assuming that the long tradition, both federal and state, which regards statutes of limitations as falling within the category of remedial rather than substantive law, necessarily must be ruled in the same way; and without conceding further that only a different jurisprudential climate or a kind of "brooding omnipresence in the sky" has dictated the hitherto unvaried policy of the federal courts in their general attitude toward the strict application of local statutes of limitations in equity causes.

Food for Thought

Where does "remedial" fit within the substance/procedure divide? Justice Rutledge seems to treat legal rules pertaining to remedies as non-substantive, thus suggesting for him that the rule of *Erie* should not apply to such rules. Are legal rules of a remedial nature within the category of legal rules that *Erie* obligates federal courts to follow in diversity cases, or is the majority here saying that it is not the label for the rule that matters? If the latter is the case, what then is the majority saying matters in determining whether a state legal rule must be followed?

If any characteristic of equity jurisprudence has descended unbrokenly from * * * "the traditional scope of equity as historically evolved in the English Court of Chancery," it is that statutes of limitations * * * have never been deemed to be rigidly applicable as absolute barriers to suits in equity as they are to actions at law. * * *

Moreover, the decision of today does not in so many words rule that Congress could not authorize the federal courts to administer equitable relief in accordance with the substantive rights of the parties, notwithstanding state courts had been forbidden by local statutes of limitations to do so. Nevertheless the implication to that effect seems strong, in view of the reliance upon *Erie R.R. Co. v. Tompkins*. In any event, the question looms more largely in the issues than the Court's opinion appears to make it. For if legislative acquiescence in long-established judicial construction can make it part of a statute, it has done so in this instance. More is at stake in the implications of the decision, if not in the words of the opinion, than simply bringing federal and local law into accord upon matters clearly and exclusively within the constitutional power of the state to determine. It is one thing to require that kind of an accord in diversity cases when the question is merely whether the federal court must follow the law of the state as to burden of proof, contributory negligence, or perhaps in application of the so-called parol evidence rule. These ordinarily involve matters of substantive law, though nominated in terms of procedure. But in some instances their application may lie along the border between procedure or remedy and substance, where the one may or may not be in fact but another name for the other. It is exactly in this borderland, where procedural or remedial rights may or may not have the effect of determining the substantive ones completely, that caution is required in extending the rule of the *Erie* case by the very rule itself.

The words "substantive" and "procedural" or "remedial" are not talismanic. Merely calling a legal question by one or the other does not resolve it otherwise than as a purely authoritarian performance. But they have come to designate in a broad way large and distinctive legal domains within the greater one of the law and to mark, though often indistinctly or with overlapping limits, many divides between such regions.

* * * The large division between adjective law and substantive law still remains, to divide the power of Congress from that of the states and consequently to determine the power of the federal courts to apply federal law or state law in diversity matters.

What's That?

Adjective law is simply a term used during this time in the 20th century to describe procedural law.

This division, like others drawn by the broad allocation of adjective or remedial and substantive, has areas of admixture of these two aspects of the law. In these areas whether a particular situation or issue presents one aspect or the other depends upon how one looks at the matter. * * *

Whenever this integration or admixture prevails in a substantial measure, so that a clean break cannot be made, there is danger either of nullifying the power of Congress to control not only how the federal courts may act, but what they may do by way of affording remedies, or of usurping that function, if the *Erie* doctrine is to be expended judicially to include such situations to the utmost extent.

It may be true that if the matter were wholly fresh the barring of rights in equity by statutes of limitation would seem to partake more of the substantive than of the remedial phase of law. But the matter is not fresh and it is not without room for debate. A long tradition, in the states and here, as well as in the common law which antedated both state and federal law, has emphasized the remedial character of statutes of limitations, more especially in application to equity causes, on many kinds of issues requiring differentiation of such matters from more clearly and exclusively substantive ones. * * * The tradition now in question is equally long and unvaried. I cannot say the tradition is clearly wrong in this case more than in that. Nor can I say, as was said in the *Erie* case, that the matter is beyond the power of Congress to control. If that be conceded, I think Congress should make the change if it is to be made. The *Erie* decision was rendered in 1938. Seven years have passed without action by Congress to extend the rule to these matters. That is long enough to justify the conclusion that Congress also regards them as not governed by *Erie* and as wishing to make no change. This should be reason enough for leaving the matter at rest until it decides to act.

* * *

Applicable statutes of limitations in state tribunals are not always the ones which would apply if suit were instituted in the courts of the state which creates the substantive rights for which enforcement is sought. The state of the forum is free to apply its own period of limitations, regardless of whether the state originating the right has barred suit upon it. Whether or not the action will be held to be barred depends therefore not upon the law of the state which creates the substantive right, but upon the law of the state where suit may be brought. This in turn will depend upon where it may be possible to secure service of process, and thus jurisdiction of the person of the defendant. It may be therefore that because of the plaintiff's inability to find the defendant in the jurisdiction which creates his substantive right, he will be foreclosed of remedy by the sheer necessity of going to the haven of refuge within which the defendant confines its "presence" for jurisdictional purposes. The law of the latter may bar the suit even though suit still would be allowed under the law of the state creating the substantive right.

It is not clear whether today's decision puts it into the power of corporate trustees, by confining their jurisdictional "presence" to states which allow their courts to give equitable remedies only within short periods of time, to defeat the purpose and intent of the law of the state creating the substantive right. If so, the "right" remains alive, with full-fledged remedy, by the law of its origin, and because enforcement must be had in

Food for Thought

Does Justice Rutledge have a valid point when he claims that it is not fair for states to be able to block a federal court's enforcement of rights created elsewhere and that diversity jurisdiction should be seen in part as being made available to prevent this type of unfairness from arising?

another state, which affords refuge against it, the remedy and with it the right are nullified. I doubt that the Constitution of the United States requires this or that the Judiciary Acts permit it. A good case can be made, indeed has been made, that the diversity jurisdiction was created to afford protection against exactly this sort of nullifying state legislation.

Points for Discussion

a. *York*'s Contribution to the *Erie* Doctrine

What are the precise contours of the *Erie* doctrine after *York*? *Erie* had instructed federal courts to follow the common law decisions of state courts in diversity cases and indicated that federal courts could not formulate and impose federal substantive legal rules in such cases. What more is *York* saying about what state legal rules federal courts sitting in diversity are bound to apply? How did the majority reach its conclusion that the federal court was obliged to adhere to the forum state's statute of limitations in this case? What guidance did the Court give for how to determine whether federal or state legal rules must be followed in future cases?

The *York* Court indicates that it does not like the fact that ignoring the state legal rule at issue here—the statute-of-limitations period—would lead to different outcomes in state versus federal court. Why is that a problem? Don't all legal rules have the potential to impact the outcome of a case? If so, does a concern with avoiding different outcomes provide good guidance for evaluating whether a certain state law should be applied by a federal court sitting in diversity?

b. Substance Versus Procedure After *York*

There was much discussion in the majority opinion and in Justice Rutledge's dissent regarding the divide between substance and procedure and whether or to what extent such characterizations of legal rules were relevant to the determination of whether certain state rules were binding on federal courts sitting in diversity. What did the Court and the dissent have to say about this issue? Are these labels considered relevant or at least helpful in an *Erie* analysis in the eyes of Justice Frankfurter, author of the Court's opinion in *York*? Should these categories be so considered or should they be discarded as useless given the inability to characterize many legal rules as either one or the other? See *Perspective & Analysis* below.

—Perspective & Analysis—

Many legal rules are not readily classifiable as either "substantive" or "procedural." Statutes of limitations, the type of legal rule involved in *York*, provides a good example of this difficulty:

> Limitations law is famously a body of rules that are neither grass nor hay, being at once both substantive and procedural. In one sense, limitations law is clearly procedural—a sibling or at least a cousin to summary judgment. It is a means of clearing dockets, of protecting both the court and the defendant from waste, and of protecting the defendant from the unjust coercion that can result simply from the threat of waste. . . .

> In another sense, however, limitations law is substantive. Repose is a social and political value with economic consequences. Limitations law is thus a means of healing and stabilizing relationships. It reduces the general level of stress and anxiety, protecting even plaintiffs from the self-injuries that result when resentments are nourished for too long. . . . To the extent that these considerations are paramount, limitations law can be characterized as substantive.

Paul D. Carrington, *"Substance" and "Procedure" in the Rules Enabling Act,* 1989 DUKE L.J. 281, 290.

c. Law Versus Equity and the *York* Decision

A central issue in *York* was whether the RDA obligated federal courts to follow state legal rules when they considered matters on their equity side. As explained earlier, historically, when plaintiffs sought remedies besides money damages, the action was one in equity. Different rules inherited from English courts govern equitable actions and one of these rules is that statutes-of-limitations periods do not apply to equitable claims. Rather, the doctrine of laches applies, which permits courts to determine whether in their judgment the plaintiff asserted its claim in a timely fashion. Thus, in *York*—an equitable proceeding—whether the state's statute of limitations had to be applied in the federal court was a big deal. Was the Court right to hold that federal courts were bound to follow the forum state's practice of imposing its statute-of-limitations period on equitable actions, even though that was contrary to traditional principles of equity?

d. The Role of Federalism in *York*

The majority opinion also focused on the relationship between federal courts sitting in diversity and their host states, indicating that federal courts are simply state courts in federal garb when hearing diversity claims. Is this a fair characterization? How does this view of federal courts sitting in diversity impact Justice Frankfurter's analysis of whether the federal court is bound to follow the forum state's statute-of-limitations rule?

Principles of federalism generally derive from the constitutional arrangement whereby states delegated limited powers to the federal government and reserved the rest for themselves. Under this arrangement, if a matter is within the sphere of authority reserved to the states and not delegated to the federal government, federal efforts to act in this area are viewed as an affront to federalism. What legitimate federalism concerns suggest that federal courts, when hearing diversity claims, must strive to achieve outcomes that would mirror those that would be reached in state courts hearing the same claims? Do any legitimate federalism concerns similarly prohibit Congress from legislating, if it so chose, to enable federal courts to ignore state legal rules of the kind the *York* Court suggests federal courts must follow? For example, could Congress constitutionally amend the RDA to empower federal courts to disregard forum states' statute-of-limitations laws in instances where application of the limitations law would yield inequitable results?

e. The Impact of *York* on the Litigants in the Case

What was the impact of the Court's decision in *York* on the claims being asserted by the plaintiffs in the case? Is that a fair result? Justice Rutledge points out in his dissent that it is not fair for litigants and the federal court to be bound by the statute-of-limitations rule of the forum state when that state is not necessarily the one in which the rights at issue were created and is simply the place where the plaintiffs were able to obtain personal jurisdiction over the defendant. Do you agree with this perspective?

f. Applying *York*

Four years after *York*, the Supreme Court decided a group of three *Erie* doctrine cases all on the same day. In brief, their holdings were as follows:

Table 5.1

Case Name	Holding
Ragan v. Merchs. Transfer & Warehouse Co., 337 U.S. 530 (1949) [*FLEX* Case 5.A]	Kansas state law (commencement of an action upon service), not Federal Rule 3 (commencement upon filing of complaint), determines the time of commencement of an action for purposes of determining when the statute-of-limitations period is tolled (stops running).
Woods v. Interstate Realty Co., 337 U.S. 535 (1949)	Mississippi state rule barring unqualified businesses from the right to appear in state court governs and prevents an unqualified business from appearing in a federal diversity action in that state.
Cohen v. Beneficial Indus. Loan Corp., 337 U.S. 541 (1949)	New Jersey state rule requiring a bond in shareholder derivative suits governs notwithstanding a provision of then-Federal Rule 23 (now Rule 23.1), which does not require a bond.

How do the holdings of these cases conform to the holding of *York*? Two of these cases involved Federal Rules of Civil Procedure. Do *York* and the cases noted above suggest the inapplicability of the Federal Rules in federal diversity cases?

Although fealty to state legal rules appeared to be at its peak in the wake of this 1949 trio, the case that follows saw the Court take a seemingly sharp turn in the direction of favoring federal over state legal rules and shows the Court apparently recasting the *Erie* doctrine in the process.

Byrd v. Blue Ridge Rural Electric Cooperative, Inc.

Supreme Court of the United States
356 U.S. 525 (1958)

MR. JUSTICE BRENNAN delivered the opinion of the Court.

This case was brought in the District Court for the Western District of South Carolina. Jurisdiction was based on diversity of citizenship. The petitioner, a resident of North Carolina, sued respondent, a South Carolina corporation, for damages for injuries allegedly caused by the respondent's negligence. He had judgment on a jury verdict. The Court of Appeals for the Fourth Circuit reversed and directed the entry of judgment for the respondent. * * *

From 1911 until 1961, the United States District Court for the District of South Carolina was divided into the United States District Courts for the Eastern and Western Districts of South Carolina.

The respondent is in the business of selling electric power to subscribers in rural sections of South Carolina. The petitioner was employed as a lineman in the construction crew of a construction contractor. The contractor, R. H. Bouligny, Inc., held a contract with the respondent in the amount of $334,300 for the building of some 24 miles of new power lines, the reconversion to higher capacities of about 88 miles of existing lines, and the construction of two new substations and a breaker station. The petitioner was injured while connecting power lines to one of the new substations.

One of respondent's affirmative defenses was that under the South Carolina Workmen's Compensation Act, the petitioner—because the work contracted to be done by his employer was work of the kind also done by the respondent's own construction and maintenance crews—had the status of a statutory employee of the respondent and was therefore barred from suing the respondent at law because [sic] obliged to accept statutory compensation benefits as the exclusive remedy for his injuries. Two questions concerning this defense are before us: (1) whether the Court of Appeals erred in directing judgment for respondent without a remand to give petitioner an opportunity to introduce further evidence; and (2) whether petitioner, state practice notwithstanding, is entitled to a jury determination of the factual issues raised by this defense. * * *

What's That?

Workers' Compensation Acts are state statutes that set up a system of fixed awards for employees who suffer employment-related injuries and serve as a mandatory substitute for proceeding with a lawsuit on such injuries in court.

[On the first issue, the Supreme Court held that the Court of Appeals did err in failing to remand the case in order to permit petitioner the opportunity to introduce further evidence regarding whether the respondent was a statutory employee.]

II.

A question is also presented as to whether on remand the factual issue is to be decided by the judge or by the jury. The respondent argues on the basis of the decision of the Supreme Court of South Carolina in *Adams v. Davison-Paxon Co.*, 230 S.C. 532, 96 S.E.2d 566 (1957), that the issue of immunity should be decided by the judge and not by the jury. That was a negligence action brought in the state trial court against a store owner by an employee of an independent contractor who operated the store's millinery department. The trial judge denied the store owner's motion for a directed verdict made upon the ground that § 72–111 [of the South Carolina Code] barred the plaintiff's action. The jury returned a verdict for the plaintiff. The South Carolina Supreme Court reversed, holding that it was for the judge and not the jury to decide on the evidence whether the owner was a statutory employer, and that the store owner had sustained his defense. * * *

* * *

The respondent argues that this state-court decision governs the present diversity case and "divests the jury of its normal function" to decide the disputed fact question of the respondent's immunity under § 72–111. This is to contend that the federal court is bound under *Erie R.R. Co. v. Tompkins*, to follow the state court's holding to secure uniform enforcement of the immunity created by the State.

First. It was decided in *Erie R.R. Co. v. Tompkins* that the federal courts in diversity cases must respect the definition of state-created rights and obligations by the state courts. We must, therefore, first examine the rule in *Adams v. Davison-Paxon Co.* to determine whether it is bound up with these rights and obligations in such a way that its application in the federal court is required.

The Workmen's Compensation Act is administered in South Carolina by its Industrial Commission. The South Carolina courts hold that, on judicial review of actions of the Commission under § 72–111, the question whether the claim of an injured workman is within the Commission's jurisdiction is a matter of law for decision by the court, which makes its own findings of fact relating to that jurisdiction. The South Carolina Supreme Court states no reasons in *Adams v. Davison-Paxon Co.* why, although the jury decides all other factual issues raised by the cause of action and defenses, the jury is displaced as to the factual issue raised by the affirmative defense under § 72–111. * * * A State may, of course, distribute the functions of its judicial machinery as it sees fit. The decisions relied upon, however, furnish no reason for selecting the judge rather than the jury to decide this single affirmative defense in the negligence action. They simply reflect a policy that administrative determination of "jurisdictional facts" should not be final but subject to judicial review. The conclusion is inescapable that the *Adams* holding is grounded in the practical consideration that the question had theretofore come before the South Carolina courts from the Industrial Commission and the courts had become accustomed to deciding the factual issue of immunity without the aid of juries. We find nothing to suggest that this rule was announced as an integral part of the special relationship created by the statute. Thus the requirement appears to be merely a form and mode of enforcing the immunity, *Guaranty Trust Co. of New York v. York*, 326 U.S. 99, 108 (1945), and not a rule intended to be bound up with the definition of the rights and obligations of the parties. * * *

Second. But cases following *Erie* have evinced a broader policy to the effect that the federal courts should conform as near as may be—in the absence of other considerations—to state rules even of form and mode where the state rules may bear substantially on the question whether the litigation would come out one way in the federal court and another way in the state court if the federal court failed to apply a particular local rule. *E.g., York.* Concededly the nature of the tribunal which tries issues may be important in the enforcement of the parcel of rights making up a cause of action or defense, and bear significantly upon achievement of uniform enforcement of the right. It may well be that in the instant personal-injury case the outcome would be substantially affected by whether the issue of immunity is decided by a judge or a jury. Therefore, were "outcome" the only consideration, a strong case might appear for saying that the federal court should follow the state practice.

But there are affirmative countervailing considerations at work here. The federal system is an independent system for administering justice to litigants who properly invoke its jurisdiction. An essential characteristic of that system is the manner in which, in civil common-law actions, it distributes trial functions between judge and jury and, under the influence—if not the command—of the Seventh Amendment, assigns the decisions of disputed questions of fact to the jury. The policy of uniform enforcement of state-created rights and obligations, see, e.g., *Guaranty Trust Co. of New York v. York, supra*, cannot in every case exact compliance with a state rule—not bound up with rights and obligations—which disrupts the federal system of allocating functions between judge and jury. *Herron v. Southern Pacific Co., 283 U.S. 91 (1931)*. Thus the inquiry here is whether the federal policy favoring jury decisions of disputed fact questions should yield to the state rule in the interest of furthering the objective that the litigation should not come out one way in the federal court and another way in the state court.

We think that in the circumstances of this case the federal court should not follow the state rule. It cannot be gainsaid that there is a strong federal policy against allowing state rules to disrupt the judge-jury relationship in the federal courts. In *Herron v. Southern Pacific Co., supra*, the trial judge in a personal-injury negligence action brought in the District Court for Arizona on diversity grounds directed a verdict for the defendant when it appeared as a matter of law that the plaintiff was guilty of contributory negligence. The federal judge refused to be bound by a provision of the Arizona Constitution which made the jury the sole arbiter of the question of contributory negligence. This Court sustained the action of the trial judge, holding

What's That?

A *directed verdict* involves the trial judge ordering the entry of a verdict without letting the jury decide because one party has failed to prove its case as a matter of law. The equivalent in the federal system, a judgment as a matter of law, is governed by Rule 50(a) and will be covered in Chapter 10.

that "state laws cannot alter the essential character or function of a federal court" because that function "is not in any sense a local matter, and state statutes which

> **FYI**
>
> The *Conformity Act of 1872* was a federal statute that instructed federal district courts to follow the procedural rules of the states in which they were located in all non-equity, non-admiralty civil causes. The Conformity Act is no longer effective in the wake of the 1938 adoption of the Federal Rules of Civil Procedure.

would interfere with the appropriate performance of that function are not binding upon the federal court under either the Conformity Act or the 'Rules of Decision' Act." Perhaps even more clearly in light of the influence of the Seventh Amendment, the function assigned to the jury "is an essential factor in the process for which the Federal Constitution provides." Concededly the *Herron* case was decided before *Erie R.R. Co. v. Tompkins*, but even when *Swift v. Tyson* was governing law and allowed federal courts sitting in diversity cases to disregard state decisional law, it was never thought that state statutes or constitutions were similarly to be disregarded. Yet *Herron* held that state statutes and constitutional provisions could not disrupt or alter the essential character or function of a federal court.

Third. We have discussed the problem upon the assumption that the outcome of the litigation may be substantially affected by whether the issue of immunity is decided by a judge or a jury. But clearly there is not present here the certainty that a different result would follow, or even the strong possibility that this would be the case. There are factors present here which might reduce that possibility. The trial judge in the federal system has powers denied the judges of many States to comment on the weight of evidence and credibility of witnesses, and discretion to grant a new trial if the verdict appears to him to be against the weight of the evidence. We do not think the likelihood of a different result is so strong as to require the federal practice of jury determination of disputed factual issues to yield to the state rule in the interest of uniformity of outcome.

* * *

Reversed and remanded.

MR. JUSTICE WHITTAKER, concurring in part and dissenting in part.

* * *

Inasmuch as the law of South Carolina, as construed by its highest court, requires its courts—not juries—to determine whether jurisdic-

> **FYI**
>
> Justice Whittaker served as an Associate Justice of the U.S. Supreme Court for only five years, reportedly suffering a nervous breakdown that led to his retirement from the bench. His appointment to the Supreme Court made him the first person to serve as a judge of a U.S. District Court, a U.S. Court of Appeals, and the U.S. Supreme Court.

tion over the subject matter of cases like this is vested in its Industrial Commission, and inasmuch as the Court's opinion concedes "that in the instant personal-injury case the outcome would be substantially affected by whether the issue of immunity is decided by a judge or a jury," it follows that in this diversity case the jurisdictional issue must be determined by the judge—not by the jury. Insofar as the Court holds that the question of jurisdiction should be determined by the jury, I think the Court departs from its past decisions. I therefore respectfully dissent from part II of the opinion of the Court.

[The dissenting opinions of MR. JUSTICE FRANKFURTER and MR. JUSTICE HARLAN are omitted.]

Points for Discussion

a. *Erie* Doctrine After *Byrd*

What approach did the Court in *Byrd* take to determine whether the federal court had to follow the state rule requiring that the factual question at issue in the case must be resolved by a judge rather than a jury? How did the *Byrd* Court integrate the approach of *York* in its analysis, if at all? Is *Byrd* consistent with *York*? How would you describe the two approaches for determining whether to follow state law exhibited in *Byrd* and *York*?

Justice Brennan seemed to be comparing the interests of the state in its "judge decides" rule with the interests of the federal government in its policy favoring jury resolution of factual disputes. What role does this balancing of interests play in his analysis and in leading him to the outcome he reaches in this case? How are federal courts to discern whether a state has a strong interest in application of its legal rule to the matter at hand? Did Justice Brennan do a good job of assessing South Carolina's interest in its rule? Is there any principled way to do this so that the analysis is predictable, uniform, and not simply open to manipulation according to the result desired by the judges engaged in the analysis?

b. Impact of the Seventh Amendment

Did Justice Brennan determine that a jury had to resolve the fact issue here because such a result was compelled by the Seventh Amendment? If not, what did he mean when he wrote that "the influence—if not the command—of the Seventh Amendment, assigns the decisions of disputed questions of fact to the jury"? *Byrd*, 356 U.S. at 537. How does the "influence" of the Seventh Amendment factor into Justice Brennan's analysis?

c.   **Substance Versus Procedure After *Byrd***

Did the familiar substance/procedure divide play a role in the outcome in this case? Justice Brennan's statement that "the [South Carolina judicial determination] requirement appears to be merely a form and mode of enforcing the immunity, and not a rule intended to be bound up with the definition of the rights and obligations of the parties" indicates his view that the South Carolina rule was more procedural ("form and mode") than substantive ("the definition of the rights and obligations of the parties"). Byrd, 356 U.S. at 536. Do you agree with this characterization? What role did this assessment play in Justice Brennan's analysis?

D. The Rules Enabling Act and Modern *Erie* Doctrine

The Court's *Erie* decisions up to this point were not a model of clarity and coherence, to say the least. The *Erie* Court said that the substance/procedure dichotomy mattered, but the *York* Court said achieving similar outcomes—not categorizing a legal rule as substantive versus procedural—is what really mattered in the analysis. The Court in *Byrd* offered a third view: The possibility of different outcomes between state and federal court does not matter as much as the importance of the policies underlying the competing legal rules under consideration. Fair enough, but how were courts to apply that approach in any consistent and predictable fashion without allowing their own subjective views of these interests to creep into the analysis?

To this confusion, add the lingering question of the relationship between *Erie* and the Federal Rules of Civil Procedure. Recall that the Court in two cases— Ragan v. Merchants Transfer & Warehouse Co., 337 U.S. 530 (1949) [FLEX Case 5.A], and Cohen v. Beneficial Industrial Loan Corp., 337 U.S. 541 (1949)—favored application of state rules over seemingly applicable Federal Rules. Although *Erie* seemed to confine itself to requiring adherence to state substantive rules, *Ragan* and *Cohen* at least suggested that the *Erie* doctrine had evolved to prohibit application of the Federal Rules of Civil Procedure in the face of a conflicting state practice.

But these cases did not provide the entire picture. First, it is important to note that the Federal Rules were enacted pursuant to authority conferred by the Rules Enabling Act ("REA"), a federal statute that was originally enacted in 1934 and is presently codified at 28 U.S.C. § 2072. The text of the REA reads as follows:

The Rules Enabling Act: 28 U.S.C. § 2072

(a)   The Supreme Court shall have the power to prescribe general rules of practice and procedure and rules of evidence for cases in the United States district courts (including proceedings before magistrate judges thereof) and courts of appeals.

(b)   Such rules shall not abridge, enlarge or modify any substantive right. All laws in conflict with such rules shall be of no further force or effect after such rules have taken effect.

* * *

Thus, the Federal Rules of Civil Procedure are the direct product of a statutorily-authorized rulemaking process, a fact that should empower the federal district courts to follow these rules in all cases, including those based on diversity jurisdiction.

Second, the Supreme Court upheld the validity of the REA and the applicability of the Federal Rules in diversity cases in *Sibbach v. Wilson & Co.,* 312 U.S. 1 (1941) [*FLEX* Case 5.B]—a post-*Erie* case—without citing to *Erie* at all. *See Sibbach,* 312 U.S. at 9–10 ("Congress has undoubted power to regulate the practice and procedure of federal courts, and may exercise that power by delegating to this or other federal courts authority to make rules not inconsistent with the statutes or Constitution of the United States . . . ."). In *Sibbach,* the Court held that Rule 35, which permits courts to order plaintiffs to submit to a physical examination, could be applied in a diversity action in Illinois federal court, even though the courts of Illinois had held that such orders could not be made (Indiana, the state in which the alleged tort had occurred, did authorize such orders, a fact that figured into the Court's willingness to favor the application of Rule 35 in this case).

How can *Sibbach*—which upheld the application of a Federal Rule in the face of a seemingly conflicting state practice—be reconciled with *Ragan* and *Cohen*—which favored state rules over certain Federal Rules of Civil Procedure—or with *York's* outcome-determinative approach? The next case, *Hanna v. Plumer,* resolved much of this confusion by deftly reconciling all of these disparate opinions and giving the *Erie* doctrine the more (but not completely) coherent shape it enjoys today.

Hanna v. Plumer

Supreme Court of the United States
380 U.S. 460 (1965)

Mr. Chief Justice Warren delivered the opinion of the Court.

The question to be decided is whether, in a civil action where the jurisdiction of the United States district court is based upon diversity of citizenship between the parties, service of process shall be made in the manner prescribed by state law or that set forth in Rule 4(d)(1)* of the Federal Rules of Civil Procedure.

On February 6, 1963, petitioner, a citizen of Ohio, filed her complaint in the District Court for the District of Massachusetts, claiming damages in excess of $10,000 for personal injuries resulting from an automobile accident in South Carolina, allegedly caused by the negligence of one Louise Plumer Osgood, a Massachusetts citizen deceased at the time of the filing of the complaint. Respondent, Mrs. Osgood's executor and also a Massachusetts citizen, was named as defendant. On February 8, service was made by leaving copies of the summons and the complaint with respondent's wife at his residence, concededly in compliance with Rule 4(d)(1), which provides:

> * * * Service shall be made as follows:

> (1) Upon an individual other than an infant or an incompetent person, by delivering a copy of the summons and of the complaint to him personally or by leaving copies thereof at his dwelling house or usual place of abode with some person of suitable age and discretion then residing therein * * *.

FYI

The terms *infant* and *incompetent* here do not have their ordinary meaning but rather are legal terms that refer to minors and those officially judged to be mentally incapacitated, respectively.

Respondent filed his answer on February 26, alleging, *inter alia*, that the action could not be maintained because it had been brought "contrary to and in violation of the provisions of Massachusetts General Laws (Ter. Ed.) Chapter 197, Section 9." That section provides:

> Except as provided in this chapter, an executor or administrator shall not be held to answer to an action by a creditor of the deceased which is not commenced within one year from the time of his giving bond for the performance of his trust, or to such an action which is commenced within said year unless before the expiration thereof the writ in such action has been served by delivery in hand upon such executor or administrator or service thereof accepted by him or a notice stating the name of the estate, the name and address of the creditor, the amount of the claim and the court in which the action has been brought has been filed in the proper registry of probate. * * *

On October 17, 1963, the District Court granted respondent's motion for summary judgment, citing *Ragan v. Merchants Transfer & Warehouse Co., 337 U.S. 530 (1949)*, and *Guaranty Trust Co. of New York v. York, 326 U.S. 99 (1945)*, in support

---

* The federal rule referred to in this opinion, Rule 4(d)(1), is now Rule 4(e). [Ed.]

of its conclusion that the adequacy of the service was to be measured by § 9, with which, the court held, petitioner had not complied. On appeal, petitioner admitted noncompliance with § 9, but argued that Rule 4(d)(1) defines the method by which service of process is to be effected in diversity actions. The <u>Court of Appeals for the First Circuit</u>, finding that "(r)elatively recent amendments (to § 9) evince a clear legislative purpose to require personal notification within the year," concluded that the conflict of state and federal rules was over "a substantive rather than a procedural matter," and unanimously affirmed. Because of the threat to the goal of uniformity of federal procedure posed by the decision below, we granted certiorari.

We conclude that the adoption of Rule 4(d)(1), designed to control service of process in diversity actions, neither exceeded the congressional mandate embodied in the Rules Enabling Act nor transgressed constitutional bounds, and that the Rule is therefore the standard against which

Practice Pointer

Note here that the Court explains why it granted certiorari in this case: the threat to the goal of uniformity of federal procedure. When an attorney petitions the Supreme Court for review of a case, it is important not just to argue that the decision made in the lower court was wrong, but that the Supreme Court needs to take the case for larger, more systemic reasons, such as to resolve an existing split of authority among the federal circuits or to address an issue that recurs with regularity in litigation throughout the country.

the District Court should have measured the adequacy of the service. Accordingly, we reverse the decision of the Court of Appeals.

* * * Under the cases construing the scope of the Enabling Act, Rule 4(d)(1) clearly passes muster. Prescribing the manner in which a defendant is to be notified that a suit has been instituted against him, it relates to the "practice and procedure of the district courts."

> The test must be whether a rule really regulates procedure,—the judicial process for enforcing rights and duties recognized by substantive law and for justly administering remedy and redress for disregard or infraction of them. <u>*Sibbach v. Wilson & Co.*, 312 U.S. 1 (1941)</u>.

In <u>*Mississippi Publ'g Corp. v. Murphree*, 326 U.S. 438 (1946)</u>, this Court upheld Rule 4(f), which permits service of a summons anywhere within the State (and not merely the district) in which a district court sits:

> We think that Rule 4(f) is in harmony with the Enabling Act * * *. Undoubtedly most alterations of the rules of practice and procedure may and often do affect the rights of litigants. Congress' prohibition of any alteration of substantive rights of litigants was obviously not addressed to such

incidental effects as necessarily attend the adoption of the prescribed new rules of procedure upon the rights of litigants who, agreeably to rules of practice and procedure, have been brought before a court authorized to determine their rights. *Sibbach v. Wilson & Co.* The fact that the application of Rule 4(f) will operate to subject petitioner's rights to adjudication by the district court for northern Mississippi will undoubtedly affect those rights. But it does not operate to abridge, enlarge or modify the rules of decision by which that court will adjudicate its rights.

Thus were there no conflicting state procedure, Rule 4(d)(1) would clearly control. *National Equipment Rental, Limited v. Szukhent, 375 U.S. 311, 316 (1964)*. However, respondent, focusing on the contrary Massachusetts rule, calls to the Court's attention another line of cases, a line which—like the Federal Rules—had its birth in 1938. *Erie R.R. Co. v. Tompkins, 304 U.S. 64 (1938)* overruling *Swift v. Tyson, 41 U.S. (16 Pet.) 1 (1842)*, held that federal courts sitting in diversity cases, when deciding questions of "substantive" law, are bound by state court decisions as well as state statutes. The broad command of *Erie* was therefore identical to that of the Enabling Act: federal courts are to apply state substantive law and federal procedural law. However, as subsequent cases sharpened the distinction between substance and procedure, the line of cases following *Erie* diverged markedly from the line construing the Enabling Act. * * *

Respondent, by placing primary reliance on *York* and *Ragan*, suggests that the *Erie* doctrine acts as a check on the Federal Rules of Civil Procedure, that despite the clear command of Rule 4(d)(1), *Erie* and its progeny demand the application of the Massachusetts rule. Reduced to essentials, the argument is: (1) *Erie*, as refined in *York*, demands that federal courts apply state law whenever application of federal law in its stead will alter the outcome of the case. (2) In this case, a determination that the Massachusetts service requirements obtain will result in immediate victory for respondent. If, on the other hand, it should be held that Rule 4(d)(1) is applicable, the litigation will continue, with possible victory for petitioner. (3) Therefore, *Erie* demands application of the Massachusetts rule. The syllogism possesses an appealing simplicity, but is for several reasons invalid.

In the first place, it is doubtful that, even if there were no Federal Rule making it clear that in-hand service is not required in diversity actions, the *Erie* rule would have obligated the District Court to follow the Massachusetts procedure. "Outcome-determination" analysis was never intended to serve as a talisman. *Byrd v. Blue Ridge Rural Elec. Cooperative, 356 U.S. 525, 537 (1958)*. Indeed, the message of *York* itself is that choices between state and federal law are to be made not by application of any automatic, "litmus paper" criterion, but rather by reference to the policies underlying the *Erie* rule. *Guaranty Trust Co. of New York v. York*.

The *Erie* rule is rooted in part in a realization that it would be unfair for the character of result of a litigation materially to differ because the suit had been brought in a federal court. * * * The decision was also in part a reaction to the practice of "forum-shopping" which had grown up in response to the rule of *Swift v. Tyson.* [*See* Erie,] 304 U.S. at 73–74. That the *York* test was an attempt to effectuate these policies is demonstrated by the fact that the opinion framed the inquiry in terms of "substantial" variations between state and federal litigation. Not only are nonsubstantial, or trivial, variations not likely to raise the sort of equal protection problems which troubled the Court in *Erie*; they are also unlikely to influence the choice of a forum. The "outcome-determination" test therefore cannot be read without reference to the twin aims of the *Erie* rule: discouragement of forum-shopping and avoidance of inequitable administration of the laws.[9]

Food for Thought

The Court here mentions "equal protection problems" that were of concern to the *Erie* Court. What was the nature of these problems? How does the question of whether to apply state versus federal law implicate the Equal Protection Clause of the Constitution?

The difference between the conclusion that the Massachusetts rule is applicable, and the conclusion that it is not, is of course at this point "outcome-determinative" in the sense that if we hold the state rule to apply, respondent prevails, whereas if we hold that Rule 4(d)(1) governs, the litigation will continue. But in this sense every procedural variation is "outcome-determinative." For example, having brought suit in a federal court, a plaintiff cannot then insist on the right to file subsequent pleadings in accord with the time limits applicable in state courts, even though enforcement of the federal timetable will, if he continues to insist that he must meet only the state time limit, result in determination of the controversy against him. So it is here. Though choice of the federal or state rule will at this point have a marked effect upon the outcome of the litigation, the

---

[9] The Court of Appeals seemed to frame the inquiry in terms of how "important" § 9 is to the State. In support of its suggestion that § 9 serves some interest the State regards as vital to its citizens, the court noted that something like § 9 has been on the books in Massachusetts a long time, that § 9 has been amended a number of times and that § 9 is designed to make sure that executors receive actual notice. The apparent lack of relation among these three observations is not surprising, because it is not clear to what sort of question the Court of Appeals was addressing itself. One cannot meaningfully ask how important something is without first asking "important for what purpose?" *Erie* and its progeny make clear that when a federal court sitting in a diversity case is faced with a question of whether or not to apply state law, the importance of a state rule is indeed relevant, but only in the context of asking whether application of the rule would make so important a difference to the character or result of the litigation that failure to enforce it would unfairly discriminate against citizens of the forum State, or whether application of the rule would have so important an effect upon the fortunes of one or both of the litigants that failure to enforce it would be likely to cause a plaintiff to choose the federal court.

difference between the two rules would be of scant, if any, relevance to the choice of a forum. Petitioner, in choosing her forum, was not presented with a situation where application of the state rule would wholly bar recovery; rather, adherence to the state rule would have resulted only in altering the way in which process was served. Moreover, it is difficult to argue that permitting service of defendant's wife to take the place of in-hand service of defendant himself alters the mode of enforcement of state-created rights in a fashion sufficiently "substantial" to raise the sort of equal protection problems to which the *Erie* opinion alluded.

Food for Thought

The Court acknowledges that applying the state versus the federal rule will likely alter the outcome but nonetheless is not "outcome determinative" in the sense that really matters to an *Erie* analysis. How does the Court describe its view of the proper understanding of outcome determinativeness and why the instant case does not implicate that concern?

There is, however, a more fundamental flaw in respondent's syllogism: the incorrect assumption that the rule of *Erie R.R. Co. v. Tompkins* constitutes the appropriate test of the validity and therefore the applicability of a Federal Rule of Civil Procedure. The *Erie* rule has never been invoked to void a Federal Rule. It is true that there have been cases where this Court has held applicable a state rule in the face of an argument that the situation was governed by one of the Federal Rules. But the holding of each such case was not that *Erie* commanded displacement of a Federal Rule by an inconsistent state rule, but rather that the scope of the Federal Rule was not as broad as the losing party urged, and therefore, there being no Federal Rule which covered the point in dispute, *Erie* commanded the enforcement of state law. * * * (Here, of course, the clash is unavoidable; Rule 4(d)(1) says—implicitly, but with unmistakable clarity—that in-hand service is not required in federal courts.) At the same time, in cases adjudicating the validity of Federal Rules, we have not applied the *York* rule or other refinements of *Erie*, but have to this day continued to decide questions concerning the scope of the Enabling Act and the constitutionality of specific Federal Rules in light of the distinction set forth in *Sibbach*.

Nor has the development of two separate lines of cases been inadvertent. The line between "substance" and "procedure" shifts as the legal context changes. * * * It is true that both the Enabling Act and the *Erie* rule say, roughly, that federal courts are to apply state "substantive" law and federal "procedural" law, but from that it need not follow that the tests are identical. For they were designed to control very different sorts of decisions. When a situation is covered by one of the Federal Rules, the question facing the court is a far cry from the typical, relatively unguided *Erie* choice: the court has been instructed to apply the Federal Rule, and can refuse to do so only if the Advisory Committee, this Court, and Congress erred in their *prima facie* judgment that the Rule in question transgresses neither the terms of the Enabling Act nor constitutional restrictions.

We are reminded by the *Erie* opinion that neither Congress nor the federal courts can, under the guise of formulating rules of decision for federal courts, fashion rules which are not supported by a grant of federal authority contained in Article I or some other section of the Constitution; in such areas state law must govern because there can be no other law. But the opinion in *Erie*, which involved no Federal Rule and dealt with a question which was "substantive" in every traditional sense (whether the railroad owed a duty of care to Tompkins as a trespasser or a licensee), surely neither said nor implied that measures like Rule 4(d)(1) are unconstitutional. For the constitutional provision for a federal court system (augmented by the <u>Necessary and Proper Clause</u>) carries with it congressional power to make rules governing the practice and pleading in those courts, which in turn includes a power to regulate matters which, though falling within the uncertain area between substance and procedure, are rationally capable of classification as either. Neither *York* nor the cases following it ever suggested that the rule there laid down for coping with situations where no Federal Rule applies is coextensive with the limitation on Congress to which *Erie* had adverted. * * *

* * *

Erie and its offspring cast no doubt on the long-recognized power of Congress to prescribe housekeeping rules for federal courts even though some of those rules will inevitably differ from comparable state rules. * * * Thus, though a court, in measuring a Federal Rule against the standards contained in the Enabling Act and the Constitution, need not wholly blind itself to the degree to which the Rule makes they character and result of the federal litigation stray from the course it would follow in state courts, it cannot be forgotten that the *Erie* rule, and the guidelines suggested in *York*, were created to serve another purpose alto-

Food for Thought

The Court here suggests that the Federal Rules of Civil Procedure are mere "housekeeping rules" for the federal courts. Is this a fair characterization? Why might the Court be using this language, which seems to downplay the importance and impact of the Rules on federal practice?

gether. To hold that a Federal Rule of Civil Procedure must cease to function whenever it alters the mode of enforcing state-created rights would be to disembowel either the Constitution's grant of power over federal procedure or Congress' attempt to exercise that power in the Enabling Act. Rule 4(d)(1) is valid and controls the instant case.

Reversed.

Mr. Justice BLACK concurs in the result.

Mr. Justice HARLAN, concurring.

* * *

Erie was something more than an opinion which worried about "forum-shopping and avoidance of inequitable administration of the laws," although to be sure these were important elements of the decision. I have always regarded that decision as one of the modern cornerstones of our federalism, expressing policies that profoundly touch the allocation of judicial power between the state and federal systems. *Erie* recognized that there should not be two conflicting systems of law controlling the primary activity of citizens, for such alternative governing authority must necessarily give rise to a debilitating uncertainty in the planning of everyday affairs. And it recognized that the scheme of our Constitution envisions an allocation of law-making functions between state and federal legislative processes which is undercut if the federal judiciary can make substantive law affecting state affairs beyond the bounds of congressional legislative powers in this regard. * * *

The shorthand formulations which have appeared in some past decisions are prone to carry untoward results that frequently arise from oversimplification. The Court is quite right in stating that the "outcome-determinative" test of <u>Guaranty Trust Co. of New York v. York, 326 U.S. 99 (1945)</u>, if taken literally, proves too much, for any rule, no matter how clearly "procedural," can affect the outcome of litigation if it is not obeyed. In turning from the "outcome" test of *York* back to the unadorned forum-shopping rationale of *Erie*, however, the Court falls prey to like oversimplification, for a simple forum-shopping rule also proves too much; litigants often choose a federal forum merely to obtain what they consider the advantages of the Federal Rules of Civil Procedure or to try their cases before a supposedly more favorable judge. To my mind the proper line of approach in determining whether to apply a state or a federal rule, whether "substantive" or "procedural," is to stay close to basic principles by inquiring if the choice of rule would substantially affect those primary decisions respecting human conduct which our constitutional system leaves to state regulation. If so, *Erie* and the Constitution require that the state rule prevail, even in the face of a conflicting federal rule.

Food for Thought

Is Justice Harlan's critique of the majority's forum-shopping rule sound? What alternative does he propose? Is his test any better or more workable?

* * *

So long as a reasonable man could characterize any duly adopted federal rule as "procedural," the Court, unless I misapprehend what is said, would have it apply no matter how seriously it frustrated a State's substantive regulation of the primary conduct and affairs of its citizens. Since the members of the Advisory Committee, the Judicial Conference, and this Court who formulated the Federal Rules are presumably reasonable men, it follows that the integrity of the Federal Rules is absolute. Whereas the unadulterated outcome and forum-shopping tests may err too far toward honoring state rules, I submit that the Court's "arguably procedural, ergo constitutional" test moves too fast and far in the other direction.

Food for Thought

Is Justice Harlan correct in concluding that the majority's standard for evaluating the Federal Rules will result in their being upheld in all cases where they apply?

* * *

It remains to apply what has been said to the present case. The Massachusetts rule provides that an executor need not answer suits unless in-hand service was made upon him or notice of the action was filed in the proper registry of probate within one year of his giving bond. The evident intent of this statute is to permit an executor to distribute the estate which he is administering without fear that further liabilities may be outstanding for which he could be held personally liable. If the Federal District Court in Massachusetts applies Rule 4(d)(1) of the Federal Rules of Civil Procedure instead of the Massachusetts service rule, what effect would that have on the speed and assurance with which estates are distributed? As I see it, the effect would not be substantial. It would mean simply that an executor would have to check at his own house or the federal courthouse as well as the registry of probate before he could distribute the estate with impunity. As this does not seem enough to give rise to any real impingement on the vitality of the state policy which the Massachusetts rule is intended to serve, I concur in the judgment of the Court.

Points for Discussion

a. The Holding of *Hanna*

The Court in *Hanna* analyzes the question before it both in terms of *Erie* and the Rules of Decision Act and in terms of the Rules Enabling Act. What is the relationship between these two strains of the analysis? Which one serves as the basis for the Court's decision in *Hanna*?

How does the Court further develop the *Erie*/Rules of Decision Act analysis in *Hanna*? What role should the *York* outcome-determinative test and the *Byrd* balancing approach play in an *Erie* analysis after *Hanna*?

What is the precise nature of the Court's analysis under the Rules Enabling Act? When does such an analysis come into play? How does the Constitution fit into this analysis?

Hypo 5.1

A pedestrian initiated a tort action in State A federal court against a driver for personal injuries he sustained from a collision with the driver's truck in State A. The pedestrian sought $50,000 in compensatory damages and $1 million in punitive damages.

Assume that in State A there is a statute that requires plaintiffs to have the court's permission before they can seek punitive damages in their complaints. Federal Rule 8(a) however, the rule governing the content of complaints in federal court, does not require such permission from federal judges and instructs pleaders to include "a demand for the relief sought." Upon receiving the complaint, the driver objected that the pedestrian's request for punitive damages was made without the court's permission and thus must be stricken from the complaint based on the State A statute.

Must the federal court adhere to the State A rule and require the pedestrian to obtain its permission to seek punitive damages?

---

b. Substance Versus Procedure After *Hanna*

Chief Justice Warren, the author of the *Hanna* opinion, discussed the distinction between substance and procedure as had been done in previous *Erie* doctrine cases. Of what relevance is the substance/procedure dichotomy to the two strains of analysis featured in *Hanna*? Do "substance" and "procedure" have the same meanings in the context of *Erie* and the Rules of Decision Act as they do in the context of the Rules Enabling Act according to Chief Justice Warren?

In *Hanna*, Chief Justice Warren stated that federal courts should apply one of the Federal Rules of Civil Procedure if it "really regulates procedure." How does one make this determination? The Court in *Sibbach v. Wilson & Co.*, 312 U.S. 1, 14 (1941) [*FLEX Case 5.B*], offered the following formulation for determining whether a legal rule was procedural: "The test must be whether a rule really regulates procedure—the judicial process for enforcing rights and duties recognized by substantive law and for justly administering remedy and redress for disregard or infraction of them." Is this test useful?

—Perspective & Analysis—

Many commentators openly deride the notion that one can clearly distinguish between procedural and substantive legal rules:

> [T]he Rules Enabling Act invests in the Supreme Court lawmaking power untied to the judicial process. It was the statute's express insulation of the authority to abridge or modify a "substantive right" that was generally assumed to preserve Congress's legislative power. The reasoning appears to have been that where the Court merely promulgates rules of "procedure," it is not overstepping its constitutionally limited bounds because procedure is, by definition, internal to the operation of the judiciary; it has no impact outside the four walls of the courthouse. We now know—and probably should have known at the time of the Act's passage—that this is political nonsense. In numerous instances, procedural choices inevitably—and often intentionally—impact the scope of substantive political choices.

Martin H. Redish & Uma M. Amuluru, *The Supreme Court, the Rules Enabling Act, and the Politicization of the Federal Rules: Constitutional and Statutory Implications*, 90 MINN. L. REV. 1303, 1305 (2006).

c. Justice Harlan's Opinion

What is Justice Harlan's quarrel with the majority in *Hanna*? Is his concern regarding the impact of the majority's holding valid?

d. "Commencement" of an Action Redux

Recall that in *Ragan v. Merchants Transfer & Warehouse Co.*, 337 U.S. 530 (1949) [*FLEX Case 5.A*]—a pre-*Hanna* case—the Court held that a Kansas state rule, not Rule 3 of the Federal Rules of Civil Procedure, determined the time of "commencement" of a civil action for purposes of determining when the relevant statute-of-limitations period tolled. Was *Ragan* still valid after *Hanna*? In other words, does the rule of *Hanna* mean that Rule 3 should indeed be held to govern the commencement of an action for purposes of tolling state statute-of-limitations periods?

The Court had the opportunity to revisit this question after *Hanna* in *Walker v. Armco Steel Corp.*, 446 U.S. 740 (1980) [*FLEX Case 5.C*]. The Court, per Justice Marshall, unanimously reaffirmed its holding in *Ragan*, writing as follows:

> Petitioner argues that the analysis and holding of *Ragan* did not survive our decision in *Hanna*. * * * Petitioner seeks to have us overrule our decision in *Ragan*. * * * This Court in *Hanna* distinguished *Ragan* rather than over-ruled it, and for good reason. Application of the *Hanna* analysis is premised on a "direct collision" between the Federal Rule and the state law. In *Hanna* itself the "clash" between Rule 4(d)(1) and the state in-hand service requirement was "unavoidable." The first question must therefore be whether the scope of the Federal Rule in fact is sufficiently broad to control the issue

before the Court. It is only if that question is answered affirmatively that the *Hanna* analysis applies.

* * * Rule 3 simply states that "[a] civil action is commenced by filing a complaint with the court." There is no indication that the Rule was intended to toll a state statute of limitations, much less that it purported to displace state tolling rules for purposes of state statutes of limitations. In our view, in diversity actions Rule 3 governs the date from which various timing requirements of the Federal Rules begin to run, but does not affect state statutes of limitations. * * *

In contrast to Rule 3, the Oklahoma statute is a statement of a substantive decision by that State that actual service on, and accordingly actual notice by, the defendant is an integral part of the several policies served by the statute of limitations.

Walker, 446 U.S. at 749–51. What does the *Walker* decision reveal about the nature of the *Hanna* Rules Enabling Act analysis and how it should be applied?

In seeking to avoid a conflict between a state rule and a Federal Rule of Civil Procedure, is the Court giving an unnecessarily narrow interpretation of Rule 3? Is there a danger that the *Hanna* analysis will lead courts to construe the scope of the Federal Rules too narrowly in order to avoid such conflicts? Conversely, because *Hanna* tends to favor the validity and application of a Federal Rule once it is deemed to be designed to govern a given situation, is there a danger under *Hanna* that courts will be encouraged to interpret the Federal Rules too broadly, finding them to control a matter as a basis for ignoring the conflicting state rule? *See, e.g., Burlington N. R.R. Co. v. Woods*, 480 U.S. 1, 4–8 (1987) (ignoring an Alabama statute entitling plaintiffs to an additional 10% on their judgments when appealing defendants lose their appeals in favor of Federal Rule of Appellate Procedure 38, which empowers appellate courts to award "just damages and single or double costs" to prevailing appellees in such situations).

e. Federal Procedural Statutes and *Hanna*

Hanna addressed itself to the applicability of the Federal Rules of Civil Procedure in the face of seemingly conflicting state legal rules. As we have seen, however, federal procedural requirements can be embodied in federal statutes rather than the Federal Rules. Does *Hanna's* analysis apply to the situation in which a federal statute presents a procedural requirement in seeming conflict with state procedural rules? If so how? *See Stewart Org., Inc. v. Ricoh Corp.*, 487 U.S. 22, 32 (1988) [*FLEX Case 5.D*] (rejecting an Alabama judge-made rule refusing to enforce forum-selection clauses in favor of the venue transfer provision of 28 U.S.C. § 1404, under which such clauses were to be given some consideration in the venue transfer analysis);* *see also Jinks v. Richard Cty.*, 538 U.S. 456 (2003) (rejecting a constitutional challenge of 28 U.S.C. § 1367(d), the tolling provision of the supplemental jurisdiction statute).

Gasperini v. Center for Humanities, Inc.

Supreme Court of the United States
518 U.S. 415 (1996)

JUSTICE GINSBURG delivered the opinion of the Court.

Under the law of New York, appellate courts are empowered to review the size of jury verdicts and to order new trials when the jury's award "deviates materially from what would be reasonable compensation." N.Y. Civ. Prac. Law and Rules (CPLR) § 5501(c). Under the Seventh Amendment, which governs proceedings in federal court, but not in state court, "the right of trial by jury shall be preserved, and no fact tried by a jury, shall be otherwise re-examined in any Court of the United States, than according to the rules of the common law." U.S. Const. amend. VII. The compatibility of these provisions, in an action based on New York law but tried in federal court by reason of the parties' diverse citizenship, is the issue we confront in this case. We hold that New York's law controlling compensation awards for excessiveness or inadequacy can be given effect, without detriment to the Seventh Amendment, if the review standard set out in CPLR § 5501(c) is applied by the federal trial court judge, with appellate control of the trial court's ruling limited to review for "abuse of discretion."

I

Petitioner William Gasperini, a journalist for CBS News and the Christian Science Monitor, began reporting on events in Central America in 1984. He earned his living primarily in radio and print media and only occasionally sold his photographic work. During the course of his seven-year stint in Central America, Gasperini took over 5,000 slide transparencies, depicting active war zones, political leaders, and scenes from daily life. In 1990, Gasperini agreed to supply his original color transparencies to The Center for Humanities, Inc. (Center) for use in an educational videotape, Conflict in Central America. Gasperini selected 300 of his slides for the Center; its videotape included 110 of them. The Center agreed

---

* The Supreme Court recently modified its position respecting the role of forum-selection clauses in the transfer analysis of 28 U.S.C. § 1404, holding that such clauses "should be given controlling weight in all but the most exceptional cases." *Atl. Marine Constr. Co. v. U.S. Dist. Court for W. Dist. of Tex.*, 134 S. Ct. 568, 579 (2013). This holding does not alter the *Hanna* analysis of *Stewart*; the holding that § 1404—not conflicting state law—governs the federal transfer determination was affirmed. [Ed.]

to return the original transparencies, but upon the completion of the project, it could not find them.

Make the Connection

Conversion is a **tort** that refers to the wrongful taking of the personal property of another.

Gasperini commenced suit in the United States District Court for the Southern District of New York, invoking the court's diversity jurisdiction pursuant to 28 U.S.C. § 1332. Hev alleged several state-law claims for relief, including breach of contract, conversion, and negligence. The Center conceded liability for the lost transparencies and the issue of damages was tried before a jury.

At trial, Gasperini's expert witness testified that the "industry standard" within the photographic publishing community valued a lost transparency at $1,500. This industry standard, the expert explained, represented the average license fee a commercial photograph could earn over the full course of the photographer's copyright * * * . He also testified that he intended to produce a book containing [some of these photographs].

After a three-day trial, the jury awarded Gasperini $450,000 in compensatory damages. This sum, the jury foreperson announced, "is [$]1500 each, for 300 slides." Moving for a new trial under Federal Rule of Civil Procedure 59, the Center attacked the verdict on various grounds, including excessiveness. Without comment, the District Court denied the motion.

The Court of Appeals for the Second Circuit vacated the judgment entered on the jury's verdict. Mindful that New York law governed the controversy, the Court of Appeals endeavored to apply CPLR § 5501(c), which instructs that, when a jury returns an itemized verdict, as the jury did in this case, the New York Appellate Division "shall determine that an award is excessive or inadequate if it deviates materially from what would be reasonable compensation." * * * Surveying Appellate Division decisions that reviewed damage awards for lost transparencies, the Second Circuit concluded that testimony on industry standard alone was insufficient to justify a verdict; prime among other factors warranting consideration were the uniqueness of the slides' subject matter and the photographer's earning level.

The New York Appellate Division refers to the intermediate appellate courts of the State of New York. New York's Appellate Division is divided into four "Departments" with geographically-based coverage. For more information on these courts, visit www.courts.state.ny.us/courts/appellatedivisions.shtml.

Guided by Appellate Division rulings, the Second Circuit held that the $450,000 verdict "materially deviates from what is reasonable compensation." Some of Gasperini's transparencies, the Second Circuit recognized, were unique, notably those capturing combat situations in which Gasperini was the only photographer present. But others "depicted either generic scenes or events at which other professional photojournalists were present." No more than 50 slides merited a $1,500 award, the court concluded, after "[g]iving Gasperini every benefit of the doubt." Absent evidence showing significant earnings from photographic endeavors or concrete plans to publish a book, the court further determined, any damage award above $100 each for the remaining slides would be excessive. Remittiturs "presen[t] difficult problems for appellate courts," the Second Circuit acknowledged, for court of appeals judges review the evidence from "a cold paper record." Nevertheless, the Second Circuit set aside the $450,000 verdict and ordered a new trial, unless Gasperini agreed to an award of $100,000.

Food for Thought

The Second Circuit here found that some of Gasperini's transparencies depicted "generic" scenes or scenes where other photojournalists were present and thus did not each warrant a $1,500 award. Is this finding a factual finding by the Second Circuit, a legal judgment, or a mixture of the two? This question is important as you think about whether following New York's rule permitting appellate reexamination of jury awards runs afoul of the Seventh Amendment's Reexamination Clause.

* * *

II

Before 1986, state and federal courts in New York generally invoked the same judge-made formulation in responding to excessiveness attacks on jury verdicts: courts would not disturb an award unless the amount was so exorbitant that it "shocked the conscience of the court." As described by the Second Circuit: "The standard for determining excessiveness and the appropriateness of remittitur in New York is somewhat ambiguous. Prior to 1986, New York law employed the same standard as the federal courts, which authorized remittitur only if the jury's verdict was so excessive that it 'shocked the conscience of the court.' "

In both state and federal courts, trial judges made the excessiveness assessment in the first instance, and appellate judges ordinarily deferred to the trial court's judgment.

In 1986, as part of a series of tort reform measures, New York codified a standard for judicial review of the size of jury awards. Placed in CPLR § 5501(c), the prescription reads:

In reviewing a money judgment . . . in which it is contended that the award is excessive or inadequate and that a new trial should have been granted unless a stipulation is entered to a different award, the appellate division shall determine that an award is excessive or inadequate if it deviates materially from what would be reasonable compensation.

As stated in Legislative Findings and Declarations accompanying New York's adoption of the "deviates materially" formulation, the lawmakers found the "shock the conscience" test an insufficient check on damage awards; the legislature therefore installed a standard "invit[ing] more careful appellate scrutiny." At the same time, the legislature instructed the Appellate Division, in amended § 5522, to state the reasons for the court's rulings on the size of verdicts, and the factors the court considered in complying with § 5501(c). In his signing statement, then-Governor Mario Cuomo emphasized that the CPLR amendments were meant to ratchet up the review standard: "This will assure greater scrutiny of the amount of verdicts and promote greater stability in the tort system and greater fairness for similarly situated defendants throughout the State."

New York state-court opinions confirm that § 5501(c)'s "deviates materially" standard calls for closer surveillance than "shock the conscience" oversight.

Although phrased as a direction to New York's intermediate appellate courts, § 5501(c)'s "deviates materially" standard, as construed by New York's courts, instructs state trial judges as well. Application of § 5501(c) at the trial level is key to this case.

To determine whether an award "deviates materially from what would be reasonable compensation," New York state courts look to awards approved in similar cases. Under New York's former "shock the conscience" test, courts also referred to analogous cases. The "deviates materially" standard, however, in design and operation, influences outcomes by tightening the range of tolerable awards.

III

In cases like Gasperini's, in which New York law governs the claims for relief, does New York law also supply the test for federal-court review of the size of the verdict? The Center answers yes. The "deviates materially" standard, it argues, is a substantive standard that must be applied by federal appellate courts in diversity cases. The Second Circuit agreed. Gasperini, emphasizing that § 5501(c) trains on the New York Appellate Division, characterizes the provision as procedural, an allocation of decisionmaking authority regarding damages, not a hard cap on the amount recoverable. Correctly comprehended, Gasperini urges, § 5501(c)'s direction to the Appellate Division cannot be given effect by federal appellate courts without violating the Seventh Amendment's Re-examination Clause.

As the parties' arguments suggest, CPLR § 5501(c), appraised under *Erie R.R. Co. v. Tompkins*, 304 U.S. 64 (1938), and decisions in *Erie*'s path, is both "substantive" and "procedural": "substantive" in that § 5501(c)'s "deviates materially" standard controls how much a plaintiff can be awarded; "procedural" in that § 5501(c) assigns decisionmaking authority to New York's Appellate Division. Parallel application of § 5501(c) at the federal appellate level would be out of sync with the federal system's division of trial and appellate court functions, an allocation weighted by the Seventh Amendment. The dispositive question, therefore, is whether federal courts can give effect to the substantive thrust of § 5501(c) without untoward alteration of the federal scheme for the trial and decision of civil cases.

Food for Thought

What does the Court mean when it says that the division of trial and appellate court functions is "weighted" by the Seventh Amendment?

A

Federal diversity jurisdiction provides an alternative forum for the adjudication of state-created rights, but it does not carry with it generation of rules of substantive law. As *Erie* read the Rules of Decision Act: "Except in matters governed by the Federal Constitution or by Acts of Congress, the law to be applied in any case is the law of the State." Under the *Erie* doctrine, federal courts sitting in diversity apply state substantive law and federal procedural law.

Classification of a law as "substantive" or "procedural" for *Erie* purposes is sometimes a challenging endeavor.[7] *Guaranty Trust Co. v. York*, an early interpretation of *Erie*, propounded an "outcome-determination" test: "[D]oes it significantly affect the result of a litigation for a federal court to disregard a law of a State that would be controlling in an action upon the same claim by the same parties in a State court?" Ordering application of a state statute of limitations to an equity proceeding in federal court, the Court said in [*York*]: "[W]here a federal court is exercising jurisdiction solely because of the diversity of citizenship of the parties, the outcome of the litigation in the federal court should be substantially the same, so far as legal rules determine the outcome of a litigation, as it would be if tried in

---

[7] Concerning matters covered by the Federal Rules of Civil Procedure, the characterization question is usually unproblematic: It is settled that if the Rule in point is consonant with the Rules Enabling Act, 28 U.S.C. § 2072, and the Constitution, the Federal Rule applies regardless of contrary state law. *See Hanna v. Plumer*, 380 U.S. 460, 469–474 (1965); *Burlington N. R.R. Co. v. Woods*, 480 U.S. 1, 4–5 (1987). Federal courts have interpreted the Federal Rules, however, with sensitivity to important state interests and regulatory policies. *See, e.g., Walker v. Armco Steel Corp.*, 446 U.S. 740, 750–752 (1980) (reaffirming decision in *Ragan v. Merchants Transfer & Warehouse Co.*, 337 U.S. 530 (1949), that state law rather than Rule 3 determines when a diversity action commences for the purposes of tolling the state statute of limitations; Rule 3 makes no reference to the tolling of state limitations, the Court observed, and accordingly found no "direct conflict").

a State court." A later pathmarking case, qualifying [*York*], explained that the "outcome-determination" test must not be applied mechanically to sweep in all manner of variations; instead, its application must be guided by "the twin aims of the *Erie* rule: discouragement of forum-shopping and avoidance of inequitable administration of the laws." *Hanna v. Plumer.*

Food for Thought

Why does the Court dive into an *Erie* analysis without first evaluating the applicability of Rule 59—the relevant federal rule competing for application—as *Hanna* instructed? Does Rule 59—which limits the conditions under which new trials may be granted—cover this situation and conflict with CPLR § 5501(c)?

Informed by these decisions, we address the question whether New York's "deviates materially" standard, codified in CPLR § 5501(c), is outcome affective in this sense: Would "application of the [standard] . . . have so important an effect upon the fortunes of one or both of the litigants that failure to [apply] it would [unfairly discriminate against citizens of the forum State, or] be likely to cause a plaintiff to choose the federal court"?

We start from a point the parties do not debate. Gasperini acknowledges that a statutory cap on damages would supply substantive law for *Erie* purposes. Although CPLR § 5501(c) is less readily classified, it was designed to provide an analogous control.

New York's Legislature codified in § 5501(c) a new standard, one that requires closer court review than the common-law "shock the conscience" test. More rigorous comparative evaluations attend application of § 5501(c)'s "deviates materially" standard. To foster predictability, the legislature required the reviewing court, when overturning a verdict under § 5501(c), to state its reasons, including the factors it considered relevant. We think it a fair conclusion that CPLR § 5501(c) differs from a statutory cap principally "in that the maximum amount recoverable is not set forth by statute, but rather is determined by case law." In sum, § 5501(c) contains a procedural instruction, but the State's objective is manifestly substantive.

Food for Thought

The Court states that the application of the federal "shock the conscience" test rather than the New York "deviates materially" standard to the review of jury damages awards could be expected to result in substantial variations in money judgments between state and federal court. Is the Court right in this assessment? Even if the Court is correct in its assessment, is that possibility alone sufficient to implicate *Erie*'s twin aims or is more needed?

It thus appears that if federal courts ignore the change in the New York standard and persist in applying the "shock the conscience" test to damage awards on claims governed by New York law, " 'substantial' variations between state and federal [money judg-ments]" may be expected. We therefore agree with the Second Circuit that New York's check on excessive damages implicates what we have called *Erie*'s "twin aims." Just as the *Erie* principle precludes a federal court from giving a state-created claim "longer life . . . than [the claim] would have had in the state court," so *Erie* precludes a recovery in federal court significantly larger than the recovery that would have been tolerated in state court.

B

CPLR § 5501(c) * * * is phrased as a direction to the New York Appellate Division. Acting essentially as a surrogate for a New York appellate forum, the Court of Appeals reviewed Gasperini's award to determine if it "deviate[d] materially" from damage awards the Appellate Division permitted in similar circumstances. The Court of Appeals performed this task without benefit of an opinion from the District Court, which had denied "without comment" the Center's Rule 59 motion. Concen-trating on the authority § 5501(c) gives to the Appellate Division, Gasperini urges that the provision shifts fact-finding responsibility from the jury and the trial judge to the appellate court. Assigning such responsibility to an appellate court, he main-tains, is incompatible with the Seventh Amendment's Reexamination Clause, and therefore, Gasperini concludes, § 5501(c) cannot be given effect in federal court. Although we reach a different conclusion than Gasperini, we agree that the Second Circuit did not attend to "[a]n essential characteristic of [the federal court] system," when it used § 5501(c) as "the standard for [federal] appellate review."

That "essential characteristic" was described in *Byrd*, a diversity suit for negli-gence in which a pivotal issue of fact would have been tried by a judge were the case in state court. The *Byrd* Court held that, despite the state practice, the plaintiff was entitled to a jury trial in federal court. In so ruling, the Court said that the *Guaranty Trust* "outcome-determination" test was an insufficient guide in cases presenting countervailing federal interests. The Court described the countervailing federal interests present in *Byrd* this way:

> "The federal system is an independent system for administering justice to
> litigants who properly invoke its jurisdiction. An essential characteristic of
> that system is the manner in which, in civil common-law actions, it distrib-
> utes trial functions between judge and jury and, under the influence—if
> not the command—of the Seventh Amendment, assigns the decisions of
> disputed questions of fact to the jury."

The Seventh Amendment, which governs proceedings in federal court, but not in state court, bears not only on the allocation of trial functions between judge and jury, the issue in *Byrd*; it also controls the allocation of authority to review verdicts, the issue of concern here. * * *

Byrd involved the first Clause of the Amendment, the "trial by jury" Clause. This case involves the second, the "Reexamination" Clause. In keeping with the historic understanding, the Reexamination Clause does not inhibit the authority of trial judges to grant new trials "for any of the reasons for which new trials have heretofore been granted in actions at law in the courts of the United States." FED. RULE CIV. PROC. 59(a). That authority is large. "The trial judge in the federal system," we have reaffirmed, "has . . . discretion to grant a new trial if the verdict appears to [the judge] to be against the weight of the evidence." This discretion includes overturning verdicts for excessiveness and ordering a new trial without qualification, or conditioned on the verdict winner's refusal to agree to a reduction (remittitur).

What's That?

A district judge may order a *new trial* when she feels that the verdict of the jury is inconsistent with the weight of the evidence. This topic will be covered in greater detail in Chapter 10.

In contrast, appellate review of a federal trial court's denial of a motion to set aside a jury's verdict as excessive is a relatively late, and less secure, development. Such review was once deemed inconsonant with the Seventh Amendment's Reexamination Clause.

Before today, we have not "expressly [held] that the Seventh Amendment allows appellate review of a district court's denial of a motion to set aside an award as excessive." * * * We now [hold]: "[N]othing in the Seventh Amendment . . . precludes appellate review of the trial judge's denial of a motion to set aside [a jury verdict] as excessive."

C

In *Byrd*, the Court faced a one-or-the-other choice: trial by judge as in state court, or trial by jury according to the federal practice. In the case before us, a choice of that order is not required, for the principal state and federal interests can be accommodated. The Second Circuit correctly recognized that when New York substantive law governs a claim for relief, New York law and decisions guide the allowable damages. But that court did not take into account the characteristic of the federal court system that caused us to reaffirm: "The proper role of the trial and appellate courts in the federal system in reviewing the size of jury verdicts is . . . a matter of federal law."

New York's dominant interest can be respected, without disrupting the federal system, once it is recognized that the federal district court is capable of performing the checking function, i.e., that court can apply the State's "deviates materially" standard in line with New York case law evolving under CPLR § 5501(c).[22] * * *

Within the federal system, practical reasons combine with Seventh Amendment constraints to lodge in the district court, not the court of appeals, primary responsibility for application of § 5501(c)'s "deviates materially" check. Trial judges have the "unique opportunity to consider the evidence in the living courtroom context," while appellate judges see only the "cold paper record."

District court applications of the "deviates materially" standard would be subject to appellate review under the standard the Circuits now employ when inadequacy or excessiveness is asserted on appeal: abuse of discretion. In light of *Erie*'s doctrine, the federal appeals court must be guided by the damage-control standard state law supplies, but as the Second Circuit itself has said: "If we reverse, it must be because of an abuse of discretion. . . . The very nature of the problem counsels restraint. . . . We must give the benefit of every doubt to the judgment of the trial judge."

IV

It does not appear that the District Court checked the jury's verdict against the relevant New York decisions demanding more than "industry standard" testimony to support an award of the size the jury returned in this case. As the Court of Appeals recognized, the uniqueness of the photographs and the plaintiff's earnings as photographer—past and reasonably projected—are factors relevant to appraisal of the award. Accordingly, we vacate the judgment of the Court of Appeals and instruct that court to remand the case to the District Court so that the trial judge, revisiting his ruling on the new trial motion, may test the jury's verdict against CPLR § 5501(c)'s "deviates materially" standard.

It is so ordered.

[The dissenting opinion of JUSTICE STEVENS is omitted.]

JUSTICE SCALIA, with whom THE CHIEF JUSTICE and JUSTICE THOMAS join, dissenting.

Today the Court overrules a longstanding and well-reasoned line of precedent that has for years prohibited federal appellate courts from reviewing refusals by

---

[22] Justice SCALIA finds in Federal Rule of Civil Procedure 59 a "federal standard" for new trial motions in " 'direct collision' " with, and " 'leaving no room for the operation of,' " a state law like CPLR § 5501(c). The relevant prescription, Rule 59(a), has remained unchanged since the adoption of the Federal Rules by this Court in 1937. 302 U.S. 783. Rule 59(a) is as encompassing as it is uncontroversial. It is indeed "Hornbook" law that a most usual ground for a Rule 59 motion is that "the damages are excessive." Whether damages are excessive for the claim-in-suit must be governed by some law. And there is no candidate for that governance other than the law that gives rise to the claim for relief—here, the law of New York.

district courts to set aside civil jury awards as contrary to the weight of the evidence. One reason is given for overruling these cases: that the Courts of Appeals have, for some time now, decided to ignore them. Such unreasoned capitulation to the nullification of what was long regarded as a core component of the Bill of Rights—the Seventh Amendment's prohibition on appellate reexamination of civil jury awards—is wrong. It is not for us, much less for the Courts of Appeals, to decide that the <u>Seventh Amendment's</u> restriction on federal-court review of jury findings has outlived its usefulness.

The Court also holds today that a state practice that relates to the division of duties between state judges and juries must be followed by federal courts in diversity cases. On this issue, too, our prior cases are directly to the contrary. * * *

* * *

II

The Court's holding that federal courts of appeals may review district court denials of motions for new trials for error of fact is not the only novel aspect of today's decision. The Court also directs that the case be remanded to the District Court, so that it may "test the jury's verdict against CPLR § 5501(c)'s 'deviates materially' standard." This disposition contradicts the principle that "[t]he proper role of the trial and appellate courts in the federal system in reviewing the size of jury verdicts is . . . a matter of federal law."

The Court acknowledges that state procedural rules cannot, as a general matter, be permitted to interfere with the allocation of functions in the federal court system. Indeed, it is at least partly for this reason that the Court rejects direct application of § 5501(c) at the appellate level as inconsistent with an " 'essential characteristic' " of the federal court system—by which the Court presumably means abuse-of-discretion review of denials of motions for new trials. But the scope of the Court's concern is oddly circumscribed. The "essential characteristic" of the federal jury, and, more specifically, the role of the federal trial court in reviewing jury judgments, apparently counts for little. The Court approves the "accommodat[ion]" achieved by having district courts review jury verdicts under the "deviates materially" standard, because it regards that as a means of giving effect to the State's purposes "without disrupting the federal system." But changing the standard by which trial judges review jury verdicts does disrupt the federal system, and is plainly inconsistent with the "strong federal policy against allowing state rules to disrupt the judge-jury relationship in federal court." *Byrd v. Blue Ridge Rural Elec. Cooperative, Inc.* The Court's opinion does not even acknowledge, let alone address, this dislocation.

* * *

* * * It seems to me quite wrong to regard this provision as a "substantive" rule for *Erie* purposes. The "analog[y]" to "a statutory cap on damages," fails utterly.

There is an absolutely fundamental distinction between a *rule of law* such as that, which would ordinarily be imposed upon the jury in the trial court's instructions, and a *rule of review*, which simply determines how closely the jury verdict will be scrutinized for compliance with the instructions. A tighter standard for reviewing jury determinations can no more plausibly be called a "substantive" disposition than can a tighter appellate standard for reviewing trial-court determinations. The one, like the other, provides additional assurance *that the law has been complied with*; but the other, like the one, *leaves the law unchanged*.

The Court commits the classic *Erie* mistake of regarding whatever changes the outcome as substantive. That is not the only factor to be considered. Outcome determination "was never intended to serve as a talisman," *Hanna v. Plumer*, and does not have the power to convert the most classic elements of the *process* of assuring that the law is observed into the substantive law itself. The right to have a jury make the findings of fact, for example, is generally thought to favor plaintiffs, and that advantage is often thought significant enough to be the basis for forum selection. But no one would argue that *Erie* confers a right to a jury in federal court wherever state courts would provide it; or that, were it not for the Seventh Amendment, *Erie* would require federal courts to dispense with the jury whenever state courts do so.

* * *

The foregoing describes why I think the Court's *Erie* analysis is flawed. But in my view, one does not even reach the *Erie* question in this case. The standard to be applied by a district court in ruling on a motion for a new trial is set forth in Rule 59 of the Federal Rules of Civil Procedure, which provides that "[a] new trial may be granted . . . for any of the reasons for which new trials have heretofore been granted in actions at law *in the courts of the United States*." (Emphasis added.) That is undeniably a federal standard.[12] Federal District Courts in the Second Circuit have interpreted that standard to permit the granting of new trials where " 'it is quite clear that the jury has reached a seriously erroneous result' " and letting the verdict stand would result in a " 'miscarriage of justice.' " Assuming (as we have no reason to question) that this is a correct interpretation of what Rule 59 requires, it is undeniable that the Federal Rule is " 'sufficiently broad' to cause a 'direct collision' with the state law or, implicitly, to 'control the issue' before the court, thereby leaving no room for the operation of that law." It is simply not possible to give controlling effect both to the federal standard and the state standard in reviewing the jury's award. That being so, the court has no choice but to apply the Federal Rule, which is an exercise of what we have called Congress's "power to regulate

---

[12] I agree with the Court's entire progression of reasoning in its footnote 22, leading to the conclusion that state law must determine "[w]hether damages are excessive." But the question whether damages are excessive is quite separate from the question of when a jury award may be set aside for excessiveness. It is the latter that is governed by Rule 59; as *Browning-Ferris* said, district courts are "to determine, by reference to federal standards developed under Rule 59, whether a new trial or remittitur should be ordered."

matters which, though falling within the uncertain area between substance and procedure, are rationally capable of classification as either," *Hanna*.

* * *

There is no small irony in the Court's declaration today that appellate review of refusals to grant new trials for error of fact is "a control necessary and proper to the fair administration of justice." It is objection to precisely that sort of "control" by federal appellate judges that gave birth to the Reexamination Clause of the Seventh Amendment. Alas, those who drew the Amendment, and the citizens who approved it, did not envision an age in which the Constitution means whatever this Court thinks it ought to mean—or indeed, whatever the courts of appeals have recently thought it ought to mean.

When there is added to the revision of the Seventh Amendment the Court's precedent-setting disregard of Congress's instructions in Rule 59, one must conclude that this is a bad day for the Constitution's distinctive Article III courts in general, and for the role of the jury in those courts in particular. I respectfully dissent.

───────

Points for Discussion

a. The *Gasperini* Court's Analysis

How does the Court in *Gasperini* apply the *Erie* line of cases to reach the conclusion that federal courts must apply the New York "deviates materially" standard for reviewing the excessiveness of jury verdicts? Was the Court correct to avoid a *Hanna* Rules Enabling Act analysis in favor of the modified-*Erie* analysis presented in *Hanna* given the existence of Rule 59, which governs grants of new trials in federal court? Did the Court sufficiently address the applicability of Rule 59 to the issue in this case?

The majority in *Gasperini* walks through each of the elements of an *Erie* analysis as modified by *Hanna*. How does each piece of the *Erie* analysis look in the hands of Justice Ginsburg, the author of the *Gasperini* opinion? *See* Robert J. Condlin, *"A Formstone of Our Federalism": The* Erie/Hanna *Doctrine & Casebook Law Reform,* 59 U. MIAMI L. REV. 475, 527–30 (2005) (arguing that the majority opinion in *Gasperini* was confused in structure and misguided in its analysis).

Substance Versus Procedure in *Gasperini*. Rather than labeling the New York rule substantive or procedural, Justice Ginsburg acknowledged that it was in some ways both substantive and procedural, and later noted that "§ 5501(c) contains a procedural instruction, but the State's objective is manifestly substantive." *Gasperini*, 518 U.S. at 429. Does this conclusion reveal the difficulty with attempts to classify any legal rule as substantive versus procedural, or at least the problem with resting a choice-of-law analysis on such a tenuous classification scheme? How does Justice Ginsburg's characterization of the rule as both substantive and procedural factor into her analysis?

Outcome Determinativeness in *Gasperini*. The Court in *Gasperini* concluded that "if federal courts ignore the change in the New York standard and persist in applying the 'shock the conscience' test to damage awards on claims governed by New York law, 'substantial' variations between state and federal money judgments may be expected." *Gasperini*, 518 U.S. at 429–30. This conclusion led the Court to find that the twin aims of *Erie* were implicated. Do you agree that the potential divergence between tolerable awards under the respective tests would be sufficiently great to encourage forum shopping among prospective litigants or to result in an inequitable administration of the laws?

Byrd Balancing in *Gasperini*. Justice Ginsburg references *Byrd* as support for the idea that outcome determination is "an insufficient guide in cases presenting countervailing federal interests." In *Byrd* the countervailing federal interest was the federal interest in preserving the jury right reflected in the Seventh Amendment. Why did Justice Ginsburg not find that similar Seventh Amendment concerns provided a countervailing federal interest warranting the rejection of the New York rule in *Gasperini*?

b. Justice Scalia's Dissent

What is Justice Scalia's main quarrel with the majority in *Gasperini*? Do you agree with some or all of his critique? How does he arrive at such a radically different conclusion than the majority?

Viewing all of the cases from *Erie* through *Gasperini*, it is possible to distill the Court's analytical framework into a workable approach that can be applied to resolve vertical choice-of-law questions. See *Perspective & Analysis* below. Generally speaking, the initial key is to figure out whether there is a Federal Rule or federal statute on point that governs the matter at hand. This initial inquiry will determine whether the *Hanna* Rules Enabling Act analysis or the modified-*Erie* analysis should be employed to make the choice between state and federal law.

—Perspective & Analysis—

Understanding the *Erie* doctrine and the *Hanna* Rules Enabling Act analysis remains challenging even given all the Court has said on the topic. Professor John Hart Ely long ago offered this view of the analysis:

> The United States Constitution . . . constitutes the relevant text only where Congress has passed a statute creating law for diversity actions, and it is in this situation alone that *Hanna's* "arguably procedural" test controls. . . . [W]here there is no relevant Federal Rule of Civil Procedure or other Rule promulgated pursuant to the Enabling Act and the federal rule in issue is therefore wholly judge-made, whether state or federal law should be applied is controlled by the Rules of Decision Act, the statute construed in *Erie* and *York*. Where the matter in issue is covered by a Federal Rule, however, the Enabling Act—and not the Rules of Decision Act itself or the line of cases construing it—constitutes the relevant standard. To say that . . . is by no means to concede the validity of all Federal Rules, for the Enabling Act contains significant limiting language of its own. . . . However, the Court's recent appreciation that the Enabling Act constitutes the only check on the Rules—that "*Erie*" does not stand there as a backstop—should lead it in an appropriate case to take the Act's limiting language more seriously than it has in the past.

John Hart Ely, *The Irrepressible Myth of* Erie, 87 HARV. L. REV. 693, 698 (1974).

Unfortunately, as the cases thus far have demonstrated, making this initial determination regarding the applicability of a Federal Rule is not an exact science and is subject to some manipulability. Although the Court has written that the Federal Rules should be given their "plain meaning" and not necessarily interpreted narrowly simply to avoid a "direct collision" with state law, *Walker v. Armco Steel Corp., 446 U.S. 740, 750 n.9 (1980)* [*FLEX Case 5.C*], the Court has also appeared to favor reading the Federal Rules in a manner that avoids a federal-state conflict. *See, e.g., Semtek Int'l Inc. v. Lockheed Martin Corp., 531 U.S. 497 (2001)* (interpreting Rule 41(b)—under which dismissals on state statute-of-limitations grounds are adjudications "on the merits"—as not governing whether such judgments were to be given preclusive effect in other states); *Ortiz v. Fibreboard Corp., 527 U.S. 815, 842 (1999)* (adopting a "limiting construction" of Rule 23(b)(1)(B) because this "construction . . . minimizes potential conflict with the Rules Enabling Act" and "avoids serious constitutional concerns"); *Walker, 446 U.S. at 750–51* (interpreting Rule 3—which indicates that a civil action commences upon the filing of a complaint—as not determining the time of commencement for purposes of a state statute-of-limitations period).

Justice Ginsburg in *Gasperini* seemed to further this approach by writing, "Federal courts have interpreted the Federal Rules . . . with sensitivity to important state interests and regulatory policies" and " 'continued since [*Hanna*] to interpret the federal rules to avoid conflict with important state regulatory policies.' " *Gasperini, 518 U.S. at 428 n.7, 438 n.22*; *see also* Thomas D. Rowe, Jr., *Not Bad For Government*

Work: Does Anyone Else Think the Supreme Court is Doing a Halfway Decent Job in its Erie-Hanna Jurisprudence?, 73 NOTRE DAME L. REV. 963, 994 (1998) (arguing that the Court in *Gasperini* suggested that it favored "more deferential interpretations of federal law to avoid federal-state conflicts"). This seeming trend was halted by the decision in the next case, in which a divided Court declined to give a Federal Rule a construction that would have avoided a conflict with state law.

Shady Grove Orthopedic Assocs. v. Allstate Insurance Co.

Supreme Court of the United States
559 U.S. 393 (2010)

JUSTICE SCALIA announced the judgment of the Court and delivered the opinion of the Court with respect to Parts I and II-A, an opinion with respect to Parts II-B and II-D, in which THE CHIEF JUSTICE, JUSTICE THOMAS, and JUSTICE SOTOMAYOR join, and an opinion with respect to Part II-C, in which THE CHIEF JUSTICE and JUSTICE THOMAS join.

New York law prohibits class actions in suits seeking penalties or statutory minimum damages.[2] We consider whether this precludes a federal district court sitting in diversity from entertaining a class action under Federal Rule of Civil Procedure 23.

I

The petitioner's complaint alleged the following: Shady Grove Orthopedic Associates, P. A., provided medical care to Sonia E. Galvez for injuries she suffered in an automobile accident. As partial payment for that care, Galvez assigned to Shady Grove her rights to insurance benefits under a policy issued in New York by Allstate Insurance Co. Shady Grove tendered a claim for the assigned benefits to Allstate, which under New York law had 30 days to pay the claim or deny it. Allstate appar-

---

[2] N.Y. Civ. Prac. Law Ann. § 901 (West 2006) provides:

"(a) One or more members of a class may sue or be sued as representative parties on behalf of all if:"

"1.   the class is so numerous that joinder of all members, whether otherwise required or permitted, is impracticable;"

"2.   there are questions of law or fact common to the class which predominate over any questions affecting only individual members;"

"3.   the claims or defenses of the representative parties are typical of the claims or defenses of the class;"

"4.   the representative parties will fairly and adequately protect the interests of the class; and"

"5.   a class action is superior to other available methods for the fair and efficient adjudication of the controversy."

"(b) Unless a statute creating or imposing a penalty, or a minimum measure of recovery specifically authorizes the recovery thereof in a class action, an action to recover a penalty, or minimum measure of recovery created or imposed by statute may not be maintained as a class action."

ently paid, but not on time, and it refused to pay the statutory interest that accrued on the overdue benefits (at two percent per month).

Shady Grove filed this diversity suit in the Eastern District of New York to recover the unpaid statutory interest. Alleging that Allstate routinely refuses to pay interest on overdue benefits, Shady Grove sought relief on behalf of itself and a class of all others to whom Allstate owes interest. The District Court dismissed the suit for lack of jurisdiction. It reasoned that N.Y. Civ. Prac. Law Ann. § 901(b), which precludes a suit to recover a "penalty" from proceeding as a class action, applies in diversity suits in federal court, despite Federal Rule of Civil Procedure 23. Concluding that statutory interest is a "penalty" under New York law, it held that § 901(b) prohibited the proposed class action. And, since Shady Grove conceded that its individual claim (worth roughly $500) fell far short of the amount-in-controversy requirement for individual suits under 28 U.S.C. § 1332(a), the suit did not belong in federal court.[3]

The Second Circuit affirmed. The court did not dispute that a federal rule adopted in compliance with the Rules Enabling Act, 28 U.S.C. § 2072, would control if it conflicted with § 901(b). But there was no conflict because * * * the Second Circuit concluded that Rule 23 and § 901(b) address different issues. Finding no federal rule on point, the Court of Appeals held that § 901(b) is "substantive" within the meaning of *Erie R. Co. v. Tompkins,* 304 U.S. 64 (1938), and thus must be applied by federal courts sitting in diversity. * * *

II

The framework for our decision is familiar. We must first determine whether Rule 23 answers the question in dispute. *Burlington Northern R. Co. v. Woods,* 480 U.S. 1, 4–5 (1987). If it does, it governs—New York's law notwithstanding—unless it exceeds statutory authorization or Congress's rulemaking power. We do not wade into *Erie*'s murky waters unless the federal rule is inapplicable or invalid.

A

The question in dispute is whether Shady Grove's suit may proceed as a class action. Rule 23 provides an answer. It states that "[a] class action may be maintained" if two conditions are met: The suit must satisfy the criteria set forth in subdivision (a) (*i.e.,* numerosity, commonality, typicality, and adequacy of representation), and it also must fit into one of the three categories described in subdivision (b). FED. RULE CIV. PROC. 23(b). By its terms this creates a categorical rule entitling a plaintiff whose suit meets the specified criteria to pursue his claim as a class action. * * * Thus, Rule 23 provides a one-size-fits-all formula for deciding the class-action question.

---

[3] Shady Grove had asserted jurisdiction under 28 U.S.C. § 1332(d)(2), which relaxes, for class actions seeking at least $5 million, the rule against aggregating separate claims for calculation of the amount in controversy. See *Exxon Mobil Corp. v. Allapattah Services, Inc.,* 545 U.S. 546, 571 (2005).

Because § 901(b) attempts to answer the same question—*i.e.,* it states that Shady Grove's suit "may *not* be maintained as a class action" (emphasis added) because of the relief it seeks—it cannot apply in diversity suits unless Rule 23 is *ultra vires.*

The Second Circuit believed that § 901(b) and Rule 23 do not conflict because they address different issues. Rule 23, it said, concerns only the criteria for determining whether a given class can and should be certified; section 901(b), on the other hand, addresses an antecedent question: whether the particular type of claim is eligible for class treatment in the first place—a question on which Rule 23 is silent. * * *

We disagree. To begin with, the line between eligibility and certifiability is entirely artificial. Both are preconditions for maintaining a class action. Allstate suggests that eligibility must depend on the "particular cause of action" asserted, instead of some other attribute of the suit. But that is not so. Congress could, for example, provide that only claims involving more than a certain number of plaintiffs are "eligible" for class treatment in federal court. In other words, relabeling Rule 23(a)'s prerequisites "eligibility criteria" would obviate Allstate's objection—a sure sign that its eligibility-certifiability distinction is made-to-order.

There is no reason, in any event, to read Rule 23 as addressing only whether claims made eligible for class treatment by some *other* law should be certified as class actions. Allstate asserts that Rule 23 neither explicitly nor implicitly empowers a federal court "to certify a class in each and every case" where the Rule's criteria are met. But that is *exactly* what Rule 23 does: It says that if the prescribed preconditions are satisfied "[a] class action *may be maintained* " (emphasis added)—not "*a class action may be permitted.*" Courts do not maintain actions; litigants do. The discretion suggested by Rule 23's "may" is discretion residing in the plaintiff: He may bring his claim in a class action if he wishes. And like the rest of the <u>Federal Rules of Civil Procedure, Rule 23</u> *automatically* applies "in all civil actions and proceedings in the United States district courts," <u>Fed. Rule Civ. Proc. 1</u>.

* * *

The dissent argues that § 901(b) has nothing to do with whether Shady Grove may maintain its suit as a class action, but affects only the *remedy* it may obtain if it wins. * * * Accordingly, the dissent says, Rule 23 and New York's law may coexist in peace.

We need not decide whether a state law that limits the remedies available in an existing class action would conflict with Rule 23; that is not what § 901(b) does. By its terms, the provision precludes a plaintiff from "maintain[ing]" a class action seeking statutory penalties. Unlike a law that sets a ceiling on damages (or puts other remedies out of reach) in properly filed class actions, § 901(b) says nothing about what remedies a court may award; it prevents the class actions it covers from coming into existence at all. Consequently, a court bound by § 901(b) could not certify a class action seeking both statutory penalties and other remedies even if it announces in advance that it will refuse to award the penalties in the event the plaintiffs prevail; to do so would violate the statute's clear prohibition on "maintain[ing]" such suits as class actions.

The dissent asserts that a plaintiff can avoid § 901(b)'s barrier by omitting from his complaint (or removing) a request for statutory penalties. Even assuming all statutory penalties are waivable, the fact that a complaint omitting them could be brought as a class action would not at all prove that § 901(b) is addressed only to remedies. If the state law instead banned class actions for fraud claims, a would-be class-action plaintiff could drop the fraud counts from his complaint and proceed with the remainder in a class action. Yet that would not mean the law provides no remedy for fraud; the ban would affect only the procedural means by which the remedy may be pursued. In short, although the dissent correctly abandons Allstate's eligibility-certifiability distinction, the alternative it offers fares no better.

The dissent all but admits that the literal terms of § 901(b) address the same subject as Rule 23—*i.e.*, whether a class action may be maintained—but insists the provision's *purpose* is to restrict only remedies. Unlike Rule 23, designed to further procedural fairness and efficiency, § 901(b) (we are told) "responds to an entirely different concern": the fear that allowing statutory damages to be awarded on a class-wide basis would "produce overkill." * * * [T]he New York Legislature's purpose * * * cannot override the statute's clear text. Even if its aim is to restrict the remedy a plaintiff can obtain, § 901(b) achieves that end by limiting a plaintiff's power to maintain a class action. * * *

* * *

But while the dissent does indeed artificially narrow the scope of § 901(b) by finding that it pursues only substantive policies, that is not the central difficulty of the dissent's position. The central difficulty is that even artificial narrowing cannot render § 901(b) compatible with Rule 23. *Whatever* the policies they pursue, they flatly contradict each other. Allstate asserts * * * that we can (and must) *interpret* Rule 23 in a manner that avoids overstepping its authorizing statute. If the Rule were susceptible of two meanings—one that would violate § 2072(b) and another that would not—we would agree. But it is not. Rule 23 unambiguously authorizes *any* plaintiff, in *any* federal civil proceeding, to maintain a class action if the Rule's prerequisites are met. We cannot contort its text, even to avert a collision with state law that might render it invalid. *See Walker v. Armco Steel Corp.*, 446 U.S. 740, 750, n. 9 (1980).[8] What the dissent's approach achieves is not the avoiding of a "conflict between Rule 23 and § 901(b)," but rather the invalidation of Rule 23 (pursuant to

---

[8] The cases chronicled by the dissent each involved a Federal Rule that we concluded could fairly be read not to "control the issue" addressed by the pertinent state law, thus avoiding a "direct collision" between federal and state law, *Walker*, 446 U.S. at 749 (internal quotation marks omitted). But here, as in *Hanna, supra* at 470, a collision is "unavoidable."

§ 2072(b) of the Rules Enabling Act) to the extent that it conflicts with the substantive policies of § 901. There is no other way to reach the dissent's destination. We must therefore confront head-on whether Rule 23 falls within the statutory authorization.

B

Erie involved the constitutional power of federal courts to supplant state law with judge-made rules. In that context, it made no difference whether the rule was technically one of substance or procedure; the touchstone was whether it "significantly affect[s] the result of a litigation." *Guaranty Trust Co. v. York, 326 U.S. 99, 109 (1945)*. That is not the test for either the constitutionality or the statutory validity of a Federal Rule of Procedure. Congress has undoubted power to supplant state law, and undoubted power to prescribe rules for the courts it has created, so long as those rules regulate matters "rationally capable of classification" as procedure. *Hanna, 380 U.S. at 472*. In the Rules Enabling Act, Congress authorized this Court to promulgate rules of procedure subject to its review, 28 U.S.C. § 2072(a), but with the limitation that those rules "shall not abridge, enlarge or modify any substantive right," § 2072(b).

We have long held that this limitation means that the Rule must "really regulat[e] procedure—the judicial process for enforcing rights and duties recognized by substantive law and for justly administering remedy and redress for disregard or infraction of them," *Sibbach, 312 U.S. at 14*. The test is not whether the rule affects a litigant's substantive rights; most procedural rules do. *Mississippi Publishing Corp. v. Murphree, 326 U.S. 438, 445 (1946)*. What matters is what the rule itself regulates: If it governs only "the manner and the means" by which the litigants' rights are "enforced," it is valid; if it alters "the rules of decision by which [the] court will adjudicate [those] rights," it is not. *Id. at 446*.

Applying that test, we have rejected every statutory challenge to a Federal Rule that has come before us. We have found to be in compliance with § 2072(b) rules prescribing methods for serving process, *see id. at 445–446* (FED. RULE CIV. PROC. 4(f)); *Hanna, supra* at 463–465 (FED. RULE CIV. PROC. 4(d)(1)), and requiring litigants whose mental or physical condition is in dispute to submit to examinations, *see Sibbach, supra* at 14–16 (FED. RULE CIV. PROC. 35); *Schlagenhauf v. Holder, 379 U.S. 104, 113–114 (1964)* (same). Likewise, we have upheld rules authorizing imposition of sanctions upon those who file frivolous appeals, *see Burlington, supra* at 8 (FED. RULE APP. PROC. 38), or who sign court papers without a reasonable inquiry into the facts asserted, *see Business Guides, Inc. v. Chromatic Communications Enterprises, Inc., 498 U.S. 533, 551–554 (1991)* (FED. RULE CIV. PROC. 11). Each of these rules had some practical effect on the parties' rights, but each undeniably regulated only the process for enforcing those rights; none altered the rights themselves, the available remedies, or the rules of decision by which the court adjudicated either.

Applying that criterion, we think it obvious that rules allowing multiple claims (and claims by or against multiple parties) to be litigated together are also valid. *See*, *e.g.*, FED. RULES CIV. PROC. 18 (joinder of claims), 20 (joinder of parties), 42(a) (consolidation of actions). Such rules neither change plaintiffs' separate entitlements to relief nor abridge defendants' rights; they alter only how the claims are processed. For the same reason, Rule 23—at least insofar as it allows willing plaintiffs to join their separate claims against the same defendants in a class action—falls within § 2072(b)'s authorization. A class action, no less than traditional joinder (of which it is a species), merely enables a federal court to adjudicate claims of multiple parties at once, instead of in separate suits. And like traditional joinder, it leaves the parties' legal rights and duties intact and the rules of decision unchanged.

Allstate contends that the authorization of class actions is not substantively neutral: Allowing Shady Grove to sue on behalf of a class "transform[s] [the] dispute over a five *hundred* dollar penalty into a dispute over a five *million* dollar penalty." Allstate's aggregate liability, however, does not depend on whether the suit proceeds as a class action. Each of the 1,000-plus members of the putative class could (as Allstate acknowledges) bring a freestanding suit asserting his individual claim. It is undoubtedly true that some plaintiffs who would not bring individual suits for the relatively small sums involved will choose to join a class action. That has no bearing, however, on Allstate's or the plaintiffs' legal rights. The likelihood that some (even many) plaintiffs will be induced to sue by the availability of a class action is just the sort of "incidental effec[t]" we have long held does not violate § 2072(b).

Allstate argues that Rule 23 violates § 2072(b) because the state law it displaces, § 901(b), creates a right that the Federal Rule abridges—namely, a "substantive right . . . not to be subjected to aggregated class-action liability" in a single suit. To begin with, we doubt that that is so. Nothing in the text of § 901(b) (which is to be found in New York's procedural code) confines it to claims under New York law; and of course New York has no power to alter substantive rights and duties created by other sovereigns. As we have said, the *consequence* of excluding certain class actions may be to cap the damages a defendant can face in a single suit, but the law itself alters only procedure. In that respect, § 901(b) is no different from a state law forbidding simple joinder. As a fallback argument, Allstate argues that even if § 901(b) is a procedural provision, it was enacted "for *substantive reasons*." Its end was not to improve "the conduct of the litigation process itself" but to alter "the outcome of that process."

The fundamental difficulty with both these arguments is that the substantive nature of New York's law, or its substantive purpose, *makes no difference*. A Federal Rule of Procedure is not valid in some jurisdictions and invalid in others—or valid in some cases and invalid in others—depending upon whether its effect is to frustrate a state substantive law (or a state procedural law enacted for substantive purposes).

* * * *Hanna* unmistakably expressed the same understanding that compliance of a Federal Rule with the Enabling Act is to be assessed by consulting the Rule itself, and not its effects in individual applications * * * .

In sum, it is not the substantive or procedural nature or purpose of the affected state law that matters, but the substantive or procedural nature of the Federal Rule. We have held since *Sibbach*, and reaffirmed repeatedly, that the validity of a Federal Rule depends entirely upon whether it regulates procedure. If it does, it is authorized by § 2072 and is valid in all jurisdictions, with respect to all claims, regardless of its incidental effect upon state-created rights.

* * *

D

We must acknowledge the reality that keeping the federal-court door open to class actions that cannot proceed in state court will produce forum shopping. That is unacceptable when it comes as the consequence of judge-made rules created to fill supposed "gaps" in positive federal law. For where neither the Constitution, a treaty, nor a statute provides the rule of decision or authorizes a federal court to supply one, "state law must govern because there can be no other law." But divergence from state law, with the attendant consequence of forum shopping, is the inevitable (indeed, one might say the intended) result of a uniform system of federal procedure. Congress itself has created the possibility that the same case may follow a different course if filed in federal instead of state court. The short of the matter is that a Federal Rule governing procedure is valid whether or not it alters the outcome of the case in a way that induces forum shopping. To hold otherwise would be to "disembowel either the Constitution's grant of power over federal procedure" or Congress's exercise of it.

* * *

The judgment of the Court of Appeals is reversed, and the case is remanded for further proceedings.

It is so ordered.

JUSTICE STEVENS, concurring in part and concurring in the judgment.

The New York law at issue, N.Y. Civ. Prac. Law Ann. (CPLR) § 901(b) (West 2006), is a procedural rule that is not part of New York's substantive law. Accordingly, I agree with Justice SCALIA that Federal Rule of Civil Procedure 23 must apply in this case and join Parts I and II-A of the Court's opinion. * * *

* * *

Because Rule 23 governs class certification, the only decision is whether certifying a class in this diversity case would "abridge, enlarge or modify" New York's substantive rights or remedies. § 2072(b). Although one can argue that class certification would enlarge New York's "limited" damages remedy, such arguments rest on extensive speculation about what the New York Legislature had in mind when it created § 901(b). But given that there are two plausible competing narratives, it seems obvious to me that we should respect the plain textual reading of § 901(b), a rule in New York's procedural code about when to certify class actions brought under any source of law, and respect Congress' decision that Rule 23 governs class certification in federal courts. In order to displace a federal rule, there must be more than just a possibility that the state rule is different than it appears.

Accordingly, I concur in part and concur in the judgment.

JUSTICE GINSBURG, with whom JUSTICE KENNEDY, JUSTICE BREYER, and JUSTICE ALITO join, dissenting.

The Court today approves Shady Grove's attempt to transform a $500 case into a $5,000,000 award, although the State creating the right to recover has proscribed this alchemy. If Shady Grove had filed suit in New York state court, the 2% interest payment authorized by New York Ins. Law Ann. § 5106(a) as a penalty for overdue benefits would, by Shady Grove's own measure, amount to no more than $500. By instead filing in federal court based on the parties' diverse citizenship and requesting class certification, Shady Grove hopes to recover, for the class, statutory damages of more than $5,000,000. The New York Legislature has barred this remedy, instructing that, unless specifically permitted, "an action to recover a penalty, or minimum measure of recovery created or imposed by statute may not be maintained as a class action." N.Y. Civ. Prac. Law Ann. (CPLR) § 901(b). The Court nevertheless holds that Federal Rule of Civil Procedure 23, which prescribes procedures for the conduct of class actions in federal courts, preempts the application of § 901(b) in diversity suits.

The Court reads Rule 23 relentlessly to override New York's restriction on the availability of statutory damages. Our decisions, however, caution us to ask, before undermining state legislation: Is this conflict really necessary? Had the Court engaged in that inquiry, it would not have read Rule 23 to collide with New York's legitimate interest in keeping certain monetary awards reasonably bounded. I would continue to interpret Federal Rules with awareness of, and sensitivity to, important state regulatory policies. Because today's judgment radically departs from that course, I dissent.

I

A

"Under the *Erie* doctrine," it is long settled, "federal courts sitting in diversity apply state substantive law and federal procedural law." *Gasperini v. Center for Humanities, Inc.,* 518 U.S. 415, 427 (1996); see *Erie R. Co. v. Tompkins,* 304 U.S. 64 (1938). Justice Harlan aptly conveyed the importance of the doctrine; he described *Erie* as "one of the modern cornerstones of our federalism, expressing policies that profoundly touch the allocation of judicial power between the state and federal systems." *Hanna v. Plumer,* 380 U.S. 460, 474 (1965) (concurring opinion). Although we have found *Erie*'s application "sometimes [to be] a challenging endeavor," *Gasperini,* 518 U.S. at 427, two federal statutes mark our way.

* * *

If a Federal Rule controls an issue and directly conflicts with state law, the Rule, so long as it is consonant with the Rules Enabling Act, applies in diversity suits. *See Hanna,* 380 U.S. at 469–474. If, however, no Federal Rule or statute governs the issue, the Rules of Decision Act, as interpreted in *Erie,* controls. That Act directs federal courts, in diversity cases, to apply state law when failure to do so would invite forum-shopping and yield markedly disparate litigation outcomes. See *Gasperini,* 518 U.S. at 428; *Hanna,* 380 U.S. at 468. Recognizing that the Rules of Decision Act and the Rules Enabling Act simultaneously frame and inform the *Erie* analysis, we have endeavored in diversity suits to remain safely within the bounds of both congressional directives.

B

In our prior decisions in point, many of them not mentioned in the Court's opinion, we have avoided immoderate interpretations of the Federal Rules that would trench on state prerogatives without serving any countervailing federal interest. "Application of the *Hanna* analysis," we have said, "is premised on a 'direct collision' between the Federal Rule and the state law." *Walker v. Armco Steel Corp.,* 446 U.S. 740, 749–750 (1980) (quoting *Hanna,* 380 U.S. at 472). To displace state law, a Federal Rule, "when fairly construed," must be "sufficiently broad" so as "to 'control the issue' before the court, thereby leaving *no room* for the operation of that law."

In pre-*Hanna* decisions, the Court vigilantly read the Federal Rules to avoid conflict with state laws. * * * [I]n *Ragan v. Merchants Transfer & Warehouse Co.,* 337 U.S. 530 (1949), the Court ruled that state law determines when a diversity suit commences for purposes of tolling the state limitations period. Although Federal Rule 3 specified that "[a] civil action is commenced by filing a complaint with the court," we held that the Rule did not displace a state law that tied an action's commencement to service of the summons. The "cause of action [wa]s created by local law," the Court explained, therefore "the measure of it [wa]s to be found only in local law."

Similarly in *Cohen v. Beneficial Industrial Loan Corp.,* 337 U.S. 541 (1949), the Court held applicable in a diversity action a state statute requiring plaintiffs, as a prerequisite to pursuit of a stockholder's derivative action, to post a bond as security for costs. At the time of the litigation, Rule 23, now Rule 23.1, addressed a plaintiff's institution of a derivative action in federal court. Although the Federal Rule specified prerequisites to a stockholder's maintenance of a derivative action, the Court found no conflict between the Rule and the state statute in question; the requirements of both could be enforced, the Court observed. Burdensome as the security-for-costs requirement may be, *Cohen* made plain, suitors could not escape the upfront outlay by resorting to the federal court's diversity jurisdiction.

In all of these cases, the Court stated in *Hanna,* "the scope of the Federal Rule was not as broad as the losing party urged, and therefore, there being no Federal Rule which covered the point in dispute, *Erie* commanded the enforcement of state law." In *Hanna* itself, the Court found the clash "unavoidable"; the petitioner had effected service of process as prescribed by Federal Rule 4(d)(1), but that "how-to" method did not satisfy the special Massachusetts law applicable to service on an executor or administrator. Even as it rejected the Massachusetts prescription in favor of the federal procedure, however, "[t]he majority in *Hanna* recognized . . . that federal rules . . . must be interpreted by the courts applying them, and that the process of interpretation can and should reflect an awareness of legitimate state interests."

Following *Hanna,* we continued to "interpre[t] the federal rules to avoid conflict with important state regulatory policies." In *Walker,* the Court took up the question whether *Ragan* should be overruled; we held, once again, that Federal Rule 3 does not directly conflict with state rules governing the time when an action commences for purposes of tolling a limitations period. Rule 3, we said, addresses only "the date from which various timing requirements of the Federal Rules begin to run," and does not "purpor[t] to displace state tolling rules." Significant state policy interests would be frustrated, we observed, were we to read Rule 3 as superseding the state rule, which required actual service on the defendant to stop the clock on the statute of limitations.

We were similarly attentive to a State's regulatory policy in *Gasperini.* That diversity case concerned the standard for determining when the large size of a jury verdict warrants a new trial. Federal and state courts alike had generally employed a "shock the conscience" test in reviewing jury awards for excessiveness. See 518 U.S. at 422. Federal courts did so pursuant to Federal Rule 59(a) which, as worded at the time of *Gasperini,* instructed that a trial court could grant a new trial "for any of the reasons for which new trials have heretofore been granted in actions at law in the courts of the United States." FED. RULE CIV. PROC. 59(a). In an effort to provide greater control, New York prescribed procedures under which jury verdicts would be examined to determine whether they "deviate[d] materially from what would be reasonable compensation." This Court held that Rule 59(a) did not inhibit federal-court accommodation of New York's invigorated test.

Most recently, in *Semtek Int'l Inc. v. Lockheed Martin Corp., 531 U.S. 497, 503–504 (2001)*, we addressed the claim-preclusive effect of a federal-court judgment dismissing a diversity action on the basis of a California statute of limitations. The case came to us after the same plaintiff renewed the same fray against the same defendant in a Maryland state court. (Plaintiff chose Maryland because that State's limitations period had not yet run.) We held that Federal Rule 41(b), which provided that an involuntary dismissal "operate[d] as an adjudication on the merits," did not bar maintenance of the renewed action in Maryland. To hold that Rule 41(b) precluded the Maryland courts from entertaining the case, we said, "would arguably violate the jurisdictional limitation of the Rules Enabling Act," and "would in many cases violate [*Erie's*] federalism principle."

* * *

C

Our decisions instruct over and over again that, in the adjudication of diversity cases, state interests—whether advanced in a statute, *e.g., Cohen,* or a procedural rule, *e.g., Gasperini*—warrant our respectful consideration. Yet today, the Court gives no quarter to New York's limitation on statutory damages and requires the lower courts to thwart the regulatory policy at stake: To prevent excessive damages, New York's law controls the penalty to which a defendant may be exposed in a single suit. * * *

* * *

D

Shady Grove contends—and the Court today agrees—that Rule 23 unavoidably preempts New York's prohibition on the recovery of statutory damages in class actions. The Federal Rule, the Court emphasizes, states that Shady Grove's suit "may be" maintained as a class action, which conflicts with § 901(b)'s instruction that it "may not" so proceed. Accordingly, the Court insists, § 901(b) "cannot apply in diversity suits unless Rule 23 is ultra vires." Concluding that Rule 23 does not violate the Rules Enabling Act, the Court holds that the federal provision controls Shady Grove's ability to seek, on behalf of a class, a statutory penalty of over $5,000,000.

The Court, I am convinced, finds conflict where none is necessary. Mindful of the history behind § 901(b)'s enactment, the thrust of our precedent, and the substantive-rights limitation in the Rules Enabling Act, I conclude * * * that Rule 23 does not collide with § 901(b). As the Second Circuit well understood, Rule 23 prescribes the considerations relevant to class certification and postcertification proceedings—but it does not command that a particular remedy be available when a party sues in a representative capacity. Section 901(b), in contrast, trains on that latter issue. Sensibly read, Rule 23 governs procedural aspects of class litigation, but allows state law to control the size of a monetary award a class plaintiff may pursue.

In other words, Rule 23 describes a method of enforcing a claim for relief, while § 901(b) defines the dimensions of the claim itself. In this regard, it is immaterial that § 901(b) bars statutory penalties in wholesale, rather than retail, fashion. The New York Legislature could have embedded the limitation in every provision creating a cause of action for which a penalty is authorized; § 901(b) operates as shorthand to the same effect. It is as much a part of the delineation of the claim for relief as it would be were it included claim by claim in the New York Code.

The Court single-mindedly focuses on whether a suit "may" or "may not" be maintained as a class action. Putting the question that way, the Court does not home in on the reason *why*. Rule 23 authorizes class treatment for suits satisfying its prerequisites because the class mechanism generally affords a fair and efficient way to aggregate claims for adjudication. Section 901(b) responds to an entirely different concern; it does not allow class members to recover statutory damages because the New York Legislature considered the result of adjudicating such claims en masse to be exorbitant. The fair and efficient *conduct* of class litigation is the legitimate concern of Rule 23; the *remedy* for an infraction of state law, however, is the legitimate concern of the State's lawmakers and not of the federal rulemakers.

* * *

The absence of an inevitable collision between Rule 23 and § 901(b) becomes evident once it is comprehended that a federal court sitting in diversity can accord due respect to both state and federal prescriptions. Plaintiffs seeking to vindicate claims for which the State has provided a statutory penalty may pursue relief through a class action if they forgo statutory damages and instead seek actual damages or injunctive or declaratory relief; any putative class member who objects can opt out and pursue actual damages, if available, and the statutory penalty in an individual action. * * * In sum, while phrased as responsive to the question whether certain class actions may begin, § 901(b) is unmistakably aimed at controlling how those actions must end. On that remedial issue, Rule 23 is silent.

Any doubt whether Rule 23 leaves § 901(b) in control of the remedial issue at the core of this case should be dispelled by our *Erie* jurisprudence, including *Hanna*, which counsels us to read Federal Rules moderately and cautions against stretching a rule to cover every situation it could conceivably reach. * * * By finding a conflict without considering whether Rule 23 rationally should be read to avoid any collision, the Court unwisely and unnecessarily retreats from the federalism principles undergirding *Erie*. * * *

II

Because I perceive no unavoidable conflict between Rule 23 and § 901(b), I would decide this case by inquiring "whether application of the [state] rule would have so important an effect upon the fortunes of one or both of the litigants that failure to [apply] it would be likely to cause a plaintiff to choose the federal court." *Hanna*, 380 U.S. at 468, n. 9. *See Gasperini*, 518 U.S. at 428.

* * *

It is beyond debate that "a statutory cap on damages would supply substantive law for *Erie* purposes." *Gasperini*, 518 U.S. at 428. In *Gasperini*, we determined that New York's standard for measuring the alleged excessiveness of a jury verdict was designed to provide a control analogous to a damages cap. The statute was framed as "a procedural instruction," we noted, "but the State's objective [wa]s manifestly substantive."

Gasperini's observations apply with full force in this case. By barring the recovery of statutory damages in a class action, § 901(b) controls a defendant's maximum liability in a suit seeking such a remedy. The remedial provision could have been written as an explicit cap: "In any class action seeking statutory damages, relief is limited to the amount the named plaintiff would have recovered in an individual suit." That New York's Legislature used other words to express the very same meaning should be inconsequential.

We have long recognized the impropriety of displacing, in a diversity action, state-law limitations on state-created remedies. Just as *Erie* precludes a federal court from entering a deficiency judgment when a State has "authoritatively announced that [such] judgments cannot be secured within its borders," *Angel v. Bullington*, 330 U.S. 183, 191 (1947), so too *Erie* should prevent a federal court from awarding statutory penalties aggregated through a class action when New York prohibits this recovery. In sum, because "New York substantive law governs [this] claim for relief, New York law . . . guide[s] the allowable damages." *Gasperini*, 518 U.S. at 437.

* * *

I would continue to approach *Erie* questions in a manner mindful of the purposes underlying the Rules of Decision Act and the Rules Enabling Act, faithful to precedent, and respectful of important state interests. I would therefore hold that the New York Legislature's limitation on the recovery of statutory damages applies in this case, and would affirm the Second Circuit's judgment.

Points for Discussion

a. Determining Federal-State Conflict After *Shady Grove*

As discussed above, prior to *Shady Grove* it had appeared that the Court might favor reading Federal Rules narrowly to avoid a conflict with competing state law. However, in *Shady Grove* the majority interpreted Rule 23 as governing the issue of whether and under what circumstances a class action may be maintained, the same issue that—in the view of the majority—was covered by the New York statute. Do you agree with that interpretation? Was there an alternative, narrower interpretation of Rule 23 that could have avoided this conflict?

Justice Ginsburg's dissent offers one way out of this seeming conflict: to interpret New York CPLR § 901(b) as addressing the *remedy* available to litigants seeking statutory damages, a matter (according to Justice Ginsburg) that Rule 23 does not—and could not, consistent with the Rules Enabling Act—address. Is Justice Ginsburg's characterization of the competing provisions convincing?

Note that in *Shady Grove*, as in the cases that preceded it in this line, the key decisions affecting the outcome are made at the threshold of the analysis: What is the relevant issue at hand and do both of the competing federal and state legal provisions cover that issue so as to create an unavoidable conflict? As the cases reveal, reasonable people can disagree about what the relevant issue is. In *Shady Grove* Justice Ginsburg thought the issue was the scope of the New York law claim and its attendant available remedy, while Justice Scalia defined the issue as whether a class action may be maintained by a litigant in federal court. After reading all of the post-*Hanna* cases through *Shady Grove*, do you have a clear sense of how to make this threshold determination in a principled and consistent fashion? Are there fundamental differences between how Justice Scalia and Justice Ginsburg approach the task of identifying the issue at hand? Is there only one "correct" answer to that question in each case or will there always be room to define the issue at hand in multiple ways?

b. *Erie/Hanna* Doctrine After *Shady Grove*

Does the holding of *Shady Grove* alter the *Erie/Hanna* doctrine in any major way, or does the case simply reflect an application of the established doctrine to a new set of facts?

Notwithstanding the Justices' divisions in *Gasperini* and *Hanna* over the proper way to formulate the issue at hand and which analysis—*Erie* or *Hanna*—applies, there does seem to be a more uniform view among the Justices of how an *Erie* or a *Hanna* analysis is conducted once one determines which of the two applies. An *Erie* analysis continue to require an assessment of whether either or both of the twin aims of *Erie* are implicated in the manner explained in *Hanna*, followed by—when necessary—a balancing of any important federal policy concerns that might underlie the competing federal approach. A *Hanna* analysis, on the other hand, focuses on whether the rule or statute in question regulates procedure—the manner and mode of enforcing substantive rights—as its lodestar for determining the validity and constitutionality of codified Federal Rules and statutes.

c.   Horizontal Choice-of-Law Questions

Once a federal court has determined under the *Erie* doctrine that it must apply state law, the horizontal choice-of-law question alluded to at the beginning of this chapter—which state's law applies to a particular issue—comes into play. Although the precise rules for determining which state's law applies to an issue are the subject of a separate law school course—Conflict of Laws—and thus beyond the scope of your basic first-year procedure course, what is important to know is that federal courts sitting in diversity that are faced with resolving such horizontal choice-of-law questions are bound to follow the choice-of-law rules of the state in which they sit. *Klaxon Co. v. Stentor Elec. Mfg. Co.*, 313 U.S. 487, 496 (1941) ("The conflict of laws rules to be applied by the federal court in Delaware must conform to those prevailing in Delaware's state courts."). For a discussion of the various approaches to choice-of-law analysis among the states, see Symeon C. Symeonides, *Choice of Law in the American Courts in 2015: Twenty-Ninth Annual Survey*, 64 Am. J. Comp. L. 221 (2016).

> **FYI**
>
> The Court has held that states are permitted to choose to apply their own substantive law in a case provided that the state has "a significant contact or significant aggregation of contacts, creating state interests, such that choice of its law is neither arbitrary nor fundamentally unfair." *Allstate Ins. Co. v. Hague*, 449 U.S. 302, 312–13 (1981).

d.   Reverse-*Erie*

The *Erie/Hanna* doctrine we have been studying concerns itself with the question of whether state or federal law applies to various matters when federal courts handle state-law claims. An inverse version of this question arises in state court: When must a state court apply federal law rather than state law? This is a relatively simple matter when Congress has explicitly or impliedly indicated that federal law preempts conflicting state law and thus binds state courts under the Constitution's Supremacy Clause. U.S. CONST. art. VI. In the absence of preemption, a federally-crafted vertical choice-of-law analysis becomes necessary:

> [I]n the absence of . . . a constitutional or congressional directive, and in the absence of binding precedent, the state courts and ultimately the U.S. Supreme Court must decide whether the existing federal law applies in state court. The courts do so by employing . . . a federally mandated judicial choice-of-law methodology similar to the *Erie* methodology. Just as the

Erie methodology itself is specialized federal common law, the reverse-*Erie* judicial choice-of-law methodology is a federal-common-law creation of the U.S. Supreme Court that the state courts must follow.

If those reverse-*Erie* methodologies yield a choice in favor of federal law, that choice is binding on the state courts under the Supremacy Clause. Thus, <u>*Hinderlider v. La Plata River & Cherry Creek Ditch Co.*, 304 U.S. 92 (1938)</u> an interstate water case decided in an opinion by Justice Brandeis on the same day as his *Erie* opinion, held that substantive federal common law, which would govern in the federal courts, also binds the state courts. But if those methodologies yield a choice in favor of state law, the state is left free to create and apply it. Thus, <u>*Oregon ex rel. State Land Board v. Corvallis Sand & Gravel Co.*, 429 U.S. 363 (1977)</u> on review of the Oregon Supreme Court, held that state law solely governed the disputed ownership of lands along a navigable river inside the state, after the lands had become riverbed because of avulsive changes in the river's course.

Kevin M. Clermont, *Federal Courts, Practice & Procedure: Reverse*-Erie, <u>82 NOTRE DAME L. REV. 1, 20–21 (2006)</u>. For a full discussion of reverse-*Erie*, see <u>id. at 20–46</u>.

Executive Summary

■ **The Context for Vertical Choice-of-Law Questions.** The issue of whether to apply federal law or a competing state legal rule is one that arises when federal courts are handling state-law claims. In general, when the claim arises under federal law, no issue about whether to apply state law to some aspect of the matter comes into play.

■ **Two Strains of Analysis.** The Court in *Hanna* clarified that there are two separate analytical frameworks for analyzing vertical choice-of-law problems depending upon the nature of the competing federal legal rule involved: A *Hanna* Rules Enabling Act analysis for circumstances in which there is a Federal Rule of Civil Procedure that governs the situation (or a simplified *Hanna* analysis for circumstances in which a federal statute supplies the competing legal rule) and a modified-*Erie* analysis to determine whether a federal court should follow the state legal rule in the absence of a governing Federal Rule or federal statute.

■ **Threshold Question.** Given these two strains, the critical point in the analysis is the threshold question of whether there is a codified Federal Rule or federal statute that can be read to govern the issue at hand. If so, a *Hanna* analysis must be pursued. Otherwise, the modified-*Erie* analysis is appropriate. As members of the

Supreme Court have demonstrated in their own efforts to resolve this threshold question, this determination is an imprecise matter about which reasonable people can disagree.

■ *Hanna* **Analysis.** The presence of a governing Federal Rule or federal statute simply requires one to determine whether the provision is constitutional, and, in the case of a Federal Rule, valid under the Rules Enabling Act.

■ **Modified-*Erie* Analysis.** In the absence of a governing federal statute or Federal Rule of Civil Procedure, courts consider whether application of the state law in federal diversity actions would implicate the twin aims of *Erie*, and, if so, whether there are any countervailing federal interests that would nonetheless suggest applying federal law.

Major Themes

The following are two key themes that emerge from the *Erie/Hanna* material:

a. ***Federalism***—federalism concerns, namely a respect for the authority of states over substantive law within their territories and adhering to the notion of a government of limited, delegated powers, animates the Court's vertical choice-of-law jurisprudence.

b. ***Forum Shopping & Fairness***—diversity jurisdiction is not intended to give litigants the opportunity to shop for a forum that will apply a more favorable body of law; thus, differences in legal rules that would cause litigants to favor one system over the other will tend to militate in favor of applying the state law in a federal court sitting in diversity. This discourages forum shopping and avoids the inequity of affording only certain litigants access to a distinct, more favorable body of law.

For More Information

Students interested in studying the *Erie/Hanna* doctrine further may consult the following resources:

- 19 C. WRIGHT, A. MILLER, & E. COOPER, FED. PRAC. & PROC. § 4501 *et seq.* (3d ed. 2016).
- Richard D. Freer, *Some Thoughts on the State of* Erie *after* Gasperini, 76 TEX. L. REV. 1637 (1998).
- Adam N. Steinman, *What Is the* Erie *Doctrine (And What Does It Mean for the Contemporary Politics of Judicial Federalism?)*, 84 NOTRE DAME L. REV. 245 (2008).

Test Your Knowledge

To assess your understanding of the material in this chapter, click here to take a quiz.

CHAPTER SIX

Pleading

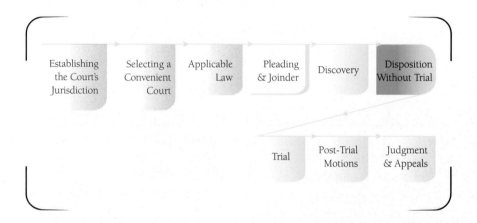

Introduction

HAVING DEALT WITH THE PRELIMINARY matters of selecting the proper court and identifying the applicable law, we now turn our attention to the process of initiating, prosecuting, and defending a civil action in the federal courts. A civil action is commenced in the federal system by the filing of a complaint by the plaintiff. FED. R. CIV. P. 3. Several questions surround this and ensuing procedures: What is a complaint and what information must it include? What are the permissible ways in which a defendant may or must respond to a complaint? Are there any means of ensuring that litigants are truthful in these submissions? And finally, is there any way to change the substance of these documents— referred to as pleadings—after they have been filed with the court and served on the parties? These are questions that this chapter will address.

What's That?

Pleadings are the documents filed with a court and served on other parties in which a litigant pleads its case, either asserting claims or raising defenses.

Before doing so, it is useful to consider the origins of our current approach to pleading and the purposes that pleadings are intended to serve. We do this to better understand why the rules governing pleadings are written as they are. Modern federal pleading rules evolved from earlier common-law pleading and code pleading systems. Under these predecessor regimes the pleadings were intended to accomplish a variety of disparate objectives:

Historical Functions of Pleading

- **Notice.** The pleadings served to notify the parties and the court of the nature of the claims and defenses raised in the case.

- **Fact Presentation.** The pleadings also set forth the facts in support of the parties' claims or defenses.

- **Screening.** The pleadings helped courts evaluate the merits of claims and weed out those that were frivolous or unmeritorious before proceeding to trial.

- **Issue Narrowing.** Finally, the process of pleading back and forth served to narrow the range of issues that would have to be resolved by the court.

What's That?

Common-law pleading refers to the *writ system* of pleading inherited from England that required plaintiffs to fit their claims within certain *forms of action* and defendants to respond either by challenging the legal entitlement to relief (a *demurrer*), challenging the facts alleged by the plaintiff (a *traverse*), or asserting additional facts that excused the defendant's actions (*confession and avoidance*). The parties would plead back and forth until a single legal or factual issue was isolated for the court or a jury to resolve. Plaintiffs choosing the wrong form of action would have their cases dismissed and would be forced to start over.

Code pleading was a mid-19th century response to common-law pleading—championed by David Dudley Field—that abolished the forms of action and emphasized the pleading of facts. For a thorough presentation of the history of pleading in the federal system, see Stephen N. Subrin, *How Equity Conquered Common Law: The Federal Rules of Civil Procedure in Historical Perspective*, 135 U. PA. L. REV. 909 (1987).

Over time, the common-law pleading system became increasingly rigid as parties and courts focused more on legal technicalities, such as issue narrowing and fitting the case within the correct form of action (common-law legal categories for certain types of claims), than on resolving the case on its merits. Further, under the common-law system, there was no discovery. As a result, pleadings took on heightened importance because they were the only pretrial mechanism through which the parties and the courts could obtain information regarding the disputed issues in the case.

Code pleading (described briefly in the accompanying *What's That?* text box)—which for the most part was the successor to common-law pleading in the United States—attempted to move the pleadings phase away from an emphasis on legal technicalities by focusing on the notice-giving function of pleadings. However, code pleading ultimately proved unworkable because of its insistence on the pleading of facts rather than legal conclusions, and because of the enduring legacy of the rigid common-law pleading system to which courts and litigants had grown accustomed. *Gillispie v. Goodyear Service Stores*, 128 S.E.2d 762 (N.C. 1963), decided under North Carolina's code pleading system, illustrates the level of factual detail expected in such systems:

> "In an action or defense based upon negligence, it is not sufficient to allege the mere happening of an event of an injurious nature and call it negligence on the part of the party sought to be charged. This is necessarily so because negligence is not a fact in itself, but is the legal result of certain facts. Therefore, the facts which constitute the negligence charged and also the facts which establish such negligence as the proximate cause * * * of the injury must be alleged." [*Shives v. Sample*, 79 S.E.2d 193 (N.C. 1953).] * * *

> The complaint states no facts upon which these legal conclusions may be predicated. Plaintiff's allegations do not disclose *what* occurred, *when* it occurred, *where* it occurred, *who* did *what*, the relationships between defendants and plaintiff or of defendants *inter se*, or any other factual data that might identify the occasion or describe the circumstances of the alleged wrongful conduct of defendants.

Gillispie, 128 S.E.2d at 765–66.

The Advent of the Federal Rules of Civil Procedure

The Federal Rules of Civil Procedure, which took effect in 1938, in part were a response to these earlier pleading regimes. The Federal Rules made no pretense of achieving all of the various functions set forth above. Rather, pleading now was to be solely concerned with providing notice to the parties of the claims and defenses in the case. Detailed fact pleading was no longer required and the forms of action were abolished. Fed. R. Civ. P. 2 ("There is one form of action—the civil action.").

Other procedural innovations of the Federal Rules were developed to achieve those additional goals that previously were the responsibility of the pleadings. For example, Rule 11

> **Take Note!**
>
> The idea that detailed fact pleading is not required under the Federal Rules has been called into question in recent years in the wake of two pleading decisions that will be covered later in this chapter, *Bell Atlantic Corp. v. Twombly*, 550 U.S. 544 (2007), and *Ashcroft v. Iqbal*, 556 U.S. 662 (2009).

(treated in Section D below) was created to impose a certification requirement intended to deter and punish the raising of frivolous claims or defenses. Rule 56 provided for summary judgment (covered in Chapter 9), which empowered courts preliminarily to dispose of cases not worthy of consideration at trial by a jury due to the absence of any genuine, material factual dispute. Rules 26 through 37 provided for extensive pretrial discovery (covered in Chapter 8) between the parties, eliminating the need for the pleadings to communicate the facts upon which each side relied for its position.

In the remainder of this chapter, we will take a look at the main rules that govern pleading in the federal system today (Rules 7, 8 and 9), the rule designed to prevent and sanction untruthful or frivolous pleading (Rule 11), and the rule that permits parties to change their pleadings if necessary (Rule 15). We will also cover the defenses and objections that defendants may raise in response to a lawsuit. The basic flow of the pleading process is illustrated in **Figure 6.1** below. *See also* FED. R. CIV. P. 7(a) (outlining the permitted pleadings).

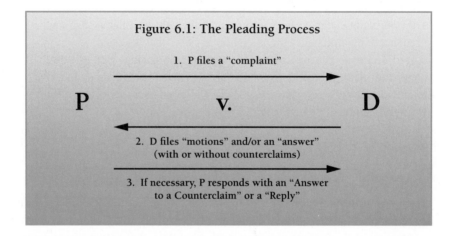

Figure 6.1: The Pleading Process

1. P files a "complaint"

P   V.   D

2. D files "motions" and/or an "answer"
   (with or without counterclaims)

3. If necessary, P responds with an "Answer
   to a Counterclaim" or a "Reply"

A. The Complaint

As mentioned earlier, a civil action is initiated in the federal system by filing a complaint. Rule 8(a) provides the basic instructions regarding what information must be included in the this document:

FRCP 8(a). General Rules of Pleading: Claim for Relief.

(a) **Claim for Relief.** A pleading that states a claim for relief must contain:

(1) a short and plain statement of the grounds for the court's jurisdiction, unless the court already has jurisdiction and the claim needs no new jurisdictional support;

(2) a short and plain statement of the claim showing that the pleader is entitled to relief; and

(3) a demand for the relief sought, which may include relief in the alternative or different types of relief.

The elements that a complaint should include are thus threefold: There must be a statement of the basis for the court's subject matter jurisdiction, the plaintiff's claim must be set forth, and the relief that the plaintiff seeks must be demanded. Establishing subject matter jurisdiction was covered in Chapter 3. Below we will focus on the statement of the claim and the prayer for relief.

1. Sufficiency of the Complaint Under the Federal Rules

Focusing first on the need to state one's claim, what does it mean to set forth a "short and plain statement of the claim showing that the pleader is entitled to relief"? FED. R. CIV. P. 8(a)(2). Must one set forth the who, what, when, where, and how that was required under code pleading as illustrated above in *Gillispie*? The Supreme Court originally answered this question in the negative in *Conley v. Gibson*, 355 U.S. 41 (1957):

In appraising the sufficiency of the complaint we follow, of course, the accepted rule that a complaint should not be dismissed for failure to state a claim unless it appears beyond doubt that the plaintiff can prove no set of facts in support of his claim which would entitle him to relief. Here, the complaint alleged, in part, that petitioners were discharged wrongfully by the Railroad and that the Union, acting according to plan, refused to protect their jobs as it did those of white employees or to help them with their grievances all because they were Negroes. If these allegations are proven there has been a manifest breach of the Union's statutory

What's That?

Dismissal for failure to state a claim is an objection that a defendant may raise under Rule 12(b)(6). The objection claims that the complaint is insufficient under the rules or that the complaint, even if true, does not entitle the plaintiff to any relief. This objection will be considered in further detail below.

duty to represent fairly and without hostile discrimination all of the employees in the bargaining unit. * * *

The respondents also argue that the complaint failed to set forth specific facts to support its general allegations of discrimination and that its dismissal is therefore proper. The decisive answer to this is that the Federal Rules of Civil Procedure do not require a claimant to set out in detail the facts upon which he bases his claim. To the contrary, all the Rules require is "a short and plain statement of the claim" that will give the defendant fair notice of what the plaintiff's claim is and the grounds upon which it rests. The illustrative forms appended to the Rules plainly demonstrate this. Such simplified "notice pleading" is made possible by the liberal opportunity for discovery and the other pretrial procedures established by the Rules to disclose more precisely the basis of both claim and defense and to define more narrowly the disputed facts and issues. Following the simple guide of Rule 8(f) that "all pleadings shall be so construed as to do substantial justice," we have no doubt that petitioners' complaint adequately set forth a claim and gave the respondents fair notice of its basis. The Federal Rules reject the approach that pleading is a game of skill in which one misstep by counsel may be decisive to the outcome and accept the principle that the purpose of pleading is to facilitate a proper decision on the merits.

Take Note!

The Conley Court referred to "illustrative forms appended to the Rules" in support of its opinion that notice pleading did not require the plaintiff to set forth specific facts supporting the allegation of discrimination. In 2015 the Supreme Court approved amendments to abrogate these forms, which formerly appeared as an Appendix to the Rules and were deemed sufficient under Rule 84, which was also abrogated. For more information on the Official Forms, their historical utility, and the arguments surrounding their abrogation, see A. Benjamin Spencer, *The Forms Had a Function: Rule 84 and the Appendix of Forms as Guardians of the Liberal Ethos in Civil Procedure*, 15 NEV. L.J. 1113 (2015).

Id. at 45–48. Thus, the Court's answer to the question of how much detail must a plaintiff include in the pleadings under the Federal Rules was not very much. Instead, the Court said that Rules "do not require a claimant to set out in detail the facts upon which he bases his claim" and that "all the Rules require is a 'short and plain statement of the claim' that will give the defendant fair notice of what the plaintiff's claim is and the ground upon which it rests."

Although the *Conley* Court emphasized that the Federal Rules impose only a simplified notice pleading regime, it has remained difficult to know with any certainty just what degree of detail is required to make a complaint sufficient. In the next two cases, the Court gave mixed messages about the level of detail required by <u>Rule 8(a)(2)</u>, ultimately leaving some doubt about the future of notice pleading.

Swierkiewicz v. Sorema N.A.

Supreme Court of the United States
<u>534 U.S. 506 (2002)</u>

JUSTICE <u>THOMAS</u> delivered the opinion of the Court.

This case presents the question whether a complaint in an employment discrimination lawsuit must contain specific facts establishing a prima facie case of discrimination under the framework set forth by this Court in <u>McDonnell Douglas Corp. v. Green, 411 U.S. 792 (1973)</u>. We hold that an employment discrimination complaint need not include such facts and instead must contain only "a short and plain statement of the claim showing that the pleader is entitled to relief." FED. RULE CIV. PROC. 8(a)(2).

What's That?

A *prima facie case* refers to the presentation of sufficient allegations that, if left unchallenged, would suffice to establish the claim.

I

Petitioner Akos Swierkiewicz is a native of Hungary, who at the time of his complaint was 53 years old. In April 1989, petitioner began working for respondent Sorema N.A., a reinsurance company headquartered in New York and principally owned and controlled by a French parent corporation. Petitioner was initially employed in the position of senior vice president and chief underwriting officer (CUO). Nearly six years later, François M. Chavel, respondent's Chief Executive Officer, demoted petitioner to a marketing and services position and transferred the bulk of his underwriting responsibilities to Nicholas Papadopoulo, a 32-year-old who, like Mr. Chavel, is a French national. About a year later, Mr. Chavel stated that he wanted to "energize" the underwriting department and appointed Mr. Papadopoulo as CUO. Petitioner claims that Mr. Papadopoulo had only one year of underwriting experience at the time he was promoted, and therefore was less experienced and less qualified to be CUO than he, since at that point he had 26 years of experience in the insurance industry.

Following his demotion, petitioner contends that he "was isolated by Mr. Chavel . . . excluded from business decisions and meetings and denied the opportunity to reach his true potential at SOREMA." Petitioner unsuccessfully attempted to meet with

Mr. Chavel to discuss his discontent. Finally, in April 1997, petitioner sent a memo to Mr. Chavel outlining his grievances and requesting a severance package. Two weeks later, respondent's general counsel presented petitioner with two options: He could either resign without a severance package or be dismissed. Mr. Chavel fired petitioner after he refused to resign.

Petitioner filed a lawsuit alleging that he had been terminated on account of his national origin in violation of Title VII of the Civil Rights Act of 1964, and on account of his age in violation of the Age Discrimination in Employment Act of 1967 (ADEA). The United States District Court for the Southern District of New York dismissed petitioner's complaint because it found that he "ha[d] not adequately alleged a prima facie case, in that he ha[d] not adequately alleged circumstances that support an inference of discrimination." The United States Court of Appeals for the Second Circuit affirmed the dismissal, relying on its settled precedent, which requires a plaintiff in an employment discrimination complaint to allege facts constituting a prima facie case of discrimination under the framework set forth by this Court in *McDonnell Douglas*. The Court of Appeals held that petitioner had failed to meet his burden because his allegations were "insufficient as a matter of law to raise an inference of discrimination." We granted certiorari to resolve a split among the Courts of Appeals concerning the proper pleading standard for employment discrimination cases, and now reverse.

Food for Thought

The Second Circuit here applied its own precedent requiring plaintiffs alleging employment discrimination to allege facts that establish a *prima facie* case. Do you think this requirement is consistent with the *Conley* Court's interpretation of Rule 8(a)(2)?

II

Applying Circuit precedent, the Court of Appeals required petitioner to plead a prima facie case of discrimination in order to survive respondent's motion to dismiss. In the Court of Appeals' view, petitioner was thus required to allege in his complaint: (1) membership in a protected group; (2) qualification for the job in question; (3) an adverse employment action; and (4) circumstances that support an inference of discrimination. McDonnell Douglas, 411 U.S. at 802.

Make the Connection

The type of claim asserted here, one alleging discrimination under Title VII of the Civil Rights Act, is something that you will study further if you take a course on **Civil Rights Litigation** or perhaps an advanced **Constitutional Law** course. Here, where the Court refers to a *prima facie* case, it is simply identifying what a plaintiff must establish at trial to create an inference of discrimination, which the defendant then must seek to rebut.

The prima facie case under *McDonnell Douglas*, however, is an evidentiary standard, not a pleading requirement. In *McDonnell Douglas*, this Court made clear that "[t]he critical issue before us concern[ed] the order and allocation of proof in a private, non-class action challenging employment discrimination." In subsequent cases, this Court has reiterated that the prima facie case relates to the employee's burden of presenting evidence that raises an inference of discrimination.

This Court has never indicated that the requirements for establishing a prima facie case under *McDonnell Douglas* also apply to the pleading standard that plaintiffs must satisfy in order to survive a motion to dismiss. For instance, we have rejected the argument that a Title VII complaint requires greater "particularity," because this would "too narrowly constric[t] the role of the pleadings." <u>McDonald v. Santa Fe Trail Transp. Co., 427 U.S. 273, 283 n.11 (1976)</u>. Consequently, the ordinary rules for assessing the sufficiency of a complaint apply. *See, e.g.,* <u>Scheuer v. Rhodes, 416 U.S. 232, 236 (1974)</u> ("When a federal court reviews the sufficiency of a complaint, before the reception of any evidence either by affidavit or admissions, its task is necessarily a limited one. The issue is not whether a plaintiff will ultimately prevail but whether the claimant is entitled to offer evidence to support the claims").

* * *

Furthermore, imposing the Court of Appeals' heightened pleading standard in employment discrimination cases conflicts with <u>Federal Rule of Civil Procedure 8(a) (2)</u>, which provides that a complaint must include only "a short and plain statement of the claim showing that the pleader is entitled to relief." Such a statement must simply "give the defendant fair notice of what the plaintiff's claim is and the grounds upon which it rests." <u>Conley v. Gibson, 355 U.S. 41, 47 (1957)</u>. This simplified notice pleading standard relies on liberal discovery rules and summary judgment motions to define disputed facts and issues and to dispose of unmeritorious claims. *See* <u>id. at 47–48</u>; <u>Leatherman v. Tarrant County Narcotics Intelligence and Coordination Unit, 507 U.S. 163, 168–69 (1993)</u>. "The provisions for discovery are so flexible and the provisions for pretrial procedure and summary judgment so effective, that attempted surprise in federal practice is aborted very easily, synthetic issues detected, and the gravamen of the dispute brought frankly into the open for the inspection of the court." 5 C. WRIGHT & A. MILLER, <u>5 FEDERAL PRACTICE AND PROCEDURE: CIVIL 3D § 1202</u>, p. 76 (2d ed. 1990).

<u>Rule 8(a)</u>'s simplified pleading standard applies to all civil actions, with limited exceptions. Rule 9(b), for example, provides for greater particularity in all averments of fraud or mistake.[3] This Court, however, has declined to extend such

---

[3] "In all averments of fraud or mistake, the circumstances constituting fraud or mistake shall be stated with particularity. Malice, intent, knowledge, and other condition of mind of a person may be averred generally."

exceptions to other contexts. In *Leatherman* we stated: "[T]he Federal Rules do address in Rule 9(b) the question of the need for greater particularity in pleading certain actions, but do not include among the enumerated actions any reference to complaints alleging municipal liability under § 1983. *Expressio unius est exclusio alterius.*" 507 U.S., at 168. Just as Rule 9(b) makes no mention of municipal liability * * *, neither does it refer to employment discrimination. Thus, complaints in these cases, as in most others, must satisfy only the simple requirements of Rule 8(a).[4]

> **It's Latin to Me!**
>
> *Expressio unius est exclusio alterius* is Latin for "the expression of one is the exclusion of others." This is a canon of statutory construction that holds that where a statute expressly mentions certain items, it should be interpreted to exclude those items not mentioned.

Other provisions of the Federal Rules of Civil Procedure are inextricably linked to Rule 8(a)'s simplified notice pleading standard. Rule 8(e)(1) states that "[n]o technical forms of pleading or motions are required," and Rule 8(f) provides that "[a]ll pleadings shall be so construed as to do substantial justice." Given the Federal Rules' simplified standard for pleading, "[a] court may dismiss a complaint only if it is clear that no relief could be granted under any set of facts that could be proved consistent with the allegations." If a pleading fails to specify the allegations in a manner that provides sufficient notice, a defendant can move for a more definite statement under Rule 12(e) before responding. Moreover, claims lacking merit may be dealt with through summary judgment under Rule 56. The liberal notice pleading of Rule 8(a) is the starting point of a simplified pleading system, which was adopted to focus litigation on the merits of a claim. *See Conley, 355 U.S. at 48* ("The Federal Rules reject the approach that pleading is a game of skill in which one misstep by counsel may be decisive to the outcome and accept the principle that the purpose of pleading is to facilitate a proper decision on the merits").

Applying the relevant standard, petitioner's complaint easily satisfies the requirements of Rule 8(a) because it gives respondent fair notice of the basis for petitioner's claims. Petitioner alleged that he had been terminated on account of his national origin in violation of Title VII and on account of his age in violation of the ADEA. His complaint detailed the events leading to his termination, provided relevant dates, and included the ages and nationalities of at least some of the relevant persons involved with his termination. These allegations give respondent fair notice

---

[4] These requirements are exemplified by the Federal Rules of Civil Procedure Forms, which "are sufficient under the rules and are intended to indicate the simplicity and brevity of statement which the rules contemplate." FED. R. CIV. P. 84. For example, Form 9 sets forth a complaint for negligence in which plaintiff simply states in relevant part: "On June 1, 1936, in a public highway called Boylston Street in Boston, Massachusetts, defendant negligently drove a motor vehicle against plaintiff who was then crossing said highway." [Form 9, referred to here, became Form 11 as a result of the 2007 restyling of the civil rules. These forms are slated to be abrogated on December 1, 2015 absent contrary action by Congress. Ed.]

of what petitioner's claims are and the grounds upon which they rest. In addition, they state claims upon which relief could be granted under Title VII and the ADEA.

Respondent argues that allowing lawsuits based on conclusory allegations of discrimination to go forward will burden the courts and encourage disgruntled employees to bring unsubstantiated suits. Whatever the practical merits of this argument, the Federal Rules do not contain a heightened pleading standard for employment discrimination suits. A requirement of greater specificity for particular claims is a result that "must be obtained by the process of amending the Federal Rules, and not by judicial interpretation." *Leatherman*, 507 U.S. at 168. Furthermore, Rule 8(a) establishes a pleading standard without regard to whether a claim will succeed on the merits. "Indeed it may appear on the face of the pleadings that a recovery is very remote and unlikely but that is not the test."

> **Take Note!**
>
> The respondent offered a policy argument here in support of the Second Circuit's fact pleading requirement. Why would the respondent bother to make such an argument? Do you think such an argument might have some value in terms of persuading the Court to reconsider its previous interpretation of Rule 8(a)(2) in *Conley*? Does this point justify imposing a heightened pleading standard?

For the foregoing reasons, we hold that an employment discrimination plaintiff need not plead a *prima facie* case of discrimination and that petitioner's complaint is sufficient to survive respondent's motion to dismiss. Accordingly, the judgment of the Court of Appeals is reversed, and the case is remanded for further proceedings consistent with this opinion.

It is so ordered.

Bell Atlantic Corp. v. Twombly

Supreme Court of the United States
550 U.S. 544 (2007)

JUSTICE SOUTER delivered the opinion of the Court.

Liability under § 1 of the Sherman Act, 15 U.S.C. § 1, requires a "contract, combination . . . , or conspiracy, in restraint of trade or commerce." The question in this putative class action is whether [the] § 1 complaint can survive a motion to dismiss. * * *

I

The upshot of the 1984 divestiture of the American Telephone & Telegraph Company's (AT&T) local telephone business was a system of regional service monopolies (variously called "Regional Bell Operating Companies," "Baby Bells," or "Incumbent Local Exchange Carriers" (ILECs)), and a separate, competitive market for long-distance service from which the ILECs were excluded. More than a decade later, Congress withdrew approval of the ILECs' monopolies by enacting the Telecommunications Act of 1996 (1996 Act), 110 Stat. 56, which "fundamentally restructure[d] local telephone markets" and "subject[ed] [ILECs] to a host of duties intended to facilitate market entry." In recompense, the 1996 Act set conditions for authorizing ILECs to enter the long-distance market.

"Central to the [new] scheme [was each ILEC's] obligation . . . to share its network with competitors," which came to be known as "competitive local exchange carriers" (CLECs). A CLEC could make use of an ILEC's network in any of three ways: by (1) "purchas[ing] local telephone services at wholesale rates for resale to end users," (2) "leas[ing] elements of the [ILEC's] network 'on an unbundled basis,' " or (3) "interconnect[ing] its own facilities with the [ILEC's] network." Owing to the "considerable expense and effort" required to make unbundled network elements available to rivals at wholesale prices, the ILECs vigorously litigated the scope of the sharing obligation imposed by the 1996 Act, with the result that the Federal Communications Commission (FCC) three times revised its regulations to narrow the range of network elements to be shared with the CLECs.

Respondents William Twombly and Lawrence Marcus (hereinafter plaintiffs) represent a putative class consisting of all "subscribers of local telephone and/or high speed internet services . . . from February 8, 1996 to present." In this action against petitioners, a group of ILECs, plaintiffs seek treble damages and declaratory and injunctive relief for claimed violations of § 1 of the Sherman Act, which prohibits "[e]very contract, combination in the form of trust or otherwise, or conspiracy, in restraint of trade or commerce among the several States, or with foreign nations."

The complaint alleges that the ILECs conspired to restrain trade in two ways, each supposedly inflating charges for local telephone and high-speed Internet services. Plaintiffs say, first, that the ILECs "engaged in parallel conduct" in their respective service areas to inhibit the growth of upstart CLECs. Their actions allegedly included making unfair agreements with the CLECs for access to ILEC networks, providing inferior connections to the networks, overcharging, and billing in ways designed to sabotage the CLECs' relations with their own customers. According to the complaint, the ILECs' "compelling common motivatio[n]" to thwart the CLECs' competitive efforts naturally led them to form a conspiracy; "[h]ad any one [ILEC] not sought to prevent CLECs . . . from competing effectively . . . , the resulting greater competitive inroads into that [ILEC's] territory would have revealed the degree to which competitive entry by CLECs would have been successful in the other territories in the absence of such conduct."

Second, the complaint charges agreements by the ILECs to refrain from competing against one another. These are to be inferred from the ILECs' common failure "meaningfully [to] pursu[e]" "attractive business opportunit[ies]" in contiguous markets where they possessed "substantial competitive advantages," and from a statement of Richard Notebaert, chief executive officer (CEO) of the ILEC Qwest, that competing in the territory of another ILEC " 'might be a good way to turn a quick dollar but that doesn't make it right.' "

The complaint couches its ultimate allegations this way:

"In the absence of any meaningful competition between the [ILECs] in one another's markets, and in light of the parallel course of conduct that each engaged in to prevent competition from CLECs within their respective local telephone and/or high speed internet services markets and the other facts and market circumstances alleged above, Plaintiffs allege upon information and belief that [the ILECs] have entered into a contract, combination or conspiracy to prevent competitive entry in their respective local telephone and/or high speed internet services markets and have agreed not to compete with one another and otherwise allocated customers and markets to one another."[2]

The <u>United States District Court for the Southern District of New York</u> dismissed the complaint for failure to state a claim upon which relief can be granted. The District Court acknowledged that "plaintiffs may allege a conspiracy by citing instances of parallel business behavior that suggest an agreement," but emphasized that "while circumstantial evidence of consciously parallel behavior may have made heavy inroads into the traditional judicial attitude toward conspiracy, 'conscious parallelism' has not yet read conspiracy out of the Sherman Act entirely." Thus, the District Court understood that allegations of parallel business conduct, taken alone, do not state a claim under <u>§ 1</u>; plaintiffs must allege additional facts that "ten[d] to exclude independent self-interested conduct as an explanation for defendants' parallel behavior." The District Court found plaintiffs' allegations of parallel ILEC actions to discourage competition inadequate because "the behavior of each ILEC in resisting the incursion of CLECs is fully explained by the ILEC's own interests in defend-

---

[2] In setting forth the grounds for <u>§ 1</u> relief, the complaint repeats these allegations in substantially similar language:

"Beginning at least as early as February 6, 1996, and continuing to the present, the exact dates being unknown to Plaintiffs, Defendants and their co-conspirators engaged in a contract, combination or conspiracy to prevent competitive entry in their respective local telephone and/or high speed internet services markets by, among other things, agreeing not to compete with one another and to stifle attempts by others to compete with them and otherwise allocating customers and markets to one another in violation of Section 1 of the Sherman Act."

ing its individual territory." As to the ILECs' supposed agreement against competing with each other, the District Court found that the complaint does not "allege facts . . . suggesting that refraining from competing in other territories as CLECs was contrary to the ILECs' apparent economic interests, and consequently does not raise an inference that the ILECs' actions were the result of a conspiracy."

The Court of Appeals for the Second Circuit reversed, holding that the District Court tested the complaint by the wrong standard. It held that "plus factors are not required to be pleaded to permit an antitrust claim based on parallel conduct to survive dismissal." Although the Court of Appeals took the view that plaintiffs must plead facts that "include conspiracy among the realm of 'plausible' possibilities in order to survive a motion to dismiss," it then said that "to rule that allegations of parallel anticompetitive conduct fail to support a plausible conspiracy claim, a court would have to conclude that there is no set of facts that would permit a plaintiff to demonstrate that the particular parallelism asserted was the product of collusion rather than coincidence."

* * *

II

A

Because § 1 of the Sherman Act "does not prohibit [all] unreasonable restraints of trade . . . but only restraints effected by a contract, combination, or conspiracy," the crucial question is whether the challenged anticompetitive conduct "stem[s] from independent decision or from an agreement, tacit or express," *Theatre Enterprises, Inc. v. Paramount Film Distributing Corp.*, 346 U.S. 537, 540 (1954). While a showing of parallel "business behavior is admissible circumstantial evidence from which the fact finder may infer agreement," it falls short of "conclusively establishing agreement or . . . . itself constituting a Sherman Act offense." Even "conscious parallelism," a common reaction of "firms in a concentrated market that recognize their shared economic interests and their interdependence with respect to price and output decisions" is "not in itself unlawful."

The inadequacy of showing parallel conduct or interdependence, without more, mirrors the ambiguity of the behavior: consistent with conspiracy, but just as much in line with a wide swath of rational and competitive business strategy unilaterally prompted by common perceptions of the market. Accordingly, we have previously hedged against false inferences from identical behavior at a number of points in the trial sequence. An antitrust conspiracy plaintiff with evidence showing nothing beyond parallel conduct is not entitled to a directed verdict, *see Theatre Enterprises*; proof of a § 1 conspiracy must include evidence tending to exclude the possibility of independent action, *see Monsanto Co. v. Spray-Rite Service Corp.*, 465 U.S. 752 (1984); and at the summary judgment stage a § 1 plaintiff's offer of conspiracy evidence must tend to rule out the possibility that the defendants were acting independently, *see Matsushita Elec. Industrial Co. v. Zenith Radio Corp.*, 475 U.S. 574 (1986).

B

This case presents the antecedent question of what a plaintiff must plead in order to state a claim under § 1 of the Sherman Act. Federal Rule of Civil Procedure 8(a)(2) requires only "a short and plain statement of the claim showing that the pleader is entitled to relief," in order to "give the defendant fair notice of what the . . . claim is and the grounds upon which it rests," *Conley v. Gibson*, 355 U.S. 41, 47 (1957). While a complaint attacked by a Rule 12(b)(6) motion to dismiss does not need detailed factual allegations, a plaintiff's obligation to provide the "grounds" of his "entitlement to relief" requires more than labels and conclusions, and a formulaic recitation of the elements of a cause of action will not do. Factual allegations must be enough to raise a right to relief above the speculative level[3] on the assumption that all the allegations in the complaint are true (even if doubtful in fact), see, e.g., *Scheuer v. Rhodes*, 416 U.S. 232, 236 (1974) (a well-pleaded complaint may proceed even if it appears "that a recovery is very remote and unlikely").

In applying these general standards to a § 1 claim, we hold that stating such a claim requires a complaint with enough factual matter (taken as true) to suggest that an agreement was made. Asking for plausible grounds to infer an agreement does not impose a probability requirement at the pleading stage; it simply calls for enough fact to raise a reasonable expectation that discovery will reveal evidence of illegal agreement. And, of course, a well-pleaded complaint may proceed even if it strikes a savvy judge that actual proof of those facts is improbable, and "that a recovery is very remote and unlikely." In identifying facts that are suggestive enough to render a § 1 conspiracy plausible, we have the benefit of the prior rulings and considered views of leading commentators * * * that lawful parallel conduct fails to bespeak unlawful agreement. It makes sense to say, therefore, that an allegation of parallel conduct and a bare assertion of conspiracy will not suffice. Without more, parallel conduct does not suggest conspiracy, and a conclusory allegation of agreement at some unidentified point does not supply facts adequate to show illegality. Hence, when allegations of parallel conduct are set out in order to make a § 1 claim, they must be placed in a context that raises a suggestion of a preceding agreement, not merely parallel conduct that could just as well be independent action.

The need at the pleading stage for allegations plausibly suggesting (not merely consistent with) agreement reflects the threshold requirement of Rule 8(a)(2) that

---

[3] The dissent greatly oversimplifies matters by suggesting that the Federal Rules somehow dispensed with the pleading of facts altogether. While, for most types of cases, the Federal Rules eliminated the cumbersome requirement that a claimant "set out *in detail* the facts upon which he bases his claim," *Conley v. Gibson*, 355 U.S. 41, 47 (1957) (emphasis added), Rule 8(a)(2) still requires a "showing," rather than a blanket assertion, of entitlement to relief. Without some factual allegation in the complaint, it is hard to see how a claimant could satisfy the requirement of providing not only "fair notice" of the nature of the claim, but also "grounds" on which the claim rests.

the "plain statement" possess enough heft to "show that the pleader is entitled to relief." A statement of parallel conduct, even conduct consciously undertaken, needs some setting suggesting the agreement necessary to make out a § 1 claim; without that further circumstance pointing toward a meeting of the minds, an account of a defendant's commercial efforts stays in neutral territory. An allegation of parallel conduct is thus much like a naked assertion of conspiracy in a § 1 complaint: it gets the complaint close to stating a claim, but without some further factual enhancement it stops short of the line between possibility and plausibility of "entitlement to relief."

We alluded to the practical significance of the Rule 8 entitlement requirement in *Dura Pharmaceuticals, Inc. v. Broudo*, 544 U.S. 336 (2005), when we explained that something beyond the mere possibility of loss causation must be alleged, lest a plaintiff with "a largely groundless claim" be allowed to "take up the time of a number of other people, with the right to do so representing an *in terrorem* increment of the settlement value." *Id., at 347* (quoting *Blue Chip Stamps v. Manor Drug Stores*, 421 U.S. 723, 741 (1975)). So, when the allegations in a complaint, however true, could not raise a claim of entitlement to relief, "this basic deficiency should . . . be exposed at the point of minimum expenditure of time and money by the parties and the court."

[P]roceeding to antitrust discovery can be expensive. As we indicated over 20 years ago in *Associated Gen. Contractors of Cal., Inc. v. Carpenters*, 459 U.S. 519, 528 n.17 (1983), "a district court must retain the power to insist upon some specificity in pleading before allowing a potentially massive factual controversy to proceed." That potential expense is obvious enough in the present case: plaintiffs represent a putative class of at least 90 percent of all subscribers to local telephone or high-speed Internet service in the continental United States, in an action against America's largest telecommunications firms * * * for unspecified (if any) instances of antitrust violations that allegedly occurred over a period of seven years.

It is no answer to say that a claim just shy of a plausible entitlement to relief can, if groundless, be weeded out early in the discovery process through "careful case management," given the common lament that the success of judicial supervision in checking discovery abuse has been on the modest side. And it is self-evident that the problem of discovery abuse cannot be solved by "careful scrutiny of evidence at the summary judgment stage," much less "lucid instructions to juries"; the threat of discovery expense will push cost-conscious defendants to settle even anemic cases before reaching those proceedings. Probably, then, it is only by taking care to require allegations that reach the level suggesting conspiracy that we can hope to avoid the potentially enormous expense of discovery in cases with no "reasonably founded hope that the [discovery] process will reveal relevant evidence" to support a § 1 claim.

Plaintiffs' * * * main argument against the plausibility standard at the pleading stage is its ostensible conflict with an early statement of ours construing Rule 8.

Justice Black's opinion for the Court in <u>Conley v. Gibson</u> spoke not only of the need for fair notice of the grounds for entitlement to relief but of "the accepted rule that a complaint should not be dismissed for failure to state a claim unless it appears beyond doubt that the plaintiff can prove no set of facts in support of his claim which would entitle him to relief." This "no set of facts" language can be read in isolation as saying that any statement revealing the theory of the claim will suffice unless its factual impossibility may be shown from the face of the pleadings; and the Court of Appeals appears to have read *Conley* in some such way when formulating its understanding of the proper pleading standard.

On such a focused and literal reading of *Conley*'s "no set of facts," a wholly conclusory statement of claim would survive a motion to dismiss whenever the pleadings left open the possibility that a plaintiff might later establish some "set of [undisclosed] facts" to support recovery. So here, the Court of Appeals specifically found the prospect of unearthing direct evidence of conspiracy sufficient to preclude dismissal, even though the complaint does not set forth a single fact in a context that suggests an agreement. It seems fair to say that this approach to pleading would dispense with any showing of a "reasonably founded hope" that a plaintiff would be able to make a case.

Seeing this, a good many judges and commentators have balked at taking the literal terms of the *Conley* passage as a pleading standard. * * * *Conley*'s "no set of facts" language has been questioned, criticized, and explained away long enough. To be fair to the *Conley* Court, the passage should be understood in light of the opinion's preceding summary of the complaint's concrete allegations, which the Court quite reasonably understood as amply stating a claim for relief. But the passage so often quoted fails to mention this understanding on the part of the Court, and after puzzling the profession for 50 years, this famous observation has earned its retirement. The phrase is best forgotten as an incomplete, negative gloss on an accepted pleading standard: once a claim has been stated adequately, it may be supported by showing any set of facts consistent with the allegations in the complaint. *Conley*, then, described the breadth of opportunity to prove what an adequate complaint claims, not the minimum standard of adequate pleading to govern a complaint's survival.

III

When we look for plausibility in this complaint, we agree with the District Court that plaintiffs' claim of conspiracy in restraint of trade comes up short. To begin with, the complaint leaves no doubt that plaintiffs rest their <u>§ 1</u> claim on descriptions of parallel conduct and not on any independent allegation of actual agreement among the ILECs. Although in form a few stray statements speak directly of agreement,[9] on fair reading these are merely legal conclusions resting on the prior allegations. Thus, the complaint first takes account of the alleged "absence of any

---

[9] *See* Complaint ¶¶ 51, 64 (alleging that ILECs engaged in a "contract, combination or conspiracy" and agreed not to compete with one another).

meaningful competition between [the ILECs] in one another's markets," "the parallel course of conduct that each [ILEC] engaged in to prevent competition from CLECs," "and the other facts and market circumstances alleged [earlier]"; "in light of" these, the complaint concludes "that [the ILECs] have entered into a contract, combination or conspiracy to prevent competitive entry into their . . . markets and have agreed not to compete with one another."[10] The nub of the complaint, then, is the ILECs' parallel behavior, consisting of steps to keep the CLECs out and manifest disinterest in becoming CLECs themselves, and its sufficiency turns on the suggestions raised by this conduct when viewed in light of common economic experience.

We think that nothing contained in the complaint invests either the action or inaction alleged with a plausible suggestion of conspiracy. As to the ILECs' supposed agreement to disobey the 1996 Act and thwart the CLECs' attempts to compete, we agree with the District Court that nothing in the complaint intimates that the resistance to the upstarts was anything more than the natural, unilateral reaction of each ILEC intent on keeping its regional dominance. * * * The economic incentive to resist was powerful, but resisting competition is routine market conduct, and even if the ILECs flouted the 1996 Act in all the ways the plaintiffs allege, there is no reason to infer that the companies had agreed among themselves to do what was only natural anyway; so natural, in fact, that if alleging parallel decisions to resist competition were enough to imply an antitrust conspiracy, pleading a § 1 violation against almost any group of competing businesses would be a sure thing. * * * We agree with the District Court's assessment that antitrust conspiracy was not suggested by the facts adduced under either theory of the complaint, which thus fails to state a valid § 1 claim.[14]

---

[10] If the complaint had not explained that the claim of agreement rested on the parallel conduct described, we doubt that the complaint's references to an agreement among the ILECs would have given the notice required by Rule 8. Apart from identifying a seven-year span in which the § 1 violations were supposed to have occurred, the pleadings mentioned no specific time, place, or person involved in the alleged conspiracies. This lack of notice contrasts sharply with the model form for pleading negligence, Form 9, which the dissent says exemplifies the kind of "bare allegation" that survives a motion to dismiss. Whereas the model form alleges that the defendant struck the plaintiff with his car while plaintiff was crossing a particular highway at a specified date and time, the complaint here furnishes no clue as to which of the four ILECs (much less which of their employees) supposedly agreed, or when and where the illicit agreement took place. A defendant wishing to prepare an answer in the simple fact pattern laid out in Form 9 would know what to answer; a defendant seeking to respond to plaintiffs' conclusory allegations in the § 1 context would have little idea where to begin.

[14] In reaching this conclusion, we do not apply any "heightened" pleading standard, nor do we seek to broaden the scope of Federal Rule of Civil Procedure 9, which can only be accomplished " 'by the process of amending the Federal Rules, and not by judicial interpretation.' " *Swierkiewicz v. Sorema N.A.*, 534 U.S. 506, 515 (2002) (quoting *Leatherman v. Tarrant County Narcotics Intelligence and Coordination Unit*, 507 U.S. 163, 168 (1993)). On certain subjects understood to raise a high risk of abusive litigation, a plaintiff must state factual allegations with greater particularity than Rule 8 requires. FED. RULES CIV. PROC. 9(b)–(c). Here, our concern is not that the allegations in the complaint were insufficiently "particular[ized]", *ibid.*; rather, the complaint warranted dismissal because it failed *in toto* to render plaintiffs' entitlement to relief plausible.

Plaintiffs say that our analysis runs counter to <u>Swierkiewicz v. Sorema N.A., 534 U.S. 506, 508 (2002)</u>, which held that "a complaint in an employment discrimination lawsuit [need] not contain specific facts establishing a prima facie case of discrimination * * * " They argue that just as the prima facie case is a "flexible evidentiary standard" that "should not be transposed into a rigid pleading standard for discrimination cases," <u>Swierkiewicz, supra, at 512</u>, "transposing 'plus factor' summary judgment analysis woodenly into a rigid Rule 12(b)(6) pleading standard . . . would be unwise." As the District Court correctly understood, however, "*Swierkiewicz* did not change the law of pleading, but simply re-emphasized . . . that the Second Circuit's use of a heightened pleading standard for Title VII cases was contrary to the Federal Rules' structure of liberal pleading requirements." Even though Swierkiewicz's pleadings "detailed the events leading to his termination, provided relevant dates, and included the ages and nationalities of at least some of the relevant persons involved with his termination," the Court of Appeals dismissed his complaint for failing to allege certain additional facts that Swierkiewicz would need at the trial stage to support his claim in the absence of direct evidence of discrimination. We reversed on the ground that the Court of Appeals had impermissibly applied what amounted to a heightened pleading requirement by insisting that Swierkiewicz allege "specific facts" beyond those necessary to state his claim and the grounds showing entitlement to relief.

Here, in contrast, we do not require heightened fact pleading of specifics, but only enough facts to state a claim to relief that is plausible on its face. Because the plaintiffs here have not nudged their claims across the line from conceivable to plausible, their complaint must be dismissed.

* * *

The judgment of the Court of Appeals for the Second Circuit is reversed, and the cause is remanded for further proceedings consistent with this opinion.

It is so ordered.

Justice Stevens, with whom Justice Ginsburg joins except as to part IV, dissenting.

In the first paragraph of its * * * opinion the Court states that the question to be decided is whether allegations that "major telecommunications providers engaged in certain parallel conduct unfavorable to competition" suffice to state a violation of § 1 of the Sherman Act. The answer to that question has been settled for more than 50 years. If that were indeed the issue, a summary reversal citing <u>Theatre Enterprises, Inc. v. Paramount Film Distributing Corp., 346 U.S. 537 (1954)</u>, would adequately resolve this case. As *Theatre Enterprises* held, parallel conduct is circumstantial evidence admissible on the issue of conspiracy, but it is not itself illegal.

Thus, this is a case in which there is no dispute about the substantive law. If the defendants acted independently, their conduct was perfectly lawful. If, however, that conduct is the product of a horizontal agreement among potential competitors, it was unlawful. Plaintiffs have alleged such an agreement and, because the complaint was dismissed in advance of answer, the allegation has not even been denied. Why, then, does the case not proceed? Does a judicial opinion that the charge is not "plausible" provide a legally acceptable reason for dismissing the complaint? I think not.

Respondents' amended complaint describes a variety of circumstantial evidence and makes the straightforward allegation that petitioners "entered into a contract, combination or conspiracy to prevent competitive entry in their respective local telephone and/or high speed internet services markets and have agreed not to compete with one another and otherwise allocated customers and markets to one another." * * *

Under rules of procedure that have been well settled since well before our decision in *Theatre Enterprises*, a judge ruling on a defendant's motion to dismiss a complaint, "must accept as true all of the factual allegations contained in the complaint." *Swierkiewicz v. Sorema N.A.*, 534 U.S. 506, 508 n.1 (2002). But instead of requiring knowledgeable executives such as Notebaert to respond to these allegations by way of sworn depositions or other limited discovery—and indeed without so much as requiring petitioners to file an answer denying that they entered into any agreement—the majority permits immediate dismissal based on the assurances of company lawyers that nothing untoward was afoot. The Court embraces the argument of those lawyers that "there is no reason to infer that the companies had agreed among themselves to do what was only natural anyway," that "there was just no need for joint encouragement to resist the 1996 Act," and that the "natural explanation for the noncompetition alleged is that the former Government-sanctioned monopolists were sitting tight, expecting their neighbors to do the same thing."

The Court and petitioners' legal team are no doubt correct that the parallel conduct alleged is consistent with the absence of any contract, combination, or conspiracy. But that conduct is also entirely consistent with the presence of the illegal agreement alleged in the complaint. And the charge that petitioners "agreed not to compete with one another" is not just one of "a few stray statements"; it is an allegation describing unlawful conduct. As such, the Federal Rules of Civil Procedure, our longstanding precedent, and sound practice mandate that the District Court at least require some sort of response from petitioners before dismissing the case.

Two practical concerns presumably explain the Court's dramatic departure from settled procedural law. Private antitrust litigation can be enormously expensive, and there is a risk that jurors may mistakenly conclude that evidence of parallel conduct has proved that the parties acted pursuant to an agreement when they in fact merely made similar independent decisions. Those concerns merit careful case management, including strict control of discovery, careful scrutiny of evidence at the summary judgment stage, and lucid instructions to juries; they do not, however, justify the dismissal of an adequately pleaded complaint without even requiring the defendants to file answers denying a charge that they in fact engaged in collective decisionmaking. * * *

I

* * * Under the relaxed pleading standards of the Federal Rules, the idea was not to keep litigants out of court but rather to keep them in. The merits of a claim would be sorted out during a flexible pretrial process and, as appropriate, through the crucible of trial. *See Swierkiewicz, 534 U.S., at 514* ("The liberal notice pleading of Rule 8(a) is the starting point of a simplified pleading system, which was adopted to focus litigation on the merits of a claim"). * * * The pleading paradigm under the new Federal Rules was well illustrated by the inclusion in the appendix of Form 9, a complaint for negligence. As relevant, the Form 9 complaint states only: "On June 1, 1936, in a public highway called Boylston Street in Boston, Massachusetts, defendant negligently drove a motor vehicle against plaintiff who was then crossing said highway." * * * [T]hat bare allegation suffices under a system that "restricts the pleadings to the task of general notice-giving and invests the deposition-discovery process with a vital role in the preparation for trial."[3]

II

It is in the context of this history that *Conley v. Gibson, 355 U.S. 41 (1957),* must be understood. Consistent with the design of the Federal Rules, *Conley*'s "no set of facts" formulation permits outright dismissal only when proceeding to discovery or beyond would be futile. Once it is clear that a plaintiff has stated a claim that, if true, would entitle him to relief, matters of proof are appropriately relegated to other stages of the trial process. * * *

Petitioners have not requested that the *Conley* formulation be retired * * * . I would not rewrite the Nation's civil procedure textbooks and call into doubt the pleading rules of most of its States without far more informed deliberation as to the costs of doing so. Congress has established a process—a rulemaking process—for revisions of that order.

* * *

Everything today's majority says would therefore make perfect sense if it were ruling on a Rule 56 motion for summary judgment and the evidence included nothing more than the Court has described. But it should go without saying in the wake

---

[3] The Federal Rules do impose a "particularity" requirement on "all averments of fraud or mistake," FED. RULE CIV. PROC. 9(b), neither of which has been alleged in this case. We have recognized that the canon of *expresio unius est exclusio alterius* applies to Rule 9(b). *See Leatherman v. Tarrant Cty. Narcotics Intelligence and Coordination Unit, 507 U.S. 163, 168 (1993).*

of *Swierkiewicz* that a heightened production burden at the summary judgment stage does not translate into a heightened pleading burden at the complaint stage. * * *This case is a poor vehicle for the Court's new pleading rule, for we have observed that "in antitrust cases, where 'the proof is largely in the hands of the alleged conspirators,' . . . dismissals prior to giving the plaintiff ample opportunity for discovery should be granted very sparingly." * * *

The same year we decided *Conley*, Judge Clark wrote, presciently,

"I fear that every age must learn its lesson that special pleading cannot be made to do the service of trial and that live issues between active litigants are not to be disposed of or evaded on the paper pleadings, i.e., the formalistic claims of the parties. Experience has found no quick and easy short cut for trials in cases generally *and antitrust cases in particular.*" Special Pleading in the "Big Case"? in Procedure—The Handmaid of Justice 147, 148 (C. Wright & H. Reasoner eds.1965)

* * *

IV

* * *

FYI

The Judge Clark referred to in the text is Charles E. Clark, the first reporter to the committee that drafted the original version of the Federal Rules of Civil Procedure. Clark's views regarding the Federal Rules are treated as persuasive, if not authoritative, by those who attempt to understand their original meaning. *See* Michael E. Smith, *Judge Charles E. Clark and the Federal Rules of Civil Procedure*, 85 YALE L.J. 914 (1976).

The transparent policy concern that drives the [majority] decision is the interest in protecting antitrust defendants—who in this case are some of the wealthiest corporations in our economy—from the burdens of pretrial discovery. * * *

If the allegation of conspiracy happens to be true, today's decision obstructs the congressional policy favoring competition that undergirds both the Telecommunications Act of 1996 and the Sherman Act itself. More importantly, even if there is abundant evidence that the allegation is untrue, directing that the case be dismissed without even looking at any of that evidence marks a fundamental—and unjustified—change in the character of pretrial practice.

Accordingly, I respectfully dissent.

Points for Discussion

a. Pleading Under Rule 8(a)(2)

Having reviewed *Conley v. Gibson, 355 U.S. 41 (1957)*, *Swierkiewicz*, and *Bell Atlantic v. Twombly*, how would you describe the ordinary pleading burden imposed by Rule 8(a)(2)? Has the Court done a good job of making the standard clear to you? For example, if a plaintiff filed a complaint that alleged simply, "I was fired from my job based on my national origin in violation of Title VII of the Civil Rights Act of 1964, and on account of my age in violation of the Age Discrimination in Employment Act of 1967 (ADEA)," would that have been enough under Rule 8(a)(2) and *Swierkiewicz*? *See Sparrow v. United Air Lines, Inc., 216 F.3d 1111, 1115 (D.C. Cir. 2000)* (stating that a complaint need only state, "I was turned down for a job because of my race" to be sufficient under the Federal Rules (citation and internal quotation marks omitted)). Would such a pleading be sufficient under *Twombly*?

b. The Holding of *Twombly*

How would you describe the holding of *Twombly*? Can you articulate the pleading standard applicable under Rule 8(a)(2) as described by the *Twombly* Court? Is the *Twombly* Court's reading of Rule 8(a)(2) consistent with the intent and language of Rule 8, particularly given the existence of Federal Rule 9(b), which provides for particularized pleading only for allegations of fraud and mistake?

What policy concerns moved the Court to interpret the general pleading standard of Rule 8(a)(2) in the way that it did in *Twombly*? Were these policy concerns sound reasons that justified the Court's new interpretation of the rule?

How do you think the decision in *Twombly* will impact future plaintiffs in antitrust cases involving allegations of conspiracy? How might *Twombly's* revised pleading standard affect plaintiffs more generally? *See, e.g., Branham v. Dolgencorp, Inc., 2009 WL 2604447, at *2 (W.D. Va. Aug. 24, 2009)* (citing *Twombly* as the basis for dismissing a negligence complaint in a slip-and-fall case because the plaintiff "failed to allege any facts that show how the liquid came to be on the floor, whether the Defendant knew or should have known of the presence of the liquid, or how the Plaintiff's accident occurred").

c. *Twombly* and the Supreme Court's Prior Pleading Cases

Is the *Twombly* Court's interpretation of the "no set of facts" language in *Conley* convincing? Did the majority adequately explain and justify its decision to abrogate that portion of the *Conley* opinion?

How does *Twombly* square with prior holdings of the Court regarding the ordinary pleading standard under Rule 8 such as *Swierkiewicz*? Had the Court previously cast any doubt on the validity of the "no set of facts" standard of *Conley*? *See* A. Benjamin Spencer, *Plausibility Pleading*, 49 B.C. L. Rev. 431, 464–65 (2008) ("In fact, until *Twombly*, the Court had consistently and repeatedly reaffirmed and applied *Conley's* 'no set of facts' admonition, including in the antitrust context." (citations omitted)).

In *Leatherman v. Tarrant County Narcotics Intelligence & Coordination Unit*, 507 U.S. 163, 168 (1993), and *Swierkiewicz*, the Court indicated that amending Rule 8 formally was the proper way to change its meaning in response to policy concerns. Was it proper for the Court in *Twombly* to reinterpret the meaning of Rule 8(a)(2) rather than rely on the rule amendment process to change its meaning? *See Ortiz v. Fibreboard Corp.*, 527 U.S. 815, 861 (1999) ("[W]e are bound to follow Rule 23 as we understood it upon its adoption, and . . . we are not free to alter it except through the process prescribed by Congress in the Rules Enabling Act."). Did the *Twombly* Court in fact reinterpret Rule 8 or does the Court's understanding of the rule remain largely unchanged? Does notice pleading survive *Twombly*?

d. *Erickson v. Pardus*

Two weeks after *Twombly* the Court decided *Erickson v. Pardus*, 551 U.S. 89 (2007), in which it seemed to reaffirm notice pleading. *Erickson* involved a *pro se* prisoner with a § 1983 claim asserting that necessary treatment for hepatitis C had been initiated and then wrongfully terminated by prison officials and that such termination endangered his life. The District Court dismissed the prisoner's complaint and the Tenth Circuit affirmed the dismissal on the ground that the complaint failed to allege whether the withdrawal of treatment exacerbated his health problems beyond the harm that the disease itself would present to the prisoner.

The Supreme Court found a dismissal on such a basis to be error. First, the Court stated the relevant pleading standard as follows:

> Federal Rule of Civil Procedure 8(a)(2) requires only "a short and plain statement of the claim showing that the pleader is entitled to relief." Specific facts are not necessary; the statement need only " 'give the defendant fair notice of what the . . . claim is and the grounds upon which it rests.' " *Bell Atlantic Corp. v. Twombly* (quoting *Conley v. Gibson*, 355 U.S. 41, 47 (1957)). In addition, when ruling on a defendant's motion to dismiss, a judge must accept as true all of the factual allegations contained in the complaint.

Erickson, 551 U.S. at 93–94. After this recitation, the Court reiterated the prisoner's allegations that the doctor's decision to terminate the hepatitis C treatment was "endangering his life," that the prisoner was "still in need of treatment for this disease," and that the prison officials continued to refuse treatment. *Id.* at 9. According to the Court, "This alone was enough to satisfy Rule 8(a)(2)." *Id.* Does *Erickson's* recitation of a notice pleading standard suggest that *Twombly* did not fundamentally alter the pleading standard of Rule 8(a)(2)? How can *Twombly's* vision of pleading be reconciled with the standard described and applied in *Erickson*? *See Swanson v. Citibank, N.A.*, 614 F.3d 400 (7th Cir. 2010) ("As *Erickson* underscored, '[s]pecific facts are not necessary.' The Court was not engaged in a *sub rosa* campaign to reinstate the old fact-pleading system called for by the Field Code or even more modern codes. We know that because it said so in *Erickson*: 'the statement need only give the defendant fair notice of what the . . . claim is and the grounds upon which it rests.' ").

In the next case, the Supreme Court had an opportunity to shed additional light on the meaning of its decision in *Twombly*.

Ashcroft v. Iqbal

Supreme Court of the United States
556 U.S. 662 (2009)

JUSTICE KENNEDY delivered the opinion of the Court.

Respondent Javaid Iqbal is a citizen of Pakistan and a Muslim. In the wake of the September 11, 2001, terrorist attacks he was arrested in the United States on criminal charges and detained by federal officials. Respondent claims he was deprived of various constitutional protections while in federal custody. To redress the alleged deprivations, respondent filed a complaint against numerous federal officials, including John Ashcroft, the former Attorney General of the United States, and Robert Mueller, the Director of the Federal Bureau of Investigation (FBI). Ashcroft and Mueller are the petitioners in the case now before us. As to these two petitioners, the complaint alleges that they adopted an unconstitutional policy that subjected respondent to harsh conditions of confinement on account of his race, religion, or national origin.

* * * This case * * * turns on a narrow[ ] question: Did respondent, as the plaintiff in the District Court, plead factual matter that, if taken as true, states a claim that petitioners deprived him of his clearly established constitutional rights. We hold respondent's pleadings are insufficient.

I

Following the 2001 attacks, the FBI and other entities within the Department of Justice began an investigation of vast reach to identify the assailants and prevent them from attacking anew. * * * In the ensuing months the FBI questioned more than 1,000 people with suspected links to the attacks in particular or to terrorism in general. Of those individuals, some 762 were held on immigration charges; and a 184-member subset of that group was deemed to be "of 'high interest' " to the investigation. The high-interest detainees were held under restrictive conditions designed to prevent them from communicating with the general prison population or the outside world.

For More Information

To read more about the attacks of September 11, 2001, visit www.9-11commission.gov.

Respondent was one of the detainees. According to his complaint, in November 2001 agents of the FBI and Immigration and Naturalization Service arrested him on charges of fraud in relation to identification documents and conspiracy to defraud the United States. Pending trial for those crimes, respondent was housed at the Metropolitan Detention Center (MDC) in Brooklyn, New York. Respondent was designated a person "of high interest" to the September 11 investigation and in January 2002 was placed in a section of the MDC known as the Administrative Maximum Special Housing Unit (ADMAX SHU). As the facility's name indicates, the ADMAX SHU incorporates the maximum security conditions allowable under Federal Bureau of Prison regulations. ADMAX SHU detainees were kept in lockdown 23 hours a day, spending the remaining hour outside their cells in handcuffs and leg irons accompanied by a four-officer escort.

Respondent pleaded guilty to the criminal charges, served a term of imprisonment, and was removed to his native Pakistan. He then filed a *Bivens* action in the United States District Court for the Eastern District of New York against 34 current and former federal officials and 19 "John Doe" federal corrections officers. See *Bivens v. Six Unknown Fed. Narcotics Agents,* 403 U.S. 388 (1971). The defendants range from the correctional officers who had day-to-day contact with respondent during the term of his confinement, to the wardens of the MDC facility, all the way to petitioners—officials who were at the highest level of the federal law enforcement hierarchy.

Make the Connection

Bivens actions are claims against federal governmental officials that allege violations of constitutional rights. You can learn more about *Bivens* actions in a **Federal Courts** or **Constitutional Law** course.

* * *

The allegations against petitioners are the only ones relevant here. The complaint contends that petitioners designated respondent a person of high interest on account of his race, religion, or national origin, in contravention of the First and Fifth Amendments to the Constitution. The complaint alleges that "the [FBI], under the direction of Defendant MUELLER, arrested and detained thousands of Arab Muslim men . . . as part of its investigation of the events of September 11."

It further alleges that "[t]he policy of holding post-September-11th detainees in highly restrictive conditions of confinement until they were 'cleared' by the FBI was approved by Defendants ASHCROFT and MUELLER in discussions in the weeks after September 11, 2001." Lastly, the complaint posits that petitioners "each knew of, condoned, and willfully and maliciously agreed to subject" respondent to harsh conditions of confinement "as a matter of policy, solely on account of [his] religion, race, and/or national origin and for no legitimate penological interest." The pleading names Ashcroft as the "principal architect" of the policy, and identifies Mueller as "instrumental in [its] adoption, promulgation, and implementation."

Petitioners moved to dismiss the complaint for failure to state sufficient allegations to show their own involvement in clearly established unconstitutional conduct. The District Court denied their motion. Accepting all of the allegations in respondent's complaint as true, the court held that "it cannot be said that there [is] no set of facts on which [respondent] would be entitled to relief as against" petitioners. [relying on *Conley v. Gibson,* 355 U.S. 41 (1957)]. Invoking the collateral-order doctrine petitioners filed an interlocutory appeal in the United States Court of Appeals for the Second Circuit. While that appeal was pending, this Court decided *Bell Atlantic Corp. v. Twombly,* 550 U.S. 544 (2007), which discussed the standard for evaluating whether a complaint is sufficient to survive a motion to dismiss.

What's That?

The *collateral-order doctrine* is a rule that permits litigants to appeal interlocutory court orders that finally determine claims of right separable from the rights asserted in the action that are too important and independent to require deferred appellate consideration after the whole case is adjudicated. *See Cohen v. Benefit Indus. Loan Corp.,* 337 U.S. 541 (1949).

The Court of Appeals considered *Twombly's* applicability to this case. Acknowledging that *Twombly* retired the *Conley* no-set-of-facts test relied upon by the District Court, the Court of Appeals' opinion discussed at length how to apply this Court's "standard for assessing the adequacy of pleadings." It concluded that *Twombly* called for a "flexible 'plausibility standard,'" which obliges a pleader to amplify a claim with some factual allegations in those contexts where such amplification is needed to render the claim *plausible.*" The court found that petitioners' appeal did not present one of "those contexts" requiring amplification. As a consequence, it held respondent's pleading adequate to allege petitioners' personal involvement in discriminatory decisions which, if true, violated clearly established constitutional law.

* * *

III

What's That?

The defense of *qualified immunity* is a defense available to government officials that protects them from suit unless the official violated a constitutional right that was clearly established at the time in question.

In *Twombly, supra,* at 553–554, the Court found it necessary first to discuss the antitrust principles implicated by the complaint. Here too we begin by taking note of the elements a plaintiff must plead to state a claim of unconstitutional discrimination against officials entitled to assert the defense of qualified immunity.

* * *

* * * Based on the rules our precedents establish, respondent correctly concedes that Government officials may not be held liable for the unconstitutional conduct of their subordinates under a theory of *respondeat superior.* Because vicarious liability is inapplicable to *Bivens* and § 1983 suits, a plaintiff must plead that each Government-official defendant, through the official's own individual actions, has violated the Constitution.

The factors necessary to establish a *Bivens* violation will vary with the constitutional provision at issue. Where the claim is invidious discrimination in contravention of the First and Fifth Amendments, our decisions make clear that the plaintiff must plead and prove that the defendant acted with discriminatory purpose. Under extant precedent purposeful discrimination requires more than "intent as volition or intent as awareness of consequences." It instead involves a decisionmaker's undertaking a course of action " 'because of,' not merely 'in spite of,' [the action's] adverse effects upon an identifiable group." It follows that, to state a claim based on a violation of a clearly established right, respondent must plead sufficient factual matter to show that petitioners adopted and implemented the detention policies at issue not for a neutral, investigative reason but for the purpose of discriminating on account of race, religion, or national origin.

* * *

IV

A

We turn to respondent's complaint. Under Federal Rule of Civil Procedure 8(a)(2), a pleading must contain a "short and plain statement of the claim showing that the pleader is entitled to relief." As the Court held in *Twombly,* 550 U.S. 544, the pleading standard <u>Rule 8</u> announces does not require "detailed factual allegations," but it demands more than an unadorned, the-defendant-unlawfully-harmed-me accusation. A pleading that offers "labels and conclusions" or "a formulaic recitation of the elements of a cause of action will not do." Nor does a complaint suffice if it tenders "naked assertion[s]" devoid of "further factual enhancement."

To survive a motion to dismiss, a complaint must contain sufficient factual matter, accepted as true, to "state a claim to relief that is plausible on its face." A claim has facial plausibility when the plaintiff pleads factual content that allows the court to draw the reasonable inference that the defendant is liable for the misconduct alleged. The plausibility standard is not akin to a "probability requirement," but it asks for more than a sheer possibility that a defendant has acted unlawfully. Where a complaint pleads facts that are "merely consistent with" a defendant's liability, it "stops short of the line between possibility and plausibility of 'entitlement to relief.' "

Two working principles underlie our decision in *Twombly*. First, the tenet that a court must accept as true all of the allegations contained in a complaint is inapplicable to legal conclusions. Threadbare recitals of the elements of a cause of action, supported by mere conclusory statements, do not suffice. <u>Rule 8</u> marks a notable and generous departure from the hyper-technical, code-pleading regime of a prior era, but it does not unlock the doors of discovery for a plaintiff armed with nothing more than conclusions. Second, only a complaint that states a plausible claim for relief survives a motion to dismiss. Determining whether a complaint states a plausible claim for relief will, as the Court of Appeals observed, be a context-specific task that requires the reviewing court to draw on its judicial experience and common sense. <u>490 F.3d, at 157–158.</u> But where the well-pleaded facts do not permit the court to infer more than the mere possibility of misconduct, the complaint has alleged—but it has not "show[n]"—"that the pleader is entitled to relief." FED. RULE CIV. PROC. <u>8(a)(2)</u>.

In keeping with these principles a court considering a motion to dismiss can choose to begin by identifying pleadings that, because they are no more than conclusions, are not entitled to the assumption of truth. While legal conclusions can provide the framework of a complaint, they must be supported by factual allegations. When there are well-pleaded factual allegations, a court should assume their veracity and then determine whether they plausibly give rise to an entitlement to relief.

Our decision in *Twombly* illustrates the two-pronged approach. There, we considered the sufficiency of a complaint alleging that incumbent telecommunications providers had entered an agreement not to compete and to forestall competitive entry, in violation of the Sherman Act, <u>15 U.S.C. § 1</u>. Recognizing that <u>§ 1</u> enjoins only anticompetitive conduct "effected by a contract, combination, or conspiracy," the plaintiffs in *Twombly* flatly pleaded that the defendants "ha[d] entered into a contract, combination or conspiracy to prevent competitive entry . . . and ha[d] agreed not to compete with one another." The complaint also alleged that the defendants' "parallel course of conduct . . . to prevent competition" and inflate prices was indicative of the unlawful agreement alleged.

The Court held the plaintiffs' complaint deficient under <u>Rule 8</u>. In doing so it first noted that the plaintiffs' assertion of an unlawful agreement was a " 'legal conclusion' " and, as such, was not entitled to the assumption of truth. * * * The Court next addressed the "nub" of the plaintiffs' complaint—the well-pleaded, non-conclusory factual allegation of parallel behavior—to determine whether it gave rise to a "plausible suggestion of conspiracy." Acknowledging that parallel conduct was consistent with an unlawful agreement, the Court nevertheless concluded that it did not plausibly suggest an illicit accord because it was not only compatible with, but indeed was more likely explained by, lawful, unchoreographed free-market behavior. Because the well-pleaded fact of parallel conduct, accepted as true, did not plausibly suggest an unlawful agreement, the Court held the plaintiffs' complaint must be dismissed.

B

Under *Twombly*'s construction of <u>Rule 8</u>, we conclude that respondent's complaint has not "nudged [his] claims" of invidious discrimination "across the line from conceivable to plausible."

We begin our analysis by identifying the allegations in the complaint that are not entitled to the assumption of truth. Respondent pleads that petitioners "knew of, condoned, and willfully and maliciously agreed to subject [him]" to harsh conditions of confinement "as a matter of policy, solely on account of [his] religion, race, and/or national origin and for no legitimate penological interest." Complaint ¶ 96. The complaint alleges that Ashcroft was the "principal architect" of this invidious policy, *id.,* ¶ 10, and that Mueller was "instrumental" in adopting and executing it, *id.,* ¶ 11. These bare assertions, much like the pleading of conspiracy in *Twombly* amount to nothing more than a "formulaic recitation of the elements" of a constitutional discrimination claim, namely, that petitioners adopted a policy " 'because of,' not merely 'in spite of,' its adverse effects upon an identifiable group." As such, the allegations are conclusory and not entitled to be assumed true. To be clear, we do not reject these bald allegations on the ground that they are unrealistic or nonsensical. We do not so character-

Food for Thought

Do you agree that the quoted allegations are nothing more than a "formulaic recitation of the elements of a constitutional discrimination claim" as opposed to factual allegations entitled to be assumed true? If so, can you think of another way such allegations could be stated in a manner that would satisfy the Court?

ize them any more than the Court in *Twombly* rejected the plaintiffs' express allega-tion of a " 'contract, combination or conspiracy to prevent competitive entry,' " because it thought that claim too chimerical to be maintained. It is the conclusory nature of respondent's allegations, rather than their extravagantly fanciful nature, that disentitles them to the presumption of truth.

We next consider the factual allegations in respondent's complaint to determine if they plausibly suggest an entitlement to relief. The complaint alleges that "the [FBI], under the direction of Defendant MUELLER, arrested and detained thousands of Arab Muslim men . . . as part of its investigation of the events of September 11." Complaint ¶ 47. It further claims that "[t]he policy of holding post-September-11th detainees in highly restrictive conditions of confinement until they were 'cleared' by the FBI was approved by Defendants ASHCROFT and MUELLER in discussions in the weeks after September 11, 2001." *Id.,* ¶ 69. Taken as true, these allegations are consistent with petitioners' purposefully designating detainees "of high interest" because of their race, religion, or national origin. But given more likely explanations, they do not plausibly establish this purpose.

The September 11 attacks were perpetrated by 19 Arab Muslim hijackers who counted themselves members in good standing of <u>al Qaeda</u>, an Islamic fundamentalist group. Al Qaeda was headed by another Arab Muslim—<u>Osama bin Laden</u>—and com-posed in large part of his Arab Muslim disciples. It should come as no surprise that a legitimate policy directing law enforce-ment to arrest and detain individuals because of their suspected link to the attacks would produce a disparate, incidental impact on Arab Muslims, even though the purpose of the policy was to target neither Arabs nor Mus-lims. On the facts respondent alleges the arrests Mueller oversaw were likely lawful and justified by his nondiscrimi-natory intent to detain aliens who were illegally present in the United States and who had potential connections to

Food for Thought

Is it appropriate for the Court to be making judgments about what might be "more likely explanations" or an "obvious alternate explanation" at the pleadings stage of a lawsuit? What ba-sis does the Court have for asserting that its surmised explanation is more likely than the alleged explanation of-fered by the defendant?

those who committed terrorist acts. As between that "obvious alternative explanation" for the arrests, *Twombly, supra, at 567,* and the purposeful, invidious discrimination respondent asks us to infer, discrimination is not a plausible conclusion.

But even if the complaint's well-pleaded facts give rise to a plausible inference that respondent's arrest was the result of unconstitutional discrimination, that inference alone would not entitle respondent to relief. It is important to recall that respondent's complaint challenges neither the constitutionality of his arrest nor his initial detention in the MDC. Respondent's constitutional claims against petitioners rest solely on their ostensible "policy of holding post-September-11th detainees" in the ADMAX SHU once they were categorized as "of high interest." Complaint ¶ 69. To prevail on that theory, the complaint must contain facts plausibly showing that petitioners purposefully adopted a policy of classifying post-September-11 detainees as "of high interest" because of their race, religion, or national origin.

This the complaint fails to do. Though respondent alleges that various other defendants, who are not before us, may have labeled him a person "of high interest" for impermissible reasons, his only factual allegation against petitioners accuses them of adopting a policy approving "restrictive conditions of confinement" for post-September-11 detainees until they were " 'cleared' by the FBI." *Ibid.* Accepting the truth of that allegation, the complaint does not show, or even intimate, that petitioners purposefully housed detainees in the ADMAX SHU due to their race, religion, or national origin. All it plausibly suggests is that the Nation's top law enforcement officers, in the aftermath of a devastating terrorist attack, sought to keep suspected terrorists in the most secure conditions available

Food for Thought

The Court here refers to Iqbal's "only factual allegation against petitioners" as being the claim that they approved "restrictive conditions of confinement." But Iqbal also alleged that petitioners "knew of, condoned, and willfully and maliciously agreed to subject [him]" to harsh conditions of confinement "as a matter of policy, solely on account of [his] religion, race, and/or national origin." Why is the Court ignoring that allegation, which, if true, would be unconstitutional?

until the suspects could be cleared of terrorist activity. Respondent does not argue, nor can he, that such a motive would violate petitioners' constitutional obligations. He would need to allege more by way of factual content to "nudg[e]" his claim of purposeful discrimination "across the line from conceivable to plausible." Twombly, 550 U.S., at 570.

To be sure, respondent can attempt to draw certain contrasts between the pleadings the Court considered in *Twombly* and the pleadings at issue here. In *Twombly,* the complaint alleged general wrongdoing that extended over a period of years, whereas here the complaint alleges discrete wrongs—for instance, beatings—by lower level Government actors. The allegations here, if true, and if condoned by petitioners, could be the basis for some inference of wrongful intent on petitioners' part. Despite these distinctions, respondent's pleadings do not suffice to state a claim. Unlike in *Twombly,* where the doctrine of *respondeat superior* could bind the corporate defendant, here, as we have noted, petitioners cannot be held liable unless they themselves acted on account of a constitutionally protected characteristic. Yet respondent's complaint does not contain any factual allegation sufficient to plausibly suggest petitioners' discriminatory state of mind. His pleadings thus do not meet the standard necessary to comply with Rule 8.

* * *

C

Respondent offers three arguments that bear on our disposition of his case, but none is persuasive.

1

Respondent first says that our decision in *Twombly* should be limited to pleadings made in the context of an antitrust dispute. This argument is not supported by *Twombly* and is incompatible with the Federal Rules of Civil Procedure. Though *Twombly* determined the sufficiency of a complaint sounding in antitrust, the decision was based on our interpretation and application of <u>Rule 8</u>. That Rule in turn governs the pleading standard "in all civil actions and proceedings in the United States district courts." <u>FED. RULE CIV. PROC. 1</u>. Our decision in *Twombly* expounded the pleading standard for "all civil actions," and it applies to antitrust and discrimination suits alike.

2

Respondent next implies that our construction of <u>Rule 8</u> should be tempered where, as here, the Court of Appeals has "instructed the district court to cabin discovery in such a way as to preserve" petitioners' defense of qualified immunity "as much as possible in anticipation of a summary judgment motion." We have held, however, that the question presented by a motion to dismiss a complaint for insufficient pleadings does not turn on the controls placed upon the discovery process.

* * *

3

Respondent finally maintains that the Federal Rules expressly allow him to allege petitioners' discriminatory intent "generally," which he equates with a conclusory allegation. Iqbal Brief 32 (citing <u>FED. RULE CIV. PROC. 9</u>). It follows, respondent says, that his complaint is sufficiently well pleaded because it claims that petitioners discriminated against him "on account of [his] religion, race, and/or national origin and for no legitimate penological interest." Complaint ¶ 96. Were we required to accept this allegation as true, respondent's complaint would survive petitioners' motion to dismiss. But the Federal Rules do not require courts to credit a complaint's conclusory statements without reference to its factual context.

Food for Thought

The majority is responding to the argument that Rule 9's admonition that malice, intent, knowledge, and other conditions of the mind may be alleged generally precludes the imposition of the stringent pleading standard of *Twombly*. Do you think Justice Kennedy adequately addressed this argument?

It is true that Rule 9(b) requires particularity when pleading "fraud or mistake," while allowing "[m]alice, intent, knowledge, and other conditions of a person's mind [to] be alleged generally." But "generally" is a relative term. In the context of Rule 9, it is to be compared to the particularity requirement applicable to fraud or mistake. Rule 9 merely excuses a party from pleading discriminatory intent under an elevated pleading standard. It does not give him license to evade the less rigid-though still operative-strictures of Rule 8. And Rule 8 does not empower respondent to plead the bare elements of his cause of action, affix the label "general allegation," and expect his complaint to survive a motion to dismiss.

V

We hold that respondent's complaint fails to plead sufficient facts to state a claim for purposeful and unlawful discrimination against petitioners. The Court of Appeals should decide in the first instance whether to remand to the District Court so that respondent can seek leave to amend his deficient complaint.

The judgment of the Court of Appeals is reversed, and the case is remanded for further proceedings consistent with this opinion.

It is so ordered.

JUSTICE SOUTER, with whom JUSTICE STEVENS, JUSTICE GINSBURG, and JUSTICE BREYER join, dissenting.

* * *

II

* * * Iqbal alleges that after the September 11 attacks the Federal Bureau of Investigation (FBI) "arrested and detained thousands of Arab Muslim men," Complaint ¶ 47, that many of these men were designated by high-ranking FBI officials as being " 'of high interest,' " *id.,* ¶¶ 48, 50, and that in many cases, including Iqbal's, this designation was made "because of the race, religion, and national origin of the detainees, and not because of any evidence of the detainees' involvement in supporting terrorist activity," *id.,* ¶ 49. The complaint further alleges that Ashcroft was the "principal architect of the policies and practices challenged," *id.,* ¶ 10, and that Mueller "was instrumental in the adoption, promulgation, and implementation of the policies and practices challenged," *id.,* ¶ 11. According to the complaint, Ashcroft and Mueller "knew of, condoned, and willfully and maliciously agreed to subject [Iqbal] to these conditions of confinement as a matter of policy, solely on account of [his] religion, race, and/or national origin and for no legitimate penological interest." *Id.,* ¶ 96. The complaint thus alleges, at a bare minimum, that Ashcroft and Mueller knew of and condoned the discriminatory policy their subordinates carried out. Actually, the complaint goes further in alleging that Ashcroft and Muller affirmatively acted to create the discriminatory detention policy. If these factual allegations are true, Ashcroft and Mueller were, at the very least, aware of the discriminatory policy being implemented and deliberately indifferent to it.

Ashcroft and Mueller argue that these allegations fail to satisfy the "plausibility standard" of *Twombly*. They contend that Iqbal's claims are implausible because such high-ranking officials "tend not to be personally involved in the specific actions of lower-level officers down the bureaucratic chain of command." But this response bespeaks a fundamental misunderstanding of the enquiry that *Twombly* demands. *Twombly* does not require a court at the motion-to-dismiss stage to consider whether the factual allegations are probably true. We made it clear, on the contrary, that a court must take the allegations as true, no matter how skeptical the court may be. See *Twombly, 550 U.S., at 555* (a court must proceed "on the assumption that all the allegations in the complaint are true (even if doubtful in fact)"); *id., at 556* ("[A] well-pleaded complaint may

Food for Thought

Did the majority adhere to the admonition to accept allegations as true "even if doubtful in fact"? Can you articulate the majority's legitimate basis for discounting some of Iqbal's allegations as not being entitled to the assumption of truth?

proceed even if it strikes a savvy judge that actual proof of the facts alleged is improbable"); see also *Neitzke v. Williams, 490 U.S. 319, 327 (1989)* ("Rule 12(b)(6) does not countenance . . . dismissals based on a judge's disbelief of a complaint's factual allegations"). The sole exception to this rule lies with allegations that are sufficiently fantastic to defy reality as we know it: claims about little green men, or the plaintiff's recent trip to Pluto, or experiences in time travel. That is not what we have here.

Under *Twombly,* the relevant question is whether, assuming the factual allegations are true, the plaintiff has stated a ground for relief that is plausible. That is, in *Twombly*'s words, a plaintiff must "allege facts" that, taken as true, are "suggestive of illegal conduct." In *Twombly,* we were faced with allegations of a conspiracy to violate § 1 of the Sherman Act through parallel conduct. The difficulty was that the conduct alleged was "consistent with conspiracy, but just as much in line with a wide swath of rational and competitive business strategy unilaterally prompted by common perceptions of the market." We held that in that sort of circumstance, "[a]n allegation of parallel conduct is . . . much like a naked assertion of conspiracy in a § 1 complaint: it gets the complaint close to stating a claim, but without some further factual enhancement it stops short of the line between possibility and plausibility of 'entitlement to relief.' " Here, by contrast, the allegations in the complaint are neither confined to naked legal conclusions nor consistent with legal conduct. The complaint alleges that FBI officials discriminated against Iqbal solely on account of his race, religion, and national origin, and it alleges the knowledge and deliberate indifference that, by Ashcroft and Mueller's own admission, are sufficient to make them liable for the illegal action. Iqbal's complaint therefore contains "enough facts to state a claim to relief that is plausible on its face."

I do not understand the majority to disagree with this understanding of "plausibility" under *Twombly*. Rather, the majority discards the allegations discussed above with regard to Ashcroft and Mueller as conclusory, and is left considering only two statements in the complaint: that "the [FBI], under the direction of Defendant MUELLER, arrested and detained thousands of Arab Muslim men . . . as part of its investigation of the events of September 11," Complaint ¶ 47, and that "[t]he policy of holding post-September-11th detainees in highly restrictive conditions of confinement until they were 'cleared' by the FBI was approved by Defendants ASHCROFT and MUELLER in discussions in the weeks after September 11, 2001," *id.,* ¶ 69. I think the majority is right in saying that these allegations suggest only that Ashcroft and Mueller "sought to keep suspected terrorists in the most secure conditions available until the suspects could be cleared of terrorist activity," and that this produced "a disparate, incidental impact on Arab Muslims." And I agree that the two allegations selected by the majority, standing alone, do not state a plausible entitlement to relief for unconstitutional discrimination.

But these allegations do not stand alone as the only significant, nonconclusory statements in the complaint, for the complaint contains many allegations linking Ashcroft and Mueller to the discriminatory practices of their subordinates. See Complaint ¶ 10 (Ashcroft was the "principal architect" of the discriminatory policy); *id.,* ¶ 11 (Mueller was "instrumental" in adopting and executing the discriminatory policy); *id.,* ¶ 96 (Ashcroft and Mueller "knew of, condoned, and willfully and maliciously agreed to subject" Iqbal to harsh conditions "as a matter of policy, solely on account of [his] religion, race, and/or national origin and for no legitimate penological interest").

The majority says that these are "bare assertions" that, "much like the pleading of conspiracy in *Twombly,* amount to nothing more than a 'formulaic recitation of the elements' of a constitutional discrimination claim" and therefore are "not entitled to be assumed true." The fallacy of the majority's position, however, lies in looking at the relevant assertions in isolation. The complaint contains specific allegations that, in the aftermath of the September 11 attacks, the Chief of the FBI's International Terrorism Operations Section and the Assistant Special Agent in Charge for the FBI's New York Field Office implemented a policy that discriminated against Arab Muslim men, including Iqbal, solely on account of their race, religion, or national origin. See Complaint ¶¶ 47–53. Viewed in light of these subsidiary allegations, the allegations singled out by the majority as "conclusory" are no such thing. Iqbal's claim is not that Ashcroft and Mueller "knew of, condoned, and willfully and maliciously agreed to subject" him to a discriminatory practice that is left undefined; his allegation is that "they knew of, condoned, and willfully and maliciously agreed to subject" him to a particular, discrete, discriminatory policy detailed in the complaint. Iqbal does not say merely that Ashcroft was the architect of some amorphous discrimination, or that Mueller was instrumental in an ill-defined constitutional violation; he alleges that they helped to create the discriminatory policy he has described. Taking the complaint as a whole, it gives Ashcroft and Mueller " 'fair notice of what the . . . claim is and the grounds upon which it rests.' "

That aside, the majority's holding that the statements it selects are conclusory cannot be squared with its treatment of certain other allegations in the complaint as nonconclusory. For example, the majority takes as true the statement that "[t]he policy of holding post-September-11th detainees in highly restrictive conditions of confinement until they were 'cleared' by the FBI was approved by Defendants ASHCROFT and MUELLER in discussions in the weeks after September 11, 2001." Complaint ¶ 69. This statement makes two points: (1) after September 11, the FBI held certain detainees in highly restrictive conditions, and (2) Ashcroft and Mueller discussed and approved these conditions. If, as the majority says, these allegations are not conclusory, then I cannot see why the majority deems it merely conclusory when Iqbal alleges that (1) after September 11, the FBI designated Arab Muslim detainees as being of " 'high interest' " "because of the race, religion, and national origin of the detainees, and not because of any evidence of the detainees' involvement in supporting terrorist activity," Complaint ¶¶ 48–50, App. to Pet. for Cert. 164a, and (2) Ashcroft and Mueller "knew of, condoned, and willfully and maliciously agreed" to that discrimination, *id.,* ¶ 96. By my lights, there is no principled basis for the majority's disregard of the allegations linking Ashcroft and Mueller to their subordinates' discrimination.

I respectfully dissent.

[A separate dissenting opinion by JUSTICE BREYER is omitted.]

Points for Discussion

a. The Court's Interpretation and Application of the *Twombly* Standard

The *Iqbal* majority interpreted *Twombly* as requiring a two-step process to determine the sufficiency of a complaint. First, "conclusory" allegations that are not "well-pleaded" must be disregarded and need not be accepted as true. Second, the remaining "factual" allegations are to be assessed to determine whether they plausibly state a claim for relief. Does the Court give good guidance on how these determinations are to be made? Do you agree with the majority's labeling of some of Iqbal's allegations as conclusory and thus unworthy of being accepted as true?

Justice Souter questions the majority's rejection of one set of allegations as conclusory given its willingness to accept another set of allegations that do not appear to have been stated with any greater degree of specificity. Does Justice Souter have a valid point? Did the majority have a sound basis for rejecting Iqbal's allegation regarding Ashcroft's and Mueller's personal involvement in the shaping of the allegedly discriminatory policy given the obligation to accept a plaintiff's factual allegations as true? Is the majority simply disregarding those allegations it subjectively doubts?

b.   Satisfying the *Twombly/Iqbal* Pleading Standard

Figuring out what level of detail is necessary to satisfy the plausibility standard can be challenging. Consider this perspective from the Judge Richard Posner of the Seventh Circuit:

> The Court said in *Iqbal* that the "plausibility standard is not akin to a 'probability requirement,' but it asks for more than a sheer possibility that a defendant has acted unlawfully." This is a little unclear because plausibility, probability, and possibility overlap. Probability runs the gamut from a zero likelihood to a certainty. What is impossible has a zero likelihood of occurring and what is plausible has a moderately high likelihood of occurring. The fact that the allegations undergirding a claim could be true is no longer enough to save a complaint from being dismissed; the complaint must establish a nonnegligible probability that the claim is valid; but the probability need not be as great as such terms as "preponderance of the evidence" connote.

Food for Thought

If Iqbal's allegations of discrimination on the part of Ashcroft and Mueller were insufficient, how could he present his allegations in a manner that would suffice? Would pleading his allegations sufficiently require him to offer additional factual information to make his claim plausible? If so, what kind of information might that be? Is Iqbal likely to have access to such factual information?

In re Text Messaging Antitrust Litig., 630 F.3d 622, 629 (7th Cir. 2010).

Justice Souter, after he retired from active service on the Supreme Court, offered his own clarification of the standard for satisfying Twombly in a First Circuit case by a teacher claiming that giving him large class sizes caused an aggravation of his medical disability that the school failed to accommodate:

> [T]he trial judge's call for allegations explaining "how" class size was significant and the change in size was actionable as a call for pleading the details of medical evidence in order to bolster the likelihood that a causal connection will prove out as fact. It may even be read as an expression of

skepticism that medical evidence would support the causal claim that increased class size damaged health. But *Twombly* cautioned against thinking of plausibility as a standard of likely success on the merits; the standard is plausibility assuming the pleaded facts to be true and read in a plaintiff's favor.

None of this is to deny the wisdom of the old maxim that after the fact does not necessarily mean caused by the fact, but its teaching here is not that the inference of causation is implausible (taking the facts as true), but that it is possible that other, undisclosed facts may explain the sequence better. Such a possibility does not negate plausibility, however; it is simply a reminder that plausibility of allegations may not be matched by adequacy of evidence. A plausible but inconclusive inference from pleaded facts will survive a motion to dismiss . . . .

Sepúlveda-Villarini v. Dep't of Educ. of P.R., 628 F.3d 25, 30 (1st Cir. 2010) (citations omitted).

More recently, in a follow up to *Iqbal*, the Supreme Court had occasion to apply its plausibility standard to allegations that remained against the warden of the detention facility. Here were the allegations against the warden, as stated by the Court:

The complaint alleges that guards routinely abused respondents; that the warden encouraged the abuse by referring to respondents as "terrorists"; that he prevented respondents from using normal grievance procedures; that he stayed away from the Unit to avoid seeing the abuse; that he was made aware of the abuse via "inmate complaints, staff complaints, hunger strikes, and suicide attempts"; that he ignored other "direct evidence of [the] abuse, including logs and other official [records]"; that he took no action "to rectify or address the situation"; and that the abuse resulted in the injuries described above.

Ziglar v. Abbasi, 137 S. Ct. 1843 (2017). Given that the standard for prevailing on a *Bivens* claim against the warden would be to show that he exhibited "deliberate indifference" to prisoner abuse, the Court concluded, "These allegations—assumed here to be true, subject to proof at a later stage—plausibly show the warden's deliberate indifference to the abuse." *Id.* at 1864. Does the Court's application of the *Twombly* standard in *Ziglar* shed additional light on the precise contours of the standard? What was it about the allegations against the warden in *Ziglar* that rendered them sufficient under *Twombly* while the allegations against the Attorney General and the FBI Director in *Iqbal* were deemed insufficient?

c. *Iqbal's* Impact

Does *Iqbal* represent a faithful application of *Twombly* or does it reflect an expansion of the approach taken in *Twombly*? In other words, can it be said that the Court modified pleading doctrine in any way in *Iqbal* beyond that which was done in *Twombly*?

—Perspective & Analysis—

Some scholars have criticized the *Iqbal* decision for permitting judges to question the truth of facts under the guise of identifying and eliminating allegations as too conclusory to be believed, thereby going beyond *Twombly* in empowering courts to block doubtful claims at the pleading stage:

> Although *Iqbal* involves the application of pleading standards developed previously in *Twombly*, the *Iqbal* Court's rejection of Iqbal's core allegations as too conclusory to be entitled to the assumption of truth reflects a disturbing extension of the *Twombly* doctrine in the direction of increased fact skepticism. *Twombly* resulted in many changes to federal civil pleading standards, including the retirement of *Conley's* "no set of facts" standard, the revival of the need to plead substantiating facts that show entitlement to relief, and the formulation of plausibility as the relevant measure of a complaint's sufficiency. But it did not cast aside the assumption-of-truth rule, which holds that a claimant's factual allegations are entitled to be believed and accepted at the pleading stage, though it arguably opened the door for a weakening of that rule.

> *Iqbal* is a clear challenge to the continuing vitality of the assumption-of-truth rule given the Court's poorly explained rejection of what were undeniably allegations that were non-conclusory and factual in nature.

A. Benjamin Spencer, Iqbal *and the Slide Toward Restrictive Procedure*, 14 LEWIS & CLARK L. REV. 185, 192 (2010).

The consequence of granting a motion to dismiss based on *Iqbal* typically is an obligation to replead one's claims with sufficient additional factual information or face a dismissal with prejudice. Is a dismissal with prejudice a fair result for plaintiffs who lack access to more detailed information about defendants' alleged wrongdoing prior to discovery? Should such plaintiffs be able to plead "upon information and belief" when they do not know certain facts that might support their allegations? *See Arista Records L.L.C. v. Doe 3*, 604 F.3d 110, 120 (2d Cir. 2010) ("The *Twombly* plausibility standard . . . does not prevent a plaintiff from pleading facts alleged 'upon information and belief' where the facts are peculiarly within the possession and control of the defendant . . . .").

How do you think the *Twombly* and *Iqbal* decisions will affect plaintiffs and defendants going forward? *See, e.g., Sanders v. Grenadier Realty, Inc.*, 367 F. App'x 173, 175 (2d Cir. 2010) (dismissing a complaint alleging that "non-black residents have been granted subsidies and re-certifications while plaintiffs have been denied the same in the same period" as not stating a plausible claim of housing discrimination and upholding denial of leave to amend); *Braden v. Wal-Mart Stores*, 588 F.3d 585, 596–97 (8th Cir. 2009) (reversing a district court's dismissal of an ERISA claim because the district court has erroneously required the plaintiff "to plead 'specific facts' explaining precisely how the defendant's conduct was unlawful," which Rule 8 does not require); *Moss v. U.S. Secret Serv.*, 572 F.3d 962, 971–72 (9th Cir. 2009) ("We conclude that Plaintiffs' complaint fails to plead facts plausibly suggesting a colorable *Bivens* claim against the Agents. The facts do not rule out the possibility of viewpoint discrimination, and thus at some level they are consistent with a viable First Amendment claim, but mere possibility is not enough."). *See also* Suzette M. Malveaux, *Front Loading And Heavy Lift-ing: How Pre-Dismissal Discovery Can Address the Detrimental Effect of* Iqbal *on Civil Rights Cases*, 14 LEWIS & CLARK L. REV. 65, 89 (2010) ("[B]ecause complaints alleging intentional discrimination will often set forth factual allegations consistent with illegal and legal conduct, such complaints are more vulnerable to dismissal under the plausibility standard.").

> **FYI**
>
> In the wake of *Iqbal*, Congress considered legislation—such as the Notice Pleading Restoration Act of 2009, S. 1504, 111th Cong. (2009) and the Open Access to Courts Act of 2009, H.R. 4115 111th Cong. (2009)—that sought to reverse the holdings of Twombly and Iqbal and restore civil pleading standards to that which prevailed prior to those cases. Do you think congressional intervention of this kind is a good idea? Is legislative reversal of these cases warranted in your view?

For a perspective arguing that *Twombly* and *Iqbal* can be read as not requiring a stricter approach to pleading than indicated by the Court's prior cases on the topic, see Adam N. Steinman, *The Pleading Problem*, 62 STAN. L. REV. 1293, 1298–1299 (2010) ("Courts should not . . . misread[ ] *Twombly* and *Iqbal* to drastically change federal pleading standards going forward. . . . [P]roperly understood, the post-*Iqbal* pleading framework is not fundamentally in conflict with notice pleading. . . ."). For an argument that the *Twombly* and *Iqbal* decisions indeed were a consequential revision of long-standing pleading principles that promoted access to justice, see A. Benjamin Spencer, *Pleading and Access to Justice: A Response to* Twiqbal *Apologists*, 60 UCLA L. REV. 1710 (2013); *see also* Arthur Miller, *Simplified Pleading, Meaningful Days in Court, and Trials on the Merits: Reflections on the Deformation of Federal Procedure*, 88 N.Y.U. L. REV. 286, 331–47 (2013).

d. Plaintiff's Pleading Obligations

Beyond understanding the minimum level of detail required, you should also be clear on which matters the plaintiff has the burden of pleading. The plaintiff's pleading burden is limited to those matters for which the plaintiff will bear the burden of introducing evidence at trial. This means that plaintiffs must plead their basic claims but ordinarily need not plead the nonexistence of various defenses.

Finally, note that Rule 8(a)(2)'s requirement of a "short and plain statement of the claim" can cut both ways: not only does it permit a relatively simple statement of the legal claim and its grounds, but it also prohibits overly lengthy hyper-pleading. Thus, although one might desire to plead in extensive detail to ensure that sufficient information is pleaded, where the complaint strays too far from being "short and plain," it may be subject to dismissal (although probably with the right to submit an amended complaint). *See, e.g.,* Ausherman v. Stump, 643 F.2d 715, 716 (10th Cir. 1981) ("The complaint, as amended, can be fairly described as prolix. It consists of sixty-three pages, with nine pages of attachments. It violates FED. R. CIV. P. 8(a) . . . ."). A dismissal on such grounds, however, should be considered extremely rare.

Take Note!

Although the plaintiff typically will not have the burden of pleading the nonexistence of all the potential defenses that the defendant may raise, exceptions to this rule occur where the defense in reality is an integral component of the claim such as the defense of payment in an action on a debt or the defense of truth in a slander action. In such cases, the plaintiff will have to plead non-payment and falsity, respectively, to plead an actionable claim.

e. Pleading Special Matters Under Rule 9(b)

Although the ordinary pleading requirement is simply a "short and plain" statement of the claim (complex as that concept may be after *Twombly* and *Iqbal*) under Rule 8(a)(2), the Federal Rules do specifically provide for heightened pleading in two contexts.

FRCP 9(b). Pleading Special Matters.

(b) Fraud or Mistake; Conditions of Mind. In alleging fraud or mistake, a party must state with particularity the circumstances constituting fraud or mistake. Malice, intent, knowledge, and other conditions of a person's mind may be alleged generally.

What additional information must claims of fraud—which are covered by Rule 9(b)'s particularity requirement—include to be sufficient under Rule 9(b)? *Denny v. Carey,* 72 F.R.D. 574 (E.D. Pa. 1976), provides a good statement of the nature of the additional pleading burden imposed by Rule 9(b):

> Defendants are incorrect when they argue that Rule 9(b) places a "rigorous" burden of pleading on plaintiff. * * * FED. R. CIV. P. 8 requires a short and plain statement of the claim which is simple, concise and direct. Rule 9(b) must be harmonized with the notice pleading mandate of Rule 8. * * * Rule 9(b) does not require nor make legitimate the pleading of detailed eviden-

tiary matter. * * * Since fraud embraces a wide variety of potential misconduct, Rule 9(b) requires slightly more notice than would be forthcoming under Rule 8. * * * But the requirement of Rule 9(b) is met when there is sufficient identification of the circumstances constituting fraud so that the defendant can prepare an adequate answer to the allegations.

72 F.R.D. at 578 (citations and internal quotation marks omitted). *See also United States ex rel. Nathan v. Takeda Pharm. of N. Am., Inc.,* 707 F.3d 451, 455–56 (4th Cir. 2013) ("To satisfy Rule 9(b), a plaintiff asserting a claim under the Act must, at a minimum, describe the time, place, and contents of the false representations, as well as the identity of the person making the misrepresentation and what he obtained thereby.") (citation and internal quotation marks omitted). How does Rule 9(b)'s heightened pleading requirement compare with the level of pleading required under

F.R.D., which appears in the citation for *Denny v. Carey*, refers to the *Federal Rules Decisions*, a reporter that publishes cases of particular relevance to the Federal Rules.

Twombly and *Iqbal*? *See McCauley v. City of Chi.,* 671 F.3d 611, 622 (7th Cir. 2011) (Hamilton, J., dissenting in part) ("*Iqbal*'s reasoning and holding conflict with Rule 9(b). . . .").

Allegations of fraud and mistake were singled out for special heightened pleading requirements in the Federal Rules based on the idea that these allegations were too easily fabricated and, in the case of fraud, too potentially detrimental to the defendant's reputation. *See* Christopher M. Fairman, *Heightened Pleading,* 81 TEX. L. REV. 551, 563 (2002) (reporting the traditional justifications for Rule 9(b)'s heightened pleadings as "protection of reputation, deterrence of frivolous or strike suits, defense of completed transactions, and providing adequate notice"). Are the reasons put forward in support of the rule valid in your view? Should the Federal Rules be amended to expand or alter the types of allegations for which heightened pleading is required? *See* Christopher M. Fairman, *The Myth of Notice Pleading,* 45 ARIZ. L. REV. 987 (2004) (describing heightened pleading requirements imposed by courts in cases involving antitrust, copyright, defamation, negligent misrepresentation, and civil RICO claims).

Take Note!

Former Form 21, which appeared in the now-abrogated Appendix of Forms, provided some indication of the level of detail required under Rule 9(b). In setting forth a fraudulent conveyance, the form merely stated, "On *date*, defendant *name* conveyed all defendant's real and personal property . . . to the defendant *name* for the purpose of defrauding the plaintiff . . . ."

Note that Rule 9(b) also indicates that "[m]alice, intent, knowledge, and other conditions of a person's mind may be alleged generally." What does this mean, particularly in light of *Iqbal? See McCauley v. City of Chi.*, 671 F.3d 611, 623 (7th Cir. 2011) (Hamilton, J., dissenting in part) ("The [Supreme] Court's application of Rule 8 to impose a more demanding pleading standard for discriminatory intent is not consistent with its stated adherence to Rule 9 and its express authorization of general pleading of discriminatory intent and most other states of mind. The Court's statement about Rule 9(b) that ' "generally" is a relative term' does not solve the problem or give practical guidance to district courts.").

> **FYI**
>
> Other of the Federal Rules of Civil Procedure provide special pleading rules for certain types of actions. *See* FED. R. CIV. P. 23.1 (providing pleading requirements for shareholder derivative actions); FED. R. CIV. P. 65(b)(1)(A) (requiring specific facts in an affidavit or verified complaint in requesting a temporary restraining order); FED. R. CIV. P. 71.1 (providing pleading requirements for condemnation proceedings).

f.   Statutorily-Imposed Heightened Pleading

Although the Federal Rules only impose heightened pleading in the aforementioned contexts, Congress has the authority to impose heightened pleading requirements for claims as it sees fit. Congress exercised this authority when it enacted the Private Securities Litigation Reform Act of 1995 (PSLRA), Pub. L. No. 104–67, 109 Stat. 737 (1995), which imposed stricter pleading requirements in private securities fraud actions that, among other things, require that a complaint "state with particularity facts giving rise to a strong inference that the defendant acted with the required [fraudulent] state of mind." *Dura Pharm., Inc. v. Broudo*, 544 U.S. 336, 345 (2005). Why do you think Congress created more stringent pleading standards for securities fraud actions?

It is worth noting that the Supreme Court has interpreted the strong inference requirement of the PSLRA to mean that the allegations in the complaint, if true, would lead a reasonable person to deem the inference of scienter "at least as strong as any opposing inference." *Tellabs, Inc. v. Makor Issues & Rights, Ltd.*, 551 U.S. 308, 326 (2007). In adopting this standard, the Court rejected the urging of Justices Scalia and Alito to require such complaints to show that "the inference of scienter . . . is *more plausible* than the inference of innocence." *Id. at 329* (Scalia, J., concurring). How does this standard, which pertains to the heightened pleading obligations under the PSLRA compare with the plausibility pleading standard for ordinary civil cases that the Court announced in *Twombly? See* Stephen B. Burbank, *Pleading and the Dilemmas of "General Rules,"* 2009 WIS. L. REV. 535, 552 ("[C]ertain language in *Twombly* can be read to mean that the Court's standard . . . is more demanding than the standard under the PSLRA [as interpreted by the Court in *Tellabs*].").

g. Pleading Alternate & Inconsistent Allegations

Note that in *Swierkiewicz* the plaintiff included multiple allegations in his complaint asserting an entitlement to relief under more than one legal theory: he argued that his termination violated federal anti-age discrimination law and that his termination violated federal law prohibiting discrimination based on national origin. The Federal Rules permit plaintiffs to include multiple allegations that assert alternate grounds for relief based on a single set of facts and also allow plaintiffs to plead inconsistent allegations. For example, a plaintiff who has been hit by a car can assert both that the driver intentionally hit the plaintiff with the vehicle and that the driver negligently hit the plaintiff. The ability to plead in this fashion derives from Rule 8(d):

> **FRCP 8(d). Pleading to Be Concise and Direct; Alternative Statements; Inconsistency.**
>
> **(1) In General.** Each allegation must be simple, concise, and direct. No technical form is required.
>
> **(2) Alternative Statements of a Claim or Defense.** A party may set out two or more statements of a claim or defense alternatively or hypothetically, either in a single count or defense or in separate ones. If a party makes alternative statements, the pleading is sufficient if any one of them is sufficient.
>
> **(3) Inconsistent Claims or Defenses.** A party may state as many separate claims or defenses as it has, regardless of consistency.

What do you think is the rationale for permitting multifarious and inconsistent pleading? Note that the inconsistent pleading cannot go too far; a pleading party must keep in mind the obligations of Rule 11, which prohibits untruthful or baseless statements (Rule 11 is considered in further detail in Section D below).

h. The Prayer for Relief

Recall that Rule 8(a) includes a requirement to contain "a demand for the relief sought." FED. R. CIV. P. 8(a)(3). Such a demand is referred to as a prayer for relief. The requirement to include such a demand is simple enough. What is worth noting, however, is the role the prayer plays in the ultimate relief that may be obtained by the plaintiff. Rule 54(c) states, "A default judgment must not differ in kind from, or exceed in amount, what is demanded in the pleadings. Every other final judgment should grant the relief to which each party is entitled, even if the party has not demanded that relief in its pleadings." Under this rule, then, a plain-

What's That?

A *default judgment* is a judgment obtained against a defendant who has failed to defend or otherwise appear in a case. Default judgments, which are governed by Rule 55, are covered fully in Chapter 9.

tiff may collect more than they seek in the prayer, so long as the evidence supports the increased amount. *See, e.g.*, *Bail v. Cunningham Bros.*, 452 F.2d 182, 187–88 (7th Cir. 1971) (affirming a jury's award of $150,000 when the plaintiff only requested $100,000 in damages in the original complaint). Why do you think plaintiffs who prevail on default judgments are denied the same privilege under Rule 54(c)?

If a plaintiff seeks so-called special damages, the Federal Rules provide that they must be "specifically stated." FED. R. CIV. P. 9(g). Special damages are damages that are unusual for the type of claim in question and are not the natural damages associated with such a claim. *See, e.g.*, *Avitia v. Metro. Club of Chi., Inc.*, 49 F.3d 1219, 1226 (7th Cir. 1995) ("Damages for personal injury are unusual in commercial cases, normal in tort cases; lost profits are normal in contract cases, unusual in personal-injury tort cases."). Ordinarily, failing to plead special damages as required by Rule 9(g) results in the plaintiff being unable to present evidence on those damages at trial and ultimately precludes recovery of the damages on

Food for Thought

Should punitive damages be considered special damages that must be specifically stated in the complaint or does Rule 54(c) permit plaintiffs to receive punitive damages, if entitled to them, regardless of whether they are requested in the complaint? See *Soltys v. Costello*, 520 F.3d 737, 742–43 (7th Cir. 2008), for a discussion of the issue and citation to relevant cases.

the verdict. However, some courts have shown a willingness to excuse the omission and permit such damages so long as there would be no unfair prejudice to the defendant. *See, e.g.*, *First Am. Corp. v. Al-Nahyan*, 17 F. Supp. 2d 10, 28–29 (D.D.C. 1998) (allowing a claim for disgorgement under Rule 54(c) notwithstanding plaintiff's failure to plead the claim explicitly because defendants had "ample notice" and "were not prejudiced" by the request). Should plaintiffs be permitted to amend their complaints to plead special damages during trial to comply with Rule 9(g) and to enable the presentation of evidence in support of those damages? *See, e.g.*, *Isuzu Motors Ltd. v. Consumers Union of U.S., Inc.*, 12 F. Supp. 2d 1035, 1047 (C.D. Cal. 1998) ("Plaintiff is granted leave to amend the Eleventh through Twenty-second claims to plead special damages specifically.").

B. Responding to the Complaint

Once served with the summons and the complaint, the defendant must respond in some way. The defendant's two main options are to file an answer—in which the defendant responds to the specific allegations contained in the complaint—or to file one or several motions raising various legal defenses that highlight legal defects in the plaintiff's action rather than addressing the merits of the plaintiff's allegations. This Section will consider these responses in the order in which they typically appear in an action by reviewing the defenses and objections presented by motion first and then considering the defendant's pleading in response to the complaint, the answer.

1. Defenses and Objections Under Rule 12

Rule 12 presents a wide array of defenses and objections that may be raised by a defendant in response to a complaint. Here, we will first review the defenses made available by Rule 12(b), after which we will consider the other objections made available in Rule 12 and the procedures governing how defenses and objections under the rule may be raised.

Rule 12(b) sets forth seven basic defects that serve as grounds for dismissing a complaint:

FRCP 12(b). Defenses and Objections—How Presented.

(b) **How to Present Defenses.** Every defense to a claim for relief in any pleading must be asserted in the responsive pleading if one is required. But a party may assert the following defenses by motion:

    (1) lack of subject-matter jurisdiction;

    (2) lack of personal jurisdiction;

    (3) improper venue;

    (4) insufficient process;

    (5) insufficient service of process;

    (6) failure to state a claim upon which relief can be granted; and

    (7) failure to join a party under Rule 19.

A motion asserting any of these defenses must be made before pleading if a responsive pleading is allowed. If a pleading sets out a claim for relief that does not require a responsive pleading, an opposing party may assert at trial any defense to that claim. No defense or objection is waived by joining it with one or more other defenses or objections in a responsive pleading or in a motion.

Most of the defenses mentioned in Rule 12(b) should be familiar to you. We have studied personal jurisdiction, subject-matter jurisdiction, venue, and service of process. The substantive aspects of these defenses have already been covered previously in other chapters. Thus, we will not rehash here the standards governing whether jurisdiction, venue, or service of process are proper.

The defect listed under 12(b)(4)—insufficient process—is different from the defect in 12(b)(5)—insufficient of service of process. The former challenge asserts that there is some technical defect in the content of the summons, while the latter asserts that process was not served in compliance with the requirements of Rule 4. *See Cranford v. United States*, 359 F. Supp. 2d 981, 984 (E.D. Cal. 2005) ("Rule 12(b)(4) was designed to challenge irregularities in the contents of a summons. Rule 12(b)(5) permits a defendant to challenge the method of service attempted by the plaintiff." (citation omitted)). The seventh defect, failure to join a party under Rule 19, simply alleges that the plaintiff has proceeded with the action without joining a party that is deemed to be indispensable to the action under the terms of Rule 19. The standards for determining whether a party must be joined under Rule 19 will be covered in Chapter 7.

Take Note!

In response to a motion to dismiss for insufficient service of process a court may either dismiss the case or simply quash process and permit the plaintiff to attempt service again, provided that remains a viable possibility. *See Hickory Travel Systems, Inc. v. TUI AG*, 213 F.R.D. 547, 553 (N.D. Cal. 2003) ("If service is insufficient, the Court may either dismiss the case or retain jurisdiction but quash service. So long as there is a chance that the plaintiff still could accomplish service, the latter remedy is preferred." (citing *Umbenhauer v. Woog*, 969 F.2d 25, 30 (3rd Cir. 1992))).

The remaining defect, failure to state a claim upon which relief can be granted (Rule 12(b)(6)), deserves more attention.

Points for Discussion

a. The Motion to Dismiss for Failure to State a Claim Under Rule 12(b)(6)

A motion to dismiss for failure to state a claim is a motion that states either, "You've failed to plead enough detail to satisfy your pleading burden" or "Even if everything you allege in your complaint is true, no legal liability attaches to the defendant." Thus, we can see that a 12(b)(6) motion challenges the sufficiency of the complaint in one (or both) of two ways. The motion can allege that the complaint is formally insufficient, meaning that it fails to give the minimum level of detail required under Rule 8(a)(2) such that the defendant is not put on notice of the claim being alleged against it. This type of challenge was presented in *Swierkiewicz* above, in which the defendant

Food for Thought

If *P*'s complaint alleged, "Last Saturday, *D* committed a battery against me by intentionally grabbing my hand and deliberately squeezing it so hard that he broke several of my bones," would this survive a 12(b)(6) motion to dismiss?

claimed that the plaintiff had not included enough information in the complaint to satisfy his pleading burden.

The other type of defect that a 12(b)(6) motion can allege is substantive or legal insufficiency, which means that the allegations in the complaint fail to say anything that would render the defendant liable for a violation of the law. For example, consider a complaint in which *P* alleged, "Last Saturday, *D* came up to me and gave me a handshake." Even if this is true, so what? *P* has no legal claim against *D* just because *D* gave *P* a handshake. So based on this complaint, taking all of the plaintiff's allegations as true, *P*'s complaint fails to state a claim upon which relief can be granted. *D* should thus file a motion to dismiss under Rule 12(b)(6) and that motion should be granted.

As alluded to in this example, when evaluating a 12(b)(6) motion, *a court must accept as true all of the facts that the plaintiff has alleged in its complaint* (the **assumption of truth rule**). A 12(b)(6) motion is not the place for challenging the factual allegations of the plaintiff or to offer some sort of explanation or defense that justifies the defendant's actions. Thus, for example, a defendant who moves to dismiss under Rule 12(b)(6) cannot say, "No, that is not true; I did not shake *P*'s hand last Saturday and I never have." That would be a denial, a response appropriate as part of the defendant's *answer*, a pleading we will consider below. Indeed, if either of the parties offers anything beyond what is in the pleadings in support of their position on the 12(b)(6) motion, such as an affidavit or some other evidence, under Rule 12(d) the 12(b)(6) motion is to be treated as a motion for summary judgment and resolved according to the terms of Rule 56, a device that will be covered in Chapter 9.

Hypo 6.1

A mother initiated an action in State A federal court against an informant in federal court for wrongful death in connection with the death of the mother's son. In the complaint, the mother stated her claim as follows: "The informant submitted a statement to members of a local gang falsely implicating my son in a recent theft of some of the informant's property and asked the gang to retaliate against my son by killing him. After this conversation with the informant, the gang members located my son and beat him to death as punishment for the theft they were told he committed. Based on these actions, the informant is liable for wrongful death under State A law."

Under State A's wrongful death law: (1) surviving parents are permitted to bring wrongful death actions; (2) wrongful death actions are permitted only against persons directly responsible for causing the death; and (3) a recent decision by the Supreme Court of State A held that persons who "expressly solicit" others to kill the decedent may be held liable under the wrongful death law.

If the informant files a motion to dismiss this action under Rule 12(b)(6) is the court likely to grant the motion?

b. *Twombly*, *Iqbal*, and the Motion to Dismiss Under Rule 12(b)(6)

Plaintiffs are supposed to be given the benefit of the doubt in the face of a motion to dismiss, with not only the plaintiff's factual allegations being accepted as true but also with *all reasonable factual inferences being made in the plaintiff's favor. See Fitzgerald v. Barnstable Sch. Comm., 555 U.S. 246, 249 (2009)* ("Because this case comes to us on a motion to dismiss under Federal Rule of Civil Procedure 12(b)(6), we assume the truth of the facts as alleged in petitioners' complaint."); *Morrow v. Balaski, 719 F.3d 160, 197 n.16 (3d Cir. 2013)* ("Because, as noted, this case comes to us from a ruling on a motion to dismiss, we must draw all reasonable inferences in the [plaintiffs'] favor"). Further, prior to *Bell Atlantic Corp. v. Twombly, 550 U.S. 544 (2007)*—discussed earlier in this chapter—the Supreme Court had indicated that a motion to dismiss for failure to state a claim should not be granted "unless it appears beyond doubt that the plaintiff can prove no set of facts in support of his claim which would entitle him to relief." *Conley v. Gibson, 355 U.S. 41, 45–46 (1957)*.

However, the Court in *Twombly* expressly abrogated the above-quoted language from *Conley*, indicating that it was no longer good law. Instead, a motion to dismiss under Rule 12(b)(6) would now be appropriate if the plaintiff failed to plead facts showing "plausible entitlement to relief." *Twombly, 550 U.S. at 559*. In *Twombly*, this standard meant that the complaint—which alleged an antitrust conspiracy based largely on the conscious parallelism of the defendants—was insufficient because it alleged facts that were merely consistent with, rather than suggestive of, liability. According to the Court, there were more plausible innocent explanations for the observed conduct of the defendants, and thus, the complaint could be dismissed. Similar results obtained in *Ashcroft v. Iqbal, 556 U.S. 662 (2009)*, where the Court applied *Twombly* to dismiss the civil rights claim of the plaintiff for lack of plausibility. How will courts go about determining, objectively, whether the facts alleged demonstrate plausible entitlement to relief? What impact do you think the *Twombly* decision and the Court's abrogation of the *Conley* "no set of facts" language will have on the granting of motions to dismiss? Take special note of Justice Kennedy's opinion in *Iqbal*, in which he identified those allegations that were conclusory, and thus, not entitled to the assumption of truth. How did Justice Kennedy distinguish between those allegations he labeled as legal conclusions and those he chose to accept as factual? Does his analysis raise any questions about the nature and continuing strength of the assumption-of-truth principle?

c. Repleading After a Motion to Dismiss

If a Rule 12(b)(6) motion is granted in a case, what do you think the effect should be? Should the plaintiff have the opportunity to replead and submit an amended complaint? Permission to amend in such circumstances is typically granted. *See, e.g.*, *Bazrowx v. Scott, 136 F.3d 1053, 1054 (5th Cir.)*, *cert. denied*, 525 U.S. 865 (1998) ("Generally a district court errs in dismissing a *pro se* complaint for failure to state a claim under Rule 12(b)(6) without giving the plaintiff an opportunity to amend."); <u>Wolff v. Rare Medium, Inc., 171 F. Supp. 2d 354, 361 (S.D.N.Y. 2001)</u> (dismissing plaintiff's original complaint with leave to replead). However, repeated failures to state a claim could be met with a dismissal with prejudice, meaning the plaintiff will be unable to submit an amended complaint. *See* <u>Rozsa v. May Davis Grp., Inc., 187 F. Supp. 2d 123, 132 (S.D.N.Y. 2002), aff'd 165 Fed. App'x 892 (2d Cir. 2006)</u> (dismissing plaintiff's claims with prejudice after granting leave to amend the complaint twice). Also, courts may deny leave to replead if they determine that granting such permission would be futile. *See, e.g.,* <u>Ruffolo v. Oppenheimer & Co., 987 F.2d 129, 131 (2d Cir. 1993)</u> ("Where it appears that granting leave to amend is unlikely to be productive, however, it is not an abuse of discretion to deny leave to amend.").

Food for Thought

Under *Twombly* and *Iqbal*, courts appear able to dismiss complaints if they lack certain facts that plaintiffs might not be able to know, such as the details regarding a conspiracy, a defendant's discriminatory intent, or the circumstances surrounding the creation of a dangerous condition. If such plaintiffs' claims are dismissed with permission to replead, how will the plaintiffs gain access to the facts that their initial complaints may have lacked? Does this difficulty suggest any problems with the *Twombly/Iqbal* standard for granting dismissals?

d. Other Defenses and Objections Under <u>Rule 12</u>

In addition to the arsenal of defenses contained within <u>Rule 12(b)</u>, there are several other responses available to the parties under <u>Rule 12</u>:

<u>Rule 12(c)</u>—Motion for Judgment on the Pleadings. Once all of the pleadings have been submitted—usually meaning after the plaintiff has filed a complaint and the defendant has filed an answer—either party may move for a judgment on the pleadings, meaning that in the movant's view, the information contained on the face of the pleadings alone reveals that there is no factual dispute and the movant is entitled to a judgment as a matter of law. *See* **Example 6.1**. *See also* 5C CHARLES ALAN WRIGHT & ARTHUR R. MILLER, <u>FED. PRAC. & PROC. § 1367 (3d ed. 2004)</u> ("The motion for a judgment on the pleadings only has utility when all material allegations of fact are admitted or not controverted in the pleadings and only questions of law remain to be decided by the district court."). Keep in mind that if a motion under Rule 12(c) or Rule 12(b)(6) is accompanied with any supporting material

---

Example 6.1

P alleges: "*D* intentionally hit my parked vehicle, causing damage to it." *D* responds in his answer, "I admit to hitting *P*'s parked car intentionally, but I was justified in doing so because *P*'s car was in my parking space." If *P* moves for a judgment on the pleadings, *P* will prevail because *D* admits to *P*'s allegations and *D*'s proffered defense does not excuse his conduct under the law.

beyond the pleadings (not including exhibits included within the pleadings under Rule 10(c), *see, e.g.*, *Gibson v. Mortg. Elec. Registration Sys.*, 2012 WL 517329, at *3 (W.D. Tenn. Feb. 15, 2012) (determining that exhibits attached to defendants' motion for judgment on the pleadings, which were attached to or referenced in the complaint, were "part of the pleadings for purposes of Rule 12 and Rule 10(c)")), it must—if the court considers the material—be converted to a motion for summary judgment under Rule 56, a topic we will cover in Chapter 9. *See* FED. R. CIV. P. 12(d).

Rule 12(e)—Motion for a More Definite Statement. If a defendant believes that the complaint is "so vague or ambiguous" that it "cannot reasonably prepare a response," the defendant may move for a more definite statement under Rule 12(e).[*] This motion is only appropriate in limited circumstances where the responding party and the court cannot understand what it is the claimant is trying to assert. *Pozarlik v. Camelback Assocs., Inc.*, 2012 WL 760582, at *2 (M.D. Pa. Mar. 8, 2012) ("[T]he class of pleadings that are appropriate subjects for a motion under Rule 12(e) is quite small—the pleading must be sufficiently unintelligible for the court to be able to make out one or more potentially viable legal theories on which the claimant might proceed." (citation omitted)).

Rule 12(f)—Motion to Strike. The final responsive motion included within Rule 12 is the motion to strike. Such a motion is appropriate when a party believes that a pleading contains an "insufficient defense or any redundant, immaterial, impertinent, or scandalous matter." Although this motion is uncommon, it is available if a pleading needlessly includes information that is clearly false, non-germane, or defamatory. *See, e.g.*, *Cobell v. Norton*, 224 F.R.D. 1, 3 (D.D.C. 2004) ("Under Rule 12(f) 'immaterial' matter consists of statements and averments bearing no essential or important relationship to the claim for relief or the defenses being pled."); *Gateway Bottling, Inc. v. Dad's Rootbeer Co.*, 53 F.R.D. 585, 588 (W.D. Pa. 1971) ("To strike material as scandalous it must be obviously false and unrelated to the subject matter of the action.").

Take Note!

The motion to strike is sometimes used to challenge pleadings that are filed beyond the time periods required by the Federal Rules. However, granting the motion based on missed deadlines is disfavored, since the consequences of striking a pleading can be severe. *See, e.g.*, *Am. S. Ins. Co. v. Buckley*, 748 F. Supp. 2d 610, 626–28 (E.D. Tex. 2010) (denying motion to strike because granting it on the sole basis that responsive pleadings were untimely "would be a drastic and harsh remedy").

The motion is also handy for plaintiffs who want to challenge the legal sufficiency of a defense raised by the defendant in its answer. This type of use mirrors the 12(b)(6) motion to dismiss for failure to state a claim except it is used to attack defenses

---

[*] Plaintiffs facing counterclaims from defendants may also avail themselves of this motion before filing an answer to a counterclaim. The answer to a counterclaim will be considered further below. [Ed.]

rather than claims. *Kaiser Aluminum & Chem. Sales, Inc. v. Avondale Shipyards, Inc.*, 677 F.2d 1045, 1057 (5th Cir. 1982) ("Although motions to strike a defense are generally disfavored, a Rule 12(f) motion to dismiss a defense is proper when the defense is insufficient as a matter of law.").

e.   Procedural Aspects of Filing Motions Under Rule 12

Rule 12 also sets forth the procedures for raising the defenses included in the rule. Regarding the defenses listed in Rule 12(b), each of these may be made either through a motion or within the answer itself. However, certain of these defenses—those enumerated in Rule 12(b)(2)–(5)—are waivable, meaning if they are not raised in the initial response to the complaint—either through a pre-answer Rule 12 motion or in the answer—they are waived and may not be raised subsequently. *See* FED. R. CIV. P. 12(h)(1). Further, these waivable defenses must be raised in a consolidated fashion; thus, if a party raises one of these waivable defenses in a pre-answer Rule 12 motion but neglects to assert one of the others, the party has waived those defenses and is barred from raising them at a later time. *See* FED. R. CIV. P. 12(g) & (h)(1). Why do you think that these waiver rules exist? Why have certain defenses been singled out as waivable while others have not? After reading Rules 12(g) & 12(h), see if you can sort through the following hypothetical problems:

Hypo 6.2

Marty sued Felix for breach of contract. Felix moved to dismiss for lack of personal jurisdiction under Rule 12(b)(2) and the motion was denied. Felix now moves to dismiss the complaint for insufficient service of process under Rule 12(b)(5). Has Felix waived this latter defense?

Hypo 6.3

Marty sued Felix for breach of contract. Felix moved to dismiss for lack of subject matter jurisdiction under Rule 12(b)(1). The motion was denied. Felix now files an answer in which he raises the defenses of a lack of personal jurisdiction and failure to state a claim upon which relief can be granted. Has Felix waived either of these two defenses?

Hypo 6.4

Marty sued Felix for breach of contract. Felix then filed an answer in which he raised the defenses of a lack of personal jurisdiction and improper venue. Both defenses were rejected. During the trial, Felix raises the defense of failure to state a claim upon which relief can be granted. Has Felix waived this defense? May the court consider this defense at this point in the proceedings?

Hypo 6.5

Marty sued Felix for breach of contract. Felix moved to dismiss for improper venue under Rule 12(b)(3). The motion was denied. Felix then filed an answer and the case proceeded to trial. After the case was submitted to the jury, Felix sought to dismiss the action for lack of subject matter jurisdiction. Has this defense been waived? May the court consider this defense at this point in the proceedings?

The remaining defenses under Rule 12 have slightly different rules regarding when they may be raised. The motion for a more definite statement under Rule 12(e) and the motion to strike under Rule 12(f) must be made before the movant's responsive pleading is filed (or, in the case of the motion to strike, within 21 days after being served with the pleading if no response is allowed). This means, for example, that if a defendant believes that the complaint is too vague, she must submit a motion for a more definite statement before filing her answer. A motion for judgment on the pleadings under Rule 12(c), on the other hand, may be made only after the pleadings are closed, which means that each party has submitted its pleadings and no more responsive pleadings are due or permitted (we will review all of the responsive pleadings below).

> **FYI**
>
> A motion to dismiss for lack of subject matter jurisdiction may be raised at any time. FED. R. CIV. P. 12(h)(3). The motions to dismiss for failure to state a claim or legal defense or for failure to join a required Rule 19 party may be raised at any time prior to the end of a trial. FED. R. CIV. P. 12(h)(2).

2. The Answer

If the case is not dismissed in response to a pre-answer motion the defendant will have to submit its pleading in response to the complaint, which is the .* FED. R. CIV. P. 7(a). One can better understand and appreciate the range of responses that an answer may contain by looking back to common law pleading. Under the common law system, there were three types of responses a defendant could give to a complaint, with the caveat that one of those three had to be selected to the exclusion of the others:

---

* Former Rule 7(c), which was abrogated in 2007, technically abolished the demurrer in the federal system, although the same function is now served by the 12(b)(6) motion. [Ed.]

Available Responses Under Common Law Pleading

- **Traverse.** The defendant could meet the allegations of the complaint with a defense challenging the facts. A trial on the merits would ensue. In modern times this is the basic *answer*.

- **Demurrer.** Alternatively, the defendant could challenge the legal sufficiency of the claim by filing a demurrer. A demurrer did not challenge the facts and precluded the defendant from subsequently challenging facts. If the demurrer prevailed, the defendant won; if it failed, the plaintiff won. The demurrer is the precursor to today's ***motion to dismiss for failure to state a claim*** under Rule 12(b)(6).*

- **Confession & Avoidance.** This response admitted the truth of the plaintiff's factual allegations but proffered additional facts that absolved the defendant from any liability. Such responses are now referred to as ***affirmative defenses*** and are included within a defendant's answer to a complaint.

Modern pleading practice under the Federal Rules permits defendants to raise each of these types of responses within the answer, although, as we have just seen, defenses of the second type may be raised separately prior to filing the answer. The Rules specifically give defendants the option of including one or more of three different types of responses to the complaint:

Components of an Answer Under the Federal Rules

- **Denials & Admissions.** Under Rule 8(b) a defendant must admit or deny all factual allegations of the complaint.

- **Defenses.** A defendant may also include any defenses it intends to raise, including the defenses found in Rule 12(b) that have not been waived and any affirmative defenses such as those listed in Rule 8(c).

- **Claims.** Finally, if the defendant has claims against the plaintiff or other parties that she wishes to assert she may do so in the answer.

Although the defenses contained within Rule 12(b) may be included in a defendant's answer if they have not been waived, if the defendant is serious about asserting these defenses they will typically be raised by motion prior to the filing of an answer. Why do you think this is so?

The heart of a defendant's answer is the series of responses to the factual allegations contained in the complaint, of which there are three types under the Federal Rules: A defendant may either admit, deny, or assert that it "lacks knowledge or information sufficient to form a belief about the truth of an allegation." FED. R. CIV. P. 8(b)(5). Admissions are plain enough to understand; this simply means that the defendant admits the truth of the plaintiff's allegation. Denials are more complicated. There are specific rules governing how denials must be made in order to be effective. Rule 8(b) sets forth these requirements:

FRCP 8(b). Defenses; Admissions and Denials.

(b) Defenses; Admissions and Denials.

(1) *In General.* In responding to a pleading, a party must:

(A) state in short and plain terms its defenses to each claim asserted against it; and

(B) admit or deny the allegations asserted against it by an opposing party.

(2) *Denials—Responding to the Substance.* A denial must fairly respond to the substance of the allegation.

(3) *General and Specific Denials.* A party that intends in good faith to deny all the allegations of a pleading—including the jurisdictional grounds—may do so by a general denial. A party that does not intend to deny all the allegations must either specifically deny designated allegations or generally deny all except those specifically admitted.

(4) *Denying Part of an Allegation.* A party that intends in good faith to deny only part of an allegation must admit the part that is true and deny the rest.

(5) *Lacking Knowledge or Information.* A party that lacks knowledge or information sufficient to form a belief about the truth of an allegation must so state, and the statement has the effect of a denial.

(6) *Effect of Failing to Deny.* An allegation—other than one relating to the amount of damages—is admitted if a responsive pleading is required and the allegation is not denied. If a responsive pleading is not required, an allegation is considered denied or avoided.

Under this language, denials may be general in the sense that they deny everything in a particular paragraph of a complaint, but only if such a complete, general denial is intended. However, if any part of a sentence or paragraph is true and worthy of admission, the defendant must specifically admit that portion of the allegation and then may generally deny the rest. Otherwise, the court may find that the defendant's general denial is ineffective because it failed to "fairly respond to the substance of the allegation." FED. R. CIV. P. 8(b)(2). What should the consequences be when a defendant fails to deny an allegation or offers an ineffective general denial? The next case addresses this issue.

Zielinski v. Philadelphia Piers, Inc.

<u>U.S. District Court for the Eastern District of Pennsylvania</u>
<u>139 F. Supp. 408 (1956)</u>

<u>Van Dusen</u>, District Judge.

Plaintiff requests a ruling that, for the purposes of this case, the motor-driven fork lift operated by Sandy Johnson on February 9, 1953, was owned by defendant and that Sandy Johnson was its agent acting in the course of his employment on that date. The following facts are established by the pleadings, interrogatories, depositions and uncontradicted portions of affidavits:

What's That?

Interrogatories are simply written questions that one party may submit, under <u>Rule 33</u>, to any other party. Receiving parties then are obliged to answer or object to each question. Interrogatories, depositions, and other discovery devices will be covered fully in <u>Chapter 8</u>.

1.   Plaintiff filed his complaint on April 28, 1953, for personal injuries received on February 9, 1953, while working on Pier 96, Philadelphia, for J. A. McCarthy, as a result of a collision of two motor-driven fork lifts.

2.   Paragraph 5 of this complaint stated that "a motor-driven vehicle known as a fork lift or chisel, owned, operated and controlled by the defendant, its agents, servants and employees, was so negligently and carelessly managed * * * that the same * * * did come into contact with the plaintiff causing him to sustain the injuries more fully hereinafter set forth."

3.   The "First Defense" of the Answer stated "Defendant * * * (c) denies the averments of paragraph 5 * * *."

4.   The motor-driven vehicle known as a fork lift or chisel, which collided with the McCarthy fork lift on which plaintiff was riding, had on it the initials "P.P.I."

5.   On February 10, 1953, Carload Contractors, Inc. made a report of this accident to its insurance company, whose policy No. CL 3964 insured Carload Contractors, Inc. against potential liability for the negligence of its employees contributing to a collision of the type described in paragraph 2 above.

6.   By letter of April 29, 1953, the complaint served on defendant was forwarded to the above-mentioned insurance company. This letter read as follows:

Gentlemen: * * *

We find that a fork lift truck operated by an employee of Carload Contractors, Inc. also insured by yourselves was involved in an accident with another chisel truck, which, was alleged, did cause injury to Frank Zielinski, and same was reported to you by Carload Contractors, Inc. at the time, and you assigned Claim Number OL 0153-94 to this claim.

Should not this Complaint in Trespass be issued against Carload Contractors, Inc. and not Philadelphia Piers, Inc.?

We forward for your handling.

7.   Interrogatories 1 to 5 and the answers thereto, which were sworn to by defendant's General Manager on June 12, 1953 * * *, read as follows:

1.   State whether you have received any information of an injury sustained by the plaintiff on February 9, 1953, South Wharves. If so, state when and from whom you first received notice of such injury. [Answer:] We were first notified of this accident on or about February 9, 1953 by Thomas Wilson.

2.   State whether you caused an investigation to be made of the circumstances of said injury and if so, state who made such investigation and when it was made. [Answer:] We made a very brief investigation on February 9, 1953 and turned the matter over to (our insurance company) for further investigation.

* * *

8.   At a deposition taken August 18, 1953, Sandy Johnson testified that he was the employee of defendant on February 9, 1953, and had been their employee for approximately fifteen years.

9.   At a pre-trial conference held on September 27, 1955,[3] plaintiff first learned that over a year before February 9, 1953, the business of moving freight on piers in Philadelphia, formerly conducted by defendant, had been sold by it to Carload Contractors, Inc. and Sandy Johnson had been transferred to the payroll of this corporation without apparently realizing it, since the nature or location of his work had not changed.

* * *

11.   Defendant now admits that on February 9, 1953, it owned the fork lift in the custody of Sandy Johnson and that this fork lift was leased to Carload Contractors, Inc. It is also admitted that the pier on which the accident occurred was leased by defendant.

12.   There is no indication of action by either party in bad faith and there is no proof of inaccurate statements being made with intent to deceive. Because defen-

---

[3]   The applicable statute of limitations prevented any suit against Carload Contractors, Inc. after February 9, 1955.

dant made a prompt investigation of the accident * * * its insurance company has been representing the defendant since suit was brought, and this company insures Carload Contractors, Inc. also, requiring defendant to defend this suit, will not prejudice it.

Under these circumstances, and for the purposes of this action, it is ordered that the following shall be stated to the jury at the trial:

It is admitted that, on February 9, 1953, the towmotor or fork lift bearing the initials "P.P.I." was owned by defendant and that Sandy Johnson was a servant in the employ of defendant and doing its work on that date.

This ruling is based on the following principles:

1. Under the circumstances of this case, the answer contains an ineffective denial of that part of paragraph 5 of the complaint which alleges that "a motor driven vehicle known as a fork lift or chisel (was) owned, operated and controlled by the defendant, its agents, servants and employees."

F. R. Civ. P. 8(b) provides:

A party shall state in short and plain terms his defenses to each claim asserted and shall admit or deny the averments upon which the adverse party relies. * * * Denials shall fairly meet the substance of the averments denied. When a pleader intends in good faith to deny only a part or a qualification of an averment, he shall specify so much of it as is true and material and shall deny only the remainder.

For example, it is quite clear that defendant does not deny the averment in paragraph 5 that the fork lift came into contact with plaintiff, since it admits, in the answers to interrogatories, that an investigation of an occurrence of the accident had been made and that a report dated February 10, 1953, was sent to its insurance company stating "While Frank Zielinski was riding on bumper of chisel and holding rope to secure cargo, the chisel truck collided with another chisel truck operated by Sandy Johnson causing injuries to Frank Zielinski's legs and hurt head of Sandy Johnson." Compliance with the above-mentioned rule required that defendant file a more specific answer than a general denial. A specific denial of parts of this paragraph and specific admission of other parts would have warned plaintiff that he had sued the wrong defendant. * * *

Under circumstances where an improper and ineffective answer has been filed, the Pennsylvania courts have consistently held that an allegation of agency in the complaint requires a statement to the jury that agency is admitted where an attempt to amend the answer is made after the expiration of the period of limitation. Although the undersigned has been able to find no federal court decisions on this point, he believes the principle of these Pennsylvania appellate court decisions may be considered in view of all the facts of this case, where jurisdiction is based on diversity of citizenship, the accident occurred in Pennsylvania, and the federal district court is sitting in Pennsylvania. * * *

2.   Under the circumstances of this case, principles of equity require that defendant be estopped from denying agency because, otherwise, its inaccurate statements and statements in the record, which it knew (or had the means of knowing within its control) were inaccurate, will have deprived plaintiff of his right of action.

Practice Pointer

When defending a *deposition*, you must be constantly aware of what is being said, intervening in an appropriate way to correct any misrepresentations that your deponent may make. Note that the court here states that the presence of attorneys for the insurance companies at the deposition where the inaccurate statement regarding company of employment was made put them on notice of the communication of inaccurate information and thus, in part, supported the sanction that the court imposed.

If Interrogatory 2 had been answered accurately by saying that employees of Carload Contractors, Inc. had turned the matter over to the insurance company, it seems clear that plaintiff would have realized his mistake. The fact that if Sandy Johnson had testified accurately, the plaintiff could have brought its action against the proper party defendant within the statutory period of limitations is also a factor to be considered, since defendant was represented at the deposition and received knowledge of the inaccurate testimony.

At least one appellate court has stated that the doctrine of equitable estoppel will be applied to prevent a party from taking advantage of the statute of limitations where the plaintiff has been misled by conduct of such party. See, <u>Peters v. Public Service Corporation, 29 A.2d 189, 195 (N.J. Ch. 1942)</u>.[12] In that case, the court said:

> Of course, defendants were under no duty to advise complainants' attorney of his error, other than by appropriate pleadings, but neither did defendants have a right, knowing of the mistake, to foster it by its acts of omission.

* * *

Since this is a pre-trial order, it may be modified at the trial if the trial judge determines from the facts which then appear that justice so requires.

————

[12] When inaccurate statements are made under circumstances where there is foreseeable danger that another will rely on them to his prejudice, and he does in fact rely thereon, such statements are sufficient to invoke this doctrine even though fraud is not present.

Points for Discussion

a. Lessons from *Zielinski*

One thing that should be clear from *Zielinski* is that general denials should only be used when every single aspect of an allegation is intended to be denied. If any component turns out to be something that the defendant had no intention of denying—like the fact of the collision itself in *Zielinski*—the court will be in a position to declare the entire denial ineffective. As *Zielinski* reveals, the consequences of an ineffective denial can be severe; Rule 8(b)(6) [formerly Rule 8(d)] provides that all allegations not properly denied are deemed to be admitted. *See, e.g.*, H.R.R. Zimmerman Co. v. Tecumseh Prods. Co., 2001 WL 184982, at *6 n.5 (N.D. Ill. Feb. 22, 2001) ("The effect of the failure to deny an allegation in a pleading to which a responsive pleading is required . . . is an admission."); Mosiman v. Warren, 2011 WL 321148, at *2 (N.D. Tex. Jan. 28, 2011) ("[C]onsidering both that Warren could not have made a good-faith denial of the jurisdictional facts in Mosiman's second amended complaint

Take Note!

The take-home message is that it is a good practice to be precise with one's denials, offering specific denials in most instances and general denials only when there is certainty that such a denial properly should apply to the entirety of the allegation to which it refers.

and that the language used is so primitive and imprecise, Warren's answer fails as a general denial and Rule 8(b)(6) demands that the allegations in the second amended complaint be deemed admitted."). Is it fair to invoke these principles to hold a party to a statement of fact that is in truth not an accurate representation of reality, as happened in *Zielinski*?

b. Denials for Lack of Information

Rule 8(b) permits a third type of response other than an admission or denial; a party may deny an allegation because it "lacks knowledge or information sufficient to form a belief about the truth of an allegation . . . ." FED. R. CIV. P. 8(b)(5). The effect of such a response is the same as a denial. FED. R. CIV. P. 8(b)(5). *See also* Grupo Mexicano de Desarrollo S.A. v. Alliance Bond Fund, Inc., 527 U.S. 308, 320 n.5 (1999) ("Petitioners' answer . . . denied knowledge or information sufficient to form a belief (which is the equivalent of a denial, see Federal Rule of Civil Procedure 8(b)). . . ."); Glater v. Eli Lilly & Co., 712 F.2d 735, 737 (1st Cir. 1983) ("It is settled law that a defendant's good faith answer that it lacks knowledge or information sufficient to form a belief as to the truth of an averment constitutes a denial."). When should a party be able to offer this type of response? Keep in mind that such responses are subject to the obligation to be truthful and demonstrate good faith in the pleadings, something we will study further in Section D below. Is this response appropriate from a defendant in response to an allegation such as, "The defendant is a Delaware corporation"? *See* Oliver v. Swiss

Club Tell, 222 Cal. App. 2d 528, 540, 35 Cal. Rptr. 324, 330–31 (1963) (treating a "without information or belief" response as an admission because the allegation being responded to—whether the defendant was an unincorporated association—was "presumptively within the defendant's knowledge").

c. Improper Forms of Denial

Note that the response of being without knowledge or information sufficient to form a belief is not the same as one that states, "*The defendant neither admits nor denies the allegations in paragraph A.*" Such a response is a non-response, and will thus be treated as an admission under Rule 8(b)(6). *Quantum Mgmt. Group v. U. of Chi. Hosps.*, 2000 WL 1221632, at *10 (N.D. Ill. Aug. 18, 2000) ("Plaintiff neither admits nor denies the accuracy of Defendant's damages amount, but such equivocation constitutes an admission."). Similarly, responding to an allegation by stating that "*it states a legal conclusion to which no response is required*" is improper as it is not one of the permitted responses under the Rules. *See State Farm Mutual Automobile Ins. v. Riley*, 199 F.R.D. 276, 278 (N.D. Ill. 2001) ("Another regular offender is the lawyer who takes it on himself or herself to decline to respond to an allegation because it 'states a legal conclusion.' That of course violates the express Rule 8(b) requirement that *all* allegations must be responded to."). Such non-responses will be disregarded, and thus, can result in the allegations being admitted. *See, e.g.*, *Thompson v. Ret. Plan for Emps. of S.C. Johnson & Sons*, 2008 WL 5377712, at *3 (E.D. Wis. Dec. 22, 2008) ("All allegations require a response permitted by Rule 8, including legal conclusions. Accordingly, the court will strike the defendant's response. . . .").

There are other improper forms of denial as well. The negative pregnant denial involves an overly specific denial that repeats every detail of the assertion, leaving the possible impression that some other form of the allegation could be true. For example, if the allegation states, "Last Saturday, *D* hit my vehicle with his vehicle," and *D*'s response was, "I deny that last Saturday I hit *P*'s vehicle with my vehicle," the denial is "pregnant" with the suggestion that *D* may have hit *P* on another day, or that he hit *P*'s vehicle with someone else's vehicle rather than his own. How should a court treat such denials? *See, e.g.*, *Freedom Nat'l Bank v. N. Ill. Corp.*, 202 F.2d 601, 605 (7th Cir. 1953). What would be a better response than the one given in this example? A variant of the negative pregnant is the conjunctive denial. This type of denial comes in response to an allegation that asserts, "The defendant did A, B, and C." If the defendant responds by saying, "I deny that I did A, B, and C," that is a conjunctive denial because it leaves open the possibility that the defendant did one or two of the three but not all three of the things alleged. These types of denials are seen as evasive and should be avoided. Nevertheless, because the prohibitions against these types of denials may be regarded as archaic holdovers from the common law pleading era, the best response to them may be a motion for a more definite statement under Rule 12(e) rather than an attempt to have them stricken as ineffective and treated as admissions.

d. Affirmative Defenses

In addition to admitting or denying the allegations of a complaint, the defendant must include any affirmative defenses it has in the answer. FED. R. CIV. P. 8(c). Professors Wright and Miller provide a good explanation of what affirmative defenses are when they write, " 'an avoidance or affirmative defense' [under Rule 8(c)] encompasses two types of defensive allegations: those that admit the allegations of the complaint but suggest some other reason why there is no right of recovery, and those that concern allegations outside of the plaintiff's prima facie case that the defendant therefore cannot raise by a simple denial in the answer." 5 C. WRIGHT & A. MILLER, FED. PRAC. & PROC. § 1271 (3d ed. 2004). For example, in some states, if the plaintiff's own negligence in any way contributed to her injuries, the plaintiff is barred from recovery in a negligence action based on that incident. The plaintiff's negligence in such an instance is referred to as contributory negligence and constitutes an affirmative defense that the defendant must specifically assert in its answer. Why would the defendant's simple denial of the plaintiff's allegations not suffice to put the contributory negligence of the plaintiff at issue in the case?

The Federal Rules instruct defendants to state their defenses as follows: "In responding to a pleading, a party must . . . state in short and plain terms its defenses to each claim asserted against it . . . ." FED. R. CIV. P. 8(b). If a party believes that an affirmative defense is not supported by the relevant law, it may file a motion to strike the defense under Rule 12(f). In the face of such a motion to strike, should courts apply the standards of *Twombly* and *Iqbal* to judge the sufficiency of any pleaded affirmative defenses? *See* Leslie Paul Machado & C. Matthew Haynes, *Do Twombly and Iqbal Apply To Affirmative Defenses?*, 59 FED. LAW. 56 (2012) (discussing the issue and relevant cases); *see also Francisco v. Verizon S., Inc.*, 2010 WL 2990159, at *6 nn.3–4 (E.D. Va. July 29, 2010) (collecting cases). Prior to its abrogation in 2015, Form 30 in the Appendix of Forms provided an example of how an affirmative defense should be pleaded.

Although Rule 8(c) enumerates eighteen affirmative defenses, the list is not exhaustive. *See* C. WRIGHT & A. MILLER, FED. PRAC. & PROC. § 1271 (3d ed. 2004) (listing several additional affirmative defenses not presented in Rule 8(c)). Rule 8(c) instructs pleaders to state "any avoidance or affirmative defenses," whether listed in the rule or not. How does a party determine whether something is an affirmative defense that must be pleaded if it is not mentioned in Rule 8(c)? Why do you think the rules require defendants to assert these defenses affirmatively rather than rely on their denials of allegations in the complaint?

The failure to plead an affirmative defense ordinarily results in the defense being waived. *See, e.g., Harris v. Sec'y, U.S. Dep't of Veterans Affairs*, 126 F.3d 339, 343 (D.C. Cir. 1997) ("[I]t is well-settled that a party's failure to plead an affirmative defense . . . generally results in the waiver of that defense and its *exclusion from the case*." (internal citations and quotation marks omitted)); *Ingraham v. United States*,

808 F.2d 1075 (5th Cir. 1987) [*FLEX Case 6.A*]. However, some courts do not treat non-pleaded affirmative defenses as forfeited in cases where there is no prejudice to the plaintiff. *See, e.g., Carter v. United States*, 333 F.3d 791, 796 (7th Cir. 2003), *cert. denied* 540 U.S. 1111 (2004) ("The failure to plead an affirmative defense in the answer works a forfeiture only if the plaintiff is harmed by the defendant's delay in asserting it."). In the event that a party mistakenly omits an affirmative defense or any other matter that it should have included or meant to include in its pleadings, the rules do permit the pleadings to be amended. Amending the pleadings is the topic we turn to in the next section of this chapter.

e.   The Answer to a Counterclaim and the Reply

As mentioned above, under the Federal Rules a defendant may include affirmative claims for relief that it wishes to assert in its answer. In the event that the defendant asserts such a claim against the plaintiff, this will be considered a counterclaim and will entitle the plaintiff to submit a further pleading referred to as "an answer to a counterclaim." FED. R. CIV. P. 7(a)(3). In the answer to the counterclaim, the plaintiff—who is now a defendant to the counterclaim—will have the same opportunity to answer the allegations lodged against it, with the obligation to admit or deny the allegations and submit any defenses or objections it may have. Failure to submit an answer to a counterclaim in response to a counterclaim will result in those allegations being confessed. *See Alloy Prods. Corp. v. United States*, 302 F.2d 528, 531 (Ct. Cl. 1962) ("Since plaintiff has filed no [answer] to defendant's counterclaim, defendant's allegations were admitted. . . ."); *Peters & Russell, Inc. v. Dorfman*, 188 F.2d 711, 712 (7th Cir. 1951) ("Such failure to reply [to Defendant's counterclaim] constitutes an admission by Plaintiff of the specific allegations of Defendants . . . .").

What's That?

The court you see referenced in the *Alloy Products* citation is the U.S. Court of Claims, today known as the U.S. Court of Federal Claims, which has jurisdiction primarily over money claims against the United States.

Plaintiffs may file a pleading called a "reply" with the permission of the court if they wish to respond to the defendant's affirmative defenses. FED. R. CIV. P. 7(a)(7) (permitting, "if the court orders one, a reply to an answer"). However, plaintiffs are under no obligation to file a reply in response to affirmative defenses and if the court does not order such a reply, all affirmative defenses are simply deemed denied. *See Radio Shack Corp. v. Radio Shack*, 180 F.2d 200, 206 (7th Cir. 1950) ("[T]the court did not order a reply to the affirmative defenses. As a matter of pleading they stand denied.").

Although common law pleading permitted subsequent pleadings after the reply, the Federal Rules close the pleadings at this stage. FED. R. CIV. P. 7(a). Because there is no further opportunity to respond, any allegations or affirmative defenses raised in the reply are automatically deemed to be denied. FED. R. CIV. P. 8(b)(6).

C. Amending the Pleadings

As the action goes forward from the initial pleadings, there are two main circumstances that would lead parties to be interested in somehow altering or amending their pleadings: the need to remedy an inadvertent omission or mistake, or the desire to add, alter, or remove claims or defenses in light of new information. In this section, we will review the basic rules governing amendments to the pleadings and then consider the more complex issue of when the pleadings may be amended at a later date, but treated as if they were amended on a previous date, the process known as "relation-back" of amendments.

1. The Basic Rules Governing Amendments

Rule 15(a) sets forth the conditions under which a party's pleading may be amended before trial. After the rule, the case that follows demonstrates its application.

FRCP 15(a). Amendments Before Trial.

(a) **Amendments Before Trial.**

(1) **Amending as a Matter of Course**. A party may amend its pleading once as a matter of course within:

(A) 21 days after serving it, or

(B) if the pleading is one to which a responsive pleading is required, 21 days after service of a responsive pleading or 21 days after service of a motion under Rule 12(b), (e), or (f), whichever is earlier.

(2) **Other Amendments**. In all other cases, a party may amend its pleading only with the opposing party's written consent or the court's leave. The court should freely give leave when justice so requires.

(3) **Time to Respond**. Unless the court orders otherwise, any required response to an amended pleading must be made within the time remaining to respond to the original pleading or within 14 days after service of the amended pleading, whichever is later.

Beeck v. Aquaslide 'N' Dive Corp.

<u>U.S. Court of Appeals for the Eighth Circuit</u>
<u>562 F.2d 537 (8th Cir. 1977)</u>

B<small>ENSON</small>, D<small>ISTRICT</small> J<small>UDGE</small>. [Sitting by designation.]

This case is an appeal from the trial court's exercise of discretion on procedural matters in a diversity personal injury action.

> **FYI**
>
> Federal judges not assigned to a particular federal court of appeals may sit on panels within a circuit and hear cases *by designation* pursuant to 28 U.S.C. §§ <u>291</u>, <u>292</u>, & <u>293</u>. For an odd case in which the entire panel consisted of judges sitting by designation—with each judge designated pursuant to a different one of the statutory provisions just mentioned—see <u>*In re Rodriguez*, 2005 WL 3843612 (D.C. Cir. Oct. 14, 2005)</u>.

Jerry A. Beeck was severely injured on July 15, 1972, while using a water slide. He and his wife, Judy A. Beeck, sued Aquaslide 'N' Dive Corporation (Aquaslide), a Texas corporation, alleging it manufactured the slide involved in the accident, and sought to recover substantial damages on theories of negligence, and breach of implied warranty.

Aquaslide initially admitted manufacture of the slide, but later moved to amend its answer to deny manufacture; the motion was resisted. The district court granted leave to amend. On motion of the defendant, a separate trial was held on the issue of "whether the defendant designed, manufactured or sold the slide in question." This motion was also resisted by the plaintiffs. The issue was tried to a jury, which returned a verdict for the defendant, after which the trial court entered summary judgment of dismissal of the case. Plaintiffs took this appeal, and stated the issues presented for review to be:

1. Where the manufacturer of the product, a water slide, admitted in its Answer and later in its Answer to Interrogatories both filed prior to the running of the statute of limitations that it designed, manufactured and sold the water slide in question, was it an abuse of the trial court's discretion to grant leave to amend to the manufacturer in order to deny these admissions after the running of the statute of limitations?

2. After granting the manufacturer's Motion for Leave to Amend in order to deny the prior admissions of design, manufacture and sale of the water slide in question, was it an abuse of the trial court's discretion to further grant the manufacturer's Motion for a Separate Trial on the issue of manufacture?

I. FACTS

A brief review of the facts found by the trial court in its order granting leave to amend, and which do not appear to have been in dispute, is essential to a full understanding of appellants' claims.

In 1971 Kimberly Village Home Association of Davenport, Iowa, ordered an Aquaslide product from one George Boldt, who was a local distributor handling defendant's products. The order was forwarded by Boldt to Sentry Pool and Chemical Supply Co. in Rock Island, Illinois, and Sentry forwarded the order to Purity Swimming Pool Supply in Hammond, Indiana. A slide was delivered from a Purity warehouse to Kimberly Village, and was installed by Kimberly employees. On July 15, 1972, Jerry A. Beeck was injured while using the slide at a social gathering sponsored at Kimberly Village by his employer, Harker Wholesale Meats, Inc. Soon after the accident investigations were undertaken by representatives of the separate insurers of Harker and Kimberly Village. On October 31, 1972, Aquaslide first learned of the accident through a letter sent by a representative of Kimberly's insurer to Aquaslide, advising that "one of your Queen Model #Q-3D slides" was involved in the accident. Aquaslide forwarded this notification to its insurer. Aquaslide's insurance adjuster made an on-site investigation of the slide in May, 1973, and also interviewed persons connected with the ordering and assembly of the slide. An inter-office letter dated September 23, 1973, indicates that Aquaslide's insurer was of the opinion the "Aquaslide in question was definitely manufactured by our insured." The complaint was filed October 15, 1973.[3] Investigators for three different insurance companies, representing Harker, Kimberly and the defendant, had concluded that the slide had been manufactured by Aquaslide, and the defendant, with no information to the contrary, answered the complaint on December 12, 1973, and admitted that it "designed, manufactured, assembled and sold" the slide in question.[4]

The statute of limitations on plaintiff's personal injury claim expired on July 15, 1974. About six and one-half months later Carl Meyer, president and owner of Aquaslide, visited the site of the accident prior to the taking of his deposition by the plaintiff.[5] From his on-site inspection of the slide, he determined it was not a product of the defendant. Thereafter, Aquaslide moved the court for leave to amend its answer to deny manufacture of the slide.

---

[3] Aquaslide 'N' Dive Corporation was the sole defendant named in the complaint.

[4] In answers to interrogatories filed on June 3, 1974, Aquaslide again admitted manufacture of the slide in question.

[5] Plaintiffs apparently requested Meyer to inspect the slide prior to the taking of his deposition to determine whether it was defectively installed or assembled.

II. LEAVE TO AMEND

Amendment of pleadings in civil actions is governed by <u>Rule 15(a), F.R.Civ.P.</u>, which provides in part that once issue is joined in a lawsuit, a party may amend his pleading "only by leave of court or by written consent of the adverse party; and leave shall be freely given when justice so requires."

In *Foman v. Davis*, 371 U.S. 178 (1962), the Supreme Court had occasion to construe that portion of <u>Rule 15(a)</u> set out above:

> <u>Rule 15(a)</u> declares that leave to amend "shall be freely given when justice so requires," this mandate is to be heeded. . . . If the underlying facts or circumstances relied upon by a plaintiff may be a proper subject of relief, he ought to be afforded an opportunity to test his claim on the merits. In the absence of any apparent or declared reason such as undue delay, bad faith or dilatory motive on the part of the movant, repeated failure to cure deficiencies by amendments previously allowed, undue prejudice to the opposing party by virtue of allowance of the amendment, futility of amendment, etc. the leave sought should, as the rules require, be "freely given." Of course, the grant or denial of an opportunity to amend is within the discretion of the District Court, ...

This Court in *Hanson v. Hunt Oil Co.*, 398 F.2d 578, 582 (8th Cir. 1968), held that "prejudice *must be shown*." (emphasis added). The burden is on the party opposing the amendment to show such prejudice. In ruling on a motion for leave to amend, the trial court must inquire into the issue of prejudice to the opposing party, in light of the particular facts of the case.

Certain principles apply to appellate review of a trial court's grant or denial of a motion to amend pleadings. First, as noted in *Foman v. Davis*, allowance or denial of leave to amend lies within the sound discretion of the trial court, and is reviewable only for an abuse of discretion. The appellate court must view the case in the posture in which the trial court acted in ruling on the motion to amend.

What's That?

Abuse of discretion is a particular type of error that is relevant to the *standard of review* that guides an appellate court's review of the district court's decision. When reviewing for an abuse of discretion, the reviewing court may not second-guess the judgment of the lower court, but rather must simply determine whether the initial court had a reasonable basis for ruling the way that it did. Standards of review will be covered more fully in <u>Chapter 11</u>.

It is evident from the order of the district court that in the exercise of its discretion in ruling on defendant's motion for leave to amend, it searched the record for evidence of bad faith, prejudice and undue delay which might be sufficient to overbalance the mandate of <u>Rule 15(a), F.R.Civ.P.</u>, and <u>*Foman v. Davis*</u>, that leave to amend should be "freely given." Plaintiffs had not at any time conceded that the slide in question had not been manufactured by the defendant, and at the time the motion for leave to amend was at issue, the court had to decide whether the defendant should be permitted to litigate a material factual issue on its merits.

In inquiring into the issue of bad faith, the court noted the fact that the defendant, in initially concluding that it had manufactured the slide, relied upon the conclusions of three different insurance companies,[6] each of which had conducted an investigation into the circumstances surrounding the accident. This reliance upon investigations of three insurance companies, and the fact that "no contention has been made by anyone that the defendant influenced this possibly erroneous conclusion," persuaded the court that "defendant has not acted in such bad faith as to be precluded from contesting the issue of manufacture at trial." The court further found "to the extent that 'blame' is to be spread regarding the original identification, the record indicates that it should be shared equally."

In considering the issue of prejudice that might result to the plaintiffs from the granting of the motion for leave to amend, the trial court held that the facts presented to it did not support plaintiffs' assertion that, because of the running of the two year Iowa statute of limitations on personal injury claims, the allowance of the amendment would sound the "death knell" of the litigation. In order to accept plaintiffs' argument, the court would have had to assume that the defendant would prevail at trial on the factual issue of manufacture of the slide, and further that plaintiffs would be foreclosed, should the amendment be allowed, from proceeding against other parties if they were unsuccessful in pressing their claim against Aquaslide. On the state of the record before it, the trial court was unwilling to make such assumptions,[7] and concluded "under these circumstances, the Court deems that the possible prejudice to the plaintiffs is an insufficient basis on which to deny the proposed amendment." The court reasoned that the amendment would merely allow the defendant to contest a disputed factual issue at trial, and further that it would be prejudicial to the defendant to deny the amendment.

---

[6] The insurer of Beeck's employer, the insurer of Kimberly Village, as well as the defendant's insurer had each concluded the slide in question was an Aquaslide.

[7] The district court noted in its order granting leave to amend that plaintiffs may be able to sue other parties as a result of the substituting of a "counterfeit" slide for the Aquaslide, if indeed this occurred. The court added:

> again, the Court is handicapped by an unclear record on this issue. If, in fact, the slide in question is not an Aquaslide, the replacement entered the picture somewhere along the Boldt to Sentry, Sentry to Purity, Purity to Kimberly Village chain of distribution. Depending upon the circumstances of its entry, a cause of action sounding in fraud or contract might lie. If so, the applicable statute of limitations period would not have run. Further, as defendant points out, the doctrine of equitable estoppel might possibly preclude another defendant from asserting the two-year statute as a defense.

The court also held that defendant and its insurance carrier, in investigating the circumstances surrounding the accident, had not been so lacking in diligence as to dictate a denial of the right to litigate the factual issue of manufacture of the slide.

On this record we hold that the trial court did not abuse its discretion in allowing the defendant to amend its answer. * * *

Points for Discussion

a. The Outcome in *Beeck*

The practical result of permitting the defendant to amend its complaint to deny manufacture of the slide was a finding in its favor on that issue and the entry of summary judgment for the defendant. Was it fair for the court to permit the defendant to amend its complaint to deny manufacture after the statute-of-limitations period had lapsed? The court seemed to think that permitting such an amendment did not doom the plaintiff's case or foreclose all options for seeking relief. What possibilities for recovery remained open to the plaintiff after the amendment in the eyes of the court? Do you think these possibilities were sufficiently realistic to save the plaintiff from being unduly prejudiced by the decision to permit the amendment?

b. The Standard for Granting Amendments Under Rule 15(a)

From *Beeck* you get a good sense that Rule 15(a) means what it says when it states that "[t]he court should freely give leave when justice so requires." Parties will generally be permitted to amend unless there is evidence of resulting *unfair* prejudice to the other parties or bad faith on the part of the party seeking the amendment. *See Foman v. Davis, 371 U.S. 178, 182 (1962)* (stating that courts should grant leave to amend unless there is evidence of "undue delay, bad faith or dilatory motive on the part of the movant, repeated failure to cure deficiencies by amendments previously allowed, undue prejudice to the opposing party by virtue of allowance of the amendment, futility of amendment, etc."). This is particularly so when

Take Note!

Although *Beeck* involved an amendment to change a response from an admission to a denial, Rule 15 also encompasses amendments to change parties named in a pleading. Why do you think Beeck did not seek to amend his complaint to name the correct manufacturer in his complaint? Below, we will study the rules governing when an amendment changing a party can relate back to the time of filing so as to avoid the effect of a lapsed statute-of-limitations period.

an amendment is necessary to conform the pleadings to reality in the wake of a previous mistake.

Do you agree with the court's conclusion in *Beeck* that the plaintiff would not be unfairly prejudiced by permitting the amendment? How is this case distinguishable from *Zielinski*, in which the court held the defendant to an erroneous statement in the pleadings because the statute of limitations had lapsed? Why do you think Rule 15(a) is written to favor amendments to the pleadings?

c.   Amendments as a Matter of Course

Do not forget that Rule 15(a) gives parties an absolute right to amend their pleadings without the court's permission if they do so within particular timeframes. If no responsive pleading is required, a party may amend once without leave within twenty-one days after serving it. FED. R. CIV. P. 15(a)(1)(A). If a responsive pleading is required, the pleading party may amend once at any time within twenty-one days after service of the responsive pleading or a motion under Rule 12(b), (e) or (f). FED. R.

Practice Pointer

In the event of an amendment to a pleading that requires a response (such as a complaint or an answer with a counterclaim), the deadline to respond to the amended pleading is either the time remaining to respond to the original pleading or within 14 days after service of the amended pleading, whichever is later. FED. R. CIV. P. 15(a)(3).

CIV. P. 15(a)(1)(B). Otherwise, the opposing party's written consent or leave of the court is required to amend. How would this rule be applied to the following hypothetical problem?

Hypo 6.6

On February 1 two homeowners filed a complaint in federal court alleging that a contractor negligently constructed their home, thereby causing them injuries. On February 15 of the same year the contractor filed and served a motion to dismiss for failure to state a claim, arguing that under the applicable state law the contractor is immune from all suits alleging negligence in the construction of homes. In response, on March 15 of that year the homeowners sought to amend their complaint to allege that the contractor was reckless in constructing their home, a claim to which the contractor would not be immune. The contractor objects to the amendment.

Should the amendment be allowed?

To help you understand Rule 15(a)(1), **Figure 6.2** illustrates the operation of the deadlines for amending a pleading as a matter of course.

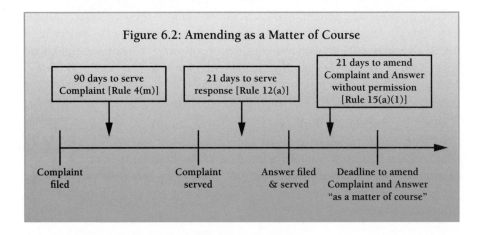

Figure 6.2: Amending as a Matter of Course

Note that in **Figure 6.2**, the answer lacks a counterclaim. How would the inclusion of a counterclaim in the answer impact the deadline to amend either the complaint or the answer as a matter of course, if at all? If a reply were ordered—perhaps because the answer contained affirmative defenses, how would that impact the relevant amendment deadlines? What would be the deadline to amend the reply?

d. Amendments During and After Trial

If a party presents evidence at trial that goes to an issue not raised in the pleadings, the opposing party may object to the presentation of such evidence. At that point, the party seeking to present the evidence can seek the court's permission to amend the pleadings under Rule 15(b); such amendments are to be "freely" allowed unless the opposing party can show unfair prejudice to its case. *See Scully Signal Co. v. Elecs. Corp. of Am.*, 570 F.2d 355, 362 (1st Cir. 1977), *cert. denied*, 436 U.S. 945 (1978) ("Although Rule 15(b) by its terms requires amendment of the pleadings whenever an issue has been tried by express or implied consent, courts have refused to grant such motions if amendment would prejudice one of the parties, such as by requiring the presentation of additional evidence."). However, if the opposing party fails to object, and the issue is tried, under Rule 15(b) the issue will be treated as if it were raised in the pleadings. *See* FED. R. CIV. P. 15(b)(2) ("When an issue not raised by the pleadings is tried by the parties' express or implied consent, it must be treated in all respects as if raised in the pleadings."); *see also Cruz v. Coach Stores, Inc.*, 202 F.3d 560, 569 (2d Cir. 2000) ("The totality of the circumstances convinces us that, despite Cruz's imprecise complaint, the district court was correct in considering

Cruz's hostile work environment claim on the merits. Under F<small>ED</small>. R. C<small>IV</small>. P. 15(b), a district court may consider claims outside those raised in the pleadings so long as doing so does not cause prejudice.").

---

2. Relation Back of Amendments

Most, if not all, causes of action have limitations periods attached to them, meaning that claims must be asserted within a certain period of time from when the alleged wrong occurred or was discovered. Sometimes parties need to amend their pleadings after the applicable statute-of-limitations period has expired. When this is the case, amendments that raise new claims or defenses or introduce new parties into the action will have to relate back to the time the initial action commenced to avoid being barred by the applicable statute of limitations. Rule 15(c) provides for the of amendments, but under tightly controlled circumstances:

FRCP 15(c): Relation Back of Amendments

(1) When an Amendment Relates Back. An amendment to a pleading relates back to the date of the original pleading when:

(A) the law that provides the applicable statute of limitations allows relation back;

(B) the amendment asserts a claim or defense that arose out of the conduct, transaction, or occurrence set out—or attempted to be set out—in the original pleading; or

(C) the amendment changes the party or the naming of the party against whom a claim is asserted, if Rule 15(c)(1)(B) is satisfied and if, within the period provided by Rule 4(m) for serving the summons and complaint, the party to be brought in by amendment:

(i) received such notice of the action that it will not be prejudiced in defending on the merits; and

(ii) knew or should have known that the action would have been brought against it, but for a mistake concerning the proper party's identity.

Rule 15(c)(1)(B) makes clear that when the amendment in question simply pertains to a claim or defense—not to the change or addition of a party—the standard for permitting relation back is straightforward: The amendment will relate back if it is transactionally related to the matters set forth in the pleading to be amended. *See* **Figure 6.3**. However, things are more complicated if the amendment seeks to change a party named in the pleading. The next two cases illustrate how Rule 15(c) is understood and applied to resolve this latter type of relation-back problem.

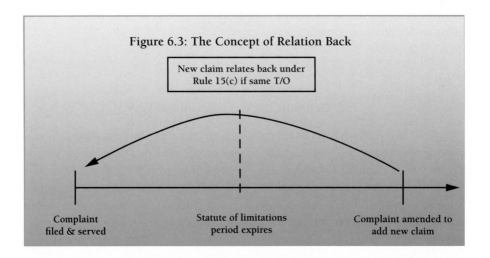

Figure 6.3: The Concept of Relation Back

New claim relates back under Rule 15(c) if same T/O

Complaint filed & served

Statute of limitations period expires

Complaint amended to add new claim

Krupski v. Costa Crociere, S.p.A.

Supreme Court of the United States
560 U.S. 538 (2010)

JUSTICE SOTOMAYOR delivered the opinion of the Court.

Rule 15(c) of the Federal Rules of Civil Procedure governs when an amended pleading "relates back" to the date of a timely filed original pleading and is thus itself timely even though it was filed outside an applicable statute of limitations. Where an amended pleading changes a party or a party's name, the Rule requires, among other things, that "the party to be brought in by amendment . . . knew or should have known that the action would have been brought against it, but for a mistake concerning the proper party's identity." Rule 15(c)(1)(C). In this case, the Court of Appeals held that Rule 15(c) was not satisfied because the plaintiff knew or should have known of the proper defendant before filing her original complaint. The court also held that relation back was not appropriate because the plaintiff had unduly delayed in seeking to amend. We hold that relation back under Rule 15(c)(1)(C) depends on what the party to be added knew or should have known, not on the amending party's knowledge or its timeliness in seeking to amend the pleading. Accordingly, we reverse the judgment of the Court of Appeals.

I

On February 21, 2007, petitioner, Wanda Krupski, tripped over a cable and fractured her femur while she was on board the cruise ship Costa Magica. Upon her return home, she acquired counsel and began the process of seeking compensation for her injuries. Krupski's passenger ticket—which explained that it was the sole

contract between each passenger and the carrier—included a variety of requirements for obtaining damages for an injury suffered on board one of the carrier's
ships. The ticket identified the carrier as

> "Costa Crociere S. p. A., an Italian corporation, and all Vessels and other
> ships owned, chartered, operated, marketed or provided by Costa Cro-
> ciere, S. p. A., and all officers, staff members, crew members, independent
> contractors, medical providers, concessionaires, pilots, suppliers, agents
> and assigns onboard said Vessels, and the manufacturers of said Vessels and
> all their component parts."

> The ticket required an injured party to submit "written notice of the claim
> with full particulars . . . to the carrier or its duly authorized agent within
> 185 days after the date of injury." The ticket further required any lawsuit to
> be "filed within one year after the date of injury" and to be "served upon the
> carrier within 120 days after filing." For cases arising from voyages depart-
> ing from or returning to a United States port in which the amount in con-
> troversy exceeded $75,000, the ticket designated the United States District
> Court for the Southern District of Florida in Broward County, Florida, as the
> exclusive forum for a lawsuit. The ticket extended the "defenses, limitations
> and exceptions . . . that may be invoked by the CARRIER" to "all persons
> who may act on behalf of the CARRIER or on whose behalf the CARRIER
> may act," including "the CARRIER's parents, subsidiaries, affiliates, succes-
> sors, assigns, representatives, agents, employees, servants, concessionaires
> and contractors" as well as "Costa Cruise Lines N. V.," identified as the "sales
> and marketing agent for the CARRIER and the issuer of this Passage Ticket
> Contract." The front of the ticket listed Costa Cruise Lines' address in Florida
> and stated that an entity called "Costa Cruises" was "the first cruise company
> in the world" to obtain a certain certification of quality.

On July 2, 2007, Krupski's counsel notified Costa Cruise Lines of Krupski's claims.
On July 9, 2007, the claims administrator for Costa Cruise requested additional
information from Krupski "[i]n order to facilitate our future attempts to achieve
a pre-litigation settlement." The parties were unable to reach a settlement, however, and on February 1, 2008—three weeks before the 1-year limitations period
expired—Krupski filed a negligence action against Costa Cruise, invoking the diversity jurisdiction of the Federal District Court for the Southern District of Florida.
The complaint alleged that Costa Cruise "owned, operated, managed, supervised
and controlled" the ship on which Krupski had injured herself; that Costa Cruise
had extended to its passengers an invitation to enter onto the ship; and that Costa
Cruise owed Krupski a duty of care, which it breached by failing to take steps that
would have prevented her accident. The complaint further stated that venue was
proper under the passenger ticket's forum selection clause and averred that, by

the July 2007 notice of her claims, Krupski had complied with the ticket's presuit requirements. Krupski served Costa Cruise on February 4, 2008.

Over the next several months—after the limitations period had expired—Costa Cruise brought Costa Crociere's existence to Krupski's attention three times. First, on February 25, 2008, Costa Cruise filed its answer, asserting that it was not the proper defendant, as it was merely the North American sales and marketing agent for Costa Crociere, which was the actual carrier and vessel operator. Second, on March 20, 2008, Costa Cruise listed Costa Crociere as an interested party in its corporate disclosure statement. Finally, on May 6, 2008, Costa Cruise moved for summary judgment, again stating that Costa Crociere was the proper defendant.

On June 13, 2008, Krupski responded to Costa Cruise's motion for summary judgment, arguing for limited discovery to determine whether Costa Cruise should be dismissed. According to Krupski, the following sources of information led her to believe Costa Cruise was the responsible party: The travel documents prominently identified Costa Cruise and gave its Florida address; Costa Cruise's Web site listed Costa Cruise in Florida as the United States office for the Italian company Costa Crociere; and the Web site of the Florida Department of State listed Costa Cruise as the only "Costa" company registered to do business in that State. Krupski also observed that Costa Cruise's claims administrator had responded to her claims notification without indicating that Costa Cruise was not a responsible party. With her response, Krupski simultaneously moved to amend her complaint to add Costa Crociere as a defendant.

On July 2, 2008, after oral argument, the District Court denied Costa Cruise's motion for summary judgment without prejudice and granted Krupski leave to amend, ordering that Krupski effect proper service on Costa Crociere by September 16, 2008. Complying with the court's deadline, Krupski filed an amended complaint on July 11, 2008, and served Costa Crociere on August 21, 2008. On that same date, the District Court issued an order dismissing Costa Cruise from the case pursuant to the parties' joint stipulation, Krupski apparently having concluded that Costa Cruise was correct that it bore no responsibility for her injuries.

Shortly thereafter, Costa Crociere—represented by the same counsel who had represented Costa Cruise—moved to dismiss, contending that the amended complaint did not relate back under Rule 15(c) and was therefore untimely. The District Court agreed. Rule 15(c), the court explained, imposes three requirements before an amended complaint against a newly named defendant can relate back to the original complaint. First, the claim against the newly named defendant must have arisen "out of the conduct, transaction, or occurrence set out-or attempted to be set out-in the original pleading." Fed. Rules Civ. Proc. 15(c)(1)(B), (C). Second, "within the period provided by Rule 4(m) for serving the summons and complaint" (which is ordinarily 120 days from when the complaint is filed, see

Rule 4(m)), the newly named defendant must have "received such notice of the action that it will not be prejudiced in defending on the merits." Rule 15(c)(1)(C) (i). Finally, the plaintiff must show that, within the Rule 4(m) period, the newly named defendant "knew or should have known that the action would have been brought against it, but for a mistake concerning the proper party's identity." Rule 15(c)(1)(C)(ii).

The first two conditions posed no problem, the court explained: The claim against Costa Crociere clearly involved the same occurrence as the original claim against Costa Cruise, and Costa Crociere had constructive notice of the action and had not shown that any unfair prejudice would result from relation back. But the court found the third condition fatal to Krupski's attempt to relate back, concluding that Krupski had not made a mistake concerning the identity of the proper party. Relying on Eleventh Circuit precedent, the court explained that the word "mistake" should not be construed to encompass a deliberate decision not to sue a party whose identity the plaintiff knew before the statute of limitations had run. Because Costa Cruise informed Krupski that Costa Crociere was the proper defendant in its answer, corporate disclosure statement, and motion for summary judgment, and yet Krupski delayed for months in moving to amend and then in filing an amended complaint, the court concluded that Krupski knew of the proper defendant and made no mistake.

The Eleventh Circuit affirmed in an unpublished *per curiam* opinion. *Krupski v. Costa Cruise Lines*, N. V., LLC, 330 Fed.Appx. 892 (2009). Rather than relying on the information contained in Costa Cruise's filings, all of which were made after the statute of limitations had expired, as evidence that Krupski did not make a mistake, the Court of Appeals noted that the relevant information was located within Krupski's passenger ticket, which she had furnished to her counsel well before the end of the limitations period. Because the ticket clearly identified Costa Crociere as the carrier, the court stated, Krupski either knew or should have known of Costa Crociere's identity as a potential party. It was therefore appropriate to treat Krupski as having chosen to sue one potential party over another. Alternatively, even assuming that she first learned of Costa Crociere's identity as the correct party from Costa Cruise's answer, the Court of Appeals observed that Krupski waited 133 days from the time she filed her original complaint to seek leave to amend and did not file an amended complaint for another month after that. In light of this delay, the Court of Appeals concluded that the District Court did not abuse its discretion in denying relation back.

We granted certiorari to resolve tension among the Circuits over the breadth of Rule 15(c)(1)(C)(ii), and we now reverse.

II

Under the Federal Rules of Civil Procedure, an amendment to a pleading relates back to the date of the original pleading when:

"(A) the law that provides the applicable statute of limitations allows relation back;

"(B) the amendment asserts a claim or defense that arose out of the conduct, transaction, or occurrence set out-or attempted to be set out-in the original pleading; or

"(C) the amendment changes the party or the naming of the party against whom a claim is asserted, if Rule 15(c)(1)(B) is satisfied and if, within the period provided by Rule 4(m) for serving the summons and complaint, the party to be brought in by amendment:

"(i) received such notice of the action that it will not be prejudiced in defending on the merits; and

"(ii) knew or should have known that the action would have been brought against it, but for a mistake concerning the proper party's identity." Rule 15(c)(1).

In our view, neither of the Court of Appeals' reasons for denying relation back under Rule 15(c)(1)(C)(ii) finds support in the text of the Rule. We consider each reason in turn.

A

The Court of Appeals first decided that Krupski either knew or should have known of the proper party's identity and thus determined that she had made a deliberate choice instead of a mistake in not naming Costa Crociere as a party in her original pleading. By focusing on Krupski's knowledge, the Court of Appeals chose the wrong starting point. The question under Rule 15(c)(1)(C)(ii) is not whether Krupski knew or should have known the identity of Costa Crociere as the proper defendant, but whether Costa Crociere knew or should have known that it would have been named as a defendant but for an error. Rule 15(c)(1)(C)(ii) asks what the prospective *defendant* knew or should have known during the Rule 4(m) period, not what the *plaintiff* knew or should have known at the time of filing her original complaint.

Information in the plaintiff's possession is relevant only if it bears on the defendant's understanding of whether the plaintiff made a mistake regarding the proper party's identity. For purposes of that inquiry, it would be error to conflate knowledge of a party's existence with the absence of mistake. A mistake is "[a]n error, misconception, or misunderstanding; an erroneous belief." *Black's Law Dictionary* 1092 (9th ed. 2009); see also *Webster's Third New International Dictionary* 1446 (2002) (defining "mistake" as "a misunderstanding of the meaning or implication of something"; "a wrong action or statement proceeding from faulty judgment, inadequate knowledge, or inattention"; "an erroneous belief"; or "a state of mind not in accordance with the facts"). That a plaintiff knows of a party's existence does not preclude her from making a mistake with respect to that party's identity. A plaintiff may know that a prospective defendant—call him party A—exists, while erroneously believing him to have the status of party B. Similarly, a plaintiff may know generally what party A does while misunderstanding the roles that party A and party B played in the "conduct, transaction, or occurrence" giving rise to her claim. If the plaintiff sues party B instead of party A under these circumstances, she has made a "mistake concerning the proper party's identity" notwithstanding her knowledge of the existence of both parties. The only question under Rule 15(c)(1)(C)(ii), then, is whether party A knew or should have known that, absent some mistake, the action would have been brought against him.

Respondent urges that the key issue under Rule 15(c)(1)(C)(ii) is whether the plaintiff made a deliberate choice to sue one party over another. We agree that making a deliberate choice to sue one party instead of another while fully understanding the factual and legal differences between the two parties is the antithesis of making a mistake concerning the proper party's identity. We disagree, however, with respondent's position that any time a plaintiff is aware of the existence of two parties and chooses to sue the wrong one, the proper defendant could reasonably believe that the plaintiff made no mistake. The reasonableness of the mistake is not itself at issue. As noted, a plaintiff might know that the prospective defendant exists but nonetheless harbor a misunderstanding about his status or role in the events giving rise to the claim at issue, and she may mistakenly choose to sue a different defendant based on that misimpression. That kind of deliberate but mistaken choice does not foreclose a finding that Rule 15(c)(1)(C)(ii) has been satisfied.

This reading is consistent with the purpose of relation back: to balance the interests of the defendant protected by the statute of limitations with the preference expressed in the Federal Rules of Civil Procedure in general, and Rule 15 in particular, for resolving disputes on their merits. A prospective defendant who legitimately believed that the limitations period had passed without any attempt to sue him has a strong interest in repose. But repose would be a windfall for a prospective defendant who understood, or who should have understood, that he escaped suit during the limitations period only because the plaintiff misunderstood a crucial fact about his identity. Because a plaintiff's knowledge of the existence of a party does not foreclose the possibility that she has made a mistake of identity about which that party should have been aware, such knowledge does not support that party's interest in repose.

Our reading is also consistent with the history of Rule 15(c)(1)(C). That provision was added in 1966 to respond to a recurring problem in suits against the Federal Government, particularly in the Social Security context. Individuals who had filed timely lawsuits challenging the administrative denial of benefits often failed to name the party identified in the statute as the proper defendant—the current Secretary of what was then the Department of Health, Education, and Welfare—and named instead the United States; the Department of Health, Education, and Welfare itself; the nonexistent "Federal Security Administration"; or a Secretary who had recently retired from office. By the time the plaintiffs discovered their mistakes, the statute of limitations in many cases had expired, and the district courts denied the plaintiffs leave to amend on the ground that the amended complaints would not relate back. Rule 15(c) was therefore "amplified to provide a general solution" to this problem. It is conceivable that the Social Security litigants knew or reasonably should have known the identity of the proper defendant either because of documents in their administrative cases or by dint of the statute setting forth the filing requirements. Nonetheless, the Advisory Committee clearly meant their filings to qualify as mistakes under the Rule.

* * *

B

The Court of Appeals offered a second reason why Krupski's amended complaint did not relate back: Krupski had unduly delayed in seeking to file, and in eventually filing, an amended complaint. The Court of Appeals offered no support for its view that a plaintiff's dilatory conduct can justify the denial of relation back under Rule 15(c)(1)(C), and we find none. The Rule plainly sets forth an exclusive list of requirements for relation back, and the amending party's diligence is not among them. Moreover, the Rule mandates relation back once the Rule's requirements are satisfied; it does not leave the decision whether to grant relation back to the district court's equitable discretion. See Rule 15(c)(1) ("An amendment . . . *relates back* . . . when" the three listed requirements are met (emphasis added)).

The mandatory nature of the inquiry for relation back under Rule 15(c) is particularly striking in contrast to the inquiry under Rule 15(a), which sets forth the circumstances in which a party may amend its pleading before trial. By its terms, Rule 15(a) gives discretion to the district court in deciding whether to grant a motion to amend a pleading to add a party or a claim. Following an initial period after filing a pleading during which a party may amend once "as a matter of course," "a party may amend its pleading only with the opposing party's written consent or the court's leave," which the court "should freely give . . . when justice so requires." Rules 15(a)(1)–(2). We have previously explained that a court may consider a movant's "undue delay" or "dilatory motive" in deciding whether to grant leave to amend under Rule 15(a). *Foman v. Davis,* 371 U.S. 178, 182 (1962). As the contrast between Rule 15(a) and Rule 15(c) makes clear, however, the speed with which a plaintiff moves to amend her complaint or files an amended complaint after obtaining leave to do so has no bearing on whether the amended complaint relates back. Cf. 6A C. Wright, A. Miller, & M. Kane, Federal Practice and Procedure § 1498, pp. 142–143, and nn. 49–50 (2d ed. 1990 and Supp. 2010).

Rule 15(c)(1)(C) does permit a court to examine a plaintiff's conduct during the Rule 4(m) period, but not in the way or for the purpose respondent or the Court of Appeals suggests. As we have explained, the question under Rule 15(c)(1)(C)(ii) is what the prospective defendant reasonably should have understood about the plaintiff's intent in filing the original complaint against the first defendant. To the extent the plaintiff's postfiling conduct informs the prospective defendant's understanding of whether the plaintiff initially made a "mistake concerning the proper party's identity," a court may consider the conduct. Cf. *Leonard v. Parry*, 219 F.3d 25, 29 (1st Cir. 2000) ("[P]ost-filing events occasionally can shed light on the plaintiff's state of mind at an earlier time" and "can inform *a defendant's* reasonable beliefs concerning whether her omission from the original complaint represented a mistake (as opposed to a conscious choice)"). The plaintiff's postfiling conduct is otherwise immaterial to the question whether an amended complaint relates back.[5]

C

Applying these principles to the facts of this case, we think it clear that the courts below erred in denying relation back under Rule 15(c)(1)(C)(ii). The District Court held that Costa Crociere had "constructive notice" of Krupski's complaint within the Rule 4(m) period. Costa Crociere has not challenged this finding. Because the complaint made clear that Krupski meant to sue the company that "owned, operated, managed, supervised and controlled" the ship on which she was injured, and also indicated (mistakenly) that Costa Cruise performed those roles, Costa Crociere should have known, within the Rule 4(m) period, that it was not named as a defendant in that complaint only because of Krupski's misunderstanding about which "Costa" entity was in charge of the ship—clearly a "mistake concerning the proper party's identity."

Respondent contends that because the original complaint referred to the ticket's forum requirement and presuit claims notification procedure, Krupski was clearly aware of the contents of the ticket, and because the ticket identified Costa Crociere as the carrier and proper party for a lawsuit, respondent was entitled to think that she made a deliberate choice to sue Costa Cruise instead of Costa Crociere. As we have explained, however, that Krupski may have known the contents of the ticket does not foreclose the possibility that she nonetheless misunderstood crucial facts regarding the two companies' identities. Especially because the face of the complaint plainly indi-

---

[5] Similarly, we reject respondent's suggestion that Rule 15(c) requires a plaintiff to move to amend her complaint or to file and serve an amended complaint within the Rule 4(m) period. Rule 15(c)(1)(C)(i) simply requires that the prospective defendant has received sufficient "notice of the action" within the Rule 4(m) period that he will not be prejudiced in defending the case on the merits. The Advisory Committee Notes to the 1966 Amendment clarify that "the notice need not be formal." Advisory Committee's 1966 Notes 122.

cated such a misunderstanding, respondent's contention is not persuasive. Moreover, respondent has articulated no strategy that it could reasonably have thought Krupski was pursuing in suing a defendant that was legally unable to provide relief.

Respondent also argues that Krupski's failure to move to amend her complaint during the Rule 4(m) period shows that she made no mistake in that period. But as discussed, any delay on Krupski's part is relevant only to the extent it may have informed Costa Crociere's understanding during the Rule 4(m) period of whether she made a mistake originally. Krupski's failure to add Costa Crociere during the Rule 4(m) period is not sufficient to make reasonable any belief that she had made a deliberate and informed decision not to sue Costa Crociere in the first instance. Nothing in Krupski's conduct during the Rule 4(m) period suggests that she failed to name Costa Crociere because of anything other than a mistake.

It is also worth noting that Costa Cruise and Costa Crociere are related corporate entities with very similar names; "crociera" even means "cruise" in Italian. *Cassell's Italian Dictionary* 137, 670 (1967). This interrelationship and similarity heighten the expectation that Costa Crociere should suspect a mistake has been made when Costa Cruise is named in a complaint that actually describes Costa Crociere's activities. Cf. *Morel v. DaimlerChrysler AG*, 565 F.3d 20, 27 (1st Cir. 2009) (where complaint conveyed plaintiffs' attempt to sue automobile manufacturer and erroneously named the manufacturer as Daimler-Chrysler Corporation instead of the actual manufacturer, a legally distinct but related entity named DaimlerChrysler AG, the latter should have realized it had not been named because of plaintiffs' mistake); *Goodman v. Praxair, Inc.*, 494 F.3d 458, 473–475 (4th Cir. 2007) (en banc) (where complaint named parent company Praxair, Inc., but described status of subsidiary company Praxair Services, Inc., subsidiary company knew or should have known it had not been named because of plaintiff's mistake). In addition, Costa Crociere's own actions contributed to passenger confusion over "the proper party" for a lawsuit. The front of the ticket advertises that "Costa Cruises" has achieved a certification of quality, without clarifying whether "Costa Cruises" is Costa Cruise Lines, Costa Crociere, or some other related "Costa" company. Indeed, Costa Crociere is evidently aware that the difference between Costa Cruise and Costa Crociere can be confusing for cruise ship passengers. See, *e.g., Suppa v. Costa Crociere, S.p.A.*, No. 07-60526-CIV, 2007 WL 4287508, *1, (S.D. Fla., Dec.4, 2007) (denying Costa Crociere's motion to dismiss the amended complaint where the original complaint had named Costa Cruise as a defendant after "find[ing] it simply inconceivable that Defendant Costa Crociere was not on notice . . . that . . . but for the mistake in the original Complaint, Costa Crociere was the appropriate party to be named in the action").

In light of these facts, Costa Crociere should have known that Krupski's failure to name it as a defendant in her original complaint was due to a mistake concerning the proper party's identity. We therefore reverse the judgment of the Court of Appeals for the Eleventh Circuit and remand the case for further proceedings consistent with this opinion.

It is so ordered.

[An opinion by JUSTICE SCALIA, concurring in part and concurring in the judgment, is omitted.]

Worthington v. Wilson

U.S. District Court for the Central District of Illinois
790 F. Supp. 829 (C.D. Ill. 1992)

MIHM, CHIEF JUDGE.

BACKGROUND

According to the amended complaint, the Plaintiff Richard Worthington ("Worthington") was arrested on February 25, 1989 by two police officers in the Peoria Heights Police Department. At the time of his arrest, Worthington was nursing an injured left hand and so advised the arresting officer. The officer responded by grabbing and twisting Worthington's injured hand and wrist, which prompted Worthington to shove the officer away and tell him to "take it easy." A second officer arrived on the scene and the two officers wrestled Worthington to the ground and handcuffed him. The officers then hoisted Worthington from the ground by the handcuffs, which caused him to suffer broken bones in his left hand. These allegations are taken as true by this court for purposes of the pending motions.

Exactly two years later, on February 25, 1991, Worthington, by his attorney Gary Morris, filed a complaint in the Circuit Court of Peoria County against the Village of Peoria Heights and "three unknown named police officers." This complaint recited the facts above and claimed that the officers' actions deprived Worthington of his constitutional rights in violation of the Civil Rights Act of 1964, 42 U.S.C. § 1983. This complaint was divided into five counts. The first three name the officers jointly and severally, and claim a variety of damages. The fourth and fifth counts name the Village, and claim that it was also responsible for the officers' conduct under the doctrine of respondeat superior. The Village removed the action to this court and moved to dismiss the claims against it on the grounds that respondeat superior is not a valid basis for municipal liability under § 1983.

It's Latin to Me!

Respondeat superior is Latin for "let the superior make answer" and refers to the **Tort** doctrine that holds an employer liable for the wrongdoing of its employee or agent, provided the subordinate was acting within the scope of employment.

The motion was set for hearing before Magistrate Judge Robert J. Kauffman on May 2, 1991. Worthington did not respond to the motion to dismiss before that date, but on the date of the hearing he voluntarily dismissed the counts against the Village. Oddly enough, three weeks later, on May 23, 1991, Mr. Morris filed a response to the Village's motion to dismiss, which had already been disposed of when Worthington voluntarily dismissed the claims against the Village. In this response, Mr. Morris confessed that the reliance upon the theory of respondeat superior in the complaint was an oversight, but stressed that there was a valid basis for the § 1983 claims against the officers. On June 4, 1991, the Village of Peoria Heights filed a motion to strike this response as improper since the motion to dismiss was no longer pending.

What's That?

A *United States Magistrate Judge* is a special type of judge created by Congress to assist U.S. District Judges with their caseloads. Magistrate Judges can be designated to manage and determine many pretrial matters and can try civil cases with party consent. See 28 U.S.C. § 636 for more information on the scope of a Magistrate Judge's authority.

This motion to strike was later granted by the Magistrate. The Village also moved for sanctions against Worthington and Mr. Morris for having filed a baseless action against it. This motion remains pending.

On June 17, 1991, Worthington filed an amended complaint which named as Defendants Dave Wilson and Jeff Wall ("the Defendants"), the two officers who arrested Worthington on February 25, 1989. This amended complaint contains no claim against the Village of Peoria Heights. These Defendants, represented by Jeanne Wysocki (the same attorney who represented the Village), moved to dismiss the amended complaint on the grounds that the statute of limitations had run and that the complaint failed to state a proper claim under § 1983. Worthington responded to this motion and a hearing was held before the Magistrate on October 31, 1991. On December 19, 1991, the Magistrate issued a recommendation that both

FYI

U.S. Magistrate Judges ordinarily issue *reports* and *recommendations* to the U.S. District Court judges that assigned them to handle a matter. The district judge may accept or reject those recommendations under standards set forth in 28 U.S.C. § 636.

the motion to dismiss and the motion for sanctions be allowed. Worthington filed an objection to this recommendation, to which the Defendants in turn responded. The Defendants also filed a motion to strike an affidavit included in Worthington's response to the motion to dismiss. This motion also remains pending. On March 17, 1992, this court held an additional hearing on the pending motions.

DISCUSSION

I. STATUTE OF LIMITATIONS/RELATION BACK

In their motion to dismiss, the Defendants first argue that the amended complaint against them must be dismissed because the statute of limitations has run. The Defendants note that the statute of limitations for § 1983 cases in Illinois is two years, and that the amended complaint was not filed until about four months after this period had expired. Moreover, the Defendants argue that the amended complaint cannot be deemed to relate back to the filing date of the original complaint because the prerequisites of relation back under Federal Rule of Civil Procedure 15(c) have not all been met. Specifically, the Defendants argue that they did not have notice of the action before the statute of limitations period had run as required by *Schiavone v. Fortune*, 477 U.S. 21 (1986), and that the renaming of fictitious parties does not constitute a "mistake" under Rule 15(c).

Worthington's primary argument in response is that relation back of his amended complaint is not governed by Rule 15(c), but rather by certain provisions in the Illinois Code of Civil Procedure, namely Ill.Rev.Stat. ch. 110, ¶¶ 2–407 and 2–413. Worthington argues that, under these provisions, his amended complaint is properly deemed to relate back to the February 25, 1991 filing of the original complaint. In the alternative, Worthington suggests that the requirements of Rule 15(c) have been met. Finally, Worthington argues that, whatever rules govern the situation, he should not be punished for omitting the arresting officers' names from the original complaint because the Peoria Heights Police Department had withheld that information from him.

In his recommendation, the Magistrate agreed with the Defendants that, under Rule 15(c) and *Schiavone*, the amended complaint naming the officers could only relate back if the officers were actually aware of the action before the limitations period expired on February 25, 1991. Since the record demonstrated that the Village was not even served until February 28, 1991, the Magistrate concluded that the Defendants did not have actual knowledge of the action on February 25, 1991 and that the amended complaint should therefore be dismissed as untimely filed. * * *

A. Schiavone *Notice Requirements*

As an initial matter, there is no doubt that the statute of limitations for a § 1983 action in Illinois is two years. Therefore, as noted by the Magistrate, Worthington's action against the Defendants must have been filed by February 25, 1991. Since the amended complaint was not filed until June 17, 1991, the only way the amended complaint can be found to be timely filed is if it relates back to the filing of the original complaint. Relation back of amendments under federal rules is covered by Rule 15(c).

The Defendants' first argument is that Rule 15(c), as interpreted by *Schiavone*, requires that the party to be brought in by amendment receives notice of the action before the expiration of the statute of limitations period. The Defendants argue that because they did not receive notice of this action within this time, the amended complaint does not relate back and is therefore untimely. Because this court finds that *Schiavone* no longer controls, it rejects the Defendants' first argument.

Until December 1, 1991, Rule 15(c) provided, in relevant part:

Whenever the claim or defense asserted in the amended pleading arose out of the conduct, transaction, or occurrence set forth or attempted to be set forth in the original pleading, the amendment relates back to the date of the original pleading. An amendment changing the party against whom a claim is asserted relates back if the foregoing provision is satisfied and, within the period provided by law for commencing the action against the party to be brought in by amendment that party (1) has received such notice of the institution of the action that the party will not be prejudiced in maintaining his defense on the merits, and (2) knew or should have known that, but for a mistake concerning the identity of the proper party, the action would have been brought against the party.

In *Schiavone*, the Supreme Court interpreted this provision to require that, in addition to the amended complaint arising out of the same conduct set forth in the original complaint, the new party must have received actual notice of the action (and that it was the proper party) before the statute of limitations period expired. As noted by the Magistrate and counsel for the Defendants, it appears that the Defendants did not receive notice of this action against them by February 25, 1991. Thus, under the old version of Rule 15(c) and *Schiavone*, the amended complaint against the officers would not relate back and would thus be untimely filed.

However, as of December 1, 1991, Rule 15(c) reads differently. As will be seen momentarily, the amendment was designed to change the requirement of *Schiavone* that the new party receives notice of the action before the expiration of the limitations period.

* * * [R]elation-back is now governed by a modified standard. An amended complaint which changes the name of the defendant will relate back to the filing of the original complaint if it arises out of the same conduct contained in the original complaint and the new party was aware of the action within 120 days of the filing of the original complaint.

Thus, under the amended version of Rule 15(c), Worthington's amended complaint, which arises out of the very same conduct in its original complaint, would relate back to February 25, 1991 if the Defendants were aware, before June 25, 1991, that they were the officers referred to as "unknown named police officers" in the original complaint. At oral argument on March 12, 1992, counsel for the Defendants conceded that they were aware of the pendency of the action within this period; thus, under the new version of Rule 15(c), the amended complaint would be timely because the Defendants received notice of the action within 120 days of the original filing. * * *

B. "Mistake"

The Defendants also argue that relation back is not permitted here under Rule 15(c) because there was no "mistake" concerning the identity of the proper party. In this regard, Rule 15(c) states that an amendment changing the naming of a party will relate back if, among other things, the party brought in by the amendment "knew or should have known that, but for a mistake concerning the identity of the proper party, the action would have been brought against the party." * * *

The Defendants argue that the failure of the original complaint to name Wilson and Wall was not due to a "mistake" but rather was due to a lack of knowledge over the proper defendant. The Defendants argue that while Rule 15(c) permits amendments which change a mistaken name in the original complaint, it does not permit a plaintiff to replace "unknown" parties with actual parties. In support of this argument, the Defendants cite *Wood v. Worachek*, 618 F.2d 1225, 1230 (7th Cir. 1980) and *Rylewicz v. Beaton Services, Ltd.*, 888 F.2d 1175, 1181 (7th Cir. 1989). These cases reflect the Seventh Circuit's view that an amended complaint which replaces fictitious names with actual names due to an initial lack of knowledge concerning the proper defendant does not involve a "mistake" and is therefore not entitled to relation back under Rule 15(c). These holdings would seem to control in this case, since Worthington concedes that he designated the Defendants as "unknown named police officers" in the original complaint because he was unaware of their identities at that time. * * * Accordingly, the court finds that, pursuant to the Seventh Circuit authority noted above, Worthington's amended complaint is not entitled to relation back.

However, this court will take this opportunity to respectfully express its disagreement with the above-noted Seventh Circuit decisions. First of all, this court is of the opinion that the "mistake" language in Rule 15(c) does not create a new, separate prerequisite for relation back, but rather merely refers back to the first portion of Rule 15(c)(3). The word "mistake" appears to this court to be a way of referencing, in one word, the phrase "change the party or the naming of the party" at the beginning of the subsection. * * *

The above is an explanation of how Rule 15(c)(3) can be rationally interpreted, under its existing language, as not having a separate "mistake" requirement. The more interesting question to be addressed now is why such a "mistake" requirement should not be included. It must be questioned whether a fourth requirement of "mistake" logically fits in with the other three requirements listed above. Those first three requirements in essence demand that the party being brought in had notice—that he knew about the action and knew that he was the one intended to be sued. The focus is on the awareness of the party to be brought in, out of concern for due process. A separate "mistake" requirement improperly shifts the focus to the state of mind of the plaintiff bringing the action—whether the plaintiff named the wrong defendant out of a mistake or because he did not have enough information to identify the proper defendant at all. Such an analysis is irrelevant in this court's view. The heart of Rule 15(c) is notice to the defendant. *See generally* 6A WRIGHT & MILLER, Federal Practice and Procedure, § 1498. The mistake requirement does nothing to further this controlling interest.

Indeed, it can plausibly be argued that a mistake requirement would actually hinder the important interest of notice to the Defendant. As is true in this case, a complaint which does not attempt to specifically identify the proper defendants leaves open the possibility that the eventual defendants are the ones being sued. If the original complaint comes to the attention of those defendants (as it did here) and the complaint uses "John Doe" or "unknown," the defendants will be on notice that they are being sued if the content of that complaint implicates them. Contrast that with the situation where the complaint actually names defendants, but names the wrong ones. Had Worthington simply randomly chosen the names of two officers in the department, the Defendants Wilson and Wall might have been lulled into the belief that they were not being sued. As a result, a separate "mistake" requirement could be detrimental to the true purpose of Rule 15(c) and should not be included in the analysis. Having said all of this, this court recognizes that it is duty bound to follow Seventh Circuit precedent on point, and accordingly reaches the result dictated by *Wood*.

Food for Thought

Why is the court bound to adhere to the Seventh Circuit's interpretation of the meaning of "mistake" in Rule 15(c)(3)? If this is the case, why has the court bothered to express its disagreement with the Seventh Circuit's view?

Accordingly, this court finds that Worthington's amended complaint does not relate back under Rule 15(c) because the amendment did not correct a "mistake," but rather corrected a lack of knowledge at the time of the original complaint.

C. State Law

This brings us to Worthington's only real argument in support of relation-back. Worthington asserts that the issue of relation-back in this case is not governed by

Rule 15(c), but rather is governed by § 2–413 of the Illinois Code of Civil Procedure. That section provides, in relevant part:

> Unknown Parties. If in any action there are persons interested therein whose names are unknown, it shall be lawful to make them parties to the action by the name and description of unknown owners, or unknown heirs or legatees of any deceased person, who may have been interested in the subject matter of the action previous to his or her death; but an affidavit shall be filed by the party desiring to make those persons parties stating that their names are unknown. Process may then issue and publication may be had against those persons by the name and description so given, and judgments entered in respect to them shall be of the same effect as though they had been designed by their proper names.

Worthington suggests that this provision would allow the amended complaint to relate back because his inability to discover the names of the arresting officers was not for want of due diligence. This court need not address the question of whether Worthington's efforts would satisfy § 2–413, because it now finds this provision to be inapplicable in this action.

In support of the notion that an Illinois procedural rule would govern the issue of relation back in this action, Worthington cites *Cabrales v. County of Los Angeles,* 644 F. Supp. 1352 (C.D. Cal. 1986), which held that relation-back of an amendment which added a new party was an issue governed by state law. 644 F. Supp. at 1360. Perhaps even more important is the Ninth Circuit's decision on the appeal of this case. *Cabrales v. County of Los Angeles,* 864 F.2d 1454 (9th Cir. 1988). In affirming the trial court's decision, the Ninth Circuit stated:

> * * * "[T]he length of the limitations period, and closely related questions of tolling and application, are to be governed by state law." The California relation back doctrine is such a tolling issue that * * * must be decided under state law. Also, as the district court noted, statutes of limitation define the substantive rights of parties. The California pleading practice allows new defendants to be named after the original complaint is filed without violating the statute of limitations is such a substantive state policy that it is applicable in the federal courts.

864 F.2d at 1463–64. The decision rests on the principle that, because federal courts borrow state statutes of limitation for § 1983 claims, they must also borrow state rules of procedure which increase or decrease those statutes of limitations, such as tolling or relation-back.

This decision seems to be at odds with Seventh Circuit authority.[2] In <u>Lewellen v. Morley, 875 F.2d 118 (7th Cir. 1989)</u>, Judge Easterbrook agreed with the Ninth Circuit's general proposition that "[w]hen state law supplies the period of limitations, it also supplies associated tolling and extension rules." However, after noting that state law rules which affect the period of limitations are often part of the state law which a federal court borrows for <u>§ 1983</u> cases, Judge Easterbrook noted a bright-line limitation on this principle: "[f]ederal courts absorb state law only when federal law neglects the topic." In other words, even though a state rule may affect the state statute of limitations, a federal court in a civil rights case does not borrow that rule unless there is no similar federal provision. In this case, there is a federal rule (<u>Rule 15(c)</u>) which addresses the issue of relation-back of unknown named defendants addressed in § 2–413. That federal rule, as interpreted by the Seventh Circuit in *Wood*, provides that parties brought in by amendment whose identities were not known at the time of the original complaint were not added due to a "mistake" and therefore, the amended filing does not relate back. To the extent that § 2–413 would dictate a contrary result, it is at odds with federal law. As noted in *Lewellen*, when there is such a clash between state and federal rules, "[f]ederal law wins these contests every time." * * *

Take Note!

The court here is referring to the conflict between a Federal Rule of Civil Procedure and conflicting state law. Such conflicts are resolved with reference to the doctrine articulated in <u>Hanna v. Plumer, 380 U.S. 460 (1965)</u>, which is covered in <u>Chapter 5</u>.

Points for Discussion

a. The Impact of Denying Relation Back

What impact did the lower court's decision in *Krupski* and the district court's decision in *Worthington* have on the plaintiffs in those cases and their ability to pursue their respective claims? Were those outcomes fair under the circumstances? In *Krupski*, the plaintiff had the benefit of a reversal by the Supreme Court in her favor, but Worthington was not so fortunate; on appeal, the Seventh Circuit affirmed that "[b]ecause Worthington's failure to name Wilson and Wall was due to a lack

---

[2] Moreover, the decision seems to represent an extension of law on this topic. Courts have struggled with the issue of the applicability of state relation back doctrines in the context of diversity cases, presumably because of the elusive substance/procedure distinction. But in federal question cases, the issue is much simpler—federal law controls. The only exception to this is that state law at times provides the statute of limitations, as is true in <u>§ 1983</u> cases. Thus, while this court borrows § 13–202 (and presumably state rules which are inextricably entwined with the statute of limitations) from Illinois for <u>§ 1983</u> cases, it does not borrow any and all state procedural rules which may have some impact on the limitations period, particularly where there is a federal rule of procedure directly on point.

of knowledge as to their identity, and not a mistake in their names, Worthington was prevented from availing himself of the relation back doctrine of Rule 15(c)." *Worthington v. Wilson,* 8 F.3d 1253, 1257 (7th Cir. 1993). What option do plaintiffs in Worthington's situation have, given the inability to relate back amendments that change unknown parties to known parties? Should the newly named defendants in *Worthington* have been estopped from raising the statute of limitations defense if the police department was responsible for Worthington's inability to obtain the names of the proper defendants in a timely fashion?

b. The Interaction Between State and Federal Relation-Back Rules

At the time of *Worthington,* Rule 15(c)(1) stated that an amendment should relate back if "permitted by the law that provides the statute of limitations applicable to the action," and offers this as an alternative to Rule 15(c)(3). Should this provision have led the court to apply the Illinois standard for relation back? Why or why not?

The First Circuit has explained the relationship between state and federal relation-back rules created by Rule 15(c)(1) as follows: "The provision cements in place a one-way ratchet; less restrictive state relation-back rules will displace federal relation-back rules, but more restrictive state relation-back rules will not." *Morel v. Daimler-Chrysler AG,* 565 F.3d 20, 26 (1st Cir. 2009). Thus, the federal rule will trump more restrictive state law that might not permit relation back under the same circumstances in state court. Is there an *Erie/Hanna* issue here regarding the conflict between state and federal law? *See id. at* 24 ("In the case at hand, Rule 15(c) is squarely on point. . . . [T]here is no credible basis for impugning its constitutionality. . . . It is a truly procedural rule because it governs the in-court dispute resolution processes rather than the dispute that brought the parties into court; consequently, it does not transgress the Rules Enabling Act." (internal quotation marks and citation omitted)).

c. The Proper Meaning of "Mistake" in Rule 15(c)

Under *Krupski,* a plaintiff can be said to have made a "mistake" under Rule 15(c) if she named the wrong defendant but had an awareness of the existence of a party who turns out to be the correct defendant. This is so, the *Krupski* Court said, because the plaintiff's awareness of the existence of those ultimately deemed to be the proper defendants was irrelevant to the mistake inquiry:

> The Court of Appeals first decided that Krupski either knew or should have known of the proper party's identity and thus determined that she had made a deliberate choice instead of a mistake in not naming Costa Crociere as a party in her original pleading. By focusing on Krupski's knowledge, the Court of Appeals chose the wrong starting point. The question under Rule 15(c)(1)(C)(ii) is not whether Krupski knew or should

have known the identity of Costa Crociere as the proper defendant, but whether Costa Crociere knew or should have known that it would have been named as a defendant but for an error. Rule 15(c)(1)(C)(ii) asks what the prospective defendant knew or should have known during the Rule 4(m) period, not what the plaintiff knew or should have known at the time of filing her original complaint.

Food for Thought

Do you think *Krupski* will have any impact on those courts holding that plaintiffs who are unaware of the identity of a party (and thus proceed against "unnamed" defendants) have not committed a "mistake" under Rule 15(c) and thus cannot relate back amendments that seek to name such defendants once their identities are discovered? *See, e.g.*, *Burdine v. Kaiser*, 2010 WL 2606257, at *2 n.2 (N.D. Ohio Jun. 25, 2010)* ("Unlike *Krupski*, the plaintiff's problem here is not that she knew the parties' identities and simply failed to sue the correct one. Here, instead, plaintiff did not know the identity of Cook, Hirt and Fligor until after the statute of limitations ran. Plaintiff therefore did not have all the requisite information to sue the correct party absent an understanding of the law's specification of whom to sue. In *Krupski*, in contrast, plaintiff had that knowledge, and the Supreme Court's resolution of her case does not affect plaintiff's here.").

Krupski v. Costa Crociere, S.p.A., 560 U.S. 538 (2010). Why do you think some lower courts had been holding that no "mistake" under Rule 15(c) was possible if the plaintiff knew or should have known the identity of the proper defendant? Was the Supreme Court right to reject this interpretation of Rule 15(c) as erroneous?

In *Worthington*, the district court felt obliged to follow Seventh Circuit precedent holding that a prior naming of unknown defendants does not constitute a "mistake" under Rule 15(c). This understanding of the rule is embraced by a majority of the circuit courts. *See, e.g.*, *Whitt v. Stephens Cty.*, 529 F.3d 278, 283 (5th Cir. 2008) ("[A]n amendment to substitute a named party for a John Doe does not relate back under rule 15(c)."); *Moore v. Tennessee*, 267 F. App'x 450, 455 (6th Cir. 2008) ("[A] plaintiff's lack of knowledge pertaining to an intended defendant's identity does not constitute a 'mistake concerning the party's identity' within the meaning of Rule 15(c)."); *Jackson v. Kotter*, 541 F.3d 688, 699 (7th Cir. 2008) ("We have consistently held that Rule 15(c)(3) does not provide for relation back under circumstances, such as here, in which the plaintiff fails to identity the proper party."); *Bell v. City of Topeka*, 279 F. App'x 689, 692 (10th Cir. 2008) ("[A] plaintiff's designation of an

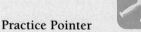

Practice Pointer

Randomly naming members of the police department to avoid the *Worthington* rule would undoubtedly violate Rule 11, which requires counsel to certify that there is a basis for the factual allegations in a complaint. However, if the names selected had some factual basis—such as the plaintiff's visual description of the officers or information gleaned from cross-checking the time and place of the incident with police records tracking officer locations—no Rule 11 concerns would arise.

unknown defendant . . . in the original complaint is not a formal defect of the type [Rule 15(c)] was meant to address and a later amendment that specifically names that defendant does not relate back to the original complaint."). Indeed, it appears that only the Third Circuit embraces a contrary interpretation. *See Singletary v. Pa. Dep't. of Corrs., 266 F.3d 186, 201 (3d Cir. 2001).* ("[T]he plaintiff's lack of knowledge of a particular defendant's identity can be a mistake under Rule 15(c).") Do you agree with the majority interpretation of the "mistake" language in Rule 15(c) that denies relation-back when the proper identity was previously unknown? Could a plaintiff, having read *Worthington*, simply use whatever names he can find rather than naming "unknown" defendants to get around this interpretation of "mistake"?

—Perspective & Analysis—

Although most federal courts of appeals have concluded that "mistake" in Rule 15(c) means an affirmative misapprehension about the identity of the proper defendant rather than ignorance or lack of knowledge as to the defendant's identity, this interpretation has been criticized by some commentators:

> [There is a] special problem created by this understanding and application of mistake in § 1983 actions. The use of John Doe or Unknown Officer pleading is most common and most necessary in these cases . . . . [The plaintiff] is unable to identify the individual officers and name them as defendants without the benefit of formal discovery, but cannot get formal discovery until after she files the lawsuit. Without the benefit of relation back, her claims against the . . . officers are barred by the statute of limitations . . . .
>
> This substantive outcome results from a narrow interpretation and application of a procedural rule, contradicting the notion that stringent procedure should not defeat substance. Rather, a civil rights plaintiff . . . should be able to discover the names of the target individual officer defendants in sufficient time that she can bring them into a federal court action and proceed to a determination of the merits of her claim, vindicating the substantive rights and interests guaranteed by § 1983 and the Constitution.

Howard M. Wasserman, *Civil Rights Plaintiffs and John Doe Defendants: A Study in Section 1983 Procedure*, 25 CARDOZO L. REV. 793, 797–99 (2003).

d. Rule 15(c)'s "Conduct, Transaction, or Occurrence" Requirement

Note that in order to relate back, the change being made to the pleadings must be part of the same "conduct, transaction, or occurrence" set forth in the original pleading. What does this language mean? *See Mayle v. Felix, 545 U.S. 644, 659 (2005)* ("[R]elation back depends on the existence of a common core of operative facts uniting the original and newly asserted claims."); *La. Wholesale Drug Co. v. Biovail Corp., 437 F. Supp. 2d 79, 86 (D.D.C. 2006), aff'd, 533 F.3d 857 (D.C. Cir. 2008)* ("An amended complaint that 'attempts to introduce a new legal theory based on facts different from those underlying the timely claims' will not relate back." (quoting *United States v. Hicks, 283 F.3d 380, 388 (D.C. Cir. 2002)*)). What do you think is the purpose of this requirement?

e. Supplemental Pleadings Under Rule 15(d)

In the event that alterations need to be made to a pleading to reflect events that take place after that pleading has been filed, the proper course is to submit a supplemental pleading under Rule 15(d), provided the court has given its permission. Alterations that pertain to pre-filing matters are the proper purview of amendments. Why might a party need to supplement its pleadings with information pertaining to events that transpired after the pleadings were filed? *See, e.g., Diaz v. City of Inkster,* 2006 WL 2192929, at *12–13 (E.D. Mich. Aug. 2, 2006) (permitting a plaintiff to add two newly arising retaliation claims to his existing discrimination claims based on the employer's failure to promote the plaintiff after the filing of his lawsuit).

> **FYI**
>
> Rule 13(e) permits a party to file a supplemental pleading to assert a counterclaim that arises after service of an earlier pleading. Counterclaims will be covered in Chapter 7.

Supplemental pleadings are available for all of the pleadings permitted by Rule 7(a), meaning the rule is not just for plaintiffs. For example, a defendant may need to supplement its answer to add an affirmative defense that has arisen after its original answer was filed. *See, e.g., Beckway v. DeShong,* 717 F. Supp. 2d 908 (N.D. Cal. 2010) (permitting claim preclusion to be alleged via a supplemental answer based on a judgment that was entered subsequent to the service of the original answer). Should supplemental pleadings be permitted to relate back under the same standards set forth in Rule 15(c)? *See, e.g., Kemper Ins. Cos. v. United States,* 2004 WL 1811390, at *3 (W.D.N.Y. Aug. 13, 2004) ("In deciding whether to grant a motion to supplement pursuant to Rule 15(d), the Court may rely on the doctrine of relation back. If the supplemental claim is sufficiently related to the prior claims, but based on transactions that occurred subsequent to the commencement of the action, then the supplemental pleadings relate back to the date the original pleadings were filed."). The Supreme Court has interpreted Rule 15(d) as permitting supplemental pleadings in which a plaintiff may correct a jurisdictional defect in its complaint by informing the court of post-complaint events. *Mathews v. Diaz,* 426 U.S. 67, 75 (1976).

D. Ensuring Truthful Allegations

From the beginning, the Federal Rules have included a provision that requires attorneys to certify or verify the truthfulness of the pleadings they file. This requirement has always been found within Rule 11, although in modern times the substance of the rule has changed dramatically from its original language. The current version of the rule consists of two main parts: provisions outlining the representations that counsel makes when submitting a filing to the court and rules governing the imposition of sanctions (punishment) when Rule 11 is violated. We will review each of these portions of the rule in turn.

Go Online

To learn more about the history of Rule 11 and the various changes that have been made to the rule over the years, see Carl Tobias, *The 1993 Revision to Federal Rule 11*, 70 IND. L.J. 171 (1994).

1. Representations to the Court

The first sections of Rule 11 concern themselves with counsel's obligation to sign all papers filed with the court and the representations to the court that counsel and unrepresented parties make by presenting such papers to the court:

FRCP 11. Signing Pleadings, Motions, and Other Papers; Representations to the Court; Sanctions

(a) Signature. Every pleading, written motion, and other paper must be signed by at least one attorney of record in the attorney's name—or by a party personally if the party is unrepresented. * * *

(b) Representations to the Court. By presenting to the court a pleading, written motion, or other paper—whether by signing, filing, submitting, or later advocating it—an attorney or unrepresented party certifies that to the best of the person's knowledge, information, and belief, formed after an inquiry reasonable under the circumstances:

(1) it is not being presented for any improper purpose, such as to harass, cause unnecessary delay, or needlessly increase the cost of litigation;

(2) the claims, defenses, and other legal contentions are warranted by existing law or by a nonfrivolous argument for extending, modifying, or reversing existing law or for establishing new law;

(3) the factual contentions have evidentiary support or, if specifically so identified, will likely have evidentiary support after a reasonable opportunity for further investigation or discovery; and

(4) the denials of factual contentions are warranted on the evidence or, if specifically so identified, are reasonably based on belief or a lack of information.

* * *

(d) Inapplicability to Discovery. This rule does not apply to disclosures and discovery requests, responses, objections, and motions under Rules 26 through 37.

Points for Discussion

a. Applicability of Rule 11

What is the scope of Rule 11's application? Does it apply only to pleadings? Does it cover oral statements made to opposing counsel? Letters exchanged between counsel? Be sure to have a clear understanding of the conduct that is covered by Rule 11. Also, be sure to sort out who is covered by the obligations of Rule 11. Finally, note that Rule 11 does not apply to actions taken under the discovery rules, Rule 26 through 37.

b. Representations Made Under Rule 11

Take note of the different representations that an attorney (or unrepresented party) makes when submitting a filing to the court. They fall into five general categories, as illustrated in **Table 6.1**:

Table 6.1

Representation	Rule
Reasonable inquiry undertaken	Rule 11(b)
Proper motivation for filing	Rule 11(b)(1)
Soundness of legal arguments	Rule 11(b)(2)
Basis for factual allegations	Rule 11(b)(3)
Basis for denials	Rule 11(b)(4)

Before Rule 11(b) sets forth the four specific representations counsel makes with every filing, the rule first imposes a general requirement that counsel has conducted a pre-filing inquiry that is "reasonable under the circumstances." What constitutes a "reasonable" pre-filing inquiry? *See, e.g.*, *Kraemer v. Grant Cty.*, 892 F.2d 686, 689 (7th Cir. 1990):

> It is not necessary that an investigation into the facts be carried to the point of absolute certainty. The investigation need merely be reasonable under the circumstances. Relevant factors for the court to consider include: Whether the signer of the documents had sufficient time for investigation; the extent to which the attorney had to rely on his or her client for the factual foundation underlying the pleading, motion, or other paper; whether the case was accepted from another attorney; the complexity of the facts and the attorney's ability to do a sufficient pre-filing investigation; and whether discovery would have been beneficial to the development of the underlying facts. (citation and internal quotation marks omitted)

After requiring a reasonable pre-filing inquiry, there are four categories of representations laid out in the rule. The first is the **motivation** for submitting a paper to the court. Under the rule, the motivation behind the filing may not be sinister in that it is meant to drive up litigation costs or needlessly delay the litigation. The second representation is concerned with the **soundness of legal arguments**. Note that the rule does not simply permit arguments soundly based on existing law, but also permits arguments that argue for a change in the law if those arguments are "nonfrivolous." Why do you think the rule makes this allowance? How is the court to determine if the argument for legal change is "nonfrivolous"? *See, e.g.,* Larez v. Holcomb, 16 F.3d 1513, 1522 (9th Cir. 1994) ("A 'frivolous'

Food for Thought

What do you think is the purpose of the pre-filing inquiry requirement? *See* Phx. Airway Inn Assocs. v. Essex Fin. Servs., 741 F. Supp. 734, 736 (N.D. Ill. 1990) ("The purpose of this timing requirement is obvious: counsel should not be permitted—without reasonable investigation—to file pleadings, motions, or other papers, and then, only if challenged (and after imposing substantial costs on the opposing party), be allowed to scramble to find facts and law justifying his original filing.").

filing is both baseless and made without reasonable and competent inquiry. But Rule 11 must be read in light of concerns that it will . . . chill vigorous advocacy.

The *certification* requirement of Rule 11 should not be confused with a *verification* requirement such as appears in Rules 23.1(b) and 65(b). *Verified* pleadings are those for which the pleader swears to the truth of the statements in the document and are not required under Rule 11. FED. R. CIV. P. 11(a) ("[A] pleading need not be verified or accompanied by an affidavit.").

If, judged by an objective standard, a reasonable basis for the position exists in both law and in fact at the time the position is adopted, then sanctions should not be imposed." (citations and internal quotation marks omitted)).

Third, the rule requires that there be some **basis for factual allegations** made in the pleadings, either in evidence known to counsel or in evidence expected to be discovered by counsel. How certain should counsel have to be to make an allegation supported only by evidence she hopes to discover later? What should happen in the event that such evidence never materializes? *See* In re Commercial Fin. Servs., Inc., 261 B.R. 49, 53–54 (N.D. Okla. 2000) (finding that law firm violated Rule 11(b)(3) because "[t]here is no evidence in the record to support the above-quoted allegations in the three complaints filed in this case" and entering the sanction of "publication" of the violation as punishment). Finally, the rule requires that there be an evidentiary **basis** *for denials* of factual allegations. <u>Pentalpha Macau Commercial Offshore, Ltd. v. Reddy, 2005 WL 2562624, at *2 (N.D. Cal. Oct. 12, 2005)</u> ("Reddy could not have had any good faith basis for denying some of the allegations in the First Amended Complaint. . . . With even the most minimal conferring with his client, Reddy's attorney should have known that he needed to admit some of these facts. Instead, Reddy chose to file a general denial. While this tactic might have spared Reddy some effort and expense, it was improper, and his continued refusal to remedy it was baseless.").

What's That?

The "B.R." that appears in the citation to *In re Commercial Financial Services* refers to West's *Bankruptcy Reporter*. This is a federal case law reporter that covers decisions issued by U.S. Bankruptcy Courts and U.S. District Courts dealing with bankruptcy matters.

2. Sanctions Under Rule 11

Now that you have a basic understanding of what it is that <u>Rule 11</u> requires of counsel filing papers with the court and the scope of these obligations, we now turn to a consideration of the consequences associated with the failure to comply with the strictures of <u>Rule 11</u>. How is <u>Rule 11</u> enforced, meaning, what are the procedures surrounding the raising and adjudication of a <u>Rule 11</u> violation before the court? The sanctioning provisions of <u>Rule 11</u> read as follows:

<u>FRCP 11(c)</u>. Sanctions.

(c) Sanctions.

(1) *In General.* If, after notice and a reasonable opportunity to respond, the court determines that <u>Rule 11(b)</u> has been violated, the court may impose an appropriate sanction on any attorney, law firm, or party that violated the rule or is responsible for the violation. Absent exceptional circumstances, a law firm must be held jointly responsible for a violation committed by its partner, associate, or employee.

(2) *Motion for Sanctions.* A motion for sanctions must be made separately from any other motion and must describe the specific conduct that allegedly violates <u>Rule 11(b)</u>. The motion must be served under <u>Rule 5</u>, but it must not be filed or be presented to the court if the challenged paper, claim, defense, contention, or denial is withdrawn or appropriately corrected within 21 days after service or within another time the court sets. If warranted, the court may award to the prevailing party the reasonable expenses, including attorney's fees, incurred for the motion.

(3) *On the Court's Initiative.* On its own, the court may order an attorney, law firm, or party to show cause why conduct specifically described in the order has not violated <u>Rule 11(b)</u>.

(4) *Nature of a Sanction.* A sanction imposed under this rule must be limited to what suffices to deter repetition of the conduct or comparable conduct by others similarly situated. The sanction may include nonmonetary directives; an order to pay a penalty into court; or, if imposed on motion and warranted for effective deterrence, an order directing payment to the movant of part or all of the reasonable attorney's fees and other expenses directly resulting from the violation.

(5) *Limitations on Monetary Sanctions.* The court must not impose a monetary sanction:

(A)   against a represented party for violating Rule 11(b)(2); or

(B)   on its own, unless it issued the show-cause order under Rule 11(c)(3) before voluntary dismissal or settlement of the claims made by or against the party that is, or whose attorneys are, to be sanctioned.

The key components to sort out here are the procedures surrounding how a Rule 11 violation can be raised with the court and what punishments or sanctions the court may impose if it determines that the rule has been violated. The next case explores these issues in detail.

Hadges v. Yonkers Racing Corp.

U.S. Court of Appeals for the Second Circuit
48 F.3d 1320 (2d Cir. 1995)

FEINBERG, CIRCUIT JUDGE:

Plaintiff George Hadges appeals from three rulings of the United States District Court for the Southern District of New York, Gerard L. Goettel, J. The first ruling * * * denied relief to Hadges in his action brought under FED. R. CIV. P. 60(b) (the Rule 60(b) action) to set aside the judgment of the court in an earlier case, *Hadges v. Yonkers Racing Corp.,* 733 F. Supp. 686 (S.D.N.Y. 1990) (*Hadges I*). In *Hadges I,* Judge Goettel had denied Hadges's application for a preliminary injunction and had granted defendant Yonkers Racing Corp. (YRC) summary judgment in Hadges's action against it. We affirmed that judgment * * *. The basis of the present Rule 60(b) action is that YRC had committed a fraud on the court in *Hadges I.*

In the second ruling on appeal * * * Judge Goettel imposed Rule 11 sanctions on Hadges and his attorney, William M. Kunstler, for misleading the court in the course of the Rule 60(b) action. The judge fined Hadges and censured Kunstler. In the third ruling * * * the judge denied Hadges and

What's That?

A *Rule 60(b) action* is an action before the district court to set aside a final judgment based on one of several reasons enumerated in the rule, including mistake, new evidence, and fraud.

Kunstler permission to reargue the sanctions issues. This appeal followed. For the reasons stated below, we affirm the denial of Rule 60(b) relief, but we reverse the sanction on Hadges and the censure of Kunstler.

I. Background

This appeal concerns the most recent dispute arising out of the efforts of plaintiff-appellant Hadges to compel various racetracks and state agencies to permit him to pursue his career as a harness racehorse driver, trainer and owner. We set forth below the factual background * * * .

A. Facts underlying *Rule 60(b)* action

Hadges was first licensed by the New York State Racing and Wagering Board (Racing Board) in 1972. His license was suspended and revoked in 1974 because he failed to disclose the full extent of his criminal arrest record in his initial license application. Hadges was relicensed in 1976. In early 1989, the Racing Board again suspended Hadges's license for six months after determining that Hadges had illegally passed wagering information to a member of the betting public at Roosevelt Raceway in 1986. According to the Racing Board, as Hadges approached the starting gate, he trailed behind the other horses and shouted, "Get the '7'," to someone in the stands. The number seven horse did in fact win, and Hadges's horse, number two, drove erratically and interfered with the other horses.

In September 1989, although the Racing Board had reissued Hadges's license, YRC denied Hadges the right to work at its racetrack, Yonkers Raceway. In response, Hadges filed an action against YRC in the district court under 42 U.S.C. § 1983,

Make the Connection

Title 42 U.S.C. § 1983 is a statute that serves as the foundation for much civil rights litigation and requires that the complained of conduct be the product of *state action* or "under color of any statute". You can study § 1983 further in a **Federal Courts** or **Civil Rights Litigation** course.

which resulted in the decision in *Hadges I*. Hadges alleged that YRC had violated his Fourteenth Amendment right to due process in banning him. In the course of the *Hadges I* litigation, YRC submitted an affidavit of its General Manager, Robert Galterio, who stated that the YRC ban did not prevent Hadges from pursuing his profession because he could still work at other regional tracks, including the Meadowlands in New Jersey.

In March 1990, the district court granted YRC's motion for summary judgment, finding that YRC's practices were not state action and thus could not give rise to liability under § 1983. In two footnotes, the district court indicated its apparent understanding that Hadges was not barred from racing at other facilities but "that proof that other tracks in the state followed YRC's decision could establish state action."

In 1992, Hadges commenced another suit against YRC, this time in New York state court. He alleged several causes of action including that all the harness tracks in New York State were engaged in a civil conspiracy and that the racetracks had blackballed him in violation of the Donnelly Act. The state court ruled against Hadges on all of his claims (the state court action). In 1993, Hadges brought another § 1983 action, this time against the Meadowlands Raceway, in federal district court in New Jersey (the Meadowlands suit). He alleged that in 1992 Meadowlands had improperly banned him from racing without a hearing. Because Meadowlands is run by a state agency, the New Jersey Sports & Exposition Authority (Sports Authority), there was no dispute as to whether the banning constituted state action. The parties settled that litigation.

In the course of that action, Meadowlands General Manager Bruce Garland submitted an affidavit stating that Meadowlands had banned Hadges based on the YRC ban. In particular, Garland said that Meadowlands had acted pursuant to a Sports Authority resolution adopted in 1992, which provided that Meadowlands would exclude those who had been "ruled off from . . . [an]other racetrack." Thus, he stated, "the fact that plaintiff has been barred at Yonkers Raceway would operate as a basis for . . . rejecting plaintiff's application for participation in [a] 1993 . . . [m]eet at the Meadowlands, had such an application been properly filed."

After successfully settling the Meadowlands suit, and with the appeal from dismissal of the New York state court action pending, Hadges brought the instant Rule 60(b) action in the Southern District of New York. He sought to vacate the court's decision in *Hadges I* on the ground that YRC had perpetrated a fraud on the court in that action by submitting the Galterio affidavit stating that Hadges could continue to work at other tracks despite the YRC ban. Hadges did not inform the district court of the then-pending state court appeal. As noted above, the district court ruled against Hadges and granted YRC's motion for summary judgment. In response to a request by YRC, the court also imposed sanctions under FED. R. CIV. P. 11 on both Hadges and Kunstler.

B. Facts underlying *Rule 11* sanctions

In support of his claim for relief in the Rule 60(b) action, Hadges submitted a sworn statement that 1993 was his "fifth year . . . out of work, with the boycott by Yonkers still in effect." In addition, he stated that "there was a secret agreement among all of the racetracks, that barring a licensee from one, will result in his being barred from all." Plaintiff's memorandum of law, signed by Kunstler, also asserted that Hadges "has not worked for more than four years." Hadges claimed that he had applied to race at other tracks in New York State, but that these tracks refused to act upon the applications, thereby barring him from racing. * * *

In response, YRC produced documents revealing that Hadges had in fact raced at Monticello Raceway five times in 1991 and seven times in 1993. The most recent race took place less than one month before Hadges submitted his affidavit stating that he had been banned from racing by all tracks in New York State for more than four years. YRC also submitted letters of current and former Racing Secretaries from race tracks in Saratoga, Batavia Downs, Fairmount Park, Vernon Downs and Buffalo who asserted that Hadges had not applied (or they had no recollection of his having applied) for racing privileges at their respective tracks in the relevant time period.

In a memorandum of law and notice of motion to dismiss the Rule 60(b) action, YRC requested that the court impose sanctions on Hadges and, if warranted, on his counsel for this misrepresentation and for failing to disclose the state court action to the district court. This method of requesting Rule 11 sanctions was, as set forth below, contrary to the procedural requirements of Rule 11 that took effect on December 1, 1993, five days before Hadges filed his complaint in the Rule 60(b) action and 15 days before YRC requested sanctions.

Practice Pointer

The Federal Rules are constantly being revised, with any amendments taking effect on December 1 of the year in which the Supreme Court approves the changes. Knowing this, one should always stay abreast of the rules amendments to determine what impact, if any, they may have on your client's case.

After YRC requested sanctions, Hadges submitted an affidavit dated December 28, 1993, admitting that he had raced in Monticello in 1991 and 1993, but explaining that he considered the races insignificant because he had earned less than $100 in the two years combined. That affidavit also described a so-called "scratching incident" that Hadges claimed had taken place at Yonkers Raceway on October 31, 1989. He stated that although his state racing license had been restored in 1989, New York State Racing Board judges "scratched" him from that race * * * . After this scratching incident, YRC informed him of its independent ban. Hadges argued to the district court that this sequence of events supported his theory that YRC was acting as a state agent in banning him and thus could be held liable in a § 1983 action. Hadges submitted to the court a "scratch sheet," purporting to document his version of the event.

YRC then submitted what the district court later described as "overwhelming proof" that the scratch sheet did not refer to an October 1989 race, but rather to a November 1987 race.

In its decision on the merits of the Rule 60(b) action, the district court found that Hadges had raced at Monticello in 1991 and 1993 but that he had made only a "minimal" amount of money. It also found that the legal basis for Hadges's Rule 60(b) action was not "so frivolous as to warrant Rule 11 sanctions." However, the court was "quite concerned" that Hadges and Kunstler had attempted "to indicate that [Hadges] had not raced in four years when, in fact, he had privileges at Monticello in both 1991 and 1993." The court stated that Hadges had "made matters worse by attempting to strengthen his claim of state involvement alleging that he was scratched * * * on October 31, 1989 by the judges of the racing board." The court further found that submission of the undated scratch sheet was a "flagrant misrepresentation . . . suggest[ing] the need for sanctions, certainly against the plaintiff and possibly against his counsel." The judge invited Hadges and Kunstler to submit papers opposing the imposition of sanctions. The court did not refer to the nondisclosure of the state court action as a possible basis for sanctions.

Thereafter, Hadges submitted an affidavit admitting that he had made a misstatement about the scratching incident but expressing his objection to sanctions. He stated that this error was the result of a simple memory loss, and that the scratch sheet involved was bona fide proof of his having been scratched in 1987 rather than in 1989. He went on to describe yet another 1989 incident in which he had been scratched from racing * * * at YRC. Hadges also submitted an affidavit of his then-assistant Erik Schulman, which also described the 1989 * * * scratching incident. Further, Hadges repeated that he had written to the General Managers * * * of the various tracks to request driving privileges but had received no reply. He attached copies of the letters along with copies of postal receipts.

Take Note!

Take note of the precise conduct that formed the basis for the court's sanctions against Hadges and Kunstler. What portions of Rule 11 do you think the court was relying on in sanctioning this conduct?

Kunstler also submitted a sworn response, which stated that he "had no idea" that the scratch sheet was from 1987 rather than 1989 * * * . Kunstler maintained that the error regarding the date of the scratch sheet was unintentional but would not have affected the outcome of the case in any event. Regardless of its date, he argued, the scratch sheet was evidence that YRC was acting as an agent of the state Racing Board and could therefore be held liable in a § 1983 action. Thus, he maintained that submission of the document was not sanctionable. Kunstler's affidavit did not describe the efforts he had undertaken to verify his client's factual claims. YRC then submitted further affidavits stating that it had no records concerning the alleged [the 1989 scratching] incident.

Thereafter, in the second ruling on appeal to us, the judge imposed a Rule 11 sanction of $2,000 on Hadges as an appropriate sanction for his misrepresentations. The judge also censured Kunstler under Rule 11 for failing to make adequate inquiry as to the truth of Hadges's affidavits and for failing to inform the court of the pending state court litigation. In the course of his opinion, the judge stated:

Mr. Kunstler is apparently one of those attorneys who believes that his sole obligation is to his client and that he has no obligations to the court or to the processes of justice. Unfortunately, he is not alone in this approach to the practice of law, which may be one reason why the legal profession is held in such low esteem by the public at this time.

Kunstler responded in a letter to the court, in which he argued that the court erred in sanctioning his client $2,000 and in censuring him. In particular, he objected to the court's characterization of him as an attorney "who believes that his sole obligation is to his client," and he objected to the court's charge that his approach to law practice was in part responsible for the low public esteem for the legal profession. Kunstler went on to state his opinion that the court's comment was "generated by an animus toward activist practitioners who, like myself, have, over the years, vigorously represented clients wholly disfavored by the establishment."

The court treated the letter as an application to reargue the sanction issues. Its order denying the application is the third ruling on appeal to us. In that order, the court quoted at length from a recent New York state court opinion criticizing Kunstler's law partner, Ronald L. Kuby in an entirely unrelated case. The judge's order further reprimanded Kunstler stating:

> Finally, Mr. Kunstler claims that he is entitled to "consideration" because of his representation of unpopular clients. Undoubtedly an attorney who assumes or is assigned the defense of an unpopular case or client and does so at risk to his practice or standing in the community (such as the fictional attorney Atticus Finch in Harper Lee's "To Kill a Mockingbird") is entitled to some consideration. However, an attorney who aggressively and repeatedly seeks to represent unpopular causes or questionable clients for personal reasons of his own is not deserving of any particular consideration. And an attorney who places himself and his causes above the interests of justice is entitled to none.

This appeal from the judgment for YRC in the Rule 60(b) action and from the two April 1994 rulings on sanctions followed.

II. Discussion

A. The *Rule 60(b)* action

* * *

* * * Since we believe that the district court was correct in concluding that there was no fraud on the court, its denial of Rule 60(b) relief must be upheld.

B. Rule 11 sanctions

As we have already noted, not only did the district court rule against Hadges regarding his claims of fraud on the court in *Hadges I*, but it went on to impose Rule 11 sanctions on both Hadges and Kunstler for their own misrepresentations and omissions. This determination was based on two principal grounds: (1) misstatement of the date of the alleged "scratching" incident and (2) misstatement regarding Hadges's lack of work in the years since the YRC ban. In addition, the court based Kunstler's censure on his failure to inform the court of the state court action. * * *

1. *Hadges's sanction*

Hadges argues that the district court abused its discretion in imposing sanctions on him. YRC argues that the sanctions were justified. We believe that Hadges is correct.

In imposing sanctions, the district court apparently did not take into account YRC's failure to comply with the revised procedural requirements of Rule 11. In this case, YRC did not submit the sanction request separately from all other requests, and there is no evidence in the record indicating that YRC served Hadges with the request for sanctions 21 days before presenting it to the court. Thus, YRC denied Hadges the "safe-harbor" period that the current version of the Rule specifically mandates.

Take Note!

Hadges himself, the plaintiff in the action, has been sanctioned here, not just his attorney. Rule 11 allows courts to sanction individual parties themselves, not simply their counsel. Is that as it should be?

If Hadges had received the benefit of the safe-harbor period, the record indicates that he would have "withdrawn or appropriately corrected" his misstatements, thus avoiding sanctions altogether. Hadges did in fact correct one of his misstatements by admitting in an affidavit * * * just 12 days after YRC asked for sanctions, that he had raced at Monticello in 1991 and 1993. Thus, this misstatement is not sanctionable.

Hadges also explained and corrected his misstatement about the 1989 date of the first scratching incident and described another scratching incident in 1989 involving another horse (Dazzling GT). This correction was supported by his own affidavit sworn to on March 17, 1994, and the affidavit of Erik Schulman, sworn to on March 16, 1994. Both were filed with the district court on March 21, 1994, just one week after the court issued its order stating that it was considering imposition of sanctions. Apparently, YRC had not previously requested sanctions on the basis of the scratching incident. Although YRC subsequently questioned whether the Dazzling GT incident described by Hadges and Schulman had taken place, the district court did not rely on this as a basis for imposing sanctions. We note that Kunstler also filed an affidavit making similar retractions.

* * *

Rule 11 also provides that a court may impose sanctions on its own initiative. FED.R.CIV.P. 11(c)(1)(B). If a court wishes to exercise its discretion to impose sanctions *sua sponte*, it must "enter an order describing the specific conduct that appears to violate subdivision (b) and directing an attorney, law firm, or party to show cause why it has not violated subdivision (b) with respect thereto." In this case, the court indicated that it was imposing sanctions in response to YRC's request and did not state that it was imposing sanctions on Hadges *sua sponte*. We doubt that *sua sponte* sanctions would have been justified here. The advisory committee note on the 1993 amendment specifically states that such sanctions "will ordinarily be [imposed] only in situations that are akin to a contempt of court." Hadges's conduct did not rise to that level.

What's That?

The committee that revises the Federal Rules of Civil Procedure, the Advisory Committee on Civil Rules, typically appends a note after a rule each time they amend it in an effort to provide some explanation of the change. What weight, if any, should such notes be given when interpreting the Federal Rules? *See Krupski v. Costa Crociere, S.p.A., 560 U.S. 538 (2010)* (Scalia, J., concurring) ("[T]he Committee's intentions have no effect on the Rule's meaning. . . . [I]t is the text of the Rule that controls.").

Thus, under all the circumstances, particularly the failure to afford Hadges the 21-day safe-harbor period provided by revised Rule 11, we believe that the sanction of Hadges should be reversed.

2. Kunstler's censure

Like Hadges, Kunstler did not receive the benefit of the safe-harbor period. The district court imposed sanctions on Kunstler for failing to adequately investigate the truth of Hadges's representations prior to submitting them to the court and for failing to disclose that Hadges had brought an action against YRC in New York state court. Kunstler argues that the court's censure of him was an abuse of discretion because the court was motivated by a personal or political animus against him and because his conduct was not sufficiently egregious to justify imposition of sanctions.

In our decisions concerning the former version of Rule 11 we have had occasion to address the reasonableness of an attorney's reliance on information provided by a client. In *Kamen v. American Tel. & Tel. Co., 791 F.2d 1006 (2d Cir. 1986)*, the plaintiff brought suit against her employer and supervisors under the Rehabilitation Act of 1973 and state law. Employers are not liable under the Rehabilitation Act unless they receive "[f]ederal financial assistance." 29 U.S.C. § 794. The employer sent letters to the plaintiff's attorney asserting that it did not receive federal financial assistance, but her attorney persisted in prosecuting the Rehabilitation Act suit. The district court agreed with the employer and dismissed the claims. Although plaintiff's attorney had submitted an affirmation stating that his client had advised him that the employer received federal grants, the district court imposed sanctions. We found that the district court abused its discretion because the attorney's reliance on his client's statements was reasonable.

A few years later, we relied on *Kamen* in holding that "[a]n attorney is entitled to rely on his or her client's statements as to factual claims when those statements are objectively reasonable." *Calloway v. Marvel Entertainment Group,* 854 F.2d 1452, 1470 (2d Cir. 1988), *rev'd in part on other grounds sub nom. Pavelic & LeFlore v. Marvel Entertainment Group,* 493 U.S. 120 (1989). This interpretation is in keeping with the advisory committee notes on former Rule 11, which indicates that the reasonableness of an inquiry depends upon the surrounding circumstances, including

> such factors as how much time for investigation was available to the signer; whether he had to rely on a client for information as to the facts underlying the pleading . . . ; or whether he depended on forwarding counsel or another member of the bar.

Advisory committee note on 1983 amendment to FED.R.CIV.P. 11.

In *Calloway*, at least one of the plaintiff's claims "was never supported by any evidence at any stage of the proceeding," and we affirmed the district court's imposition of sanctions. However, we went on to set forth a procedure for district courts to follow in analyzing whether an attorney has conducted a reasonable inquiry into the facts underlying a party's position.

> In considering sanctions regarding a factual claim, the initial focus of the district court should be on whether an objectively reasonable evidentiary basis for the claim was demonstrated in pretrial proceedings or at trial. Where such a basis was shown, no inquiry into the adequacy of the attorney's pre-filing investigation is necessary.

The new version of Rule 11 makes it even clearer that an attorney is entitled to rely on the objectively reasonable representations of the client. No longer are attorneys required to certify that their representations are "well grounded in fact." FED.R.CIV.P. 11 (1983) amended 1993. The current version of the Rule requires only that an attorney conduct "an inquiry reasonable under the circumstances" into whether "factual contentions have evidentiary support." FED.R.CIV.P. 11(b) & (b)(3). Thus, the new version of Rule 11 is in keeping with the emphasis in *Calloway* on looking to the record before imposing sanctions.

In its first sanction decision in April 1994, the district court here stated:

> With respect to plaintiff's counsel, William M. Kunstler, the situation is not quite as clear. There is nothing to indicate that, on the serious factual

misrepresentations made in plaintiff's papers, Mr. Kunstler had independent knowledge of their falsity. However, it is equally clear that he made no attempt to verify the truth of the plaintiff's representations prior to submitting them to the court.

Apparently, the district court did not focus, as Rule 11 now requires, on whether the pretrial proceedings provided "evidentiary support" for the factual misrepresentations with which the court was concerned.

It is clear that the record before the district court contained evidentiary support for Kunstler's incorrect statements. As to the scratching incident, the record included a sworn statement by Hadges describing an October 1989 incident in which he claimed to have been scratched from driving the horse "Me Gotta Bret." A scratch sheet, which did not reveal the year in which it was made out, was also part of the record. Kunstler later submitted an affidavit admitting the error and stating that he had no idea that the 1989 date was wrong. He further maintained that regardless of its date, the scratch sheet was relevant to show collaboration between the Racing Board and YRC in 1987, which would subject the latter to § 1983 liability. Moreover, it appears to be undisputed that most of the evidence YRC produced to persuade the court that the event had taken place in 1987 was within its possession, not Hadges's. *See Kamen, 791 F.2d at 1012* (noting reasonableness of relying on client representations where "the relevant information [is] largely in the control of the defendants").

We also believe that the record contained evidentiary support for the claim that Hadges had not worked for four years. At the time the district court granted YRC summary judgment in Hadges's Rule 60(b) action, it had before it Hadges's affidavit asserting that he had written to racetrack General Managers asking for driving privileges and had not received any replies. The record also contained attorney Faraldo's affidavit asserting that Hadges had followed his advice in writing these letters. Moreover, Kunstler represented Hadges in the Meadowlands suit in which Meadowlands admitted banning Hadges based upon the YRC ban. We believe that in light of his familiarity with the Meadowlands litigation and the sworn statements of his client and another attorney, Kunstler had sufficient evidence to support a belief that Hadges had not participated in harness horseracing in New York since the YRC ban.

The district court also believed that censure of Kunstler was justified because "he had to be aware of the recent state court litigation, still on appeal, but made no mention of it in his initial papers." Kunstler concedes that he was aware of this litigation but maintains that he did not believe that it was necessary to bring the proceedings to the court's attention because the New York Supreme Court had not ruled on the merits of the state law blackballing claim. As noted above, we agree with the view that the state court opinion was not a decision on the merits of that issue. Even if it were, there would be no tactical advantage in not mentioning the state court ruling to the district court since YRC was a party to both actions (indeed, it was represented by the same law firm and the same attorney in both actions) and could be expected to inform the district court of the state court action if it were helpful.

Moreover, the portion of the court's opinion in the Rule 60(b) action that listed the possible bases for imposition of sanctions omitted any reference to Kunstler's nondisclosure of the state court action. Rule 11 specifically requires that those facing sanctions receive adequate notice and the opportunity to respond. *See* Fed.R.Civ.P. 11(c)(1)(A) & (B). Although YRC had requested sanctions on this ground, as discussed above, that request was procedurally improper. Thus, although Kunstler would have been wiser to alert the court to the state court proceedings, the nondisclosure was not a proper ground for sanctioning him.

* * *

Finally, the remarks of the district court, which we have quoted in substantial part above, contribute to our conclusion that the sanction of Kunstler was unjustified. These remarks have the appearance of a personal attack against Kunstler, and perhaps more broadly, against activist attorneys who represent unpopular clients or causes. We find the court's criticism of Kunstler's law partner, Ronald L. Kuby, for his activities in another case, especially unwarranted. For all these reasons, we reverse the imposition of the sanction of censure on Kunstler.

Take Note!

The court takes time here to express its stern disapproval of the district court's personal attack on the attorneys in this case. This type of reprimand of a district court judge is rare.

* * *

Points for Discussion

a. Sanctioning Procedures Under Rule 11

In *Hadges*, the appeals court struck down the sanctions imposed against Hadges because of the failure to comply with the procedures surrounding the imposition of sanctions under Rule 11, particularly its so-called "safe harbor" provision. What steps should YRC or the district court have taken to comply with the rule? The safe harbor provision at the center of *Hadges* refers to the following language from Rule 11: "The motion [for sanctions] must not be filed or presented to the court if the challenged paper, claim, defense, contention, or denial is withdrawn or appropriately corrected within 21 days after service [of the motion]." FED. R. CIV. P. 11(c)(2). What do you think is the purpose of this provision?

Rule 11 additionally imposes a **separate motion requirement**, which requires parties seeking sanctions under Rule 11 to make such motions "separately from any other motion . . . ." FED. R. CIV. P. 11(c)(2); *see also Boyce v. Interbake Foods, 2012 WL 112295, at *3 (D.S.D. Jan. 12, 2012)* (denying motion for Rule 11 sanctions in part because "Interbake did not separately move for sanctions. Instead, it combined its motion for sanctions with its motion for attorney's fees, which violates Rule 11").

Rule 11 does permit courts to impose sanctions on its own initiative (*sua sponte*), without a motion, provided the court gives the party to be sanctioned notice and the opportunity to be heard on the matter prior to imposing sanctions. FED. R. CIV. P. 11(c)(3). Why was the court's *sua sponte* issuance of sanctions in *Hadges* rejected by the appellate court?

b.   Available Sanctions Under Rule 11

Sanctions under Rule 11 are discretionary, meaning the court is not obligated to impose sanctions in the face of a violation of the rule. If the court chooses to impose sanctions, they can range from a minor warning or reprimand to significant monetary sanctions in rare cases. Does the rule offer any guidance that can help courts determine what type of punishment is appropriate in a given case?

> **FYI**
>
> Federal courts have split over the question of whether magistrate judges are authorized to impose Rule 11 sanctions on attorneys practicing in matters referred to them or may only recommend that a district judge do so. *See Kiobel v. Millson*, 592 F.3d 78, 106–07 (2d Cir. 2010) (Jacobs, C.J., concurring) (discussing the issue and related circuit split).

Be sure to note that if a court seeks to impose sanctions on its own initiative, it may not award attorneys' fees to the aggrieved party; those are only available in response to a motion for sanctions. FED. R. CIV. P. 11(c)(4). Further, regardless of whether the sanctions are imposed on motion or *sua sponte*, no monetary sanctions may be imposed against a represented party for violating Rule 11(b)(2), which pertains to certifications regarding the legal contentions contained within a filing. FED. R. CIV. P. 11(b)(2).

c.   The History of Rule 11

The court in *Hadges* provides a brief glimpse into the history of Rule 11, the main components of which involve a major amendment to the Rule in 1983, and a subsequent overhaul of the Rule in 1993. Without going too deeply into this history, the 1983 version of the rule was strict, holding counsel to an objective standard of reasonableness rather than a good-faith standard, making sanctions mandatory upon the finding of a violation, and failing to provide for the safe harbor found within the current version of the rule. Because that version of the rule led to a dramatic upswing in Rule 11 motions and spawned too much "satellite" litigation regarding whether Rule 11 had been violated (plus because many viewed the rule as imposing too onerous a burden on claimants' efforts to bring legitimate but disfavored claims such as civil rights actions), the rule was amended in 1993 to its current form. *See* Carl Tobias, *The 1993 Revision to Federal Rule 11,* 70 IND. L.J. 171 (1994). What interest groups do you think favored amending the rule to its strict 1983 version and why? What interests do you think promoted amending the rule again in 1993? Which version of the rule is better? *See Perspective & Analysis* below.

—Perspective & Analysis—

The Supreme Court must approve amendments to the Federal Rules of Civil Procedure before they can take effect. Justice Scalia dissented to the adoption of the 1993 amendment with the following comments:

> It is undeniably important to the Rules' goal of "the just, speedy, and inexpensive determination of every action," FED. RULE CIV. PROC. 1, that frivolous pleadings and motions be deterred. The current Rule 11 achieves that objective by requiring sanctions when its standards are violated . . . and by allowing compensation for the moving party's expenses and attorney's fees. The proposed revision would render the Rule toothless, by allowing judges to dispense with sanction, by disfavoring compensation for litigation expenses, and by providing a 21-day "safe harbor" within which, if the party accused of a frivolous filing withdraws the filing, he is entitled to escape with no sanction at all.

> . . . In my view, those who file frivolous suits and pleadings should have no "safe harbor." The Rules should be solicitous of the abused (the courts and the opposing party), and not of the abuser. Under the revised Rule, parties will be able to file thoughtless, reckless, and harassing pleadings, secure in the knowledge that they have nothing to lose: If objection is raised, they can retreat without penalty. The proposed revision contradicts what this Court said only three years ago: "Baseless filing puts the machinery of justice in motion, burdening courts and individuals alike with needless expense and delay. Even if the careless litigant quickly dismisses the action, the harm triggering Rule 11's concerns has already occurred. Therefore, a litigant who violates Rule 11 merits sanctions even after a dismissal." *Cooter & Gell v. Hartmarx Corp.*, 496 U.S. 384, 398 (1990).

Order of the Supreme Court Amending the Federal Rules of Civil Procedure (Apr. 22, 1993), *reprinted in* 146 F.R.D. 401, 507–08 (1993) **(Scalia, J., dissenting).**

d. Purpose of and Need for Rule 11

Why do we need a rule like Rule 11? After all, attorneys are subject to the ethical rules of the bar,* and can get into trouble on that front if they are found to have been dishonest in their advocacy before a court. The answer lies, in part, in the fact that ours is nominally a notice pleading system. Because so little has traditionally been required to satisfy the pleading standard imposed by Rule 8(a), it has been quite easy to commence an action in federal court and initiate discovery, which sometimes can be both intrusive and expensive for the opposing party. The seeming ease with which this machinery of the federal judiciary can be employed means that it might otherwise be subject to abuse were no controls or limitations in place.

One means of controlling abusive litigation of course would be to require litigants to plead their causes with specificity and factual support, so a court could determine in advance whether there was any merit to the claims. Although that appears not to have been the choice the drafters of the Federal Rules made, after the Supreme Court's decisions in *Bell Atlantic v. Twombly, 550 U.S. 544 (2007)* and *Ashcroft v. Iqbal, 556 U.S. 662 (2009)*, it seems that the pleadings may now be used to screen for frivolous claims. Rule 11, then, is in place as an additional part of our system's attempt to weed out claims by deterring and punishing those who abuse the pleading system by filing claims and other court documents that lack merit.

Given the purpose of Rule 11, how strict do you think courts should be in its enforcement? How strictly should the rule itself be written? As already noted, a prior version of the rule made sanctions mandatory for violations and lacked any safe harbor provision. Indeed, on multiple occasions Congress has considered a proposal to return these attributes to the rule. *See* Lawsuit Abuse Reduction Act of 2013, H.R. 2655, 113th Cong. (1st Sess. 2013); Lawsuit Abuse Reduction Act of 2005, H.R. 420, 109th Cong. (1st Sess. 2005). Most recently, the U.S. House of Representatives passed the Lawsuit Abuse Reduction Act of 2017, H.R. 720, 115th Cong. (1st Sess. 2017), on March 10, 2017, although the Senate never took up the version of the Act that was introduced there, S. 237, 115th Cong. (1st Sess. 2017). What impact would a stricter version of the rule have on litigants seeking to press their claims? *See Perspective and Analysis* below.

---

* For a good sense of these rules, see MODEL RULES OF PROF'L CONDUCT r. 3.1, r. 3.2, r. 3.3, r. 4.1 (AM. BAR ASS'N, 1983). [Ed.]

—Perspective & Analysis—

As alluded to earlier, the relative strictness or laxity of Rule 11 has an impact on litigants and the claims that they are able to pursue in court. Many scholars have commented on this impact; the comments of one such scholar were as follows:

> [T]he sanctions debate is a distributional political battle that has some unavoidable aspects of a zero-sum game. If Rule 11 is written or interpreted stringently, some claims are sacrificed in the name of efficiency, deterring the unfounded or abusive, and thinning court dockets. If Rule 11's text or application is made more forgiving, some of these values are sacrificed in favor of zealous advocacy, innovative lawyering, and claimants' rights. Because some lawyers tend to favor the access/advocacy/innovation goals while others prefer the efficiency/expense/deterrence goals, no theory of Rule 11 can hope to satisfy all sides of the sanctions debate completely.

Jeffrey W. Stempel, *Sanctions, Symmetry, and Safe Harbors: Limiting Misapplications of Rule 11 by Harmonizing It with Pre-Verdict Dismissal Devices*, 60 FORDHAM L. REV. 257, 260–61 (1991).

e. Other Sanctioning Provisions

Beyond Rule 11, there are several other sources of authority for regulating the conduct of attorneys and parties litigating in the federal courts:

Other Sources of Authority for Ensuring Truthful Allegations and Controlling Litigant Conduct

- **Rule 23.1**. Requires plaintiffs in shareholder derivative suits to verify their pleadings, meaning that they must affirm the truth of their allegations.

- **28 U.S.C. § 1927**. Holds counsel financially responsible for "unreasonably and vexatiously" multiplying proceedings. No safe harbor provision or separate motion requirement but harder to prove. Applies to all litigation conduct, not just filings.

- **18 U.S.C.A. § 401**. Gives courts the power to fine or imprison any person for contempt of court based on misbehavior that obstructs the administration of justice or for disobedience of lawful orders, rules, or commands.

- **Rules 26(g) and 37**. Together, these rules set forth the certifications required for the discovery process, impose obligations similar to those in Rule 11, and provide the court with sanctioning authority for any violations.

- **Federal Statutes**. In some instances Congress has written certification standards into federal statutes. An example is the Private Securities Litigation Reform Act (PSLRA) of 1995, Pub. L. No. 104–67, 109 Stat. 737 (1995).

- **Inherent Power**. Courts retain an "inherent power" to sanction parties for objectionable conduct.

If counsel pursues sanctions under more than one of these provisions, which sanctioning authority should courts use if they determine that conduct is sanctionable under several of the above sources? If the objectionable conduct may not be sanctioned under Rule 11, should a court be able to use its inherent authority to impose sanctions? *See Chambers v. NASCO, Inc.*, 501 U.S. 32, 44–46 (1991) (upholding a district court's use of its inherent power to impose sanctions for a party's bad-faith conduct).

One commentator has criticized courts' use of other sanctioning authority as Rule 11 has been made less strict. Danielle Kie Hart, *And the Chill Goes on—Federal Civil Rights Plaintiffs Beware: Rule 11 vis-à-vis 28 U.S.C. § 1927 and the Court's Inherent Power*, 37 Loy. L.A. L. Rev. 645, 646–47 (2004) ("[W]hile Rule 11 use appears to be declining in the federal courts after the 1993 amendments to the Rule, imposing of sanctions under § 1927 and the court's inherent power may be increasing . . . . [Courts may be doing so] to circumvent the procedural requirements of Rule 11 when those procedural requirements have not been or could not be met."). The same commentator notes that civil rights plaintiffs have disproportionately been targeted for Rule 11 sanctions. Danielle Kie Hart, *Still Chilling after All These Years: Rule 11 of the Federal Rules of Civil Procedure and Its Impact on Federal Civil Rights Plaintiffs after the 1993 Amendments*, 37 Val. U.L. Rev. 1, 3 (2002) ("Civil rights plaintiffs are still targeted for Rule 11 sanctions more frequently than other litigants in the federal courts . . . ."). Is this fair?

For a thorough discussion of the impact of Rule 11 and other Federal Rules on civil rights litigants and other public law litigation, see Carl Tobias, *Public Law Litigation and the Federal Rules of Civil Procedure*, 74 Cornell L. Rev. 270, 296 (1989) ("Judicial application of numerous Rules has adversely affected public interest litigants.").

————

Executive Summary

■ **Sufficiency of the Complaint.** Rule 8(a) requires only a short and plain statement of entitlement to relief, which the *Twombly* Court interpreted as requiring the pleading of facts suggestive of liability in most cases. In the case of allegations of mistake or fraud, however, Rule 9(b) additionally requires that the circumstances of the mistake or fraud be pleaded with particularity, meaning the "who, what, when, where, and how" of the misconduct charged must be articulated.

■ **Responding to a Complaint.** A defendant can raise numerous defenses by pre-answer motion in response to a complaint. However, certain of these must be consolidated and raised initially or they are waived. *See* Rules 12(g) & (h). The defendant is ultimately obliged to submit an answer in response to the complaint if it is not dismissed, which can include the non-waived defenses and objections of <u>Rule 12</u>, but also must include admissions or denials of all factual allegations, as well as any affirmative defenses the defendant intends to raise. The answer is also the appropriate vehicle for asserting any counterclaims the defendant may wish to assert.

Major Themes

Keep in mind two overarching themes at work within the pleadings area:

a. ***Shift away from Notice Pleading***—although <u>Rule 8(a)</u> had traditionally been interpreted to impose only a notice pleading standard, the Supreme Court's decision in <u>Bell Atlantic v. Twombly</u> marked a major shift away from mere notice toward a system that requires the pleading of facts showing plausible entitlement to relief.

b. ***From Access to Restrictiveness***—after <u>Bell Atlantic v. Twombly</u> and <u>Ashcroft v. Iqbal</u> the historical policy that favored litigant access to the federal courts by requiring only simplified notice pleading seems to be giving way to a policy focused on screening out meritless claims at the very front end in an effort to protect defendants from the perceived high costs of modern complex litigation. *See* A. Benjamin Spencer, Iqbal *and the Slide Toward Restrictive Procedure*, <u>14 LEWIS & CLARK L. REV. 185 (2010)</u>.

■ **Amending the Pleadings.** The parties are generally free to amend their pleadings once without permission within 21 days of serving it, or within 21 days of service of a responsive pleading, if one is due. Beyond that time period, permission of the court is needed, which is to be freely given unless there is some evidence of undue delay or unfair prejudice to the party opposing the amendment. *See* <u>Rule 15(a)</u>.

■ **Relation-Back of Amendments.** Whether amendments will relate back to the time the original pleading was filed is governed by <u>Rule 15(c)</u>. If the amendment asserts a claim or defense that arose out of the conduct, transaction, or occurrence set out in the original pleading, it will relate back. If the amendment seeks to change the naming of a party against whom a claim is asserted, to relate back the party to be named (1) must have known of the action within 90 days of its filing, (2) must have known or should have known that they were the intended party, and (3) would have been named originally but for a mistake by the pleader.

■ **Certification & Sanctions.** <u>Rule 11</u> requires that attorneys sign all filings with the court and represent that the substance of the filings have a good basis in law or fact and are not being submitted for any improper purpose. Violations of this rule subject a party to a risk of sanctions, but opposing parties may only seek sanctions with the court 21 days after submitting a separate motion for sanctions to the alleged violator of the rule.

For More Information

Students interested in studying pleading further may consult the following resources:

- 5 C. WRIGHT & A. MILLER, FED. PRAC. & PROC. § 1201 *et seq.* (3d ed. 2004) (pleadings generally).

- A. Benjamin Spencer, *Understanding Pleading Doctrine*, 108 MICH. L. REV. 1 (2009).

- 5B C. WRIGHT & A. MILLER, FED. PRAC. & PROC. § 1341 *et seq.* (3d ed. 2004) (defenses and objections).

- 6 C. WRIGHT, A. MILLER & M. KANE, FED. PRAC. & PROC. CIV. 3d § 1471 *et seq.* (amendments and supplemental pleadings).

- 5A C. WRIGHT & A. MILLER, FED. PRAC. & PROC. § 1331 *et seq.* (3d ed. 2004) (Rule 11).

Test Your Knowledge

To assess your understanding of the material in this chapter, click here to take a quiz.

CHAPTER SEVEN

Joinder of Claims and Parties

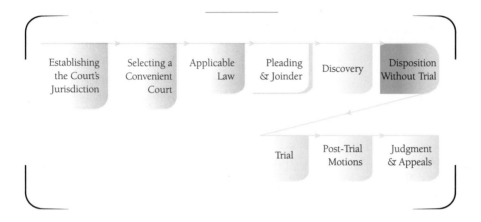

THE SIMPLE MODEL OF A lawsuit involves a single plaintiff asserting a single claim against a single defendant. Although this model is useful for learning the basic concepts of civil procedure studied thus far, in reality litigation is often much more complex. For example, a plaintiff may have multiple claims that it wishes to assert in one civil action. Or, the plaintiff may want to assert its claim along with several other plaintiffs, all against multiple defendants. As a third possibility, a defendant may want to assert its own claims, either against the plaintiff, against other defendants, or against nonparties. The possible scenarios of claims and parties could go on. When may claims and parties be joined within a single action? When *must* such joinder occur? This chapter focuses on the set of rules governing how additional claims and parties may be joined within or added to an action.

A. Claim Joinder

Turning first to claim joinder, this section will review the rules determining when a party may assert multiple claims against its opponent and the rules governing when defending parties may assert whatever claims they may have. As you go through the material, think about why the rules permit or limit claim joinder in the way that they do and what policy interests are served by permitting joinder of claims in the federal system.

1. Joinder of Multiple Claims

Let us begin our consideration of the joinder material by looking at the simple case involving a single plaintiff who wishes to assert multiple claims against a single defendant. Rule 18(a) covers this situation:

FRCP 18(a). Joinder of Claims.

(a) In General. A party asserting a claim, counterclaim, crossclaim, or third-party claim may join, as independent or alternative claims, as many claims as it has against an opposing party.

Points for Discussion

a.   The Scope of Rule 18(a)

Given the language of Rule 18(a), there are no limitations on what claims a plaintiff may join against a defendant. Further, there need not be any relationship between the claims joined. Why do you think the rule is written as broadly as it is? *See* John McCoid, *A Single Package for Multiparty Disputes*, 28 STAN. L. REV. 707, 707 (1976) ("The resources devoted to any lawsuit . . . are scarce. . . . Either repetitive litigation requires the expenditure of additional resources on adjudication, or . . . it diverts those resources from resolution of other controversies of significance."). Why would a party want to assert multiple, unrelated claims in a single action? Are there any negatives that you can think of that might be associated with joining unrelated claims in one action?

Although Rule 18(a) is liberal in its permissiveness, courts retain the authority to sever claims under Rule 21 if any inconvenience or unfairness would arise from having the claims proceed together. *See* Advisory Committee Note, 1966 Amendment ("[A] claim properly joined as a matter of pleading need not be proceeded with together with the other claims if fairness or convenience justifies separate treatment.").

Note that the rule is permissive; it states that a party "may join" claims as it sees fit. Should the rule be rewritten to identify certain claims that the party is required to join in a single action? Although Rule 18(a) does not require joinder, rules deriving from preclusion doctrine (covered in Chapter 11) may compel a party to do so nonetheless. *See* Richard D. Freer, *Avoiding Duplicative Litigation: Rethinking Plaintiff Autonomy and the Court's Role in Defining the Litigative Unit*, 50 U. PITT. L. REV. 809, 822 (1989) ("[Rule 18(a)] is merely the carrot, for it is not mandatory. The stick is claim preclusion, which . . . impels the claimant to assert all transactionally related elements of recovery in a single suit.").

b.   Subject Matter Jurisdiction over Joined Claims

Keep in mind that Rule 18(a) and all the joinder rules are only pleading rules. They do not concern themselves with whether a court would have subject matter jurisdiction over the claims pleaded. Thus, although the pleading rules may allow the claims to be joined, separate subject-matter-jurisdiction determinations will have to be made for each claim to see if the court has the authority to hear those claims. The same is true—as will be highlighted below—of cases involving the joinder of multiple or additional parties. **Example 7.1** illustrates how subject-matter-jurisdiction questions arise in the claim-joinder context.

Example 7.1

Paul (NY) sues DSX Corp. (NY) in federal district court for wrongful discharge in firing him based on his age in violation of federal civil rights law. Paul wishes to join a state-law conversion claim based on the company's unrelated towing and destruction of his vehicle from the company parking lot earlier this year.

Paul may join these claims under Rule 18(a), but the court will not have subject matter jurisdiction over the additional conversion claim because there is no diversity, it is a state-law claim that does not involve a federal question, and the claim does not appear to qualify for supplemental jurisdiction because it does not share a common nucleus of fact with the civil rights claim that does qualify for federal question jurisdiction. Were the parties from two different states, there would be no jurisdictional problem, provided the total amount in controversy exceeded $75,000.

---

2. Counterclaims

As discussed in Chapter 6, the defendant in an action has an array of responses that it may make to a complaint. Beyond asserting various defenses and objections and filing an answer responding to the complaint, the defendant is also permitted—and sometimes compelled—to file claims that it has against the plaintiff. These claims by the defendant against the plaintiff are called counterclaims.

Rules 13(a) and (b) set forth the basic rules governing the assertion of counterclaims:

FRCP 13. Counterclaim and Crossclaim.

(a) Compulsory Counterclaim.

(1) *In General.* A pleading must state as a counterclaim any claim that—at the time of its service—the pleader has against an opposing party if the claim:

(A) arises out of the transaction or occurrence that is the subject matter of the opposing party's claim; and

(B) does not require adding another party over whom the court cannot acquire jurisdiction.

(2) *Exceptions.* The pleader need not state the claim if:

(A) when the action was commenced, the claim was the subject of another pending action; or

(B) the opposing party sued on its claim by attachment or other process that did not establish personal jurisdiction over the pleader on that claim, and the pleader does not assert any counterclaim under this rule.

(b) Permissive Counterclaim. A pleading may state as a counterclaim against an opposing party any claim that is not compulsory.

Notice that the rule divides counterclaims into two kinds: compulsory and permissive. How do courts determine whether a party is required to assert a claim as a compulsory counterclaim? The next case addresses that issue.

United States v. Heyward-Robinson Co.

U.S. Court of Appeals for the Second Circuit
430 F.2d 1077 (2d Cir. 1970)

FREDERICK VAN PELT BRYAN, DISTRICT JUDGE.[*]

This is an appeal from a judgment for the plaintiff entered in the United States District Court for the District of Connecticut upon a jury verdict after trial before Chief Judge J. Edward Lumbard, of the Court of Appeals of this Circuit, sitting by designation.

Take Note!

Note that the circuit court opinion is authored by a district judge, while the trial court judgment on review was issued by a circuit judge, both of whom were sitting by designation. This was done pursuant to 28 U.S.C. §§ 292 & 291, respectively.

---

[*] Of the Southern District of New York, sitting by designation. [Footnote by the court.]

The action involves two subcontracts for excavation work between D'Agostino Excavators, Inc. (D'Agostino) and The Heyward-Robinson Company, Inc. (Heyward) as prime contractor on two construction jobs in Connecticut. One of the prime contracts, for the construction of barracks at the Naval Submarine Base in New London, Groton, was with the federal government (the Navy job). The other, a non-federal job, was for the construction of a plant for Stelma, Inc. at Stamford (the Stelma job).

D'Agostino brought this action against Heyward and its surety, Maryland Casualty Company (Maryland) under the Miller Act, <u>40 U.S.C. §§ 270a and 270b</u>, to recover payments alleged to be due on the Navy job. Heyward answered, denying liability on the Navy job and counterclaiming for alleged over-payments and extra costs of completing both the Navy job and the Stelma job. In reply, D'Agostino denied liability on the Heyward counterclaims and interposed a reply counterclaim to recover from Heyward monies alleged to be due on the Stelma job.

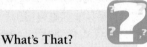

What's That?

A *surety* is someone who is responsible for the payment of another's debt.

At the trial, the two subcontracts in suit were treated together. D'Agostino claimed that Heyward had breached both subcontracts by failing to make progress payments as required and that substantial sums were owing to it from Heyward on both jobs. Heyward claimed that D'Agostino had breached both subcontracts by permitting its compensation and employee liability insurance to lapse; that, as a result, Heyward on October 19, 1965 had terminated both; and that D'Agostino was liable for overpayments and costs of completion on both.

The issue as to whether Heyward had breached the subcontracts prior to October 19, 1965, when Heyward claimed to have terminated them, was submitted to the jury as a special question. The jury found that Heyward had breached the subcontracts prior to that date.

What's That?

Submitting something to a jury as a *special question* simply means that the jury is asked to resolve that isolated issue prior to having to resolve the entire case.

After amendment of the complaint by D'Agostino to allege a claim in quantum meruit for the work performed on both jobs, special questions then were submitted to the jury as to the reasonable value of the work performed by D'Agostino on each project and the net amount owed by Heyward to D'Agostino on both. The jury found, in answer to these questions, that the net amount owed by Heyward to D'Agostino on both jobs was $63,988.36. Judgment against Heyward was rendered accordingly. Under a formula agreed to by the parties, it was determined that the amount due to D'Agostino on the Navy job was $40,771.46 and judgment was entered against Maryland in that sum.

It's Latin to Me!

Quantum meruit is Latin for "as much as he has deserved" and refers to an action seeking reasonable compensation for services rendered, due not based on an actual contract but based on an obligation created by law for the sake of justice.

The trial court denied motions for judgment notwithstanding the verdict and for a new trial pursuant to Rules 50(b) and 59, Fed.R.Civ.P. Heyward and Maryland appeal from the judgment against them, raising a variety of questions which will be dealt with seriatim.

I.

Appellants' initial contention is that the District Court had no jurisdiction over the counterclaims on the Stelma job. They therefore contend that the Stelma claims must be dismissed and that since D'Agostino's claims on the Navy and Stelma jobs were presented to the jury as inseparable, the judgment below must be reversed.

Appellants urge that the Stelma counterclaims are not compulsory counterclaims over which the federal court acquired jurisdiction ancillary to the jurisdiction which it had over D'Agostino's Miller Act claim stated in the complaint. They say that these are permissive counterclaims over which the court had no ancillary jurisdiction and which lacked the required independent basis of federal jurisdiction.

This jurisdictional issue is raised for the first time in this Court. In the Court below appellants affirmatively urged that the Stelma counterclaims were compulsory. Nevertheless, it is well settled that lack of federal jurisdiction may be raised for the first time on appeal, even by a party who originally asserted that jurisdiction existed or by the Court sua sponte. We turn, then, to the jurisdictional issue.

It is apparent from the record that there is no independent basis of federal jurisdiction over the Stelma counterclaims. Both D'Agostino and Heyward are New York corporations with offices in New York. There is thus no diversity jurisdiction. Clearly there is no jurisdiction under the Miller Act over these counterclaims since the Stelma contract did not involve public work for the federal government.

The question is whether the Stelma counterclaims are compulsory or are permissive. Under the rule in this circuit, if they are permissive there is no Federal jurisdiction over them unless they rest on independent jurisdictional grounds. On the other hand, if they are compulsory counterclaims, they are ancillary to the claim asserted in the complaint and no independent basis of Federal jurisdiction is required.

Under Rule 13(a) FED.R.CIV.P. a counterclaim is compulsory "if it arises out of the transaction or occurrence that is the subject matter of the opposing party's claim." In *United Artists Corp. v. Masterpiece Productions*, 221 F.2d 213 (2d Cir. 1955), Chief Judge Clark said:

> In practice this criterion has been broadly interpreted to require not an absolute identity of factual backgrounds for the two claims, but only a logical relationship between them. *Lesnik v. Public Industrials Corp.*, 2 Cir., 144 F.2d 968, 975 (1944), citing and quoting, inter alia, *Moore v. New York Cotton Exchange*, 270 U.S. 593 (1926), thus: " 'Transaction' is a word of flexible meaning. It may comprehend a series of many occurrences, depending not so much upon the immediateness of their connection as upon their logical relationship."

Thus " * * * courts should give the phrase 'transaction or occurrence that is the subject matter' of the suit a broad realistic interpretation in the interest of avoiding a multiplicity of suits." As the Supreme Court said in [*Southern Construction Co. v.*] *Pickard*:

> The requirement that counterclaims arising out of the same transaction or occurrence as the opposing party's claim 'shall' be stated in the pleadings was designed to prevent multiplicity of actions and to achieve resolution in a single lawsuit of all disputes arising out of common matters. 371 U.S. 57, 60 (1962).

In the case at bar the counterclaims were compulsory within the meaning of Rule 13(a). There was such a close and logical relationship between the claims on the Navy and Stelma jobs that the Stelma counterclaims arose out of the same "transaction or occurrence" as those terms are now broadly defined. Both subcontracts were entered into by the same parties for the same type of work and carried on during substantially the same period. Heyward had the right to terminate both subcontracts in the event of a breach by D'Agostino of either. Heyward also had the right to withhold monies due on one to apply

Take Note!

Here and below Judge Bryan is explaining his conclusion that the counterclaims were compulsory. Take note of the analysis he uses to support that conclusion and the facts that led him to this result.

against any damages suffered on the other. Progress payments made by Heyward were not allocated as between jobs and were made on a lump sum basis for both as though for a single account.

A single insurance policy covered both jobs. The letters of Heyward to D'Agostino of October 8 and 19, 1965 threatening termination and terminating both jobs, allegedly because of the cancellation by D'Agostino of this joint insurance coverage and failure to properly man both projects, treated both jobs together. These letters formed the basis of one of Heyward's major claims at the trial.

The controversy between the parties which gave rise to this litigation was with respect to both jobs and arose from occurrences affecting both. Indeed, it would seem to have been impossible for Heyward to have fully litigated the claims against it on the Navy job without including the Stelma job, because the payments it made to D'Agostino could not be allocated between the two jobs.

As the appellants themselves point out in their brief, the "Stelma and Navy claims were so interwoven at the trial that they are now absolutely incapable of separation." The proof as to payments and alleged defaults in payments was made without any differentiation between the two claims and neither of the parties was able to offer any evidence of apportionment. Finally, the evidence as to the breaches of contract claimed by the respective parties related in the main to both contracts rather than to one or the other.

The jurisdictional question so belatedly raised by the appellants must be viewed in light of the record as a whole. So viewed, it is plain that the Stelma counterclaims bare a logical and immediate relationship to the claims on the Navy job. Thus they arose out of the 'transaction or occurrence which is the subject matter' of the suit instituted by D'Agostino on the Navy job and are compulsory counterclaims under Rule 13(a). The Stelma counterclaims were thus ancillary to the claims asserted in the complaint over which the Federal Court had acquired jurisdiction under the Miller Act, and there is jurisdiction over them. To require that the closely related Navy and Stelma claims must be litigated separately would result in fragmentation of litigation and multiplicity of suits contrary to one of the major purposes of Rule 13(a).

* * *

The judgment below is affirmed.

FRIENDLY, CIRCUIT JUDGE (concurring).

I cannot agree that, as maintained in Part I of the majority opinion, the counterclaim relating to the Stelma job was compulsory under F.R.Civ.P. 13(a). Of course, it is tempting to stretch a point when a jurisdictional objection is so belatedly raised by the very party who clamored for the exercise of jurisdiction until the decision went against it. But we must consider the question as if Heyward had not pleaded the Stelma counterclaim and proceeded to sue D'Agostino in some other court for failure to perform that subcontract, and D'Agostino then claimed that Heyward's failure to bring the Stelma transaction into this Miller Act suit barred the later action. Despite the desirability of requiring that all claims which in fact arise "out of the transaction or occurrence that is the subject matter of the opposing party's claim" be litigated in a single action, courts must be wary of extending these words in a way that could cause unexpectedly harsh results.

Food for Thought

Judge Friendly says that the issue of whether the Stelma counterclaim is compulsory must be resolved by asking whether a separate, later suit on that claim would have been barred. The bar to which he refers is the doctrine of *res judicata*, which will be taken up in Chapter 11. Why do you think he analyzes the compulsory counterclaim question in terms of *res judicata*? How does Judge Friendly's analysis differ from the majority's analysis of the issue?

Even on a liberal notion of "logical relation," I am unable to perceive how Heyward's claim for breach of the Stelma subcontract arose "out of the transaction or occurrence" to wit, the Navy subcontract, that was the subject matter of D'Agostino's Miller Act claim. Whatever historical interest there may be in the circumstances that the two subcontracts were entered into between the same parties for the same type of work and were carried on during substantially the same period, these facts seem to me to be lacking in legal significance. So likewise do D'Agostino's having furnished a single insurance policy to cover both jobs and Heyward's having cancelled the subcontracts in one letter rather than two. The boiler-plate in each subcontract, whereby "if one or more other contracts, now or hereafter, exist between the parties," a breach of any such contract by D'Agostino might, at Heyward's option, be considered a breach of the contract at issue and Heyward might terminate any or all contracts so breached and withhold moneys due on any contract and apply these to damages on any other, might meet the test if Heyward had availed itself of these rights, but it did not.

All that is left is that, as the trial proceeded, it turned out that some of Heyward's payments were not earmarked as between the two subcontracts. However, the determination whether a counterclaim is compulsory must be made at the pleading stage. The complaint was specific on how much Heyward owed on the Navy subcontract, and the counterclaims were equally so on how much D'Agostino owed for failure to complete this and how much it owed for failure to complete the Stelma subcontract. To say that the failure to earmark some payments made it impossible to try the claims separately ignores the law on application of payments. If Heyward did not specify the application of its payments, as it could, and D'Agostino had not made an application of them, as it could in default of specification by Heyward, the court would do this.

* * *

Take Note!

Judge Friendly is writing prior to the adoption of the supplemental jurisdiction statute, which governs jurisdiction over ancillary claims. Would his analysis hold true if that statute, 28 U.S.C. § 1367, were applied to the facts of this case?

Nevertheless I think the court below had jurisdiction of the Stelma counterclaim. I would now reject the conventional learning, which I followed too readily in *O'Connell v. Erie Lackawanna R.R.*, 391 F.2d 156, 163 (1968), that the permissive counterclaim 'needs independent jurisdictional grounds to support it * * * .'
* * *

The reasons why the conventional view is wrong * * * is that at least since *United Mine Workers v. Gibbs*, 383 U.S. 715 (1966), it is no longer thought the heavens will fall if a federal court deals with a non-federal claim when it is convenient to do so. * * *

If the decision were mine, I would therefore ask that the court sit in banc and overrule the holding in O'Connell, supra, 391 F.2d at 163, that a permissive counterclaim requires independent jurisdictional grounds. Since my brothers find themselves able to affirm without doing this, I join in the result and leave the issue for another day. On all other points I concur in Judge Bryan's thorough opinion.

What's That?

In banc—more properly spelled *en banc*—refers generally to the full circuit court hearing a case rather than a panel of three of its judges. *En banc* hearings are typically necessary for a circuit to overrule one of its own precedents; panels are not empowered to do this.

Points for Discussion

a.   The Meaning of "Transaction or Occurrence"

Between Rule 13(a) and Rule 13(b), a defending party can assert any claim as a counterclaim without regard to whether it bears any relationship to the claim asserted against it. The critical issue, then, is to determine when a defendant has a counterclaim that it must assert under the rules. Figuring out whether a defendant's counterclaim is compulsory requires a determination of whether the claim "arises out of the transaction or occurrence that is the subject matter of the opposing party's claim." FED. R. CIV. P. 13(a).

What does "transaction or occurrence" mean? *See, e.g.*, *Moore v. N.Y. Cotton Exch.*, 270 U.S. 593, 610 (1926) (" 'Transaction' is a word of flexible meaning. It may comprehend a series of many occurrences, depending not so much upon the immediateness of their connection as upon their logical relationship."). How does the majority in *Heyward-Robinson* define this concept? What other ways can "transaction or occurrence" be conceptualized? *See* 6 C. WRIGHT, A. MILLER & M. KANE, FED. PRAC. & PROC. § 1410

Food for Thought

The concept of a transaction or occurrence is used elsewhere in the Federal Rules. For example, Rule 15(c) permits relation back of amendments if there is a transactional relationship between the new material and what is contained in the original pleadings. Should the concept of transaction or occurrence mean the same thing throughout the Federal Rules, or should its meaning depend on the purpose and role of the rule in which the concept appears? See Mary Kay Kane, *Original Sin and the Transaction in Federal Civil Procedure*, 76 TEX. L. REV. 1723 (1998), for a discussion of this issue.

(3d ed. 2010) (discussing four inquiries to determine whether a counterclaim is compulsory); *see also* *Painter v. Harvey*, 863 F.2d 329, 331 (4th Cir. 1988) (same).

b. Subject Matter Jurisdiction over Counterclaims

As was the case with basic claim joinder, the rules permitting and requiring counterclaims are pleading rules that indicate what types of claims may and must be pleaded. A separate question is whether the court will have jurisdiction to hear the claims. Determining whether there is federal subject matter jurisdiction over a counterclaim involves the same analysis you learned in Chapter 3. The first step is to evaluate the claim to determine whether there is diversity or federal question jurisdiction. **Hypo 7.1** provides a scenario in which such an analysis is necessary.

Hypo 7.1

Plato (VA) asserted a claim against Diogenes (FL) in Florida federal court for copyright infringement under the federal Copyright Act seeking $20,000 in damages. Diogenes responded by asserting a counterclaim for defamation under state law, seeking $76,000 in damages, and a separate counterclaim for copyright infringement under the Copyright Act for $55,000. Diogenes's defamation counterclaim arose out of Plato's circulation of a letter to colleagues asserting that Diogenes had plagiarized Plato's writings and used vast portions of those writings without permission or proper attribution. Diogenes's copyright infringement counterclaim asserts that Plato's writings referred to above were in fact unauthorized reproductions of Diogenes's writings.

Are Diogenes's counterclaims permitted under the Federal Rules? If allowed, are the counterclaims permissive or compulsory? Does the federal court have subject matter jurisdiction over the counterclaims?

If the counterclaim does not qualify for federal subject matter jurisdiction on its own based on diversity or federal question jurisdiction, a supplemental jurisdiction analysis will be necessary. See **Hypo 7.2** below.

Hypo 7.2

Same facts as Hypo 7.1 except Plato and Diogenes are both from Florida. Does the federal court have subject matter jurisdiction over Diogenes's defamation counterclaim?

Recall that in order for state-law claims to qualify for supplemental jurisdiction they must "form part of the same case or controversy" under Article III. 28 U.S.C. § 1367(a). Given the "transaction or occurrence" standard for identifying compulsory counterclaims, will compulsory counterclaims always satisfy the "case or controversy" requirement of § 1367(a)? What about permissive counterclaims; can they ever satisfy the same case or controversy standard of the supplemental jurisdiction statute? *See Jones v. Ford Motor Credit Co.*, 358 F.3d 205, 213–14 (2d Cir. 2004) (holding that the permissive debt-collection counterclaim under state law bore "a sufficient factual relationship" to the federal Equal Credit Opportunity claim "to constitute the same 'case' within the meaning of Article III and hence of section 1367"); *Campos v. W. Dental Servs., Inc.*, 404 F. Supp. 2d 1164, 1168 (N.D. Cal. 2005). ("While it appears that the Ninth Circuit has not addressed the issue, this court agrees with the Second and Seventh Circuit that it may exercise supplemental jurisdiction over some permissive counterclaims."). *But see, e.g., Ramirez v. Amazing Home Contractors, Inc*, No. JKB–14–2168, 2014 WL 6845555, at *5 (D. Md. Nov.

Food for Thought

If a plaintiff asserts a jurisdictionally insufficient claim against a diverse defendant, and that defendant responds with a compulsory counterclaim in an amount that—if added to the plaintiff's claim—would total more than the jurisdictional amount required for diversity jurisdiction, should such aggregation be permitted to satisfy the amount-in-controversy requirement to confer jurisdiction over the plaintiff's claim? Two circuits have suggested that the answer is yes. *See Spectacor Mgmt. Grp. v. Brown*, 131 F.3d 120, 125 (3rd Cir. 1997) (compulsory counterclaim filed by defendant will satisfy jurisdictional amount if defendant elects not to file a motion to dismiss); *Geoffrey E. Macpherson, Ltd. v. Brinecell, Inc.*, 98 F.3d 1241, 1245 n.2 (10th Cir. 1996) (the amount of defendant's compulsory counterclaim may provide a basis for jurisdiction).

25, 2014) ("The Court holds that, until the United States Court of Appeals for the Fourth Circuit abrogates its decisions [pre-dating the supplemental jurisdiction statute], federal courts may not exercise supplemental jurisdiction over permissive counterclaims.").

Although subject matter jurisdiction must be separately evaluated, is there a similar need to analyze whether personal jurisdiction and venue are appropriate with respect to counterclaims? Why or why not? *See, e.g.,* <u>*Volvo N. Am. Corp. v. Men's Int'l Prof'l Tennis Council,* 839 F.2d 69, 72 (2d Cir. 1988)</u> ("[P]laintiffs [can] not . . . simultaneously invoke the jurisdiction of the district court as plaintiffs and avoid personal jurisdiction as counterclaim defendants."); *see also* 14D C. WRIGHT, A. MILLER, E. COOPER, & R. FREER, <u>FED. PRAC. & PROC. § 3808</u> (4th ed. 2013) (arguing that when "additional claims are asserted against parties to the original suit, the better view is that no venue objection should be entertained. . . . [V]enue should not be lost by the subsequent expansion of the case among the same parties").

c. The Consequences of Failing to Plead a Counterclaim

Although <u>Rule 13(a)(1)</u> states that a pleading "must" state any transactionally-related counterclaim, it does not specify the consequences of a failure to do so. What do you think the penalty should be for litigants who fail to assert compulsory counterclaims? Should they be permitted to raise these claims in separate or subsequent legal proceedings, or should they be barred from doing so? *See* <u>*Stone v. Dep't of Aviation,* 453 F.3d 1271, 1275 (10th Cir. 2006)</u> ("A defendant's failure to assert a counterclaim will preclude him from asserting that claim in a later action if '[t]he counterclaim is required to be interposed by a compulsory counterclaim statute or rule of court.'" (quoting RESTATEMENT (SECOND) OF JUDGMENTS § 22(2)(a))); <u>*Twin Disc, Inc. v. Lowell,* 69 F.R.D. 64, 68 (E.D. Wis. 1975)</u> (holding that as "a matter of waiver and estoppel," compulsory counterclaims may not be subsequently litigated). What would be the basis for prohibiting a party that fails to assert a compulsory counterclaim from raising that claim in the future? *See* 6 C. WRIGHT, A. MILLER & M. KANE, <u>FED. PRAC. & PROC. § 1417</u> (3d ed. 2010) ("A

Take Note!

Prior to the 2009 amendments to the Federal Rules, a separate rule—Rule 13(f)—addressed the ability to add previously omitted counterclaims. This rule created confusion regarding the proper standards for amending to assert counterclaims and the relation back of such amendments. *Compare* <u>*Harrison v. Grass,* 304 F. Supp. 2d 710, 715 (D. Md. 2004)</u> ("[T]he counterclaims, being compulsory, relate back to the filing date of the complaint . . . ."), *with* <u>*Am. Annuity Grp., Inc. v. Guar. Reassurance Corp.,* 140 F. Supp. 2d 859, 872 (S.D. Ohio 2001)</u> ("[A]nomitted counterclaim under <u>Rule 13(f)</u> does not relate back to the time of the original action." (citing <u>*Stoner v. Terranella,* 372 F.2d 89, 91 (6th Cir. 1967)</u>)). It was this confusion—and the redundancy with Rule 15—that the 2009 amendment sought to clarify by eliminating Rule 13(f).

failure to plead a compulsory counterclaim bars a party from bringing a later independent action on that claim. Although this result is well established by the cases, . . . it is not clear precisely on what authority it is based."). Preclusion doctrine, the doctrine that governs the preclusive effect of prior adjudication on subsequent claims, controls the extent to which a previously unasserted claim will be barred in a future action; that topic is covered in Chapter 11.

> **FYI**
>
> Some states may expressly provide for such tolling with respect to compulsory counterclaims. See, e.g., Mass. Gen Laws ch. 260, § 36 (1973) ("Notwithstanding the provisions of the first paragraph of this section, a counterclaim arising out of the same transaction or occurrence that is the subject matter of the plaintiff's claim, to the extent of the plaintiff's claim, may be asserted without regard to the provisions of law relative to limitations of actions.").

Recall that Rule 15(a) permits parties to amend their pleadings under certain circumstances. This rule also governs parties' ability to amend their pleadings to assert previously omitted counterclaims. When the amendment to assert the counterclaim comes after the relevant statute-of-limitations period covering the claim has expired, whether the amendment will be permitted to relate back depends on satisfaction of the requirements of Rule 15(c). Additionally, even in the absence of an amendment, when a party is asserting a compulsory counterclaim for the first time after the expiration an applicable statute of limitations, courts generally will permit compulsory counterclaims to relate back to the time that the plaintiff's claim was made. *See Giordano v. Claudio*, 714 F. Supp. 2d 508, 522–23 (E.D. Pa. 2010) ("Although Rule 13 does not provide for relation back, the majority view is that the institution of plaintiff's suit tolls or suspends the running of the statute of limitations governing a compulsory counterclaim." (citation and internal quotation marks omitted)). See **Figure 7.1**.

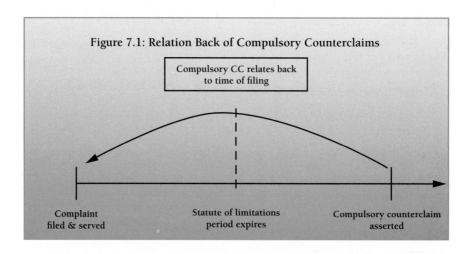

Figure 7.1: Relation Back of Compulsory Counterclaims

Compulsory CC relates back to time of filing

Complaint filed & served

Statute of limitations period expires

Compulsory counterclaim asserted

3. Crossclaims

As we will see in the next section below, the Federal Rules permit multiple parties to sue or be sued simultaneously within a single action. When this happens, the Federal Rules allow coparties to assert claims against each other, such as when a defendant has claims it wishes to assert against a fellow defendant in an action. Rule 13(g) covers this situation:

FRCP 13(g). Crossclaim Against a Coparty.

(g) Crossclaim Against a Coparty. A pleading may state as a crossclaim any claim by one party against a coparty if the claim arises out of the transaction or occurrence that is the subject matter of the original action or of a counterclaim, or if the claim relates to any property that is the subject matter of the original action. The crossclaim may include a claim that the coparty is or may be liable to the crossclaimant for all or part of a claim asserted in the action against the crossclaimant.

Points for Discussion

a. Types of Claims Permitted Under Rule 13(g)

What limits does this rule place on the types of claims that a party may assert against a coparty? Note that the rule does not make any crossclaims compulsory, even though claims asserted under Rule 13(g) will be related to other claims asserted in the action. Why do you think the rule does not make related crossclaims compulsory as is the case with sufficiently related counterclaims?

Even though Rule 13(g) limits the types of claims that may be asserted as crossclaims, recall that Rule 18(a) permits a party asserting any claim, including a crossclaim, to join any other claim that it may have to its claim regardless of the claim's relationship to the initial claim. Does Rule 18(a) eviscerate the limitations of Rule 13(g), or do the limits of the latter rule still have some effect on a party's ability to assert claims against a coparty?

b. Subject Matter Jurisdiction over Crossclaims

Subject matter jurisdiction must exist over crossclaims even if they may be pleaded under Rule 13(g). Given the relationship that crossclaims must have with the claims asserted in the original action, how will such claims generally be treated under the supplemental jurisdiction statute, 28 U.S.C. § 1367? Will they tend to form part of the same Article III "case or controversy" as required by § 1367(a)?

Note that Rule 13(g) does not only apply to claims by defendants; plaintiffs similarly may avail themselves of the rule to assert crossclaims against co-plaintiffs if the claims satisfy the requirements of the rule. If a co-plaintiff asserts a claim against a non-diverse fellow co-plaintiff, or against a co-plaintiff for a jurisdictionally insufficient amount, will § 1367(b) present any obstacles to the assertion of supplemental jurisdiction over such crossclaims? *See Exxon Mobil Corp. v. Allapattah Servs., Inc., 545 U.S. 546, 560 (2005)* ("Nothing in the text of § 1367(b), however, withholds supplemental jurisdiction over the claims of plaintiffs permissively joined under Rule 20."); *Ryan ex rel. Ryan v. Schneider Nat'l Carriers, Inc., 263 F.3d 816, 820 (8th Cir. 2001)* (finding supplemental jurisdiction over the claims by several co-plaintiffs against a non-diverse co-plaintiff).

Food for Thought

The Third Circuit has held that plaintiff crossclaims are permissible only if related to claims being asserted against the plaintiff asserting the crossclaim, not if related simply to the original claim asserted by that plaintiff. *Danner v. Anskis, 256 F.2d 123, 124 (3d Cir. 1958)*. Is such a limitation consistent with the language of the Rule?

B. Party Joinder

Thus far we have been studying the rules that permit or require parties to join multiple claims within a single action. Now we move to the slightly more complex matter of joining multiple parties in an action. There are many variations on party joinder. Plaintiffs may wish to unite with other plaintiffs and proceed jointly against a common defendant. Alternatively, a single plaintiff may wish to assert claims against multiple defendants in one lawsuit rather than suing each of them separately. A defendant may find that it is defending against claims for which a nonparty is liable and would like to join that nonparty to the action to hold it responsible. Nonparties may find that their interests are going to be affected by an existing lawsuit and wish to interpose themselves in the action by joining themselves as parties. Or, there may be nonparties that are so integral to the interests being litigated in an action that the court will determine that they must be joined as parties regardless of their interest in being so joined. This section will consider each of the rules that address these various forms of party joinder.

1. Permissive Party Joinder

Within a single action, parties may voluntarily join together as plaintiffs, or a plaintiff may choose to join several parties together as defendants, provided the requirements of Rule 20(a) are satisfied:

FRCP 20(a). Permissive Joinder of Parties.

(a) **Persons Who May Join or Be Joined.**

(1) *Plaintiffs.* Persons may join in one action as plaintiffs if:

(A) they assert any right to relief jointly, severally, or in the alternative with respect to or arising out of the same transaction, occurrence, or series of transactions or occurrences; and

(B) any question of law or fact common to all plaintiffs will arise in the action.

(2) *Defendants.* Persons—as well as a vessel, cargo, or other property subject to admiralty process in rem—may be joined in one action as defendants if:

(A) any right to relief is asserted against them jointly, severally, or in the alternative with respect to or arising out of the same transaction, occurrence, or series of transactions or occurrences; and

(B) any question of law or fact common to all defendants will arise in the action.

(3) *Extent of Relief.* Neither a plaintiff nor a defendant need be interested in obtaining or defending against all the relief demanded. The court may grant judgment to one or more plaintiffs according to their rights, and against one or more defendants according to their liabilities.

What limitations are imposed on party joinder by this rule? How does it differ from the rule providing for permissive claim joinder, Rule 18(a)? The next case illustrates an interpretation and application of the permissive party joinder provision of Rule 20(a).

Mosley v. General Motors Corp.

U.S. Court of Appeals for the Eighth Circuit
497 F.2d 1330 (8th Cir. 1974)

Ross, CIRCUIT JUDGE.

Nathaniel Mosley and nine other persons joined in bringing this action individually and as class representatives alleging that their rights guaranteed under 42 U.S.C. § 2000e *et seq.* and 42 U.S.C. § 1981 were denied by General Motors and Local 25, United Automobile, Aerospace and Agriculture Implement Workers of America (Union) by reason of their color and

What's That?

A *class representative* is a plaintiff who sues on behalf of herself and all similarly situated others who belong to a class. Rule 23 sets forth the requirements for proceeding as a class and for serving as a class representative. This rule will be discussed in Section E below.

race. Each of the ten named plaintiffs had, prior to the filing of the complaint, filed a charge with the Equal Employment Opportunity Commission (EEOC) asserting the facts underlying these claims. Pursuant thereto, the EEOC made a reasonable cause finding that General Motors, Fisher Body Division and Chevrolet Division, and the Union had engaged in unlawful employment practices in violation of Title VII of the Civil Rights Act of 1964. Accordingly, the charging parties were notified by EEOC of their right to institute a civil action in the appropriate federal district court, pursuant to § 706(e) of Title VII, 42 U.S.C. § 2000e–5(e).

In each of the first eight counts of the twelve-count complaint, eight of the ten plaintiffs alleged that General Motors, Chevrolet Division, had engaged in unlawful employment practices by: 'discriminating against Negroes as regards promotions, terms and conditions of employment'; 'retaliating against Negro employees who protested actions made unlawful by Title VII of the Act and by discharging some because they protested said unlawful acts'; 'failing to hire Negro employees as a class on the basis of race'; 'failing to hire females as a class on the basis of sex'; 'discharging Negro employees on the basis of race'; and 'discriminating against Negroes and females in the granting of relief time.' Each additionally charged that the defendant Union had engaged in unlawful employment practices 'with respect to the granting of relief time to Negro and female employees' and 'by failing to pursue 6a grievances.' The remaining two plaintiffs made similar allegations against General Motors, Fisher Body Division. All of the individual plaintiffs requested injunctive relief, back pay, attorneys fees and costs. Counts XI and XII of the complaint were class action counts against the two individual divisions of General Motors. They also sought declaratory and injunctive relief, back pay, attorneys fees and costs.

Go Online

Note that the litigants had to obtain a notice of a right to sue from the EEOC before proceeding in federal district court. For more information on this process, visit the EEOC's website at http://www.eeoc.gov/employees/charge.cfm.

General Motors moved to strike portions of each count of the twelve-count complaint, to dismiss Counts XI and XII, to make portions of Counts I through XII more definite, to determine the propriety of Counts XI and XII as class actions, to limit the scope of the class purportedly represented, and to determine under which section of Rule 23 Counts XI and XII were maintainable as class actions. The district court ordered that 'insofar as the first ten counts are concerned, those ten counts shall be severed into ten separate causes of action,' and each plaintiff was directed to bring a separate action based upon his complaint, duly and separately filed. The court also ordered that the class action would not be dismissed, but rather would be left open 'to each of the plaintiffs herein, individually or collectively . . . to allege a separate cause of action on behalf of any class of persons which such plaintiff or plaintiffs may separately or individually represent.'

In reaching this conclusion on joinder, the district court followed the reasoning of _Smith v. North American Rockwell Corp., 50 F.R.D. 515 (N.D. Okla. 1970)_, which, in a somewhat analogous situation, found there was

Take Note!

Take note of the procedural motions made by General Motors here. We studied these motions in Chapter 6. What do you think GM's motivation is for seeking to have each plaintiff proceed individually? Wouldn't GM benefit from consolidated litigation, which presumably would be more cost effective?

no right to relief arising out of the same transaction, occurrence or series of transactions or occurrences, and that there was no question of law or fact common to all plaintiffs sufficient to sustain joinder under Federal Rule of Civil Procedure 20(a). Similarly, the district court here felt that the plaintiffs' joint actions against General Motors and the Union presented a variety of issues having little relationship to one another; that they had only one common problem, i.e. the defendant; and that as pleaded the joint actions were completely unmanageable. Upon entering the order, and upon application of the plaintiffs, the district court found that its decision involved a controlling question of law as to which there is a substantial ground for difference of opinion and that any of the parties might make application for appeal under 28 U.S.C. § 1292(b). We granted the application to permit this interlocutory appeal and for the following reasons we affirm in part and reverse in part.

Rule 20(a) of the Federal Rules of Civil Procedure provides:

> All persons may join in one action as plaintiffs if they assert any right to relief jointly, severally, or in the alternative in respect of or arising out of the same transaction, occurrence, or series of transactions or occurrences and if any question of law or fact common to all these persons will arise in the action . . .

Additionally, Rule 20(b) and Rule 42(b) vest in the district court the discretion to order separate trials or make such other orders as will prevent delay or prejudice. In this manner, the scope of the civil action is made a matter for the discretion of the district court, and a determination on the question of joinder of parties will be reversed on appeal only upon a showing of abuse of that discretion. To determine whether the district court's order was proper herein, we must look to the policy and law that have developed around the operation of Rule 20.

The purpose of the rule is to promote trial convenience and expedite the final determination of disputes, thereby preventing multiple lawsuits. 7 C. Wright, Federal Practice and Procedure § 1652 at 265 (1972). Single trials generally tend to lessen the delay, expense and inconvenience to all concerned. Reflecting this policy, the Supreme Court has said:

> Under the Rules, the impulse is toward entertaining the broadest possible scope of action consistent with fairness to the parties; joinder of claims, parties and remedies is strongly encouraged.

United Mine Workers of America v. Gibbs, 383 U.S. 715, 724 (1966).

Permissive joinder is not, however, applicable in all cases. The rule imposes two specific requisites to the joinder of parties: (1) a right to relief must be asserted by, or against, each plaintiff or defendant relating to or arising out of the same *transaction or occurrence, or series of transactions or occurrences*; and (2) some *question of law or fact common* to all the parties must arise in the action.

In ascertaining whether a particular factual situation constitutes a single transaction or occurrence for purposes of Rule 20, a case by case approach is generally pursued. No hard and fast rules have been established under the rule. However, construction of the terms 'transaction or occurrence' as used in the context of Rule 13(a) counterclaims offers some guide to the application of this test. For the purposes of the latter rule,

> "Transaction" is a word of flexible meaning. It may comprehend a series of many occurrences, depending not so much upon the immediateness of their connection as upon their logical relationship.

Moore v. New York Cotton Exchange, 270 U.S. 593, 610 (1926). Accordingly, all "logically related" events entitling a person to institute a legal action against another generally are regarded as comprising a transaction or occurrence. 7 C. Wright, Federal Practice and Procedure § 1653 at 270 (1972). The analogous interpretation of the terms as used in Rule 20 would permit all reasonably related claims for relief by or against different parties to be tried in a single proceeding. Absolute identity of all events is unnecessary.

This construction accords with the result reached in *United States v. Mississippi*, 380 U.S. 128 (1965) of which depended to a large extent upon "question(s) of law or fact common to all of them." The election commissioners, and six voting registrars of the State, charging them with engaging in acts and practices hampering and destroying the right of black citizens of Mississippi to vote. The district court concluded that the complaint improperly attempted to hold the six county registrars jointly liable for what amounted to nothing more than individual torts committed by them separately against separate applicants. In reversing, the Supreme Court said:

But the complaint charged that the registrars had acted and were continuing to act as part of a state-wide system designed to enforce the registration laws in a way that would inevitably deprive colored people of the right to vote solely because of their color. On such an allegation the joinder of all the registrars as defendants in a single suit is authorized by <u>Rule 20(a) of the Federal Rules of Civil Procedure</u>. . . . These registrars were alleged to be carrying on activities which were part of a series of transactions or occurrences the validity of which depended to a large extent upon 'question(s) of law or fact common to all of them.'

<u>Id.</u> at 142–143.

Here too, then, the plaintiffs have asserted a right to relief arising out of the same transactions or occurrences. Each of the ten plaintiffs alleged that he had been injured by the same general policy of discrimination on the part of General Motors and the Union. Since a 'state-wide system designed to enforce the registration laws in a way that would inevitably deprive colored people of the right to vote' was determined to arise out of the same series of transactions or occurrences, we conclude that a company-wide policy purportedly designed to discriminate against blacks in employment similarly arises out of the same series of transactions or occurrences. Thus the plaintiffs meet the first requisite for joinder under <u>Rule 20(a)</u>.

The second requisite necessary to sustain a permissive joinder under the rule is that a question of law or fact common to all the parties will arise in the action. The rule does not require that *all* questions of law and fact raised by the dispute be common. Yet, neither does it establish any qualitative or quantitative test of commonality. For this reason, cases construing the parallel requirement under <u>Federal Rule of Civil Procedure 23(a)</u> provide a helpful framework for construction of the commonality required by <u>Rule 20</u>. In general, those cases that have focused on <u>Rule 23(a)(2)</u> have given it a permissive application so that common questions have been found to exist in a wide range of context. 7 C. Wright, Federal Practice and Procedure § 1763 at 604 (1972). Specifically, with respect to employment discrimination cases under Title VII, courts have found that the discriminatory character of a defendant's conduct is basic to the class, and the fact that the individual class members may have suffered different effects from the alleged discrimination is immaterial for the purposes of the prerequisite. <u>Hicks v. Crown Zellerbach Corp.</u>, 49 F.R.D. 184, 187–88 (E.D. La. 1968). In this vein, one court has said:

Take Note!

Note that here and above the court refers to case law interpreting other rules (<u>Rules 13(a)</u> & <u>23(a)</u>) to aid in the interpretation of similar language used in <u>Rule 20</u>. Is this "intratextualist" approach to rule interpretation appropriate considering the different contexts of claim and party joinder?

Although the actual effects of a discriminatory policy may thus vary throughout the class, the existence of the discriminatory policy threatens the entire class. And whether the Damoclean threat of a racially discriminatory policy hangs over the racial class is a question of fact common to all the members of the class.

Hall v. Werthan Bag Corp., 251 F. Supp. 184, 186 (M.D. Tenn. 1966).

The right to relief here depends on the ability to demonstrate that each of the plaintiffs was wronged by racially discriminatory policies on the part of the defendants General Motors and the Union. The discriminatory character of the defendants' conduct is thus basic to each plaintiff's recovery. The fact that each plaintiff may have suffered different effects from the alleged discrimination is immaterial for the purposes of determining the common question of law or fact. Thus, we conclude that the second requisite for joinder under Rule 20(a) is also met by the complaint.

For the reasons set forth above, we conclude that the district court abused its discretion in severing the joined actions. The difficulties in ultimately adjudicating damages to the various plaintiffs are not so overwhelming as to require such severance. If appropriate, separate trials may be granted as to any particular issue after the determination of common questions.

The judgment of the district court disallowing joinder of the plaintiffs' individual actions is reversed and remanded with directions to permit the plaintiffs to proceed jointly. * * *

———————————

Points for Discussion

a.   The Holding in *Mosley*

Did the court in *Mosley* reach the right result regarding joinder? *Cf. Howard Motor Co. v. Swint*, 448 S.E.2d 713, 714 (Ga. App. 1994) (preventing five female employees asserting sexual harassment claims against the president of their employer from joining their claims under Georgia's similarly worded permissive joinder rule).

b.   The Requirements of Rule 20(a)

Although, as the *Mosley* court indicated, Rule 20(a) shares similar language with Rule 13(a), there is a difference in the standard articulated in Rule 20(a) for permitting party joinder. In addition to providing that claims asserted by or against the joined parties that arise out of the same transaction or occurrence can satisfy the first part of the rule, Rule 20(a) also permits party joinder when the asserted claims arise out of the same "series of transactions or occurrences." Does this language make Rule 20(a) broad-er than Rule 13(a), which lacks this language?

Note also that Rule 20(a) imposes an additional requirement beyond requiring a transactional relationship: the Rule adds that party joinder will be permitted only if "any question of law or fact common to all defendants will arise in the action." FED. R. CIV. P. 20(a). Does this additional limita-tion make the provision narrower than Rule 13(a)? What do you think accounts for the different language used in the two rules?

Take Note!

In 2011, the Supreme Court nar-rowed the meaning of a similar com-mon question requirement found in Rule 23, the class action rule. *Wal-Mart Stores, Inc. v. Dukes*, 564 U.S. 338 (2011) (requiring the common question to be one whose determi-nation "will resolve an issue that is central to the validity of each one of the claims in one stroke"). Should the *Wal-Mart* interpretation apply to common-question requirements found in other Federal Rules such as Rule 20?

c. Tactical Considerations and Permissive Joinder

General Motors opposed joinder of the plaintiffs in *Mosley*. Tactical consider-ations likely motivated GM to do this, even though consolidated litigation involving all of the claims may have been more efficient and cost effective. What do you think those tactical considerations were? What would have been the practical impact on the plaintiffs' claims had GM ultimately prevailed and the cases remained severed? How would severance of the claims affect GM and its ability to defend itself against those claims?

From a plaintiff's perspective, is it always going to be advantageous to proceed with other plaintiffs or against multiple defendants under Rule 20(a)? *See, e.g.*, *Dan-ner v. Anskis*, 256 F.2d 123 (3d Cir. 1958) (involving a driver and passenger of one car jointly suing the driver of another car that rear-ended them, followed by an attempted crossclaim by the passenger of the first car against her co-plaintiff, the driver of the first car). What advantages are there to plaintiffs who join with others or who assert their claims against multiple defendants in a single action?

d. Severance Under Rule 21 & Separate Trials Under Rule 20(b)

In the event that the judge in a case feels that the Rule 20 joinder attempted by the plaintiff is improper, that judge is empowered by Rule 21 to sever the claims so that they may proceed separately. *See* FED. R. CIV. P. 21 ("On motion or on its own, the court may at any time, on just terms, add or drop a party. The court may also sever any claim against a party."). Note also that, as the court in *Mosley* pointed out, Rule 20(b) permits courts to order separate trials to avoid any undue expense, delay, or prejudice that might come from the joinder proposed by parties in an action. Rule 42(b) contains a similar provision.

e. Consolidation Under Rule 42(a)

Take a look at <u>Rule 42(a)</u>, a rule that permits a court to consolidate related multiple actions pending before it (or within the same federal judicial district) into a single action. How do the standards governing the permissibility of consolidation under <u>Rule 42(a)</u> differ from the standards for permissive party joinder under <u>Rule 20(a)</u>? Why do you think these rules employ different standards for what appears to be a similar joinder device?

----

2. Third-Party Practice

<u>Rule 20</u> enables plaintiffs to shape the litigation by determining whether to assert their claims along with others or to assert their claims against multiple defendants within a single action. Defendants are afforded the opportunity to join parties to the litigation through Rule 14, which provides for the joinder of and assertion of claims against nonparties:

<u>FRCP 14(a)(1)</u>. Third-Party Practice.

(a) When a Defending Party May Bring in a Third Party.

(1) *Timing of the Summons and Complaint.* A defending party may, as third-party plaintiff, serve a summons and complaint on a nonparty who is or may be liable to it for all or part of the claim against it. But the third-party plaintiff must, by motion, obtain the court's leave if it files the third-party complaint more than 14 days after serving its original answer.

Joinder by defendants under this rule is referred to as impleader. **Figure 7.2** illustrates, in the abstract, the arrangement of parties when a defendant impleads a nonparty into the action under Rule 14.

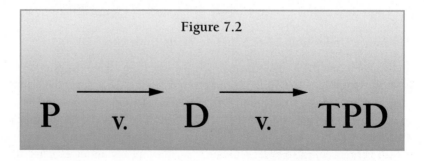

Figure 7.2

P v. D v. TPD

Note the placement of the newly joined party, who formerly was a nonparty and now is referred to as the "third-party defendant." The third-party defendant creates a new adversarial relationship between it and the original defendant but is not opposed to the original plaintiff as a coparty with the original defendant. The next case demonstrates how Rule 14 is used by parties and interpreted by the courts.

Lehman v. Revolution Portfolio L.L.C.

<u>U.S. Court of Appeals for the First Circuit</u>
<u>166 F.3d 389 (1st Cir. 1999)</u>

SELYA, CIRCUIT JUDGE.

This appeal grows out of a triangular 1987 financial transaction that involved the Farm Street Trust (the Trust), its beneficiaries (Barry Lehman and Stuart A. Roffman), and First Mutual Bank for Savings (the Bank). In the ensuing eleven years, the transaction imploded, litigation commenced, the Bank and Lehman became insolvent, parties came and went, and the case was closed and partially reopened. In the end, only a third-party complaint proved ripe for adjudication. Even then, the district court dismissed two of its three counts, but entered summary judgment on the remaining count. The third-party defendant, Roffman, now appeals. After sorting through the muddled record and the case's serpentine procedural history, we affirm.

I. BACKGROUND

The historical facts are not seriously disputed. On or about October 19, 1987, the Trust, acting through its trustee, executed a promissory note for $2,800,000 in favor of the Bank in order to fund the purchase of property in Dover, Massachusetts. Lehman and Roffman, each of whom enjoyed a 50% beneficial interest in the Trust, personally guaranteed the note, and Lehman proffered two parcels of real estate as additional collateral. In short order, the Trust defaulted on the loan and the Bank foreclosed on Lehman's properties. Lehman responded by suing the Bank in a Massachusetts state court seeking restraint or rescission of the imminent sale of his real estate. The gravamen of

Take Note!

Try to keep track of what has happened here. On what grounds is Lehman, who is a guarantor of the debt owed to the Bank, suing the Bank to prevent it from collecting on the collateral? What is Lehman alleging that the Bank did wrong?

his suit was a claim that Roffman had fraudulently introduced a sham investor to the Bank in order to gull it into making the loan, and that the Bank, in swallowing this spurious bait hook, line, and sinker, had failed to exercise due diligence.

Roughly one year after answering the complaint, the Bank failed. The Bank was a federally-insured financial institution. Consequently, the <u>Federal Deposit Insurance Corporation</u> (FDIC), acting as receiver under <u>12 U.S.C. § 1821(c)(3)(A)</u>, removed the action to the federal district court and successfully asked to be substituted as defendant. Six months later, it moved for leave to amend its answer to include a counterclaim against Lehman, *qua* guarantor, for the outstanding loan balance. At the same time, it moved for leave to serve a third-party complaint against Roffman. A magistrate judge granted the motion to amend on July 14, 1992, and granted the impleader motion on January 21, 1993.

It's Latin to Me!

Qua is a Latin term meaning "as" or "in the capacity of."

The FDIC's third-party complaint contained three counts. The first two sought indemnification and contribution, respectively, in regard to the claims advanced by Lehman. The third sought judgment against Roffman, *qua* guarantor, for the outstanding loan balance.

After Roffman answered the third-party complaint, the FDIC moved for summary judgment. Roffman not only objected, but also moved to strike the third-party complaint in its entirety. The FDIC opposed that motion. Meanwhile, Lehman entered bankruptcy and requested a stay of proceedings in the civil suit. [The district court dismissed Lehman's action without prejudice, indicating that the parties were free to reinstate the case after completion of the bankruptcy.]

Eight months later, and periodically thereafter during the next few years, the FDIC's counsel wrote to the district court soliciting action in respect to its summary judgment motion. * * * Judge Wolf * * * set a motions hearing (presumably encompassing both the FDIC's summary judgment motion and Roffman's related motion to strike). At that hearing, rescheduled and eventually held on April 28, 1998, the court entered an order reinstating the third-party complaint. It simultaneously denied Roffman's motion to strike, granted the FDIC's motion for *brevis* disposition on count 3, and dismissed the remainder of the third-party complaint without prejudice. On June 1, 1998, Roffman filed a notice of appeal.

What's That?

The term "*brevis* disposition" simply is another way that courts sometimes refer to an abbreviated resolution of a case via summary judgment.

Later the same month, the FDIC moved to substitute Revolution Portfolio LLC (RP) as the real party in interest, averring that it previously had assigned its interest in certain of the Bank's assets (including the Trust's indebtedness and Roffman's guaranty) to RP. Roffman timely filed an opposition. He also moved for relief from the April 28 judgment, see FED.R.CIV.P. 60(b) asserting that the district court, at the time it entered summary judgment, did not have the real party in interest before it. The court granted the motion to substitute, see FED.R.CIV.P. 25(c) and denied the motion for relief from judgment. Roffman did not file a second notice of appeal at that juncture.

II. DISCUSSION

Roffman asseverates that the district court never should have reopened the case in the first place; that, even if the court appropriately reinstated the third party complaint, it erred in entertaining the third-party complaint and granting summary judgment on count 3; and that the court impermissibly permitted an untimely substitution of parties. We consider these arguments *seriatim*.

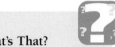

What's That?

Asseverate means to assert seriously or positively.

A. Reinstatement.

* * *

* * * Judge Wolf opted to reopen the case to permit litigation of the third-party complaint after the FDIC's repeated correspondence brought the matter to his attention and further study convinced him that he had swept too broadly in closing the entire file. This decision falls comfortably within the realm of the court's discretion * * * . Hence, we uphold the district court's reinstatement order.

B. Joinder.

Resolution of the reinstatement question only begins the work of disentangling the imbricated strands of Roffman's appeal. We next must answer the question whether the FDIC's deployment of a third-party complaint against Roffman was proper. In this regard, Roffman asserts that the district court should not have entertained the impleader, and that, therefore, the joined claim on the guaranty should fall of its own weight. We review a district court's decision to permit the filing of a third-party complaint under FED.R.CIV.P. 14(a) for abuse of discretion.

As previously explained, the FDIC impleaded Roffman as a third-party defendant on theories of indemnification and contribution (counts 1 and 2, respectively), maintaining, in essence, that if it were found to be liable to Lehman, then Roffman would in turn be liable to hold it harmless or, at least, contribute to any damages assessed against it. In the same pleading, the FDIC asserted an independent claim for the outstanding loan balance, premised on Roffman's guaranty (count 3). RP (which now stands in the FDIC's shoes) acknowledges that the FDIC could not have brought count 3 as a stand-alone third-party claim under Rule 14(a), but asserts that count 3 was validly joined with counts 1 and 2 under FED.R.CIV.P. 18(a) (providing for permissive joinder). To parry this thrust, Roffman contends that the FDIC's claims for indemnification and contribution were not viable under state law, and thus, since the use of Rule 14(a) admittedly hinged on the propriety of those claims, the FDIC should not have been allowed to implead him at all.

Food for Thought

RP acknowledged that count 3, the action against Roffman as guarantor for the loan balance, could not by itself have been asserted as a third-party claim under Rule 14(a). Why do you think this is so?

We doubt that Roffman has preserved this argument inasmuch as he did not raise it below in his opposition to the FDIC's summary judgment motion. *See Teamsters, Chauffeurs, Warehousemen & Helpers Union, Local No. 59 v. Superline Transp. Co., 953 F.2d 17, 21 (1st Cir.1992)* ("If any principle is settled in this circuit, it is that, absent the most extraordinary circumstances, legal theories not raised squarely in the lower court cannot be broached for the first time on appeal."). We prefer not to inquire into this apparent waiver, however, for we conclude, without serious question, that the FDIC was entitled to implead Roffman under Rule 14(a) and that it appropriately joined the guaranty claim under Rule 18(a).

A defendant, acting as a third-party plaintiff, may implead any non-party "who is or may be liable to the third-party plaintiff for all or part of the plaintiff's claim against the third-party plaintiff." FED.R.CIV.P. 14(a) (emphasis supplied). If the defendant acts within ten days of submitting his answer, he may bring a third party into the suit without leave of court. Otherwise, the court's permission must be obtained.[6] In that event, the determination is left to the informed discretion of the district court, which should allow impleader on any colorable claim of derivative liability that will not unduly delay or otherwise prejudice the ongoing proceedings. Under this liberal standard, a party accused of passive negligence (here, the FDIC) assuredly is entitled to implead the party who allegedly committed the relevant active conduct (here, Roffman) on a theory of indemnification.

The FDIC's third-party claim for contribution against Roffman similarly passes muster because Roffman and the Bank (the FDIC's predecessor in interest) were putative joint tortfeasors (i.e., according to the complaint, Roffman's fraudulent acts

---

[6] In this case, the FDIC obtained leave of court through an order duly entered by a magistrate judge. Roffman did not appeal that order to the district judge within the time prescribed by law, and thus cannot be heard to complain about it here.

combined with the Bank's negligent omissions to create harm). See Mass. Gen. Laws ch. 231B, § 1(a) (1986) (providing a right of contribution among persons who are jointly liable in tort for the same injury); see also Wolfe v. Ford Motor Co., 386 Mass. 95, 100, 434 N.E.2d 1008 (1982) (allowing contribution even though the two joint tortfeasors were liable under different theories of tort liability).

To be sure, Roffman argues that because Lehman's complaint sought only restraint or rescission of the property sales, and not damages, a third-party claim for contribution should not lie. But this argument gains him no ground. Even though Lehman's complaint did not explicitly seek money damages, that omission did not eliminate the possibility that damages might be awarded to him. See FED.R.CIV.P. 54(c) (providing that "every final judgment [except those by default] shall grant the relief to which the party in whose favor it is rendered is entitled, even if the party has not demanded such relief in the party's pleadings"). Rule 54(c) is particularly apt in this situation, for a party may pray for rescission and be entitled to it, yet only receive damages. As long as damages may be awarded in lieu of rescission, impleader properly may be used to seek contribution toward those potential damages. It follows inexorably that the district court did not err in denying Roffman's motion to strike and allowing the FDIC's Rule 14(a) claims to stand.

Against this backdrop, the court properly assumed jurisdiction over count 3 of the third-party complaint. Rule 18(a) authorizes a third-party plaintiff to "join, either as independent or as alternative claims, as many claims, legal, equitable, or maritime, as the [third-party plaintiff] has against an opposing party." This authorization is subject only to the usual requirements of jurisdiction and venue (none of which are implicated here) and the district court's discretionary power to "direct an appropriate procedure for trying the claims." Given Rule 18(a)'s broad expanse, misjoinder of claims has become an anachronism in federal civil practice.

In this instance, Roffman signed an unconditional personal guaranty of a loan, and the borrower later defaulted. As a holder in due course of the note, the FDIC had an independent claim for the outstanding balance against Roffman. There is absolutely no reason why the FDIC could not append its independent claim on the guaranty to its other claims against Roffman.

Make the Connection

A *holder in due course* is one who has given value for a negotiable instrument that appears complete and regular on its face. This is a concept you will study further if you take a course on **Commercial Paper**. It is also a concept that is typically tested on state bar exams.

As a fallback position, Roffman suggests that the third-party complaint against him should have been dismissed because the FDIC had a complete defense under

12 U.S.C. § 1823(e) (1994) to the claims brought by Lehman.[7] We do not agree. Even if section 1823(e) offered the FDIC a potentially strong defense against Lehman's claims, the record fails to show that the mere existence of that statute rendered Lehman's complaint a nullity.

There is, moreover, a broader point. A district court must oversee third-party practice with the core purpose of Rule 14(a) in mind: avoiding unnecessary duplication and circuity of action. Requiring a district court to determine the merits of all defenses potentially available to the original defendant as a precondition to allowing that defendant to file a third-party complaint would frustrate this purpose and countervail the efficient allocation of judicial resources. Thus, as long as a third-party action falls within the general contours limned by Rule 14(a), does not contravene customary jurisdictional and venue requirements, and will not work unfair prejudice, a district court should not preclude its prosecution. So here. [The court went on to affirm summary judgment on count 3 and held that it lacked jurisdiction to hear Roffman's challenge to the substitution of parties.]

Take Note!

Note the court's reference to the core purpose of Rule 14(a). Wouldn't the same purpose justify a more broadly written Rule 14(a) that permitted more than derivative liability claims? Why do you think Rule 14(a) is so limited?

Points for Discussion

a. Permissible Claims Under Rule 14(a)

What types of claims may defendants assert under Rule 14(a)? What relationship must those claims have with the claim being asserted against the defendant? Notice that Rule 14(a) does not permit the assertion of claims simply based on being part of the same transaction or occurrence as the original claim, the standard in some of the other joinder rules. Why do you

Take Note!

If a defendant seeks to implead a nonparty under Rule 14 more than 14 days after serving its original answer, it must first obtain the court's permission.

---

[7] The statute that Roffman mentions reflects the Court's decision in *D'Oench, Duhme & Co. v. FDIC*, 315 U.S. 447 (1942), and prohibits a litigant from relying upon any agreement that tends to diminish or defeat the interest of the FDIC in any asset acquired by it from a failed bank, unless the agreement was written, executed contemporaneously with the bank's acquisition of the asset, approved by the bank's board of directors or loan committee, reflected in the bank's minutes, and continuously maintained as an official record.

think Rule 14(a) has been written with narrower criteria than the transaction-or-occurrence standard?

b. Subsequent Joinder Under Rule 14

Under what circumstances may third-party defendants assert claims against the third-party plaintiff or the original plaintiff? Rule 14(a) addresses this issue as well:

FRCP 14(a)(2). Third-Party Practice:
Third-Party Defendant's Claims and Defenses.

(a)   When a Defending Party May Bring in a Third Party. * * *

(2)   *Third-Party Defendant's Claims and Defenses.* The person served with the summons and third-party complaint—the "third-party defendant":

(A)   must assert any defense against the third-party plaintiff's claim under Rule 12;

(B)   must assert any counterclaim against the third-party plaintiff under Rule 13(a), and may assert any counterclaim against the third-party plaintiff under Rule 13(b) or any crossclaim against another third-party defendant under Rule 13(g);

(C)   may assert against the plaintiff any defense that the third-party plaintiff has to the plaintiff's claim; and

(D)   may also assert against the plaintiff any claim arising out of the transaction or occurrence that is the subject matter of the plaintiff's claim against the third-party plaintiff.

What happens if the third-party defendant avails itself of the opportunity to assert a claim against the plaintiff as provided in Rule 14(a); how may the plaintiff respond? May the plaintiff assert counterclaims under Rule 13? Third-party claims under Rule 14(a)? Even if the third-party defendant does not assert any claims against the plaintiff, Rule 14(a) states, "The plaintiff may assert any claim against the third-party defendant arising out of the transaction or occurrence that is the subject matter of the plaintiff's claim against the third-party plaintiff." FED. R. CIV. P. 14(a)(3).

Take Note!

Notice that the joinder rules must be considered as a whole because once one party asserts a claim under a rule that may permit her adversary to assert various claims under other rules, which in turn could permit still other parties to assert further claims. This process can become quite convoluted, so diagramming the parties and ensuing claims can be helpful.

In the background of all of this, you must keep in mind Rule 18(a). As was shown in *Lehman*, once a party is able to assert a claim by satisfying the requirements of a particular joinder rule, that party may then assert any additional claims it has—related or unrelated—under Rule 18(a). Thus, it is important not to forget this possibility in the event that joinder of a claim under another rule will not work. **Hypo 7.3** illustrates this point.

Hypo 7.3

Parker (MA) asserted a claim against Douglass (VT) for negligence in causing an automobile accident. Douglass asserted a third-party claim against Tina (VT) seeking contribution on the negligence claim against him. Parker then asserted a claim against Tina for negligence in the same accident that was the basis for his claim against Douglass. Parker also asserted a claim against Tina seeking damages for an unrelated breach of contract. Do the Federal Rules allow Douglass to assert his claim against Tina? May Parker assert his claims against Tina under the Federal Rules?

---

c. Subject Matter Jurisdiction and Third-Party Claims

A constant theme throughout the joinder material has been the distinction between joinder rules and rules governing jurisdiction. Thus, even though joinder may be permissible under the joinder rules, it is still necessary to consider separately whether there is proper subject matter jurisdiction and personal jurisdiction over the claims and parties sought to be joined.

How will subject matter jurisdiction questions generally be resolved in the case of third-party claims, given the relationship such claims must have with original claims and given the language of the federal supplemental jurisdiction statute, 28 U.S.C. § 1367? See, e.g., *Grimes v. Mazda N. Am. Operations*, 355 F.3d 566, 572 (6th Cir. 2004) ("It is well settled that supplemental jurisdiction exists over a properly brought third-party complaint."). As noted above, plaintiffs may assert claims against third-party defendants under Rule 14(a) provided there is a basis for subject matter jurisdiction. What does the supplemental jurisdiction statute have to say about such claims by plaintiffs?

Remember that even though third-party claims will enjoy supplemental jurisdiction, additional joined claims under Rule 18(a)—such as was present in *Lehman*—require their own subject matter jurisdiction analysis in light of the fact that such claims need not bear any relationship to the claims to which they are joined. **Hypo 7.4** gives you an opportunity to deal with these issues.

Hypo 7.4

Same facts as Hypo 7.3. Parker (MA) seeks $100,000 in damages in his negligence claim against Douglass (VT), while Douglass seeks $50,000 in contribution from Tina (VT) on his third-party claim. Parker seeks $100,000 in damages on his negligence claim against Tina and $25,000 in damages on the breach of contract claim. The action is brought in Vermont federal district court. Does the court have subject matter jurisdiction over each of these claims?

d. The Real Party in Interest Rule

In *Lehman*, the FDIC substituted a different party for itself as the real party in interest in its action against Roffman. Rule 17(a) requires that "[a]n action must be prosecuted in the name of the real party in interest." FED. R. CIV. P. 17(a)(1). What made Revolution Portfolio LLC—the substituted party in this case—the real party in interest rather than the FDIC? Why do you think it is important to substitute Revolution Portfolio as the real party in interest? Whose interests do you think Rule 17(a) protects, those of the real party in interest or those of the defendant here, Mr. Roffman? What would happen in the event that Revolution Portfolio were not substituted as the proper party here; could it subsequently come along and initiate an action against Roffman seeking recovery against him as guarantor on the debt? Note that under Rule 17(a)(3), "The court may not dismiss an action for failure to prosecute in the name of the real party in interest until, after an objection, a reasonable time has been allowed for the real party in interest ratify, join, or be substituted into the action."

Does Rule 17(a) also apply to defendants, requiring that defendants identify and join parties that should be viewed as the real party in interest on the defendant's side of the action? The Supreme Court has said no. *Lincoln Prop. Co. v. Roche*, 546 U.S. 81, 91 (2005) ("Rule 17(a) applies only to joinder of parties who assert claims . . . .").

e. Fourth-Party Claims Under Rule 14(a)

Can a third-party defendant make use of Rule 14(a) to turn around and assert a derivative liability claim against a fourth-party? *See* FED. R. CIV. P. 14(a)(5) ("A third-party defendant may proceed under this rule against a nonparty who is or may be liable to the third-party defendant for all or part of any claim against it."); *see also Bank of India v. Trendi Sportswear, Inc.*, 239 F.3d 428 (2d Cir. 2000) (discussing a fourth-party claim).

---

3. Compulsory Party Joinder

Thus far we have considered mechanisms by which the parties may join additional parties to the action if they so choose. Under certain circumstances, however, whether a nonparty should be joined is not a matter of choice but one of compulsion. Such compulsory party joinder is provided for in Rule 19. The rule consists of two parts. First, Rule 19(a) sets forth the criteria for determining whether a party is "needed for just adjudication," a status that would make it a necessary party in the common parlance under the rule:

FRCP 19(a). Required Joinder of Parties.

(a) Persons Required to Be Joined if Feasible.

(1) *Required Party.* A person who is subject to service of process and whose joinder will not deprive the court of subject-matter jurisdiction must be joined as a party if:

(A) in that person's absence, the court cannot accord complete relief among existing parties; or

(B) that person claims an interest relating to the subject of the action and is so situated that disposing of the action in the person's absence may:

(i) as a practical matter impair or impede the person's ability to protect the interest; or

(ii) leave an existing party subject to a substantial risk of incurring double, multiple, or otherwise inconsistent obligations because of the interest.

(2) *Joinder by Court Order.* If a person has not been joined as required, the court must order that the person be made a party. A person who refuses to join as a plaintiff may be made either a defendant or, in a proper case, an involuntary plaintiff.

(3) *Venue.* If a joined party objects to venue and the joinder would make venue improper, the court must dismiss that party.

Second, if a person is determined to be a required party under Rule 19(a), Rule 19(b) governs the determination of whether the action may proceed in the required party's absence. Before considering Rule 19(b), however, let us take a look at a case that illustrates how Rule 19(a) is used to make necessary party determinations.

MasterCard International v. Visa International Service Ass'n

U.S. Court of Appeals for the Second Circuit
471 F.3d 377 (2d Cir. 2006)

POOLER, CIRCUIT JUDGE.

Non-party movant-appellant Visa International Service Association ("Visa") moved to dismiss the underlying action contending that it is a necessary and indispensable party under Federal Rule of Civil Procedure 19. Visa also moved to intervene in the action under Federal Rule of Civil Procedure 24. Both motions were denied by the United States District Court for the Southern District of New York. The district court concluded that Visa was neither necessary nor indispensable to the underlying breach of contract action between plaintiff-appellee MasterCard International Incorporated ("MasterCard") and defendant Fédération Internationale de Football Association ("FIFA"). The district court further concluded that Visa failed to satisfy the conditions for intervention under Rule 24.

BACKGROUND

FIFA is the worldwide governing body of soccer (or football, as it is known outside the United States), and the organizer of the World Cup soccer tournament held every four years. The underlying lawsuit is a breach of contract action brought by MasterCard against FIFA seeking enforcement of an alleged contractual provision giving MasterCard "first right to acquire" exclusive sponsorship rights in its product category for the FIFA World Cup event in 2010 and 2014. * * *

* * * On March 30, 2006, MasterCard learned that FIFA had decided to finalize an agreement with Visa. On April 5, 2006, MasterCard received a letter from FIFA's president stating that FIFA had entered into a contract with Visa granting Visa the exclusive sponsorship rights to FIFA competitions, including the World Cup, through 2014 ("the Visa Contract"). The Visa Contract becomes effective January 1, 2007. Upon learning of the FIFA-Visa deal, MasterCard notified both FIFA and Visa that it considered FIFA's actions a violation of the right of first refusal provision in the MasterCard Contract and MasterCard would seek legal redress if FIFA went forward with the Visa Contract.

What's That?

A *right of first refusal* is the right of a potential contracting party to meet the terms of a third party's offer and enter into the contract itself.

On April 10, 2006, Visa issued a press release announcing its contract with FIFA for exclusive sponsorship rights in the World Cup through 2014. On April 20, 2006, MasterCard filed suit in the Southern District of New York for breach of contract and sought injunctive relief "enjoining FIFA from consummating, effectuating or performing" any terms of the Visa Contract and ordering FIFA to perform its obligations under the alleged contract granting MasterCard exclusive rights through 2014. Federal jurisdiction is premised solely on diversity of citizenship.

On June 15, 2006, MasterCard filed a motion for a preliminary injunction. After FIFA's motion to dismiss for lack of personal jurisdiction and motion to compel arbitration were both denied, the district court scheduled the preliminary injunction hearing for September 18, 2006, and later adjourned it to September 26, 2006. Email communication produced in this case indicates that Visa has been in contact with FIFA regarding this litigation since the time it was filed. On September 11, 2006, two weeks before the preliminary injunction hearing, Visa sent a letter to the district court stating that it was a necessary and indispensable party to the litigation because of its contractual entitlement to the FIFA sponsorship rights. Visa claimed that because it was an indispensable party, the case must be dismissed for lack of subject matter jurisdiction. Since MasterCard and Visa are both incorporated under the laws of Delaware, Visa's joinder would destroy diversity jurisdiction—the sole basis for federal jurisdiction.

Make the Connection

Subject matter jurisdiction was covered in Chapter 3. Be sure you understand how the addition of Visa as a defendant in this action would undermine diversity jurisdiction, which in turn would require the dismissal of the entire action.

The district court construed Visa's letter submission as a motion to dismiss under Federal Rule of Civil Procedure 19 and scheduled a hearing for September 21, 2006. At the conclusion of that hearing, the district court denied Visa's motion, finding that Visa was not a necessary party under Rule 19(a), and even assuming that it were, Visa was not an indispensable party under Rule 19(b) requiring dismissal of the action ("Rule 19 Order"). The district court reasoned that because the underlying litigation involved the MasterCard Contract and whether FIFA had breached that contract, Visa's presence was unnecessary to decide the dispute between Master-Card and FIFA. Moreover, even if MasterCard prevailed in this lawsuit, Visa's right to sue FIFA for breach of the warranty provision in the Visa Contract would not be prejudiced. Finally, since Visa conceded that it had no knowledge of the negotiations between MasterCard and FIFA or the MasterCard Contract, it would have nothing to contribute to the outcome of that lawsuit. Thus, the district court found that the case could proceed without Visa. [The district court also denied Visa's motion to intervene under Rule 24; the appeal of both denials ensued.]

* * *

II. Rule 19 Order

We review the district court's failure to join a party under Rule 19 only for abuse of discretion. * * * A party is "necessary" under Rule 19 if:

(1) in the person's absence complete relief cannot be accorded among those already parties, or (2) the person claims an interest relating to the subject of the action and is so situated that the disposition of the action in the person's absence may (i) as a practical matter impair or impede the person's ability to protect that interest or (ii) leave any of the persons already par-

ties subject to a substantial risk of incurring double, multiple, or otherwise inconsistent obligations by reason of the claimed interest.

Fed.R.Civ.P. 19(a). Visa contends that it fits within all three of these categories. We disagree.

A. Rule 19(a)(1)[*]

A party is necessary under Rule 19(a)(1) only if in that party's absence "complete relief cannot be accorded among *those already parties.*" Fed.R.Civ.P. 19(a)(1) (emphasis added). Visa's absence will not prevent the district court from granting complete relief between MasterCard and FIFA. Visa argues that without it in the case, MasterCard can receive only partial relief because Visa still holds contractual rights to the sponsorship rights and will file suit against FIFA to enforce the Visa Contract. While there is no question that further litigation between Visa and FIFA, and perhaps MasterCard and Visa, is inevitable if MasterCard prevails in this lawsuit, Rule 19(a)(1) is concerned only with those who are already parties. MasterCard can obtain complete relief *as to FIFA* without Visa's presence in the case. If MasterCard prevails and is granted its requested relief, FIFA will be enjoined from awarding the sponsorship rights to another party, including Visa. This will resolve the dispute between MasterCard and FIFA, and Visa's presence is unnecessary to decide those questions. Thus, Visa is not a necessary party under Rule 19(a)(1).

B. Rule 19(a)(2)(i)

We find no abuse of discretion in the district court's conclusion that Visa was not a necessary party under Rule 19(a)(2)(i). Visa claims that because MasterCard seeks to enjoin FIFA from performing the Visa Contract, its interests are clearly implicated and it is therefore entitled to appear in this litigation. Visa relies primarily on this court's decision in *Crouse-Hinds Co. v. InterNorth, Inc.*, 634 F.2d 690 (2d Cir.1980), which it characterizes as controlling here. In *Crouse-Hinds*, the defendant asserted a counterclaim alleging that a proposed merger between the plaintiff and a third party, Belden, was unfair under the business judgment rule because it lacked any legitimate business purpose and was entered into solely to defeat the defendant's tender offer. The counterclaim sought to enjoin the merger. On appeal of the district court's grant of a preliminary injunction, this court noted its disagreement with the district court's conclusion that Belden was not a necessary party to the action because "Belden's rights [under the merger agreement] would clearly be prejudiced if the relief sought by InterNorth were to be granted." *Id.* at 700–01 (citing *Lomay-ahtewa v. Hathaway*, 520 F.2d 1324, 1325 (9th Cir. 1975) ("No procedural principle is more deeply imbedded in the common law than that, in an action to set aside a

---

[*] The numbering employed in this opinion predates the renumbering of Rule 19 that occurred in 2007. Rule 19(a)(1) referred to here is now Rule 19(a)(2)(i)(A). Former Rule 19(a)(1)(B)(i) and former Rule 19(a)(2)(ii) is now Rule 19(a)(1)(B)(ii). [Ed.]

lease or a contract, all parties who may be affected by the determination of the action are indispensable.")).

Visa's reliance on this case is misplaced. In *Crouse-Hinds*, the actual contract involving the absent third party was the basis of the claim. The counterclaim specifically challenged the validity of the merger agreement and sought to set aside that agreement. If the defendant prevailed on this counterclaim, the merger agreement would be deemed invalid, which would presumably affect Belden's ability to then sue for breach of that agreement or invoke any of the protections in that agreement. Thus, non-party Belden was faced with the possibility of having its contract terminated in its absence. In contrast, in this case, while the Visa Contract may be affected by this litigation, it is not the contract at issue in MasterCard's lawsuit. The underlying litigation involves the MasterCard Contract and whether MasterCard had a right of first refusal to the World Cup sponsorship rights. Even if MasterCard prevails and receives the relief it seeks, that does not render the Visa Contract invalid. It means that FIFA likely has breached the warranty provision of that contract, and Visa has the right to sue FIFA for that breach.

Furthermore, in *Crouse-Hinds*, because the absent non-party was a party to the contract at issue, its ability to protect its interest in that contract would have been seriously impaired if it were not made a party to the action. This places the absentee non-party in *Crouse-Hinds* in a distinctly different position from Visa, whose contract with FIFA is not at issue here. As the district court correctly found, Visa's ability to protect its interest in its contract with FIFA will not be impaired if it is not joined here. The primary flaw in Visa's argument is that it has construed Rule 19(a)(2)(i) to extend to any party whose interests would be impaired or impeded by a litigation. This overlooks a key element of the definition of "necessary" party under Rule 19(a)(2)(i). It is not enough under Rule 19(a)(2)(i) for a third party to have an interest, even a very strong interest, in the litigation. Nor is it enough for a third party to be adversely affected by the outcome of the litigation. Rather, necessary parties under Rule 19(a)(2)(i) are only those parties whose ability to protect their interests would be impaired *because of that party's absence from the litigation. See* Fed.R.Civ.P. 19(a) (2) (defining necessary party as one with an "interest relating to the subject of the action and is so situated that the disposition of the action *in the person's absence may* . . . as a practical matter impair or impede the person's ability to protect that interest" (emphasis added)). Thus, while Visa may have an interest that would be impaired by the outcome of this litigation, Visa still does not qualify as a necessary party under Rule 19(a)(2)(i) because the harm Visa may suffer is *not caused by Visa's absence* from this litigation. Any such harm would result from FIFA's alleged conduct in awarding Visa sponsorship rights. We would be significantly broadening both Rule 19(a)(2)(i) and the principle discussed in *Crouse-Hinds* if we found that because the outcome of this case may impact a separate contract involving a different party, that finding would transform the action into "an action to set aside a lease or a contract." *Crouse-Hinds,* 634 F.2d at 701 (quoting *Lomayaktewa,*

520 F.2d at 1325]. *Crouse-Hinds* involved an actual action to set aside a contract; here we have an action that could in the future impact a third party's rights under a separate contract. We, therefore, do not find *Crouse-Hinds* controlling here and decline to broaden its scope to reach the facts before us, particularly since doing so would read a key element out of the text of Rule 19(a)(2)(i).

Visa also relies on several cases that recite the general proposition that a party who claims title to a piece of property that is the subject of an action has sufficient interest in the action to justify compulsory joinder, and urges us to follow that reasoning here. Visa attempts to characterize this case as if it were a proceeding to determine the rightful owner of a piece of property to which MasterCard and Visa have competing claims. While we have held in cases involving this factual scenario that all claimants to the property at issue are necessary parties to the action, see, e.g., *Brody v. Village of Port Chester*, 345 F.3d 103, 117–19 (2d Cir.2003) (holding that in action by property owner to recover land taken by eminent domain, current titleholder to land might be necessary party if district court were to restore land to plaintiff); *Kulawy v. United States*, 917 F.2d 729, 736 (2d Cir.1990) (holding that in an action to quiet title by aggrieved tax payer against government seeking to recover automobiles sold to satisfy tax lien, purchasers of automobiles were necessary parties), we do not find this reasoning applicable here. In *Brody* and *Kulawy*, the district courts were required to determine who among several parties had title to a piece of property. Thus, the district court could not grant the relief sought—declaring the plaintiff the titleholder—in the absence of the current or competing titleholders to that piece of property. As Master-Card correctly notes, the MasterCard-FIFA dispute is not an *in rem* proceeding between competing claimants with the district court tasked with deciding who has superior rights to a piece of property. The district court need only decide whether MasterCard has a right of first refusal under its prior contract with FIFA. While this has the *effect* of determining who will get the sponsorship rights, that does not transform this case into an *in rem* proceeding nor does it place Visa in the same position as MasterCard as a competing claimant. Unfortunately for Visa, there is nothing it can do about the fact that MasterCard's prior contractual rights with FIFA may preclude FIFA's ability to grant the sponsorship rights to Visa. Visa's problems here are due to FIFA's alleged actions, not Visa's absence from this litigation. Nor will its absence prevent Visa from seeking the only remedy available to it if MasterCard indeed has a right of first refusal to the sponsorship rights: Visa can sue FIFA for breach of the warranty provision in the Visa Contract. For these reasons, we find the district court properly rejected Visa's contention that it is a necessary party under Rule 19(a)(2)(i).

C. Rule 19(a)(2)(ii)

The district court's conclusion that Visa does not satisfy Rule 19(a)(2)(ii) is also not an abuse of discretion. Visa presents us with the following scenario: MasterCard prevails in the underlying lawsuit and is granted injunctive relief that prohibits FIFA from performing its obligations under the Visa Contract; Visa then sues FIFA for breach of the warranty provision in the Visa Contract seeking specific performance; Visa prevails and is granted specific performance requiring FIFA to perform its obligations under the Visa Contract. According to Visa, the possibility exists that FIFA could be under court order to perform the Visa Contract and under court order not to perform the Visa Contract, and this potential for inconsistent obligations renders Visa a necessary party to this litigation. Once again, Visa is ignoring a critical element in Rule 19(a)(2)(ii): the substantial risk of inconsistent obligations must be *caused by* the nonparty's absence in the case. *See* Fed.R.Civ.P. 19(a)(2) (defining necessary party as one with an interest related to the action who "is so situated that the disposition of the action in *the person's absence* may . . . leave any of the persons already parties subject to a substantial risk of incurring double, multiple, or otherwise inconsistent obligations by reason of the claimed interest" (emphasis added)). FIFA's risk of multiple obligations to different parties is not a result of Visa's absence in this lawsuit; it is the result of FIFA allegedly breaching its contract with MasterCard and awarding Visa sponsorship rights it was contractually prohibited from granting. Visa's presence in this lawsuit will not remedy that fact. Whether Visa is or is not a party in the underlying lawsuit, FIFA and Visa will litigate *their* dispute under *their* contract later on down the road if MasterCard prevails here. Visa cannot re-litigate and undo a finding in this case that the MasterCard Contract contains a right of first refusal or that FIFA breached its contract with MasterCard since these issues admittedly have nothing to do with Visa.

We are also not persuaded that the scenario envisioned by Visa, in which the court below enjoins FIFA from performing the Visa Contract while a subsequent court orders FIFA to perform the Visa Contract, presents a "substantial risk" of inconsistent obligations, as required by Rule 19(a)(2)(ii). It is difficult to believe that a subsequent tribunal faced with a party under a prior court-ordered injunction will nevertheless order that party to perform the very obligations a prior court has prohibited it from performing. While Visa

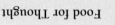

Food for Thought

Given that FIFA did not raise the Rule 19 defense and did not join in Visa's motion to dismiss for failure to join a party under Rule 19, should nonparties like Visa be permitted to raise such challenges or should they be limited to seeking to intervene under Rule 24 (discussed in this chapter below)?

is correct that it will not be bound by any injunction entered in the underlying litigation in its absence, FIFA is certainly bound by any such injunction and a subsequent proceeding will have to recognize and respect the injunction ordered by the district court in this case. It is worth noting that FIFA, the party supposedly facing this grave predicament, has not advanced the argument that it would be prejudiced by Visa's absence from this case. FIFA never raised the Rule 19 defense before the district court, it did not join in Visa's motion below, and it has not participated in any way in the proceedings before this court. If FIFA actually believed it would suffer prejudice if Visa is not a party in this case, it surely would have had something to say on this point.

For these reasons, we cannot say that the district court's conclusion that Visa is not a necessary party under Rule 19(a)(2)(ii) was an abuse of discretion. Having found that Visa satisfies none of the three criteria for compulsory joinder, we affirm the district court's decision that Visa is not a necessary party under Rule 19(a).

* * *

CONCLUSION

For the foregoing reasons, we dismiss the appeal originally filed by Visa of the district court's Rule 19 Order [and] reject Visa's argument that the district court lacks subject matter jurisdiction because Visa is a necessary and indispensable party. * * *

Points for Discussion

a. The Requirements of Rule 19(a)

There are three ways that a nonparty can be deemed a required or "necessary" party under Rule 19(a). The court in *MasterCard* found none of these circumstances to apply to Visa. Do you agree with the court's application of each of the Rule 19(a) categories? Would the district court have been abusing its discretion if it had found that Visa did qualify as a required party under one of the provisions? *MasterCard* serves as an example of how difficult it is to satisfy the standards for being deemed a required party under Rule 19(a).

Indeed, determining whether an absent party is a necessary party that should be joined if feasible is a difficult, fact-specific determination that will depend on the circumstances of each case:

There is no precise formula for determining whether a particular nonparty must be joined under Rule 19(a). The decision has to be made in terms of the general policies of avoiding multiple litigation, providing the parties with complete and effective relief in a single action, and protecting the absent persons from the possible prejudicial effect of deciding the case without them. Account also must be taken of whether other alternatives are available to the litigants. By its very nature Rule 19(a) calls for determinations that are heavily influenced by the facts and circumstances of individual cases . . . .

7 C. Wright, A. Miller & M. Kane, Fed. Prac. & Proc. § 1604 (3d ed. 2001).

Additionally, the standards are difficult to satisfy and narrowly interpreted generally speaking; the Federal Reporters and Supplements are much more full of decisions finding that an absentee is *not* a necessary party (or appellate decisions reversing district court findings that an absentee is a necessary party) than decisions finding that Rule 19(a)'s standards have been satisfied. Let's look at each of the three Rule 19(a) categories in a bit more detail.

Rule 19(a)(1)(A): No complete relief in nonparty's absence. This category is potentially applicable when nonmonetary relief is at stake and any ensuing court order would be ineffective or incomplete unless certain nonparties were brought before the court as parties. For example, Rule 19(a)(1)(A) has been found to be satisfied in cases involving a dispute over rights to a piece of property when one of the owners of the property is not joined in the action. *See, e.g., Shell W. E & P Inc. v. Dupont,* 152 F.R.D. 82, 85 (M.D. La. 1993) (finding that co-owners of real property were persons who must be joined under Rule 19(a) in an action seeking a declaration of an oil company's right under a mineral lease to conduct operations on the property); *Weaver v. Mid-Century Ins.,* 690 F. Supp. 845, 846 (E.D. Mo. 1988) (determining that plaintiff's ex-husband was a necessary party to a quiet title action since he remained liable on a promissory note encumbering real property). Keep in mind, though, that substantive law defining the legal relationship between joined and unjoined parties may also bear on the compulsory joinder decision, further complicating the analysis. *See, e.g., Americontainer Ltd. P'ship v. Rankin,* 25 F.3d 1053 (Table), 1994 WL 209897, at *5 (7th Cir. May 24, 1994) (noting that because under Indiana law cotenants can lease their undivided interest in the common property without the consent of the other cotenants and such leases are not binding on them, the other cotenants are not necessary parties to a dispute involving the terms of the lease). Finally, note that the existence of multiple parties who are jointly and severally liable to a plaintiff will not require that each be joined because a court may order any single party to pay the full monetary damages. *Janney Montgomery Scott, Inc. v. Shepard Niles, Inc.,* 11 F.3d 399, 404–13 (3d Cir. 1993) ("If the Agreement in question can be construed or interpreted as a contract imposing joint and several liability on its co-obligors, . . . complete relief may be granted in a suit against only one of them," and so the other is not a necessary party).

What's That?

Joint and several liability is a Torts concept that refers to liability that may be apportioned either among multiple parties or to only one of them at the adversary's discretion.

Rule 19(a)(1)(B)(i): Absence will impair nonparty's ability to protect its interests. Under this provision, it is not enough that an absent party have an interest in the action. Rather, its ability to protect that interest must, "as a practical matter," be impaired by its absence. Satisfying this provision requires "that some outcome of the federal case that is reasonably likely can preclude the absent party with respect to an issue material to the absent party's rights or duties under standard principles governing the effect of prior judgments." *Janney Montgomery Scott, Inc. v. Shepard Niles, Inc.,*

11 F.3d 399, 409 (3d Cir. 1993). However, the rule has been interpreted as not requiring that a judgment be binding on the absent party for practical impairment to occur; courts have found that the persuasive effect of a prior judgment can suffice to create the practical impairment necessary to satisfy Rule 19(a)(1)(B)(i). See, e.g., *Pulitzer-Polster v. Pulitzer*, 784 F.2d 1305 (5th Cir. 1986) (finding that the judgment in the federal action might have a precedent-setting effect in a subsequent state-court action involving the absent party and involving similar arguments raised in the federal case). Further, courts have indicated that there is no risk of impairment if the nonparty is "adequately represented" in the action. *Salt River Project Agric. Imp. & Power Dist. v. Lee*, 672 F.3d 1176, 1180 (9th Cir. 2012). Courts tend to discount interests that are merely financial or speculative, see, e.g., *Cachil Dehe Band of Wintun Indians v. California*, 547 F.3d 962, 970 (9th Cir. 2008) ("[T]he interest must be more than a financial stake, and more than speculation about a future event." (citation and internal quotation marks omitted)), although the threatened depletion of a limited fund to which the absentee lays claim can be considered a sufficient interest at risk of impairment, see, e.g., *id.* at 970–71 ("An interest in a fixed fund or limited resource that the court is asked to allocate may also be protected.").

Rule 19(a)(1)(B)(ii): Existing party subject to risk of multiple or inconsistent obligations. The key understanding to have regarding this provision is that logically inconsistent or conflicting judgments are not the same thing as subjecting a party to a risk of "inconsistent obligations" under Rule 19:

> [I]nconsistent obligations are not . . . the same as inconsistent adjudications or results, because inconsistent obligations occur when a party is unable to comply with one court's order without breaching another court's order concerning the same incident. In contrast, inconsistent adjudications or results occur when a party wins on a claim in one forum and loses on another claim from the same incident in another forum.

Bacardi Int'l Ltd. v. V. Suarez & Co., 719 F.3d 1, 12 (1st Cir. 2013) (citation and internal quotation marks omitted); *see also Broad. Music, Inc. v. Armstrong*, 2013 WL 3874082, at *7 (W.D. Tex. July 24, 2013) ("Inconsistent obligations occur when an existing party cannot comply with one court's order without breaching the order of another court that pertains to the same incident."). Thus, if a plaintiff asserts a claim against one of two joint tortfeasors, "the defendant does not face 'multiple liability' because it may lose in the original action and then lose in the subsequent action for contribution against the other joint tortfeasor." *In re DBSI Inc.*, 2013 WL 1498365, at *8 (Bankr. D. Idaho Apr. 11, 2013); *see also Temple v. Synthes Corp.*, 498 U.S. 5, 7 (1990) ("It has long been the rule that it is not necessary for all joint tortfeasors to be named as defendants in a single lawsuit."). Rule 19(a)(1)(B)(ii) addresses "the more fundamental clash of court orders that occurs when a party is subject to two judgments which it cannot obey simultaneously—such as being ordered to give the same property to two different people." *Wheeler Peak, L.L.C. v. L.C.I.2, Inc.*, 2009 WL 2982817, at *12 (D.N.M. Aug. 15, 2009).

For a useful review of the types of claims for which absent parties should qualify as necessary parties under Rule 19, see Richard D. Freer, *Rethinking Compulsory Joinder: A Proposal to Restructure Fed. Rule 19*, 60 N.Y.U. L. Rev. 1061, 1082–96 (1985). For a discussion of the historical roots of the principles that animate compulsory party joinder doctrine, see Geoffrey Hazard, *Indispensable Party: The Historical Origin of a Procedural Phantom*, 61 Colum. L. Rev. 1254 (1961).

Take Note!

Prior to the 2007 restyling of the Federal Rules, the numbering of Rule 19 was different, with Rule 19(a)(2) housing the provisions that now appear in Rule 19(a)(1). This is important to know if you are re-searching Rule 19 case law prior to 2007.

—Perspective & Analysis—

Is Rule 19 well crafted to achieve its goals? At least one commentator thinks not:

Rule 19 of the Federal Rules of Civil Procedure, which implements the doctrine of compulsory party joinder, is intended to promote packaging. It has two basic goals: to identify nonparties whose joinder is necessary for a just adjudication and to secure that joinder. Rule 19 fails to accomplish either goal adequately.

First, Rule 19 does a poor job of identifying nonparties whose joinder should be compelled. It describes three situations in which an absentee should be joined: (1) when, without joinder, complete relief cannot be accorded among those already parties; (2) when the absentee's ability to protect an interest relating to the subject of the action may be impaired unless she is joined in the litigation; and (3) when the defendant may be subjected to multiple liability or inconsistent obligations if the absentee is not joined. The first situation describes a null set; that part of Rule 19 lacks independent significance and ought to be jettisoned. The second situation need not be addressed by Rule 19; an absentee threatened with practical impairment may protect her interest by intervening under Rule 24(a)(2). The third situation is too broadly defined and should be narrowed.

Richard D. Freer, *Rethinking Compulsory Joinder: A Proposal to Restructure Fed. Rule 19*, 60 N.Y.U. L. Rev. 1061, 1061–63 (1985).

b. Feasibility Under Rule 19(a)

Once a nonparty is deemed to be a necessary party under Rule 19(a), the court is required to join that party to the action "if feasible." Joinder of the party is feasible if: (1) the court is able to exercise personal jurisdiction over the party, (2) joinder would not undermine the subject matter jurisdiction of the court, and (3) the party to be joined makes no valid objection to venue. *See* Fed. R. Civ. P. 19(a). How might the joinder of a party undermine the court's subject matter jurisdiction? Hypo 7.5 provides an illustration:

Hypo 7.5

Pedro (SC) asserted a conversion claim against Laurel (NC) in North Carolina federal court to recover a stolen coin collection worth $100,000. Laurel is alleged to have stolen the collection along with Hardy (SC). The two currently are holding the collection in a safe deposit box. It takes a key both from Laurel and from Hardy to open the box. Should Hardy be treated as a necessary party under Rule 19(a)? If so, is his joinder feasible?

The proper mechanism for challenging an opposing party's failure to join a party under Rule 19 is either to move for the court to join the party under Rule 19 or to file a motion to dismiss under Rule 12(b)(7) for failure to join a party under Rule 19. Rule 19(b) permits courts to dismiss actions where it is not feasible to join important necessary parties to the action:

FRCP 19(b). Required Joinder of Parties:
When Joinder Is Not Feasible.

(b) When Joinder Is Not Feasible. If a person who is required to be joined if feasible cannot be joined, the court must determine whether, in equity and good conscience, the action should proceed among the existing parties or should be dismissed. The factors for the court to consider include:

(1) the extent to which a judgment rendered in the person's absence might prejudice that person or the existing parties;

(2) the extent to which any prejudice could be lessened or avoided by:

    (A) protective provisions in the judgment;

    (B) shaping the relief; or

    (C) other measures;

(3) whether a judgment rendered in the person's absence would be adequate; and

(4) whether the plaintiff would have an adequate remedy if the action were dismissed for nonjoinder.

If a necessary party's presence in an action is so important that the case must be dismissed in its absence based on a Rule 19(b) analysis, that party is referred to as an indispensable party. The following case illustrates how the Supreme Court interprets and applies Rule 19(b).

Republic of The Philippines v. Pimentel

Supreme Court of the United States
553 U.S. 851 (2008)

JUSTICE KENNEDY delivered the opinion of the Court.

This case turns on the interpretation and proper application of Rule 19 of the Federal Rules of Civil Procedure and requires us to address the Rule's operation in the context of foreign sovereign immunity.

This interpleader action was commenced to determine the ownership of property allegedly stolen by Ferdinand Marcos when he was the President of the Republic of the Philippines. Two entities named in the suit invoked sovereign immunity. They are the Republic of the Philippines and the Philippine Presidential Commission on Good Governance, referred to in turn as the Republic and the Commission. They were dismissed, but the interpleader action proceeded to judgment over their objection. Together with two parties who remained in the suit, the Republic and the Commission now insist it was error to allow the litigation to proceed. Under Rule 19, they contend, the action should have been dismissed once it became clear they could not be joined as parties without their consent.

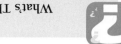

What's That?

An *interpleader* action is one in which a person in possession of property subject to the conflicting ownership claims of others brings those parties into court to obtain a judgment resolving the ownership question among them. This is a party joinder device that is covered in Section B.5 below.

The United States Court of Appeals for the Ninth Circuit, agreeing with the District Court, held the action could proceed without the Republic and the Commission as parties. Among the reasons the Court of Appeals gave was that the absent, sovereign entities would not prevail on their claims. We conclude the Court of Appeals gave insufficient weight to the foreign sovereign status of the Republic and the Commission, and that the court further erred in reaching and discounting the merits of their claims.

I

* * *

B

In 1972, Ferdinand Marcos, then President of the Republic, incorporated Arelma, S.A. (Arelma), under Panamanian law. Around the same time, Arelma opened a brokerage account with Merrill Lynch, Pierce, Fenner & Smith Inc. (Merrill Lynch) in New York, in which it deposited $2 million. As of the year 2000, the account had grown to approximately $35 million.

Alleged crimes and misfeasance by Marcos during his presidency became the subject of worldwide attention and protest. A class action by and on behalf of some 9,539 of his human rights victims was filed against Marcos and his estate, among others. The class action was tried in the United States District Court for the District of Hawaii and resulted in a nearly $2 billion judgment for the class. We refer to that litigation as the Pimentel case and to its class members as the Pimentel class. In a related action, the Estate of Roger Roxas and Golden Budha [sic] Corporation (the Roxas claimants) claim a right to execute against the assets to satisfy their own judgment against Marcos' widow, Imelda Marcos.

The Pimentel class claims a right to enforce its judgment by attaching the Arelma assets held by Merrill Lynch. The Republic and the Commission claim a right to the assets under a 1955 Philippine law providing that property derived from the misuse of public office is forfeited to the Republic from the moment of misappropriation.

After Marcos fled the Philippines in 1986, the Commission was created to recover any property he wrongfully took. Almost immediately the Commission asked the Swiss Government for assistance in recovering assets—including shares in Arelma—that Marcos had moved to Switzerland. In compliance the Swiss Government froze certain assets and, in 1990, that freeze was upheld by the Swiss Federal Supreme Court. In 1991, the Commission asked the Sandiganbayan, a Philippine court of special jurisdiction over corruption cases, to declare forfeited to the Repub-lic any property Marcos had obtained through misuse of his office. That litigation is still pending in the Sandiganbayan.

The Swiss assets were transferred to an escrow account set up by the Commis-sion at the Philippine National Banc (PNB), pending the Sandiganbayan's decision as to their rightful owner. The Republic and the Commission requested that Merrill Lynch follow the same course and transfer the Arelma assets to an escrow account at PNB. Merrill Lynch did not do so. Facing claims from various Marcos credi-tors, including the Pimentel class, Merrill Lynch instead filed an interpleader action under 28 U.S.C. § 1335. The named defendants in the interpleader action were, among others, the Republic and the Commission, Arelma, PNB, and the Pimentel class (the respondents here).

The Pimentel case had been tried as a class action before Judge Manuel Real of the United States District Court for the Central District of California, who was sit-ting by designation in the District of Hawaii after the Judicial Panel on Multidistrict Litigation consolidated the various human rights complaints against Marcos in that court. Judge Real directed Merrill Lynch to file the interpleader action in the District of Hawaii, and he presided over the matter.

After being named as defendants in the interpleader action, the Republic and the Commission asserted sovereign immunity under the Foreign Sovereign Immunities Act of 1976 (FSIA), 28 U.S.C. § 1604. They moved to dismiss pursuant to Rule 19(b), based on the premise that the action could not proceed without them. Aretma and PNB also moved to dismiss pursuant to Rule 19(b). Without addressing whether they were entitled to sovereign immunity, Judge Real initially rejected the request by the Republic and the Commission to dismiss the interpleader action. They appealed, and the Court of Appeals reversed. It held the Republic and the Commission are entitled to sovereign immunity and that under Rule 19(a) they are required parties (or "necessary" parties under the old terminology). The Court of Appeals entered a stay pending the outcome of the litigation in the Sandiganbayan over the Marcos assets.

After concluding that the pending litigation in the Sandiganbayan could not determine entitlement to the Aretma assets, Judge Real vacated the stay, allowed the action to proceed, and awarded the assets to the Pimentel class. A week later, in the case initiated before the Sandiganbayan in 1991, the Republic asked that court to declare the Aretma assets forfeited, arguing the matter was ripe for decision. The Sandiganbayan has not yet ruled.

In the interpleader case the Republic, the Commission, Aretma, and PNB appealed the District Court's judgment in favor of the Pimentel claimants. This time the Court of Appeals affirmed. Dismissal of the interpleader suit, it held, was not warranted under Rule 19(b) because, though the Republic and the Commission were required ("necessary") parties under Rule 19(a), their claim had so little likelihood of success on the merits that the interpleader action could proceed without them. One of the reasons the court gave was that any action commenced by the Republic and the Commission to recover the assets would be barred by New York's 6-year statute of limitations for claims involving the misappropriation of public property. The court thus found it unnecessary to consider whether any prejudice to the Republic and the Commission might be lessened by some form of judgment or interim decree in the interpleader action. The court also considered the failure of the Republic and the Commission to obtain a judgment in the Sandiganbayan—despite the Aretma share certificates having been located and held in escrow at the PNB since 1997–1998—to be an equitable consideration counseling against dismissal of the interpleader suit. The court further found it relevant that allowing the interpleader case to proceed would serve the interests of the Pimentel class, which, at this point, likely has no other available forum in which to enforce its judgment against property belonging to Marcos.

This Court granted certiorari.

* * *

III

We turn to the question whether the interpleader action could proceed in the District Court without the Republic and the Commission as parties.

Subdivision (a) of Rule 19 states the principles that determine when persons or entities must be joined in a suit. The Rule instructs that nonjoinder even of a required person does not always result in dismissal. Subdivision (a) opens by noting that it addresses joinder "if Feasible." Where joinder is not feasible, the question whether the action should proceed turns on the factors outlined in subdivision (b). The considerations set forth in subdivision (b) are nonexclusive, as made clear by the introductory statement that "[t]he factors for the court to consider include." Fed. Rule Civ. Proc. 19(b). The general direction is whether "in equity and good conscience, the action should proceed among the existing parties or should be dismissed." The design of the Rule, then, indicates that the determination whether to proceed will turn upon factors that are case specific, which is consistent with a Rule based on equitable considerations. This is also consistent with the fact that the determination of who may, or must, be parties to a suit has consequences for the persons and entities affected by the judgment; for the judicial system and its interest in the integrity of its processes and the respect accorded to its decrees; and for society and its concern for the fair and prompt resolution of disputes. See, e.g., Illinois Brick Co. v. Illinois, 431 U.S. 720, 737–739 (1977). For these reasons, the issue of joinder can be complex, and determinations are case specific. See, e.g., Provident Tradesmens Bank & Trust Co. v. Patterson, 390 U.S. 102, 118–119 (1968).

* * *

IV

We turn to Rule 19 as it relates to this case. The application of subdivision (a) of Rule 19 is not contested. The Republic and the Commission are required entities because "[w]ithout [them] as parties in this interpleader action, their interests in the subject matter are not protected." See Fed. Rule Civ. Proc. 19(a)(1)(B)(i). All parties appear to concede this. The disagreement instead centers around the application of subdivision (b), which addresses whether the action may proceed without the Republic and the Commission, given that the Rule requires them to be parties.

* * *

The Court of Appeals erred in not giving the necessary weight to the absent entities' assertion of sovereign immunity. The court in effect decided the merits of the Republic and the Commission's claims to the Arelma assets. Once it was recognized that those claims were not frivolous, it was error for the Court of Appeals to address them on their merits when the required entities had been granted sovereign immunity. The court's consideration of the merits was itself an infringement on foreign sovereign immunity; and, in any event, its analysis was flawed. We discuss these errors first in the context of how they affected the Court of Appeals' analysis under the first factor of Rule 19(b). We then explain that the outcome suggested by the first factor is confirmed by our analysis under the other provisions of Rule 19(b). The action may not proceed.

A

As to the first Rule 19(b) factor—the extent to which a judgment rendered in the person's absence might prejudice that person or the existing parties, Fed. Rule Civ. Proc. 19(b)(1)—the judgment of the Court of Appeals is incorrect.

In considering whether the Republic and the Commission would be prejudiced if the action were to proceed in their absence, the Court of Appeals gave insufficient weight to their sovereign status. The doctrine of foreign sovereign immunity has been recognized since early in the history of our Nation. It is premised upon the "perfect equality and absolute independence of sovereigns, and th[e] common interest impelling them to mutual intercourse." *Schooner Exchange v. McFaddon,* 7 Cranch 116, 137, 3 L.Ed. 287 (1812). The Court has observed that the doctrine is designed to "give foreign states and their instrumentalities some protection from the inconvenience of suit," *Dole Food Co. v. Patrickson,* 538 U.S. 468, 479 (2003).

* * * Immunity in this case * * * is uncontested; and pursuant to the Court of Appeals' earlier ruling on the issue, the District Court dismissed the Republic and the Commission from the action on this ground.

The District Court and the Court of Appeals failed to give full effect to sovereign immunity when they held the action could proceed without the Republic and the Commission. Giving full effect to sovereign immunity promotes the comity interests that have contributed to the development of the immunity doctrine.

Comity and dignity interests take concrete form in this case. The claims of the Republic and the Commission arise from events of historical and political significance for the Republic and its people. The Republic and the Commission have a unique interest in resolving the ownership of or claims to the Arelma assets and in determining if, and how, the assets should be used to compensate those persons who suffered grievous injury under Marcos. There is a comity interest in allowing a foreign state to use its own courts for a dispute if it has a right to do so. The dignity of a foreign state is not enhanced if other nations bypass its courts without right or good cause. Then, too, there is the more specific affront that could result to the Republic and the Commission if property they claim is seized by the decree of a foreign court.

Though this Court has not considered a case posing the precise question pre-sented here, there are some authorities involving the intersection of joinder and the governmental immunity of the United States. *See, e.g., Mine Safety Appliances Co. v. Forrestal*, 326 U.S. 371, 373–375 (1945) (dismissing an action where the Under Secretary of the Navy was sued in his official capacity, because the Government was a required entity that could not be joined when it withheld consent to be sued); *Minnesota v. United States*, 305 U.S. 382, 386–388 (1939) (dismissing the action for nonjoinder of a required entity where the United States was the owner of the land in question but had not consented to suit). The analysis of the joinder issue in those cases was somewhat perfunctory, but the holdings were clear: A case may not pro-ceed when a required-entity sovereign is not amenable to suit. These cases instruct us that where sovereign immunity is asserted, and the claims of the sovereign are not frivolous, dismissal of the action must be ordered where there is a potential for injury to the interests of the absent sovereign.

The Court of Appeals accordingly erred in undertaking to rule on the merits of the Republic and the Commission's claims. There may be cases where the person who is not joined asserts a claim that is frivolous. In that instance a court may have leeway under both Rule 19(a)(1), defining required parties, and Rule 19(b), addressing when a suit may go forward nonetheless, to disregard the frivolous claim. Here, the claims of the absent entities are not frivolous; and the Court of Appeals should not have proceeded on the premise that those claims would be determined against the sovereign entities that asserted immunity.

* * *

As these comments indicate, Rule 19 cannot be applied in a vacuum, and it may require some preliminary assessment of the merits of certain claims. For example, the Rule directs a court, in determining who is a required person, to consider whether complete relief can be afforded in their absence. *See* Fed. Rule Civ. Proc. 19(a)(1)(A). Likewise, in the Rule 19(b) inquiry, a court must examine, to some extent, the claims presented and the interests likely to be asserted both by the joined parties and the absent entities or persons. Here, however, it was improper to issue a definitive holding regarding a nonfrivolous, substantive claim made by an absent, required entity that was entitled by its sovereign status to immunity from suit. That privilege is much diminished if an important and consequential ruling affecting the sovereign's substantial interest is determined, or at least assumed, by a federal court in the sovereign's absence and over its objection.

As explained above, the decision to proceed in the absence of the Republic and the Commission ignored the substantial prejudice those entities likely would incur. This most directly implicates Rule 19(b)'s first factor, which directs consideration of prejudice both to absent persons and those who are parties. We have discussed the absent entities. As to existing parties, we do not discount the Pimentel class' interest in recovering damages it was awarded pursuant to a judgment. Furthermore, combating public corruption is a significant international policy. * * * This policy does support the interest of the Pimentel class in recovering damages awarded to it. But it also under-scores the important comity concerns implicated by the Republic and the Commission in asserting foreign sovereign immunity. The error is not that the District Court and the Court of Appeals gave too much weight to the interest of the Pimentel class, but that it did not accord proper weight to the compelling claim of sovereign immunity.

Based on these considerations we conclude the District Court and the Court of Appeals gave insufficient weight to the likely prejudice to the Republic and the Commission should the interpleader proceed in their absence.

B

As to the second Rule 19(b) factor—the extent to which any prejudice could be lessened or avoided by relief or measures alternative to dismissal, Fed. Rule Civ. Proc. 19(b)(2)—there is no substantial argument to allow the action to proceed. No alternative remedies or forms of relief have been proposed to us or appear to be available. If the Marcos estate did not own the assets, or if the Republic owns them now, the claim of the Pimentel class likely fails; and in all events, if there are equally valid but competing claims, that too would require adjudication in a case where the Republic and the Commission are parties. *See State Farm Fire & Casualty Co. v. Tashire,* 386 U.S. 523, 534, and n. 16 (1967).

C

As to the third Rule 19(b) factor—whether a judgment rendered without the absent party would be adequate, Fed. Rule Civ. Proc. 19(b)(3)—the Court of Appeals understood "adequacy" to refer to satisfaction of the Pimentel class' claims. But adequacy refers to the "public stake in settling disputes by wholes, whenever possible." *Provident Bank,* 390 U.S., at 111. This "social interest in the efficient administration of justice and the avoidance of multiple litigation" is an interest that has "traditionally been thought to support compulsory joinder of absent and poten-tially adverse claimants." *Illinois Brick Co.,* 431 U.S., at 737–738. Going forward with the action without the Republic and the Commission would not further the public interest in settling the dispute as a whole because the Republic and the Commission would not be bound by the judgment in an action where they were not parties.

D

As to the fourth Rule 19(b) factor—whether the plaintiff would have an adequate remedy if the action were dismissed for nonjoinder, Fed. Rule Civ. Proc. 19(b)(4)— the Court of Appeals made much of what it considered the tort victims' lack of an alternative forum should this action be dismissed. This seems to assume the plaintiff in this interpleader action was the Pimentel class. It is Merrill Lynch, however, that has the statutory status of plaintiff as the stakeholder in the interpleader action.

It is true that, in an interpleader action, the stakeholder is often neutral as to the outcome, while other parties press claims in the manner of a plaintiff. That is insufficient, though, to overcome the statement in the interpleader statute that the stakeholder is the plaintiff. See 28 U.S.C. § 1335(a) (conditioning jurisdiction in part upon whether "the plaintiff has deposited such money or property" at issue with the district court or has "given bond payable to the clerk of the court in such amount and with such surety as the court or judge may deem proper"). We do not ignore that, in context, the Pimentel class (and indeed all interpleader claimants) are to some extent comparable to the plaintiffs in noninterpleader cases. Their interests are not irrelevant to the Rule 19(b) equitable balance; but the other provisions of the Rule are the relevant ones to consult.

Merrill Lynch, as the stakeholder, makes the point that if the action is dismissed it loses the benefit of a judgment allowing it to disburse the assets and be done with the matter. Dismissal of the action, it urges, leaves it without an adequate remedy, for it "could potentially be forced . . . to defend lawsuits by the various claimants in different jurisdictions, possibly leading to inconsistent judgments." A dismissal of the action on the ground of nonjoinder, however, will protect Merrill Lynch in some respects. That disposition will not provide Merrill Lynch with a judgment determining the party entitled to the assets, but it likely would provide Merrill Lynch with an effective defense against piecemeal litigation and inconsistent, conflicting judgments. As matters presently stand, in any later suit against it Merrill Lynch may seek to join the Republic and the Commission and have the action dismissed under Rule 19(b) should they again assert sovereign immunity. Dismissal for nonjoinder to some extent will serve the purpose of interpleader, which is to prevent a stakeholder from having to pay two or more parties for one claim.

Any prejudice to Merrill Lynch in this regard is outweighed by prejudice to the absent entities invoking sovereign immunity. Dismissal under Rule 19(b) will mean, in some instances, that plaintiffs will be left without a forum for definitive resolution of their claims. But that result is contemplated under the doctrine of foreign sovereign immunity.

V

The Court of Appeals' failure to give sufficient weight to the likely prejudice to the Republic and the Commission should the interpleader proceed in their absence would, in the usual course, warrant reversal and remand for further proceedings. In this case, however, that error and our further analysis under the additional provisions of Rule 19(b) lead us to conclude the action must be dismissed. This leaves the Pimentel class, which has waited for years now to be compensated for grievous wrongs, with no immediate way to recover on its judgment against Marcos. And it leaves Merrill Lynch, the stakeholder, without a judgment.

The balance of equities may change in due course. One relevant change may occur if it appears that the Sandiganbayan cannot or will not issue its ruling within a reasonable period of time. Other changes could result when and if there is a ruling. If the Sandiganbayan rules that the Republic and the Commission have no right to the assets, their claims in some later interpleader suit would be less substantial than they are now. If the ruling is that the Republic and the Commission own the assets, then they may seek to enforce a judgment in our courts; or consent to become parties in an interpleader suit, where their claims could be considered; or file in some other forum if they can obtain jurisdiction over the relevant persons. We do not note that if Merrill Lynch, or other parties, elect to commence further litigation in light of changed circumstances, it would not be necessary to file the new action in the District Court where this action arose, provided venue and jurisdictional requirements are satisfied elsewhere. The present action, however, may not proceed.

* * *

The judgment of the Court of Appeals for the Ninth Circuit is reversed, and the case is remanded with instructions to order the District Court to dismiss the interpleader action.

It is so ordered.

[An opinion by JUSTICE STEVENS concurring in part and dissenting in part is omitted.]

[An opinion by JUSTICE SOUTER concurring in part and dissenting in part is omitted.]

Points for Discussion

a.   The Consequences of a Failure to Join a Party Under Rule 19

As illustrated in *Pimentel*, the consequences of being unable to join a party deemed necessary under Rule 19(a) can be severe: The case is dismissed. Why do you think the rule provides for such a drastic remedy? Should the severity of the remedy lead courts to be sparing in their application of Rule 19(b), or are the interests being protected so important that courts should not hesitate to dismiss an action under the rule? What interests are being protected by this rule?

is indispensable?

particularly given the consequences associated with a finding that an absent party

Court in *Pimentel*? Does that phrase give courts too much discretion in this area,

and good conscience." Do you have a sense of what this means in the eyes of the

Rule 19(b) instructs the court to make its dismissal determination "in equity

---

Hypo 7.6

Phyllis (NC) entered into a contract to buy a painting worth $1 million from Smith (SC) and Deborah (NC), joint owners of the painting. After Phyllis transferred the agreed upon amount of money to Smith and Deborah's bank account as the purchase price of the painting, Smith, and Deborah failed to deliver the painting to Phyllis. Phyllis initiated an action in North Carolina federal court against Smith, seeking a decree ordering a transfer of the painting pursuant to the terms of the agreement. Smith responds by filing a motion to dismiss under Rule 12(b)(7) for failure to join Deborah as a party under Rule 19.

How should the judge rule? Is Deborah a necessary party? If so, is her joinder feasible? If her joinder is not feasible, should the action be dismissed?

---

b. Applying the Factors of Rule 19(b)

How should courts apply the four factors listed in Rule 19(b) when making their dismissal determinations? See *Provident Tradesmens Bank & Tr. v. Patterson*, 390 U.S. 102 (1968) [FLEX Case 7.A] (applying the four factors). Do any of the factors deserve more weight than the others? For example, if the plaintiff would be unable to obtain the sought relief anywhere else, should that weigh heavily against the court dismissing the action under Rule 19(b)? See, e.g., *Extra Equipamentos E Exportacao Lida. v. Case Corp.*, 361 F.3d 359, 361 (7th Cir. 2004) ("Rule 19(b) lists several factors as bearing on this determination, of which the two most important in this case are 'to what extent a judgment rendered in the person's absence might be prejudicial to' him and 'whether the plaintiff will have an adequate remedy if the action is dismissed for nonjoinder.' "); *Confederated Tribes of Chehalis Indian Reservation v. Lujan*, 928 F.2d 1496, 1505 (9th Cir. 1991) (O'Scannlain, J., concurring in part and dissenting in part) ("Given the absence of an alternative forum, proceeding to the merits in this action is the plaintiffs' only hope of obtaining an adequate remedy. In my view, this single factor makes dismissal of the suit so harsh that it may outweigh the other three factors combined."). But see *Wilbur v. Locke*, 423 F.3d 1101, 1114 (9th Cir. 2005) ("[E]ven assuming the Wilburs have no other forum in which to pursue a remedy, we have 'regularly held that the tribal interest in immunity overcomes the lack of an alternative remedy or forum for the plaintiffs.' "), *overruled on other grounds*, *Levin v. Commerce Energy, Inc.*, 560 U.S. 413 (2010).

How should courts evaluate the prejudice factor of Rule 19(b)? What type of prejudice should be sufficient to warrant a dismissal under the rule? In *Helzberg's Diamond Shops, Inc. v. Valley West Des Moines Shopping Center Inc.*, 564 F.2d 816 (8th Cir. 1977), Helzberg's sued its landlord, Valley West, claiming that the landlord had violated the terms of their lease by permitting another tenant in the mall, Lord's Jewelers, to operate a competing store. When Valley West moved to dismiss claiming that Lord's was an indispensable party, the court disagreed:

Rule 19(b) requires the court to look first to the extent to which a judgment rendered in Lord's absence might be prejudicial to Lord's or to Valley West. Valley West argues that the District Court's order granting preliminary in-junctive relief does prejudice Lord's and may prejudice Valley West. We do not agree.

It seems axiomatic that none of Lord's rights or obligations will be ultimate-ly determined in a suit to which it is not a party. Even if, as a result of the District Court's granting of the preliminary injunction, Valley West should attempt to terminate Lord's leasehold interest in space 261 in the Valley West Mall, Lord's will retain all of its rights under its Lease Agreement with Valley West. None of its rights or obligations will have been adjudicated as a result of the present proceedings, proceedings to which it is not a party. Therefore, we conclude that Lord's will not be prejudiced in a way contem-plated by Rule 19(b) as a result of this action.

Likewise, we think that Lord's absence will not prejudice Valley West in a way contemplated by Rule 19(b). Valley West contends that it may be subjected to inconsistent obligations as a result of a determination in this action and a determination in another forum that Valley West should pro-ceed in a fashion contrary to what has been ordered in these proceedings.

It is true that the obligations of Valley West to Helzberg, as determined in these proceedings, may be inconsistent with Valley West's obligations to Lord's. However, we are of the opinion that any inconsistency in those obligations will result from Valley West's voluntary execution of two Lease Agreements which impose inconsistent obligations rather than from Lord's absence from the present proceedings.

Id. at 819. Do you agree with this analysis?

c. Using Other Joinder Devices

Recall each of the other joinder devices provided for in the Federal Rules. Defendants who feel that certain absent parties should be joined in the action need not always rely upon compulsory joinder under Rule 19. For example, if a defendant feels that a joint tortfeasor should be joined in an action, it can implead that party as a third-party defendant under Rule 14(a), even though that party would not qualify for compulsory joinder under Rule 19(a) as we saw in the note on *Temple v. Synthes* above. Note also a defendant's ability to join nonparties through Rule 13(h), which permits defendants that assert counterclaims or cross-claims to join nonparties to those claims pursuant to Rules 19 or 20. **Example 7.2** illustrates this point.

> **Example 7.2**
>
> Lou sues Mike for causing damage to his car as a result of a recent accident. Mike counterclaims against Lou for damage to his own car, asserting that Lou was to blame for the accident along with the driver of another car, Sue. Under Rule 13(h), Mike may bring Sue into the action as an additional defendant to his counterclaim based on the permissive party joinder rule of Rule 20.

4. Intervention

If neither of the existing parties to an action make an effort to draw in nonparties, such outsiders are not without recourse if they nonetheless wish to become a party to the action. Rule 24 permits outsiders to intervene in a case, provided certain requirements are met. Rule 24(a) sets forth the standards under which nonparties have a *right* to intervene:

FRCP 24(a). Intervention: Intervention of Right.

(a) **Intervention of Right.** On timely motion, the court must permit anyone to intervene who:

(1) is given an unconditional right to intervene by a federal statute; or

(2) claims an interest relating to the property or transaction that is the subject of the action, and is so situated that disposing of the action may as a practical matter impair or impede the movant's ability to protect its interest, unless existing parties adequately represent that interest.

The next case, *Natural Resources Defense Council v. U.S. Nuclear Regulatory Commission*, demonstrates the application of this rule.

NRDC v. U.S. Nuclear Regulatory Commission

U.S. Court of Appeals for the Tenth Circuit
578 F.2d 1341 (10th Cir. 1978)

WILLIAM E. DOYLE, CIRCUIT JUDGE.

The American Mining Congress and Kerr-McGee Nuclear Corporation seek review of the order of the United States District Court for the District of New Mexico denying their motions to intervene [as] a matter of right or on a permissive basis, pursuant to Rule 24(a)(2) and (b), Fed. R. Civ. P.

The underlying action in which the movants requested intervention was instituted by the Natural Resources Defense Council, Inc., and others. In the action, declaratory and injunctive relief is directed to the United States Nuclear Regulatory Commission (NRC) and the New Mexico Environmental Improvement Agency (NMEIA), prohibiting those agencies from issuing licenses for the operation of uranium mills in New Mexico without first preparing environmental impact statements. Kerr-McGee and United Nuclear are potential recipients of the licenses.

What's That?

An *environmental impact statement is* a report that federal agencies must prepare before they undertake major projects or regulatory efforts. *See* 42 U.S.C. § 4332(2)(C).

Congress, in the Atomic Energy Act of 1954, 42 U.S.C. §§ 2011–2296, has authorized the NRC to issue such licenses. NMEIA is involved because under § 274(b) of the Act, 42 U.S.C. § 2021(b) (1970), the NRC is authorized to enter into agreements with the states allowing the states to issue licenses. Such agreements have been made with about 25 states including New Mexico. Thus, the action below in effect seeks to prevent the use of § 274(b) of the Act so as to avoid the requirement of an impact statement for which provision is made in the National Environmental Policy Act.

42 U.S.C. § 4332(2)(C) (1970) requires that a detailed environmental impact statement must be prepared by all federal agencies "in every recommendation or report on proposals for legislation and other major Federal actions significantly affecting the quality of the human environment." The complaint cites this requirement and alleges that an environmental impact statement would ordinarily be required here as a prerequisite to the issuance of licenses for the operation of uranium mills were it not for the arrangement which gives jurisdiction to the state. It further alleges that such statements are now prepared by the NRC in states that have not entered into agreements with the NRC, but that the NRC does not prepare such statements where there is an agreement with a state such as New Mexico. Plaintiff contends that the granting of licenses by state agencies predicated on delegation of authority from the

NRC causes the NRC to consider the aspect of "major federal action" to be thereby eliminated. The New Mexico agency, NMEIA, which grants the license, does not prepare environmental impact statements since it is not a federal agency and is not required either by its agreement with NRC or by state law to prepare such a statement.

The relief sought by the plaintiffs' complaint is, First, that NRC's involvement in the licensing procedure in New Mexico is, notwithstanding the delegation to the state, sufficient to constitute major federal action, whereby the impact statement requirement is not eliminated. Second, that if an impact statement is not required in connection with the granting of licenses, the New Mexico program is in conflict with § 274(d)(2) of the Atomic Energy Act of 1954, 42 U.S.C. § 2021(d)(2) (1970).

The motion of United Nuclear Corporation to intervene is not opposed by the parties and was granted. On May 3, 1977, the date that the complaint herein was filed, NMEIA granted a license to United Nuclear to operate a uranium mill at Church Rock, New Mexico. The complaint seeks to enjoin the issuance of the license thus granted.

It was after that that Kerr-McGee Nuclear Corporation, Anaconda Company, Gulf Oil Corporation, Phillips Petroleum Company, and the American Mining Congress filed motions to intervene. These motions, insofar as they sought intervention as of right, were denied on the ground that the interests of the parties or movants would be adequately represented by United Nuclear. Permissive intervention was also denied. Kerr-McGee and the American Mining Congress both appeal denial of both intervention as of right and permissive intervention.

Our issue is a limited one. We merely construe and weigh Rule 24(a) of the FED. R. CIV. P. (intervention as of right) and decide in light of the facts and considerations presented whether the denial of intervention was correct. The Rule provides as follows:

> *Permissive intervention* is provided for under Rule 24(b), which states, "(1) On timely motion, the court may permit anyone to intervene who . . . (B) has a claim or defense that shares with the main action a common question of law or fact. . . . (3) In exercising its discretion, the court must consider whether the intervention will unduly delay or prejudice the adjudication of the original parties' rights." FED. R. CIV. P. 24(b).

[The court quoted Rule 24(a).]

We do not have a subsection (1) situation involving a statutory conferring of right to intervene. Accordingly, we must consider the standards set forth in subsection (2), which are:

1. Whether the applicant claims an interest relating to the property or transaction which is the subject of the action.

2.   Whether the claimants are so situated that the disposition of the action may as a practical matter impair or impede their ability to protect that interest.

3.   Whether their interest is not adequately represented by existing parties.

The district court's order denying intervention by the several corporations focused on whether the interest of the party seeking to intervene was adequately represented by a fellow member of the industry. Our relatively recent decision in National Farm Lines v. ICC, 564 F.2d 381 (10th Cir. 1977), was held not determinative because the movants for intervention would be represented by a fellow member of the industry rather than by the United States Government, whose interests were different in *National Farm Lines*. The court decided that the interests of the movants were adequately protected by United Nuclear, which possessed the necessary experience and knowledge in a complex area of business, whereby the representative's capability was competent to meet the demands. The court thought that to allow the intervention would engender delay and produce unwieldy procedure; and that the movants' requirements were met by allowing the filing of amicus curiae briefs.

It's Latin to Me!

Amicus curiae is Latin for "friend of the court." *Amicus curiae* briefs are briefs submitted by those who are not parties to the action, but nonetheless are permitted to submit briefs in support of whatever position they favor. Why do you think the outsiders here favor actual intervention over simply being permitted to file *amicus* briefs?

Our conclusion is that the interests of movants in the subject matter is sufficient to satisfy the requirements of Rule 24 and that the threat of loss of their interest and inability to participate is of such magnitude as to impair their ability to advance their interest.

I.

The position adopted by the trial court that Kerr-McGee was adequately represented dispensed with the need for the court to consider the question whether Kerr-McGee had an interest in the litigation before the court. Plaintiffs-appellees maintain that the appellants do not have the requisite interest because they are not directly involved; that the controversy centers on the effort of Natural Resources Defense Council, Inc. to prevent the issuance of a license to United Nuclear unless and until an environmental impact statement is issued. The question then is whether the contention made is a correct concept of interest. Strictly to require that the movant in intervention have a *direct* interest in the outcome of the lawsuit strikes us as being too narrow a construction of Rule 24(a)(2). Kerr-McGee argues that the meaning of interest is one which, if they do not prevail in the intervention, threatens them with a disposition of the action which may, as a practical matter, impair or impede their efforts to protect the interest. Thus, we are asked to interpret interest in relationship to the second criterion in Rule 24(a)(2), impairment or impeding ability to protect the interest.

The Supreme Court has said that the interest must be a significantly protectable interest. *See Donaldson v. United States*, 400 U.S. 517 (1971). The Supreme Court held that a taxpayer did not have a right to intervene in a judicial enforcement proceeding seeking issuance of an Internal Revenue summons ordering production of business records of his employer. The narrowness of the *summons proceeding* was noted, and it was said that an objection of the taxpayer could be raised at the proper time in a subsequent trial.

Food for Thought

Notice that this language regarding the impairment to the nonparties' interest is similar to the language regarding outsider impairment found in Rule 19(a)(1)(B)(i). Does that mean that the standards for being deemed a necessary party under Rule 19(a) and having a right to intervene under Rule 24 are the same, or are there relevant differences between the two rules and how they should be analyzed?

Cascade Natural Gas Corp. v. El Paso Natural Gas Co., 386 U.S. 129, 135–36 (1967), held that the interest claimed by the applicant in intervention did not have to be a direct interest in the property or transaction at issue provided that it was an interest that would be impaired by the outcome. There Cascade's source of supply would have been a new company created by an antitrust divestiture, a significant change. In view of this consequence of the litigation, it was held that Cascade had a sufficient interest. * * *

In our case the matter of immediate interest is, of course, the issuance and delivery of the license sought by United Nuclear. However, the consequence of the litigation could well be the imposition of the requirement that an environmental impact statement be prepared before granting any uranium mill license in New Mexico, or, secondly, it could result in an injunction terminating or suspending the agreement between NRC and NMEIA. Either consequence would be felt by United Nuclear and to some degree, of course, by Kerr-McGee, which is said to be one of the largest holders of uranium properties in New Mexico. It operates a uranium mill in Grants, New Mexico, pursuant to an NMEIA license, which application for renewal is pending. A decision in favor of the plaintiffs, which is not unlikely, could have a profound effect upon Kerr-McGee. Hence, it does have an interest within the meaning of Rule 24(a)(2). This interest of Kerr-McGee is in sharp contrast to the minimal interest which was present in *Allard*, wherein it was an interest of environmental groups in the protection of living birds. This was considered insufficient to justify intervention in a case involving feathers which are part of Indian artifacts. Their interest was said to be limited to a general interest in the public. The interest asserted on behalf of Kerr-McGee and the American Mining Congress is one which is a genuine threat to Kerr-McGee and the members of the American Mining Congress to a substantial degree.

We do not suggest that Kerr-McGee could expect better treatment from state authorities than federal. We do recognize that a change in procedure would produce impairing complications.

II.

The next question is whether, assuming the existence of an interest, the chance of impairment is sufficient to fulfill the requirement of <u>Rule 24(a)(2)</u>.

As already noted, the question of impairment is not separate from the question of existence of an interest. The appellants both claim an interest in licenses that are now before NMEIA or will be in the future. If the relief sought by the plaintiffs is granted, there can be little question but that the interests of the American Mining Congress and of Kerr-McGee would be affected. Plaintiffs contend, however, that appellants would not be bound by such a result if they are not participants. Kerr-McGee points out that even though it may not be *res judicata*, still it would have a *stare decisis* effect. Moreover, with NRC and NMEIA as parties, the result might be more profound than *stare decisis*.

Take Note!

What is Kerr-McGee arguing here when it says that the effect would not be *res judicata* but would still have a *stare decisis* effect? *Res judicata* refers to the binding effect of a prior judgment in a subsequent case. *Stare decisis* refers to the judicial practice of adhering to legal precedent in subsequent cases. Given those meanings, what point is Kerr-McGee trying to make here?

It should be pointed out that the Rule refers to impairment "as a practical matter." Thus, the court is not limited to consequences of a strictly legal nature. The court may consider any significant legal effect in the applicant's interest and it is not restricted to a rigid *res judicata* test. Hence, the *stare decisis* effect might be sufficient to satisfy the requirement. * * *

Finally, the considerations for requiring an environmental impact statement will be relatively the same in respect to the issuance of a uranium mining license in every instance. Hence, to say that it can be repeatedly litigated is not an answer, for the chance of getting a contrary result in a case which is substantially similar on its facts to one previously adjudicated seems remote.

We are of the opinion, therefore, that appellants have satisfied the impairment criterion.

III.

The final question is whether the trial court was correct in its conclusion that United Nuclear would adequately represent Kerr-McGee and the American Mining Congress.

The finding and conclusion was that the representation would be adequate because United Nuclear, a fellow member of the industry, has interests which were the same as those of the appellants and possessed the same level of knowledge and experience with the ability and willingness to pursue the matter and could adequately represent Kerr-McGee and the members of the American Mining Congress.

We have held in accordance with *Trbovich v. UMW*, 404 U.S. 528, 538 n.10 (1972), that the burden continues to be on the petitioner or movant in intervention to show that the representation by parties may be inadequate. *National Farm Lines v. ICC*, 564 F.2d 381, 383 (10th Cir. 1977). We have also recognized the holding in *Trbovich* that the burden is minimal; that it is enough to show that the representation "may be" inadequate.

United Nuclear is situated somewhat differently in this case than are the other members of the industry since it has been granted its license. From this it is urged by Kerr-McGee that United Nuclear may be ready to compromise the case by obtaining a mere declaration that while environmental impact statements should be issued, this requirement need be prospective only, whereby it would not affect them. While we see this as a remote possibility, we gravely doubt that United Nuclear would opt for such a result. It is true, however, that United Nuclear has a defense of laches that is not available to Kerr-McGee or the others.

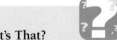

What's That?

Laches is an equitable defense that alleges that the plaintiff has unreasonably delayed the assertion of its rights in a way that prejudices the opposing party. It is similar to raising a statute-of-limitations defense, except there is not a specifically identified time period that must lapse for the defense of laches to apply.

7A C. Wright & A. Miller, Federal Practice & Procedure, § 1909, at 524 (1972), says:

> [I]f [an applicant's] interest is similar to, but not identical with, that of one of the parties, a discriminating judgment is required on the circumstances of the particular case, but he ordinarily should be allowed to intervene unless it is clear that the party will provide adequate representation for the absentee.

While the interest of the two applicants may appear similar, there is no way to say that there is no possibility that they will not be different and the possibility of divergence of interest need not be great in order to satisfy the burden of the applicants * * * .

Practice Pointer

Note that the court is discussing additional reasons to allow intervention—the ability to bind more parties to the result—and, in the next paragraph, discrediting the notion that adding these additional parties would make the case unwieldy. These are not considerations that you will find in Rule 24(a)(2). However, they are considerations that are important to this court and probably others as well. As a practitioner, it is thus always a good practice to argue not simply that the black-letter terms of the rule apply (or do not apply) to the situation, but also to argue to the court that there are other more practical or policy-oriented reasons to permit or refuse intervention.

There are other reasons for allowing intervention. There is some value in having the parties before the court so that they will be bound by the result. American Mining Congress represents a number of companies having a wide variety of interests. This can, therefore, provide a useful supplement to the defense of the case. The same can be said of Kerr-McGee.

The trial court was concerned that the addition of these movants would make the litigation unwieldy. If the intervenors are limited to this group, unwieldiness does not become a problem which the trial court cannot control. It does not appear that there would be a need for additional parties in view of the presence of the American Mining Congress. While we do not express an opinion on the possibilities of further additions, we wish to make clear that the present holdings that the two applicants should be allowed to intervene does not say that others should be added. The two appellants here have satisfied their burden of the three requirements of Rule 24(a)(2). Consequently, they should be and they are hereby allowed to intervene. Accordingly, we need not determine whether the district court erred in denying permissive intervention under Rule 24(b).

The order of the district court is reversed and the cause is remanded with instructions to the trial court to grant the appellants, Kerr-McGee's and American Mining Congress', motions to intervene.

Points for Discussion

a. The Meaning of "Interest" Under Rule 24(a)(2)

How did the court define the interests of Kerr-McGee and members of the American Mining Congress? What type of interest must a party have in litigation to satisfy the interest requirement of Rule 24(a)(1)(B)? Is the nature of the interest needed similar to the interest required to identify those parties who should be joined under Rule 19(a)(1)(B)? The Supreme Court in *Donaldson v. United States*, 400 U.S. 517 (1971), established that the interest must be a "significantly protectable interest." What does that mean? Is prospective economic impairment sufficient?

What about having a property interest, such as an interest in protecting property values from declining as a result of construction of an abortion clinic, that might be impaired by existing litigation? In *Planned Parenthood of Minnesota Inc. v. Citizens for Community Action*, 558 F.2d 861 (8th Cir. 1977), opponents to an abortion clinic sought to intervene in an action by a family planning organization against the city, which had passed an ordinance banning the construction of abortion facilities. Should the clinic opponents be viewed as having a sufficient interest in the dispute to be permitted to intervene? How would the interests of the clinic opponents be impaired were Planned Parenthood to be victorious in overturning the ordinance? What if the clinic opponents were permitted to intervene, and then the city dropped out of the case on appeal; would the opponents of the clinic have standing to continue their defense of the ordinance? *See Diamond v. Charles*, 476 U.S. 54, 68 (1986) (holding that an intervenor's right to continue a suit in the absence of the party on whose side intervention was permitted depends on the intervenor independently meeting the standing requirement of Article III).

How would you analyze the interests of environmental groups seeking to intervene in an action between a company seeking to convert an area into a housing development and the federal Environmental Protection Agency claiming that the area is protected wetlands? *See, e.g.*, *Allard v. Frizzell*, 536 F.2d 1332, 1333 (10th Cir. 1976) (denying intervention by an environmental group in action by sellers of Indian artifacts challenging a statute prohibiting the use of feathers of protected birds).

When there is litigation challenging the use of race in employment decisions or college admissions, should people who benefit from those policies be treated as having an interest sufficient to qualify for intervention as a matter of right? *See, e.g.*, *Grutter v. Bollinger*, 188 F.3d 394, 399 (6th Cir. 1999) (identifying the interest in gaining admission to the University as sufficient to give student groups a right to intervene); *Jansen v. City of Cincinnati*, 904 F.2d 336, 342 (6th Cir. 1990) (finding that black applicants and employees of the city's fire department had a sufficient interest in litigation challenging the fire department's use of an affirmative action program to have a right to intervene).

b. Intervention "of Right" Versus Permissive Intervention

In *Natural Resources Defense Council* the court was considering the application of Rule 24(a)(2), which refers to "intervention of right." The other portion of the rule, Rule 24(b), refers to "permissive intervention." What is the difference between these two rules? How do the considerations relevant to each rule differ from one another? *See Stringfellow v. Concerned Neighbors in Action*, 480 U.S. 370, 381–83 (1987) (Brennan, J., concurring) (distinguishing permissive intervention from intervention of right). When deciding whether to grant permissive intervention, in addition to finding a common question of law or fact, courts are supposed to "consider whether the intervention will unduly delay or prejudice the adjudication of the original parties' rights." Fᴇᴅ. R. Cɪᴠ. P. 24(b)(3). Courts may also weigh a number of efficiency considerations, including the degree of overlap of the two actions, the extent of progress in the original action, the impact that intervention would have on the original action, and the availability of alternatives to intervention such as consolidation under Rule 42(a). *See generally* 7C C. Wʀɪɢʜᴛ, A. Mɪʟʟᴇʀ & M. Kᴀɴᴇ, Fᴇᴅ. Pʀᴀᴄ. & Pʀᴏᴄ. § 1913 (3d ed. 2007) (discussing how courts exercise their discretion when making permissive intervention determinations and citing illustrative cases).

Note that intervention of right does not mean that intervention is compulsory. The determination of whether to attempt intervention is within the discretion of the outsiders, meaning that even if they satisfy the standards of Rule 24(a)(2), they are not under any obligation to intervene. *See Martin v. Wilks*, 490 U.S. 755, 763 (1989) ("[A] party seeking a judgment binding on another cannot obligate that person to intervene; he must be joined."). If existing parties are interested in mandating the joinder of a nonparty, then they must avail themselves of the compulsory joinder rule, Rule 19, if its terms can be satisfied.

That said, in some circumstances principles of preclusion doctrine will treat a party's failure to intervene in a prior action when it had the opportunity to do so as a basis for binding the party to a determination made in the prior action. *See, e.g.*, *Swayne v. Capitol Indem. Corp.*, 2010 WL 2663209, at *3 (July 1, 2010) ("[Capitol] had notice on July 12, 2007, prior to the entry of the final judgment on September 17, 2007. Capitol could then have filed a motion to intervene pursuant to Ohio Rule of Civil Procedure 24, but it did not. Capitol made no effort to involve itself in the suit, despite notice, until Mrs. Swayne brought this action. Therefore, privity does apply in this case, and Capitol is bound by res judicata."); *see also* 18A C. Wʀɪɢʜᴛ, A. Mɪʟʟᴇʀ & E. Cᴏᴏᴘᴇʀ, Fᴇᴅ. Pʀᴀᴄ. & Pʀᴏᴄ. § 4452 (2d ed. 2002). ("Preclusion may extend to a nonparty who did not participate in an action on the ground that the nonparty should have participated.").

Make the Connection

Res judicata (claim preclusion) and *collateral estoppel* (issue preclusion) are preclusion doctrine concepts referring to the binding effect of prior judgments on subsequent litigation. Preclusion doctrine will be studied in detail in Chapter 11.

Further, parties that fail to intervene may face obstacles to their later attempts to take advantage of favorable issue determinations in prior cases via the offensive use of issue preclusion (collateral estoppel). *See Parklane Hosiery Co. v. Shore,* 439 U.S. 322, 331 (1979) ("The general rule should be that in cases where a plaintiff could easily have joined in the earlier action . . . a trial judge should not allow the use of offensive collateral estoppel.").

c.   Adequacy of Representation Under Rule 24(a)(2)

As we saw in *Natural Resources Defense Council,* if the interests of the outsider are not sufficiently aligned with any of the existing parties, the court will conclude that the outsider's interests are not adequately represented in the action. However, some courts have found adequate representation even though the interests of the prospective intervenor and existing parties were not exactly aligned. *See, e.g., Nat. Res. Def. Council, Inc. v. N.Y. State Dep't of Envtl. Conservation,* 834 F.2d 60, 61–62 (2d Cir. 1987):

> A putative intervenor does not have an interest not adequately represented by a party to a lawsuit simply because it has a motive to litigate that is different from the motive of an existing party. So long as the party has demonstrated sufficient motivation to litigate vigorously and to present all colorable contentions, a district judge does not exceed the bounds of discretion by concluding that the interests of the intervenor are adequately represented.

The standard for showing the inadequacy of representation is not supposed to be high; the Supreme Court has itself so indicated: "The requirement of the Rule is satisfied if the applicant shows that representation of his interest 'may be' inadequate; and the burden of making that showing should be treated as minimal." *Trbovich v. United Mine Workers,* 404 U.S. 528, 538 n.10 (1972); *see also Grutter v. Bollinger,* 188 F.3d 394, 399 (6th Cir. 1999) ("The proposed intervenors need show only that there is a potential for inadequate representation.").

What other circumstances might provide grounds for concluding that the interests of the prospective intervenor are not adequately represented by existing parties? *See Commonwealth of Va. v. Westinghouse Elec. Corp.,* 542 F.2d 214, 216 (4th Cir. 1976) ("When the party seeking intervention has the same ultimate objective as a party to the suit, a presumption arises that its interests are adequately represented, against which the petitioner must demonstrate adversity of interest, collusion, or nonfeasance.").

In cases where a governmental entity is a party, should it be deemed to adequately represent the interests of its citizens such that public interest organizations may not intervene on their behalf? Does the answer depend on what position the governmental entity is asserting in the case or on the type of case (e.g., antitrust, environmental, civil rights)? *See, e.g., United States ex rel. Richards v. De Leon Guerrero, 4 F.3d 749, 756 (9th Cir. 1993)* (denying permissive intervention where the government party to the case made the same arguments as the taxpayer intervenors and would adequately represent the intervenors' privacy interests).

d. Timeliness of Intervention Under Rule 24

Both Rule 24(a) and Rule 24(b) have timeliness requirements. These rules impose no fixed time limit for intervention; rather, courts evaluate timeliness by considering whether the parties and the court will suffer from the fact that the effort to intervene did not come earlier, and whether the intervenor can be faulted for seeking to intervene at a late stage in the process. *Staley v. Harris Cnty., 160 Fed. App'x 410 (5th Cir. 2005)*, provides one example of how courts evaluate the timeliness of an effort to intervene:

> **FYI**
>
> Rule 24(a)(1) provides that courts must permit intervention by parties "given an unconditional right to intervene by a federal statute." Under 28 U.S.C. § 2403(a) the United States has an unconditional right to intervene in an action challenging the constitutionality of federal statutes. States are given a similar right under 28 U.S.C. § 2403(b).

The timeliness requirement is measured based on four factors: (1) the length of time during which the would-be intervenor actually knew or reasonably should have known of its interest in the action before petitioning for leave to intervene, (2) the extent of the prejudice that the existing parties to the litigation may suffer as a result of the would-be intervenor's failure to apply for intervention as soon as it actually knew or reasonably should have known of its interest in the action, (3) the extent of the prejudice that the would-be intervenor may suffer if its petition for leave to intervene is denied, [and] (4) the existence of unusual circumstances militating either for or against a determination that the application is timely.

Id. at 412 (quoting *Stallworth v. Monsanto Co., 558 F.2d 257, 264–66 (5th Cir. 1977)*).

e. Subject Matter Jurisdiction

As in other joinder contexts, the claims asserted by or against intervenors must satisfy subject-matter-jurisdiction requirements. If no independent basis for subject matter jurisdiction exists, supplemental jurisdiction may be available under the terms of 28 U.S.C. § 1367. In a diversity action, how would § 1367(b) affect claims by non-diverse intervening plaintiffs asserting state-law claims?

Take Note!

In *Town of Chester, N.Y. v. Laroe Estates, Inc., 137 S. Ct. 1645 (2017)*, the Court held that "an intervenor of right must have Article III standing in order to pursue relief that is different from that which is sought by a party with standing," resolving a circuit split that had previously existed on this question.

5. Interpleader

Interpleader is a unique procedural device that permits a party in possession of property that it does not claim to own—referred to as the stakeholder—to join all prospective claimants to the property—referred to as the stake—in a single action in which a court can conclusively resolve ownership of the property. **Example 7.3** illustrates such a scenario. Current interpleader rules also permit stakeholders who claim a right to the stake for themselves to institute interpleader actions as well.

Example 7.3

B is the seller of a home that *C* wants to buy. *A* is in possession of $1000, which was given as a deposit by *C* on a contract to purchase the house from *B*. After the housing contract fell through, both *B* and *C* claimed entitlement to the deposit held by *A*. *A* can institute an action and *interplead B* and *C* as parties to that action, enabling the court to resolve who is entitled to the funds.

Interpleader is a necessary device because otherwise a stakeholder facing multiple claimants could be sued by each claimant in separate actions, with the result that the stakeholder could be subjected to multiple and inconsistent liability (for example, each case could reach the result that a different claimant is entitled to the stake).

In the federal system, there are two means by which stakeholders can institute interpleader actions. The first is **rule interpleader**, which is provided for by Rule 22 of the Federal Rules of Civil Procedure. It reads as follows:

FRCP 22. Interpleader.

(a) Grounds.

(1) *By a Plaintiff.* Persons with claims that may expose a plaintiff to double or multiple liability may be joined as defendants and required to interplead. Joinder for interpleader is proper even though:

(A) the claims of the several claimants, or the titles on which their claims depend, lack a common origin or are adverse and independent rather than identical; or

(B) the plaintiff denies liability in whole or in part to any or all of the claimants.

(2) *By a Defendant.* A defendant exposed to similar liability may seek interpleader through a crossclaim or counterclaim.

(b) Relation to Other Rules and Statutes. This rule supplements—and does not limit—the joinder of parties allowed by Rule 20. The remedy this rule provides is in addition to—and does not supersede or limit—the remedy provided by 28 U.S.C. §§ 1335, 1397, and 2361. An action under those statutes must be conducted under these rules.

When interpleader is attempted under Rule 22, ordinary subject matter jurisdiction, venue, and personal jurisdiction restrictions apply, meaning that the stake in question would have to be worth more than $75,000 and the stakeholder would have to hail from a different state than each of the various claimants.

However, an alternative to rule interpleader exists. Congress has enacted legislation providing for **statutory interpleader** under 28 U.S.C. § 1335:

28 U.S.C. § 1335. Interpleader.

(a) The district courts shall have original jurisdiction of any civil action of interpleader * * * filed by any person, firm, or corporation, association, or society having in his or its custody or possession money or property of the value of $500 or more * * * if

(1) Two or more adverse claimants, of diverse citizenship as defined in subsection (a) or (d) of section 1332 of this title, are claiming or may claim to be entitled to such money or property * * * ; and if

(2) the plaintiff has deposited such money or property or has paid the amount of or the loan or other value of such instrument or the amount due under such obligation into the registry of the court * * * .

* * *

Statutory interpleader thus permits an interpleader action to go forward in the federal courts on the basis of a claim equal to or exceeding only $500, rather than the $75,000-plus amount required under rule interpleader. Note also that statutory interpleader only requires two or more of the adverse claimants to be of diverse citizenship rather than requiring complete diversity between the stakeholder and all adverse claimants. Is such a requirement consistent with the diversity limitations of Article III to the Constitution discussed in Chapter 3? *See State Farm Fire & Cas. Co. v. Tashire*, 386 U.S. 523 (1967) [*FLEX* Case 7.B]; *Treinies v. Sunshine Mining Co.*, 308 U.S. 66 (1939) (holding that subject matter jurisdiction under 28 U.S.C. § 1335 was appropriate even though the stakeholder and one of the claimants were from the same state).

Further differences between the two devices exist. Under 28 U.S.C. § 1397, venue in statutory inter-pleader actions is appropriate in any judicial district where any claimant resides. Rule interpleader actions are subject to the general venue statute, 28 U.S.C. § 1391, which is more limited in the range of venues it approves. Personal jurisdiction requirements are also more generous for statutory interpleader actions, with 28 U.S.C. § 2361 authorizing nationwide personal jurisdiction over claimants in statutory interpleader actions. Rule interpleader actions are subject to the ordinary rules surrounding personal jurisdiction.

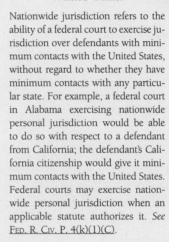

What's That?

Nationwide jurisdiction refers to the ability of a federal court to exercise jurisdiction over defendants with minimum contacts with the United States, without regard to whether they have minimum contacts with any particular state. For example, a federal court in Alabama exercising nationwide personal jurisdiction would be able to do so with respect to a defendant from California; the defendant's California citizenship would give it minimum contacts with the United States. Federal courts may exercise nationwide personal jurisdiction when an applicable statute authorizes it. *See* FED. R. CIV. P. 4(k)(1)(C).

Finally, 28 U.S.C. § 2361 also permits courts entertaining statutory interpleader actions to restrain claimants from pursuing any action affecting the stake in any other state or federal court. Courts overseeing rule interpleader cases may not make use of

What's That?

The Anti-Injunction Act is a statute that prohibits federal courts from enjoining state-court proceedings unless one of three exceptions applies. Its text is as follows: "A court of the United States may not grant an injunction to stay proceedings in a State court except as expressly authorized by Act of Congress, or where necessary in aid of its jurisdiction, or to protect or effectuate its judgments." 28 U.S.C. § 2283.

this statute but rather must operate under the strictures of the Anti-Injunction Act, 28 U.S.C. § 2283, and Federal Rule 65 governing injunctions. *See Life Ins. Co. of N. Am. v. Thorngren*, 2005 WL 2387596, at *4 (D. Idaho Sept. 27, 2005) ("When a restraining order is sought in a Rule 22 interpleader action, the court looks to the standards of 28 U.S.C § 2283, and FED.R.CIV.P. 65, and not to those of statutory interpleader. As such, the court may restrain a party from filing a duplicative action only when there is an actual threat to either the stakeholder or the proceedings currently before the court." (citations omitted)). **Table 7.1** summarizes the differences between rule and statutory interpleader.

Table 7.1—Distinctions Between Rule and Statutory Interpleader

	Rule Interpleader	Statutory Interpleader
Diversity Requirement	Complete diversity between stakeholder and claimants	Minimal diversity among adverse claimants
Amount-in-Controversy Requirement	Greater than $75,000	At least $500
Personal Jurisdiction	Governed by Rule 4(k) [typically tied to the reach of the forum state]	Nationwide
Venue	Limited according to 28 U.S.C. § 1391	Anywhere any claimant resides
Enjoining Claimants	Governed by the Anti-Injunction Act and Rule 65	Authorized under 28 U.S.C. § 2361

Given the immense advantages of statutory interpleader to stakeholders wishing to initiate federal interpleader actions, why would one ever opt for rule interpleader over statutory interpleader? Most likely, proceeding under rule interpleader would not be a choice, but would be the result of the unavailability of statutory interpleader. Look again at the requirements for statutory interpleader; can you think of instances when it would be unavailable, but rule interpleader would apply?

C. Class Actions

Each of the previous party joinder devices involved the actual joinder of persons or entities as parties to the action. When an action proceeds as a class action, however, multiple parties become involved in a case without being individually joined. Rather, a class action is a representative action, where one or several persons prosecute (or defend) an action on behalf of others who are not present in the action but who have claims or defenses similar to those of the class representatives. Such collective, representative actions are provided for in the federal system by Rule 23.

FYI For a detailed account of the history and purpose behind class actions, see Stephen C. Yeazell, *The Past and Future of Defendant and Settlement Classes in Collective Litigation*, 39 Ariz. L. Rev. 687 (1997).

Class actions are a complex topic to which entire law school courses are dedicated. Most complex litigation courses will focus heavily on the class action device and many law school casebooks are exclusively concerned with class actions. *See, e.g.*, R. Klonoff, Class Actions and Other Multi-Party

LITIGATION (4th ed. West 2017). Legal journals overflow with articles commenting on just about every aspect of class action litigation, so much so that they are too numerous to cite. *See* David L. Shapiro, *Class Actions: The Class as Party and Client*, 73 NOTRE DAME L. REV. 913, 914 n.2 (1998) (citing the numerous law journal publications on class actions). Thus, the goal here is not to cover the topic of class actions in its entirety. Rather, we will review the types of class actions that exist and the basic elements required for obtaining class certification. Special problems, such as choice of law, jurisdiction, settlement, and the Class Action Fairness Act of 2005 will be discussed as well.

1. Certifying a Class Under Rule 23

To proceed as a class action, there are several requirements that must be satisfied under the terms of Rule 23. The plaintiff must prove that the class satisfies the prerequisites for class certification and that the class fits within one of the four types of class actions described in the rule. *Halliburton Co. v. Erica P. John Fund, Inc.*, 134 S. Ct. 2398, 2412 (2014) ("Those decisions have made clear that plaintiffs wishing to proceed through a class action must actually prove—not simply plead—that their proposed class satisfies each requirement of Rule 23, including (if applicable) the predominance requirement of Rule 23(b)(3)."). The basic prerequisites to class certification are found in Rule 23(a):

FRCP 23. Class Actions: Prerequisites.

(a) Prerequisites. One or more members of a class may sue or be sued as representative parties on behalf of all members only if:

(1) the class is so numerous that joinder of all members is impracticable;

(2) there are questions of law or fact common to the class;

(3) the claims or defenses of the representative parties are typical of the claims or defenses of the class; and

(4) the representative parties will fairly and adequately protect the interests of the class.

These four requirements for class certification are generally referred to as numerosity, commonality, typicality, and adequacy of representation. The commonality requirement of Rule 23(a)(2) had previously been a straightforward standard comparable to the requirement found in Rule 20—a requirement that there are identical legal or factual questions that would arise in each case were they to be litigated separately. However, in 2011 the Supreme Court reinterpreted the provision to make it more robust. Specifically, in *Wal-Mart Stores, Inc. v. Dukes*, 564 U.S. 33 (2011), the Court set forth a new standard for commonality with three requirements. First, claimants must "have suffered the same injury." *Id.* at 350. Second, the common question must be "central to the validity of each one of the claims." *Id.* Third, the common question must be one whose determination will resolve a central issue "in one stroke" by "generat[ing] common answers apt to drive the resolution of the litigation." *Id. See also* A. Benjamin Spencer, *Class Actions, Heightened Commonality, and Declining Access to Justice*, 93 B.U. L. Rev. 441, 464 (2013) (discussing and critiquing the *Wal-Mart* commonality decision).

Regarding the other requirements, how numerous does a class have to be before joinder becomes "impracticable"? What makes a class representative's claims "typical" of the claims of the rest of the class? And how do courts determine whether the class representative will "fairly and adequately" protect the interests of the class? These issues will be addressed in *Hubler Chevrolet, Inc. v. General Motors Corp.*, 193 F.R.D. 574 (2000), below.

In addition to meeting the four prerequisites for class certification, a class action must fit within one of four categories of class actions outlined in Rule 23(b).

Rule 23(b)(1)(A): The Incompatible-Standards Class. The first category, often referred to as an *incompatible-standards class*, is provided for in Rule 23(b)(1)(A) and is maintainable if "prosecuting separate actions by or against individual class members would create a risk of . . . inconsistent or varying adjudications with respect to individual class members that would establish incompatible standards of conduct for the party opposing the class." Fed. R. Civ. P. 23(b)(1)(A). **Example 7.4** illustrates a situation that would qualify for class treatment under this rule.

Note that the rule requires the party opposing the class to be subjected to a risk of incompatible standards of *conduct*. Under such language, would the possibility of having to pay damages to some victims but not others of a common mass accident suffice to qualify an action for class treatment under Rule 23(b)(1)(A)?

Example 7.4

City issued bonds pursuant to an ordinance its city council passed last year. Several citizens believe that this bond issuance violates the state's constitution. If individual citizens file separate lawsuits, one court may rule that the bond issuance is valid and another may rule that the bond issuance is invalid, resulting in City being subject to inconsistent determinations on the question of whether the bonds could be issued.

Rule 23(b)(1)(B): The Limited-Fund Class. The second type of class action is permitted when separate actions would create a risk of "adjudications with respect to individual class members that, as a practical matter, would be dispositive of the interests of the other members not parties to the individual adjudications or would substantially impair or impede their ability to protect their interests." Fed. R. Civ. P. 23(b)(1)(B). This type of class action is sometimes referred to as a *limited-fund class* because it is often used to certify actions involving multiple claims that exceed the amount available to satisfy them. *See* **Example 7.5**. Why do you think class treatment is warranted in such circumstances? How should courts determine whether an action fits within this category? *See Ortiz v. Fibreboard Corp.*, 527 U.S. 815, 838–39 (1999) (holding that to qualify for Rule 23(b)(1)(B) treatment there must be an insufficient fund available to pay claims, the entirety of the fund must be dedicated to the payment of claims, and all claimants against the fund must be treated equitably).

> **Example 7.5**
>
> Nuke 'Em, Inc. operates a nuclear power plant that had a major accident. Local affected citizens seek compensation from Nuke 'Em for personal injuries that resulted from the accident. A federal statute places a cap ($500 million) on aggregate damages that may be collected against nuclear power plant operators whose accidents cause harm. The action by the victims against Nuke 'Em could proceed as a Rule 23(b)(1)(B) class provided their total claims are expected to exceed the statutorily-limited amount.

Rule 23(b)(2): The Injunctive-Relief Class. Third among the categories of class actions is the class action seeking injunctive or declaratory relief, which is appropriate when "the party opposing the class has acted or refused to act on grounds that apply generally to the class, so that final injunctive relief or corresponding declaratory relief is appropriate respecting the class as a whole." FED. R. CIV. P. 23(b)(2). Examples of suits qualifying as this type of class are easy to imagine, such as when a group of citizens complain that the State is dumping waste products into their neighborhoods and they seek an injunction ordering the dumping to stop. What should courts do when monetary relief is sought along with injunctive relief? Can such an action still qualify as an injunctive-relief class, or should it be treated as the next type of class, a damages class?

What's That?

Injunctive relief refers to remedies pursued when money damages are inadequate to redress the alleged injury. Such remedies are those historically awarded by courts of equity such as injunctions, decrees of specific performance, rescission of contracts, and the imposition of constructive trusts. For more information about the type of injunctive relief that qualifies an action for certification under Rule 23(b)(2), see 7AA C. WRIGHT, A. MILLER & M. KANE, FED. PRAC. & PROC. CIV. § 1775 (3d ed. 2005).

Rule 23(b)(3): The Damages Class. The final category of class actions consists of those in which class members are seeking money damages against a common defendant or group of defendants. Under Rule 23(b)(3), a damages class is only proper when "the court finds that the questions of law or fact common to class members predominate over any questions affecting only individual members, and that a class action is superior to other available methods for fairly and efficiently adjudicating the controversy." FED. R. CIV. P. 23(b)(3). These two requirements have been termed *predominance* and *superiority*. The Rule goes on to identify four factors relevant to the predominance and superiority determinations: (1) the class members' interests in individually controlling separate actions; (2) the extent and nature of litigation concerning the controversy already begun involving class members; (3) the desirability of concentrating the litigation in a particular forum; and (4) the likely difficulties in managing the class action. *Id.*

Table 7.2 summarizes these categories of class actions:

Table 7.2—Categories of Class Actions	
Category	**Rule**
Incompatible-standards class	Rule 23(b)(1)(A)
Limited-fund class	Rule 23(b)(1)(B)
Injunctive-relief class	Rule 23(b)(2)
Damages class	Rule 23(b)(3)

The next case brings many of these concepts together by illustrating the application of the certification standards to a concrete set of facts, as well as showing us how courts engage in the predominance and superiority analyses required under Rule 23(b)(3). The case after that, *Wal-Mart Stores, Inc. v. Dukes*, shows the Supreme Court's current approach to certifying classes seeking both injunctive and monetary relief, as well as how it interprets the common question requirement found in Rule 23(a).

Hubler Chevrolet, Inc. v. General Motors Corp.

U.S. District Court for the Southern District of Indiana
193 F.R.D. 574 (2000)

BARKER, CHIEF JUDGE.

Plaintiffs, a group of Indiana automobile dealers who sell vehicles manufactured by General Motors (GM), a Delaware corporation, brought this action against GM on behalf of all Indiana dealers alleging that GM's marketing scheme violates the Indiana Deceptive Franchise Practices Act (IDFPA, Ind. Code 23–2–2.7–2(1)) and constitutes criminal conversion and unjust enrichment. Plaintiffs claim that GM unlawfully altered its marketing program, under which it collects from dealers an extra one (1) percent of the Manufacturer's Suggested Retail Price (MSRP) of new cars sold. Formerly, the dealers authorized GM's collection of the one percent charge because GM redistributed the money to regional dealer marketing groups (DMGs) for use in local advertising campaigns. In April of 1999, GM began to retain the monies previously earmarked for local marketing efforts, announcing that it would now spend this money on national advertising. Plaintiffs' Complaint seeks to enjoin

GM from assessing the alleged marketing charge against Indiana GM dealers, a declaration that the marketing funds in question belong to the dealers, disgorgement of illegal benefits that GM has derived from its marketing program since April of 1999, treble damages for conversion, and attorney fees under the IDFPA and Ind. Code 9–23–6–9. Pursuant to Federal Rule of Civil Procedure 23, Plaintiffs moved for certification of a class defined as all GM dealers located in Indiana. * * *

Take Note!

Take note of the type of relief the dealers are seeking here. Is it injunctive, money damages, or both? Given the type of relief being sought, into which Rule 23(b) category does this class action fit?

DISCUSSION

1. *Rule 23(a)*

* * * Federal Rule of Civil Procedure 23 establishes a two-step procedure for determining whether a class can be certified. *See* 7A Charles Alan Wright, Arthur R. Miller & Mary Kay Kane, Federal Practice and Procedure: Civil 2d § 1753, at 44 (1986). The first step is to satisfy the prerequisites of Rule 23(a) * * * . The party seeking class certification bears the burden of proving that these prerequisites have been met and that class certification is appropriate. *See General Tel. Co. of Southwest v. Falcon, 457 U.S. 147, 161 (1982)*. Because each element is a prerequisite to certification, failure to meet any one of them precludes certification as a class.

a. Numerosity

As discussed above, Plaintiffs must show that the putative class is so numerous that "joinder of all [class] members is *impracticable*." FED. R. CIV. P. 23(a)(1) (emphasis added). While there is no magic number held to satisfy this requirement, classes of forty or more members have generally been found to be sufficiently numerous. *See Swanson v. Am. Consumer Indus., 415 F.2d 1326, 1333 n. 9 (7th Cir. 1969)*; Charles Alan Wright, Arthur R. Miller & Mary Kay Kane § 1762, at 159. By GM's own account, there are 258 current GM dealers in the state of Indiana. General Motors argues that joinder is not impracticable because all proposed class members' identities and addresses are readily ascertainable. The authority it cites in support of its position represents a minority view; we rely instead on the established principle that "a showing of strong litigational hardship or inconvenience should be sufficient" to establish numerosity. See Herbert Newberg & Alba Conte, Newberg on Class Actions § 3.04 (3d ed. 1992). In light of the circumstances of this action, including the geographic dispersion of the dealers and the difficulties of administering a case involving over 200 plaintiffs, we believe that joinder is impracticable and that Plaintiffs have satisfied the numerosity requirement.

Food for Thought

Was GM's argument that a class consisting of 258 members did not satisfy the numerosity requirement plausible? What was GM's basis for arguing that joinder of such a number was practicable? Will joinder ever be practicable in a case where the class membership numbers in the hundreds? *See Bd. of Educ. v. Climatemp, Inc.*, 1981 WL 2033 (N.D. Ill. Feb. 20, 1981) (finding the joinder of 350 Chicago-area governmental entities to be sufficiently practicable to defeat numerosity).

b. Commonality and Typicality

Rule 23(a)(2) requires that "there are questions of law or fact common to the class," and Rule 23(a)(3) requires that the plaintiff's claim be typical of those of the class. FED. R. CIV. P. 23(a)(2), (3). These two requirements are "closely related." *Rosario v. Livaditis*, 963 F.2d 1013, 1018 (7th Cir. 1992). Commonality does not require that all questions of fact or law be identical. Factual variation among class grievances does not defeat a finding of commonality. Rather, this requirement is satisfied as long as "the class claims arise out of the same legal or remedial theory." It is enough to satisfy commonality that there be a "common question . . . at the heart of the case. . . ." *Rosario*, 963 F.2d at 1018.

GM's argument that Plaintiffs' claims are based on a variety of differing oral and written communications cannot defeat commonality and typicality, though it may be relevant in determining whether common issues predominate. Plaintiffs readily fulfill the element of commonality in this case. All members of the proposed class share an identical legal claim: that the one percent charge collected by GM, formerly distributed to the DMGs, belongs to them. The legality in Indiana of General Motors' marketing practices, namely its retention of the assessment against all new cars sold by its dealers, forms the common basis of the suit.

Similarly, typicality is shown if the named plaintiff's claim "arises from the same . . . practice or course of conduct that gives rise to the claims of other class members and his or her claims are based on the same legal theory." *De La Fuente v. Stokely-Van Camp, Inc.*, 713 F.2d 225, 232 (7th Cir. 1983). Plaintiffs have alleged that General Motors requires dealers to pay a marketing fee of one percent of the sales price for all new cars sold, without regard to the brand of GM vehicles purchased by the dealer, the dealer's marketing strategy, the size or geographic location of the dealership, or the local economic conditions in the dealership's area. This is easily characterized as a "single practice or course of conduct." *De La Fuente*, 713 F.2d at 232. As we have previously noted, all of the class members' claims are based on the same legal theory regarding the marketing charge and Rule 23(a)(3) is satisfied.

c. Adequacy of Representation

Rule 23(a)(4) requires that the representative parties fairly and adequately protect the interests of the class. This element reflects concerns about the competency of class counsel and potential conflicts of interest: "(a) the plaintiffs' attorney must be qualified, experienced, and generally able to conduct the proposed litigation; and (b) the plaintiffs must not have interests antagonistic to those of the class." *Rosario, 963 F.2d at 1018; see General Tel. Co. v. Falcon, 457 U.S. at 157 n.13.* Courts generally presume competency of class counsel at the outset of the litigation "in the absence of specific proof to the contrary by the defendant." See Newberg & Conte, Newberg on Class Actions at § 3.42. General Motors provides no evidence that Plaintiffs' counsel is inadequate and we believe the briefs filed in this Court by class counsel support a presumption of competency. General Motor's allegation that a conflict of interest arises from counsel's representation of a local association of automobile dealers lacks merit as GM does not demonstrate that an actual conflict exists, nor does it cogently explain how the alleged conflict might harm class interests.

Similarly unavailing are GM's suggestions that the named plaintiffs are not adequate representatives of the class. General Motors presents deposition testimony excerpts of proposed class representatives to establish that the named plaintiffs have differing goals in the litigation. While the named plaintiffs may prefer different marketing strategies, it is clear that they share a common view that GM has unlawfully appropriated the one percent marketing charge at issue in this case for use in national advertising efforts. General Motors further alleges that some of the named plaintiffs provided "no input" in drafting the Complaint and are not willing to personally finance this litigation in its entirety. We think GM's arguments overstate the responsibilities of class representatives; the proposed representatives are not lawyers expected to understand intimately the legal nuances of the case. They may not comprehend perfectly their legal obligations as class representatives, but their testimony reveals genuine interest in the outcome of this litigation: one dealer expressed willingness to bear the entire costs of the action, while the others said they would pay their fair share.

Food for Thought

GM is vigorously opposing certification by making at times seemingly implausible arguments against satisfaction of each of the four prerequisites to class certification. Why do you think GM is so against class certification here? Would GM prefer that the 258 dealers sue it independently in separate litigation? Or is GM hoping that by not getting certified as a class the dealers will not be able to sue GM at all?

The fact that these businessmen made time to appear for scheduled depositions (one individual cut short a trip to attend his) also indicates commitment to this lawsuit and an understanding of the importance of their role. Furthermore, the plaintiffs' willingness to represent the class against GM, potentially damaging their franchise relationships with GM, demonstrates keen desire to pursue this cause. We disagree with GM's contention that these putative class representatives have "so little involvement in the class action that they would be unable or unwilling to protect the interests of the class against the possibly competing interests of the attorneys." They appear willing and able to preserve class interests against any adverse concerns.

Despite GM's speculative-but-thorough description of the ways in which the interests of Indiana GM dealers could vary, we reject GM's argument that these differences constitute antagonistic interests that should prevent class certification. The interests of the class members need not be identical; the only conflicts relevant to our inquiry are those that relate materially to Plaintiffs' claims. In addition, as will be addressed in our discussion of (b)(3) certification, if members of the putative class believe that the named plaintiffs do not adequately represent their interests, they may choose to opt out of the suit. We find that Plaintiffs have met the requirement of adequacy of representation. Plaintiffs have established that they meet all of Rule 23(a)'s prerequisites; thus, we turn to consideration of 23(b).

Take Note!

Note that the plaintiffs are claiming that their action qualifies as each of the three types of class actions maintainable under Rule 23(b). Is this really possible? In what ways might their action satisfy each of the three Rule 23(b) standards?

2. *Rule 23(b)*

It is not enough that the threshold requirements of Rule 23(a) are met; the action must also be maintainable under one of Rule 23(b)'s subparts. Plaintiffs seek certification under Rule 23(b)(1), 23(b)(2) and 23(b)(3).

a. *Rule 23(b)(1)*

Class certification under Rule 23(b)(1) is typically appropriate in cases where there exists either a common fund that may limit recovery to individual plaintiffs or a risk of establishing inconsistent standards of conduct for the defendant. *See Jefferson v. Ingersoll Int'l Inc., 195 F.3d 894, 897 (7th Cir. 1999)* (commenting that "domain of Rule 23(b)(1)" is "limited fund that must be distributed ratably," citing *Ortiz v. Fibreboard Corp., 527 U.S. 815 (1999)*). We discern no allegation of a limited fund that would demonstrate why this type of certification should apply in the instant case. Plaintiffs note that "the prosecution of separate actions will create the risk of varying adjudications with respect to individual dealers" that could "be dispositive of the interests of other GM dealers in the State of Indiana who are not parties to this action or will substantially impair

Take Note!

Note that the possibility of inconsistent results in separate litigation against multiple plaintiffs does not support certification as a Rule 23(b)(1)(A) class. Do you understand why this is so?

or impede their ability to protect their interests." However, "that some plaintiffs may ultimately be successful against a defendant while others may not is simply not a ground for invoking Rule 23(b)(1)(A)." *Hurd v. Monsanto Co.*, 164 F.R.D. 234, 239 (S.D. Ind. 1995).

b. *Rule 23(b)(2)*

Under Rule 23(b)(2), a class may be certified when "the party opposing the class has acted or refused to act on grounds generally applicable to the class," and the representatives are seeking "final injunctive relief or corresponding declaratory relief." FED. R. CIV. P. 23(b)(2); *Doe v. Guardian Life Ins. Co. of Am.*, 145 F.R.D. 466, 477 (N.D. Ill. 1992); Charles Alan Wright, Arthur R. Miller & Mary Kay Kane § 1775, at 477. The primary limitation imposed by this subsection is that injunctive or declaratory relief must predominate as the remedy being sought on behalf of the class. *See Clay v. Am. Tobacco Co.*, 188 F.R.D. 483, 494 (S.D. Ill. 1999); *Doe*, 145 F.R.D. at 477; Wright, Miller & Kane § 1775, at 444–48. The subsection is not fulfilled where the plaintiffs are seeking predominantly money damages.

Plaintiffs have alleged conduct by General Motors clearly applicable to all members of the class: illegal conversion of one percent of the price of new vehicles, an amount formerly contributed to local advertising funds, for use in its own national marketing efforts. Thus, any obstacle to Plaintiffs' attempt to certify this class action under Rule 23(b)(2) would come from the type of relief they are seeking, that is, whether it is a form of final injunctive or corresponding declaratory relief. To determine whether the relief sought is primarily equitable or money damages, "the plaintiffs' specific request for relief must be closely scrutinized and consideration must be given to whether the 'crux of the action is for money damages.' " *Clay*, 188 F.R.D. at 494 (quoting *Dhamer v. Bristol-Myers Squibb Co.*, 183 F.R.D. 520, 528 (N.D. Ill. 1998)).

Deciding whether Plaintiffs' case fits the (b)(2) paradigm presents a close issue because Plaintiffs want to prevent future economic harm and would be entitled to equitable recovery of the amounts paid under an unjust enrichment theory, but they also pursue treble damages on the conversion count and an award of attorney fees as provided for by Indiana statute. In one sense Plaintiffs seek a declaration that the one percent is their money, and relief would seem to flow directly from that proposition. Declaratory relief only "correspond[s]" to final injunctive relief when "as a practical purpose it affords injunctive relief or serves as a basis for later injunctive relief." 1966 Advisory Committee Note to Rule 23. Declaratory relief is not to be used simply to "lay the basis for a later damage award." *Sarafin v. Sears, Roebuck and Co.*, 446 F. Supp. 611, 615 (N.D. Ill. 1978); Wright, Miller & Kane § 1775, at 463. "The use of a declaratory judgment in a class action where the real goal is a damage award undermines the purpose of Rule 23(b)(2)." *Sarafin*, 446 F. Supp. at 615. We do not think that Plaintiffs' prayer for declaratory relief is presented only to lay the basis for an award of treble damages and attorneys fees, but we cannot ignore the large amount of money involved in the potential recovery to class members.

In *Jefferson v. Ingersoll International*, Judge Easterbrook offered guidance to district courts deciding between 23(b)(2) and (b)(3) class certification. 195 F.3d 894, 898 (7th Cir. 1999). Questioning whether Rule 23(b)(2) may ever be used to certify a no-notice, no-opt-out class when compensatory or punitive damages are at issue, he pointed out that Rule 23

> does not say that the class must be certified under the first matching subsection. A court should endeavor to select the most appropriate one in the list. When substantial damages have been sought, the most appropriate approach is that of Rule 23(b)(3), because it allows notice and an opportunity to opt out.

Food for Thought

What is a "no-notice, no-opt-out class," and why would certifying one involving compensatory or punitive damages be an issue? Rule 23(b)(2) classes are mandatory, meaning that plaintiffs may not opt out of the class and are not entitled to notice. Damages classes, however, do permit opting out and have stringent notice requirements. What issues might arise if a class pursuing both injunctive relief and money damages were certified under Rule 23(b)(2) without the accompanying notice and opt-out rights ordinarily afforded when money damages are pursued by a class?

Jefferson, 195 F.3d at 898. Plaintiffs' argument (regarding (b)(1) certification) recognizing that a decision that could "be dispositive of the interests of other GM dealers in the State of Indiana" who did not participate in that action might "substantially impair or impede their ability to protect their interests" reflects the disadvantage of (b)(2) certification: that Indiana GM dealers would be bound to a judgment or settlement in this case without notice or the opportunity to opt out. Because of the importance of money damages to Plaintiffs' claims, we believe that class members should have the opportunity to receive notice and opt out. We therefore decline to certify a (b)(2) class, though we recognize that any grant of injunctive relief may affect those who choose not to participate in the suit.

c. Rule 23(b)(3)

A class action is maintainable under Rule 23(b)(3) if we find that "the questions of law or fact common to the members of the class *predominate* over any questions affecting only individual members, and that a class action is *superior* to other available methods for the fair and efficient adjudication of the controversy." FED. R. CIV. P. 23(b)(3) (emphasis added). The underlying purpose of Rule 23(b)(3)'s requirements is to assure that a class action has "practical utility" in the suit. *Hylaszek v. Aetna Life Ins. Co.*, 1998 WL 381064, at *3 (N.D. Ill. July 1, 1998). Rule 23(b)(3) lays out four factors which we consider in analyzing these issues:

(A) the interest of members of the class in individually controlling the prosecution . . . of separate actions; (B) the extent and nature of any litigation concerning the controversy already commenced by . . . members of the class; (C) the desirability or undesirability of concentrating the litigation of the claims in the particular forum; (D) the difficulties likely to be encountered in the management of a class action.

FED. R. CIV. P. 23(b)(3).

i. Predominance

Predominance is met when "one or more of the central issues in the action are common to the class and can be said to predominate. . . ." Satisfying this criterion "normally turns on the answer to one basic question: is there an essential factual link between all class members and the defendant for which the law provides a remedy?" We have determined that putative class members share a common basis for their suit: the issue of whether GM's marketing practices violate Indiana law. Each of the plaintiffs involved herein alleges that a one percent charge that he or she formerly agreed to pay for use in local advertising has been diverted to GM's national marketing without his or her consent. The legality of this alleged marketing assessment program under Indiana law is the "dominant, central focus" of the proposed class action. While their objections to General Motors' various marketing initiatives may differ, every member of the proposed class shares the desire to reassert control over what it believes is its marketing money and a common belief that General Motors has in essence stolen its money by exerting exclusive control over the marketing funds.

The essence of Defendant's claim that this class cannot be maintained under Rule 23(b)(3) is that the common issue of the legality of the one percent charge will require individual determination of many unique fact issues as well as legal issues arising from oral representations made to some but not all putative class members. In addition, GM maintains that the plaintiffs want different kinds of relief and that their damages must be individually calculated, thus overshadowing any common issues: "In this action, plaintiffs' goals and remedies are as varied and diverse as the named plaintiffs themselves and, indeed, as diverse as every putative class member."

Rule 23(b)(3) class actions commonly involve numerous levels of damages and injury for different class members. In [*Johns v. DeLeonardis*, 145 F.R.D. 480 (N.D. Ill. 1992)] the court certified a class action despite dissimilar damage amounts because "the extent of damages is not an issue" when certifying the class, rather it is a question for the merits of the lawsuit. * * * Finally, determining damages in this case will not necessitate minitrials because damages can be calculated easily from General Motors computer records tracking the number of vehicles sold by dealers.

The only possibility that Plaintiffs will need to present individualized proof lies in their IDFPA claim, an element of which is "coercion." Assuming that actual coercion must be shown to establish the IDFPA violation, Plaintiffs need not present individualized proof if coercion can be proven on a classwide basis, for example through contracts, agreements and promotional materials uniformly applicable to all members of the proposed class. Other courts addressing this issue under similar fact patterns have held that the need to find coercion will not defeat class certification where it is based upon conduct applicable to the class as a whole.

We conclude that the common legal questions affecting General Motors' liability predominate over any individualized factual and legal questions involved in this case; however, we note that a class could be decertified if it became evident that Plaintiffs must rely upon facts unique to each dealer to show GM forced dealers to participate in the marketing scheme. To the extent the relevant communications differed according to GM division (e.g., different contracts or letters sent to Oldsmobile versus Pontiac dealers) we can create subclasses if material differences prevent their consideration as a single group, with the exception of Buick dealers unless the communications received by them resemble those sent to another type of dealer. (None of the named plaintiffs is a Buick dealer.)

Food for Thought

Won't damages determinations usually be individualized? If so, then is it a good argument to point to damages determinations as undermining predominance? Under what circumstances might the need for individualized damages determinations suffice to overwhelm the common issues that unite the class such that the predominance requirement would not be satisfied?

ii. *Superiority*

Rule 23(b)(3) also requires Plaintiffs to establish that a class action would be the "superior" manner in which to resolve the controversy. It does not appear that individual class members have any particular interest in pursuing separate actions, and we are unaware of any other litigation surrounding this issue already commenced by class members. Thus, the two most relevant issues regarding the superiority of the class action form highlighted by Rule 23(b)(3) are the desirability of concentrating the actions in this forum and the difficulty that management of such a class action would impose upon us. See FED. R. CIV. P. 23(b)(3)(C), (D).

One reason to favor a class action is to avoid duplicative lawsuits, which would thereby waste the parties' and the courts' time and resources. It is without question that allowing this case to proceed as a class action would allow economies of scale to operate and ultimately reduce the overall burden on the courts associated with pursuing the claims versus maintaining individual actions. Assuming for the moment that all of the potential plaintiffs filed suit individually, the federal courts would be open to an avalanche of suits involving duplicitous discovery and a repetition of legal determinations.

A class action allows discovery to proceed on all of the potential claims jointly. A class action also eliminates the potential that the defendants will be subject to contradictory resolutions of the ultimate legal issue; to wit, the validity of the marketing program, because the issue is resolved vis-à-vis all class members at once. A class action simplifies discovery because the defendants and the court will have to deal with only one plaintiffs' counsel, rather than a separate attorney for each individual plaintiff. Discovery disputes can be resolved and legal determinations made with respect to all of the parties at once instead of one plaintiff at a time.

Food for Thought

Are these benefits of class treatment unique to this case, or are they simply the benefits that apply to class actions generally? If the latter is the case, should the court have focused its analysis on what makes class treatment a superior method in this case?

While class actions may present undue pressure upon defendants to settle cases, this factor alone does not outweigh the advantages we have discussed. For these reasons, we hold that Plaintiffs' putative class action is superior to alternative methods of adjudicating the claims and thus this class action may be maintained under Rule 23(b)(3).

CONCLUSION

Plaintiffs' proposed class satisfies the demands of Rule 23(a) and is maintainable under Rule 23(b)(3). Plaintiffs' motion for class certification is therefore GRANTED.

Wal-Mart Stores, Inc. v. Dukes

Supreme Court of the United States
564 U.S. 338 (2011)

JUSTICE SCALIA delivered the opinion of the Court, in which ROBERTS, C.J., and KENNEDY, THOMAS, and ALITO, JJ., joined, and in which GINSBURG, BREYER, SOTOMAYOR, and KAGAN, JJ., joined as to Parts I and III.

We are presented with one of the most expansive class actions ever. The District Court and the Court of Appeals approved the certification of a class comprising about one and a half million plaintiffs, current and former female employees of petitioner Wal-Mart who allege that the discretion exercised by their local supervisors over pay and promotion matters violates Title VII by discriminating against women. In addition to injunctive and declaratory relief, the plaintiffs seek an award of backpay. We consider whether the certification of the plaintiff class was consistent with Federal Rules of Civil Procedure 23(a) and (b)(2).

I

A

Petitioner Wal-Mart is the Nation's largest private employer. * * * In all, Wal-Mart operates approximately 3,400 stores and employs more than one million people.

Pay and promotion decisions at Wal-Mart are generally committed to local managers' broad discretion, which is exercised "in a largely subjective manner." Local store managers may increase the wages of hourly employees (within limits) with only limited corporate oversight. As for salaried employees, such as store managers and their deputies, higher corporate authorities have discretion to set their pay within preestablished ranges.

Promotions work in a similar fashion. Wal-Mart permits store managers to apply their own subjective criteria when selecting candidates as "support managers," which is the first step on the path to management. Admission to Wal-Mart's management training program, however, does require that a candidate meet certain objective criteria, including an above-average performance rating, at least one year's tenure in the applicant's current position, and a willingness to relocate. But except for those requirements, regional and district managers have discretion to use their own judgment when selecting candidates for management training. Promotion to higher office—*e.g.,* assistant manager, co-manager, or store manager—is similarly at the discretion of the employee's superiors after prescribed objective factors are satisfied.

B

The named plaintiffs in this lawsuit, representing the 1.5 million members of the certified class, are three current or former Wal-Mart employees who allege that the company discriminated against them on the basis of their sex by denying them equal pay or promotions, in violation of Title VII of the Civil Rights Act of 1964, 78 Stat. 253, as amended, 42 U.S.C. § 2000e–1 *et seq.*

Betty Dukes began working at a Pittsburgh, California, Wal-Mart in 1994. She started as a cashier, but later sought and received a promotion to customer service manager. After a series of disciplinary violations, however, Dukes was demoted back to cashier and then to greeter. Dukes concedes she violated company policy, but contends that the disciplinary actions were in fact retaliation for invoking internal complaint procedures and that male employees have not been disciplined for similar infractions. Dukes also claims two male greeters in the Pittsburgh store are paid more than she is.

Christine Kwapnoski has worked at Sam's Club stores in Missouri and California for most of her adult life. She has held a number of positions, including a supervisory position. She claims that a male manager yelled at her frequently and screamed at female employees, but not at men. The manager in question "told her to 'doll up,' to wear some makeup, and to dress a little better."

The final named plaintiff, Edith Arana, worked at a Wal-Mart store in Duarte, California, from 1995 to 2001. In 2000, she approached the store manager on more than one occasion about management training, but was brushed off. Arana concluded she was being denied opportunity for advancement because of her sex. She initiated internal complaint procedures, whereupon she was told to apply directly to the district manager if she thought her store manager was being unfair. Arana, however, decided against that and never applied for management training again. In 2001, she was fired for failure to comply with Wal-Mart's timekeeping policy.

These plaintiffs, respondents here, do not allege that Wal-Mart has any express corporate policy against the advancement of women. Rather, they claim that their local managers' discretion over pay and promotions is exercised disproportionately in favor of men, leading to an unlawful disparate impact on female employees, see 42 U.S.C. § 2000e–2(k). And, respondents say, because Wal-Mart is aware of this effect, its refusal to cabin its managers' authority amounts to disparate treatment. Their complaint seeks injunctive and declaratory relief, punitive damages, and backpay. It does not ask for compensatory damages.

Importantly for our purposes, respondents claim that the discrimination to which they have been subjected is common to *all* Wal-Mart's female employees. The basic theory of their case is that a strong and uniform "corporate culture" permits bias against women to infect, perhaps subconsciously, the discretionary decisionmaking of each one of Wal-Mart's thousands of managers—thereby making every woman at the company the victim of one common discriminatory practice. Respondents therefore wish to litigate the Title VII claims of all female employees at Wal-Mart's stores in a nationwide class action.

C

Class certification is governed by Federal Rule of Civil Procedure 23. * * * Invoking th[is] provision[ ], respondents moved the District Court to certify a plaintiff class consisting of " '[a]ll women employed at any Wal-Mart domestic retail store at any time since December 26, 1998, who have been or may be subjected to Wal-Mart's challenged pay and management track promotions policies and practices.' " As evidence that there were indeed "questions of law or fact common to" all the women of Wal-Mart, as Rule 23(a)(2) requires, respondents relied chiefly on three forms of proof: statistical evidence about pay and promotion disparities between men and women at the company, anecdotal reports of discrimination from about 120 of Wal-Mart's female employees, and the testimony of a sociologist, Dr. William Bielby, who conducted a "social framework analysis" of Wal-Mart's "culture" and personnel practices, and concluded that the company was "vulnerable" to gender discrimination. 603 F.3d 571, 601 (9th Cir. 2010) (en banc).

* * *

II

The class action is "an exception to the usual rule that litigation is conducted by and on behalf of the individual named parties only." In order to justify a departure from that rule, "a class representative must be part of the class and 'possess the same interest and suffer the same injury' as the class members." Rule 23(a) ensures that the named plaintiffs are appropriate representatives of the class whose claims they wish to litigate. The Rule's four requirements—numerosity, commonality, typicality, and adequate representation—"effectively 'limit the class claims to those fairly encompassed by the named plaintiff's claims.'"

A

The crux of this case is commonality—the rule requiring a plaintiff to show that "there are questions of law or fact common to the class." Rule 23(a)(2). That language is easy to misread, since "[a]ny competently crafted class complaint literally raises common 'questions.'" Nagareda, Class Certification in the Age of Aggregate Proof, 84 N.Y.U. L. Rev. 97, 131–132 (2009). For example: Do all of us plaintiffs indeed work for Wal-Mart? Do our managers have discretion over pay? Is that an unlawful employment practice? What remedies should we get? Reciting these questions is not sufficient to obtain class certification. Commonality requires the plaintiff to demonstrate that the class members "have suffered the same injury," *General Telephone Co. of Southwest v. Falcon*, 457 U.S. 147, 157 (1982). This does not mean merely that they have all suffered a violation of the same provision of law. Title VII, for example, can be violated in many ways—by intentional discrimination, or by hiring

Food for Thought

Read Justice Scalia's analysis of the commonality requirement carefully. What is the basis for his assertions regarding the meaning of "common questions"? Is his view sound? Do you agree with his analysis? What should be the proper understanding of the common-question requirement of Rule 23(a)(2)? *See* A. Benjamin Spencer, *Class Actions, Heightened Commonality, and Declining Access to Justice,* 93 B.U. L. Rev. 441, 464 (2013).

and promotion criteria that result in disparate impact, and by the use of these practices on the part of many different superiors in a single company. Quite obviously, the mere claim by employees of the same company that they have suffered a Title VII injury, or even a disparate-impact Title VII injury, gives no cause to believe that all their claims can productively be litigated at once. Their claims must depend upon a common contention—for example, the assertion of discriminatory bias on the part of the same supervisor. That common contention, moreover, must be of such a nature that it is capable of classwide resolution—which means that determination of its truth or falsity will resolve an issue that is central to the validity of each one of the claims in one stroke.

> "What matters to class certification . . . is not the raising of common 'questions'—even in droves—but, rather the capacity of a classwide proceeding to generate common *answers* apt to drive the resolution of the litigation. Dissimilarities within the proposed class are what have the potential to impede the generation of common answers." Nagareda, *supra,* at 132.

Rule 23 does not set forth a mere pleading standard. A party seeking class certification must affirmatively demonstrate his compliance with the Rule—that is, he must be prepared to prove that there are *in fact* sufficiently numerous parties, common questions of law or fact, etc. We recognized in *Falcon* that "sometimes it may be necessary for the court to probe behind the pleadings before coming to rest on the certification question," and that certification is proper only if "the trial court is satisfied, after a rigorous analysis, that the prerequisites of Rule 23(a) have been satisfied." Frequently that "rigorous analysis" will entail some overlap with the merits of the plaintiff's underlying claim. That cannot be helped. " '[T]he class determination generally involves considerations that are enmeshed in the factual and legal issues comprising the plaintiff's cause of action.' " *Falcon, supra, at 160, 102 S.Ct. 2364*. Nor is there anything unusual about that consequence: The necessity of touching aspects of the merits in order to resolve preliminary matters, *e.g.,* jurisdiction and venue, is a familiar feature of litigation. * * *

In this case, proof of commonality necessarily overlaps with respondents' merits contention that Wal-Mart engages in a *pattern or practice* of discrimination. That is so because, in resolving an individual's Title VII claim, the crux of the inquiry is "the reason for a particular employment decision." Here respondents wish to sue about literally millions of employment decisions at once. Without some glue holding the alleged *reasons* for all those decisions together, it will be impossible to say that examination of all the class members' claims for relief will produce a common answer to the crucial question *why was I disfavored.*

B

This Court's opinion in *Falcon* describes how the commonality issue must be approached. There an employee who claimed that he was deliberately denied a promotion on account of race obtained certification of a class comprising all employees wrongfully denied promotions and all applicants wrongfully denied jobs. We rejected that composite class for lack of commonality and typicality, explaining:

> "Conceptually, there is a wide gap between (a) an individual's claim that he has been denied a promotion [or higher pay] on discriminatory grounds, and his otherwise unsupported allegation that the company has a policy of discrimination, and (b) the existence of a class of persons who have suffered the same injury as that individual, such that the individual's claim and the class claim will share common questions of law or fact and that the individual's claim will be typical of the class claims."

Falcon suggested two ways in which that conceptual gap might be bridged. First, if the employer "used a biased testing procedure to evaluate both applicants for employment and incumbent employees, a class action on behalf of every applicant or employee who might have been prejudiced by the test clearly would satisfy the commonality and typicality requirements of Rule 23(a)." Second, "[s]ignificant proof that an employer operated under a general policy of discrimination conceivably could justify a class of both applicants and employees if the discrimination manifested itself in hiring and promotion practices in the same general fashion, such as through entirely subjective decisionmaking processes." We think that statement precisely describes respondents' burden in this case. The first manner of bridging the gap obviously has no application here; Wal-Mart has no testing procedure or other companywide evaluation method that can be charged with bias. The whole point of permitting discretionary decisionmaking is to avoid evaluating employees under a common standard.

The second manner of bridging the gap requires "significant proof" that Wal-Mart "operated under a general policy of discrimination." That is entirely absent here. Wal-Mart's announced policy forbids sex discrimination, and as the District Court recognized the company imposes penalties for denials of equal employment opportunity. The only evidence of a "general policy of discrimination" respondents produced was the testimony of Dr. William Bielby, their sociological expert. Relying on "social framework" analysis, Bielby testified that Wal-Mart has a "strong corporate culture," that makes it " 'vulnerable' " to "gender bias." He could not, however, "determine with any specificity how regularly stereotypes play a meaningful role in employment decisions at Wal-Mart. At his deposition . . . Dr. Bielby conceded that he could not calculate whether 0.5 percent or 95 percent of the employment decisions at Wal-Mart might be determined by stereotyped thinking." * * * Bielby's testimony does nothing to advance respondents' case. "[W]hether 0.5 percent or

95 percent of the employment decisions at Wal-Mart might be determined by stereotyped thinking" is the essential question on which respondents' theory of commonality depends. If Bielby admittedly has no answer to that question, we can safely disregard what he has to say. It is worlds away from "significant proof" that Wal-Mart "operated under a general policy of discrimination."

C

The only corporate policy that the plaintiffs' evidence convincingly establishes is Wal-Mart's "policy" of *allowing discretion* by local supervisors over employment matters. On its face, of course, that is just the opposite of a uniform employment practice that would provide the commonality needed for a class action; it is a policy *against having* uniform employment practices. It is also a very common and presumptively reasonable way of doing business—one that we have said "should itself raise no inference of discriminatory conduct."

To be sure, we have recognized that, "in appropriate cases," giving discretion to lower-level supervisors can be the basis of Title VII liability under a disparate-impact theory—since "an employer's undisciplined system of subjective decision-making [can have] precisely the same effects as a system pervaded by impermissible intentional discrimination." But the recognition that this type of Title VII claim "can" exist does not lead to the conclusion that every employee in a company using a system of discretion has such a claim in common. To the contrary, left to their own devices most managers in any corporation—and surely most managers in a corporation that forbids sex discrimination—would select sex-neutral, performance-based criteria for hiring and promotion that produce no actionable disparity at all. Others may choose to reward various attributes that produce disparate impact—such as scores on general aptitude tests or educational achievements. And still other managers may be guilty of intentional discrimination that produces a sex-based disparity. In such a company, demonstrating the invalidity of one manager's use of discretion will do nothing to demonstrate the invalidity of another's. A party seeking to certify a nationwide class will be unable to show that all the employees' Title VII claims will in fact depend on the answers to common questions.

Respondents have not identified a common mode of exercising discretion that pervades the entire company—aside from their reliance on Dr. Bielby's social frameworks analysis that we have rejected. In a company of Wal-Mart's size and geographical scope, it is quite unbelievable that all managers would exercise their discretion in a common way without some common direction. Respondents attempt to make that showing by means of statistical and anecdotal evidence, but their evidence falls well short.

The statistical evidence consists primarily of regression analyses performed by Dr. Richard Drogin, a statistician, and Dr. Marc Bendick, a labor economist. Drogin conducted his analysis region-by-region, comparing the number of women promoted into management positions with the percentage of women in the available pool of hourly workers. After considering regional and national data, Drogin concluded that "there are statistically significant disparities between men and women at Wal-Mart . . . [and] these disparities . . . can be explained only by gender discrimination. Bendick compared work-force data from Wal-Mart and competitive retailers and concluded that Wal-Mart "promotes a lower percentage of women than its competitors."

Even if they are taken at face value, these studies are insufficient to establish that respondents' theory can be proved on a classwide basis. In *Falcon,* we held that one named plaintiff's experience of discrimination was insufficient to infer that "discriminatory treatment is typical of [the employer's employment] practices." A similar failure of inference arises here. "Information about disparities at the regional and national level does not establish the existence of disparities at individual stores, let alone raise the inference that a company-wide policy of discrimination is implemented by discretionary decisions at the store and district level." A regional pay disparity, for example, may be attributable to only a small set of Wal-Mart stores, and cannot by itself establish the uniform, store-by-store disparity upon which the plaintiffs' theory of commonality depends.

There is another, more fundamental, respect in which respondents' statistical proof fails. Even if it established (as it does not) a pay or promotion pattern that differs from the nationwide figures or the regional figures in *all* of Wal-Mart's 3,400 stores, that would still not demonstrate that commonality of issue exists. Some managers will claim that the availability of women, or qualified women, or interested women, in their stores' area does not mirror the national or regional statistics. And almost all of them will claim to have been applying some sex-neutral, performance-based criteria—whose nature and effects will differ from store to store. In the landmark case of ours which held that giving discretion to lower-level supervisors can be the basis of Title VII liability under a disparate-impact theory, the plurality opinion *conditioned* that holding on the corollary that merely proving that the discretionary system has produced a racial or sexual disparity *is not enough.* "[T]he plaintiff must begin by identifying the specific employment practice that is challenged." <u>Watson v. Fort Worth Bank & Trust, 487 U.S. 977, 994 (1988)</u>, accord, <u>Wards Cove Packing Co. v. Atonio, 490 U.S. 642, 656 (1989)</u> (approving that statement), superseded by statute on other grounds, <u>42 U.S.C. § 2000e–2(k)</u>. That is all the more necessary when a class of plaintiffs is sought to be certified. Other than the bare existence of delegated discretion, respondents have identified no "specific employment practice"—much less one that ties all their 1.5 million claims together. Merely showing that Wal-Mart's policy of discretion has produced an overall sex-based disparity does not suffice.

Respondents' anecdotal evidence suffers from the same defects, and in addition is too weak to raise any inference that all the individual, discretionary personnel decisions are discriminatory. * * * Here * * * respondents filed some 120 affidavits reporting experiences of discrimination—about 1 for every 12,500 class members—relating to only some 235 out of Wal-Mart's 3,400 stores. More than half of these reports are concentrated in only six States (Alabama, California, Florida, Missouri, Texas, and Wisconsin); half of all States have only one or two anecdotes; and 14 States have no anecdotes about Wal-Mart's operations at all. Even if every single one of these accounts is true, that would not demonstrate that the entire company "operate[s] under a general policy of discrimination," *Falcon, supra,* at 159, n. 15, which is what respondents must show to certify a companywide class.

* * *

III

We also conclude that respondents' claims for backpay were improperly certified under Federal Rule of Civil Procedure 23(b)(2). Our opinion in *Ticor Title Ins. Co. v. Brown,* 511 U.S. 117, 121 (1994) *(per curiam)* expressed serious doubt about whether claims for monetary relief may be certified under that provision. We now hold that they may not, at least where (as here) the monetary relief is not incidental to the injunctive or declaratory relief.

A

Rule 23(b)(2) allows class treatment when "the party opposing the class has acted or refused to act on grounds that apply generally to the class, so that final injunctive relief or corresponding declaratory relief is appropriate respecting the class as a whole." One possible reading of this provision is that it applies *only* to requests for such injunctive or declaratory relief and does not authorize the class certification of monetary claims at all. We need not reach that broader question in this case, because we think that, at a minimum, claims for *individualized* relief (like the backpay at issue here) do not satisfy the Rule. The key to the (b)(2) class is "the indivisible nature of the injunctive or declaratory remedy warranted—the notion that the conduct is such that it can be enjoined or declared unlawful only as to all of the class members or as to none of them." Nagareda, 84 N.Y.U. L. Rev., at 132. In other words, Rule 23(b)(2) applies only when a single injunction or declaratory judgment would provide relief to each member of the class. It does not authorize class certification when each individual class member would be entitled to a *different* injunction or declaratory judgment against the defendant. Similarly, it does not authorize class certification when each class member would be entitled to an individualized award of monetary damages.

That interpretation accords with the history of the Rule. Because Rule 23 "stems from equity practice" that predated its codification, in determining its meaning we have previously looked to the historical models on which the Rule was based. As we observed in *Amchem Products, Inc. v. Windsor,* 521 U.S. 591 (1997), "[c]ivil rights cases against parties charged with unlawful, class-based discrimination are prime examples" of what (b)(2) is meant to capture. 521 U.S., at 614. In particular, the Rule reflects a series of decisions involving challenges to racial segregation—conduct that was remedied by a single classwide order. In none of the cases cited by the Advisory Committee as examples of (b)(2)'s antecedents did the plaintiffs combine any claim for individualized relief with their classwide injunction. See Advisory Committee's Note, 39 F.R.D. 69, 102 (1966) (citing cases).

Permitting the combination of individualized and classwide relief in a (b)(2) class is also inconsistent with the structure of Rule 23(b). Classes certified under (b)(1) and (b)(2) share the most traditional justifications for class treatment—that individual adjudications would be impossible or unworkable, as in a (b)(1) class, or that the relief sought must perforce affect the entire class at once, as in a (b)(2) class. For that reason these are also mandatory classes: The Rule provides no opportunity for (b)(1) or (b)(2) class members to opt out, and does not even oblige the District Court to afford them notice of the action. Rule 23(b)(3), by contrast, is an "adventuresome innovation" of the 1966 amendments, *Amchem,* 521 U.S., at 614, framed for situations "in which 'class-action treatment is not as clearly called for'," id., at 615, 117 S.Ct. 2231. It allows class certification in a much wider set of circumstances but with greater procedural protections. Its only prerequisites are that "the questions of law or fact common to class members predominate over any questions affecting only individual members, and that a class action is superior to other available methods for fairly and efficiently adjudicating the controversy." Rule 23(b)(3). And unlike (b)(1) and (b)(2) classes, the (b)(3) class is not mandatory; class members are entitled to receive "the best notice that is practicable under the circumstances" and to withdraw from the class at their option. See Rule 23(c)(2)(B).

Given that structure, we think it clear that individualized monetary claims belong in Rule 23(b)(3). The procedural protections attending the (b)(3) class— predominance, superiority, mandatory notice, and the right to opt out—are missing from (b)(2) not because the Rule considers them unnecessary, but because it considers them unnecessary *to a (b)(2) class.* When a class seeks an indivisible injunction benefitting all its members at once, there is no reason to undertake a case-specific inquiry into whether class issues predominate or whether class action is a superior method of adjudicating the dispute. Predominance and superiority are self-evident. But with respect to each class member's individualized claim for money, that is not so—which is precisely why (b)(3) requires the judge to make findings about predominance and superiority before allowing the class. Similarly, (b)(2) does not require that class members be given notice and optout rights, presumably because it is thought (rightly or wrongly) that notice has no purpose when the class is mandatory, and that depriving people of their right to sue in this manner complies with the Due Process Clause. In the context of a class action predominantly for money damages we have held that absence of notice and opt-out violates due process. See *Phillips Petroleum Co. v. Shutts,* 472 U.S. 797, 812 (1985). While we have never held that to be so where the monetary claims do not predominate, the serious possibility that it may be so provides an additional reason not to read Rule 23(b)(2) to include the monetary claims here.

B

Against that conclusion, respondents argue that their claims for backpay were appropriately certified as part of a class under Rule 23(b)(2) because those claims do not "predominate" over their requests for injunctive and declaratory relief. They rely upon the Advisory Committee's statement that Rule 23(b)(2) "does not extend to cases in which the appropriate final relief relates *exclusively or predominantly* to money damages." 39 F.R.D., at 102 (emphasis added). The negative implication, they argue, is that it *does* extend to cases in which the appropriate final relief relates only partially and nonpredominantly to money damages. Of course it is the Rule itself, not the Advisory Committee's description of it, that governs. And a mere negative inference does not in our view suffice to establish a disposition that has no basis in the Rule's text, and that does obvious violence to the Rule's structural features. The mere "predominance" of a proper (b)(2) injunctive claim does nothing to justify elimination of Rule 23(b)(3)'s

Food for Thought

Notice Justice Scalia's admonition that it is the Rule's text that governs their interpretation of it. This is a frequent refrain of his. Is he faithful to that creed in his interpretation of the common-question requirement of Rule 23(a)?

procedural protections: It neither establishes the superiority of *class* adjudication over *individual* adjudication nor cures the notice and opt-out problems. We fail to see why the Rule should be read to nullify these protections whenever a plaintiff class, at its option, combines its monetary claims with a request—even a "predominating request"—for an injunction.

Respondents' predominance test, moreover, creates perverse incentives for class representatives to place at risk potentially valid claims for monetary relief. In this case, for example, the named plaintiffs declined to include employees' claims for compensatory damages in their complaint. That strategy of including only backpay claims made it more likely that monetary relief would not "predominate." But it also created the possibility (if the predominance test were correct) that individual class members' compensatory-damages claims would be *precluded* by litigation they had no power to hold themselves apart from. If it were determined, for example, that a particular class member is not entitled to backpay because her denial of increased pay or a promotion was *not* the product of discrimination, that employee might be collaterally estopped from independently seeking compensatory damages based on that same denial. That possibility underscores the need for plaintiffs with individual monetary claims to decide *for themselves* whether to tie their fates to the class representatives' or go it alone—a choice Rule 23(b)(2) does not ensure that they have.

* * *

Finally, respondents argue that their backpay claims are appropriate for a (b)(2) class action because a backpay award is equitable in nature. The latter may be true, but it is irrelevant. The Rule does not speak of "equitable" remedies generally but of injunctions and declaratory judgments. As Title VII itself makes pellucidly clear, backpay is neither. See 42 U.S.C. § 2000e–5(g)(2)(B)(i) and (ii) (distinguishing between declaratory and injunctive relief and the payment of "backpay," see § 2000e–5(g)(2)(A)).

C

In *Allison v. Citgo Petroleum Corp.*, 151 F.3d 402, 415 (5th Cir. 1998), the Fifth Circuit held that a (b)(2) class would permit the certification of monetary relief that is "incidental to requested injunctive or declaratory relief," which it defined as "damages that flow directly from liability to the class *as a whole* on the claims forming the basis of the injunctive or declaratory relief." In that court's view, such "incidental damage should not require additional hearings to resolve the disparate merits of each individual's case; it should neither introduce new substantial legal or factual issues, nor entail complex individualized determinations." *Ibid.* We need not decide in this case whether there are any forms of "incidental" monetary relief that are consistent with the interpretation of Rule 23(b)(2) we have announced and that comply with the Due Process Clause. Respondents do not argue that they can satisfy this standard, and in any event they cannot.

* * *

The judgment of the Court of Appeals is

Reversed.

JUSTICE GINSBURG, with whom JUSTICE BREYER, JUSTICE SOTOMAYOR, and JUSTICE KAGAN join, concurring in part and dissenting in part.

The class in this case, I agree with the Court, should not have been certified under Federal Rule of Civil Procedure 23(b)(2). The plaintiffs, alleging discrimination in violation of Title VII, 42 U.S.C. § 2000e *et seq.*, seek monetary relief that is not merely incidental to any injunctive or declaratory relief that might be available. A putative class of this type may be certifiable under Rule 23(b)(3), if the plaintiffs show that common class questions "predominate" over issues affecting individuals— *e.g.*, qualification for, and the amount of, backpay or compensatory damages—and that a class action is "superior" to other modes of adjudication.

Whether the class the plaintiffs describe meets the specific requirements of Rule 23(b)(3) is not before the Court, and I would reserve that matter for consideration and decision on remand. The Court, however, disqualifies the class at the starting gate, holding that the plaintiffs cannot cross the "commonality" line set by Rule 23(a)(2). In so ruling, the Court imports into the Rule 23(a) determination concerns properly addressed in a Rule 23(b)(3) assessment.

I

A

Rule 23(a)(2) establishes a preliminary requirement for maintaining a class action: "[T]here are questions of law or fact common to the class." The Rule "does not require that all questions of law or fact raised in the litigation be common," 1 H. Newberg & A. Conte, Newberg on Class Actions § 3.10, pp. 3–48 to 3–49 (3d ed.1992); indeed, "[e]ven a single question of law or fact common to the members of the class will satisfy the commonality requirement," Nagareda, The Preexistence Principle and the Structure of the Class Action, 103 Colum. L.Rev. 149, 176, n.110 (2003). See Advisory Committee's 1937 Notes on FED. RULE CIV. PROC. 23, 28 U.S.C.App., p. 138 (citing with approval cases in which "there was only a question of law or fact common to" the class members).

A "question" is ordinarily understood to be "[a] subject or point open to controversy." American Heritage Dictionary 1483 (3d ed.1992). See also Black's Law Dictionary 1366 (9th ed.2009) (defining "question of fact" as "[a] disputed issue to be resolved . . . [at] trial" and "question of law" as "[a]n issue to be decided by the judge"). Thus, a "question" "common to the class" must be a dispute, either of fact or of law, the resolution of which will advance the determination of the class members' claims.

* * *

C

The District Court's identification of a common question, whether Wal-Mart's pay and promotions policies gave rise to unlawful discrimination, was hardly infirm. The practice of delegating to supervisors large discretion to make personnel decisions, uncontrolled by formal standards, has long been known to have the potential to produce disparate effects. Managers, like all humankind, may be prey to biases of which they are unaware. The risk of discrimination is heightened when those managers are predominantly of one sex, and are steeped in a corporate culture that perpetuates gender stereotypes.

* * *

We have held that "discretionary employment practices" can give rise to Title VII claims, not only when such practices are motivated by discriminatory intent

670 CIVIL PROCEDURE *A Contemporary Approach*

but also when they produce discriminatory results. See *Watson v. Fort Worth Bank & Trust*, 487 U.S. 977, 988, 991 (1988). In *Watson*, as here, an employer had given its managers large authority over promotions. An employee sued the bank under Title VII, alleging that the "discretionary promotion system" caused a discriminatory effect based on race. 487 U.S., at 984 (internal quotation marks omitted). Four different supervisors had declined, on separate occasions, to promote the employee. *Id., at 982*. Their reasons were subjective and unknown. The employer, we noted "had not developed precise and formal criteria for evaluating candidates"; "[i]t relied instead on the subjective judgment of supervisors." *Ibid.*

Aware of "the problem of subconscious stereotypes and prejudices," we held that the employer's "undisciplined system of subjective decisionmaking" was an "employment practic[e]" that "may be analyzed under the disparate impact approach." *Id., at 990–991*. See also *Wards Cove Packing Co. v. Atonio*, 490 U.S. 642, 657 (1989) (recognizing "the use of 'subjective decision making' " as an "employment practic[e]" subject to disparate-impact attack).

The plaintiffs' allegations state claims of gender discrimination in the form of biased decisionmaking in both pay and promotions. The evidence reviewed by the District Court adequately demonstrated that resolving those claims would necessitate examination of particular policies and practices alleged to affect, adversely and globally, women employed at Wal-Mart's stores. Rule 23(a)(2), setting a necessary but not a sufficient criterion for class-action certification, demands nothing further.

II

A

The Court gives no credence to the key dispute common to the class: whether Wal-Mart's discretionary pay and promotion policies are discriminatory. "What matters," the Court asserts, "is not the raising of common 'questions,' " but whether there are "[d]issimilarities within the proposed class" that "have the potential to impede the generation of common answers."

The Court blends Rule 23(a)(2)'s threshold criterion with the more demanding criteria of Rule 23(b)(3), and thereby elevates the (a)(2) inquiry so that it is no longer "easily satisfied," 5 J. Moore et al., Moore's Federal Practice § 23.23[2], p. 23–72 (3d ed. 2011).[7] Rule 23(b)(3) certification requires, in addition to the four 23(a)

---

[7] The Court places considerable weight on *General Telephone Co. of Southwest v. Falcon*, 457 U.S. 147 (1982). That case has little relevance to the question before the Court today. The lead plaintiff in *Falcon* alleged discrimination evidenced by the company's failure to promote him and other Mexican-American employees and failure to hire Mexican-American applicants. There were "*no* common questions of law or fact" between the claims of the lead plaintiff and the applicant class. 457 U.S., at 162 (Burger, C.J., concurring in part and dissenting in part) (emphasis added). The plaintiff-employee alleged that the defendant-employer had discriminated against him intentionally. The applicant class claims, by contrast, were "advanced under the 'adverse impact' theory," *ibid.*, appropriate for facially neutral practices.

findings, determinations that "questions of law or fact common to class members predominate over any questions affecting only individual members" and that "a class action is superior to other available methods for . . . adjudicating the controversy."

The Court's emphasis on differences between class members mimics the Rule 23(b)(3) inquiry into whether common questions "predominate" over individual issues. And by asking whether the individual differences "impede" common adjudication, the Court duplicates 23(b)(3)'s question whether "a class action is superior" to other modes of adjudication. Indeed, Professor Nagareda, whose "dissimilarities" inquiry the Court endorses, developed his position in the context of Rule 23(b)(3). See 84 N.Y.U. L. Rev., at 131 (Rule 23(b)(3) requires "some decisive degree of similarity across the proposed class" because it "speaks of common 'questions' that 'predominate' over individual ones"). "The Rule 23(b)(3) predominance inquiry" is meant to "tes[t] whether proposed classes are sufficiently cohesive to warrant adjudication by representation." *Amchem Products, Inc. v. Windsor,* 521 U.S. 591, 623 (1997). If courts must conduct a "dissimilarities" analysis at the Rule 23(a)(2) stage, no mission remains for Rule 23(b)(3).

Because Rule 23(a) is also a prerequisite for Rule 23(b)(1) and Rule 23(b)(2) classes, the Court's "dissimilarities" position is far reaching. Individual differences should not bar a Rule 23(b)(1) or Rule 23(b)(2) class, so long as the Rule 23(a) threshold is met. See *Amchem Products,* 521 U.S., at 623, n. 19 (Rule 23(b)(1)(B) "does not have a predominance requirement"); *Yamasaki,* 442 U.S., at 701 (Rule 23(b)(2) action in which the Court noted that "[i]t is unlikely that differences in the factual background of each claim will affect the outcome of the legal issue"). For example, in *Franks v. Bowman Transp. Co.,* 424 U.S. 747 (1976), a Rule 23(b)(2) class of African-American truckdrivers complained that the defendant had discriminatorily refused to hire black applicants. We recognized that the "qualification[s] and performance" of individual class members might vary. *Id., at 772* (internal quotation marks omitted). "Generalizations concerning such individually applicable evidence," we cautioned, "cannot serve as a justification for the denial of [injunctive] relief to the entire class." *Ibid.*

B

The "dissimilarities" approach leads the Court to train its attention on what distinguishes individual class members, rather than on what unites them. Given the lack of standards for pay and promotions, the majority says, "demonstrating the invalidity of one manager's use of discretion will do nothing to demonstrate the invalidity of another's."

Wal-Mart's delegation of discretion over pay and promotions is a policy uniform throughout all stores. The very nature of discretion is that people will exercise it in

---

"[T]he only commonality [wa]s that respondent is a Mexican-American and he seeks to represent a class of Mexican-Americans." *Ibid.* Here the same practices touch and concern all members of the class.

various ways. A system of delegated discretion, *Watson* held, is a practice actionable under Title VII when it produces discriminatory outcomes. A finding that Wal-Mart's pay and promotions practices in fact violate the law would be the first step in the usual order of proof for plaintiffs seeking individual remedies for company-wide discrimination. *Teamsters v. United States*, 431 U.S. 324, 359 (1977); see *Albemarle Paper Co. v. Moody*, 422 U.S. 405, 415–423 (1975). That each individual employee's unique circumstances will ultimately determine whether she is entitled to backpay or damages, § 2000e–5(g)(2)(A) (barring backpay if a plaintiff "was refused . . . advancement . . . for any reason other than discrimination"), should not factor into the Rule 23(a)(2) determination.

* * *

The Court errs in importing a "dissimilarities" notion suited to Rule 23(b)(3) into the Rule 23(a) commonality inquiry. I therefore cannot join Part II of the Court's opinion.

Points for Discussion

a. Injunctive-Relief Versus Damages Class Actions

In *Hubler Chevrolet*, the court faced a dilemma in classifying the class under Rule 23(b). The heart of the issue was whether this action, which was seeking both injunctive and money damages relief, should be classified as an injunctive-relief class under Rule 23(b)(2) or a damages class under Rule 23(b)(3). What standard did the court use to make this determination? After *Wal-Mart*, is there any ability to certify "hybrid" cases that seek both monetary and injunctive relief as injunctive relief classes under Rule 23(b)(2)? *See Wal-Mart, 564 U.S. at 360* ("Rule 23(b)(2) . . . does not authorize class certification when each class member would be entitled to an individualized award of monetary damages."). Classes that seek truly class-wide injunctive relief should have no difficulty obtaining certification. *See, e.g., Ligon v. City of New York*, 288 F.R.D. 72, 77 (S.D.N.Y. 2013) (certifying class seeking "an order requiring the NYPD to create and implement new policies, training programs, and monitoring and supervisory procedures that specifically address the problem of unconstitutional trespass stops").

Why does it matter how the class action is categorized under Rule 23(b)? Because Rule 23(b)(3) damages class actions are historically disfavored, a number of additional requirements apply to such class actions that are not applicable to the remaining categories. First, absent members of the class have the right to *opt out* of the action so that they remain free to pursue their claims individually. The other three types of class actions do not afford opt-out rights to absent class members. Second, there are more rigorous notice requirements for Rule 23(b)(3) classes due to the need to afford each absent class member the opportunity to take advantage of these opt-out rights. *See Eisen v. Carlisle & Jacquelin, 417 U.S. 156, 173, 177 (1974)* (holding that *Mullane* notice—notice reasonably calculated under the circumstances to apprise absent class members of the pendency of the action—applies to notice of opt-out rights in Rule 23(b)(3) classes, and that plaintiffs rather than defendants have to bear the cost of such notice). Third, as noted above, damages class actions have two additional requirements not applicable to the other categories—predominance and superiority—making it more difficult to achieve class certification as a damages class.

b. Mandatory Class Actions

Each of the types of class actions except for the damages class provided for in Rule 23(b)(3) are mandatory classes because, as just mentioned, class members are not permitted to opt out of the class. Why do you think opting out is not permitted in these types of class actions? Take another look at the standards for mandatory class actions. Are there any similarities between these standards and those for compulsory party joinder under Rule 19(a)?

c. Predominance and Superiority for Rule 23(b)(3) Classes

How did the court in *Hubler Chevrolet* determine whether the common issues predominated over individual matters? Why did the court reject the assertion that individual damages determination would predominate over the common legal issues? In *Jenkins v. Raymark Industries, Inc., 782 F.2d 468 (5th Cir. 1986)*, the court certified an asbestos class action notwithstanding the fact that individual issues— such as individual exposure and applicability of a statute-of-limitations defense to various claims—were substantial. According to the *Jenkins* court, resolution of the "core liability" of the defendant with respect to the harmfulness of the product united the class and predominated over individual issues. Part of what enabled the court to make this determination was the plan to use "phased trials" to try the class-wide issues first, followed by individual "mini-trials" of the claims of several plaintiffs. Do you think that difficulties with predominance should be overcome by such a phased or bifurcated trial approach that defers treatment of the separate issues to a later point in the process? Is such an approach consistent with Rule 23? *See Amchem Products, Inc. v. Windsor, 521 U.S. 591, 625 (1999)* ("Even mass tort cases arising from a common cause or disaster may, depending upon the circumstances, satisfy the predominance requirement" even though "'mass accident' cases are likely to present 'significant questions, not only of damages but of liability and defenses of liability, . . . affecting the individuals in different ways.'" (quoting FED. R. CIV. P. 23 advisory committee's note (1966))).

Two recent Supreme Court cases provide more guidance regarding the predominance inquiry. In *Comcast Corp. v. Behrend, 133 S. Ct. 1426 (2013)*, the Court indicated that the need for individualized damages determinations can undermine the predominance required for class certification:

> [I]t is clear that, under the proper standard for evaluating certification, respondents' [damages] model falls far short of establishing that damages are capable of measurement on a classwide basis. Without presenting another methodology, respondents cannot show Rule 23(b)(3) predominance: Questions of individual damage calculations will inevitably overwhelm questions common to the class.

Id. at 1433. *Comcast* has the potential to make it more difficult to satisfy the predominance requirement when there are differences among class members relating to the extent of individual damages. In another recent Supreme Court case, <u>*Amgen Inc. v. Connecticut Retirement Plans & Trust Funds*, 133 S. Ct. 1184 (2013)</u>, the Court rejected an attempt to require the putative class to prove aspects of their claims at the class certification stage to establish predominance: "While Connecticut Retirement certainly must prove materiality to prevail on the merits, we hold that such proof is not a prerequisite to class certification. Rule 23(b)(3) requires a showing that questions common to the class predominate, not that those questions will be answered, on the merits, in favor of the class." *Id.* at 1191.

Regarding superiority, what made proceeding as a class superior to individual lawsuits in *Hubler Chevrolet*? *See also, e.g.,* <u>*Young v. Nationwide Mut. Ins. Co.*, 693 F.3d 532, 545 (6th Cir. 2012)</u> (noting that superiority is satisfied "[w]here it is not economically feasible to obtain relief within the traditional framework of a multiplicity of small individual suits for damages"). Will class treatment always be superior to individual actions or can you imagine a situation in which aggregate litigation is less preferable? *See, e.g.,* <u>*In re Herald*, 2013 WL 5048291, at *9 (2d Cir. Sept. 16, 2013)</u> (holding that class litigation in the U.S. federal courts was not superior to litigating claims along with other actions pending in Ireland); <u>*Vassalle v. Midland Funding L.L.C.*, 708 F.3d 747, 758 (6th Cir. 2013)</u> (holding that class litigation was not superior to individual actions because, in part, "the class members could have collected damages under state law claims that would exceed the value of monetary relief in this settlement").

<u>Rule 23</u> outlines several factors relevant to the superiority determination, including class members' interests in prosecuting and controlling separate actions, the extent of any existing related litigation, the desirability of concentrating the litigation of the claims in the chosen forum, and any likely difficulties in managing the class action. Fed. R. Civ. P. 23(b)(3). The last factor is referred to a *manageability* and can undermine class certification if the class is so large and internally distinctive as to render class treatment unmanageable. *See, e.g.,* <u>*Arch v. Am. Tobacco Co.*, 175 F.R.D. 469, 492 (E.D. Pa. 1997)</u> (refusing to certify the class because "there are simply too many individual issues and class members to try this class efficiently. The manageability problems . . . are staggering").

d. Adequacy of Representation Under Rule 23

To satisfy Rule 23(a)(4), a class representative must, among other factors, be someone who will vigorously pursue the case. 7A C. WRIGHT, A. MILLER & M. KANE, FED. PRAC. & PROC. § 1776 (3d ed. 2005) ("[T]he general standard is that the representatives must be of such a character as to assure the vigorous prosecution or defense of the action so that the members' rights are certain to be protected."). What facts would support a court's finding that the class representative was not adequate to represent the class? Consider *Dubin v. Miller*, 132 F.R.D. 269, 273–74 (D. Colo. 1990) (finding inadequate representation by the class representative based on his demonstrated bias, lack of diligence in prosecuting the action, and lack of credibility), and *Monroe v. City of Charlottesville, Va.*, 579 F.3d 380, 385 (4th Cir. 2009) ("Findings that a representative lacks sufficient interest, credibility, or either knowledge or an understanding of the case—although a knowledge or understanding of all the intricacies of the litigation is not required—are grounds for denying class certification.").

Why does Rule 23 concern itself with the adequacy of the named class representative? Because it is the class counsel, more so than the class representative, that prosecutes the action on behalf of the class, should the rulemakers do away with the adequacy of representation requirement, at least to the extent that it requires scrutiny of class representatives? *See* Jean Wegman Burns, *Decorative Figureheads: Eliminating Class Representatives in Class Action*, 42 HASTINGS L.J. 165 (1990). Rule 23(g) empowers the court to scrutinize the quality of appointed class counsel by considering his or her experience in handling class actions, the work counsel has done to investigate potential claims in the proposed action, counsel's knowledge of the applicable law, and the resources counsel has available to commit to the representation. FED. R. CIV. P. 23(g). If these standards have been satisfied, should that make the qualifications of the class representative less important?

Would due process concerns arise if an absent class member were not adequately represented by the named class representative? What if the interests of the class representative were antagonistic to absent class members; would it be fair to bind them to a judgment obtained by one who did not truly share their interests? *See Hansberry v. Lee*, 311 U.S. 32 (1940) [*FLEX* Case 7.C].

FYI

Rule 23(c)(2) provides that members of mandatory classes "may" be given "appropriate notice" at the discretion of the court, whereas members of damages classes under Rule 23(b)(3) must be given "the best notice that is practicable under the circumstances, including individual notice" if possible. The Supreme Court has held that the cost of such notice—which can be expensive—must be borne by the party seeking class certification. *Eisen v. Carlisle & Jacquelin*, 417 U.S. 156 (1974). What might be the practical impact of placing the expense of providing notice on class members whose claims may be of little monetary value?

Should the class representative simply be the first person who steps forward to initiate the suit, or should the class representative be the "best" person for that role? In the securities context, Congress has determined that the "lead plaintiff" presumptively should be the party who has the greatest financial stake in the outcome of the case. *See* 1995 Private Securities Litigation Reform Act (PSLRA), 15 U.S.C. § 78u–4(a)(3)(B).

e.   Typicality Under Rule 23

Under what circumstances might a class representative's claims not be typical of those claims held by absent class members? In *General Telephone Co. of the Southwest v. Falcon*, 457 U.S. 147 (1982), the Court found an absence of typicality because the class representative—who was asserting a claim of discrimination in promotions against his employer—sought to represent all those who had been discriminated against in hiring by the same employer, a harm the class representative did not allege that he suffered. *See id. at 156* ("[A] class representative must be part of the class and 'possess the same interest and suffer the same injury' as the class members.").

f.   Appealing the Certification Decision

In modern class litigation, the certification stage is the critical battle in the dispute. Failure to attain class certification often means the death of the action, as individual suits are typically not economically viable. Conversely, success at the certification stage can make the threat of large damages more palpable to defendants and can thus lead many of them to settle once the certification battle has been lost.

In the event that either party is dissatisfied with the certification decision, Rule 23(f) permits them to appeal the decision with the permission of the appellate court. *See* Michael E. Solimine & Christine Oliver Hines, *Deciding to Decide: Class Action Certification and Interlocutory Review by the United States Courts of Appeals Under Rule 23(f)*, 41 WM. & MARY L. REV. 1531 (2000) (discussing appeals of certification decisions under Rule 23(f)). Discretion to grant such appeals is exercised by the circuit courts in various ways. *See, e.g., Blair v. Equifax Check Servs., Inc.*, 181 F.3d 832 (7th Cir. 1999) (describing three circumstances in which an appeal is warranted—when a denial of class certification effectively ends the case, when the certification of a class raises the stakes sufficiently to make the pressure on the defendant to settle irresistible, and when an appeal will

FYI

When plaintiffs have damages that are not sufficiently high to warrant individual prosecution of the action, their claims are referred to as *negative value claims*. For example, a bank may have overcharged all of its customers $1.00 a month over the course of 5 years. Each plaintiff's claim would be worth $60, hardly enough to hire an attorney and file suit in federal court. The class action device was created in part to provide plaintiffs having such claims the ability to unite with others and bring suit. Thus, the certification determination is critical because non-certification will mean the end of a case consisting of negative value claims.

lead to clarification of a fundamental question of law); *Chamberlan v. Ford Motor Co., 402 F.3d 952 (9th Cir. 2005)* ("The most notable modification of the *Blair* trilogy has been the development of a fourth category of cases in which review is warranted: when the district court's decision is manifestly erroneous.").

g. Defendant Class Actions

Note that Rule 23 states that persons may sue "or be sued" as representative parties on behalf of a class. This language indicates that defendant class actions are proper under the Rule, meaning that plaintiffs may sue a class of defendants without joining each of them individually. Under what conditions do you think a defendant class action would be appropriate? *See, e.g., Thillens, Inc. v. Community Currency Exchange Ass'n of Illinois, 97 F.R.D. 668 (N.D. Ill. 1983).* ("Defendant classes seldom are certified. If at all, such certification most commonly occurs (1) in patent infringement cases . . . (2) in suits against local public officials challenging the validity of state laws . . . or (3) in securities litigation."). Who can serve as an adequate representative for a defendant class? *See, e.g.*, Note, *Defendant Class Actions*, 91 HARV. L. REV. 630, 642 (1978) (arguing that trade or labor organizations are ideal adequate representatives for classes of defendants belonging to the organizations).

---

2. Special Issues Pertaining to Class Actions

Certification of a class is only one of the myriad issues surrounding class actions in the federal system. Below, we will review a few of the more important of these issues, focusing on jurisdiction, choice of law, arbitration, and settlement in the class action context. This section concludes with an overview of the Class Action Fairness Act of 2005, legislation that has significantly altered the class action landscape.

a. Subject Matter Jurisdiction

The jurisdictional questions relevant in other joinder contexts apply here as well, but are magnified in significance given the large scale of class actions and the potentially high stakes involved in such litigation. Because Rule 23 is simply a joinder device, the claims asserted must enjoy federal subject matter jurisdiction to be entertained by the federal courts. When the claims asserted arise under federal law, subject matter jurisdiction is not a problem. *See* 28 U.S.C. § 1331.

Difficulties arise when the plaintiffs assert state-law claims and seek to invoke the diversity jurisdiction of the federal courts. The federal diversity statute requires that all of the plaintiffs be from different states than all of the defendants (meaning there must be "complete diversity"), and the amount in controversy must exceed $75,000. *See* 28 U.S.C. § 1332. Recall, however, that the claims of multiple plaintiffs ordinarily may not be aggregated to reach the jurisdictional amount. *See Snyder v. Harris, 394 U.S. 332 (1969)* (discussed in Chapter 3). Thus, the Supreme Court ruled that even where one class member's claim did exceed the jurisdictionally-required amount, other class members could not simply piggyback on the qualifying claims if their own claims were jurisdictionally insufficient. *See* Zahn v. Int'l Paper Co., 414 U.S. 291, 301 (1973). The enactment of the supplemental jurisdiction statute, 28 U.S.C. § 1367, combined with the Supreme Court's more recent decision in *Exxon Mobil Corp. v. Allapattah Services, Inc.*, 545 U.S. 546 (2005), overturned the *Zahn* rule. In *Exxon Mobil*, the Court determined that jurisdictionally insufficient claims may be appended to a jurisdictionally sufficient claim when proceeding as a class under Rule 23 under the terms of § 1367. Note also, as discussed in Chapter 3, that diversity of citizenship for class actions is determined with reference to the citizenship of the class representatives, not absent class members.

b. Personal Jurisdiction

To render a binding judgment against defendants, courts must have personal jurisdiction over them. Ordinarily, when a plaintiff relies on specific jurisdiction, he must establish that jurisdiction is proper for "each claim asserted against a defendant." *Action Embroidery Corp. v. Atl. Embroidery, Inc.*, 368 F.3d 1174, 1180 (9th Cir. 2004); *see also* Phillips Exeter Academy v. Howard Phillips Fund, 196 F.3d 284, 289 (1st Cir. 1999) ("Questions of specific jurisdiction are always tied to the particular claims asserted."); 5B C. WRIGHT & A. MILLER, FED. PRAC. & PROC. § 1351 n.30 (3d ed. 2004) ("There is no such thing as supplemental specific personal jurisdiction; if separate claims are pled, specific personal jurisdiction must independently exist for each claim and the existence of personal jurisdiction for one claim will not provide the basis for another claim."). Thus, in the class action context, the court hearing the case should be required to have personal jurisdiction over the defendant with respect to the claims of each class member. *See* Bristol-Myers Squibb Co. v. Superior Court, 137 S. Ct. 1773 (2017) (holding that due process does not permit the exercise of specific personal jurisdiction in California over the claims of nonresident co-plaintiffs whose claims had no connection with California).

However, there are courts that—at least prior to the certification of the class—assess personal jurisdiction exclusively with regard to the claims of the named class representatives. *See, e.g.,* Ambriz v. Coca Cola Co., 2014 WL 296159 at *6 (N.D. Cal. Jan. 27, 2014) ("[I]t is the named plaintiff's claim that 'must arise out of or result from the defendant's forum-related activities,' not the claims of the unnamed members of the proposed class, who are not party to the litigation absent class certification." (citation omitted)); Williams v. FirstPlus Home Loan Trust 1996–2, 209 F.R.D. 404, 410 n. 4 (W.D. Tenn. 2002) (indicating that on a Rule 12(b)(2) motion to dismiss a class action, the court assesses whether the named plaintiffs, rather than the class members, have themselves established personal jurisdiction over the defendants). Although this approach may be sensible prior to class certification, in light of *Bristol-Myers Squibb Co.*, 137 S. Ct. 1773 (2017), courts should be wary of attempting to assert personal jurisdiction over the defendant with respect to class claims lacking any connection with the forum state, unless there is some basis for nationwide jurisdiction.

What about absent plaintiffs in class actions; because judgments in class actions will bind them and conclude their rights, should courts also be required to have personal jurisdiction over absent class plaintiffs before they can render a judgment that is binding on them? *See Phillips Petroleum Co. v. Shutts, 472 U.S. 797 (1985)* [*FLEX Case 7.D*] (holding that absent class plaintiffs need not have minimum contacts with the forum but rather need only be afforded minimal procedural due process protection of notice and the opportunity to be heard). How does the personal jurisdiction requirement apply to members absent of defendant classes? *See, e.g., Pennsylvania v. Local Union 542, Int'l Union of Operating Eng'rs, 469 F. Supp. 329, 419–20 (E.D. Pa. 1978)* ("[T]here is no room for argument that the named defendant Glasgow, Inc., was unrepresentative. I must also reiterate that notice was provided to the unnamed members of the defendant class by certified mail two years prior to the trial in this case. In these circumstances and given full compliance with Rule 23 there seems little doubt that through the defendant class device personal jurisdiction over the defendant class was achieved.").

c. Choice of Law

Choice of law can be a confounding matter for class litigation when the class harm cuts across state boundaries, requiring courts to determine whether one or several states' laws should apply and whether the need to apply different state law to the claims of class members undermines the predominance requirement of Rule 23(b)(3). Regarding the first issue, the Supreme Court has held that a state's law can only apply to a dispute if it has a sufficient nexus with that dispute. *See Phillips Petroleum Co. v. Shutts, 472 U.S. 797 (1985)* [*FLEX Case 7.D*]. Thus, a court may not simply apply one state's law to adjudicate claims completely unconnected with that state.

The *Shutts* rule presents an obstacle to the certification of multistate or nationwide classes in cases where there are substantive differences in the content of applicable law from one state to another because

Food for Thought

If a nationwide or multistate class action is more difficult to certify after *Shutts*, what alternative should a plaintiff's attorney consider in order to move her case forward? Is there any type of class that would minimize the *Shutts* choice-of-law problem or are individual actions the only solution?

these differences are viewed by courts as undermining the predominance of the common issues and thus precluding class certification. *See, e.g., Castano v. Am. Tobacco Co., 84 F.3d 734 (5th Cir. 1996)* (finding that a nationwide class could not be certified in the nicotine addiction suit due in part to the differences in state law applicable to each claim).

d. Class Arbitration

Parties to contracts are free to reach agreements that disputes between them will be subject to arbitration rather than litigation in court, and these agreements are generally enforceable under the Federal Arbitration Act, 9 U.S.C.A. § 2, *et seq.* Such agreements may further indicate that arbitration may not be pursued on a class-wide basis. The Supreme Court recently articulated the latter principle in *AT&T Mobility L.L.C. v. Concepcion*, 563 U.S. 333 (2011), in which it held that the Federal Arbitration Act preempted California's judicial rule regarding the unconscionability of class arbitration waivers, preventing the attempted class action from proceeding in federal court. The Court further held, in *American Express Co. v. Italian Colors Restaurant*, 570 U.S. 228 (2013), that class arbitration waivers are enforceable under the Federal Arbitration Act notwithstanding the fact that a plaintiff's cost of individually arbitrating a federal statutory claim would exceed the potential recovery. What is the practical consequence of permitting class arbitration waivers to be enforceable, even in the context of negative value claims for which individual arbitration would be cost prohibitive?

Take Note!

In *Shady Grove Orthopedic Associates v. Allstate Insurance Co.*, 559 U.S. 393 (2010), the Supreme Court addressed a vertical choice of law question, whether a state law prohibiting class actions for the recovery of a state statutory penalty trumped Rule 23, which permitted class certification under the circumstances. Based on a *Hanna* analysis, the Court held that Rule 23 applied to the issue, was valid, and thus controlled the certification question. Vertical choice of law analysis, as well as the *Shady Grove* case, are covered in Chapter 5.

Note that if an arbitrator interprets an arbitration agreement as permitting classwide arbitration, courts will not ordinarily be permitted to reverse that determination. *Oxford Health Plans L.L.C. v. Sutter*, 569 U.S. 654 (2013) (holding that an arbitrator's determination that a contract permits class arbitration must stand as long as it is "arguably construing or applying the contract . . . , regardless of a court's view of its (de)merits").

On July 10, 2017, the Consumer Financial Protection Board (CFPB) issued a rule prohibiting regulated financial services providers from "rely[ing] in any way on a pre-dispute arbitration agreement . . . with respect to any aspect of a class action that concerns any of the [covered] consumer financial products or services." 12 C.F.R. § 1040.4 (2017). This rule was disapproved (revoked) by an act of Congress, effective November 22, 2017. 82 F.R. 55500.

e. Settlement Classes

Should parties be able to use the class action device in a pure settlement context? If so, should the standards for certifying the class be more lax given that there will not be a trial, making considerations of predominance and manageability less important? In *Amchem Products, Inc. v. Windsor*, 521 U.S. 591 (1997) [*FLEX Case 7.E*]—an asbestos case—the Supreme Court held that settlement-only classes must satisfy all of the requirements of Rule 23 as would apply to any other class action. In *Amchem*, certification was denied based on the predominance of individual issues such as exposure, injury, and medical history. *Id. at 624*. However, if the settlement is fair to all prospective class members and offers the only hope of delivering compensation to the class, should a court find a way to permit settlement-only certification under Rule 23? The Supreme Court thought not:

> Federal courts, in any case, lack authority to substitute for Rule 23's certification criteria a standard never adopted—that if a settlement is "fair," then certification is proper.

* * *

> Rule 23, which must be interpreted with fidelity to the Rules Enabling Act and applied with the interests of absent class members in close view, cannot carry the large load [that the parties] and the District Court heaped upon it.

Id. at 622, 629. The Court decertified another asbestos class two years later in *Ortiz v. Fibreboard Corp., 527 U.S. 815 (1999)*, refusing again to let the fairness of the settlement preempt proper compliance with the certification standards of Rule 23:

> Here, just as in [*Amchem*], the proponents of the settlement are trying to rewrite Rule 23; each ignores the fact that Rule 23 requires protections under subdivisions (a) and (b) against inequity and potential inequity at the precertification stage, quite independently of the required determination at postcertification fairness review under subdivision (e) that any settlement is fair in an overriding sense. A fairness hearing under subdivision (e) can no more swallow the preceding protective requirements of Rule 23 in a subdivision (b)(1)(B) action than in one under subdivision (b) (3).

> **FYI**
>
> Rule 23(h)(2) authorizes courts to award attorneys' fees in any certified class action, though such fees must be authorized by law or the parties' agreement. This complements the authority to appoint and monitor class counsel under Rule 23(g), giving courts powerful tools to ensure that counsel act in the best interest of the class.

Id. at 858–59. If such settlement-only classes are not certifiable because of their presentation of individual issues, what is the practical alternative for the plaintiffs involved in these cases? Justice Breyer, dissenting in *Ortiz*, wrote, "[T]he alternative to class-action settlement is not a fair opportunity for each potential plaintiff to have his or her own day in court. Unusually high litigation costs, unusually long delays, and limitations upon the total amount of resources available for payment together mean that most potential plaintiffs may not have a realistic alternative." Id. at 867–68 (Breyer, J., dissenting). What is your view of the matter?

f.   The Class Action Fairness Act of 2005

The Class Action Fairness Act (CAFA), codified at 28 U.S.C. §§ 1332(d), 1453, 1711–1715, became effective on February 18, 2005, and contains several provisions that substantially alter the class action landscape. Numerous law review articles have already been written analyzing and describing CAFA in detail. *See e.g.*, Edward F. Sherman, *Class Actions After the Class Action Fairness Act of 2005,* 80 TUL. L. REV. 1593 (2006); Adam N. Steinman, *Sausage-Making, Pigs' Ears, and Congressional Expansions of Federal Jurisdiction:* Exxon Mobil v. Allapattah *and its Lessons for the Class Action Fairness Act,* 81 WASH. L. REV. 279 (2006); Anna Andreeva, *Class Action Fairness Act of 2005: The Eight-Year Saga is Finally Over,* 59 U. MIAMI L. REV. 385 (2005). Here, we only want to sketch out the basics of its provisions pertaining to federal subject matter jurisdiction over certain types of class actions.

Expanded Subject Matter Jurisdiction. CAFA expanded the jurisdiction of federal courts over class actions by providing that class actions involving at least 100 class members whose claims aggregate to greater than $5 million may proceed as a class in federal court, provided that at least one member of the class is diverse from at least one defendant (minimal diversity). 28 U.S.C. § 1332(d) (2). The class action provisions of CAFA should not be confused with its "mass action" provision, which permits the removal of "any civil action . . . in which monetary relief claims of 100 or more persons are proposed to be tried jointly on the ground that the plaintiffs' claims involve common questions of law or fact," limited to those plaintiffs whose claims can individually satisfy the ordinary jurisdictional amount required under § 1332(a) ($75,000-plus). 28 U.S.C. § 1332(d) (11)(B)(i). Unlike for class actions under CAFA, mass actions must involve at least 100 *named* plaintiffs who propose to join in a single action. *See Mississippi ex rel. Hood v. AU Optronics Corp.,* 134 S. Ct. 736, 742 (2014) (holding that CAFA's "100 or more persons" phrase in 28 U.S.C. § 1332(d)(11)(B)(i) does not encompass unnamed persons who are real parties in interest to claims brought by named plaintiffs.").

However, there is what might be called a "local action" exception to CAFA that requires district courts to decline jurisdiction over a class action under § 1332(d) when more than two-thirds of the class is from the forum state, a principal defendant is from the same state, and the harm alleged was suffered mainly

within that state. 28 U.S.C. § 1332(d)(4).[*] Also, it is worth noting that CAFA permits the aggregation of jurisdictionally insufficient claims to reach the $5 million jurisdictional amount, something that may not ordinarily be done under the normal diversity provision, 28 U.S.C. § 1332(a). Why do you think Congress sought to increase the number of class actions that could be filed in federal court?

"Red-Carpet" Removal. CAFA importantly includes relaxed standards for removing cases that qualify for jurisdiction under CAFA into federal court. As discussed in Chapter 3, removal ordinarily requires that all defendants agree to remove the case. For CAFA cases, only one defendant need be interested in removal. 28 U.S.C.A. § 1453(b). Further, under the normal rules for removal, removal is unavailable if any defendant is a citizen of the forum state. Not so for CAFA removals; removal is available "without regard to whether any defendant is a citizen of the State in which the action is brought." 28 U.S.C.A. § 1453(b). These and additional variations from normal removal procedure are highlighted in **Table 7.3**.

Table 7.3—"Red-Carpet" Removal Under CAFA	
Ordinary Removal	**CAFA Removal**
Unanimous defendant consent	Single defendant may remove
No defendant may be a forum citizen	Citizenship of the defendant is irrelevant
No removal of diversity cases after one year	One-year time limitation does not apply
No review of remand orders	Remand orders are reviewable

These removal provisions are so facilitative of moving state-filed class actions into federal court that one commentator has dubbed them "red-carpet removal" provisions. *See* Steinman, *supra*, 81 WASH. L. REV. 279, 290 (2006). Coupled with the expanded subject matter jurisdiction provisions, the result of these red-carpet removal provisions is that even plaintiffs who wish to try their cases in state court will be easily swept into federal court and forced to litigate their cases there. This is so even if the class representative is willing to stipulate that the aggregate amount in controversy will not exceed $5 million. *See Standard Fire Ins. Co. v. Knowles*, 568 U.S. 588 (2013) [*FLEX Case 3.D*] ("The question presented concerns a class-action plaintiff who stipulates, prior to certification of the class, that he, and the class he seeks to represent, will not seek damages that exceed $5 million in total. Does that stipulation remove the case from CAFA's scope? In our view, it does not.").

---

[*] CAFA also provides that when the proportion of the class from the forum state ranges from one-third to two-thirds, courts have the discretion to decline jurisdiction. *See* 28 U.S.C. § 1332(d)(3). Jurisdiction based on other grounds, such as the presence of a federal question, is not affected by the local action exception. *See Blevins v. Aksut*, 849 F.3d 1016, 1020 (11th Cir. 2017) ("[Section] 1332(d)(4) does not affect a district court's ability to exercise jurisdiction under § 1331.").

Why do you think Congress wanted to force these cases into federal court? Was this done to benefit plaintiffs or defendants? It may help to know that states have their own class certification standards and Congress apparently felt that these standards were more relaxed than what one finds in the federal system.

Executive Summary

- **Basic Claim Joinder.** Rule 18(a) can be used to add related or unrelated claims to claims asserted under any of the other rules, including counterclaims, crossclaims, and third-party claims.

- **Counterclaims.** Counterclaims that arise out of the same transaction or occurrence that is the subject of the opposing party's claim are compulsory. All other counterclaims are merely permissive. *See* Rules 13(a) & (b).

- **Crossclaims.** Although no crossclaims are compulsory, they may be asserted only if they relate to the same transaction, occurrence, or property that is the subject of the original action. *See* Rule 13(g).

Major Themes

Keep in mind these two themes relevant to the joinder material:

a. *Subject Matter Jurisdiction*— after satisfying the terms of a joinder rule, do not forget to assess whether the claim qualifies for federal subject matter jurisdiction.

b. *Complexity*—these rules are numerous, and they combine to make joinder a very complex topic. Look out for the change in status that joinder can bring about for a party (*e.g.*, making them a defending party or a coparty). This can place such parties in a new position that may entitle them to joinder rights they may have previously lacked.

- **Premissive Party Joinder.** Plaintiffs may proceed jointly if their claims are transactionally related and share a common question of law or fact. Defendants may be sued jointly if the claims asserted against them are transactionally related and share a common question of law or fact. *See* Rule 20(a).

- **Third-Party Claims.** Any defending party may implead a nonparty to assert that the nonparty is liable for all or part of the liability being asserted against the defending party. *See* Rule 14(a).

- **Compulsory Party Joinder.** Under Rule 19(a), if a nonparty's absence from an action will adversely affect the interests of existing parties or of the nonparty in certain specified ways, the nonparty is a necessary party and must be joined if there are no jurisdictional or venue problems. If joinder is not feasible, courts must determine, under the terms of Rule 19(b), whether the party is so essential to the case that it must be dismissed in its absence.

■   **Intervention**. Nonparties have a right to intervene in an action where their interests will be impaired, provided their interests are not adequately represented by existing parties. *See* Rule 24(a). Nonparties may be permitted to intervene if their claim or defense shares a common question of law or fact with the main action. *See* Rule 24(b). In both instances, the effort to intervene must be timely, meaning done within a reasonable time without undue and prejudicial delay.

■   **Class Actions**. A class may be certified if it satisfies the numerosity, commonality, typicality, and adequacy of representation requirements of Rule 23(a) and if it fits within one of the class categories found within Rule 23(b). Damages classes under Rule 23(b)(3) must satisfy additional predominance and superiority requirements.

For More Information

Students interested in studying joinder further may consult the following resources:

- 6 C. WRIGHT, A. MILLER & M. KANE, FED. PRAC. & PROC. § 1401 *et seq.* (3d ed. 2010) (Counterclaims & Crossclaims) and § 1441 *et seq.* (third-party claims).

- 7 C. WRIGHT, A. MILLER & M. KANE, FED. PRAC. & PROC. § 1601 *et seq.* (3d ed. 2001) (Compulsory Party Joinder) and § 1651, *et seq.* (permissive party joinder).

- John Bronsteen & Owen Fiss, *The Class Action Rule*, 78 NOTRE DAME L. REV. 1419 (2003).

Test Your Knowledge

To assess your understanding of the material in this chapter, click here to take a quiz.

CHAPTER EIGHT

Discovery

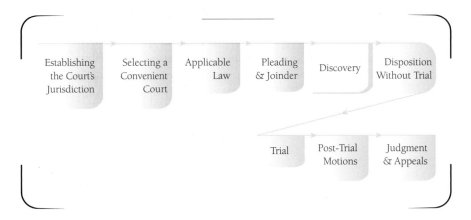

AFTER INITIATING THE ACTION AND getting beyond the pleadings stage, the parties ultimately will have to turn to the discovery phase of litigation. Discovery refers to the process of compelled information exchange that occurs among the parties before trial. What is the purpose of discovery? Litigants typically need to engage in some measure of discovery in order to obtain information germane to their claims or defenses. This information in turn helps each party build its legal case and prepare for trial or, in most cases, a summary judgment battle or settlement negotiations. It is only through the exploration of all the facts that the parties can develop a fuller understanding of the disputed events and issues and formulate how they intend to make their case before the court.

The Federal Rules provide for extensive discovery, granting parties access to virtually all information their adversaries have in their possession (or under their control) that is relevant to a dispute. In this chapter, we will take a closer look at the scope of discovery under the Federal Rules, which will include a look at the extent to which some materials are protected from discovery and the challenges surrounding the discovery of electronically stored information. We will also review each of the discovery devices made available in the Federal Rules such as depositions, document inspection, and interrogatories. The chapter will conclude with a consideration of the measures that may be taken to sanction litigants who fail to comply with their discovery obligations or who abuse the discovery process.

A. The Scope of Discovery: Relevance

Discovery in the federal system is traditionally regarded as quite broad. Ours is a system in which litigants, in theory, do not rely on surprise and ambush to prevail, but rather on the full exchange of information so that resolution on the merits is possible. In reality, although parties certainly seek as much information as possible from their adversaries through discovery, they tend to be less enthusiastic about sharing information with their opponents. Notwithstanding the obstructionist impulses of some litigants, the rules entitle all parties to a substantial amount of information in the name of discovery. What type of information may be sought through discovery and what information is beyond the reach of discovery? The general scope of discovery is set forth in Rule 26(b)(1).

Food for Thought

Do you think reticence in producing information—to the degree that such a sentiment exists among litigants—is more likely to characterize the attitude of plaintiffs or defendants? Does the answer depend on the specific case or would you suppose that generalization is possible here?

FRCP 26(b)(1). Discovery Scope and Limits: Scope in General.

(1) *Scope in General*. Unless otherwise limited by court order, the scope of discovery is as follows: Parties may obtain discovery regarding any nonprivileged matter that is relevant to any party's claim or defense and proportional to the needs of the case, considering the importance of the issues at stake in the action, the amount in controversy, the parties' relative access to relevant information, the parties' resources, the importance of the discovery in resolving the issues, and whether the burden or expense of the proposed discovery outweighs its likely benefit. Information within this scope of discovery need not be admissible in evidence to be discoverable.

There are several aspects of this Rule. First, the basic scope of discovery is all information relevant to a claim or defense of any party. Second, relevant material that is privileged is not discoverable. Third, relevant material under the rule does not have to be "admissible" to be discoverable. Finally, there are proportionality limitations applicable to discovery.

The core requirement here, then, is that the information must be relevant to a claim or defense of any party. It is worth noting that this language is of relatively recent origin. Prior to the 2000 amendments to the Federal Rules, this provision permitted discovery of any "matter relevant to the subject matter involved in the pending action," something that the rule no longer permits. The next case demonstrates how courts interpret and apply this rule. Subsequent parts of this chapter will take a look at the limitations on discovery found in Rule 26(b)(2) and the privilege limitations referred to in Rule 26(b)(1).

Cormack v. United States

<u>U.S. Court of Federal Claims</u>
<u>117 Fed. Cl. 392 (Ct. Fed. Cl. 2014)</u>

Lettow, Judge.

In this patent case, plaintiff, Cameron Lanning Cormack ("Mr. Cormack"), filed a motion to compel discovery responses from defendant-intervenor, Northrop Grumman Systems Corporation ("Northrop Grumman Systems" or "Systems"), pursuant to <u>Rule 37 of the Rules of the Court of Federal Claims</u> ("RCFC"). * * *

> The Rules of the Court of Federal Claims and the Federal Rules of Civil Procedure track one another, making the interpretation and application of each body of rules instructive of the interpretation and application of the other. *See Pac. Nat'l Cellular v. United States*, 41 Fed. Cl. 20, 24 n.3 (1998). ("In general, the rules of this court are patterned on the Federal Rules of Civil Procedure. Therefore, precedent under the Federal Rules of Civil Procedure is relevant to interpret the rules of this court.").

BACKGROUND

On April 3, 2013, Mr. Cormack filed his complaint in this court, alleging that the United States Postal Service ("Postal Service") engaged in an unlicensed procurement and authorization of manufacture and use of patented inventions, a claim arising under <u>28 U.S.C. § 1498</u>. In August 2010, Mr. Cormack had been granted <u>United States Patent No. 7,781,693 ("the '693 Patent")</u>, entitled "Method and System for Sorting Incoming Mail." Mr. Cormack alleged that the Postal Service infringed this patent when it contracted with Northrop Grumman Systems for the manufacture and delivery of Flats Sequencing Systems ("FSS"), a mail sorting device. Mr. Cormack further averred that, pursuant to the contract, Northrop Grumman Systems actually manufactured and delivered 102 such machines and that the Postal Service continues to use them.

Shortly after Mr. Cormack filed his complaint, the court granted the government's unopposed motion to notify Northrop Grumman Systems as an interested party pursuant to <u>RCFC 14(b)</u>. The government advised the court that its contract with Northrop Grumman Systems contains an indemnity clause whereby Systems is obligated to indemnify the government against liability for patent infringement. Subsequently, Northrop Grumman Systems filed a motion to intervene as a defendant-intervenor, which this court granted the same day.

* * *

II. THE MOTION TO COMPEL

A. Documents Possessed by Solystic, S.A.S.

Mr. Cormack has requested that Systems produce documents in the apparent possession of Solystic, S.A.S. ("Solystic"), a wholly owned but indirect French subsidiary of the Northrop Grumman Corporation that designs and develops mail sorting systems and products. These documents, he contends, are relevant because Northrop Grumman Systems jointly developed the FSS machine with Solystic and incorporated components of Solystic's TOP 2000, an automated flat sorting machine that preceded the FSS, into the FSS. Moreover, Mr. Cormack argues that Solystic is familiar with his '693 patent because Solystic had to recognize and differentiate its work from the '693 patent to receive its own European method patent for sorting postal items. The requested information, he avers, is relevant to his infringement contentions.

Simply stated, the issue is whether Systems can be compelled to produce documents currently in the possession of its parent corporation's foreign indirect subsidiary, a nonparty in this action. RCFC 34(a) provides that a party may serve a request for production of documents "in the responding party's possession, custody, or control." RCFC 34(a)(1). Control is construed broadly, and it "does not require that the party have legal ownership or actual physical possession of the documents at issue, but rather the right, authority, or practical ability to obtain the documents from a nonparty to the action." *E.I. DuPont de Nemours & Co. v. Kolon Indus., Inc.,* 286 F.R.D. 288, 292 (E.D.Va.2012) (internal quotation marks omitted) (quoting *Bush v. Ruth's Chris Steak House, Inc.,* 286 F.R.D. 1, 5–6 (D.D.C.2012)). In essence, the inquiry is whether the party has access to the nonparty's documents. *See Gerling Int'l Ins. Co. v. Commissioner,* 839 F.2d 131, 141 (3d Cir.1988).

Mr. Cormack contends that Solystic's documents are within Systems's control. Denominating Systems and Solystic as sister corporations, he argues that common parentage provides Systems with the requisite control to obtain the documents. He further alleges that because Systems and Solystic jointly developed and manufactured the FSS, the court can require Systems to comply with his discovery requests.

Systems, however, insists that it does not have the requisite control over or access to the documents. * * * Systems * * * contends that because it has no ownership interest in Solystic, Mr. Cormack must present evidence akin to that required to pierce the corporate veil or to establish Solystic as an "alter ego" of Systems to establish control and compel production. This argument reaches too far. While an "alter ego" relationship is indicative of control, it is not required for control to be found. *See, e.g., Gerling,* 839 F.2d at 141 ("The requisite control has been found only where the sister corporation was found to be the alter ego of the litigating entity *. . . or where the litigating corporation had acted with its sister in effecting the transaction giving rise to suit and is litigating on its behalf.*" (emphasis added) (internal citations omitted)). Rather, courts consider a variety of factors when determining whether a party has sufficient control over a nonparty for the purpose of RCFC 34 and 37, including (1) the corporate structure of the party and nonparty; (2) the nonparty's connection to the transaction at issue in the litigation; and (3) the degree that the nonparty will benefit from the outcome of the case. *See Steele Software Sys. Corp. v. DataQuick Info. Sys., Inc.,* 237 F.R.D. 561, 564–65 (D.Md.2006); *Afros S.P.A. v. Krauss-Maffei Corp.,* 113 F.R.D. 127, 130 (D.Del.1986). Here, Mr. Cormack argues that both the corporate structure of Systems and Solystic and Solystic's involvement in the development of the FSS support a finding of control.

* * *

Taken together, the recitations in the proposal to the Postal Service, the agreement between Systems and Solystic, and the related e-mails support plaintiff's contention that Systems and Solystic collaborated on the FSS design and show that Solystic was critical to the project. The court finds that this collaboration equips Systems both with access to Solystic's documents and with the requisite power to obtain them, rendering Systems able and required to comply with Mr. Cormack's discovery requests in accordance with an order by the court.

B. Documents Related to Non-Infringing Products

Mr. Cormack seeks discovery into nonaccused products that fall within his definition of "mail sorting product;" which, as specified, would include both FSS and non-FSS products. RCFC 26 provides that "[p]arties may obtain discovery regarding any nonprivileged matter that is relevant to any party's claim or defense." RCFC 26(b)(1). This rule should be applied no differently in patent cases than in other types of cases. *See SRI Int'l v. Matsushita Elec. Corp. of Am.,* 775 F.2d 1107, 1116. Mr. Cormack seeks information related to the development and functionality of non-FSS mail sorting products because, "[t]o the extent that these products function in a manner that infringes the '693 Patent and were sold to the [g]overnment, Mr. Cormack would be entitled to amend his [c]omplaint to add those products to this case." Pl.'s Mem. Supporting Mot. to Compel at 17. Additionally, Mr. Cormack asserts that information related to "non-FSS products that do not practice the method taught by the '693 Patent [is] useful to show the advantages and utility gained through the FSS's use of Mr. Cormack's patented invention," which is relevant for determining damages in the form of a reasonable royalty. * * *

Northrop Grumman Systems opposes Mr. Cormack's request, stating that " '[n]on-FSS mail sorting products'—i.e., all [Systems] products *not accused of infringement* in this action—have little or no relevance to the claims and defenses in this case." Systems describes Mr. Cormack's request as "an unprecedented expansion of the scope of this litigation and . . . highly prejudicial."

As a preliminary matter, the court cannot accept Northrop Grumman Systems's characterization of Mr. Cormack's request. The court does not read Mr. Cormack's document requests or interrogatories to be requesting "discovery of *all* of [the] company's products that [have] not been accused of infringement." That said, the court finds Mr. Cormack's definition of "Mail Sorting Product" to be overly broad and not sufficiently tailored to discovery of relevant documents. In his First Set of Interrogatories, Mr. Cormack defined "Mail Sorting Product" to mean:

> any product, including without limitation, equipment, hardware products, firmware products, or software products, relating to a Mail Sorting System, including without limitation, flats sorting machine (FSM), flats sorting equipment (FSE), flats sequencing system (FSS) equipment, mail sorting machine, mail sorting equipment, automatic induction equipment, in-feed equipment, image processing equipment, carousel equipment, integrated tray converter equipment, electrical components, components of the same, combinations of the same, and hardware, firmware or software related to the same.

The other extreme position is equally untenable. Courts have not required plaintiffs to name specifically the products respecting which they seek discovery to establish their relevance to the patent at issue. Instead, a plaintiff must "identify those systems and the components, characteristics, or elements allegedly causing infringement with requisite specificity." *Tesseron, Ltd. v. R.R. Donnelley & Sons Co.,* No. 1:06 CV 2909, 2007 WL 2034286, at *1 (N.D.Ohio July 10, 2007). In summarizing existing precedent, a district court recently explained that "[c]ases that have examined the issue of the discoverability concerning nonaccused products have concluded that the scope of discovery may include products that are 'reasonably similar' to those accused in a party's preliminary infringement chart." *AGA Medical Corp. v. W.L. Gore & Assocs., Inc.,* No. 10–3734, 2011 WL 11023511, at * 7 (D.Minn. Oct. 19, 2011) (permitting discovery into a product closely related in function to the accused product). In some instances, while recognizing the permissibility of discovery into nonaccused products, courts have required the requesting party to narrow the request. For example, in *Tessera Inc. v. Sony Elecs., Inc.,* No. 10–0838–RMB–KMW, 2012 U.S. Dist. LEXIS 180771, at *8–*11 (D.Del. Aug. 6, 2012), a magistrate judge determined that the plaintiff's attempts to compel the defendant to identify all of their "multi-chip stacked semiconductor products, and provide information about them" was too broad because it would require production of information related to numerous products that were not alleged to have infringed upon the patent-in-suit. The court directed the plaintiff to narrow the applicable definition of "Your Products" to one limited to a relevant time frame and sufficiently pertinent in function to the alleged infringement of the patents-in-suit.

Northrop Grumman Systems relies on a series of decisions in support of its overarching contention that discovery of nonaccused products is disfavored by courts, Def.-Intervenor's Opp'n to Mot. to Compel at 7–8, but these cases are of limited usefulness. For example, in *Tesseron*, the court expressly recognized that "a party claiming patent infringement may obtain discovery of unidentified and unaccused systems under certain circumstances," but that the plaintiff had failed to make the required showing in that particular instance. *Tesseron*, 2007 WL 2034286, at *1; cf. *Biax Corp. v. Nvidia Corp*, 271 F.R.D. 200, 205 (D.Colo.2010) (denying plaintiff's discovery requests regarding nonaccused products without a "more specific showing of need or relevance."). Here, Mr. Cormack has specifically pointed to the TOP 2000, produced by Solystic, as being the prototype for the accused FSS machine. Northrop Grumman Systems has not responded, even in part, to Mr. Cormack's requests to the extent that there are products similar in function to the FSS, such as the TOP 2000. Information related to the TOP 2000, as a precursor to the FSS machine, is relevant to the determination of whether it or other similar machines infringe upon Mr. Cormack's patent, as well as relevant to the calculation of damages.

In other respects, Mr. Cormack is directed to more narrowly tailor his definition of "mail sorting products" to those reasonably similar in function to the FSS, and Northrop Grumman Systems is directed to respond to the document requests as so amended. Mr. Cormack should take care to specifically identify the elements or components of a machine that would render it similar in function to the FSS machine and thus potentially infringing on the '693 patent.

C. Documents Related to Damages

Mr. Cormack alleges that the damages he seeks in this case may be measured using several different well-known methodologies: "(1) cost-savings to the [g]overnment; (2) lost profits; or (3) a reasonable royalty." He argues that Northrop Grumman Systems has not "provided full and complete responses to Mr. Cormack's discovery requests, nor has it produced documents related to these three damages theories." Mr. Cormack seeks information related to "[Systems's] revenues, costs of goods sold, and profits related to the sale of mail sorting systems," and information related to the government's cost-savings realized by using the FSS machines as contrasted to human sorters.

Northrop Grumman Systems contends that Mr. Cormack's motion to compel documents related to damages is moot because Systems produced over 30,000 pages of such material on the same date that the motion to compel was filed. Mr. Cormack concedes that this production resolved certain issues but maintains that it has not rendered the motion to compel wholly moot on this issue. Nonetheless, Mr. Cormack has withdrawn his requests for production seeking documents related to "revenues, costs of goods sold, and profits for FSS," pending Mr. Cormack's review of the produced documents.[18] The motion to compel remains extant, however, respecting two items. First, Mr. Cormack seeks production regarding the revenues, costs of goods sold, and profit related to non-FSS mail sorting products and systems sold within the United States. Second, Mr. Cormack maintains that Northrop Grumman Systems's production of documents related to cost-savings to the government resulting from using the FSS is deficient. The court will address each of Mr. Cormack's contentions in turn.

First, Mr. Cormack, as already discussed, is entitled to discovery of revenues, costs of goods sold, and profits for non-FSS mail sorting machines to the extent that "non-FSS mail sorting machines" is limited to mail sorting machines that are functionally equivalent to the FSS machine, such as a precursor to the FSS. At the very least, this information would be directly relevant to *Georgia-Pacific* factors 8 and 9, *viz.,* "[t]he established profitability of the product made under the patent; its commercial success; and its current popularity" and "[t]he utility and advantages of the patent property over the old modes or devices, if any, that had been used for working out similar results," respectively. *Georgia-Pacific,* 318 F.Supp. at 1120.

Second, while acknowledging some production responsive to his request for documents related to cost-savings for the government, Mr. Cormack avers that more responsive documents must be in Systems's possession. Systems's production consists of four documents, all originally created by the Postal Service, related to cost-savings to the government. In support of the contention that more documents must exist, Mr. Cormack points to the ongoing breach-of-contract suit pending in this court between the United States and Northrop Grumman Systems related to the same FSS contract at issue in this case. In that case, the Postal Service is seeking reimbursement for cost-savings it did not realize due to delayed delivery of the FSS machines by Northrop Grumman Systems. In Mr. Cormack's view, because cost-savings are at the heart of the government's counterclaim against Northrop Grumman Systems in that suit, Systems must possess more documents related to projected government cost-savings. Systems counters that the government's projected cost-savings were calculated by the government and Northrop Grumman Systems has no responsive documents other than those already produced.

At the hearing, counsel for Systems reiterated that no other responsive documents exist and that Mr. Cormack is mistaken in believing that Northrop Grumman Systems ever produced marketing materials intended to convince the Postal Service

---

[18] Mr. Cormack has not, however, withdrawn his motion to compel a further response by Systems to a related interrogatory seeking an analysis and summary of the documents provided. * * * The court cannot compel Northrop Grumman Systems to produce documents or submissions that do not exist. *See Tech v. United States,* 284 F.R.D. 192, 198 (M.D.Pa.2012) ("It is clear that the court cannot compel the production of things that do not exist. Nor can the court compel the creation of evidence by parties who attest that they do not possess the materials sought by an adversary in litigation."); *see also United States v. Capitol Supply, Inc.,* 2014 WL 1046006, at *9 (D.D.C. Mar. 19, 2014) (quoting *Tech,* 284 F.R.D. at 198). In the circumstances, the court has no reason to believe that Systems possesses a readily available narrative responsive to the pertinent interrogatory.

of the cost-savings it could realize by use of FSS machines. He explained that the contract with the Postal Service was a fixed-price government contract. "The [Postal Service] was the one who identified the need. Northrop [Grumman Systems] did not have to sell the [Postal Service] on the idea that the FSS would be a beneficial device to have. What [Systems] had to do was competitively bid on the contract, and it won it, and it had to fulfill it." Second, counsel has represented that the Postal Service made the statements regarding cost-savings, and Systems asked the Postal Service how it arrived at the amount of alleged cost savings. In response, Systems received the four documents that it has produced to Mr. Cormack. *Id.* The court cannot compel Northrop Grumman Systems to produce documents that it insists do not exist. Mr. Cormack's motion to compel is denied as to this issue.[19]

CONCLUSION

* * *Mr. Cormack's motion to compel is GRANTED IN PART and DENIED IN PART. The motion to compel is GRANTED insofar as Northrop Grumman Systems is directed to produce documents in the possession of Solystic that relate to the FSS and other mail sorting machines that have a function similar to the FSS, such as the TOP 2000. Northrop Grumman Systems is also directed to produce documents related to nonaccused products to the extent they are encompassed by a revised and narrowed definition of "mail sorting product." The motion to compel is DENIED insofar as Mr. Cormack seeks further documents or interrogatory responses related to the "profits" or "costs of goods sold" for FSS products or related to the government's projected cost-savings by use of the FSS.

It is so ORDERED.

Points for Discussion

a. The Scope of Discovery Under Rule 26(b)(1)

As mentioned previously, the 2000 amendments to the Federal Rules of Civil Procedure narrowed the scope of discoverable information from that relevant to the "subject matter" of the action to information relevant to "a claim or defense" raised in the action. Courts have varied in their view of the revised language, with some arguing that the change was meant to be substantial, *see, e.g., Thompson v. Dep't of Hous. and Urban Dev.*, 199 F.R.D. 168, 172 (D. Md. 2001) ("It . . . is clear . . . that the new rule represents a change from the old version, and that . . . it is intended that the scope of discovery be narrower than it was, in some meaningful way."), and others regarding the change as minor, *see, e.g., Johnson v. Mundy Indus. Contractors, Inc.*, 2002 WL 31464984, at *3 (E.D.N.C. Mar. 15, 2002) (stating that the 2000

---

[19] The court notes that this subject may be a proper matter for deposition testimony by a designee of Systems pursuant to RCFC 30(b)(6).

Amendments to Rule 26(b)(1) are "basically a semantic change unlikely to have much salutary effect on the conduct of discovery").

Often, plaintiffs may not have a full picture of the wrongdoing that may have been perpetrated by the defendant when a suit is filed and thus they hope to use discovery to obtain information that may permit them to add additional claims to their complaints. Under the old "subject matter" language of the rule, such "fishing expeditions" were allowed. *See Hickman v. Taylor,* 329 U.S. 495, 507 (1947) ("[T]he deposition-discovery rules are to be accorded a broad and liberal treatment. No longer can the time-honored cry of 'fishing expedition' serve to preclude a party from inquiring into the facts underlying his opponent's case."). The 2000 version of Rule 26(b)(1) retained the ability to obtain subject matter discovery "for good cause" shown. However, the 2015 amendments to the rule eliminated that possibility entirely. Why do you think such a change was made?

Given that the scope of discovery is tied to the claims or defenses asserted in the pleadings, do you think litigants will be encouraged to assert additional claims or raise additional defenses to ensure that they are able to seek broad discovery on those matters?

b. Determining Relevance

Prior to the 2015 amendments, Rule 26(b)(1) permitted discovery of information "relevant" to a claim or defense and elaborated that "[r]elevant information need not be admissible at trial if the discovery appears reasonably calculated to lead to the discovery of admissible evidence." This was meant to be a broad standard. 8 C. WRIGHT, A. MILLER & R. MARCUS, FED. PRAC. & PROC. § 2008, n. 31 (3d ed. 2010). ("Discovery requests should be considered relevant if there is any possibility that the information sought is relevant to any issue in the case, and should ordinarily be allowed unless it is clear that the information sought can have no possible bearing on the subject matter of the action." (citing *Brown Bear v. Cuna Mut. Grp.,* 266 F.R.D. 310 (D.S.D. 2009))).

As of December 1, 2015, the previously quoted sentence from Rule 26(b)(1) now reads, "Information within this scope of discovery need not be admissible in evidence to be discoverable," deleting the "reasonably calculated to lead to the discovery of admissible evidence" language. Additionally, the 2015 amendment deleted explicit authorization for discovery of information relating to "the existence, description, nature, custody, condition, and location of any documents or other tangible things and the identity and location of persons who know of any discoverable matter." Why do you think these changes were made? Have they narrowed the scope of discoverable information? The Advisory Committee Note accompanying the amendment makes clear that such information will remain within the scope of discovery so long as it is relevant to a claim or defense raised in the action. In the

Committee's words, "Discovery of such matters is so deeply entrenched in practice that it is no longer necessary to clutter the long text of Rule 26 with these examples."

In its note accompanying the 2000 amendments to Rule 26, the Advisory Committee acknowledged that making the relevance determination is not an exact science:

> The dividing line between information relevant to the claims and defenses and that relevant only to the subject matter of the action cannot be defined with precision. A variety of types of information not directly pertinent to the incident in suit could be relevant to the claims or defenses raised in a given action. For example, other incidents of the same type, or involving the same product, could be properly discoverable under the revised standard. Information about organizational arrangements or filing systems of a party could be discoverable if likely to yield or lead to the discovery of admissible information. Similarly, information that could be used to impeach a likely witness, although not otherwise relevant to the claims or defenses, might be properly discoverable. In each instance, the determination whether such information is discoverable because it is relevant to the claims or defenses depends on the circumstances of the pending action.

Take Note!

Federal Rule of Evidence 401 defines as relevant evidence having "any tendency to make a fact more or less probable than it would be without the evidence; and the fact is of consequence in determining the action." Should relevance under Rule 26(b)(1) mean the same thing as it does under Evidence Rule 401? *See Oppenheimer Fund v. Sanders, 437 U.S. 340, 351 (1978)* (indicating that the standard for relevance under Rule 26(b)(1) is "construed broadly to encompass any matter that bears on, or that reasonably could lead to other matter that could bear on, any issue . . . in the case").

What about information relating to sexual promiscuity beyond the workplace in a workplace sexual harassment suit? Or information regarding how the plaintiff dressed in the workplace? Could such information be viewed as relevant to defending against a harassment claim? *See Mitchell v. Hutchings, 116 F.R.D. 481, 484 (D. Utah 1987)* (holding that evidence of plaintiffs' sexual conduct which was remote in time and place to plaintiffs' working environment was irrelevant to defendant's defense that his advances were welcomed by plaintiffs). Often, one's ability to determine if information will lead to the discovery of admissible evidence requires some understanding of what types of information will ultimately be admissible for a given type of substantive claim, a topic covered in Evidence courses.

> ### Hypo 8.1
>
> Michael sues Guns, Inc. for creating a defective product—their JK-57 rifle—which backfired and caused Michael serious injuries. As part of his discovery efforts, Michael seeks to discover information relating to the design of Guns, Inc.'s JK-56 rifle, which was the predecessor to the JK-57 and was the basis on which the JK-57 was designed. Michael wants to know whether there were any documented defects with the previous model in order to figure out whether such defects were incorporated into the JK-57. Does such discovery fall within the permissible scope of discovery under Rule 26(b)(1)?

c. Protective Orders

Rule 26(c) permits the targets of discovery efforts to seek a protective order from the court if they object to the production of requested information based on relevance or other concerns. Under Rule 26(c), persons who seek protective orders must first *meet and confer* with the requesting party and make a good-faith effort to resolve the discovery dispute without court action. Then, "good cause" must be shown and the rule indicates that such orders are appropriate "to protect a party or person from annoyance, embarrassment, oppression, or undue burden or expense . . . ." FED. R. CIV. P. 26(c). *See, e.g.*, *Seattle Times Co. v. Rhinehart*, 467 U.S. 20, 36–37 (1984) (holding that a protective order entered to protect a litigant from the release and publication of a religious organization's membership lists and financial donations does not violate the First Amendment when the court has concluded that dissemination of such information would result in annoyance, embarrassment, and oppression). What should constitute "good cause" under this rule? *See, e.g.*, *Pansy v. Borough of Stroudsburg*, 23 F.3d 772, 786–87 (3d Cir. 1994) (holding that good cause exists when a party shows that disclosure will result in a clearly defined, specific and serious injury, but broad allegations of harm are not sufficient to establish good cause).

Beyond this list of concerns, protective orders are also appropriate when the court determines that the discovery request seeks information that lies beyond the scope of discovery under Rule 26(b)(1), *see, e.g.*, *Zappia Middle E. Constr. Co., Ltd. v. Emirate of Abu Dhabi*, 1995 WL 559445 (S.D.N.Y. Sept. 19, 1995) (granting a protective order foreclosing disclosure of an international loan transaction based on the grounds that it was outside the scope of the agreed-upon discovery and not relevant to plaintiff's case), or if the court needs to impose some of the limitations found within Rule 26(b)(2) (*see* Section B below).

The remedies that the court can provide through a protective order can include ordering that the information be kept confidential, an order narrowing the scope of the request, an order permitting the responding party to produce the information in a particular format, or an order denying the discovery of the information altogether. Courts also have the ability to order that the costs of producing information be shifted to or shared with the requesting party. *See, e.g.*, <u>CBT Flint Partners, LLC v. Return Path, Inc., 737 F.3d 1320, 1338 (Fed. Cir. 2013)</u> (O'Malley, J., dissenting) ("Rule 26(b)(2)(B) limits discovery on electronically stored information from sources not 'reasonably accessible,' and provides the court discretion to order discovery and specify cost-shifting to obtain that discovery."). When the 2015 amendments to Rule 26 took effect, this authority became explicit in the rule. *See* <u>FED. R. CIV. P. 26(c)(1)(B)</u> ("The court may, for good cause, issue an order to protect a party or person from . . . undue burden or expense, including one or more of the following: . . . (B) specifying terms, including time and place or the allocation of expenses, for the disclosure or discovery."). Courts have enormous discretion in this area to shape protective orders to work out the wide array of discovery disputes that arise between parties during the course of a lawsuit.

———————————

B. Limits on the Scope of Discovery

As we saw in <u>Rule 26(b)(1)</u>, although one generally is entitled to discovery of any material relevant to a claim or defense raised in an action, there are several limitations on this grant to keep in mind. One limitation—which the 2015 amendments relocated from <u>Rule 26(b)(2)(C)(iii)</u> into Rule 26(b)(1) as a component of the scope of discovery itself—is the requirement that any discovery sought be proportional to the needs of the case. Another limitation on the scope of discovery is found at <u>Rule 26(b)(2)(C)(ii)</u>, which provides special protections against having to produce electronically stored information that is "not reasonably accessible." Each of these two limitations will be reviewed below.

1. Burden and Proportionality Limits Generally

In brief, <u>Rule 26(b)</u> enables the court to limit discovery if the court finds that the discovery is too burdensome in relation to its utility to the litigation. The concern reflected in this rule is one of *proportionality*, meaning that although discovery is broad and the parties are entitled to certain information, discovery of information whose cost and burden far outweigh the contribution the information can make to the case need not be permitted. Heretofore, <u>Rule 26(b)(2)(C)(iii)</u> supplied this proportionality limitation. However, as of December 1, 2015, it is located within Rule 26(b)(1), although the requirements remain the same: Discovery must be "proportional to the needs of the case, considering the importance of the issues at stake in the action, the amount in controversy, the parties' relative access to relevant information, the parties' resources, the importance of the discovery in resolving the issues, and whether the burden or expense of the proposed discovery outweighs its likely benefit."

Rule 26(b)(2)(C) outlines additional limitations on discovery that may be imposed either on motion or on the court's own initiative. Discovery can be opposed if it "is unreasonably cumulative or duplicative, or can be obtained from some other source that is more convenient, less burdensome, or less expensive," or if "the party seeking discovery has had ample opportunity to obtain the information by discovery in the action." Rule 26(b)(2)(C)(i) & (ii).

Because parties are ordinarily required to cover their own costs of producing information in response to discovery requests (costs that can include the time and expense of retrieving and reviewing information before it is produced), if the costs or burdens appear to be prohibitive or unreasonable, or if these other limitations are being breached, responding parties can and often do seek protective orders from the court under the terms of Rule 26(c). The following case provides an example of a court's application of these limitations.

Gonzales v. Google, Inc.

U.S. District Court for the Northern District of California
234 F.R.D. 674 (N.D. Cal. 2006)

WARE, DISTRICT JUDGE.

I. INTRODUCTION

What's That?

A *subpoena* is a document in which a court commands a person to appear or produce documents or other items. Rule 45 governs the issuance of subpoenas in the federal system. The rule formerly indicated that subpoenas must issue from the court where the documents were to be produced. However, 2013 amendments changed the rule to make the court where the action is pending the issuing court.

This case raises three vital interests: (1) the national interest in a judicial system to reach informed decisions through the power of a subpoena to compel a third party to produce relevant information; (2) the third-party's interest in not being compelled by a subpoena to reveal confidential business information and devote resources to a distant litigation; and (3) the interest of individuals in freedom from general surveillance by the Government of their use of the Internet or other communications media.

In aid of the Government's position in the case of *ACLU v. Gonzales*, Civil Action No. 98-CV-5591 pending in the Eastern District of Pennsylvania, United States Attorney General Alberto R. Gonzales has subpoenaed Google, Inc., ("Google") to compile and produce a massive amount of information from Google's search index, and to turn over a significant number of search queries entered by Google users. Google timely objected to the Government's request. Following the requisite meet and confer, the Government filed the present Miscellaneous Action in this District to compel Google to comply with the subpoena. On March 14, 2006, this Court held a hearing on the Government's Motion. At that hearing, the Government made a significantly scaled-down request from the information it originally sought. For the reasons explained in this Order, the motion to compel, as modified, is GRANTED as to the sample of URLs from Google search index and DENIED as to the sample of users' search queries from Google's query log.

What's That?

A *meet and confer* is the meeting that discovery disputants are required to have before the disgruntled party seeks a motion to compel under Rule 37(a)(3) (sought by requesting parties) or a motion for a protective order under Rule 26(c) (sought by responding parties).

II. PROCEDURAL BACKGROUND

In 1998, Congress enacted the Child Online Protection Act ("COPA"), which is now codified as 47 U.S.C. § 231. COPA prohibits the knowing making of a communication by means of the World Wide Web, "for commercial purposes that is available to any minor and that includes material that is harmful to minors," subject to certain affirmative defenses. 47 U.S.C. § 231(a)(1). * * *

Upon enactment of COPA, the American Civil Liberties Union and several other plaintiffs ("Plaintiffs") filed an action in the Eastern District of Pennsylvania, challenging the constitutionality of the Act. The district court granted Plaintiffs' motion for a preliminary injunction on the grounds that COPA is likely to be found unconstitutional on its face for violating the First Amendment rights of adults. *ACLU v. Reno*, 31 F. Supp. 2d 473 (E.D. Pa. 1999). The United States Court of Appeals for the Third Circuit affirmed the grant of the preliminary injunction. *ACLU v. Reno*, 217 F.3d 162 (3d Cir. 2000). After granting certiorari, the Supreme Court of the United States vacated the judgment of the Third Circuit, and remanded the case to that court for further review of the district court's grant of preliminary injunction in favor of Plaintiffs. The Third Circuit again affirmed the preliminary injunction, *ACLU v. Ashcroft*, 322 F.3d 240 (3d Cir. 2003), and the Supreme Court again granted certiorari.

The Supreme Court affirmed the preliminary injunction and held that there was an insufficient record before it by which the Government could carry its burden to show that less restrictive alternatives may be more effective than the provisions of COPA. *Ashcroft v. ACLU*, 542 U.S. 656, 673 (2004). Of these alternatives directed at preventing minors from viewing "harmful to minors" material on the Internet, the Court focused on blocking and filtering software programs which "impose selective restrictions on speech at the receiving end, not universal restrictions at the source." <u>Id. at 667</u>. To "allow the parties to update and supplement the factual record to reflect current technological realities," the Court remanded the case for a trial on the merits.

Following remand, Plaintiffs filed a First Amended Complaint ("FAC"). Apparently, in preparing its defense, the Government initiated a study designed to somehow test the effectiveness of blocking and filtering software. To provide it with data for its study, the Government served a subpoena on Google, <u>America Online, Inc.</u> ("AOL"), <u>Yahoo! Inc.</u> ("Yahoo"), and <u>Microsoft, Inc.</u> ("Microsoft"). The subpoena required that these companies produce a designated listing of the URLs which would be available to a user of their services. The subpoena also required the companies to produce the text of users' search queries. AOL, Yahoo, and Microsoft appear to be producing data pursuant to the Government's request. Google, however, objected.

Google is a Delaware corporation headquartered in Mountain View, CA, that, like AOL, Yahoo, and Microsoft, also provides search engine capabilities. Based on the Government's estimation, and uncontested by Google, <u>Google's search engine</u> is the most widely used search engine in the world, with a market share of about 45%. The search engine at Google yields URLs in response to a search query entered by a user. The search queries entered may be of varying lengths, and incorporate a number of terms and connectors. Upon receiving a search query, Google produces a responsive list of URLs from its search index in a particular order based on algorithms proprietary to Google.

FYI
Google's market share has grown since this case was decided. As of July 2017, Google's share of the global online desktop search market was 81.12%, while its share of the mobile market hovered around 96%. Current market share data is available <u>here</u>.

The initial subpoena to Google sought production of an electronic file containing two general categories. First, the subpoena requested "[a]ll URLs that are available to be located to a query on your company's search engine as of July 31, 2005." In negotiations with Google, this request was later narrowed to a "multi-stage random" sampling of one million URLs in Google's indexed database. As represented to the Court at oral argument, the Government now seeks only 50,000 URLs from Google's search index. Second, the government also initially sought "[a]ll queries that have been entered on your company's search engine between June 1, 2005 and July 31, 2005 inclusive." Following further negotiations with Google, the Government narrowed this request to all queries that have been entered on the Google search engine during a one-week period. During the course of the present Miscellaneous Action, the Government further restricted the scope of its request, and now represents that it only requires 5,000 entries from Google's query log in order to meet its discovery needs.

Despite these modifications in the scope of the subpoena, Google maintained its objection to the Government's requests. Before the Court is a <u>motion to compel</u>* Google to comply with the modified subpoena, namely, for a sample of 50,000 URLs from Google's search index and 5,000 search queries entered by Google's users from Google's query log.

III. STANDARDS

<u>Rule 45 of the Federal Rules of Civil Procedure</u> governs discovery of nonparties by subpoena. <u>FED. R. CIV. P. 45</u> ("<u>Rule 45</u>"). The Advisory Committee Notes to the 1970 Amendment to <u>Rule 45</u> state that the "scope of discovery through a subpoena is the same as that applicable to Rule 34 and other discovery rules." <u>Rule 45</u> advisory committee's note (1970). Under Rule 34, the rule governing the production of documents between parties, the proper scope of discovery is as specified in <u>Rule 26(b)</u>. <u>FED. R. CIV. P. 34</u>.

<u>Rule 26(b)</u>, in turn, permits the discovery of any non-privileged material "relevant to the claim or defense of any party," where "relevant information need not be admissible at trial if the discovery appears reasonably calculated to lead to the discovery of admissible evidence." <u>Rule 26(b)(1)</u>. Relevancy, for the purposes of discovery, is defined broadly, although it is not without "ultimate and necessary boundaries." <u>Rule 26</u> also specifies that "[a]ll discovery is subject to the limitations imposed by Rule 26(b)(2)(i), (ii), and (iii)."* The Advisory Committee Notes to the 1983 amendments to <u>Rule 26</u> state that "[t]he objective is to guard against redundant or disproportionate discovery by giving the court authority to reduce the amount of discovery that may be directed to matters that are otherwise proper subjects of inquiry." However, the commentators also caution that "the court must be careful not to deprive a party of discovery that is reasonably necessary to afford a fair opportunity to defend and prepare the case." <u>Rule 26</u> advisory committee's note (1983).

In addition to the discovery standards under <u>Rule 26</u> incorporated by <u>Rule 45</u>, Rule 45 itself provides that "on timely motion, the court by which a subpoena was issued shall quash or modify the subpoena if it . . . subjects a person to undue burden." <u>Rule 45(3)(A)</u>. Of course, "if the sought-after documents are not relevant, nor calculated to lead to the discovery of admissible evidence, then any burden whatsoever imposed would be by definition 'undue.' " <u>Compaq Computer Corp. v. Packard Bell Elec., Inc., 163 F.R.D. 329, 335–36 (N.D. Cal. 1995)</u>. Underlying the protections of <u>Rule 45</u> is the recognition that "the word 'nonparty' serves as a

---

* After the 2015 amendments to the Federal Rules, the proportionality limitations that formerly appeared in Rule 26(b)(2)(C)(iii) now appear within Rule 26(b)(1). [Ed.]

constant reminder of the reasons for the limitations that characterize 'third-party' discovery." <u>Dart Indus. Co. v. Westwood Chem. Co., 649 F.2d 646, 649 (9th Cir. 1980)</u> (citations omitted). Thus, a court determining the propriety of a subpoena balances the relevance of the discovery sought, the requesting party's need, and the potential hardship to the party subject to the subpoena.

IV. DISCUSSION

Google primarily argues that the information sought by the subpoena is not reasonably calculated to lead to evidence admissible in the underlying litigation, and that the production of information is unduly burdensome. The Court discusses each of these objections in turn, as well as the Court's own concerns about the potential interests of Google's users.

A. Relevance

Any information sought by means of a subpoena must be relevant to the claims and defenses in the underlying case. More precisely, the information sought must be "reasonably calculated to lead to admissible evidence." <u>Rule 26(b)</u>. This requirement is liberally construed to permit the discovery of information which ultimately may not be admissible at trial. * * *

1. Sample of URLs

As narrowed by negotiations with Google and through the course of this Miscellaneous Action, the Government now seeks a sample of 50,000 URLs from Google's search index. In determining whether the information sought is reasonably calculated to lead to admissible evidence, the party seeking the information must first provide the Court with its plans for the requested information. The Government's disclosure of its plans for the sample of URLs is incomplete. The actual methodology disclosed in the Government's papers as to the search index sample is, in its entirety, as follows: "A human being will browse a random sample of 5,000–10,000 URLs from Google's index and categorize those sites by content" and from this information, the Government intends to "estimate . . . the aggregate properties of the websites that search engines have indexed." The Government's disclosure only describes its methodology for a study to categorize the URLs in Google's search index, and does not disclose a study regarding the effectiveness of filtering software. Absent any explanation of how the "aggregate properties" of material on the Internet is germane to the underlying litigation, the Government's disclosure as to its planned categorization study is not particularly helpful in determining whether the sample of Google's search index sought is reasonably calculated to lead to admissible evidence in the underlying litigation. * * *

* * * [I]t is difficult for a court to determine the relevance of information where the party seeking the information does not concretely disclose its plans for the infor-

mation sought. Given the broad definition of relevance in <u>Rule 26</u>, and the
current narrow scope of the subpoena,
despite the vagueness with which the
Government has disclosed its study,
the Court gives the Government the
benefit of the doubt. The Court finds
that 50,000 URLs randomly selected
from Google's data base for use in a
scientific study of the effectiveness of
filters is relevant to the issues in the
case of *ACLU v. Gonzales.*

Food for Thought

After criticizing the Government
for not explaining the relevance of
the information, the court gives the
Government the benefit of the doubt
and allows the discovery anyway.
Was that decision warranted?

2. Search Queries

In its original subpoena the Government sought a listing of the text of all search
queries entered by Google users over a two month period. As defined in the Government's subpoena, "queries" include only the text of the search string entered by a
user, and not "any additional information that may be associated with such a text
string that would identify the person who entered the text string into the search
engine, or the computer from which the text string was entered." The Government
has narrowed its request so that it now seeks only a sample of 5,000 such queries
from Google's query log. The Government discloses its plans for the query log information as follows: "A random sample of approximately 1,000 Google queries from a
one-week period will be run through the Google search engine. A human being will
browse the top URLs returned by each search and categorize the sites by content."
To the extent that the URLs obtained by the researchers as a result of running the
search queries provided are then used to create "a sample of a relevant population
of websites that can be categorized and used to test filtering software" similar to the
sample created from URLs from Google's search index, the Court finds that were
the Government to run these URLs through the filtering software and analyze the
results, the information sought would be reasonably calculated to lead to admissible
evidence.

Google's arguments challenging the relevance of the search queries to the Government's study center around its contention that a number of additional factors exist
which may mitigate the correlation between a search query and the search result. In
particular, Google cites to the presence of a safe search filter, customized searches,
or advanced preferences all potentially activated at the user end and not reflected
in the user's search string. Google also argues that the list of search queries does not
distinguish between sources of the queries such as adults, minors, automatic queries
generated by a program, known as "bot" queries, and artificial queries generated by
individual users. Contrary to Google's belief, the broad standard of relevance under
<u>Rule 26</u> does not require that the information sought necessarily be directed at the

ultimate fact in issue, only that the information sought be reasonably calculated to lead to admissible evidence in the underlying litigation. Thus, the presence of these additional factors may impact the probative value of the Government's expert report in the Eastern District of Pennsylvania on the effectiveness of filtering software in preventing minors from accessing "harmful to minors" material on the Internet, but at this stage, the Court does not find the search queries to be entirely irrelevant to the creation of a test set on which to test the effectiveness of search filters in general.

B. Undue Burden

This Court is particularly concerned anytime enforcement of a subpoena imposes an economic burden on a nonparty. Under Rule 45(c)(3)(A), a court may modify or quash a subpoena even for relevant information if it finds that there is an undue burden on the nonparty. Undue burden to the nonparty is evaluated under both Rule 26 and Rule 45.

1. Technological Burden of Production

Google argues that it faces an undue burden because it does not maintain search query or URL information in the ordinary course of business in the format requested by the Government. As a general rule, non-parties are not required to create documents that do not exist, simply for the purposes of discovery. In this case, however, Google has not represented that it is unable to extract the information requested from its existing systems. Google contends that it must create new code to format and extract query and URL data from many computer banks, in total requiring up to eight full time days of engineering time. Because the Government has agreed to compensate Google for the reasonable costs of production, and given the extremely scaled-down scope of the subpoena as modified, the Court does not find that the technical burden of production excuses Google from complying with the subpoena. Later in this Order, the Court addresses other concerns with respect to this information, however.

Google also argues that even if the Government compensates Google for its engineering time, if the Government plans on executing a high volume of searches on Google, such searches would lead to an interference with Google's search engine and disrupt use by users and advertisers. The Government only intends to run 1,000 to 5,000 of the search queries through the Google search engine. Furthermore, these searches will be run by humans who will then categorize the search results and record their findings. Given the volume and rate of the proposed study, the Court finds that the additional burden on Google's search engine caused by the Government's study as represented to the Court, is likely to be *de minimus*.

It's Latin to Me!

De minimus is a Latin term meaning minimal.

2. Potential for Loss of User Trust

Google also argues that it will be unduly burdened by loss of user trust if forced to produce its users' queries to the Government. Google claims that its success is attributed in large part to the volume of its users and these users may be attracted to its search engine because of the privacy and anonymity of the service. According to Google, even a perception that Google is acquiescing to the Government's demands to release its query log would harm Google's business by deterring some searches by some users.

Go Online

The government's pursuit of this information was controversial at the time it occurred. ZDNet published a news report of the issues raised by this request that is viewable at its website.

Google's own privacy statement indicates that Google users could not reasonably expect Google to guard the query log from disclosure to the Government. Google's privacy statement at www.google.com/privacypolicy.html states only that Google will protect "personal information" of users. "Personal information" is expressly defined for users at www.google.com/privacy_faq.html as "information that you provide to us which personally identifies you, such as your name, email address or billing information, or other data which can be reasonably linked to such information by Google." Google's privacy policy does not represent to users that it keeps confidential any information other than "personal information." Neither Google's URLs nor the text of search strings with "personal information" redacted, are reasonably "personal information" under Google's stated privacy policy. Google's privacy policy indicates that it has not suggested to its users that non-"personal information" such as that sought by the Government is kept confidential.

Food for Thought

Do you think most users of Google's search services have ever read Google's privacy policy? Have you ever read the policy? Is it appropriate to refer to the policy as indicating the reasonable expectations of Google's users?

However, even if an expectation by Google users that Google would prevent disclosure to the Government of its users' search queries is not entirely reasonable, the statistic cited by Dr. Stark that over a quarter of all Internet searches are for pornography indicates that at least some of Google's users expect some sort of privacy in their searches. The expectation of privacy by some Google users may not be reasonable, but may nonetheless have an appreciable impact on the way in which Google is perceived, and consequently the frequency with which users use Google. Such an expectation does not rise to the level of an absolute privilege, but does indicate that there is a potential burden as to Google's loss of goodwill if Google is forced to disclose search queries to the Government.

3. Trade Secret

Rule 45(c)(3)(B) provides additional protections where a subpoena seeks trade secret or confidential commercial information from a nonparty. Once the

What's That?

A *trade secret* is a formula, process, device, software program, or other business information that is kept confidential to maintain an advantage over competitors.

nonparty shows that the requested information is a trade secret or confidential commercial information, the burden shifts to the requesting party to show a "substantial need for the testimony or material that cannot be otherwise met without undue hardship and assures that the person to whom the subpoena is addressed will be reasonably compensated." Rule 45(c)(3)(B). Upon such a showing, "the court may order appearance or production only upon specified conditions."

a. Search Index and Query Log as Trade Secrets

Trade secret or commercially sensitive information must be "important proprietary information" and the party challenging the subpoena must make "a strong showing that it has historically sought to maintain the confidentiality of this information." A statistically significant sample of Google's search index and Google's query log would have independent economic value from not being known generally to the public. The

Take Note!

The court refers to the trade secret protection offered under Rule 45(c)(3)(B) (now 45(d)(3)(B)) because this case involves nonparty discovery. However, you should note that the same protection is available in the context of party discovery under Rule 26(c)(1)(G).

disclosure of a statistically significant sample of Google's search index or query log may permit competitors to estimate information about Google's indexing methods or Google's users. By declaration, Google represents that it does not share this information with third parties and it has security procedures to maintain the confidentiality of this information.

* * * Because Google still continues to claim information about its entire search index and entire query log as confidential, the Court will presume that the requested information, as a small sample of proprietary information, may be somewhat commercially sensitive, albeit not independently commercially sensitive. Successive disclosures, whether in this lawsuit or pursuant to subsequent civil subpoenas, in the aggregate could yield confidential commercial information about Google's search index or query log. * * *

* * *

c. Substantial Need

The burden thus shifts to the Government to demonstrate that the requested discovery is relevant and essential to a judicial determination of its case. Because "there is no absolute privilege for trade secrets and similar confidential information," the district court's role in this inquiry is to balance the need for the trade secrets against the claim of injury resulting from disclosure. The determination of substantial need is particularly important in the context of enforcing a subpoena when discovery of trade secret or confidential commercial information is sought from non-parties.

Google contends that it should not be compelled to produce its search index or query log because the information sought by the Government is readily available from open URL databases such as Alexa and transparent search engines such as Dogpile, or that the Government already has sufficient information from AOL, Yahoo, and Microsoft. * * * [A]t oral argument, the Government's counsel likened its discovery goals to a team of researchers studying an elephant by separately viewing the trunk, the ears, the tail, etc., and piecing the research together to get a picture of the elephant as whole.

In this case, the Government has demonstrated a substantial need for some information from Google in creating a set of URLs to run through filtering software. It is uncontested that Google is the market leader with over 45% of the search engine market. Because Google has the greatest market share, the Government's study may be significantly hampered if it did not have access to some information from the most often used search engine.

4. Cumulative and Duplicative Discovery

What the Government has not demonstrated, however, is a substantial need for both the information contained in the sample of URLs and sample of search query text. Furthermore, even if the information requested is not a trade secret, a district court may in its discretion limit discovery on a finding that "the discovery sought is unreasonably cumulative or duplicative, or is obtainable from some other source that is more convenient, less burdensome, or less expensive." Rule 26(b)(2)(i).* *See In re Sealed Case (Medical Records), 381 F.3d 1205, 1215 (D.C. Cir. 2004)* (citing the advisory committee's notes to Rule 26 and finding that "the last sentence of Rule 26(b)(1) was added in 2000 'to emphasize the need for active judicial use of subdivision (b)(2) to control excessive discovery' "). From this Court's interpretation of the Government's general statements of purpose for the information requested, both the sample of URLs and the set of search queries are aimed at providing a list of URLs which will be categorized and run through the filtering software in an effort to

---

* This limitation currently appears at Rule 26(b)(2)(C)(i). [Ed.]

determine the effectiveness of filtering software as to certain categories. * * * [T]he actual similarity of the two categories of information sought in their presumed utility to the Government's study indicates that it would be unreasonably cumulative and duplicative to compel Google to hand over both sets of proprietary information. To borrow the Government's vivid analogy, in order to aid the Government in its study of the entire elephant, the Court may burden a nonparty to require production of a picture of the elephant's tail, but it is within this Court's discretion to not require a nonparty to produce another picture of the same tail.

Faced with duplicative discovery, and with the Government not expressing a preference as to which source of the test set of URLs it prefers, this Court exercises its discretion pursuant to Rule 26(b)(2) and determines that the marginal burden of loss of trust by Google's users based on Google's disclosure of its users' search queries to the Government outweighs the duplicative disclosure's likely benefit to the Government's study. Accordingly, the Court grants the Government's motion to compel only as to the sample of 50,000 URLs from Google's search index.

C. Protective Order

As trade secret or confidential business information, Google's production of a list of URLs to the Government shall be protected by protective order. Generally, "the selective disclosure of protectable trade secrets is not per se 'unreasonable and oppressive,' when appropriate protective measures are imposed." The Court recognizes that Google was unable to negotiate the particular provisions of the protective order in the underlying litigation, but since Google's filing of its Opposition, the Government has considerably narrowed its request for Google's information from its proprietary search index such that the risk of trade secret disclosure is substantially mitigated.

The Court grants the motion to compel as to a set of 50,000 URLs from Google's search index and orders the parties to show cause, if any, on or before April 3, 2006, why a designation of the produced information as "Confidential" under the existing protective order is insufficient protection for Google's confidential commercial information.

D. Privacy

Take Note!

Note that the court raised this issue *sua sponte* but ultimately decided that the issue was irrelevant because it was denying the Government's request for the log of search queries. Why then do you think the court bothered to address these issues at all?

The Court raises, *sua sponte*, its concerns about the privacy of Google's users apart from Google's business goodwill argument. In *Gill v. Gulfstream Park Racing Assoc.*, the First Circuit held that "considerations of the public interest, the need for confidentiality, and privacy interests are relevant factors to be balanced" in a

Rule 26(c) determination regarding the subpoena of documents used to prepare an allegedly defamatory report issued by a nonparty trade association. 399 F.3d 391, 402 (1st Cir. 2005).

* * * Although the Government has only requested the text strings entered, basic identifiable information may be found in the text strings when users search for personal information such as their social security numbers or credit card numbers through Google in order to determine whether such information is available on the Internet. The Court is also aware of so-called "vanity searches," where a user queries his or her own name perhaps with other information. * * * Thus, while a user's search query reading "[user name] stanford glee club" may not raise serious privacy concerns, a user's search for "[user name] third trimester abortion san jose," may raise certain privacy issues as of yet unaddressed by the parties' papers. This concern, combined with the prevalence of Internet searches for sexually explicit material—generally not information that anyone wishes to reveal publicly—gives this Court pause as to whether the search queries themselves may constitute potentially sensitive information. * * *

In the end, the Court need not express an opinion on this issue because the Government's motion is granted only as to the sample of URLs and not as to the log of search queries.

V. CONCLUSION

As expressed in this Order, the Court's concerns with certain aspects of the Government's subpoena have been mitigated by the reduced scope the Government's present requests. * * *

* * * [U]nless the parties agree otherwise on or before April 3, 2006, Google is ordered to confer with the Government to develop a protocol for the random selection and afterward immediate production of a listing of 50,000 URLs in Google's database on the following conditions:

1.   In the development or implementation of the protocol, Google shall not be required to disclose proprietary information with respect to its database;

2.   The Government shall pay the reasonable cost incurred by Google in the formulation and implementation of the extraction protocol;

3.   Any information disclosed in response to this Order shall be subject to the protective order in the underlying case;

To the extent the motion seeks an order compelling Google to disclose search queries of its users the motion is DENIED. The Court retains jurisdiction to enforce this Order.

Points for Discussion

a. Undue Burden & Proportionality

In addition to issues of privilege and relevance, the concepts of proportionality and undue burden may fairly be characterized as being at the heart of many, if not most, disputes concerning the propriety of discovery in the federal system. Because parties are entitled to all relevant information as they develop their claims or defenses, if there is no serious burden on the person being asked to produce the information, then there is no real basis for denying the discovery of relevant, non-privileged information. However, when a serious burden would result from having to comply with a discovery request, the issue becomes whether the burden is sufficiently substantial to warrant protecting the responding party from having to produce the desired information.

What qualifies as undue burden can vary widely depending upon the circumstances of the case. Responding to discovery requests involves financial expense, opportunity costs, and the commitment of human and other resources to the response effort. How substantial must these costs be to rise to the level of undue burden? Does the answer depend on what is at stake in the litigation? *See In re New England Carpenter Health Benefits Fund*, 2006 WL 3050806, at *2 (C.D. Ill. Oct. 24, 2006) (holding that requiring a nonparty to incur the significant costs of complying with the served subpoena constitutes an undue burden); *Auto-Owners Ins. Co. v. Se. Floating Docks, Inc.*, 231 F.R.D. 426, 429 (M.D. Fla. 2005) ("To the extent that Defendants would be required to incur third party discovery costs that rise to the level of an undue burden for Defendants, Defendants have standing to quash on those grounds.").

How are courts to make difficult determinations such as whether the "the burden or expense of the proposed discovery outweighs its likely benefit" or whether the cost of certain discovery is justifiable in relation to the amount in controversy? Is there a ratio between cost and the amount in controversy that should guide the courts? Rule 26(b) instructs courts to take into account the "parties' resources" in making these determinations. Does that mean wealthy litigants have to provide more discovery than less well-heeled parties? *See Perspective & Analysis* below.

—Perspective & Analysis—

Proportionality determinations involve case-by-case determinations and the application of multiple factors in what is inherently a subjective inquiry. How are courts to engage in such analyses in any principled way? Here is one framing of the issue:

> [T]he proposed amendment gives the court discretion to limit the frequency and invocation of particular discovery methods under specified circumstances. . . .
>
> This list of circumstances invokes cost-benefit principles which contemplate both achieving an optimal level of discovery beyond which additional discovery would not be cost-effective and restricting discovery when the dollar amount or values at stake are low. . . .
>
> A potential difficulty with this approach is in finding principled criteria for differentiating between various types of cases. What values should be used in deciding whether, for example, the plaintiff in a $10,000 personal injury case should be limited in the number of depositions he may take, or the plaintiff seeking reinstatement in an employment discrimination case should be prohibited from discovering documents only tangentially related to the claim, or the defendant in a $10,000,000 product liability case should be allowed to require answers to voluminous interrogatories involving the most searching details of the plaintiff's past life? Where, one may ask, are judges expected to find the criteria and analytical structure for making such judgments?

Edward F. Sherman & Stephen O. Kinnard, *Federal Court Discovery in the 80's—Making the Rules Work*, 95 F.R.D. 245, 276 (1983).

Burden can also be measured by negative consequences that will result from compliance with the requested discovery, such as bad publicity or the disclosure of confidential or protected trade information. When should these type of considerations prevent a party from obtaining information relevant to its case? *See, e.g.*, *Cardenas v. Dorel Juvenile Grp., Inc.*, 230 F.R.D. 635, 638 (D. Kan. 2005) (issuing a protective order for trade secrets and commercial information). Was the court in *Gonzales v. Google* right to consider the potential loss of user trust in determining whether an undue burden would result from Google having to hand over sample search strings to the Government?

b. Cumulative & Duplicative Discovery

Rule 26(b)(2)(C) indicates that courts may limit discovery if it is "unreasonably cumulative or duplicative." What makes discovery "unreasonably" cumulative? Why did the Court in *Gonzales v. Google* find that the Government's request of the information contained in the sample of URLs *and* samples of search query text was unreasonably duplicative? Do you agree with that conclusion?

c. Cost-Shifting

In *Gonzales v. Google* the Government agreed to compensate Google for the reasonable costs of production, and the court memorialized this agreement in its

Order. If the Government had not agreed to do so, could the court have ordered the Government to cover Google's costs as a condition of obtaining the discovery?

The general rule in discovery is that the responding party must pay the expenses associated with responding to a discovery request. *Oppenheimer Fund, Inc. v. Sanders, 437 U.S. 340, 358 (1978)* ("[T]he presumption is that the responding party must bear the expense of complying with discovery requests . . . ."). However, the Supreme Court in *Oppenheimer* also stressed that courts do have discretion under Rule 26(c) to condition discovery upon the requesting party paying the costs of producing the information. *See id.* ("[T]he responding party . . . may invoke the district court's discretion under Rule 26(c) to grant orders protecting him from 'undue burden or expense' . . . including orders conditioning discovery on the requesting party's payment of the costs of discovery."). The authority to condition discovery on "the allocation of expenses" became explicit in Rule 26(c)(1)(B) as of December 1, 2015. Should responding parties be presumptively required to pay the cost of producing information in response to a discovery request? *See* A. Benjamin Spencer, *Rationalizing Cost Allocation in Civil Discovery*, 34 REV. LITIG. 769 (2015).

d.   Discovery from Nonparties

In *Gonzales v. Google*, we saw that discovery was being sought from nonparties to the action. Rule 45 governs discovery from nonparties, which is done via subpoenas. Subpoenas must issue from the court where the action is pending, FED. R. CIV. P. 45(a)(2), but may only compel attendance at a hearing or deposition within 100 miles of where the subpoenaed nonparty resides or anywhere within their state of residence, FED. R. CIV. P. 45(c)(1).

When nonparties are the object of discovery, the mechanisms for obtaining information from them are more limited under the Federal Rules because not all of the discovery mechanisms are applicable to nonparties. For example, the rules providing for interrogatories and physical examinations may not be used to obtain information from nonparties. However, Rule 45 permits nonparties to be subjected to depositions and document inspection via subpoenas. FED. R. CIV. P. 45(a)(1)(A). Further, when discovery is sought from nonparties, requesting parties are under an affirmative obligation not to impose "undue burden or expense" on the responding nonparty. FED. R. CIV. P. 45(d)(1). Finally, it is worth noting that witness fees and mileage must be paid when a subpoena requires the nonparty's attendance. FED. R. CIV. P. 45(b)(1); *see also* 28 U.S.C. § 1821 (providing for a per diem and mileage for witnesses in actions pending in a court of the United States). Subpoenaed persons may resist a subpoena on the ground that any applicable limitations were not honored via a motion to quash filed in the district where compliance is required. FED. R. CIV. P. 45(d)(3).

————————————

2. Proportionality Limits on Electronic Discovery

As we have just seen, the Federal Rules are concerned with protecting litigants from discovery that is unduly burdensome in relation to the importance of the information to the issues in the case, the stakes in the litigation, and the ability of the requesting party to obtain the information through other means. Historically, the undue burden determination occurred in the context of the production of physical paper documents on a large scale and the expenses associated with identifying, reviewing, and producing such material to the requesting party. However, over the past couple of decades information storage has increasingly migrated from print to digital sources. The past decade and a half in particular has been witness to an explosion in the amount of data that is not only retained but created in an electronic format. Modern innovations in computing, programming, and storage have made it increasingly preferable to operate almost exclusively on a digital plane.

The advent of the Internet compounded the effect of these changes by permitting instantaneous electronic communications to supplant slower off-line methods as the primary means by which individuals and entities transmit information, both for personal and for business or governmental purposes. As a result of these developments, litigants—particularly sophisticated commercial concerns—possess an enormous volume of material in electronic format. Because electronically stored material occupies dramatically less physical space than its predecessor formats, much more of it can be kept at less expense for longer periods of time.

When the liberal discovery regime of the federal system was overlain with this technological reality, a problem occurred. With massive volumes of electronically stored information ("ESI") in one's possession, responding to a discovery request became a much more burdensome affair in several

Go Online

For a good overview of the history of the Internet written by one of the creators of the Internet, Dr. Vinton Cerf, visit the Internet Society's website at http://www.isoc.org/internet/history/brief.shtml.

ways. Reviewing an exponentially larger universe of documents itself provides a source of increased expense associated with the discovery of ESI. More important, however, is the fact that various electronic formats can differ in the degree to which they can be accessed and searched. For example, active data on one's hard drive is relatively easy to access while information stored on archival backup tapes may require time-consuming and costly restoration processes before the information can be reviewed. When the costs of retrieval and review escalate into the tens of thousands of dollars or beyond, legitimate questions arise as to whether such expense is proportional to the need for the information and its potential value to the litigation.

Because of the unique challenges that ESI presents to the discovery process, in 2006 the Federal Rules were amended in several respects. Pertinent to our present discussion are the changes to the Rules that sought to adapt the undue burden and proportionality standards discussed above to the electronic information context. Under the 2006 amendments the core measure of burdensomeness and proportionality is a new concept—accessibility. Revised Rule 26(b)(2)(B) protects parties against having to produce ESI that they deem to be "not reasonably accessible." The rule reads as follows:

FRCP 26(b)(2)(B). Discovery Scope & Limits: Limitations on Frequency and Extent.

(B) *Specific Limitations on Electronically Stored Information*: A party need not provide discovery of electronically stored information from sources that the party identifies as not reasonably accessible because of undue burden or cost. On motion to compel discovery or for a protective order, the party from whom discovery is sought must show that the information is not reasonably accessible because of undue burden or cost. If that showing is made, the court may nonetheless order discovery from such sources if the requesting party shows good cause, considering the limitations of Rule 26(b)(2)(C). The court may specify conditions for the discovery.

This rule makes otherwise relevant information not discoverable based on the responding party's declaration and ultimate showing that it is "not reasonably accessible." How are courts to interpret the phrase "not reasonably accessible"? What type of ESI should qualify as being not reasonably accessible? The next case presents the approach one district court took to this issue before the 2006 amendments took effect.

Zubulake v. UBS Warburg L.L.C. ("Zubulake I")

U.S. District Court for the Southern District of New York
217 F.R.D. 309 (S.D.N.Y. 2003)

Scheindlin, District Judge.

* * * The issue presented here is * * * : To what extent is inaccessible electronic data discoverable, and who should pay for its production?

Take Note!

Judge Scheindlin's comments regarding "simplified notice pleading" are no longer apt in the wake of *Twombly* and *Iqbal*. Think about whether the advent of plausibility pleading has any bearing on the court's analysis of the discovery issues in this case.

I. Introduction

The Supreme Court recently reiterated that our "simplified notice pleading standard relies on liberal discovery rules and summary judgment motions to define disputed facts and issues and to dispose of unmeritorious claims."[2] Thus, it is now beyond dispute that "[b]road discovery is a cornerstone of the litigation process contemplated by the Federal Rules of Civil Procedure." The Rules contemplate a minimal burden to bringing a claim; that claim is then fleshed out through vigorous and expansive discovery.[4]

In one context, however, the reliance on broad discovery has hit a roadblock. As individuals and corporations increasingly do business electronically—using computers to create and store documents, make deals, and exchange e-mails—the universe of discoverable material has expanded exponentially.[6] The more information there is to discover, the more expensive it is to discover all the relevant information until, in the end, "discovery is not just about uncovering the truth, but also about how much of the truth the parties can afford to disinter."

This case provides a textbook example of the difficulty of balancing the competing needs of broad discovery and manageable costs. Laura Zubulake is suing UBS Warburg LLC, UBS Warburg, and UBS AG (collectively, "UBS" or the "Firm") under Federal, State and City law for gender discrimination and illegal retaliation. Zubulake's case is certainly not frivolous[8] and if she prevails, her damages may be substantial.[9] She contends that key evidence is located in various e-mails exchanged among UBS employees that now exist only on backup tapes and perhaps other archived media. According to UBS, restoring those e-mails would cost approximately $175,000.00, exclusive of attorney time in reviewing the e-mails. Zubulake now moves for an order compelling UBS to produce those e-mails at its expense.

II. BACKGROUND

A. Zubulake's Lawsuit

UBS hired Zubulake on August 23, 1999, as a director and senior salesperson on its U.S. Asian Equities Sales Desk (the "Desk"), where she reported to Dominic Vail, the Desk's manager. At the time she was hired, Zubulake was told that she would be considered for Vail's position if and when it became vacant.

In December 2000, Vail indeed left his position to move to the Firm's London office. But Zubulake was not considered for his position, and the Firm instead hired Matthew Chapin as director of the Desk. Zubulake alleges that from the

---

[2] *Swierkiewicz v. Sorema, N.A.*, 534 U.S. 506, 512 (2002).

[4] *See Hickman v. Taylor*, 329 U.S. 495, 500–01 (1947).

[6] *Rowe Entm't, Inc. v. William Morris Agency, Inc.*, 205 F.R.D. 421, 429 (S.D.N.Y. 2002) (explaining that electronic data is so voluminous because, unlike paper documents, "the costs of storage are virtually nil. Information is retained not because it is expected to be used, but because there is no compelling reason to discard it"), *aff'd*, 2002 WL 975713 (S.D.N.Y. May 9, 2002).

[8] Indeed, Zubulake has already produced a sort of "smoking gun": an e-mail suggesting that she be fired "ASAP" after her EEOC charge was filed, in part so that she would not be eligible for year-end bonuses.

[9] At the time she was terminated, Zubulake's annual salary was approximately $500,000. Were she to receive full back pay and front pay, Zubulake estimates that she may be entitled to as much as $13,000,000 in damages, not including any punitive damages or attorney's fees.

outset Chapin treated her differently than the other members of the Desk, all of whom were male. In particular, Chapin "undermined Ms. Zubulake's ability to perform her job by, *inter alia*: (a) ridiculing and belittling her in front of co-workers; (b) excluding her from work-related outings with male co-workers and clients; (c) making sexist remarks in her presence; and (d) isolating her from the other senior salespersons on the Desk by seating her apart from them." No such actions were taken against any of Zubulake's male co-workers.

Make the Connection

The claim of *retaliation* here refers to an allegation that the employer has discharged Zubulake in retaliation for her filing of a gender discrimination complaint with the EEOC. Such a retaliatory discharge is unlawful under Title VII of the Civil Rights Act of 1964, something you can study further in a **Civil Rights Litigation** course.

Zubulake ultimately responded by filing a Charge of (gender) Discrimination with the EEOC [Equal Employment Opportunity Commission] on August 16, 2001. On October 9, 2001, Zubulake was fired with two weeks' notice. On February 15, 2002, Zubulake filed the instant action, suing for sex discrimination and retaliation under Title VII, the New York State Human Rights Law, and the Administrative Code of the City of New York. UBS timely answered on March 12, 2002, denying the allegations. UBS's argument is, in essence, that Chapin's conduct was not unlawfully discriminatory because he treated everyone equally badly. On the one hand, UBS points to evidence that Chapin's anti-social behavior was not limited to women: a former employee made allegations of national origin discrimination against Chapin, and a number of male employees on the Desk also complained about him. On the other hand, Chapin was responsible for hiring three new females employees to the Desk.

B. The Discovery Dispute

Discovery in this action commenced on or about June 3, 2002, when Zubulake served UBS with her first document request. At issue here is request number twenty-eight for "[a]ll documents concerning any communication by or between UBS employees concerning Plaintiff." The term document in Zubulake's request "includ[es], without limitation, electronic or computerized data compilations." On July 8, 2002, UBS responded by producing approximately 350 pages of documents, including approximately 100 pages of e-mails. UBS also objected to a substantial portion of Zubulake's requests.

What's That?

A *document request* is a request to produce documents as part of discovery pursuant to Rule 34. It is one of the discovery devices we will discuss below in Section C of this chapter.

On September 12, 2002 * * * the parties reached an agreement. With respect to document request twenty-eight, the parties reached the following agreement:

Defendants will [ ] ask UBS about how to retrieve e-mails that are saved in the firm's computer system and will produce responsive e-mails if retrieval is possible and Plaintiff names a few individuals.

Pursuant to the Agreement, UBS agreed unconditionally to produce responsive e-mails from the accounts of five individuals named by Zubulake * * * . UBS was to produce such e-mails sent between August 1999 (when Zubulake was hired) and December 2001 (one month after her termination), to the extent possible.

UBS, however, produced no additional e-mails and insisted that its initial production (the 100 pages of e-mails) was complete. As UBS's opposition to the instant motion makes clear—although it remains unsaid—UBS never searched for responsive e-mails on any of its backup tapes. To the contrary, UBS informed Zubulake that the cost of producing e-mails on backup tapes would be prohibitive (estimated at the time at approximately $300,000.00).

Zubulake, believing that the 9/12/02 Agreement included production of e-mails from backup tapes, objected to UBS's nonproduction. In fact, Zubulake knew that there were additional responsive e-mails that UBS had failed to produce because she herself had produced approximately 450 pages of e-mail correspondence. Clearly, numerous responsive e-mails had been created and deleted[19] at UBS, and Zubulake wanted them.

* * *

C. UBS's E-Mail Backup System

In the first instance, the parties agree that e-mail was an important means of communication at UBS during the relevant time period. Each salesperson, including the salespeople on the Desk, received approximately 200 e-mails each day. Given this volume, and because Securities and Exchange Commission regulations require it, UBS implemented extensive e-mail backup and preservation protocols. In particular, e-mails were backed up in two distinct ways: on backup tapes and on optical disks.

---

[19] The term "deleted" is sticky in the context of electronic data. " 'Deleting' a file does not actually erase that data from the computer's storage devices. Rather, it simply finds the data's entry in the disk directory and changes it to a 'not used' status—thus permitting the computer to write over the 'deleted' data. Until the computer writes over the 'deleted' data, however, it may be recovered by searching the disk itself rather than the disk's directory. Accordingly, many files are recoverable long after they have been deleted—even if neither the computer user nor the computer itself is aware of their existence. Such data is referred to as 'residual data.' " Shira A. Scheindlin & Jeffrey Rabkin, *Electronic Discovery in Federal Civil Litigation: Is Rule 34 Up to the Task?*, 41 B.C. L. REV. 327, 337 (2000) (footnotes omitted). Deleted data may also exist because it was backed up before it was deleted. Thus, it may reside on backup tapes or similar media. Unless otherwise noted, I will use the term "deleted" data to mean residual data, and will refer to backed-up data as "backup tapes."

1. Backup Tape Storage

UBS employees used a program called HP OpenMail, manufactured by Hewlett-Packard, for all work-related e-mail communications. With limited exceptions, all e-mails sent or received by any UBS employee are stored onto backup tapes. To do so, UBS employs a program called Veritas NetBackup, which creates a "snapshot" of all e-mails that exist on a given server at the time the backup is taken. Except for scheduling the backups and physically inserting the tapes into the machines, the backup process is entirely automated.

UBS used the same backup protocol during the entire relevant time period, from 1999 through 2001. Using NetBackup, UBS backed up its e-mails at three intervals: (1) daily, at the end of each day, (2) weekly, on Friday nights, and (3) monthly, on the last business day of the month. Nightly backup tapes were kept for twenty working days, weekly tapes for one year, and monthly tapes for three years. After the relevant time period elapsed, the tapes were recycled.[25]

Once e-mails have been stored onto backup tapes, the restoration process is lengthy. Each backup tape routinely takes approximately five days to restore, although resort to an outside vendor would speed up the process (at greatly enhanced costs, of course). Because each tape represents a snapshot of one server's hard drive in a given month, each server/month must be restored separately onto a hard drive. Then, a program called Double Mail is used to extract a particular individual's e-mail file. That mail file is then exported into a Microsoft Outlook data file, which in turn can be opened in Microsoft Outlook, a common e-mail application. A user could then browse through the mail file and sort the mail by recipient, date or subject, or search for key words in the body of the e-mail.

Fortunately, NetBackup also created indexes of each backup tape. Thus, [UBS] was able to search through the tapes from the relevant time period and determine that the e-mail files responsive to Zubulake's requests are contained on a total of ninety-four backup tapes.

2. Optical Disk Storage

In addition to the e-mail backup tapes, UBS also stored certain e-mails on optical disks. For certain "registered traders," probably including the members of the Desk, a copy of all e-mails sent to or received from outside sources (i.e., e-mails from a "registered trader" at UBS to someone at another entity, or vice versa) was

---

[25] Of course, periodic backups such as UBS's necessarily entails the loss of certain e-mails. Because backups were conducted only intermittently, some e-mails that were deleted from the server were never backed up. For example, if a user both received and deleted an e-mail on the same day, it would not reside on any backup tape. Similarly, an e-mail received and deleted within the span of one month would not exist on the monthly backup, although it might exist on a weekly or daily backup, if those tapes still exist. As explained below, if an e-mail was to or from a "registered trader," however, it may have been stored on UBS's optical storage devices.

simultaneously written onto a series of optical disks. Internal e-mails, however, were not stored on this system.

UBS has retained each optical disk used since the system was put into place in mid-1998. Moreover, the optical disks are neither erasable nor rewritable. Thus, UBS has every e-mail sent or received by registered traders (except internal e-mails) during the period of Zubulake's employment, even if the e-mail was deleted instantaneously on that trader's system.

The optical disks are easily searchable using a program called Tumbleweed. Using Tumbleweed, a user can simply log into the system with the proper credentials and create a plain language search. Search criteria can include not just "header" information, such as the date or the name of the sender or recipient, but can also include terms within the text of the e-mail itself. For example, UBS personnel could easily run a search for e-mails containing the words "Laura" or "Zubulake" that were sent or received * * * .

III. LEGAL STANDARD

Federal Rules of Civil Procedure 26 through 37 govern discovery in all civil actions. * * * Rule 26(b)(2) imposes general limitations on the scope of discovery in the form of a "proportionality test" * * * . * * * "Under [the discovery] rules, the presumption is that the responding party must bear the expense of complying with discovery requests, but [it] may invoke the district court's discretion under Rule 26(c) to grant orders protecting [it] from 'undue burden or expense' in doing so, including orders conditioning discovery on the requesting party's payment of the costs of discovery."[32]

The application of these various discovery rules is particularly complicated where electronic data is sought because otherwise discoverable evidence is often only available from expensive-to-restore backup media. That being so, courts have devised creative solutions for balancing the broad scope of discovery prescribed in Rule 26(b)(1) with the cost-consciousness of Rule 26(b)(2). By and large, the solution has been to consider cost-shifting: forcing the requesting party, rather than the answering party, to bear the cost of discovery.

By far, the most influential response to the problem of cost-shifting relating to the discovery of electronic data was given by United States Magistrate Judge James C. Francis IV of this district in *Rowe Entertainment, Inc. v. William Morris Agency, Inc.*, 205 F.R.D. 421, 429 (S.D.N.Y. 2002). Judge Francis utilized an eight-factor test to determine whether discovery costs should be shifted. Those eight factors are:

---

[32] *Oppenheimer Fund, Inc. v. Sanders*, 437 U.S. 340, 358 (1978).

(1) the specificity of the discovery requests; (2) the likelihood of discovering critical information; (3) the availability of such information from other sources; (4) the purposes for which the responding party maintains the requested data; (5) the relative benefits to the parties of obtaining the information; (6) the total cost associated with production; (7) the relative ability of each party to control costs and its incentive to do so; and (8) the resources available to each party.

Both Zubulake and UBS agree that the eight-factor *Rowe* test should be used to determine whether cost-shifting is appropriate.

IV. Discussion

A. *Should Discovery of UBS's Electronic Data Be Permitted?*

Under Rule 34, a party may request discovery of any document, "including writings, drawings, graphs, charts, photographs, phonorecords, and other data compilations. . . ." The "inclusive description" of the term document "accord[s] with changing technology." "It makes clear that Rule 34 applies to *electronics* [sic] data compilations." Thus, "[e]lectronic documents are no less subject to disclosure than paper records." This is true not only of electronic documents that are currently in use, but also of documents that may have been deleted and now reside only on backup disks.

That being so, Zubulake is entitled to discovery of the requested e-mails so long as they are relevant to her claims, which they clearly are. As noted, e-mail constituted a substantial means of communication among UBS employees. To that end, UBS has already produced approximately 100 pages of e-mails, the contents of which are unquestionably relevant.

Nonetheless, UBS argues that Zubulake is not entitled to any further discovery because it already produced all responsive documents, to wit, the 100 pages of e-mails. This argument is unpersuasive for two reasons. First, because of the way that UBS backs up its e-mail files, it clearly could not have searched all of its e-mails without restoring the ninety-four backup tapes (which UBS admits that it has not done). UBS therefore cannot represent that it has produced all responsive e-mails. Second, Zubulake herself has produced over 450 pages of relevant e-mails, including e-mails that would have been responsive to her discovery requests but were never produced by UBS. These two facts strongly suggest that there are e-mails that Zubulake has not received that reside on UBS's backup media.

B. *Should Cost-Shifting Be Considered?*

Because it apparently recognizes that Zubulake is entitled to the requested discovery, UBS expends most of its efforts urging the court to shift the cost of production to "protect [it] . . . from undue burden or expense." Faced with similar applications, courts generally engage in some sort of cost-shifting analysis * * * . The first question, however, is whether cost-shifting must be considered in every case involving the discovery of electronic data, which—in today's world—includes virtually all cases. In light of the accepted principle, stated above, that electronic evidence is no less discoverable than paper evidence, the answer is, "No." The Supreme Court has instructed that "the presumption is that the responding party must bear the expense of complying with discovery requests. . . ." Any principled approach to electronic evidence must respect this presumption.

Courts must remember that cost-shifting may effectively end discovery, especially when private parties are engaged in litigation with large corporations. As large companies increasingly move to entirely paper-free environments, the frequent use of cost-shifting will have the effect of crippling discovery in discrimination and retaliation cases. This will both undermine the "strong public policy favor[ing] resolving disputes on their merits," and may ultimately deter the filing of potentially meritorious claims.

Food for Thought

Why do you think that the Supreme Court has maintained the presumption that responding parties bear the expense of responding to discovery requests? Is it fair to make a responding party bear the costs of requests imposed by their adversary? Does such a presumption enable a requesting party to impose painful expense on their adversary in an effort to pressure them to settle the case? *See* Martin H. Redish, *Electronic Discovery and the Litigation Matrix*, 51 Duke L.J. 561 (2001).

Thus, cost-shifting should be considered only when electronic discovery imposes an "undue burden or expense" on the responding party. The burden or expense of discovery is, in turn, "undue" when it "outweighs its likely benefit, taking into account the needs of the case, the amount in controversy, the parties' resources, the importance of the issues at stake in the litigation, and the importance of the proposed discovery in resolving the issues." Fed.R.Civ.P. 26(b)(2)(iii).*

Many courts have automatically assumed that an undue burden or expense may arise simply because electronic evidence is involved. This makes no sense. Electronic evidence is frequently cheaper and easier to produce than paper evidence because it can be searched automatically, key words can be run for privilege checks, and the production can be made in electronic form obviating the need for mass photocopying.

In fact, whether production of documents is unduly burdensome or expensive turns primarily on whether it is kept in an accessible or inaccessible format (a distinction that corresponds closely to the expense of production). In the world of

---

* After the 2015 amendments, this provision is now found in Rule 26(b)(1). [Ed.]

paper documents, for example, a document is accessible if it is readily available in a usable format and reasonably indexed. Examples of inaccessible paper documents could include (a) documents in storage in a difficult to reach place; (b) documents converted to microfiche and not easily readable; or (c) documents kept haphazardly, with no indexing system, in quantities that make page-by-page searches impracticable. But in the world of electronic data, thanks to search engines, any data that is retained in a machine readable format is typically accessible.

Whether electronic data is accessible or inaccessible turns largely on the media on which it is stored. Five categories of data, listed in order from most accessible to least accessible, are described in the literature on electronic data storage:

1. *Active, online data*: "On-line storage is generally provided by magnetic disk. It is used in the very active stages of an electronic record's life—when it is being created or received and processed, as well as when the access frequency is high and the required speed of access is very fast * * *." Examples of online data include hard drives.

Food for Thought

As you review the court's classification of electronic storage formats, consider whether this categorization is likely to be enduring or instead will become less pertinent as the technology of electronic information storage evolves over time. Is it possible that technological advances will eventually result in the elimination of "inaccessible" formats?

2. *Near-line data*: "This typically consists of a robotic storage device (robotic library) that houses removable media, uses robotic arms to access the media, and uses multiple read/write devices to store and retrieve records. Access speeds can range from as low as milliseconds if the media is already in a read device, up to 10–30 seconds for optical disk technology, and between 20–120 seconds for sequentially searched media, such as magnetic tape." Examples include optical disks.

3. *Offline storage/archives*: "This is removable optical disk or magnetic tape media, which can be labeled and stored in a shelf or rack. Off-line storage of electronic records is traditionally used for making disaster copies of records and also for records considered 'archival' in that their likelihood of retrieval is minimal. Accessibility to off-line media involves manual intervention and is much slower than on-line or near-line storage. Access speed may be minutes, hours, or even days, depending on the access-effectiveness of the storage facility." * * *.

4. *Backup tapes*: "A device, like a tape recorder, that reads data from and writes it onto a tape. * * * The disadvantage of tape drives is that they are sequential-access devices, which means that to read any particular block of data, you need to read all

the preceding blocks." As a result, "[t]he data on a backup tape are not organized for retrieval of individual documents or files" * * *. Backup tapes also typically employ some sort of data compression, permitting more data to be stored on each tape, but also making restoration more time-consuming and expensive * * *.

5.   *Erased, fragmented or damaged data*: "When a file is first created and saved, it is laid down on the [storage media] in contiguous clusters . . . As files are erased, their clusters are made available again as free space. Eventually, some newly created files become larger than the remaining contiguous free space. These files are then broken up and randomly placed throughout the disk." Such broken-up files are said to be "fragmented," and along with damaged and erased data can only be accessed after significant processing.

Of these, the first three categories are typically identified as accessible, and the latter two as inaccessible. The difference between the two classes is easy to appreciate. Information deemed "accessible" is stored in a readily usable format. Although the time it takes to actually access the data ranges from milliseconds to days, the data does not need to be restored or otherwise manipulated to be usable. "Inaccessible" data, on the other hand, is not readily usable. Backup tapes must be restored using a process similar to that previously described, fragmented data must be defragmented, and erased data must be reconstructed, all before the data is usable. That makes such data inaccessible.

The case at bar is a perfect illustration of the range of accessibility of electronic data. As explained above, UBS maintains e-mail files in three forms: (1) active user e-mail files; (2) archived e-mails on optical disks; and (3) backup data stored on tapes. The active (HP OpenMail) data is obviously the most accessible: it is online data that resides on an active server, and can be accessed immediately. The optical disk (Tumbleweed) data is only slightly less accessible, and falls into either the second or third category. The e-mails are on optical disks that need to be located and read with the correct hardware, but the system is configured to make searching the optical disks simple and automated once they are located. For these sources of e-mails—active mail files and e-mails stored on optical disks—it would be wholly inappropriate to even consider cost-shifting. UBS maintains the data in an accessible and usable format, and can respond to Zubulake's request cheaply and quickly. Like most typical discovery requests, therefore, the producing party should bear the cost of production.

E-mails stored on backup tapes (via NetBackup), however, are an entirely different matter. Although UBS has already identified the ninety-four potentially responsive backup tapes, those tapes are not currently accessible. In order to search the tapes for responsive e-mails, UBS would have to engage in the costly and time-consuming process detailed above. It is therefore appropriate to consider cost shifting.

C. What Is the Proper Cost-Shifting Analysis?

In order to maintain the presumption that the responding party pays, the cost-shifting analysis must be neutral; close calls should be resolved in favor of the presumption. The *Rowe* factors, as applied, undercut that presumption for three reasons. First, the *Rowe* test is incomplete. Second, courts have given equal weight to all of the factors, when certain factors should predominate. Third, courts applying the *Rowe* test have not always developed a full factual record. * * *

Set forth below is a new seven-factor test based on * * * modifications to *Rowe*:

1. The extent to which the request is specifically tailored to discover relevant information;

2. The availability of such information from other sources;

3. The total cost of production, compared to the amount in controversy;

4. The total cost of production, compared to the resources available to each party;

5. The relative ability of each party to control costs and its incentive to do so;

6. The importance of the issues at stake in the litigation; and

7. The relative benefits to the parties of obtaining the information.

* * * When evaluating cost-shifting, the central question must be, does the request impose an "undue burden or expense" on the responding party? Put another way, "how important is the sought-after evidence in comparison to the cost of production?" The seven-factor test articulated above provides some guidance in answering this question, but the test cannot be mechanically applied at the risk of losing sight of its purpose.

Weighting the factors in descending order of importance may * * * avoid a mechanistic application of the test. The first two factors—comprising the marginal utility test—are the most important. These factors include: (1) The extent to which the request is specifically tailored to discover relevant information and (2) the availability of such information from other sources. * * *

The second group of factors addresses cost issues: "How expensive will this production be?" and, "Who can handle that expense?" These factors include: (3) the total cost of production compared to the amount in controversy, (4) the total cost of production compared to the resources available to each party and (5) the relative ability of each party to control costs and its incentive to do so. The third "group"— (6) the importance of the litigation itself—stands alone, and as noted earlier will only rarely come into play. But where it does, this factor has the potential to predominate over the others. Collectively, the first three groups correspond to the three explicit considerations of Rule 26(b)(2)(iii). Finally, the last factor—(7) the relative benefits of production as between the requesting and producing parties—is the least important because it is fair to presume that the response to a discovery request generally benefits the requesting party. But in the unusual case where production will also provide a tangible or strategic benefit to the responding party, that fact may weigh against shifting costs.

Food for Thought

After considering each of the factors in this "test," how is the court supposed to make its decision? For example, if the information is unavailable elsewhere but the cost of producing it is disproportionately high for a litigant to pay given the amount in controversy and their financial condition, what does that mean? Shift all of the costs to the requesting party? Half of the costs? Isn't the ultimate decision here still just a matter of the court's discretion, the seven-factored test notwithstanding? What role, then, do you see the test playing here?

D. A Factual Basis Is Required to Support the Analysis

Courts applying *Rowe* have uniformly favored cost-shifting largely because of assumptions made concerning the likelihood that relevant information will be found. * * * But such proof will rarely exist in advance of obtaining the requested discovery. The suggestion that a plaintiff must not only demonstrate that probative evidence exists, but also prove that electronic discovery will yield a "gold mine," is contrary to the plain language of <u>Rule 26(b)(1)</u>, which permits discovery of "any matter" that is "relevant to [a] claim or defense." * * *

Requiring the responding party to restore and produce responsive documents from a small sample of backup tapes will inform the cost-shifting analysis laid out above. When based on an actual sample, the marginal utility test will not be an exercise in speculation—there will be tangible evidence of what the backup tapes may have to offer. There will also be tangible evidence of the time and cost required to restore the backup tapes, which in turn will inform the second group of cost-shifting factors. Thus, by requiring a sample restoration of backup tapes, the entire cost-shifting analysis can be grounded in fact rather than guesswork.

V. CONCLUSION AND ORDER

In summary, deciding disputes regarding the scope and cost of discovery of electronic data requires a three-step analysis:

First, it is necessary to thoroughly understand the responding party's computer system, both with respect to active and stored data. For data that is kept in an accessible format, the usual rules of discovery apply: the responding party should pay the costs of producing responsive data. A court should consider cost-shifting only when electronic data is relatively inaccessible, such as in backup tapes.

Second, because the cost-shifting analysis is so fact-intensive, it is necessary to determine what data may be found on the inaccessible media. Requiring the responding party to restore and produce responsive documents from a small sample of the requested backup tapes is a sensible approach in most cases.

Third, and finally, in conducting the cost-shifting analysis, the [seven] factors [above] should be considered, weighted more-or-less in the * * * order [presented]. * * *

Accordingly, UBS is ordered to produce all responsive e-mails that exist on its optical disks or on its active servers * * * at its own expense. UBS is also ordered to produce, at its expense, responsive e-mails from any five backups tapes selected by Zubulake. UBS should then prepare an affidavit detailing the results of its search, as well as the time and money spent. After reviewing the contents of the backup tapes and UBS's certification, the Court will conduct the appropriate cost-shifting analysis.

————————

Points for Discussion

a. Accessibility Under Rule 26(b)(2)(B)

Zubulake predates the current version of Rule 26(b)(2), which includes standards governing the production of electronically stored information or ESI. However, it is clear that the rule's embrace of the concept of accessibility is a legacy of the *Zubulake* court's adept use of the concept to resolve the electronic discovery dispute before it. Should accessibility under Rule 26(b)(2)(B) be construed to have the same meaning as the term was given in *Zubulake*? The rule ties inaccessibility to "undue burden or cost," familiar concepts within the discovery rules. The question is, should such a burden and cost analysis proceed along the lines suggested by *Zubulake*, guided by the categorization of electronic storage formats outlined in that case? For example, is all data kept on backup tapes presumptively inaccessible?

b. Dispute Resolution Procedure Under Rule 26(b)(2)(B)

Rule 26(b)(2)(B) permits the responding party not to produce relevant, responsive ESI that is contained within not reasonably accessible formats based on its own judgment regarding accessibility. After the responding party identifies the sources that are not reasonably accessible, the requesting party may then file a motion to compel production of the information, which in turn obligates the responding party to demonstrate inaccessibility based on undue burden and cost. If undue burden is established, the requesting party must show "good cause" to obtain a court order forcing the responding party to produce the information.

Food for Thought

What other types of ESI might be inaccessible beyond those categories identified by the *Zubulake* court (backup tapes and fragmentary data)? One example is *legacy data*, which refers to data that can only be retrieved or understood by software and/or hardware that no longer exists or has become obsolete.

Several questions are prompted by this procedure. Are responding parties likely to lean towards claiming that information is inaccessible if it is something they do not want to produce? Will requesting parties be likely to accept responding parties' representations about accessibility without putting them to proof via a motion to compel? In an effort to buttress their prospective inaccessibility claims and thereby render information undiscoverable, are litigants likely—as an ordinary business practice—to migrate information to less accessible formats than they otherwise might? If so, is anything wrong with such a practice?

c. Relevance and Inaccessible ESI

The discovery questions that we are considering generally involve a two-part inquiry: (1) is the information relevant and (2) if so, would it be unduly burdensome to produce it? What should courts do when the inaccessibility of ESI prevents any initial determination of relevance without great expense? Is the sampling approach of the court in *Zubulake* the wisest course of action? *See* McPeek v. Ashcroft, 202 F.R.D. 31 (D.D.C. 2001) (ordering a random sampling of requested backup tapes to determine relevance and cost of retrieval).

d. Cost-Shifting and Inaccessible ESI

The *Zubulake* court articulated what has become the predominant approach to evaluating who should bear the costs associated with the retrieval and restoration of inaccessible ESI by setting forth a weighted seven-factor test. These factors are basically elaborations of the considerations found within Rule 26(b)(1).

Does cost-shifting have to be an all-or-nothing matter or should courts that engage in this analysis be permitted to split the costs among the requesting and responding parties? In Zubulake v. UBS Warburg L.L.C., 216 F.R.D. 280 (S.D.N.Y. 2003) (*Zubulake III*), a follow-up to the first *Zubulake* case (now referred to as *Zubulake I*), the court ruled that the plaintiff would be required to pay 25% of the costs associated with restoring UBS backup tapes based on its application of the seven-factor test. Was this fair given the substantially larger financial resources possessed by UBS compared with Zubulake? If costs are regularly shifted in whole or in part to requesting parties, will that place additional barriers in front of efforts to discover information contained within inaccessible formats? In other words, even though parties may be able to get at inaccessible ESI, if the court makes them pay for it are they less likely to pursue it? This would seem to be a possibility of particular concern to individual plaintiffs who may lack the resources to absorb such costs.

---

3. Privilege and Work-Product Protection

The Attorney-Client Privilege. Recall that the rule governing the permissible scope of discovery, Rule 26(b)(1), indicates that all relevant matters that are "non-privileged" are discoverable. A matter is privileged if it is covered by a privilege rule that gives certain persons the right to withhold the information from disclosure for various reasons. According to the general rule on privileges in the federal courts—Rule 501 of the Federal Rules of Evidence—privilege rules can come from various sources:

> The common law—as interpreted by United States courts in the light of reason and experience—governs a claim of privilege unless any of the following provides otherwise: the United States Constitution; a federal statute; or rules prescribed by the Supreme Court. But in a civil case, state law governs privilege regarding a claim or defense for which state law supplies the rule of decision.

FED. R. EVID. 501.

Make the Connection

Privileges are a matter of the law of evidence and you will have the opportunity to study the various evidentiary privileges in detail in an **Evidence** course. The attorney-client privilege may also be treated in your **Professional Responsibility/Ethics** course.

Although there are several widely accepted privileges, our purpose here is not to catalogue and explain each of them but rather to discuss the most basic and widely recognized privilege—the attorney-client privilege—and how that privilege is asserted and protected in the context of discovery. As an initial matter, it is worth asking why we have certain privileges against disclosure that are recognized in our system. The main answer given to this question is that society values the relationships protected by privileges and prioritizes free communication in the context of these relationships more than the contribution such information could make to improved accuracy of litigation outcomes were it obtainable. This is particularly so in the context of the attorney-client relationship. The right to the representation of legal counsel is a deeply embedded value in American society and a critical component of protecting that relationship is enabling clients to be completely candid with their attorneys so that they might be better able to represent their clients' interests.

For More Information

Other privileges besides the attorney-client privilege include executive privilege, the doctor-patient privilege, and the priest-penitent privilege. For a discussion of the rationale behind testimonial privileges with a particular focus on the marital privilege, see Amanda H. Frost, *Updating the Marital Privileges: A Witness-Centered Rationale*, 14 WIS. WOMEN'S L.J. 1 (1999).

Generally speaking, the elements of the attorney-client privilege are as follows:

(1) the asserted holder of the privilege is or sought to become a client; (2) the person to whom the communication was made (a) is a member of the bar of a court, or his or her subordinate, and (b) in connection with this communication is acting as a lawyer; (3) the communication relates to a fact of which the attorney was informed (a) by his client (b) without the presence of strangers (c) for the purpose of securing primarily either (i) an opinion of law or (ii) legal services or (iii) assistance in some legal proceeding, and (d) not for the purpose of committing a crime or tort; and (4) the privilege has been (a) claimed and (b) not waived by the client.

Montgomery Cty. v. MicroVote Corp., 175 F.3d 296, 301 (3d Cir. 1999) (citing *Rhone-Poulenc Rorer Inc. v. Home Indem. Co.*, 32 F.3d 851, 862 (3d Cir. 1994)). *See also, e.g., Brennan Ctr. for Justice at N.Y. Univ. Sch. of Law v. DOJ*, 697 F.3d 184, 207 (2d Cir. 2012) ("The attorney-client privilege protects communications (1) between a client and his or her attorney (2) that are intended to be, and in fact were, kept confidential (3) for the purpose of obtaining or providing legal assistance.") (citation omitted). Note that the attorney in question must be licensed and acting in the capacity of a lawyer, not some other non-legal professional, for the privilege to attach. *See, e.g., United States v. Gurtner*, 474 F.2d 297, 299 (9th Cir. 1973) (no attorney-client privilege when attorney was acting in capacity

Take Note!

Communications with existing clients *and* prospective clients fall within the attorney-client privilege. *Dempsey v. Bucknell University*, 296 F.R.D. 323, 332 (E.D. Pa. 2013) ("The attorney-client privilege protects communications between prospective clients and counsel as well as retained counsel.").

of an accountant); *Wultz v. Bank of China Ltd., 979 F. Supp. 2d 479, 487 (S.D.N.Y. 2013)* (must be licensed attorney).

The key portions of the privilege to understand are that it protects *communications* rather than information or facts, the client must be communicating with the attorney for the purposes of securing legal—not business—advice, *see, e.g., United States v. ChevronTexaco Corp., 241 F. Supp. 2d 1065, 1076 (N.D. Cal. 2002)* ("The privilege does not protect an attorney's business advice. Corporations may not conduct their business affairs in private simply by staffing a transaction with attorneys."), and the privilege does not hold if it has been waived, *see, e.g., New Phoenix Sunrise Corp. v. C.I.R., 408 F. App'x 908, 918 (6th Cir. 2010)* ("Both the attorney-client privilege and work-product protection are waived by voluntary disclosure of private communications to third parties."). Disclosure to third parties who are vital to the attorney's provision of legal services, such as secretaries, paralegal assistants, outside document vendors, etc., will not typically be treated as a waiver. *See, e.g., Ross v. UKI Ltd., 2003 WL 22319573, at *1 (S.D.N.Y. Oct. 9, 2003)* ("[T]he involvement of the third party [must] be nearly indispensable or serve some specialized purpose in facilitating the attorney-client communications"); *U.S. v. Pepper's Steel & Alloys, Inc., 1991 WL 1302864, at *3 (S.D. Fla. Mar. 20, 1991)* ("The only recognized exception to the rule which requires that communications be directly between the client and the attorney is for essential ministerial agents of the attorney or client.").

Although we may be most familiar with an individual client's assertion of the attorney-client privilege, how does the privilege apply in the corporate context? Does it cover communications between attorneys and all employees of the corporation or just legal communications with a corporation's managers? In *Upjohn Co. v. United States, 449 U.S. 383 (1981)* [*FLEX Case 8.A*], the Supreme Court explained that the privilege applied throughout the organization, not just to communications with key managers. Specifically, the Court held that the privilege applied to internal employee communications engaged in for the purpose of supplying the corporate counsel with a basis for legal advice, so long as the communications concerned matters within the scope of the employees' duties and was treated as confidential within the corporation:

> The communications at issue were made by Upjohn employees to counsel for Upjohn acting as such, at the direction of corporate superiors in order to secure legal advice from counsel. * * * Information, not available from upper-echelon management, was needed to supply a basis for legal advice concerning compliance with securities and tax laws, foreign laws, currency regulations, duties to shareholders, and potential litigation in each of these areas. The communications concerned matters within the scope of the employees' corporate duties, and the employees themselves were sufficiently aware that they were being questioned in order that the corporation could

obtain legal advice. * * * Pursuant to explicit instructions from the Chairman of the Board, the communications were considered "highly confidential" when made, and have been kept confidential by the company. Consistent with the underlying purposes of the attorney-client privilege, these communications must be protected against compelled disclosure.

Many courts hold that the *Upjohn* privilege also extends to former employees, *see, e.g.*, <u>In re Refco Inc. Sec. Litig., 2012 WL 678139, at *2 (S.D.N.Y. Feb. 28, 2012)</u> ("[C]onversations between corporate counsel and *former* employees of the corporation, so long as the discussion related to the former employee's conduct and knowledge gained during employment." (emphasis added)); some also extend that privilege to independent contractors, *see, e.g.*, <u>In re Bieter Company, 16 F.3d 929, 937 (8th Cir. 1994)</u> ("[W]hen applying the attorney-client privilege to a corporation or partnership, it is inappropriate to distinguish between those on the client's payroll and those who are instead, and for whatever reason, employed as independent contractors."). *But see* <u>Chubb Integrated Sys., Ltd. v. Nat'l Bank of Washington, D.C., 103 F.R.D. 52, 66 (D.D.C. 1984)</u> (noting that *Upjohn*, which limited an attorney's 'corporate client' to employees of corporation, did not apply to independent contractors, and finding that foreign patent agent was not an employee of the corporation, but was more akin to independent contractor, so his communications with principal's United States counsel were not covered by attorney-client privilege).

Take Note!

The Supreme Court has held that court orders to disclose information protected by the attorney-client privilege do not qualify for immediate appeal under the collateral order doctrine. <u>Mohawk Indus., Inc. v. Carpenter, 558 U.S. 100 (2009)</u>. This doctrine is covered in <u>Chapter 11</u>.

Notwithstanding the privileged status of attorney communications with an entity's employees under the circumstances outlined in *Upjohn*, the privilege belongs to the represented entity—not the employee—and thus attorneys for the entity should inform those employees that they (the attorneys) represent the entity, not the individual employees (the so-called "*Upjohn* warning"). *See* AMERICAN BAR ASSOCIATION MODEL RULE OF PROFESSIONAL CONDUCT 1.13(f).

The Work-Product Doctrine. Separate from the attorney-client privilege is another similar doctrine that protects materials prepared in anticipation of litigation from being disclosed to a certain extent: the work-product doctrine. The next case discusses that doctrine at a time when the Federal Rules did not cover this issue [the doctrine today is also covered in <u>Rules 26(b)(3) & (4)</u>].

Hickman v. Taylor

Supreme Court of the United States
329 U.S. 495 (1947)

MR. JUSTICE MURPHY delivered the opinion of the Court.

This case presents an important problem under the Federal Rules of Civil Procedure as to the extent to which a party may inquire into oral and written statements of witnesses, or other information, secured by an adverse party's counsel in the course of preparation for possible litigation after a claim has arisen. Examination into a person's files and records, including those resulting from the professional activities of an attorney, must be judged with care. It is not without reason that various safeguards have been established to preclude unwarranted excursions into the privacy of a man's work. At the same time, public policy supports reasonable and necessary inquiries. Properly to balance these competing interests is a delicate and difficult task.

On February 7, 1943, the tug "J. M. Taylor" sank while engaged in helping to tow a car float of the Baltimore & Ohio Railroad across the Delaware River at Philadelphia. The accident was apparently unusual in nature, the cause of it still being unknown. Five of the nine crew members were drowned. Three days later the tug owners and the underwriters employed a law firm, of which respondent Fortenbaugh is a member, to defend them against potential suits by representatives of the deceased crew members and to sue the railroad for damages to the tug.

FYI

The *Steamboat Inspection Service* was created by an Act of Congress in 1871 for the safeguarding of lives and property at sea. After a series of departmental reassignments and name changes, the Steamboat Inspectors were placed under the authority of the U.S. Coast Guard, by Executive Order of President Franklin Roosevelt. For more information, visit https://www.coastguardmodeling. com/index.php/cg-history/steamboat -inspection-service/.

A public hearing was held on March 4, 1943, before the United States Steamboat Inspectors, at which the four survivors were examined. This testimony was recorded and made available to all interested parties. Shortly thereafter, Fortenbaugh privately interviewed the survivors and took statements from them with an eye toward the anticipated litigation; the survivors signed these statements on March 29. Fortenbaugh also interviewed other persons believed to have some information relating to the accident and in some cases he made memoranda of what they told him. At the time when Fortenbaugh secured the statements of the survivors, representatives of two of the deceased crew members had been in communication with him. Ultimately claims were presented by representatives of all five of the deceased; four of the claims, however, were settled without litigation. The fifth claimant, petitioner herein, brought suit in a federal court under the Jones Act on November 26, 1943, naming as defendants the two tug owners, individually and as partners, and the railroad.

One year later, petitioner filed 39 interrogatories directed to the tug owners. The 38th interrogatory read:

What's That?

The *Jones Act*, which was also known as the Merchant Marine Act, allowed injured seamen to recover damages for their injuries in a negligence action against their employer. *See* 46 App. U.S.C. § 688(a), *repealed by* Pub. L. 109–304, § 19, 120 Stat. 1710 (2006).

> State whether any statements of the members of the crews of the Tugs "J. M. Taylor" and "Philadelphia" or of any other vessel were taken in connection with the towing of the car float and the sinking of the Tug "John M. Taylor." Attach hereto exact copies of all such statements if in writing, and if oral, set forth in detail the exact provisions of any such oral statements or reports.

Supplemental interrogatories asked whether any oral or written statements, records, reports or other memoranda had been made concerning any matter relative to the towing operation, the sinking of the tug, the salvaging and repair of the tug, and the death of the deceased. If the answer was in the affirmative, the tug owners were then requested to set forth the nature of all such records, reports, statements or other memoranda.

The tug owners, through Fortenbaugh, answered all of the interrogatories except No. 38 and the supplemental ones just described. While admitting that statements of the survivors had been taken, they declined to summarize or set forth the contents. They did so on the ground that such requests called "for privileged matter obtained in preparation for litigation" and constituted "an attempt to obtain indirectly counsel's private files." It was claimed that answering these requests "would involve practically turning over not only the complete files, but also the telephone records and, almost, the thoughts of counsel."

In connection with the hearing on these objections, Fortenbaugh made a written statement and gave an informal oral deposition explaining the circumstances under which he had taken the statements. But he was not expressly asked in the deposition to produce the statements. The District Court for the Eastern District of Pennsylvania * * * held that the requested matters were not privileged. The court then decreed that the tug owners and Fortenbaugh, as counsel and agent for the tug owners forthwith "Answer Plaintiff's 38th interrogatory and supplemental interrogatories; produce all written statements of witnesses obtained by Mr. Fortenbaugh, as counsel and agent for Defendants; state in substance any fact concerning this case which Defendants learned through oral statements made by witnesses to Mr. Fortenbaugh whether or not included in his private memoranda and produce Mr. Fortenbaugh's memoranda containing statements of fact by witnesses or to submit these memoranda to the Court for determination of those portions which should be revealed to Plaintiff." Upon their refusal, the court adjudged them in contempt and ordered them imprisoned until they complied.

What's That?

Contempt is conduct that defies the authority of a court. Under 18 U.S.C. § 401 federal courts have the power to imprison those who disobey its commands.

The Third Circuit Court of Appeals, also sitting *en banc*, reversed the judgment of the District Court. It held that the information here sought was part of the "work product of the lawyer" and hence privileged from discovery under the Federal Rules of Civil Procedure. The importance of the problem, which has engendered a great divergence of views among district courts, led us to grant certiorari.

The pre-trial deposition-discovery mechanism established by Rules 26 to 37 is one of the most significant innovations of the Federal Rules of Civil Procedure. Under the prior federal practice, the pre-trial functions of notice-giving issue-formulation and fact-revelation were performed primarily and inadequately by the pleadings. Inquiry into the issues and the facts before trial was narrowly confined and was often cumbersome in method. The new rules, however, restrict the pleadings to the task of general notice-giving and invest the deposition-discovery process with a vital role in the preparation for trial. The various instruments of discovery now serve (1) as a device, along with the pre-trial hearing under Rule 16, to narrow and clarify the basic issues between the parties, and (2) as a device for ascertaining the facts, or information as to the existence or whereabouts of facts, relative to those issues. Thus civil trials in the federal courts no longer need be carried on in the dark. The way is now clear, consistent with recognized privileges, for the parties to obtain the fullest possible knowledge of the issues and facts before trial. * * *

In urging that he has a right to inquire into the materials secured and prepared by Fortenbaugh, petitioner emphasizes that the deposition-discovery portions of the Federal Rules of Civil Procedure are designed to enable the parties to discover the true facts and to compel their disclosure wherever they may be found. It is said that inquiry may be made under these rules, epitomized by Rule 26, as to any relevant matter which is not privileged; and since the discovery provisions are to be applied as broadly and liberally as possible, the privilege limitation must be restricted to its narrowest bounds. On the premise that the attorney-client privilege is the one involved in this case, petitioner argues that it must be strictly confined to confidential communications made by a client to his attorney. And since the materials here in issue were secured by Fortenbaugh from third persons rather than from his clients, the tug owners, the conclusion is reached that these materials are proper subjects for discovery under Rule 26.

As additional support for this result, petitioner claims that to prohibit discovery under these circumstances would give a corporate defendant a tremendous advantage in a suit by an individual plaintiff. Thus in a suit by an injured employee against a railroad or in a suit by an insured person against an insurance company the corporate defendant could pull a dark veil of secrecy over all the pertinent facts it can collect after the claim arises merely on the assertion that such facts were gathered by its large staff of attorneys and claim agents. At the same time, the individual plaintiff, who often has direct knowledge of the matter in issue and has no counsel until some time after his claim arises could be compelled to disclose all the intimate details of his case. By endowing with immunity from disclosure all that a lawyer discovers in the course of his duties, it is said, the rights of individual litigants in such cases are drained of vitality and the lawsuit becomes more of a battle of deception than a search for truth.

But framing the problem in terms of assisting individual plaintiffs in their suits against corporate defendants is unsatisfactory. Discovery concededly may work to the disadvantage as well as to the advantage of individual plaintiffs. Discovery, in other words, is not a one-way proposition. It is available in all types of cases at the behest of any party, individual or corporate, plaintiff or defendant. The problem thus far transcends the situation confronting this petitioner. And we must view that problem in light of the limitless situations where the particular kind of discovery sought by petitioner might be used.

We agree, of course, that the deposition-discovery rules are to be accorded a broad and liberal treatment. No longer can the time-honored cry of "fishing expedition" serve to preclude a party from inquiring into the facts underlying his opponent's case. Mutual knowledge of all the relevant facts gathered by both parties is essential to proper litigation. To that end, either party may compel the other to disgorge whatever facts he has in his possession. The deposition-discovery procedure simply advances the stage at which the disclosure can be compelled from the time of trial to the period preceding it, thus reducing the possibility of surprise. But discovery, like all matters of procedure, has ultimate and necessary boundaries. As indicated by Rules 30(b) and (d) and 31(d), limitations inevitably arise

Food for Thought

The Court here articulates its support for broad discovery and a liberal interpretation of the discovery rules. What makes broad discovery so "essential to proper litigation" as the Court claims? Could it be argued that broad, liberal discovery has made modern litigation more expensive and time-consuming, thus warranting the imposition of limits on the process that have been engrafted onto the discovery rules?

when it can be shown that the examination is being conducted in bad faith or in such a manner as to annoy, embarrass or oppress the person subject to the inquiry. And as Rule 26(b) provides, further limitations come into existence when the inquiry touches upon the irrelevant or encroaches upon the recognized domains of privilege.

We also agree that the memoranda, statements and mental impressions in issue in this case fall outside the scope of the attorney-client privilege and hence are not protected from discovery on that basis. It is unnecessary here to delineate the content and scope of that privilege as recognized in the federal courts. For present purposes, it suffices to note that the protective cloak of this privilege does not extend to information which an attorney secures from a witness while acting for his client in anticipation of litigation. Nor does this privilege concern the memoranda, briefs, communications and other writings prepared by counsel for his own use in prosecuting his client's case; and it is equally unrelated to writings which reflect an attorney's mental impressions, conclusions, opinions or legal theories.

But the impropriety of invoking that privilege does not provide an answer to the problem before us. Petitioner has made more than an ordinary request for relevant, non-privileged facts in the possession of his adversaries or their counsel. He has sought discovery as of right of oral and written statements of witnesses whose identity is well known and whose availability to petitioner appears unimpaired. He has sought production of these matters after making the most searching inquiries of his opponents as to the circumstances surrounding the fatal accident, which inquiries were sworn to have been answered to the best of their information and belief. Interrogatories were directed toward all the events prior to, during and subsequent to the sinking of the tug. Full and honest answers to such broad inquiries would necessarily have included all pertinent information gleaned by Fortenbaugh through his interviews with the witnesses. Petitioner makes no suggestion, and we cannot assume, that the tug owners or Fortenbaugh were incomplete or dishonest in the framing of their answers. In addition, petitioner was free to examine the public testimony of the witnesses taken before the United States Steamboat Inspectors. We are thus dealing with an attempt to secure the production of written statements and mental impressions contained in the files and the mind of the attorney Fortenbaugh without any showing of necessity or any indication or claim that denial of such production would unduly prejudice the preparation of petitioner's case or cause him any hardship or injustice. For aught that appears, the essence of what petitioner seeks either has been revealed to him already through the interrogatories or is readily available to him direct from the witnesses for the asking.

The District Court, after hearing objections to petitioner's request, commanded Fortenbaugh to produce all written statements of witnesses and to state in substance any facts learned through oral statements of witnesses to him. Fortenbaugh was to submit any memoranda he had made of the oral statements so that the court might determine what portions should be revealed to petitioner. All of this was ordered without any showing by petitioner, or any requirement that he make a proper showing, of the necessity for the production of any of this material or any demonstration that denial of production would cause hardship or injustice. The court simply ordered production on the theory that the facts sought were material and were not privileged as constituting attorney-client communications.

In our opinion, neither Rule 26 nor any other rule dealing with discovery contemplates production under such circumstances. That is not because the subject matter is privileged or irrelevant, as those concepts are used in these rules. Here is simply an attempt, without purported necessity or justification, to secure written statements, private memoranda and personal recollections prepared or formed by an adverse party's counsel in the course of his legal duties. As such, it falls outside the arena of discovery and contravenes the public policy underlying the orderly prosecution and defense of legal claims. Not even the most liberal of discovery theories can justify unwarranted inquiries into the files and the mental impressions of an attorney.

Historically, a lawyer is an officer of the court and is bound to work for the advancement of justice while faithfully protecting the rightful interests of his clients. In performing his various duties, however, it is essential that a lawyer work with a certain degree of privacy, free from unnecessary intrusion by opposing parties and their

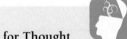

Food for Thought

If the material sought is not privileged, and it is clearly relevant to the dispute, what is the Court's basis for declaring that the material "falls outside the arena of discovery"?

counsel. Proper preparation of a client's case demands that he assemble information, sift what he considers to be the relevant from the irrelevant facts, prepare his legal theories and plan his strategy without undue and needless interference. That is the historical and the necessary way in which lawyers act within the framework of our system of jurisprudence to promote justice and to protect their clients' interests. This work is reflected, of course, in interviews, statements, memoranda, correspondence, briefs, mental impressions, personal beliefs, and countless other tangible and intangible ways—aptly though roughly termed by the Circuit Court of Appeals in this case as the "work product of the lawyer." Were such materials open to opposing counsel on mere demand, much of what is now put down in writing would remain unwritten. An attorney's thoughts, heretofore inviolate, would not be his own. Inefficiency, unfairness and sharp practices would inevitably develop in the giving of legal advice and in the preparation of cases for trial. The effect on the legal profession would be demoralizing. And the interests of the clients and the cause of justice would be poorly served.

We do not mean to say that all written materials obtained or prepared by an adversary's counsel with an eye toward litigation are necessarily free from discovery in all cases. Where relevant and non-privileged facts remain hidden in an attorney's file and where production of those facts is essential to the preparation of one's case, discovery may properly be had. Such written statements and documents might, under certain circumstances, be admissible in evidence or give clues as to the existence or location of relevant facts. Or they might be useful for purposes of impeachment or corroboration. And production might be justified where the witnesses are no longer available or can be reached only with difficulty. Were production of written statements and documents to be precluded under such circumstances, the liberal ideals of the deposition-discovery portions of the Federal Rules of Civil Procedure would be stripped of much of their meaning. But the general policy against invading the privacy of an attorney's course of preparation is so well recognized and so essential to an orderly working of our system of legal procedure that a burden rests on the one who would invade that privacy to establish adequate reasons to justify production through a subpoena or court order. That burden, we believe, is necessarily implicit in the rules as now constituted.

Take Note!

Note the conditions under which the Court indicates that counsel can be forced to disclose attorney work product. Do these "exceptions" to the work-product doctrine make sense?

Rule 30(b), as presently written, gives the trial judge the requisite discretion to make a judgment as to whether discovery should be allowed as to written statements secured from witnesses. But in the instant case there was no room for that discretion to operate in favor of the petitioner. No attempt was made to establish any reason why Fortenbaugh should be forced to produce the written statements. There was only a naked, general demand for these materials as of right and a finding by the District Court that no recognizable privilege was involved. That was insufficient to justify discovery under these circumstances and the court should have sustained the refusal of the tug owners and Fortenbaugh to produce.

But as to oral statements made by witnesses to Fortenbaugh, whether presently in the form of his mental impressions or memoranda, we do not believe that any showing of necessity can be made under the circumstances of this case so as to justify production. Under ordinary conditions, forcing an attorney to repeat or write out all that witnesses have told him and to deliver the account to his adversary gives rise to

Food for Thought

What distinction is the Court making between the written statements secured from witnesses and the oral statements they made to Fortenbaugh? Why are the two classes of information treated differently?

grave dangers of inaccuracy and untrustworthiness. No legitimate purpose is served by such production. The practice forces the attorney to testify as to what he remembers or what he saw fit to write down regarding witnesses' remarks. Such testimony could not qualify as evidence; and to use it for impeachment or corroborative purposes would make the attorney much less an officer of the court and much more an ordinary witness. The standards of the profession would thereby suffer.

Denial of production of this nature does not mean that any material, non-privileged facts can be hidden from the petitioner in this case. He need not be unduly hindered in the preparation of his case, in the discovery of facts or in his anticipation of his opponents' position. Searching interrogatories directed to Fortenbaugh and the tug owners, production of written documents and statements upon a proper showing and direct interviews with the witnesses themselves all serve to reveal the facts in Fortenbaugh's possession to the fullest possible extent consistent with public policy. Petitioner's counsel frankly admits that he wants the oral statements only to help prepare himself to examine witnesses and to make sure that he has overlooked nothing. That is insufficient under the circumstances to permit him an exception to the policy underlying the privacy of Fortenbaugh's professional activities. If there should be a rare situation justifying production of these matters, petitioner's case is not of that type.

We fully appreciate the wide-spread controversy among the members of the legal profession over the problem raised by this case. It is a problem that rests on what has been one of the most hazy frontiers of the discovery process. But until some rule or statute definitely prescribes otherwise, we are not justified in permitting discovery in a situation of this nature as a matter of unqualified right. When Rule 26 and the other discovery rules were adopted, this Court and the members of the bar in general certainly did not believe or contemplate that all the files and mental processes of lawyers were thereby opened to the free scrutiny of their adversaries. And we refuse to interpret the rules at this time so as to reach so harsh and unwarranted a result.

We therefore affirm the judgment of the Circuit Court of Appeals.

Affirmed.

Mr. Justice Jackson, concurring.

* * *

The primary effect of the practice advocated here would be on the legal profession itself. But it too often is overlooked that the lawyer and the law office are indispensable parts of our administration of justice. Law-abiding people can go nowhere else to learn the ever changing and constantly multiplying rules by which they must behave and to obtain redress for their wrongs. The welfare and tone of the legal profession is therefore of prime consequence to society, which would feel the consequences of such a practice as petitioner urges secondarily but certainly. * * *

It seems clear and long has been recognized that discovery should provide a party access to anything that is evidence in his case. It seems equally clear that discovery should not nullify the privilege of confidential communication between attorney and client. But those principles give us no real assistance here because what is being sought is neither evidence nor is it a privileged communication between attorney and client.

To consider first the most extreme aspect of the requirement in litigation here, we find it calls upon counsel, if he has had any conversations with any of the crews of the vessels in question or of any other, to "set forth in detail the exact provision of any such oral statements or reports." Thus the demand is not for the production of a transcript in existence but calls for the creation of a written statement not in being. But the statement by counsel of what a witness told him is not evidence when written plaintiff could not introduce it to prove his case. What, then, is the purpose sought to be served by demanding this of adverse counsel?

Counsel for the petitioner candidly said on argument that he wanted this information to help prepare himself to examine witnesses, to make sure he overlooked nothing. He bases his claim to it in his brief on the view that the Rules were to do away with the old situation where a law suit developed into "a battle of wits between counsel." But a common law trial is and always should be an adversary proceeding. Discovery was hardly intended to enable a learned profession to perform its functions either without wits or on wits borrowed from the adversary.

The real purpose and the probable effect of the practice ordered by the district court would be to put trials on a level even lower than a "battle of wits." I can conceive of no practice more demoralizing to the Bar than to require a lawyer to write out and deliver to his adversary an account of what witnesses have told him. Even if his recollection were perfect, the statement would be his language permeated with his inferences. Every one who has tried it knows that it is almost impossible so fairly to record the expressions and emphasis of a witness that when he testifies in the environment of the court and under the influence of the leading question there will not be departures in some respects. Whenever the testimony of the witness would differ from the "exact" statement the lawyer had delivered, the lawyer's statement would be whipped out to impeach the witness. Counsel producing his adversary's "inexact" statement could lose nothing by saying, "Here is a contradiction, gentlemen of the jury. I do not know whether it is my adversary or his witness who is not telling the truth, but one is not." Of course, if this practice were adopted, that scene would be repeated over and over again. The lawyer who delivers such statements often would find himself branded a deceiver afraid to take the stand to support his own version of the witness's conversation with him, or else he will have to go on the stand to defend his own credibility—perhaps against that of his chief witness, or possibly even his client.

Every lawyer dislikes to take the witness stand and will do so only for grave reasons. This is partly because it is not his role; he is almost invariably a poor witness. But he steps out of professional character to do it. He regrets it; the profession discourages it. But the practice advocated here is one which would force him to be a witness, not as to what he has seen or done but as to other witnesses' stories, and not because he wants to do so but in self-defense.

And what is the lawyer to do who has interviewed one whom he believes to be a biased, lying or hostile witness to get his unfavorable statements and know what to meet? He must record and deliver such statements even though he would not vouch for the credibility of the witness by calling him. Perhaps the other side would not want to call him either, but the attorney is open to the charge of suppressing evidence at the trial if he fails to call such a hostile witness even though he never regarded him as reliable or truthful. * * *

It is true that the literal language of the Rules would admit of an interpretation that would sustain the district court's order. * * * But all such procedural measures have a background of custom and practice which was assumed by those who wrote and should be by those who apply them. * * * Certainly nothing in the tradition or practice of discovery up to the time of these Rules would have suggested that they would authorize such a practice as here proposed.

The question remains as to signed statements or those written by witnesses. Such statements are not evidence for the defendant. Nor should I think they ordinarily could be evidence for the plaintiff. But such a statement might be useful for impeachment of the witness who signed it, if he is called and if he departs from the statement. There might be circumstances, too, where impossibility or difficulty of access to the witness or his refusal to respond to requests for information or other facts would show that the interests of justice require that such statements be made available. Production of such statements are governed by Rule 34 and on "Showing good cause therefore" the court may order their inspection, copying or photographing. No such application has here been made; the demand is made on the basis of right, not on showing of cause.

I agree to the affirmance of the judgment of the Circuit Court of Appeals which reversed the district court.

MR. JUSTICE FRANKFURTER joins in this opinion.

Points for Discussion

a. Work-Product Protection Under the Federal Rules

Rule 26(b)(3) was added to the Federal Rules in 1970 to set forth rules governing the discovery of work product:

FRCP 26(b)(3). Discovery Scope and Limits;
Trial Preparation: Materials.

(3) Trial Preparation: Materials.

(A) *Documents and Tangible Things.* Ordinarily, a party may not discover documents and tangible things that are prepared in anticipation of litigation or for trial by or for another party or its representative (including the other party's attorney, consultant, surety, indemnitor, insurer, or agent). But, subject to Rule 26(b)(4), those materials may be discovered if:

(i)   they are otherwise discoverable under Rule 26(b)(1); and

(ii)   the party shows that it has substantial need for the materials to prepare its case and cannot, without undue hardship, obtain their substantial equivalent by other means.

(B) *Protection Against Disclosure.* If the court orders discovery of those materials, it must protect against disclosure of the mental impressions, conclusions, opinions, or legal theories of a party's attorney or other representative concerning the litigation.

Does this rule fairly encapsulate the work-product protection set forth in *Hickman*? Is there a difference between the two iterations of the work-product doctrine? Rule 26(b)(3) limits its applicability to "documents and tangible things." Is *Hickman* similarly limited?

Take Note!

Note that the rule does not require that the material have been prepared by an attorney. Rather, protection extends to material prepared by non-attorney representatives or even the party itself so long as the material was prepared "in anticipation of litigation or for trial." Is the work-product protection provided by the rule, as written, too broad? Why extend protection to material prepared by non-lawyers? Did *Hickman* suggest such a scope for the work-product doctrine?

As set forth in Rule 26(b)(3), documentary materials prepared in anticipation of litigation or for trial by or for another party or that party's representative are protected from discovery unless the requesting party can show a substantial need for the materials. However, "mental impressions, conclusions, opinions, or legal theories" of a party's representative are never discoverable. Why is that the case?

b. Asserting Privilege and Work-Product Protection

Although the Federal Rules exclude privileged and work-product-protected materials from the scope of discovery, responding parties are obliged to indicate the material that is being withheld based on assertions of privilege or work-product protection in a privilege log. Rule 26(b)(5) provides that parties asserting such protections "must: (i) expressly make the claim; and (ii) describe the nature of the documents, communications, or tangible things not produced or disclosed—and do so in a manner that, without revealing information itself privileged or protected, will enable other parties to assess the claim." FED. R. CIV. P. 26(b)(5). This requirement must be taken seriously, as the court in *Breon v. Coca-Cola Bottling Co. of New England*, 232 F.R.D. 49 (D. Conn. 2005), made clear:

> Defendant has provided the court with no privilege log. However, in its response to plaintiff's requests for production defendant did provide a skeletal argument outlining the documents it claims are privileged, including titles, dates and the names of authors and recipients. The court cannot, however, conclude that either the attorney-client privilege or work-product immunity applies on the basis of such little information. Having failed to provide adequate information for such a determination, the defendant has not perfected its claim of privilege. Since the documents are not privileged, they are discoverable. Therefore, the defendant is ordered to provide plaintiff's counsel with the documents requested in [its] production requests . . . .

Id. at 55. **Table 8.1** provides a hypothetical example of what a typical privilege log would look like, although in practice attorneys may have additional categories of information they would report such as the date or subject matter of the protected document.

Practice Pointer

Protecting client privileges is one of the most important responsibilities of an attorney engaged in the discovery process. In addition to the harsh consequences potentially associated with privilege waivers (see below), the disclosure of privileged material may reveal sensitive and damaging information to adversaries that they otherwise were not entitled to receive. Thus, when you enter practice, you should take your obligation to conduct a privilege review and prepare a privilege log very seriously.

Table 8.1: Hypothetical Privilege Log

Author	Recipients	Doc. Type	Privilege	Description
Jim Smith, Esq. (JS)	Ike Biggs (IB) Don Ivan (DI)	Letter	A/C	Letter from outside counsel to CEO and CFO conveying legal advice.
IB	JS & DI	Email	A/C	Letter from CEO to outside counsel requesting legal advice.
Wendy Ng (WN)	Stacy Reeves (SR)	Memo	A/C	Memo from supervisor to subordinate requesting data for purposes of responding to request from counsel as part of his effort to provide legal advice.
SR	n/a	Spreadsheet	W/P	Data compilation prepared in anticipation of litigation involving customer dispute.

c. The Meaning of "In Anticipation of Litigation"

The work-product rule—Rule 26(b)(3)—uses the phrase "in anticipation of litigation." How far in advance can a party anticipate litigation and thereby obtain work-product protection for the material? Can a company determine that litigation surrounding a particular matter will always be an ongoing possibility and thus perpetually anticipate litigation? Imagine that a company prepares a litigation analysis in order to inform a business decision that turns on an assessment of the likely outcome of potential litigation. Should such an analysis receive work-product protection?

Courts have reached two different conclusions regarding how the phrase "in anticipation of litigation" should be interpreted. Some courts adhere to the notion that documents are protected by work-product privilege if they are prepared "primarily or exclusively to assist in litigation." *See, e.g.*, *United States v. El Paso Co.*, 682 F.2d 530, 542–44 (5th Cir. 1982), *cert. denied*, 466 U.S. 944 (1984) (denying work-product protection over documents because they were not prepared to "ready" the defendant for litigation). The majority of courts, however, reject such a definition as unsupported by the language of the rule and follow the "prepared because of litigation" approach. Under this formulation of the work-product rule, a document should be deemed prepared "in anticipation of litigation," if "in light of the nature of the document and the factual situation in the particular case, the document can fairly be said to have been prepared or obtained because of the prospect of litigation." *United States v. Adlman*, 134 F.3d 1194, 1202 (2d Cir. 1998) (quoting 8 C. WRIGHT, A. MILLER, & R. MARCUS, FED. PRAC. & PROC. § 2024, 323 (2d ed. 1994)). Which definition is most consistent with the language of the Rule? *See United States v. Textron, Inc.*, 577 F.3d 21, 29 (1st Cir. 2009) (en banc):

It is not enough to trigger work product protection that the *subject matter* of a document relates to a subject that might conceivably be litigated. Rather, as the Supreme Court explained, "the literal language of [Rule 26(b)(3)] protects materials *prepared for* any litigation or trial as long as they were prepared by or for a party to the subsequent litigation." (quoting *Fed. Trade Comm'n v. Grolier Inc.*, 462 U.S. 19, 25 (1983) (emphases and alteration in original)).

Hypo 8.2

Parker Brothers, Inc. was preparing its annual financial statements. The CEO asked the company's General Counsel (GC) to provide an assessment of the value of all pending litigation as well as potential litigation over the course of the next year and estimate the outcomes in each case in order to identify a proper amount for the company's litigation reserves. The GC prepared such a document, which includes a comprehensive analysis of disputes that may mature into lawsuits, their likely value, and the likelihood of the company prevailing in each.

Mark Five, Ltd. brought an action against Parker Brothers and has requested production of the GC's litigation assessment prepared for the company's annual financial statements. Is the report protected by either the attorney-client privilege or the work-product doctrine?

---

d. The Meaning of "Substantial Need"

To overcome work-product protection, a requesting party must show a "substantial need" for the information. What type of showing should be necessary to demonstrate substantial need? Is the inability to get the information from any other sources sufficient of itself to meet this standard? Is need measured by the importance of the information to the requesting party's claims or defenses? *See Jinks-Umstead v. England*, 232 F.R.D. 142, 147 (D.D.C. 2005) (holding that no substantial need was shown when plaintiff claimed she needed a document covered under work-product privilege to determine the precise scope of a third party's responsibilities in responding to plaintiff's discovery requests); *see also In re Nat. Gas Commodities Litig.*, 232 F.R.D. 208, 212–13 (S.D.N.Y. 2005):

> Plaintiffs failed to demonstrate a substantial need for the requested documents. Defendants have produced all of the factual documents underlying the work product analysis provided to the government agencies, with the exception of any documentation underlying the interview memoranda. Therefore, Plaintiffs can perform their own analysis of the trading data. Furthermore, Plaintiffs failed to show substantial need for the interview memoranda. To demonstrate substantial need, a party must demonstrate an inabil-

ity to obtain equivalent evidence without undue hardship. Plaintiffs have not demonstrated that they would be unable to acquire the data underlying the interview memoranda without undue hardship, as Plaintiffs have not demonstrated why they would not be able to depose the individuals interviewed during the internal investigation.

e. The Consequences of Privilege Waiver

The attorney-client privilege only holds up if it has not been waived, which can occur whenever the protected communication is disclosed to third parties. It is important to note, however, that if a waiver occurs, that can jeopardize not only the confidentiality of the disclosed communication but the confidentiality of all communications relating to the same subject matter. *See, e.g., In re Sealed Case,* 877 F.2d 976, 980–81 (D.C. Cir. 1989) ("[A] waiver of the privilege in an attorney-client communication extends 'to all other communications relating to the same subject matter.' " (quoting *In re Sealed Case,* 676 F.2d 793, 809 (D.C. Cir. 1982))). *But see, e.g., In re von Bulow,* 828 F.2d 94, 102 (2d Cir. 1987) (holding that the disclosure of privileged information would not result in unfairness to the adversary and thus a subject matter waiver was not warranted).

Food for Thought

Why do you think some courts treat the waiver of privilege with respect to certain material as a waiver of the privilege with respect to all other communications relating to the same subject matter?

The breadth of a subject matter waiver can be compounded by the fact that once a waiver occurs with respect to one party, the communication typically can no longer be claimed as privileged with respect to others. Federal Rule of Evidence 502—which will be covered in the next section—was promulgated, in large part, to address this issue. Nevertheless, because subject matter waivers—when they occur—can result in the permanent loss of privilege protection and in the resultant required disclosure of significant amounts of otherwise privileged information in current and future litigation, attorneys rightly take great care when conducting a privilege review of material before it is disclosed to requesting parties during discovery.

Such understandable conservatism, however, has its costs. It takes many expensive hours of attorney review to cull through thousands if not millions of pages of documents to identify privileged or work-product-protected material. These costs are only exacerbated when the volume of material increases as is the case with large amounts of electronically stored information. *See, e.g., Rowe Entm't, Inc. v. William Morris Agency,* 205 F.R.D. 421, 425–26 (S.D.N.Y. 2002) (finding that in a case involving the production of email, the cost of pre-production review for privileged and work-product material would cost one defendant $120,000 and another defendant $247,000). This issue will be addressed further in Section B.4 below.

f.   Experts and Trial Preparation

In some litigation it may be necessary for the parties to retain the assistance and testimony of experts on technical matters pertinent to the lawsuit. For example, in a complex accounting dispute each side may want an accounting expert to testify as to the details of how a particular transaction was accounted for or should have been accounted for. In a products-liability case each side may want certain types of engineering experts to assist in the preparation and defense of a case alleging a product defect and to testify to certain facts at trial. When technical matters require the assistance of experts in the preparation of a case and the development of trial strategy, the expert functions as a part of the party's litigation team. When testifying at trial or in depositions, however, the expert serves as a witness. How should such experts be treated for purposes of discovery?

Make the Connection

The Federal Rules of Evidence permit qualified experts to testify with respect to scientific, technical, or other specialized knowledge that will assist fact-finders' understanding of the evidence. FED. R. EVID. 702. Courts determine whether a person may testify as an expert under the standards set forth in *Daubert v. Merrell Dow Pharm., Inc.*, 509 U.S. 579 (1993). You will study qualification and admission of expert testimony in an **Evidence** course.

Rule 26(a)(2) requires the disclosure of the identity of all experts that a party intends to call at trial and requires the expert to prepare a report detailing her expected testimony, the basis for her opinions, the facts or data "considered" in forming those opinions, her qualifications, experience as an expert witness, and level of compensation to be received for serving as a witness in the present case. FED. R. CIV. P. 26(a)(2)(A)–(B). What is the purpose of requiring the disclosure of such information by expert witnesses?

Experts who will appear at trial may be deposed, FED. R. CIV. P. 26(b)(4)(A), and any facts or data that serve as a basis for their opinions must be disclosed, FED. R. CIV. P. 26(a)(2)(B). However, any draft reports by the expert are protected from discovery as are most communications between a party's attorney and expert witnesses. FED. R. CIV. P. 26(b)(4)(B) & (C). Experts who will

Practice Pointer

Because Rule 26(b)(4) protects non-testifying experts from discovery to some extent, it may be advisable to use two separate experts in litigation, one as a trial consultant and the other as a trial witness. This approach of course will be more expensive, but it may enable the consulting expert to have access to more information without subjecting the information to the disclosure obligations of Rule 26(a)(2). Material prepared by the consulting expert also will typically be protected by the work-product doctrine. However, keep in mind that disclosing privileged information to outside consulting experts can waive the privilege since they are not part of the confidential attorney-client relationship.

not be called as witnesses at trial may not be deposed or served with interrogatories in most circumstances. FED. R. CIV. P. 26(b)(4)(D). Finally, Rule 45(d)(3)(B)(ii) protects "unretained experts" from depositions that seek expertise unconnected with specific occurrences in dispute; this provision prevents litigants from using depositions to obtain "free" expert opinions via the subpoena power.

———————————

4. Electronic Discovery & Protected Materials

As you can see, privilege review is a major element of responding to document discovery requests. The dramatic increase in the volume of material associated with electronically stored information or "ESI" has only exacerbated the time and costs of conducting a thorough privilege review. More alarming, however, is the impact that voluminous ESI has on the mere ability to conduct a privilege review. With millions of documents at issue, it becomes a physical impossibility for attorneys to engage in a comprehensive privilege review before documents are handed over to their adversaries. *See* Report to the Judicial Conference Standing Committee on Rules of Practice and Procedure by the Advisory Committee on the Federal Rules of Civil Procedure, September 2005, at 26–27 ("The volume of [such data] . . . may make privilege determinations more difficult, and privilege review correspondingly more expensive and time-consuming . . . .").

As a result of these conditions, it is virtually inevitable that both sides will end up inadvertently disclosing material that is privileged or protected by the work-product doctrine. However, the consequences of such disclosures typically are a waiver of the privilege, and in the worst case a waiver of privilege with respect to the subject matter covered by the material. With the consequences of inadvertent disclosure being potentially so severe, attorneys have to be meticulous about privilege review, which ultimately drives up the time and expense associated with screening material before it is produced. These costs and such delays have come to dominate modern litigation. *See* Kenneth J. Withers, *Electronically Stored Information: The December 2006 Amendments to the Federal Rules of Civil Procedure*, 7 SEDONA CONF. J. 1, 11 (2006) ("Of all the costs associated with electronic discovery, screening electronically stored information for privilege before production is emerging as the greatest."). To address this situation, reform efforts have proceeded on two fronts, both of which will be discussed in turn.

a. 2006 Amendments to the Federal Rules of Civil Procedure

First, the Federal Rules of Civil Procedure were amended in 2006 to encourage parties to enter into various "non-waiver" agreements by which they agree not to treat certain disclosures as privilege waivers. One type of non-waiver agreement has been referred to as a ***"claw-back" agreement***, so labeled because under such agreements parties are entitled to reclaim (or "claw-back") material that they produced but should have withheld based on privilege or work-product protection. *Zubulake v. UBS Warburg L.L.C.*, 216 F.R.D. 280, 290 (S.D.N.Y. 2003) (*Zubulake III*) ("Indeed, many parties to document-intensive litigation enter into so-called 'claw-back' agreements that allow the parties to forego privilege review altogether in favor of an agreement to return inadvertently produced privileged documents."). Such agreements can be useful because the party receiving the inadvertently disclosed material agrees not to treat the disclosure as a waiver and they agree to return the material to the producing party, or at least to sequester the material until the court decides on the merits of the claims of privilege.

The other major type of agreement concerning privilege reviews are so-called **"quick peek" agreements**. These agreements permit requesting parties to review a body of material in possession of the responding party prior to a privilege review by the responding party in order to identify the subset of material that the requesting party is actually interested in having produced. The responding party then conducts a full-scale privilege review for that smaller subset of material rather than the entire universe of material they would have otherwise been obliged to review. The benefit of this approach is that the time and expense of privilege review can be dramatically reduced by permitting parties to focus on the material that actually matters in the case.

Food for Thought

What potential problems or shortcomings do you see with either of these types of agreements? Do you think that such agreements can prevent third-parties from claiming that disclosures protected by the agreements nonetheless constituted waivers? If not, is it wise to be any less diligent in pre-screening material for privilege before disclosing it to requesting parties pursuant to such agreements?

What's That?

A *discovery plan* is a document the parties formulate under Rule 26(f) that sets forth agreements regarding the timing and scope of discovery as well as agreements pertaining to confidentiality and privilege and the form of production of ESI. These agreements in turn may be incorporated into an order that the court issues under Rule 16(b) that makes them binding called a *scheduling order*.

Rule 26(f)(3)(D) instructs the parties to include any agreements they reach on matters pertaining to privilege and inadvertent disclosures within their **discovery plan**, while Rule 16(b) permits courts to incorporate such agreements into their pretrial **scheduling orders**. However, to the extent there is no party agreement in place, Rule 26(b)(5)(B) opts for the claw-back approach to resolving disputes related to inadvertent disclosure:

> ### FRCP 26(b)(5)(B). Discovery Scope and Limits
>
> (B) *Information Produced.* If information produced in discovery is subject to a claim of privilege or of protection as trial-preparation material, the party making the claim may notify any party that received the information of the claim and the basis for it. After being notified, a party must promptly return, sequester, or destroy the specified information and any copies it has; must not use or disclose the information until the claim is resolved; must take reasonable steps to retrieve the information if the party disclosed it before being notified; and may promptly present the information to the court under seal for a determination of the claim. The producing party must preserve the information until the claim is resolved.

Although Rule 26(b)(5)(B) provides for the orderly resolution of privilege waiver disputes in the context of inadvertent disclosures, the rule does not alter the substantive law governing whether privilege has been waived by a disclosure because it is merely a federal procedural rule. (As we learned in Chapter 5 when discussing the *Erie/Hanna* doctrine, under the Rules Enabling Act a Federal Rule of Civil Procedure enacted pursuant to the REA process must be procedural, and it may not "abridge, enlarge or modify any substantive right." 28 U.S.C.A. § 2072.) Neither does the fact that Rule 16(b) permits the court to bless any non-waiver agreements the parties may reach affect substantive privilege waiver law. Thus, these rules, on their own, have not been able to prevent nonparties to any non-waiver agreements from claiming that disclosures made pursuant to the agreement resulted in a waiver of privilege. *See Westinghouse Elec. Corp. v. Republic of the Philippines*, 951 F.2d 1414, 1426–27 (3d Cir. 1991) (holding that an agreement between litigant and DOJ that documents produced in response to investigation would not waive privilege does not preserve privilege against different entity in unrelated civil proceeding); *Bowne of N.Y. City, Inc. v. AmBase Corp.*, 150 F.R.D. 465, 478–79 (S.D.N.Y. 1993) (holding that a non-waiver agreement between producing party in one case is not applicable to a third-party in another civil case). That issue is something Congress addressed through the enactment of Federal Rule of Evidence 502.

Make the Connection

Connect this discussion with what you learned about the *Erie/Hanna* doctrine. If Rule 26(b)(5)(B) read, "No waiver of privilege shall result from the inadvertent disclosure of privileged material," but the forum state's law read, "Any disclosure of privileged material—intentional or unintentional—shall result in a waiver of privilege," which legal rule would a federal court sitting in diversity be obliged to apply? Would Rule 26(b)(5)(B)—if so written—violate either the Constitution or the Rules Enabling Act?

b.   Federal Rule of Evidence 502

In response to the concerns surrounding the cost of pre-production privilege review, and in view of the inability of the Federal Rules of Civil Procedure to address the underlying problem driving such costs (substantive privilege waiver law), in 2008 Congress enacted an amendment to the Federal Rules of Evidence (FRE) that alters substantive privilege waiver law in several respects.

FRE Rule 502. Attorney-Client Privilege and Work Product; Limitations on Waiver

(a) Disclosure Made in a Federal Proceeding or to a Federal Office or Agency; Scope of a Waiver. When the disclosure is made in a federal proceeding or to a federal office or agency and waives the attorney-client privilege or work-product protection, the waiver extends to an undisclosed communication or information in a federal or state proceeding only if:

    (1) the waiver is intentional;

    (2) the disclosed and undisclosed communications or information concern the same subject matter; and

    (3) they ought in fairness to be considered together.

(b) Inadvertent Disclosure. When made in a federal proceeding or to a federal office or agency, the disclosure does not operate as a waiver in a federal or state proceeding if:

    (1) the disclosure is inadvertent;

    (2) the holder of the privilege or protection took reasonable steps to prevent disclosure; and

    (3) the holder promptly took reasonable steps to rectify the error, including (if applicable) following Federal Rule of Civil Procedure 26(b)(5)(B). * * *

(d) Controlling Effect of a Court Order. A federal court may order that the privilege or protection is not waived by disclosure connected with the litigation pending before the court—in which event the disclosure is also not a waiver in any other federal or state proceeding.

(e) Controlling Effect of a Party Agreement. An agreement on the effect of disclosure in a federal proceeding is binding only on the parties to the agreement, unless it is incorporated into a court order.

* * *

This rule does what the 2006 amendments to the Federal Rules of Civil Procedure could not do by altering the law of waiver with respect to inadvertent disclosures and with respect to subject matter waivers. Under Evidence Rule 502, inadvertent disclosures do not result in waiver so long as the disclosing party took "reasonable steps to prevent disclosure" and "promptly took reasonable steps to rectify the error . . . ." FED. R. EVID. 502(b). See, e.g., *Oasis Int'l Waters, Inc. v. United States,* 110 Fed. Cl. 87, 116 (Fed. Cl. 2013) ("Defefendant's production of four copies of the partially redacted version of the Memorandum to plaintiff after examining the Memorandum for privileged information and applying only some redactions to the document suggests that defendant took inadequate precautions against disclosure."); *Stewart Title Guar. Co. v. Owlett & Lewis, P.C.,* 297 F.R.D. 232, 234 (M.D. Pa. 2013) (finding that the defendant failed to take reasonable steps to rectify the inadvertent disclosure of privileged material by failing to object to its use on privilege grounds when used by opposing counsel during a deposition).

Food for Thought

What should qualify as reasonable precautions to preserve a privilege? *See, e.g., In re Nat. Gas Commodity Litig.,* 229 F.R.D. 82, 86 (S.D.N.Y. 2005) ("Generally, precautions will be reasonable if the procedure followed in maintaining the confidentiality of the document [is] not . . . so lax, careless, inadequate or indifferent to consequences as to constitute a waiver.").

Further, to the extent the court does conclude that a waiver has occurred, the scope of the waiver will be limited to the disclosed material, not the subject matter it embraces, unless fairness dictates that other related but undisclosed privileged material should be disclosed as well. FED. R. EVID. 502(a)(3). See, e.g., *Oasis Int'l Waters, Inc. v. United States,* 110 Fed. Cl. 87, 118 (Fed. Cl. 2013) (holding that defendant's intentional disclosure of privileged material did not result in subject matter waiver "because defendant's partial disclosure does not appear to give defendant a tactical advantage over plaintiff"). Thus, if courts determine that a disclosure was not inadvertent but rather done for tactical advantage, they will not hesitate to impose subject matter waivers under the Rule. See, e.g., *Century Aluminum Co. v. AGCS Marine Ins. Co.,* 285 F.R.D. 468, 472 (N.D. Cal. 2012) ("AGCS has attempted to use the disclosed document as both a shield and a sword, that is, to reveal a limited aspect of privileged communications in order to gain a tactical advantage in litigation. The Court finds that by voluntarily producing a privileged document concerning 'significant development in the weather investigation' drafted by Robb, AGCS has waived the attorney-client privilege and work product protection as to all Robb communications concerning defendants' weather investigation.").

Finally, although the Rule maintains the idea that non-waiver agreements are ordinarily not binding on third-parties, it makes such agreements binding on all others if the agreements are incorporated into a court order declaring that disclosures within the litigation do not constitute waiver. FED. R. EVID. 502(d).

If litigants and their attorneys draw comfort from the protections offered by Evidence Rule 502, it has the potential to have a real impact

Take Note!

Revisions to Rule 26(f)(3)(D) that took effect on December 1, 2015 require litigants to include in their discovery plan their views on whether to ask the court to incorporate any FRE 502 agreement into a court order under the rule. Further, the 2015 amendment to Rule 16(b)(3)(B)(iv) authorizes courts to include any FRE 502 agreements in their scheduling orders. Court activities under Rule 16 will be covered in Chapter 9.

on relieving parties from the sometimes crushing burdens associated with the preproduction privilege review of voluminous materials. However, if attorneys charged with protecting their clients' privileges continue to feel compelled to engage in the level of pre-production privilege review that was warranted prior to the enactment of FRE 502, few of the Rule's intended benefits will be realized.

C. Discovery Devices

We now come to the specifics of discovery, the various devices by which parties may seek and obtain relevant material from their adversaries or other parties during the discovery process. Below, we review each of the discovery devices and some of the various issues pertaining to their use.

1. Rule 26(a): Initial Disclosures

Rule 26(a)(1) requires the parties to disclose certain information to one another at the beginning of the action without awaiting a specific request for the material:

FRCP 26(a)(1). Duty to Disclose; General Provisions Governing Discovery.

(a) **Required Disclosures.**

(1) *Initial Disclosure.*

(A) *In General.* Except as exempted by Rule 26(a)(1)(B) or as otherwise stipulated or ordered by the court, a party must, without awaiting a discovery request, provide to the other parties:

(i) the name and, if known, the address and telephone number of each individual likely to have discoverable information—along with the subjects of that information—that the disclosing party may use to support its claims or defenses, unless the use would be solely for impeachment;

(ii) a copy—or a description by category and location—of all documents, electronically stored information, and tangible things that the disclosing party has in its possession, custody, or control and may use to support its claims or defenses, unless the use would be solely for impeachment;

(iii) a computation of each category of damages claimed by the disclosing party—who must also make available for inspection and copying as under Rule 34 the documents or other evidentiary material, unless privileged or protected from disclosure, on which each computation is based, including materials bearing on the nature and extent of injuries suffered; and

(iv) for inspection and copying as under Rule 34, any insurance agreement under which an insurance business may be liable to satisfy all or part of a possible judgment in the action or to indemnify or reimburse for payments made to satisfy the judgment.

Food for Thought

What do you think is the purpose of the requirement of <u>Rule 26(a)(1)(A)</u> to disclose a list of "each individual likely to have discoverable information"?

Do these initial disclosure obligations seem onerous to you? Will a party easily be able to describe "all documents" that it may use to support its claims or defenses at such an early stage in the lawsuit? <u>Rule 37(c)(1)</u> provides that information that is not disclosed as required under <u>Rule 26(a)(1)</u> may not be used as evidence at trial. Is such a penalty unnecessarily harsh?

The topic of initial disclosures is something that the parties are supposed to discuss at the ***discovery conference*** provided for in <u>Rule 26(f)</u>. At this conference, if the parties do not actually make the required initial disclosures, they are to make arrangements for doing so. These arrangements may include an agreement to alter the default timing applicable to initial disclosures or any of the requirements surrounding initial disclosures. Absent any agreement to the contrary, the disclosures required under <u>Rule 26(a)(1)</u> are to be made within fourteen days of the discovery conference.

Take Note!

Note that the rule only obligates a party to disclose documents that it may use "to *support* its claims or defenses." This means that documents that might prove harmful to the disclosing parties claims or defenses do not fall within the scope of the initial disclosure obligation. Why do you think such documents are not mentioned by the rule?

After initial disclosures are made, parties are under an ongoing obligation to supplement or correct the information. FED. R. CIV. P. 26(e)(1) (requiring supplementation or correction "in a timely manner if the party learns that in some material respect the disclosure or response is incomplete or incorrect, and if the additional or corrective information has not otherwise been made known to the other parties during the discovery process or in writing"). Failure to do so may result in sanctions under Rule 37(c)(1), including an order to pay expenses caused by the failure, informing the jury of the party's failure, and imposing other sanctions authorized by Rule 37(b)(2)(A)(i)–(vi).

2. Rule 34: Production of Documents, ESI, and Things

Under <u>Rule 34</u> parties may request that other parties produce documents, electronically stored information, or tangible things in their possession that fall within the scope of <u>Rule 26(b)</u>. The rule reads as follows:

FRCP 34(a). Producing Documents, Electronically Stored Information, and Tangible Things.

(a) In General. A party may serve on any other party a request within the scope of Rule 26(b):

(1) to produce and permit the requesting party or its representative to inspect, copy, test, or sample the following items in the responding party's possession, custody, or control:

(A) any designated documents or electronically stored information * * * stored in any medium from which information can be obtained either directly or, if necessary, after translation by the responding party into a reasonably usable form; or

(B) any designated tangible things * * * .

Document requests can either be specifically focused on particular known documents or may more broadly seek information in categorical terms. Although requesting parties certainly want as much relevant information that they can get from their adversaries, that does not necessarily mean it is wise to draft categorical requests in overly broad terms (*e.g.*, "all documents and electronically stored information relating to the shipment of the defendant's products to customers worldwide"). The problem with less-focused document requests is that the responsive material may be so voluminous that it will be difficult for the receiving party to identify the truly relevant information that may be found therein. This is particularly so if the documents are produced "as they are kept in the usual course of business," rather than being organized by reference to the categories in the request, as is permitted under Rule 34(b)(2)(E)(i).

Take Note!

Pursuant to Rule 45(a)(1)(A)(iii) a party can also request the production of documents, ESI, and tangible things from nonparties by serving subpoenas on them.

After being served with a request for documents, parties have 30 days to respond, in writing. FED. R. CIV. P. 34(b)(2)(A). Under amendments to Rules 26(d) and 34(b) that took effect on December 1, 2015, requests for documents under Rule 34 may be delivered to one's adversary as early as 21 days after service of the complaint and summons, in which case a response will be due 30 days after the first Rule 26(f) discovery conference. Once in receipt of a document request, the responding party may either produce the requested material or object on any applicable grounds such as relevance or privilege. When disagreements arise, the parties must meet and attempt to resolve their differences before either of them petitions the court for a forced resolution of the matter, a dispute resolution process that we will cover in more detail below in Section D.

The dominance of electronically stored information (ESI) among the universe of potentially discoverable material has brought three issues to the fore that will be discussed below: (1) the exact form in which responding parties must produce ESI—such as in printed-out hard copies, in *native format*, or in a converted, easier to use format of some sort; (2) whether *metadata*—data about data—that accompanies ESI must be produced; and (3) the extent to which computer-aided review techniques including predictive coding may be used to satisfy one's obligation to review and produce ESI responsive to Rule 34 requests.

What's That?

Native format simply refers to producing ESI in the format in which it is normally read, accessed, and manipulated. For example, the native format of a Microsoft Word document would be a Microsoft Word file. If that same document were migrated into a PDF file, then it would not be in its native format.

a.   Form of Production

From the beginning, the fact that certain information was maintained in an electronic format raised the question of whether responding parties were obligated to produce the information in an electronic format or were permitted simply to print out the information and produce it in that manner. As ESI proliferated and expanded beyond simple word processing documents, this question grew into the more sophisticated issue of which electronic format parties had to use when producing the information.

For example, does a document produced in WordPerfect have to be produced in its "native format" as a WordPerfect file or may it be produced in (1) <u>Portable Document Format</u> ("PDF"), (2) <u>Tagged Image File Format</u> ("TIFF"), (3) Microsoft Word format, or (4) some other format? Each side might have its own preference for how the information should be produced. The requesting party may want the information produced in its native format or in Microsoft Word format so that it is completely word-searchable, a feature that would facilitate document review. Conversely, the producing party may prefer production in a

Food for Thought

Should the "Golden Rule" apply here, meaning that you should produce the information in the format you would want if you were receiving the information? Or, do you have an obligation to produce information in the format that is most advantageous to your client, which may be the format that imposes the most cost on the receiving party and lengthens the time needed to review the material? Is the latter approach ethical? Is the former approach, which favors your client's adversary more than your own client, ethical in light of the duty of zealous advocacy that attorneys have towards their clients?

PDF or TIFF format because those formats are less subject to manipulation or can make word searches more difficult or impossible.

Under the Federal Rules as revised by the 2006 amendments, form of production issues are front and center in the discovery process from the discovery conference through the actual production of information. Parties are explicitly instructed to discuss "any issues about disclosure, discovery, or preservation of electronically stored information, including the form or forms in which it should be produced," *see* FED. R. CIV. P. 26(f)(3)(C), and any agreements regarding form of production may be incorporated into the court's scheduling order under Rule 16(b).

If no agreement regarding form of production is reached, then requesting parties may specify the form in which they would like ESI to be produced. FED. R. CIV. P. 34(b). The responding party may object to the requested form of producing ESI and must then specify the form that it intends to use. Even if the requesting party does not specify form of production, the responding party must indicate the form in which it intends to produce the information. Either party who is dissatisfied with the form of production requested or supplied may petition the court for an order resolving the matter.

Finally, if there is no agreement and no court order on the issue, the rule sets forth a default standard:

> **FRCP 34(b)(2)(E)(ii). Producing Documents, Electronically Stored Information, and Tangible Things: Procedure.**
>
> (ii)   If a request does not specify a form for producing electronically stored information, a party must produce it in a form or forms in which it is ordinarily maintained or in a reasonably usable form or forms * * * .

What does the rule mean by "a form . . . in which it is ordinarily maintained"? Does that mean native format? Imagine a situation in which the native format of a producing party's ESI is a format that is only readable by software that has been discontinued and is now obsolete. Is producing such "legacy data" useful to the requesting party if they will have to engage in expensive efforts to translate the data into a readable format? Should the producing party in such circumstances be required to translate the data into a form that is "reasonably usable"? *See* FED. R. CIV. P. 34(a)(1)(A). The Advisory Committee indicated that this question should be resolved under Rule 26(b)(2)(B), which addresses the production of difficult to access information and permits courts to specify the conditions of discovery. *See* FED. R. CIV. P. 34 advisory committee's notes to 2006 amendment ("The questions whether a producing party should be required to convert [inaccessible legacy data] to a more usable form, or should be required to produce it at all, should be addressed under Rule 26(b)(2)(B).").

What makes a format "reasonably usable" under the rule? The Advisory Committee Notes to the 2006 amendments suggest that searchability may, in certain instances, be one hallmark of the usability of any given format. *See id.* ("If the responding party ordinarily maintains the information it is producing in a way that makes it searchable by electronic means, the information should not be produced in a form that removes or significantly degrades this feature."). But the rule does not necessarily require a producing party to convert ESI to a searchable format for it to be deemed "reasonably usable." *In re Jemsek Clinic, P.A., 2013 WL 3994663, at *7 (Bkrtcy. W.D.N.C. Aug. 2, 2013)* ("Use of TIFF images [which are not searchable] is a 'reasonably usable form' for the production of ESI under Rule 34(b)(2)(E) when the parties have never discussed a particular format for production of electronic documents."). If data of some kind is contained within the ESI, "reasonably usable" will likely mean whether the requesting party is able to analyze and perhaps manipulate the data in needed ways. *See, e.g., Positive Tech., Inc. v. Sony Elecs., Inc., 2013 WL 525031, at *1–2 (N.D. Cal. Feb. 11, 2013)* ("In order to view an entire row, the pages of the spreadsheet would have to be lined up along a long table or across the floor. The Court finds that this is not a reasonably usable form. . . . [T]he Court finds it more efficient to order the production of all of the spreadsheets in their native form."); *Capacchione v. Charlotte-Mecklenburg Sch., 186 F.R.D. 335, 337 (W.D.N.C. 1998)* ("[The] Intervenors were not given this information in reasonably usable form. In order for the database information to be meaningful and useful for the preparation of expert witness reports, the [ ] Intervenors must be able to research, compile, and manipulate the database with the same ease and efficiency as the [Defendant].").

Food for Thought

Because form of production issues can get thorny—as there is no precision to what is "reasonably usable"—it is ideal for parties to reach an explicit agreement on these issues as part of the discovery plan. What obstacles can you envision to the parties reaching an agreement regarding form of production?

b.   Metadata

Another issue surrounding the production of ESI is whether parties have an obligation to produce such information with its metadata intact. The Committee Note to Rule 26(f) defines metadata as "[i]nformation describing the history, tracking, or management of an electronic document" and indicates that it "is usually not apparent to the reader viewing a hard copy or a screen image." FED. R. CIV. P. 26(f) advisory committee's note to 2006 amendment. An example of metadata would be the information that appears when a Microsoft Word user opens the "Properties" dialog box for a document. In that box one can find information such as the date on which the document was created, when it was last modified, printed, or accessed, and the identity of the author of the document. Metadata can prove quite useful in tracking the manipulation of documents, which may be a concern in instances where there is some question as to the authenticity or integrity of documents that have been produced. *See, e.g., Plasse v. Tyco Elecs. Corp., 448 F. Supp. 2d 302 (D. Mass. 2006)* (using metadata to discover that certain files had been accessed and deleted by plaintiff employee). Do requesting parties have any right to receive such metadata when printed versions of the documents would not have conveyed this type of information?

Under the Federal Rules, parties are supposed to discuss this issue at the Rule 26(f) conference and reach an agreement on the matter if possible. Generally speaking, though, the pertinent question here is whether the information falls within the scope of discovery set forth in Rule 26(b)(1), which is that the information be relevant to a claim or defense asserted in the action. Thus, there is no blanket obligation to produce or permission to withhold metadata just because it is metadata. Rather, a responding party has an obligation to produce nonprivileged metadata within the scope of a discovery request if the metadata meets the relevance standard of Rule 26(b)(1), which one can easily imagine being the case in many instances given the type of information that metadata can reveal. That said, courts have held that if parties do not explicitly request metadata in their Rule 34 requests, they are not entitled to receive it. *See, e.g., Aguilar v. Immigration & Customs Enf't Div., 255 F.R.D. 350, 357 (S.D.N.Y. 2008)* ("[I]f a party wants metadata, it should 'Ask for it. Up front. Otherwise, if the party asks too late or has already received the document in another form, it may be out of luck.' " (citation omitted)); *D'Onofrio v. SFX Sports Grp., Inc., 247 F.R.D. 43, 48 (D.D.C. 2008)* (denying motion to compel metadata that was not included in initial request).

Take Note!

For an example of case in which the duty to produce relevant metadata was emphasized, see *Williams v. Sprint/United Mgmt. Co., 230 F.R.D. 640, 656 (D. Kan. 2005)* ("When the Court orders a party to produce an electronic document in the form in which it is regularly maintained, *i.e.*, in its native format or as an active file, that production must include all metadata unless that party timely objects to production of the metadata, the parties agree that the metadata should not be produced, or the producing party requests a protective order.").

The duty to produce responsive and relevant metadata has its limits just as there are limits to the production obligations in general. If the information reported by the metadata is privileged, it is not discoverable. That means that counsel will have to be sure to review metadata for privilege before producing ESI with its metadata intact. Further, if metadata exists, but for technical reasons is "not reasonably accessible" or is unduly burdensome to retrieve and produce under the terms of Rule 26(b)(2), the court may conclude that a responding party need not produce the information. The critical point to remember here is that these are not determinations that responding parties should make on their own without informing their adversaries and the court; to the extent a party feels that responsive metadata should not be produced, it must make that assertion and either convince the requesting party or the court to agree.

c. Technology-Assisted Review and Predictive Coding

The immense volume of electronically stored information (ESI) possessed by most business entities makes comprehensive human review of documents for responsiveness a near practical impossibility. In addition to the inordinate amount of time and expense that can be associated with a large-scale human document review, human review of massive document sets—particularly that carried out by paralegals and contract attorneys—leaves much to be desired in terms of accurately identifying and retrieving all responsive documents. In light of the proportionality limitations on discovery, the costs of manual review in large-data cases will typically be prohibitive in relation to the amount in controversy in the dispute.

Today, litigants are increasingly turning to technology-assisted review methods to cull through large documents for responsive material. Studies have shown that such methods are equal or superior to human review in terms of accuracy and can complete the task in dramatically less time at a fraction of the cost. *See, e.g.*, Herb Roitblatt, Ann Kershaw, & Patrick Oot, *Document Categorization in Legal Electronic Discovery: Computer Classification vs. Manual Review*, 61 J. OF AM. SOC'Y FOR INFO. SCI. & TECH. 70, 79 (2010) ("On every measure, the performance of the two computer systems was at least as accurate (measured against the original review) as that of human re-review."); Maura R. Grossman & Gordon V. Cormack, *Technology-Assisted Review in E-Discovery Can Be More Effective and More Efficient Than Exhaustive Manual Review*, 17 RICHMOND J. L. & TECH. 11, 61 (2011) ("[T]he myth that exhaustive manual review is the most effective—and therefore the most defensible—approach to document review is strongly refuted. Technology-assisted review can (and does) yield more accurate results than exhaustive manual review, with much lower effort.").

When speaking of technology-assisted review, one must note that there are different kinds of such review, each of which has varying degrees of effectiveness. The most rudimentary form of computer-aided review—keyword searches—is notoriously ineffective. With this method, attorneys attempt to develop a list of keywords that will recover relevant and responsive documents and then run searches to retrieve documents containing those terms. The problems with this approach are that developing a list of appropriate and comprehensive keywords is difficult without familiarity with the documents, the use of keywords will be both under- and over-inclusive (missing relevant documents while also retrieving irrelevant documents), and many people will create documents that discuss concepts without using the selected keywords or with misspellings, abbreviations, etc. United States Magistrate Judge Andrew Peck pointed to studies demonstrating the ineffectiveness of keyword searching in a 2012 article:

> In 1985, scholars David Blair and M.E. Maron collected 40,000 documents from a Bay Area Rapid Transit accident, and instructed experienced attorney and paralegal searchers to use keywords and other review techniques to retrieve at least 75% of the documents relevant to 51 document requests.

Searchers believed they met the goals, but their average recall was just 20%. This result has been replicated in the TREC Legal Track studies over the past few years.

Andrew Peck, *Search, Forward: Will Manual Document Review and Keyword Searches Be Replaced by Computer-Assisted Coding?*, L. TECH. NEWS, Oct. 1, 2011, at 26. Several judicial opinions have expressed the same view. *See, e.g.*, *United States v. O'Keefe*, 537 F. Supp. 2d 14, 24 (D.D.C. 2008) (Facciola, M.J.); *Equity Analytics, L.L.C. v. Lundin*, 248 F.R.D. 331, 333 (D.D.C. 2008) (Facciola, M.J.); *Victor Stanley, Inc. v. Creative Pipe, Inc.*, 250 F.R.D. 251, 260, 262 (D. Md. 2008) (Grimm, M.J.). Judge Peck advised that "where counsel are using keyword searches for retrieval of ESI, they at a minimum must carefully craft the appropriate keywords, with input from the ESI's custodians as to the words and abbreviations they use, and the proposed methodology must be quality control tested to assure accuracy in retrieval and elimination of 'false positives.' " *William A. Gross Constr. Assocs., Inc. v. Am. Mfrs. Mut. Ins. Co.*, 256 F.R.D. 134, 134, 136 (S.D.N.Y. 2009) (Peck, M.J.).

The more effective type of technology-assisted review that has been embraced by many is referred to as **predictive coding**. Judge Peck has explained predictive coding as:

> [T]ools . . . that use sophisticated algorithms to enable the computer to determine relevance, based on interaction with (i.e., training by) a human reviewer.

> Unlike manual review, where the review is done by the most junior staff, computer-assisted coding involves a senior partner (or team) who review and code a "seed set" of documents. The computer identifies properties of those documents that it uses to code other documents. As the senior reviewer continues to code more sample documents, the computer predicts the reviewer's coding. (Or, the computer codes some documents and asks the senior reviewer for feedback.)

> When the system's predictions and the reviewer's coding sufficiently coincide, the system has learned enough to make confident predictions for the remaining documents. Typically, the senior lawyer (or team) needs to review only a few thousand documents to train the computer.

Peck, *supra* at 29. Although this basic definition can provide a general sense of what predictive coding is, there is much more detail involved in actually designing and engaging in predictive coding for a document retrieval effort. Several vendors provide this service and many law firms have in-house specialists who are experts at this type of process.

Having written favorably on the value of predictive coding, Judge Peck has approved of its use in the case of *Da Silva Moore v. Publicis Groupe*, 287 F.R.D. 182 (S.D.N.Y. 2012) (Peck, M.J.) [*FLEX* Case 8.B]. See also *Davine v. Golub Corp.*, 2017 WL 549151, at *1 (D. Mass. Feb. 8, 2017) ("Defendants are entitled to rely on their predictive coding model for purposes of identifying relevant responsive documents, and may cease their review of the documents identified as possibly relevant when they made a good faith determination that the burden of continuing the review outweighs the benefit in terms of identifying relevant documents."). Approving of the use of predictive coding, however, is not the same as ordering it; courts have not been willing to order technology-assisted review ("TAR") or predictive coding. See *In re Viagra (Sildenafil Citrate) Prod. Liab. Litig.*, 2016 WL 7336411, *2 (N.D. Cal. Oct. 14, 2016) ("Plaintiffs do not cite to any case law in support of their proposal to require Pfizer, over its objection, to use TAR

Food for Thought

How transparent should the computer training process be between adversaries in litigation? For example, should requesting parties have access to the "seed set" of documents and accompanying relevance determinations that the producing party used to train the computer to identify relevant documents? John M. Facciola & Philip J. Favro, *Safeguarding the Seed Set: Why Seed Set Documents May Be Entitled To Work Product Protection*, 8 FED. CTS. L. REV. 1 (2015).

and/or predictive coding. At the hearing on this matter, Plaintiffs conceded that no court has ordered a party to engage in TAR and/or predictive coding over the objection of the party. The few courts that have considered this issue have all declined to compel predictive coding." (citing cases)). Courts opt instead to have the parties come to an agreement on the most appropriate search method. *See, e.g., Kleen Prods. L.L.C. v. Packaging Corp. of Am.*, 2012 WL 4498465, at *5 (N.D. Ill. Sept. 28, 2012) ("[T]he Court observed that under Sedona Principle 6, '[r]esponding parties are best situated to evaluate the procedures, methodologies, and techniques appropriate for preserving and producing their own electronically stored information.' " (quoting The Sedona Conference, The Sedona Conference Best Practices Commentary on the Use of Search and Information Retrieval Methods in E-Discovery, 8 SEDONA CONFERENCE J. 189, 193 (Fall 2007))). More decisions touching on predictive coding are certain to come from other courts in the future. For an excellent overview of predictive coding and the legal issues that arise in this context, see Charles Yablon & Nick Landsman-Roos, Predictive Coding: Emerging Questions and Concerns, 64 S.C. L. REV. 633 (2013).

3. Rule 33: Interrogatories

Under Rule 33 a party may send written questions or interrogatories that the receiving party must answer "under oath." FED. R. CIV. P. 33(a)(1) & (b)(3). For example, an interrogatory might read, "Identify all individuals who have applied for employment within your organization in the past ten years, specifying the age, race, and gender of each." Parties issuing interrogatories are free to inquire into any area that falls within the scope of discovery as outlined in Rule 26(b)(1) and can seek opinions, contentions, or even the application of law to facts. FED. R. CIV. P. 33(a)(2). The parties are limited to 25 of these questions unless the court grants permission to issue additional interrogatories. FED. R. CIV. P. 33(a)(1).

Although it is relatively easy to craft interrogatories, it can be quite expensive and burdensome to respond to them. To answer some questions fully and truthfully, parties may have to undertake an extensive investigation and review of their own internal files, which could take a significant amount of employee or attorney time.

The Federal Rules also provide for issuing **requests for admission** to one's adversary. FED. R. CIV. P. 36. Such requests are like interrogatories except they make affirmative assertions and ask the defendant to admit or deny them. For example, a request to admit might read, "Admit that you were not wearing your eyeglasses at the time of the accident." The responding party must then admit or deny the statement. If the assertion is admitted, the issue is eliminated as a disputed matter in the case. A denial obligates the adversary to try to prove the assertion with the evidence before the trier of fact.

If responding to the interrogatory appears likely to be too burdensome, responding parties may object on any ground applicable to other discovery requests such as privilege, relevance, or undue burden under Rule 26(b)(2). However, Rule 33 also gives responding parties the option to permit a questioning party to view the responding party's business records to figure out the answers for itself:

FRCP 33(d). Interrogatories to Parties.

(d) Option to Produce Business Records. If the answer to an interrogatory may be determined by examining, auditing, compiling, abstracting, or summarizing a party's business records (including electronically stored information), and if the burden of deriving or ascertaining the answer will be substantially the same for either party, the responding party may answer by:

(1) specifying the records that must be reviewed, in sufficient detail to enable the interrogating party to locate and identify them as readily as the responding party could; and

(2) giving the interrogating party a reasonable opportunity to examine and audit the records and to make copies, compilations, abstracts, or summaries.

Subparagraph (1) of this provision was added in 1980 to prevent parties from simply giving their adversaries access to a mass of undifferentiated business records without any guidance as to how the sought information might be found. What are the advantages and disadvantages to the responding party of taking this approach rather than undertaking the review and response effort itself?

Something to keep in mind when crafting interrogatories or responding to them is the goose-gander rule: What's good for the goose is good for the gander; you should only dish out as much as you are prepared to get in return. This flip axiom simply means that if you issue overly-broad and unduly burdensome interrogatories to your adversaries, you may receive such interrogatories in return. Similarly, if you are unhelpful and evasive in your responses to interrogatories it is not likely that you will get very useful answers to your own set of questions. The key to a peaceful discovery process (if such a thing is possible) is early discussion of issues and cooperation where possible. *See* The Sedona Conference Cooperation Proclamation, *available at* www. TheSedonaConference.org (urging legal advocates to cooperate in discovery matters as a path to a more cost-effective and beneficial discovery process). That said, your task as an advocate is to represent your client's interests, not to give your client's adversary a key and welcome mat to all information that will undermine your client's case. Finding the right balance here is a challenge all litigators face, particularly when confronted with a combative, obstructionist opposing counsel seemingly unconcerned with facilitating an efficient and cost-effective discovery process.

Food for Thought

What risks do you think might be associated with this approach from the responding party's perspective? As an advocate, would you want your adversary at your client's site nosing around looking for information? It is probably advisable to assign people to accompany your adversary as it reviews your client's files and systems for the relevant information. However, if that is the case, isn't your client spending a similar amount of time and money providing such oversight as it would have had it simply done the review itself?

4. Rule 30: Oral Depositions

Through oral depositions, parties may question, under oath, any person thought to have testimony relevant to their dispute, without the court's permission. FED. R. CIV. P. 30(a)(1). These witnesses or deponents do not have to be parties to the action and—under Rule 30(b)(2)—they may be required to produce documents at the deposition (a request known as a *subpoena duces tecum*). The format for depositions mirrors the format of witness examinations during a trial, except no judge is present. The attorney conducting the deposition examines the deponent by asking a series of prepared or extemporaneous questions.

The deponent will typically have her own legal counsel representing her at the deposition who may make objections to questions based either on the confusing or harrassing nature of the question or based on a view that the question delves into an area protected by privilege, confidentiality, or some other similar ground. Objections are also proper based on relevance.

In the event that the deponent's counsel has an objection, the objection "must be stated concisely in a nonargumentative and nonsuggestive manner." FED. R. CIV. P. 30(c)(2). This is a prohibition against "speaking objections," in which objecting counsel attempts to use the objection as a vehicle for coaching the witness. *Specht v. Google, Inc.,* 268 F.R.D. 596, 598 (N.D. Ill. 2010) ("Objections that are argumentative or that suggest an answer to a witness are called 'speaking objections' and are improper under Rule 30(c)(2).").

Take Note!

Note that the Federal Rules also provide for **depositions on written questions**, which involve the presentation of a set of typed questions to a witness who proceeds to answer them orally, under oath, before a stenographer who records the answers. FED R. CIV. P. 31. When might a party be interested in using a written versus an oral deposition?

After an attorney makes an objection, the deponent still must answer the question and the questioning continues. FED. R. CIV. P. 30(c)(2); *Breaux v. Haliburton Energy Servs.,* 2006 WL 2460748, at *4 (E.D. La. Aug. 22, 2006) ("[O]nce the objection is made, the witness answers the question and the parties move on."). However, the objecting counsel may ask for the question to be rephrased, or—

Practice Pointer

"Defending" a deposition, which is the term used to refer to serving as counsel for a deponent, is a very important task. In addition to objecting to improper questions, it is vital that counsel for the deponent pay close attention to the testimony elicited by the questioning. If you are defending a deposition and the elicited testimony leaves a negative or mistaken impression of the facts from your client's perspective, you should ask clarifying questions that can set the record straight when it is your turn to examine the deponent.

under certain circumstances—may direct the deponent not to respond to the question. These circumstances are limited: "A person may instruct a deponent not to answer only when necessary to preserve a privilege, to enforce a limitation directed by the court, or to present a motion under Rule 30(d)(3)," which is a motion to terminate the deposition because it is proceeding in bad faith. FED. R. CIV. P. 30(c)(2).

Given that no judge is present during the deposition, what should the questioning attorney do in the event that a deponent refuses to answer a question? The attorney may continue with the deposition and

later seek an order compelling a response from the court or, if the matter is vital to the attorney's subsequent line of questioning, the attorney may suspend the deposition and seek the court's intervention. Once the attorney is finished examining the deponent, the deponent's attorney may then question the deponent as well.

Depositions are limited to one day of seven hours unless otherwise stipulated by the parties or the court allows additional time. FED. R. CIV. P. 30(d)(1). Further, after ten depositions, leave of the court is required to conduct a deposition. FED. R. CIV. P. 30(a)(2) & 31(a)(2). A stenographic, audio, or audiovisual record is kept of the deposition and upon its completion a transcript is produced, which the deponent or a party may request a copy of to review and correct if necessary. FED. R. CIV. P. 30(e). The uses of depositions at trial are limited, such as to impeach a witness or if a witness becomes unavailable. FED. R. CIV. P. 32(a).

5. Rule 35: Physical or Mental Examinations

In actions where a party makes his own physical or mental health an issue, the need may arise for the opposing party to conduct its own examination of the physical or mental condition of that person. This is a sensitive area in which to compel discovery, however, because physical and mental examinations touch on privacy concerns and can be intrusive and sometimes painful. Under what circumstances should parties be permitted to compel this type of discovery? Rule 35 addresses the issue:

> **FRCP 35. Physical and Mental Examinations:**
> **Order for an Examination.**
>
> **(a) Order for an Examination.**
>
> **(1) *In General.*** The court where the action is pending may order a party whose mental or physical condition * * * is in controversy to submit to a physical or mental examination by a suitably licensed or certified examiner. The court has the same authority to order a party to produce for examination a person who is in its custody or under its legal control.
>
> **(2) *Motion and Notice; Contents of the Order.*** The order:
>
> (A) may be made only on motion for good cause and on notice to all parties and the person to be examined * * * .

Take Note!

Employees are not in an employer's custody or legal control for purposes of Rule 35; the type of control intended is akin to that of a parent or guardian in relation to a child, although that is not necessarily the full extent of the scope of rule's reach. *See* 8B C. WRIGHT, A. MILLER & R. MARCUS, FED. PRAC. & PROC. § 2233 (3d ed. 2010).

Under the terms of the rule, the critical requirements are that the person to be examined must be a "party" (or someone under the control of a party), that party's mental or physical condition must be "in controversy," and the party seeking the examination must demonstrate "good cause" to justify the examination. How can requesting parties demonstrate "good cause" and what puts a party's physical or mental condition "in controversy"? The Supreme Court addressed these questions in *Schlagenhauf v. Holder*, 379 U.S. 104 (1964), a case involving the alleged negligence of a bus driver involved in an accident, as follows:

> Rule 35, therefore, requires discriminating application by the trial judge, who must decide, as an initial matter in every case, whether the party requesting a mental or physical examination or examinations has adequately demonstrated the existence of the Rule's requirements of "in controversy" and "good cause," which requirements * * * are necessarily related. * * *
>
> Of course, there are situations where the pleadings alone are sufficient to meet these requirements. A plaintiff in a negligence action who asserts mental or physical injury * * * places that mental or physical injury clearly in controversy and provides the defendant with good cause for an examination to determine the existence and extent of such asserted injury. This is not only true as to a plaintiff, but applies equally to a defendant who asserts his mental or physical condition as a defense to a claim, such as, for example, where insanity is asserted as a defense to a divorce action. * * *
>
> The "good cause" and "in controversy" requirements of Rule 35 make it very apparent that sweeping examinations of a party who has not affirmatively put into issue his own mental or physical condition are not to be automatically ordered merely because the person has been involved in an accident—or, as in this case, two accidents—and a general charge of negligence is lodged. Mental and physical examinations are only to be ordered upon a discriminating application by the district judge of the limitations prescribed by the Rule. To hold otherwise would mean that such examinations could be ordered routinely in automobile accident cases.

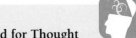

Food for Thought

Under the *Schlagenhauf* standard, if an employee sues her employer for sexual harassment and claims emotional distress as one of the harms for which she seeks money damages, should the defendant employer be able to compel her to submit to a psychiatric examination under Rule 35? See *Valencia v. By the Bay Invs., Inc.*, 2006 WL 2792866, at *1 (N.D. Cal. Sept. 28, 2006).

Id. at 118–22.

After examinations are conducted under the rule, the examined party may request a copy of a detailed written report of the examiner's findings. FED. R. CIV. P. 35(b)(1). However, if the examined party requests such a report, the party that caused the Rule 35 examination to take place is entitled to receive a copy of the reports arising from any similar examinations the examined party has been subjected to for the same condition. FED. R. CIV. P. 35(b)(3). Further, if the party examined under Rule 35 requests a copy of the examiner's report, that party waives any doctor-patient privilege "concerning testimony about all examinations of the same condition." FED. R. CIV. P. 35(b)(4).

> **FYI**
>
> Failure to comply with an order to produce a person for examination under Rule 35(a) is punishable by all but one of the sanctions enumerated in Rule 37(b)(2); a court may not treat such a failure as contempt of court. FED. R. CIV. P. 37(b)(2)(B).

D. Discovery Disputes

Although the parties are obligated to comply with the initial disclosure requirements of the Federal Rules and must respond to all proper discovery requests from other parties, disputes often arise over many discovery-related issues, including the proper scope of discovery, whether a request seeks information that is due under the rules, whether efforts to comply with discovery requests or discovery orders have been sufficient, and whether parties who have failed to meet their discovery obligations should be penalized in some way as a result.

Indeed, these disputes can be major battles between the parties as they fight to avoid what they may perceive to be inordinately costly or extremely intrusive discovery seeking information that they would otherwise prefer not to have to produce. Battles can also surround form of production, who pays for costly discovery, and the failure to preserve information for discovery in the face of a legal duty to preserve. In this section, we will take a look at various types of discovery disputes and how litigants and courts can deal with such disputes, as well as the challenging issue of preservation of information pending litigation and sanctions for failing to preserve.

1. Discovery Offenses and Sanctions

The paradigmatic discovery dispute is that a requesting party wants certain information to be produced and the responding party refuses to produce it. The refusal might be justified based on privilege, work-product protection, undue burden, or a belief that the information is electronically stored information that is not reasonably accessible. The refusal might also be unjustified either because the responding party erroneously believes that the material is protected or not discoverable, or worse, because the party is trying to hide the information from its opponent. When the parties are at loggerheads over a discovery issue, the rules provide that they must meet and confer to try to negotiate a resolution of the dispute before they can seek intervention from the court. *See* FED. R. CIV. P. 26(c); 37(a)(1).

Orders to Compel & Protective Orders. After the parties meet and confer, intervention from the court can then be solicited in two ways. First, the requesting party can file a motion to compel the production of information at issue pursuant to Rule 37(a):

FRCP 37. Failure to Make Disclosures or to Cooperate in Discovery; Sanctions.

(a) Motion for an Order Compelling Disclosure or Discovery.

(1) *In General.* On notice to other parties and all affected persons, a party may move for an order compelling disclosure or discovery. The motion must include a certification that the movant has in good faith conferred or attempted to confer with the person or party failing to make disclosure or discovery in an effort to obtain it without court action.

* * *

(3) *Specific Motions.*

(A) *To Compel Disclosure.* If a party fails to make a disclosure required by Rule 26(a), any other party may move to compel disclosure and for appropriate sanctions.

(B) *To Compel a Discovery Response.* A party seeking discovery may move for an order compelling an answer, designation, production, or inspection. This motion may be made if:

    (i) a deponent fails to answer a question asked under Rule 30 or 31;

    (ii) a corporation or other entity fails to make a designation under Rule 30(b)(6) or 31(a)(4);

    (iii) a party fails to answer an interrogatory submitted under Rule 33; or

    (iv) a party fails to produce documents or fails to respond that inspection will be permitted—or fails to permit inspection—as requested under Rule 34.

Motions to compel are particularly appropriate when the requesting party feels that the responding party is not legitimately claiming protection for the withheld material or if the responding party has dragged its feet in complying with the production request and appears to be stonewalling rather than making a good-faith effort to produce the requested material.

Alternatively, the responding party who feels that it should not be required to comply with a particular discovery request and disclose certain information may file a motion seeking a protective order under Rule 26(c):

FRCP 26. General Provisions Governing Discovery.

(c) **Protective Orders.**

(1) *In General.* A party or any person from whom discovery is sought may move for a protective order in the court where the action is pending—or as an alternative on matters relating to a deposition, in the court for the district where the deposition will be taken. The motion must include a certification that the movant has in good faith conferred or attempted to confer with other affected parties in an effort to resolve the dispute without court action. The court may, for good cause, issue an order to protect a party or person from annoyance, embarrassment, oppression, or undue burden or expense, including one or more of the following:

(A) forbidding the disclosure or discovery;

* * *

(D) forbidding inquiry into certain matters, or limiting the scope of disclosure or discovery to certain matters * * *.

Protective orders are particularly useful to protect responding parties against abusive discovery requests, such as those that seek a large amount of unnecessary information that it would cost the responding party great expense to produce. In our system, we follow the "American Rule," which means that litigants are responsible for their own litigation expenses, including the cost of producing information in response to discovery requests. As a result of this rule, however, requesting parties are able to inflict costs on their adversaries through discovery requests. Unfortunately, some advocates have been known to take advantage of this ability to make discovery requests more for the purpose of inflicting cost and bringing about delay than for the value the sought information would actually provide to the party's claims or defenses. Protective orders give responding parties a way to combat this practice.

Discovery Certification Requirement. In an effort to discourage abusive discovery practices, such as those mentioned above, parties requesting or producing information must certify that their disclosures are complete, FED. R. CIV. P. 26(g)(1), and that the discovery request or response is consistent with the following provision:

FRCP 26(g)(1). Signing Disclosures and Discovery Requests, Responses, and Objections.

(1) *Signature Required; Effect of Signature.* Every disclosure under Rule 26(a)(1) or (a)(3) and every discovery request, response, or objection must be signed by at least one attorney of record in the attorney's own name—or by the party personally, if unrepresented—and must state the signer's address, e-mail address, and telephone number. By signing, an attorney or party certifies that to the best of the person's knowledge, information, and belief formed after a reasonable inquiry: (A) with respect to a disclosure, it is complete and correct as of the time it is made; and

(B)   with respect to a discovery request, response, or objection, it is:

(i)   consistent with these rules and warranted by existing law or by a nonfrivolous argument for extending, modifying, or reversing existing law, or for establishing new law;

(ii)   not interposed for any improper purpose, such as to harass, cause unnecessary delay, or needlessly increase the cost of litigation; and

(iii)   neither unreasonable nor unduly burdensome or expensive, considering the needs of the case, prior discovery in the case, the amount in controversy, and the importance of the issues at stake in the action.

This certification requirement is akin to that imposed by Rule 11 (recall that Rule 11 is inapplicable to discovery). Parties found to have violated the Rule may be sanctioned as deemed appropriate by the court. FED. R. CIV. P. 26(g)(3).

Sanctions. In most instances, it is knowledge of the court's authority to impose sanctions that incentivizes compliance with parties' discovery obligations. When parties persist in non-compliance, however, courts can and have imposed a wide range of sanctions on those parties, some of which are set forth in **Table 8.2**.

Table 8.2

Sanction	Rule
An order that designated facts shall be taken to be established for purposes of the action	Rule 37(b)(2)(A)(i)
An order preventing the disobedient party from introducing certain documents, or supporting or opposing designated claims or defenses	Rule 37(b)(2)(A)(ii)
The entry of dismissal or default	Rule 37(b)(2)(A)(v) & (vi)
The striking of the pleadings of the offending party	Rule 37(b)(2)(A)(iii)
The award of reasonable expenses, including attorneys' fees	Rule 37(b)(2)(C)

These sanctions, which are authorized under various portions of Rule 37, are not an exhaustive list. Rule 37 itself states that courts are empowered to impose "further just orders." FED. R. CIV. P. 37(b)(2). *See also Scovin v. Great W. Life & Annuity Ins. Co.*, 2006 WL 2828428, at *6 (D. Conn. Sept. 29, 2006) ("There is no indication in Rule 37 that this list of sanctions was intended to be exhaustive."). Further, courts have inherent power to impose sanctions for discovery abuses, authority that supplements courts' sanctioning power under Rule 37. *See, e.g., Leon v. IDX Sys. Corp.*, 464 F.3d 951, 958 (9th Cir. 2006) ("There are two sources of authority under which a district court can sanction a party who has despoiled evidence: the inherent power of federal courts to levy sanctions in response to abusive litigation practices, and the availability of sanctions under Rule 37 against a party who 'fails to obey an order to provide or permit discovery.' " (quoting *Fjelstad v. Am. Honda Motor Co., 762 F.2d 1334, 1337 (9th Cir. 1985)*)).

Although courts have inherent authority to sanction parties for discovery misconduct, there are limits on such power. In *Goodyear Tire & Rubber Co. v. Haeger, 137 S. Ct. 1178 (2017)*, the Supreme Court reversed a district court's imposition of sanctions issued pursuant to its inherent authority because the Court concluded that such sanctions for bad-faith conduct in discovery must be limited to the attorney fees the innocent party incurred solely because of the misconduct. The district court had imposed sanctions in the amount of $2.7 million, which included expenses incurred since the time of the misconduct. The Supreme Court indicated that sanctions beyond those connected in a "but-for" fashion to the misconduct could only be imposed if additional procedural protections akin to those given criminal defendants were afforded to the party to be sanctioned; "When (as in this case) those criminal-type protections are missing, a court's shifting of fees is limited to reimbursing the victim." *Id.* at 1186. The next case illustrates a court's exercise of its sanctioning authority in the discovery context.

FYI

When courts impose severe sanctions such as dismissal, factors that bear on the propriety of such a sanction include "(1) the willfulness of the non-compliant party or the reason for noncompliance; (2) the efficacy of lesser sanctions; (3) the duration of the period of noncompliance; and (4) whether the non-compliant party had been warned of the consequences of noncompliance." *Agiwal v. Mid Island Mortg. Corp., 555 F.3d 298, 302 (2d Cir. 2009)*.

Poole ex rel. Elliott v. Textron

U.S. District Court for the District of Maryland
192 F.R.D. 494 (D. Md. 2000)

GAUVEY, UNITED STATES MAGISTRATE JUDGE.

I. INTRODUCTION

This is a product liability case in which the plaintiff, Ryan W. Poole ("Poole"), has sued Textron, Inc. ("Textron") for alleged defects in a golf car, which resulted in serious injuries to him. * * *

It's Latin to Me!

The term *ex rel.* that appears in the name of this case refers to the Latin phrase *ex relatione*, which in turn means "by or on the relation of." Suits prosecuted *ex rel.* are those brought by an interested party on behalf of the plaintiff. Here, who is the "Elliott" referred to in the caption and why do you think she is bringing this case on Poole's behalf?

Before the Court is plaintiff's request for attorneys' fees and other expenses related to the three substantive discovery motions and other sanctions: the motion for sanctions raising six instances of discovery abuse,[1] the motion to compel production of documents and the motion to determine sufficiency of answers and objections to requests for admissions. * * *

Textron acknowledges this Court's authority to assess sanctions to punish discovery abuses under FED.R.CIV.P. 37, FED.R.CIV.P. 26(g) and the inherent authority of the Court. However, Textron argues that an award of fees is inappropriate for several reasons. Chiefly, Textron argues that its collection and investigative efforts to comply with the Court's May 20, 1999 Order were both extensive and expensive—costing Textron $23,260 in attorneys' fees and expenses. That "sanction" is, in Textron's view, sufficient. Alternatively, Textron argues that plaintiff's request for expenses, including fees, in the amount of $50,346.89 is grossly excessive, under governing law. Specifically, Textron objects to the hourly rate charged by the plaintiff's counsel as not in line with those prevailing in the community for similar services by lawyers of reasonably comparable skill, experience and reputation.

II. GOVERNING LAW ON ENTITLEMENT TO SANCTIONS AND EXPENSES, INCLUDING ATTORNEYS' FEES

As Textron acknowledged, this Court has authority to redress discovery misconduct under the Federal Rules as well as under its inherent powers, and can impose a range of sanctions from award of expenses against both a party and its

---

[1] These instances of discovery abuse are incomplete document production, failure to provide accurate interrogatory answers, lack of diligent search for documents and failure to provide a corporate designee able to address all specified areas of inquiry, defendants' refusal to answer questions at the deposition, defendants' lack of candor with the Court and counsel and Textron's attempt to conceal the existence of the 1998 GX-440 golf car in its possession.

counsel to an entry of a default judgment. The sanction, of course, depends on the nature of the discovery abuse.

The Court's inherent authority is not displaced or limited by the sanctioning scheme of the Federal Rules. *Chambers v. NASCO, Inc.*, 501 U.S. 32, 46 (1991). * * *

What's That?

Inherent powers of a court refer to the intrinsic authority that courts are thought to have to deal with certain matters essential to the carrying out of their judicial function, such as procedural rulemaking, regulation of the practice of law, and the imposition of sanctions for misconduct.

The Supreme Court has cautioned restraint in the exercise of the inherent powers "[b]ecause of their very potency," *Chambers, 501 U.S. at 44* and "[b]ecause inherent powers are shielded from direct democratic controls." *Roadway Express, Inc. v. Piper, 447 U.S. 752, 764 (1980)*. Accordingly, whether default judgment or some lesser punitive sanction, such as an award of attorneys' fees, is imposed under the inherent powers, courts require evidence of misconduct, usually characterized as "contumacious," "fraudulent" or "bad faith," with some courts requiring that the misconduct be shown by "clear and convincing" evidence. As will be more fully discussed below, this Court finds the sanctioning scheme of Rules 37 and 26 of the Federal Rules of Civil Procedure sufficient to redress the violations here without exercise of the inherent powers.

As to plaintiff's motions to compel and to test the sufficiency of the answers and objections to the request for admission, FED.R.CIV.P. 37 governs both the entitlement to expenses and the amount of such expenses. If such a motion is granted, the Rule provides, in pertinent part:

> [T]he Court *shall* . . . require the party or deponent whose conduct necessitated the motion or the party or attorney advising such conduct or both of them to pay to the moving party the *reasonable expenses* incurred in making the motion, *including attorneys' fees*, unless the Court finds that the motion was filed without the movant's first making a good faith effort to obtain the disclosure or discovery without court action, or that the opposing party's non-disclosure, response or objection was substantially justified, or that other circumstances make an award of expenses unjust.

FED.R.CIV.P. 37(a)(4)(A) (emphasis added). Where, as here, the motion is granted in part and denied in part, the court shall "apportion the reasonable expenses incurred in relation to the motion among the parties and persons in a just manner." FED.R.CIV.P. 37(a)(4). The Court has determined that there was no substantial justification for Textron's non-disclosure, responses and objections and that there were no circumstances that made an award of expenses unjust.

Similarly, Rule 26(g)(3) provides, in pertinent part, that "if without substantial justification a certification is made in violation of the rule, the Court, upon motion or upon its own initiative *shall* impose upon the person who made the certification, the party on whose behalf the disclosure request, response, or objection is made, or both, an *appropriate sanction* which *may* include an order to pay the amount of *reasonable expenses* incurred because of the violation, *including a reasonable attorney's fee*." (emphasis added). By its language, Rule 26(g)(3) does not limit a court to the award of expenses only, but gives the Court latitude to fashion an "appropriate sanction," in addition to an award of expenses. Nevertheless, an award of attorneys' fees appear to be the sanction most commonly imposed in reported decisions. The Court has determined that while counsel for Textron signed the various discovery responses, counsel had not conducted the requisite "reasonable inquiry" and that the quality of the responses suggested an improper purpose, specifically "to cause unnecessary delay or needless cost of litigation." FED.R.CIV.P. 26(g). Accordingly, there was no substantial justification for the certifications in violation of the rule. Thus, in the absence of certain findings (which the court does not make here), the rules direct the imposition of a sanction. * * *

III. PLAINTIFF'S MOTION FOR DETERMINATION OF SUFFICIENCY OF ANSWERS AND OBJECTIONS TO PLAINTIFF'S REQUEST FOR ADMISSIONS

Regarding plaintiff's motion for determination of the sufficiency of Textron's answers and objections to plaintiff's request for admissions, the Court finds under Rule 37, in conjunction with Rule 36, that Textron's responses or objections were not substantially justified. To the contrary, with one exception, the responses and objections appeared crafted to sabotage the legitimate use of request for admissions. Under the plain language of the rule, a party must either lodge an objection or an answer to a request, but cannot do both.

Pursuant to the requirements of Rule 36(a), the answering party that objects to a request for admissions does so at its own peril. That is, Rule 36(a) mandates that a "*matter is admitted unless* . . . a written answer or objection" is served on the requesting party. (Emphasis added). Rule 36 also states, in detail, the requirements for denials, objections, partial admissions, and qualified answers. Failure to adhere to the plain language of this statute requires that the fact in question be admitted.

Rule 36 expressly permits a party to qualify an answer, but only "when good faith requires." In almost every response, Textron impermissibly lodged both an objection and an answer. Moreover, when Textron filed an answer, its complexity "undermine[d] the efficacy of the rule by crediting disingenuous, hair-splitting distinctions whose unarticulated goal is unfairly to burden an opposing party."

Accordingly, this Court believes the defendant's responses and objections lacked substantial justification. As the Court granted relief as to 12 out of the

13 contested requests (or 92% of the requests), the Court grants that percentage of the attorney time and expenses reasonably related to this motion. See FED.R.CIV.P. 37(a)(4).

IV. PLAINTIFF'S MOTION FOR SANCTIONS

In his motion for sanctions filed pursuant to Rule 37 and the inherent powers of the Court, plaintiff charged that defendant Textron engaged in "improper discovery tactics [which] were willful, inexcusable and not in good faith" and asked for a finding of liability, or alternatively certain relief tailored to each of the alleged instances of discovery abuse. The Court found that many of plaintiff's complaints of discovery abuse were meritorious, and ordered considerable relief in terms of further investigation and production of discovery responses.

A. Textron's Lack of Diligence in Providing Key, Requested Information

The conduct this Court has found sanctionable violates FED.R.CIV.P. 37, and, in some instances, FED.R.CIV.P. 26(g) as well. Particularly egregious was Textron's lack of diligence in providing key, requested information, such as prior litigation involving the golf car model or testing whether in its response to requests for production of documents or its identification of designees for the corporation's deposition on these same subjects.

1. Textron's Responses to Plaintiff's Requests for Production

This Court has concluded, as plaintiff states, that "Textron did not perform an even minimally-adequate search for documents prior to Plaintiff's Motion for Sanctions." At the Court's request, Textron described its efforts to locate documents and information requested by plaintiff. Review of Textron's seven page single space letter showed half-hearted, scatter-shot inquiries prior to the court-ordered investigation and inquiry efforts—often times only reacting to leads that plaintiff's counsel provided about Textron's prior litigation involving the same or similar golf cars or testing of the golf car type at issue. That letter did not dispel the Court's previously held impression that Textron's initial inquiry in response to written discovery requests (as well as Rule 30(b)(6) corporate designation) started and largely, if not entirely, stopped with an inquiry to Mr. Gerald W. Powell, a Textron reliability engineer and E-Z-Go's designee in golf car litigation since 1981 and with a review of the official corporate records of Textron. It appears that Textron did not even contact its own employees in other corporate departments, such as the manager of Textron's Commercial and Media Relations, to respond to the document requests or requests attached to the corporate designee notice. * * *

However, another and perhaps greater proof of the inadequacy of the initial inquiry was the productivity of the additional efforts mandated by the Court which conformed with the demands of the rules and case law on the level of inquiry and the broad definition of "control" under <u>Rule 34</u>. First, the sheer volume of documents produced after plaintiff's motions and court order compared to that produced in response to discovery demands under the rules demonstrates the inadequacy of Textron's initial efforts. Textron initially produced a single page in response to plaintiff's document request. After plaintiff served motions to compel and filed one such motion with the Court (which was granted), Textron produced a total of 470 pages of documents. After plaintiff filed his Motion for Sanctions, Textron produced 20 videotapes and more than 2,900 additional pages of documents that are responsive to the discovery requests. Given the results of court-mandated efforts, it is clear that these documents were in the control of Textron and that a reasonable search would have located them.

Second, a review of Textron's responses to certain of plaintiff's specific discovery requests likewise demonstrates the lack of an adequate inquiry. For example, plaintiff had propounded a request for "[a]ll advertisements and promotional materials that concern or refer to the GX-440, X-440, GX-444, and X-444 for model years 1978 through 1990." (Request No. 23). * * * In response, Textron produced a single brochure. When plaintiff moved to compel further production on the basis that it was inconceivable that Textron had only used a single brochure to advertise and promote its golf cars, Textron responded curiously that: "[a]n inspection of plaintiff's own exhibits demonstrates that Textron has already produced all such materials concerning this discontinued model line."

After the Court-ordered investigation, Textron produced 229 pages of advertising and promotional materials, including photos of the golf cars on grassy slopes much like that on which the accident occurred here. * * *

Rule 26(g) of the Federal Rules of Procedure defines the duty of counsel in responding to discovery requests. That is, counsel must make "a reasonable effort to assure that the client has provided all the information and documents responsive to the discovery demand." * * * In this case, it is clear that defendant's counsel did not make a reasonable effort under the Rule to assure that its client had complied fully with plaintiff's discovery requests and obtained all documents within its possession, custody and control.

* * *

VI. An Award of Reasonable Attorneys' Fees and Costs Is the Appropriate Sanction

In an attempt to ward off any sanction, Textron represents to this Court that its counsel spent at least 154.6 hours on document collection and investigation efforts to comply with the Court's May 22, 1999 Order, at a cost to Textron of $23,260, and argues that "it has now cured (at considerable expense) all deficiencies found by the Court and that an award of sanctions could, under the circumstances, be unjust."

Such an interpretation of the rules would encourage sharp practices and dilatory responses to legitimate discovery demands. If the only sanction for failing to comply with the discovery rules is having to comply with the discovery rules if you are caught, the diligent are punished and the less than diligent, rewarded. Indeed, Rule 37 itself defeats such an interpretation, as it provides, *inter alia*, that the Court shall award the moving party fees if the discovery is provided by ruling or simply after the motion is filed. FED.R.CIV.P. 37(a)(4)(A).

This is clearly not a situation where justice should be tempered by mercy, given the comparative resources of the plaintiff and defendant, and the inescapable conclusion that Textron's stonewalling on discovery played on that disparity. Sanctions are to be awarded "against parties or persons unjustifiably resisting discovery." Advisory Committee Notes to the 1970 Amendments to FED.R.CIV.P. 37. Rule 37 sanctions must be applied diligently both "to penalize those whose conduct may be deemed to warrant such a sanction, [and] to deter those who might be tempted to such conduct in the absence of such a deterrent." *Nat'l Hockey League v. Metropolitan Hockey Club*, 427 U.S. 639, 643 (1976). Likewise, "Rule 26(g) is designed to curb discovery abuse by explicitly encouraging imposition of sanctions." Advisory Committee Notes to 1983 Amendments to FED.R.CIV.P. 26.

However, * * * [i]n the absence of a bad faith finding, the Court is not justified in awarding sanctions beyond the relief afforded by Rule 37(a)(4)(A) and Rule 26(g), and certainly not entry of default judgment, as plaintiff repeatedly requested. Moreover, with the exception of the Court's finding of a Rule 26(g) violation, for which imposition of an "appropriate sanction" is permitted (in addition to, or in lieu of an award of expenses), the individual discovery abuses represent violations of Rule 37(a)(4)(A), as Textron did not violate any order of the Court. The remedy available to the Court is thus limited to an award of the "reasonable expenses incurred in making the motion, including attorneys' fees." FED.R.CIV.P. 37(a)(4)(A).

However, the fact that the Court did not find bad faith does not minimize the wrongheadedness of the conduct of Textron and its counsel or suggest lenience in the imposition of the Rule-delineated sanctions. The Court recognizes there is an unquantifiable but real prejudice to plaintiff in the motions practice that Textron's conduct necessitated and the litigation disadvantages of the delayed and staged receipt of discovery that was its consequence. For example, depositions are taken without the benefit of later received discovery. That later received discovery might have eliminated whole areas of inquiry or suggested entirely different questioning at deposition. In that situation, a lawyer is faced with the dilemma of whether to spend the time and expense to seek another deposition session or "to make do." Or, belatedly received information may impact an expert's opinion, requiring additional analysis and a further report and even a further deposition.

Textron argues that its (costly) compliance with the Court's May 20 Order is "punishment" enough. The Court disagrees. A significant sanction award is crucial to vindicate the important principles of fair play in the largely private world of civil discovery. In complex litigation such as this, cases are shaped, if not won or lost, in the discovery phase. * * * The integrity of the discovery process rests on the faithfulness of parties and counsel to the rules—both the spirit and the letter. * * *

VII. CONCLUSION

For all these reasons, the Court imposes a monetary sanction of $37,258.39 jointly and severally against Andrew Gendron of Goodell, DeVries, Leech and Gray and Textron, Inc.[24] Mr. Thomas M. Goss is jointly and severally liable with Mr. Gendron and Textron for $4,206.24 of that $37,258.39, which are the fees and costs associated with the motion to determine the sufficiency of answers and objections to requests for admission.

* * *

Points for Discussion

a. Over-Discovery and Stonewalling

It is difficult to convey in the context of a law school classroom the degree to which many litigants and their counsel engage in counterproductive and obstructionist tactics during the discovery process. To appreciate this phenomenon, it is important to understand the dynamics of modern litigation. Generally speaking, the vast majority of cases do not proceed to trial but rather are resolved through pretrial dismissals, summary judgment, or through settlement. From the time a case is filed through its resolution by one of these means, time and effort—in more complicated cases—can be expended principally on a lengthy and costly discovery process. Often, this can become a war of attrition where some defendants prefer an extended pretrial phase during which maximum cost is inflicted on their opponents, all in the hopes of nudging them towards giving up on a trial in favor of settling the matter. Part of inflicting expense on the other side is *over-discovery*: Making discovery requests that fall within the scope of discovery but solicit material that is not really of any great interest to the requesting party. Because the responding party must pay for the cost of locating, reviewing, and producing material to the requesting party, its expenses can quickly become prohibitive in relation to the value of its claim.

---

[24] While the Court would have preferred to award the expenses against the firm and its client, the language of Rules 37 and 26 does not permit that. Unlike FED.R.CIV.P. 11 which specifically authorizes the imposition of the sanction on the law firm, in addition to or in lieu of the individual lawyer, neither Rule 37 nor Rule 26 contains such a specific authorization. In light of that fact and the precedent of *Pavelic & LeFlore v. Marvel Entertainment Group*, 493 U.S. 120 (1989), this Court is constrained to award the expenses against the specific lawyers representing Textron and/or Textron itself.

Coupled with such burdensome requests, defendants who would rather delay the arrival of judgment day than hasten its arrival by offering full cooperation inevitably turn to the practice of *stonewalling* by delaying the production of responsive material as long as possible without attracting the ire of the court.

Make the Connection

The ethical questions that arise in the context of making and responding to discovery requests—including how you should balance your duty of zealous advocacy on behalf of your client with a duty to avoid needless over-discovery or stonewalling—may be covered in a **Professional Responsibility** course.

Consider the ethics of these tactics. Isn't it counsel's obligation to request all relevant material and then determine whether it will be helpful to the case rather than trim discovery requests out of a concern for the cost it will impose on one's adversary? Can counsel legitimately request information but quietly relish in the fact that it will cost the responding party dearly to comply with the request? Is counsel obligated to manage the pace and sequence of a client's production in response to discovery requests in a manner that is to their client's advantage rather than to the advantage of the client's adversary?

b. Dump-Truck Tactics

A related approach to causing delay, expense, and general aggravation for one's adversaries through over-discovery or stonewalling is to produce massive amounts of information in response to a discovery request with critical or even harmful information buried deep within it. The idea is that the requesting party will have to spend large amounts of money paying

Take Note!

Keep in mind that Rule 34(b) requires that documents be produced "as they are kept in the usual course of business" or organized according to the categories in the document request. Do you think that this requirement can effectively prevent dump-truck tactics?

attorneys to review the material carefully, a task that will take a long time and one that the producing party might hope will be insufficiently diligent to locate the problematic document. Are such "dump-truck" or "needle-in-the-haystack" tactics ethical? If your client receives an extremely broad document request, are you permitted to produce only a narrow set of documents in response to avoid overburden-

Practice Pointer

To avoid getting hit with dump-truck tactics, carefully tailor your discovery request so that you are only getting information that you are truly interested in to build your case. Be careful, however, to avoid being too narrow; if you fail to ask for something important, you won't get it.

ing your adversary with too many documents or are you obligated to produce everything covered by the request? If the answer is the latter, then whose fault is it if a requesting party gets overwhelmed with too many documents?

---

2. Preservation Obligations & Spoliation

In order for discovery to work, discoverable information in the possession of the parties must be available and preserved for the litigation. Clearly, if parties were free to destroy harmful documents once litigation initiated, that would frustrate the effort of the court to resolve the dispute on the merits. To forestall this possibility, the courts have devised a preservation obligation that binds parties once they have notice of a dispute that is in litigation or likely to result in litigation.

Although the duty to preserve information relevant to pending litigation has been in place for some time, the advent of electronically stored information and the accompanying practice of frequently deleting or overwriting such information as a standard element of a business's information management policies has resulted in the issue of preservation (and the related issue of spoliation) taking center stage in contemporary litigation. In this section, we will review how the Federal Rules and the courts have addressed the new challenges pertaining to preservation and spoliation that massive amounts of ESI have introduced into the discovery process.

Rimkus Consulting Group, Inc. v. Cammarata

U.S. District Court for the Southern District of Texas
688 F. Supp. 2d 598 (S.D. Tex. 2010)

LEE H. ROSENTHAL, DISTRICT JUDGE.

Spoliation of evidence—particularly of electronically stored information—has assumed a level of importance in litigation that raises grave concerns. * * * Much of the recent case law on sanctions for spoliation has focused on failures by litigants and their lawyers to take adequate steps to preserve and collect information in discovery. The spoliation allegations in the present case are different. They are allegations of willful misconduct: the intentional destruction of emails

> **FYI**
>
> At the time of this opinion, its author, Judge Rosenthal, was serving as the Chair of the Judicial Conference Committee on Rules of Practice and Procedure, also known as the Standing Committee. This committee oversees and coordinates the promulgation and amendment of the federal civil, criminal, evidence, bankruptcy, and appellate rules. Prior to serving in that capacity, Judge Rosenthal was the Chair of the Advisory Committee on Civil Rules, the committee directly charged with developing and amending the Federal Rules of Civil Procedure.

and other electronic information at a time when they were known to be relevant to anticipated or pending litigation. * * * The allegations include that * * * the defendants concealed and delayed providing information in discovery that would have revealed their spoliation. The case law recognizes that such conduct is harmful in ways that extend beyond the parties' interests and can justify severe sanctions.

* * *

I. The Pending Motions

In November 2006, Rimkus Consulting Group, Inc. ("Rimkus") was sued in Louisiana state court by Nickie G. Cammarata and Gary Bell, who had just resigned from the Rimkus office in Louisiana. Cammarata, Bell, and other ex-Rimkus employees had begun a new company, U.S. Forensic, L.L.C., to compete with Rimkus in offering investigative and forensic engineering services primarily for insurance disputes and litigation. In the Louisiana suit, Cammarata and Bell sought a declaratory judgment that the forum-selection, choice-of-law, noncompetition, and nonsolicitation provisions in agreements they had signed with Rimkus were unenforceable. In January and February 2007, Rimkus sued Cammarata and Bell in separate suits in Texas, alleging that they breached the noncompetition and nonsolicitation covenants in their written employment agreements and that they used Rimkus's trade secrets and proprietary information in setting up and operating U.S. Forensic. U.S. Forensic is a defendant in the *Cammarata* case. The Texas *Cammarata* and *Bell* cases were consolidated in this court.

* * * Rimkus moves for sanctions against the defendants and their counsel and asks that they be held in contempt. Rimkus alleges that the defendants and their counsel "conspiratorially engaged" in "wholesale discovery abuse" by destroying evidence, failing to preserve evidence after a duty to do so had arisen, lying under oath, failing to comply with court orders, and significantly delaying or failing to produce requested discovery. Rimkus asks this court to strike the defendants' pleadings and to enter a default judgment against them or give an adverse inference jury instruction. Rimkus also seeks monetary sanctions in the form of the costs and attorneys' fees it incurred because of the defendants' discovery abuses.

In response, the defendants acknowledge that they did not preserve "some arguably relevant emails" but argue that Rimkus cannot show prejudice because the missing emails "would be merely cumulative of the evidence already produced." * * *

* * *

II. THE FRAMEWORK FOR ANALYZING SPOLIATION ALLEGATIONS

In her recent opinion in *Pension Committee of the University of Montreal Pension Plan v. Banc of America Securities, LLC*, 2010 WL 184312 (S.D.N.Y. Jan.15, 2010), Judge Scheindlin has again done the courts a great service by laying out a careful analysis of spoliation and sanctions issues in electronic discovery. The focus of *Pension Committee* was on when negligent failures to preserve, collect, and produce documents—including electronically stored information—in discovery may justify the severe sanction of a form of adverse inference instruction. Unlike *Pension Committee*, the present case does not involve allegations of negligence in electronic discovery. Instead, this case involves allegations of intentional destruction of electronically stored evidence. But there are some common analytical issues between this case and *Pension Committee* that deserve brief discussion.

A. The Source of Authority to Impose Sanctions for Loss of Evidence

Allegations of spoliation, including the destruction of evidence in pending or reasonably foreseeable litigation, are addressed in federal courts through the inherent power to regulate the litigation process if the conduct occurs before a case is filed or if, for another reason, there is no statute or rule that adequately addresses the conduct. *See Chambers v. NASCO, Inc.*, 501 U.S. 32, 43–46 (1991). If an applicable statute or rule can adequately sanction the conduct, that statute or rule should ordinarily be applied, with its attendant limits, rather than a more flexible or expansive "inherent power." *Chambers*, 501 U.S. at 50.

* * *

Rule 37(b)(2)(A) provides:

> If a party or a party's officer, director, or managing agent—or a witness designated under Rule 30(b)(6) or 31(a)(4)—fails to obey an order to provide or permit discovery, including an order under Rule 26(f), 35, or 37(a), the court where the action is pending may issue further just orders. * * *

FED. R. CIV. P. 37(b)(2)(A). In addition, a court has statutory authority to impose costs, expenses, and attorneys' fees on "any attorney . . . who so multiplies the proceedings in any case unreasonably and vexatiously." 28 U.S.C. § 1927.

* * *

The alleged spoliation and proposed sanctions in this case implicate the court's inherent authority, including for spoliation occurring before this case was filed or before discovery orders were entered and <u>Rule 37</u>, for failures to comply with discovery orders.

> **FYI**
>
> Judge Rosenthal is relying on the court's inherent authority because at the time the Rules did not address sanctions for breaches of the duty to preserve information relevant to anticipated litigation. Under an amendment to Rule 37(e) that took effect on December 1, 2015, the Rules explicitly deal with this issue. Rule 37(e) will be discussed in the Points for Discussion following this case.

B. When Deletion Can Become Spoliation

Spoliation is the destruction or the significant and meaningful alteration of evidence. Electronically stored information is routinely deleted or altered and affirmative steps are often required to preserve it. Such deletions, alterations, and losses cannot be spoliation unless there is a duty to preserve the information, a culpable breach of that duty, and resulting prejudice.

Generally, the duty to preserve arises when a party " 'has notice that the evidence is relevant to litigation or . . . should have known that the evidence may be relevant to future litigation.' " Generally, the duty to preserve extends to documents or tangible things (defined by <u>Federal Rule of Civil Procedure 34</u>) by or to individuals "likely to have discoverable information that the disclosing party may use to support its claims or defenses." *See, e.g., <u>Zubulake IV, 220 F.R.D. at 217–18</u>* (footnotes omitted).

* * *

C. Culpability

As a general rule, in this circuit, the severe sanctions of granting default judgment, striking pleadings, or giving adverse inference instructions may not be imposed unless there is evidence of "bad faith." " 'Mere negligence is not enough' to warrant an instruction on spoliation." <u>*Russell v. Univ. of Tex. of Permian Basin,* 234 F. App'x 195, 208 (5th Cir. 2007)</u> (unpublished) (quoting <u>*Vick v. Tex. Employment Comm'n,* 514 F.2d 734, 737 (5th Cir. 1975)</u>.

Other circuits have also held negligence insufficient for an adverse inference instruction. The Eleventh Circuit has held that bad faith is required for an adverse inference instruction. The Seventh, Eighth, Tenth, and D.C. Circuits also appear to require bad faith. The First, Fourth, and Ninth Circuits hold that bad faith is not essential to imposing severe sanctions if there is severe prejudice, although the cases often emphasize the presence of bad faith. In the Third Circuit, the courts balance the degree of fault and prejudice.

The court in *Pension Committee* imposed a form of adverse inference instruction based on a finding of gross negligence in preserving information and in collecting it in discovery. The court applied case law in the Second Circuit, including the language in <u>Residential Funding Corp. v. DeGeorge Financial Corp., 306 F.3d 99, 108 (2d Cir. 2002)</u>, stating that "[t]he sanction of an adverse inference may be appropriate in some cases involving the negligent destruction of evidence because each party should bear the risk of its own negligence." That language has been read to allow severe sanctions for negligent destruction of evidence. In the Fifth Circuit and others, negligent as opposed to intentional, "bad faith" destruction of evidence is not sufficient to give an adverse inference instruction and may not relieve the party seeking discovery of the need to show that missing documents are relevant and their loss prejudicial. The circuit differences in the level of culpability necessary for an adverse inference instruction limit the applicability of the *Pension Committee* approach. And to the extent sanctions are based on inherent power, the Supreme Court's decision in *Chambers* may also require a degree of culpability greater than negligence.

Take Note!

Notice that Judge Rosenthal is differing with Judge Scheindlin's conclusions in *Pension Committee* by indicating that culpability greater than negligence is required for an adverse inference instruction. Do you understand the basis for her disagreement?

D. Relevance and Prejudice: The Burden of Proof

It is well established that a party seeking the sanction of an adverse inference instruction based on spoliation of evidence must establish that: (1) the party with control over the evidence had an obligation to preserve it at the time it was destroyed; (2) the evidence was destroyed with a culpable state of mind; and (3) the destroyed evidence was "relevant" to the party's claim or defense such that a reasonable trier of fact could find that it would support that claim or defense. *See* <u>Zubulake v. UBS Warburg LLC (Zubulake IV), 220 F.R.D. 212, 220 (S.D.N.Y. 2003)</u>. The "relevance" and "prejudice" factors of the adverse inference analysis are often broken down into three subparts: "(1) whether the evidence is relevant to the lawsuit; (2) whether the evidence would have supported the inference sought; and (3) whether the nondestroying party has suffered prejudice from the destruction of the evidence." * * *

* * *

In *Pension Committee,* the court followed the approach that even for severe sanctions, relevance and prejudice may be presumed when the spoliating party acts in a grossly negligent manner. * * * When the level of culpability is "mere" negligence, the presumption of relevance and prejudice is not available; the *Pension Committee* court imposed a limited burden on the innocent party to present some extrinsic evidence.

The Fifth Circuit has not explicitly addressed whether even bad-faith destruction of evidence allows a court to presume that the destroyed evidence was relevant or its loss prejudicial. Case law in the Fifth Circuit indicates that an adverse inference instruction is not proper unless there is a showing that the spoliated evidence would have been relevant. * * * In the present case, the party seeking sanctions for deleting emails after a duty to preserve had arisen presented evidence of their contents. The evidence included some recovered deleted emails and circumstantial evidence and deposition testimony relating to the unrecovered records. There is neither a factual nor legal basis, nor need, to rely on a presumption of relevance or prejudice.

E. Remedies: Adverse Inference Instructions

Courts agree that a willful or intentional destruction of evidence to prevent its use in litigation can justify severe sanctions. Courts also agree that the severity of a sanction for failing to preserve when a duty to do so has arisen must be proportionate to the culpability involved and the prejudice that results. Such a sanction should be no harsher than necessary to respond to the need to punish or deter and to address the impact on discovery. * * * A measure of the appropriateness of a sanction is whether it "restore[s] the prejudiced party to the same position he would have been in absent the wrongful destruction of evidence by the opposing party." Extreme sanctions—dismissal or default—have been upheld when "the spoliator's conduct was so egregious as to amount to a forfeiture of his claim" and "the effect of the spoliator's conduct was so prejudicial that it substantially denied the defendant the ability to defend the claim."

When a party is prejudiced, but not irreparably, from the loss of evidence that was destroyed with a high degree of culpability, a harsh but less extreme sanction than dismissal or default is to permit the fact finder to presume that the destroyed evidence was prejudicial. * * *

* * *

IV. RIMKUS'S MOTION FOR SANCTIONS AND CONTEMPT

A. The Parties' Contentions

Rimkus argues that the defendants intentionally deleted emails "in direct contravention of their legal duty to preserve electronically stored information when they anticipated they would be engaged in litigation with Rimkus." Rimkus contends that the duty to preserve arose before November 2006, when Bell, Cammarata, and DeHarde planned to sue Rimkus in Louisiana. Rimkus points to the November 11, 2006 email that Bell sent to Cammarata, DeHarde, and Janowsky stating that they needed to file suit in Louisiana and "serve [Rimkus] on Monday to prevent them from filing in Texas." Rimkus argues that the defendants understood that their Louisiana suit seeking to invalidate the noncompetition and nonsolicitation clauses would be met with a countersuit seeking to enforce the provisions as well as the contractual and common-law duty not to misappropriate propriety and confidential information.

Rimkus alleges that the defendants "scheme[d]" to destroy evidence showing the extent to which they took confidential information from Rimkus to use to set up, operate, and solicit business for U.S. Forensic. The scheme, and the attempt to conceal it, included deleting emails showing that the defendants took information from Rimkus and used it for U.S. Forensic, donating or throwing away laptop computers from which such emails might be recovered, and lying about personal email accounts. According to Rimkus, the cover-up unraveled when DeHarde testified about the defendants' agreement to delete all emails more than two weeks old. Rimkus also points to the April 2008 email Gary Bell sent himself containing attachments with confidential Rimkus customer-contact information and the reports Cammarata produced containing language and data copied from Rimkus. Rimkus argues that these documents, withheld from production until recently, combined with Cammarata's and Bell's prior testimony, provide evidence of intentional, bad-faith efforts to withhold or destroy relevant information.

As a sanction for spoliation, Rimkus asks this court to strike the defendants' pleadings and enter a default judgment or, in the alternative, to give an adverse inference jury instruction at trial. Rimkus also seeks reimbursement of the costs and fees it incurred in discovering or attempting to discover spoliated evidence and in moving for sanctions.

* * *

[1.] The Duty to Preserve

The record shows that no later than November 11, 2006, when the defendants were about to "preemptively" sue Rimkus, they had an obligation to preserve documents and information—including electronically stored information—relevant to these disputes. The disputes included whether Bell breached the fiduciary duty he owed Rimkus as an officer, whether Bell or Cammarata breached enforceable obligations under the noncompete and nonsolicitation provisions in the parties' contracts, and whether Bell or Cammarata breached contractual or common-law duties not to take or use Rimkus's confidential and proprietary information.

Bell sought the advice of counsel before leaving Rimkus. The November 11, 2006 email from Bell to Cammarata, DeHarde, and Janowsky discussing the final steps of the plan to sue Rimkus in Louisiana to challenge the noncompete and nonsolicitation provisions shows that the defendants knew that they would be suing Rimkus within days. The duty to preserve electronically stored information and documents relevant to that suit and reasonably anticipated related litigation was triggered no later than November 11, 2006.

The defendants' argument that their preservation obligation was limited to documents or emails related to breach of fiduciary obligation claims against Bell is unpersuasive. Bell, Cammarata, and DeHarde sued Rimkus in Louisiana seeking a declaratory judgment that the noncompetition and nonsolicitation clauses were unenforceable so that they could operate U.S. Forensic to compete with Rimkus. It was reasonable for Bell and Cammarata to anticipate that Rimkus would seek to enforce those contractual provisions as to all the U.S. Forensic employees who left Rimkus, as well as the contractual and common-law duty not to disclose Rimkus's confidential and proprietary information. Emails and attachments and other documents relating to U.S. Forensic and its related company, to soliciting Rimkus clients or employees, and to obtaining or using Rimkus information were subject to a preservation obligation. Such records were relevant to the claims involved in the Louisiana state court action that Cammarata, Bell, and DeHarde filed and to the reasonably anticipated claims that Rimkus would file, and involved the key players in the parties' litigation.

Rule 37(e), which precludes sanctions if the loss of the information arises from the routine operation of the party's computer system, operated in good faith, does not apply here. The evidence in the record shows that the defendants and other U.S. Forensic founders did not have emails deleted through the routine, good-faith operation of the U.S. Forensic computer system. DeHarde testified that he, Bell, Cammarata, and Janowsky decided on a "policy" of deleting emails more than two weeks old. Putting aside for the moment other evidence in the record inconsistent with this testimony, a policy put into place after a duty to preserve had arisen, that applies almost exclusively to emails subject to that duty to preserve, is not a routine, good-faith operation of a computer system. Moreover, the evidence shows that the founders of U.S. Forensic manually and selectively deleted emails, after the duty to preserve arose. The selective, manual deletions continued well after Rimkus filed suit in January and February 2007.

Despite the fact that the founders of U.S. Forensic had sought and obtained legal advice on many aspects of their departure from Rimkus and their formation and operation of the competing business, they made *no* effort to preserve relevant documents, even after the Louisiana and Texas suits had been filed. To the contrary, the evidence shows affirmative steps to delete potentially relevant documents. Even assuming that there was an email destruction policy as DeHarde testified, it was selectively implemented. The deleted documents included emails and attachments relevant to the disputes with Rimkus—the emails and attachments showing what information U.S. Forensic's founders took from Rimkus to use in the competing business, including to solicit business from Rimkus clients, and how they solicited those clients.

The record shows that the electronically stored information that the defendants deleted or destroyed after the duty to preserve arose was relevant to the issues involving both Bell and Cammarata, not limited to a breach of fiduciary claim against Bell. The deleted emails and attachments related not only to setting up U.S. Forensic but also to obtaining information from Rimkus, including copyrighted materials, financial documents, and customer lists; using at least some of that information to operate U.S. Forensic in competition with Rimkus; and soliciting business for U.S. Forensic. The evidence shows that by deleting emails relating to forming U.S. Forensic and to using information from Rimkus for U.S. Forensic, by failing to preserve such emails, and by giving away or destroying laptops with such emails, the defendants destroyed potentially relevant evidence.

[2.] The Degree of Culpability

Destruction or deletion of information subject to a preservation obligation is not sufficient for sanctions. Bad faith is required. A severe sanction such as a default judgment or an adverse inference instruction requires bad faith and prejudice.

The defendants' proffered reasons and explanations for deleting or destroying the emails and attachments are inconsistent and lack record support. Bell testified that he deleted emails for "space concerns," Janowsky testified that he deleted emails on a weekly basis because he got a lot of emails and they "fill up [his] box," and DeHarde testified in his first deposition that he deleted emails on an ad hoc basis because he was concerned about storage capacity in his in-box. The defendants also asserted that they deleted emails about preparations to form U.S. Forensic for fear of retaliation by Rimkus if they ended up staying on at Rimkus. Allen Bostick, the IT consultant, testified that lack of space on U.S. Forensic's server and external hard drives did not become an issue until late 2007, well after this litigation began. The fact that DeHarde did not reveal the "policy" of deleting all emails more than two weeks old until after Rimkus was able to subpoena DeHarde's Yahoo! account is another reason for questioning the truthfulness of this explanation. Fear of retaliation by Rimkus might explain the deletions that occurred before the defendants resigned, but not after.

Some of the emails the defendants deleted were obtained from a Rule 45 subpoena issued to one of the internet service providers, Homestead. These emails show the defendants making preparations to form U.S. Forensic in September, October, and November 2006, and soliciting clients with whom they worked while at Rimkus in late November and early December 2006. Other emails, obtained not from the defendants but through forensic analysis of the laptop Bell used at Rimkus, show that Bell downloaded and transmitted financial spreadsheets for specific Rimkus offices *after* his resignation. Emails obtained from Homestead show that Cammarata forwarded language in Rimkus reports from his home email account to his U.S. Forensic email account; Cammarata admitted giving the language from a Rimkus report to a U.S. Forensic Associates engineer for use on a project. Still another email from Bell to himself, which the defendants did not originally produce with the attachments, shows that Bell was in possession of Rimkus client-contact information in April 2008.

The evidence that the defendants knew about the litigation with Rimkus when they deleted the emails; the inconsistencies in the explanations for deleting the emails; the failure to disclose information about personal email accounts that were later revealed as having been used to obtain and disseminate information from Rimkus; and the fact that some of the emails reveal what the defendants had previously denied—that they took information from Rimkus and used at least some of it in competing with Rimkus—support the conclusion that there is sufficient evidence for a reasonable jury to find that the defendants intentionally and in bad faith deleted emails relevant to setting up and operating U.S. Forensic, to obtaining information from Rimkus and using it for U.S. Forensic, and to soliciting Rimkus clients, to prevent the use of these emails in litigation in Louisiana or Texas.

[3.] Relevance and Prejudice

Despite the evidence of spoliation and efforts to conceal it, the record also shows that Rimkus was able to obtain a significant amount of evidence. * * * Between the records the defendants did produce, the deleted records Rimkus obtained from other sources, and other evidence of the contents of deleted lost records, Rimkus has extensive evidence it can present. The evidence of the contents of the lost records shows that some would have been favorable to Rimkus. There is prejudice to Rimkus, but it is far from irreparable. Rimkus's demand that this court strike the defendants' pleadings and enter a default judgment is not appropriate. The sanction of dismissal or default judgment is appropriate only if the spoliation or destruction of evidence resulted in "irreparable prejudice" and no lesser sanction would suffice.

Although a terminating sanction is not appropriate, a lesser sanction of a form of adverse inference instruction is warranted to level the evidentiary playing field and sanction the improper conduct. The evidence of the contents of the deleted emails and attachments shows that deleted and unrecoverable emails and attachments were relevant and that some would have been helpful to Rimkus. * * * The emails that have been recovered by Rimkus, through great effort and expense, include some that support Rimkus's claims, contradict testimony the defendants gave, and are unfavorable to the defendants. Rimkus has shown that it has been prejudiced by the inability to obtain the deleted emails for use in the litigation. To level the evidentiary playing field and to sanction the defendants' bad-faith conduct, Rimkus is entitled to a form of adverse inference instruction with respect to deleted emails.

At the same time, it is important that Rimkus has extensive evidence to use in this case. And some of the emails that the defendants deleted and that were later recovered are *consistent* with their positions in this lawsuit and *helpful* to their defense. * * *

Given this record, it is appropriate to allow the jury to hear the evidence about the deletion of emails and attachments and about discovery responses that concealed and delayed revealing the deletions. The jury will receive an instruction that in and after November 2006, the defendants had a duty to preserve emails and other information they knew to be relevant to anticipated and pending litigation. If the jury finds that the defendants deleted emails to prevent their use in litigation with Rimkus, the jury will be instructed that it may, but is not required to, infer that the content of the deleted lost emails would have been unfavorable to the defendants. In making this determination, the jury is to consider the evidence about the conduct of the defendants in deleting emails after the duty to preserve had arisen and the evidence about the content of the deleted emails that cannot be recovered.

The record also supports the sanction of requiring the defendants to pay Rimkus the reasonable costs and attorneys' fees required to identify and respond to the spoliation. The defendants agree that this sanction is appropriate. Rimkus has spent considerable time and money attempting to determine the existence and extent of the spoliation, hampered by the defendants' inconsistent and untruthful answers to questions about internet accounts and retention and destruction practices. The defendants failed to produce documents in compliance with court orders. Rimkus also expended significant time and effort to obtain some of the deleted emails and attachments.

* * *

E. Conclusion

There is evidence in the record showing that the defendants intentionally deleted emails after a duty to preserve had clearly arisen. There is evidence in the record showing that at least some of this lost evidence would have been relevant and favorable to Rimkus's case. The loss of the evidence prejudiced Rimkus, though not irreparably. These failures have imposed significant costs on the parties and the court. Sanctions are appropriate. Accordingly, the court will allow the jury to hear the evidence of the defendants' deletion of emails and attachments, and inconsistent testimony about the emails, the concealment of email accounts, and the delays in producing records and information sought in discovery. The jury will be instructed that if it decides that the defendants intentionally deleted emails to prevent their use in litigation against Rimkus, the jury may, but need not, infer that the deleted emails that cannot be produced would have been adverse to the defendants. Rimkus is also entitled to an award of attorneys' fees and costs reasonably incurred in investigating the spoliation, obtaining emails from third-party subpoenas, taking additional depositions of Cammarata and Bell, and moving for sanctions based on the deleted emails and on Bell's false testimony.

Points for Discussion

a. The Common Law Duty to Preserve & Spoliation

The duty to preserve information because it is potentially relevant to pending or future litigation is a common law duty that courts have devised in aid of the need to encourage litigants to retain material that their adversaries will have a right to discover as the case unfolds. A breach of this duty is referred to as **spoliation**. As noted in *Rimkus Consulting*, this duty attaches once a party receives notice of a dispute or can reasonably anticipate future litigation. When can a party be expected to anticipate future litigation?

An example comes from <u>*Zubulake v. UBS Warburg L.L.C.* ("*Zubulake IV*"), 220 F.R.D. 212 (S.D.N.Y. 2003)</u>, in which Judge Scheindlin determined that the "trigger date" for UBS's duty to preserve was April of 2001—four months before Zubulake filed her EEOC complaint—because emails showed and deposition testimony confirmed that in April of 2001 Zubulake's co-workers were concerned about the possibility that Zubulake might sue. <u>*Id.* at 216–17</u>. What other types of evidence might be relevant to determining whether a party should have reasonably anticipated litigation sufficient to trigger a preservation obligation? *See, e.g.,* <u>*In re Napster, Inc. Copyright Litig.,* 462 F. Supp. 2d 1060, 1067–70 (N.D. Cal. 2006)</u> (explaining that one of the defendants should have known that litigation was probable once he was threatened with a lawsuit in the event of his noncompliance with an existing injunction).

Food for Thought

Should prospective litigants' duty to preserve be solely a matter of common law? The lack of a federal rule or statute that addresses this issue undermines uniformity and predictability, as prospective litigants are subject to varying standards for anticipating litigation across the circuits. Would it be possible to craft a Federal Rule that addresses the trigger for parties' preservation obligations? *See* A. Benjamin Spencer, *The Preservation Obligation: Regulating and Sanctioning Pre-Litigation Spoliation in Federal Court,* 79 FORDHAM L. REV. 2005 (2011) (proposing amendments to the Federal Rules to address pre-litigation preservation obligations).

Once a party reasonably anticipates litigation, a prudent practice is to impose a *litigation hold*, which is a notification from an attorney to a person or entity in possession of material potentially relevant to anticipated or pending litigation, giving instructions to preserve that material so that it can be available for discovery.

Although the duty to preserve ordinarily arises as a matter of common law, courts retain inherent authority to issue orders to preserve documents once litigation ensues. *See, e.g.,* <u>*Am. LegalNet, Inc. v. Davis,* 673 F. Supp. 2d 1063, 1071 (C.D. Cal. 2013)</u> ("Federal courts have the implied or inherent power to issue preservation orders as part of their general authority to manage their own affairs so as to achieve the orderly and expeditious disposition of cases.") (citation and internal quotation marks omitted). Further, litigants are encouraged to develop discovery plans that address preservation and courts are encouraged to include matters pertaining to preservation in their Rule 16 scheduling orders. *See* FED. R. CIV. P. 26(f)(3)(C); FED. R. CIV. P. 16(b)(3)(B)(iii).

b. Statutory Duties to Preserve

In addition to the common law duty to preserve, many statutes and regulations impose legal obligations to preserve certain documents or materials. *See, e.g.*, 17 C.F.R. § 240.17a–4(b)(4) ("Every . . . broker and dealer . . . shall preserve for a period of not less than three years, the first two years in an easily accessible place, . . . [o]riginals of all communications received and copies of all communications sent . . . by the member, broker or dealer (including inter-office memoranda and communications) relating to its business as such . . . ."); *King Lincoln Bronzeville Neighborhood Ass'n v. Blackwell*, 448 F. Supp. 2d 876, 878 (S.D. Ohio 2006) ("Ohio's statutory scheme provides for the retention and disposition of ballots following elections." (citing OHIO REV. CODE § 3505.31)). Violations of such statutory duties to preserve may carry their own penalties under their respective statutes.

Should the violation of a duty to preserve imposed by rule or statute be able to serve as the basis for a finding of spoliation in a pending lawsuit? Although some courts have held that violations of statutory duties give rise to an inference of spoliation, *see, e.g.*, *Latimore v. Citibank Fed. Sav. Bank*, 151 F.3d 712, 716 (7th Cir. 1998) ("The violation of a record-retention regulation creates a presumption that the missing record contained evidence adverse to the violator."), the better view seems to be that a breach of a statutory or rule-based duty to preserve may only be the basis for a spoliation finding when "the party seeking the inference [is] a

Practice Pointer

Producing ESI can be particularly challenging for large corporations possessed of thousands of backup tapes sprawled across many different storage facilities. Counsel must be exceedingly diligent and thorough in attempting to track down all possibly relevant material and see to their preservation. The failure to do so, and the failure to be candid with the court and one's adversary regarding the difficulties faced in such efforts, can lead to fairly substantial and cataclysmic consequences for counsel and the producing party. *See, e.g.*, *Coleman Holdings, Inc. v. Morgan Stanley & Co.*, 2005 WL 679071 (Fla. Cir. Ct. Mar. 1, 2005) (imposing sanctions including an adverse inference instruction, a shifting of the burden of proof to the defendant, and costs); *Coleman Holdings, Inc. v. Morgan Stanley & Co.*, 2005 WL 674885 (Fla. Cir. Ct. Mar. 23, 2005) (entering a default judgment against the defendant as sanctions for the deliberate and willful failure to comply with discovery orders and come clean about production challenges and deficiencies).

member of the general class of persons that the regulatory agency sought to protect in promulgating the rule," *Byrnie v. Town of Cromwell*, 243 F.3d 93, 109 (2d Cir. 2001). Which approach do you think is more sound? For a comprehensive review of duties to preserve and spoliation, see Steffen Nolte, *The Spoliation Tort: An Approach to Underlying Principles*, 26 St. Mary's L.J. 351 (1995).

c. Sanctions for Spoliation and Non-Production

The sanctioning authority of courts can vary depending on the circumstances of the spoliation; specifically, whether the spoliation is of tangible things or electronically stored information and whether the spoliation occurs in violation of a court order to preserve material or in the absence of such an order.

A court may impose sanctions under Rule 37(b) when a party spoliates evidence in violation of a court order. *See, e.g., John B. Hull, Inc. v. Waterbury Petroleum Prods., Inc.*, 845 F.2d 1172, 1176 (2d Cir. 1988). Such sanctions range from adverse inference instructions, prohibiting the offending party from supporting or opposing designated claims or defenses, striking pleadings, dismissing the action, or entering default judgment. FED. R. CIV. P. 37(b)(2)(A). In the absence of a court order, when it turns out that a litigant failed to preserve tangible documents or things relevant to reasonably anticipated litigation, courts have inherent authority to impose sanctions for spoliation. *Silvestri v. Gen. Motors Corp.*, 271 F.3d 583, 590 (4th Cir. 2001) ("The right to impose sanctions for spoliation arises from a court's inherent power to control the judicial process and litigation . . . ."). This power is supposed to be limited to what is necessary to redress conduct that impairs the judicial process, with sanctions being confined to those that "serve the prophylactic, punitive, and remedial rationales underlying the spoliation doctrine." *Id.* Courts exercising this authority must find some degree of fault in the party to be sanctioned, *see id.*, and the ultimate sanction of dismissal "should be avoided if a lesser sanction will perform the necessary function." *Id.*

In determining the appropriate type of sanctions to impose for the non-production of evidence due to a breach of the duty to preserve, courts typically exercise their discretion in the following manner:

> Appropriate sanctions should (1) deter the parties from engaging in spoliation; (2) place the risk of an erroneous judgment on the party who wrongfully created the risk; and (3) restore the prejudiced party to the same position it would have been in absent the wrongful destruction of evidence by the opposing party.
>
> It is well accepted that a court should always impose the least harsh sanction that can provide an adequate remedy. The choices include—from least harsh to most harsh—further discovery, cost-shifting, fines, special jury instructions, preclusion, and the entry of default judgment or dis-

missal (terminating sanctions). The selection of the appropriate remedy is a delicate matter requiring a great deal of time and attention by a court.

Pension Comm. of Univ. of Montreal Pension Plan v. Banc of Am. Secs., LLC, 685 F. Supp. 2d 456, 469 (S.D.N.Y. 2010) (citations and internal quotation marks omitted).

d. Regulating Preservation and Spoilation Under Rule 37(e)

With regard to the spoliation of electronically stored information, the 2015 amendment to Rule 37 overhauled how courts may respond. The 2006 version of Rule 37(e) was scrapped in favor of the following:

FRCP 37(e). Failure to Make Disclosures or to Cooperate in Discovery; Sanctions.

(e) Failure to Preserve Electronically Stored Information. If electronically stored information that should have been preserved in the anticipation or conduct of litigation is lost because a party failed to take reasonable steps to preserve it, and it cannot be restored or replaced through additional discovery, the court:

(1) upon finding prejudice to another party from loss of the information, may order measures no greater than necessary to cure the prejudice; or

(2) only upon finding that the party acted with the intent to deprive another party of the information's use in the litigation may.

(A) presume that the lost information was unfavorable to the party;

(B) instruct the jury that it may or must presume the information was unfavorable to the party; or

(C) dismiss the action or enter a default judgment.

The amended version of Rule 37(e) expands protection to parties against sanctions for preservation obligation violations in several ways. First, the amendment favors the resort to curative measures by limiting the imposition of sanctions to circumstances in which the spoliating party acted "with the intent to deprive another party of the information's use in the litigation." The amended rule thus would overturn cases like *Residential Funding Corp. v. DeGeorge Fin. Corp.,* 306 F.3d 99 (2d Cir. 2002), and its progeny that treat negligence or gross negligence as sufficient to support sanctions.

Second, when an intent to deprive has not been shown, the innocent party will be required to show prejudice rather than having any prejudice presumed. This would be a departure from those cases that previously had endorsed such presumptions. *See, e.g., Sekisui Am. Corp. v. Hart,* 945 F. Supp. 2d 494, 504–05 (S.D.N.Y. 2013) ("When evidence is destroyed willfully or through gross negligence, prejudice to the innocent party may be presumed because that party is deprived of what the court can assume would have been evidence relevant to the innocent party's claims or defenses.") (citation and internal quotation marks omitted). Is this a good change? Will it be difficult for innocent parties to demonstrate the requisite prejudice if the documents at issue are no longer available? How is a party supposed to make a showing of prejudice when the evidence is now missing? Is this standard tilted too much in favor of spoliating parties?

Finally, amended Rule 37(e) limits its applicability to information losses that result from a failure to "take reasonable steps to preserve it." According to the Committee Note accompanying the amended rule, this limitation should be understood as follows:

> Because the rule calls only for reasonable steps to preserve, it is inapplicable when the loss of information occurs despite the party's reasonable steps to preserve. For example, the information may not be in the party's control. Or information the party has preserved may be destroyed by events outside the party's control — the computer room may be flooded, a "cloud" service may fail, a malign software attack may disrupt a storage system, and so on. Courts may, however, need to assess the extent to which a party knew of and protected against such risks.
>
> Another factor in evaluating the reasonableness of preservation efforts is proportionality. The court should be sensitive to party resources; aggressive preservation efforts can be extremely costly, and parties (including governmental parties) may have limited staff and resources to devote to those efforts.
>
> The precise contours of the "reasonable steps" standard will need to be further refined out as courts interpret and apply the rule.

Go Online

In light of the significant changes that have been made to the discovery rules, you may be interested in learning more about the process through which such amendments are made. The federal civil rulemaking process consists of many levels, beginning with development of the proposal by the Advisory Committee on Civil Rules, followed by approvals by the Committee on Rules of Practice and Procedure (commonly referred to as the "Standing Committee"), the Judicial Conference of the U.S., and the Supreme Court of the United States. After Supreme Court approval, the amendment is sent to Congress, which has until December 1 of that year to enact legislation vetoing it. If that does not happen, the rule amendment takes effect. *See* 28 U.S.C. §§ 2073–2075. This entire process usually takes three years. You can learn more about the rulemaking process by visiting http://www.uscourts.gov/RulesAndPolicies/rules/about-rulemaking.aspx.

e. Document Retention Policies

To keep track of their various preservation obligations, corporations and other entities tend to rely on written document retention policies. Such policies will typically refer to types of information such as tax records, board records, employment records, intellectual property records, contracts, etc., and ascribe appropriate retention periods for each. These periods generally are based upon a mixture of business needs and legal requirements. Comprehensive document retention policies should also provide for the process of destroying information once its retention period has expired and should provide for the suspension of the destruction process when the need to preserve for anticipated litigation arises. Indeed, if a party has a routine document destruction policy, "reasonable steps to preserve" information under Rule 37(e) require that such a policy be suspended so that relevant documents can be preserved. *See* Fed. R. Civ. P. 37(e) advisory committee's note to 2015 amendment ("[T]he routine, good-faith operation of an electronic information system would be a relevant factor for the court to consider in evaluating whether a party failed to take reasonable steps to preserve lost information, although the prospect of litigation may call for reasonable steps to preserve information by intervening in that routine operation."); *see also, e.g.*, *Weitzman v. Maywood, Melrose Park, Broadview School District 89*, 2014 WL 4269074, at *3 (N.D. Ill. Aug. 29, 2014) ("District 89's failure to suspend normal document destruction policies, for closed session board meetings, was a bad faith breach of its discovery obligations.").

Executive Summary

■ **The Scope & Limits of Discovery.** Parties have a right to discovery of all non-privileged information that is relevant to a claim or defense raised in the action. *See* Rule 26(b)(1). Parties may resist unduly burdensome or duplicative discovery requests by seeking a protective order from the court. *See* Rule 26(b)(2) & 26(c).

■ **Not Reasonably Accessible ESI.** Parties are not under an obligation to produce electronically stored information that is not reasonably accessible but they must inform the requesting party that such information is being withheld. *See* Rule 26(b)(2)(B).

■ **Privilege.** Confidential communications between attorneys and clients regarding legal advice are privileged and non-discoverable unless the privilege has been waived. Material withheld on the basis of privilege must be indicated in a document such as a privilege log. *See* Rule 26(b)(5).

■ **Work-Product Protection.** Any material prepared by or for a party in anticipation of litigation is protected by the work-product doctrine and need not be produced (but must be logged) unless the requesting party can demonstrate a substantial need for the information. *See* Rule 26(b)(3).

Major Themes

Keep in mind these themes relevant to the discovery material:

a. *Cooperation*—the rules push parties toward discussing discovery matters early and often. It is better to negotiate discovery protocols initially than to fight endlessly about these matters later before the court.

b. *The ESI Effect*—the rules require attorneys to pay attention to issues that present special challenges for electronically stored information such as data accessibility, production format, privilege protection, and information preservation.

c. *Preservation & Spoliation*—counsel and parties must take extreme care to ensure that relevant material is not destroyed pending litigation or once litigation is reasonably anticipated or they may face harsh sanctions.

d. *Proportionality*—an overarching theme and growing concern is that discovery and its costs remain proportional to the stakes of litigation.

■ **Motions to Compel.** Requesting parties who disagree with the responding party's basis for withholding information may seek a court order compelling the production, after they have conferred with the responding party. *See* Rule 37(a)(3)(A).

■ **Sanctions.** Parties found to have improperly refused to comply with discovery requests or who have otherwise engaged in abusive discovery practices may be sanctioned for their misconduct. *See* Rule 37(b).

■ **Preservation Obligations & Spoliation.** Parties must preserve information relevant to litigation that is pending or reasonably foreseeable. The failure to do so can result in a range of spoliation sanctions. FED. R. CIV. P. 37(e).

For More Information

Students interested in studying discovery further may consult the following resources:

- 8 C. WRIGHT, A. MILLER & R. MARCUS, FED. PRAC. & PROC. § 2001 *et seq.* (3d ed. 2010). (discovery).

- Adam N. Steinman, *The End of an Era? Federal Civil Procedure after the 2015 Amendments*, 66 EMORY L.J. 1 (2016).

- Paul W. Grimm, *Are We Insane? The Quest for Proportionality in the Discovery Rules of The Federal Rules of Civil Procedure*, 36 REV. LITIG. 117 (2017).

Test Your Knowledge

To assess your understanding of the material in this chapter, click here to take a quiz.

CHAPTER NINE

Disposition Without Trial

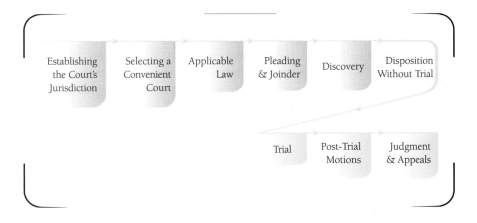

Establishing the Court's Jurisdiction → Selecting a Convenient Court → Applicable Law → Pleading & Joinder → Discovery → Disposition Without Trial → Trial → Post-Trial Motions → Judgment & Appeals

MOST LAW STUDENTS PROBABLY ARRIVE at law school with the idea that the typical consummation of a lawsuit is a trial before a jury that is resolved by a verdict. Many may be surprised to learn that this is hardly the case at all. To the contrary, the vast majority of actions filed in the federal courts are disposed of without trial. For the twelve-month period ending June 30, 2017, out of a total of 298,656 civil cases that were resolved during that period, only 2,752 were disposed of during or after a trial, a trial rate of 0.9%. This compares with a 6.1% trial rate in 1982 and an 11.5% rate in 1962. The decline of trials in our courts is such a stark reality that commentators have dubbed the phenomenon "The Vanishing Trial." *See, e.g.*, Marc Galanter, *The Vanishing Trial: An Examination of Trials and Related Matters in Federal and State Courts*, 1 J. EMPIRICAL LEGAL STUD. 459 (2004).

Go Online

To view the raw data behind these and many other statistics about the federal courts, you can access the Federal Judicial Caseload Statistics (Table C-4) at the U.S. Courts website (www.uscourts.gov/statistics-reports/caseload-statistics-data-tables).

Given the paucity of cases going to trial, it is perhaps now more understandable to the reader why first-year civil procedure courses dedicate most of their time to the pretrial phase of civil litigation. In this chapter, we will turn our attention to the processes through which most cases are resolved, which include defaults, dismissals, summary judgments, and settlements. Each of these mechanisms will be reviewed below.

A. Default & Dismissal

Once a lawsuit is initiated, both plaintiffs and defendants are under an obligation to prosecute and defend the case, meaning that defendants must diligently respond to the complaint and plaintiffs must move forward with the development of their respective cases and pursue an ultimate resolution of their claims by the court. When either side fails to do its part—either by failing to answer a complaint as a defendant or failing to prosecute one's claims as a plaintiff—the Federal Rules provide for a way to terminate the action against the party who has dropped the ball. In this section, we will look at the mechanisms for addressing these issues: default and involuntary dismissal.

1. Default & Default Judgment

As we saw when studying the pleadings material, after the plaintiff files its complaint, the defendant is then obliged to respond to the complaint in some way. Either the defendant can file an answer raising various defenses and admitting or denying the allegations of the complaint, FED. R. CIV .P. 7(a) & 8(b), or the defendant may simply raise certain objections by motion—such as a motion to dismiss for lack of personal jurisdiction or improper venue—before filing an answer to the complaint. FED. R. CIV. P. 12(b). After being served with the summons and complaint, the defendant then has 21 days to serve the responsive pleading, FED. R. CIV. P. 12(a)(1)(A), unless it has waived formal service, in which case the defendant may respond within 60 days (90 days for overseas defendants), FED. R. CIV. P. 4(d)(3). What happens if the defendant fails to respond within the prescribed time or at all? Rule 55 addresses this situation:

Take Note!

Although default and default judgment are generally thought of as risks facing defendants in civil actions, note that plaintiffs facing counterclaims—or any party facing crossclaims or third-party claims—may also be subjected default and default judgment if they fail to defend themselves against the claims asserted against them.

FRCP 55. Default; Default Judgment.

(a) **Entering a Default.** When a party against whom a judgment for affirmative relief is sought has failed to plead or otherwise defend, and that failure is shown by affidavit or otherwise, the clerk must enter the party's default.

(b) **Entering a Default Judgment.**

(1) *By the Clerk.* If the plaintiff's claim is for a sum certain or a sum that can be made certain by computation, the clerk—on the plaintiff's request, with an affidavit showing the amount due—must enter judgment for that amount and costs against a defendant who has been defaulted for not appearing and who is neither a minor nor an incompetent person.

(2) *By the Court.* In all other cases, the party must apply to the court for a default judgment. A default judgment may be entered against a minor or incompetent person only if represented by a general guardian, conservator, or other like fiduciary who has appeared. If the party against whom a default judgment is sought has appeared personally or by a representative, that party or its representative must be served with written notice of the application at least 7 days before the hearing. * * *

The next case illustrates the interpretation and application of Rule 55.

Colleton Preparatory Academy, Inc. v. Hoover Universal, Inc.

U.S. Court of Appeals for the Fourth Circuit
616 F.3d 413 (4th Cir. 2010)

DAVIS, CIRCUIT JUDGE:

Hoover Universal, Inc. ("Hoover Universal") timely appeals from an adverse judgment awarding substantial damages in this diversity action, contending that the judgment is tainted by the district court's refusal to set aside the clerk's entry of default against it. Hoover Universal's default resulted when its resident agent for service of process failed to deliver the summons and complaint to Hoover Universal. We are persuaded, for the reasons stated within, that the district court abused its discretion in refusing to vacate the entry of default. Accordingly, we vacate the judgment and remand the case for further proceedings consistent with this opinion.

I.

Colleton Preparatory Academy, Inc. ("Colleton"), which operates a small private school in Walterboro, South Carolina, filed suit in the United States District Court for the District of South Carolina on March 24, 2003, against two non-parties to this appeal, Beazer East, Inc. ("Beazer") and Hoover Treated Wood Products, Inc. ("Hoover Wood"), alleging claims for negligence and for violation of the South Carolina Unfair Trade Practices Act ("UTPA"). All the claims arose from alleged damage to the roof trusses and sheathing on several Colleton buildings allegedly caused by fire-retardant substances produced and sold by the defendants or their predecessors-in-interest. Beazer timely filed an answer denying liability and asserting affirmative defenses; Hoover Wood failed to answer, and Colleton promptly obtained an entry of default against Hoover Wood.

In fact, Colleton had sued the incorrect defendant in joining Hoover Wood. Accordingly, on or about June 6, 2003, Colleton filed an amended complaint substituting Hoover Universal for Hoover Wood. The district court issued an order vacating the entry of default and dismissing Hoover Wood without prejudice. Colleton served a copy of the summons and amended complaint on Hoover Universal by certified mail through service on the latter's registered agent for service of process, The Corporation Company ("TCC"), and received a certified mail receipt showing that TCC had accepted service on June 23, 2003. Unbeknownst to the parties, however, TCC negligently failed to forward the suit papers or otherwise to notify Hoover Universal of the existence of the lawsuit. As a result of TCC's error, Hoover Universal failed to file a timely answer to the amended complaint. Colleton moved in due course for entry of default, *see* FED.R.CIV.P. 55(a), and the clerk entered default against Hoover Universal two days later, on August 5, 2003. The district court also ordered Colleton to set a date for a trial on damages, but no such proceeding had been calendared by the time Hoover Universal learned of the lawsuit less than two months later.

As the district court found, one of Hoover Universal's lawyers learned of the lawsuit "by coincidence," *see Colleton Preparatory Academy, Inc. v. Beazer East, Inc., 223 F.R.D. 401, 406 (D.S.C. 2004)* (denying motion to set aside entry of default), during an October 8, 2003, conversation about a separate case with a paralegal working in the office of one of Colleton's lawyers. On October 17, 2003, nine days later, Hoover Universal filed a motion to quash service of process and to set aside the entry of default. The district court held a hearing and denied both motions by order entered on December 1, 2003, as amended on September 8, 2004. The district court also ordered that a trial on damages take place within 60 days.

Before the damages trial occurred, with the consent of all parties, the district court "bifurcated" Colleton's claims against Beazer (relating to two buildings) from those against Hoover Universal (relating to only one building) in order to deal with a conflict of interest discovered by one of Colleton's attorneys. Colleton filed a new complaint on February 20, 2004 naming Hoover Universal as the sole defendant and the clerk assigned a new case number to the newly-filed action.[2] When Hoover Universal filed an answer to the newly-filed complaint, however, the district court struck the answer, at Colleton's request, concluding that the newly-filed complaint was a mere administrative formality, and that any judgment awarded to Colleton

---

[2] Colleton and Beazer settled the initial case and a stipulation of dismissal was entered on May 6, 2004.

would be based on the first amended complaint as to which Hoover Universal was in default.

* * * [T]he district court conducted a two-day, non-jury damages trial beginning on January 31, 2005. * * * The district court found in favor of Colleton on the UTPA claim and in favor of Hoover Universal on the negligence claim * * *.

[After receiving answers from the South Carolina Supreme Court on certified questions of state law,] [o]n March 25, 2009, the district court amended its findings of fact and conclusions of law to incorporate the South Carolina Supreme Court's answers to the certified questions and awarded judgment in favor of Colleton under both common law negligence and UTPA. The court affirmed its previous damages award of $871,690.15, and awarded Colleton $290,563.38 in costs and attorney's fees.

Hoover Universal timely appeals, vassigning error in the district court's* * * denial of its motion to set aside the order of default * * * .

What's That?

A federal court may certify questions of state law for clarification by the highest court of the relevant state, provided the solicited state court is empowered and willing to give answers to such questions. The purpose of such certification is for the federal district court to get an authoritative answer on an unclear matter of state law rather than attempting to resolve the state legal question on its own. *See Tobin v. Mich. Mut. Ins. Co.*, 398 F.3d 1267, 1274 (11th Cir. 2005) ("Where there is doubt in the interpretation of state law, a federal court may certify the question to the state supreme court to avoid making unnecessary *Erie* guesses and to offer the state court the opportunity to interpret or change existing law.").

II.

A.

We review a district court's refusal to set aside an entry of default for abuse of discretion. *Payne ex rel. Estate of Calzada v. Brake*, 439 F.3d 198, 203 (4th Cir. 2006). As we stated in *Payne*, 439 F.3d at 204–05:

When deciding whether to set aside an entry of default, a district court should consider whether the moving party has a meritorious defense, whether it acts with reasonable promptness, the personal responsibility of the defaulting party, the prejudice to the party, whether there is a history of dilatory action, and the availability of sanctions less drastic.

See FED.R.CIV.P. 55(c) (providing that "[f]or good cause shown the court may set aside an entry of default").

We have repeatedly expressed a strong preference that, as a general matter, defaults be avoided and that claims and defenses be disposed of on their merits. * * *

B.

In denying the motion to vacate the entry of default, the district court forthrightly acknowledged our strong policy in favor of merits-based adjudication and applied the *Payne* factors * * * . Specifically, the district court correctly found that Hoover Universal presented evidence of a meritorious defense. Furthermore, the district court found that Hoover Universal acted with the requisite promptness and diligence in seeking to set aside the entry of default when it acted within nine days after its counsel learned of the existence of the case. Furthermore, the district court found "no other instances of dilatory action [by Hoover Universal]." Moreover, the district court acknowledged its awareness that a less drastic sanction than maintaining the entry of default must be considered, although it neither explained, nor even mentioned in its order, why an award of attorney's fees and costs to Colleton in opposing the motion to set aside the entry of default, as Hoover Universal suggested, would be inappropriate. Thus, fully four of the six factors identified in *Payne* as informing the exercise of discretion whether to vacate an entry of default weighed significantly in favor of Hoover Universal.

As to a fifth factor, the district court found that any "further delay" in the action would unduly prejudice Colleton. This finding is highly suspect.

In the context of a motion to set aside an entry of default, as in other contexts, delay in and of itself does not constitute prejudice to the opposing party. *See, e.g., Indigo America, Inc. v. Big Impressions, LLC*, 597 F.3d 1, 4 (1st Cir. 2010). As we noted in *Payne*, the issue is one of *prejudice to the adversary*, not merely the existence of delay. Our review of the record does not sustain the district court's view that undue prejudice would have been visited upon Colleton if the entry of default had been set aside in November 2003, less than three months after a timely answer to the complaint would have been filed and the case made ready for the commencement of discovery. We by no means impose on the district court a duty of 20/20 foresight, but the course of the trial court proceedings in this case, even with the default left in place, from the damages trial in January 2005 to final judgment in March 2009 (more than four years) was reasonably foreseeable in November 2003, given the magnitude of Colleton's claims (against what was then two distinct defendants) and the character of the defenses asserted. Discovery (including expert discovery) and related pretrial proceedings surely would be expected to consume a reasonable period of time.[5]

---

[5] Indeed, * * * critical legal issues, including those surrounding the application of the economic loss doctrine and the necessity *vel non* of privity in respect to the statutory claim under UTPA, surfaced in the case only in the context of post-verdict motions, prompting considerable delay in bringing the case to conclusion. Thus, had Hoover Universal been permitted to file pre-answer motions pursuant to Fed.R.Civ.P. 12, there is strong reason to believe that those legal issues would have been aired in a more timely and efficient manner, and the overall delay in bringing the case to conclusion greatly lessened.

Furthermore, we have not heretofore countenanced as a factor deserving weight in the analysis of a <u>Rule 55(c)</u> motion to set aside an entry of default, whether a "plaintiff could . . . have confidence in its service of process and . . . the timing of its legal actions," and we decline to do so under the circumstances presented here. Moreover, as obvious as it may be, it bears mention that no cognizable prejudice inheres in requiring a plaintiff *to prove* a defendant's liability, a burden every plaintiff assumes in every civil action filed in every federal court.

At bottom, therefore, regarding the issue of prejudice to Colleton from setting aside the entry of default as of November 2003, we conclude that the record is, at best, neutral.

Ultimately, in refusing to set aside the entry of default, the district court placed overarching emphasis on a single *Payne* factor: the "personal responsibility of the defaulting party." *See* <u>223 F.R.D. at 406</u> ("This court finds that the most important factor . . . [is] the responsibility of the default [.]"). The court seemed particularly bewildered that although the summons and complaint (and a letter accompanying them) all clearly stated that the process was intended for Hoover Universal, TCC sent the amended summons and complaint to Beazer (for whom TCC was also a resident agent, and whose name was listed first among the defendants in the caption of the action) and not Hoover Universal. As the district court correctly explained, here was a situation where TCC, Hoover Universal's agent, hired for the sole purpose of being the company's registered agent for service of process, was clearly at fault.

As framed by the district court, consideration under the *Payne* factor of whether a defaulting party bore "personal responsibility" for the default required it to attribute the actions of a corporation's non-attorney agents directly to the corporation. Accordingly, the court concluded that Hoover Universal was "personally responsible" for the default. *Id.* (citing <u>*Park Corp. v. Lexington Ins. Co.*, 812 F.2d 894, 897 (4th Cir. 1987)</u>; cf. <u>*Lolatchy v. Arthur Murray, Inc.*, 816 F.2d 951, 953 (4th Cir. 1987)</u> (vacating default where the attorneys were at fault, not the defendants).

We need not examine here whether and under what circumstances an agent's mishandling of process should be charged to a defendant. Rather, we are satisfied that the district court abused its discretion when, in the face of our time-worn commitment to the resolution of disputes on their merits, and in light of overwhelming evidence supporting "good cause" to vacate the entry of default under Fed.R.Civ.P. 55(c), it relied too heavily on *Park Corp.* in denying Hoover Universal's motion to vacate the entry of default.

In *Park Corp.*, the defaulting party, Lexington Insurance, lost the summons and complaint after they had been received in its *own mailroom* as a result of mishandling by its *own employees*. Moreover, Lexington Insurance could not rationally explain the disappearance of the summons and complaint or offer evidence of its procedures for handling such important legal mail. 812 F.2d at 897.

The situation in *Park Corp.* is clearly distinguishable from the situation here and the district court's heavy reliance on that case is misplaced. In *Park Corp.*, unlike here, the defaulting party offered *no explanation* for the disappearance of the summons and complaint, and made no showing that its internal procedures were designed to avoid such occurrences. Here, TCC admitted to its mishandling of process, and offered some explanation of why the suit papers were forwarded to Beazer rather than to Hoover Universal.

Equally pertinent, the *Park Corp.* court reviewed the denial of a FED.R.CIV.P. 60(b) motion for relief from a *default judgment,* not, as in this case, a Rule 55(c) motion to set aside entry of default. Although we have analyzed Rule 55(c) and Rule 60(b) motions using the same factors, *see United States v. Moradi,* 673 F.2d 725, 727–28 (4th Cir.1982), the burden on a movant seeking relief under the two rules is not the same. As the district court recognized, Rule 60(b) motions request relief from judgment, which implicates an interest in "finality and repose," a situation that is not present when default has been entered under Rule 55(a) and no judgment has been rendered.

Make the Connection

The motion for relief from a judgment, which is governed by Rule 60(b), is discussed in Chapter 10.

Therefore, while an analysis under each rule employs similar factors, Rule 60(b)'s "excusable neglect" standard is a more onerous standard than Rule 55(c)'s "good cause" standard, which is more forgiving of defaulting parties because it does not implicate any interest in finality.

In sum, we adhere to our long-held view that Rule 55(c) motions must be "liberally construed in order to provide relief from the onerous consequences of defaults and default judgments. *Tolson v. Hodge,* 411 F.2d 123, 130 (4th Cir. 1969)."

III.

For the reasons set forth herein * * * we hold that the district court abused its discretion when it denied the motion filed by Hoover Universal to set aside the entry of default. Under the circumstances, the entire course of the district court proceedings, resting on the district court's flawed view that liability against Hoover Universal had been reliably established by the entry of default, is undermined. Accordingly, the judgment in favor of Colleton is affirmed in part, reversed in part, vacated in part, and the case is remanded for further proceedings consistent with this opinion, including pretrial proceedings and, if appropriate, a new trial on liability and damages.

Points for Discussion

a. Procedures for Obtaining Default and Default Judgment

Rule 55 sets up a two-stage process for obtaining a default judgment. First, once the defendant fails to plead as required by the Rules or fails to otherwise defend itself via motion, the opposing party may bring that fact to the attention of the court clerk and seek the clerk's entry of the defendant's "default." An entry of default is distinct from the second step in this process, a default judgment. After the clerk has entered a default, the opposing party may then seek a default judgment from the court (although clerks themselves may enter default judgments against *non-appearing* defendants if "the plaintiff's claim is for a sum certain" and if the defendant is "neither a minor nor an incompetent person").

What's That?

The *clerk* referred to here is not a judicial law clerk of the kind that works for a judge shortly after graduating from law school but rather is a full-time court officer responsible for processing all of the paperwork and records of a particular court and for managing and overseeing court operations and personnel.

Food for Thought

What constitutes an "appearance" under Rule 55(b) so as to entitle the defaulting party the right to notice of the hearing on the application for a default judgment? *Compare Zuelzke Tool & Eng'g Co. v. Anderson Die Castings, Inc.*, 925 F.2d 226, 230 (7th Cir. 1991) (construing the term "appearance" to require a party to make "some presentation or submission to the district court in the pending action"), *with H.F. Livermore Corp. v. Aktiengesellschaft Gebruder Loepfe*, 432 F.2d 689, 691 (D.C. Cir. 1970) (stating that an appearance is made by "those parties who, although delaying in a formal sense by failing to file pleadings within the [required] period, have otherwise indicated to the moving party a clear purpose to defend the suit").

In cases where the defaulting party has made an "appearance" in the case—for example, by filing a preliminary motion but subsequently failing to file its required pleading in response to the complaint—the court must notify that party at least seven days in advance of a hearing on the opposing party's application for default judgment. The defendant may then appear at that hearing and raise arguments demonstrating why the court should not enter a default judgment against it. What arguments might a defendant raise to avoid a judgment by default? *Cf. Peralta v. Heights Med. Ctr., Inc.*, 485 U.S. 80, 84 (1988) (reversing a state-court default judgment because the defendant argued that he had not been properly served and had no notice of the judgment).

b. Standards for Granting Default and Default Judgment

What type of delay or failure to respond warrants an entry of default or a default judgment? As you can see from *Colleton Preparatory Academy*, once the defendant fails to respond, the entry of default can be proper; the appeals court in *Colleton* did not find that the entry of default was erroneous (it was the failure to *set aside* the default that was an error). Although default is technically available upon the requisite failure to respond, default judgments are not likely to result purely from a *de minimus* failure to make the response deadline. *See, e.g., Goodwin v. Libbey Glass, Inc.,* 176 F. App'x 588, 593 n.6 (5th Cir. 2006) (finding no abuse of discretion where the magistrate judge set aside entry of default because "default judgments . . . should not be granted on the claim, without more, that the defendant had failed to meet a procedural time requirement").

Practice Pointer

Be careful in being too quick to seek a default judgment. Courts have at times reacted harshly to overzealous efforts to rush to obtain a default judgment against an adversary too soon. *See, e.g., First Interstate Bank of Okla., N.A. v. Serv. Stores of Am., Inc.,* 128 F.R.D. 679, 680 (W.D. Okla. 1989) ("Resisting a motion to vacate, where entry of default was secured without notice to opposing counsel on the first day after the time to answer had lapsed, is in the Court's view a practice inconsistent with the standards of professionalism which this Court desires and expects to be observed on the part of its officers in the bar.").

How long must an attorney representing a plaintiff in an action where a defendant has failed to respond to the complaint wait before pursuing an entry of default? Should attorneys make efforts to contact their adversaries to see if they have received the summons and complaint? Because courts generally disfavor default judgments, *see, e.g., Harad v. Aetna Cas. & Sur. Co.,* 839 F.2d 979, 982 (3d Cir. 1988) ("[T]his Court has adopted a policy disfavoring default judgments and encouraging decisions on the merits . . . ."), advocates probably should not be too overzealous in pursuing them.

Has a defendant defaulted if it answers the complaint but fails to appear for the trial? The court in *Bass v. Hoagland,* 172 F.2d 205 (5th Cir. 1949), *cert. denied,* 338 U.S. 816 (1949), addressed this point:

> Rule 55(a) authorizes the clerk to enter a default "When a party against whom a judgment for affirmative relief is sought has failed to plead or otherwise defend as provided by these rules." This does not require that to escape default the defendant must not only file a sufficient answer to the merits, but must also have a lawyer or be present in court when the case is called for a trial. The words "otherwise defend" refer to attacks on the service, or motions to dismiss, or for better particulars, and the like, which may prevent default without presently pleading to the merits. When Bass by his attorney filed a denial of the plaintiff's case neither the clerk nor the

judge could enter a default against him. The burden of proof was put on the plaintiff in any trial. When neither Bass nor his attorney appeared at the trial, no default was generated; the case was not confessed. The plaintiff might proceed, but he would have to prove his case.

172 F.2d at 210. The *Bass v. Hoagland* view appears to be a minority position, as most circuits have rejected its approach. *See, e.g., City of New York v. Mickalis Pawn Shop, LLC*, 645 F.3d 114, 131 (2d Cir. 2011) ("[The *Bass v. Hoagland*] interpretation of Rule 55 has not been embraced by this Court. Nor has it found favor in a majority of our sister circuits." (citing cases)); *Hoxworth v. Blinder, Robinson & Co.*, 980 F.2d 912, 918 (3d Cir. 1992) ("Although we acknowledge that some courts have stated that a Rule 55 default cannot be based on a failure to appear at trial, *see, e.g., Bass v. Hoagland*, we are not persuaded by their reasoning and decline to follow it. The failure to plead is no greater an impediment to the orderly progress of a case than is the failure to appear at trial or meet other required time schedules, and we see no reason why the former would be subject to a sanction not equally applicable to the latter.").

A defendant can also default by failing to file a timely answer after removing a case from state court to federal court. After removal, a defendant has the longer of 21 days after service of the initial complaint or 7 days after filing the notice of removal to answer or raise defenses in response to the complaint. FED. R. CIV. P. 81(c)(2). Missing the operative deadline will subject defendants to the possibility of default, although the filing of the notice of removal will count as having made an "appearance" for purposes of Rule 55(b). *See, e.g., Martha Stewart Living Omnimedia LLC v. Beers Flower Shop, Inc.*, 1998 WL 646648, at *3 (S.D.N.Y. Sept. 21, 1998) ("Beers' . . . filing of a Notice of Removal constitutes an appearance. MSLO was thus required to give notice before entry of the default.").

Although entry of default might follow from the missing of a procedural deadline, entry of a default *judgment* is a more serious matter and typically requires more. As already noted, courts disfavor default judgments, and thus for some courts "default judgment usually is available 'only when the adversary process has been halted because of an essentially unresponsive party . . . as the diligent party must be protected lest he be faced with inter-

Take Note!

Under the Foreign Sovereign Immunities Act ("FSIA"), no default judgment may be entered by a court unless the claimant establishes his right to relief or claim by evidence satisfactory to the court. 28 U.S.C. § 1608(e). That means the court must be satisfied that the plaintiff has presented a *prima facie* case supporting its entitlement to relief. Because Congress could always modify the default judgment requirements associated with claims under any given federal statute, it may be prudent to check for the existence of such a provision before seeking a default judgment on a federal law claim.

minable delay and continued uncertainty as to his rights.' " *Int'l Painters and Allied Trades Indus. Pension Fund v. Rose City Glass Co.*, 729 F. Supp. 2d 336, 338 (D.D.C. 2010) (quoting *Jackson v. Beech*, 636 F.2d 831, 836 (D.C. Cir. 1980)). Further, obtaining a default does not mean that a plaintiff is automatically entitled to prevail via a default judgment. Many courts will engage in an independent inquiry into whether the plaintiff has alleged facts that entitle it to relief and the amount of damages. *See, e.g., Nicholes v. Advanced Credit Mgmt., Inc.*, 2010 WL 2998625, at *1 (D. Md. July 27, 2010) ("It, however, remains for the court to determine whether these unchallenged factual allegations constitute a legitimate cause of action. . . . If the court determines that liability is established, the court must then determine the appropriate amount of damages."); *see also* 10A C. WRIGHT, A. MILLER & M. KANE, FED. PRAC. & PROC. § 2688 (4th ed. 2016) ("[L]iability is not deemed established simply because of the default, although it may not be necessary to present testimony to obtain a judgment on the liability issue.").

c.   **Setting Aside an Entry of Default**

Once default has been entered a party may petition the court to set aside the default under Rule 55(c). The court will do so if the petitioner shows "good cause," a determination courts have typically made based on multiple factors, including: (1) whether the default was willful or the result of the defendant's culpable conduct, (2) whether the set-aside will prejudice the plaintiff, and (3) whether the defendant had a meritorious defense. *See O.J. Distrib., Inc. v. Hornell Brewing Co.*, 340 F.3d 345, 353 n.3 (6th Cir. 2003); *see also Payne ex rel. Estate of Calzada v. Brake*, 439 F.3d 198, 203 (4th Cir. 2006) (employing a similar, but six-factored, test that adds consideration of the availability of alternative, less drastic sanctions and whether the defendant has had a history of dilatory behavior in the case). As might be expected, evidence of improper service of process requires that an entry of default be set aside. *See O.J. Distrib.*, 340 F.3d at 353 ("[I]f service of process was not proper, the court must set aside an entry of default."). What other reasons do you think might establish good cause for setting aside entry of default? What was the court's basis for setting aside default in *Colleton Preparatory Academy*?

d.   **Setting Aside a Default Judgment**

Rule 55(c) also indicates that a final default judgment may be set aside, but in such a case it may only be set aside in accordance with the standards of Rule 60(b). *See* FED. R. CIV. P. 55(c); *Weiss v. St. Paul Fire & Marine Ins. Co.*, 283 F.3d 790 (6th Cir. 2002). The standards for setting aside a judgment under Rule 60(b) will be discussed in Chapter 10, but generally speaking, courts are more willing to set aside default judgments than judgments reached after some consideration of the merits, provided there is no evidence of willful conduct on the part of the defendant. *See,* *e.g., Bonney v. Roelle,* 117 F.3d 1413 (Table), 1997 WL 407831, at *6 (4th Cir. 1997) ("In the case of a Rule 60(b) motion seeking to set aside a default judgment, our judicial preference for trials on the merits demands that courts resolve any doubt as to the propriety of giving relief in favor of the moving party." (citation omitted)). Note that in *Colleton* the appeals court emphasized the difference between the Rule 60(b) and Rule 55(c) contexts, instructing that the latter requires more leniency on the part of courts.

e. Damages for Default Judgments

In the event that a plaintiff successfully obtains a default judgment, Rule 54(c) limits her recovery to the amount prayed for in the complaint. FED. R. CIV. P. 54(c) ("A default judgment must not differ in kind from, or

Food for Thought

Should a party be relieved of a default judgment if the failure to defend the case was due to the negligence of its attorney? Compare *S.E.C. v. McNulty,* 137 F.3d 732, 739 (2d Cir. 1998) ("[I]n the context of a default judgment, we have rather consistently refused to relieve a client of the burdens of a final judgment entered against him due to the mistake or omission of his attorney.") with *Augusta Fiberglass Coatings, Inc. v. Fodor Contracting, Corp.,* 843 F.2d 808, 811 (4th Cir. 1988) ("[W]hen the party is blameless, his attorney's negligence qualifies as a "mistake" or as "excusable neglect" under Rule 60(b)(1)."). Note that in such a case, the party may be able to pursue a malpractice action against its attorney.

exceed in amount, what is demanded in the pleadings."). In such a case, the court may hold a hearing to establish the appropriate amount of damages if the court feels that doing so is necessary. FED. R. CIV. P. 55(b)(2) ("The court may conduct hearings or make referrals—preserving any federal statutory right to a jury trial—when, to enter or effectuate judgment, it needs to: (A) conduct an accounting; (B) determine the amount of damages; (C) establish the truth of any allegation by evidence; or (D) investigate any other matter.").

f. Protections Against Default Judgments for Certain Parties

Rule 55 provides that default judgments may not be entered against minors or incompetent persons by the clerk at all, nor by the court unless a representative for such persons has appeared in the case. FED. R. CIV. P. 55(b)(1) & (b)(2). Default judgments may be entered against the United States, its officers, or its agencies but only if the plaintiff actually proves its claim to the satisfaction of the court. FED. R. CIV. P. 55(d). Finally, the Servicemembers Civil Relief Act protects members of the military against default judgments by requiring courts to stay proceedings for at least 90 days if the defendant's military service prevents an appearance in the case. 50 U.S.C. § 3931.

2. Involuntary & Voluntary Dismissals

In addition to dismissals based on one of the several grounds found in Rule 12(b), such as lack of subject matter jurisdiction or failure to state a claim upon which relief can be granted, there are involuntary and voluntary dismissals under Rule 41. Each of these two types of dismissals will be reviewed in turn.

Involuntary Dismissals. The defendant is not the only party obligated to pursue its case with diligence. Plaintiffs, too, must move their case forward in a timely fashion and respond as obligated to various orders of the court. Rule 41(b) provides, "If the plaintiff fails to prosecute or to comply with these rules or a court order, a defendant may move to dismiss the action or any claim against it." FED. R. CIV. P. 41(b). Courts may also involuntarily dismiss an action for failure to prosecute sua sponte, pursuant to their inherent authority. *Link v. Wabash R.R. Co., 370 U.S. 626, 630–31 (1962)* ("The authority of a court to dismiss sua sponte for lack of prosecution has generally been considered an 'inherent power,' governed not by rule or statute but by the control necessarily vested in courts to manage their own affairs so as to achieve the orderly and expeditious disposition of cases.").

What do you think is the purpose of such a rule? *See Link, 370 U.S. at 629–30* ("The power to invoke this sanction is necessary in order to prevent undue delays in the disposition of pending cases and to avoid congestion in the calendars of the District Courts."). What circumstances warrant an involuntary dismissal of the plaintiff's case? *See id.* (upholding the *sua sponte* dismissal of the plaintiff's action based on the failure of the plaintiff and his counsel to attend a pretrial conference).

Unless the court states otherwise in its order, the effect of an involuntary dismissal is a dismissal with prejudice, meaning that the matter is deemed to have been adjudicated on the merits. FED. R. CIV. P. 41(b) ("Unless the dismissal order states otherwise, a dismissal under this subdivision (b) and any dismissal not under this rule—except one for lack of jurisdiction, improper venue, or failure to join a party under Rule 19—operates as an adjudication on the merits."). An adjudication on the merits is ordinarily entitled to *res judicata* preclusive effect, which means that the plaintiff will not be able to refile the dismissed claims—or in some cases related claims—in the future. *See, e.g., Owens v. Kaiser Found. Health Plan, Inc., 244 F.3d 708, 714 (9th Cir. 2001)* (upholding the district court's finding that *res judicata* barred the plaintiff's federal discrimination claim in the wake of the prior dismissal of a related set of state law claims for failure to prosecute under Rule 41(b)). However, the Supreme Court has made clear

What's That?

Res judicata, also referred to as *claim preclusion*, prohibits lawsuits on any claims that were raised or could have been raised in a prior action. The specific requirements for applying the doctrine of *res judicata* will be covered in Chapter 11.

that the claim-preclusive effect of a Rule 41(b) dismissal is limited to the refiling of that same claim in the same district from which it was dismissed; an analysis of claim-preclusion principles not found in Rule 41(b) would be necessary to determine any further preclusive effect in any given case. *See Semtek Int'l Inc. v. Lockheed Martin Corp., 531 U.S. 497, 506 (2001)* ("[T]he effect of the 'adjudication upon the merits' default provision of Rule 41(b) . . . is simply that . . . the dismissal in the present case barred refiling of the same claim in the [district where the case was dismissed]. That is undoubtedly a necessary condition, but it is not a sufficient one, for claim-preclusive effect in other courts.").*

Voluntary Dismissals. If a plaintiff determines that it is better to terminate the action rather than proceed, the Federal Rules provide the plaintiff with the ability to dismiss its own case voluntarily. The plaintiff may do this without the court's permission or the consent of the other parties in the suit if the plaintiff files a "notice of dismissal" prior to the filing of an answer or a summary judgment motion, whichever comes first. FED. R. CIV. P. 41(a)(1)(A)(ii); *see In re Bath & Kitchen Fixtures Antitrust Litig., 535 F.3d 161 (3d Cir. 2008)* (holding that prior to the filing of an answer or summary judgment motion, the plaintiff has an absolute right to file a notice a voluntary dismissal, notwithstanding the filing and pendency of a motion to dismiss under Rule 12(b)(6)). After such time the plaintiff must obtain the consent of the parties, evidenced by a "stipulation of dismissal," FED. R. CIV. P. 41(a)(1)(A)(ii), or the permission of the court, FED. R. CIV. P. 41(a)(2).

What criteria should a court use to determine whether to grant permission for a voluntary dismissal under Rule 41(a)(2)? *See, e.g., Hamm v. Rhone-Poulenc Rorer Pharm., Inc., 187 F.3d 941, 950 (8th Cir. 1999)* ("A decision whether to allow a party to voluntarily dismiss a case rests upon the sound discretion of the court. In exercising that discretion, a court should consider factors such as whether the party has presented a proper explanation for its desire to dismiss, whether a dismissal would result in a waste of judicial time and effort, and whether a dismissal will prejudice the defendants." (citations omitted)).

Why would a plaintiff want to dismiss its own case voluntarily? Is it a proper motive to seek a voluntary dismissal because the plaintiff wishes to avoid an adverse determination of its case before the present tribunal? *Compare Hamm, 187 F.3d at 950* ("[A] party is not permitted to dismiss merely to escape an adverse decision nor to seek a more favorable forum."), *with McCants v. Ford Motor Co., 781 F.2d 855, 857–59 (11th Cir. 1986)* (upholding a Rule 41(a)(2) dismissal based on the plaintiff's desire to avoid summary judgment on statute-of-limitations grounds and refile her case in a different jurisdiction where the statute-of-limitations period had not expired). Keep in mind that before an answer or summary judgment motion is filed or with the consent of all the parties, a plaintiff may voluntarily dismiss the

---

* *Semtek* appears as a principal case in Chapter 11 of this book. [Ed.]

case without the court's permission, for any reason. The plaintiff only must justify the dismissal in the event that she requires the court's approval.

Unlike involuntary dismissals, voluntary dismissals under Rule 41(a) are without prejudice (unless otherwise stated by the court), meaning that the plaintiff is free to pursue the claims again in the future. FED. R. CIV. P. 41(a)(1)(B) ("Unless the notice or stipulation states otherwise, the dismissal is without prejudice."). There is an important caveat, however: The plaintiff may only voluntarily dismiss its case without a court order under Rule 41(a)(1) without prejudice once. A subsequent voluntary dismissal by the plaintiff of an action based on the same claims that were previously voluntarily dismissed will operate as an adjudication on the merits entitled to preclusive effect. FED. R. CIV. P. 41(a)(1)(B) ("But if the plaintiff previously dismissed any federal- or state-court action based on or including the same claim, a notice of dismissal operates as an adjudication on the merits."); *see also* Commercial Space Mgmt. Co. v. Boeing Co., 193 F.3d 1074, 1076 (9th Cir. 1999) ("[A] voluntary dismissal of a second action operates as a dismissal on the merits if the plaintiff has previously dismissed an action involving the same claims. This is known as the 'two dismissal rule.' "); *Cooter & Gell v. Hartmarx Corp.*, 496 U.S. 384, 394 (1990) ("If the plaintiff invokes Rule 41(a)(1) a second time for an 'action based on or including the same claim,' the action must be dismissed with prejudice."). Why do you think the rule limits plaintiffs to one voluntary dismissal without prejudice?

> **FYI**
>
> The voluntary dismissal made available under Rule 41(a) is the descendant of a common law procedure known as a *nonsuit*. A plaintiff wishing voluntarily to dismiss its suit would file a nonsuit to withdraw the case, which typically could be done with fewer restrictions and at a later stage in the proceedings than permitted under Rule 41(a).

Rule 41(a)(2), which provides for voluntary dismissals with permission of the court, treats court-approved voluntary dismissals as dismissals without prejudice but does not include the proviso that a subsequent dismissal of this sort involving the same claim must be dismissed with prejudice. Why in your view does Rule 41(a) seemingly permit limitless repetitive voluntary dismissals with court approval but treat non-court-approved dismissals differently? Is there room for abuse here? Should plaintiffs have to pay costs or attorneys' fees to defendants who face repetitive filings of claims after they have been voluntarily dismissed? Rule 41(d) provides courts with the authority to impose costs on plaintiffs under such circumstances:

> If a plaintiff who previously dismissed an action in any court files an action based on or including the same claim against the same defendant, the court: (1) may order the plaintiff to pay all or part of the costs of that previous action; and (2) may stay the proceedings until the plaintiff has complied.

FED. R. CIV. P. 41(d). May such costs include attorneys' fees? *Compare Rogers v. Wal-Mart Stores, Inc.*, 230 F.3d 868, 874 (6th Cir. 2000), *cert. denied*, 532 U.S. 953 (2001) (holding that "costs" under Rule 41(d) does not include attorneys' fees) *and Esposito v. Piatrowski*, 223 F.3d 497, 501 (7th Cir. 2000) (holding that attorneys' fees are available under Rule 41(d) only in "those instances where the underlying statute that is the basis of the original action permits the recovery of fees as costs"), *with Evans v. Safeway Stores*, 623 F.2d 121, 122 (8th Cir. 1980) (affirming the award of attorneys' fees under Rule 41(d)).

—Perspective & Analysis—

One commentator has taken issue with the holdings of *Rogers* and *Esposito* limiting the availability of attorneys' fees under Rule 41(d):

> [T]hese rulings are unsound, primarily because they are based on a flawed plain meaning analysis of Rule 41(d). In holding that Rule 41(d) does not confer power upon district courts to award attorneys' fees, the Sixth and Seventh Circuits appear to have (i) largely ignored a long line of caselaw which had resolved that Rule 41(d) does provide for attorneys' fees, and (ii) overlooked entirely the rule's purpose of curing vexatious and bad faith litigation conduct. By withholding attorneys' fees from Rule 41(d) cost awards, the Sixth and Seventh Circuits have signaled that they are willing to countenance both repetitive filings and, more importantly, only partial and incomplete reimbursement to defendants for those litigation expenses wasted because of such filings. * * *
>
> This article contends that Rule 41(d) implicitly authorizes district courts to grant attorneys' fees as part of the "costs" of a previously filed action, but nevertheless requires clarification based on the Sixth and Seventh Circuits' abandonment of standard Rule 41(d) practice.

Thomas Southard, *Increasing the "Costs" of Nonsuit: A Proposed Clarifying Amendment to Federal Rule of Civil Procedure 41(d)*, 32 SETON HALL L. REV. 367, 369 (2002).

B. Case Management, Settlement & ADR

Beyond disposition by default or dismissal there remain several ways that claims may be resolved short of a trial on the merits. Contested matters that proceed with discovery ultimately are placed under the supervision of a federal district court judge or U.S. Magistrate Judge who manages the case using the techniques provided for in Rule 16 and other parts of the Federal Rules. Pursuant to Rule 16, supervising judges may dispose of certain issues or claims during this process, thereby removing them from consideration during trial. Further, as more information is revealed during the course of discovery, the parties may begin settlement discussions to come to a negotiated agreement regarding the resolution of the claims, a process that may involve or even be at the urging of the presiding judge. Finally, judges may direct the parties to participate in alternative dispute resolution ("ADR") to resolve the case without having to hold a formal trial before the court. Each of these aspects of the pretrial process will be discussed below.

1. Case Management

A basic first-year course in civil procedure is not the place to review the full range of topics that falls within the subject of judicial case management or managerial judging, as the process through which judges actively manage and direct litigation before trial has come to be called. *See* Judith Resnik, *Managerial Judges*, 96 HARV. L. REV. 374 (1982). Here, we will only touch on the topic to reveal the ways in which judges may use their managerial authority to narrow and resolve issues in a case prior to trial.

The basis for a court's authority to engage in case management comes from an array of sources but primarily can be found in Rule 16. Under Rule 16, the court may hold a pretrial conference in which the parties are to discuss—and the court may issue orders with respect to—several matters relevant to resolving the action expeditiously:

FRCP 16. Pretrial Conferences; Scheduling; Management.

(c) **Attendance and Matters for Consideration at a Pretrial Conference.**

(1) *Attendance.* A represented party must authorize at least one of its attorneys to make stipulations and admissions about all matters that can reasonably be anticipated for discussion at a pretrial conference. If appropriate, the court may require that a party or its representative be present or reasonably available by other means to consider possible settlement.

(2) *Matters for Consideration.* At any pretrial conference, the court may consider and take appropriate action on the following matters:

(A) formulating and simplifying the issues, and eliminating frivolous claims or defenses;

(B) amending the pleadings if necessary or desirable;

(C) obtaining admissions and stipulations about facts and documents to avoid unnecessary proof, and ruling in advance on the admissibility of evidence;

(D) avoiding unnecessary proof and cumulative evidence * * * ;

(E) determining the appropriateness and timing of summary adjudication under Rule 56;

(F)   controlling and scheduling discovery, including orders affecting disclosures and discovery under Rule 26 and Rules 29 through 37;

(G)   identifying witnesses and documents, scheduling the filing and exchange of any pretrial briefs, and setting dates for further conferences and for trial;

(H)   referring matters to a magistrate judge or a master;

(I)   settling the case and using special procedures to assist in resolving the dispute when authorized by statute or local rule;

(J)   determining the form and content of the pretrial order;

(K)   disposing of pending motions;

(L)   adopting special procedures for managing potentially difficult or protracted actions that may involve complex issues, multiple parties, difficult legal questions, or unusual proof problems;

(M)   ordering a separate trial under Rule 42(b) of a claim, counterclaim, crossclaim, third-party claim, or particular issue;

(N)   ordering the presentation of evidence early in the trial on a manageable issue that might, on the evidence, be the basis for a judgment as a matter of law under Rule 50(a) or a judgment on partial findings under Rule 52(c);

(O)   establishing a reasonable limit on the time allowed to present evidence; and

(P)   facilitating in other ways the just, speedy, and inexpensive disposition of the action.

As can be seen, the range of matters that the parties and the court may address during a pretrial conference is broad. What these provisions share is a commitment to driving the litigation toward a paring down of issues, claims, and defenses in the interests of focusing the litigation on those matters truly in dispute and not wasting any time with remaining matters that are more suitable for dismissal, settlement, or summary judgment.

Most important for our present purposes are those subparagraphs in Rule 16(c) that enable the court to eliminate issues and move the case toward settlement or summary adjudication. Among these are subparagraph (2)(A), which empowers the court to take action related to "simplifying the issues, and eliminating frivolous claims or defenses"; subparagraph

Under Rule 16(c)(1), courts have the authority to compel a party or its representative to participate in pretrial conferences. Further, represented parties must authorize their attorneys "to make stipulations and admissions about all matters that can reasonably be anticipated for discussion at a pretrial conference." FED. R. CIV. P. 16(c)(1).

(2)(I), which authorizes the court to take action with respect to "settling the case and using special procedures to assist in resolving the dispute when authorized by statute or local rule"; subparagraph (2)(E), which permits the court to consider the "appropriateness" of summary adjudication; and subparagraphs (2)(M) and (2)(N), which permit the court to try and hear evidence separately or early in the trial on certain matters or threshold issues the resolution of which may result in an early disposition of the case.

Clearly, the power to eliminate claims or defenses before trial is substantial. How are courts to go about exercising this authority?

CompuServe Inc. v. Saperstein

U.S. Court of Appeals for the Sixth Circuit
172 F.3d 47 (Table), 1999 WL 16481 (6th Cir. 1999)

KAREN NELSON MOORE, CIRCUIT JUDGE.

CompuServe sued Saperstein in federal district court for declaratory and other relief regarding particular agreements and certain business torts. Saperstein counterclaimed seeking damages for the same business torts and for violations of state business practices acts. At a pretrial conference hearing the district court, pursuant to CompuServe's motion, struck certain of Saperstein's counterclaims and *sua sponte* dismissed the others without prejudice. At a later date the district court granted a motion by CompuServe to dismiss its claims with prejudice, ending the action in full. Saperstein appeals both the dismissal of his original four counterclaims and the dismissal of CompuServe's claims.

For the reasons stated below, we AFFIRM the order of the district court dismissing CompuServe's claims with prejudice, and REVERSE and REMAND the order dismissing Saperstein's counterclaims.

I. BACKGROUND AND PROCEDURAL POSTURE

Jerry Saperstein is the sole shareholder of FontBank, Inc. The actions underlying this appeal stem from a contractual dispute between CompuServe and Font-Bank. The original agreement was for FontBank to manage and handle marketing and distribution for an electronic marketing device offered through CompuServe to its subscribers. In 1996 FontBank sued CompuServe in state court for breach of contract.

CompuServe then filed this federal action against both FontBank and Saperstein in an alleged attempt to combine all the relevant issues in one proceeding. The action was for declaratory judgment regarding the parties' agreements, defamation, intentional interference with contractual relations, and violations of the Ohio Deceptive Trade Practices Act. The district court found CompuServe's requests for a declaratory judgment to be compulsory counterclaims in the state court action.

Saperstein filed an answer that included counterclaims for defamation, intentional interference with business and contractual relations, and violations of Ohio and Illinois business practices acts. The claims as set forth were basically conclusory allegations without any factual support. Both parties moved for more definite statements. Saperstein filed an amended answer, adding somewhat to his original counterclaims. Shortly thereafter, without seeking leave of the court as required under FED. R. CIV. P. 15(a), Saperstein refiled essentially the same answer with the addition of six new counterclaims.

Make the Connection

Intentional interference with business relations is a **Tort** involving the intentional damaging of another's potential business relationship. *Intentional interference with contract* is also a **Tort** and involves the intentional inducement of a contracting party to break a contract.

Two days after holding a conference hearing the district judge issued an order *sua sponte* dismissing without prejudice Saperstein's original four counterclaims, ostensibly under authority from Rule 16(c) of the Federal Rules of Civil Procedure, and granting CompuServe's motion to strike the six counterclaims added in the Second Amended Answer.

CompuServe's belief that FontBank had no authority to sue it in state court fell through when FontBank registered as a foreign corporation in Ohio, and thereafter CompuServe aborted its attempt to consolidate actions in federal court by filing a motion to dismiss its federal court complaint without prejudice. The district court denied this motion but granted CompuServe's later motion to dismiss its action with prejudice.

Saperstein challenges the dismissal of both his and CompuServe's claims.

II. ANALYSIS

A. Dismissal of CompuServe's Claims With Prejudice

Saperstein argues that the district judge should not have granted CompuServe's motion to dismiss its own action with prejudice and should have instead allowed CompuServe's case to go forward. Saperstein claims that he is prejudiced by this because it may prevent him from maintaining future state-law claims. We have jurisdiction over the dismissals as final orders of the district court pursuant to 28 U.S.C. § 1291.

* * *

Saperstein does not show substantial injustice, nor does he clearly indicate why he opposes the dismissal with prejudice at all. Saperstein argues only that dismissal of CompuServe's action at this time would prevent him from maintaining a suit for malicious prosecution, abuse of process, and spoliation of evidence. The district court found this argument unconvincing, and we agree. Saperstein's interpretation of Ohio and Illinois case law is mistaken. In sum we conclude that the district court properly dismissed CompuServe's action with prejudice.

* * *

C. Dismissal of Saperstein's Counterclaims Without Prejudice

The district judge denied Saperstein leave to amend and dismissed Saperstein's claims after a FED. R. CIV. P. 16 pretrial conference because he "amended his counterclaims on two occasions subsequent to [CompuServe's] motion for a more definite statement and . . . failed to cure the defects." We normally review for abuse of discretion a district court's refusal to grant leave to amend.

Saperstein's counterclaims were originally set out as conclusory allegations. In response to CompuServe's motion for a more definite statement with respect to two of Saperstein's counterclaims, he added the names of alleged culprits, and supplemented each with the language:

> [t]o date, however, my efforts to identify those [defamatory] statements have been frustrated by plaintiff/counter-defendant CompuServe's refusal to comply with Requests for Interrogatories and Production of Documents. A true and accurate copy of CompuServe's reply to my Interrogatories and Request for Production of Documents is attached as Exhibit A.

Saperstein did not set forth any specific facts or examples. He claims that he had the facts all along, but did not want to burden the court or his opposition at the pleading stage.

The district court dismissed all four of Saperstein's counterclaims, stating that he amended his claims twice after the motion for a more definite statement and still failed to state claims on which relief could be granted. However, Saperstein amended two of his four counterclaims once, as indicated above. His second amended answer added six new counterclaims, but was submitted without leave of court and did not offer any changes to the first four counterclaims.[6] Indeed, CompuServe had not responded to the changes he had made to Counts One and Two in the first amended answer, and Saperstein believed he had complied with the motion for a

---

[6] Saperstein admits he made a mistake by not seeking leave and asks for leniency as a *pro se* party.

more definite statement. Moreover, CompuServe never asked for a more definite statement with respect to the third and fourth counts. CompuServe never objected to the third and fourth counts.

CompuServe also never filed a motion to dismiss. The district judge *sua sponte* denied Saperstein's request for further leave to amend and dismissed his original four counterclaims after one opportunity to amend in response to a motion for a more definite statement. Rule 15(a) of the Federal Rules of Civil Procedure provides that leave to amend "shall be freely given when justice so requires."[7] Whether to grant or deny such a request is typically within the discretion of the district court, but "cases should be tried on their merits rather than the technicalities of pleadings." Abuse of discretion occurs when a district court fails to state the basis for its denial or fails to consider the competing interests of the parties and likelihood of prejudice to the opponent. "[O]utright refusal to grant the leave without any justifying reason appearing for the denial is not an exercise of discretion; it is merely abuse of that discretion and inconsistent with the spirit of the Federal Rules." *Foman v. Davis*, 371 U.S. 178, 182 (1962).

Here the district court, citing authority to rid the proceedings of frivolous claims under Rule 16,[8] dismissed *sua sponte* four of Saperstein's counterclaims without leave to amend. Given that CompuServe neither moved for a more definite statement of the counterclaims nor for their dismissal, that the counterclaims were not found to be frivolous, that Saperstein is a *pro se* party, and that leave to amend is to be freely granted under FED. R. CIV. P. 15(a), the court should have afforded Saperstein one more opportunity to amend. While the question is a close one, this error constitutes an abuse of discretion. * * *

It's Latin to Me!

A *pro se* party is one who represents himself and appears in a matter without the assistance of legal counsel.

III. CONCLUSION

For the reasons stated above, we AFFIRM the district court's dismissal of CompuServe's claims with prejudice, REVERSE the district court's dismissal of Saperstein's counterclaims without prejudice, and REMAND for further proceedings consistent with this opinion.

---

[7] Saperstein also properly points out that courts have been traditionally more lenient with *pro se* plaintiffs than with pleadings from experienced counsel. *See Estelle v. Gamble*, 429 U.S. 97, 106 (1976) (stating "a pro se complaint, 'however inartfully pleaded,' must be held to 'less stringent standards than formal pleadings drafted by lawyers' and can only be dismissed for failure to state a claim if it appears 'beyond doubt that the plaintiff can prove no set of facts in support of his claim which would entitle him to relief' " (citing *Haines v. Kerner*, 404 U.S. 519, 520–21 (1972)).

[8] FED. R. CIV. P. 16(a) gives the district court discretion to call multiple pretrial conferences at which the district judge assists the parties in distilling the important issues and eliminates unmeritorious or frivolous claims.

Points for Discussion

a. Elimination of Claims & Defenses Under Rule 16(c)(2)(A)

In *CompuServe*, it appears that the district judge dismissed Saperstein's counterclaims because he "amended his counterclaims on two occasions subsequent to CompuServe's motion for a more definite statement and . . . failed to cure the defects." Was the district court justified in using its power under Rule 16(c)(2)(A) to eliminate the claims at that point since it appeared that Saperstein would be unable to plead his claims properly? Is the fact that Saperstein was proceeding without the assistance of legal counsel the reason why the circuit court felt that the district court's dismissal was in error?

If the facts of *CompuServe* were insufficient to warrant the elimination of Saperstein's claims under Rule 16(c)(2)(A), what other circumstances might warrant the court's dismissal using this mechanism? Consider the court's dismissal under Rule 16(c)(2)(A) (which was numbered (c)(1) at the time) in *MacArthur v. San Juan County*, 416 F. Supp. 2d 1098 (D. Utah 2005):

Accepting the Proposed Amended Complaint as the best articulation of the * * * [p]laintiffs' claims as of the time of pretrial, it becomes apparent that many of plaintiffs' theories of liability had already failed as a matter of law—one because the statute in question simply does not afford plaintiffs a private civil remedy, the others because they are legally meritless: either the essential elements of the cause of action have no bearing upon the specific facts alleged by these plaintiffs (even if those facts are taken as true and all reasonable inferences are drawn in their favor), or because the plaintiffs have pleaded the claims in conclusory terms, without alleging any specific facts that would provide a viable factual footing for these claims, that is, without a plain statement of the claim showing that they are entitled to relief. See FED. R. CIV. P. 8(a)(2). * * * [The plaintiffs'] claims may properly be dismissed as frivolous pursuant to FED. R. CIV. P. 16(c)(1) because they are based upon an indisputably meritless legal theory, or are footed upon conclusory assertions rather than specific facts * * * .

Id. at 1198–99.

Should courts be able to eliminate matters under this Rule only if the dismissal standards of other rules such as Rule 12(b)(6) (failure to state a claim) or Rule 56 (summary judgment) are satisfied, or does Rule 16(c)(2) give courts an independent authority for the dismissal of claims and defenses? *See MacArthur v. San Juan Cty.*, 2005 WL 2716300, at *5 (D. Utah Oct. 21, 2005) ("Pretrial identification of triable issues under Rule 16(c)(1) [now numbered 16(c)(2)(A)] proceeds under its own power, without reference to summary judgment under Rule 56 or any 'pleadings-only' analysis of legal sufficiency under Rule 12(b)(6).").

How does Rule 16(c)(2)(A) interact with the pleading regime established by Rule 8? Should parties be subject to a dismissal of their claims or defenses under Rule 16(c)(2)(A) simply because they fail to plead with sufficient specificity, particularly in light of the revised pleading standards of *Bell Atlantic Corp. v. Twombly*, 550 U.S. 544 (2007), and *Ashcroft v. Iqbal*, 556 U.S. 662 (2009)?

b. Summary Adjudication Under Rule 16(c)(2)(E)

Rule 16(c)(2)(E) indicates that the court may take appropriate action with respect to "the appropriateness and timing of summary adjudication under Rule 56." Make a note that although a court may enter summary judgment on its own initiative without awaiting a motion from a party, *see* 3 James W. Moore et al., Moore's Federal Practice ¶ 16.11, at 16–49 (2d ed., rev. 1994) ("Rule 16(c) has confirmed the court's power to identify the litigable issues, and to eliminate frivolous claims or defenses without awaiting the making of a summary judgment or other motion by the parties."), the court's consideration of the propriety of summary judgment via its authority under Rule 16(c)(2)(E) does not supplant the need to comply with the minimum procedural requirements surrounding the imposition of summary judgment under Rule 56. *See* Fed. R. Civ. P. 56(f) (requiring courts to give "notice and a reasonable time to respond" prior to considering summary judgment on its own initiative).

Specifically, courts at a minimum must notify the party against whom summary judgment may be entered of the possibility of the court's *sua sponte* grant of summary judgment, and courts must permit discovery to advance to a point such that that party has had the opportunity to explore the evidence and determine what additional evidence is likely to be discovered. *Rogan v. Menino*, 175 F.3d 75, 80 (1st Cir. 1999) ("To be sure, Rule 16 permits a court to dispose of marginal claims or issues that do not warrant a full-dress trial. Nevertheless, when the district court employs summary judgment as the vehicle for the elimination of such detritus, Rule 16 does not trump the procedural prophylaxis of Rule 56.").

c. Distinguishing Rule 16(c)(2)(A) Dismissals from Summary Adjudication Under Rule 16(c)(2)(E)

Note the difference between a dismissal under Rule 16(c)(2)(A) and a *sua sponte* grant of summary judgment under Rule 16(c)(2)(E). Dismissals under Rule 16(c)(2)(A) proceed on their own authority and need not have an independent basis in another rule to be appropriate. *See MacArthur*, 2005 WL 2716300 at *10 (noting that in the face of a Rule 16(c)(1) [now numbered 16(c)(2)(A)] dismissal based on frivolousness, "objections based upon Rule 56 summary judgment procedures have no bearing"). The Rule 16(c)(2)(A) standard is the court's own determination that the claim or defense is "frivolous." As mentioned above, however, summary adjudications under Rule 16(c)(2)(E) must comply with the standards of Rule 56 and are not a determination that a party's claim or defense is frivolous, but rather that there is no genuine dispute over any material issue of fact, thereby entitling a party to a judgment as a matter of law. The standards for summary judgment under Rule 56 will be covered in full detail in Section C below.

d. Scheduling Orders

A major piece of business to take care of at the pretrial conference is the development of a scheduling order, which the court issues after consultation with the parties and receipt of their Rule 26(f) discovery plans. Scheduling orders will set forth a timetable for joinder, amendments, motions, and the completion of discovery. FED. R. CIV. P. 16(b)(3)(A). They may also address the timing of various components of the discovery process, protocols governing the discovery and preservation of electronically stored information ("ESI"), the nature of agreements reached between the parties on the protection of privilege and work product against inadvertent disclosures (including agreements reached under Federal Rule of Evidence 502), and dates for other pretrial conferences. FED. R. CIV. P. 16(b)(3)(B). Scheduling orders must be issued within the earlier of 60 days after any defendant has appeared or 90 days after any defendant has been served. FED. R. CIV. P. 16(b)(2).

———————

2. Settlement

A major element of the court's authority under Rule 16 is the power to require parties to engage in discussions to settle the case without proceeding to summary judgment or trial. As was already mentioned, at the pretrial conference, the parties may consider and the court may take appropriate action with respect to "settling the case." FED. R. CIV. P. 16(c)(2)(I). In addition, Rule 16 empowers the court to compel the attendance of litigants and their counsel at pretrial conferences to discuss settlement:

FRCP 16. Pretrial Conferences; Scheduling; Management.

(a) **Purposes of a Pretrial Conference.** In any action, the court may order the attorneys and any unrepresented parties to appear for one or more pretrial conferences for such purposes as * * * (5) facilitating settlement.

* * *

(c) **Attendance and Matters for Consideration at a Pretrial Conference.**

(1) *Attendance.* * * * If appropriate, the court may require that a party or its representative be present or reasonably available by other means to consider possible settlement.

* * *

How extensive is the court's power to facilitate settlement of the case? What happens if a party declines to participate in a pretrial conference called for the purpose of discussing settlement? Can her attendance be compelled? Once in attendance, can the court force the parties to agree to a settlement? The next case illustrates how courts construe the scope of their authority to compel the parties to attend and participate in pretrial settlement conferences and engage in settlement discussions.

Olson v. Alick

U.S. Court of Appeals for the Seventh Circuit
234 F.3d 1273 (7th Cir. 2000)

Before Hon. JOHN L. COFFEY, Hon. DANIEL A. MANION, and Hon. DIANE P. WOOD, CIRCUIT JUDGES.

ORDER

Donn Olson filed suit in May 1998, alleging that Alick's Drugs, Inc. fired him from his job as a pharmacist due to a disability and his age. The district court set the case for trial commencing on December 13, 1999 and scheduled the final pretrial conference for November 30, 1999. After Olson withdrew his consent to participate in a settlement conference and apparently arrived five minutes late to the November 30 conference, the district court dismissed his complaint and denied his subsequent motion to reconsider. Olson now appeals. We vacate and remand.

Olson filed his complaint *pro se,* but several months later obtained counsel. The lawsuit then progressed without incident until virtually the eve of trial. The parties engaged in pretrial discovery in substantial compliance with the court's initial scheduling order. A pretrial conference in April 1999 resulted in a two-month extension of the original discovery deadline, and the district court also granted the parties' joint request for three additional weeks to file expert witness reports. Despite these extensions, the case was still on track for its mid-December trial date.

Circumstances changed, however. The parties' private settlement negotiations stalled and Olson's counsel requested that the court hold a settlement conference. On November 9, 1999, the district court in South Bend, where Olson resides, referred the matter to a magistrate judge in Fort Wayne, and, during a conference call later that day, Olson's lawyers agreed to participate in a settlement conference to take place on Friday, November 12. At 6:15 a.m. on the conference date, however, Olson's lawyers notified opposing counsel that Olson had decided not to attend the settlement conference. Counsel for the parties then informed the magistrate judge that Olson "did not choose to attend" the conference, and so the magistrate judge cancelled it. Olson's lawyers moved to withdraw that afternoon, citing a breakdown in communication, disagreement with Olson about how the litigation should proceed, and Olson's withdrawal of his consent to participate in the settlement conference. In their motion, Olson's lawyers also sought to postpone the trial date to give Olson time to obtain new counsel, a request that the defendants said they did not oppose.

The district court granted the motion to withdraw, but deferred ruling on Olson's request for a continuance until the November 30 pretrial conference, which, in its written order, the court "advised" Olson to attend in person or by new counsel. When the conference commenced at 1:05 p.m., neither Olson nor a new lawyer was present. Asked whether he knew if Olson was coming, the defendants' lawyer replied that Olson had made a hurried telephone call from work the previous evening that left him "with the distinct impression that there would not be anybody here." Asked then if he had "any motion," counsel replied that "the defense is always agreeable to a dismissal" and said he would "be more than happy to move for that." Concluding that anything less than dismissal would reward Olson "for his failures to appear," the district court dismissed under Rule 16(f) of the Federal Rules of Civil Procedure with the explanation that "Olson failed to appear with virtually no notice at the settlement conference . . . and has now failed to appear at the final pretrial conference, despite having been advised to do so in the court's order."

The very next day, Olson wrote a letter to the court, explaining that he tried to attend the pretrial conference but did not arrive at the courthouse in South Bend until 1:10 p.m. Olson was late, he said, because that day he had been working at a hospital pharmacy in Sturgis, Michigan, and, as he was leaving for court, an order came in for a chemotherapy prescription that the replacement pharmacist, a nursing mother, could not safely fill. He also explained that he had not refused to attend the settlement conference, but rather that his attorneys scheduled it without first consulting him about his work schedule. Olson advised that he was working as a "float pharmacist" at 30 different K-Mart stores, and that his schedule was set three to four weeks in advance. The day of the Fort Wayne settlement conference, he added, he was working in Chesterton, Indiana. Though he tried to find a replacement, said Olson, he was unsuccessful and thus had informed his lawyers the day *before* the conference that he could not attend because he feared losing his job. In addition to this correspondence, on December 3 Olson also filed a motion to set aside the dismissal, repeating what he had said in his letter and adding that he tried to warn the defendants' counsel that he would be late for the pretrial conference, but learned when he called the lawyer's Elkhart, Indiana, office that he had already left for South Bend. Olson later supplied the court with billing records evidencing that indeed he had told his lawyers on November 11 that he could not find a replacement for work, and yet his lawyers waited until the next day to notify opposing counsel and the magistrate judge that Olson had elected not to attend the settlement conference.

Although Olson cited no rule, the defendants interpreted his motion as one pursuant to Federal Rule of Civil Procedure 60(b), which permits a court to relieve a party from a judgment because of mistake, inadvertence, surprise or excusable neglect. *See* FED.R.CIV.P. 60(b). Following the defendants' lead and applying the Rule 60(b) standard, the district court denied the motion, concluding that Olson had offered "neither a showing of excusable neglect nor hope for better performance in the future." The court explained—incorrectly—that the defendants had opposed continuing the trial date and reasoned that Olson should not be permitted effectively to win a contested motion by intentionally missing the pretrial conference and then expecting it to be rescheduled.

* * * Though Olson's notice of appeal identifies the denial of his postjudgment motion as the order from which he appeals, his motion sought reconsideration of the Rule 16(f) dismissal and was filed within ten days after entry of the dismissal. The motion, therefore, is properly viewed as one seeking to alter or amend the judgment pursuant to Federal Rule of Civil Procedure Rule 59(e). In contrast, Rule 60(b) is an "extraordinary remedy." * * * In essence, then, this appeal poses the single question of whether, based on the record as it stood when the district court's judgment became final, the Rule 16(f) dismissal was an abuse of discretion.

* * * Dismissal is a harsh sanction to be employed only in extreme situations of delay or contumacious conduct, depending on the egregiousness of the plaintiff's conduct, the frequency and magnitude of the plaintiff's errors, and the meritorious nature of the plaintiff's case. The district court may impose the sanction of dismissal for "ordinary misconduct" only after a warning and a determination that dismissal is an appropriate sanction in the circumstances.

We conclude that the district court abused its discretion in dismissing Olson's lawsuit. First, the district court should not have construed his withdrawal of consent to participate in the settlement conference as a form of delinquency. Olson may have inconvenienced the defendants and the magistrate judge, but we see nothing in this record—and the defendants point us to nothing—suggesting that the district court intended the November 12 settlement conference to be anything but consensual. Indeed, the defendants tell us that they *"agreed to attend* a settlement conference," not that they or anyone else was ordered to do so. And if the court did not compel the conference, then neither was Olson precluded from changing his mind about participating. Moreover, even if the conference became mandatory once requested and scheduled, we find no evidence in the record that the district court exercised its authority to compel Olson, rather than just his lawyers, to attend. *Compare G. Heileman Brewing Co. v. Joseph Oat Corp., 871 F.2d 648, 653–54 (7th Cir.1989)* (en banc) (upholding sanctions for violating court order to appear at settlement conference).

In addition, the dismissal for arriving five minutes late one time in the 22-month history of the case was improper. Where, as here, Olson recently found himself without counsel and the defendants had no objection to the pending motion, "one missed hearing should rarely form an adequate basis for [dismissal]." *Stafford v. Mesnik, 63 F.3d 1445, 1449 (7th Cir. 1995)* (holding that entry of default judgment for failure to appear at one hearing was abuse of discretion where defendant's counsel had temporarily withdrawn and plaintiff's counsel did not object to counsel's reappearance). Furthermore, Olson was entitled to, but did not receive, a direct and explicit warning of the possible consequences of his failure to appear, particularly in light of his lawyers' recent withdrawal. Olson's late arrival for the pretrial conference was an isolated incident that alone "does not satisfy the threshold showing of delay, contumacious conduct, or failed prior sanctions" to justify denying him the opportunity to have his case decided on the merits. *See Long v. Steepro,* 213 F.3d 983, 986 (7th Cir. 2000) (dismissal was error where *pro se* litigant's only misstep during 12-month litigation was untimely filing of evidentiary lists).

The dismissal in this instance was particularly inappropriate given that the case had been proceeding on schedule and was nearly ready for trial, that no prior continuances of the trial date had been requested, and that Olson's counsel had withdrawn just two weeks prior to the final pretrial conference. *See Long,* 213 F.3d at 986 (dismissal was error where *pro se* plaintiff's failure to file list of witnesses, exhibits and contentions was first missed deadline and plaintiff had "prosecuted his complaint without incident for over one year"). *Compare 3 Penny Theater Corp. v. Plitt Theatres, Inc.,* 812 F.2d 337, 339–40 (7th Cir. 1987) (dismissal not abuse of discretion where plaintiff repeatedly failed to attend status hearings and had received five extensions of pretrial deadlines). The defendants now try to tell us that the case was not so ready for trial after all, and that we should uphold the dismissal because Olson had failed to file his proposed jury instructions or assist the defendants in preparing a pretrial order. But the district court did not rest the dismissal on these grounds, and so they are not before us. Even so, Olson's lawyers failed to timely file these materials prior to their withdrawal, conduct for which Olson should not be sanctioned, and regardless, the district court had suspended substantially all pretrial deadlines when it granted the motion to withdraw. Furthermore, the district court dismissed Olson's case on the mistaken belief that the defendants opposed continuing the trial date; the court instead could have granted the motion for a continuance at the pretrial conference, Olson's late arrival notwithstanding.

Finally, the record indicates that the district court failed to consider the likely merits of Olson's claims before dismissing the case. *See Bolt v. Loy,* No. 00-1280, 2000 WL 1286255, at *2 (7th Cir. Sept. 13, 2000) (district court must consider whether suit has any possible merit before dismissing for ordinary misconduct). Significantly, prior to the final pretrial conference, the defendants never moved for dismissal or summary judgment, and were willing participants in settlement negotiations. Their conduct of the litigation was enough to put the district court on notice that at least the defendants thought Olson's case was more than baseless, and the court should have inquired further before inviting a hasty motion to dismiss from defendants who were "more than happy" to comply.

VACATED AND REMANDED.

————

Points for Discussion

a. Facilitating Settlement Under Rule 16

Although courts may compel litigants to attend settlement conferences, courts may not compel them to settle or accept certain settlement terms. <u>G. Heileman Brewing Co. v. Joseph Oat Corp., 871 F.2d 648, 653 (7th Cir. 1989) (en banc)</u> ("If this case represented a situation where Oat Corporation had sent a corporate representative and was sanctioned because that person refused to make an offer to pay money—that is, refused to submit to settlement coercion—we would be faced with a decidedly different issue—a situation we would not countenance."). What purpose does the settlement conference serve if the court does not have the authority to compel settlement? *See* <u>Abney v. Patten, 696 F. Supp. 567, 568 (W.D. Okla. 1987)</u> ("Obviously the Rule does not permit compelled settlements . . . . However, . . . 'A settlement conference is appropriate at any time.' The horses may be led to water. Whether they drink is up to them." (quoting Report of the Advisory Committee on <u>Federal Civil Rules, 97 F.R.D. 165, 211 (1983)</u>)).

Given that courts may not compel parties to settle a case, what "appropriate action" may a judge take with respect to settlement under <u>Rule 16(c)(2)(I)</u> and how can a pretrial conference contribute to facilitating a settlement under <u>Rule 16(a)(5)</u>? *Heileman* provides one answer: Judges may compel authorized representatives to participate in settlement talks with the hope that doing so will lead to an actual settlement (indeed the parties ultimately settled the case in *Heileman*).

Other possibilities exist, however. Assume you represented the defendant in this case and were attending the settlement conference where the judge told you that he thought that your client did not have much of a defense and that its chances of prevailing in this case were slim. Would knowing this perspective of the judge persuade you to suggest to your client that it consider settling the case?

In reality, judges likely engage in this practice with some regularity. *See, e.g.,* <u>Sloan v. State Farm Mut. Auto. Ins. Co., 360 F.3d 1220, 1227 (10th Cir. 2004)</u>("[W]e do not find that the district court's comments in this case . . . rendered the trial unfair. The district court repeatedly expressed its views

Food for Thought

Is it appropriate for a judge to comment on the merits of the case as suggested here, particularly if it is done to motivate your client into settling? Should such commentary be grounds for having the judge disqualified from hearing the case? *See, e.g.,* <u>Rocha v. Great Am. Ins. Co., 850 F.2d 1095, 1100 (6th Cir. 1988)</u> ("When the remarks of the judge . . .clearly indicate . . . an unwarranted prejudgment of the merits of the case . . . the judge indicates, whether consciously or not, a personal bias and prejudice which renders invalid any resulting judgment in favor of the party so favored." (quoting <u>Knapp v. Kinsey, 232 F.2d 458, 466 (6th Cir. 1956)</u>, *cert. denied,* <u>352 U.S. 892</u>)).

that the parties should settle the case (and what the case was worth), but it did this outside the presence of the jury.").

Judges may also impose a deadline by which the parties must reach any settlement in a case, and impose sanctions in the event that a settlement occurs at a later time as a means of facilitating settlement. *See* <u>Newton v. A.C. & S., Inc., 918 F.2d 1121, 1126 (3d Cir. 1990)</u> (holding that a district court has the authority under <u>Rule 16(f)</u> to impose fines upon a party or its counsel for failure to settle by a certain date prior to the commencement of trial).

The ability of judges to facilitate settlement does not go so far as to extend to other outstanding disputes that the parties in an action have with each other that have not been asserted as claims. Even if the parties wish to incorporate a resolution of these other unasserted claims into a global settlement, the court may not use a <u>Rule 16</u> pretrial conference as the forum for resolving all of these matters in one setting. *See* <u>In re Asbestos Litig., 90 F.3d 963, 1015 (5th Cir. 1996)</u> (Smith, J., dissenting) ("[R]ule [16] allows judges to schedule conferences only to settle 'the case,' which surely must mean the case filed and pending before the judge. <u>Rule 16</u> cannot permit a judge to order settlement conferences over cases that are not before him—that would be an exercise of power the Constitution does not permit.").

—Perspective & Analysis—

Some commentators have criticized the active role that many judges take in encouraging parties to settle their cases:

> [The] [p]rivacy and informality [of pretrial conferences] have some genuine advantages; attorneys and judges can discuss discovery schedules and explore settlement proposals without the constraints of the formal courtroom environment. But substantial dangers also inhere in such activities. The extensive information that judges receive during pretrial conferences has not been filtered by the rules of evidence. Some of this information is received *ex parte*, a process that deprives the opposing party of the opportunity to contest the validity of information received. Moreover, judges are in close contact with attorneys during the course of management. Such interactions may become occasions for the development of intense feelings—admiration, friendship, or antipathy. Therefore, management becomes a fertile field for the growth of personal bias. * * *
>
> Having supervised case preparation and pressed for settlement, judges can hardly be considered untainted if they are ultimately asked to find the facts and adjudicate the merits of a dispute.

Judith Resnik, *Managerial Judges*, 96 HARV. L. REV. 374, 426–27, 430 (1982).

b. Sanctions Under <u>Rule 16</u>

As we saw in *Olson*, courts have the authority to impose sanctions on litigants who do not comply with a court's pretrial orders. This authority is spelled out in <u>Rule 16(f)</u>:

FRCP 16(f). Pretrial Conferences; Scheduling; Management: Sanctions.

(f) Sanctions.

(1) *In General.* On motion or on its own, the court may issue any just orders, including those authorized by Rule 37(b)(2)(A)(ii)–(vii), if a party or its attorney:

(A) fails to appear at a scheduling or other pretrial conference;

(B) is substantially unprepared to participate—or does not participate in good faith—in the conference; or

(C) fails to obey a scheduling or other pretrial order.

(2) *Imposing Fees and Costs.* Instead of or in addition to any other sanction, the court must order the party, its attorney, or both to pay the reasonable expenses—including attorney's fees—incurred because of any noncompliance with this rule, unless the noncompliance was substantially justified or other circumstances make an award of expenses unjust.

An example of the imposition of monetary sanctions can be found in *G. Heileman Brewing Co. v. Joseph Oat Corp.*, 871 F.2d 648, 653 (7th Cir. 1989) (en banc), a case in which the district court required the party that failed to appear at the settlement conference to pay the costs and attorneys' fees of its adversaries associated with attending the pretrial conference. *See also Official Airline Guides, Inc. v. Goss*, 6 F.3d 1385, 1396 (9th Cir. 1993) (finding that it was not an abuse of discretion to award a sanction of attorneys' fees and costs for failure to obey the court's order regarding participation in a settlement conference). Under Rule 16(f), however, the sanctions imposed can be much more severe, up to and including dismissal of the offending party's case. *See, e.g.*, *Bud Brooks Trucking, Inc. v. Bill Hodges Trucking Co.*, 909 F.2d 1437, 1440 (10th Cir. 1990) (refusing to disturb a judgment of dismissal imposed as sanction for failure to comply with discovery orders and failure to appear at a settlement conference); *see also Griffin v. Wilshire Credit Corp.*, 2010 WL 2301743 (N.D. Tex. May 14, 2010) ("Plaintiff failed to comply with two orders requiring her to participate in a Rule 26(f) conference and the preparation of a joint status report and proposed scheduling plan, and an order requiring her to attend a show cause hearing on May 14, 2010—all without justification or excuse. As a result, her pleadings should be stricken and her claims dismissed with prejudice.").

Practice Pointer

In light of the consequences that may result from disobeying a court's pretrial orders, clearly it is advisable to comply with those orders. When you as counsel or your client disagree with the court's order, the proper remedy is to make an objection, comply with the order, and then raise the matter on an appeal of the final judgment if it comes to that.

c.   Offers of Judgment Under Rule 68

In addition to equipping courts with the ability to facilitate settlements through the Rule 16 pretrial conference, the Federal Rules express a preference for settlement through a completely separate rule, Rule 68:

FRCP 68. Offer of Judgment.

(a)   Making an Offer; Judgment on an Accepted Offer. At least 14 days before the date set for trial, a party defending against a claim may serve on an opposing party an offer to allow judgment on specified terms, with the costs then accrued. If, within 14 days after being served, the opposing party serves written notice accepting the offer, either party may then file the offer and notice of acceptance, plus proof of service. The clerk must then enter judgment.

(b)   Unaccepted Offer. An unaccepted offer is considered withdrawn, but it does not preclude a later offer. Evidence of an unaccepted offer is not admissible except in a proceeding to determine costs.

(c)   Offer After Liability Is Determined. When one party's liability to another has been determined but the extent of liability remains to be determined by further proceedings, the party held liable may make an offer of judgment. It must be served within a reasonable time— but at least 14 days—before the date set for a hearing to determine the extent of liability.

(d)   Paying Costs After an Unaccepted Offer. If the judgment that the offeree finally obtains is not more favorable than the unaccepted offer, the offeree must pay the costs incurred after the offer was made.

The practical import of this Rule is that a party who receives an offer to settle a case but refuses that offer, and then later collects a lesser amount after a trial, will ultimately have to cover the costs of the party that made the offer. What impact do you think such a rule has on influencing parties to accept settlement offers before going to trial? Is the Rule too coercive, meaning that it might encourage parties to accept settlement offers well below what they could get at trial?

Experience has revealed that defendants rarely take advantage of Rule 68, rendering questions about its potential coerciveness virtually a moot point. *See* Harold S. Lewis, Jr. & Thomas A. Eaton, *Of Offers Not (Frequently) Made and (Rarely) Accepted: The Mystery of Rule 68*, 57 MERCER L. REV. 723, 724 (2006) (noting that

Food for Thought

Should the cost-shifting of Rule 68 be triggered only when the defendant's settlement offer is reasonable and made in good faith? *See Delta Air Lines, Inc. v. August*, 450 U.S. 346, 369 (1981) (Rehnquist, J., dissenting) ("To import into the mandatory language of Rule 68 a requirement that the tender of judgment must be 'reasonable' or made in 'good faith' not only rewrites Rule 68, but also puts a district court in the impossible position of having to evaluate such uncertain and nebulous concepts in the context of an 'offer of judgment.' ").

Rule 68 "is seldom used"). Further, the costs referred to in the rule do not ordinarily include attorneys' fees, which means that the threatened costs are typically not sufficiently large to have too coercive an effect on settlement where large dollar amounts are at stake. However, if the underlying statute on which the action is based includes attorneys' fees within the scope of "costs" that may be awarded to prevailing parties, then such fees are properly awardable under Rule 68. *See Marek v. Chesny*, 473 U.S. 1, 9 (1985) [*FLEX Case 9.A*] ("[A]ll costs properly awardable in an action are to be considered within the scope of Rule 68 'costs.' Thus, absent congressional expressions to the contrary, where the underlying statute defines 'costs' to include attorney's fees, we are satisfied such fees are to be included as costs for purposes of Rule 68.").

> Although there was some controversy regarding the point for several years, in 2016 the Supreme Court held that an unaccepted Rule 68 offer of judgment does not moot a plaintiff's case. *Campbell-Ewald Co. v. Gomez*, 136 S. Ct. 663, 670 (2016).

3. Alternative Dispute Resolution

In recent times there has been a movement to migrate disputes away from the courts and into alternative forums that might be able to provide a more amicably reached resolution of a dispute at less cost and with better results. This alternative-dispute-resolution or ADR movement has resulted in the advent of numerous private dispute-resolution service providers that enable parties to arbitrate their disputes or have them mediated by a neutral third party, without having to litigate the matter formally in the public court system. With the delay and expense of litigation apparently on the rise—particularly in complex commercial matters—it is thought that a private arbitration will enable the parties to resolve their dispute much more quickly and cheaply, typically with the added benefit of confidentiality. Such private, extrajudicial arbitration is generally a process that the parties have agreed to *ex ante* through contract and usually produces binding, non-reviewable decisions.

What's That?

Arbitration is a process in which disputants present their case to a neutral third party or panel of third parties who then render a (typically binding) decision. *Mediation* involves a neutral third party who tries to help the parties reach a mutually agreeable resolution of their dispute instead of deciding the matter for them.

The Federal Arbitration Act

Under the Federal Arbitration Act ("FAA"), 9 U.S.C. § 1 et seq., private arbitration agreements are rigorously enfo rced. Thus, if a party attempts to litigate a matter in state or federal court that is subject to an agreement to arbitrate, its adversary can move to compel arbitration under the FAA and the case will be dismissed. *Nitro-Lift Techs., L.L.C. v. Howard*, 568 U.S. 17, 20 (2012) ("It is well settled that the substantive law the Act created is applicable in state and federal courts." (citation and internal quotation marks omitted)). There has been a spate of recent Supreme Court decisions interpreting the FAA, each of which reaffirm the strength of the federal policy in favor of the enforcement of private arbitration agreements. *See, e.g.*, *Am. Express Co. v. Italian Colors Rest.*, 570 U.S. 228, 238 (2013) (holding that the FAA does not permit courts to invalidate a contractual waiver of class arbitration on the ground that the plaintiff's cost of individually arbitrating a federal statutory claim exceeds the potential recovery); *Oxford Health Plans L.L.C. v. Sutter*, 569 U.S. 564, 568 (2013) (holding that an arbitrator's determination that a contract permits class arbitration must stand as long as it is "arguably construing or applying the contract . . . , regardless of a court's view of its (de)merits"); *Marmet Health Care Ctr., Inc. v. Brown*, 565 U.S. 530, 531–534 (2012) (holding that state law prohibiting outright the arbitration of a particular type of claim conflicts with the FAA and is preempted); *CompuCredit Corp. v. Greenwood*, 565 U.S. 95, 97 (2012) (noting that the FAA "requires courts to enforce agreements to arbitrate according to their terms . . . even when the claims at issue are federal statutory claims, unless the FAA's mandate has been overridden by a contrary congressional command" (citation and internal quotation marks omitted)); *AT&T Mobility L.L.C. v. Concepcion*, 563 U.S. 333, 343 (2011) (holding that the FAA preempts California's judicial rule regarding the unconscionability of class arbitration waivers in consumer contracts); *Stolt-Nielsen S.A. v. AnimalFeeds Int'l Corp.*, 559 U.S. 662 (2009) (holding that an arbitrator may employ class procedures only if the parties have authorized them).

Court-Annexed ADR

We turn now to the phenomenon of court-annexed ADR. Federal district courts have the authority to require litigants before them to submit their dispute to an ADR process in an effort to arrive at a disposition of the matter without having to go through the trial or much of the pretrial process. This authority resides in part in Rule 16(c)(2)(I): "At any pretrial conference, the court may consider and take appropriate action . . . (I) settling the case and using special procedures to assist in resolving the dispute when authorized by statute or local rule." Fed. R. Civ. P. 16(c)(2)(I). The next case spells out in further detail the source and nature of federal courts' authority to order parties to participate in court-annexed ADR.

In re Atlantic Pipe Corp.

U.S. Court of Appeals for the First Circuit
304 F.3d 135 (1st Cir. 2002)

SELYA, CIRCUIT JUDGE.

This mandamus proceeding[1] requires us to resolve an issue of importance to judges and practitioners alike: Does a district court possess the authority to compel an unwilling party to participate in, and share the costs of, non-binding mediation conducted by a private mediator? We hold that a court may order mandatory mediation pursuant to an explicit statutory provision or local rule. We further hold that where, as here, no such authorizing medium exists, a court nonetheless may order mandatory mediation through the use of its inherent powers as long as the case is an appropriate one and the order contains adequate safeguards. Because the mediation order here at issue lacks such safeguards (although it does not fall far short), we vacate it and remand the matter for further proceedings.

I. BACKGROUND

In January 1996, Thames-Dick Superaqueduct Partners (Thames-Dick) entered into a master agreement with the Puerto Rico Aqueduct and Sewer Authority (PRASA) to construct, operate, and maintain the North Coast Superaqueduct Project (the Project). Thames-Dick granted subcontracts for various portions of the work, including a subcontract for construction management to Dick Corp. of Puerto Rico (Dick-PR), a subcontract for the operation and maintenance of the Project to Thames Water International, Ltd. (Thames Water), and a subcontract for the fabrication of pipe to Atlantic Pipe Corp. (APC). After the Project had been built, a segment of the pipeline burst. Thames-Dick incurred significant costs in repairing the damage. Not surprisingly, it sought to recover those costs from other parties. In response, one of PRASA's insurers filed a declaratory judgment action in a local court to determine whether Thames-Dick's claims were covered under its policy. The litigation ballooned, soon involving a number of parties and a myriad of issues above and beyond insurance coverage.

---

[1] Although the petition seeks the issuance of a writ of mandamus, the relief sought is more in the nature of a writ of prohibition. Because the two writs have much in common—one is merely the obverse of the other—we follow past practice and make no distinction between them.

On April 25, 2001, the hostilities spilled over into federal court. Two entities beneficially interested in the master agreement—CPA Group International and Chiang, Patel & Yerby, Inc. (collectively CPA)—sued Thames-Dick, Dick-PR, Thames Water, and various insurers in the <u>United States District Court for the District of Puerto Rico</u>, seeking remuneration for consulting services rendered in connection with repairs to the Project. A googol of claims, counterclaims, cross-claims, and third-party complaints followed. Some of these were brought against APC (the petitioner here). To complicate matters, one of the defendants moved to dismiss on grounds that, *inter alia*, (1) CPA had failed to join an indispensable party whose presence would destroy diversity jurisdiction, and (2) the existence of the parallel proceeding in the local court counseled in favor of abstention.

> **FYI**
>
> Puerto Rico, although not a U.S. state, is a territory of the United States that falls within the jurisdiction of the First Circuit. Appeals from the U.S. district court in Puerto Rico are heard by the First Circuit, and one of the Judges of the First Circuit, Judge <u>Juan R. Torruella</u>, sits in and is from Puerto Rico.

While this motion was pending before the district court, Thames-Dick asked that the case be referred to mediation and suggested Professor Eric Green as a suitable mediator. The district court granted the motion over APC's objection and ordered nonbinding mediation to proceed before Professor Green. The court pronounced mediation likely to conserve judicial resources; directed all parties to undertake mediation in good faith; stayed discovery pending completion of the mediation; and declared that participation in the mediation would not prejudice the parties' positions vis-à-vis the pending motion or the litigation as a whole. The court also stated that if mediation failed to produce a global settlement, the case would proceed to trial.

After moving unsuccessfully for reconsideration of the mediation order, APC sought relief by way of mandamus. Its petition alleged that the district court did not have the authority to require mediation (especially in light of unresolved questions as to the court's subject-matter jurisdiction) and, in all events, could not force APC to pay a share of the expenses of the mediation. * * *

Prior to argument in this court, two notable developments occurred. First, the district court considered and rejected the challenges to its exercise of jurisdiction. Second, APC rejected an offer by Thames-Dick to pay its share of the mediator's fees.

II. JURISDICTION

In an effort to shut off further debate, the respondents asseverate that mandamus is improper because APC will not suffer irreparable harm in the absence of such relief. * * * We believe that this case is fit for * * * mandamus because the extent of a trial court's power to order mandatory mediation presents a systemically important issue as to which this court has not yet spoken. * * * We turn, then, to the merits.

III. THE MERITS

There are four potential sources of judicial authority for ordering mandatory non-binding mediation of pending cases, namely, (a) the court's local rules, (b) an applicable statute, (c) the Federal Rules of Civil Procedure, and (d) the court's inherent powers. Because the district court did not identify the basis of its assumed authority, we consider each of these sources.

A. The Local Rules.

A district court's local rules may provide an appropriate source of authority for ordering parties to participate in mediation. In Puerto Rico, however, the local rules contain only a single reference to any form of alternative dispute resolution (ADR). That reference is embodied in the district court's Amended Civil Justice Expense and Delay Reduction Plan (CJR Plan).

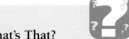

What's That?

Local rules are rules promulgated by individual federal districts to govern various procedural matters not covered by the Federal Rules of Civil Procedure. Federal Rule 83(a) authorizes each district court to make such rules as long as they do not duplicate or contradict the Federal Rules. For an example of local rules, visit http://www.vaed.uscourts.gov.

The district court adopted the CJR Plan on June 14, 1993, in response to the directive contained in the Civil Justice Reform Act of 1990 (CJRA), 28 U.S.C. §§ 471–482. Rule V of the CJR Plan states:

Pursuant to 28 U.S.C. § 473(b)(4), this Court shall adopt a method of Alternative Dispute Resolution ("ADR") through mediation by a judicial officer.

Such a program would allow litigants to obtain from an impartial third party—the judicial officer as mediator—a flexible non-binding, dispute resolution process to facilitate negotiations among the parties to help them reach settlement.

What's That?

The *Civil Justice Reform Act* ("CJRA") was a statute that required the federal districts to develop plans aimed at reducing the expense and delay associated with litigation. For more information on the CJRA, see Lauren Robel, *Fractured Procedure: The Civil Justice Reform Act of 1990*, 46 STAN. L. REV. 1447 (1994).

In addition to specifying who may act as a mediator, Rule V also limns the proper procedure for mediation sessions and assures confidentiality.

The respondents concede that the mediation order in this case falls outside the boundaries of the mediation program envisioned by Rule V. It does so most noticeably because it involves mediation before a private mediator, not a judicial officer. Seizing upon this discrepancy, APC argues that the local rules limit the district court in this respect, and that the court exceeded its authority thereunder * * * . The respondents counter by arguing that the rule does not bind the district court because, notwithstanding the unambiguous promise of the CJR Plan (which declares that the district court "shall adopt a method of Alternative Dispute Resolution"), no such program has been adopted to date.

This is a powerful argument. APC does not contradict the respondents' assurance that the relevant portion of the CJR Plan has remained unimplemented, and

What's That?

Judicial notice involves a court's acceptance of something as true based not on any evidentiary presentation, but rather simply because the matter involves a well-known and indisputable fact, such as the fact that Spain shares a border with Portugal.

we take judicial notice that there is no formal, ongoing ADR program in the Puerto Rico federal district court. Because that is so, we conclude that the District of Puerto Rico has no local rule in force that dictates the permissible characteristics of mediation orders. Consequently, APC's argument founders.[2]

B. The ADR Act.

There is only one potential source of statutory authority for ordering mandatory non-binding mediation here: the Alternative Dispute Resolution Act of 1998 (ADR Act), 28 U.S.C. §§ 651–658. Congress passed the ADR Act to promote the utilization of alternative dispute resolution methods in the federal courts and to set appropriate guidelines for their use. The Act lists mediation as an appropriate ADR process. Moreover, it sanctions the participation of "professional neutrals from the private sector" as mediators. Finally, the Act requires district courts to obtain litigants' consent only when they order arbitration, not when they order the use of other ADR mechanisms (such as non-binding mediation).

Despite the broad sweep of these provisions, the Act is quite clear that some form of the ADR procedures it endorses must be adopted in each judicial district by local rule. In the absence of such local rules, the ADR Act itself does not authorize any specific court to use a particular ADR mechanism. Because the District of Puerto Rico has not yet complied with the Act's mandate, the mediation order here at issue cannot be justified under the ADR Act.

* * *

---

[2] This holding renders it unnecessary for us to discuss the respondents' alternate contention that the CJR Plan is a dead letter because the legislation that prompted its enactment—the CJRA—expired in 1997. *See, e.g.*, Carl Tobias, *Did the Civil Justice Reform Act of 1990 Actually Expire?*, 31 U. MICH. J.L. REFORM 887, 892 (1998) (exploring the uncertainty regarding whether the CJRA expired and whether local plans adopted pursuant to it are still effective).

We add, however, that although the respondents cannot use the ADR Act as a justification, neither can APC use it as a nullification. Noting that the Act requires the adoption of local rules establishing a formal ADR program, APC equates the absence of such rules with the absence of power to employ an ADR procedure (say, mediation) in a specific case. But that is wishful thinking: if one assumes that district judges possessed the power to require mediation prior to the passage of the ADR Act, there is nothing in the Act that strips them of that power. * * *

* * * Hence, we conclude that where, as here, there are no implementing local rules, the ADR Act neither authorizes nor prohibits the entry of a mandatory mediation order.

C. The Civil Rules.

The respondents next argue that the district court possessed the authority to require mediation by virtue of the Federal Rules of Civil Procedure. They concentrate their attention on <u>FED.R.CIV.P. 16</u>, which states in pertinent part that "the court may take appropriate action[ ] with respect to . . . (9) settlement and the use of special procedures to assist in resolving the dispute when authorized by statute or local rule." But the words "when authorized by statute or local rule" are a frank limitation on the district courts' authority to order mediation thereunder, and we must adhere to that circumscription. Because there is no statute or local rule authorizing mandatory private mediation in the District of Puerto Rico, <u>Rule 16(c)(9)</u> [currently numbered Rule 16(c)(2)(I)] does not assist the respondents' cause.

D. Inherent Powers.

Even apart from positive law, district courts have substantial inherent power to manage and control their calendars. This inherent power takes many forms. By way of illustration, a district court may use its inherent power to compel represented clients to attend pretrial settlement conferences, even though such a practice is not specifically authorized in the Civil Rules. *See <u>G. Heileman Brewing Co. v. Joseph Oat Corp., 871 F.2d 648, 650 (7th Cir. 1989) (en banc)</u>.*

>
>
> **Take Note!**
>
> As we saw above, Rule 16 now empowers district judges to compel represented parties to attend settlement conferences. *See <u>FED. R. CIV. P. 16(c)(1)</u>.*

Of course, a district court's inherent powers are not infinite. There are at least four limiting principles. First, inherent powers must be used in a way reasonably suited to the enhancement of the court's processes, including the orderly and expeditious disposition of pending cases. Second, inherent powers cannot be exercised in a manner that contradicts an applicable statute or rule. Third, the use of inherent powers must comport with procedural fairness. And, finally, inherent powers "must be exercised with restraint and discretion."

At one time, the inherent power of judges to compel unwilling parties to participate in ADR procedures was a hot-button issue for legal scholars. Although many federal district courts have forestalled further debate by adopting local rules that authorize specific ADR procedures and outlaw others, the District of Puerto Rico is not among them. Thus, we have no choice but to address the question head-on.

We begin our inquiry by examining the case law. In <u>*Strandell v. Jackson County,* 838 F.2d 884 (7th Cir. 1987)</u>, the Seventh Circuit held that a district court does not possess inherent power to compel participation in a summary jury trial. In the court's view, <u>FED.R.CIV.P. 16</u> occupied the field and prevented a district court from forcing "an unwilling litigant [to] be sidetracked from the normal course of litigation." But the group that spearheaded the subsequent revision of <u>Rule 16</u> explicitly rejected that interpretation. *See* <u>FED.R.CIV.P. 16</u>, advisory committee's note (1993 Amendment) ("The [amended] rule does not attempt to resolve questions as to the extent a court would be authorized to require [ADR] proceedings as an exercise of its inherent powers."). Thus, we do not find *Strandell* persuasive on this point. * * *

What's That?

A *summary jury trial* is a settlement technique where parties present their case before a mock jury, which renders a nonbinding verdict that gives the parties an indication of the strength or weakness of their respective positions.

* * * When mediation is forced upon unwilling litigants, it stands to reason that the likelihood of settlement is diminished. Requiring parties to invest substantial amounts of time and money in mediation under such circumstances may well be inefficient.

The fact remains, however, that none of these considerations establishes that mandatory mediation is always inappropriate. There may well be specific cases in which such a protocol is likely to conserve judicial resources without significantly burdening the objectors' rights to a full, fair, and speedy trial. Much depends on the idiosyncracies of the particular case and the details of the mediation order.

In some cases, a court may be warranted in believing that compulsory mediation could yield significant benefits even if one or more parties object. After all, a party may resist mediation simply out of unfamiliarity with the process or out of fear that a willingness to submit would be perceived as a lack of confidence in her legal position. In such an instance, the party's initial reservations are likely to evaporate as the mediation progresses, and negotiations could well produce a beneficial outcome, at reduced cost and greater speed, than would a trial. While the possibility that parties will fail to reach agreement remains ever present, the boon of settlement can be worth the risk.

This is particularly true in complex cases involving multiple claims and parties. The fair and expeditious resolution of such cases often is helped along by creative solutions—solutions that simply are not available in the binary framework of traditional adversarial litigation. Mediation with the assistance of a skilled facilitator gives parties an opportunity to explore a much wider range of options, including those that go beyond conventional zero-sum resolutions. Mindful of these potential advantages, we hold that it is within a district court's inherent power to order non-consensual mediation in those cases in which that step seems reasonably likely to serve the interests of justice.

E. The Mediation Order.

Our determination that the district courts have inherent power to refer cases to non-binding mediation is made with a recognition that any such order must be crafted in a manner that preserves procedural fairness and shields objecting parties from undue burdens. We thus turn to the specifics of the mediation order entered in this case. As with any exercise of a district court's inherent powers, we review the entry of that order for abuse of discretion.

As an initial matter, we agree with the lower court that the complexity of this case militates in favor of ordering mediation. At last count, the suit involves twelve parties, asserting a welter of claims, counterclaims, cross-claims, and third-party claims predicated on a wide variety of theories. The pendency of nearly parallel litigation in the Puerto Rican courts, which features a slightly different cast of characters and claims that are related to but not completely congruent with those asserted here, further complicates the matter. Untangling the intricate web of relationships among the parties, along with the difficult and fact-intensive arguments made by each, will be time-consuming and will impose significant costs on the parties and the court. Against this backdrop, mediation holds out the dual prospect of advantaging the litigants and conserving scarce judicial resources.

* * *

* * * APC posits that the appointment of a private mediator proposed by one of the parties is *per se* improper (and, thus, invalidates the order). We do not agree. The district court has inherent power to "appoint persons unconnected with the court to aid judges in the performance of specific judicial duties." In the context of non-binding mediation, the mediator does not decide the merits of the case and has no authority to coerce settlement. Thus, in the absence of a contrary statute or rule, it is perfectly acceptable for the district court to appoint a qualified and neutral private party as a mediator. The mere fact that the mediator was proposed by one of the parties is insufficient to establish bias in favor of that party. We hasten to add that the litigants are free to challenge the qualifications or neutrality of any suggested mediator.

* * *

APC also grouses that it should not be forced to share the costs of an unwanted mediation. We have held, however, that courts have the power under FED.R.CIV.P. 26(f) to issue pretrial cost-sharing orders in complex litigation. Given the difficulties facing trial courts in cases involving multiple parties and multiple claims, we are hesitant to limit that power to the traditional discovery context. This is especially true in complicated cases, where the potential value of mediation lies not only in promoting settlement but also in clarifying the issues remaining for trial.

The short of the matter is that, without default cost-sharing rules, the use of valuable ADR techniques (like mediation) becomes hostage to the parties' ability to agree on the concomitant financial arrangements. This means that the district court's inherent power to order private mediation in appropriate cases would be rendered nugatory absent the corollary power to order the sharing of reasonable mediation costs. To avoid this pitfall, we hold that the district court, in an appropriate case, is empowered to order the sharing of reasonable costs and expenses associated with mandatory non-binding mediation.

The remainder of APC's arguments are not so easily dispatched. Even when generically appropriate, a mediation order must contain procedural and substantive safeguards to ensure fairness to all parties involved. The mediation order in this case does not quite meet that test. In particular, the order does not set limits on the duration of the mediation or the expense associated therewith.

* * * As entered, the order simply requires the parties to mediate; it does not set forth either a timetable for the mediation or a cap on the fees that the mediator may charge. The figures that have been bandied about in the briefs—$900 per hour or $9,000 per mediation day—are quite large and should not be left to the mediator's whim. Relatedly, because the mediator is to be paid an hourly rate, the court should have set an outside limit on the number of hours to be devoted to mediation. Equally as important, it is trite but often true that justice delayed is justice denied. An unsuccessful mediation will postpone the ultimate resolution of the case—indeed, the district court has stayed all discovery pending the completion of the mediation—and, thus, prolong the litigation. For these reasons, the district court should have set a definite time frame for the mediation.

The respondents suggest that the district court did not need to articulate any limitations in its mediation order because the mediation process will remain under the district court's ultimate supervision; the court retains the ability to curtail any excessive expenditures of time or money; and a dissatisfied party can easily return to the court at any time. While this might be enough of a safeguard in many instances, the instant litigation is sufficiently complicated and the mediation efforts are likely to be sufficiently expensive that, here, reasonable time limits and fee constraints, set in advance, are appropriate.

A court intent on ordering non-consensual mediation should take other precautions as well. For example, the court should make it clear * * * that participation in mediation will not be taken as a waiver of any litigation position. The important point is that the protections we have mentioned are not intended to comprise an exhaustive list, but, rather, to illustrate that when a district court orders a party to participate in mediation, it should take care to assuage legitimate concerns about the possible negative consequences of such an order.

To recapitulate, we rule that a mandatory mediation order issued under the district court's inherent power is valid in an appropriate case. We also rule that this is an appropriate case. We hold, however, that the district court's failure to set reasonable limits on the duration of the mediation and on the mediator's fees dooms the decree. * * *

Points for Discussion

a. Ordering Court-Annexed ADR

Courts do not automatically have the authority to order unwilling litigants to participate in court-annexed ADR unless a statute or the court's local rules authorize such an order (pursuant to 28 U.S.C. § 651), or unless doing so is consistent with an exercise of the court's inherent authority. *See e.g.*, *In re African-American Slave Descendants' Litig.*, 272 F. Supp. 2d 755, 759 (N.D. Ill. 2003) ("Because the Northern District of Illinois has not adopted a local rule giving the court authority to compel mediation on an unwilling litigant, the court cannot, pursuant to the ADR Act, order mediation where one party objects."). What limits did the *Atlantic Pipe* court describe as constraining a court's use of its inherent authority to compel participation in court-annexed ADR?

Why would a court be interested in mandating that parties in a case participate in mediation or some other form of ADR? What factors should courts use to determine whether referring the parties to ADR is a good idea? What factors did the appeals court in *Atlantic Pipe* think were relevant to the decision?

A variety of ADR options exist, including mediation, non-binding arbitration, summary jury trials, or early neutral evaluation. How should a court determine which among the universe of options is the best approach to utilize when ordering parties to engage in court-annexed ADR? Where local rules or a statute provide the source of authority, those provisions may themselves indicate the type of ADR available to the court.

What's That?

Early neutral evaluation is a process whereby the parties present their cases to a neutral person selected by them or the court. The neutral evaluator then candidly shares with the parties an assessment of the strengths and weaknesses of their respective positions, with the hope that this information will encourage the parties to move closer to settling their dispute.

b. Policy Concerns

The purported purpose of court-annexed ADR is to reduce the time and expense associated with formal litigation. However, because court-annexed ADR is typically non-binding, the parties may get nowhere through the ADR process and ultimately end up before the court again, having wasted time and expense in the process. Does that possibility make the authority of courts to *compel* participation in court-annexed ADR more questionable, at least from a policy perspective?

Is it fair that litigants who have opted to use the public courts system are forcibly routed into an ADR process in which they do not want to participate? The *Atlantic Pipe* court held that courts can force the parties to bear the cost of court-annexed ADR. Is that appropriate?

c. The Impact of Court-Annexed ADR

Has court-annexed ADR been successful in achieving the goal of reducing the cost and time associated with litigation? Studies of court-annexed ADR programs have reached varying results. A 1996 study authored by the RAND Corporation reported the following:

> Our evaluation provided no strong statistical evidence that the mediation or neutral evaluation programs as implemented in these districts significantly affected time to disposition, litigation costs, or attorney views of fairness or satisfaction with case management. * * * Our only statistically significant finding is that the mediation programs appear to increase the likelihood of a monetary settlement.

JAMES S. KAKALIK ET AL., JUST, SPEEDY, AND INEXPENSIVE? AN EVALUATION OF MEDIATION AND EARLY NEUTRAL EVALUATION UNDER THE CIVIL JUSTICE REFORM ACT (RAND ICJ 1996). However, other studies have reported more favorable results. For example, according to a study done by the Federal Judicial Center ("FJC") for the Judicial Conference, a high proportion of the attorneys responding to questions about their experience with court-annexed ADR in several pilot districts reported a positive impact on reducing the time and expense associated with litigation. *See* Donna Stienstra et al., Report to the Judicial Conference Committee on Court Administration and Case Management: A Study of Five Demonstration Programs Established Under the Civil Justice Reform Act of 1990 (Fed. Jud. Ctr. 1997).

Although these studies and others are imperfect, they do not offer resounding affirmation of the benefits of court-annexed ADR. Should courts or Congress be obligated to demonstrate the effectiveness of court-annexed ADR before they can embrace it as a pretrial case-management technique that parties are forced to participate in and finance?

C. Summary Judgment

Matters that are not disposed of during the pretrial phase through default, dismissal, settlement, or resolution via a court-annexed ADR process may alternatively be disposed of without a trial through the mechanism of summary judgment. Summary judgment is the means by which courts may dispose of claims that plaintiffs cannot prove. It is also the vehicle through which courts may hand a pretrial victory to plaintiffs having claims that defendants cannot refute. In the federal system, the process for seeking and the standard for granting summary judgment are set forth in Rule 56:

FRCP 56. Summary Judgment.

(a) Motion for Summary Judgment or Partial Summary Judgment. A party may move for summary judgment, identifying each claim or defense—or the part of each claim or defense—on which summary judgment is sought. The court shall grant summary judgment if the movant shows that there is no genuine dispute as to any material fact and the movant is entitled to judgment as a matter of law. The court should state on the record the reasons for granting or denying the motion.

(b) Time to File a Motion. Unless a different time is set by local rule or the court orders otherwise, a party may file a motion for summary judgment at any time until 30 days after the close of all discovery.

(c) Procedures.

(1) *Supporting Factual Positions.* A party asserting that a fact cannot be or is genuinely disputed must support the assertion by:

(A) citing to particular parts of materials in the record, including depositions, documents, electronically stored information, affidavits or declarations, stipulations (including those made for purposes of the motion only), admissions, interrogatory answers, or other materials; or

(B) showing that the materials cited do not establish the absence or presence of a genuine dispute, or that an adverse party cannot produce admissible evidence to support the fact.

(2)   *Objection That a Fact Is Not Supported by Admissible Evidence.* A party may object that the material cited to support or dispute a fact cannot be presented in a form that would be admissible in evidence.

* * *

To understand the significance and role of summary judgment, it is critical to understand the purpose of a trial and of juries in our system of civil justice. (Trials and juries are considered more fully in Chapter 10.) The main purpose of a trial is to resolve factual disputes between the parties, something that is typically done by a jury (in actions at law). If the court is able to determine that there is "no genuine dispute as to any material fact," then there is no factual dispute for a jury to resolve, meaning that a trial would be pointless. In the absence of any genuine factual dispute, resolution of the action becomes simply a matter of applying the relevant law to the facts, something that the court itself may do without the aid of a jury.

Partial summary judgment can be sought respect to issues within a claim if there is no genuine dispute as to the facts pertaining to an issue in a case. Under such circumstances, the court may resolve that issue without the jury, leaving the remaining issues for which there is a factual dispute for the jury to resolve.

Take Note!

To understand these questions regarding the movant's showing and the respondent's burden, one must understand the concept of burden of production. The party asserting a claim has the burden of coming forward with evidence sufficient to support a finding in that party's favor. When the opposing party makes a summary judgment motion, the question is what information, if any, should the opposing party have to produce to establish its entitlement to summary judgment?

Either plaintiffs or defendants may seek summary judgment if they believe that there are no genuine disputes of any material facts and that the law entitles them to judgment as a matter of law. What constitutes a "material fact" has been spelled out by the Supreme Court: "As to materiality, the substantive law will identify which facts are material. Only disputes over facts that might affect the outcome of the suit under the governing law will properly preclude the entry of summary judgment." *Anderson v. Liberty Lobby, Inc.*, 477 U.S. 242, 248 (1986). Further, when evaluating a summary judgment motion, "courts are required to view the facts and draw reasonable inferences in the light most favorable to the party opposing the motion." *Scott v. Harris*, 550 U.S. 372, 378 (2007) (citation, internal quotation marks, and emendation omitted). Finally, although this motion may be made at any time, if the nonmovant feels that a summary judgment motion has been made prematurely—before there has been sufficient opportunity to discover facts that would enable it to oppose the motion—it may move to defer consideration of the motion pending further discovery. Fed. R. Civ. P. 56(d).

When seeking summary judgment, what type of showing is the movant required to make to the court? Must the movant adduce evidence demonstrating the absence of a material fact or can the movant simply assert that such is the case? Once a summary judgment motion is made, what is the respondent's burden in opposing the motion? Does the federal jury trial right enshrined in the Seventh Amendment require courts to be hesitant in rendering summary judgment or is there no warrant for such restraint?

An initial answer to these questions came from the Supreme Court in *Adickes v. S.H. Kress & Co.*, 398 U.S. 144 (1970). In this case, Adickes was a white woman and "Freedom School" teacher who had been denied service in Kress's restaurant because she was in the company of several of her African-American students. After she left Kress's restaurant, she was arrested by the Hattiesburg, Mississippi police for vagrancy. She brought suit in federal court under 42 U.S.C. § 1983 for a violation of her constitutional rights under the Equal Protection Clause of the Fourteenth Amendment. Adickes alleged that the refusal of service and her subsequent arrest were the product of a conspiracy between Kress and the Hattiesburg police. Kress moved for summary judgment, claiming that Adickes had "failed to allege any facts from which a conspiracy might be inferred." The district court granted the motion and the appeals court affirmed.

Freedom Schools were a component of the Mississippi Freedom Summer Project of 1964. The aim of the schools was to "provide Black children and teenagers with a richer educational experience than was offered in Mississippi public schools," and the schools "were structured to motivate young people to become critically engaged in their communities and to help them identify and design authentic solutions to local problems." The overall goal of the Summer Project was "to engage Black students and community volunteers in a variety of strategic activities to ensure basic citizenship rights for all Mississippians." For more information about this important part of American history, visit http://en.wikipedia.org/wiki/Freedom_Schools.

The Supreme Court reversed, writing:

> We think that on the basis of this record, it was error to grant summary judgment. As the moving party, respondent [Kress] had the burden of showing the absence of a genuine issue as to any material fact, and for these purposes the material it lodged must be viewed in the light most favorable to the opposing party [Adickes]. Respondent here did not carry its burden because of its failure to foreclose the possibility that there was a policeman in the Kress store while petitioner was awaiting service, and that this policeman reached an understanding with some Kress employee that petitioner not be served.
>
> It is true that Mr. Powell, the store manager, claimed in his deposition that he had not seen or communicated with a policeman prior to his tacit signal to Miss Baggett, the supervisor of the food counter. But respondent did not submit any affidavits from Miss Baggett, or from Miss Freeman, the waitress who actually refused petitioner service, either of whom might well have seen and communicated with a policeman in the store. Further, we find it particularly noteworthy that the two officers involved in the arrest each failed in his affidavit to foreclose the possibility (1) that he was in the store while petitioner was there; and (2) that, upon seeing petitioner with Negroes, he communicated his disapproval to a Kress employee, thereby influencing the decision not to serve petitioner.
>
> Given these unexplained gaps in the materials submitted by respondent, we conclude that respondent failed to fulfill its initial burden of demonstrating what is a critical element in this aspect of the case—that there was no policeman in the store. If a policeman were present, we think it would be open to a jury, in light of the sequence that followed, to infer from the circumstances that the policeman and a Kress employee had a 'meeting of the minds' and thus reached an understanding that petitioner should be refused service. Because '(o)n summary judgment the inferences to be drawn from the underlying facts contained in (the moving party's) materials must be viewed in the light most favorable

Food for Thought

The Court faults Kress for not producing enough evidence to establish that there was no police officer present in the store who conspired with its staff to discriminate against Adickes. However, because Adickes is the one asserting the claim, she is the person with the burden of producing evidence that there was a conspiracy. Is it appropriate, then, for the Court to invert that burden in the summary judgment context and require Kress to produce evidence *disproving* a conspiracy?

to the party opposing the motion,' we think respondent's failure to show there was no policeman in the store requires reversal.

* * * The Advisory Committee note on the amendment states * * * "(w)here the evidentiary matter in support of the motion does not establish the absence of a genuine issue, summary judgment must be denied even if no opposing evidentiary matter is presented." Because respondent did not meet its initial burden of establishing the absence of a policeman in the store, petitioner here was not required to come forward with suitable opposing affidavits.

Take Note!

Note that here the Court says that the party responding to a summary judgment motion has *no burden* of coming forward with any information if the movant does not establish the absence of a genuine issue of material fact. Keep this point in mind as you read *Celotex Corp. v. Catrett* below.

If respondent had met its initial burden by, for example, submitting affidavits from the policemen denying their presence in the store at the time in question, Rule 56(e) would then have required petitioner to have done more than simply rely on the contrary allegation in her complaint. To have avoided conceding this fact for purposes of summary judgment, petitioner would have had to come forward with either (1) the affidavit of someone who saw the policeman in the store or (2) an affidavit under Rule 56(f) explaining why at that time it was impractical to do so. * * *

Adickes, 398 U.S. at 157–60.

In the wake of *Adickes*, it appeared that a summary judgment movant had the burden of coming forward with evidence that established the correctness of its position in a case and refuted the opposing party's case, regardless of who bore the burden of producing such information at trial. In practical terms, this meant that defendants seeking summary judgment would have to carry an evidentiary burden that they would not carry if the case were tried, something that made it more difficult for defendants to seek and obtain summary judgment in their favor. In 1986, the Supreme Court decided three cases that altered this post-*Adickes* understanding of summary judgment. Primary among these cases was *Celotex Corp. v. Catrett*, our next case.

Celotex Corp. v. Catrett

Supreme Court of the United States
477 U.S. 317 (1986)

JUSTICE REHNQUIST delivered the opinion of the Court.

The United States District Court for the District of Columbia granted the motion of petitioner Celotex Corporation for summary judgment against respondent Catrett because the latter was unable to produce evidence in support of her allegation in her wrongful-death complaint that the decedent had been exposed to petitioner's asbestos products. A divided panel of the Court of Appeals for the District of Columbia Circuit reversed, however, holding that petitioner's failure to support its motion with evidence tending to negate such exposure precluded the entry of summary judgment in its favor. This view conflicted with that of the Third Circuit * * * . We granted certiorari to resolve the conflict, and now reverse the decision of the District of Columbia Circuit.

Respondent commenced this lawsuit in September 1980, alleging that the death in 1979 of her husband, Louis H. Catrett, resulted from his exposure to products containing asbestos manufactured or distributed by 15 named corporations. Respondent's complaint sounded in negligence, breach of warranty, and strict liability. Two of the defendants filed motions challenging the District Court's *in personam* jurisdiction, and the remaining 13, including petitioner, filed motions for summary judgment. Petitioner's motion, which was first filed in September 1981, argued that summary judgment was proper because respondent had "failed to produce evidence that any [Celotex] product . . . was the proximate cause of the injuries alleged within the jurisdictional limits of [the District] Court." In particular, petitioner noted that respondent had failed to identify, in answering interrogatories specifically requesting such information, any witnesses who could testify about the decedent's exposure to petitioner's asbestos products. In response to petitioner's summary judgment motion, respondent then produced three documents which she claimed "demonstrate that there is a genuine material factual dispute" as to whether the decedent had ever been exposed to petitioner's asbestos products. The three documents included a transcript of a deposition of the decedent, a letter from an official of one of the decedent's former employers whom petitioner planned to call as a trial witness, and a letter from an insurance company to respondent's attorney, all tending to establish that the decedent had been exposed to petitioner's asbestos products in Chicago during 1970–1971. Petitioner, in turn, argued that the three documents were inadmissible hearsay and thus could not be considered in opposition to the summary judgment motion.

Make the Connection

Hearsay refers to any out-of-court statement introduced to prove the matter asserted. Such statements are generally inadmissible because of the inability of opposing counsel to cross-examine the declarant. You will study hearsay in an **Evidence** course.

In July 1982, almost two years after the commencement of the lawsuit, the District Court granted all of the motions filed by the various defendants. The court explained that it was granting petitioner's summary judgment motion because "there [was] no showing that the plaintiff was exposed to the defendant Celotex's product in the District of Columbia or elsewhere within the statutory period." Respondent appealed only the grant of summary judgment in favor of petitioner, and a divided panel of the District of Columbia Circuit reversed. The majority of the Court of Appeals held that petitioner's summary judgment motion was rendered "fatally defective" by the fact that petitioner "made no effort to adduce *any* evidence, in the form of affidavits or otherwise, to support its motion." According to the majority, Rule 56(e),[3] and this Court's decision in *Adickes v. S.H. Kress & Co.* establish that "the party opposing the motion for summary judgment bears the burden of responding *only after* the moving party has met its burden of coming forward with proof of the absence of any genuine issues of material fact." The majority therefore declined to consider petitioner's argument that none of the evidence produced by respondent in opposition to the motion for summary judgment would have been admissible at trial. * * *

We think that the position taken by the majority of the Court of Appeals is inconsistent with the standard for summary judgment set forth in Rule 56(c) * * *. In our view, the plain language of Rule 56(c) mandates the entry of summary judgment, after adequate time for discovery and upon motion, against a party who fails

---

[3] Rule 56(e) provides:

"Supporting and opposing affidavits shall be made on personal knowledge, shall set forth such facts as would be admissible in evidence, and shall show affirmatively that the affiant is competent to testify to the matters stated therein. Sworn or certified copies of all papers or parts thereof referred to in an affidavit shall be attached thereto or served therewith. The court may permit affidavits to be supplemented or opposed by depositions, answers to interrogatories, or further affidavits. When a motion for summary judgment is made and supported as provided in this rule, an adverse party may not rest upon the mere allegations or denials of his pleading, but his response, by affidavits or as otherwise provided in this rule, must set forth specific facts showing that there is a genuine issue for trial. If he does not so respond, summary judgment, if appropriate, shall be entered against him." [This text has been modified and reorganized significantly by subsequent amendments to Rule 56. Ed.]

to make a showing sufficient to establish the existence of an element essential to that party's case, and on which that party will bear the burden of proof at trial. * * *

What's That?

The *burden of proof* is a party's duty to prove a disputed assertion. Plaintiffs typically have the burden of proof with respect to the elements of their claims. Included in this burden are both the burden of production, a concept discussed above, and the burden of persuasion, which is the party's duty to convince the fact-finder that its version of the facts is correct.

Of course, a party seeking summary judgment always bears the initial responsibility of informing the district court of the basis for its motion, and identifying those portions of "the pleadings, depositions, answers to interrogatories, and admissions on file, together with the affidavits, if any," which it believes demonstrate the absence of a genuine issue of material fact. But unlike the Court of Appeals, we find no express or implied requirement in <u>Rule 56</u> that the moving party support its motion with affidavits or other similar materials *negating* the opponent's claim. On the contrary, Rule 56(c), which refers to "the affidavits, *if any*" (emphasis added), suggests the absence of such a requirement. And if there were any doubt about the meaning of Rule 56(c) in this regard, such doubt is clearly removed by Rules 56(a) and (b), which provide that claimants and defendants, respectively, may move for summary judgment "*with or without supporting affidavits*" (emphasis added). The import of these subsections is that, regardless of whether the moving party accompanies its summary judgment motion with affidavits, the motion may, and should, be granted so long as whatever is before the district court demonstrates that the standard for the entry of summary judgment, as set forth in Rule 56(c), is satisfied. One of the principal purposes of the summary judgment rule is to isolate and dispose of factually unsupported claims or defenses, and we think it should be interpreted in a way that allows it to accomplish this purpose.

Respondent argues, however, that Rule 56(e), by its terms, places on the nonmoving party the burden of coming forward with rebuttal affidavits, or other specified kinds of materials, only in response to a motion for summary judgment "made and supported as provided in this rule." According to respondent's argument, since petitioner did not "support" its motion with

Take Note!

The 2007 amendments to Rule 56 eliminated the "affidavits, if any" language cited by Justice Rehnquist and replaced it with "any affidavits." Further, the 2010 amendments to Rule 56 got rid of this language altogether, simply referring to affidavits as one of the types of record materials that may be cited in support of one's position in a summary judgment fight. The 2010 amendments also eliminated the "with or without supporting affidavits" language from Rule 56. Would Justice Rehnquist's analysis hold up under the 2010 version of Rule 56, or does its language cease to support his views?

affidavits, summary judgment was improper in this case. But as we have already explained, a motion for summary judgment may be made pursuant to Rule 56 "with or without supporting affidavits." In cases like the instant one, where the nonmoving party will bear the burden of proof at trial on a dispositive issue, a summary judgment motion may properly be made in reliance solely on the "pleadings, depositions, answers to interrogatories, and admissions on file." Such a motion, whether or not accompanied by affidavits, will be "made and supported as provided in this rule," and Rule 56(e) therefore requires the nonmoving party to go beyond the pleadings and by her own affidavits, or by the "depositions, answers to interrogatories, and admissions on file," designate "specific facts showing that there is a genuine issue for trial."

We do not mean that the nonmoving party must produce evidence in a form that would be admissible at trial in order to avoid summary judgment. Obviously, Rule 56 does not require the nonmoving party to depose her own witnesses. Rule 56(e) permits a proper summary judgment motion to be opposed by any of the kinds of evidentiary materials listed in Rule 56(c), except the mere pleadings themselves, and it is from this list that one would normally expect the nonmoving party to make the showing to which we have referred.

The Court of Appeals in this case felt itself constrained, however, by language in our decision in *Adickes v. S.H. Kress & Co.* There we held that summary judgment had been improperly entered in favor of the defendant restaurant in an action brought under 42 U.S.C. § 1983. In the course of its opinion, the *Adickes* Court said that "both the commentary on and the background of the 1963 amendment conclusively show that it was not intended to modify the burden of the moving party . . . to show initially the absence of a genuine issue concerning any material fact." We think that this statement is accurate in a literal sense, since we fully agree with the *Adickes* Court that the 1963 amendment to Rule 56(e) was not designed to modify the burden of making the showing generally required by Rule 56(c). It also appears to us that, on the basis of the showing before the Court in *Adickes*, the motion for summary judgment in that case should have been denied. But we do not think the *Adickes* language quoted above should be construed to mean that the burden is on the party moving for summary judgment to produce evidence showing the absence of a genuine issue of material fact, even with respect to an issue on which the nonmoving party bears the burden of proof. Instead, as we have explained, the burden on the

Food for Thought

The Court here states that *Adickes* should not be interpreted as having said that the movant must "produce evidence showing the absence of a genuine issue of material fact." Is that an honest reading of *Adickes*, or is the Court trying to revise its meaning without overruling the case? Didn't the *Adickes* Court explicitly fault the movant there for failing to produce evidence that disproved Adickes's allegations?

moving party may be discharged by "showing"—that is, pointing out to the district court—that there is an absence of evidence to support the nonmoving party's case.

The last two sentences of Rule 56(e) were added, as this Court indicated in *Adickes*, to disapprove a line of cases allowing a party opposing summary judgment to resist a properly made motion by reference only to its pleadings. While the *Adickes* Court was undoubtedly correct in concluding that these two sentences were not intended to reduce the burden of the moving party, it is also obvious that they were not adopted to add to that burden. Yet that is exactly the result which the reasoning of the Court of Appeals would produce; in effect, an amendment to Rule 56(e) designed to facilitate the granting of motions for summary judgment would be interpreted to make it more difficult to grant such motions. Nothing in the two sentences themselves requires this result, for the reasons we have previously indicated, and we now put to rest any inference that they do so.

Our conclusion is bolstered by the fact that district courts are widely acknowledged to possess the power to enter summary judgments *sua sponte*, so long as the losing party was on notice that she had to come forward with all of her evidence. It would surely defy common sense to hold that the District Court could have entered summary judgment *sua sponte* in favor of petitioner in the instant case, but that petitioner's filing of a motion requesting such a disposition precluded the District Court from ordering it.

Take Note!

Note the reference to Rule 56(f), which, after the 2010 amendments, now appears under Rule 56(d). This rule enables a party responding to a summary judgment motion to request a delay in consideration of the motion while additional discovery is taken to support its case.

Respondent commenced this action in September 1980, and petitioner's motion was filed in September 1981. The parties had conducted discovery, and no serious claim can be made that respondent was in any sense "railroaded" by a premature motion for summary judgment. Any potential problem with such premature motions can be adequately dealt with under Rule 56(f), which allows a summary judgment motion to be denied, or the hearing on the motion to be continued, if the nonmoving party has not had an opportunity to make full discovery.

In this Court, respondent's brief and oral argument have been devoted as much to the proposition that an adequate showing of exposure to petitioner's asbestos products was made as to the proposition that no such showing should have been required. But the Court of Appeals declined to address either the adequacy of the showing made by respondent in opposition to petitioner's motion for summary judgment, or the question whether such a showing, if reduced to admissible evidence, would be sufficient to carry respondent's burden of proof at trial. We think the Court of Appeals with its superior knowledge of local law is better suited than we are to make these determinations in the first instance.

The Federal Rules of Civil Procedure have for almost 50 years authorized motions for summary judgment upon proper showings of the lack of a genuine, triable issue of material fact. Summary judgment procedure is properly regarded not as a disfavored procedural shortcut, but rather as an integral part of the Federal Rules as a whole, which are designed "to secure the just, speedy and inexpensive determination of every action." FED. R. CIV. PROC. 1. Before the shift to "notice pleading" accomplished by the Federal Rules, motions to dismiss a complaint or to strike a defense were the principal tools by which factually insufficient claims or defenses could be isolated and prevented from going to trial with the attendant unwarranted consumption of public and private resources. But with the advent of "notice pleading," the motion to dismiss seldom fulfills this function any more, and its place has been taken by the motion for summary judgment. Rule 56 must be construed with due regard not only for the rights of persons asserting claims and defenses that are adequately based in fact to have those claims and defenses tried to a jury, but also for the rights of persons opposing such claims and defenses to demonstrate in the manner provided by the Rule, prior to trial, that the claims and defenses have no factual basis.

Food for Thought

Having resolved the case, Justice Rehnquist goes on to express a view in this paragraph regarding the role of Rule 56 in what was referred to as the notice pleading system. What is the connection between notice pleading and the summary judgment standards articulated in *Celotex,* and why did Justice Rehnquist feel the need to explain this connection? After the Court's refinement (or retirement) of notice pleading in Bell Atlantic Corp. v. Twombly, 550 U.S. 544 (2007), and Ashcroft v. Iqbal, 556 U.S. 662 (2009), do you think that the motion to dismiss will start to serve as more of a tool for weeding out factually insufficient claims?

The judgment of the Court of Appeals is accordingly reversed, and the case is remanded for further proceedings consistent with this opinion.

It is so ordered.

JUSTICE WHITE, concurring.

I agree that the Court of Appeals was wrong in holding that the moving defendant must always support his motion with evidence or affidavits showing the absence of a genuine dispute about a material fact. I also agree that the movant may rely on depositions, answers to interrogatories, and the like, to demonstrate that the plaintiff has no evidence to prove his case and hence that there can be no factual dispute. But the movant must discharge the burden the Rules place upon him: It is not enough to move for summary judgment without supporting the motion in any way or with a conclusory assertion that the plaintiff has no evidence to prove his case.

* * *

Petitioner Celotex does not dispute that if respondent has named a witness to support her claim, summary judgment should not be granted without Celotex somehow showing that the named witness' possible testimony raises no genuine issue of material fact. It asserts, however, that respondent has failed on request to produce any basis for her case. Respondent, on the other hand, does not contend that she was not obligated to reveal her witnesses and evidence but insists that she has revealed enough to defeat the motion for summary judgment. Because the Court of Appeals found it unnecessary to address this aspect of the case, I agree that the case should be remanded for further proceedings.

JUSTICE BRENNAN, with whom THE CHIEF JUSTICE and JUSTICE BLACKMUN join, dissenting.

This case requires the Court to determine whether Celotex satisfied its initial burden of production in moving for summary judgment on the ground that the plaintiff lacked evidence to establish an essential element of her case at trial. I do not disagree with the Court's legal analysis. The Court clearly rejects the ruling of the Court of Appeals that the defendant must provide affirmative evidence disproving the plaintiff's case. Beyond this, however, the Court has not clearly explained what is required of a moving party seeking summary judgment on the ground that the non-moving party cannot prove its case. This lack of clarity is unfortunate: district courts must routinely decide summary judgment motions, and the Court's opinion will very likely create confusion. For this reason, even if I agreed with the Court's result, I would have written separately to explain more clearly the law in this area. However, because I believe that Celotex did not meet its burden of production under Federal Rule of Civil Procedure 56, I respectfully dissent from the Court's judgment.

I

Summary judgment is appropriate where the Court is satisfied "that there is no genuine issue as to any material fact and that the moving party is entitled to a judgment as a matter of law." The burden of establishing the nonexistence of a "genuine issue" is on the party moving for summary judgment. This burden has two distinct components: an initial burden of production, which shifts to the nonmoving party if satisfied by the moving party; and an ultimate burden of persuasion, which always remains on the moving party. The court need not decide whether the moving party has satisfied its ultimate burden of persuasion[2] unless and until the Court finds that the moving party has discharged its initial burden of production.

The burden of production imposed by Rule 56 requires the moving party to make a prima facie showing that it is entitled to summary judgment. The manner in which this showing can be made depends upon which party will bear the burden of persuasion on the challenged claim at trial. If the moving party will bear the burden of persuasion at trial, that party must support its motion with credible evidence—using any of the materials specified in Rule 56(c)—that would entitle it to a directed verdict if not controverted at trial. Such an affirmative showing shifts the burden of production to the party opposing the motion and requires that party either to produce evidentiary materials that demonstrate the existence of a "genuine issue" for trial or to submit an affidavit requesting additional time for discovery.

What's That?

A *directed verdict* is a ruling by the trial judge taking the case from the jury because the evidence will only support one result. The modern version of this procedure in the federal system, *judgment as a matter of law*, will be discussed in Chapter 10.

If the burden of persuasion at trial would be on the *non-moving* party, the party moving for summary judgment may satisfy Rule 56's burden of production in either of two ways. First, the moving party may submit affirmative evidence that negates an essential element of the nonmoving party's claim. Second, the moving party may demonstrate to the Court that the nonmoving party's evidence is insufficient to establish an essential element of the nonmoving party's claim. If the nonmoving party cannot muster sufficient evidence to make out its claim, a trial would be useless and the moving party is entitled to summary judgment as a matter of law. *Anderson v. Liberty Lobby, Inc.,* 477 U.S. 242, 249 (1986).

Where the moving party adopts this second option and seeks summary judgment on the ground that the nonmoving party—who will bear the burden of persuasion at trial—has no evidence, the mechanics of discharging Rule 56's burden of production are somewhat trickier. Plainly, a conclusory assertion that the nonmov-

---

[2] The burden of persuasion imposed on a moving party by Rule 56 is a stringent one. Summary judgment should not be granted unless it is clear that a trial is unnecessary, *Anderson v. Liberty Lobby, Inc.,* 477 U.S. 242, 255 (1986), and any doubt as to the existence of a genuine issue for trial should be resolved against the moving party, *Adickes v. S.H. Kress & Co.,* 398 U.S. 144, 158–159 (1970). In determining whether a moving party has met its burden of persuasion, the court is obliged to take account of the entire setting of the case and must consider all papers of record as well as any materials prepared for the motion. As explained by the Court of Appeals for the Third Circuit in *In re Japanese Electronic Products Antitrust Lit.,* 723 F.2d 238 (1983), rev'd on other grounds sub nom. *Matsushita Electric Industrial Co. v. Zenith Radio Corp.,* 475 U.S. 574 (1986), "[i]f . . . there is any evidence in the record from any source from which a reasonable inference in the [nonmoving party's] favor may be drawn, the moving party simply cannot obtain a summary judgment . . . ." 723 F.2d, at 258.

ing party has no evidence is insufficient. Such a "burden" of production is no burden at all and would simply permit summary judgment procedure to be converted into a tool for harassment. Rather, as the Court confirms, a party who moves for summary judgment on the ground that the nonmoving party has no evidence must affirmatively show the absence of evidence in the record. This may require the moving party to depose the nonmoving party's witnesses or to establish the inadequacy of documentary evidence. If there is literally no evidence in the record, the moving party may demonstrate this by reviewing for the court the admissions, interrogatories, and other exchanges between the parties that are in the record. Either way, however, the moving party must affirmatively demonstrate that there is no evidence in the record to support a judgment for the nonmoving party.

If the moving party has not fully discharged this initial burden of production, its motion for summary judgment must be denied, and the Court need not consider whether the moving party has met its ultimate burden of persuasion. Accordingly, the nonmoving party may defeat a motion for summary judgment that asserts that the nonmoving party has no evidence by calling the Court's attention to supporting evidence already in the record that was overlooked or ignored by the moving party. In that event, the moving party must respond by making an attempt to demonstrate the inadequacy of this evidence, for it is only by attacking all the record evidence allegedly supporting the nonmoving party that a party seeking summary judgment satisfies Rule 56's burden of production.[3] Thus, if the record disclosed that the moving party had overlooked a witness who would provide relevant testimony for the nonmoving party at trial, the Court could not find that the moving party had discharged its initial burden of production unless the moving party sought to demonstrate the inadequacy of this witness' testimony. Absent such a demonstration, summary judgment would have to be denied on the ground that the moving party had failed to meet its burden of production under Rule 56.

* * *

II

I do not read the Court's opinion to say anything inconsistent with or different than the preceding discussion. My disagreement with the Court concerns the application of these principles to the facts of this case.

---

[3] Once the moving party has attacked whatever record evidence—if any—the nonmoving party purports to rely upon, the burden of production shifts to the nonmoving party, who must either (1) rehabilitate the evidence attacked in the moving party's papers, (2) produce additional evidence showing the existence of a genuine issue for trial as provided in Rule 56(e), or (3) submit an affidavit explaining why further discovery is necessary as provided in Rule 56(f). Summary judgment should be granted if the nonmoving party fails to respond in one or more of these ways, or if, after the nonmoving party responds, the court determines that the moving party has met its ultimate burden of persuading the court that there is no genuine issue of material fact for trial. *See, e.g., First Nat'l Bank of Ariz. v. Cities Serv. Co.*, 391 U.S. 253, 289 (1968).

Defendant Celotex sought summary judgment on the ground that plaintiff had "failed to produce" any evidence that her decedent had ever been exposed to Celotex asbestos. Celotex supported this motion with a two-page "Statement of Material Facts as to Which There is No Genuine Issue" and a three-page "Memorandum of Points and Authorities" which asserted that the plaintiff had failed to identify any evidence in responding to two sets of interrogatories propounded by Celotex and that therefore the record was "totally devoid" of evidence to support plaintiff's claim.

Food for Thought

Is Justice Brennan correct to claim that there is no light between his view of the burdens surrounding a summary judgment motion and the view of the majority, or is the majority's stated understanding qualitatively different from the view Justice Brennan articulates?

Approximately three months earlier, Celotex had filed an essentially identical motion. Plaintiff responded to this earlier motion by producing three pieces of evidence which she claimed "[a]t the very least . . . demonstrate that there is a genuine factual dispute for trial": (1) a letter from an insurance representative of another defendant describing asbestos products to which plaintiff's decedent had been exposed, *id., at 160*; (2) a letter from T.R. Hoff, a former supervisor of decedent, describing asbestos products to which decedent had been exposed; and (3) a copy of decedent's deposition from earlier workmen's compensation proceedings. Plaintiff also apparently indicated at that time that she intended to call Mr. Hoff as a witness at trial.

Celotex subsequently withdrew its first motion for summary judgment. However, as a result of this motion, when Celotex filed its second summary judgment motion, the record did contain evidence—including at least one witness—supporting plaintiff's claim. Indeed, counsel for Celotex admitted to this Court at oral argument that Celotex was aware of this evidence and of plaintiff's intention to call Mr. Hoff as a witness at trial when the second summary judgment motion was filed. Moreover, plaintiff's response to Celotex' second motion pointed to this evidence— noting that it had already been provided to counsel for Celotex in connection with the first motion—and argued that Celotex had failed to "meet its burden of proving that there is no genuine factual dispute for trial."

On these facts, there is simply no question that Celotex failed to discharge its initial burden of production. Having chosen to base its motion on the argument that there was no evidence in the record to support plaintiff's claim, Celotex was not free to ignore supporting evidence that the record clearly contained. Rather, Celotex was required, as an initial matter, to attack the adequacy of this evidence. Celotex' failure to fulfill this simple requirement constituted a failure to discharge its initial burden of production under Rule 56, and thereby rendered summary judgment improper.

This case is indistinguishable from *Adickes*. Here, as there, the defendant moved for summary judgment on the ground that the record contained no evidence to support an essential element of the plaintiff's claim. Here, as there, the plaintiff responded by drawing the court's attention to evidence that was already in the record and that had been ignored by the moving party. Consequently, here, as there, summary judgment should be denied on the ground that the moving party failed to satisfy its initial burden of production.

Food for Thought

Does the majority disagree with this application of the summary judgment standard to the facts? Why did the Court remand the case rather than apply its summary judgment analysis to the facts as Justice Brennan does here? Which approach seems more appropriate?

[A dissenting opinion by JUSTICE STEVENS is omitted.]

Points for Discussion

a. Summary Judgment After *Celotex*

How would you articulate the respective burdens that movants and opposing parties have in the context of a summary judgment motion after *Celotex*? In *Celotex*, the majority wrote, "[T]he burden on the moving party may be discharged by 'showing'—that is, pointing out to the district court—that there is an absence of evidence to support the nonmoving party's case." Does "pointing out" the absence of evidence to support the nonmoving party's case require anything more than a mere statement by the movant that the opposing party has failed to produce sufficient evidence in support of her case? Or does the movant have to demonstrate this fact to the court by going through the evidence and articulating and explaining its deficiencies? Justice Brennan seems to think that the latter is the case:

> Plainly, a conclusory assertion that the nonmoving party has no evidence is insufficient. Such a "burden" of production is no burden at all and would simply permit summary judgment procedure to be converted into a tool for harassment. Rather, as the Court confirms, a party who moves for summary judgment on the ground that the nonmoving party has no evidence must affirmatively show the absence of evidence in the record.

Celotex, 477 U.S. at 332 (Brennan, J., dissenting). Does the above accurately reflect the majority's view, or is this merely wishful thinking on the part of Justice Brennan?

It appears that most lower courts read *Celotex* as being closer to the view that the movant lacking the burden of proof at trial lacks any real burden at the summary judgment phase. *See Adler v. Wal-Mart Stores, Inc., 144 F.3d 664, 671 (10th Cir. 1998)* ("In [showing the absence of a genuine issue of material fact], a movant that will not bear the burden of persuasion at trial need not negate the nonmovant's claim. Such a movant may make its prima facie demonstration simply by pointing out to the court a lack of evidence for the nonmovant on an essential element of the nonmovant's claim." (citations omitted)); *Nat'l State Bank v. Fed. Reserve Bank, 979 F.2d 1579, 1581–82 (3d Cir. 1992)* ("Where the movant is the defendant, or the party without the burden on the underlying claim . . . [t]he moving party merely has to point to the lack of any evidence supporting the non-movant's claim."). Is the holding of *Celotex* consistent with the Court's view of the parties' burdens expressed in *Adickes*? The following hypothetical problem tests your understanding of the holding of *Celotex*.

When the Court of Appeals applied the *Celotex* approach on remand, it again found that summary judgment was inappropriate because the plaintiff had produced sufficient evidence of asbestos exposure. *See Catrett v. Johns-Manville Sales Corp., 826 F.2d 33 (D.C. Cir. 1987), cert. denied, 484 U.S. 1066 (1988)*.

Hypo 9.1

Ace, a contractor who worked on Sally's summer home, filed suit in federal court against Sally claiming that she owed him $100,000 for home improvement work Ace completed last month. In support of his claim, Ace has produced an email in which Sally offered to pay Ace $100,000 for work on her summer home. Sally moved for summary judgment, attaching her own affidavit stating that Ace never responded to the email offer and that she neither knew of nor approved of Ace's working on her summer home. Assume that the applicable contract law requires proof of an offer and acceptance in order for there to be a binding contract. Assume further that to hold Sally liable under a quasi-contract theory there must be proof that she had knowledge that Ace was working on her home but failed to put a stop to it.

Has Sally satisfied her burden of production for making a summary judgment motion under *Celotex*? If so, what is Ace's burden in response to Sally's motion? Was it even necessary for Sally to submit her affidavit along with her motion for summary judgment in light of *Celotex*?

b. The *Celotex* "Trilogy"

During the same Term in which *Celotex* was decided, the Court decided two other summary judgment cases that made it more difficult for plaintiffs to oppose summary judgment motions:

Anderson v. Liberty Lobby, Inc., <u>477 U.S. 242 (1986)</u>. In *Anderson*, decided on the same day as *Celotex*, the Court decided that the substantive evidentiary standard of proof applicable to a matter at trial is the standard by which a summary judgment motion should be judged. *Anderson* involved a libel suit by a publisher and his organization, Liberty Lobby, against a magazine and its publisher, Jack Anderson. Under established Supreme Court precedent,[*] a plaintiff in a defamation suit involving public figures could only prevail if he could establish that, by clear and convincing evidence, the defendants acted with actual malice, meaning they knew that their statements were false or were reckless with respect to whether they were true or false. The question for the *Anderson* Court was whether a court determining if summary judgment is appropriate in such a case should evaluate the evidence before it in light of the clear and convincing evidence standard of proof or should deny summary judgment simply if the plaintiff is able to make a *prima facie* showing that it is entitled to relief.

What's That?

Standard of proof refers to the degree to which a party carrying the burden must prove its case. There are several different standards of proof applicable in different contexts:

- *Prima Facie Evidence*—sufficient evidence that, when standing alone, supports a claim for the party asserting it.

- *Preponderance of Evidence*—convincing the factfinder that, given competing evidence, it is more likely than not that the facts alleged by the party bearing the burden are true.

- *Clear and Convincing Evidence*—evidence that the thing to be proved is highly probable or reasonably certain.

- *Beyond a Reasonable Doubt*—the most stringent standard, used in criminal cases, requiring that there can be no reasonable doubt about the outcome; a likelihood or substantial likelihood that the outcome is correct is not enough.

The district court in *Anderson* granted summary judgment on the basis of its view that the plaintiff's evidence did not meet the clear and convincing standard of proof. The appeals court reversed, holding that the clear and convincing standard was irrelevant to the summary judgment decision. The Supreme Court reversed the appeals court, writing as follows:

---

[*] <u>*N.Y. Times Co. v. Sullivan*, 376 U.S. 254 (1964)</u>. [Ed.]

When determining if a genuine factual issue as to actual malice exists in a libel suit brought by a public figure, a trial judge must bear in mind the actual quantum and quality of proof necessary to support liability under *New York Times* [*v. Sullivan*, 376 U.S. 254 (1964)]. For example, there is no genuine issue if the evidence presented in the opposing affidavits is of insufficient caliber or quantity to allow a rational finder of fact to find actual malice by clear and convincing evidence.

Thus, in ruling on a motion for summary judgment, the judge must view the evidence presented through the prism of the substantive evidentiary burden. This conclusion is mandated by the nature of this determination. The question here is whether a jury could reasonably find either that the plaintiff proved his case by the quality and quantity of evidence required by the governing law or that he did not. Whether a jury could reasonably find for either party, however, cannot be defined except by the criteria governing what evidence would enable the jury to find for either the plaintiff or the defendant: It makes no sense to say that a jury could reasonably find for either party without some benchmark as to what standards govern its deliberations and within what boundaries its ultimate decision must fall, and these standards and boundaries are in fact provided by the applicable evidentiary standards.

Our holding that the clear-and-convincing standard of proof should be taken into account in ruling on summary judgment motions does not denigrate the role of the jury. It by no means authorizes trial on affidavits. Credibility determinations, the weighing of the evidence, and the drawing of legitimate inferences from the facts are jury functions, not those of a judge, whether he is ruling on a motion for summary judgment or for a directed verdict. The evidence of the non-movant is to be believed, and all justifiable inferences are to be drawn in his favor.

* * *

Take Note!

The Court here instructs judges evaluating summary judgment to do so with reference to the substantive evidentiary standard of proof that will apply to the issue at trial. What is the alternative to such an approach? Justice Brennan, dissenting in *Anderson*, suggests that the approach prior to *Anderson*, and the proper approach in his view, is to require a plaintiff opposing summary judgment only to make out a *prima facie* case. See *Anderson*, 477 U.S. at 264 (Brennan, J.,dissenting).

In sum, we conclude that the determination of whether a given factual dispute requires submission to a jury must be guided by the substantive evidentiary standards that apply to the case. This is true at both the directed verdict and summary judgment stages. Consequently, where the

New York Times "clear and convincing" evidence requirement applies, the trial judge's summary judgment inquiry as to whether a genuine issue exists will be whether the evidence presented is such that a jury applying that evidentiary standard could reasonably find for either the plaintiff or the defendant. Thus, where the factual dispute concerns actual malice, clearly a material issue in a *New York Times* case, the appropriate summary judgment question will be whether the evidence in the record could support a reasonable jury finding either that the plaintiff has shown actual malice by clear and convincing evidence or that the plaintiff has not.

Anderson, 477 U.S. at 254–56.

Weighing the evidence and making credibility determinations is traditionally the province of the factfinder, which in most cases is the jury. Does the *Anderson* decision improperly invade the province of the jury by permitting judges to determine whether the evidence presented satisfies the substantive evidentiary standard of proof? How can a judge make such a determination without weighing the evidence? *See id. at 266* (Brennan, J., dissenting) ("[T]he Court's opinion is also full of language which could surely be understood as an invitation—if not an instruction—to trial courts to assess and weigh evidence much as a juror would . . . ."); *see also* Suja A. Thomas, *Why Summary Judgment is Unconstitutional*, 93 VA. L. REV. 139, 140, 143 (2007) ("Summary judgment is unconstitutional. . . . Cases that would have been decided by a jury under the common law are now dismissed by a judge under summary judgment."). *But see J.R. Simplot v. Chevron Pipeline Co.*, 563 F.3d 1102, 1117 (10th Cir. 2009) ("The law is well-settled that summary judgment does not violate the Seventh Amendment." (citing *Fidelity & Deposit Co. v. United States*, 187 U.S. 315, 319–21 (1902))). How does *Anderson* impact summary judgment determinations in cases in which the standard of proof is a preponderance of the evidence?

One thing *Anderson* made clear is that a nonmovant bearing the burden of proof at trial will not be able to defeat a summary judgment motion simply by offering its own testimony contradicting the evidence of the moving party. *See Anderson*, 477 U.S. at 249–50 (stating that no issue remains for trial "unless there is sufficient evidence favoring the non-moving party for a jury to return a verdict for that party. If the evidence is merely colorable, or is not sufficiently probative, summary judgment may be granted." (citations omitted)); *see also Weeks v. Samsung Heavy Indus. Co.*, 126 F.3d 926, 939 (7th Cir. 1997) ("[Nonmovant's] own uncorroborated testimony is insufficient to defeat a motion for summary judgment."). Further, no genuine issue of fact can be created based on a factual conflict that arises only as a result of an affiant's self-serving contradiction of his own previous testimony. *See, e.g., Mack v. United States*, 814 F.2d 120, 124–25 (2d Cir. 1987) ("It is well settled in this circuit that a party's affidavit which contradicts his own prior deposition testimony should be disregarded on a motion for summary judgment.").

Matsushita Elec. Indus. Co. v. Zenith Radio Corp., <u>475 U.S. 574 (1986)</u>. In *Matsushita*, two American television manufacturers sued a collection of twenty-one Japanese-controlled television manufacturers claiming that the Japanese group had illegally conspired to drive the American firms from the American consumer electronics products market. The heart of the conspiracy alleged was a "scheme to raise, fix and maintain artificially *high* prices for television receivers sold by [the Japanese defendants] in Japan and, at the same time, to fix and maintain *low* prices for television receivers exported to and sold in the United States."

After several years of discovery, the defendants moved for summary judgment. The district court found that the admissible evidence did not raise a genuine issue of material fact as to the existence of the alleged conspiracy because in its view, any inference of a conspiracy based on the evidence was unreasonable. The court felt this way based on its belief that some portions of the evidence suggested that the defendants conspired in ways that did not injure the plaintiffs, and that the evidence that bore directly on the alleged price-cutting conspiracy did not rebut the more plausible inference that the defendants were cutting prices to compete in the American market and not to monopolize it. The court thus granted summary judgment for the defendants on the plaintiffs' claims. The <u>Third Circuit</u> reversed, finding that there was direct evidence that could support an inference of a conspiracy to monopolize the American market by the defendants.

The Supreme Court reversed the appeals court and held that the entry of summary judgment was appropriate:

> To survive petitioners' motion for summary judgment, respondents must establish that there is a genuine issue of material fact as to whether petitioners entered into an illegal conspiracy that caused respondents to suffer a cognizable injury. * * * Second, the issue of fact must be "genuine." When the moving party has carried its burden under <u>Rule 56(c)</u>, its opponent must do more than simply show that there is some metaphysical doubt as to the material facts. * * *

> It follows from these settled principles that if the factual context renders respondents' claim implausible—if the claim is one that simply makes no economic sense—respondents must come forward with more persuasive evidence to support their claim than would otherwise be necessary. * * *

> * * * To survive a motion for summary judgment or for a directed verdict, a plaintiff seeking damages for a violation of § 1 [of the Sherman Act] must present evidence "that tends to exclude the possibility" that the alleged conspirators acted independently. Respondents in this case, in other words, must show that the inference of conspiracy is reasonable in light of the

competing inferences of independent action or collusive action that could not have harmed respondents.

* * *

[P]etitioners had no motive to enter into the alleged conspiracy. To the contrary, as presumably rational businesses, petitioners had every incentive not to engage in the conduct with which they are charged, for its likely effect would be to generate losses for petitioners with no corresponding gains. The Court of Appeals did not take account of the absence of a plausible motive to enter into the alleged predatory pricing conspiracy. It focused instead on whether there was "direct evidence of concert of action." The Court of Appeals erred in two respects: (i) the "direct evidence" on which the court relied had little, if any, relevance to the alleged predatory pricing conspiracy; and (ii) the court failed to consider the absence of a plausible motive to engage in predatory pricing. * * *

* * * [T]he absence of any plausible motive to engage in the conduct charged is highly relevant to whether a "genuine issue for trial" exists within the meaning of Rule 56(e). Lack of motive bears on the range of permissible conclusions that might be drawn from ambiguous evidence: if petitioners had no rational economic motive to conspire, and if their conduct is consistent with other, equally plausible explanations, the conduct does not give rise to an inference of conspiracy. * * * [I]n light of the absence of any rational motive to conspire, neither petitioners' pricing practices, nor their conduct in the Japanese market, nor their agreements respecting prices and distribution in the American market, suffice to create a "genuine issue for trial."

Food for Thought

The Court cites the "absence of any plausible motive" to enter into the alleged conspiracy as the basis for its conclusion that it is unreasonable to infer a conspiracy from the evidence. Is the Court saying that judges evaluating summary judgment motions must be persuaded by the evidence and that they may reach judgments about whether various theories are plausible? If so, would it have been more appropriate to reserve such judgments for the jury?

Matsushita, 475 U.S. at 585–97.

To understand the impact of *Matsushita*, one must consider a previous Supreme Court case, *Poller v. Columbia Broadcasting System, Inc.*, 368 U.S. 464 (1962), in which the Court wrote:

We look at the record on summary judgment in the light most favorable to Poller, the party opposing the motion, and conclude here that it should not have been granted. We believe that summary procedures should be used sparingly in complex antitrust litigation where motive and intent play leading roles, the proof is largely in the hands of the alleged conspirators, and hostile witnesses thicken the plot. It is only when the witnesses are present and subject to cross-examination that their credibility and the weight to be given their testimony can be appraised. Trial by affidavit is no substitute for trial by jury which so long has been the hallmark of "even handed justice."

Id. at 473. In light of *Poller*, was the Supreme Court wrong in *Matsushita* to discount the inference of conspiracy that could be drawn from the evidence on the basis of its view regarding the absence of a plausible motive for the conspiracy? Should the Court have permitted a jury to evaluate motive and reach its own conclusion about what inferences to draw from the evidence?

Food for Thought

Is summary judgment ever appropriate in cases where a critical issue is the defendant's intent or state of mind? Does *Matsushita* improperly permit the judge to evaluate state-of-mind evidence more properly reserved for the jury?

c. The Impact of the *Celotex* Trilogy

Although each case addressed a different aspect of summary judgment practice, the cases that comprise the 1986 trilogy did have a collective impact both doctrinally and perhaps practically. How would you describe the specific doctrinal changes wrought by each case in the 1986 trilogy? Professor David Shapiro nicely summarized some of the additional work that the trilogy did on the doctrinal side when he wrote:

Food for Thought

Might there be a benefit to the changes in the summary judgment process for plaintiffs? Although it makes it more difficult for some plaintiffs to proceed to trial, are those who survive summary judgment in a strengthened position with respect to negotiating a settlement of the case? Further, one could argue that those plaintiffs who do not survive summary judgment are spared the expense of conducting a trial they ultimately would lose. Is there merit to this point?

[E]ach case, in addition to expressing a general view more favorable to summary judgment than the Court had expressed in the past, laid aside some specific shibboleths that had long affected summary judgment practice, e.g., that the moving party (even one who did not have the ultimate burden of proof) had to support its motion with evidence negating the fact or facts to be proved; that summary judgment was to be avoided in complex cases; that the faintest possibility that the opponent on summary judgment might come up with sufficient evidence by the time of trial was enough to warrant the denial of the motion; and that certain subjective matters that may be especially hard for a party to prove (like the adversary's state of mind) are always inappropriate subjects for summary judgment against that party.

David L. Shapiro, *The Story of* Celotex: *The Role of Summary Judgment in the Administration of Justice, in* CIVIL PROCEDURE STORIES (Kevin M. Clermont ed. 2004).

Together, the *Celotex* trilogy of cases places on nonmovants bearing the burden of proof at trial the obligation to demonstrate—at the summary judgment stage—more than "some metaphysical doubt as to material facts." *Matsushita*, 475 U.S. at 586. A "genuine" dispute as to those facts must be shown, and if the record "blatantly contradict[s]" the nonmovant's version of events, the court is under no duty to accept that version and permit the case to proceed to a jury. *Scott v. Harris*, 550 U.S. 372, 380 (2007).

In light of the major changes in summary judgment doctrine, one might expect that the use of summary judgment at the behest of defendants would have increased. Commentators have expressed the view that this indeed has been the case, *see* Martin H. Redish, *Summary Judgment and the Vanishing Trial: Implications of the Litigation Matrix*, 57 STAN. L. REV. 1329, 1330 (2005) ("Changes in the law of summary judgment quite probably explain at least a large part of the dramatic reduction in federal trials."), but others have claimed that the evidence indicating an impact is "hard to come by" and "sparse," *see* Shapiro, *The Story of* Celotex, *supra*, at 365–66. See *Perspective & Analysis* below.

—Perspective & Analysis—

Patricia M. Wald, a former judge on the U.S. Court of Appeals for the D.C. Circuit, aptly summarized much of the critical response to the *Celotex* trilogy:

> A few [commentators] protested that . . . it was defendants who brought summary judgment motions and thus, the more freely these motions were granted, the harder it would be for plaintiffs—who are typically less privileged than their adversaries—to get a fair hearing, since they often depend upon discovery and trial to flesh out their cases. Simply stated, to these critics the 1986 cases appeared to have sharply tilted the playing field, forcing the more disadvantaged parties to run uphill. These critics also worried that this trio of decisions invaded the province of the factfinder by blocking trials even when material facts were contested, on the basis of judges' predictions as to whether sustainable inferences could be drawn from the few pieces of evidence that were available at this early stage. What almost everyone in the academic and legal communities agreed on was that the Supreme Court had moved summary judgment out of left field and onto first base, where it began shortening the innings by taking out runners before they could even begin

to make the rounds. From 1986 to the present day, summary judgment has remained at first base and, some would say, it is getting progressively better at tagging runners out.

Patricia M. Wald, *Summary Judgment at Sixty*, 76 TEX. L. REV. 1897, 1914– 15 (1998).

One commentator has gone as far as to conclude that the trilogy was not a key turning point in the use of the summary judgment device. *See* Stephen B. Burbank, *Vanishing Trials and Summary Judgment in Federal Civil Cases: Drifting Toward Bethlehem or Gomorrah?*, 1 J. EMPIRICAL LEGAL STUD. 591, 620 (2004) ("Such reliable empirical evidence as we have, however, does not support the claims of those who see a turning point in the Supreme Court's 1986 trilogy. Rather, the evidence suggests that summary judgment started to assume a greater role in the 1970s."); *see also* Joe S. Cecil, Rebecca Eyre, Dean Miletich & David Rindskopf, *A Quarter Century of Summary Judgment Practice in Six Federal District Courts*, 4 J. EMPIRICAL LEGAL STUD. 861 (2007). Clearly, even though the evidence of the trilogy's impact may be scarce or inconclusive, the fact remains that the trilogy made the summary judgment motion a tool that is more available to defendants and something that is more difficult for plaintiffs to oppose. Is that a positive development?

> **FYI**
>
> Several scholars have moved beyond the debate over the impact of the *Celotex* trilogy to turn their attention to more fundamental questions about the validity and utility of the summary judgment device. *See, e.g.*, Suja A. Thomas, *Why Summary Judgment Is Unconstitutional*, 93 VA. L. REV. 139 (2007) (arguing that summary judgment impermissibly intrudes upon the Seventh Amendment right to jury); John Bronsteen, *Against Summary Judgment*, 75 GEO. WASH. L. REV. 522 (2007) (arguing that rather than facilitating systemic efficiency, the summary judgment device imposes large costs on the system by discouraging the early settlement of disputes).

d. The Timing of a Summary Judgment Motion

A motion for summary judgment is typically sought after the litigants have had the opportunity to engage in discovery. Although Rule 56 sets a deadline of 30 days after the close of discovery for filing a motion for summary judgment, it does not require parties to wait until the close of discovery to do so. Indeed, a party may seek summary judgment "at any time" prior to the stated deadline FED. R. CIV. P. 56(b). If summary judgment is sought at a time thought to be premature from the perspective of the nonmovant, Rule 56(d)—formerly Rule 56(f)—permits the nonmovant to stay the motion pending further discovery.

This may be especially appropriate if a party seeks summary judgment at the outset of the case. This can occur if a summary judgment motion is made after the close of the pleadings prior to discovery but can also occur if a party seeks a dismissal for failure to state a claim (under Rule 12(b)(6)) or seeks a judgment on the pleadings (under Rule 12(c)) but accompanies either motion with material beyond the pleadings. Under such circumstances, if the court considers the material Rule 12(d) indicates that the motion is converted to a motion for summary judgment under Rule 56. FED. R. CIV. P. 12(d). The adverse party must then be given a reasonable opportunity to present all material pertinent to the motion in response. *Id.* Keep in mind that under Rule 10(c), a "written instrument that is an exhibit to a pleading is part of the pleading for all purposes"; thus, reference to such exhibits will not ordinarily trigger the Rule 12(d) conversion. *See, e.g., Gibson v. Mortg. Elec. Registration Sys., Inc.*, No. 11–2173–STA, 2012 WL 517329, at *3 (W.D. Tenn. Feb. 15, 2012) (determining that exhibits attached to defendants' motion for judgment on the pleadings, which were attached to or referenced in the complaint, were "part of the pleadings for purposes of Rule 12 and Rule 10(c)").

Executive Summary

- **Default Judgments.** A party who fails to "plead or otherwise defend" its case is subject to an entry of default against it. The opposing party may then seek a default judgment against the defaulting party from the court. *See* Rule 55.

- **Voluntary Dismissal.** If a plaintiff determines that it is better to terminate the action rather than proceed, the plaintiff may voluntarily dismiss its own case without permission prior to an answer or summary judgment motion. Otherwise, consent of the other parties or the court is required. *See* Rule 41(a).

- **Involuntary Dismissal.** A defendant may move for dismissal of an action or of any claim against it if the plaintiff fails to prosecute the claim or to comply with the rules or any order of the court. *See* Rule 41(b).

- **Case Management.** At any pretrial conference, courts have the authority to take action to formulate the issues in the case and eliminate claims or defenses they deem to be frivolous. *See* Rule 16(c)(2)(A).

■ **Settlement Promotion.** Courts are also empowered to promote settlement negotiations among the parties and in certain circumstances direct the parties to participate in court-annexed ADR processes such as mediation or non-binding arbitration. *See* Rule 16(c)(2)(I).

■ **Summary Judgment.** Summary judgment is appropriate when there is no genuine dispute as to any material fact and one party is entitled to judgment as a matter of law. Parties not bearing the burden of proof at trial may seek summary judgment by simply indicating the absence of a genuine issue of material fact to the court, which then obligates the responding party to produce evidence in support of its claim sufficient to support a reasonable jury verdict in its favor at trial. See Rule 56; *Celotex Corp. v. Catrett, 477 U.S. 317 (1986)*.

Major Themes

Keep in mind these three themes relevant to the disposition without trial material:

a. *Diligence*—insufficient diligence on the part of the plaintiff or defendant in pursuing his or her case before the court can result in dismissal or default.

b. *Managerial Judging*—judges have a good deal of authority to manage cases by formulating the issues, eliminating frivolous claims or defenses, pushing the parties toward settlement, and forcing the parties to engage in court-annexed ADR.

c. *Plaintiffs & Summary Judgment*—the standards surrounding summary judgment that the Court articulated in the *Celotex* trilogy of cases made it more difficult for plaintiffs to resist a summary judgment motion by relaxing defendants' burden in making the motion, applying the substantive evidentiary standard of proof to the summary judgment determination, and endorsing summary judgment even where the dispositive issue is a party's intent or state of mind.

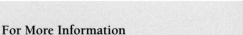

For More Information

Students interested in studying disposition without trial further may consult the following resources:

- 9 C. WRIGHT & A. MILLER, FED. PRAC. & PROC. § 2361 *et seq.* (3d ed. 2008) (dismissal of actions).

- 6A C. WRIGHT, A. MILLER & M. KANE, FED. PRAC. & PROC. § 1521 *et seq.* (3d ed. 2010) (Rule 16).

- 10A C. WRIGHT, A. MILLER & M. KANE, FED. PRAC. & PROC. § 2711 *et seq.* (4th ed. 2016) (summary judgment).

- David L. Shapiro, *The Story of* Celotex: *The Role of Summary Judgment in the Administration of Justice, in* CIVIL PROCEDURE STORIES (Kevin M. Clermont ed. 2004).

Test Your Knowledge

To assess your understanding of the material in this chapter, <u>click here</u> to take a quiz.

CHAPTER TEN

Trials

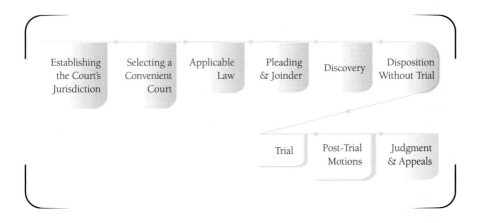

Establishing the Court's Jurisdiction	Selecting a Convenient Court	Applicable Law	Pleading & Joinder	Discovery	Disposition Without Trial

			Trial	Post-Trial Motions	Judgment & Appeals

IN THE PREVIOUS CHAPTER, WE began by dispelling the myth that trials are the means by which a large proportion of cases are resolved. Given the reality that less than two percent of all federal civil filings result in a trial each year, it should come as no surprise then that civil procedure does not focus on trials or the conduct of trials. That does not mean, however, that trials should be ignored. In this chapter, we will focus on two important aspects of the trial phase of civil litigation: issues surrounding the right to a jury trial and judicial control over jury decisionmaking.

Make the Connection

Specific instruction on how to conduct a trial—including eliciting testimony, the presentation of evidence, and the making of opening and closing arguments—is something you will receive in a course on **Trial Practice** or **Trial Advocacy**.

A. Trial by Jury

In the American federal judicial system, civil trials—when they occur—are typically conducted before a jury. Drawn from the local community, the civil jury is an institution that has been an important part of our system of civil justice from the colonial era through the present day. So important was the civil jury that a right to trial by jury in civil suits was preserved—in the federal courts—through the adoption of the Seventh Amendment to the U.S. Constitution. In this section, we will consider the scope of the constitutional right to a jury trial and how juries are constituted and impaneled. We will also briefly review the phases of a trial conducted before a jury.

1. The Seventh Amendment Right to a Jury Trial

Any consideration of the federal jury trial right must begin with reference to the Seventh Amendment. Although the original Constitution did not protect a right to trial by jury in civil cases, once the Bill of Rights was ratified the Seventh Amendment extended such protection as follows:

U.S. Const. Amend. VII: Trial by Jury in Civil Cases

In Suits at common law, where the value in controversy shall exceed twenty dollars, the right of trial by jury shall be preserved, and no fact tried by a jury, shall be otherwise re-examined in any Court of the United States, than according to the rules of the common law.

Three aspects of this provision are particularly worth highlighting. First, the amendment begins by indicating that it applies to "[s]uits at common law." Second, it declares that the right of trial by jury is to be "preserved." Third, under the amendment no facts tried by a jury may be "re-examined" other than in accordance with "the rules of the common law."

The first and third of the highlighted aspects of the Seventh Amendment—both references to the "common law"—pertain to the difference between law and equity that was introduced in the <u>Overview</u> to this casebook. *See* <u>*Parsons v. Bedford, Breedlove & Robeson*, 28 U.S. (3 Pet.) 433, 446 (1830)</u> ("The phrase 'common law,' found in [the Seventh Amendment], is used in contradistinction to equity, and admiralty, and maritime jurisprudence."). The system of law inherited from England made distinctions between actions at law, equity, and admiralty. Although historically the right to a jury attached to actions at law, the same could not be said for suits in equity or admiralty. *See id.* ("It is well known, that . . . in courts of equity and admiralty, juries do not intervene . . . ."). Thus, the Seventh Amendment maintains this distinction by protecting the jury right only in the context of actions at law.

Food for Thought

Does a historical approach to interpreting the jury trial right make sense? Is it possible to determine for every issue whether it would have been considered legal versus equitable in 1791? What about issues or claims—such as statutorily created actions—that did not exist in 1791; is it possible to apply a historical approach to determining whether those matters fall on the law or equity side of history?

The "preserved" language of the amendment relates to its "common law" references: The Seventh Amendment preserves a jury right instead of affirmatively granting one, and what is preserved is the right to a jury trial for matters that enjoyed such a right when the amendment was adopted. The Supreme Court has indicated that by using the term "preserved," the amendment calls for a historical analysis; courts are to determine the scope of the jury trial right as it existed at the time of the ratification of the amendment (1791) and make determinations about the availability of a jury right today on that basis. *See Dimick v. Schiedt, 293 U.S. 474, 476 (1935)* ("In order to ascertain the scope and meaning of the Seventh Amendment, resort must be had to the appropriate rules of the common law established at the time of the adoption of that constitutional provision in 1791.").

Together, the concept of preserving the jury right as it existed in 1791, combined with the idea that the jury right is limited to actions at law, provide the basic analytical framework for determining in what circumstances a party is entitled to have a matter tried to a jury. In the cases that follow, we will review how the Supreme Court has developed its Seventh Amendment jurisprudence and how it has dealt with the challenging issue of determining the applicability of the jury right in new contexts not extant at the time the Bill of Rights was adopted.

> **FYI**
>
> Although the Constitution preserves the jury right for certain claims, under the Federal Rules a party must demand a trial by jury within 14 days of service of the last pleading on the issue or a jury trial is waived. *See* FED. R. CIV. P. 38(b), (d).

Beacon Theatres, Inc. v. Westover

Supreme Court of the United States
359 U.S. 500 (1959)

MR. JUSTICE BLACK delivered the opinion of the Court.

Petitioner, Beacon Theatres, Inc., sought by mandamus to require a district judge in the Southern District of California to vacate certain orders alleged to deprive it of a jury trial of issues arising in a suit brought against it by Fox West Coast Theatres, Inc. The Court of Appeals for the Ninth Circuit refused the writ, holding that the trial judge had acted within his proper discretion in denying petitioner's request for a jury. We granted certiorari because "Maintenance of the jury as a fact-finding body is of such importance and occupies so firm a place in our history and jurisprudence that any seeming curtailment of the right to a

> **Take Note!**
>
> Note that the respondent in this case is someone named Westover, not Fox West Coast Theatres. Can you figure out who Westover is?

jury trial should be scrutinized with the utmost care." <u>Dimick v. Schiedt, 293 U.S. 474, 486</u>.

Fox had asked for declaratory relief against Beacon alleging a controversy arising under the <u>Sherman Antitrust Act, 26 Stat. 209</u>, as amended, 15 U.S.C. §§ <u>1</u>, <u>2</u>, and under the <u>Clayton Act, 15 U.S.C.A. § 15</u>, which authorizes suits for treble damages against Sherman Act violators. According to the complaint Fox operates a movie theatre in San Bernardino, California, and has long been exhibiting films under contracts with movie distributors. These contracts grant it the exclusive right to show 'first run' pictures in the 'San Bernardino competitive area' and provide for 'clearance'—a period of time during which no other theatre can exhibit the same pictures. After building a drive-in theatre about 11 miles from San Bernardino, Beacon notified Fox that it

What's That?

Declaratory relief refers to a judgment of a court that declares the legal rights of the parties without ordering any affirmative relief such as an injunction or damages. For example, a plaintiff seeking declaratory relief might ask the court for a declaration that its conduct does not violate the defendant's rights under a particular statute.

considered contracts barring simultaneous exhibitions of first-run films in the two theatres to be overt acts in violation of the antitrust laws. Fox's complaint alleged that this notification, together with threats of treble damage suits against Fox and its distributors, gave rise to 'duress and coercion' which deprived Fox of a valuable property right, the right to negotiate for exclusive first-run contracts. Unless Beacon was restrained, the complaint continued, irreparable harm would result. Accordingly, while its pleading was styled a 'Complaint for Declaratory Relief,' Fox prayed both for a declaration that a grant of clearance between the Fox and Beacon theatres is reasonable and not in violation of the antitrust laws, and for an injunction, pending final resolution of the litigation, to prevent Beacon from instituting any action under the antitrust laws against Fox and its distributors arising out of the controversy alleged in the complaint. Beacon filed an answer, a counterclaim against Fox, and a crossclaim against an exhibitor who had intervened. These denied the

Make the Connection

The *Sherman Antitrust Act* is a federal statute that polices monopolizing and anticompetitive conduct. The *Clayton Act* amended the Sherman Act and prohibits specific anticompetitive practices such as exclusive-dealing contracts and tying arrangements. You can study the federal antitrust laws in detail in an **Antitrust** course.

threats and asserted that there was no substantial competition between the two theatres, that the clearances granted were therefore unreasonable, and that a conspiracy existed between Fox and its distributors to manipulate contracts and clearances so as to restrain trade and monopolize first-run pictures in violation of the antitrust laws. Treble damages were asked.

Beacon demanded a jury trial of the factual issues in the case as provided by Federal Rule of Civil Procedure 38(b). The District Court, however, viewed the issues raised by the 'Complaint for Declaratory Relief,' including the question of competition between the two theatres, as essentially equitable. Acting under the pur-

Food for Thought

Having studied counterclaims in Chapter 7, do you think Beacon's counterclaim is a compulsory counterclaim? Does it assert equitable or legal relief or both?

ported authority of Rules 42(b) and 57, it directed that these issues be tried to the court before jury determination of the validity of the charges of antitrust violations made in the counterclaim and crossclaim. A common issue of the 'Complaint for Declaratory Relief,' the counterclaim, and the crossclaim was the reasonableness of the clearances granted to Fox, which depended, in part, on the existence of competition between the two theatres. Thus the effect of the action of the District Court could be, as the Court of Appeals believed, 'to limit the petitioner's opportunity fully to try to a jury every issue which has a bearing upon its treble damage suit,' for determination of the issue of clearances by the judge might 'operate either by way of *res judicata* or collateral estoppel so as to conclude both parties with respect thereto at the subsequent trial of the treble damage claim.'

Take Note!

What is the nature of the potential problem that the Court is highlighting here? Be sure to understand this issue because it is an integral part of what the Court has been called upon to resolve in this case.

The District Court's finding that the Complaint for Declaratory Relief presented basically equitable issues draws no support from the Declaratory Judgment Act, 28 U.S.C. §§ 2201, 2202; FED. RULES CIV. PROC. 57. That statute, while allowing prospective defendants to sue to establish their nonliability, specifically preserves the right to jury trial for both parties. It follows that if Beacon would have been entitled to a jury trial in a treble damage suit against Fox it cannot be deprived of that right merely because Fox took advantage of the availability of declaratory relief to sue Beacon first. Since the right to trial by jury applies to treble damage suits under the antitrust laws, and is, in fact, an essential part of the congressional plan for making competition rather than monopoly the rule of trade, the Sherman and Clayton Act issues on which Fox sought a declaration were essentially jury questions.

Nevertheless the Court of Appeals refused to upset the order of the district judge. It held that the question of whether a right to jury trial existed was to be judged by Fox's complaint read as a whole. In addition to seeking a declaratory judgment, the court said, Fox's complaint can be read as making out a valid plea for injunctive relief, thus stating a claim traditionally cognizable in equity. A party who is entitled to maintain a suit in equity for an injunction, said the court, may have all the issues in his suit determined by the judge without a jury regardless of whether legal rights are involved. The court then rejected the argument that equitable relief, traditionally available only when legal remedies are inadequate, was rendered unnecessary in this case by the filing of the counterclaim and crossclaim which presented all the issues necessary to a determination of the right to injunctive relief. Relying on *American Life Ins. Co. v. Stewart*, 300 U.S. 203, 215, decided before the enactment of the Federal Rules of Civil Procedure, it invoked the principle that a court sitting in equity could retain jurisdiction even though later a legal remedy became available. In such instances the equity court had discretion to enjoin the later lawsuit in order to allow the whole dispute to be determined in one case in one court. Reasoning by analogy, the Court of Appeals held it was not an abuse of discretion for the district judge, acting under Federal Rule of Civil Procedure 42(b), to try the equitable cause first even though this might, through collateral estoppel, prevent a full jury trial of the counterclaim and crossclaim which were as effectively stopped as by an equity injunction.

Beacon takes issue with the holding of the Court of Appeals that the complaint stated a claim upon which equitable relief could be granted. As initially filed the complaint alleged that threats of lawsuits by petitioner against Fox and its distributors were causing irreparable harm to Fox's business relationships. The prayer for relief, however, made no mention of the threats but asked only that pending litigation of the claim for declaratory judgment, Beacon be enjoined from beginning any lawsuits under the antitrust laws against Fox and its distributors arising out of the controversy alleged in the complaint. Evidently of the opinion that this prayer did not state a good claim for equitable relief, the Court of Appeals construed it to include a request for an injunction against threats of lawsuits. * * * Assuming that the pleadings can be construed to support such a request and assuming additionally that the complaint can be read as alleging the kind of harassment by a multiplicity of lawsuits which would traditionally have justified equity to take jurisdiction and settle the case in one suit, we are nevertheless of the opinion that, under the Declaratory Judgment Act and the Federal Rules of Civil Procedure, neither claim can justify denying Beacon a trial by jury of all the issues in the antitrust controversy.

The basis of injunctive relief in the federal courts has always been irreparable harm and inadequacy of legal remedies. At least as much is required to justify a trial court in using its discretion under the Federal Rules to allow claims of equitable origins to be tried ahead of legal ones, since this has the same effect as an equitable injunction of the legal claims. And it is immaterial, in judging if that discretion is properly employed, that before the Federal Rules and the Declaratory Judgment Act were passed, courts of equity, exercising a jurisdiction separate from courts of law, were, in some cases, allowed to enjoin subsequent legal actions between the same parties involving the same controversy. This was because the subsequent legal action, though providing an opportunity to try the case to a jury, might not protect the right of the equity plaintiff to a fair and orderly adjudication of the controversy.

Under such circumstances the legal remedy could quite naturally be deemed inadequate. Inadequacy of remedy and irreparable harm are practical terms, however. As such their existence today must be determined, not by precedents decided under discarded procedures, but in the light of the remedies now made available by the Declaratory Judgment Act and the Federal Rules.

Viewed in this manner, the use of discretion by the trial court under <u>Rule 42(b)</u> to deprive Beacon of a full jury trial on its counterclaim and crossclaim, as well as on Fox's plea for declaratory relief, cannot be justified. Under the Federal Rules the same court may try both legal and equitable causes in the same action. Thus any defenses, equitable or legal, Fox may have to charges of antitrust violations can be raised either in its suit for declaratory relief or in answer to Beacon's counterclaim. On proper showing, harassment by threats of other suits, or other suits actually brought, involving the issues being tried in this case, could be temporarily enjoined pending the outcome of this litigation. Whatever permanent injunctive relief Fox might be entitled to on the basis of the decision in this case could, of course, be given by the court after the jury renders its verdict. In this way the issues between these parties could be settled in one suit giving Beacon a full jury trial of every antitrust issue. By contrast, the holding of the court below while granting Fox no additional protection unless the avoidance of jury trial be considered as such, would compel Beacon to split his antitrust case, trying part to a judge and part to a jury. Such a result, which involves the postponement and subordination of Fox's own legal claim for declaratory relief as well as of the counterclaim which Beacon was compelled by the Federal Rules to bring, is not permissible.

Our decision is consistent with the plan of the Federal Rules and the Declaratory Judgment Act to effect substantial procedural reform while retaining a distinction between jury and nonjury issues and leaving substantive rights unchanged. Since in the federal courts equity has always acted only when legal remedies were inadequate, the expansion of adequate legal remedies provided by the Declaratory Judgment Act and the Federal Rules necessarily affects the scope of equity. Thus, the justification for equity's deciding legal issues once it obtains jurisdiction, and refusing to dismiss a case, merely because subsequently a legal remedy becomes available, must be re-evaluated in the light of the liberal joinder provisions of the Federal Rules which allow legal and equitable causes to be brought and resolved in one civil action. Similarly the need for, and therefore, the availability of such equitable remedies as Bills of Peace, Quia Timet and Injunction must be reconsidered in view of the existence of the Declaratory Judgment Act as well as the liberal joinder provision of the Rules. * * *

>
>
> ### It's Latin to Me!
>
> *Quia timet* is a Latin phrase meaning "because he fears" and refers to a legal doctrine that permits a party to seek equitable protection against an anticipated future injury.

If there should be cases where the availability of declaratory judgment or joinder in one suit of legal and equitable causes would not in all respects protect the plaintiff seeking equitable relief from irreparable harm while affording a jury trial in the legal cause, the trial court will necessarily have to use its discretion in deciding whether the legal or equitable cause should be tried first. Since the right to jury trial is a constitutional one, however, while no similar requirement protects trials by the court, that discretion is very narrowly limited and must, wherever possible, be exercised to preserve jury trial. As this Court said in <u>Scott v. Neely, 140 U.S. 106, 109–10</u>: 'In the Federal courts this (jury) right cannot be dispensed with, except by the assent of the parties entitled to it; nor can it be impaired by any blending with a claim, properly cognizable at law, of a demand for equitable relief in aid of the legal action, or during its pendency.' This long-standing principle of equity dictates that only under the most imperative circumstances, circumstances which in view of the flexible procedures of the Federal Rules we cannot now anticipate, can the right to a jury trial of legal issues be lost through prior determination of equitable claims. We as have shown, this is far from being such a case.

* * *

The judgment of the Court of Appeals is reversed.

MR. JUSTICE FRANKFURTER took no part in the consideration or decision of this case.

MR. JUSTICE STEWART, with whom MR. JUSTICE HARLAN and MR. JUSTICE WHITTAKER[*] concur, dissenting.

> **FYI**
>
> Justice John Marshall Harlan, one of the Justices joining in Justice Stewart's opinion here, had a grandfather whose name was John Marshall Harlan and who also sat as an Associate Justice on the U.S. Supreme Court from 1877 to 1911. The younger Justice Harlan served from 1955 through retirement in 1971.

There can be no doubt that a litigant is entitled to a writ of mandamus to protect a clear constitutional or statutory right to a jury trial. But there was no denial of such a right here. The district judge simply exercised his inherent discretion, now explicitly confirmed by the Federal Rules of Civil Procedure, to schedule the trial of an equitable claim in advance of an action at law. Even an abuse of such discretion could not, I think, be attacked by the extraordinary writ of mandamus. In any event no abuse of discretion is apparent in this case.

---

[*] Justice Whittaker, the other dissenter here, served on the Supreme Court for only 5 years; he had a nervous breakdown while serving and retired under his doctor's orders. [Ed.]

The complaint filed by Fox stated a claim traditionally cognizable in equity. That claim, in brief, was that Beacon had wrongfully interfered with the right of Fox to compete freely with Beacon and other distributors for the licensing of films for first-run exhibition in the San Bernardino area. The complaint alleged that the plaintiff was without an adequate remedy at law and would be irreparably harmed unless the defendant were restrained from continuing to interfere—by coercion and threats of litigation—with the plaintiff's lawful business relationships.

The Court of Appeals found that the complaint, although inartistically drawn, contained allegations entitling the petitioner to equitable relief. That finding is accepted in the prevailing opinion today. If the complaint had been answered simply by a general denial, therefore, the issues would under traditional principles have been triable as a proceeding in equity. Instead of just putting in issue the allegations of the complaint, however, Beacon filed pleadings which affirmatively alleged the existence of a broad conspiracy among the plaintiff and other theatre owners to monopolize the first-run exhibition of films in the San Bernardino area to refrain from competing among themselves, and to discriminate against Beacon in granting film licenses. Based upon these allegations, Beacon asked damages in the amount of $300,000. Clearly these conspiracy allegations stated a cause of action triable as of right by a jury. What was demanded by Beacon, however, was a jury trial not only of this cause of action, but also of the issues presented by the original complaint.

Upon motion of Fox the trial judge ordered the original action for declaratory and equitable relief to be tried separately to the court and in advance of the trial of the defendant's counter-claim and crossclaim for damages. The court's order, which carefully preserved the right to trial by jury upon the conspiracy and damage issues raised by the counterclaim and crossclaim, was in conformity with the specific provisions of the Federal Rules of Civil Procedure. *Rule 42(b).* Yet it is decided today that the Court of Appeals must compel the district judge to rescind it.

Assuming the existence of a factual issue common both to the plaintiff's original action and the defendant's counterclaim for damages, I cannot agree that the District Court must be compelled to try the counterclaim first. It is, of course, a matter of no great moment in what order the issues between the parties in the present litigation are tried. What is disturbing is the process by which the Court arrives at its decision—a process which appears to disregard the historic relationship between equity and law.

I.

The Court suggests that 'the expansion of adequate legal remedies provided by the Declaratory Judgment Act * * * necessarily affects the scope of equity.' Does the Court mean to say that the mere availability of an action for a declaratory judgment operates to furnish 'an adequate remedy at law' so as to deprive a court of equity of the power to act? That novel line of reasoning is at least implied in the Court's opinion. But the Declaratory Judgment Act did not 'expand' the substantive law. That Act merely provided a new statutory remedy, neither legal nor equitable, but available in the areas of both equity and law. When declaratory relief is sought, the right to trial by jury depends upon the basic context in which the issues are presented. If the basic issues in an action for declaratory relief are of a kind traditionally cognizable in equity, e.g., a suit for cancellation of a written instrument, the declaratory judgment is not a 'remedy at law.' If, on the other hand, the issues arise in a context traditionally cognizable at common law, the right to a jury trial of course remains unimpaired, even though the only relief demanded is a declaratory judgment.

Food for Thought

Do you agree that availability of the jury trial right for actions under the Declaratory Judgment Act (28 U.S.C. § 2201) depends on the equitable or legal nature of the underlying issues or does an action seeking declaratory relief have its own (equitable?) character that must be considered when determining entitlement to a jury? Does the majority clearly address this question?

Thus, if in this case the complaint had asked merely for a judgment declaring that the plaintiff's specified manner of business dealings with distributors and other exhibitors did not render it liable to Beacon under the antitrust laws, this would have been simply a 'juxtaposition of parties' case in which Beacon could have demanded a jury trial. But the complaint in the present case, as the Court recognizes, presented issues of exclusively equitable cognizance, going well beyond a mere defense to any subsequent action at law. Fox sought from the court protection against Beacon's allegedly unlawful interference with its business relationships—protection which this Court seems to recognize might not have been afforded by a declaratory judgment, unsupplemented by equitable relief. The availability of a declaratory judgment did not, therefore, operate to confer upon Beacon the right to trial by jury with respect to the issues raised by the complaint.

II.

The Court's opinion does not, of course, hold or even suggest that a court of equity may never determine 'legal rights.' For indeed it is precisely such rights which the Chancellor, when his jurisdiction has been properly invoked, has often been called upon to decide. Issues of fact are rarely either 'legal' or 'equitable.' All depends upon the context in which they arise. * * *

Though apparently not disputing these principles, the Court holds, quite apart from its reliance upon the Declaratory Judgment Act, that Beacon by filing its counterclaim and crossclaim acquired a right to trial by jury of issues which otherwise would have been properly triable to the court. Support for this position is found in the principle that, "in the federal courts equity has always acted only when legal remedies were inadequate. * * * " Yet that principle is not employed in its traditional sense as a limitation upon the exercise of power by a court of equity. This is apparent in the Court's recognition that the allegations of the complaint entitled Fox to equitable relief—relief to which Fox would not have been entitled if it had had an adequate remedy at law. Instead, the principle is employed today to mean that because it is possible under the counterclaim to have a jury trial of the factual issue of substantial competition, that issue must be tried by a jury, even though the issue was primarily presented in the original claim for equitable relief. This is a marked departure from long-settled principles.

It has been an established rule 'that equitable jurisdiction existing at the filing of a bill is not destroyed because an adequate legal remedy may have become available thereafter.' <u>American Life Ins. Co. v. Stewart,</u> <u>300 U.S. 203, 215</u>. It has also been long settled that the District Court in its discretion may order the trial of a suit in equity in advance of an action at law between the same parties, even if there is a factual issue common to both. * * *

What's That?

A *bill* is a term that refers to the pleading in which a party asserts an equitable claim in a court of equity. This is a historical term in the federal system, since all claims are asserted via a *complaint*, though the term is still used in various states that preserve the distinction between law and equity.

III.

The Court today sweeps away these basic principles as 'precedents decided under discarded procedures.' It suggests that the Federal Rules of Civil Procedure have somehow worked an 'expansion of adequate legal remedies' so as to oust the District Courts of equitable jurisdiction, as well as to deprive them of their traditional power to control their own dockets. But obviously the Federal Rules could not and did not 'expand' the substantive law one whit.

Like the Declaratory Judgment Act, the Federal Rules preserve inviolate the right to trial by jury in actions historically cognizable at common law, as under the Constitution they must. They do not create a right of trial by jury where that right "does not exist under the Constitution or statutes of the United States." Rule 39(a). Since Beacon's counterclaim was compulsory under the Rules, *see* Rule 13(a), it is apparent that by filing it Beacon could not be held to have waived its jury rights. But neither can the counterclaim be held to have transformed Fox's original complaint into an action at law.

The Rules make possible the trial of legal and equitable claims in the same proceeding, but they expressly affirm the power of a trial judge to determine the order in which claims shall be heard. Rule 42(b). Certainly the Federal Rules were not intended to undermine the basic structure of equity jurisprudence, developed over the centuries and explicitly recognized in the United States Constitution.

For these reasons I think the petition for a writ of mandamus should have been dismissed.

———

Points for Discussion

a. The Impact of *Beacon Theatres*

As noted in the text before *Beacon Theatres*, the Supreme Court had interpreted the Seventh Amendment's "preserved" language to indicate that the jury right was to be interpreted according to the scope of the right as it existed in 1791. Does *Beacon Theatres* reflect a rejection of that approach or simply a modification of it?

b. The Reasoning of *Beacon Theatres*

The Court in *Beacon Theatres* held that when there are factual issues to be decided that pertain both to legal and to equitable claims within a single action, a jury must be permitted to decide those facts and related legal claims before the equitable matters are resolved by the judge. However, the equitable claim was raised here first, and the district court determined that it would resolve the equitable claim before the subsequently raised legal claims asserted by the defendant. Why did the *Beacon Theatres* majority determine that it was inappropriate for the district court to do this? On what basis did the Court determine that the jury had to have the initial opportunity to resolve the common factual issues underlying the equitable and legal claims?

What impact is the Court claiming that the Declaratory Judgment Act or the Federal Rules of Civil Procedure have on determining the scope of the jury right in this case? Recall that the Federal Rules achieved the merger of law and equity. FED. R. CIV. P. 2. Is that merger the culprit behind the problem of resolving factual issues that pertain both to equitable and legal claims within a single action? Is the *Beacon Theatres* Court saying that such merger has necessarily altered the analysis of whether the jury trial right is available in a case?

Hypo 10.1

Howard sued Joe for breach of contract, seeking specific performance [equitable relief] and money damages. Assuming a timely jury demand, is Howard entitled to a jury trial? If so, which issues will the jury be entitled to resolve?

c. Determining Whether Issues Are "Legal" or "Equitable"

Does the *Beacon Theatres* Court articulate a clear standard for distinguishing between legal issues, which are entitled to jury resolution, and equitable matters, which are not? In <u>Dairy Queen, Inc. v. Wood, 369 U.S. 469 (1962)</u>, the Court again addressed the availability of the jury trial right in the context of a case raising both equitable and legal claims, and in the process clarified how to identify legal versus equitable claims. *Dairy Queen* involved a dispute surrounding a contract under which the petitioner agreed to pay the owners of the "Dairy Queen" trademark $150,000 for the exclusive use of the trademark in certain portions of Pennsylvania. When the petitioner allegedly defaulted on its payment obligations, the respondent owners of the trademark brought suit:

> The complaint filed in the District Court alleged, among other things, that petitioner had "ceased paying * * * as required in the contract;" that the default "under the said contract * * * [was] in excess of $60,000.00;" that this default constituted a "material breach" of that contract; that petitioner had been notified by letter that its failure to pay as alleged made it guilty of a material breach of contract which if not "cured" would result in an immediate cancellation of contract; that the breach had not been cured but that petitioner was contesting the cancellation and continuing to conduct business as an authorized dealer; that to continue such business after the cancellation of the contract constituted an infringement of the respondents' trademark; that petitioner's financial condition was unstable; and that because of the foregoing allegations, respondents were threatened with irreparable injury for which they had no adequate remedy at law. The complaint then prayed for both temporary and permanent relief, including: (1) temporary and permanent injunctions to restrain petitioner from any future use of or dealing in the franchise and the trademark; (2) an accounting to determine the exact amount of money owing by petitioner and a judgment for that amount; and (3) an injunction pending accounting to prevent petitioner from collecting any money from 'Dairy Queen' stores in the territory.

> In its answer to this complaint, petitioner * * * [included] a demand for trial by jury in accordance with <u>Rule 38(b) of the Federal Rules of Civil Procedure</u>. [The district court granted a motion to strike the petitioner's demand for a jury trial because the action was "purely equitable" or alternatively because the legal issues raised were "incidental" to the equitable issues. The <u>Third Circuit</u> refused to grant mandamus relief compelling the district judge to vacate that order.]

> Petitioner's contention, as set forth in its petition for mandamus to the Court of Appeals and reiterated in its briefs before this Court, is that insofar as the complaint requests a money judgment it presents a claim which

is unquestionably legal. We agree with that contention. The most natural construction of the respondents' claim for a money judgment would seem to be that it is a claim that they are entitled to recover whatever was owed them under the contract as of the date of its purported termination plus damages for infringement of their trademark since that date. * * * As an action on a debt allegedly due under a contract, it would be difficult to conceive of an action of a more traditionally legal character. And as an action for damages based upon a charge of trademark infringement, it would be no less subject to cognizance by a court of law.

The respondents' contention that this money claim is 'purely equitable' is based primarily upon the fact that their complaint is cast in terms of an "accounting," rather than in terms of an action for "debt" or "damages." But the constitutional right to trial by jury cannot be made to depend upon the choice of words used in the pleadings. The necessary prerequisite to the right to maintain a suit for an equitable accounting, like all other equitable remedies, is, as we pointed out in Beacon Theatres, the absence of an adequate remedy at law. Consequently, in order to maintain such a suit on a cause of action cognizable at law, as this one is, the plaintiff must be able to show that the 'accounts between the parties' are of such a 'complicated nature' that only a court of equity can satisfactorily unravel them. In view of the powers given to District Courts by Federal Rule of Civil Procedure 53(b) to appoint masters to assist the jury in those exceptional cases where the legal issues are too complicated for the jury adequately to handle alone, the burden of such a showing is considerably increased and it will indeed be a rare case in which it can be met. But be that as it may, this is certainly not such a case. A jury, under proper instructions from the court, could readily determine the recovery, if any, to be had here, whether the theory finally settled upon is that of breach of contract, that of trademark infringement, or any combination of the two. The

What's That?

An *accounting* is an action asking a court to require the defendant to account for money owed to the plaintiff and to pay the money owed.

What's That?

A *master* is a person appointed by the district court to assist it with its proceedings. The authority that masters have depends on the court's order and is limited by Rule 53.

legal remedy cannot be characterized as inadequate merely because the measure of damages may necessitate a look into petitioner's business records.

369 U.S. at 475–79.

In *Dairy Queen*, the Court looked past the traditional equitable classification of an action for an accounting and equated it with an action on a debt for purposes of determining the availability of the jury trial right. On what basis did the Court do this? Did the *Dairy Queen* Court articulate a clear standard for determining whether an action for relief is truly legal such that the jury right attaches? If so, what is that standard?

The Court offered additional guidance on this matter in *Ross v. Bernhard*, 396 U.S. 531 (1970), when it wrote:

> As our cases indicate, the "legal" nature of an issue is determined by considering, first, the pre-merger custom with reference to such questions; second, the remedy sought; and, third, the practical abilities and limitations of juries. Of these factors, the first, requiring extensive and possibly abstruse historical inquiry, is obviously the most difficult to apply.

Id. at 538 n.10. Is this approach helpful? How is a court to measure the "practical abilities and limitations of juries," and on what basis do limits in that regard permit courts to treat an issue as non-legal and thus not entitled to jury determination?

—Perspective & Analysis—

Under the rationale offered by the Court in *Ross v. Bernhard*, limitations on the "practical abilities" of jurors are relevant to whether a jury trial right exists. Does that mean that no jury right should attach to legal issues in complex cases? Would it be advisable, then, to consider seeking out a more qualified and "intelligent" group of citizens to comprise the jury in such cases? Some commentators have advanced such a proposal:

> The case for special juries in complex civil cases depends upon acceptance of a rather straightforward proposition: All people are not equally capable of learning about new concepts and applying them to the solution of difficult problems . . . . [T]he purposeful selection of more capable citizen-jurors would seem to be a natural and positive step.

> The plan [proposed by the authors] would involve the use of modified jury selection procedures in those limited civil cases where the average jury seems unequal to its task. Juror qualification standards would be keyed to educational background, and a specified level of education—probably college graduation—would be a prerequisite to service

on a special jury. Though not a perfect measure of juror ability, level of education does have a bearing on an individual's ability to function as a juror, especially in a complex, technical case. Furthermore, reliance upon educational background can result not only in an administrable system, but one that, in this time of rather general educational opportunities, produces reasonably representative panels.

William V. Luneburg & Mark A. Nordenberg, _Specially Qualified Juries and Expert Nonjury Tribunals: Alternatives for Coping with the Complexities of Modern Civil Litigation_, 67 VA. L. REV. 887, 899–900 (1981).

d. The "Clean-Up" Doctrine

The other basis for the district court's denial of a jury trial in *Dairy Queen* was that the legal issues raised were "incidental" to the equitable issues. The practice of denying jury consideration of legal issues on the ground that they were incidental to equitable matters under consideration by the judge has been referred to as the "clean-up" doctrine, because it allowed equity courts to resolve legal issues that were ancillary to what was predominately an equitable dispute. *See, e.g., N.L.R.B. v. Jones & Laughlin Steel Corp., 301 U.S. 1, 48 (1937)* ("[The Seventh Amendment] has no application to cases where recovery of money damages is an incident to equitable relief even though damages might have been recovered in an action at law."). The Supreme Court in *Dairy Queen* rejected the use of the "clean-up" doctrine and denied a jury trial for the legal issues in that case:

> At the outset, we may dispose of one of the grounds upon which the trial court acted in striking the demand for trial by jury—that based upon the view that the right to trial by jury may be lost as to legal issues where those issues are characterized as "incidental" to equitable issues—for our previous decisions make it plain that no such rule may be applied in the federal courts. * * * The holding in *Beacon Theatres* was that where both legal and equitable issues are presented in a single case, "only under the most imperative circumstances, circumstances which in view of the flexible procedures of the Federal Rules we cannot now anticipate, can the right to a jury trial of legal issues be lost through prior determination of equitable claims." That holding, of course, applies whether the trial judge chooses to characterize the legal issues presented as "incidental" to equitable issues or not. Consequently, in a case such as this where there cannot even be a contention of such "imperative circumstances," *Beacon Theatres* requires that any legal issues for which a trial by jury is timely and properly demanded be submitted to a jury.

369 U.S. at 470–73. What do you think is the Court's basis for rejecting use of the "clean-up" doctrine here?

e. "Imperative Circumstances" Under *Beacon Theatres* & *Dairy Queen*

The Court, both in *Beacon Theatres* and *Dairy Queen*, indicated that only "imperative circumstances" could permit the right to a jury trial of legal issues to be lost due to their presentation in a single case with equitable claims. Such imperative circumstances—which the Court admitted it could not predict in *Beacon Theatres*—were found to exist in <u>Katchen v. Landy, 382 U.S. 323 (1966)</u>. In *Katchen*, a bankruptcy trustee pursued a money damages claim of the debtor against one of its creditors (who was already seeking to collect money from the debtor's estate) in the context of the non-jury bankruptcy proceedings rather than via a separate legal action. The Supreme Court held that the creditor was not entitled to a jury trial on the trustee's claim, even though the money damages claim would have been entitled to determination by a jury had it been brought outside of the bankruptcy context. The Court so held on the basis of its view that making a jury available to hear such claims would be too disruptive to the statutory bankruptcy scheme developed by Congress, which had the aim of facilitating "the prompt trial of a disputed claim without the intervention of a jury." <u>Id. at 339</u>.

> **Food for Thought**
>
> Could it be said that the bankruptcy court's authority to resolve "incidental" legal issues in the context of a bankruptcy dispute without a jury is an affirmation of the "clean-up" doctrine discussed above, at least in this context?

f. Shareholder Derivative Suits

Prior to the merger of law and equity, shareholder derivative suits were litigated in courts of equity, meaning that there was no jury right even for clearly legal issues involved in such cases. Post-merger, does the jury right now attach to the legal issues in shareholder derivative suits? The Court answered this question in <u>Ross v. Bernhard, 396 U.S. 531 (1970)</u>:

> We have noted that the derivative suit has dual aspects: first, the stockholder's right to sue on behalf of the corporation, historically an equitable matter; second, the claim of the corporation against directors or third parties on which, if the corporation had sued and the claim presented legal issues, the company could demand a jury trial. . . . [L]egal claims are not magically converted into equitable issues by their presentation to a court of equity in a derivative suit. The claim pressed by the stockholder against directors or third parties "is not his own but the corporation's." * * * The heart of the action is the corporate claim. If it presents a legal issue, one entitling the corporation to a jury trial under the Seventh Amendment, the right to a jury is not forfeited merely because the stockholder's right to sue must first be adjudicated as an equitable issue triable to the court. *Beacon* and *Dairy Queen* require no less.

* * *

> In the instant case we have no doubt that the corporation's claim is, at least in part, a legal one. The relief sought is money damages. There are allegations in the complaint of a breach of fiduciary duty, but there are also allegations of ordinary breach of contract and gross negligence. The corporation, had it sued on its own behalf, would have been entitled to a jury's determination, at a minimum, of its damages against its broker under the brokerage contract and of its rights against its own directors because of their negligence. Under these circumstances it is unnecessary to decide whether the corporation's other claims are also properly triable to a jury. *Dairy Queen, Inc. v. Wood*, 369 U.S. 469 (1962).

Ross, 396 U.S. at 538–39, 542–43.

2. The Jury Right and New Statutory Rights to Relief

The claims presented in the cases just discussed represented attempts to vindicate well-established common law or equitable rights. Thus, courts were familiar with whether certain claims were to be regarded as legal or equitable—at least *as a historical matter*—and could take that understanding as the starting point for an analysis of whether the Seventh Amendment's jury right attached to the claim.

As Congress has enacted statutes that create new rights and private rights of action in areas such as civil rights, securities fraud, and environmental protection, the question of whether lawsuits brought to vindicate such rights were entitled to be resolved by a jury came to the fore. In *Curtis v. Loether*, 415 U.S. 189 (1974) [*FLEX Case 10.A*], the Supreme Court squarely dealt with this issue in the context of a housing discrimination claim:

> Petitioner * * * argues that the [Seventh] Amendment is inapplicable to new causes of action created by congressional enactment. * * * Although the Court has apparently never discussed the issue at any length, we have often found the Seventh Amendment applicable to causes of action based on statutes. Whatever doubt may have existed should now be dispelled. The Seventh Amendment does apply to actions enforcing statutory rights, and requires a jury trial upon demand, if the statute creates legal rights and remedies, enforceable in an action for damages in the ordinary courts of law.

* * *

[W]hen Congress provides for enforcement of statutory rights in an ordinary civil action in the district courts, * * * a jury trial must be available if the action involves rights and remedies of the sort typically enforced in an action at law.

Id. at 193–94, 195 (citations omitted). In the Court's view, a claim for damages under the fair housing provisions of the Civil Rights Act of 1968, 42 U.S.C. § 3612, "sounds basically in tort" because "the statute merely defines a new legal duty, and authorizes the courts to compensate a plaintiff for the injury caused by the defendant's wrongful breach. . . . [T]his cause of action is analogous to a number of tort actions recognized at common law. More important, the relief sought here—actual and punitive damages—is the traditional form of relief offered in the courts of law." Curtis, 415 U.S. at 195–96. Keep the approach of Curtis in mind as you read the next case.

Chauffeurs, Teamsters and Helpers, Local No. 391 v. Terry

Supreme Court of the United States
494 U.S. 558 (1990)

JUSTICE MARSHALL delivered the opinion of the Court, except as to Part III-A.

This case presents the question whether an employee who seeks relief in the form of backpay for a union's alleged breach of its duty of fair representation has a right to trial by jury. We hold that the Seventh Amendment entitles such a plaintiff to a jury trial.

I

McLean Trucking Company and the Chauffeurs, Teamsters, and Helpers Local No. 391 (Union) were parties to a collective-bargaining agreement that governed the terms and conditions of employment at McLean's terminals. The 27 respondents were employed by McLean as truckdrivers in bargaining units covered by the agreement, and all were members of the Union. In 1982 McLean implemented a change in operations that resulted in the elimination of some of its terminals and the reorganization of others. As part of that change, McLean transferred respondents to the terminal located in Winston-Salem and agreed to give them special seniority rights in relation to "inactive" employees in Winston-Salem who had been laid off temporarily.

After working in Winston-Salem for approximately six weeks, respondents were alternately laid off and recalled several times. Respondents filed a grievance with the Union, contesting the order of the layoffs and recalls. * * * After these proceedings, the grievance committee ordered McLean to recall any respondent who was then laid off * * *. On the basis of this decision, McLean recalled respondents and laid off the drivers who had been on the inactive list when respondents transferred to Winston-Salem. Soon after this, though, McLean recalled the inactive employees, thereby allowing them to regain seniority rights over respondents. In the next round of layoffs, then, respondents had lower priority than inactive drivers and were laid off first. Accordingly, respondents filed another grievance * * * . * * * At the conclusion of the hearing, the committee held that McLean had not violated the committee's first decision.

McLean continued to engage in periodic layoffs and recalls of the workers at the Winston-Salem terminal. Respondents filed a third grievance with the Union, but the Union declined to refer the charges to a grievance committee on the ground that the relevant issues had been determined in the prior proceedings.

In July 1983, respondents filed an action in District Court, alleging * * * that the Union had violated its duty of fair representation. Respondents * * * sought, *inter alia*, compensatory damages for lost wages and health benefits. * * *

Respondents had requested a jury trial in their pleadings. The Union moved to strike the jury demand on the ground that no right to a jury trial exists in a duty of fair representation suit. The District Court denied the motion to strike. After an interlocutory appeal, the Fourth Circuit affirmed the trial court, holding that the Seventh Amendment entitled respondents to a jury trial of their claim for monetary relief. We granted the petition for certiorari to resolve a Circuit conflict on this issue, and now affirm the judgment of the Fourth Circuit.

II

The duty of fair representation is inferred from unions' exclusive authority under the National Labor Relations Act (NLRA), 49 Stat. 449, 29 U.S.C. § 159(a), to represent all employees in a bargaining unit. The duty requires a union "to serve the interests of all members without hostility or discrimination toward any, to exercise its discretion with complete good faith and honesty, and to avoid arbitrary conduct." * * *

III

* * * To determine whether a particular action will resolve legal rights, we examine both the nature of the issues involved and the remedy sought. "First, we compare the statutory action to 18th-century actions brought in the courts of England prior to the merger of the courts of law and equity. Second, we examine the remedy sought and determine whether it is legal or equitable in nature." *Tull v. United States*, 481 U.S. 412, 417–18. The second inquiry is the more important in our analysis. *Granfinanciera, S.A. v. Nordberg*, 492 U.S. 33, 42 (1989).

A

An action for breach of a union's duty of fair representation was unknown in 18th-century England; in fact, collective bargaining was unlawful. We must therefore look for an analogous cause of action that existed in the 18th century to determine whether the nature of this duty of fair representation suit is legal or equitable.

The Union contends that this duty of fair representation action resembles a suit brought to vacate an arbitration award because respondents seek to set aside the result of the grievance process. In the 18th century, an action to set aside an arbitration award was considered equitable. * * *

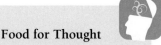

Food for Thought

If the Seventh Amendment only has "preserved" the jury right to the extent it existed in 1791, does it make any sense to apply the right to a claim that didn't even exist at that time? Is searching for an analogous 18th-century claim a sensible approach?

The arbitration analogy is inapposite, however, to the Seventh Amendment question posed in this case. No grievance committee has considered respondents' claim that the Union violated its duty of fair representation; the grievance process was concerned only with the employer's alleged breach of the collective-bargaining agreement. Thus, respondents' claim against the Union cannot be characterized as an action to vacate an arbitration award * * * .

The Union next argues that respondents' duty of fair representation action is comparable to an action by a trust beneficiary against a trustee for breach of fiduciary duty. Such actions were within the exclusive jurisdiction of courts of equity. This analogy is far more persuasive than the arbitration analogy. Just as a trustee must act in the best interests of the beneficiaries, a union, as the exclusive representative of the workers, must exercise its power to act on behalf of the employees in good faith. Moreover, just as a beneficiary does not directly control the actions of a trustee, an individual employee lacks direct control over a union's actions taken on his behalf.

Make the Connection

The duties of a *trustee* in relation to a *trust* and to trust *beneficiaries* are matters you can study further in a **Trusts & Estates** course. *Fiduciary duty* is also a concept you may cover in a **Corporations** or **Business Associations** course.

The trust analogy extends to a union's handling of grievances. In most cases, a trustee has the exclusive authority to sue third parties who injure the beneficiaries' interest in the trust, including any legal claim the trustee holds in trust for the beneficiaries. The trustee then has the sole responsibility for determining whether to settle, arbitrate, or otherwise dispose of the claim. Similarly, the union typically has broad discretion in its decision whether and how to pursue an employee's grievance against an employer. Just as a trust beneficiary can sue to enforce a contract entered into on his behalf by the trustee only if the trustee "improperly refuses or neglects to bring an action against the third person," so an employee can sue his employer for a breach of the collective-bargaining agreement only if he shows that the union breached its duty of fair representation in its handling of the grievance.

Respondents contend that their duty of fair representation suit is less like a trust action than an attorney malpractice action, which was historically an action at law. * * * The attorney malpractice analogy is inadequate in several respects. Although an attorney malpractice suit is in some ways similar to a suit alleging a union's breach of its fiduciary duty, the two actions are fundamentally different. The nature of an action is in large part controlled by the nature of the underlying relationship between the parties. Unlike employees represented by a union, a client controls the significant decisions concerning his representation. Moreover, a client can fire his attorney if he is dissatisfied with his attorney's performance. This option is not available to an individual employee who is unhappy with a union's representation, unless a majority of the members of the bargaining unit share his dissatisfaction. Thus, we find the malpractice analogy less convincing than the trust analogy.

What's That?

Attorney malpractice is a tort claim, based on state law, that typically requires proving four elements (these vary among the states): (1) the existence of an attorney-client relationship giving rise to duty on the attorney's part, (2) a negligent breach of that duty, (3) proximate cause establishing that but for the attorney's negligence, the plaintiff-client would have prevailed in the underlying action, and (4) actual damages.

Nevertheless, the trust analogy does not persuade us to characterize respondents' claim as wholly equitable. The Union's argument mischaracterizes the nature of our comparison of the action before us to 18th-century forms of action. As we observed in *Ross v. Bernhard*, 396 U.S. 531 (1970), "The Seventh Amendment question depends on the nature of the issue to be tried rather than the character of the overall action." *Id.* at 538 (emphasis added). As discussed above, to recover from the Union here, respondents must prove both that McLean violated § 301 by breaching the collective-bargaining agreement and that the Union breached its duty of fair representation. When viewed in isolation, the duty of fair representation issue is analogous to a claim against a trustee for breach of fiduciary duty. The § 301 issue, however, is comparable to a breach of contract claim—a legal issue.

Respondents' action against the Union thus encompasses both equitable and legal issues. The first part of our Seventh Amendment inquiry, then, leaves us in equipoise as to whether respondents are entitled to a jury trial.

B

Our determination under the first part of the Seventh Amendment analysis is only preliminary. *Granfinanciera, S.A. v. Nordberg*, 492 U.S., at 47. In this case, the only remedy sought is a request for compensatory damages representing backpay and benefits. Generally, an action for money damages was "the traditional form of relief offered in the courts of law." *Curtis v. Loether*, 415 U.S. 189, 196 (1974). This Court has not, however, held that "any award of monetary relief must *necessarily* be 'legal' relief." *Ibid.* (emphasis added). Nonetheless, because we conclude that the remedy respondents seek has none of the attributes that must be present before we will find an exception to the general rule and characterize damages as equitable, we find that the remedy sought by respondents is legal.

First, we have characterized damages as equitable where they are restitutionary, such as in "action[s] for disgorgement of improper profits," *Tull*, 481 U.S., at 424. The backpay sought by respondents is not money wrongfully held by the Union, but wages and benefits they would have received from McLean had the Union processed the employees' grievances properly. Such relief is not restitutionary.

Second, a monetary award "incidental to or intertwined with injunctive relief" may be equitable. *Tull*, supra, 481 U.S., at 424. Because respondents seek only money damages, this characteristic is clearly absent from the case.

Food for Thought

Restitutionary relief involves the return of something to its rightful owner. The example given here, disgorgement of improper profits, is restitutionary because it gives profits to the party who was entitled to them instead of the defendant. Do you understand why the Court states that the backpay relief sought here is not restitutionary?

The Union argues that the backpay relief sought here must nonetheless be considered equitable because this Court has labeled backpay awarded under Title VII, of the Civil Rights Act of 1964, 42 U.S.C. § 2000e *et seq.*, as equitable. * * * We are not convinced.

The Court has never held that a plaintiff seeking backpay under Title VII has a right to a jury trial. *See Lorillard v. Pons*, 434 U.S. 575, 581–582 (1978). Assuming, without deciding, that such a Title VII plaintiff has no right to a jury trial, the Union's argument does not persuade us that respondents are not entitled to a jury trial here. Congress specifically characterized backpay under Title VII as a form of "equitable relief." 42 U.S.C. § 2000e-5(g) (1982 ed.) ("[T]he court may . . . order such affirmative action as may be appropriate, which may include, but is not limited to, reinstatement or hiring of employees, with or without back pay . . . , or any other equitable relief as the court deems appropriate"). Congress made no similar pronouncement regarding the duty of fair representation. Furthermore, the Court has noted that backpay sought from an employer under Title VII would generally be restitutionary in nature, *see Curtis v. Loether*, in contrast to the damages sought here from the Union. Thus, the remedy sought in this duty of fair representation case is clearly different from backpay sought for violations of Title VII. * ≈* *

We hold, then, that the remedy of backpay sought in this duty of fair representation action is legal in nature. Considering both parts of the Seventh Amendment inquiry, we find that respondents are entitled to a jury trial on all issues presented in their suit.

IV

On balance, our analysis of the nature of respondents' duty of fair representation action and the remedy they seek convinces us that this action is a legal one. Although the search for an adequate 18th-century analog revealed that the claim includes both legal and equitable issues, the money damages respondents seek are the type of relief traditionally awarded by courts of law. Thus, the Seventh Amendment entitles respondents to a jury trial, and we therefore affirm the judgment of the Court of Appeals.

It is so ordered.

JUSTICE BRENNAN, concurring in part and concurring in the judgment.

I agree with the Court that respondents seek a remedy that is legal in nature and that the Seventh Amendment entitles respondents to a jury trial on their duty of fair representation claims. I therefore join Parts I, II, III-B, and IV of the Court's opinion. I do not join that part of the opinion which reprises the particular historical analysis this Court has employed to determine whether a claim is a "Sui[t] at common law" under the Seventh Amendment because I believe the historical test can and should be simplified.

The current test, first expounded in *Curtis v. Loether*, 415 U.S. 189, 194 (1974), requires a court to compare the right at issue to 18th-century English forms of action to determine whether the historically analogous right was vindicated in an action at law or in equity, and to examine whether the remedy sought is legal or equitable in nature.

However, this Court, in expounding the test, has repeatedly discounted the significance of the analogous form of action for deciding where the Seventh Amendment applies. I think it is time we dispense with it altogether. I would decide Seventh Amendment questions on the basis of the relief sought. If the relief is legal in nature, i.e., if it is the kind of relief that historically was available from courts of law, I would hold that the parties have a constitutional right to a trial by jury—unless Congress has permissibly delegated the particular dispute to a non-Article III decisionmaker and jury trials would frustrate Congress' purposes in enacting a particular statutory scheme.

Take Note!

Justice Brennan is proposing a revised analysis for determining the availability of the jury trial right. What are the precise contours of his proposed analysis? Does his approach present a viable or even superior alternative to the Court's modified historical approach? Revisit this question once you have reviewed Justice Brennan's arguments in favor of his approach below.

I believe that our insistence that the jury trial right hinges in part on a comparison of the substantive right at issue to forms of action used in English courts 200 years ago needlessly convolutes our Seventh Amendment jurisprudence. For the past decade and a half, this Court has explained that the two parts of the historical test are not equal in weight, that the nature of the remedy is more important than the nature of the right. Since the existence of a right to jury trial therefore turns on the nature of the remedy, absent congressional delegation to a specialized decisionmaker, there remains little purpose to our rattling through dusty attics of ancient writs. * * *

We have long acknowledged that, of the factors relevant to the jury trial right, comparison of the claim to ancient forms of action, "requiring extensive and possibly abstruse historical inquiry, is obviously the most difficult to apply." *Ross v. Bernhard, 396 U.S. 531, 538 (1970)*. Requiring judges, with neither the training nor time necessary for reputable historical scholarship, to root through the tangle of primary and secondary sources to determine which of a hundred or so writs is analogous to the right at issue has embroiled courts in recondite controversies better left to legal historians. * * *

* * *

To rest the historical test required by the Seventh Amendment solely on the nature of the relief sought would not, of course, offer the federal courts a rule that is in all cases self-executing. Courts will still be required to ask which remedies were traditionally available at law and which only in equity. But this inquiry involves fewer variables and simpler choices, on the whole, and is far more manageable than the scholasticist debates in which we have been engaged. Moreover, the rule I propose would remain true to the Seventh Amendment, as it is undisputed that, historically, "[j]urisdictional lines [between law and equity] were primarily a matter of remedy." McCoid, *Procedural Reform and the Right to Jury Trial: A Study of Beacon Theaters, Inc. v. Westover,* 116 U. PA. L. REV. 1 (1967).

This is not to say that the resulting division between claims entitled to jury trials and claims not so entitled would exactly mirror the division between law and equity in England in 1791. But it is too late in the day for this Court to profess that the Seventh Amendment preserves the right to jury trial only in cases that would have been heard in the British law courts of the 18th century.

Indeed, given this Court's repeated insistence that the nature of the remedy is always to be given more weight than the nature of the historically analogous right, it is unlikely that the simplified Seventh Amendment analysis I propose will result in different decisions than the analysis in current use. In the unusual circumstance that the nature of the remedy could be characterized equally as legal or equitable, I submit that the comparison of a contemporary statutory action unheard of in the 18th century to some ill-fitting ancient writ is too shaky a basis for the resolution of an issue as significant as the availability of a trial by jury. If, in the rare case, a tie breaker is needed, let us break the tie in favor of jury trial. * * *

JUSTICE STEVENS, concurring in part and concurring in the judgment.

Because I believe the Court has made this case unnecessarily difficult by exaggerating the importance of finding a precise common-law analogue to the duty of fair representation, I do not join Part III-A of its opinion. * * *

As I have suggested in the past, I believe the duty of fair representation action resembles a common-law action against an attorney for malpractice more closely than it does any other form of action. * * *

* * * Duty of fair representation suits are for the most part ordinary civil actions involving the stuff of contract and malpractice disputes. There is accordingly no ground for excluding these actions from the jury right.

In my view, the evolution of this doctrine through suits tried to juries, the useful analogy to common-law malpractice cases, and the well-recognized duty to scrutinize any proposed curtailment of the right to a jury trial "with the utmost care," provide a plainly sufficient basis for the Court's holding today. I therefore join its judgment and all of its opinion except for Part III-A.

JUSTICE KENNEDY, with whom JUSTICE O'CONNOR and JUSTICE SCALIA join, dissenting.

This case asks whether the Seventh Amendment guarantees the respondent union members a jury trial in a duty of fair representation action against their labor union. The Court is quite correct, in my view, in its formulation of the initial premises that must govern the case. * * * To determine whether rights and remedies in a duty of fair representation action are legal in character, we must compare the action to the 18th-century cases permitted in the law courts of England, and we must examine the nature of the relief sought. I agree also with those Members of the Court who find that the duty of fair representation action resembles an equitable trust action more than a suit for malpractice.

I disagree with the analytic innovation of the Court that identification of the trust action as a model for modern duty of fair representation actions is insufficient to decide the case. The Seventh Amendment requires us to determine whether the duty of fair representation action "is more similar to cases that were tried in courts of law than to suits tried in courts of equity." *Tull v. United States*, 481 U.S. 412, 417 (1987). Having made this decision in favor of an equitable action, our inquiry should end. Because the Court disagrees with this proposition, I dissent. * * *

II

The Court relies on two lines of precedents to overcome the conclusion that the trust action should serve as the controlling model. The first consists of cases in which the Court has considered simplifications in litigation resulting from modern procedural reforms in the federal courts. Justice MARSHALL asserts that these cases show that the Court must look at the character of individual issues rather than claims as a whole. The second line addresses the significance of the remedy in determining the equitable or legal nature of an action for the purpose of choosing the most appropriate analogy. Under these cases, the Court decides that the respondents have a right to a jury because they seek money damages. These authorities do not support the Court's holding.

A

In three cases we have found a right to trial by jury where there are legal claims that, for procedural reasons, a plaintiff could have or must have raised in the courts of equity before the systems merged. [*Beacon Theatres, Inc. v. Westover*; *Dairy Queen, Inc. v. Wood*; *Ross v. Bernhard*.] * * *

These three cases responded to the difficulties created by a merged court system. They stand for the proposition that, because distinct courts of equity no longer exist, the possibility or necessity of using former equitable procedures to press a legal claim no longer will determine the right to a jury. Justice MARSHALL reads these cases to require a jury trial whenever a cause of action contains legal issues and would require a jury trial in this case because the respondents must prove a breach of the collective-bargaining agreement as one element of their claim.

I disagree. The respondents, as shown above, are asserting an equitable claim. Having reached this conclusion, the *Beacon*, *Dairy Queen*, and *Ross* cases are inapplicable. Although we have divided self-standing legal claims from equitable declaratory, accounting, and derivative procedures, we have never parsed legal elements out of equitable claims absent specific procedural justifications. Actions which, beyond all question, are equitable in nature may involve some predicate inquiry that would be submitted to a jury in other contexts. For example, just as the plaintiff in a duty of fair representation action against his union must show breach of the collective-bargaining agreement as an initial matter, in an action against a trustee for failing to pursue a claim the beneficiary must show that the claim had some merit. But the question of the claim's validity, even if the claim raises contract issues, would not bring the jury right into play in a suit against a trustee. * * *

B

The Court also rules that, despite the appropriateness of the trust analogy as a whole, the respondents have a right to a jury trial because they seek money damages. The nature of the remedy remains a factor of considerable importance in determining whether a statutory action had a legal or equitable analog in 1791, but we have not adopted a rule that a statutory action permitting damages is by definition more analogous to a legal action than to any equitable suit. In each case, we look to the remedy to determine whether, taken with other factors, it places an action within the definition of "Suits at common law."

In *Curtis, 415 U.S., at 195–196*, for example, we ruled that the availability of actual and punitive damages made a statutory antidiscrimination action resemble a legal tort action more than any equitable action. We made explicit that we did not "go so far as to say that any award of monetary relief must necessarily be 'legal' relief." Although monetary damages might cause some statutory actions to resemble tort suits, the presence of monetary damages in this duty of fair representation action does not make it more analogous to a legal action than to an equitable action. Indeed, as shown above, the injunctive and monetary remedies available make the duty of fair representation suit less analogous to a malpractice action than to a suit against a trustee. * * *

III

Food for Thought

Justice Kennedy here insists that the Court should "adhere to the historical test" when determining the availability of the jury trial right. Does the majority disagree? If so, in what ways does the approach endorsed by the majority opinion depart from the historical test? Is the departure warranted?

The Court must adhere to the historical test in determining the right to a jury because the language of the Constitution requires it. The Seventh Amendment "preserves" the right to jury trial in civil cases. We cannot preserve a right existing in 1791 unless we look to history to identify it. * * * If we abandon the plain language of the Constitution to expand the jury right, we may expect Courts with opposing views to curtail it in the future.

It is true that a historical inquiry into the distinction between law and equity may require us to enter into a domain becoming less familiar with time. Two centuries have passed since the Seventh Amendment's ratification, and the incompleteness of our historical records makes it difficult to know the nature of certain actions in 1791. The historical test, nonetheless, has received more criticism than it deserves. * * * The historical test, in fact, resolves most cases without difficulty.

I would hesitate to abandon or curtail the historical test out of concern for the competence of the Court to understand legal history. We do look to history for the answers to constitutional questions. Although opinions will differ on what this history shows, the approach has no less validity in the Seventh Amendment context than elsewhere.

If Congress has not provided for a jury trial, we are confined to the Seventh Amendment to determine whether one is required. Our own views respecting the wisdom of using a jury should be put aside. Like Justice BRENNAN, I admire the jury process. Other judges have taken the opposite view. But the judgment of our own times is not always preferable to the lessons of history. Our whole constitutional experience teaches that history must inform the judicial inquiry. Our obligation to the Constitution and its Bill of Rights, no less than the compact we have with the generation that wrote them for us, do not permit us to disregard provisions that some may think to be mere matters of historical form.

Points for Discussion

a. The Court's Two-Part Test

In its opinion, the *Terry* Court indicates that it uses a two-part test to determine whether legal versus equitable rights are involved in an action asserting statutory rights: "First, we compare the statutory action to 18th-century actions brought in the courts of England prior to the merger of the courts of law and equity. Second, we examine the remedy sought and determine whether it is legal or equitable in nature." *Terry, 494 U.S. at 565*. The Court then went on to state, "The second inquiry is the more important in our analysis," *id.*, a view the Court first clearly articulated in *Tull v. United*

Take Note!

Recall that in *Ross v. Bernhard* (quoted in the Points for Discussion section following *Beacon Theatres*) the Court included a third part in the analysis, "the practical abilities and limitations of juries." What has happened to this part of the test? In an omitted footnote in *Terry*, Justice Marshall indicated that this consideration "is relevant only to the determination whether Congress has permissibly entrusted the resolution of certain disputes to an administrative agency or specialized court of equity, and whether jury trials would impair the functioning of the legislative scheme." *Terry, 494 U.S. at 565 n.4*.

States, 481 U.S. 412, 421 (1987) ("We need not rest our conclusion on what has been called an 'abstruse historical' search for the nearest 18th-century analog. We reiterate our previously expressed view that characterizing the relief sought is '[m]ore important' than finding a precisely analogous common-law cause of action in determining whether the Seventh Amendment guarantees a jury trial." (citation omitted)).

Why should the second inquiry be considered to be "more important" than the first? Is this two-part test and its emphasis on the nature of the remedy sought consistent with the "preserved" language of the Seventh Amendment, which would seem to require emphasis on the more historically-oriented first part of the test? What are Justice Brennan's and Justice Kennedy's views on this point as expressed in their respective opinions? Regardless of its merits, the Court has stood by its view that the two prongs of the test are unevenly weighed. *See City of Monterey v. Del Monte Dunes*, 526 U.S. 687, 708–11 (1999).

Hypo 10.2

The federal government initiated an action in federal court against a company for violating the Clean Water Act, seeking a civil monetary penalty for each day of violation (as permitted under the Act) and an injunction ordering the company to cease violating the Act. Assume the statute does not provide for a jury trial right.

The company responded to the complaint with an answer demanding a jury trial. Should the district court permit a jury to hear any aspect of this case?

---

b. Historical Analysis and the Seventh Amendment Jury Right

To the extent that the historical analysis remains a component of the Court's two-part inquiry and has some impact on determinations of the availability of the jury right, is such an analysis useful? Is Justice Brennan correct when he highlights the disparate historical analyses of the Justices as an indication that the effort is not very useful or accurate? Is the purported inaccuracy of the historical analysis a sufficient basis for abandoning it if the Seventh Amendment calls for such an analysis? Does the Seventh Amendment call for a historical analysis? Is there any wisdom that you can see to tying the scope of the jury right to its historical availability

Food for Thought

In *Terry*, of the three circa-1791 claims presented as analogous to the action against the union—a suit to vacate an arbitration award, an action against a trustee, and an attorney malpractice claim—the Court thought that the trustee analogy was the most appropriate. Do you agree?

rather than permitting it to be applied according to judges' views of the nature of the relief sought? What does Justice Kennedy have to say about this question? For more recent examples of courts engaging in the jury right analysis, see *Pereira v. Farace*, 413 F.3d 330, 341 (2d Cir. 2005) ("We thus hold that the district court improperly characterized the Trustee's damages as restitution. Plaintiff's claim is for compensatory damages—a legal claim. . . . [W]e conclude that defendants were entitled to a jury trial on the Trustee's breach of fiduciary duty claims."); *Taylor Corp. v. Four Seasons Greetings, LLC*, 403 F.3d 958, 969 (8th Cir. 2005) (holding that there is no right to a jury trial in a copyright action seeking only injunctive relief); *Lutz v. Glendale Union High Sch.*, 403 F.3d 1061, 1069 (9th Cir. 2005) ("[W]e hold that there is no right to have a jury determine the appropriate amount of back pay under Title VII, and thus the ADA . . . .").

c. Congressional Power over the Jury Right

In addition to the Court's ability to determine that the jury right attaches to the trial of certain statutorily created claims, Congress has the authority to provide for a statutory right to a jury trial. Can Congress similarly restrict the availability of the jury right for statutorily created claims as it sees fit? *See Granfinanciera, S.A. v. Nordberg*, 492 U.S. 33, 36 (1989) (holding that a person who has not submitted a claim against a bankruptcy estate has a right to a jury trial when sued by the trustee in bankruptcy to recover an allegedly fraudulent monetary transfer, "notwithstanding Congress' designation of fraudulent conveyance actions as 'core proceedings'" resolvable by the bankruptcy judge). Can Congress limit the jury right for legal claims asserted against the United States government? *See Lehman v. Nakshian*, 453 U.S. 156, 160 (1981) ("It has long been settled that the Seventh Amendment right to trial by jury does not apply in actions against the Federal Government."). Against federal officials? *See Carlson v. Green*, 446 U.S. 14, 20–22 (1980) (holding that the plaintiff can maintain a *Bivens* action despite the availability of an FTCA claim—thus entitling the plaintiff to a jury).

Although Congress is limited in its authority to remove a traditionally legal claim from the province of the jury, the Supreme Court has held that Congress has a limited ability to do so if it assigns the adjudication of "new statutory 'public rights'" to an administrative agency:

> At least in cases in which "public rights" are being litigated—*e.g.*, cases in which the Government sues in its sovereign capacity to enforce public rights created by statutes within the power of Congress to enact—the Seventh Amendment does not prohibit Congress from assigning the factfinding function and initial adjudication to an administrative forum with which the jury would be incompatible.

Atlas Roofing Co., Inc. v. Occupational Safety & Health Review Comm'n, 430 U.S. 442, 450 (1977). Given that such litigation, had it occurred in federal court, would have required a jury trial, does it make sense for the Court to say that no such right exists for the same claims simply because Congress has assigned them to an administrative agency for initial resolution?

---

3. The Role of the Jury

Once it is determined that there will be a jury trial, important questions remain regarding which matters may be decided by the jury as opposed to the judge. Generally speaking, the jury is tasked with making findings of fact, while the judge is charged with determining the law and instructing the jury on the law. But this law/fact distinction is not as clear as one might hope: There are grey areas in which it is difficult to characterize a matter as one or the other, making the law/fact distinction at times a not very helpful basis for assigning tasks in a trial to a jury. In the next case, the Court touches on the law/fact distinction and illustrates how other factors can help resolve the question of whether a matter is more appropriately handled by the judge or the jury.

Markman v. Westview Instruments, Inc.

Supreme Court of the United States
517 U.S. 370 (1996)

JUSTICE SOUTER delivered the opinion of the Court.

The question here is whether the interpretation of a so-called patent claim, the portion of the patent document that defines the scope of the patentee's rights, is a matter of law reserved entirely for the court, or subject to a Seventh Amendment guarantee that a jury will determine the meaning of any disputed term of art about which expert testimony is offered. We hold that the construction of a patent, including terms of art within its claim, is exclusively within the province of the court.

I

* * * It has long been understood that a patent must describe the exact scope of an invention and its manufacture to "secure to [the patentee] all to which he is entitled, [and] to apprise the public of what is still open to them." Under the modern American system, these objectives are served by two distinct elements of a patent document. First, it contains a specification describing the invention "in such full, clear, concise, and exact terms as to enable any person skilled in the art . . . to make and use the same." Second, a patent includes one or more "claims," which "particularly poin[t] out and distinctly clai[m] the subject matter which the applicant regards as his invention." 35 U.S.C. § 112. "A claim covers and secures a process, a

machine, a manufacture, a composition of matter, or a design, but never the function or result of either, nor the scientific explanation of their operation." The claim "define[s] the scope of a patent grant," and functions to forbid not only exact copies of an invention, but products that go to "the heart of an invention but avoids the literal language of the claim by making a noncritical change," In this opinion, the word "claim" is used only in this sense peculiar to patent law.

Characteristically, patent lawsuits charge what is known as infringement, and rest on allegations that the defendant "without authority ma[de], use[d] or [sold the] patented invention, within the United States during the term of the patent therefor . . . ." 35 U.S.C. § 271(a). Victory in an infringement suit requires a finding that the patent claim "covers the alleged infringer's product or process," which in turn necessitates a determination of "what the words in the claim mean."

Make the Connection

You can learn more about patents, patent construction, infringement actions, and special terminology related to patents (such as *reissue patent* and *patent claim*) in a **Patent Law** or **Intellectual Property** course.

Petitioner in this infringement suit, Markman, owns United States Reissue Patent No. 33,054 for his "Inventory Control and Reporting System for Drycleaning Stores." The patent describes a system that can monitor and report the status, location, and movement of clothing in a dry-cleaning establishment. The Markman system consists of a keyboard and data processor to generate written records for each transaction, including a bar code readable by optical detectors operated by employees, who log the progress of clothing through the dry-cleaning process. Respondent Westview's product also includes a keyboard and processor, and it lists charges for the dry-cleaning services on bar-coded tickets that can be read by portable optical detectors.

Markman brought an infringement suit against Westview and Althon Enterprises, an operator of dry-cleaning establishments using Westview's products (collectively, Westview). Westview responded that Markman's patent is not infringed by its system because the latter functions merely to record an inventory of receivables by tracking invoices and transaction totals, rather than to record and track an inventory of articles of clothing. Part of the dispute hinged upon the meaning of the word "inventory," a term found in Markman's independent claim 1, which states that Markman's product can "maintain an inventory total" and "detect and localize spurious additions to inventory." The case was tried before a jury, which heard, among others, a witness produced by Markman who testified about the meaning of the claim language.

After the jury compared the patent to Westview's device, it found an infringement of Markman's independent claim 1 and dependent claim 10. The District Court nevertheless granted Westview's deferred motion for judgment as a matter of law, one of its reasons being that the term "inventory" in Markman's patent encompasses "both cash inventory and the actual physical inventory of articles of clothing." Under the trial court's construction of the patent, the production, sale, or use of a tracking system for dry cleaners would not infringe Markman's patent unless the product was capable of tracking articles of clothing throughout the cleaning process and generating reports about their status and location. Since Westview's system cannot do these things, the District Court directed a verdict * * * .

Markman appealed, arguing it was error for the District Court to substitute its construction of the disputed claim term 'inventory' for the construction the jury had presumably given it. The United States Court of Appeals for the Federal Circuit affirmed, holding the interpretation of claim terms to be the exclusive province of the court and the Seventh Amendment to be consistent with that conclusion. Markman sought our review on each point, and we granted certiorari. We now affirm.

II

The Seventh Amendment provides that "[i]n Suits at common law, where the value in controversy shall exceed twenty dollars, the right of trial by jury shall be preserved . . . ." Since Justice Story's day, we have understood that "[t]he right of trial by jury thus preserved is the right which existed under the English common law when the Amendment was adopted." In keeping with our longstanding adherence to this "historical test," we ask, first, whether we are dealing with a cause of action that either was tried at law at the time of the founding or is at least analogous to one that was, see, e.g., *Tull v. United States*, 481 U.S. 412, 417 (1987). If the action in question belongs in the law category, we then ask whether the particular trial decision must fall to the jury in order to preserve the substance of the common-law right as it existed in 1791.

A

As to the first issue, going to the character of the cause of action, "[t]he form of our analysis is familiar. 'First we compare the statutory action to 18th-century actions brought in the courts of England prior to the merger of the courts of law and equity.'" *Granfinanciera, S.A. v. Nordberg*, 492 U.S. 33, 42 (1989) (citation omitted). Equally familiar is the descent of today's patent infringement action from the infringement actions tried at law in the 18th century, and there is no dispute that infringement cases today must be tried to a jury, as their predecessors were more than two centuries ago.

B

This conclusion raises the second question, whether a particular issue occurring within a jury trial (here the construction of a patent claim) is itself necessarily a jury issue, the guarantee being essential to preserve the right to a jury's resolution of the ultimate dispute. In some instances the answer to this second question may be easy because of clear historical evidence that the very subsidiary question was so regarded under the English practice of leaving the issue for a jury. But when, as here, the old practice provides no clear answer, we are forced to make a judgment about the scope of the Seventh Amendment guarantee without the benefit of any foolproof test.

The Court has repeatedly said that the answer to the second question "must depend on whether the jury must shoulder this responsibility as necessary to preserve the '*substance of the common-law right of trial by jury*.'" *Tull v. United States, supra, at 426* (emphasis added) (quoting *Colgrove v. Battin, 413 U.S. 149, 156 (1973)*). "Only those incidents which are regarded as fundamental, as inherent in and of the essence of the system of trial by jury, are placed beyond the reach of the legislature." *Tull v. United States, supra, at 426* (citations omitted).

The "substance of the common-law right" is, however, a pretty blunt instrument for drawing distinctions. We have tried to sharpen it, to be sure, by reference to the distinction between substance and procedure. We have also spoken of the line as one between issues of fact and law.

But the sounder course, when available, is to classify a mongrel practice (like construing a term of art following receipt of evidence) by using the historical method, much as we do in characterizing the suits and actions within which they arise. Where there is no exact antecedent, the best hope

Take Note!

Notice the Court's language here: "pretty blunt instrument," "We have tried," "the best hope," and "seeking the best analogy we can." Such language does not inspire much confidence in its analysis. Should something so important as the jury right be based on such a seemingly imprecise approach?

lies in comparing the modern practice to earlier ones whose allocation to court or jury we do know, seeking the best analogy we can draw between an old and the new.

C

"Prior to 1790 nothing in the nature of a claim had appeared either in British patent practice or in that of the American states," and we have accordingly found no direct antecedent of modern claim construction in the historical sources. Claim practice did not achieve statutory recognition until the passage of the Act of July 4, 1836, and inclusion of a claim did not become a statutory requirement until 1870. * * *

The closest 18th-century analogue of modern claim construction seems, then, to have been the construction of specifications, and as to that function the mere smattering of patent cases that we have from this period shows no established jury practice sufficient to support an argument by analogy that today's construction of a claim should be a guaranteed jury issue. * * *

III

Since evidence of common-law practice at the time of the framing does not entail application of the Seventh Amendment's jury guarantee to the construction of the claim document, we must look elsewhere to characterize this determination of meaning in order to allocate it as between court or jury. We accordingly consult existing precedent[10] and consider both the relative interpretive skills of judges and juries and the statutory policies that ought to be furthered by the allocation.

A

The two elements of a simple patent case, construing the patent and determining whether infringement occurred, were characterized by the former patent practitioner, Justice Curtis. "The first is a question of law, to be determined by the court, construing the letters-patent, and the description of the invention and specification of claim annexed to them. The second is a question of fact, to be submitted to a jury."

In arguing for a different allocation of responsibility for the first question, Markman relies primarily on two cases, *Bischoff v. Wethered*, 9 Wall. 812 (1870), and *Tucker v. Spalding*, 13 Wall. 453 (1872). These are said to show that evidence of the meaning of patent terms was offered to 19th-century juries, and thus to imply that the meaning of a documentary term was a jury issue whenever it was subject to evidentiary proof. That is not what Markman's cases show, however. * * * [N]either *Bischoff* nor *Tucker* indicates that juries resolved the meaning of terms of art in construing a patent, and neither case undercuts Justice Curtis's authority.

B

Where history and precedent provide no clear answers, functional considerations also play their part in the choice between judge and jury to define terms of art. We said in *Miller v. Fenton*, 474 U.S. 104, 114 (1985), that when an issue "falls somewhere between a pristine legal standard and a simple historical fact, the fact/law distinction at times has turned on a determination that, as a matter of the

---

[10] Because we conclude that our precedent supports classifying the question as one for the court, we need not decide either the extent to which the Seventh Amendment can be said to have crystallized a law/fact distinction, or whether post-1791 precedent classifying an issue as one of fact would trigger the protections of the Seventh Amendment if (unlike this case) there were no more specific reason for decision.

sound administration of justice, one judicial actor is better positioned than another to decide the issue in question." So it turns out here, for judges, not juries, are the better suited to find the acquired meaning of patent terms.

Take Note!

Recall that in determining whether the jury trial right attached, the Court in *Ross v. Bernhard* indicated that an analysis of the "practical abilities and limitations of juries" was relevant to the analysis. Is that consideration making an appearance here as the Court determines that "judges, not juries, are better suited" to resolve the patent construction issue?

The construction of written instruments is one of those things that judges often do and are likely to do better than jurors unburdened by training in exegesis. Patent construction in particular "is a special occupation, requiring, like all others, special training and practice. The judge, from his training and discipline, is more likely to give a proper interpretation to such instruments than a jury; and he is, therefore, more likely to be right, in performing such a duty, than a jury can be expected to be." Such was the understanding nearly a century and a half ago, and there is no reason to weigh the respective strengths of judge and jury differently in relation to the modern claim; quite the contrary, for "the claims of patents have become highly technical in many respects as the result of special doctrines relating to the proper form and scope of claims that have been developed by the courts and the Patent Office."

Markman would trump these considerations with his argument that a jury should decide a question of meaning peculiar to a trade or profession simply because the question is a subject of testimony requiring credibility determinations, which are the jury's forte. It is, of course, true that credibility judgments have to be made about the experts who testify in patent cases * * * . But our own experience with document construction leaves us doubtful that trial courts will run into many cases like that. In the main, we expect, any credibility determinations will be subsumed within the necessarily sophisticated analysis of the whole document, required by the standard construction rule that a term can be defined only in a way that comports

Food for Thought

What is the basis for relying on juror competence as a means of determining whether the jury right applies? Should the right apply irrespective of the jury's ability to handle the question? Is there warrant for such a consideration in the Seventh Amendment?

with the instrument as a whole. Thus, in these cases a jury's capabilities to evaluate demeanor, to sense the "mainsprings of human conduct," or to reflect community standards, are much less significant than a trained ability to evaluate the testimony in relation to the overall structure of the patent. The decisionmaker vested with the task of construing the patent is in the better position to ascertain whether an expert's proposed definition fully comports with the specification and claims and so will preserve the patent's internal coherence. We accordingly think there is sufficient reason to treat construction of terms of art like many other responsibilities that we cede to a judge in the normal course of trial, notwithstanding its evidentiary underpinnings.

C

Finally, we see the importance of uniformity in the treatment of a given patent as an independent reason to allocate all issues of construction to the court. As we noted in *General Elec. Co. v. Wabash Appliance Corp.*, 304 U.S. 364, 369 (1938), "[t]he limits of a patent must be known for the protection of the patentee, the encouragement of the inventive genius of others and the assurance that the subject of the patent will be dedicated ultimately to the public." Otherwise, a "zone of uncertainty which enterprise and experimentation may enter only at the risk of infringement claims would discourage invention only a little less than unequivocal foreclosure of the field," and "[t]he public [would] be deprived of rights supposed to belong to it, without being clearly told what it is that limits these rights." It was just for the sake of such desirable uniformity that Congress created the Court of Appeals for the Federal Circuit as an exclusive appellate court for patent cases, observing that increased uniformity would "strengthen the United States patent system in such a way as to foster technological growth and industrial innovation."

Uniformity would, however, be ill served by submitting issues of document construction to juries. Making them jury issues would not, to be sure, necessarily leave evidentiary questions of meaning wide open in every new court in which a patent might be litigated, for principles of issue preclusion would ordinarily foster uniformity. *Cf. Blonder-Tongue Laboratories, Inc. v. University of Ill. Foundation,* 402 U.S. 313 (1971). But whereas issue preclusion could not be asserted against new and independent infringement defendants even within a given jurisdiction, treating interpretive issues as purely legal will promote (though it will not guarantee) intra-jurisdictional certainty through the application of stare decisis on those questions not yet subject to interjurisdictional uniformity under the authority of the single appeals court.

Accordingly, we hold that the interpretation of the word "inventory" in this case is an issue for the judge, not the jury, and affirm the decision of the Court of Appeals for the Federal Circuit.

It is so ordered.

————————

Points for Discussion

a. The Law/Fact Distinction

In the federal system, legal questions are reserved for the judge. *United States v. Gaudin*, 515 U.S. 506, 513 (1995) ("In criminal cases, as in civil, we held, the judge must be permitted to instruct the jury on the law and to insist that the jury follow his instructions."). Conversely, questions of fact are reserved for the jury. *Edmonson v. Leesville Concrete Co.*, 500 U.S. 614, 624–25 (1991) ("In the federal system, the Constitution itself commits the trial of facts in a civil cause to the jury."); *Byrd v. Blue Ridge Rural Elec. Coop.*, 356 U.S. 525, 538 (1958) (identifying a "federal policy favoring jury decisions of disputed fact questions"). So-called mixed questions of law and fact that involve the application of a legal standard to a jury-determined set of facts are ordinarily the province of the jury. *Hana Fin. Inc. v. Hana Bank*, 135 S. Ct. 907, 911 (2015) ("[T]he application-of-legal-standard-to-fact sort of question . . . commonly called a 'mixed question of law and fact,' has typically been resolved by juries.") (quoting *Gaudin*, 515 U.S. at 512)). However, it is more challenging to figure out who should resolve matters that cannot be readily characterized as either a question of fact or a question of law. What approach does the *Markman* Court offer for figuring out who should decide such "mongrel" issues?

b. The *Markman* Court's Analysis

The holding in *Markman* relies heavily upon the conclusion that judges are better suited than juries to construe the meaning of terms in a patent. Do you agree with that conclusion? Even if that is true, is that a proper basis for deciding the question of whether the jury should resolve the issue? Is the *Markman* analysis one that can easily be applied in other cases? How is one to determine whether a jury or a judge is more qualified to resolve a question? Does the *Markman* Court provide some guidance on how to make such a determination?

c. *Dobson v. Masonite Corp.*

In *Dobson v. Masonite Corp.*, 359 F.2d 921 (5th Cir. 1966), Dobson sued the defendant for breach of an oral agreement calling on him to clear timber from lands owned by the defendant and sell it, giving the defendant a certain amount of the proceeds of the sale. The parties did not dispute the existence or terms of the agreement. The sole issue disputed was whether the agreement was a contract for service or a contract for timber. Under the applicable statute of frauds, a contract of the latter kind would have to be in writing to be enforceable. The question was presented to the jury as follows:

(1) Was the agreement of March 1, 1963, between Dobson and * * * Masonite one:

(a) Solely and alone for a service to be performed by Dobson to lands of Masonite by his salvage cuttings on its lands? Answer: (Yes or No)

OR

(b) In whole or in part for the sale by Masonite to Dobson of felled or standing timber on its lands?

Id. at 923 n.2.

The jury decided the issue in favor of the plaintiff (by finding that the contract was one for services), but the trial judge disagreed and entered a judgment for the defendant (by finding as a matter of law that the contract was for the sale of timber). Was it appropriate for the trial court to substitute its view of the matter for that of the jury? The appeals court said no:

> [The case] calls for an interpretation of the agreement between the parties to determine what they meant by the terms of that agreement. Interpretation is always a question of fact. As a question of fact, this issue was properly presented to, and determined by, the jury; and unless there was no evidence which, if believed, would authorize the jury's conclusions, they must stand. * * *

> The district court, apparently because there was no dispute regarding the existence of the oral contract or its terms, felt that only a legal question, what was the legal effect of the contract, was involved. But "legal effect" is the result of applying rules of law to the facts; necessarily this determination must await a determination of all the facts. And, as we have stated, deciding what is the meaning of the contract is a question of fact.

<u>*Id.* at 923–24</u> (citations omitted). How does *Dobson* fit with *Markman*? Are the two cases consistent with one another?

———

4. Selecting the Jury

After a jury is demanded—which, under Rule 38(b)(2), must be done within 14 days of service of the last pleading directed to the issue—and it is determined that a jury trial is appropriate, a jury must be selected. Initially, the court will send out a notice to randomly selected voters from the local community who must appear to be considered for jury service. *See* 28 U.S.C. §§ 1863, 1864. From this group of prospective jurors (called a *venire panel*), the parties and the court must select a subset to serve on the jury. Under the Federal Rules, a federal civil jury must be composed of at least six jurors and cannot have more than twelve. FED. R. CIV. P. 48.

Practice Pointer

If the 14-day deadline is missed, a litigant may file a motion for a jury trial under Rule 39(b), although circuits vary in the approach their constituent district courts may take to granting such motions. *Compare, e.g.*, *Andrews v. Columbia Gas Transmission Corp.*, 544 F.3d 618, 632 (6th Cir. 2008) ("A district court has broad discretion in deciding whether to grant a Rule 39(b) motion."), *with BCCI Holdings (Lux.), S.A. v. Khalil*, 214 F.3d 168, 172–73 (D.C. Cir. 2000) (noting that a district court is "not required to grant a Rule 39(b) request based on nothing but inadvertence" and examining the reason for the late demand and the prejudice to the other party).

The final jurors are selected from among the venire panel through a process referred to as *voir dire*, in which the court disqualifies the jurors on certain statutory grounds, *see* 28 U.S.C. § 1865, and then the court and the parties dismiss

FYI

Examples of cause to eliminate prospective jurors are evidence of bias or partiality, such as through having a close relationship with one of the parties or based on having deeply held beliefs that would prevent them from serving impartially.

various prospective jurors for cause, or the litigants can eliminate up to three prospective jurors without cause through peremptory challenges. 28 U.S.C. § 1870. The next case discusses constitutional limitations on the use of peremptory challenges to remove prospective members of a jury.

Edmonson v. Leesville Concrete Co.

Supreme Court of the United States
500 U.S. 614 (1991)

JUSTICE KENNEDY delivered the opinion of the Court.

We must decide in the case before us whether a private litigant in a civil case may use peremptory challenges to exclude jurors on account of their race. Recognizing the impropriety of racial bias in the courtroom, we hold the race-based exclusion violates the equal protection rights of the challenged jurors. This civil case originated in a United States District Court, and we apply the equal protection component of the Fifth Amendment's Due Process Clause. *See Bolling v. Sharpe, 347 U.S. 497 (1954)*.

Food for Thought

Take a look at the Fifth Amendment's Due Process Clause. Does it say anything that refers to an "equal protection component"? What, then, does the Court mean when it refers to the Fifth Amendment's "equal protection component"?

I

Thaddeus Donald Edmonson, a construction worker, was injured in a jobsite accident at Fort Polk, Louisiana, a federal enclave. Edmonson sued Leesville Concrete Company for negligence in the United States District Court for the Western District of Louisiana, claiming that a Leesville employee permitted one of the company's trucks to roll backward and pin him against some construction equipment. Edmonson invoked his Seventh Amendment right to a trial by jury.

During voir dire, Leesville used two of its three peremptory challenges authorized by statute to remove black persons from the prospective jury. Citing our decision in *Batson v. Kentucky, 476 U.S. 79 (1986)*, Edmonson, who is himself black, requested that the District Court require Leesville to articulate a race-neutral explanation for striking the two jurors. The District Court denied the request on the ground that *Batson* does not apply in civil proceedings. As empaneled, the jury included 11 white persons and 1 black person. The jury rendered a verdict for Edmonson, assessing his total damages at $90,000. It also attributed 80% of the fault to Edmonson's contributory negligence, however, and awarded him the sum of $18,000.

FYI

Bolling v. Sharpe, cited above in the text, is a companion case to *Brown v. Board of Education, 347 U.S. 483 (1954)*. *Bolling* invalidated racial discrimination in public schools in the District of Columbia as a violation of the Fifth Amendment's Due Process Clause. Recourse to the Fourteenth Amendment, the basis for the ruling in *Brown*, was unavailable because that amendment applies only to the states.

Edmonson appealed, and a divided panel of the <u>Court of Appeals for the Fifth Circuit</u> reversed, holding that our opinion in *Batson* applies to a private attorney representing a private litigant and that peremptory challenges may not be used in a civil trial for the purpose of excluding jurors on the basis of race. * * *

The full court then ordered rehearing *en banc*. A divided *en banc* panel affirmed the judgment of the District Court, holding that a private litigant in a civil case can exercise peremptory challenges without accountability for alleged racial classifications. <u>895 F.2d 218 (1990)</u>. * * * We granted certiorari, and now reverse the Court of Appeals.

II

A

In <u>*Powers v. Ohio*, 499 U.S. 400 (1991)</u>, we held that a criminal defendant, regardless of his or her race, may object to a prosecutor's race-based exclusion of persons from the petit jury. Our conclusion rested on a two-part analysis. First, following our opinions in *Batson* and in <u>*Carter v. Jury Commission of Greene County*, 396 U.S. 320 (1970)</u>, we made clear that a prosecutor's race-based peremptory challenge violates the equal protection rights of those excluded from jury service. Second, we relied on well-established rules of third-party standing to hold that a defendant may raise the excluded jurors' equal protection rights.

What's That?

A *petit jury* is simply the formal term for the jury of six to twelve persons that hears a case in a trial.

Powers relied upon over a century of jurisprudence dedicated to the elimination of race prejudice within the jury selection process. While these decisions were for the most part directed at discrimination by a prosecutor or other government officials in the context of criminal proceedings, we have not intimated that race discrimination is permissible in civil proceedings. Indeed, discrimination on the basis of race in selecting a jury in a civil proceeding harms the excluded juror no less than discrimination in a criminal trial. In either case, race is the sole reason for denying the excluded venireperson the honor and privilege of participating in our system of justice.

That an act violates the Constitution when committed by a government official, however, does not answer the question whether the same act offends constitutional guarantees if committed by a private litigant or his attorney. The Constitution's protections of individual liberty and equal protection apply in general only to action by the government. Racial discrimination, though invidious in all contexts, violates the Constitution only when it may be attributed to state action. Thus, the legality of the exclusion at issue here turns on the extent to which a litigant in a civil case may be subject to the Constitution's restrictions.

The Constitution structures the National Government, confines its actions, and, in regard to certain individual liberties and other specified matters, confines the actions of the States. With a few exceptions, such as the provisions of the Thirteenth Amendment, constitutional guarantees of individual liberty and equal protection do not apply to the actions of private entities. * * *

To implement these principles, courts must consider from time to time where the governmental sphere ends and the private sphere begins. Although the conduct of private parties lies beyond the Constitution's scope in most instances, governmental authority may dominate an activity to such an extent that its participants must be deemed to act with the authority of the government and, as a result, be subject to constitutional constraints. This is the jurisprudence of state action, which explores the "essential dichotomy" between the private sphere and the public sphere, with all its attendant constitutional obligations.

We begin our discussion within the framework for state-action analysis set forth in *Lugar v. Edmondson Oil Co.*, 457 U.S. 922, 937 (1982). There we considered the state-action question in the context of a due process challenge to a State's procedure allowing private parties to obtain prejudgment attachments. We asked first whether the claimed constitutional deprivation resulted from the exercise of a right or privilege having its source in state authority; and second, whether the private party charged with the deprivation could be described in all fairness as a state actor.

There can be no question that the first part of the *Lugar* inquiry is satisfied here. By their very nature, peremptory challenges have no significance outside a court of law. Their sole purpose is to permit litigants to assist the government in the selection of an impartial trier of fact. While we have recognized the value of peremptory challenges in this regard, particularly in the criminal context, there is no constitutional obligation to allow them. Peremptory challenges are permitted only when the government, by statute or decisional law, deems it appropriate to allow parties to exclude a given number of persons who otherwise would satisfy the requirements for service on the petit jury.

Legislative authorizations, as well as limitations, for the use of peremptory challenges date as far back as the founding of the Republic; and the common-law origins of peremptories predate that. Today in most jurisdictions, statutes or rules make a limited number of peremptory challenges available to parties in both civil and criminal proceedings. In the case before us, the challenges were exercised under * * * 28 U.S.C. § 1870. Without this authorization, granted by an Act of Congress itself, Leesville would not have been able to engage in the alleged discriminatory acts.

Given that the statutory authorization for the challenges exercised in this case is clear, the remainder of our state-action analysis centers around the second part of the *Lugar* test, whether a private litigant in all fairness must be deemed a government actor in the use of peremptory challenges. Although we have recognized that this aspect of the analysis is often a factbound inquiry, our cases disclose certain principles of general application. Our precedents establish that, in determining whether a particular action or course of conduct is governmental in character, it is relevant to examine the following: the extent to which the actor relies on governmental assistance and benefits, whether the actor is performing a traditional governmental function, and whether the injury caused is aggravated in a unique way by the incidents of governmental authority. Based on our application of these three principles to the circumstances here, we hold that the exercise of peremptory challenges by the defendant in the District Court was pursuant to a course of state action.

Although private use of state-sanctioned private remedies or procedures does not rise, by itself, to the level of state action, our cases have found state action when private parties make extensive use of state procedures with "the overt, significant assistance of state officials." It cannot be disputed that, without the overt, significant participation of the government, the peremptory challenge system, as well as the jury trial system of which it is a part, simply could not exist. As discussed above, peremptory challenges have no utility outside the jury system, a system which the government alone administers. In the federal system, Congress has established the qualifications for jury service, see 28 U.S.C. § 1865, and has outlined the procedures by which jurors are selected. To this end, each district court in the federal system must adopt a plan for locating and summoning to the court eligible prospective jurors. 28 U.S.C. § 1863. This plan, as with all other trial court procedures, must implement statutory policies of random juror selection from a fair cross section of the community, 28 U.S.C. § 1861, and non-exclusion on account of race, color, religion, sex, national origin, or economic status, 18 U.S.C. § 243; 28 U.S.C. § 1862. Statutes prescribe many of the details of the jury plan, 28 U.S.C. § 1863, defining the jury wheel, § 1863(b)(4), voter lists, §§ 1863(b)(2), 1869(c), and jury commissions, § 1863(b)(1). A statute also authorizes the establishment of procedures for assignment to grand and petit juries, § 1863(b)(8), and for lawful excuse from jury service, §§ 1863(b)(5), (6).

At the outset of the selection process, prospective jurors must complete jury qualification forms as prescribed by the Administrative Office of the United States Courts. See 28 U.S.C. § 1864. Failure to do so may result in fines and imprisonment, as might a willful misrepresentation of a material fact in answering a question on the form. In a typical case, counsel receive these forms and rely on them when exercising their peremptory strikes. The clerk of the United States district court, a federal official, summons potential jurors from their employment or other pursuits. They are required to travel to a United States courthouse, where they must report to juror lounges, assembly rooms, and courtrooms at the direction of the court and its officers. Whether or not they are selected for a jury panel, summoned jurors receive a per diem fixed by statute for their service. 28 U.S.C. § 1871.

The trial judge exercises substantial control over *voir dire* in the federal system. See FED. RULE CIV. PROC. 47. The judge determines the range of information that may be discovered about a prospective juror, and so affects the exercise of both challenges for cause and peremptory challenges. In some cases, judges may even conduct the entire *voir dire* by themselves, a common practice in the District Court where the instant case was tried. The judge oversees the exclusion of jurors for cause, in this way determining which jurors remain eligible for the exercise of peremptory strikes. In cases involving multiple parties, the trial judge decides how peremptory challenges shall be allocated among them. 28 U.S.C. § 1870. When a lawyer exercises a peremptory challenge, the judge advises the juror he or she has been excused.

As we have outlined here, a private party could not exercise its peremptory challenges absent the overt, significant assistance of the court. The government summons jurors, constrains their freedom of movement, and subjects them to public scrutiny and examination. The party who exercises a challenge invokes the formal authority of the court, which must discharge the prospective juror, thus effecting the "final and practical denial" of the excluded individual's opportunity to serve on the petit jury. Without the direct and indispensable participation of the judge, who beyond all question is a state actor, the peremptory challenge system would serve no purpose. By enforcing a discriminatory peremptory challenge, the court "has not only made itself a party to the [biased act], but has elected to place its power, property and prestige behind the [alleged] discrimination." * * *

In determining Leesville's state-actor status, we next consider whether the action in question involves the performance of a traditional function of the government. A traditional function of government is evident here. The peremptory challenge is used in selecting an entity that is a quintessential governmental body, having no attributes of a private actor. The jury exercises the power of the court and of the government that confers the court's jurisdiction. As we noted in *Powers*, the jury system performs the critical governmental functions of guarding the rights of litigants and "ensur[ing] continued acceptance of the laws by all of the people." In the federal system, the Constitution itself commits the trial of facts in a civil cause to the jury. Should either party to a cause invoke its Seventh Amendment right, the jury becomes the principal factfinder, charged with weighing the evidence, judging the credibility of witnesses, and reaching a verdict. The jury's factual determinations as a general rule are final. * * * These are traditional functions of government, not of a select, private group beyond the reach of the Constitution. * * *

Finally, we note that the injury caused by the discrimination is made more severe because the government permits it to occur within the courthouse itself. Few places are a more real expression of the constitutional authority of the government than a courtroom, where the law itself unfolds. Within the courtroom, the government invokes its laws to determine the rights of those who stand before it. In full view of the public, litigants press their cases, witnesses give testimony, juries render verdicts, and judges act with the utmost care to ensure that justice is done.

Race discrimination within the courtroom raises serious questions as to the fairness of the proceedings conducted there. Racial bias mars the integrity of the judicial system and prevents the idea of democratic government from becoming a reality. In the many times we have addressed the problem of racial bias in our system of justice, we have not "questioned the premise that racial discrimination in the qualification or selection of jurors offends the dignity of persons and the integrity of the courts." To permit racial exclusion in this official forum compounds the racial insult inherent in judging a citizen by the color of his or her skin.

B

Having held that in a civil trial exclusion on account of race violates a prospective juror's equal protection rights, we consider whether an opposing litigant may raise the excluded person's rights on his or her behalf. As we noted in *Powers*: "In the ordinary course, a litigant must assert his or her own legal rights and interests, and cannot rest a claim to relief on the legal rights or interests of third parties." We also noted, however, that this fundamental restriction on judicial authority admits of "certain, limited exceptions," and that a litigant may raise a claim on behalf of a third party if the litigant can demonstrate that he or she has suffered a concrete, redressable injury, that he or she has a close relation with the third party, and that there exists some hindrance to the third party's ability to protect his or her own interests. All three of these requirements for third-party standing were held satisfied in the criminal context, and they are satisfied in the civil context as well. * * *

* * * Civil juries, no less than their criminal counterparts, must follow the law and act as impartial factfinders. And, as we have observed, their verdicts, no less than those of their criminal counterparts, become binding judgments of the court. Racial discrimination has no place in the courtroom, whether the proceeding is civil or criminal. Congress has so mandated by prohibiting various discriminatory acts in the context of both civil and criminal trials. The Constitution demands nothing less. We conclude that courts must entertain a challenge to a private litigant's racially discriminatory use of peremptory challenges in a civil trial.

It may be true that the role of litigants in determining the jury's composition provides one reason for wide acceptance of the jury system and of its verdicts. But if race stereotypes are the price for acceptance of a jury panel as fair, the price is too high to meet the standard of the Constitution. Other means exist for litigants to satisfy themselves of a jury's impartiality without using skin color as a test. If our society is to continue to progress as a multiracial democracy, it must recognize that the automatic invocation of race stereotypes retards that progress and causes continued hurt and injury. By the dispassionate analysis which is its special distinction, the law dispels fears and preconceptions respecting racial attitudes. The quiet rationality of the courtroom makes it an appropriate place to confront race-based fears or hostility by means other than the use of offensive stereotypes. Whether the race generality employed by litigants to challenge a potential juror derives from open hostility or from some hidden and unarticulated fear, neither motive entitles the litigant to cause injury to the excused juror. And if a litigant believes that the prospective juror harbors the same biases or instincts, the issue can be explored in a rational way that consists with respect for the dignity of persons, without the use of classifications based on ancestry or skin color.

III

It remains to consider whether a prima facie case of racial discrimination has been established in the case before us, requiring Leesville to offer race-neutral explanations for its peremptory challenges. In *Batson*, we held that determining whether a prima facie case has been established requires consideration of all relevant circumstances, including whether there has been a pattern of strikes against members of a particular race. The same approach applies in the civil context, and we leave it to the trial courts in the first instance to develop evidentiary rules for implementing our decision.

The judgment is reversed, and the case is remanded for further proceedings consistent with our opinion.

It is so ordered.

JUSTICE O'CONNOR, with whom THE CHIEF JUSTICE and JUSTICE SCALIA join, dissenting.

The Court concludes that the action of a private attorney exercising a peremptory challenge is attributable to the government and therefore may compose a constitutional violation. This conclusion is based on little more than that the challenge occurs in the course of a trial. Not everything that happens in a courtroom is state action. A trial, particularly a civil trial is by design largely a stage on which private parties may act; it is a forum through which they can resolve their disputes in a peaceful and ordered manner. The government erects the platform; it does not thereby become responsible for all that occurs upon it. As much as we would like to eliminate completely from the courtroom the specter of racial discrimination, the Constitution does not sweep that broadly. Because I believe that a peremptory strike by a private litigant is fundamentally a matter of private choice and not state action, I dissent. * * *

The peremptory challenge "allow[s] parties," in this case private parties, to exclude potential jurors. It is the nature of a peremptory that its exercise is left wholly within the discretion of the litigant. The purpose of this longstanding practice is to establish for each party an "arbitrary and capricious species of challenge" whereby the "sudden impressions and unaccountable prejudices we are apt to conceive upon the bare looks and gestures of another" may be acted upon. By allowing the litigant to strike jurors for even the most subtle of discerned biases, the peremptory challenge fosters both the perception and reality of an impartial jury. In both criminal and civil trials, the peremptory challenge is a mechanism for the exercise of private choice in the pursuit of fairness. The peremptory is, by design, an enclave of private action in a government-managed proceeding. * * * The entirety of the government's actual participation in the peremptory process boils down to a single fact: "When a lawyer exercises a peremptory challenge, the judge advises the juror he or she has been excused." This is not significant participation. The judge's action in "advising" a juror that he or she has been excused is state action to be sure. It is, however, if not de minimis, far from what our cases have required in order to hold the government "responsible" for private action or to find that private actors "represent" the government. The government "normally can be held responsible for a private decision only when it has exercised coercive power or has provided such significant encouragement, either overt or covert, that the choice must in law be deemed to be that of the State." * * *

Racism is a terrible thing. It is irrational, destructive, and mean. Arbitrary discrimination based on race is particularly abhorrent when manifest in a courtroom, a forum established by the government for the resolution of disputes through "quiet rationality." But not every opprobrious and inequitable act is a constitutional violation. The Fifth Amendment's Due Process Clause prohibits only actions for which the Government can be held responsible. The Government is not responsible for everything that occurs in a courtroom. The Government is not responsible for a peremptory challenge by a private litigant. I respectfully dissent.

[The dissenting opinion of JUSTICE SCALIA is omitted.]

Points for Discussion

a. State Action in *Edmonson*

In order for there to be an equal protection violation, the allegedly violating conduct must be the product of governmental or "state" action. In *Edmonson*, the majority found the exercise of peremptory challenges by litigants to be state action, while the dissenting Justices felt that the government bears no responsibility for how a litigant uses a peremptory challenge. What support for these views does each opinion offer and which has the better of the two arguments?

b. Peremptory Challenges

As noted earlier, a peremptory challenge is supposed to enable a litigant to remove prospective jurors for any reason at all. Why should litigants have such an opportunity to exclude qualified jurors in this way? Does it enable the litigants to ensure that the case is tried by an impartial jury? Are there any arguments against permitting the use of peremptory challenges at all? *See, e.g.*, Vivien Toomey Montz & Craig Lee Montz, *The Peremptory Challenge: Should It Still Exist? An Examination of Federal and Florida Law*, 54 U. Miami L. Rev. 451, 491–94 (2000) (exploring whether peremptory challenges should be abolished).

Keep in mind that the availability of peremptory challenges is a longstanding tradition, but not a constitutional right. *See Georgia v. McCollum*, 505 U.S. 42, 57 (1992) ("[I]t is important to recall that peremptory challenges are not constitutionally protected fundamental rights; rather, they are but one state-created means to the constitutional end of an impartial jury and a fair trial."). However, federal litigants do have a *statutory* entitlement to three peremptory challenges. 28 U.S.C. § 1870.

c. Enforcing *Edmonson*

Although peremptory challenges need not be explained, if the adversary party suspects that a challenge has been exercised for discriminatory reasons, that party can require the party making the peremptory challenge to offer a non-discriminatory basis for exercising the challenge. *See Johnson v. California*, 545 U.S. 162, 168 (2005). The judge then will determine whether the proffered non-discriminatory reason is authentic or simply a pretext to cover up intended discrimination. *Batson v. Kentucky*, 476 U.S. 79, 96–97 (1986). How should the court go about determining whether the offered justification is pretextual? *See Miller-El v. Dretke*, 545 U.S. 231, 239–40 (2005).

d. Gender Discrimination in Jury Selection

Edmonson prohibited the use of race as a basis for exercising a peremptory challenge. Does the reasoning of *Edmonson* apply with equal force to the use of such challenges to exclude prospective jurors based on their gender? *See J.E.B. v. Alabama ex rel. T.B.*, 511 U.S. 127, 130–31 (1994) (holding that peremptory challenges based on gender are impermissible). What about other traits like religion? *See, e.g., Card v. United States*, 776 A.2d 581, 593 (D.C. 2001) (upholding the use of a peremptory challenge to remove a juror because he appeared to be Muslim), *vacated*, 863 A.2d 821 (D.C. 2004).

5. The Phases of a Trial

After the jury has been selected, the trial may commence. The trial begins with the opening statements of each party, which is their opportunity to introduce the jury to what the case is all about and to present a general overview of the big picture before getting into the detailed evidence during the main part of the case. No evidence is presented during these statements.

Next, plaintiff presents its case-in-chief, calling and examining witnesses and introducing evidence as it sees fit. The defendant's counsel has the opportunity to cross-examine the plaintiff's witnesses, after which time the plaintiff may re-examine the witness to address issues raised during the cross-examination. The opposing counsel also has the opportunity to raise any objections it has to the introduction of evidence or to any improper questions. Once the plaintiff finishes presenting all of its evidence, the plaintiff rests its case.

Make the Connection

Learning about the various grounds for objecting to evidence, testimony, or questioning is largely beyond the scope of a basic first-year Civil Procedure course. You will learn more about making evidentiary objections in an **Evidence** course.

After the plaintiff rests, the defendant may seek the entry of judgment as a matter of law in its favor if it feels that the plaintiff has failed to present sufficient evidence to carry its burden of proof. FED. R. CIV. P. 50(a)(1). The standards for evaluating such a motion are reviewed in Section B below. If that motion is rejected or not made, the defendant proceeds with the presentation of its evidence in an effort to rebut the plaintiff's case. Like the plaintiff, the defendant may call witnesses and examine them, with the plaintiff having the opportunity for cross-examination. When the defendant has presented all of its evidence, it rests its case. Both parties at this point may raise motions for judgment as a matter of law. The plaintiff will also have the opportunity for a rebuttal, to call witnesses and introduce evidence pertaining to new matters raised in the defendant's case-in-chief.

After all parties have rested their cases, the parties present their closing arguments in which they summarize the evidence for the jury and argue why the jury should reach a particular result. Of course, no new evidence may be presented at this stage, and counsel are limited to commenting on the evidence that has been admitted, urging the jury to reach a result on the basis of a particular view of that evidence. The judge then instructs the jury on the law to be applied once they resolve any factual disputes (see Section B.2 below) and the case is submitted to the jury. The jury then deliberates in private and renders its verdict if it reaches one. After the verdict is announced in open court, the trial is complete and the jury is discharged.

FYI

When the trial proceeds without a jury, that is referred to as *a bench trial*. The phases of the trial are generally the same as for a jury trial, although the judge may dispense with opening and closing arguments. Of course, with a bench trial no jury instructions are necessary. In an action tried without a jury, "the court must find the facts specially and state its conclusions of law separately." FED. R. CIV. P. 52(a). These factual findings may only be set aside if they are clearly erroneous. FED. R. CIV. P. 52(a)(6). *See also Teva Pharm. USA, Inc. v. Sandoz, Inc.*, 135 S. Ct. 831, 836–37 (2015) (indicating that Rule 52(a)(6) "sets forth a clear command" and "applies to both subsidiary and ultimate facts").

B. Judicial Control of the Verdict

As mentioned above, if the evidence is insufficient to support a verdict in favor of one party, the opposing party may move the court to enter judgment as a matter of law, something that either preempts or reverses a jury's verdict. If the case is to be submitted to the jury, the judge has some ability to control the jury's decision through the instructions to the jury and through special verdicts or general verdicts with interrogatories. Finally, the judge also exercises control over the verdict through her ability to throw out the jury's verdict and order a new trial or grant relief from judgment under Rule 60. Each of these devices will be reviewed in turn.

1. Judgment as a Matter of Law

At various points in the trial the Federal Rules permit either party to seek judgment as a matter of law ("JMOL") if they believe that their adversary has failed to present evidence sufficient to meet its evidentiary burden of proof. If the court agrees with the movant, judgment in their favor is entered and, depending

FYI

Rule 50 was amended in 1991 to change the term *directed verdict* to judgment as a matter of law. Thus, you may come across the former term when reading pre-1991 federal cases. Many states continue to refer to their similar device as a directed verdict.

upon the timing of the motion, the jury never gets the opportunity to render a verdict or its previously rendered verdict is disregarded. Rule 50(a) governs the making and granting of such motions:

FRCP 50(a). Judgment as a Matter of Law in a Jury Trial.

(a) Judgment as a Matter of Law.

(1) *In General*. If a party has been fully heard on an issue during a jury trial and the court finds that a reasonable jury would not have a legally sufficient evidentiary basis to find for the party on that issue, the court may:

(A)   resolve the issue against the party; and

(B)   grant a motion for judgment as a matter of law against the party on a claim or defense that, under the controlling law, can be maintained or defeated only with a favorable finding on that issue.

(2) *Motion*. A motion for judgment as a matter of law may be made at any time before the case is submitted to the jury. The motion must specify the judgment sought and the law and facts that entitle the movant to the judgment.

What does it mean for there to have been an absence of "a legally sufficient evidentiary basis" such that the jury's verdict can be preempted or reversed? The basic meaning is that the jury's conclusion is not supported by the evidence presented in the case. For example, if the jury rules in favor of a plaintiff in a contract dispute after the plaintiff failed to present any evidence of the defendant's breach, the verdict would be insupportable. The plaintiff will have failed to carry its burden of production.

What's That?

The *burden of production* is the duty of a party to produce admissible evidence that the judge or jury could use as a basis for reaching a conclusion of material fact on a claim or affirmative defense it has asserted. Failures in this regard can make a party vulnerable to judgment as a matter of law.

When a court makes this determination, it is not supposed to weigh the evidence or make credibility determinations—the same limitations courts face in the summary judgment context. The court is simply to determine whether evidence exists in support of the party against whom judgment as a matter of law has been sought.

The next two cases illustrate the Supreme Court's understanding and application of the standards for directed verdicts, now referred to as judgments as a matter of law.

Pennsylvania R. Co. v. Chamberlain

Supreme Court of the United States
288 U.S. 333 (1933)

MR. JUSTICE SUTHERLAND delivered the opinion of the Court.

This is an action brought by respondent against petitioner to recover for the death of a brakeman, alleged to have been caused by petitioner's negligence. The complaint alleges that the deceased, at the time of the accident resulting in his death, was assisting in the yard work of breaking up and making up trains and in the classifying and assorting of cars operating in interstate commerce; that in pursuance of such work, while riding a cut of cars, other cars ridden by fellow employees were negligently caused to be brought into violent contact with those upon which deceased was riding, with the result that he was thrown therefrom to the railroad track and run over by a car or cars, inflicting injuries from which he died.

At the conclusion of the evidence, the trial court directed the jury to find a verdict in favor of petitioner. Judgment upon a verdict so found was reversed by the Court of Appeals, Judge Swan dissenting.

That part of the yard in which the accident occurred contained a lead track and a large number of switching tracks branching therefrom. The lead track crossed a 'hump,' and the work of car distribution consisted of pushing a train of cars by means of a locomotive to the top of the 'hump,' and then allowing the cars, in separate strings, to descend by gravity, under the control of hand brakes, to their respective destinations in the various branch tracks. Deceased had charge of a string of two gondola cars, which he was piloting to track 14. Immediately ahead of him was a string of seven cars, and behind him a string of nine cars, both also destined for track 14. Soon after the cars ridden by deceased had passed to track 14, his body was found on that track some distance beyond the switch. He had evidently fallen onto the track and been run over by a car or cars.

The case for respondent rests wholly upon the claim that the fall of deceased was caused by a violent collision of the string of nine cars with the string ridden by deceased. Three employees, riding the nine-car string, testified positively that no such collision occurred. They were corroborated by every other employee in a position to see, all testifying that there was no contact between the nine-car string and that of the deceased. The testimony of these witnesses, if believed, establishes beyond doubt that there was no collision between these two strings of cars, and that the nine-car string contributed in no way to the accident. The only witness who testified for the respondent was one Bainbridge; and it is upon his testimony alone that respondent's right to recover is sought to be upheld. His testimony is concisely stated, in its most favorable light for respondent, in the prevailing opinion below by Judge Learned Hand, as follows:

The plaintiff's only witness to the event, one Bainbridge, then employed by the road, stood close to the yardmaster's office, near the 'hump.' He professed to have paid little attention to what went on, but he did see the deceased riding at the rear of his cars, whose speed when they passed him he took to be about eight or ten miles. Shortly thereafter a second string passed which was shunted into another track and this was followed by the nine, which, according to the plaintiff's theory, collided with the deceased's. After the nine cars had passed at a somewhat greater speed than the deceased's, Bainbridge paid no more attention to either string for a while, but looked again when the deceased, who was still standing in his place, had passed the switch and onto the assorting track where he was bound. At that time his speed had been checked to about three miles, but the speed of the following nine cars had increased. They were just passing the switch, about four or five cars behind the deceased. Bainbridge looked away again and soon heard what he described as a 'loud crash,' not however an unusual event in a switching yard. Apparently this did not cause him at once to turn, but he did so shortly thereafter, and saw the two strings together, still moving, and the deceased no longer in sight. Later still his attention was attracted by shouts and he went to the spot and saw the deceased between the rails. Until he left to go to the accident, he had stood fifty feet to the north of the track where the accident happened, and about nine hundred feet from where the body was found.

The court, although regarding Bainbridge's testimony as not only 'somewhat suspicious in itself, but its contradiction . . . so manifold as to leave little doubt,' held, nevertheless, that the question was one of fact depending upon the credibility of the witnesses, and that it was for the jury to determine, as between the one witness and the many, where the truth lay. The dissenting opinion of Judge Swan proceeds upon the theory that Bainbridge did not testify that in fact a collision had taken place, but inferred it because he heard a crash, and because thereafter the two strings of cars appeared to him to be moving together. It is correctly pointed out in that opinion, however, that the crash might have come from elsewhere in the busy yard and that Bainbridge was in no position to see whether the two strings of cars were actually together; that Bainbridge repeatedly said he was paying no particular attention; and that his position was such, being 900 feet from the place where the body was found and less than 50 feet from the side of the track in question, that he necessarily saw the strings of cars at such an acute angle that it would be physically impossible even for an attentive observer to tell whether the forward end of the nine-car cut was actually in contact with the rear end of the two-car cut. The dissenting opinion further points out that all the witnesses who were in a position to see testified that there was no collision; that respondent's evidence was wholly circumstantial, and the inferences which might otherwise be drawn from it were shown to be utterly erroneous unless all of petitioner's witnesses were willful perjurers. 'This is not a case,' the opinion proceeds, 'where direct testimony to an essential fact is contradicted by direct testimony of other witnesses, though even there it is conceded a directed verdict might be proper in some circumstances. Here, when all the testimony was in, the circumstantial evidence in support of negligence was thought by the trial judge to be so insubstantial and insufficient that it did not justify submission to the jury.'

We thus summarize and quote from the prevailing and dissenting opinions, because they present the divergent views to be considered in reaching a correct determination of the question involved. It, of course, is true, generally, that where there is a direct conflict of testimony upon a matter of fact, the question must be left to the jury to determine, without regard to the number of witnesses upon either side. But here there really is no conflict in the testimony as to the facts. The witnesses for petitioner flatly testified that there was no collision between the nine-car and the two-car strings. Bainbridge did not say there was such a collision. What he said was that he heard a 'loud crash,' which did not cause him at once to turn, but that shortly thereafter he did turn and saw the two strings of cars moving together with the deceased no longer in sight; that there was nothing unusual about the crash of cars—it happened every day; that there was nothing about this crash to attract his attention except that it was extra loud; that he paid no attention to it; that it was not sufficient to attract his attention. The record shows that there was a continuous movement of cars over and down the 'hump,' which were distributed among a large number of branch tracks within the yard, and that any two strings of these cars moving upon the same track might have come together and caused the crash which Bainbridge heard. There is no direct evidence that in fact the crash was occasioned by a collision of the two strings in question; and it is perfectly clear that no such fact was brought to Bainbridge's attention as a perception of the physical sense of sight or of hearing. At most there was an inference to that effect drawn from observed facts which gave equal support to the opposite inference that the crash was occasioned by the coming together of other strings of cars entirely away from the scene of the accident, or of the two-car string ridden by deceased and the seven-car string immediately ahead of it.

We, therefore, have a case belonging to that class of cases where proven facts give equal support to each of two inconsistent inferences; in which event, neither of them being established, judgment, as a matter of law, must go against the party upon whom rests the necessity of sustaining one of these inferences as against the other, before he is entitled to recover.

The rule is succinctly stated in *Smith v. First National Bank in Westfield*, 99 Mass. 605, 611–612, 97 Am.Dec. 59, quoted in [*United States F. & G. Co. v. Des Moines Nat. Bank*, 145 F. 273, 279, 280 (8th Cir. 1906)]:

There being several inferences deducible from the facts which appear, and equally consistent with all those facts, the plaintiff has not maintained the proposition upon which alone he would be entitled to recover. There is strictly no evidence to warrant a jury in finding that the loss was occasioned by negligence and not by theft. When the evidence tends equally to sustain either of two inconsistent propositions, neither of them can be said to have been established by legitimate proof. A verdict in favor of the party bound to maintain one of those propositions against the other is necessarily wrong.

That Bainbridge concluded from what he himself observed that the crash was due to a collision between the two strings of cars in question is sufficiently indicated by his statements. But this, of course, proves nothing, since it is not allowable for a witness to resolve the doubt as to which of two equally justifiable inferences shall be adopted by drawing a conclusion, which, if accepted, will result in a purely gratuitous award in favor of the party who has failed to sustain the burden of proof cast upon him by the law.

And the desired inference is precluded for the further reason that respondent's right of recovery depends upon the existence of a particular fact which must be inferred from proven facts, and this is not permissible in the face of the positive and otherwise uncontradicted testimony of unimpeached witnesses consistent with the facts actually proved, from which testimony it affirmatively appears that the fact sought to be inferred did not exist. * * * A rebuttable inference of fact, as said by the court in [*Wabash R. Co. v. De Tar*, 141 F. 932, 935 (8th Cir. 1905)], 'must necessarily yield to credible evidence of the actual occurrence.' And, as stated by the court in [*George v. Mo. Pac. R.R. Co.*, 251 S.W. 729, 732 (Mo. App. 1923)], 'It is well settled that, where plaintiff's case is based upon an inference or inferences, the case must fail upon proof of undisputed facts inconsistent with such inferences.' In *Southern Ry. Co. v. Walters*, [284 U.S. 190 (1931)], the negligence charged was failure to stop a train and flag a crossing before proceeding over it. The court concluded that the only support for the charge was an inference sought to be drawn from certain facts proved. In rejecting the inference, this court said:

It is argued that it may be inferred from the speed of the train when some of the witnesses observed it crossing other streets as well as Bond avenue, and from a guess of the engineer as to the time required to get up such speed after a full stop, that none could have been made at Bond avenue. But the argument amounts to mere speculation in view of the limited scope of the witnesses' observation, the down grade of the railway tracks at the point, and the time element involved. Five witnesses for defendant (employees) testified that a full stop was made and the crossing flagged, and that no one was hit by the rear of the tender, which was the front of the train.

An examination of the record requires the conclusion that the evidence on the issue whether the train was stopped before crossing Bond avenue was so insubstantial and insufficient that it did not justify a submission of that issue to the jury.

Not only is Bainbridge's testimony considered as a whole suspicious, insubstantial, and insufficient, but his statement that when he turned shortly after hearing the crash the two strings were moving together is simply incredible, if he meant thereby to be understood as saying that he saw the two in contact; and if he meant by the words 'moving together' simply that they were moving at the same time in the same direction but not in contact, the statement becomes immaterial. As we have already seen he was paying slight and only occasional attention to what was going on. The cars were eight or nine hundred feet from where he stood and moving almost directly away from him, his angle of vision being only 3° 33′ from a straight line. At that sharp angle and from that distance, near dusk of a misty evening (as the proof shows), the practical impossibility of the witness being able to see whether the front of the nine-car string was in contact with the back of the two-car string is apparent. And, certainly, in the light of these conditions, no verdict based upon a statement so unbelievable reasonably could be sustained as against the positive testimony to the contrary of unimpeached witnesses, all in a position to see, as this witness was not, the precise relation of the cars to one another. The fact that these witnesses were employees of the petitioner, under the circumstances here disclosed, does not impair this conclusion. *Chesapeake & Ohio Ry. v. Martin*, 283 U.S. 209, 216-220 (1931).

We think, therefore, that the trial court was right in withdrawing the case from the jury. It repeatedly has been held by this court that before evidence may be left to the jury, 'there is a preliminary question for the judge, not whether there is literally no evidence, but whether there is any upon which a jury can properly proceed to find a verdict for the party producing it, upon whom the onus of proof is imposed.' And where the evidence is 'so overwhelmingly on one side as to leave no room to doubt what the fact is, the court should give a peremptory instruction to the jury.' The rule is settled for the federal courts, and for many of the state courts, that whenever in the trial of a civil case the evidence is clearly such that if a verdict were rendered for one of the parties the other would be entitled to a new trial, it is the duty of the judge to direct the jury to find according to the views of the court. Such a practice, this court has said, not only saves time and expense, but 'gives scientific certainty to the law in its application to the facts and promotes the ends of justice.' The scintilla rule has been definitely and repeatedly rejected so far as the federal courts are concerned.

Leaving out of consideration, then, the inference relied upon, the case for respondent is left without any substantial support in the evidence, and a verdict in her favor would have rested upon mere speculation and conjecture. This, of course, is inadmissible.

The judgment of the Circuit Court of Appeals is reversed and that of the District Court is affirmed.

MR. JUSTICE STONE and MR. JUSTICE CARDOZO concur in the result.

Reeves v. Sanderson Plumbing Products, Inc.

Supreme Court of the United States
530 U.S. 133 (2000)

JUSTICE O'CONNOR delivered the opinion of the Court.

This case concerns the kind and amount of evidence necessary to sustain a jury's verdict that an employer unlawfully discriminated on the basis of age. Specifically, we must resolve whether a defendant is entitled to judgment as a matter of law when the plaintiff's case consists exclusively of a prima facie case of discrimination and sufficient evidence for the trier of fact to disbelieve the defendant's legitimate, nondiscriminatory explanation for its action. We must also decide whether the employer was entitled to judgment as a matter of law under the particular circumstances presented here.

I

In October 1995, petitioner Roger Reeves was 57 years old and had spent 40 years in the employ of respondent, Sanderson Plumbing Products, Inc., a manufacturer of toilet seats and covers. Petitioner worked in a department known as the "Hinge Room," where he supervised the "regular line." Joe Oswalt, in his mid-thirties, supervised the Hinge Room's "special line," and Russell Caldwell, the manager of the Hinge Room and age 45, supervised both petitioner and Oswalt. Petitioner's responsibilities included recording the attendance and hours of those under his supervision, and reviewing a weekly report that listed the hours worked by each employee.

In the summer of 1995, Caldwell informed Powe Chesnut, the director of manufacturing and the husband of company president Sandra Sanderson, that "production was down" in the Hinge Room because employees were often absent and were "coming in late and leaving early." Because the monthly attendance reports did not indicate a problem, Chesnut ordered an audit of the Hinge Room's timesheets for July, August, and September of that year. According to Chesnut's testimony, that investigation revealed "numerous timekeeping errors and misrepresentations on the part of Caldwell, Reeves, and Oswalt." Following the audit, Chesnut, along with Dana Jester, vice president of human resources, and Tom Whitaker, vice president of operations, recommended to company president Sanderson that petitioner and Caldwell be fired. In October 1995, Sanderson followed the recommendation and discharged both petitioner and Caldwell.

In June 1996, petitioner filed suit in the United States District Court for the Northern District of Mississippi, contending that he had been fired because of his age in violation of the Age Discrimination in Employment Act of 1967 (ADEA), 81 Stat. 602, as amended, 29 U.S.C. § 621 *et seq.* At trial, respondent contended that it had fired petitioner due to his failure to maintain accurate attendance records, while petitioner attempted to demonstrate that respondent's explanation was pretext for age discrimination. Petitioner introduced evidence that he had accurately recorded the attendance and hours of the employees under his supervision, and that Chesnut, whom Oswalt described as wielding "absolute power" within the company, had demonstrated age-based animus in his dealings with petitioner.

> **Non constat**
> an aequus et bonus
> **jus civile**
> a posteriori
>
> ### It's Latin to Me!
>
> *Et seq.* is an abbreviation for *et sequentia*, which is a Latin phrase meaning "and the following ones." It is used after citations to refer the reader also to the related sections that follow the one cited without having to list each of them.

During the trial, the District Court twice denied oral motions by respondent for judgment as a matter of law under Rule 50 of the Federal Rules of Civil Procedure, and the case went to the jury. The court instructed the jury that "[i]f the plaintiff fails to prove age was a determinative or motivating factor in the decision to terminate him, then your verdict shall be for the defendant." So charged, the jury returned a verdict in favor of petitioner, awarding him $35,000 in compensatory damages, and found that respondent's age discrimination had been "willfu[l]." The District Court accordingly entered judgment for petitioner in the amount of $70,000, which included $35,000 in liquidated damages based on the jury's finding of willfulness. Respondent then renewed its motion for judgment as a matter of law and alternatively moved for a new trial, while petitioner moved for front pay. The District Court denied respondent's motions and granted petitioner's, awarding him $28,490.80 in front pay for two years' lost income.

The Court of Appeals for the Fifth Circuit reversed, holding that petitioner had not introduced sufficient evidence to sustain the jury's finding of unlawful discrimination. * * *

We granted certiorari to resolve a conflict among the Courts of Appeals as to whether a plaintiff's prima facie case of discrimination (as defined in *McDonnell*

Douglas Corp. v. Green, 411 U.S. 792, 802 [(1973)]), combined with sufficient evidence for a reasonable factfinder to reject the employer's nondiscriminatory explanation for its decision, is adequate to sustain a finding of liability for intentional discrimination.

II

Under the ADEA, it is "unlawful for an employer . . . to fail or refuse to hire or to discharge any individual or otherwise discriminate against any individual with respect to his compensation, terms, conditions, or privileges of employment, because of such individual's age." 29 U.S.C. § 623(a)(1). When a plaintiff alleges disparate treatment, "liability depends on whether the protected trait (under the ADEA, age) actually motivated the employer's decision." That is, the plaintiff's age must have "actually played a role in [the employer's decisionmaking] process and had a determinative influence on the outcome." Recognizing that "the question facing triers of fact in discrimination cases is both sensitive and difficult," and that "[t]here will seldom be 'eyewitness' testimony as to the employer's mental processes," the Courts of Appeals, including the Fifth Circuit in this case, have employed some variant of the framework articulated in *McDonnell Douglas* to analyze ADEA claims that are based principally on circumstantial evidence. * * *

McDonnell Douglas and subsequent decisions have "established an allocation of the burden of production and an order for the presentation of proof in . . . discriminatory-treatment cases." First, the plaintiff must establish a prima facie case of discrimination. It is undisputed that petitioner satisfied this burden here: (i) at the time he was fired, he was a member of the class protected by the ADEA ("individuals who are at least 40 years of age," 29 U.S.C. § 631(a)), (ii) he was otherwise qualified for the position of Hinge Room supervisor, (iii) he was discharged by respondent, and (iv) respondent successively hired three persons in their thirties to fill petitioner's position. The burden therefore shifted to respondent

Make the Connection

The elements of an ADEA claim and the burdens associated with establishing such claims and other employment discrimination claims will likely be covered in an **Employment Discrimination** course, or possibly in an **Employment Law** course.

to "produc[e] evidence that the plaintiff was rejected, or someone else was preferred, for a legitimate, nondiscriminatory reason." This burden is one of production, not persuasion; it "can involve no credibility assessment." Respondent met this burden by offering admissible evidence sufficient for the trier of fact to conclude that petitioner was fired because of his failure to maintain accurate attendance records. Accordingly, "the *McDonnell Douglas* framework—with its presumptions and burdens"—disappeared and the sole remaining issue was "discrimination *vel non.*"

Although intermediate evidentiary burdens shift back and forth under this framework, "[t]he ultimate burden of persuading the trier of fact that the defendant intentionally discriminated against the plaintiff remains at all times with the plaintiff." And in attempting to satisfy this burden, the plaintiff—once the employer produces sufficient evidence to support a nondiscriminatory explanation for its decision—must be afforded the "opportunity to prove by a preponderance of the evidence that the legitimate reasons offered by the defendant were not its true reasons, but were a pretext for discrimination." That is, the plaintiff may attempt to establish that he was the victim of intentional discrimination "by showing that the employer's proffered explanation is unworthy of credence." Moreover, although the presumption of discrimination "drops out of the picture" once the defendant meets its burden of production, the trier of fact may still consider the evidence establishing the plaintiff's prima facie case "and inferences properly drawn therefrom . . . on the issue of whether the defendant's explanation is pretextual."

In this case, the evidence supporting respondent's explanation for petitioner's discharge consisted primarily of testimony by Chesnut and Sanderson and documentation of petitioner's alleged "shoddy record keeping." Chesnut testified that a 1993 audit of Hinge Room operations revealed "a very lax assembly line" where employees were not adhering to general work rules. As a result of that audit, petitioner was placed on 90 days' probation for unsatisfactory performance. In 1995, Chesnut ordered another investigation of the Hinge Room, which, according to his testimony, revealed that petitioner was not correctly recording the absences and hours of employees. Respondent introduced summaries of that investigation documenting several attendance violations by 12 employees under petitioner's supervision, and noting that each should have been disciplined in some manner. Chesnut testified that this failure to discipline absent and late employees is "extremely important when you are dealing with a union" because uneven enforcement across departments would keep the company "in grievance and arbitration cases, which are costly, all the time." He and Sanderson also stated that petitioner's errors, by failing to adjust for hours not worked, cost the company overpaid wages. Sanderson testified that she accepted the recommendation to discharge petitioner because he had "intentionally falsif[ied] company pay records."

Petitioner, however, made a substantial showing that respondent's explanation was false. First, petitioner offered evidence that he had properly maintained the attendance records. Most of the timekeeping errors cited by respondent involved employees who were not marked late but who were recorded as having arrived at the plant at 7 a.m. for the 7 a.m. shift. Respondent contended that employees arriving at 7 a.m. could not have been at their workstations by 7 a.m., and therefore must have been late. But both petitioner and Oswalt testified that the company's automated timeclock often failed to scan employees' timecards, so that the timesheets would not record any time of arrival. On these occasions, petitioner and Oswalt would visually check the workstations and record whether the employees were present at the start of the shift. They stated that if an employee arrived promptly but the timesheet contained no time of arrival, they would reconcile the two by marking "7 a.m." as the employee's arrival time, even if the employee actually arrived at the plant earlier. On cross-examination, Chesnut acknowledged that the timeclock sometimes malfunctioned, and that if "people were there at their work station[s]" at the start of the shift, the supervisor "would write in seven o'clock." * * *

Petitioner similarly cast doubt on whether he was responsible for any failure to discipline late and absent employees. Petitioner testified that his job only included reviewing the daily and weekly attendance reports, and that disciplinary writeups were based on the monthly reports, which were reviewed by Caldwell. Sanderson admitted that Caldwell, and not petitioner, was responsible for citing employees for violations of the company's attendance policy. Further, Chesnut conceded that there had never been a union grievance or employee complaint arising from petitioner's recordkeeping, and that the company had never calculated the amount of overpayments allegedly attributable to petitioner's errors. Petitioner also testified that, on the day he was fired, Chesnut said that his discharge was due to his failure to report as absent one employee, Gina Mae Coley, on two days in September 1995. But petitioner explained that he had spent those days in the hospital, and that Caldwell was therefore responsible for any overpayment of Coley. Finally, petitioner stated that on previous occasions that employees were paid for hours they had not worked, the company had simply adjusted those employees' next paychecks to correct the errors.

Based on this evidence, the Court of Appeals concluded that petitioner "very well may be correct" that "a reasonable jury could have found that [respondent's] explanation for its employment decision was pretextual." Nonetheless, the court held that this showing, standing alone, was insufficient to sustain the jury's finding of liability: "We must, as an essential final step, determine whether Reeves presented sufficient evidence that his age motivated [respondent's] employment decision." And in making this determination, the Court of Appeals ignored the evidence supporting petitioner's prima facie case and challenging respondent's explanation for its decision. The court confined its review of evidence favoring petitioner to that evidence showing that Chesnut had directed derogatory, age-based comments at petitioner, and that Chesnut had singled out petitioner for harsher treatment than younger employees. It is therefore apparent that the court believed that only this additional evidence of discrimination was relevant to whether the jury's verdict should stand. That is, the Court of Appeals proceeded from the assumption that a prima facie case of discrimination, combined with sufficient evidence for the trier of fact to disbelieve the defendant's legitimate, nondiscriminatory reason for its decision, is insufficient as a matter of law to sustain a jury's finding of intentional discrimination.

In so reasoning, the Court of Appeals misconceived the evidentiary burden borne by plaintiffs who attempt to prove intentional discrimination through indirect evidence. This much is evident from our decision in St. Mary's Honor Center v. Hicks, 509 U.S. 502 (1993). There we held that the factfinder's rejection of the employer's legitimate, nondiscriminatory reason for its action does not compel judgment for the plaintiff. The ultimate question is whether the employer intentionally discriminated, and proof that "the employer's proffered reason is unpersuasive, or even obviously contrived, does not necessarily establish that the plaintiff's proffered reason . . . is correct." In other words, "[i]t is not enough . . . to disbelieve the employer; the factfinder must believe the plaintiff's explanation of intentional discrimination."

In reaching this conclusion, however, we reasoned that it is *permissible* for the trier of fact to infer the ultimate fact of discrimination from the falsity of the employer's explanation. Specifically, we stated:

> "The factfinder's disbelief of the reasons put forward by the defendant (particularly if disbelief is accompanied by a suspicion of mendacity) may, together with the elements of the prima facie case, suffice to show intentional discrimination. Thus, rejection of the defendant's proffered reasons will permit the trier of fact to infer the ultimate fact of intentional discrimination."

Proof that the defendant's explanation is unworthy of credence is simply one form of circumstantial evidence that is probative of intentional discrimination, and it may be quite persuasive. In appropriate circumstances, the trier of fact can reasonably infer from the falsity of the explanation that the employer is dissembling to cover up a discriminatory purpose. Such an inference is consistent with the general principle of evidence law that the factfinder is entitled to consider a party's dishonesty about a material fact as "affirmative evidence of guilt." Moreover, once the employer's justification has been eliminated, discrimination may well be the most likely alternative explanation, especially since the employer is in the best position to put forth the actual reason for its decision. Thus, a plaintiff's prima facie case, combined with sufficient evidence to find that the employer's asserted justification is false, may permit the trier of fact to conclude that the employer unlawfully discriminated.

This is not to say that such a showing by the plaintiff will *always* be adequate to sustain a jury's finding of liability. Certainly there will be instances where, although the plaintiff has established a prima facie case and set forth sufficient evidence to reject the defendant's explanation, no rational factfinder could conclude that the action was discriminatory. For instance, an employer would be entitled to judgment as a matter of law if the record conclusively revealed some other, nondiscriminatory reason for the employer's decision, or if the plaintiff created only a weak issue of fact as to whether the employer's reason was untrue and there was abundant and uncontroverted independent evidence that no discrimination had occurred. To hold otherwise would be effectively to insulate an entire category of employment discrimination cases from review under Rule 50, and we have reiterated that trial courts should not "treat discrimination differently from other ultimate questions of fact."

Whether judgment as a matter of law is appropriate in any particular case will depend on a number of factors. Those include the strength of the plaintiff's prima facie case, the probative value of the proof that the employer's explanation is false, and any other evidence that supports the employer's case and that properly may be considered on a motion for judgment as a matter of law. For purposes of this case, we need not—and could not—resolve all of the circumstances in which such factors would entitle an employer to judgment as a matter of law. It suffices to say that, because a prima facie case and sufficient evidence to reject the employer's explanation may permit a finding of liability, the Court of Appeals erred in proceeding from the premise that a plaintiff must always introduce additional, independent evidence of discrimination.

III

A

The remaining question is whether, despite the Court of Appeals' misconception of petitioner's evidentiary burden, respondent was nonetheless entitled to judgment as a matter of law. Under Rule 50, a court should render judgment as a matter of law when "a party has been fully heard on an issue and there is no legally sufficient evidentiary basis for a reasonable jury to find for that party on that issue." FED. RULE CIV. PROC. 50(a). The Courts of Appeals have articulated differing formulations as to what evidence a court is to consider in ruling on a Rule 50 motion. Some decisions have stated that review is limited to that evidence favorable to the nonmoving party, while most have held that review extends to the entire record, drawing all reasonable inferences in favor of the nonmovant.

On closer examination, this conflict seems more semantic than real. Those decisions holding that review under Rule 50 should be limited to evidence favorable to the nonmovant appear to have their genesis in *Wilkerson v. McCarthy, 336 U.S. 53 (1949)*. See 9A C. Wright & A. Miller, Federal Practice and Procedure § 2529, pp. 297–301 (2d ed. 1995) (hereinafter Wright & Miller). In *Wilkerson*, we stated that "in passing upon whether there is sufficient evidence to submit an issue to the jury we need look only to the evidence and reasonable inferences which tend to support the case of" the nonmoving party. But subsequent decisions have clarified that this passage was referring to the evidence to which the trial court should give credence, not the evidence that the court should review. In the analogous context of summary judgment under Rule 56, we have stated that the court must review the record "taken as a whole." *Matsushita Elec. Industrial Co. v. Zenith Radio Corp., 475 U.S. 574, 587 (1986)*. And the standard for granting summary judgment "mirrors" the standard for judgment as a matter of law, such that "the inquiry under each is the same." *Anderson v. Liberty Lobby, Inc., 477 U.S. 242, 250–251 (1986)*; see also *Celotex Corp. v. Catrett,* 477 U.S. 317, 323 (1986). It therefore follows that, in entertaining a motion for judgment as a matter of law, the court should review all of the evidence in the record.

In doing so, however, the court must draw all reasonable inferences in favor of the nonmoving party, and it may not make credibility determinations or weigh the evidence. "Credibility determinations, the weighing of the evidence, and the drawing of legitimate inferences from the facts are jury functions, not those of a judge." Thus, although the court should review the record as a whole, it must disregard all evidence favorable to the moving party that the jury is not required to believe. That is, the court should give credence to the evidence favoring the nonmovant as well as that "evidence supporting the moving party that is uncontradicted and unimpeached, at least to the extent that that evidence comes from disinterested witnesses."

Food for Thought

Why do you think this is the appropriate standard that courts must follow when evaluating the propriety of granting a motion for judgment as a matter of law? Although the Supreme Court indicates that this analysis mirrors the summary judgment analysis, do you imagine there being any difference in how courts actually engage in these analyses given the different points in the proceedings at which the two motions are made?

B

Applying this standard here, it is apparent that respondent was not entitled to judgment as a matter of law. In this case, in addition to establishing a prima facie case of discrimination and creating a jury issue as to the falsity of the employer's explanation, petitioner introduced additional evidence that Chesnut was motivated by age-based animus and was principally responsible for petitioner's firing. Petitioner testified that Chesnut had told him that he "was so old [he] must have come over on the Mayflower" and, on one occasion when petitioner was having difficulty starting a machine, that he "was too damn old to do [his] job." According to petitioner, Chesnut would regularly "cuss at me and shake his finger in my face." Oswalt, roughly 24 years younger than petitioner, corroborated that there was an "obvious difference" in how Chesnut treated them. He stated that, although he and Chesnut "had [their] differences," "it was nothing compared to the way [Chesnut] treated Roger." Oswalt explained that Chesnut "tolerated quite a bit" from him even though he "defied" Chesnut "quite often," but that Chesnut treated petitioner "[i]n a manner, as you would . . . treat . . . a child when . . . you're angry with [him]." Petitioner also demonstrated that, according to company records, he and Oswalt had nearly identical rates of productivity in 1993. Yet respondent conducted an efficiency study of only the regular line, supervised by petitioner, and placed only petitioner on probation. Chesnut conducted that efficiency study and, after having testified to the contrary on direct examination, acknowledged on cross-examination that he had recommended that petitioner be placed on probation following the study.

Further, petitioner introduced evidence that Chesnut was the actual decision-maker behind his firing. Chesnut was married to Sanderson, who made the formal decision to discharge petitioner. Although Sanderson testified that she fired petitioner because he had "intentionally falsif[ied] company pay records," respondent only introduced evidence concerning the inaccuracy of the records, not their falsification. A 1994 letter authored by Chesnut indicated that he berated other company directors, who were supposedly his coequals, about how to do their jobs. Moreover, Oswalt testified that all of respondent's employees feared Chesnut, and that Chesnut had exercised "absolute power" within the company for "[a]s long as [he] can remember."

In holding that the record contained insufficient evidence to sustain the jury's verdict, the Court of Appeals misapplied the standard of review dictated by <u>Rule 50</u>. Again, the court disregarded critical evidence favorable to petitioner—namely, the evidence supporting petitioner's prima facie case and undermining respondent's nondiscriminatory explanation. The court also failed to draw all reasonable inferences in favor of petitioner. For instance, while acknowledging "the potentially damning nature" of Chesnut's age-related comments, the court discounted them on the ground that they "were not made in the direct context of Reeves's termination." And the court discredited petitioner's evidence that Chesnut was the actual decisionmaker by giving weight to the fact that there was "no evidence to suggest that any of the other decision makers were motivated by age." Moreover, the other evidence on which the court relied—that Caldwell and Oswalt were also cited for poor recordkeeping, and that respondent employed many managers over age 50—although relevant, is certainly not dispositive. In concluding that these circumstances so overwhelmed the evidence favoring petitioner that no rational trier of fact could have found that petitioner was fired because of his age, the Court of Appeals impermissibly substituted its judgment concerning the weight of the evidence for the jury's.

The ultimate question in every employment discrimination case involving a claim of disparate treatment is whether the plaintiff was the victim of intentional discrimination. Given the evidence in the record supporting petitioner, we see no reason to subject the parties to an additional round of litigation before the Court of Appeals rather than to resolve the matter here.

The District Court plainly informed the jury that petitioner was required to show "by a preponderance of the evidence that his age was a determining and motivating factor in the decision of [respondent] to terminate him." The court instructed the jury that, to show that respondent's explanation was a

Take Note!

These quoted statements of the court to the jury are examples of jury instructions, a topic that will be discussed briefly below.

pretext for discrimination, petitioner had to demonstrate "1, that the stated reasons were not the real reasons for [petitioner's] discharge; and 2, that age discrimination was the real reason for [petitioner's] discharge." Given that petitioner established a prima facie case of discrimination, introduced enough evidence for the jury to reject respondent's explanation, and produced additional evidence of age-based animus, there was sufficient evidence for the jury to find that respondent had intentionally discriminated. The District Court was therefore correct to submit the case to the jury, and the Court of Appeals erred in overturning its verdict.

For these reasons, the judgment of the Court of Appeals is reversed.

It is so ordered.

[The concurring opinion of JUSTICE GINSBURG is omitted.]

Points for Discussion

a. The Standard for Granting Judgment as a Matter of Law

What standard does the Court articulate for granting judgment as a matter of law? *See also Lavender v. Kurn, 327 U.S. 645 (1946)* [*FLEX Case 10.B*]. Does this standard appear to be influenced by a concern for the constitutional jury trial right?

As a general matter, judgment as a matter of law is appropriate when the party opposing it lacks "substantial evidence" to support a jury verdict. All evidence before the court at the time is relevant to this determination, with all reasonable inferences being drawn in the nonmovant's favor. Further, as the court is not supposed to be weighing evidence, all evidence in favor of the moving party that the jury is not obligated to believe must be disregarded.

If there is evidence in favor of the movant's position that is uncontroverted—or incontrovertible—the court should give credence to that as well. This was the situation in *Chamberlain. See also Delano-Pyle v. Victoria Cnty., Tex., 302 F.3d 567, 572 (5th Cir. 2002):*

> [The court determines whether] reasonable and fair-minded jurors in the exercise of impartial judgment might reach different conclusions. A mere scintilla is insufficient to present a question for the jury. However, it is the function of the jury as the traditional finder of facts, and not the Court, to weigh conflicting evidence and inferences, and determine the credibility of witnesses. (citation and emendations omitted).

Thus, when there is evidence in the record that "blatantly contradict[s]" the non-movant's version of events—such as clear, unimpeached, and properly authenticated videotape evidence—the court is under no duty to accept the nonmovant's version and may direct a verdict in favor of the movant rather than permit the case to be decided by the jury. *See Scott v. Harris*, 550 U.S. 372, 380 (2007). Test your understanding of the Rule 50 standard by answering the following hypothetical question:

Hypo 10.3

Martha sued Denise asserting that she was negligent in causing a car accident in which the two were involved. Martha filed the action in federal court seeking $100,000 in damages for personal injuries and damage to her vehicle. During her case-in-chief, Martha presented evidence of the damage to her vehicle, evidence establishing that the damage resulted from a collision with Denise, and evidence of her injuries. Martha also testified that when the two vehicles entered the intersection where they collided, her traffic signal was green. During Denise's presentation of her evidence, she introduced a videotape showing that her traffic signal was green as she entered the intersection and Martha's signal was red as she entered the intersection. During her rebuttal, Martha took the testimony of a witness who was a pedestrian at the time of the accident, who testified that Martha's signal was green as she entered the intersection.

After Martha rested her case, Denise moved for judgment as a matter of law, arguing that Martha has failed to put forward evidence carrying her burden of demonstrating that Denise was negligent and thus responsible for causing the accident. How should the court rule?

---

b. The Renewed Motion for Judgment as a Matter of Law

As we saw in *Reeves*, an unsuccessful motion for judgment as a matter of law may be renewed after the jury returns its verdict. Rule 50(b) permits the renewal of such motions:

FRCP 50(b). Judgment as a Matter of Law in a Jury Trial.

(b) Renewing the Motion After Trial; Alternative Motion for a New Trial. If the court does not grant a motion for judgment as a matter of law made under Rule 50(a), the court is considered to have submitted the action to the jury subject to the court's later deciding the legal questions raised by the motion. No later than 28 days after the entry of judgment—or if the motion addresses a jury issue not decided by a verdict, no later than 28 days after the jury was discharged—the movant may file a renewed motion for judgment as a matter of law and may include an alternative or joint request for a new trial under Rule 59. In ruling on the renewed motion, the court may:

(1)   allow judgment on the verdict, if the jury returned a verdict;

(2)   order a new trial; or

(3)   direct the entry of judgment as a matter of law.

Note the wording of the rule: it only speaks of permitting the movant to "renew" its request for judgment as a matter of law. Thus, any post-verdict consideration of a motion for judgment as a matter of law may only be on the basis of a pre-verdict motion that is now being reconsidered. No such motion may be made for the first time after the verdict. Why do you think such is the case? Why would a court deny a motion for judgment as a matter of law prior to submitting the case to the jury but grant the motion—based on no new evidence—after the jury has issued its verdict?

Regarding the standard for granting a renewed motion for judgment as a matter of law, it parallels the standard for granting such motions prior to submission of the case to the jury. The evidence is not to be weighed nor are credibility determinations to be made; courts will not disregard a verdict on a motion for judgment as a matter of law unless the jury's findings are not supported by substantial evidence. *See, e.g. E.E.O.C. v. Boh Bros. Constr. Co., 731 F.3d 444, 452 (5th Cir. 2013)* ("[W]e must draw all reasonable inferences in the light most favorable to the verdict and cannot substitute other inferences that we might regard as more reasonable. For it is the function of the jury as the traditional finder of the facts, and not for the Court, to weigh conflicting evidence and inferences, and determine the credibility of witnesses. The jury is free to choose among reasonable constructions of the evidence. Thus, we cannot reverse a denial of a motion for judgment as a matter of law unless the jury's factual findings are not supported by substantial evidence, or if the legal conclusions implied

FYI

As noted previously, Rule 50 was amended in 1991. In addition to the change from use of the term *directed verdict* to "judgment as a matter of law," the term *judgment notwithstanding the verdict* (abbreviated as *j.n.o.v.* for its Latin version, *judgment non obstante verdicto*) was changed to refer to the "renewal of a motion for judgment as a matter of law." Many states retain use of the term *j.n.o.v.*

from the jury's verdict cannot in law be supported by those findings." (citations and internal quotation marks omitted)).

c.   Timing of the Motion

As Rule 50 states, "A motion for judgment as a matter of law may be made at any time before the case is submitted to the jury." FED. R. CIV. P. 50(a)(2). When can such a motion be renewed? In 2006, Rule 50 was amended to permit a motion for judgment as a matter of law to be renewed after the entry of judgment so long as a motion had previously been made under Rule 50(a), which may have been made at any time before the case was submitted to the jury. Prior to the 2006 amendment, Rule 50(b) indicated that in order to be renewed, a motion for judgment as a matter of law had to have been made "at the close of all the evidence." Thus, if a party moved for judgment as a matter of law at the end of the plaintiff's case but not after each side had rested their cases, the movant was typically not permitted to renew the motion after judgment or challenge the sufficiency of the evidence on appeal, although circuits differed on how strictly to interpret this aspect of Rule 50(b). *See Szmaj v. AT&T Co.*, 291 F.3d 955 (7th Cir. 2002). The 2006 amendment was intended to eliminate this issue by permitting the renewal of any motion that has been raised under Rule 50(a), regardless of when it was raised so long as it was raised prior to the submission of the case to the jury but after the opposing party has been fully heard on the issue.

d.   The Constitutionality of Entering Judgment as a Matter of Law

In light of the Seventh Amendment right to a jury trial, how is it that courts are constitutionally permitted to take a case away from a jury by preempting their decision with an entry of judgment as a matter of law? When it had the chance to consider this question, the Supreme Court felt that the practice was consistent with the Seventh Amendment and thus affirmed its constitutionality in *Galloway v. United States*, 319 U.S. 372 (1943) [*FLEX Case 10.C*]. Relatedly, the second clause of the Seventh Amendment indicates that "no fact tried by a jury, shall be otherwise re-examined in any Court of the United States, than according to the rules of common law." Does the entry of judgment as a matter of law *post-verdict* present any difficulties under this aspect of the Seventh Amendment? As the Committee Note accompanying the revised rule suggests, Rule 50(b)'s requirement of a motion for judgment as a matter of law prior to submission of the case to the jury as a prerequisite to the court's consideration of the motion after the verdict is seen to be necessary to the constitutionality of a post-verdict entry of a judgment on the motion. *See* advisory committee's note to 2006 amendment FED. R. CIV. P. 50(b) (citing *Balt. & Carolina Line, Inc. v. Redman*, 295 U.S. 654 (1935)).

e.   *Sua Sponte* Entry of Judgment as a Matter of Law

Reread Rule 50(a) and Rule 50(b). Is a motion required for the court to enter judgment as a matter of law prior to submission of the case to the jury? What about for the court to enter judgment as a matter of law after a jury verdict? In either circumstance, may the court enter judgment as a matter of law *sua sponte*? *See, e.g., A. H. Lundberg Assocs., Inc. v. TSI, Inc.*, 2016 WL 5477524, at *2 n.3 (W.D. Wash. Sept. 29, 2016) ("Converting a Rule 50(a) motion into a Rule 50(b) motion without requiring the movant to renew the motion would contravene the requirement that the movant 'file a renewed motion for judgment as a matter of law' '[n]o later than 28 days after the entry of judgment.' " (quoting FED. R. CIV. P. 50)). *See also Doe v. Celebrity Cruises, Inc.*, 394 F.3d 891, 903–904 (11th Cir. 2004) ("[A] district court does not have the authority under Rule 50(b) to rule *sua sponte* on issues not raised by the parties.").

———————————

In the event that a party seeks but fails to obtain judgment as a matter of law prior to the submission of the case to the jury but then fails to renew its motion after the verdict is announced and judgment is entered, can that party assert on appeal that the motion was improperly denied? The next case squarely addresses that question.

Unitherm Food Systems, Inc. v. Swift-Eckrich, Inc.

Supreme Court of the United States
546 U.S. 394 (2006)

JUSTICE THOMAS delivered the opinion of the Court.

Take Note!

As a non-regional appeals court, there are issues for which the Federal Circuit is bound to follow the law of the circuit from which the case originated, here the Tenth Circuit. That is typically the case when the issue is not one that pertains uniquely to patent law, the specialty of the Federal Circuit.

Ordinarily, a party in a civil jury trial that believes the evidence is legally insufficient to support an adverse jury verdict will seek a judgment as a matter of law by filing a motion pursuant to Federal Rule of Civil Procedure 50(a) before submission of the case to the jury, and then (if the Rule 50(a) motion is not granted and the jury subsequently decides against that party) a motion pursuant to Rule 50(b). In this case, however, the respondent filed a Rule 50(a) motion before the verdict, but did not file a Rule 50(b) motion after the verdict. Nor did respondent request a new trial under Rule 59. The Court of Appeals nevertheless proceeded to review the sufficiency of the evidence and, upon a finding that the evidence was insufficient, remanded the case for a new trial. Because our cases addressing the requirements of Rule 50 compel a contrary result, we reverse.

I

The genesis of the underlying litigation in this case was ConAgra's attempt to enforce its patent for "A Method for Browning Precooked Whole Muscle Meat Products," U.S. Patent No. 5,952,027 ('027 patent). In early 2000, ConAgra issued a general warning to companies who sold equipment and processes for browning precooked meats explaining that it intended to "aggressively protect all of [its] rights under [the '027] patent." Petitioner Unitherm sold such processes, but did not receive ConAgra's warning. ConAgra also contacted its direct competitors in the precooked meat business, announcing that it was "making the '027 Patent and corresponding patents that may issue available for license * * * ." Jennie-O, a direct competitor, received ConAgra's correspondence and undertook an investigation to determine its rights and responsibilities with regard to the '027 patent. Jennie-O determined that the browning process it had purchased from Unitherm was the same as the process described in the '027 patent. Jennie-O further determined that the '027 patent was invalid because Unitherm's president had invented the process described in that patent six years before ConAgra filed its patent application.

Consistent with these determinations, Jennie-O and Unitherm jointly sued ConAgra in the Western District of Oklahoma. As relevant here, Jennie-O and Unitherm sought a declaration that the '027 patent was invalid and unenforceable, and alleged that ConAgra had violated § 2 of the Sherman Act, 15 U.S.C. § 2, by attempting to enforce a patent that was obtained by committing fraud on the Patent and Trademark Office (PTO). *See Walker Process Equipment, Inc. v. Food Machinery & Chemical Corp., 382 U.S. 172, 174 (1965).* The District Court construed the '027 patent and determined that it was invalid based on Unitherm's prior public use and sale of the process described therein. 35 U.S.C. § 102(b). After dismissing Jennie-O for lack of * * * standing, the District Court allowed Unitherm's [antitrust] claim to proceed to trial. Prior to the court's submission of the case to the jury, ConAgra moved for a directed verdict under Rule 50(a) based on legal insufficiency of the evidence. The District Court denied that motion. The jury returned a verdict for Unitherm, and ConAgra neither renewed its motion for judgment as a matter of law pursuant to Rule 50(b), nor moved for a new trial on antitrust liability pursuant to Rule 59.

On appeal to the Federal Circuit, ConAgra maintained that there was insufficient evidence to sustain the jury's [antitrust] verdict. Although the Federal Circuit has concluded that a party's "failure to present the district court with a post-verdict motion precludes appellate review of sufficiency of the evidence," in the instant case it was bound to apply the law of the Tenth Circuit. Under Tenth Circuit law, a party that has failed to file a postverdict motion challenging the sufficiency of the evidence may nonetheless raise such a claim on appeal, so long as that party filed a Rule 50(a) motion prior to submission of the case to the jury. *Cummings v. General Motors Corp.*, 365 F.3d 944, 950–951 (2004). Notably, the only available relief in such a circumstance is a new trial.

Freed to examine the sufficiency of the evidence, the Federal Circuit concluded that, although Unitherm had presented sufficient evidence to support a determination that ConAgra had attempted to enforce a patent that it had obtained through fraud on the PTO, Unitherm had failed to present evidence sufficient to support the remaining elements of its antitrust claim. Accordingly, it vacated the jury's judgment in favor of Unitherm and remanded for a new trial. We granted certiorari, and now reverse.

II

Federal Rule of Civil Procedure 50 sets forth the procedural requirements for challenging the sufficiency of the evidence in a civil jury trial and establishes two stages for such challenges—prior to submission of the case to the jury, and after the verdict and entry of judgment. Rule 50(a) allows a party to challenge the sufficiency of the evidence prior to submission of the case to the jury, and authorizes the District Court to grant such motions at the court's discretion * * * .

Rule 50(b), by contrast, sets forth the procedural requirements for renewing a sufficiency of the evidence challenge after the jury verdict and entry of judgment. * * *

This Court has addressed the implications of a party's failure to file a postverdict motion under Rule 50(b) on several occasions and in a variety of procedural contexts. This Court has concluded that, "[i]n the absence of such a motion" an "appellate court [is] without power to direct the District Court to enter judgment contrary to the one it had permitted to stand." *Cone v. West Virginia Pulp & Paper Co.*, 330 U.S. 212, 218 (1947). This Court has similarly concluded that a party's failure to file a Rule 50(b) motion deprives the appellate court of the power to order the entry of judgment in favor of that party where the district court directed the jury's verdict, and where the district court expressly reserved a party's preverdict motion for a directed verdict and then denied that motion after the verdict was returned. A postverdict motion is necessary because "[d]etermination of whether a new trial should be granted or a judgment entered under Rule 50(b) calls for the judgment in the first instance of the judge who saw and heard the witnesses and has the feel of the case which no appellate printed transcript can impart."[3] Moreover, the "requirement of a

---

[3] Neither *Neely v. Martin K. Eby Constr. Co.*, 386 U.S. 317 (1967), nor *Weisgram v. Marley Co.*, 528 U.S. 440 (2000), undermine our judgment about the benefit of postverdict input from the district court. In those cases this Court determined that an appellate court may, in certain circumstances, direct the entry of judgment when it reverses the district court's denial of a Rule 50(b) motion. But in such circumstances the district court will have had an opportunity to consider the propriety of entering judgment or ordering a new trial by virtue of the postverdict motion. Moreover, these cases reiterate the value of the district

timely application for judgment after verdict is not an idle motion" because it "is . . . an essential part of the rule, firmly grounded in principles of fairness."

The foregoing authorities lead us to reverse the judgment below. Respondent correctly points out that these authorities address whether an appellate court may enter judgment in the absence of a postverdict motion, as opposed to whether an appellate court may order a new trial (as the Federal Circuit did here). But this distinction is immaterial. This Court's observations about the necessity of a postverdict motion under Rule 50(b), and the benefits of the district court's input at that stage, apply with equal force whether a party is seeking judgment as a matter of law or simply a new trial. In *Cone*, this Court concluded that, because Rule 50(b) permits the district court to exercise its discretion to choose between ordering a new trial and entering judgment, its "appraisal of the bona fides of the claims asserted by the litigants is of great value in reaching a conclusion as to whether a new trial should be granted." Similarly, this Court has determined that a party may only pursue on appeal a particular avenue of relief available under Rule 50(b), namely the entry of judgment or a new trial, when that party has complied with the Rule's filing requirements by requesting that particular relief below.[4]

Despite the straightforward language employed in *Cone*, *Globe Liquor [v. San Roman*, 332 U.S. 571 (1948)], and *Johnson [v. New York, N.H. & H.R. Co.*, 344 U.S. 48 (1952)], respondent maintains that those cases dictate affirmance here, because in each of those cases the litigants secured a new trial. But in each of those cases the appellants moved for a new trial postverdict in the District Court, and did not seek to establish their entitlement to a new trial solely on the basis of a denied Rule 50(a) motion. Indeed, *Johnson* concluded that respondent was only entitled to a new trial by virtue of its motion for such "within the time required by Rule 50(b)." Accordingly, these outcomes merely underscore our holding today—a party is not entitled

---

court's input, cautioning the courts of appeals to be "'constantly alert' to 'the trial judge's first-hand knowledge of witnesses, testimony, and issues.'" *Id.*, at 443 (quoting *Neely, supra*, at 325).

[4] The dissent's suggestion that 28 U.S.C. § 2106 permits the Courts of Appeals to consider the sufficiency of the evidence underlying a civil jury verdict notwithstanding a party's failure to comply with Rule 50 is foreclosed by authority of this Court. * * * [T]he broad grant of authority to the Courts of Appeals in § 2106 must be exercised consistent with the requirements of the Federal Rules of Civil Procedure as interpreted by this Court.

The dissent's approach is not only foreclosed by authority of this Court, it also may present Seventh Amendment concerns. The implication of the dissent's interpretation of § 2106 is that a court of appeals would be free to examine the sufficiency of the evidence regardless of whether the appellant had filed a Rule 50(a) motion in the district court and, in the event the appellant had filed a Rule 50(a) motion, regardless of whether the district court had ever ruled on that motion. The former is squarely foreclosed by *Slocum v. New York Life Ins. Co.*, 228 U.S. 364 (1913), and the latter is inconsistent with this Court's explanation of the requirements of the Seventh Amendment in *Baltimore & Carolina Line, Inc. v. Redman*, 295 U.S. 654, 658 (1935) (explaining that "under the pertinent rules of the common law the court of appeals could set aside the verdict for error of law, such as the trial court's ruling respecting the sufficiency of the evidence, and direct a new trial, but could not itself determine the issues of fact and direct a judgment for the defendant, for this would cut off the plaintiff's unwaived right to have the issues of fact determined by a jury" (emphasis added)). Indeed, Rule 50 was drafted with such concerns in mind.

to pursue a new trial on appeal unless that party makes an appropriate postverdict motion in the district court.

Our determination that respondent's failure to comply with Rule 50(b) forecloses its challenge to the sufficiency of the evidence is further validated by the purported basis of respondent's appeal, namely the District Court's denial of respondent's preverdict Rule 50(a) motion. As an initial matter, *Cone, Globe Liquor,* and *Johnson* unequivocally establish that the precise subject matter of a party's Rule 50(a) motion—namely, its entitlement to judgment as a matter of law—cannot be appealed unless that motion is renewed pursuant to Rule 50(b). Here, respondent does not seek to pursue on appeal the precise claim it raised in its Rule 50(a) motion before the District Court—namely, its entitlement to judgment as a matter of law. Rather, it seeks a new trial based on the legal insufficiency of the evidence. But if, as in *Cone, Globe Liquor,* and *Johnson,* a litigant that has failed to file a Rule 50(b) motion is foreclosed from seeking the relief it sought in its Rule 50(a) motion—i.e., the entry of judgment—then surely respondent is foreclosed from seeking a new trial, relief it did not and could not seek in its preverdict motion. In short, respondent never sought a new trial before the District Court, and thus forfeited its right to do so on appeal.

The text of Rule 50(b) confirms that respondent's preverdict Rule 50(a) motion did not present the District Court with the option of ordering a new trial. That text provides that a district court may only order a new trial on the basis of issues raised in a preverdict Rule 50(a) motion when "ruling on a renewed motion" under Rule 50(b). Accordingly, even if the District Court was inclined to grant a new trial on the basis of arguments raised in respondent's preverdict motion, it was without the power to do so under Rule 50(b) absent a postverdict motion pursuant to that Rule. Consequently, the Court of Appeals was similarly powerless.

Similarly, the text and application of Rule 50(a) support our determination that respondent may not challenge the sufficiency of the evidence on appeal on the basis of the District Court's denial of its Rule 50(a) motion. The Rule provides that "the court *may* determine" that "there is no legally sufficient evidentiary basis for a reasonable jury to find for [a] party on [a given] issue," and "may grant a motion for judgment as a matter of law against that party . . . ." (Emphasis added.) Thus, while a district court is permitted to enter judgment as a matter of law when it concludes that the evidence is legally insufficient, it is not required to do so. To the contrary, the district courts are, if anything, encouraged to submit the case to the jury, rather than granting such motions. * * *

Thus, the District Court's denial of respondent's preverdict motion cannot form the basis of respondent's appeal, because the denial of that motion was not error. It was merely an exercise of the District Court's discretion, in accordance with the text of the Rule and the accepted practice of permitting the jury to make an initial judgment about the sufficiency of the evidence. The only error here was counsel's failure to file a postverdict motion pursuant to <u>Rule 50(b)</u>.

* * *

For the foregoing reasons, we hold that since respondent failed to renew its preverdict motion as specified in <u>Rule 50(b)</u>, there was no basis for review of respondent's sufficiency of the evidence challenge in the Court of Appeals. The judgment of the Court of Appeals is reversed.

It is so ordered.

Practice Pointer

Justice Thomas describes counsel's failure to file a postverdict motion under Rule 50(b) as an error. If you make a motion under Rule 50(a) that is rejected by the court preverdict, be sure to renew that motion under Rule 50(b) postverdict to preserve your right to seek such relief on appeal.

Justice Stevens, with whom Justice Kennedy joins, dissenting.

Murphy's law applies to trial lawyers as well as pilots. Even an expert will occasionally blunder. For that reason Congress has preserved the federal appeals courts' power to correct plain error, even though trial counsel's omission will ordinarily give rise to a binding waiver. This is not a case, in my view, in which the authority of the appellate court is limited by an explicit statute or controlling rule. The spirit of the Federal Rules of Civil Procedure favors preservation of a court's power to avoid manifestly unjust results in exceptional cases. Moreover, we have an overriding duty to obey statutory commands that unambiguously express the intent of Congress even in areas such as procedure in which we may have special expertise.

Today, relying primarily on a case decided in March 1947, *Cone v. West Virginia Pulp & Paper Co.*, 330 U.S. 212, and a case decided in January 1948, *Globe Liquor Co. v. San Roman*, 332 U.S. 571, the Court holds that the Court of Appeals was "powerless" to review the sufficiency of the evidence supporting the verdict in petitioner's favor because respondent failed to file proper postverdict motions pursuant to Rules 50(b) and 59 of the Federal Rules of Civil Procedure in the trial court. The majority's holding is inconsistent with a statute enacted just months after *Globe Liquor* was decided. That statute, which remains in effect today, provides:

> "The Supreme Court or any other court of appellate jurisdiction may affirm, modify, vacate, set aside or reverse any judgment, decree, or order of a court lawfully brought before it for review, and may remand the cause and direct the entry of such appropriate judgment, decree, or order, or require such further proceedings to be had as may be just under the circumstances."

28 U.S.C. § 2106.

Nothing in Rule 50(b) limits this statutory grant of power to appellate courts; while a party's failure to make a Rule 50(b) motion precludes the district court from directing a verdict in that party's favor, the Rule does not purport to strip the courts of appeals of the authority to review district court judgments or to order such relief as "may be just under the circumstances." Nor do general principles of waiver or forfeiture have that effect. It is well settled that a litigant's waiver or forfeiture of an argument does not, in the absence of a contrary statutory command, preclude the courts of appeals from considering those arguments. Arguments raised for the first time on appeal may be entertained, for example, if their consideration would prevent manifest injustice.*

For the reasons articulated by the Court in *Cone*, it may be unfair or even an abuse of discretion for a court of appeals to direct a verdict in favor of the party that lost below if that party failed to make a timely Rule 50(b) motion. Likewise, it may not be "just under the circumstances" for a court of appeals to order a new trial in the absence of a proper Rule 59 motion. Finally, a court of appeals has discretion to rebuff, on grounds of waiver or forfeiture, a challenge to the sufficiency of the evidence absent a proper Rule 50(b) or Rule 59 motion made in the district court. None of the foregoing propositions rests, however, on a determination that the courts of appeals lack "power" to review the sufficiency of the evidence and order appropriate relief under these circumstances, and I can divine no basis for that determination.

I respectfully dissent.

Points for Discussion

a. The Holding of *Unitherm*

The defendant in *Unitherm* made a motion for judgment as a matter of law under Rule 50(a) before the case was submitted to the jury, and the district court denied the motion. After the verdict was issued, the defendant failed to renew its motion for judgment as a matter of law under Rule 50(b), or to seek a new trial under Rule 59 (a device that we will consider below). On appeal, the defendant sought and obtained a new trial order from the circuit court, but the Supreme Court

---

* The Court suggests that the Seventh Amendment limits appellate courts' power to review judgments under 28 U.S.C. § 2106. I disagree with the Court's analysis in two respects. First, although the right to trial by jury might be implicated if no Rule 50(a) motion had been made, such a motion was made in this case. The Rule 50(a) motion triggered the automatic reservation of "legal questions," FED. RULE CIV. PROC. 50(b), and that reservation, in turn, averted any Seventh Amendment problem, see *Baltimore & Carolina Line, Inc. v. Redman*, 295 U.S. 654 (1935). Second, the Seventh Amendment imposes no greater restriction on appellate courts than it does on district courts in these circumstances; "[a]s far as the Seventh Amendment's right to jury trial is concerned, there is no greater restriction on the province of the jury when an appellate court enters judgment n.o.v. than when a trial court does." *Neely v. Martin K. Eby Constr. Co.*, 386 U.S. 317, 322 (1967). [Footnote by Justice Stevens.]

reversed that order. Why did the Supreme Court conclude that the circuit court lacked the power to order a new trial under these circumstances?

Unitherm only prohibits appeals courts from considering sufficiency of the evidence challenges when such challenges have not first been raised postverdict before the trial court. *Unitherm* does not, however, make postverdict challenges before the district court a precondition for appellate review of trial errors and the ordering of new trials by appeals courts. *See, e.g.*, *Fuesting v. Zimmer, Inc.*, 448 F.3d 936, 940–41 (7th Cir. 2006), *cert. denied*, 549 U.S. 1180 (2007):

> [T]he *Unitherm* decision does not purport to undermine those cases which explicitly state that a post-judgment motion is not a prerequisite to an appeal. * * *

> "A renewed motion for judgment as a matter of law under Rule 50(b) is not a condition precedent to appeal from a final judgment. If there have been errors at the trial, duly objected to, dealing with matters *other than the sufficiency of the evidence*, they may be raised on appeal from the judgment even though there has not been either a renewed motion for judgment as a matter of law or a motion for a new trial, although it is better practice for the parties to give the trial court an opportunity to correct its errors in the first instance." (emphasis added) (quoting 11 C. Wright & A. Miller, FED. PRAC. & PROC. § 2818 (2d ed. 1995)).

b. The Impact of 28 U.S.C. § 2106

The text of 28 U.S.C. § 2106, cited by Justice Stevens in his dissent, reads as follows:

> The Supreme Court or any other court of appellate jurisdiction may affirm, modify, vacate, set aside or reverse any judgment, decree, or order of a court lawfully brought before it for review, and may remand the cause and direct the entry of such appropriate judgment, decree, or order, or require such further proceedings to be had as may be just under the circumstances.

Which side do you think had the better argument regarding the impact of this provision on the issue before the Court? Should § 2106 be read to authorize the appeals court's grant of a new trial in *Unitherm* or is Justice Thomas's argument to the contrary—that the statute must be read in conjunction with the Court's precedents prohibiting such a practice—correct?

c.   **The Seventh Amendment and *Unitherm***

What role did the Seventh Amendment play in the *Unitherm* Court's analysis, if any? How did Justice Stevens respond to the majority's point regarding the Seventh Amendment's impact on the question before the Court? Which opinion's arguments on this issue were more convincing?

———————

2. Instructions & Verdicts

a.   **Jury Instructions**

Before a case is submitted to the jury for a decision, the court must first instruct the jury on the law that it is to apply to the facts as it decides them. Juries are not free to interpret the law themselves or to apply their own sense of what the law should be. Rather, the jury is constrained to follow the law as given to them by the judge, having the freedom only to render their judgment as to the facts and how the law should be applied to those facts. The shaping and giving of these instructions are governed by Rule 51:

FRCP 51. Instructions to the Jury.

(a)   **Requests.**

(1)   *Before or at the Close of the Evidence.* At the close of the evidence or at any earlier reasonable time that the court orders, a party may file and furnish to every other party written requests for the jury instructions it wants the court to give.

* * *

(b)   **Instructions.** The court:

(1)   must inform the parties of its proposed instructions and proposed action on the requests before instructing the jury and before final jury arguments;

(2)   must give the parties an opportunity to object on the record and out of the jury's hearing before the instructions and arguments are delivered; and

(3)   may instruct the jury at any time before the jury is discharged.

* * *

As can be seen, the litigants have the opportunity to shape the content of the jury instructions through their proposals, but it is ultimately the court's decision as to what instructions will actually be given. What considerations do you think are relevant to how litigants craft their proposed jury instructions? Is there any incentive to state the applicable law in a way that is particularly favorable to one's own case? Is there any disincentive to do so?

FYI

If the jury instructions misstate the law *and* are overly prejudicial to one side in the case, the resulting judgment is vulnerable to being reversed on appeal. See, e.g., *Huff v. Sheahan*, 493 F.3d 893, 899 (7th Cir. 2007) ("[W]e shall reverse when the instructions misstate the law or fail to convey the relevant legal principles in full and when those shortcomings confuse or mislead the jury and prejudice the objecting litigant.") (citation and internal quotation marks omitted).

A party may object to its adversary's proposed instructions and to the instructions that the court intends to give (or omit). FED. R. CIV. P. 51(c)(1) ("A party who objects to an instruction or the failure to give an instruction must do so on the record, stating distinctly the matter objected to and the grounds for the objection."). Although a court is supposed to inform parties of the instructions it intends to give prior to giving them, FED. R. CIV. P. 51(b)(1), if the court fails to do so, the party must object "promptly after learning that the instruction . . . will be, or has been, given or refused." FED. R. CIV. P. 51(c)(2)(B). Any unraised objections will be waived, meaning that the offended party will not have the opportunity to challenge an instruction (or the failure to give a certain instruction) on appeal. FED. R. CIV. P. 51(d) ("A party may assign as error: (A) an error in an instruction actually given, if that party properly objected; or (B) a failure to give an instruction, if that party properly requested it and . . . also properly objected.").

Take Note!

Although unobjected to instructions (or omissions) may not form the basis for assignments of error, Rule 51(d)(2) provides an exception to this waiver rule when a "plain error in the instructions . . . affects substantial rights." The Advisory Committee Notes to the 2003 Amendments that resulted in this provision indicate that four factors are relevant to the plain error analysis: the "obviousness of the mistake," the "importance of the error," the "cost of correcting" the error, and the "impact . . . on nonparties." FED. R. CIV. P. 51(d)(2) advisory committee's note to 2003 amendment.

b. Verdicts

After receiving instructions from the court, the jury retires to deliberate in order to reach a verdict. These deliberations are in private and the discussions are kept confidential. In the federal system, the verdict in civil trials must be unanimous and returned by a jury of at least six members unless the parties agree to the contrary on either point. FED. R. CIV. P. 48(b). The unanimity requirement makes it possible that the jury will deadlock and not be able to reach a verdict. In the event that the jury persists in being unable to arrive at a verdict, a mistrial must be declared. In the event of a mistrial, the jury is dismissed and the court will have to order a new trial in front of a new jury. Clearly, doing so involves additional costs and delay that neither the court nor the parties would like to endure; nevertheless, holdout jurors cannot be coerced into agreeing with other jurors and thus there is little a court can do if the jurors remain at an impasse.

Practice Pointer

If you believe that the announced verdict was not unanimously reached, you may request that the jury be polled individually *before it is discharged*. If the poll reveals a lack of unanimity, the court may direct the jury to deliberate further or may order a new trial. FED. R. CIV. P. 48(c).

If the jury is able to reach a verdict, the typical form of the verdict is ordinarily a simple finding either in favor of the plaintiff or the defendant. This type of verdict is referred to as a general verdict. There are two potential problems with general verdicts, however. First, juries are carefully instructed on the law and told of each of the issues they must resolve to reach a particular result. With a general verdict, it is not possible to determine whether the jury properly considered and resolved each of the necessary issues to reach its result or if they simply found in favor for a particular party based on their own instincts, emotions, or general sense of the case. Second, and more importantly, general verdicts make it more difficult to discern whether an erroneous instruction tainted the verdict when multiple grounds for a given result exist. If there are three potential bases for finding the defendant liable, for example, and the court's instructions on one of those bases is erroneous, a general verdict will leave unclear whether the jury's finding against the defendant was based on the erroneous basis or one of the other two.

It is with these issues in mind that the Federal Rules provide for other types of verdicts that vary to some extent from the basic general verdict:

FRCP 49. Special Verdict; General Verdict and Questions.

(a) Special Verdict.

(1) *In General.* The court may require a jury to return only a special verdict in the form of a special written finding on each issue of fact. The court may do so by:

(A) submitting written questions susceptible of a categorical or other brief answer;

(B) submitting written forms of the special findings that might properly be made under the pleadings and evidence; or

(C) using any other method that the court considers appropriate.

* * *

(b) General Verdict with Answers to Written Questions.

(1) *In General.* The court may submit to the jury forms for a general verdict, together with written questions on one or more issues of fact that the jury must decide. * * *

(3) *Answers Inconsistent with the Verdict.* When the answers are consistent with each other but one or more is inconsistent with the general verdict, the court may:

(A) approve, for entry under Rule 58, an appropriate judgment according to the answers, notwithstanding the general verdict;

(B) direct the jury to further consider its answers and verdict; or

(C) order a new trial.

If the jury is asked to answer questions in conjunction with issuing a general verdict, the Federal Rules empower the court to take action if the answers are inconsistent with the verdict. Rule 49(b)(3) permits the court to enter a verdict consistent with the answers or ask the jury to consider further its answers and verdict, or in the alternative, the court may order a new trial. *See also Gallick v. Balt. & Ohio R.R., 372 U.S. 108 (1963)* ("The power to enter judgment on findings consistent with each other but inconsistent with the general verdict is a constitutional one and does not violate the Seventh Amendment . . . ."). However, if the answers are inconsistent with *each other* and the verdict, the court may not enter a judgment; rather, the court's only options are to ask the jury to reconsider or to enter a new trial. FED. R. CIV. P. 49(b)(4). Attorneys should keep an eye out for such inconsistencies so they can prompt the court to take appropriate action.

Given the potential difficulties surrounding general verdicts, should courts regularly require special verdicts or general verdicts accompanied by interrogatories? Why would a court permit a simple general verdict when these options are available? Is there any downside to ordering special verdicts or answers to interrogatories? *See Perspective & Analysis.*

—Perspective & Analysis—

Justices Hugo Black and William O. Douglas had strong views against Rule 49 and the ability of federal judges to force juries to give special verdicts or answer interrogatories:

> One of the ancient, fundamental reasons for having general jury verdicts was to preserve the right of trial by jury as an indispensable part of a free government. Many of the most famous constitutional controversies in England revolved around litigants' insistence, particularly in seditious libel cases, that a jury had the right to render a general verdict without being compelled to return a number of subsidiary findings to support its general verdict. Some English jurors had to go to jail because they insisted upon their right to render general verdicts over the repeated commands of tyrannical judges not to do so.
>
> Rule 49 is but another means utilized by courts to weaken the constitutional power of juries and to vest judges with more power to decide cases according to their own judgments. A scrutiny of the special verdict and written interrogatory cases in appellate courts will show the confusion that necessarily results from the employment of these devices and the ease with which judges can use them to take away the right to trial by jury. We believe that Rule 49 should be repealed, not amplified.

Statement of Mr. Justice Black and Mr. Justice Douglas on the Rules of Civil Procedure and the Proposed Amendments, 31 F.R.D. 587, 618–19 (1963).

3. New Trials

Once a verdict is announced, the court has the authority to throw out the jury's verdict and order a new trial. Rule 59 speaks to this authority:

FRCP 59. New Trial.

(a) **In General.**

(1) *Grounds for New Trial.* The court may, on motion, grant a new trial on all or some of the issues—and to any party—as follows:

(A) after a jury trial, for any reason for which a new trial has heretofore been granted in an action at law in federal court; or

(B) after a nonjury trial, for any reason for which a rehearing has heretofore been granted in a suit in equity in federal court. * * *

Notice that the rule itself does not state the grounds on which a new trial may be ordered but rather refers to "any reason for which a new trial has heretofore been granted in an action at law in federal court." What does this mean? And how does the court's authority to order a new trial differ from its authority to disregard a jury's verdict and enter judgment as a matter of law? The next case addresses these points.

Dadurian v. Underwriters at Lloyd's, London

U.S. Court of Appeals for the First Circuit
787 F.2d 756 (1st Cir. 1986)

CAMPBELL, CHIEF JUDGE.

This diversity case arose out of the refusal of defendant-appellant Lloyd's, London ("Lloyd's") to indemnify plaintiff-appellee Paul Dadurian after he claimed the loss of certain jewelry that he allegedly owned and that had been insured under a Lloyd's insurance policy. As affirmative defenses to the suit for nonpayment, Lloyd's asserted that Dadurian's claim was fraudulent and that Dadurian had knowingly made false statements about facts material to his claim. The jury entered special verdicts favorable to Dadurian, resulting in his recovering $267,000 plus interest. Lloyd's moved for judgment notwithstanding the verdict, or alternatively, for a new trial. The United States District Court for the District of Rhode Island denied the motion, and Lloyd's now appeals. As we find the jury's verdict was against the great weight of the evidence, we vacate and remand for a new trial.

>
>
> **Take Note!**
>
> Remember that the motion for judgment notwithstanding the verdict (or *j.n.o.v.*) was renamed as the renewed motion for judgment as a matter of law after Rule 50 was amended in 1991.

I.

Dadurian claimed that he purchased 12 pieces of "specialty" jewelry for investment purposes over a period of 30 months, from August 1977 to January 1980. The pieces allegedly ranged in price from $12,000 to $35,000, costing him $233,000 in total. Dadurian testified that he purchased all the jewelry from James Howe, a jeweler in Providence, Rhode Island, and paid for each item in cash. Dadurian did not present any sales slips, receipts or other documents of transfer reflecting any of his alleged purchases; and Howe not only presented no records of his sale of the jewelry to Dadurian, but he could not remember from whom he had originally obtained the jewelry and had no records showing that the jewelry had ever actually been in his possession.

On or about March 2, 1980, Dadurian purchased a "Jewelry Floater" policy from Lloyd's, which insured him against loss of the 12 items of jewelry. The jewelry pieces were described on an attached schedule, which also set forth the maximum amount recoverable for each piece. The maximum recoverable under the policy was $267,000. Dadurian obtained the insurance coverage on the strength of eight appraisal certificates for the jewelry, which were prepared by Howe at Dadurian's request. Some certificates were dated on the same day as certain of the alleged purchases, while the others were dated months later.

Dadurian claimed that on or about April 12, 1980, armed robbers entered his home and forced him to open his safe, where the jewelry was kept. He was shot in the right shoulder, allegedly by one of the robbers, and was taken to the hospital. It is Dadurian's contention that the insured pieces of jewelry were stolen during the robbery. After preliminary investigation by an adjuster representing Lloyd's, Dadurian was asked to appear for a formal examination under oath by counsel for Lloyd's. The examination took place on September 10, 1980, and again on May 28, 1981. Because of alleged false and fraudulent statements made under oath by Dadurian at this examination, Lloyd's refused to indemnify Dadurian for the claimed losses.

On March 31, 1982, Dadurian brought this action in the district court seeking compensation for his losses under the jewelry insurance policy issued by Lloyd's. The action was tried before a jury from October 29 through November 5, 1984. The jury rendered four special verdicts, all favorable to Dadurian: that Dadurian had been robbed on April 12, 1980; that he had not given false answers or information on any material subject when he was examined under oath before the commencement of this suit; that he had not made any false statement or fraudulent claims as to any of the 12 jewelry items for which he claimed a loss; and that the total fair market value of all the jewelry on April 12, 1980, was $267,000. Judgment was entered for plaintiff in the amount of $267,000 with interest.

Pursuant to Fed.R.Civ.P. 50, Lloyd's moved for judgment n.o.v. or, in the alternative, for a new trial. The district court denied defendant's motion, and this appeal followed.

II.

Lloyd's argues on appeal that Dadurian swore falsely, and necessarily knowingly, with respect to at least two key issues, and that either instance of false swearing was sufficient to void the insurance policy. First, Dadurian is said to have clearly lied in asserting that he purchased and owned the 12 pieces of jewelry for which he later obtained the insurance; and second, he is said to have knowingly lied in telling Lloyd's, at the formal examination under oath conducted before this action was begun, that the cash he used to purchase the jewelry came from certain bank loans. Lloyd's contends that evidence presented at trial was so overwhelmingly against Dadurian on both these issues that no reasonable jury could have rendered a verdict in his favor.

A. The Purchase of the Jewelry

Pointing to the suspicious absence of documentation for any of the jewelry purchases, Lloyd's asserts that the record shows that Dadurian had sworn falsely when he testified to having purchased the jewelry at all. Dadurian procured the Lloyd's insurance on the basis of written appraisals executed by Howe, the man from whom he allegedly purchased all 12 pieces. But he obtained no receipts nor did Howe have any records of the alleged sales to Dadurian. Moreover, although Dadurian testified to specific dates and prices paid for each of his jewelry purchases, in support of his story of ownership, his testimony that he had obtained that information from Howe's records was contradicted by testimony that Howe kept no such records.

But whatever may be thought of Dadurian's story, we cannot say, as a matter of law, that no jury could have properly found that Dadurian had purchased the jewelry as he claimed. Nor can we say the verdict on this issue was so far contrary to the clear weight of the evidence as, by itself, to provide grounds for our ordering the district court to grant a new trial. Not only did Howe testify at trial that he sold each one of the jewelry pieces to Dadurian at the prices Dadurian claimed, but Howe's employees, Cheryl Cousineau and Edward Proulx, gave testimony which, in material respects, tended to support the story that Dadurian purchased at least some jewelry items from Howe with cash. And Howe and Cousineau testified that they did not usually give receipts for cash purchases of "investment jewelry" or of jewelry sold "on consignment," thus tending to explain why Dadurian had no receipts. Despite extensive cross-examination by counsel for Lloyd's, the jury apparently chose to credit the testimony of Dadurian and his witnesses, and the jury was entitled to overlook the lack of any documentation for the purchases.

B. The Source of the Funds

Lloyd's also argues that Dadurian knowingly lied under oath at the formal examination when he swore that certain specific bank loans were the source of the cash he used to buy the jewelry. If Dadurian swore falsely and knowingly on this issue, he is not entitled to recover under the insurance contract. This is so because under the Lloyd's policy Dadurian was required to give "such information and evidence as to the property lost and the circumstances of the Loss as the Underwriters may reasonably require and as may be in the Assured's power"—and it is undisputed that under the policy, as well as under established case law, knowingly false testimony by Dadurian as to any fact considered "material" to his claim voids the policy.

The district court instructed the jury, and Dadurian does not dispute, that the issue of where he obtained the cash used for his jewelry purchases was "material" to his claim. To be considered material, a statement need not "relate[ ] to a matter or subject which ultimately proves to be decisive or significant in the ultimate disposition of the claim"; rather, it is sufficient if the statement was reasonably relevant to the insurance company's investigation of a claim. We agree that where Dadurian got the cash was material to his insurance claim, since Dadurian insisted that he paid Howe a total of $233,000 in cash over a 30-month period for the jewelry, and the credibility of this story, and hence of Dadurian's ownership of the insured items, turned in part on his ability to explain plausibly where he obtained such large sums of cash.[5]

The details of Dadurian's testimony about the bank loans are as follows: Soon after the alleged robbery of the jewelry items in April 1980, Dadurian was interviewed by an adjuster for Lloyd's. At this initial interview Dadurian, to explain the sources of his cash, stated that he "may have borrowed from the bank for the purchase of certain of the personal items of jewelry and [would] check [his] records in this regard." He later submitted to Lloyd's certain promissory notes which he contended represented the bank loans used to finance many of his purchases. Apparently still dissatisfied with the information provided by Dadurian, Lloyd's notified Dadurian in a letter dated August 18, 1980, that he would be required to appear at a formal examination under oath for further questioning at which time he "should be prepared to produce . . . all documents in any way relating to the occurrence of the loss. . . ."

At the first examination session on September 10, 1980, and again at the second session on May 28, 1981, when he was examined under oath by counsel for Lloyd's, Dadurian testified to the effect that most of his cash had come from loans from the Rhode Island Hospital Trust National Bank ("Hospital Trust").[7] During the two sessions, Dadurian was specifically questioned in turn about the sources of the cash used to purchase each one of the jewelry pieces. For 11 of the 12 items, Dadurian identified the individual promissory notes of his—by date and by loan amount—that purportedly represented the bank loans he said was used to finance his purchases. In total, he identified 13 specific bank loans as the source of $166,000 of the $233,000 which he claimed to have paid to Howe.

At trial, however, Richard Niedzwiadek, an employee of the bank, testified that the loans associated with four of the jewelry pieces, totaling $49,500, were simply renewals of earlier loans which could not have generated any cash for Dadurian. He also produced bank statements for Dadurian's accounts at Hospital Trust showing that the proceeds from several other loans which Dadurian had identified as having financed a number of the jewelry pieces had been deposited in those accounts and

---

[5] Lloyd's was understandably interested in hearing Dadurian's explanation of the source of his cash, particularly when it discovered that in 1978, the year Dadurian allegedly bought four of the twelve jewelry items for a total of $90,000 in cash, his income as reported in his federal tax return was only about $3,000.

[7] Dadurian testified during his September 1980 examination as follows:

If you want to know how I wound up with the cash, how all this jewelry was paid up in cash, how I got all the cash for the jewelry, the insurance company has copies of these. (indicating) These are all bank notes. When a good piece of jewelry came along for the right price, which I had to pay for in cash, I went to the bank. I borrowed from the bank, borrowed the money on notes, and the [insurance] company has these copies which you may take them if you like, and you may make copies of them. That's how I purchased the jewelry.

* * *

I have a quarter of a million dollars loss, and the money came from here from bank notes. I still owe this bank. I borrowed this money, and it's as simple as that.

then withdrawn in too small amounts over a period of time to have been used for purchasing the jewelry as Dadurian claimed. Niedzwiadek further testified that the proceeds of yet another loan supposedly associated with a jewelry item had been deposited in the corporate account of a company named U.S. Enterprises, Inc., and that Dadurian had stated the purpose of the loan as "real estate investment." Confronted with this cumulative evidence, Dadurian essentially conceded that some, if not most, of the promissory notes he had selected had been the wrong ones, and that his testimony as to the sources of the funds was therefore in part false. He insisted, however, that he had selected the notes "to the best of [his] recollection" and that he had been honestly mistaken.

Since it is thus uncontroverted that a substantial number of Dadurian's representations under oath about the sources of his cash were untrue, the only remaining question is whether Dadurian made these false statements knowingly or whether he was simply mistaken in good faith as he claims. False swearing is "swearing knowingly and intentionally false and not through mere mistake." Black's Law Dictionary 725 (rev. 5th ed. 1979). Lloyd's forcefully contends that where Dadurian testified with such certainty, yet incorrectly, about so many of his own promissory notes and bank loans, the inference of intentional falsehood is so compelling as to render the jury's finding contrary, at very least, to the great weight of the evidence.

After carefully considering the entire record, we find that the great weight of the evidence indicates overwhelmingly that Dadurian knew he was giving false testimony. At the formal examination under oath Dadurian specifically identified 13 promissory notes, apparently from those he had given Lloyd's sometime before the examination, and explicitly linked each note to a particular jewelry purchase. He did not qualify his identifications, but rather couched his testimony in terms of misleading certainty. Only when confronted at trial with the patent falsity of his earlier testimony did Dadurian testify, by way of explanation, that he had made his selections only to the "best of his recollection" in order to satisfy the insurance company's inquiries. It was only then that he explained that because he had "files and files" of such notes in his possession, he must have simply selected the wrong ones under pressure of time and circumstances.

This explanation strains credulity. This was not a case where Dadurian was confronted for the first time at the examination with "files and files" of his promissory notes and asked to come up with correct ones "on the spot." Rather it was Dadurian himself who originated and put forward the story that most of his cash had come from bank loans, and it was Dadurian who apparently first tendered the supposedly relevant promissory notes to Lloyd's at some time before the formal examination. Dadurian admitted at trial that he had known before the first examination session that he would be questioned further about the bank loans. He apparently marked each of the notes before the examination sessions with the number of the jewelry piece with which it was supposedly associated. By the first session in September

1980, and certainly by the May 1981 session, Dadurian had had ample notice as well as opportunity to discover the correct promissory notes or, if he found he was wrong or in doubt, to say so. The uncontested facts simply belie Dadurian's excuse that he was pressured into making identifications prematurely.

Dadurian had much to gain by providing a plausible explanation for the sources of his cash. By piecing together notes executed on dates close to the times of the alleged purchases, he could hope to create an impression of credibility. That he linked the notes to the jewelry purchases so positively—without bothering to ascertain readily available information showing that they were not so related—indicates, at the least, a wilful misrepresentation as to the state of his own knowledge concerning the matters to which he was testifying. We think the only fair inference from this kind of total indifference to the truth or falsity of his assertions was that Dadurian knew that he was not telling the truth.

It follows, we believe, that the jury's verdict was against the clear weight of the evidence insofar as it found that Dadurian did not knowingly give false answers or information on any material subject when he was examined under oath before commencement of this suit.[11] We emphasize that Dadurian himself conceded that some of his answers were incorrect, and it is clear the district court properly found them "material." This leaves open only the question of their possible innocence, which, to be sure, Dadurian attested to—but with implausible explanations as to why he put forward these patently unfounded and incorrect assertions. We conclude that the jury's finding that Dadurian did not give knowingly false answers was contrary to the great weight of the evidence. For that aspect of the verdict to stand would, in our view, amount to a manifest miscarriage of justice. We hold, therefore, that the district court abused its discretion in denying defendant's motion for a new trial, and remand the case for retrial by a new jury.

We are mindful of the alternative plea by Lloyd's that we should reverse the court's refusal to grant a judgment n.o.v. and, in effect, direct a finding for Lloyd's rather than order a new trial. Whether to do so is a very close question. A factor weighing against this alternative is that Lloyd's had the burden of proving that Dadurian was lying, and this circuit, like most courts, is reluctant to direct a verdict for the party having the burden of proof. The issue, moreover, involves a determination of credibility. Hence, even though we find it hard to see how a reasonable jury could reach any result other than that Dadurian was knowingly lying, we believe that the more appropriate relief is a new trial.

---

[11] It strikes us that the jury may not have paid sufficient attention to determining whether Dadurian had knowingly lied as to the sources of his cash. There were many issues raised at trial. Once the jury concluded that Dadurian had indeed purchased the jewelry as he alleged, it could have thought that the issue of Dadurian's false swearing as to the bank loans was a mere technicality. But, as we discussed, a finding that Dadurian had knowingly given false testimony as to any material fact voids the policy just as a finding that Dadurian had not owned the jewelry would have voided it. It is possible that the jury, despite instructions in the jury charge to the contrary, decided on its own that since Lloyd's had insured the jewelry it should pay for its loss, regardless of whether Dadurian lied as to the source of his funds.

A remaining question is whether the new trial should encompass both the issue of Dadurian's ownership of the jewelry and the issue of his knowingly false testimony as to the sources of his funds. We hold that it should, even though it was on the latter issue that the district court erred. Dadurian's credibility is cast into serious doubt by our finding that the clear weight of the evidence shows that he must have knowingly lied about a material issue. It follows that this loss of credibility necessarily affects the jury finding in Dadurian's favor on the issue of his jewelry purchases, since Dadurian was his own main witness for all aspects of his story. A new trial as to both issues also makes sense since the issue of where Dadurian obtained the cash to make his purchases is so interrelated with the question of whether Dadurian bought the jewelry he claimed as to make it difficult to hold a meaningful trial on the first without the second.

Food for Thought

After *Unitherm*, studied previously in this chapter, would an appeals court be permitted to direct a verdict based on its view of the sufficiency of the evidence? *See Unitherm Food Sys., Inc. v. Swift-Eckrich, Inc., 546 U.S. 394, 400–01 (2006)* ("This Court has concluded that, in the absence of [a Rule 50(b)] motion an appellate court is without the power to direct the District Court to enter judgment contrary to the one it had permitted to stand." (citation and internal quotation marks omitted)).

Vacated and remanded for a new trial.

Points for Discussion

a. The Standard for Granting a New Trial

In *Dadurian*, the court granted a new trial because the jury's verdict was against the great weight of the evidence, even though the court acknowledged that there was sufficient evidence to prevent the court from entering judgment as a matter of law. What does that tell you about the difference between the standard for entering judgment as a matter of law and the standard for ordering a new trial?

The key difference is between concepts of "legal sufficiency" of the evidence and the "weight of the evidence." Courts may not weigh the evidence when considering whether to enter judgment as a matter of law, out of deference to the jury right. Their task in this context is to determine whether there is evidence on which a reasonable jury could base a verdict. *See* 9B C. WRIGHT & A. MILLER, FED. PRAC. & PROC. § 2521 (3d ed. 2008) ("[Rule 50] allows the court to remove from the jury's consideration cases or issues when the facts are sufficiently clear that the law requires a particular result."). However, when considering whether to grant a new trial, courts are permitted to weigh the evidence and judge the credibility of the witnesses. *See,* *e.g., Pierce v. Moore,* No. 1:11-CV-132, 2015 WL 10906058, at *1 (E.D. Mo. Apr. 2, 2015) ("When addressing a motion for new trial, the court can weigh the evidence, disbelieve witnesses, and grant a new trial even where there is substantial evidence to sustain the verdict." (citation and internal quotation marks omitted)). If the court concludes that a mistake has been made because the weight of the evidence is against the jury's verdict, it can order a new trial. 11 C. WRIGHT & A. MILLER, FED. PRAC. & PROC. § 2806 (3d ed. 2012) ("If, having given full respect to the jury's findings, the judge on the entire evidence is left with the definite and firm conviction that a mistake has

> **FYI**
>
> Like the renewed motion for judgment as a matter of law, a motion for a new trial must be sought no later than 28 days after entry of judgment. FED. R. CIV. P. 50(b). Unlike the renewed motion for JMOL, a court may order a new trial *sua sponte,* without a previous motion, so long as it is done within 28 days of the entry of judgment. FED. R. CIV. P. 59(d).

been committed, it is to be expected that the judge will grant a new trial."). Ordering a new trial does not offend the jury right because the result is the grant of a new jury trial, not the entry of judgment.

Other grounds for ordering a new trial exist: The court may feel that the damages awarded are excessive, that the conduct of the trial itself was somehow unfair to the moving party, or that there were substantial legal errors pertaining to the admission or exclusion of evidence or the content of instructions to the jury. *See Montgomery Ward & Co. v. Duncan,* 311 U.S. 243, 251 (1940). *See also Advance Sign Grp., L.L.C. v. Optec Displays, Inc.,* 722 F.3d 778, 787 (6th Cir. 2013) ("We have interpreted Rule 59 to require a new trial only when a jury has reached a seriously erroneous result as evidenced by (1) the verdict being against the weight of the evidence; (2) the damages being excessive; or (3) the trial being unfair to the moving party in some fashion, i.e., the proceedings being influenced by prejudice or bias." (citations and internal quotation marks omitted)); *United States v. Thompson,* 908 F.2d 648, 650 (10th Cir. 1990) (new trial warranted where jury was exposed to prejudicial external information). The

> **Take Note!**
>
> Under a principle known as "Mansfield's Rule" a jury verdict may not be impeached by juror testimony as to internal deliberations. This traditional common-law rule is now codified in Federal Rule of Evidence 606(b). See also *Warger v. Shauers,* 135 S. Ct. 521, 527 (2014) ("As enacted, Rule 606(b) prohibited the use of *any* evidence of juror deliberations, subject only to the express exceptions for extraneous information and outside influences."). However, in *Pena-Rodriguez v. Colorado,* 137 S. Ct. 855 (2017), the Supreme Court permitted affidavits from jurors testifying to the racial bias of another fellow juror to be admitted as evidence in support of a new trial motion in a criminal case, holding that the Sixth Amendment right to an impartial jury in criminal cases trumped Rule 606(b).

discovery of new evidence may also provide grounds for ordering a new trial provided the evidence existed at the time of trial, was not previously overlooked due to a lack of diligence, and would have been admissible and material. *See* <u>Henley v. FMC Corp., 189 F.R.D. 340, 349–50 (S.D. W. Va. 1999)</u> (ordering new trial on grounds of newly discovered evidence).

b. Harmless Error

What may not serve as grounds for a new trial is the presence of evidentiary errors that do not cause substantial harm to a party, so-called "harmless errors." This is a limitation set forth in <u>Federal Rule 61</u>: "Unless justice requires otherwise, no error in admitting or excluding evidence . . . is ground for granting a new trial, for setting aside a verdict, or for vacating, modifying, or otherwise disturbing a judgment or order. At every stage of the proceeding, the court must disregard all errors and defects that do not affect any party's substantial rights." *See, e.g.*, <u>Tesser v. Bd. of Educ., 370 F.3d 314, 319 (2d Cir. 2004)</u> ("[A]n evidentiary error in a civil case is harmless unless the appellant demonstrates that it is likely that in some material respect the factfinder's judgment was swayed by the error." (citation and internal quotation marks omitted)); <u>Peat, Inc. v. Vanguard Research, Inc., 378 F.3d 1154, 1162 (11th Cir. 2004)</u> ("Our cases, consistent with Rule 61 of the Federal Rules of Civil Procedure, hold that a new trial is warranted only where [an] error has caused substantial prejudice to the affected party . . . .").

c. Remittitur & Additur

When the court feels that the damages award is so excessive that it "shocks the conscience," rather than ordering a new trial the court can give the prevailing party the option of accepting a reduced, more appropriate damages award or face a new trial. In such a situation, the prevailing party is faced with a difficult choice: take less than a jury has awarded or face a new trial in which it may lose entirely. This practice is referred to as remittitur. The converse practice—asking a losing defendant to accept a verdict for a *higher amount* or face a new trial because the court feels that the damages are shockingly inadequate—has been declared unconstitutional in the federal system. *See* <u>Dimick v. Schiedt, 293 U.S. 474, 486–87 (1935)</u>. This prohibited practice is called additur. Why do you think additur is unconstitutional? Why isn't remittitur unconstitutional? *See* <u>Hetzel v. Prince William Cnty., 523 U.S. 208 (1998)</u>; *see also* Suja A. Thomas, *Re-Examining the Constitutionality of Remittitur Under the Seventh Amendment*, <u>64 Ohio St. L.J. 731 (2003)</u> (suggesting the unconstitutionality of remittitur).

Although additur may be unconstitutional in the federal system, there is no prohibition against its use in state court, and some states have empowered courts to increase jury awards deemed to be inadequate. *See, e.g.*, <u>Fla. Stat. § 768.74(2)</u> ("If the court finds that the amount awarded is excessive or inadequate, it shall order a remittitur or additur, as the case may be.").

Because of the need to respect the jury right and the trial court's superior knowledge of the evidence in a case, interesting issues surround appellate review of trial court judgments for sufficiency or weight of the evidence issues. In the next case, the Supreme Court had to address an appellate court's ability to enter a new trial or a judgment as a matter of law itself without having to remand the case to the trial court to make that determination.

Weisgram v. Marley Co.

Supreme Court of the United States
528 U.S. 440 (2000)

JUSTICE GINSBURG delivered the opinion of the Court.

This case concerns the respective authority of federal trial and appellate courts to decide whether, as a matter of law, judgment should be entered in favor of a verdict loser. The pattern we confront is this. Plaintiff in a product liability action gains a jury verdict. Defendant urges, unsuccessfully before the federal district court but successfully on appeal, that expert testimony plaintiff introduced was unreliable, and therefore inadmissible, under the analysis required by *Daubert v. Merrell Dow Pharmaceuticals, Inc.*, 509 U.S. 579 (1993). Shorn of the erroneously admitted expert testimony, the record evidence is insufficient to justify a plaintiff's verdict. May the court of appeals then instruct the entry of judgment as a matter of law for defendant, or must that tribunal remand the case, leaving to the district court's discretion the choice between final judgment for defendant or a new trial of plaintiff's case?

Make the Connection

The admissibility of expert testimony and the *Daubert* standard referenced in the text are matters one would study in a basic **Evidence** course.

Our decision is guided by Federal Rule of Civil Procedure 50, which governs the entry of judgment as a matter of law, and by the Court's pathmarking opinion in *Neely v. Martin K. Eby Constr. Co.*, 386 U.S. 317 (1967). As *Neely* teaches, courts of appeals should "be constantly alert" to "the trial judge's first-hand knowledge of witnesses, testimony, and issues"; in other words, appellate courts should give due consideration to the first-instance decisionmaker's "'feel' for the overall case." But the court of appeals has authority to render the final decision. If, in the particular case, the appellate tribunal determines that the district court is better positioned to decide whether a new trial, rather than judgment for defendant, should be ordered, the court of appeals should return the case to the trial court for such an assessment.

But if, as in the instant case, the court of appeals concludes that further proceedings are unwarranted because the loser on appeal has had a full and fair opportunity to present the case, including arguments for a new trial, the appellate court may appropriately instruct the district court to enter judgment against the jury-verdict winner. Appellate authority to make this determination is no less when the evidence is rendered insufficient by the removal of erroneously admitted testimony than it is when the evidence, without any deletion, is insufficient.

I

Firefighters arrived at the home of Bonnie Weisgram on December 30, 1993, to discover flames around the front entrance. Upon entering the home, they found Weisgram in an upstairs bathroom, dead of carbon monoxide poisoning. Her son, petitioner Chad Weisgram, individually and on behalf of Bonnie Weisgram's heirs, brought a diversity action in the United States District Court for the District of North Dakota seeking wrongful death damages. He alleged that a defect in an electric baseboard heater, manufactured by defendant * * * Marley Company and located inside the door to Bonnie Weisgram's home, caused both the fire and his mother's death.

At trial, Weisgram introduced the testimony of three witnesses, proffered as experts, in an endeavor to prove the alleged defect in the heater and its causal connection to the fire. The District Court overruled defendant Marley's objections, lodged both before and during the trial, that this testimony was unreliable and therefore inadmissible under Federal Rule of Evidence 702 as elucidated by *Daubert*. At the close of Weisgram's evidence, and again at the close of all the evidence, Marley unsuccessfully moved under Federal Rule of Civil Procedure 50(a) for judgment as a matter of law on the ground that plaintiffs had failed to meet their burden of proof on the issues of defect and causation. The jury returned a verdict for Weisgram.

Marley again requested judgment as a matter of law, and additionally requested, in the alternative, a new trial, pursuant to Rules 50 and 59; among arguments in support of its post-trial motions, Marley reasserted that the expert testimony essential to prove Weisgram's case was unreliable and therefore inadmissible. The District Court denied the motions and entered judgment for Weisgram. Marley appealed.

The Court of Appeals for the Eighth Circuit held that Marley's motion for judgment as a matter of law

Practice Pointer

Notice that Marley sought judgment as a matter of law on three occasions: at the close of the plaintiff's case, at the close of all the evidence before the case went to the jury, and after the jury returned its verdict. This is the best practice under the rules because, as we have learned, failure to seek judgment as a matter of law at the appropriate times can result in a waiver of sufficiency of evidence challenges after the verdict and on appeal.

should have been granted. Writing for the panel majority, Chief Judge Bowman first examined the testimony of Weisgram's expert witnesses, the sole evidence supporting plaintiffs' product defect charge. Concluding that the testimony was speculative and not shown to be scientifically sound, the majority held the expert evidence incompetent to prove Weisgram's case. The court then considered the remaining evidence in the light most favorable to Weisgram, found it insufficient to support the jury verdict, and directed judgment as a matter of law for Marley. In a footnote, the majority "reject[ed] any contention that [it was] required to remand for a new trial." It recognized its discretion to do so under Rule 50(d), but stated: "[W]e can discern no reason to give the plaintiffs a second chance to make out a case of strict liability . . . . This is not a close case. The plaintiffs had a fair opportunity to prove their claim and they failed to do so." The dissenting judge disagreed on both points, concluding that the expert evidence was properly admitted and that the appropriate remedy for improper admission of expert testimony is the award of a new trial, not judgment as a matter of law.

Courts of Appeals have divided on the question whether Federal Rule of Civil Procedure 50 permits an appellate court to direct the entry of judgment as a matter of law when it determines that evidence was erroneously admitted at trial and that the remaining, properly admitted evidence is insufficient to constitute a submissible case. We granted certiorari to resolve the conflict, and we now affirm the Eighth Circuit's judgment.

II

Federal Rule of Civil Procedure 50 * * * governs motions for judgment as a matter of law in jury trials. It allows the trial court to remove cases or issues from the jury's consideration "when the facts are sufficiently clear that the law requires a particular result." 9A C. Wright & A. Miller, Federal Practice and Procedure § 2521, p. 240 (2d ed.1995) (hereinafter Wright & Miller). Subdivision (d) controls when, as here, the verdict loser appeals from the trial court's denial of a motion for judgment as a matter of law:

> "[T]he party who prevailed on that motion may, as appellee, assert grounds entitling the party to a new trial in the event the appellate court concludes that the trial court erred in denying the motion for judgment. If the appellate court reverses the judgment, nothing in this rule precludes it from determining that the appellee is entitled to a new trial, or from directing the trial court to determine whether a new trial shall be granted."

Under this Rule, Weisgram urges, when a court of appeals determines that a jury verdict cannot be sustained due to an error in the admission of evidence, the appellate court may not order the entry of judgment for the verdict loser, but must instead remand the case to the trial court for a new trial determination. Nothing in Rule 50 expressly addresses this question.

In a series of pre-1967 decisions, this Court refrained from deciding the question, while emphasizing the importance of giving the party deprived of a verdict the opportunity to invoke the discretion of the trial judge to grant a new trial. Then, in *Neely*, the Court reviewed its prior jurisprudence and ruled definitively that if a motion for judgment as a matter of law is erroneously denied by the district court, the appellate court does have the power to order the entry of judgment for the moving party.

Neely first addressed the compatibility of appellate direction of judgment as a matter of law (then styled "judgment n.o.v.") with the Seventh Amendment's jury trial guarantee. It was settled, the Court pointed out, that a trial court, pursuant to Rule 50(b), could enter judgment for the verdict loser without offense to the Seventh Amendment. 386 U.S., at 321 (citing *Montgomery Ward & Co. v. Duncan, 311 U.S. 243 (1940)*). "As far as the Seventh Amendment's right to jury trial is concerned," the Court reasoned, "there is no greater restriction on the province of the jury when an appellate court enters judgment n.o.v. than when a trial court does"; accordingly, the Court concluded, "there is no constitutional bar to an appellate court granting judgment n.o.v." 386 U.S., at 322 (citing *Baltimore & Carolina Line v. Redman, 295 U.S. 654 (1935)*). The Court next turned to "the statutory grant of appellate jurisdiction to the courts of appeals [in 28 U.S.C. § 2106],"[6] which it found "certainly broad enough to include the power to direct entry of judgment n.o.v. on appeal." The remainder of the *Neely* opinion effectively complements Rules 50(c) and 50(d), providing guidance on the appropriate exercise of the appellate court's discretion when it reverses the trial court's denial of a defendant's Rule 50(b) motion for judgment as a matter of law.

Neely represents no *volte-face* in the Court's understanding of the respective competences of trial and appellate forums. Immediately after declaring that appellate courts have the power to order the entry of judgment for a verdict loser, the Court cautioned:

"Part of the Court's concern has been to protect the rights of the party whose jury verdict has been set aside on appeal and who may have valid grounds for a new trial, some or all of which should be passed upon by the district court, rather than the court of appeals, because of the trial judge's

---

[6] Section 2106 reads:

"The Supreme Court or any other court of appellate jurisdiction may affirm, modify, vacate, set aside or reverse any judgment, decree, or order of a court lawfully brought before it for review, and may remand the cause and direct the entry of such appropriate judgment, decree, or order, or require such further proceedings to be had as may be just under the circumstances."

first-hand knowledge of witnesses, testimony, and issues—because of his 'feel' for the overall case. These are very valid concerns to which the court of appeals should be constantly alert." 386 U.S., at 325.

Nevertheless, the Court in *Neely* continued, due consideration of the rights of the verdict winner and the closeness of the trial court to the case "do[es] not justify an ironclad rule that the court of appeals should never order dismissal or judgment for the defendant when the plaintiff's verdict has been set aside on appeal." "Such a rule," the Court concluded, "would not serve the purpose of Rule 50 to speed litigation and to avoid unnecessary retrials." *Neely* ultimately clarified that if a court of appeals determines that the district court erroneously denied a motion for judgment as a matter of law, the appellate court may (1) order a new trial at the verdict winner's request or on its own motion, (2) remand the case for the trial court to decide whether a new trial or entry of judgment for the defendant is warranted, or (3) direct the entry of judgment as a matter of law for the defendant.

III

The parties before us—and Court of Appeals opinions—diverge regarding *Neely*'s scope. Weisgram, in line with some appellate decisions, posits a distinction between cases in which judgment as a matter of law is requested based on plaintiff's failure to produce enough evidence to warrant a jury verdict, as in *Neely*, and cases in which the proof introduced becomes insufficient because the court of appeals determines that certain evidence should not have been admitted, as in the instant case. Insufficiency caused by deletion of evidence, Weisgram contends, requires an "automatic remand" to the district court for consideration whether a new trial is warranted.

Food for Thought

Neely clearly permits an appellate court to enter judgment as a matter of law in favor of the verdict loser if it feels that the trial court erroneously denied the motion. Why should appeals courts be unable to do so when they determine that the evidence is insufficient because certain evidence should have been excluded, as Weisgram argues here?

Weisgram relies on cases holding that, in fairness to a verdict winner who may have relied on erroneously admitted evidence, courts confronting questions of judgment as a matter of law should rule on the record as it went to the jury, without excising evidence inadmissible under Federal Rule of Evidence 702. These decisions are of questionable consistency with Rule 50(a)(1), which states that in ruling on a motion for judgment as a matter of law, the court is to inquire whether there is any "legally sufficient evidentiary basis for a reasonable jury to find for [the opponent of the motion]." Inadmissible evidence contributes nothing to a "legally sufficient evidentiary basis."[10]

As *Neely* recognized, appellate rulings on post-trial pleas for judgment as a matter of law call for the exercise of "informed discretion," and fairness to the parties is surely key to the exercise of that discretion. But fairness concerns should loom as large when the verdict winner, in the appellate court's judgment, failed to present sufficient evidence as when the appellate court declares inadmissible record evidence essential to the verdict winner's case. In both situations, the party whose verdict is set aside on appeal will have had notice, before the close of evidence, of the alleged evidentiary deficiency. *See* <u>FED. RULE CIV. PROC. 50(a)(2)</u> (motion for judgment as a matter of law "shall specify . . . the law and facts on which the moving party is entitled to the judgment"). On appeal, both will have the opportunity to argue in support of the jury's verdict or, alternatively, for a new trial. And if judgment is instructed for the verdict loser, both will have a further chance to urge a new trial in a rehearing petition.[11]

What's That?

The *rehearing petition* referred to here is the petition that the losing party before the appeals court may file to have their matter reconsidered by the circuit court *en banc*. *See* <u>FED. R. APP. P. 35</u>.

Since *Daubert*, moreover, parties relying on expert evidence have had notice of the exacting standards of reliability such evidence must meet. It is implausible to suggest, post-*Daubert*, that parties will initially present less than their best expert evidence in the expectation of a second chance should their first try fail. We therefore find unconvincing Weisgram's fears that allowing courts of appeals to direct the entry of judgment for defendants will punish plaintiffs who could have shored up their cases by other means had they known their expert testimony would be found inadmissible. In this case, for example, although Weisgram was on notice every step

---

[10] Weisgram additionally urges that the Seventh Amendment prohibits a court of appeals from directing judgment as a matter of law on a record different from the one considered by the jury. *Neely* made clear that a court of appeals may order entry of judgment as a matter of law on sufficiency-of-the-evidence grounds without violating the Seventh Amendment. Entering judgment for the verdict loser when all of the evidence was properly before the jury is scarcely less destructive of the jury's verdict than is entry of such a judgment based on a record made insufficient by the removal of evidence the jury should not have had before it.

[11] We recognize that it is awkward for an appellee, who is wholeheartedly urging the correctness of the verdict, to point out, in the alternative, grounds for a new trial. A petition for rehearing in the court of appeals, however, involves no conflicting tugs. We are not persuaded by Weisgram's objection that the 14 days allowed for the filing of a petition for rehearing is insufficient time to formulate compelling grounds for a new trial. This time period is longer than the ten days allowed a verdict winner to move for a new trial after a trial court grants judgment as a matter of law. *See* <u>FED. RULE CIV. PROC. 50(c)(2)</u>. Nor do we foreclose the possibility that a court of appeals might properly deny a petition for rehearing because it pressed an argument that plainly could have been formulated in a party's brief. [Rule 50 has since been amended to provide, in Rule 50(d), for 28 days to file a new trial motion. Rule 59(b) contains the same requirement. Ed.]

of the way that Marley was challenging his experts, he made no attempt to add or substitute other evidence.

After holding Weisgram's expert testimony inadmissible, the Court of Appeals evaluated the evidence presented at trial, viewing it in the light most favorable to Weisgram, and found the properly admitted evidence insufficient to support the verdict. Weisgram offered no specific grounds for a new trial to the Eighth Circuit. Even in the petition for rehearing, Weisgram argued only that the appellate court had misapplied state law, did not have the authority to direct judgment, and had failed to give adequate deference to the trial court's evidentiary rulings. The Eighth Circuit concluded that this was "not a close case." In these circumstances, the Eighth Circuit did not abuse its discretion by directing entry of judgment for Marley, instead of returning the case to the District Court for further proceedings.

* * *

Neely recognized that there are myriad situations in which the determination whether a new trial is in order is best made by the trial judge. *Neely* held, however, that there are also cases in which a court of appeals may appropriately instruct the district court to enter judgment as a matter of law against the jury-verdict winner. We adhere to *Neely*'s holding and rationale, and today hold that the authority of courts of appeals to direct the entry of judgment as a matter of law extends to cases in which, on excision of testimony erroneously admitted, there remains insufficient evidence to support the jury's verdict.

For the reasons stated, the judgment of the Court of Appeals for the Eighth Circuit is

Affirmed.

Points for Discussion

a. *Weisgram* and *Unitherm*

Recall that in *Unitherm Food Sys., Inc. v. Swift-Eckrich, Inc.*, 546 U.S. 394 (2006), the Court held that appellate courts were without power to enter judgment or to order a new trial in the absence of a postverdict renewal of a motion for judgment as a matter of law under Rule 50(b). *Weisgram* seems to affirm the authority of appellate courts to enter such orders under certain circmstances. Can you identify the distinction between the two cases or are they inconsistent with one another? *See Unitherm*, 546 U.S. at 401 n.3.

b. **The Relationship Between Rule 50 and Rule 59 Motions**

As *Weisgram* and other previous cases illustrate, the renewed motion for judgment as a matter of law and the motion for a new trial are frequently made together. More importantly, Rule 50 indicates that when faced with both motions, the district court must decide both of them. Subsections (c) and (e) of Rule 50 then specify how the court should proceed depending upon whether it grants or denies the motion for judgment as a matter of law:

> **FRCP 50(c) & (e). Judgment as a Matter of Law in a Jury Trial; Related Motion for a New Trial; Conditional Ruling.**
>
> (c) **Granting the Renewed Motion; Conditional Ruling on a Motion for a New Trial.**
>
> (1) *In General.* If the court grants a renewed motion for judgment as a matter of law, it must also conditionally rule on any motion for a new trial by determining whether a new trial should be granted if the judgment is later vacated or reversed. The court must state the grounds for conditionally granting or denying the motion for a new trial.
>
> * * *
>
> (e) **Denying the Motion for Judgment as a Matter of Law; Reversal on Appeal.** If the court denies the motion for judgment as a matter of law, the prevailing party may, as appellee, assert grounds entitling it to a new trial should the appellate court conclude that the trial court erred in denying the motion. If the appellate court reverses the judgment, it may order a new trial, direct the trial court to determine whether a new trial should be granted, or direct the entry of judgment.

Weisgram presented the latter situation. Indeed, the appeals court in *Weisgram* concluded that the trial court erred in denying the motion for judgment as a matter of law and then entered judgment without remanding the case to the trial court. It was that act that the Supreme Court in *Weisgram* upheld. Was that the right decision or is there a principled basis for distinguishing *Neely* from the situation presented in *Weisgram*?

c. **Appellate Review of New Trial Rulings**

If a litigant is interested in obtaining a new trial, one must be sought first in the district court. *Unitherm Food Sys., Inc. v. Swift-Eckrich, Inc.*, 546 U.S. 394, 404 (2006) ("[A] party is not entitled to pursue a new trial on appeal unless that party makes an appropriate postverdict motion in the district court."). To what extent should appeals courts be permitted to scrutinize district court decisions regarding whether to order a new trial? Appeals courts may review district court decisions to grant a new trial—either after the completion of the new trial or immediately if certified for interlocutory appeal under 28 U.S.C. § 1292(b)*—but such review is for abuse of

---

* Section 1292(b) "is to be used only in extraordinary cases where decision of an interlocutory appeal might avoid protracted and expensive litigation." *U.S. Rubber Co. v. Wright*, 359 F.2d 784, 785 (9th. Cir. 1966). [Ed.]

discretion, a highly deferential standard of review. *See Browning-Ferris Indus. of Vt., Inc. v. Kelco Disposal, Inc.*, 492 U.S. 257, 279 (1989) ("[T]he role of the district court is to determine whether the jury's verdict is within the confines set by state law, and to determine, by reference to federal standards developed under Rule 59, whether a new trial or remittitur should be ordered. The court of appeals should then review the district court's determination under an abuse-of-discretion standard."). *See also Christopher v. Florida*, 449 F.3d 1360, 1365 (11th Cir. 2006) ("We review the trial court's grant of a new trial for abuse of discretion."); *Mayhue v. St. Francis Hosp. of Wichita, Inc.*, 969 F.2d 919, 922 (10th Cir. 1992) ("[W]e will reverse the court's decision only if we have a definite and firm conviction that the lower court made a clear error of judgment or exceeded the bounds of permissible choice in the circumstances." (citation and internal quotation marks omitted)).

What about trial court decisions to deny a new trial? Should appeals courts be able to review and reverse such decisions? The Supreme Court has indicated that such review is possible, at least when assessing the excessiveness of the award, under the Seventh Amendment. *See Gasperini v. Ctr. for Humanities, Inc.*, 518 U.S. 415, 436 (1996) ("[N]othing in the Seventh Amendment precludes appellate review of the trial judge's denial of a motion to set aside a jury verdict as excessive." (citation omitted)). The circuit courts permit review of new trial denial in other contexts, although reversals of district court denials of new trials should be rare. *Weed v. City of Seattle*, No. 12-35191, 2013 WL 4620426, at *1 (9th Cir. Aug. 30, 2013) ("We review a district court's denial of a motion for a new trial for abuse of discretion and generally only reverse if the record contains no evidence in support of the verdict or if the district court made a mistake of law." (citing *Molski v. M.J. Cable, Inc.*, 481 F.3d 724, 728–29 (9th Cir. 2007))); *Howard v. Mo. Bone & Joint Ctr., Inc.*, 615 F.3d 991, 995 (8th Cir. 2010) ("Where the basis of the motion for a new trial is that the jury's verdict is against the weight of the evidence, the district court's denial of the motion is virtually unassailable on appeal." (citation and internal quotation marks omitted)). Are there any Seventh Amendment concerns that arise if an appeals court is able to throw out a jury verdict that the trial court has accepted? *See Gasperini v. Ctr. for Humanities, Inc.*, 518 U.S. 415, 461 (1996) (Scalia, J., dissenting) ("[I]t is not possible to review such a claim [an appeal of a denial of a new trial] without engaging in a 'reexamin[ation]' of the 'facts tried by the jury' in a manner 'otherwise' than allowed at common law.").

---

4. Relief from Judgment Under Rule 60(b)

Recall that Rule 59(b) requires that a new trial be sought "no later than 28 days after entry of the judgment." After that time has elapsed, the Federal Rules provide another means of getting the trial court to reconsider its decision—the motion for relief from judgment under Rule 60(b):

FRCP 60(b) & (c). Relief from a Judgment or Order.

(b) Grounds for Relief from a Final Judgment, Order, or Proceeding. On motion and just terms, the court may relieve a party or its legal representative from a final judgment, order, or proceeding for the following reasons:

(1) mistake, inadvertence, surprise, or excusable neglect;

(2) newly discovered evidence that, with reasonable diligence, could not have been discovered in time to move for a new trial under Rule 59(b);

(3) fraud (whether previously called intrinsic or extrinsic), misrepresentation, or misconduct by an opposing party;

(4) the judgment is void;

(5) the judgment has been satisfied, released, or discharged; it is based on an earlier judgment that has been reversed or vacated; or applying it prospectively is no longer equitable; or

(6) any other reason that justifies relief.

(c) Timing and Effect of the Motion.

(1) *Timing.* A motion under Rule 60(b) must be made within a reasonable time— and for reasons (1), (2), and (3) no more than a year after the entry of the judgment or order or the date of the proceeding. * * *

Relief under Rule 60(b) is rare. Once a court has entered a final judgment, our system's interest in finality weighs heavily against reopening the decision for reconsideration. *Gonzalez v. Crosby*, 545 U.S. 524, 535 (2005) ("[O]ur cases have required a movant seeking relief under Rule 60(b)(6) to show 'extraordinary circumstances' justifying the reopening of a final judgment." (citations omitted)). Thus, courts understand the provisions of Rule 60(b) in that light when interpreting and applying them. *See, e.g., Scutieri v. Paige*, 808 F.2d 785, 793 (11th Cir. 1987) ("A motion for a new trial under Rule 60(b)(2) is an extraordinary motion and the requirements of the rule must be strictly met.").

> **FYI**
>
> An example of a circumstance when relief under Rule 60(b)(5) would be appropriate is where there has been a substantial subsequent change in the law. *See, e.g., Prudential Ins. Co. of Am. v. Nat'l Park Med. Ctr., Inc.*, 413 F.3d 897 (8th Cir. 2005).

a. Timing for the Motion

Movants seeking relief for any of the first three reasons under Rule 60(b) must do so within a "reasonable time" and no more than one year after the entry of the final judgment. This time limit is jurisdictional, meaning that courts are not at liberty to extend it. *See Arrieta v. Battaglia*, 461 F.3d 861, 864–65 (7th Cir. 2006). However, motions for relief based on the remaining reasons need be made only within a "reasonable time." What constitutes a reasonable time under Rule 60(b)? *See Thai-Lao Lignite (Thailand) Co., v. Government of Lao People's Democratic Republic, 864 F.3d 172 (2d Cir. 2017)* (indicating that "reasonable time" in which a party must make a motion for relief from judgment "is to be determined based on the particular circumstances of the case, taking into account the reason for any delay, the possible prejudice to the non-moving party, and the interests of finality" (citation and internal quotation marks omitted)).

b. Mistake or Excusable Neglect

What considerations should warrant relief from judgment under Rule 60(b)(1), which permits relief from judgment in the face of mistake or excusable neglect? In *Pioneer Investment Services Co. v. Brunswick Associates Ltd. Partnership*, 507 U.S. 380 (1993), the Supreme Court identified several factors relevant to a Rule 60(b)(1)* determination in the context of a party's lack of diligence in prosecuting or defending an action: the risk of prejudice to the nonmovant, the length of the delay, the reason for the delay, including whether it was in the control of the movant, and whether the movant acted in good faith. *Id.* at 395–97. How should these factors be applied? *See, e.g.*, *FG Hemisphere Assocs., LLC v. Democratic Republic of Congo*, 447 F.3d 835, 839–40 (D.C. Cir. 2006) (finding that the defendant's two-month delay in responding to a motion to execute on a default judgment constituted excusable neglect in light of the delay inherent in international delivery of notice to the Democratic Republic of Congo); *Bateman v. U.S. Postal Serv.*, 231 F.3d 1220, 1225 (9th Cir. 2000) (finding excusable neglect when the delay was over one month because the plaintiff left the country on a family emergency).

c. Newly Discovered Evidence

Courts have also developed a multi-factored analysis for determining whether relief from judgment should be granted under Rule 60(b)(2) on the basis of newly discovered evidence. *See, e.g.*, *Daeda v. Sch. Dist. of Lee Cnty.*, 214 Fed. App'x 888, 889 (11th Cir. 2006) (articulating the following five-part test for granting a motion for relief from judgment under Rule 60(b)(2): "(1) the evidence must be newly discovered since the trial; (2) due diligence on the part of the movant to discover the new evidence must be shown; (3) the evidence must not be merely cumulative or impeaching; (4) the evidence must be material; and (5) the evidence must be such that a new trial would probably produce a new result." (quoting *Toole v. Baxter Healthcare Corp.*, 235 F.3d 1307, 1316 (11th Cir. 2000))); *see also U.S. Steel v. M. DeMatteo Constr. Co.*, 315 F.3d 43, 52 (1st Cir. 2002) (articulating a similar list of factors). Why do you think courts have articulated factors that go beyond those mentioned in Rule 60(b)(2)? Is such an interpretation of the rule legitimate?

---

* The *Pioneer* Court was articulating factors relevant to a relief from judgment analysis under Bankruptcy Rule 9006(b)(1) but the circuit courts have subsequently held that these factors are equally applicable to determinations under Federal Rule 60(b)(1). *See, e.g.*, *FG Hemisphere Assocs., LLC v. Democratic Republic of Congo*, 447 F.3d 835, 838 (D.C. Cir. 2006). [Ed.]

d. Fraud

To obtain relief under Rule 60(b)(3) courts have held that there must be clear and convincing evidence that the adverse party obtained the verdict through fraud and that the fraud prevented the movant from fully presenting its case. *See Waddell v. Hendry Cnty. Sheriff's Office*, 329 F.3d 1300, 1309 (11th Cir. 2003); *see also Yapp v. Excel Corp.*, 186 F.3d 1222, 1231 (10th Cir. 1999) (stating that under Rule 60(b)(3), the moving party "must prove [the opposing party's] alleged misconduct by clear and convincing evidence. This he can do only by showing that [the opposing party] acted with an intent to deceive or defraud the court by means of a deliberately planned and carefully executed scheme." (citations and internal quotation marks omitted)). What circumstances might you imagine would provide grounds for relief under Rule 60(b)(3) for fraud? *See, e.g.*, *Green v. Foley*, 856 F.2d 660, 661–62 (4th Cir. 1988) (granting Rule 60(b)(3) motion because one party failed to disclose evidence essential to an adversary's position).

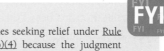

Parties seeking relief under Rule 60(b)(4) because the judgment is void generally claim a jurisdictional defect or defective notice. *See, e.g.*, *Recreational Props., Inc. v. S.W. Mortg. Serv. Corp.*, 804 F.2d 311, 314 (5th Cir. 1986) ("If a court lacks jurisdiction over the parties because of insufficient service of process, the judgment is void and the district court must set it aside.").

e. Other Reasons

As you might imagine, judgments are not often set aside under Rule 60(b)(6); "the Rule is used sparingly as an equitable remedy to prevent manifest injustice and is to be utilized only where extraordinary circumstances prevented a party from taking timely action to prevent or correct an erroneous judgment." *Latshaw v. Trainer Wortham & Co.*, 452 F.3d 1097, 1103 (9th Cir. 2006) (citations and internal quotation marks omitted). What do you think would qualify as "sufficient justification to grant relief" under Rule 60(b)(6)? *See, e.g.*, *Cmty. Dental Servs. v. Tani*, 282 F.3d 1164, 1168–69 (9th Cir. 2002) (holding that where the plaintiff's attorney ignored court orders, neglected motions, missed hearings and other court appearances, and failed to file pleadings or serve them on opposing counsel, the plaintiff was entitled to Rule 60(b)(6) relief from a default judgment on account of his counsel's gross negligence). See also *Liljeberg v. Health Servs. Acquisi-*

Food for Thought

Although reserved for extraordinary situations, is the rule as formulated too open-ended, leaving courts free to grant relief under Rule 60(b)(6) for any reason? What constraints exist to check district court discretion in this area?

tion Corp., 486 U.S. 847 (1988) (holding that the judge's failure to recuse himself pursuant to 28 U.S.C. § 455 was sufficient grounds for granting relief from judgment under Rule 60(b)(6)).

Note that "if the asserted ground for relief falls within one of the enumerated grounds for relief subject to the one-year time limit of Rule 60[(c)(1)], relief under the residual provision of Rule 60(b)(6) is not available." *Arrieta v. Battaglia*, 461 F.3d 861, 865 (7th Cir. 2006); *see also Satterfield v. Pfizer, Inc.*, 208 Fed. App'x 59, 61 (2d Cir. 2006) ("To allow Satterfield to challenge the first Southern District judgment under Rule 60(b)(6) would improperly ignore the requirement of Rule 60(b)(3) that motions based on allegations of fraud by an adversary be filed within one year of judgment.").

———————

Executive Summary

■ **The Right to a Jury Trial.** The Seventh Amendment preserves a right to a trial by jury in the federal system to the extent it existed at the time the Seventh Amendment was adopted, 1791. The jury right only extends to those matters traditionally falling on the law side of the law/equity divide. When the jury right attaches, decisions made by the jury are constitutionally protected—to a limited extent—from re-examination.

■ **Actions Asserting Statutory Rights.** The Supreme Court uses a two-part test to determine whether there is a jury right in an action asserting statutory rights: (1) a historical comparison of the statutory action to 18th-century actions brought in England prior to the merger of the courts of law and equity, and (2) an examination of the remedy sought to determine whether it is legal or equitable in nature.

■ **Judgment as a Matter of Law.** After a party has been heard on an issue— but before the matter is submitted to the jury—if the court finds that a reasonable jury would not have a legally sufficient evidentiary basis to find for the party on that issue, the court may enter judgment against that party on the issue or grant a motion requesting the same. After the jury returns its verdict, the court may only enter judgment as a matter of law on a renewed motion for judgment made by a party who made such a motion before the case went to the jury. *See* Rule 50.

■ **Jury Instructions.** Before a case is submitted to the jury for a decision, the court must first instruct the jury on the law that it is to apply to the facts as it decides them. The parties are free to submit suggested instructions and object to those that the court intends to give. Parties may challenge erroneous instructions on appeal provided they object to those instructions at the district court. *See* Rule 51.

■ **Verdicts.** Besides general verdicts in which juries announce whether the defendant is liable in general, the court may require the jury to return only a special verdict in the form of a special written finding on each issue of fact or to return a general verdict with answers to written interrogatories. *See* Rule 49.

■ **New Trials.** The district court may order a new trial if it believes that the verdict is against the great weight of the evidence, that the damages awarded are excessive, that the conduct of the trial itself was somehow unfair to the moving party, or that there were substantial legal errors pertaining to the admission or exclusion of evidence or the content of instructions to the jury. *See* Rule 59.

Major Themes

Keep in mind several themes arising from the jury trial material:

a. *Importance of History*—when studying the constitutional jury right, it is important to understand the central role that history plays in the analysis. The right is heavily rooted in the scope of the jury right that existed at the time the Seventh Amendment was adopted in 1791.

b. *Law versus Equity*—understanding the difference between law and equity is critical in this area as well, given that whether a jury right applies to the determination of certain matters depends upon whether those matters traditionally have been characterized as legal or equitable in nature.

c. *Impact of the Jury Right*—the importance of the jury right and the constitutional protection against re-examination of jury decisions gives shape to the limitations on the court's authority to enter judgment as a matter of law or to order a new trial.

■ **Relief from Judgment.** After a final judgment is entered, a party may seek relief from judgment for one of the enumerated reasons in Rule 60(b)(1)–(5)—such as excusable neglect, fraud, or newly discovered evidence—or for other reasons under Rule 60(b)(6) when extraordinary circumstances warrant such relief. *See* Rule 60(b).

For More Information

Students interested in studying trials and judicial control over jury verdicts further may consult the following resources:

- 9 C. WRIGHT & A. MILLER, FED. PRAC. & PROC. § 2301, *et seq.* (3d ed. 2008) (right to jury trial).

- 9B C. WRIGHT & A. MILLER, FED. PRAC. & PROC. § 2521, *et seq.* (3d ed. 2008) (judgment as a matter of law).

- 9C C. WRIGHT & A. MILLER, FED. PRAC. & PROC. § 2551, *et seq.* (3d ed. 2008) (jury instructions).

- 11 C. WRIGHT, A. MILLER & M. KANE, FED. PRAC. & PROC. § 2801, *et seq.* (3d ed. 2012) (new trial).

Test Your Knowledge

To assess your understanding of the material in this chapter, click here to take a quiz.

CHAPTER ELEVEN

Judgment & Appeals

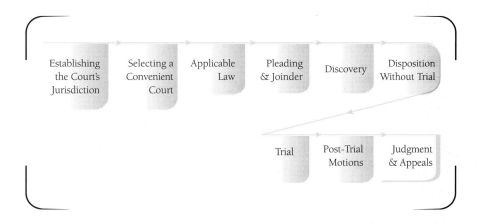

Now THAT WE HAVE COMPLETED our review of civil litigation from the point of selecting a proper court through the completion of the trial and consideration of post-trial motions, we turn to matters concerning the enforcement and effect of judgments and the issues surrounding appeals of civil judgments.

A. Securing & Enforcing Judgments

A litigant pursuing and obtaining a civil judgment faces two distinct but related questions concerning his hoped-for or received judgment. The first question is: How can a litigant who anticipates obtaining a judgment at the conclusion of the litigation secure that judgment against being rendered moot or unenforceable by the intervening actions of his adversary during the litigation? For example, you can imagine a defendant transferring all of her assets to overseas accounts in an effort to make it more difficult or impossible for the prevailing plaintiff to collect on a judgment. The second and related question is: How does a prevailing party enforce a judgment and collect damages once a final judgment is obtained? Both of these matters will be considered below.

1. Provisional Remedies

Due to the passage of time or in some cases the evasive efforts of the defendant, resources available to satisfy a prospective judgment at the outset of a suit may not be available once the suit concludes and a judgment is entered several months or years later. One can imagine how great a waste of time it would be for the courts and litigants if a matter were litigated to a conclusion only to find that the judgment is ineffective due to changed circumstances or the dissipation of assets that could have satisfied the judgment.

Rule 64 makes available, within the federal system, a number of prejudgment or provisional remedies that enable a party to secure a prospective judgment:

> ### <u>FRCP 64</u>. Seizing a Person or Property.
>
> **(a) Remedies Under State Law—In General.** At the commencement of and throughout an action, every remedy is available that, under the law of the state where the court is located, provides for seizing a person or property to secure satisfaction of the potential judgment. But a federal statute governs to the extent it applies.
>
> **(b) Specific Kinds of Remedies.** The remedies available under this rule include the following—however designated and regardless of whether state procedure requires an independent action:
>
> - arrest;
>
> - attachment;
>
> - garnishment;
>
> - replevin;
>
> - sequestration; and
>
> - other corresponding or equivalent remedies.

Most of the provisional remedies expressly mentioned in the Rule involve the encumbrance of property, with civil arrest* being the exception. Let's look at the remedies that encumber property. **Table 11.1** provides a brief description of these remedies:

---

* Civil arrest will not be discussed at all in this chapter because it is not practically available as a provisional remedy in private civil actions in federal courts today. [Ed.]

Table 11.1

Remedy	Description
Attachment	Real or personal property is seized to prevent the defendant from disposing of it pending litigation.
Garnishment	The defendant's assets in the possession of a third party are turned over to the plaintiff to satisfy an alleged debt.
Replevin	Wrongfully taken or held personal property is returned to the plaintiff pending resolution of an ownership dispute.
Sequestration	Property whose ownership is disputed is taken from the possessor and held by a neutral third party pending resolution of an ownership dispute.

To this list could be added the notice of pendency, also known as *lis pendens*, which is a notice filed and recorded with respect to real property that warns all persons that the property is the subject of litigation and that interests taken in the property after the notice are subject to its outcome. Because these remedies encumber property, the protections of the Due Process Clauses of the Fifth and Fourteenth Amendments are implicated. Both of these provisions state that no person may be deprived of "property, without due process of law," meaning that each of these provisional remedies must be accompanied by certain procedural protections before they may lawfully be used. The Supreme Court clarified exactly what due process means in this context in a series of cases culminating in its decision in *Connecticut v. Doehr*, our next case.

Connecticut v. Doehr

Supreme Court of the United States
501 U.S. 1 (1991)

JUSTICE WHITE delivered an opinion, Parts I, II, and III of which are the opinion of the Court.[1]

This case requires us to determine whether a state statute that authorizes prejudgment attachment of real estate without prior notice or hearing, without a showing of extraordinary circumstances, and without a requirement that the person seeking the attachment post a bond, satisfies the Due Process Clause of the Fourteenth Amendment. We hold that, as applied to this case, it does not.

---

[1] THE CHIEF JUSTICE, JUSTICE BLACKMUN, JUSTICE KENNEDY, and JUSTICE SOUTER join Parts I, II, and III of this opinion, and JUSTICE SCALIA joins Parts I and III.

I

On March 15, 1988, petitioner John F. DiGiovanni submitted an application to the Connecticut Superior Court for an attachment in the amount of $75,000 on respondent Brian K. Doehr's home in Meriden, Connecticut. DiGiovanni took this step in conjunction with a civil action for assault and battery that he was seeking to institute against Doehr in the same court. The suit did not involve Doehr's real estate, nor did DiGiovanni have any pre-existing interest either in Doehr's home or any of his other property.

What's That?

The *bond* referred to here is an amount of money that a person seeking a prejudgment attachment must pay to the court to be available as compensation for the defendant in the event that he suffers damages as the result of a wrongful attachment.

Connecticut law authorizes prejudgment attachment of real estate without affording prior notice or the opportunity for a prior hearing to the individual whose property is subject to the attachment. The State's prejudgment remedy statute provides * * * :

> "The court or a judge of the court may allow the prejudgment remedy to be issued by an attorney without hearing * * * upon verification by oath of the plaintiff or of some competent affiant, that there is probable cause to sustain the validity of the plaintiff's claims and (1) that the prejudgment remedy requested is for an attachment of real property. . . ." Conn.Gen. Stat. § 52–278e (1991).

The statute does not require the plaintiff to post a bond to insure the payment of damages that the defendant may suffer should the attachment prove wrongfully issued or the claim prove unsuccessful.

As required, DiGiovanni submitted an affidavit in support of his application. In five one-sentence paragraphs, DiGiovanni stated that the facts set forth in his previously submitted complaint were true; that "I was willfully, wantonly and maliciously assaulted by the defendant, Brian K. Doehr"; that "[s]aid assault and battery broke my left wrist and further caused an ecchymosis to my right eye, as well as other injuries"; and that "I have further expended sums of money for medical care and treatment." The affidavit concluded with the statement, "In my opinion, the foregoing facts are sufficient to show that there is probable cause that judgment will be rendered for the plaintiff."

On the strength of these submissions the Superior Court Judge, by an order dated March 17, found "probable cause to sustain the validity of the plaintiff's claim" and ordered the attachment on Doehr's home "to the value of $75,000." The sheriff attached the property four days later, on March 21. Only after this did Doehr receive notice of the attachment. He also had yet to be served with the complaint, which is ordinarily necessary for an action to commence in Connecticut. As the statute further required, the attachment notice informed Doehr that he had the right to a hearing: (1) to claim that no probable cause existed to sustain the claim; (2) to request that the attachment be vacated, modified, or dismissed or that a bond be substituted; or (3) to claim that some portion of the property was exempt from execution.

Rather than pursue these options, Doehr filed suit against DiGiovanni in Federal District Court, claiming that § 52–278e(a)(1) was unconstitutional under the Due Process Clause of the Fourteenth Amendment. The District Court upheld the statute and granted summary judgment in favor of DiGiovanni. On appeal, a divided panel of the United States Court of Appeals for the Second Circuit reversed.[3] * * *

Food for Thought

Although you likely have not yet taken a constitutional law course, you should at this point be able to articulate why Doehr asserted a violation of the Fourteenth Amendment's Due Process Clause rather than the Due Process Clause of the Fifth Amendment. What is the reason?

II

With this case we return to the question of what process must be afforded by a state statute enabling an individual to enlist the aid of the State to deprive another of his or her property by means of the prejudgment attachment or similar procedure. Our cases reflect the numerous variations this type of remedy can entail. In *Sniadach v. Family Finance Corp. of Bay View*, 395 U.S. 337 (1969), the Court struck down a Wisconsin statute that permitted a creditor to effect prejudgment garnishment of wages without notice and prior hearing to the wage earner. In *Fuentes v. Shevin*, 407 U.S. 67 (1972), the Court likewise found a due process violation in state replevin provisions that permitted vendors to have goods seized through an *ex parte* application to a court clerk and the posting of a bond. Conversely, the Court upheld a Louisiana *ex parte* pro-

It's Latin to Me!

Ex parte is a Latin phrase used to refer to proceedings that occur by and for one party without notice to or the participation of the other party. This is to be contrasted with proceedings that occur *inter partes*, which means with the involvement of two or more parties.

---

[3] The Court of Appeals invited Connecticut to intervene pursuant to 28 U.S.C. § 2403(b) after oral argument. The State elected to intervene in the appeal and has fully participated in the proceedings before this Court.

cedure allowing a lienholder to have disputed goods sequestered in *Mitchell v. W.T. Grant Co.*, [416 U.S. 600 (1974)]. *Mitchell*, however, carefully noted that *Fuentes* was decided against "a factual and legal background sufficiently different . . . that it does not require the invalidation of the Louisiana sequestration statute." Those differences included Louisiana's provision of an immediate post-deprivation hearing along with the option of damages; the requirement that a judge rather than a clerk determine that there is a clear showing of entitlement to the writ; the necessity for a detailed affidavit; and an emphasis on the lienholder's interest in preventing waste or alienation of the encumbered property. In *North Georgia Finishing, Inc. v. Di-Chem, Inc.*, 419 U.S. 601 (1975), the Court again invalidated an *ex parte* garnishment statute that not only failed to provide for notice and prior hearing but also failed to require a bond, a detailed affidavit setting out the claim, the determination of a neutral magistrate, or a prompt post-deprivation hearing.

Take Note!

The Court has just reviewed a series of prior cases in which it faced various prejudgment remedial schemes each with their own accompanying procedures. Can you discern a coherent analysis that the Court is applying to reach the result in each of these cases?

These cases "underscore the truism that '"[d]ue process," unlike some legal rules, is not a technical conception with a fixed content unrelated to time, place and circumstances.'" *Mathews v. Eldridge*, 424 U.S. 319, 334 (1976) (quoting *Cafeteria & Restaurant Workers v. McElroy*, 367 U.S. 886, 895 (1961)). In *Mathews*, we drew upon our prejudgment remedy decisions to determine what process is due when the government itself seeks to effect a deprivation on its own initiative. That analysis resulted in the now familiar threefold inquiry requiring consideration of "the private interest that will be affected by the official action"; "the risk of an erroneous deprivation of such interest through the procedures used, and the probable value, if any, of additional or substitute safeguards"; and lastly "the Government's interest, including the function involved and the fiscal and administrative burdens that the additional or substitute procedural requirement would entail." *Id. at 335.*

Here the inquiry is similar, but the focus is different. Prejudgment remedy statutes ordinarily apply to disputes between private parties rather than between an individual and the government. Such enactments are designed to enable one of the parties to "make use of state procedures with the overt, significant assistance of state officials," and they undoubtedly involve state action "substantial enough to implicate the Due Process Clause." Nonetheless, any burden that increasing procedural safeguards entails primarily affects not the government, but the party seeking control of the other's property. For this type of case, therefore, the relevant inquiry requires, as in *Mathews*, first, consideration of the private interest that will be affected by the prejudgment measure; second, an examination of the risk of erroneous deprivation through the procedures under attack and the probable value of additional or alternative safeguards; and third, in contrast to *Mathews*, principal attention to the interest of the party seeking the prejudgment remedy, with, nonetheless, due regard for any ancillary interest the government may have in providing the procedure or forgoing the added burden of providing greater protections.

We now consider the *Mathews* factors in determining the adequacy of the procedures before us, first with regard to the safeguards of notice and a prior hearing, and then in relation to the protection of a bond.

III

We agree with the Court of Appeals that the property interests that attachment affects are significant. For a property owner like Doehr, attachment ordinarily clouds title; impairs the ability to sell or otherwise alienate the property; taints any credit rating; reduces the chance of obtaining a home equity loan or additional mortgage; and can even place an existing mortgage in technical default where there is an insecurity clause. Nor does Connecticut deny that any of these consequences occurs.

Instead, the State correctly points out that these effects do not amount to a complete, physical, or permanent deprivation of real property; their impact is less than the perhaps temporary total deprivation of household goods or wages. But the Court has never held that only such extreme deprivations trigger due process concern. *See Buchanan v. Warley*, 245 U.S. 60, 74 (1917). To the contrary, our cases show that even the temporary or partial impairments to property rights that attachments, liens, and similar encumbrances entail are sufficient to merit due process protection. Without doubt, state procedures for creating and enforcing attachments, as with liens, "are subject to the strictures of due process."

We also agree with the Court of Appeals that the risk of erroneous deprivation that the State permits here is substantial. By definition, attachment statutes premise a deprivation of property on one ultimate factual contingency—the award of damages to the plaintiff which the defendant may not be able to satisfy. For attachments before judgment, Connecticut mandates that this determination be made by means of a procedural inquiry that asks whether "there is probable cause to sustain the validity of the plaintiff's claim." The statute elsewhere defines the validity of the claim in terms of the likelihood "that judgment will be rendered in the matter in favor of the plaintiff." What probable cause means in this context, however, remains obscure. The State initially took the position * * * that the statute requires a plaintiff to show the objective likelihood of the suit's success. Doehr * * * reads the provision as requiring no more than that a plaintiff demonstrate a subjective good-faith belief that the suit will succeed. At oral argument, the State shifted its position to argue that the statute requires something akin to the plaintiff stating a claim with sufficient facts to survive a motion to dismiss.

We need not resolve this confusion since the statute presents too great a risk of erroneous deprivation under any of these interpretations. If the statute demands inquiry into the sufficiency of the complaint, or, still less, the plaintiff's good-faith belief that the complaint is sufficient, requirement of a complaint and a factual affidavit would permit a court to make these minimal determinations. But neither inquiry adequately reduces the risk of erroneous deprivation. Permitting a court to authorize attachment merely because the plaintiff believes the defendant is liable, or because the plaintiff can make out a facially valid complaint, would permit the deprivation of the defendant's property when the claim would fail to convince a jury, when it rested on factual allegations that were sufficient to state a cause of action but which the defendant would dispute, or in the case of a mere good-faith standard, even when the complaint failed to state a claim upon which relief could be granted. The potential for unwarranted attachment in these situations is self-evident and too great to satisfy the requirements of due process absent any countervailing consideration.

Food for Thought

What is the Court saying here? Is it ever appropriate to permit a pre-judgment attachment based on a one-sided presentation by the plaintiff to a judge? What "countervailing consideration[s]," mentioned by the Court above, can you imagine would make an *ex parte* presentation a sufficient basis for such provisional relief?

Even if the provision requires the plaintiff to demonstrate, and the judge to find, probable cause to believe that judgment will be rendered in favor of the plaintiff, the risk of error was substantial in this case. As the record shows, and as the State concedes, only a skeletal affidavit need be, and was, filed. The State urges that the reviewing judge normally reviews the complaint as well, but concedes that the complaint may also be conclusory. It is self-evident that the judge could make no realistic assessment concerning the likelihood of an action's success based upon these one-sided, self-serving, and conclusory submissions. And as the Court of Appeals said, in a case like this involving an alleged assault, even a detailed affidavit would give only the plaintiff's version of the confrontation. Unlike determining the existence of a debt or delinquent payments, the issue does not concern "ordinarily uncomplicated matters that lend themselves to documentary proof." *Mitchell, 416 U.S., at 609*. The likelihood of error that results illustrates that "fairness can rarely be obtained by secret, one-sided determination of facts decisive of rights. . . . [And n]o better instrument has been devised for arriving at truth than to give a person in jeopardy of serious loss notice of the case against him and opportunity to meet it."

What safeguards the State does afford do not adequately reduce this risk. Connecticut points out that the statute also provides an "expeditiou[s]" postattachment adversary hearing, notice for such a hearing, judicial review of an adverse decision, and a double damages action if the original suit is commenced without probable cause. Similar considerations were present in *Mitchell*, where we upheld Louisiana's sequestration statute despite the lack of pre-deprivation notice and hearing. But in Mitchell the plaintiff had a vendor's lien to protect, the risk of error was minimal because the likelihood of recovery involved uncomplicated matters that lent them-selves to documentary proof, and the plaintiff was required to put up a bond. None of these factors diminishing the need for a predeprivation hearing is present in this case. It is true that a later hearing might negate the presence of probable cause, but this would not cure the temporary deprivation that an earlier hearing might have prevented. * * *

What's That?

A *vendor's lien* is a seller's lien on property as the security for the purchase price. A lien is simply an interest that a creditor has in another's property until the debt is paid.

Finally, we conclude that the interests in favor of an *ex parte* attachment, particularly the interests of the plaintiff, are too minimal to supply such a consideration here. The plaintiff had no existing interest in Doehr's real estate when he sought the attachment. His only interest in attaching the property was to ensure the availability of assets to satisfy his judgment if he prevailed on the merits of his action. Yet there was no allegation that Doehr was about to transfer or encumber his real estate or take any other action during the pendency of the action that would render his real estate unavailable to satisfy a judgment. Our cases have recognized such a properly supported claim would be an exigent circumstance permitting postponing any notice or hearing until after the attachment is effected. *See Mitchell, supra, 416 U.S., at 609; Fuentes, supra, 407 U.S., at 90–92; Sniadach, 395 U.S., at 339.* Absent such allegations, however, the plaintiff's interest in attaching the property does not justify the burdening of Doehr's ownership rights without a hearing to determine the likelihood of recovery.

No interest the government may have affects the analysis. The State's substantive interest in protecting any rights of the plaintiff cannot be any more weighty than those rights themselves. Here the plaintiff's interest is de minimis. Moreover, the State cannot seriously plead additional financial or administrative burdens involving pre-deprivation hearings when it already claims to provide an immediate post-deprivation hearing.

Historical and contemporary practices support our analysis. Prejudgment attachment is a remedy unknown at common law. Instead, "it traces its origin to the Custom of London, under which a creditor might attach money or goods of the defendant either in the plaintiff's own hands or in the custody of a third person, by proceedings in the mayor's court or in the sheriff's court." Generally speaking, attachment measures in both England and this country had several limitations that reduced the risk of erroneous deprivation which Connecticut permits. Although attachments ordinarily did not require prior notice or a hearing, they were usually authorized only where the defendant had taken or threatened to take some action that would place the satisfaction of the plaintiff's potential award in jeopardy. Attachments, moreover, were generally confined to claims by creditors. As we and the Court of Appeals have noted, disputes between debtors and creditors more readily lend themselves to accurate ex parte assessments of the merits. Tort actions, like the assault and battery claim at issue here, do not. Finally, as we will discuss below, attachment statutes historically required that the plaintiff post a bond.

Food for Thought

What is the relevance of the Court's historical discussion here? Are contemporary attachment practices bound in some way by the character of antecedent procedures employed in England hundreds of years ago?

Connecticut's statute appears even more suspect in light of current practice. A survey of state attachment provisions reveals that nearly every State requires either a pre-attachment hearing, a showing of some exigent circumstance, or both, before permitting an attachment to take place. * * *

We do not mean to imply that any given exigency requirement protects an attachment from constitutional attack. Nor do we suggest that the statutory measures we have surveyed are necessarily free of due process problems or other constitutional infirmities in general. We do believe, however, that the procedures of almost all the States confirm our view that the Connecticut provision before us, by failing to provide a preattachment hearing without at least requiring a showing of some exigent circumstance, clearly falls short of the demands of due process.

IV

[Justice White, joined only by Justices Marshall, Stevens, and O'Connor, went on to conclude that due process requires a party to file a bond when obtaining prejudgment attachment to protect defendants against possible damages that could result from an improper attachment.]

V

Because Connecticut's prejudgment remedy provision violates the requirements of due process by authorizing prejudgment attachment without prior notice or a hearing, the judgment of the Court of Appeals is affirmed, and the case is remanded to that court for further proceedings consistent with this opinion.

It is so ordered.

CHIEF JUSTICE REHNQUIST, with whom JUSTICE BLACKMUN joins, concurring in part and concurring in the judgment.

I agree with the Court that the Connecticut attachment statute, "as applied to this case," fails to satisfy the Due Process Clause of the Fourteenth Amendment. I therefore join Parts I, II, and III of its opinion. Unfortunately, the remainder of the opinion does not confine itself to the facts of this case, but enters upon a lengthy disquisition as to what combination of safeguards are required to satisfy due process in hypothetical cases not before the Court. I therefore do not join Part IV.

As the Court's opinion points out, the Connecticut statute allows attachment not merely for a creditor's claim, but for a tort claim of assault and battery; it affords no opportunity for a predeprivation hearing; it contains no requirement that there be "exigent circumstances," such as an effort on the part of the defendant to conceal assets; no bond is required from the plaintiff; and the property attached is one in which the plaintiff has no pre-existing interest. The Court's opinion is, in my view, ultimately correct when it bases its holding of unconstitutionality of the Connecticut statute as applied here on our cases [*Sniadach*, *Fuentes*, *Mitchell*, and *Di-Chem*]. But I do not believe that the result follows so inexorably as the Court's opinion suggests. All of the cited cases dealt with personalty—bank deposits or chattels—and each involved the physical seizure of the property itself, so that the defendant was deprived of its use. These cases, which represented something of a revolution in the jurisprudence of procedural due process, placed substantial limits on the methods by which creditors could obtain a lien on the assets of a debtor prior to judgment. But in all of them the debtor was deprived of the use and possession of the property. In the present case, on the other hand, Connecticut's prejudgment attachment on real property statute, which secures an incipient lien for the plaintiff, does not deprive the defendant of the use or possession of the property.

Food for Thought

Should this distinction that Chief Justice Rehnquist is highlighting make a difference in the constitutional analysis? In other words, does the fact that the imposition on the defendant's property rights is less than was the case in the Court's prior cases mean that due process should require fewer procedural protections?

The Court's opinion therefore breaks new ground, and I would point out, more emphatically than the Court does, the limits of today's holding. * * * I agree with the Court, however, that upon analysis the deprivation here is a significant one, even though the owner remains in undisturbed possession. * * *

[A concurring opinion by JUSTICE SCALIA is omitted.]

Points for Discussion

a. The Road to *Doehr*

Doehr featured quite heavily a line of cases that the Supreme Court had previously decided that addressed the constitutionality of various prejudgment remedy statutes. Take another look at these cases—*Sniadach v. Family Finance Corp. of Bay View*, 395 U.S. 337 (1969), *Fuentes v. Shevin*, 407 U.S. 67 (1972) [*FLEX Case 11.A*], *Mitchell v. W.T. Grant Co.*, 416 U.S. 600 (1974), and *North Georgia Finishing, Inc. v. Di-Chem, Inc.*, 419 U.S. 601 (1975)—as described in the Court's opinion and see if for each case you can identify the type of provisional remedy involved, the various procedural protections in place to protect defendants, and the Court's conclusion regarding the constitutional validity of the statutes at issue. Is the holding of *Doehr* consistent with this line of cases? Can a consistent approach to analyzing prejudgment remedy statutes be discerned from these cases, including *Doehr*?

b. Due Process Requirements for Provisional Remedies After *Doehr*

In *Doehr* the Court identifies a slightly modified version of the analysis of *Mathews v. Eldridge*, 424 U.S. 319, 334 (1976), as the proper framework for evaluating whether a prejudgment attachment or other provisional remedy comports with due process:

> [F]irst, consideration of the private interest that will be affected by the prejudgment measure; second, an examination of the risk of erroneous deprivation through the procedures under attack and the probable value of additional or alternative safeguards; and third, in contrast to *Mathews*, principal attention to the interest of the party seeking the prejudgment remedy, with, nonetheless, due regard for any ancillary interest the government may have in providing the procedure or forgoing the added burden of providing greater protections.

Doehr, 501 U.S. at 11. Be sure to understand the prongs of the *Doehr* test as applied to provisional remedies pursued by private parties and how that test should be applied to the facts in any given case. Can any general statement be made regarding what procedural elements (e.g., a judge, a pre-deprivation hearing, a bond, etc.) seem to be required to make a prejudgment deprivation constitutional? Does the Court say that there must always be a pre-deprivation hearing where the defendant can oppose the deprivation? What conditions might permit a state to dispense with a pre-deprivation hearing? *See, e.g., United States v. James Daniel Good Real Prop.*, 510 U.S. 43, 62 (1993) (invalidating a government seizure that occurred without notice and a pre-deprivation hearing because of the absence of exigent circumstances). Must a bond always be required to make a provisional attachment constitutional? *See Result Shipping Co. v. Ferruzzi Trading USA Inc.*, 56 F.3d 394, 402 (2d Cir. 1995) ("[B]ecause only a plurality of the Justices addressed this issue in *Doehr*, this Circuit has continued to adhere to our previously established position that a security bond need not be posted in connection with a prejudgment attachment in order to satisfy the requirements of due process."); *see also* <u>Shaumyan v. O'Neill, 987 F.2d 122 (2d Cir. 1993)</u> (upholding Connecticut prejudgment attachment statute that did not require pre-deprivation hearing or posting of security bond).

The Court noted that in *Doehr* the plaintiff lacked any pre-existing interest in the property to be attached. How should that consideration affect the due process analysis? The Court also emphasized that *Doehr* involved a tort claim rather than a claim on a debt. Is the Court saying that the nature of the underlying claim is relevant to the constitutionality of prejudgment deprivation procedures? Finally, in *Doehr* the prejudgment attachment would leave the defendant in possession of his property, while in other cases in this line the defendant was deprived entirely of the use of the property. Should that distinction affect the constitutional analysis at all? *See* <u>Mitchell v. W.T. Grant Co., 416 U.S. 600 (1974)</u> (holding that a Louisiana procedure that makes available to a mortgage lien holder a writ of sequestration to forestall alienation of secured property on *ex parte* application without notice to the debtor or an opportunity for hearing and under which the debtor may immediately seek dissolution of the writ is constitutional); <u>Diaz v. Paterson, 547 F.3d 88, 100 (2d Cir. 2008)</u> (upholding New York's *lis pendens* statute, which permitted claimants to file such notices *ex parte* without a hearing, based on application of the *Doehr* framework).

Hypo 11.1

State A has a statute that permits prejudgment attachment in any action involving claims of conspiracy, fraud, or breach of contract. To obtain the attachment, the plaintiff must present to a judge evidence establishing its claim, the plaintiff must post a bond sufficient to cover any damages suffered by the defendant in the event the attachment turns out to be improper, and there is a requirement that within two days of the attachment there must be a hearing at which the defendant may appear to contest the attachment.

An investor has filed a claim against a landowner for fraud in State A state court, seeking $65,000 in damages. The investor used State A's attachment statute to attach the landowner's house for the amount sought in the lawsuit and paid an appropriate bond as ordered by the judge. At the post-attachment hearing, the landowner appeared and sought to set aside the attachment by challenging State A's prejudgment attachment statute as unconstitutional in violation of the Due Process Clause.

What would be an appropriate decision of the court with respect to the landowner's challenge?

Do not forget that in addition to the constitutional analysis set forth in *Doehr* with respect to evaluating the sufficiency of the opportunity to be heard that must accompany provisional remedies, there is also the constitutional notice requirement, which finds its source in <u>Mullane v. Central Hanover Bank & Trust Co., 339 U.S. 306 (1950)</u>, and its progeny. The general requirement is notice reasonably calculated under the circumstances to apprise the interested party of the pendency of the action. The constitutional notice requirement is covered in <u>Chapter 2</u>.

c. State Law and Provisional Remedies in the Federal System

<u>Rule 64</u>, excerpted above, makes available in federal court all the provisional remedies that are available in the state in which the federal court is located, to the extent that such remedies are consistent with due process. The terms of obtaining such remedies in federal court are governed for the most part by the relevant state's law. That means that there will be uneven availability of provisional remedies within the federal system. Is such variation appropriate? Is it unique or can you identify other contexts in which there are variations among the federal courts rooted in differences between the states?

Take Note!

The ability to obtain provisional relief under state law is going to be limited to property within the state. Thus, for example, you will not be able to use Ohio's prejudgment attachment procedure in Ohio federal court to attach the defendant's property in Texas. What do you think is the basis for this limitation?

---

2. Interim Injunctive Relief

The provisional remedies just discussed are those used to secure potential money damages judgments in actions at law. When equitable relief is sought—meaning that the plaintiff is seeking a decree from the court ordering the defendant to do or refrain from doing something—prejudgment remedies like attachment are of little to no use if no money is at stake. In the equitable relief context, the plaintiff's concern is preserving the status quo during the litigation so that the ultimate judgment is not rendered moot by the defendant's intervening harmful conduct. In other words, if the plaintiff seeks a judgment ordering the defendant not to do something, such a judgment is useless if the defendant is free to go ahead and do the act in question while the court is considering the matter.

The solution to this problem is interim injunctive relief, which can take the form of a temporary restraining order or a preliminary injunction.

Temporary Restraining Orders. A temporary restraining order ("TRO") is interim injunctive relief issued to preserve the status quo pending the consideration of a preliminary injunction (discussed below). Rule 65 authorizes the issuance of a TRO as follows:

FRCP 65(b). Injunctions and Restraining Orders.

(b) Temporary Restraining Order.

(1) *Issuing Without Notice.* The court may issue a temporary restraining order without written or oral notice to the adverse party or its attorney only if:

(A) specific facts in an affidavit or a verified complaint clearly show that immediate and irreparable injury, loss, or damage will result to the movant before the adverse party can be heard in opposition; and

(B) the movant's attorney certifies in writing any efforts made to give notice and the reasons why it should not be required.

(2) *Contents; Expiration.* Every temporary restraining order issued without notice * * * expires at the time after entry—not to exceed 14 days—that the court sets, unless before that time the court, for good cause, extends it for a like period or the adverse party consents to a longer extension. * * * .

(3) *Expediting the Preliminary-Injunction Hearing.* If the order is issued without notice, the motion for a preliminary injunction must be set for hearing at the earliest possible time * * * . At the hearing, the party who obtained the order must proceed with the motion; if the party does not, the court must dissolve the order.

(4) *Motion to Dissolve.* On 2 days' notice to the party who obtained the order without notice * * * the adverse party may appear and move to dissolve or modify the order. The court must then hear and decide the motion as promptly as justice requires.

From the Rule we see that a TRO may be issued *ex parte*, meaning without notice to the adversary whom the TRO will bind. To obtain a TRO, however, the Rule requires that the party seeking it demonstrate a likelihood of immediate, irreparable harm that will result if the TRO is not issued, coupled with an explanation as to why prior notice to the adversary should not be required. The Rule also makes clear that the TRO is a very brief remedy that is only intended to preserve the status quo until the court can determine whether a preliminary injunction is appropriate. *See also Granny Goose Foods, Inc. v. Teamsters,* 415 U.S. 423, 438–39 (1974) ("Ex parte temporary restraining orders are no doubt necessary in certain circumstances, but under federal law they should be restricted to serving their underlying purpose of preserving the status quo and preventing irreparable harm just so long as is necessary to hold a hearing, and no longer."). A TRO must expire no more than 14 days after it is issued, with the court being permitted to extend it once for a similar length of time for good cause shown. FED. R. CIV. P. 65(b)(2). Rule 65(b) does provide for swift post-issuance hearings either to dissolve the TRO or to consider the plaintiff's request for a preliminary injunction, and Rule 65(c) requires the applicant to provide security (i.e., a bond) in an amount (as determined by the court) sufficient "to pay the costs and damages sustained by any party found to have been wrongfully enjoined or restrained." FED. R. CIV. P. 65(c). However, the grant or denial of a TRO ordinarily is not immediately appealable absent extraordinary circumstances. *See, e.g.*, *Ingram v. Ault,* 50 F.3d 898, 900 (11th Cir. 1995) ("[W]hen a grant or denial of a TRO might have a serious, perhaps irreparable, consequence, and can be effectually challenged only by immediate appeal, we may exercise appellate jurisdiction."). Do these procedural protections render the federal TRO remedy compliant with the requirements of due process as articulated in the *Sniadach/Doehr* line of cases discussed above?

Preliminary Injunctions. A preliminary injunction is a provisional equitable remedy that preserves the status quo pending a full trial on the merits in the underlying dispute. It is sought when the requesting party needs some protection against irreparable harm that could result if its adversary is left free to act in a certain way pending the litigation. Although Rule 65 sets forth the standard for issuing a TRO, the Rule authorizes, but does not articulate, the standard for issuing preliminary injunctions. However, the Supreme Court has described the requirements for obtaining a preliminary injunction as follows: "A plaintiff seeking a preliminary injunction must establish that he is likely to succeed on the merits, that he is likely to suffer irreparable harm in the absence of preliminary relief, that the balance of equities tips in his favor, and that an injunction is in the public interest." *Winter v. Nat. Res. Def. Council,* 555 U.S. 7, 20 (2008). The Court added that "[a] preliminary injunction is an extraordinary remedy" and that courts must "pay particular regard for the public consequences in employing the extraordinary remedy of injunction." *Id.* at 24.

Unlike the TRO, a preliminary injunction may only be issued after notice to the defendant. *See* FED. R. CIV. P. 65(a)(1) ("The court may issue a preliminary injunction only on notice to the adverse party."). However, as with the TRO, the grant of a preliminary injunction must be accompanied by a payment of some security by the plaintiff—in an amount the court considers proper—to compensate the defendant for any harm that might result from a wrongful injunction. *See* FED. R. CIV. P. 65(c).

Take Note!

Note that the requirement that the party seeking the preliminary injunction demonstrate irreparable harm is reflective of the tradition that interim injunctive relief is unavailable in actions at law where the plaintiff merely seeks money damages. Demonstrating irreparable harm requires showing some irreversible, harmful prospective change in circumstances that money damages will not be able to compensate, such as the imminent tearing down of a house sought to be preserved.

Under 28 U.S.C. § 1292(a)(1), a circuit court may exercise interlocutory appellate jurisdiction over a district court's decision to grant or deny a preliminary injunction. Such review is conducted under multiple standards, depending upon which aspect of the decision granting the injunction is being reviewed. *See, e.g., B.H. ex rel. Hawk v. Easton Area Sch. Dist.,* 725 F.3d 293,

301–02 (3d Cir. 2013) ("We review the District Court's factual findings for clear error, its legal conclusions *de novo*, and its ultimate decision to grant the preliminary injunction for abuse of discretion.").

There are limits to the types of injunctions that federal courts may issue. *See, e.g.*, *Grupo Mexicano de Desarrollo, S.A. v. All. Bond Fund, Inc.*, 527 U.S. 308, 333 (1999) (holding that federal courts have "no authority to issue a preliminary injunction preventing petitioners from disposing of their assets pending adjudication of respondents' contract claim for money damages"); *see also* Jonathan Greenblatt & A. Benjamin Spencer, *Obtaining* Mareva-*type Provisional Relief in New York State and Federal Courts*, in COMMERCIAL INJUNCTIONS 809–15 (Steven Gee, QC, ed., 5th ed. 2004) (discussing the *Grupo Mexicano* case).

3. Enforcing the Judgment

After the entry of judgment, the prevailing plaintiff's concern shifts from preserving assets or the status quo pending litigation to actually collecting on the judgment or enforcing an injunction. The latter is a simpler affair, given that a losing party's failure to comply with a judgment of injunctive relief will subject that party to the sanction of contempt. A court may retain jurisdiction over a case in order to enforce its injunctive orders and can impose fines to compel compliance. *See, e.g.*, *Spallone v. United States*, 493 U.S. 265 (1990) (upholding the imposition of a daily fine on the City of Yonkers for failure to comply with a consent decree).

Enforcing and collecting a judgment awarding money damages can be more difficult. Of course, if the losing party willingly pays the prevailing party the amount of the judgment, then there is no need for enforcement and collection. However, if the losing party (referred to as the *judgment debtor*) is reluctant to pay and has to be forced, how does the prevailing party (now termed a *judgment creditor*) go about accomplishing this? Enforcement and collection is accomplished through a process called execution, which is governed by Rule 69 in the federal system:

FRCP 69(a). Execution: In General.

(a) **In General.**

   (1) *Money Judgment; Applicable Procedure.* A money judgment is enforced by a writ of execution, unless the court directs otherwise. The procedure on execution—and in proceedings supplementary to and in aid of judgment or execution—must accord with the procedure of the state where the court is located, but a federal statute governs to the extent it applies.

   (2) *Obtaining Discovery.* In aid of the judgment or execution, the judgment creditor or a successor in interest whose interest appears of record may obtain discovery from any person—including the judgment debtor—as provided in these rules or by the procedure of the state where the court is located.

As was the case with provisional remedies like attachment and sequestration, the procedures surrounding execution are tied to the state in which the district court is located unless there is an applicable federal statute. Thus, because state execution procedures can only reach assets and property within the state's jurisdiction, judgment creditors will have to seek execution of a judgment in the state in which property is located. This can be done in federal or state court (28 U.S.C. § 1963 permits judgments from one district to be registered and enforced in another district), but Rule 69(a) ensures that the procedures will be the same regardless of whether a state or federal forum is chosen.

In most states, when execution is sought against real or personal property, the relevant official (a sheriff, or a U.S. Marshal in the federal system) will levy on the property and sell it if necessary, delivering the appropriate amount of proceeds to the judgment creditor and any remaining balance to the judgment debtor. The judgment debtor has a chance to contest this process but to a very limited extent; challenges to the underlying judgment will be impermissible if the judgment debtor appeared and raised or waived the available challenges in the lawsuit. *See, e.g., United States v. Straits Steel & Wire Co.,* 810 F. Supp. 208, 211 (W.D. Mich. 1992) ("[O]nce jurisdiction has attached, 'mere errors or irregularities in the proceedings, however grave . . .

What's That?

Levy is a term that means seizure (or it can mean seizure and sale) pursuant to a writ of execution.

cannot be collaterally attacked.'" (quoting *Bowie v. Arder,* 441 Mich. 23, 49 (1992))). If the judgment debtor never appeared in the prior suit, limited collateral attacks on jurisdictional grounds will be allowed. *See, e.g., United States v. Bigford,* 365 F.3d 859, 866 (10th Cir. 2004) ("[A] defendant against whom a default judgment has been entered has a due process right to launch a collateral attack of that judgment in another jurisdiction on the basis that it was rendered in violation of . . . jurisdictional principles.").

When monetary assets are the object of execution, garnishment is a remedy most states make available. This mechanism can involve the garnishment of the wages of a judgment debtor or her accounts at financial institutions. However, various state and federal laws may operate to limit the percentage of a judgment debtor's wages that may be subjected to garnishment. *See, e.g.,* 15 U.S.C. § 1673(a) (limiting garnishment to one quarter of a worker's disposable income, unless certain exceptions apply). Why do you think such limits are imposed?

Similar restrictions can apply in the real or personal property context in order to protect persons against being deprived of certain essential needs. Thus, states extend a homestead exemption that will shield a person's home up to a fixed dollar amount. New York's Civil Practice Law and Rules (C.P.L.R.) provides an example:

> ### N.Y.C.P.L.R. § 5206. Real property exempt from application to the satisfaction of money judgments.
>
> **(a) Exemption of homestead.** Property of one of the following types, not exceeding [$75,000 to $150,000 depending on county] in value above liens and encumbrances, owned and occupied as a principal residence, is exempt from application to the satisfaction of a money judgment, unless the judgment was recovered wholly for the purchase price thereof:
>
> 1. a lot of land with a dwelling thereon,
>
> 2. shares of stock in a cooperative apartment corporation,
>
> 3. units of a condominium apartment, or
>
> 4. a mobile home.
>
> * * *

New York's C.P.L.R. also contains a similar provision protecting personal property such as stoves, sewing machines, school books, family Bibles, and wedding rings from the reach of executions. N.Y.C.P.L.R. § 5205.

B. Appellate Review

As we learned in the Overview at the beginning of this book, within the federal system and every state judicial system, there are appellate courts that dedicate all of their time to reviewing the decisions of lower courts within their respective jurisdictions. Such review may occur not only potentially at the end of a trial reaching a verdict, but also potentially at various other points in the process while a case is before a trial court. Recall that there are numerous decisions that trial courts render as a case is litigated before it goes to trial, decisions such as whether to dismiss a case for lack of personal jurisdiction or failure to state a claim, decisions regarding the discoverability of certain material, or the propriety of summary judgment. During the trial there are many rulings made as well, most notably evidentiary rulings, but also rulings on the propriety of judgment as a matter of law or the appropriateness of certain jury instructions.

To what extent are these rulings appealable to another tribunal empowered to review and reverse the decisions? If appealable, when can such appeals be pursued, immediately after the ruling or after a final judgment is entered in the entire case? Once properly before an appellate court, what standard do such courts apply to determine whether the lower court's decision must be reversed? These questions and others pertaining to appellate review will be considered below.

1. The Final-Judgment Rule

In the federal system, the jurisdiction of the U.S. Courts of Appeals is limited by the final-judgment rule, which is codified at 28 U.S.C § 1291:

28 U.S.C. § 1291. Final decisions of district courts.

The courts of appeals * * * shall have jurisdiction of appeals from all final decisions of the district courts of the United States * * * .

The key component of this provision is its reference to "final decisions." What constitutes a final decision for purposes of § 1291? Generally speaking, a final decision is a final resolution of the case such that nothing remains to be done at the trial level (except enforcement). Although judgments entered on verdicts clearly fit this definition, what about the many pre-verdict or interlocutory decisions mentioned above? Dispositions of a case, for example, through a dismissal for lack of personal jurisdiction, are pre-verdict resolutions that end all proceedings in the trial court. Thus, such a ruling would seem to qualify as a final decision appealable under § 1291. On the other hand, interlocutory rulings, meaning those that do not bring the matter to a close but rather are intermediate decisions that must be made during the litigation—such as a discovery ruling—by definition appear not to qualify as final decisions and thus would not ordinarily be appealable. The general rule then is that any trial court decision that conclusively resolves a case and brings it to a close will be an appealable final decision. Pretrial and trial rulings that do not end the case are generally not appealable until the end of all trial and post-trial proceedings, or until the matter is brought to a close by a final pretrial decision such as the entry of summary judgment.

Food for Thought

What do you think is the rationale behind the final-judgment rule? In other words, why does our system generally preclude litigants from immediately appealing interlocutory decisions such as discovery or evidentiary rulings?

The next case illustrates the application of the final-judgment rule.

Liberty Mutual Insurance Co. v. Wetzel

Supreme Court of the United States
424 U.S. 737 (1976)

MR. JUSTICE REHNQUIST delivered the opinion of the Court.

Respondents filed a complaint in the United States District Court for the Western District of Pennsylvania in which they asserted that petitioner's employee insurance benefits and maternity leave regulations discriminated against women in violation of Title VII of the Civil Rights Act of 1964 * * * . The District Court ruled in favor of respondents on the issue of petitioner's liability under that Act, and petitioner appealed to the Court of Appeals for the Third Circuit. That court held that it had jurisdiction of petitioner's appeal under 28 U.S.C. § 1291, and proceeded to affirm on the merits the judgment of the District Court. We granted certiorari, and heard argument on the merits. Though neither party has questioned the jurisdiction of the Court of Appeals to entertain the appeal, we are obligated to do so on our own motion if a question thereto exists. Because we conclude that the District Court's order was not appealable to the Court of Appeals, we vacate the judgment of the Court of Appeals with instructions to dismiss petitioner's appeal from the order of the District Court.

> ### Take Note!
>
> Notice that the Court takes up the question of appealability on its own, or *sua sponte*, even though neither party challenged the Third Circuit's jurisdiction. Appellate courts may always take up jurisdictional questions on their own initiative, as jurisdiction is a matter fundamental to the power of a court to render a valid and binding judgment.

Respondents' complaint, after alleging jurisdiction and facts deemed pertinent to their claim, prayed for a judgment against petitioner embodying the following relief:

(a)   requiring that defendant establish non-discriminatory hiring, payment, opportunity, and promotional plans and programs;

(b)   enjoining the continuance by defendant of the illegal acts and practices alleged herein;

(c)   requiring that defendant pay over to plaintiffs and to the members of the class the damages sustained by plaintiffs and the members of the class by reason of defendant's illegal acts and practices, including adjusted back-pay, with interest, and an additional equal amount as liquidated damages, and exemplary damages;

(d)   requiring that defendant pay to plaintiffs and to the members of the class the costs of this suit and a reasonable attorneys' fee, with interest; and

(e)   such other and further relief as the Court deems appropriate.

After extensive discovery, respondents moved for partial summary judgment only as to the issue of liability. FED. RULE CIV. PROC. 56(c). The District Court on

What's That?

A motion for reconsideration is a motion asking the court to reconsider its decision, and is ordinarily treated as a motion under Rule 59(e) "to alter or amend a judgment" unless otherwise specified. *Fed. Kemper Ins. Co. v. Rauscher*, 807 F.2d 345, 348 (3d Cir. 1986) ("[W]e view a motion characterized only as a motion for reconsideration as the 'functional equivalent' of a Rule 59(e) motion to alter or amend a judgment.").

January 9, 1974, finding no issues of material fact in dispute, entered an order to the effect that petitioner's pregnancy-related policies violated Title VII of the Civil Rights Act of 1964. It also ruled that Liberty Mutual's hiring and promotion policies violated Title VII. Petitioner thereafter filed a motion for reconsideration which was denied by the District Court. Its order of February 20, 1974, denying the motion for reconsideration, contains the following concluding language:

"In its Order the court stated it would enjoin the continuance of practices which the court found to be in violation of Title VII. The Plaintiffs were invited to submit the form of the injunction order and the Defendant has filed Notice of Appeal and asked for stay of any injunctive order. Under these circumstances the court will withhold the issuance of the injunctive order and amend the Order previously issued under the provisions of FED. R. CIV. P. 54(b), as follows:

"And now this 20th day of February, 1974, it is directed that final judgment be entered in favor of Plaintiffs that Defendant's policy of requiring female employees to return to work within three months of delivery of a child or be terminated is in violation of the provisions of Title VII of the Civil Rights Act of 1964; that Defendant's policy of denying disability income protection plan benefits to female employees for disabilities related to pregnancies or childbirth are [sic] in violation of Title VII of the Civil Rights Act of 1964 and that it is expressly directed that Judgment be entered for the Plaintiffs upon these claims of Plaintiffs' Complaint; there being no just reason for delay."

It is obvious from the District Court's order that respondents, although having received a favorable ruling on the issue of petitioner's liability to them, received none of the relief which they expressly prayed for in the portion of their complaint set

La Buy v. Howes Leather Co., 352 U.S. 249, 258 (1957). In approving the practice, the Court wrote that "mandamus should be resorted to only in extreme cases" where there are "exceptional circumstances," but gave little specific guidance as to when mandamus is appropriate.

In a subsequent case, however, the Court stated, "The writ is appropriately issued . . . when there is 'usurpation of judicial power' or a clear abuse of discretion." *Schlagenhauf v. Holder*, 379 U.S. 104, 110 (1964) (upholding the use of mandamus to review an order requiring a defendant to submit to a mental and physical examination); *see also Beacon Theatres, Inc. v. Westover*, 359 U.S. 500, 511 (1959) ("[T]he right to grant mandamus to require jury trial where it has been improperly denied is settled."). Generally speaking, case law has reflected that the remedy is appropriate when the adversely affected party requires immediate review to forestall some irreparable harm resulting from a district court's abuse of discretion that will not be remediable on appeal from an ultimate final judgment. *See, e.g., Nixon v. Sirica*, 487 F.2d 700, 707 (D.C. Cir. 1973) ("[I]f indeed the only avenue of direct appellate review open to the President requires that he first disobey the court's order, appeal seems to be 'a clearly inadequate remedy.' These circumstances, we think, warrant the exercise, at the instance of the President, of our review power under the All Writs Act." (citations omitted)).

> **FYI**
>
> Rule 81(b) reads, "The writs of scire facias and mandamus are abolished. Relief previously available through them may be obtained by appropriate action or motion under these rules." FED. R. CIV. P. 81(b). Courts have interpreted this Rule either to be trumped by the All Writs Act, 28 U.S.C. § 1651(a), *see Stevens v. Colt*, 2011 WL 1500599, at *1 n.2 (11th Cir. Apr. 20, 2011), or have read the rule to permit relief "in the nature of mandamus" from district courts via their power to issue injunctions ordering a thing to be done, the effective equivalent of mandamus relief, *see In re Cheney*, 406 F.3d 723, 728–29 (D.C. Cir. 2005).

f. Appeals from Contempt Orders

When no appeal is available of an interim order and none of the exceptions or special circumstances warranting interlocutory or mandamus review are present, it may be possible to obtain review by disobeying the order and appealing the ensuing finding of contempt. *See United States v. Ryan*, 402 U.S. 530, 532 (1971) ("[O]ne to whom a subpoena is directed may not appeal the denial of a motion to quash that subpoena but must either obey its commands or refuse to do so and contest the validity of the subpoena if he is subsequently cited for contempt on account of his failure to obey."). This is a strategy that is only available for parties found in criminal contempt and nonparties in all instances of contempt. Civil contempt orders against parties are not immediately appealable. *See Fox v. Capital Co.*, 299 U.S. 105, 107 (1936) ("The rule is settled in this Court that except in connection with an appeal from a final judgment or decree, a party to a suit may not review upon appeal an order fining or imprisoning him for the commission of a civil contempt."); *Byrd v. Reno*, 180 F.3d 298, 300 (D.C. Cir. 1999) ("[W]e hold that the traditional rule still applies: a civil contempt order against a party in a pending proceeding is not appealable as a final order under 28 U.S.C. § 1291.").

g. Time to Appeal

As previously mentioned, litigants have ten days to appeal interlocutory decisions under 28 U.S.C. § 1292(b). The time to appeal final judgments is governed by the Federal Rules of Appellate Procedure, specifically Rule 4 of those rules. The general rule is as follows: "In a civil case . . . the notice of appeal . . . must be filed with the district clerk within 30 days after entry of the judgment or order appealed from." FED. R. APP. P. 4(a)(1)(A). Post-trial motions such as a motion for judgment under Rule 50(b) of the Federal Rules of Civil Procedure or for a new trial under Rule 59 will postpone the running of this 30-day period until the time when the district court rules on such motions. FED. R. APP. P. 4(a)(4)(A). The district court is empowered to extend the 30-day time period at the request of a party or, if 30 days have expired, if the party can demonstrate "excusable neglect" or "good cause." FED. R. APP. P. 4(a)(5)(A).

The Supreme Court has offered its view of how to evaluate excusable neglect, writing,

> [T]he determination is at bottom an equitable one, taking account of all relevant circumstances surrounding the party's omission. These include . . . the danger of prejudice to the [non-moving party], the length of the delay and its potential impact on judicial proceedings, the reason for the delay, including whether it was within the reasonable control of the movant, and whether the movant acted in good faith.

Pioneer Inv. Servs. Co. v. Brunswick Assocs. Ltd. P'ship, 507 U.S. 380, 395 (1993); *see also Virella-Nieves v. Briggs & Stratton Corp.*, 53 F.3d 451, 454 n.3 (1st Cir. 1995) ("Pioneer's exposition of excusable neglect, though made in the context of late bankruptcy filings, applies equally to FED. R. APP. P. 4(a)(5).").

---

2. Scope of Review

If a decision has the requisite finality to be appealable or is treated as appealable under an exception to the final judgment rule, the appellate court is limited in the scope of its review. There are two aspects to an appellate court's scope of review.

Reviewability. The first aspect of an appellate court's scope of review is the *reviewability* of decisions within a case presented to the appellate court. Not all decisions that a trial court has made with respect to an action are reviewable once the case makes its way to one of the courts of appeals. Adverse interlocutory rulings by the trial court are not reviewable on appeal when those rulings went against the party who ultimately prevailed on the final verdict. Relatedly, when a verdict-loser challenges certain interlocutory rulings on appeal, if those rulings are found not to have impacted the verdict and thus can be described as harmless errors, appeals courts will treat those decisions as unreviewable. *See Kotteakos v. United States, 328 U.S. 750, 764–65 (1946)* ("If, when all is said and done, the conviction is sure that the error did not influence the jury, or had but very slight effect, the verdict and the judgment should stand, except perhaps where the departure is from a constitutional norm or a specific command of Congress.").

Another way in which an interlocutory decision can be rendered unreviewable is through the failure of the adversely-affected party to enter a timely objection to the ruling before the trial court. This contemporaneous-objection rule applies to purportedly erroneous evidentiary rulings; the disgruntled party is obligated to challenge the ruling before the trial court to preserve the right to raise the challenge on appeal. *See* FED. R. EVID. 103(a). The same principle applies, for example, to challenges to jury instructions, FED. R. CIV. P. 51, or even erroneous verdicts, FED. R. CIV. P. 50; in most instances in these and other contexts, the dissatisfied litigant must first raise the objection with the trial court in order to make such matters reviewable on appeal (unless, in the case of erroneous jury instructions, there is "plain error . . . affecting substantial rights"). *See* FED R. CIV P. 51(d)(2).

> **Food for Thought**
>
> What do you think are the rationales behind these various reviewability principles? For example, why are the adverse rulings made against a verdict-winner unreviewable? Why are litigants required to raise objections with the trial court before being permitted to present the matter to an appeals court?

The Seventh Amendment prohibits the reexamination of factual determinations made by juries, so jury findings of fact are unreviewable on appeal. However, when a judge rather than a jury has been responsible for findings of fact at trial, those findings are reviewable by the appeals court. Rule 52(a) of the Federal Rules of Civil Procedure provides that such findings may not be set aside unless they are "clearly erroneous" (see Standards of Review below).

Standards of Review. Once it is determined that an issue is reviewable on appeal, the federal appeals court is not simply charged with determining whether the decision at issue was right or wrong. Rather, appellate courts are concerned with correcting errors, particularly those errors that affected the outcome. In evaluating an appealed case for errors, federal appeals courts apply three differing standards of review depending upon the nature of the issue being reviewed and how much deference the appeals court is thought to owe to the district court's decision.

a. *De Novo* Review

De novo review is the least deferential standard of review; indeed, when an appellate court exercises *de novo* review it is not giving any deference to the trial court's decision. When this standard applies, the appeals court is considering the question anew without regard to what the lower court had to say about the matter. Because *de novo* review completely second-guesses the trial court's determination, it is a level of review that is only appropriate when the appellate court is reviewing matters for which it is in as good a position to determine the correct answer as was the district court. That means that *de novo* review is inappropriate when appellate courts are reviewing trial court determinations that involve to some degree any level of factual determination or any decisions that are the result of a very fact-specific inquiry. Rather, *de novo* review is reserved for those questions of law decided by the trial court. Why do you think we permit appeals courts to substitute their own judgment on questions of law decided by district courts?

b. Review for Clear Error

When trial judges themselves make factual determinations—either because they have conducted a trial without a jury or because they have to make factual determinations in order to rule on various motions—those factual determinations may be scrutinized by the appeals courts, but such scrutiny is deferential. Specifically, appeals courts may not reverse such determinations simply because they would have made a different finding; rather, reversal in such instances is only permissible if the appeals court believes that the district court's decision is clearly erroneous. *See* FED. R. CIV. P. 52(a)(6).

A reversal on clear error review means that it is not really a close question; the district court is clearly quite wrong. *See Anderson v. City of Bessemer City, N.C.*, 470 U.S. 564, 565 (1985) ("[A] finding is 'clearly erroneous' when although there is evidence to support it, the reviewing court on the entire evidence is left with the definite and firm conviction that a mistake has been committed." (quoting *United States v. U.S. Gypsum Co.*, 333 U.S.

> **FYI**
>
> Sometimes a matter is not purely a question of law or purely a question of fact but rather is a mixed question of law and fact. What standard applies to the review of such questions? *See, e.g., Blackledge v. Blackledge*, 866 F.3d 169 (3d Cir. 2017) ("For mixed questions of law and fact, we must separate the issue into its respective parts, applying the clearly erroneous test to the factual component, and the plenary standard to the legal." (citation and internal quotation marks omitted)).

364, 395 (1948))). Note that clear error review is to be distinguished from the "plain error" review that is sometimes called for, *see, e.g.*, FED. R. CIV. P. 51(d)(2)

("A court may consider a plain error in the instructions that has not been preserved as required by Rule 51(d)(1) if the error affects substantial rights."). *See Dupree v. Warden,* 715 F.3d 1295, 1301 (11th Cir. 2013) ("[P]lain error review is an extremely stringent form of review, and the clear error standard is easier to satisfy because a party does not have to prove that the error affected substantial rights or the fairness, integrity, or reputation of the judicial proceeding.").

c. Review for Abuse of Discretion

Finally, there are those trial court decisions that are reviewed for an abuse of discretion. This level of review is the most deferential because it permits the trial judge's decision to stand as long as there is some rational basis for the decision and the proper legal standard was used, even if the appeals court disagrees with the decision and would have gone the other way. Decisions subject to this level of review include most decisions connected with the conduct and management of the pretrial and the trial process but also include provisional decisions such as whether to grant a preliminary injunction.

C. Preclusion Doctrine

Once a final judgment has been obtained, the question of the scope of its preclusive effect arises. The preclusive effect of a judgment refers to the extent to which a judgment prevents parties to the action that resulted in the judgment—or other persons—from relitigating the claims, defenses, or issues raised in the prior action. For example, if *A* obtains a final judgment in an action finding *B* negligent for causing a car accident, could *B* go to another court and challenge the first judgment? If *A* sought and obtained a judgment only for personal injury damages in the first action against *B*, could *A* initiate an action against *B* based on the same car accident seeking damages for property damage to *A*'s vehicle? If *C* had been a passenger in *A*'s car, could *C* initiate a negligence action against *B*, or would *C* be barred by the judgment in the matter of *A v. B*? If *B* had been found negligent in the initial action, would *B* be free to challenge negligence in an action by *C* against *B*, or would *B* somehow be bound by the finding of negligence in *A v. B*?

These questions and others are the province of preclusion doctrine (also known by the terms *merger* and *bar* or *former adjudication*), the topic that will be addressed in this section. Below, the two main wings of preclusion doctrine—claim preclusion and issue preclusion—are discussed in detail.

1. Claim Preclusion

The doctrine of claim preclusion prohibits the relitigation of claims that have been conclusively resolved between the same parties. Because claim preclusion is a common law doctrine, its details can vary across jurisdictions. However, the states are bound by the Constitution's Full Faith and Credit Clause—Article IV, section 1—and its implementing statute, 28 U.S.C. § 1738, to give the judgments of other American jurisdictions the same pre-clusive effect that those judgments would enjoy in the jurisdictions where they were rendered. In the federal sys-tem, whether claim preclusion applies to prevent litigation in a particular case is ordinarily determined by refer-ence to the preclusion law of the state where the initial state-court judgment was issued. *Migra v. Warren City Sch. Dist. Bd. of Educ.*, 465 U.S. 75, 81 (1984) ("Indeed, though the federal courts may look to the common law or to the policies supporting res judicata and collateral estoppel in assessing the preclu-sive effect of decisions of other federal courts, Congress has specifically required all federal courts to give preclusive effect to state-court judgments whenever the courts of the State from which the judgments emerged would do so . . . ." (quoting *Allen v. McCurry*, 449 U.S. 90, 96 (1980))).

Take Note!

The terms *claim preclusion* and *issue preclusion* are modern terms for con-cepts previously referred to as *res ju-dicata* and *collateral estoppel*, respec-tively. Many courts will still use the latter terms rather than the former; just be sure to understand the ter-minology so you can keep up with which doctrine a court is discussing.

There are several requisites to finding a matter barred by claim preclusion. The next case provides an illustration of these requirements and provides insight into how federal courts engage in claim preclusion analysis.

Nestor v. Pratt & Whitney

U.S. Court of Appeals for the Second Circuit
466 F.3d 65 (2d Cir. 2006)

JACOBS, CHIEF JUDGE

Plaintiff-Appellant Gale Nestor ("Nestor") filed a complaint with the Con-necticut Commission on Human Rights and Opportunities ("CCHRO") against her former employer, United Technologies Corporation, Pratt & Whitney Division ("Pratt"), alleging that her employment had been terminated by reason of her sex. She prevailed in the CCHRO, prevailed as well on the appeals taken by Pratt in the Connecticut state courts, and collected damages of back pay and interest. She later filed this action in the United States District Court for the District of Connecticut, pursuant to Title VII of the Civil Rights Act of 1964, 42 U.S.C. § 2000e *et seq.*, as amended by the Civil Rights Act of 1991 ("Title VII"), seeking damages that were unavailable in the CCHRO proceedings: attorney's fees, compensatory damages for emotional distress, and punitive damages (collectively referred to as "additional relief").

Pratt successfully moved for summary judgment on the ground that Nestor's action is barred by Connecticut's doctrine of *res judicata* (or "claim preclusion"). We vacate the judgment and remand for further proceedings consistent with this opinion.

I.

Gale Nestor worked as a machinist for Pratt from 1973 until September 2, 1992, when she was fired after she allegedly had an altercation with a male employee. Nestor was reinstated, without back pay, in 1993 pursuant to a labor arbitration. On November 5, 1992, Nestor filed a complaint against Pratt with the CCHRO, claiming that her employment had been terminated on account of her sex, in violation of Title VII and the Connecticut Fair Employment Practices Act, Conn. Gen. Stat. § 46a–60 et seq. See 42 U.S.C. § 2000e–5(c) (requiring notification of state or local authorities). Her complaint was automatically cross-filed with the United States Equal Employment Opportunity Commission ("EEOC").

The CCHRO apparently advised Nestor that it could not award compensatory damages, but that full damages could be awarded in state court. At that point, Nestor had a choice: she could pursue the CCHRO proceeding, or after passage of a "deferral" period, she could have requested a "right-to-sue" letter and brought an action in state or federal court to recover full relief. Nestor went ahead with the CCHRO proceeding, which offered her certain advantages:

> representation by CCHRO staff counsel (at a fee below the cost of private counsel), flexible evidentiary rules, no requirement of discovery, and speedy proceedings (though this last advantage was not realized in Nestor's case).

The CCHRO conducted the public hearing on Nestor's claim in June 1998, and decided the case on September 20, 1999, finding that Pratt terminated Nestor's employment based on her sex, and awarding Nestor back pay.

Pratt appealed to the Connecticut Superior Court, which affirmed the CCHRO decision on February 20, 2001. Pratt further appealed to the Connecticut Appellate Court, which also affirmed on September 10, 2001. Pratt's timely petition for certification to the Connecticut Supreme Court was denied. Pratt thereafter paid Nestor back pay, with interest.

On February 19, 2003, the EEOC issued Nestor a right-to-sue letter. Nestor promptly filed this action in the District of Connecticut, seeking as sole relief those remedies that are available to Title VII claimants, but that the CCHRO was not authorized to award, including compensatory damages (presumably in addition to—and not duplicative of—the back pay already received), punitive damages, attorney's fees, and prejudgment interest.

Pratt moved for summary judgment in March 2004, arguing that Connecticut's doctrine of *res judicata* bars Nestor's action. The district court agreed, and granted summary judgment to Pratt on March 31, 2005. Nestor timely appealed.

II.

The issue presented on appeal is whether a Title VII plaintiff who prevailed on her discrimination claims before a state administrative agency and in appeals of the agency decision to state court can subsequently file suit in federal court seeking relief that was unavailable in the state proceedings. This issue has split our sister circuit courts. Compare *Jones v. Am. State Bank*, 857 F.2d 494 (8th Cir. 1988) (holding that Title VII plaintiff may bring suit to recover attorney's fees after successfully litigating before a state administrative body) . . . with *Chris v. Tenet*, 221 F.3d 648 (4th Cir. 2000) (holding that federal court lacked jurisdiction to hear plaintiff's suit solely seeking attorney's fees incurred in a prior administrative action).

> **FYI**
>
> The federal circuits are split on innumerable matters of law. Although it is the place of the Supreme Court to resolve such circuit splits, the sheer number of such splits overwhelms the Court's ability to do so in most instances. Nevertheless, the Court does regularly act to resolve the most important circuit splits and thus tracking such splits is a good means of identifying what matters the Court might take up for review.

It is undisputed that the relief Nestor seeks under Title VII was unavailable in the state administrative proceedings. *See Bridgeport Hosp. v. Comm'n on Human Rights & Opportunities*, 653 A.2d 782 (Conn. 1995). It is also undisputed that Nestor could have filed her federal action at any time after the 210-day deferral period required by Connecticut law had passed in her CCHRO proceeding. If Nestor had filed an action seeking additional relief while the CCHRO proceeding was pending, the CCHRO would have been required to relinquish its jurisdiction, and she would have lost the benefits of adjudication in that forum. Conn. Gen. Stat. Ann. § 46a–100. If Nestor had filed her action in federal court (or state court) while Pratt's appeals from the CCHRO determination was still pending, the issue presented on this appeal would likely not arise: A federal court will typically stay the action pending the state appeals and (when the appeals are decided) give *res judicata* effect to the result.

Pratt urges, however, that after the state administrative decision withstood appeal and became final, additional relief was no longer available. Pratt offers two reasons: [i] subject matter jurisdiction does not exist over a "damages only" action;

and [ii] the doctrine of *res judicata* bars relitigation, including relitigation of different claims to relief. We disagree with both arguments, and reverse the district court's grant of summary judgment.

A. Jurisdiction

In <u>North Carolina Dept. of Transp. v. Crest Street Cmty. Council, Inc., 479 U.S. 6 (1986)</u>, the Supreme Court held that a district court lacked jurisdiction over an action seeking nothing but attorney's fees brought by Title VI plaintiffs who had prevailed in administrative proceedings. The Fourth Circuit has ruled that *Crest* applies likewise to Title VII plaintiffs and Pratt urges that this Court take a similar approach.

In the present action, however, not only does Nestor seek attorney's fees—which are specifically provided for in Title VII—she also seeks compensatory damages unavailable in the CCHRO proceeding, such as emotional distress and punitive damages. Her federal action thus entails litigation of substantive issues: for example, whether Nestor suffered any emotional distress caused by Pratt's discrimination and whether Pratt's conduct was malicious. Thus, it is not simply that Nestor seeks to recover for expenses incurred elsewhere; Nestor's federal action seeks to adjudicate substantive issues regarding Pratt's discriminatory conduct and its consequences.

In light of these distinctions, *Crest* neither compels nor supports the dismissal of Nestor's action for lack of subject matter jurisdiction.

B. Res judicata

We review *de novo* a district court decision as to whether a federal action is precluded by a prior adjudication. The doctrine of *res judicata* bears on "the effect of a judgment in foreclosing litigation of a matter that never has been litigated, because of a determination that it should have been advanced in an earlier suit." <u>Migra v. Warren City School Dist. Bd. of Education, 465 U.S. 75, 77, n. 1 (1984)</u>.[5] It is a rule against the splitting of actions that could be brought and resolved together. *See* Restatement (Second) of Judgments § 24 (providing "General Rule Concerning 'Splitting'").

> **Take Note!**
>
> Note that the court is applying a *de novo* standard of review to the lower court's determination that *res judicata* bars the federal action. Why do you think *de novo* review is appropriate here?

---

[5] The terminology of preclusion law can be confusing. As the Supreme Court explained in *Migra*, some commentators refer to the general preclusive effects of a judgment as "res judicata," encompassing both "issue preclusion" (also known as "collateral estoppel" or "direct estoppel") and "claim preclusion." See <u>465 U.S. at 77 n. 1, 104 S.Ct. 892</u>. "Issue preclusion refers to the effect of a judgment in foreclosing relitigation of a matter that has been litigated and decided." *Id.* "Claim preclusion" refers to the effect of a judgment in foreclosing litigation of a matter that was never litigated. We use the term "res judicata" in its narrow sense, as a synonym for "claim preclusion."

The doctrine varies in its effect from jurisdiction to jurisdiction, depending chiefly on how courts define the claims that have or could have been litigated, and on how much weight is put on the goals of preclusion (e.g., finality and efficiency). The parties to this appeal vigorously dispute whether the issue of preclusion is governed by federal law or Connecticut law; however, since Nestor's action survives either way, we do not decide the question, which implicates difficult issues of federalism. *Marrese v. American Acad. of Orthopaedic Surgeons*, 470 U.S. 373, 383 (1985); *see Lyng v. N.W. Indian Cemetery Protective Ass'n*, 485 U.S. 439, 445 (1988) ("A fundamental and long-standing principle of judicial restraint requires that courts avoid reaching constitutional questions in advance of the necessity of deciding them."); *Ashwander v. Tenn. Valley Auth.*, 297 U.S. 288, 347 (1936) (Brandeis, J., concurring) ("[I]f a case can be decided on either of two grounds, one involving a constitutional question, the other a question of statutory construction or general law, the Court will decide only the latter.").

> **FYI**
>
> The practice of avoiding the resolution of unnecessary constitutional questions is sometimes referred to as the constitutional avoidance doctrine. What do you think is the rationale behind the doctrine? Do you understand why the court here is able to employ it to avoid having to decide whether federal or Connecticut preclusion law should apply?

1. Federal Preclusion Law

In considering the preclusive effect of a state court judgment on a subsequent federal action, under the Full Faith and Credit Act, 28 U.S.C. § 1738, we usually consult the preclusion laws of the state in which the judgment was issued. *See Migra, 465 U.S. at 81; see also Marrese, 470 U.S. at 380* ("Section 1738 embodies concerns of comity and federalism that allow the States to determine, subject to the requirements of the statute and the Due Process Clause, the preclusive effect of judgments in their own courts."). We consider whether the statute creating the federal cause of action (i.e., Title VII) preempted the application of state preclusion law only if the action would be barred under state law. *See Marrese, 470 U.S. at 381*.

Our usual approach to preemption is, however, seemingly inapplicable here. The Supreme Court held in *New York Gaslight Club, Inc. v. Carey*, 447 U.S. 54 (1980) that a complainant who succeeds on a discrimination claim that is filed in a state administrative agency and that is upheld on appeal can sue in federal court under Title VII to recover attorney's fees that were incurred in the state proceedings but that are not awardable under state law. In holding that Congress intended to authorize a suit under Title VII "solely to obtain an award of attorney's fees for legal work done in state and local proceedings" irrespective of whether such a claim for fees would be permissible under state law, the Court did not consider Title VII to have preempted the application of state law, but rather considered the federal action for damages to be a "supplement" to state remedies "when the State does not provide prompt or complete relief." As the Court explained, allowing recovery in federal court of fees incurred in the state proceedings furthers the goals of Congress * * * . * * *

Pratt argues that *Carey* has been eroded by <u>Kremer v. Chem. Const. Corp., 456 U.S. 461 (1982)</u>, in which the Supreme Court held that a state court judgment affirming the denial of a Title VII claim precluded the claimant from bringing a federal action to relitigate the liability determination. *Kremer* explained that, in enacting Title VII, Congress did not intend "to override the historic respect that federal courts accord state court judgments."[7] However, nothing in *Kremer* (or in any subsequent Supreme Court holdings) overturns *Carey*, and we can read the two cases together as holding that a state court's decision on the merits of a discrimination claim is entitled to full faith and credit, but that Title VII permits a claimant to seek—in federal court—"supplemental" relief that was unavailable in the state court.

Admittedly, there are two main distinctions between *Carey* and the case on appeal: (1) Nestor seeks compensatory and punitive damages as well as attorney's fees; and (2) this federal action was filed after the state court judgment affirming the agency's determinations became final, rather than (as in *Carey*) during the pendency of the appeals from the agency's decision. Neither point seems critical: As in *Carey*, Nestor's federal action affords a victim of employment discrimination no more than the relief she is entitled to get under Title VII and it in no way impedes the state's exercise of its regulatory powers. * * *

Pratt contends that it is unfair to allow the plaintiff to (in effect) relitigate damages while binding the defendant to liability findings, particularly when (as here) liability was decided in an administrative forum that did not afford such basic procedures as discovery. There is force to this argument. However, the same detriment was inflicted in *Carey* * * *. Moreover, the preclusive effect of the state ruling on liability does not depend wholly on the proceedings of the state administrative agency. In Title VII cases, federal courts do not give preclusive effect to state agency decisions unless they have been reviewed in court. *See* <u>Univ. of Tennessee v. Elliott, 478 U.S. 788 (1986)</u>; <u>Kremer, 456 U.S. at 470 n. 7</u>. The CCHRO's liability determination binds Pratt only because Pratt appealed and lost in state court.

2. Connecticut Preclusion Law

Even if state preclusion law controls, Nestor's action survives. In Connecticut, "under the doctrine of *res judicata*, or claim preclusion, a former judgment on a claim, if rendered on the merits, is an absolute bar to a subsequent action [between the same parties or those in privity with them] on the same claim . . . or any claim

---

[7] Under *Kremer*, therefore, Pratt cannot contest the Connecticut state court's determination that Nestor was dismissed by reason of illegal sex discrimination—a point which Pratt uses to support its fairness argument regarding why Nestor should also not be permitted to "relitigate" damages.

based on the same operative facts *that might have been made*." <u>Connecticut National Bank v. Rytman, 694 A.2d 1246, 1256–57 (Conn. 1997)</u> (emphasis in original; internal quotation marks omitted). "The doctrine of *res judicata* is one of rest and is enforced on the ground of public policy. . . . To prevent a multiplicity of actions, equity will enjoin further litigation. . . ." <u>Corey v. Avco-Lycoming Division, 307 A.2d 155, 159–60 (Conn. 1972)</u> (internal citation omitted).

In determining what claims were or could have been litigated in a prior action, Connecticut law applies the "transactional" test described in <u>Section 24 of the Restatement (Second) of Judgments</u>:

> The claim that is extinguished includes all rights of the plaintiff to remedies against the defendant with respect to all or any part of the transaction, or series of connected transactions, out of which the action arose.

See also <u>Orselet v. DeMatteo, 539 A.2d 95, 97 (Conn. 1988)</u> (quoting Restatement (Second) Judgments § 24); *see also* <u>Duhaime v. American Reserve Life Ins. Co., 511 A.2d 333, 334–35 (Conn. 1986)</u>. Therefore, Pratt contends, *res judicata* in Connecticut operates to extinguish all rights regarding the transaction, even if claims for additional remedies could not have been made in the prior proceeding. This argument overlooks an exception.

<u>Section 26(1)(c) of the Restatement (Second) of Judgments</u> provides an exception to the rule against splitting an action where

> [t]he plaintiff was unable to rely on a certain theory of the case or to seek a certain remedy or form of relief in the first action because of the limitations on the subject matter jurisdiction of the courts or restrictions on their authority to entertain multiple theories or demands for multiple remedies or forms of relief in a single action, and the plaintiff desires in the second action to rely on that theory or to seek that remedy or form of relief. . . .

This Restatement provision has been adopted as Connecticut law, *see* <u>Connecticut Water Company v. Beausoleil, 526 A.2d 1329, 1335 (Conn. 1987)</u>, and as the law of other jurisdictions that employ the transaction test of the Restatement.[10]

The defendant in *Beausoleil* had been found liable in an administrative enforcement proceeding for contaminating the public water supply system, and was later

---

[10] *See, e.g.*, <u>Davidson v. Capuano, 792 F.2d 275 (2d Cir. 1986)</u> (noting that New York, which uses the transaction test for judgments, does not apply *res judicata* where "the initial forum did not have the power to award the full measure of relief sought in the later litigation"); <u>Delaware Valley Transplant Program v. Coye, 722 F.Supp. 1188, 1196 (D.N.J. 1989)</u> ("Under New Jersey law of claim preclusion, if the claim was one that could not have been brought, it cannot be precluded."); <u>Esslinger v. Baltimore City, 95 Md.App. 607, 622 A.2d 774, 783 (Md.Ct.Spec.App. 1993)</u> (holding that, under Maryland law, claim for damages was not precluded because it could not have been asserted in the prior action); <u>Lien v. Couch, 993 S.W.2d 53, 56 (Tenn.Ct.App. 1998)</u> (adopting Section 26(c)(1)'s exception to *res judicata*).

sued in tort for damaging the private reservoir of a landowner who had intervened in the enforcement action. The Connecticut Supreme Court held that the private suit for damages was not precluded, because the plaintiff had been unable to seek damages in the administrative enforcement proceeding. The Connecticut Supreme Court recognized the exception to *res judicata* for later actions that assert claims or seek relief that could not have been pressed or recovered in the prior proceeding.

We see no reason why this exception is not equally applicable in the Title VII context. The Connecticut Supreme Court has explained that "doctrines of preclusion . . . should be flexible and must give way when their mechanical application would frustrate other social policies based on values equally or more important than the convenience afforded by finality in legal controversies." Isaac v. Truck Service, Inc., 752 A.2d 509, 513 (Conn. 2000), (internal quotation marks omitted) (holding that a prior small claims court action for recovery of property damages was not *res judicata* in a subsequent lawsuit for personal injury). Connecticut and the federal government share an interest in having employment discrimination claims adjudicated in state agencies. Thus Connecticut set up the CCHRO as a faster and less expensive alternative to litigation in the trial courts; we doubt that Connecticut would apply *res judicata* in a way that would limit the relief available to claimants who use the CCHRO, and thereby furnish an incentive to litigate in court. * * *

The judgment is vacated, and the case is remanded for further proceedings.

Points for Discussion

a. The Doctrine of Claim Preclusion

As previously mentioned, claim preclusion is a common law doctrine that can vary slightly across jurisdictions. Nonetheless, the basic contours of the doctrine are as the *Nestor* court described them when it articulated the Connecticut version of the rule. That is, there are three basic requirements for claim preclusion to apply: (1) the prior action must have concluded in a valid, final judgment on the merits; (2) the claim in the subsequent action must be the same as the claim that was raised or should have been raised in the previous action; and (3) the parties in the subsequent action must be

Take Note!

Although courts look to federal law when determining the preclusive effect of federal court judgments, the Supreme Court has held that in federal diversity cases the claim-preclusive effect to be given is determined by "the law that would be applied by state courts in the State in which the federal diversity court sits," but only to the extent there is no conflict with important federal interests. Semtek Int'l Inc. v. Lockheed Martin Corp., 531 U.S. 497, 508–09 (2001).

identical to—or in privity with—the parties in the first action (we will discuss the meaning of the term privity below). Each of these requirements has its own nuances and complications. However, when satisfied, the doctrine operates to bar subsequent litigation of the claim at issue.

b. Same-Claim Requirement & the "Transactional" Test

Determining whether the same-claim requirement has been satisfied is a simple matter when the claim asserted in the subsequent action is identical to the claim asserted in the previous action. But such a bald reassertion of identical claims that have already been resolved by prior judgments is not a common occurrence given the clarity of the prohibition against relitigation in such cases.

More common are disputes over the applicability of claim preclusion in the context of the subsequent assertion of non-identical, but related claims. Most courts have come to embrace the view that claim preclusion should operate to bar the litigation of certain claims simply because they are closely related to claims asserted in prior litigation, even though the newly raised claims were not necessarily asserted previously. This approach to the same-claim requirement is referred to as the transactional test. The *Nestor* court referred to this transactional test, which is described in Section 24 of the Restatement (Second) of Judgments. The Fifth Circuit provided a useful summary of the Restatement's transactional test in *Petro-Hunt, L.L.C. v. United States*, 365 F.3d 385 (5th Cir. 2004):

Make the Connection

The concepts behind the transactional test should be familiar to you from your study of compulsory counterclaims. As we saw there, claims that arise out of the same transaction or occurrence as the plaintiff's claim must be asserted as counterclaims or are waived. FED. R. CIV. P. 13(a). The transaction or occurrence standard of the compulsory counterclaim rule is reflective of the transactional test for applying claim preclusion to subsequent claims that is being described in the main text here. One could also connect this standard to the "common nucleus of operative fact" test used in the context of a supplemental jurisdiction analysis under 28 U.S.C. § 1367.

To determine whether two suits involve the same claim or cause of action, this court has adopted the transactional test of the Restatement (Second) of Judgments, § 24. Under that test, the preclusive effect of a prior judgment extends to all rights the original plaintiff had with respect to all or any part of the transaction, or series of connected transactions, out of which the [original] action arose. . . . The critical issue is whether the two actions under consideration are based on the *same nucleus of operative facts*.

Id. at 395–96 (alteration in original) (citations and internal quotation marks omitted). Other federal circuits generally adhere to the transactional test as well. *See, e.g., Berrey v. Asarco Inc.*, 439 F.3d 636, 646 n.8 (10th Cir. 2006) ("Under Tenth Circuit law, claim preclusion prevents a party from raising a legal claim in a second lawsuit if . . . the causes of action in both suits arise from the same transaction . . . ."); *Interoceanica Corp. v. Sound Pilots, Inc.*, 107 F.3d 86, 90 (2d Cir. 1997) ("To ascertain whether two actions spring from the same 'transaction' or 'claim,' we look to whether the underlying facts are 'related in time, space, origin, or motivation, whether they form a convenient trial unit, and whether their treatment as a unit conforms to the parties' expectations or business understanding or usage.'" (quoting RESTATEMENT (SECOND) OF JUDGMENTS § 24(b))); *Porn v. Nat'l Grange Mut. Ins. Co.*, 93 F.3d 31, 34 (1st Cir. 1996) (applying the Restatement's transactional test).

To test your understanding of the transactional test, try the following hypothetical problem:

Hypo 11.2

A driver was injured when the driver's vehicle hit a huge pothole that caused it to collide with the side guardrail on the highway. The driver filed an action in a state court in State A against the City for damage to the vehicle, alleging that the City negligently maintained the highway involved in the accident and seeking $50,000 in damages. The court concluded that the City was negligent and awarded the driver $50,000.

The driver then commenced a new action against the City in a State A federal court seeking $100,000 in damages for personal injuries the driver suffered in the accident involving the pothole. State A has adopted the Second Restatement of Judgments' approach to res judicata. The City moved for summary judgment on the basis of claim preclusion, asserting that the judgment in the state court action bars the present federal court action. How is the court likely to rule on the motion?

Because the transactional test prevents parties from dividing what is in effect a single claim into multiple actions to be litigated separately, the rule is sometimes referred to as a "rule against claim splitting." Consol. Edison Co. of N.Y. v. Bodman, 445 F.3d 438, 450–51 (D.C. Cir. 2006). There are exceptions to this rule, however. The one worth mentioning here is the exception discussed by the court in Nestor: The prohibition against claim splitting does not apply if it was not actually possible to have raised the claim in the previous action. *See*

Food for Thought

What are the policy goals behind the doctrine of claim preclusion? *See Allen v. McCurry*, 449 U.S. 90, 94 (1980) ("[R]es judicata and collateral estoppel relieve parties of the cost and vexation of multiple lawsuits, conserve judicial resources, and, by preventing inconsistent decisions, encourage reliance on adjudication."). How does the transactional test further those goals?

Restatement (Second) of Judgments § 26(1)(c). What is the rationale for this exception? Under what circumstances might a party not be able to raise a transactionally related claim in a previous action?

c.   Raising a Claim Preclusion Challenge

Claim preclusion is an affirmative defense that must be set forth in a responsive pleading if a party intends to challenge a claim on preclusion grounds or it may be waived. FED. R. CIV. P. 8(c). However, courts have permitted the defense to be raised for the first time in a motion to dismiss or for summary judgment if the tardy assertion of the defense does not unfairly prejudice the claimant. *Lafreniere Park Found. v. Broussard*, 221 F.3d 804, 808 (5th Cir. 2000) ("[W]here the matter is raised in the trial court in a manner that does not result in unfair surprise, . . . technical failure to comply precisely with Rule 8(c) is not fatal." (quoting *United States v. Shanbaum*, 10 F.3d 305, 312 (5th Cir. 1994))). As just alluded to and as seen in *Nestor*, after raising the defense in a responsive pleading, litigants may press their preclusion defense by seeking dismissal or summary judgment on preclusion grounds, demanding a judgment in their favor on the basis that the current action is barred by a judgment in a prior action.

Courts may consider whether claim preclusion bars a claim *sua sponte*. *See, e.g.*, *Burrell v. Armijo*, 456 F.3d 1159, 1176 (10th Cir. 2006) ("It is well established that a court may raise the issue of preclusion on its own motion, in appropriate cases."). But the Supreme Court has suggested that doing so is warranted only under "special circumstances":

> Judicial initiative of this sort might be appropriate in special circumstances. Most notably, if a court is on notice that it has previously decided the issue presented, the court may dismiss the action *sua sponte*, even though the defense has not been raised. This result is fully consistent with the policies underlying *res judicata*: it is not based solely on the defendant's interest in avoiding the burdens of twice defending a suit, but is also based on the avoidance of unnecessary judicial waste.

Arizona v. California, 530 U.S. 392, 412 (2000) (citation and internal quotation marks omitted); *see also, e.g.*, *Energy Dev. Corp. v. St. Martin*, 296 F.3d 356, 363 (5th Cir. 2002) ("Our cases allowing consideration of *res judicata* or collateral estoppel on appeal do so only if all of the relevant facts are contained in the record and are uncontroverted." (internal quotation marks omitted)). However, courts have no obligation to raise the defense *sua sponte* because preclusion bars are not jurisdictional defects. *See Scherer v. Equitable Life Assurance Soc'y*, 347 F.3d 394, 398 n.4 (2d Cir. 2003) (stating that, unlike jurisdictional defects, a court is not required to apply res judicata *sua sponte*). In other words, the fact that a claim may be precluded does not deprive a court of jurisdiction over the claim, similar to the effect of an expired statute of limitations period. Rather, these are defenses that the litigants are obligated to raise.

The Same-Parties Requirement

As mentioned earlier, in addition to involving the same or transactionally related claims, subsequent actions must involve the same parties as were involved in the prior action—as adversaries—to be barred by claim preclusion. Like the same-claim requirement, whether the same-parties requirement has been satisfied is a no-brainer when the parties in both actions are identical, assuming those parties were adversaries in the previous action. The more challenging question is the extent to which nonparties may be bound by prior actions. Although binding nonparties appears to contravene directly the same-parties requirement, claim preclusion has been extended to embrace subsequent actions involving different parties when they are in "privity" with those who were parties to the previous action, meaning they have a sufficiently close relationship such that it is fair to bind them to the earlier judgment. What type of relationship must a person have with a party to a prior action to be bound by the results obtained therein? The next case explores this concept of privity.

Taylor v. Sturgell

Supreme Court of the United States
553 U.S. 880 (2008)

GINSBURG, J., delivered the opinion for a unanimous Court.

"It is a principle of general application in Anglo-American jurisprudence that one is not bound by a judgment *in personam* in a litigation in which he is not designated as a party or to which he has not been made a party by service of process." *Hansberry v. Lee,* 311 U.S. 32, 40 (1940). Several exceptions, recognized in this Court's decisions, temper this basic rule. In a class action, for example, a person not named as a party may be bound by a judgment on the merits of the action, if she was adequately represented by a party who actively participated in the litigation. In this case, we consider for the first time whether there is a "virtual representation" exception to the general rule against precluding nonparties. * * *

The virtual representation question we examine in this opinion arises in the following context. Petitioner Brent Taylor filed a lawsuit under the Freedom of Information Act seeking certain documents from the Federal Aviation Administration. Greg Herrick, Taylor's friend, had previously brought an unsuccessful suit seeking the same records. The two men have no legal relationship, and there is no evidence that Taylor controlled, financed, participated in, or even had notice of Herrick's earlier suit. Nevertheless, the D.C. Circuit held Taylor's suit precluded by the judgment against Herrick because, in that court's assessment, Herrick qualified as Taylor's "virtual representative."

We disapprove the doctrine of preclusion by "virtual representation," and hold, based on the record as it now stands, that the judgment against Herrick does not bar Taylor from maintaining this suit.

I

The Freedom of Information Act (FOIA) accords "any person" a right to request any records held by a federal agency. 5 U.S.C. § 552(a)(3)(A) (2006 ed.). No reason need be given for a FOIA request, and unless the requested materials fall within one of the Act's enumerated exemptions, see § 552(a)(3)(E), (b), the agency must "make the records promptly available" to the requester, § 552(a)(3)(A). If an agency refuses to furnish the requested records, the requester may file suit in federal court and obtain an injunction "order[ing] the production of any agency records improperly withheld." § 552(a)(4)(B).

The courts below held the instant FOIA suit barred by the judgment in earlier litigation seeking the same records. Because the lower courts' decisions turned on the connection between the two lawsuits, we begin with a full account of each action.

A

The first suit was filed by Greg Herrick, an antique aircraft enthusiast and the owner of an F-45 airplane, a vintage model manufactured by the Fairchild Engine and Airplane Corporation (FEAC) in the 1930's. In 1997, seeking information that would help him restore his plane to its original condition, Herrick filed a FOIA request asking the Federal Aviation Administration (FAA) for copies of any technical documents about the F-45 contained in the agency's records.

To gain a certificate authorizing the manufacture and sale of the F-45, FEAC had submitted to the FAA's predecessor, the Civil Aeronautics Authority, detailed specifications and other technical data about the plane. Hundreds of pages of documents produced by FEAC in the certification process remain in the FAA's records. The FAA denied Herrick's request, however, upon finding that the documents he sought are subject to FOIA's exemption for "trade secrets and commercial or financial information obtained from a person and privileged or confidential," 5 U.S.C. § 552(b)(4) (2006 ed.). In an administrative appeal, Herrick urged that FEAC and its successors had waived any trade-secret protection. The FAA thereupon contacted FEAC's corporate successor, respondent Fairchild Corporation (Fairchild). Because Fairchild objected to release of the documents, the agency adhered to its original decision.

Herrick then filed suit in the U.S. District Court for the District of Wyoming. Challenging the FAA's invocation of the trade-secret exemption, Herrick placed heavy weight on a 1955 letter from FEAC to the Civil Aeronautics Authority. The letter authorized the agency to lend any documents in its files to the public "for use in making repairs or replacement parts for aircraft produced by Fairchild." This broad authorization, Herrick maintained, showed that the F-45 certification records held by the FAA could not be regarded as "secre[t]" or "confidential" within the meaning of § 552(b)(4).

Rejecting Herrick's argument, the District Court granted summary judgment to the FAA. The 1955 letter, the court reasoned, did not deprive the F-45 certification documents of trade-secret status, for those documents were never in fact released pursuant to the letter's blanket authorization. The court also stated that even if the 1955 letter had waived trade-secret protection, Fairchild had successfully "reversed" the waiver by objecting to the FAA's release of the records to Herrick.

On appeal, the Tenth Circuit agreed with Herrick that the 1955 letter had stripped the requested documents of trade-secret protection. But the Court of Appeals upheld the District Court's alternative determination—*i.e.,* that Fairchild had restored trade-secret status by objecting to Herrick's FOIA request. On that ground, the appeals court affirmed the entry of summary judgment for the FAA.

* * *

B

The Tenth Circuit's decision issued on July 24, 2002. Less than a month later, on August 22, petitioner Brent Taylor—a friend of Herrick's and an antique aircraft enthusiast in his own right—submitted a FOIA request seeking the same documents Herrick had unsuccessfully sued to obtain. When the FAA failed to respond, Taylor filed a complaint in the U.S. District Court for the District of Columbia. Like Herrick, Taylor argued that FEAC's 1955 letter had stripped the records of their trade-secret status. But Taylor also sought to litigate the two issues concerning recapture of protected status that Herrick had failed to raise in his appeal to the Tenth Circuit.

After Fairchild intervened as a defendant, the District Court in D.C. concluded that Taylor's suit was barred by claim preclusion; accordingly, it granted summary judgment to Fairchild and the FAA. The court acknowledged that Taylor was not a party to Herrick's suit. Relying on the Eighth Circuit's decision in *Tyus v. Schoemehl,* 93 F.3d 449 (1996), however, it held that a nonparty may be bound by a judgment if she was "virtually represented" by a party. [The district court went on to conclude that Herrick was Taylor's virtual representative under the Eighth Circuit test.] * * * The D.C. Circuit affirmed. * * *

We granted certiorari to resolve the disagreement among the Circuits over the permissibility and scope of preclusion based on "virtual representation."

II

The preclusive effect of a federal-court judgment is determined by federal common law. See *Semtek Int'l Inc. v. Lockheed Martin Corp., 531 U.S. 497, 507–508 (2001).* For judgments in federal-question cases—for example, Herrick's FOIA suit—federal courts participate in developing "uniform federal rule[s]" of res judicata, which this Court has ultimate authority to determine and declare.[4]

What's That?

Federal common law refers to the area of decisional law derived from federal courts on matters of federal concern that are not covered by a codified rule or statute.

Taylor's case presents an issue of first impression in this sense: Until now, we have never addressed the doctrine of "virtual representation" adopted (in varying forms) by several Circuits and relied upon by the courts below. Our inquiry, however, is guided by well-established precedent regarding the propriety of nonparty preclusion. We review that precedent before taking up directly the issue of virtual representation.

A

* * * Under the doctrine of claim preclusion, a final judgment forecloses "successive litigation of the very same claim, whether or not relitigation of the claim raises the same issues as the earlier suit." *New Hampshire v. Maine, 532 U.S. 742, 748 (2001).* Issue preclusion, in contrast, bars "successive litigation of an issue of fact or law actually litigated and resolved in a valid court determination essential to the prior judgment," even if the issue recurs in the context of a different claim. *Id., at 748–749.* * * *

A person who was not a party to a suit generally has not had a "full and fair opportunity to litigate" the claims and issues settled in that suit. The application of claim and issue preclusion to nonparties thus runs up against the "deep-rooted historic tradition that everyone should have his own day in court." Indicating the strength of that tradition, we have often repeated the general rule that "one is not bound by a judgment *in personam* in a litigation in which he is not designated as a party or to which he has not been made a party by service of process." *Hansberry, 311 U.S., at 40.*

---

[4] For judgments in diversity cases, federal law incorporates the rules of preclusion applied by the State in which the rendering court sits. See *Semtek Int'l Inc. v. Lockheed Martin Corp., 531 U.S. 497, 508 (2001).*

B

Though hardly in doubt, the rule against nonparty preclusion is subject to exceptions. For present purposes, the recognized exceptions can be grouped into six categories.

First, "[a] person who agrees to be bound by the determination of issues in an action between others is bound in accordance with the terms of his agreement." 1 Restatement (Second) of Judgments § 40, p. 390 (1980) (hereinafter Restatement). For example, "if separate actions involving the same transaction are brought by different plaintiffs against the same defendant, all the parties to all the actions may agree that the question of the defendant's liability will be definitely determined, one way or the other, in a 'test case.'"

Second, nonparty preclusion may be justified based on a variety of pre-existing "substantive legal relationship[s]" between the person to be bound and a party to the judgment. Qualifying relationships include, but are not limited to, preceding and succeeding owners of property, bailee and bailor, and assignee and assignor. These exceptions originated "as much from the needs of property law as from the values of preclusion by judgment." 18A C. Wright, A. Miller, & E. Cooper, Federal Practice and Procedure § 4448, p. 329 (2d ed. 2002) (hereinafter Wright & Miller).[8]

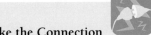

> **Make the Connection**
>
> The terms *bailor* and *bailee* refer to the giving and receiving parties, respectively, to a *bailment*, which refers to the delivery of personal property for a certain purpose without transferring ownership or title. You may study bailments in a basic **Property** course.

Third, we have confirmed that, "in certain limited circumstances," a nonparty may be bound by a judgment because she was "adequately represented by someone with the same interests who [wa]s a party" to the suit. Representative suits with preclusive effect on nonparties include properly conducted class actions and suits brought by trustees, guardians, and other fiduciaries.

Fourth, a nonparty is bound by a judgment if she "assume[d] control" over the litigation in which that judgment was rendered. Because such a person has had "the opportunity to present proofs and argument," he has already "had his day in court" even though he was not a formal party to the litigation.

---

[8] The substantive legal relationships justifying preclusion are sometimes collectively referred to as "privity." The term "privity," however, has also come to be used more broadly, as a way to express the conclusion that nonparty preclusion is appropriate on any ground. To ward off confusion, we avoid using the term "privity" in this opinion.

Fifth, a party bound by a judgment may not avoid its preclusive force by relitigating through a proxy. Preclusion is thus in order when a person who did not participate in a litigation later brings suit as the designated representative of a person who was a party to the prior adjudication. And although our decisions have not addressed the issue directly, it also seems clear that preclusion is appropriate when a nonparty later brings suit as an agent for a party who is bound by a judgment.

It's Latin to Me!

Quo warranto is Latin for "by what warrant" or "by what authority." A *quo warranto* action inquires into the authority by which a public office is held or official action is taken. It might also be used to challenge the legality of a corporate charter or some corporate activity.

Sixth, in certain circumstances a special statutory scheme may "expressly foreclos[e] successive litigation by nonlitigants . . . if the scheme is otherwise consistent with due process." Examples of such schemes include bankruptcy and probate proceedings and *quo warranto* actions or other suits that, "under [the governing] law, [may] be brought only on behalf of the public at large."

III

Reaching beyond these six established categories, some lower courts have recognized a "virtual representation" exception to the rule against nonparty preclusion. Decisions of these courts, however, have been far from consistent. Some Circuits use the label, but define "virtual representation" so that it is no broader than the recognized exception for adequate representation. *See, e.g., Becherer v. Merrill Lynch, Pierce, Fenner & Smith, Inc., 193 F.3d 415, 423, 427 (6th Cir. 1999)*. But other courts, including the Eighth, Ninth, and D.C. Circuits, apply multifactor tests for virtual representation that permit nonparty preclusion in cases that do not fit within any of the established exceptions.

The D.C. Circuit, the FAA, and Fairchild have presented three arguments in support of an expansive doctrine of virtual representation. We find none of them persuasive.

A

The D.C. Circuit purported to ground its virtual representation doctrine in this Court's decisions stating that, in some circumstances, a person may be bound by a judgment if she was adequately represented by a party to the proceeding yielding that judgment. But the D.C. Circuit's definition of "adequate representation" strayed from the meaning our decisions have attributed to that term.

In *Richards v. Jefferson County, 517 U.S. 793 (1996)*, we reviewed a decision by the Alabama Supreme Court holding that a challenge to a tax was barred by a judgment upholding the same tax in a suit filed by different taxpayers. The plaintiffs in the first suit "did not sue on behalf of a class," their complaint "did not purport to assert any claim against or on behalf of any nonparties," and the judgment "did not purport to bind" nonparties. There was no indication, we emphasized, that the court in the first suit "took care to protect the interests" of absent parties, or that the parties to that litigation "understood their suit to be on behalf of absent [parties]." In these circumstances, we held, the application of claim preclusion was inconsistent with "the due process of law guaranteed by the Fourteenth Amendment."

The D.C. Circuit stated, without elaboration, that it did not "read *Richards* to hold a nonparty . . . adequately represented only if special procedures were followed [to protect the nonparty] or the party to the prior suit understood it was representing the nonparty. As the D.C. Circuit saw this case, Herrick adequately represented Taylor for two principal reasons: Herrick had a strong incentive to litigate; and Taylor later hired Herrick's lawyer, suggesting Taylor's "satisfaction with the attorney's performance in the prior case."

The D.C. Circuit misapprehended *Richards*. As just recounted, our holding that the Alabama Supreme Court's application of res judicata to nonparties violated due process turned on the lack of either special procedures to protect the nonparties' interests or an understanding by the concerned parties that the first suit was brought in a representative capacity. *Richards* thus established that representation is "adequate" for purposes of nonparty preclusion only if (at a minimum) one of these two circumstances is present.

We restated *Richards'* core holding in <u>South Central Bell Telephone Co. v. Alabama, 526 U.S. 160 (1999)</u>. In that case, as in *Richards* the Alabama courts had held that a judgment rejecting a challenge to a tax by one group of taxpayers barred a subsequent suit by a different taxpayer. In *South Central Bell,* however, the nonparty had notice of the original suit and engaged one of the lawyers earlier employed by the original plaintiffs. Under the D.C. Circuit's decision in Taylor's case, these factors apparently would have sufficed to establish adequate representation. Yet *South Central Bell* held that the application of res judicata in that case violated due process. Our inquiry came to an end when we determined that the original plaintiffs had not understood themselves to be acting in a representative capacity and that there had been no special procedures to safeguard the interests of absentees.

Our decisions recognizing that a nonparty may be bound by a judgment if she was adequately represented by a party to the earlier suit thus provide no support for the D.C. Circuit's broad theory of virtual representation.

B

Fairchild and the FAA do not argue that the D.C. Circuit's virtual representation doctrine fits within any of the recognized grounds for nonparty preclusion. Rather, they ask us to abandon the attempt to delineate discrete grounds and clear rules altogether. Preclusion is in order, they contend, whenever "the relationship between a party and a non-party is 'close enough' to bring the second litigant within the judgment." Courts should make the "close enough" determination, they urge, through a "heavily fact-driven" and "equitable" inquiry. Only this sort of diffuse balancing, Fairchild and the FAA argue, can account for all of the situations in which nonparty preclusion is appropriate.

We reject this argument for three reasons. First, our decisions emphasize the fundamental nature of the general rule that a litigant is not bound by a judgment to which she was not a party. Accordingly, we have endeavored to delineate discrete exceptions that apply in "limited circumstances." Respondents' amorphous balancing test is at odds with the constrained approach to nonparty preclusion our decisions advance.

* * *

Our second reason for rejecting a broad doctrine of virtual representation rests on the limitations attending nonparty preclusion based on adequate representation. A party's representation of a nonparty is "adequate" for preclusion purposes only if, at a minimum: (1) the interests of the nonparty and her representative are aligned and (2) either the party understood herself to be acting in a representative capacity or the original court took care to protect the interests of the nonparty. In addition, adequate representation sometimes requires (3) notice of the original suit to the persons alleged to have been represented. In the class-action context, these limitations are implemented by the procedural safeguards contained in Federal Rule of Civil Procedure 23.

An expansive doctrine of virtual representation, however, would "recogniz[e], in effect, a common-law kind of class action." That is, virtual representation would authorize preclusion based on identity of interests and some kind of relationship between parties and nonparties, shorn of the procedural protections prescribed in *Hansberry*, *Richards*, and Rule 23. These protections, grounded in due process, could be circumvented were we to approve a virtual representation doctrine that allowed courts to "create *de facto* class actions at will."

Third, a diffuse balancing approach to nonparty preclusion would likely create more headaches than it relieves. Most obviously, it could significantly complicate the task of district courts faced in the first instance with preclusion questions. An all-things-considered balancing approach might spark wide-ranging, time-consuming, and expensive discovery tracking factors potentially relevant under seven- or five-prong tests. And after the relevant facts are established, district judges would be called upon to evaluate them under a standard that provides no firm guidance. Preclusion doctrine, it should be recalled, is intended to reduce the burden of litigation on courts and parties. "In this area of the law," we agree, "'crisp rules with sharp corners' are preferable to a round-about doctrine of opaque standards."

C

Finally, relying on the Eighth Circuit's decision in *Tyus, 93 F.3d, at 456,* the FAA maintains that nonparty preclusion should apply more broadly in "public-law" litigation than in "private-law" controversies. * * * The [Freedom of Information] Act, however, instructs agencies receiving FOIA requests to make the information available not to the public at large, but rather to the "person" making the request. § 552(a)(3)(A). Thus, in contrast to the public-law litigation contemplated in *Richards*, a successful FOIA action results in a grant of relief to the individual plaintiff, not a decree benefiting the public at large.

* * *

The FAA next argues that "the threat of vexatious litigation is heightened" in public-law cases because "the number of plaintiffs with standing is potentially limitless." FOIA does allow "any person" whose request is denied to resort to federal court for review of the agency's determination. Thus it is theoretically possible that several persons could coordinate to mount a series of repetitive lawsuits.

But we are not convinced that this risk justifies departure from the usual rules governing nonparty preclusion. First, *stare decisis* will allow courts swiftly to dispose of repetitive suits brought in the same circuit. Second, even when *stare decisis* is not dispositive, "the human tendency not to waste money will deter the bringing of suits based on claims or issues that have already been adversely determined against others." This intuition seems to be borne out by experience: The FAA has not called our attention to any instances of abusive FOIA suits in the Circuits that reject the virtual representation theory respondents advocate here.

IV

For the foregoing reasons, we disapprove the theory of virtual representation on which the decision below rested. The preclusive effects of a judgment in a federal-question case decided by a federal court should instead be determined according to the established grounds for nonparty preclusion described in this opinion.

* * * We now turn back to Taylor's action to determine whether his suit is such a case, or whether the result reached by the courts below can be justified on one of the recognized grounds for nonparty preclusion.

A

It is uncontested that four of the six grounds for nonparty preclusion have no application here: There is no indication that Taylor agreed to be bound by Herrick's litigation, that Taylor and Herrick have any legal relationship, that Taylor exercised any control over Herrick's suit, or that this suit implicates any special statutory scheme limiting relitigation. Neither the FAA nor Fairchild contends otherwise.

It is equally clear that preclusion cannot be justified on the theory that Taylor was adequately represented in Herrick's suit. Nothing in the record indicates that Herrick understood himself to be suing on Taylor's behalf, that Taylor even knew of Herrick's suit, or that the Wyoming District Court took special care to protect Taylor's interests. Under our pathmarking precedent, therefore, Herrick's representation was not "adequate." See *Richards, 517 U.S., at 801–802*.

That leaves only the fifth category: preclusion because a nonparty to an earlier litigation has brought suit as a representative or agent of a party who is bound by the prior adjudication. Taylor is not Herrick's legal representative and he has not purported to sue in a representative capacity. He concedes, however, that preclusion would be appropriate if respondents could demonstrate that he is acting as Herrick's "undisclosed agen[t]."

Respondents argue here, as they did below, that Taylor's suit is a collusive attempt to relitigate Herrick's action. The D.C. Circuit considered a similar question in addressing the "tactical maneuvering" prong of its virtual representation test. The Court of Appeals did not, however, treat the issue as one of agency, and it expressly declined to reach any definitive conclusions due to "the ambiguity of the facts." We therefore remand to give the courts below an opportunity to determine whether Taylor, in pursuing the instant FOIA suit, is acting as Herrick's agent. Taylor concedes that such a remand is appropriate.

We have never defined the showing required to establish that a nonparty to a prior adjudication has become a litigating agent for a party to the earlier case. Because the issue has not been briefed in any detail, we do not discuss the matter elaboratively here. We note, however, that courts should be cautious about finding preclusion on this basis. A mere whiff of "tactical maneuvering" will not suffice; instead, principles of agency law are suggestive. They indicate that preclusion is appropriate only if the putative agent's conduct of the suit is subject to the control of the party who is bound by the prior adjudication.

B

On remand, Fairchild suggests, Taylor should bear the burden of proving he is not acting as Herrick's agent. When a defendant points to evidence establishing a close relationship between successive litigants, Fairchild maintains, "the burden [should] shif[t] to the second litigant to submit evidence refuting the charge" of agency. Fairchild justifies this proposed burden-shift on the ground that "it is unlikely an opposing party will have access to direct evidence of collusion."

We reject Fairchild's suggestion. Claim preclusion, like issue preclusion, is an affirmative defense. *See* Fed. Rule Civ. Proc. 8(c). Ordinarily, it is incumbent on the defendant to plead and prove such a defense and we have never recognized claim preclusion as an exception to that general rule. We acknowledge that direct evidence justifying nonparty preclusion is often in the hands of plaintiffs rather than defendants. But "[v]ery often one must plead and prove matters as to which his adversary has superior access to the proof." In these situations, targeted interrogatories or deposition questions can reduce the information disparity. We see no greater cause here than in other matters of affirmative defense to disturb the traditional allocation of the proof burden.

* * *

For the reasons stated, the judgment of the United States Court of Appeals for the District of Columbia Circuit is vacated, and the case is remanded for further proceedings consistent with this opinion.

It is so ordered.

Points for Discussion

a.   Defining Privity

In *Taylor*, Justice Ginsburg helpfully sets forth the six circumstances under which courts may consider nonparties to be bound by judgments issued in prior litigation. First, those who agree to be bound by the determination in litigation involving others may be held to that agreement. Second, successors-in-interest, meaning those who are the successive owners of property, for example, are bound by former adjudication respecting that property to the same extent the previous owner would have been bound. What do you think is the basis for such a rule?

The fourth circumstance Justice Ginsburg discusses is that nonparties may be bound by former adjudication because they in fact controlled the prior suit. *See, e.g.*, *Benson & Ford, Inc. v. Wanda Petroleum Co.*, 833 F.2d 1172, 1174–75 (5th Cir. 1987):

> There is no evidence that Ford had control of the *Shelby* litigation. Enterprise argues that Ford had the same attorney, and urges the same facts on the same issues, that Ford was a witness at the *Shelby* trial and that there were meetings about their common interest which Ford and Shelby's president attended. That evidence, however, would not warrant a finding that Ford had actual control over the *Shelby* case. Absent evidence that Ford directly exercised some actual control over Shelby's cause of ac-

tion, the control theory cannot apply. We reject Enterprise's argument that because Ford's attorney was the same attorney who "controlled" the *Shelby* litigation, Ford controlled that case. A plaintiff cannot be precluded from bringing his own suit because he chose an attorney who participated in a prior suit.

What degree of control seems to be necessary to bind the allegedly controlling non-party to the results of a prior suit? *See, e.g., Montana v. United States, 440 U.S. 147, 155 (1979)* (binding the United States to the outcome of a previous suit to which it was not a party because it had required that the suit be pursued by the plaintiff-contractor, scrutinized the complaint, covered legal fees and expenses, and directed the appeal).

The third and fifth circumstances mentioned by Justice Ginsburg in which non-parties are bound because they were adequately represented in the prior litigation is perhaps the most expansive basis for binding nonparties. This category can refer both to situations in which the nonparty was actually represented in a prior case and to situations in which nonparties are found to be sufficiently aligned with parties to be treated as if they were represented in the previous action. The former set of circumstances are summarized in the Restatement (Second) of Judgments:

Restatement (Second) of Judgments § 41.
Person Represented by a Party.

(1) A person who is not a party to an action but who is represented by a party is bound by and entitled to the benefits of a judgment as though he were a party. A person is represented by a party who is:

(a) The trustee of an estate or interest of which the person is a beneficiary; or

(b) Invested by the person with authority to represent him in an action; or

(c) The executor, administrator, guardian, conservator, or similar fiduciary manager of an interest of which the person is a beneficiary; or

(d) An official or agency invested by law with authority to represent the person's interests; or

(e) The representative of a class of persons similarly situated, designated as such with the approval of the court, of which the person is a member.

The latter basis for nonparty preclusion—a sufficient alignment with the parties to a previous action—was asserted (unsuccessfully) in *Cooper v. Harris, 137 S. Ct. 1455 (2017)*. In *Cooper*, the Supreme Court rejected an attempt to preclude two voters from litigating a racial gerrymandering claim that was identical to one previously litigated (and lost) by the North Carolina NAACP. The preclusion theory was that the voters were members of the NAACP, but it turned out that they had paid dues or made financial contributions to the national NAACP and the county NAACP, respectively, which did not make them members of the state branch of the NAACP, and thus could not be treated as having a special relationship with the previous litigant sufficient to permit binding them to the prior result under *Taylor v. Sturgell,* 553 U.S. 880 (2008). Do any exceptions to the rule against nonparty preclusion apply to the facts of the following hypothetical problems?

Hypo 11.3

Polly is the widow of Jake, who died when a truck driven by an employee of ABC, Inc., collided with Jake's car. Before he died, Jake initiated a lawsuit against ABC, Inc. for personal injuries he sustained in the accident. A jury concluded that ABC's driver was not negligent and thus issued a verdict in ABC's favor. After Jake passed away from injuries he sustained in the accident, Polly initiated a wrongful-death action against ABC in Pennsylvania federal court. ABC moves to dismiss the action, asserting that the previous personal injury action involving Jake precludes Polly's wrongful-death suit. How should the court rule?

Hypo 11.4

Smith hired Plumber to do some plumbing work on her home. The plumbing work was subpar and resulted in leaks and damage to the home. Smith sued Plumber for negligence and lost on a jury verdict. The court entered a final judgment in favor of Plumber.

Smith subsequently sold the home to Valdez, who then initiated an action against Plumber seeking damages on a negligence claim against Plumber for the same allegedly faulty plumbing work that was the subject of the aforementioned lawsuit. Plumber seeks summary judgment based on the defense of res judicata (claim preclusion). How should the court rule?

The sixth and final category for nonparty preclusion discussed by Justice Ginsburg is when a statutory or regulatory scheme mandates nonparty preclusion, such as in the case of bankruptcy or probate. Can you understand why nonparty preclusion would be important in these contexts?

b. Privity and Due Process

The requirement of privity is one that is rooted in due process. Specifically, it is a violation of due process to conclude someone's rights through judicial action to which that person was not a party. The Supreme Court restated this long-held principle in <u>Martin v. Wilks, 490 U.S. 755 (1989)</u>:

> All agree that "[i]t is a principle of general application in Anglo-American jurisprudence that one is not bound by a judgment *in personam* in a litigation in which he is not designated as a party or to which he has not been made a party by service of process." <u>Hansberry v. Lee, 311 U.S. 32, 40 (1940)</u>. This rule is part of our "deep-rooted historic tradition that everyone should have his own day in court." A judgment or decree among parties to a lawsuit resolves issues as among them, but it does not conclude the rights of strangers to those proceedings.

<u>Id. at 761–62</u>. The Court went on to indicate, in a footnote, that it had recognized various exceptions to this principle in instances where a person was adequately represented in or had control over the prior litigation. <u>Id. at 762 n.2</u>. However, as the *Taylor* Court made clear, the concept of virtual representation as had been approved by many lower courts went too far.

The Requirement of a Valid Final Judgment

Finally we come to the third requirement for claim preclusion, that only valid, final judgments will be accorded claim-preclusive effect. Although we have already discussed finality in the context of our discussion of appellate review above, finality for purposes of claim preclusion requires more specificity. In particular, traditional formulations of this requirement have alluded to three aspects of the rule: validity, finality, and the need for the judgment to be "on the merits."

Validity simply means that the rendering court was a court with proper jurisdiction over the matter and over the parties, not that the prior judgment was legally correct. *See* <u>Federated Dep't Stores, Inc. v. Moitie, 452 U.S. 394, 398 (1981)</u>. *Finality* is not a complex concept here either; the Supreme Court has defined a final decision as one that "ends the litigation on the merits and leaves nothing for the court to do but execute the judgment." <u>Firestone Tire & Rubber Co. v. Risjord, 449 U.S. 368, 373 (1981)</u> (internal quotation marks omitted). The more nettlesome issue can be whether the resolution of the matter was one "*on the merits.*" Although judgments entered on verdicts after trial—or even summary judgments—can easily be deemed to be on-the-merits resolutions, what about various dismissals of actions such as for lack of jurisdiction or for failure to state a claim? How should these decisions be regarded for purposes of preclusion doctrine?

Semtek International Inc. v. Lockheed Martin Corp.

Supreme Court of the United States
531 U.S. 497 (2001)

JUSTICE SCALIA delivered the opinion of the Court.

This case presents the question whether the claim-preclusive effect of a federal judgment dismissing a diversity action on statute-of-limitations grounds is determined by the law of the State in which the federal court sits.

I

Petitioner filed a complaint against respondent in California state court, alleging inducement of breach of contract and various business torts. Respondent removed the case to the United States District Court for the Central District of California on the basis of diversity of citizenship, see 28 U.S.C. §§ 1332, 1441 (1994 ed. and Supp. IV), and successfully moved to dismiss petitioner's claims as barred by California's 2-year statute of limitations. In its order of dismissal, the District Court, adopting language suggested by respondent, dismissed petitioner's claims "in [their] entirety on the merits and with prejudice." Without contesting the District Court's designation of its dismissal as "on the merits," petitioner appealed to the Court of Appeals for the Ninth Circuit, which affirmed the District Court's order. Petitioner also brought suit against respondent in the State Circuit Court for Baltimore City, Maryland, alleging the same causes of action, which were not time barred under Maryland's 3-year statute of limitations. Respondent sought injunctive relief against this action from the California federal court under the All Writs Act, 28 U.S.C. § 1651, and removed the action to the United States District Court for the District of Maryland on federal-question grounds (diversity grounds were not available because Lockheed "is a Maryland citizen," *Semtek Int'l, Inc. v. Lockheed Martin Corp.*, 988 F. Supp. 913, 914 (1997)). The California federal court denied the relief requested, and the Maryland federal court remanded the case to state court because the federal question arose only by way of defense. Following a hearing, the Maryland state court granted respondent's motion to dismiss on the ground of res judicata. Petitioner then

Make the Connection

The Court notes that removal to Maryland federal court on the basis of diversity jurisdiction was unavailable because the defendant was a Maryland citizen. Recall our study of removal jurisdiction in Chapter 3. Why was such removal not possible but removal based on federal question jurisdiction was possible?

The Court then notes that the matter was remanded to Maryland state court because "the federal question arose only by way of defense." Why was that an issue that undermined the existence of federal question jurisdiction?

returned to the California federal court and the Ninth Circuit, unsuccessfully moving both courts to amend the former's earlier order so as to indicate that the dismissal was not "on the merits." Petitioner also appealed the Maryland trial court's order of dismissal to the Maryland Court of Special Appeals. The Court of Special Appeals affirmed, holding that, regardless of whether California would have accorded claim-preclusive effect to a statute-of-limitations dismissal by one of its own courts, the dismissal by the California federal court barred the complaint filed in Maryland, since the res judicata effect of federal diversity judgments is prescribed by federal law, under which the earlier dismissal was on the merits and claim preclusive. After the Maryland Court of Appeals declined to review the case, we granted certiorari.

II

Petitioner contends that the outcome of this case is controlled by *Dupasseur v. Rochereau*, 21 Wall. 130, 135, 22 L. Ed. 588 (1875), which held that the res judicata effect of a federal diversity judgment "is such as would belong to judgments of the State courts rendered under similar circumstances," and may not be accorded any "higher sanctity or effect." Since, petitioner argues, the dismissal of an action on statute-of-limitations grounds by a California state court would not be claim preclusive, it follows that the similar dismissal of this diversity action by the California federal court cannot be claim preclusive. While we agree that this would be the result demanded by *Dupasseur*, the case is not dispositive because it was decided under the Conformity Act of 1872, 17 Stat. 196, which required federal courts to apply the procedural law of the forum State in nonequity cases. That arguably affected the outcome of the case. *See* Restatement (Second) of Judgments § 87, Comment a, p. 315 (1980) (hereinafter Restatement) ("Since procedural law largely determines the matters that may be adjudicated in an action, state law had to be considered in ascertaining the effect of a federal judgment").

What's That?

The citation to *Dupasseur* contains references with which you may be unfamiliar. The first citation refers to "Wall." That is an abbreviation that refers to the Reporter of Decisions at the time, John William Wallace. The second citation includes "L. Ed." This is an abbreviation for *Lawyers' Edition*, which is an unofficial source for Supreme Court opinions.

Respondent, for its part, contends that the outcome of this case is controlled by Federal Rule of Civil Procedure 41(b), which provides as follows:

"Involuntary Dismissal: Effect Thereof. For failure of the plaintiff to prosecute or to comply with these rules or any order of court, a defendant may move for dismissal of an action or of any claim against the defendant. Unless the court in its order for dismissal otherwise specifies, a dismissal under this subdivision and any dismissal not provided for in this rule, other than a dismissal for lack of jurisdiction, for improper venue, or for failure to join a party under Rule 19, operates as an adjudication upon the merits."

Since the dismissal here did not "otherwise specif[y]" (indeed, it specifically stated that it was "on the merits"), and did not pertain to the excepted subjects of jurisdiction, venue, or joinder, it follows, respondent contends, that the dismissal "is entitled to claim preclusive effect."

Implicit in this reasoning is the unstated minor premise that all judgments denominated "on the merits" are entitled to claim-preclusive effect. That premise is not necessarily valid. The original connotation of an "on the merits" adjudication is one that actually "pass[es] directly on the substance of [a particular] claim" before the court. Restatement § 19, Comment a, at 161. That connotation remains common to every jurisdiction of which we are aware. *See* ibid. ("The prototyp[ical] [judgment on the merits is] one in which the merits of [a party's] claim are in fact adjudicated [for or] against the [party] after trial of the substantive issues"). And it is, we think, the meaning intended in those many statements to the effect that a judgment "on the merits" triggers the doctrine of res judicata or claim preclusion. *See, e.g.*, _Parklane Hosiery Co. v. Shore, 439 U.S. 322, 326, n.5 (1979)_ ("Under the doctrine of res judicata, a judgment on the merits in a prior suit bars a second suit involving the same parties or their privies based on the same cause of action").

But over the years the meaning of the term "judgment on the merits" "has gradually undergone change," and it has come to be applied to some judgments (such as the one involved here) that do not pass upon the substantive merits of a claim and hence do not (in many jurisdictions) entail claim-preclusive effect. That is why the Restatement of Judgments has abandoned the use of the term—"because of its possibly misleading connotations," Restatement § 19, Comment a, at 161.

In short, it is no longer true that a judgment "on the merits" is necessarily a judgment entitled to claim-preclusive effect; and there are a number of reasons for believing that the phrase "adjudication upon the merits" does not bear that meaning in Rule 41(b). To begin with, Rule 41(b) sets forth nothing more than a default rule for determining the import of a dismissal (a dismissal is "upon the merits," with the three stated exceptions, unless the court "otherwise specifies"). This would be a highly peculiar context in which to announce a federally prescribed rule on the complex question of claim preclusion, saying in effect, "All federal dismissals (with three specified exceptions) preclude suit elsewhere, unless the court otherwise specifies."

And even apart from the purely default character of Rule 41(b), it would be peculiar to find a rule governing the effect that must be accorded federal judgments by other courts ensconced in rules governing the internal procedures of the rendering court itself. Indeed, such a rule would arguably violate the jurisdictional limitation of the Rules Enabling Act: that the Rules "shall not abridge, enlarge or modify any substantive right," 28 U.S.C. § 2072(b). *Cf. Ortiz v. Fibreboard Corp., 527 U.S. 815, 842 (1999)* (adopting a "limiting construction" of Federal Rule of Civil Procedure 23(b)(1)(B) in order to "minimiz[e] potential conflict with the Rules Enabling Act, and [to] avoi[d] serious constitutional concerns"). In the present case, for example, if California law left petitioner free to sue on this claim in Maryland even after the California statute of limitations had expired, the federal court's extinguishment of that right (through Rule 41(b)'s mandated claim-preclusive effect of its judgment) would seem to violate this limitation.

Moreover, as so interpreted, the Rule would in many cases violate the federalism principle of *Erie R.R. Co. v. Tompkins, 304 U.S. 64, 78–80 (1938)*, by engendering "'substantial' variations [in outcomes] between state and federal litigation" which would "[l]ikely . . . influence the choice of a forum," *Hanna v. Plumer, 380 U.S. 460, 467–468 (1965). See also Guaranty Trust Co. v. York, 326 U.S. 99, 108–110 (1945). Cf. Walker v. Armco Steel Corp., 446 U.S. 740, 748–753 (1980)*. With regard to the claim-preclusion issue involved in the present case, for example, the traditional rule is that expiration of the applicable statute of limitations merely bars the remedy and does not extinguish the substantive right, so that dismissal on that ground does not have claim-preclusive effect in other jurisdictions with longer, unexpired limitations periods. *See* Restatement (Second) of Conflict of Laws §§ 142(2), 143 (1969); Restatement of Judgments § 49, Comment a (1942). Out-of-state defendants sued on stale claims in California and in other States adhering to this traditional rule would systematically remove state-law suits brought against them to federal court—where, unless otherwise specified, a statute-of-limitations dismissal would bar suit everywhere.

Take Note!

Notice how the Court is invoking the analysis from *Hanna v. Plumer* and *Erie R.R. Co. v. Tompkins* to aid in its interpretation of Rule 41(b). How is the Court using the *Hanna/Erie* doctrine to affirm its view that Rule 41(b) does not prescribe the rule of finality for federal dismissals for purposes of preclusion doctrine?

Finally, if Rule 41(b) did mean what respondent suggests, we would surely have relied upon it in our cases recognizing the claim-preclusive effect of federal judgments in federal-question cases. Yet for over half a century since the promulgation of Rule 41(b), we have not once done so.

We think the key to a more reasonable interpretation of the meaning of "operates as an adjudication upon the merits" in Rule 41(b) is to be found in Rule 41(a), which, in discussing the effect of voluntary dismissal by the plaintiff, makes clear that an "adjudication upon the merits" is the opposite of a "dismissal without prejudice":

> "Unless otherwise stated in the notice of dismissal or stipulation, the dismissal is without prejudice, except that a notice of dismissal operates as an adjudication upon the merits when filed by a plaintiff who has once dismissed in any court of the United States or of any state an action based on or including the same claim."

See also 18 WRIGHT & MILLER § 4435, at 329, n. 4 ("Both parts of Rule 41 . . . use the phrase 'without prejudice' as a contrast to adjudication on the merits"); 9 id., § 2373, at 396, n. 4 ("'[W]ith prejudice' is an acceptable form of shorthand for 'an adjudication upon the merits'"). The primary meaning of "dismissal without prejudice," we think, is dismissal without barring the plaintiff from returning later, to the same court, with the same underlying claim. That will also ordinarily (though not always) have the consequence of not barring the claim from other courts, but its primary meaning relates to the dismissing court itself. Thus, BLACK'S LAW DICTIONARY (7th ed. 1999) defines "dismissed without prejudice" as "removed from the court's docket in such a way that the plaintiff may refile the same suit on the same claim," and defines "dismissal without prejudice" as "[a] dismissal that does not bar the plaintiff from refiling the lawsuit within the applicable limitations period."

We think, then, that the effect of the "adjudication upon the merits" default provision of Rule 41(b)—and, presumably, of the explicit order in the present case that used the language of that default provision—is simply that, unlike a dismissal "without prejudice," the dismissal in the present case barred refiling of the same claim in the United States District Court for the Central District of California. That is undoubtedly a necessary condition, but it is not a sufficient one, for claim-preclusive effect in other courts.[2]

III

Having concluded that the claim-preclusive effect, in Maryland, of this California federal diversity judgment is dictated neither by *Dupasseur v. Rochereau,* as petitioner contends, nor by Rule 41(b), as respondent contends, we turn to consideration of what determines the issue. Neither the Full Faith and Credit Clause, U.S. Const., Art. IV,

---

[2] We do not decide whether, in a diversity case, a federal court's "dismissal upon the merits" (in the sense we have described), under circumstances where a state court would decree only a "dismissal without prejudice," abridges a "substantive right" and thus exceeds the authorization of the Rules Enabling Act. We think the situation will present itself more rarely than would the arguable violation of the Act that would ensue from interpreting Rule 41(b) as a rule of claim preclusion; and if it is a violation, can be more easily dealt with on direct appeal.

§ 1,[3] nor the full faith and credit statute, 28 U.S.C. § 1738,[4] addresses the question. By their terms they govern the effects to be given only to state-court judgments (and, in the case of the statute, to judgments by courts of territories and possessions). And no other federal textual provision, neither of the Constitution nor of any statute, addresses the claim-preclusive effect of a judgment in a federal diversity action.

It is also true, however, that no federal textual provision addresses the claim-preclusive effect of a federal-court judgment in a federal-question case, yet we have long held that States cannot give those judgments merely whatever effect they would give their own judgments, but must accord them the effect that this Court prescribes. *See Deposit Bank v. Frankfort,* 191 U.S. 499, 514–515 (1903) [and other cases]. The reasoning of that line of cases suggests, moreover, that even when States are allowed to give federal judgments (notably, judgments in diversity cases) no more than the effect accorded to state judgments, that disposition is by direction of this Court, which has the last word on the claim-preclusive effect of all federal judgments: "It is true that for some purposes and within certain limits it is only required that the judgments of the courts of the United States shall be given the same force and effect as are given the judgments of the courts of the States wherein they are rendered; but it is equally true that whether a Federal judgment has been given due force and effect in the state court is a Federal question reviewable by this court, which will determine for itself whether such judgment has been given due weight or otherwise. . . .

> "When is the state court obliged to give to Federal judgments only the force and effect it gives to state court judgments within its own jurisdiction? Such cases are distinctly pointed out in the opinion of Mr. Justice Bradley in *Dupasseur v. Rochereau* [which stated that the case was a diversity case, applying state law under state procedure]." *Ibid.*

In other words, in *Dupasseur* the State was allowed (indeed, required) to give a federal diversity judgment no more effect than it would accord one of its own judgments only because reference to state law was *the federal rule that this Court deemed appropriate.* In short, federal common law governs the claim-preclusive effect of a dismissal by a federal court sitting in diversity. *See generally* R. FALLON, D. MELTZER, & D. SHAPIRO, HART AND WECHSLER'S THE FEDERAL COURTS AND THE FEDERAL SYSTEM 1473 (4th ed. 1996); Degnan, *Federalized Res Judicata,* 85 YALE L.J. 741 (1976).

---

[3] Article IV, § 1, provides as follows:

"Full Faith and Credit shall be given in each State to the public Acts, Records, and judicial Proceedings of every other State. And the Congress may by general Laws prescribe the Manner in which such Acts, Records and Proceedings shall be proved, and the Effect thereof."

[4] Title 28 U.S.C. § 1738 provides in relevant part as follows:

"The records and judicial proceedings of any court of any . . . State, Territory or Possession . . . shall have the same full faith and credit in every court within the United States and its Territories and Possessions as they have by law or usage in the courts of such State, Territory or Possession from which they are taken."

It is left to us, then, to determine the appropriate federal rule. And despite the sea change that has occurred in the background law since *Dupasseur* was decided— not only repeal of the Conformity Act but also the watershed decision of this Court in *Erie*—we think the result decreed by *Dupasseur* continues to be correct for diversity cases. Since state, rather than federal, substantive law is at issue there is no need for a uniform federal rule. And indeed, nationwide uniformity in the substance of the matter is better served by having the same claim-preclusive rule (the state rule) apply whether the dismissal has been ordered by a state or a federal court. This is, it seems to us, a classic case for adopting, as the federally prescribed rule of decision, the law that would be applied by state courts in the State in which the federal diversity court sits. *See Gasperini v. Center for Humanities, Inc.*, 518 U.S. 415, 429–431 (1996); *Walker v. Armco Steel Corp.*, 446 U.S., at 752–753; *Klaxon Co. v. Stentor Elec. Mfg. Co.*, 313 U.S. 487, 496 (1941). As we have alluded to above, any other rule would produce the sort of "forum-shopping . . . and . . . inequitable administration of the laws" that *Erie* seeks to avoid, *Hanna*, 380 U.S., at 468, since filing in, or removing to, federal court would be encouraged by the divergent effects that the litigants would anticipate from likely grounds of dismissal. *See Guaranty Trust Co. v. York*, 326 U.S., at 109–110.

Take Note!

Note the difference between *federal common law*, referred to here, and *general federal common law*, something that was rejected by the Supreme Court in *Erie R.R. Co. v. Tompkins*, 304 U.S. 64 (1938). Can you articulate the distinction between the two?

This federal reference to state law will not obtain, of course, in situations in which the state law is incompatible with federal interests. If, for example, state law did not accord claim-preclusive effect to dismissals for willful violation of discovery orders, federal courts' interest in the integrity of their own processes might justify a contrary federal rule. No such conflict with potential federal interests exists in the present case. Dismissal of this state cause of action was decreed by the California federal court only because the California statute of limitations so required; and there is no conceivable federal interest in giving that time bar more effect in other courts than the California courts themselves would impose.

* * *

Because the claim-preclusive effect of the California federal court's dismissal "upon the merits" of petitioner's action on statute-of-limitations grounds is governed by a federal rule that in turn incorporates California's law of claim preclusion (the content of which we do not pass upon today), the Maryland Court of Special

Appeals erred in holding that the dismissal necessarily precluded the bringing of this action in the Maryland courts. The judgment is reversed, and the case remanded for further proceedings not inconsistent with this opinion.

It is so ordered.

———————————

Points for Discussion

a. The Holding of *Semtek*

What is the *Semtek* Court's holding regarding the preclusive effect of dismissals in federal diversity actions? The Court dismisses the notion that Rule 41(b) addresses the preclusive effect that should be given under such circumstances. *See, e.g.,* *Styskal v. Weld Cty. Bd. of Comm'rs*, 365 F.3d 855, 858 (10th Cir. 2004) ("The [*Semtek*] court concluded that the phrase 'adjudication upon the merits' in Rule 41(b) does not mean that the judgment must result in claim preclusion."). Does the *Semtek* Court's interpretation of Rule 41(b) make sense? *See* Stephen B. Burbank, Semtek, *Forum Shopping, and Federal Common Law*, 77 NOTRE DAME L. REV. 1027, 1042 (2002) (referring to the Court's interpretation as "a transparently dubious interpretation").

More significantly, *Semtek* stands for the proposition that federal common law governs the preclusive effect of federal court judgments and that in diversity actions, the common law rule is to give judgments the same effect as would state courts in the state where the federal court sits. For judgments actually rendered by state courts, federal courts are bound to give them the same effect as would the states that rendered those judgments under the Full Faith and Credit Act. 28 U.S.C. § 1738 ("[J]udicial proceedings or copies thereof . . . shall have the same full faith and credit in every court within the United States . . . as they have by law or usage in the courts of [the] State . . . from which they are taken."); *see also* *Baker v. Gen. Motors Corp.*, 522 U.S. 222, 246 (1998) (noting that federal courts "give the same preclusive effect to state court judgments that those judgments would be given in the courts of the State from which the judgments emerged.").

Hypo 11.5

Felix (VA) filed a suit for defamation seeking $100,000 in damages against Miguel (NC) in North Carolina federal court. Miguel filed a motion to dismiss the claim under Rule 12(b)(6) because under North Carolina's statute of limitations the claim would be time barred in North Carolina state court. The court agrees with Miguel and dismisses the action "with prejudice."

Felix then went to Virginia state court and filed an action asserting the same defamation claim against Miguel seeking $100,000. Miguel removed the case to Virginia federal court on the basis of diversity and then moved to dismiss the claim based on claim preclusion, pointing to the previous dismissal of the same claim in North Carolina federal court. Felix responded by pointing out that Virginia's statute-of-limitations period has not expired and that Virginia state courts would not give the prior North Carolina dismissal claim preclusive effect because it was a dismissal based on a procedural bar that is inapplicable in Virginia. Miguel replies by pointing out that North Carolina state courts give preclusive effect to dismissals based on the expiration of a statute-of-limitations period. How should the court rule on Miguel's motion?

b. The Meaning of a Judgment "On the Merits"

Semtek also made the point that what ultimately matters in determining the preclusive effect of a dismissal is not the label placed on the dismissal by Rule 41(b) but rather the underlying basis for the dismissal. *See Styskal*, 365 F.3d at 859 ("The state court's decision regarding whether claim preclusion prevents a state lawsuit will depend upon the basis of the federal court's dismissal, not the nomenclature employed by the federal court to describe the dismissal."). As the Tenth Circuit in *Styskal* further explained in the context of the dismissal of civil RICO claims,

[I]f the federal court's ruling is based on the substance of the claim (what has often been termed an "adjudication on the merits,") the doctrine of claim preclusion would ordinarily prevent further proceedings on the claim in a later state action. But if the federal court's dismissal is based on a procedural ground, the federal ruling is unlikely to have any preclusive effect in state court, even though the dismissal may bar the plaintiff from returning to federal court.

Id. at 859 n.1 (citations omitted).

What's That?

RICO is an abbreviation that refers to the Racketeer Influenced and Corrupt Organizations Act. The statute provides, in part, "It shall be unlawful for any person who has received any income derived, . . . from a pattern of racketeering activity or through collection of an unlawful debt . . . to use or invest . . . any part of such income . . . in acquisition of any interest in, or the establishment or operation of, any enterprise." 18 U.S.C. § 1962(a). Those who have been "injured in [their] business or property by reason of a violation of section 1962" may initiate civil actions against the alleged violators. 18 U.S.C. § 1964(c).

So the basic rule of thumb is that a judgment based on the substance of the claim will be regarded as a judgment "on the merits." Judgments on verdicts certainly qualify; summary judgments and judgments as a matter of law will tend to be on the merits in this sense as well. On the other hand, dismissals based on jurisdictional defects, failures of notice, or improper venue are procedural grounds for terminating a case that will not bar subsequent relitigation. *See Haywood v. Drown*, 556 U.S. 729, 766 (2009) ("[B]ecause the dismissal . . . is for lack of subject-matter jurisdiction it has no preclusive effect on claims refiled in federal court."); *Sewell v. Merrill Lynch Pierce Fenner & Smith*, 94 F.3d 1514, 1518 (11th Cir. 1996) ("[O]rdinarily a judgment dismissing an action or otherwise denying relief for want of jurisdiction, venue, or related reasons does not preclude a subsequent action in a court of competent jurisdiction on the

Practice Pointer

Keep in mind that these are general statements about how courts will treat various outcomes for purposes of claim preclusion. Each state has its own preclusion doctrine that may vary in some manner from these generalizations; for example, some states may take varying positions with respect to questions such as whether statute-of-limitations-based dismissals are entitled to preclusive effect. Thus, you must consult the applicable jurisdiction's preclusion law to determine the precise contours of the relevant doctrine when you are in practice.

merits of the cause of action originally involved." (citing 1B JAMES W. MOORE ET AL., MOORE'S FEDERAL PRACTICE ¶ 0.405[5] (2d ed. 1996))).

Although whether a judgment is "on the merits" is clear when the resolution of the case is the result of some consideration of the substance of a dispute, many courts have expanded their understanding of what counts as a merits dismissal to judicial resolutions less clearly connected to substance, such as statute-of-limitations-based dismissals. *See, e.g., Plaut v. Spendthrift Farm, Inc.*, 514 U.S. 211, 228 (1995) ("The rules of finality, both statutory and judge made, treat a dismissal on statute-of-limitations grounds . . . as a judgment on the merits.").

c. Preclusion in Non-Diversity Cases

Semtek addressed the preclusive effect of dismissals in federal diversity cases. What is the relevant standard for determining the preclusive effect of dismissals in non-diversity cases in federal court? It is federal law that applies in this context. *See Maher v. GSI Lumonics, Inc.*, 433 F.3d 123, 126 (1st Cir. 2005) ("[B]ecause the judgment in [the previous case] was rendered by a federal court exercising federal question jurisdiction, the applicability of res judicata is a matter of federal law."). The federal standard applied is a federal common law standard that is virtually identical to the version of claim preclusion prevalent among the states: "Before res judicata will apply, three factors must be present: (1) a final judgment on the merits in the earlier action; (2) an identity of the cause of action in both the earlier and later suits; and (3) an identity of parties or privies in the two suits." *Id. at 127* (internal quotation marks omitted).

d. Preclusive Effect of State Judgments in Federal Court

The full faith and credit statute compels federal courts to look to the rendering state's law to ascertain a judgment's preclusive effect. 28 U.S.C. § 1738 ("[J]udicial proceedings . . . shall have the same full faith and credit in every court within the United States . . . as they have by law or usage in the courts of such State, Territory or Possession from which they are taken."). This is true even if the preclusion determination is being made in the context of a subsequent lawsuit involving claims based on federal law. *See Marrese v. Am. Acad. of Orthopaedic Surgeons, 470 U.S. 373, 383 (1985)* (holding that the full faith and credit statute can apply in the context of a subsequent federal antitrust claim and that whether an exception applies depends on congressional intent).

e. The Preclusive Effect of Rule 12(b)(6) Dismissals

The Supreme Court has stated, "The dismissal for failure to state a claim under Federal Rule of Civil Procedure 12(b)(6) is a 'judgment on the merits.'" *Federated Dep't Stores, Inc. v. Moitie, 452 U.S. 394, 399 n.3 (1981)*. Should the *Federated Department Stores* position on the preclusive effect of 12(b)(6) dismissals be reconsidered in light of *Ashcroft v. Iqbal, 556 U.S. 662, 678 (2009)*, and *Bell Atlantic v. Twombly, 550 U.S. 544, 570 (2007)*, which made it possible for 12(b)(6) dismissals to result from the pleading of insufficient factual detail? Such dismissals arguably would be on procedural grounds and many pleaders are given the opportunity to replead. If courts render 12(b)(6) dismissals and indicate that the dismissal is "without prejudice," that designation typically will suffice to deprive the dismissal of the preclusive effect that *Federated Department Stores* would otherwise attach to it. *See, e.g., Lawson v. Toney, 169 F. Supp. 2d 456, 462 (M.D.N.C. 2001)* (holding that a Rule 12(b)(6) dismissal does not reach the merits but acts as an adjudication on the merits and precludes refiling of a claim unless the dismissal was without prejudice). However, successive failed attempts to plead a claim can result in 12(b)(6) dismissals "with prejudice" that will fall within the *Federated Department Stores* rule.

Practice Pointer

If your client is facing a 12(b)(6) dismissal, you should ask the court to designate the dismissal as "without prejudice" so that you will have the opportunity to replead in that court or file the claim in another jurisdiction. Failure to make such a request may result in your client being bound by the court's determination of factual insufficiency. *See, e.g., Wagh v. Metris Direct, Inc., 363 F.3d 821, 831–32 (9th Cir. 2003), overruled on other grounds, Odom v. Microsoft Corp., 486 F.3d 541, 551 (9th Cir. 2007)* (en banc).

f. Judgments on Appeal

Do judgments that are on appeal have preclusive effect or must all appeals be exhausted before a judgment may bar a subsequent suit? The general rule is that a pending appeal does not impact the preclusive effect of a judgment unless the appeals court reverses or alters the judgment. *See* 18A C. Wright, A. Miller & E. Cooper, Fed. Prac. & Proc. § 4432 (2d ed. 2002) ("Although preclusion is not affected by the fact that an appeal has been taken, the nature of the ultimate final judgment in a case ordinarily is controlled by the actual appellate disposition.").

g. Default Judgments and Settlements

Default judgments, although not the product of fully contested litigation, are nonetheless given full claim-preclusive effect so long as they are valid from a juris-dictional perspective. *Morris v. Jones, 329 U.S. 545, 550–51 (1947)* ("A judgment of a court having jurisdiction of the parties and of the subject matter operates as res judicata, in the absence of fraud or collusion, even if obtained upon a default."). *See also Whitaker v. Ameritech Corp., 129 F.3d 952, 957 (7th Cir. 1997)* ("[A] default judgment in Illinois is a judgment on the merits and has the same preclusive effect as a judgment resulting from arduous litigation." (citing *Hous. Auth. for La Salle Cty. v. YMCA, 461 N.E.2d 959, 963 (Ill. 1984)*))).

Settlements that are reduced to judgments are given claim-preclusive (but not issue-preclusive) effect. *Arizona v. California, 530 U.S. 392, 414 (2000)* ("In most circumstances, it is recognized that consent agreements ordinarily are intended to preclude any further litigation on the claim presented but are not intended to pre-clude further litigation on any of the issues presented. Thus consent judgments ordi-narily support claim preclusion but not issue preclusion."); *see also* 18A C. Wright, A. Miller, & E. Cooper, Fed. Prac. & Proc. § 4443 (2d ed. 2002).

h. Foreign Judgments

To what extent should the judgments rendered by courts in foreign countries be given claim-preclusive effect in U.S. jurisdictions? *See, e.g., Black Clawson Co., Inc. v. Kroenert Corp., 245 F.3d 759 (8th Cir. 2001)*:

> Foreign adjudication of an issue may preclude its relitigation in our courts. A foreign judgment is recognized, enforced, and given preclusive effect by a court of this country if the court finds five factors to be present. *Shen v. Leo A. Daly Co., 222 F.3d 472, 476 (8th Cir. 2000)* (citing *Hilton v. Guyot, 159 U.S. 113 (1895)*). Previously litigated claims should not be retried if the reviewing court finds that the foreign court provided a full and fair trial of the issues in a court of competent jurisdiction, the foreign forum ensured the impartial administration of justice, the foreign forum ensured that the trial was conducted without prejudice or fraud, the foreign court

had proper jurisdiction over the parties, and the foreign judgment does not violate public policy. *Shen, 222 F.3d at 476* (citing *Hilton, 159 U.S. at 202–03*).

Black Clawson, 245 F.3d at 763.

---

2. Issue Preclusion

Issue preclusion (also referred to as collateral estoppel) refers to the preclusive effect that prior judicial determinations have on the relitigation of certain issues rather than claims. Classically speaking, to invoke the doctrine of issue preclusion, four requirements must be met: (1) the issue to be precluded in subsequent litigation must be the same issue that was raised in the prior litigation that resulted in a valid final judgment; (2) the issue must have been actually litigated and determined in the first case; (3) resolution of that issue must have been necessary to the judgment in the initial action; and (4) the subsequent action must involve the same parties or their privies. *See S. Pac. R.R. Co. v. United States, 168 U.S. 1, 48–49 (1897)*. The modern view of the doctrine embraced in the federal system and in most state jurisdictions no longer holds completely to the same-parties requirement, a matter that will be taken up in greater detail below.

The contours of issue preclusion doctrine differ in several important respects from the contours of claim prelusion but they also have areas of commonality. Dealing with the common matters first, whether the parties in subsequent litigation are the same or in privity with those who were parties to prior litigation is determined according to the same principles discussed above in the context of claim preclusion. Similarly, determining whether the previous action culminated in a valid final judgment is accomplished by the same analysis in both contexts.

Issue preclusion typically does not flow from a default judgment. *See* Restatement (Second) of Judgments § 27; *Stephan v. Rocky Mountain Chocolate Factory, Inc., 136 F.3d 1134, 1136 (7th Cir. 1998)* ("[A] majority of federal courts, the *Restatement (Second) of Judgments § 27*, and commentators such as Charles Wright, Arthur Miller, and Edward Cooper have rejected the notion that a default judgment results in issue preclusion."). *But see Ortega v. Board of County Comm'rs, 683 P.2d 819 (Colo. Ct. App. 1984)* (finding that a default judgment resulted in collateral estoppel).

The differences between the two doctrines lie within the same-issue requirement for issue preclusion. The same-claim requirement for claim preclusion has been broadly conceived to encompass all transactionally related claims that could have been asserted but were not. In contrast, issue preclusion requires that the issues be identical—not merely transactionally related* —and that the issues have actually been raised and litigated; having had the opportunity to raise an issue but failing to do so is not enough to trigger issue preclusion. Thus, while there are complications to figuring out whether the same claim is involved in two successive actions arising from the need to consult the transactional test, because issue preclusion requires identical issues, whether the same-issue requirement has been met will not be difficult to determine. More complicated will be the effort to figure out whether the issue was actually litigated in the prior suit. A further unique aspect of issue preclusion is the requirement that the resolution of the issue in the prior action must have been necessary to the outcome in the case, another matter that can sometimes be difficult to determine. The next case highlights application of the actually-litigated requirement.

Cromwell v. County of Sac

Supreme Court of the United States
94 U.S. (4 Otto) 351 (1876)

MR. JUSTICE FIELD delivered the opinion of the court.

This was an action on four bonds of the county of Sac, in the State of Iowa, each for $1,000, and four coupons for interest, attached to them, each for $100. The bonds were issued in 1860, and were made payable to bearer, in the city of New York, in the years 1868, 1869, 1870, and 1871, respectively, with annual interest at the rate of ten per cent a year.

What's That?

Coupons are certificates attached to bonds that entitle the bearer to interest payments.

To defeat this action, the defendant relied upon the estoppel of a judgment rendered in favor of the county in a prior action brought by one Samuel C. Smith upon certain earlier maturing coupons on the same bonds, accompanied with proof that the plaintiff Cromwell was at the time the owner of the coupons in that action, and that the action was prosecuted for his sole use and benefit.

The questions presented for our determination relate to the operation of this judgment as an estoppel against the prosecution of the present action, and the

---

* *See Comm'r of Internal Revenue v. Sunnen, 333 U.S. 591, 599–600 (1948)* ("[C]ollateral estoppel must be used with its limitations carefully in mind so as to avoid injustice. It must be confined to situations where the matter raised in the second suit is identical in all respects with that decided in the first proceeding and where the controlling facts and applicable legal rules remain unchanged."). [Ed.]

admissibility of the evidence to connect the present plaintiff with the former action as a real party in interest.

In considering the operation of this judgment, it should be borne in mind, as stated by counsel, that there is a difference between the effect of a judgment as a bar or estoppel against the prosecution of a second action upon the same claim or demand, and its effect as an estoppel in another action between the same parties upon a different claim or cause of action. In the former case, the judgment, if rendered upon the merits, constitutes an absolute bar to a subsequent action. It is a finality as to the claim or demand in controversy, concluding parties and those in privity with them, not only as to every matter

Food for Thought

The previous action was brought by a different party, Samuel C. Smith, than the party in this case, Cromwell. On what basis is the County asserting that Cromwell should be bound by issues determined in a prior action prosecuted by Smith?

which was offered and received to sustain or defeat the claim or demand, but as to any other admissible matter which might have been offered for that purpose. Thus, for example, a judgment rendered upon a promissory note is conclusive as to the validity of the instrument and the amount due upon it, although it be subsequently alleged that perfect defences actually existed, of which no proof was offered, such as forgery, want of consideration, or payment. If such defences were not presented in the action, and established by competent evidence, the subsequent allegation of their existence is of no legal consequence. The judgment is as conclusive, so far as future proceedings at law are concerned, as though the defences never existed. The language, therefore, which is so often used, that a judgment estops not only as to every ground of recovery or defence actually presented in the action, but also as to every ground which might have been presented, is strictly accurate, when applied to the demand or claim in controversy. Such demand or claim, having passed into judgment, cannot again be brought into litigation between the parties in proceedings at law upon any ground whatever.

But where the second action between the same parties is upon a different claim or demand, the judgment in the prior action operates as an estoppel only as to those matters in issue or points controverted, upon the determination of which the finding or verdict was rendered. In all cases, therefore, where it is sought to apply the estoppel of a judgment rendered upon one cause of action to matters arising in a suit upon a different cause of action, the inquiry must always be as to the point or question actually litigated and determined in the original action, not what might have been thus litigated and determined. Only upon such matters is the judgment conclusive in another action.

The difference in the operation of a judgment in the two classes of cases mentioned is seen through all the leading adjudications upon the doctrine of estoppel. Thus, in the case of *Outram v. Morewood*, 3 East, 346 [1803], the defendants were held estoped from averring title to a mine, in an action of trespass for digging out coal from it, because, in a previous action for a similar trespass, they had set up the same title, and it had been determined against them. In commenting upon a decision cited in that case, Lord Ellenborough, in his elaborate opinion, said: 'It is not the recovery, but the matter alleged by the party, and upon which the recovery proceeds, which creates the estoppel. The recovery of itself in an action of trespass is only a bar to the future recovery of damages for the same injury; but the estoppel precludes parties and privies from contending to the contrary of that point or matter of fact, which, having been once distinctly put in issue by them, or by those to whom they are privy in estate or law, has been, on such issue joined, solemnly found against them.' And in the case of *Gardner v. Buckbee*, 3 Cowen, 120 [N.Y. 1824], it was held by the Supreme Court of New York that a verdict and judgment in the Marine Court of the city of New York, upon one of two notes given upon a sale of a vessel, that the sale was fraudulent, the vessel being at the time unseaworthy, were conclusive upon the question of the character of the sale in an action upon the other note between the same parties in the Court of Common Pleas. * * *

> **FYI**
>
> *Outram v. Morewood*, the case cited in the text, is an English case and its citation is to the English Reports in the form that was used for cases published before 1865 (similar to the name-based citation form used for Supreme Court cases through the mid-1870s). Why is the Court citing to an English case in its opinion?

These cases, usually cited in support of the doctrine that the determination of a question directly involved in one action is conclusive as to that question in a second suit between the same parties upon a different cause of action, negative the proposition that the estoppel can extend beyond the point actually litigated and determined. The argument in these cases, that a particular point was necessarily involved in the finding in the original action, proceeded upon the theory that, if not thus involved, the judgment would be inoperative as an estoppel. * * *

Various considerations, other than the actual merits, may govern a party in bringing forward grounds of recovery or defence in one action, which may not exist in another action upon a different demand, such as the smallness of the amount or the value of the property in controversy, the difficulty of obtaining the necessary evidence, the expense of the litigation, and his own situation at the time. A party acting upon considerations like these ought not to be precluded from contesting in a subsequent action other demands arising out of the same transaction. A judgment by default only admits for the purpose of the action the legality of the demand or claim in suit: it does not make the allegations of the declaration or complaint evidence in an action upon a different claim. The declaration may contain different statements of the cause of action in different counts. It could hardly be pretended that a judgment by default in such a case would make the several statements evidence in any other proceeding. * * *

If, now, we consider the main question presented for our determination by the light of the views thus expressed and the authorities cited, its solution will not be difficult. It appears from the findings in the original action of Smith, that the county of Sac, by a vote of its people, authorized the issue of bonds to the amount of $10,000, for the erection of a court-house; that bonds to that amount were issued by the county judge, and delivered to one Meserey, with whom he had made a contract for the erection of the court-house; that immediately upon receipt of the bonds the contractor gave one of them as a gratuity to the county judge; and that the court-house was never constructed by the contractor, or by any other person pursuant to the contract. It also appears that the plaintiff had become, before their maturity, the holder of twenty-five coupons, which had been attached to the bonds; but there was no finding that he had ever given any value for them. The court below held, upon these findings, that the bonds were void as against the county, and gave judgment accordingly. The case coming here on writ of error, this court held that the facts disclosed by the findings were sufficient evidence of fraud and illegality in the inception of the bonds to call upon the holder to show that he had given value for the coupons; and, not having done so, the judgment was affirmed. Reading the record of the lower court by the opinion and judgment of this court, it must be considered that the matters adjudged in that case were these: that the bonds were void as against the county in the hands of parties who did not acquire them before maturity and give value for them, and that the plaintiff, not having proved that he gave such value, was not entitled to recover upon the coupons. Whatever illegality or fraud there was in the issue and delivery to the contractor of the bonds affected equally the coupons for interest attached to them. The finding and judgment upon the invalidity of the bonds, as against the county, must be held to estop the plaintiff here from averring to the contrary. But as the bonds were negotiable instruments, * * * they would be held as valid obligations against the county in the hands of a *bona fide* holder taking them for value before maturity, according to repeated decisions of this court upon the character of such obligations. If, therefore, the plaintiff received the bond and coupons in suit before maturity for value, as he offered to prove, he should have been permitted to show that fact. There was nothing adjudged in the former action in the finding that the plaintiff had not made such proof in that case which can

Make the Connection

This discussion of fraud in the inception of the bonds and being a holder who has given value pertains to concepts that you can study in a **Negotiable Instruments** or **Commercial Paper** course.

preclude the present plaintiff from making such proof here. The fact that a party may not have shown that he gave value for one bond or coupon is not even presumptive, much less conclusive, evidence that he may not have given value for another and different bond or coupon. The exclusion of the evidence offered by the plaintiff was erroneous, and for the ruling of the court in that respect the judgment must be reversed and a new trial had.

Upon the second question presented, we think the court below ruled correctly. Evidence showing that the action of Smith was brought for the sole use and benefit of the present plaintiff was, in our judgment, admissible. The finding that Smith was the holder and owner of the coupons in suit went only to this extent, that he held the legal title to them, which was sufficient for the purpose of the action, and was not inconsistent with an equitable and beneficial interest in another.

Judgment reversed, and cause remanded for a new trial.

[The dissenting opinion of JUSTICE CLIFFORD is omitted.]

Points for Discussion

a. The Actually-Litigated Requirement

As the Court clearly stated in *Cromwell*, in order to be given preclusive effect, a previously raised issue must have been actually been litigated and decided. What rationale does the Court give for this requirement? Does the requirement make sense or should it be relaxed? *See Perspective & Analysis* below.

How are courts in subsequent actions to go about determining whether an issue was actually litigated and decided in a previous case? *See* 18A C. WRIGHT, A. MILLER & E. COOPER, FED. PRAC. & PROC. § 4420 (2d ed. 2002):

Food for Thought

Rather than requiring that an issue have been actually litigated and decided, the doctrine could instead embrace a requirement simply that the party to be bound had the incentive and a fair opportunity to litigate the matter. What would be the advantages and disadvantages of such an approach?

The major practical problem posed by the actual decision requirement lies in the need to discover what it was that has been actually decided. In cases tried to a judge, express findings of fact and conclusions of law often show clearly what has been—and what has not been—decided. Special verdicts or interrogatories may bring equal clarity to decisions reached by a jury.

At times, a court also may take pains to make it clear that specific issues are not being decided so as to remove any doubts as to possible issue preclusion. So too, in conjunction with the actual litigation requirement it may be determined that an issue was never decided because it was never raised or was withdrawn before decision. Help also may be found by asking whether the court in the first action lacked authority to decide a particular issue, reasoning that it was not likely to have actually decided an issue it lacked authority to decide. In other cases, a prior judgment may not indicate clearly what issues were resolved. Although this problem may be most common with respect to a jury's general verdict, it also can arise with respect to decisions by a judge. A variety of techniques have been adopted to identify the issues decided; to the extent that they fail, the result is that the opaque judgment fails to preclude relitigation.

—Perspective & Analysis—

One critic of the actually-litigated requirement has written as follows:

[One rationale behind] the "actually litigated" requirement . . . [is] that an [earlier] action may involve so small an amount that litigation of the issue may cost more than the value of the lawsuit. This . . . rationale . . . supports a rejection of issue preclusion in any circumstances. If there is insufficient incentive to litigate a matter, then there should be no issue preclusion. . . .

[The actually-litigated requirement is also justified] on the ground that "the forum may be an inconvenient one in which to produce the necessary evidence . . . ." . . . As the forum choice of the plaintiff, it is proper to hold that the plaintiff should be bound by any adverse decision of the court. . . .

[Also given] as a reason for the "actually litigated" rule is that a rule to the contrary "might serve to discourage compromise, to decrease the likelihood that the issues in an action would be narrowed by stipulation, and thus to intensify litigation." . . . If there is going to be a refusal to stipulate and thus narrow issues, in all probability it will be because of the importance of the instant suit and not because of the issue preclusion that may flow from the decision.

Allan D. Vestal, *The Restatement (Second) of Judgments: A Modest Dissent,* 66 CORNELL L. REV. 464, 473–74 (1981).

b. The Necessarily-Decided Requirement

The *Cromwell* Court also alluded to an equally important and closely related aspect of issue preclusion: The resolution of the issue must have been necessary to the result reached in the previous action. The Supreme Court articulated this principle more clearly in the same Term that it decided *Cromwell* in *Russell v. Place,* 94 U.S. (4 Otto) 606 (1876):

It is undoubtedly settled law that a judgment of a court of competent jurisdiction, upon a question directly involved in one suit, is conclusive as to that question in another suit between the same parties. But to this operation of the judgment it must appear, either upon the face of the record or be shown by extrinsic evidence, that the precise question was raised and determined in the former suit. If there be any uncertainty on this head in the record,—as, for example, if it appear that several distinct matters may have been litigated, upon one or more of which the judgment may have passed, without indicating which of them was thus litigated, and upon which the judgment was rendered,—the whole subject-matter of the action will be at large, and open to a new contention, unless this uncertainty be removed by extrinsic evidence showing the precise point involved and determined.

Id. at 608. What is the rationale behind this requirement?

Hypo 11.6

A driver of a car collided with a motorcyclist on the highway, causing the motorcyclist to fly through the air and suffer serious physical injuries. The motorcyclist sued the car driver in State A federal court for negligence. The car driver responded by alleging that the motorcyclist was contributorily negligent in causing the accident. State A is a contributory negligence state in which the plaintiff's negligence will serve as a complete bar to relief. Both sides presented evidence and testimony on the issues of the car driver's alleged negligence and the motorcyclist's alleged negligence.

Before submitting the case to the jury, the judge instructed it that it must return a verdict in favor of the car driver if they find either (1) that the car driver was not negligent at all, or (2) that the motorcyclist was negligent. The jury returned a general verdict in favor of the car driver.

The car driver subsequently initiated an action in State B federal court against the motorcyclist for negligence based on the same accident that was involved in the previous State B action. The car driver sought summary judgment on the issue of the motorcyclist's negligence, citing the determination of the motorcyclist's negligence in the previous State B action as precluding the motorcyclist from denying negligence, and as barring the motorcyclist from asserting the car driver's negligence. The motorcyclist responded by asserting the previous action as barring the car driver's claim entirely. Which of these assertions of preclusion, if any, have merit?

The Same-Parties Requirement and Nonmutuality

Only parties to a prior action or their privies may be bound by issue preclusion. Does the same limitation apply to who can invoke issue preclusion? Although the classic statement of the doctrine of issue preclusion includes the idea that only parties and their privies can invoke the issue-preclusive effect of a prior determination—a concept known as mutuality—it can no longer be definitively asserted that this requirement is an absolute. To the contrary, the mutuality doctrine has long been excised from the heart of the doctrine at the federal level.

Initially the rule of mutuality was thought to be necessary to achieve fairness: It did not seem fair to permit a nonparty to the previous action to invoke an adverse determination on an issue in that action against a party to that action. For example, if *A* sued *B* for negligence and it was determined in that action that *B* was negligent for crossing the double yellow line in the street, mutuality held that in an action by *C* (the driver of another vehicle) against *B* for negligence arising out of the same accident, *C* could not invoke the decision in *A v. B* regarding *B*'s negligence as conclusive against *B* in *C v. B*. Thus, *B* would traditionally have been able to challenge *C*'s assertions of negligence even though *B* had previously done so and lost in the first action. In the next case we review the Supreme Court's decision in which the mutuality doctrine was effectively slain in favor of nonmutuality.

Parklane Hosiery Co. v. Shore

Supreme Court of the United States
439 U.S. 322 (1979)

MR. JUSTICE STEWART delivered the opinion of the Court.

This case presents the question whether a party who has had issues of fact adjudicated adversely to it in an equitable action may be collaterally estopped from relitigating the same issues before a jury in a subsequent legal action brought against it by a new party.

The respondent brought this stockholder's class action against the petitioners in a Federal District Court. The complaint alleged that the petitioners, Parklane Hosiery Co., Inc. (Parklane), and 13 of its officers, directors, and stockholders, had issued a materially false and misleading proxy statement in connection with a merger. The proxy statement, according to the complaint, had violated §§ 14(a), 10(b), and 20(a) of the Securities Exchange Act of 1934, 48

Make the Connection

These topics, including the obligations imposed on issuers of securities under the Securities Exchange Act of 1934, are topics you would cover in a **Securities Law** or **Securities Regulation** course.

Stat. 895, 891, 899, as amended, 15 U.S.C. §§ 78n(a), 78j(b), and 78t(a), as well as various rules and regulations promulgated by the Securities and Exchange Commission (SEC). The complaint sought damages, rescission of the merger, and recovery of costs.

Before this action came to trial, the SEC filed suit against the same defendants in the Federal District Court, alleging that the proxy statement that had been issued by Parklane was materially false and misleading in essentially the same respects as those that had been alleged in the respondent's complaint. Injunctive relief was requested. After a 4-day trial, the District Court found that the proxy statement was materially false and misleading in the respects alleged, and entered a declaratory judgment to that effect. The Court of Appeals for the Second Circuit affirmed this judgment.

The respondent in the present case then moved for partial summary judgment against the petitioners, asserting that the petitioners were collaterally estopped from relitigating the issues that had been resolved against them in the action brought by the SEC.[2] The District Court denied the motion on the ground that such an application of collateral estoppel would deny the petitioners their Seventh Amendment right to a jury trial. The Court of Appeals for the Second Circuit reversed, holding that a party who has had issues of fact determined against him after a full and fair opportunity to litigate in a nonjury trial is collaterally estopped from obtaining a subsequent jury trial of these same issues of fact. The appellate court concluded that "the Seventh Amendment preserves the right to jury trial only with respect to issues of fact, [and] once those issues have been fully and fairly adjudicated in a prior proceeding, nothing remains for trial, either with or without a jury." Because of an inter-circuit conflict, we granted certiorari.

I

The threshold question to be considered is whether, quite apart from the right to a jury trial under the Seventh Amendment, the petitioners can be precluded from relitigating facts resolved adversely to them in a prior equitable proceeding with another party under the general law of collateral estoppel. Specifically, we must determine whether a litigant who was not a party to a prior judgment may nevertheless use that judgment "offensively" to prevent a defendant from relitigating issues resolved in the earlier proceeding.[4]

---

[2] A private plaintiff in an action under the proxy rules is not entitled to relief simply by demonstrating that the proxy solicitation was materially false and misleading. The plaintiff must also show that he was injured and prove damages. Since the SEC action was limited to a determination of whether the proxy statement contained materially false and misleading information, the respondent conceded that he would still have to prove these other elements of his prima facie case in the private action. The petitioners' right to a jury trial on those remaining issues is not contested.

[4] In this context, offensive use of collateral estoppel occurs when the plaintiff seeks to foreclose the defendant from litigating an issue the defendant has previously litigated unsuccessfully in an action with another party. Defensive use occurs when a defendant seeks to prevent a plaintiff from asserting a claim the plaintiff has previously litigated and lost against another defendant.

A

Collateral estoppel, like the related doctrine of res judicata, has the dual purpose of protecting litigants from the burden of relitigating an identical issue with the same party or his privy and of promoting judicial economy by preventing needless litigation. *Blonder-Tongue Laboratories, Inc. v. University of Illinois Foundation*, 402 U.S. 313, 328–329. Until relatively recently, however, the scope of collateral estoppel was limited by the doctrine of mutuality of parties. Under this mutuality doctrine, neither party could use a prior judgment as an estoppel against the other unless both parties were bound by the judgment. Based on the premise that it is somehow unfair to allow a party to use a prior judgment when he himself would not be so bound,[7] the mutuality requirement provided a party who had litigated and lost in a previous action an opportunity to relitigate identical issues with new parties.

By failing to recognize the obvious difference in position between a party who has never litigated an issue and one who has fully litigated and lost, the mutuality requirement was criticized almost from its inception.[8] Recognizing the validity of this criticism, the Court in *Blonder-Tongue Laboratories, Inc. v. University of Illinois Foundation, supra*, abandoned the mutuality requirement, at least in cases where a patentee seeks to relitigate the validity of a patent after a federal court in a previous lawsuit has already declared it invalid. The "broader question" before the Court, however, was "whether it is any longer tenable to afford a litigant more than one full and fair opportunity for judicial resolution of the same issue." The Court strongly suggested a negative answer to that question:

> "In any lawsuit where a defendant, because of the mutuality principle, is forced to present a complete defense on the merits to a claim which the plaintiff has fully litigated and lost in a prior action, there is an arguable misallocation of resources. To the extent the defendant in the second suit may not win by asserting, without contradiction, that the plaintiff had fully and fairly, but unsuccessfully, litigated the same claim in the prior suit, the defendant's time and money are diverted from alternative uses—productive or otherwise—to relitigation of a decided issue. And, still assuming that the issue was resolved correctly in the first suit, there is reason to be concerned about the plaintiff's allocation of resources. Permitting repeated litigation of the same issue as long as the supply of unrelated defendants holds out

---

[7]   It is a violation of due process for a judgment to be binding on a litigant who was not a party or a privy and therefore has never had an opportunity to be heard. *Blonder-Tongue Laboratories, Inc. v. University of Illinois Foundation*, 402 U.S. 313, 329; *Hansberry v. Lee*, 311 U.S. 32, 40.

[8]   This criticism was summarized in the Court's opinion in *Blonder-Tongue Laboratories, Inc. v. University of Illinois Foundation, supra*, 402 U.S., at 322–327. The opinion of Justice Traynor for a unanimous California Supreme Court in *Bernhard v. Bank of America Nat. Trust & Savings Assn.*, 122 P.2d 892, 895, made the point succinctly:

> "No satisfactory rationalization has been advanced for the requirement of mutuality. Just why a party who was not bound by a previous action should be precluded from asserting it as res judicata against a party who was bound by it is difficult to comprehend."

reflects either the aura of the gaming table or 'a lack of discipline and of disinterestedness on the part of the lower courts, hardly a worthy or wise basis for fashioning rules of procedure.' *Kerotest Mfg. Co. v. C-O-Two Co., 342 U.S. 180, 185 (1952)*. Although neither judges, the parties, nor the adversary system performs perfectly in all cases, the requirement of determining whether the party against whom an estoppel is asserted had a full and fair opportunity to litigate is a most significant safeguard."

Id. at 329.

B

The *Blonder-Tongue* case involved defensive use of collateral estoppel—a plaintiff was estopped from asserting a claim that the plaintiff had previously litigated and lost against another defendant. The present case, by contrast, involves offensive use of collateral estoppel—a plaintiff is seeking to estop a defendant from relitigating the issues which the defendant previously litigated and lost against another plaintiff. In both the offensive and defensive use situations, the party against whom estoppel is asserted has litigated and lost in an earlier action. Nevertheless, several reasons have been advanced why the two situations should be treated differently.[11]

First, offensive use of collateral estoppel does not promote judicial economy in the same manner as defensive use does. Defensive use of collateral estoppel precludes a plaintiff from relitigating identical issues by merely "switching adversaries." Thus defensive collateral estoppel gives a plaintiff a strong incentive to join all potential defendants in the first action if possible. Offensive use of collateral estoppel, on the other hand, creates precisely the opposite incentive. Since a plaintiff will be able to rely on a previous judgment against a defendant but will not be bound by that judgment if the defendant wins, the plaintiff has every incentive to adopt a "wait and see" attitude, in the hope that the first action by another plaintiff will result in a favorable judgment. Thus offensive use of collateral estoppel will likely increase rather than decrease the total amount of litigation, since potential

Food for Thought

As the Court goes through these arguments against permitting offensive collateral estoppel, be sure to understand them and to determine whether you find the arguments persuasive.

---

[11] Various commentators have expressed reservations regarding the application of offensive collateral estoppel. Currie, *Mutuality of Estoppel: Limits of the Bernhard Doctrine*, 9 STAN. L. REV. 281 (1957); Semmel, *Collateral Estoppel, Mutuality and Joinder of Parties*, 68 COLUM. L. REV. 1457 (1968); Note, *The Impacts of Defensive and Offensive Assertion of Collateral Estoppel by a Nonparty*, 35 GEO. WASH. L. REV. 1010 (1967). Professor Currie later tempered his reservations. *Civil Procedure The Tempest Brews*, 53 CALIF. L. REV. 25 (1965).

plaintiffs will have everything to gain and nothing to lose by not intervening in the first action.[13]

A second argument against offensive use of collateral estoppel is that it may be unfair to a defendant. If a defendant in the first action is sued for small or nominal damages, he may have little incentive to defend vigorously, particularly if future suits are not foreseeable. *The Evergreens v. Nunan,* 141 F.2d 927, 929 (CA2); *cf. Berner v. British Commonwealth Pac. Airlines,* 346 F.2d 532 (CA2) (application of offensive collateral estoppel denied where defendant did not appeal an adverse judgment awarding damages of $35,000 and defendant was later sued for over $7 million). Allowing offensive collateral estoppel may also be unfair to a defendant if the judgment relied upon as a basis for the estoppel is itself inconsistent with one or more previous judgments in favor of the defendant.[14] Still another situation where it might be unfair to apply offensive estoppel is where the second action affords the defendant procedural opportunities unavailable in the first action that could readily cause a different result.[15]

C

We have concluded that the preferable approach for dealing with these problems in the federal courts is not to preclude the use of offensive collateral estoppel, but to grant trial courts broad discretion to determine when it should be applied. The general rule should be that in cases where a plaintiff could easily have joined in the earlier action or where, either for the reasons discussed above or for other reasons, the application of offensive estoppel would be unfair to a defendant, a trial judge should not allow the use of offensive collateral estoppel.

Food for Thought

Is giving trial courts discretion truly the preferable approach here? What difficulties can you foresee in making the offensive use of collateral estoppel a matter of trial court discretion? Is the Court clear enough in its articulation of the factors courts should consider in exercising this discretion? And finally, is it appropriate to use plaintiffs' failure to join the prior action as a basis for preventing them from using collateral estoppel offensively?

---

[13] The Restatement (Second) of Judgments § 88(3) (Tent. Draft No. 2, Apr. 15, 1975) provides that application of collateral estoppel may be denied if the party asserting it "could have effected joinder in the first action between himself and his present adversary."

[14] In Professor Currie's familiar example, a railroad collision injures 50 passengers all of whom bring separate actions against the railroad. After the railroad wins the first 25 suits, a plaintiff wins in suit 26. Professor Currie argues that offensive use of collateral estoppel should not be applied so as to allow plaintiffs 27 through 50 automatically to recover. Currie, *supra,* 9 STAN. L. REV., at 304.

[15] If, for example, the defendant in the first action was forced to defend in an inconvenient forum and therefore was unable to engage in full scale discovery or call witnesses, application of offensive collateral estoppel may be unwarranted. Indeed, differences in available procedures may sometimes justify not allowing a prior judgment to have estoppel effect in a subsequent action even between the same parties, or where defensive estoppel is asserted against a plaintiff who has litigated and lost. The problem of unfairness is particularly acute in cases of offensive estoppel, however, because the defendant against whom estoppel is asserted typically will not have chosen the forum in the first action.

In the present case, however, none of the circumstances that might justify reluctance to allow the offensive use of collateral estoppel is present. The application of offensive collateral estoppel will not here reward a private plaintiff who could have joined in the previous action, since the respondent probably could not have joined in the injunctive action brought by the SEC even had he so desired.[17] Similarly, there is no unfairness to the petitioners in applying offensive collateral estoppel in this case. First, in light of the serious allegations made in the SEC's complaint against the petitioners, as well as the foreseeability of subsequent private suits that typically follow a successful Government judgment, the petitioners had every incentive to litigate the SEC lawsuit fully and vigorously. Second, the judgment in the SEC action was not inconsistent with any previous decision. Finally, there will in the respondent's action be no procedural opportunities available to the petitioners that were unavailable in the first action of a kind that might be likely to cause a different result.[19]

Food for Thought

Look at footnote 19. Do you agree with the Court's sentiment that "the presence or absence of a jury as factfinder is basically neutral"?

We conclude, therefore, that none of the considerations that would justify a refusal to allow the use of offensive collateral estoppel is present in this case. Since the petitioners received a "full and fair" opportunity to litigate their claims in the SEC action, the contemporary law of collateral estoppel leads inescapably to the conclusion that the petitioners are collaterally estopped from relitigating the question of whether the proxy statement was materially false and misleading.

II

The question that remains is whether, notwithstanding the law of collateral estoppel, the use of offensive collateral estoppel in this case would violate the petitioners' Seventh Amendment right to a jury trial.

A

"[T]he thrust of the [Seventh] Amendment was to preserve the right to jury trial as it existed in 1791." *Curtis v. Loether, 415 U.S. 189, 193.* At common law, a

---

[17] *SEC v. Everest Management Corp., 475 F.2d 1236, 1240 (CA2)* ("[T]he complicating effect of the additional issues and the additional parties outweighs any advantage of a single disposition of the common issues"). Moreover, consolidation of a private action with one brought by the SEC without its consent is prohibited by statute. 15 U.S.C. § 78u(g).

[19] It is true, of course, that the petitioners in the present action would be entitled to a jury trial of the issues bearing on whether the proxy statement was materially false and misleading had the SEC action never been brought—a matter to be discussed in Part II of this opinion. But the presence or absence of a jury as factfinder is basically neutral, quite unlike, for example, the necessity of defending the first lawsuit in an inconvenient forum.

litigant was not entitled to have a jury determine issues that had been previously adjudicated by a chancellor in equity.

Recognition that an equitable determination could have collateral-estoppel effect in a subsequent legal action was the major premise of this Court's decision in *Beacon Theatres, Inc. v. Westover*, 359 U.S. 500. * * *

It is thus clear that the Court in the *Beacon Theatres* case thought that if an issue common to both legal and equitable claims was first determined by a judge, relitigation of the issue before a jury might be foreclosed by res judicata or collateral estoppel. * * *

Both the premise of *Beacon Theatres*, and the fact that it enunciated no more than a general prudential rule were confirmed by this Court's decision in <u>Katchen v. Landy, 382 U.S. 323</u>. In that case the Court * * * recognized that an equitable determination can have collateral-estoppel effect in a subsequent legal action and that this estoppel does not violate the Seventh Amendment.

B

Despite the strong support to be found both in history and in the recent decisional law of this Court for the proposition that an equitable determination can have collateral-estoppel effect in a subsequent legal action, the petitioners argue that application of collateral estoppel in this case would nevertheless violate their Seventh Amendment right to a jury trial. The petitioners contend that since the scope of the Amendment must be determined by reference to the common law as it existed in 1791, and since the common law permitted collateral estoppel only where there was mutuality of parties, collateral estoppel cannot constitutionally be applied when such mutuality is absent.

The petitioners have advanced no persuasive reason, however, why the meaning of the Seventh Amendment should depend on whether or not mutuality of parties is present. A litigant who has lost because of adverse factual findings in an equity action is equally deprived of a jury trial whether he is estopped from relitigating the factual issues against the same party or a new party. In either case, the party against whom estoppel is asserted has litigated questions of fact, and has had the facts determined against him in an earlier proceeding. In either case there is no further factfinding function for the jury to perform, since the common factual issues have been resolved in the previous action.

The Seventh Amendment has never been interpreted in the rigid manner advocated by the petitioners. On the contrary, many procedural devices developed since 1791 that have diminished the civil jury's historic domain have been found not to be inconsistent with the Seventh Amendment. *See* <u>Galloway v. United States, 319 U.S. 372, 388–393</u>, (directed verdict does not violate the Seventh Amendment);

<u>*Gasoline Products Co. v. Champlin Refining Co.,* 283 U.S. 494, 497–498</u> (retrial limited to question of damages does not violate the Seventh Amendment even though there was no practice at common law for setting aside a verdict in part); <u>*Fidelity & Deposit Co. v. United States,* 187 U.S. 315, 319–321</u> (summary judgment does not violate the Seventh Amendment).

The *Galloway* case is particularly instructive. There the party against whom a directed verdict had been entered argued that the procedure was unconstitutional under the Seventh Amendment. In rejecting this claim, the Court said:

> "The Amendment did not bind the federal courts to the exact procedural incidents or details of jury trial according to the common law in 1791, any more than it tied them to the common-law system of pleading or the specific rules of evidence then prevailing. Nor were 'the rules of the common law' then prevalent, including those relating to the procedure by which the judge regulated the jury's role on questions of fact, crystalized in a fixed and immutable system. . . .

> "The more logical conclusion, we think, and the one which both history and the previous decisions here support, is that the Amendment was designed to preserve the basic institution of jury trial in only its most fundamental elements, not the great mass of procedural forms and details, varying even then so widely among common-law jurisdictions."

The law of collateral estoppel, like the law in other procedural areas defining the scope of the jury's function, has evolved since 1791. Under the rationale of the *Galloway* case, these developments are not repugnant to the Seventh Amendment simply for the reason that they did not exist in 1791. Thus if, as we have held, the law of collateral estoppel forecloses the petitioners from relitigating the factual issues determined against them in the SEC action, nothing in the Seventh Amendment dictates a different result, even though because of lack of mutuality there would have been no collateral estoppel in 1791.

The judgment of the Court of Appeals is

Affirmed.

Mr. Justice Rehnquist, dissenting.

It is admittedly difficult to be outraged about the treatment accorded by the federal judiciary to petitioners' demand for a jury trial in this lawsuit. Outrage is an emotion all but impossible to generate with respect to a corporate defendant in a securities fraud action, and this case is no exception. But the nagging sense of unfairness as to the way petitioners have been treated, engendered by the imprimatur placed by the Court of Appeals on respondent's "heads I win, tails you lose" theory of this litigation, is not dispelled by this Court's antiseptic analysis of the issues in the case. It may be that if this Nation were to adopt a new Constitution today, the Seventh Amendment guaranteeing the right of jury trial in civil cases in federal courts would not be included among its provisions. But any present sentiment to that effect cannot obscure or dilute our obligation to enforce the Seventh Amendment, which was included in the Bill of Rights in 1791 and which has not since been repealed in the only manner provided by the Constitution for repeal of its provisions.

The right of trial by jury in civil cases at common law is fundamental to our history and jurisprudence. Today, however, the Court reduces this valued right, which Blackstone praised as "the glory of the English law," to a mere "neutral" factor and in the name of procedural reform denies the right of jury trial to defendants in a vast number of cases in which defendants, heretofore, have enjoyed jury trials. Over 35 years ago, Mr. Justice Black lamented the "gradual process of judicial erosion which in one hundred fifty years has slowly worn away a major portion of the essential guarantee of the Seventh Amendment." *Galloway v. United States*, 319 U.S. 372, 397 (1943) (dissenting opinion). Regrettably, the erosive process continues apace with today's decision.

> **FYI**
>
> *Sir William Blackstone*, referred to in the text, was an English jurist who authored a four-volume treatise entitled *Commentaries on the Laws of England*. The work remains an important source for discerning historical understandings of common law principles adopted in the United States during the Founding Era.

* * *

* * * I think it is clear that petitioners were denied their Seventh Amendment right to a jury trial in this case. Neither respondent nor the Court doubts that at common law as it existed in 1791, petitioners would have been entitled in the private action to have a jury determine whether the proxy statement was false and misleading in the respects alleged. The reason is that at common law in 1791, collateral estoppel was permitted only where the parties in the first action were identical to, or in privity with, the parties to the subsequent action. It was not until 1971 that the doctrine of mutuality was abrogated by this Court in certain limited circumstances. *Blonder-Tongue Laboratories, Inc. v. University of Illinois Foundation*, 402 U.S. 313. But developments in the judge-made doctrine of collateral estoppel, however salutary, cannot, consistent with the Seventh Amendment, contract in any material fashion the right to a jury trial that a defendant would have enjoyed in 1791. In the instant case, resort to the doctrine of collateral estoppel does more than merely contract the right to a jury trial: It eliminates the right entirely and therefore contravenes the Seventh Amendment.

The Court responds, however, that at common law "a litigant was not entitled to have a jury [in a subsequent action at law between the same parties] determine issues that had been previously adjudicated by a chancellor in equity," and that "petitioners have advanced no persuasive reason . . . why the meaning of the Seventh Amendment should depend on whether or not mutuality of parties is present." But that is tantamount to saying that since a party would not be entitled to a jury trial if he brought an equitable action, there is no persuasive reason why he should receive a jury trial on virtually the same issues if instead he chooses to bring his lawsuit in the nature of a legal action. The persuasive reason is that the Seventh Amendment requires that a party's right to jury trial which existed at common law be "preserved" from incursions by the government or the judiciary. Whether this Court believes that use of a jury trial in a particular instance is necessary, or fair or repetitive is simply irrelevant. If that view is "rigid," it is the Constitution which commands that rigidity. To hold otherwise is to rewrite the Seventh Amendment so that a party is guaranteed a jury trial in civil cases unless this Court thinks that a jury trial would be inappropriate.

* * * [T]he Court's actions today constitute a far greater infringement of the defendant's rights than it ever before has sanctioned. In *Galloway*, the Court upheld the modern form of directed verdict against a Seventh Amendment challenge, but it is clear that a similar form of directed verdict existed at common law in 1791. The modern form did not materially alter the function of the jury. Similarly, the modern device of summary judgment was found not to violate the Seventh Amendment because in 1791 a demurrer to the evidence, a procedural device substantially similar to summary judgment, was a common practice. The procedural devices of summary judgment and directed verdict are direct descendants of their common-law antecedents. They accomplish nothing more than could have been done at common law, albeit by a more cumbersome procedure. * * *

By contrast, the development of nonmutual estoppel is a substantial departure from the common law and its use in this case completely deprives petitioners of their right to have a jury determine contested issues of fact. I am simply unwilling to accept the Court's presumption that the complete extinguishment of petitioners' right to trial by jury can be justified as a mere change in "procedural incident or detail." * * *

Even accepting, *arguendo*, the majority's position that there is no violation of the Seventh Amendment here, I nonetheless would not sanction the use of collateral estoppel in this case. * * *

In my view, it is "unfair" to apply offensive collateral estoppel where the party who is sought to be estopped has not had an opportunity to have the facts of his case determined by a jury. Since in this case petitioners were not entitled to a jury trial in the Securities and Exchange Commission (SEC) lawsuit. I would not estop them from relitigating the issues determined in the SEC suit before a jury in the private action. * * *

The ultimate irony of today's decision is that its potential for significantly conserving the resources of either the litigants or the judiciary is doubtful at best. That being the case, I see absolutely no reason to frustrate so cavalierly the important federal policy favoring jury decisions of disputed fact questions. The instant case is an apt example of the minimal savings that will be accomplished by the Court's decision. As the Court admits, even if petitioners are collaterally estopped from relitigating whether the proxy was materially false and misleading, they are still entitled to have a jury determine whether respondent was injured by the alleged misstatements and the amount of damages, if any, sustained by respondent. Thus, a jury must be impaneled in this case in any event. The time saved by not trying the issue of whether the proxy was materially false and misleading before the jury is likely to be insubstantial. It is just as probable that today's decision will have the result of coercing defendants to agree to consent orders or settlements in agency enforcement actions in order to preserve their right to jury trial in the private actions. In that event, the Court, for no compelling reason, will have simply added a powerful club to the administrative agencies' arsenals that even Congress was unwilling to provide them.

Food for Thought

Now that you have had a chance to consider the Court's and Justice Rehnquist's competing views on whether permitting offensive non-mutual collateral estoppel in this case violates the Seventh Amendment jury right, which side do you think has the better argument? In thinking about this issue, you should refer back to our discussion of the jury right in Chapter 10.

Points for Discussion

a. The Holdings of *Parklane Hosiery*

In affirming the permissibility of offensive nonmutual collateral estoppel, what framework did the Court establish for determining whether such estoppel is appropriate in a given case? Does the Court's approach seem sound to you, or can you anticipate problems that might arise using this analysis?

The Court also ruled that invoking collateral estoppel to preclude a party from being able to have a jury resolve an issue that was previously decided by a judge in an earlier equitable proceeding did not violate the Seventh Amendment. On what basis was it asserted by the petitioner and by Justice Rehnquist that using estoppel in that way did violate the Seventh Amendment's jury right? What explanation did the majority offer for its view of this matter?

> **FYI**
>
> The Court has held that offensive nonmutual collateral estoppel may not be invoked against the United States. *See United States v. Mendoza, 464 U.S. 154, 157–58 (1984)*. What do you think is the rationale of this exception to the *Parklane Hosiery* rule?

b. Issue Preclusion in Mass Torts

If one defendant is responsible for an accident that harms multiple persons, those victims may opt to proceed against the defendant separately in various courts. Those cases coming to a resolution first may reach competing conclusions respecting key issues in the case such as the negligence of the defendant. In subsequent cases involving new plaintiffs, which of the prior inconsistent findings on an issue should be afforded preclusive effect, if any? Does the *Parklane* analysis aid in this determination?

> **Hypo 11.7**
>
> Five people were killed when a helicopter operated by Heliscape crashed as it tried to land on a building in Manhattan. The survivors of three of the victims each initiated separate wrongful-death suits against Heliscape in federal courts in New York, Connecticut, and Ohio. In each case the jury found that Heliscape was not negligent in its operation of the helicopter at the time of the crash. The survivor of a fourth victim filed a wrongful-death suit in Vermont federal court against Heliscape and obtained a verdict in which the jury found that Heliscape was negligent.
>
> Patricia, the widow of the fifth victim of the crash, subsequently filed a wrongful-death lawsuit in Massachusetts federal court against Heliscape. On the issue of Heliscape's negligence, Patricia asserts that the previous determination of the issue against Heliscape in the Vermont action precludes Heliscape from challenging the assertion of negligence in the present case. Should the court permit Patricia's attempted use of collateral estoppel?

c. Offensive Versus Defensive Use of Issue Preclusion

The Court in *Parklane* discusses the distinction between offensive and defensive use of issue preclusion. Be sure to understand the nature of this distinction. *Parklane* addressed facts involving offensive issue preclusion. In a previous case, <u>Blonder-Tongue Laboratories, Inc. v. University of Illinois Foundation, 402 U.S. 313 (1971)</u>, the Court rejected the need for mutuality when issue preclusion was used defensively. That decision was preceded by the California Supreme Court's influential decision in <u>Bernhard v. Bank of America National Trust & Savings Ass'n, 122 P.2d 892 (Cal. 1942)</u>. In *Bernhard*, Justice <u>Traynor</u> permitted the defendant Bank to use the finding on an issue in a previous case involving the plaintiff and another party to bind the plaintiff in her action against the Bank.

Hypo 11.8

Martha told Bill that he can write a check drawn on her account for $100,000 and deposit it in his bank account as a gift. Bill did so. Two months later, Martha died and Bill became the executor of her estate. Veronica, Martha's daughter, challenged Bill's accounting of Martha's estate, claiming that the transfer of funds from Martha to Bill was void and should be returned to the estate. A court ruled that Martha intended and properly authorized the transfer to be a gift.

Bill steps aside as the executor and now Veronica assumes that role. She initiates an action against Newtown Savings & Loan, the bank on which Martha's check was drawn, seeking payment of the funds from the bank on the theory that her mother never authorized the withdrawal. Newton asserts the previous determination that Martha had authorized the transfer to preclude Veronica from asserting in the present action that the withdrawal was not authorized. May Newton assert issue preclusion in this way?

---

d. Binding Nonparties

Do not allow the relaxation of the mutuality doctrine to lead you to conclude that issue preclusion can be invoked against those who were not parties to the previous action. It is a fundamental violation of due process to bind someone to a determination arising from proceedings to which they were not a party. *See* <u>Martin v. Wilks, 490 U.S. 755, 762 (1989)</u> ("A judgment or decree among parties to a lawsuit resolves issues as among them, but it does not conclude the rights of strangers to those proceedings."). Thus, in Hypo 11.7 above Heliscape would not be able to use prior determinations of non-negligence against future plaintiffs to preclude them from asserting Heliscape's negligence in the accident.

e. "Law of the Case" Doctrine

Preclusion can operate between the parties to bind them to prior determinations made within the confines of the same case, just as they may be bound in subsequent cases by determinations made in previous cases. The doctrine that binds litigants within a case to prior rulings on matters and treats such decisions as controlling throughout the litigation is referred to as the "law of the case" doctrine. *See Christianson v. Colt Indus. Operating Corp., 486 U.S. 800, 815–16 (1988)* ("As most commonly defined, the doctrine of the 'law of the case' posits that when a court decides upon a rule of law, that decision should continue to govern the same issues in subsequent stages in the same case."). Under the doctrine, reexamination of prior determinations is typically appropriate only in limited circumstances:

> **FYI**
>
> The Supreme Court has described a similar doctrine known as judicial estoppel: "Where a party assumes a certain position in a legal proceeding, and succeeds in maintaining that position, he may not thereafter, simply because his interests have changed, assume a contrary position, especially if it be to the prejudice of the party who has acquiesced in the position formerly taken by him. This rule, known as judicial estoppel, generally prevents a party from prevailing in one phase of a case on an argument and then relying on a contradictory argument to prevail in another phase." *New Hampshire v. Maine, 532 U.S. 742, 749 (2001)* (citation and internal quotation marks omitted).

The law of the case "must be followed in all subsequent proceedings in the same case in the trial court or on a later appeal in the appellate court, unless the evidence on a subsequent trial was substantially different, controlling authority has since made a contrary decision of the law applicable to such issues, or the decision was clearly erroneous and would work a manifest injustice."

18B C. Wright, A. Miller & E. Cooper, Fed. Prac. & Proc. § 4478 (2d ed. 2002) (quoting *White v. Murtha, 377 F.2d 428, 431–32 (5th Cir. 1967)*).

Executive Summary

■ **Provisional Remedies.** Evaluating whether the imposition of a provisional remedy comports with due process requires consideration of the private interest that will be affected by the prejudgment measure, an examination of the risk of erroneous deprivation through the challenged procedures and of the probable value of additional or alternative safeguards, and consideration of the interest of the party seeking the prejudgment remedy.

■ **Interim Injunctive Relief.** Rule 65 empowers courts to issue temporary restraining orders and preliminary injunctions. The standards for granting a preliminary injunction typically include (1) the likelihood of success on the merits at trial, (2) the likelihood of irreparable harm in the absence of an injunction, (3) the inadequacy of remedies at law (money damages) to protect against this harm, and (4) a demonstration that the balance of hardships facing the parties favors issuance of the injunction.

■ **Enforcement of Judgments.** The procedures surrounding execution of judgments are tied to the state in which the district court is located unless there is an applicable federal statute.

■ **Appellate Review.** Under 28 U.S.C. § 1291 the courts of appeals have jurisdiction of appeals from all final decisions of the district courts of the United States. Title 28 U.S.C. § 1292 provides two exceptions to this rule, permitting appeals of interlocutory orders concerning injunctions and appeals of interlocutory orders concerning matters that the trial court certifies are sufficiently contentious

Major Themes

Keep in mind three overarching themes within the area of judgments and appeals:

a. *Due Process*—the Due Process Clause protects persons from wrongful prejudgment deprivations by requiring the provision of certain safeguards—such as the posting of a bond or consideration of the matter by a judicial officer—aimed at reducing the likelihood that an erroneous deprivation will occur. These protections help insure that powerful prejudgment remedies are not abused by litigants.

b. *Finality*—through the final-judgment rule, the civil justice system promotes efficiency by preventing interim appeals from disrupting the litigation process and by preventing litigants from wasting appellate court time with many harmless errors that turn out not to have an impact on the ultimate outcome in a case.

c. *Repose*—the policy behind preclusion doctrine is that litigants at some point must be able to know that an issue has been conclusively resolved such that they should not expect to have to deal with that matter again. This assurance permits parties to move forward and order their personal or business affairs accordingly and with greater certainty.

and important to the case to warrant immediate review. Civil Rule 23(f) additionally permits interlocutory appeals from orders granting or denying class-action certification.

■ **Preclusion Doctrine.** The doctrine of claim preclusion (*res judicata*) prohibits the relitigation of claims that have been conclusively resolved between the same parties. Issue prelusion (collateral estoppel) refers to the preclusive effect that prior judicial determinations have on the relitigation of certain issues rather than claims.

For More Information

Students interested in obtaining more information about judgments and appeals may consult the following resources:

- 18–18B Charles A. Wright, Arthur R. Miller & Edward H. Cooper, Fed. Prac. & Proc. § 4401 *et seq.* (2d ed. 2002).
- Restatement (Second) of Judgments §§ 17, 24, 26, 27, 28, 29, 41.

———————————

Test Your Knowledge

To assess your understanding of the material in this chapter, click here to take a quiz.

Index

References are to page numbers